JUDICIAL POLITICS
Readings from *Judicature*
Second Edition

Elliot E. Slotnick, Editor

The Ohio State University

AJS

American
Judicature
Society

Since 1913

Library of Congress Catalog Card Number 99-73258
Copyright: American Judicature Society, 1999
ISBN 0-938870-91-2

American Judicature Society
180 N. Michigan, Suite 600
Chicago, IL 60601
(312) 558-6900
www.ajs.org

For information about ordering, contact:
Burnham Inc. Publishers
111 N. Canal St.
Chicago, IL 60606

Contents

The Courts and Their Publics
Public Opinion and the Media 426

Courts, Congress, and the Presidency 477

States and State Courts 525

Alternatives to Traditional Litigation 552

Judicial Policy Making and Judicial Independence in the United States 591

Contributors 644

Preface

In drafting the preface for the first edition of *Judicial Politics*, I wrote that, "editing this volume has been, from the outset, a labor of love. Instructors of courses on judicial politics have recognized for quite some time that some of the most important, interesting, current, and accessible research in our domain has appeared in the pages of *Judicature.*" Those sentiments are as true today, perhaps even more so, than when they were initially written.

The most difficult task, of course, in putting together a volume such as this, is the selection of the "right" articles for inclusion within the constraints imposed by limited space and the demands of numerous topic areas that all stake claims for coverage. In making what were often very difficult choices, I have had an unusual amount of excellent guidance and advice. In the initial stages of this revision Wendy Watson and Eileen Braman, graduate students in judicial politics at Ohio State (and attorneys to boot!), provided me with extensive memos and cogent arguments about why all of the pieces I was considering made (or didn't make) sense for this volume. Their assistance was extraordinarily valuable. Towards the end of the selection process, equally valuable advice and assistance came from Julie-Anne Seeds, another Ohio State graduate student, as well as four valued colleagues and friends, Larry Baum and Greg Caldeira at Ohio State, Sheldon Goldman at Massachusetts, and Jennifer Segal at Kentucky. David Richert and Ira Pilchen of the American Judicature Society, utilizing a somewhat different set of critical eyeglasses, also offered several gentle suggestions about the contents and structure of this anthology that have, in my view and without question, resulted in a better book. For that, and for their full support of the project, I owe them my gratitude. Finally, my thanks are also owed to Emily Fogel for her excellent work in typing large portions of the manuscript and to Stan Kowalski of the American Judicature Society for his display of typesetting excellence that is amply revealed in the pages before you.

Users of the first edition of *Judicial Politics* will notice that there is much that has been changed in this revision. For one, nearly 60 percent of the articles reprinted here are "new" entries in the collection. Wholesale changes have occurred in several sections of the book including, especially, those on "Judges: Judicial Selection Systems and Their Consequences," "Trial Courts: Civil and Criminal Justice Processes," "Internal Court Processes and Decisions on the Merits," "Public Opinion and the Media," and "The Courts, Congress, and the Presidency." Considerably broader coverage has been given to "Alternatives to Traditional Litigation" and, in addition, the collection's final chapter on judicial policy making in the United States has been expanded to include several provocative readings on the issue of judicial independence.

In the preface to the first edition I wrote that, "the ultimate test of this volume's success will, of course, be determined by its utility in the classroom." That still remains the measure by which this volume should be judged. Looking towards the future, I continue to "urge colleagues and students to drop me a note about those selections that have been working well and those (hopefully few) that have been less successful.... Perhaps most important, I look forward to hearing from colleagues as we collectively monitor future editions of *Judicature* with an eye towards articles we would like our students to read in the years to come. In this sense, the responsibility is ours to continue the kind of scholarly work that, under David Richert's editorial direction, has contributed to *Judicature's* excellence."

As before, I must underscore that this book has been prepared for our students, and it is my hope that these readings will give them a great deal to think about regarding our system of justice. It is to our students—past, present, and future—and their efforts to improve that system, that this book is dedicated.

The American Constitutional System and the Role of the Supreme Court in the American Polity

INTRODUCTION

In every society some mechanism is established for adjudicating disputes and performing a judicial function. In the United States the American judiciary is a uniquely powerful one from a policy-making perspective. Much of the unusual authority of American courts stems from their exercise of the power of judicial review, the ability to invalidate the acts and actions of other governmental entities because of their failure to meet the guidelines set by the U.S. Constitution, the fundamental charter of American government. While judicial review may give American courts the "final" say in legitimating policy choices made elsewhere, it is a power that has always been exercised amid great controversy. Indeed, considerable historical scholarship exists that debates the fundamental question of whether judicial review was actually "intended" by the framers of the Constitution since this potentially awesome power is not explicitly mentioned within the written document itself.

Our first section of readings examines several facets of the dilemma of judicial review and judicial authority within the fabric of American democracy. In "The place of judicial review in the American tradition: the emergence of an eclectic power," Elliot Slotnick takes the reviewing power as a given and examines why the American political context was a uniquely hospitable one for such an extraordinary judicial prerogative to take hold.

In addition to underlying concerns about the historical legitimacy of judicial review and its place in the American scheme of things, it has been commonplace for analysts to debate the question of judicial review's consistency with democracy. After all, critics have contended, isn't there something fundamentally undemocratic when a group of nine justices, appointed for life and largely unaccountable, invalidate (sometimes by a 5-4 vote), the will of popular majorities enacted into law by representative legislative bodies? Others are quick to respond, however, that American democracy means more than simply majority rule and, in fact, is equally concerned about questions of minority rights. For such analysts judicial review can serve as a bulwark for democracy in the protection of minority rights. In "Judicial review: the usurpation and democracy questions," puzzles such as these are explored by Albert Melone and George Mace. The authors recognize that one cannot turn back the clock and that judicial review is a fact of American life. Further, they argue, concern over whether judicial review is democratic or undemocratic begs an equally important question, the compatibility of judicial review with a "good" democracy, one that "operates to guard against threats to liberty and human happiness."

While scholarly questions about the legitimacy of judicial review and its relationship to democracy are interesting and important ones, their exploration does not "solve" the problem faced by American judges who must come to grips with their reviewing authority and make decisions about the scope of its exercise. In "Interpreting the Constitution," opposing perspectives are offered in companion articles by federal Judge J. Clifford Wallace and law professor Jeffrey Shaman. Wallace's article presents, "The case for judicial restraint," premised on the judge's reliance on "interpretivism...the principle that judges, in resolving constitutional questions, should rely on the express provisions of the Constitution or upon those norms that are clearly implicit in its text." Shaman's answer, however, in "The Supreme Court's proper and historic function," is that such interpretivism is both impossible and unwise. Indeed, "The Court's role, when all is said and done, is to create meaning for a Constitution that otherwise would be a hollow document."

In reading the articles in this section, one is struck by the frequent use of terms such as "strict construction," "interpretivism," "noninterpretivism," "judicial restraint," "judicial activism," and others in the parlance of authors making a case for the "appropriate" exercise of judicial power. In much writing about the judiciary, such terms are ill-defined or, even worse, not defined at all. In reading pieces here and elsewhere on the controversial issues of the exercise and scope of judicial power, one must examine the arguments with a critical and cautious eye.

The place of judicial review in the American tradition: the emergence of an eclectic power

Whether judicial review was "intended" by the framers or not, it developed as a pragmatic response to the American experience, consistent with main currents of our political history.

by Elliot E. Slotnick

Traditionally, historical analyses of the American doctrine of judicial review have gone through a series of elaborate manipulations of memoirs and documents in an effort to decide whether judicial review was "intended" by the framers of the Constitution. The question of whether such "intentions" existed could be viewed as a peripheral one having little contemporary importance, except for the reality that emerges whenever there is any discussion of the role of the Supreme Court. As one scholar has noted:

A doubt that the whole package of present judicial power was legitimately conferred . . . lurks in the background of American politics and emerges to help convert grievance into passion when any sector of the population is greatly disappointed with the behavior of the Supreme Court in Constitutional cases.[1]

The question of the validity of judicial review has not been solely academically inspired, but was a great concern of many of the Constitution's framers and their contemporaries. The precedent for judicial review was established in the landmark case of *Marbury v. Madison* in an opinion by Chief Justice John Marshall. Yet the precedent was not, in reality, actively supported by all or even the great majority of his contemporaries. Thomas Jefferson raised what has since become a common argument against the judiciary's "proud preeminence."

. . . Yet this case of Marbury and Madison is continually cited by bench and bar as if it were settled law without any animadversion on its being merely an *obiter* dissertation of the Chief Justice.[2]

Despite the arguments of Jefferson and others, judicial review was here to stay. The inability of its critics to eliminate judicial review has traditionally been traced to two major factors: the contemporary political situation, and Marshall's judicial craftsmanship. While establishing a precedent for judicial review in *Marbury v. Madison*, Marshall did, in fact, decide the case as the Jeffersonians wanted. What better means of obtaining acquiescence in the *entire* decision? While the Jeffersonians won the case, the price they paid was substantially greater than they had anticipated.

. . . This decision bears many of the earmarks of a deliberate partisan coup. The court was bent on reading the President a lecture on his legal and moral duty to recent Federalist appointees to judicial office, whose commissions the last Administration had not had time to deliver, but at the same time hesitated to (initiate opposition) by actually asserting jurisdiction of the matter. It therefore took the engaging position of declining to exercise power which the Constitution withheld from it by making the occasion an opportunity to assert a far more transcendent power.[3]

The role of Marshall in this coup has rarely been underestimated.

The problem was given no answer by the Constitution. A hole was left where the Court might drive in the peg of judicial supremacy if it could. And this is what John Marshall did. He drove it in, so firmly that no one yet has been able to pull it out.[4]

While the question of whether judicial review was "provided" for by the framers is an interesting one, our verdict shall not be added to the countless others already in. Rather, for the most part, the existence of judicial review will be accepted as a "given." Beginning with the existence of judicial review, we shall attempt to relate what was a peculiarly American phenomenon to a number of undercurrents in American political thought.

Several facets of the American political experience are, at least, consistent with the Court's review power. Among these factors we shall examine the following: precedents relating to judicial review, colonial notions about the "common law," colonial notions about "natural law," limited government and constitutionalism, American pragmatism and the fear of legislative omnipotence, and the prevalence of "magical" conceptions of the judicial function and the role of justices.

Finally, we shall attempt to relate the ambivalence of many of these factors to the emergence of an American tradition of "judicial self-restraint." In essence, we shall attempt to view judicial review as a "composite" power and take an eclectic approach. Judicial review may be seen as consistent with a number of modes of constitutional thought which otherwise have not been seen as consistent with each other. Although Hamilton and Jefferson stood on opposite sides of the judicial review question, there was no inherent reason why both Hamiltonians and Jeffersonians could not support the power. The foundations of judicial review were simply that broad.

The primary principles formulated as a basis for the American doctrine were: first, that a written Constitution is fundamental and paramount and therefore superior to common and statutory law; second, that the powers of the legislature are limited, a written constitution being in the nature of a commission to the legislature by which its powers are delegated and its limitations defined; third, that judges are the special guardians of the provisions of written constitutions which are in the nature of mandatory instructions to the judges, who must uphold these provisions and refuse to enforce any legislative enactment in conflict therewith. To understand the nature of these principles it is necessary to examine the notion of a higher law . . . During the seventeenth and eighteenth centuries this idea of a higher law became the basis in England and France for laws which were held to be fundamental and unalterable and for a theory of the supremacy of courts.[5]

It is to a consideration of these and other themes and their relationship to judicial review that the bulk of this article will be addressed. First, we shall consider some of the precedents pointed to by the "headcounters" of the Constitutional Convention as evidence of the "intention " of the framers.

Not a new doctrine

The enunciations of the doctrine of judicial review by Marshall in *Marbury v. Madison* was not the first time that America was confronted with its existence. The review power had previously been recognized numerous times by colonial and state practices, debates held in the Constitutional and state conventions, and by specific clauses in state constitutions. Clearly, the notion of judicial review was not foreign to the American ear. Jefferson, it may be asserted, opposed judicial review, but he clearly recognized its existence in states other than his native Virginia.

In Virginia, where a great proportion of the legislature considers the constitution but as other acts of legislation, laws have been frequently passed which controlled its effects. I have not heard that in the other states they have ever infringed their Constitutions, and I suppose they have not done it, as the judges would consider any law void which was contrary to the Constitution.[6]

Jefferson is attesting to the existence of conceptions of judicial review in states other than his own. Yet, for an earlier period, there even exists evidence of judicial review in Jefferson's Virginia.

In Virginia . . . the Supreme Court of the colony, having been put the question, early in 1766, whether officers of the law would incur a penalty if they did not use stamped paper in conformance with the prescription of the Stamp Act, answered that the act did not bind the inhabitants of Virginia, "inasmuch as they conceived" it "to be unconstitutional."[7]

Similar words were used in many of the state courts and courts of the colonies. On the very eve of the Declaration of Independence, Judge Cushing, later one of the original members of the Supreme Court of the United States, charged a Massachusetts jury to ignore certain acts of Parliament as "void" and "inoperative."[8] Further, it is interesting to note that many of the opponents of the federal Constitution, and particularly its provisions relating to the judiciary, were critics simply because they felt that the power of judicial review, exercised so well by the state courts, would be weakened by the new system. Patrick Henry's remarks stand out.

The honorable gentleman did our judiciary honor in

saying that they had the firmness to counteract the legislature in some cases. Yes, sir, our judges opposed the acts of the legislature. We have this landmark to guide us. They had fortitude to declare that they were the judiciary, and would oppose unconstitutional acts. Are you sure that your federal judiciary will act thus?[9]

It is obvious that the framers knew of precedents for courts exercising an authority analogous to judicial review. There even exists a great deal of evidence to support the view that many people felt that judicial review had, in fact, been *included* in the federal Constitution. The Convention spent much time on a proposal for a Council of Revision that would review constitutionality. When discussing the court's role in such a council, there was a general fear of giving the courts a *double* power.

It is clear, then, that one of the reasons why the Council of Revision proposal was rejected was that some of the members assumed that the courts would exercise the power of judicial review, and they doubted the wisdom of conferring any further power of a similar character upon the judiciary.[10]

And, discussing the Council of Revision, Elbridge Gerry expressed his doubts.

. . . Whether the Judiciary ought to form a part of it, as they will have a sufficient check against encroachments . . . by their exposition of the laws which involved a power of deciding on their constitutionality.[11]

Other pronouncements by various Framers can also serve as further evidence for the fact that judicial review, in their eyes, was not unprecedented. Rufus King simply stated in the Convention that, ". . . Judges will have the expounding of those Laws when they come before them, and they will, no doubt, stop the operation of such as shall appear repugnant to the Constitution."[12] Similar remarks were made at state ratifying conventions. When George Nicholas was asked in the Virginia convention who would determine the extent of legislative powers, he replied directly, ". . . the same power which, in all well-regulated communities determines the extent of legislative powers. If they exceed these powers, the judiciary will declare it void."[13]

Similarly, in the Massachusetts convention, Samuel Adams said that, "any law . . . beyond the power granted by the proposed constitution . . . (will be) adjudged by the courts of law to be void." Oliver Ellsworth told the Connecticut convention

that if the general legislature should at any time overleap their limits, the judicial department is a constitutional check; "a law which the constitution does not authorize is 'void,' and the judges 'will declare it to be void.' " Similar statements were made by Wilson in Pennsylvania and by John Marshall in Virginia.[14]

A few remarks made by Wilson can serve to illustrate the extent to which judicial review, in some minds, was regarded as an integral part of the judicial function. When the suggestion arose in the Pennsylvania ratification convention that judges might be impeached if they were to "decide against the law," Wilson retorted, "The judges are to be impeached because they decide an act null and void, that was made in defiance of the Constitution! What House of Representatives would dare to impeach, or Senate to commit, judges for performance of their duty?"[15]

Supporters of judicial review often relied on more than simply their word as evidence of its existence. Specifically, two clauses in the Constitution, the "arising under" clause and the "supremacy clause" were cited as "proof" of the framers' intentions. Admittedly, these clauses do not, in and of themselves, furnish undeniable proof of the intended existence of judicial review. But our purpose in this survey of precedents is not to "prove" the "intention" of the framers but, rather, to show that, at worst, the power was not unheard of and inconceivable. To a certain extent, we can readily endorse Corwin's view of *Marbury v. Madison* as a logical culmination of events preceding it in the American experience.

Upon the latent talent the problem of the time acted as incentive and stimulant, eliciting from it suggestion after suggestion which it needed but the ripe occasion to erect into institutions composing a harmonious whole.[16]

Common law and Coke

In discussing the relationship between judicial review and the American experience we may take as a starting point the American conception of the English common law and our particular reverence of the juridical philosophy of Sir Edward Coke. In part, Coke's doctrine, pronounced in the *Dr. Bonham's Case*, was seen as a precedent of judicial review; in part, it served as inspiration for it. In Coke's view, adjudication was a very special function, with the common law courts standing above all else, including the Crown, in matters of law.

According to Haines, Coke sought "to erect the judges into a tribunal of arbitration between the king and the nation."[17] At bottom, Coke attempted to revive what he conceived were the limits imposed upon all authority by the Magna Carta. In his view, sovereignty had little meaning in England because "Magna Carta is such a fellow that he will have no sovereign." As a result, parliamentary acts that were "contrary to common right and reason" were to be declared "void."[18] The common law, however, and "common right and reason" were the peculiar province of judges.[19]

Coke's conception of judicial function as pronounced in *Dr. Bonham's Case* would be echoed in almost identical form in many arguments raised by American colonial judges. As early as 1688, during the short reign of the Stuart despotism, there is evidence that "the men of Massachusetts . . . did much quote Lord Coke."[20] In 1761, allegedly on Coke's authority, James Otis at Boston—in the Writs of Assistance case—plunged at once into the most fundamental issues. His argument was, that whether such writs were warranted by Act of Parliament or not, was a matter of indifference, since such Act of Parliament would be "against the Constitution" and "against natural equity" and therefore "void."[21]

Others followed Coke even more closely.

Governor Hutchinson, referring to the opposition to the Stamp Act, wrote, "The prevailing reason at this time is that the Act of Parliament is against Magna Carta, and the natural rights of Englishmen, and therefore according to Lord Coke, null and void." As late, indeed, as 1766, Judge Cushing, who was destined to become 20 years later a member of the first bench of the United States Supreme Court, charged a Massachusetts jury to ignore certain acts of Parliament as void and inoperative, and was felicitated by John Adams for his courage in doing so.[22]

Coke's doctrine had quite a different status in England than it did in the colonies, and this is the source of an interesting paradox related to the American readiness to accept judicial review. "The conception of a fundamental law as a rule to guide common law courts whose duty it is to keep both King and Parliament within bounds seems to have existed, so far as England is concerned, chiefly in the mind of Coke and a few of his very willing followers."[23]

Yet acceptance of Coke in America could be seen as a pragmatic coup; a means of accepting the common law and at the same time rejecting Great Britain. As Carr notes,

Coke's thesis was never really accepted in England, . . . but the *Dr. Bonham Case* was known in the American colonies . . . Accordingly, when in the second half of the 18th century the great controversy between the colonies and England began, and became centered in opposition in Parliament, Americans could not resist the temptation to use Coke's reasoning in the *Dr. Bonham's Case* . . . Thus, on the eve of the writing of the American constitution, and long after England had repudiated the idea of a legislature's dependence upon a higher law enforced by the Courts, the idea was known and accepted in this country, in part at least, for a very practical reason.[24]

What better method could the colonies employ than invoking a doctrine which had had its birth in the mother country? No argument was likely to be as persuasive for the colonies as the accusation that England no longer subscribed to limitations she, herself, had formulated. Unquestionably, "At the moment when Americans were beginning to lay about them for weapons with which to resist the pretensions of Parliament," Coke's doctrine "met with a degree of success—enough at least to make it a permanent memory with the men of the time."[25] It would be difficult for a country professedly founded in idealism not to adopt this doctrine as its own.

A reductionist view

The relationship between Coke's doctrine and American development has even been extended into a reductionist explanation of the American revolution itself. Such a view goes far beyond merely using Coke to justify opposition to Britain. According to Boudin, the theory is "nothing less than the assertion that the American Revolution was but a lawyers' revolution, designed to revive and perpetuate in America Lord Coke's doctrine of Judicial Power which seems to have fallen upon evil days in England just about that time." The theory "first took definite form in the special committee appointed by the New York State Bar Association." As stated in the Committee Report, "In short, the American Revolution was a lawyer's revolution to enforce Lord Coke's theory of the invalidity of Acts of Parliament in derogation of common right and the rights of Englishmen."[26]

We need not accept such an obviously incomplete and simplistic explanation of the Revolution to assert simply that the views held of Coke's jurisprudence in America were consistent with the development of the power of judicial review in this country. When Perry Miller speaks of the "ambivalence" in the American experience towards the common law, to a certain extent this ambivalence may be viewed simply as an acceptance of Coke (who was rejected in Britain) and a xenophobia towards and rejection of things that were British. This corresponds to the paradox already noted.

Indeed, it is fascinating to consider how, during these and subsequent decades, the ambivalence persisted between hostility to the intricacy of the Common Law and at the same time reluctance to abandon it as constituting the bulwark of rights and liberties.[27]

Miller's "ambivalence" seems less of a paradox, and is more understandable when we trace back our acceptance of the "bulwark of rights and liberties" to Coke, and our rejection of the remaining intricacies of the common law to our xenophobia towards basically British accoutrements.

Natural law thinking

A second factor which may be seen as totally consistent with the American doctrine of judicial review and as related to our conception of the common law is the prevalence of natural law thinking in America at the time of the country's founding. Natural law reasoning, in fact, emerges as the basic argument for why judicial review was consistent with Jeffersonian thought and could be supported by his followers even while Jefferson himself opposed the doctrine. The natural law thinking of the era was not, in any sense, a contemporary invention, but reverted back to an earlier mode of thought. "The enthusiasm which manifested itself in the fight for human rights on both sides of the Atlantic gave new life and vigor to the Roman and medieval conception of a law of nature."[28] According to this regeneration of natural law thought, there were certain things which even government could not do, and the judiciary would serve as an overseer to guard against unwarranted governmental usurpation. Thus, according to Corwin, the idea of a "universally valid code of justice which is knowable to all men in the form given it in seventeenth century England by Locke and others, of a code of individual rights prior to government and available against it, this idea is basic to all . . . conceptions of judicial review."[29]

There is much evidence that serves to link natural law thinking with judicial review, including even the somewhat questionable assertion that the very reasoning used by Marshall in *Marbury v. Madison* stemmed from ideas about natural law.

Like Marshall in *Marbury v. Madison*, (Gouverneur) Morris believed that judicial authority to void such legislation was "derived from higher authority than this Constitution. They derive it from the Constitution of man, from the nature of things, from the necessary progress of human affairs."[30]

Perhaps Dewey does stretch a point unnecessarily when he cites Morris to make an assertion about Marshall. Nevertheless, we are satisfied by the notion that judicial review (or some form of review) was, indeed, linked by some with natural law thinking. Further, this linkage was by no means limited to Morris.

The influence of the notion of an overruling law of nature is clearly apparent at an early period in the American colonies . . . George Mason in a Virginia case argued: "The laws of nature are the laws of God, whose authority can be superseded by no power on earth . . . All human constitutions which contradict his laws we are in conscience bound to disobey." Basing its judgement on a similar doctrine, a Connecticut court said: "The fundamental law which God and nature have given to the people cannot be infringed . . ." The analytical theory which deems positive law an independent of moral consideration and as based on a sovereign will, was not accepted at the time; in fact the colonies were so impressed with the idea of an overruling law of nature that the laws of God and so-called natural laws were regarded "As the true law, and all temporal legislation was to be considered binding only insofar as it was an expression of this natural law."[31]

Natural law doctrine did not simply appeal to the Americans on an intellectual level, but was also used from a pragmatic standpoint, sometimes serving to bring an end to troublesome debates. As Perry Miller notes, "it was in order that the first efforts to manufacture a doctrine of American law after the Revolution should devote long sections to the law of nature, particularly because in 1790 . . . there was so little accurate information about what constituted law in America."[32] It is unnecessary to assert that all justices or adherents of judicial review justified it on the basis of natural law, yet such an argument could and did certainly aid in adding a mystical aura to the function which removed it, to a certain degree, from reproach.

In reality, strict natural law doctrine was in no sense the major thrust of specific judicial review arguments, but natural law did serve to bolster judicial review in the abstract. Essentially, natural law arguments were used most often in the formative stages of the development and ascendance of judicial review, and served to make the judicial power a bit more palatable to a wider spectrum of citizens. As Haines notes, "The idea of rejecting laws contrary to natural justice or as infractions of the law of nature though frequently repeated by justices was, in the beginning of judicial review, seldom regarded as sufficient grounds to declare legislative acts void."[33] Nevertheless, natural law did place a cloak of idealism over the judicial function, and could serve as ample incentive to mobilize one line of support for judicial review.

Other justifications

Closely linked to natural law thought supporting judicial review were various strands of thought centering upon constitutionalism and limited government as the justification for the doctrine.

It may be remarked here that the doctrine of declaring legislative Acts void as being contrary to the Constitution was probably helped into existence by a theory . . . that Courts might disregard such acts if they were contrary to the fundamental maxims of morality, or . . . the laws of nature.[34]

Arguments for judicial review based on constitutionalism and limited government would appeal to a somewhat different segment of the population than did assertions based solely on the "mystical" natural law. The Constitution loomed as something more concrete than the heavens and the soul of man.

One of the most important principles which led to the acceptance of the American doctrine was the theory that a Constitution is a fundamental or paramount enactment. At the same time that the idea of a superior law of nature was prevalent the conception that a written constitution is a fundamental act was acquiring new meaning . . . in America.[35]

At the same time, however, judicial review's natural law constituency remained enticed by the apparent congruence between natural law, limited government, and constitutionalism.

Many historians have felt that in favoring judicial review the men of the Convention were influenced by a strong belief in certain fundamental principles . . . Accordingly they established a written constitution as the fundamental law and authorized judges to act as guardians of this Constitution by enforcing it against the im-

proper laws which the legislature might enact.[36]

Written constitutions were alleged to be reflections of the natural law and, consequently, were viewed as fundamental, fixed, immutable, and permanent. Linking natural law with constitutionalism we are faced with, in Cahn's terms, "A change from higher-than-positive law to higher, positive law."

This, of course, is the very change that Marshall consummated in *Marbury v. Madison*; by legitimizing the appeal to the Courts he presumedly bastardized any possible "appeal to heaven" . . . "Appeal to heaven" having served its historic purpose, had nothing to offer toward meeting the need of a new era, i.e., the day to day enforcement of a written constitution.[37]

Once constitutions replace natural law, upholding the documents becomes as serious a task as meeting the earlier moral code.

It is easy to smile at the vagaries of ancient political practice, and to reflect with pleasure on modern superiority—but perhaps not wholly justified. For we are about to see a strange phenomenon: the typical political theorist of seventeenth century England proceeds in a sensible fashion to secularize and naturalize the process of drafting a fundamental law; he transmutes the obsolete supernatural code into a product of human ingenuity and intellect; yet—the moment the draft has been formulated—incontinently he assumes the prostrate attitude of the ancients, invests the document with the same reverential awe he declares for its source, and declares . . . that every part and the whole of it shall remain immutable forever and in perpetuity![38]

The general notion of written constitutions as a reflection of basic fundamental law can be traced to several threads in the American fabric. Haines attributes such a notion primarily to the French, and to the English conception of Magna Carta. Even in the very early American experience we have evidence of the theme repeatedly; it appears in Puritan writings where, perhaps, notions of the primacy or importance of secular law would be expected to be muted. Winthrop writes, however,

The deputies having conceived great danger to our State, we regard that our magistrates, for want of positive laws, in many cases, might proceed according to their discretions, it was agreed that some men should be appointed to frame a body of grounds of laws, in resemblance to a Magna Carta, which, being allowed by some of the ministers, and the general Court, should be received for fundamental laws.[39]

Thus, charters were written in the early Pilgrim

settlements and these served as useful precedents for the American colonies. The courts were to play a significant role in elucidating the charters.

These charters were in the strict sense written law: As their restraints upon the colonial legislatures were enforced by the English Courts of last resort, so might they be enforced through the colonial courts, by disregarding as null what went counter to them.[40]

These charters were also significant in that they were self-imposed by "the people." What greater reason could exist for treating them as "fundamental?"

. . . there was no longer an external sovereign. Our conception now was that "the people" took his place . . . So far as existing institutions were left untouched they were construed by translating the name and style of the English sovereign into that of our new rules—ourselves, the People. After this the charters, and still more obviously the new constitutions, were not so many orders from without, backed by an organized outside government, which simply performed an ordinary function enforcing them; they were precepts from the people themselves who were to be governed, addressed . . . especially to those who were charged with the duty of conducting the government.[41]

Thus, judicial review emerges as being consistent with theories of constitutionalism aimed at establishing the rule of law over the rule of men. "The basic antithesis . . . remains substantially what it was in the period between Coke and Locke, that is, the antithesis between . . . legal precept and executive prerogative, between wise rules and exercise of wide discretion . . ."[42]

The link between judicial review and constitutionalism only maintains clarity and consistency if, somehow, judges are a different breed than executives and legislators, and adjudication does not imply wide discretion and the "rule of men," but, rather, reinforces a rule of law. We will return to this point later but, for the moment, can conclude with Andrew McLaughlin that judicial review was consistent with and was an extension of American views on constitutionalism and limited government.

The doctrine of what is now called "judicial review" is the last word, logically and historically speaking, in the attempt of a free people to establish and maintain a non-autocratic government. It is the culmination of the essentials of Revolutionary thinking and, indeed, of the thinking of those who a hundred years or more before the Revolution called for a government of laws and not men.[43]

John Marshall incorporated these views of constitutionalism in *Marbury v. Madison*. Between the lines one can read of "the Constitution" as "fundamental" law, but there remains a sense of linkage with natural law as well. Marshall, like McLaughlin, skirts the issue of why judges alone can "know" the Constitution and, as will be developed, this becomes a crucial point in the American genesis of judicial review.

Between the alternatives there is no middle ground. The constitution is either a superior paramount law, unchangeable by ordinary means, or it is on a level with ordinary legislative acts, and, like other acts, is alterable when the legislature shall please to alter it. If the former part of the alternative be true, then a legislative act, contrary to the Constitution, is not law; if the latter part be true then written constitutions are absurd attempts on the part of the people to limit a power, in its own nature, illimitable. Certainly, all those who have framed written constitutions contemplate them as forming the fundamental and paramount law of the nation, and consequently, the theory of every such government must be, that an act of the legislature, repugnant to the Constitution is void.[44]

The fear of legislative omnipotence has been a major part of the American political tradition, and this is another crucial area where judicial review served as a doctrine which could be supported by both Federalists and Jeffersonians. While the followers of Hamilton and Jefferson were rarely found on the same side of basic constitutional questions, it is crucial to an understanding of the place of judicial review in the American tradition to see how politically antagonistic groups could support the same doctrine for essentially diametrically opposed reasons. Thus, it can be demonstrated that the Hamiltonian Federalists feared that the popularly elected legislatures might not respect the prerogatives of property rights; the Jeffersonian conception, on the other hand, stressed the threat of legislatures to other minorities with the assertion that a multitude of despots were as bad as one. Approaching the problem of legislative omnipotence from different perspectives, it is instructive that judicial review was a doctrine that could serve several masters. According to Haines, "The right of the judiciary to declare law invalid, and thus to check the rapacity of legislative assemblies, was in the opinion of many to be the chief cornerstone of a governmental structure planned with particular reference to preserving property rights inviolate and to assuring special sanction for individual liberties."[45] In its utility for the preservation of property rights, judicial review became a primary Federalist doctrine; similarly, the stress on individual liberties made it acceptable to the Jeffersonians.

State legislative power

Federalist support for the doctrine of judicial review and fear of the legislature grew out of two closely related phenomena observable under the Articles of Confederation: the vast scope of state legislative power, and the use of that power against the interests of private property rights. In their framework for a new federal government, the Federalist's view of state legislatures would be instrumental in the call for both a separation and a division of powers emphasizing a new balance. Clearly, their view of the state legislatures was not a benevolent one. As Corwin notes of the "constitutional reaction" culminating in the formation of a new government, "The reaction embraced two phases, that of nationalism against State sovereignty, that of private rights against uncontrolled legislative power; but the point of attack in both instances was the State legislature."[46]

Suspicion of the post-1776 legislatures arose, in large part, as a result of their nearly unlimited powers. With virtually unchecked power in their possession, abuses followed and, as Madison noted, "Experience in all the States had evinced a powerful tendency in the Legislature to absorb all power into its real vortex. This was the real source of danger to the American Constitution, and suggested the necessity of giving every defensive authority to the other departments that was consistent with republican principles."[47] Hamilton raises a similar argument in *Federalist 78* in presenting his rationale for the judicial power.

The complete independence of the courts of justice is peculiarly essential in a limited constitution. By a limited constitution I understand one which contains certain specified exceptions to the legislative authority; . . . Limitations of this kind can be preserved in practice no other way than through the medium of courts of justice, whose duty it must be to declare all acts contrary to the manifest tenor of the Constitution void. Without this, all the reservations of particular rights or privileges would amount to nothing.[48]

The insistence upon further checks on Congress became the rallying cry of the Constitutional Convention for many Federalists. Yet by and large the checks they sought were not to protect the populace but, rather, to seek protection *from* the popularly elected legislatures. Much of this argument is articulated in the work of Charles Beard.

This very system of checks and balances, which is undeniably the essential element of the Constitution, is built upon the doctrine that the popular branch of the government cannot be allowed full sway, and least of all in the enactment of laws touching the rights of property.[49]

In seeking to avert "legislative tyranny" the Federalists sought a judiciary which would be the bastion of property, in Gouverneur Morris' words, "aristocracy, men who from pride will support consistency and permanency . . . Such an aristocratic body will keep down the turbulence of democracy."[50] Thus, as Paul notes, "The right wing Federalists . . . led by Hamilton and later by Marshall, had early regarded the judiciary as potentially the key bulwark of conservative defense."[51] Yet just as judicial review could serve the propertied Federalist interests, the doctrine could also be found in the arguments of anti-Federalists. Fear of legislatures was clearly a two-edged sword.

One who would understand the significance of judicial review for the Founders does well to start from the fact that in 1787 there was widespread fear of oppression by a remote federal government centered largely in dread of 'legislative despotism.'[52]

Jeffersonian support

Support for judicial review by Jeffersonians can trace its roots to the existence of natural law doctrine and its espousal by the Puritans as seen in the work of Winthrop. Winthrop notes the deficiencies of positive law as pronounced by *legislatures.*

Those who make laws . . . are also men subjecte to Temptations, and may also miscarrye through Ignorance, headlessnesse, or sinister respects: And it is not hard, to prove, that the Lawe makers, in all States, have Committed more and more pernitious errors than the Judges.[53]

Winthrop's characterization of the unique features of the judiciary are central to any understanding of judicial review in the American political tradition, and while Jefferson himself did not support judicial review, he often echoed the bulk of Winthrop's argument.

All of the powers of government, legislative, executive and judiciary, result to the legislative body. The concentrating of these in the same hands is precisely the definition of despotic government. It will be no alleviation that these powers will be exercised by a plurality of hands . . . 173 despots would surely be as oppressive as one . . . An elective despotism was not the government we fought for.[54]

To the extent that Jeffersonians could subscribe to Winthrop's conception of the nature of judicial power, judicial review could serve as a means to avert despotic government. Clearly Jefferson himself was not "mystified" by the judicial robes, yet "judicial magic" did serve to ingratiate judicial review to many Jeffersonians. Thus, the doctrine created strange bedfellows, serving as a rallying cry for both Federalists and Jeffersonians; the former supporting the doctrine as a protection from the excesses of mass democracy, and the latter supporting it as the very means by which to maintain such a mass democracy.

Pragmatic support

That judicial review could serve so many masters attests to the underlying pragmatic nature of support for the doctrine. Such "pragmatism" may, in fact, be seen as a manifestation of the seemingly "theoretical" American approach to politics, particularly as demonstrated during the formative years of our constitutional development. The basic pragmatism inherent in the doctrine of judicial review follows directly from the consequences of possible judge-made errors as compared to the much more severe societal consequences of legislative errors. Thus, John Winthrop noted,

If a Judge should sometymes erre in his Sentence; through misprision, or Temptation; the error or fault is his owne: and the injurye or damage extends not farr: but an error in the Lawe resteth upon the Ordinance it selfe, and the hurt of it may reache far, even to posteritye, there is more unrighteousness, and dishonor, in one unjust Lawe than in many unjust Sentences.[55]

Further, it was legislative despotism the founders feared, and not necessarily the despotism of courts. The work of Charles Beard becomes instructive in viewing judicial review as a pragmatic, non-doctrinaire response to the need the founders saw for a firmly founded, economically based government. In Beard's formulation, judicial review was just one of several bulwarks against populism. In a similar vein, Corwin notes that "judicial review was expedient, since the judiciary had control of neither the purse nor the sword; it was the substitute

offered by political wisdom for the destructive right of revolution."[56] Some authoritative organ was clearly needed to interpret the meaning of the vague formulations of the Constitution and, in large measure, judicial review can be seen as a "peculiarly" pragmatic, non-ideological American response to a glaring need.

What is the basis of this power . . . of . . . no limit save self-restraint? Why did the country let the court—let it?—insist that it should have this power? What is the magic? There is no magic. It is the most commonplace of situations. When a great people finds that there are certain things they want done, and no one specifically appointed to do the work, a job to be done and no one named to do it, they look around. When an applicant appears, shovel on his shoulder, they take him. He proves quiet, industrious, and discreet. What if he does go on a drunk now and then? He sobers off and goes to work again. Before you know it, John is a fixture. He likes his job. He is a good worker. He's a member of the family. No one else seems to know how to do the work so well.[57]

Curtis aptly portrays the importance of tradition and the basic pragmatism inherent in delineating a constitutional system out of a largely unspecified constitutional framework. Yet pragmatism cannot be the whole answer, for pragmatic men could have looked elsewhere to delegate a reviewing authority in governmental affairs. Such was, in fact, the reasoning behind demands for a Council of Revision in the original constitutional convention. While Chief Justice Marshall argued against the wisdom of allowing the legislature to be limited by limits they set for themselves, Bickel has noted that the Constitution limits "the power of the Courts as well, and it may be equally absurd, therefore, to allow the courts to set the limits."[58]

We are finally ready to address the question, then, of why *judicial* review? To this point we have attempted to demonstrate that review of some sort followed in the tradition of several different strands of American political thought. Yet to more fully understand the implications of and for *judicial* review, we must begin to view the peculiar role played by courts, judges, and the gloss of legality in American political thought.

A necessary principle

The principle of fundamental and superior constitutions, as well as defined and limited legislative powers, was necessary but not sufficient for the establishment of the American doctrine of judicial review. The role of "judicial magic" and the American conception of "the people" were both crucial to the assertion of the judicial review power in America. For the origin of the review power and its special relationship with the judiciary we may return again to the common law view of courts as outlined by Lord Coke. In his doctrine, the source of judicial power was not strictly based on or limited by constitutionalism but, rather, was inherent in the judicial office itself. "Common right and reason" were talents peculiarly held by judges and enforceable by them. That law was the special province of judges went far towards legitimizing judicial review.

As the law derives a semblance of eternal stability from this idea of Coke's that the law is over all government, so tradition lends a feeling of ancient stability to the Court. As the laws we enact are felt to be only a part of Law itself, so the Court feels that it belongs in a judicial lineage that is far older than the Constitution which it is interpreting and expounding. The Court, in fact, was already sitting and had been sitting for centuries before the Constitution was entrusted to its keeping, and Marshall's announcement of the doctrine of judicial review was, in one sense, the most natural thing in the world.[59]

Behind the common law conception of the judicial function there often lay an implicit intricate interrelationship between the role of the judge, and his position on earth as a representative of God; this corresponds to the natural law input of the common law. As early as the work of John Winthrop in America we get a clear portrayal of the place of the judiciary. Winthrop writes of special "parts and gifts, as the word of God requires in a judge,"[60] and implores, ". . . may we not . . . trust him (God) to give . . . muche wisdom . . . to such Judges as he shall sett up after us?"[61] While American legality is not simply the reflection of the common law, as we have argued, it is clear that the "religious" nature of the judicial calling survived well beyond the era of our Constitution's framing, and served for many as sufficient justification for the legitimacy of judicial review. Thus, Perry Miller notes of the legal profession in general that it "operated under a religious sanction, even when engaged in the most hairsplitting disputation."[62]

For some, the connection between religion and adjudication has been quite a direct link. Theodore

Dwight Woolsey, an ex-President of Yale, said in the post-Civil War period that, "Judges . . . are in no sense representatives of the people or the king, or of any will whatever . . . In a higher sense they are not representatives of the community nor of its chief magistrates, but of justice and of God! . . . They are in fact more immediately servants of God than any other men who manage the affairs of a country."[63] Similarly, Perry Miller cites the words of Jesse Bledsoe in 1827. "An able and upright judge does, among men, perform the office of God's viceregent. The ministers of religion, as is their duty, may show the divine anathema pointed against crime and unrighteousness; but it is the sword of law, wielded by the judge, which, from its nearness and immediate effect, operates most strongly to deter from their commission."[64]

We need not assert that all of America saw judges as the representatives of God on earth to make the more important and general point that judges have been viewed, in a sense, as a special breed of men. The "high priest" status of members of the Bar may, in part, be traced to the use of complex legalisms and "mystical" Latin phraseologies by judges and lawyers. While not accepting the "divine" element of judging, most Americans have at least been willing to grant the judicial process a peculiarly nonpolitical status.

This is a country that has most emphatically rejected the divine origin of government . . . To tell the truth, this leaves a void, which we seek somehow to fill, disguising what we are doing under different names . . . Likewise the Court's power seems to be more than can rationally be ascribed to its competence in its work. There seems to be some undisclosed factor in the equation, and its presence is indicated by excessive admiration.[65]

In the American conception, "men" were viewed as subject to acts that were arbitrary and capricious, yet "law" was seen as stable and enduring. "'Equal Justice Under Law,' we read as we enter the . . . home of the United States Supreme Court . . . In our minds takes shape a picture of impartial, impersonal judges applying traditional and immutable principles of law so as to render absolute justice to all men. Here there is no uncertainty, no mere whim or caprice, no arbitrary edict by man over man."[66] We need not look very far before seeing countless instances of the "peculiar" role of the American judiciary in our system of government.

Hamilton, for example, asserts in *Federalist 78*

that the Court, "may truly be said to have neither Force nor Will, but merely judgment."[67] Similarly, Madison stated in the Virginia convention, "Were I to select a power which might be given with confidence, it would be the judicial power."[68] Largely due to a mysticism of their own making, judges and lawyers were able to take a unique place in the American scheme of things. As Miller notes, "The figure of John Marshall loomed as the paragon of reason, as vivid a symbol to the American imagination as Natty Bumppo."[69]

Miller also notes that:

Again and again the lawyers impressed upon the democracy the idea that to attain distinction at the Bar required so severe an intellectual discipline that few could ever even hope to measure up to it. They devised a litany in which the awesome terms were regularly flung out. The law "demands the energies of the most powerful minds, and exhausts all the stores of learning." The profession is allied to every department of human knowledge: it must with the metaphysician explore the mysterious powers of the mind, with the logician it must master the rules of evidence, with the moral philosophers ascertain the duties and obligations of men, with the artisan it must learn methods and processes. In short, said Warren Dutton, "it calls to its aid all that the wisdom and experience of past times has recorded, and, in its highest exercises, becomes a model of all that is captivating or powerful in eloquence."[70]

In the landmark case of *Marbury v. Madison* Chief Justice Marshall asserted that it was "emphatically the province and duty of the judicial department to say what the law is,"[71] and we may cite with great understanding John Randolph's reaction to another of Marshall's opinions: "All wrong, all wrong, but no man in the United States can tell why or wherein."[72]

Thus, in large part, the acceptance of judicial review and the unique potential of America for the development of the doctrine rested upon "an act of faith" that judges alone "knew" the law. As evidence that this was indeed the case Americans relied upon a myriad of diverse authorities from the common law to the founding fathers themselves.

Says Montesquieu: "Judges are no more than the mouth that pronounces the words of the Law." Mr. Pope in his article in the Harvard Law Review . . . insists upon the belief in 1787 that judges knew the law, while others had only opinions on it.[73]

Further, as Daniel Webster noted:

The president may say a law is unconstitutional, but he is not the judge . . . If it were otherwise, then there would

be not a government of law, but we should all live under the government, the rule, the caprices of individuals.[74]

And, finally, we return to Hamilton in *Federalist 22*: "Laws are a dead letter without Courts to expound and define their true meaning and operation."[75]

The final link

Only one more link remains to be established to answer the question, why *judicial* review? While we have demonstrated that judges were invested by the populace with God-like qualities, it would be oversimplistic to equate them directly with God's will on earth. (Although this reasoning process was practiced by some.) The "missing link" may be found in the place of "the people" in American political thought and the acceptance of the judiciary as the representative not necessarily of God on earth but, perhaps more importantly, as the surrogate for "the people." Like so many other constructs, the importance of "the people" in the American system may be traced to the common law whose very name notes the locus of sovereignty in lawmaking. Sovereignty in America was identified with "the people" who were viewed both as the source of, as well as the location of, ultimate governing power. When Jefferson critiques judicial review, the role of "the people" becomes his primary argument. "But the Chief Justice says, 'there must be an ultimate arbiter somewhere.' True, there must, but does that prove it is either party? The ultimate arbiter is the people of the Union . . ."[76] Yet in his opposition to judicial review, Jefferson fails to take note of the ultimate coup which the Court has accomplished; that is, the identification of its pronouncements with the will of "the people." Bickel notes the apparent paradox involved.

The root difficulty is that judicial review is a countermajoritarian force in our system. There are various ways of sliding over this ineluctable reality. Marshall did so when he spoke of enforcing, in behalf of "the people," the limits that they have ordained for the institution of a limited government.[77]

Marshall, and several other justices, simply exercised the potential of the mystique that contemporary attitudes toward the judiciary afforded them. He disavowed any desire for judicial supremacy nor, alternatively did he support legislative supremacy. Rather, the will of "the people" was superior to both and the judges were the "oracles" of this "will." This theme is not unique to Marshall, but was widely echoed in the constitutional era and has reappeared with regularity ever since. Byrce states, "the Supreme Court is the living voice of the Constitution . . . that is, of the will of the people expressed in the fundamental law they have enacted."[78] The argument was stated most precisely in its pre-*Marbury v. Madison* form by Hamilton in *Federalist 78.*

It is not . . . to be supposed that the Constitution could intend to enable the representatives of the people to substitute their will to that of their constituents. It is far more rational to suppose that the Courts were designed to be an intermediate body between the people and the legislature, in order, among other things, to keep the latter within the limits assigned to their authority. The interpretation of the laws is the proper and peculiar province of the courts. A Constitution is, in fact, and must be regarded by the judges as a fundamental law . . . That which has superior obligation and validity ought, of course, to be preferred . . . The Constitution ought to be preferred to the statute. The intention of the people to the intention of their agents. Nor does this conclusion by any means suppose a superiority of the judicial to the legislative power. It only supposes that the power of the People is superior to both; and that when the will of the legislature, declared in its statutes, stands in opposition to that of the people, declared in the Constitution, the judges ought to be governed by the latter rather than the former.[79]

Hamilton's argument, and its virtual repetition by Marshall in *Marbury v. Madison,* successfully performed an admirable "sleight of hand." Until their pronouncements, the representatives of the people were, by and large, viewed as "the people." Yet as the judicial version of the Constitution became accepted as "the Constitution," likewise did the judiciary substitute itself as "the people." Alpheus T. Mason succinctly states the essence of the "judicial magic" through which the Court interposed itself as the representatives of "the people" of 1789, a position which it apparently still holds in the eyes of many Americans.

The fiction is that constitutional interpretation consists in finding meanings that can be clear only to judges. To them the purport of the Constitution is obvious; to the President and Congress, its meaning is hidden and obscure. The only final and authoritative voice of the Constitution is a majority of the Supreme Court, and its every version, gleaned from a sort of brooding omnipresence, has the special virtue of never mangling, distorting, or changing the original instrument. The continuing myth is that the Court does not govern, nor

does it affect those who do. What really controls is the immortal, unchanging instrument of 1789.[80]

In the final analysis, the American concept of the judicial function was and is a somewhat more "acceptable" version of the earlier Puritan conception. "The Puritan covenant had been that of God with his elect; the American covenant was an act of the people" speaking with their original, collective voice.[81] For the Puritans, "Judges are Gods upon earthe: Therefore, in the Administrations, they are to holde forthe the wisdome and mercye of God."[82] While not necessarily the manifestation of God on earth, early on the American judiciary interposed itself between "the people" who had ratified the American covenant and the current government. In such a way the judiciary became the living voice of "the people." In asserting this role, opposition to the judicial branch strong enough to deny it its coup could never be mounted. Largely, this could be credited to the unique position that judges were able to command in the American mind, traceable to the Common Law, the Puritans, and the trappings of legality in early American society. The consequences of this for the American doctrine of judicial review are telling, as the doctrine could be more readily accepted, and more easily legitimized and justified when the substantial powers were held by a body lacking both "force" and "will."

A continuing role

We have demonstrated that American pragmatism played a key part in the genesis of the doctrine of judicial review. Such pragmatism has also played a critical role in the doctrine's exercise and continued legitimacy. In a government based on separation of powers and checks and balances, the need arises for checking the potentially awesome power of judicial review. Yet any external check on this aspect of judicial power would fly in the face of the entire rationale for the legitimacy of judicial review. If justices were a "peculiar" breed of men how could an external check be justified? American pragmatism again supplies what has proven to be, at most times, a workable answer. In balancing the checks, the Court must simply check itself. As Justice Iredell stated, "That such a power in the Judge may be abused is very certain; that it will be, is not very probable."[83]

Advocates of "judicial supremacy" have often

criticized the Court for what they feel is excessive exercise of judicial self-restraint. Such arguments stress that it is the Constitution, and not the questionable statute that should be given the benefit of the doubt. Some have gone so far as to say that judicial self-restraint is, "Plainly a betrayal of the very basis on which the whole doctrine of judicial review has been based. A betrayal of the rights of the litigant, and the judicial duty owed him by the Court."[84] Nevertheless, it is essential to any discussion of judicial review to recognize that judicial self-restraint has had a long and honored history, and to the extent that judicial review was, and has been legitimized, its limits have always been implicitly recognized.

An essential maneuver in the exquisite strategy by which the Courts maintained their cause, despite the rising tide of democracy, was a prolongation of their advocacy of the Common Law into fervent adherence to the principle of judicial restraint. As long as they insisted upon this self-limitation, who could attack them?[85]

In the very next breath, after advocates had argued for the necessity of judicial review, they argued coincidingly for judicial self-restraint. Indeed, Hamilton himself, for example, stressed the importance of precedents for the courts, the very touchstone of judicial self-restraint.

To avoid an arbitrary discretion in the Courts, it is indispensable that they should be bound down by strict rules and precedents which serve to define and point out their duty in every particular case that comes before them.[86]

The same theme was continually sounded by a majority of the early members of the American judiciary.

Justice Iredell said in 1798 that because the authority to declare a legislative act, federal or state, "void, is of a delicate and awful nature, the Court will never resort to that authority but in a clear and unjust case." "A very clear case," said Justice Chase. In *McCulloch v. Maryland*, Marshall indicated that something like a "bold and plain usurpation, to which the Constitution gave no countenance," was required to invoke the exercise of judicial annulment. In *Fletcher v. Peck* . . . Marshall said, "The question whether a law be void for its repugnancy to the Constitution, is, at all times, a question of much delicacy which ought seldom, if ever, to be decided in the affirmative, in a doubtful case . . . The opposition between the Constitution and the law should be such that the judge feels a clear and strong conviction of their incompatibility with each other." This attitude carried over, as is evidenced by the remark of Justice Bushrod Washington in 1827, "It is but a decent respect due to

the wisdom, the integrity, and the patriotism of the legislative body by which any law is passed to presume in favor of its validity until its violation of the Constitution is proved beyond all reasonable doubt." (*Ogden v. Saunders*)[87]

What is demonstrated by the above statements is the final pragmatic thrust at making the doctrine of judicial review a palatable one. In essence, the logic of the doctrine itself has been turned around and the ultimate question being addressed becomes one not of ascertaining the "true" meaning of the Constitution, but rather of deciding whether specific legislation can be sustained. Judicial review when aligned with the doctrine of judicial self-restraint becomes primarily a "negative" and/or defensive power, as opposed to a much more problematical and less acceptable positive initiating power. When viewed from this perspective, the review power can be seen as amenable to several opposing schools of governmental philosophy in America.

Marbury v. Madison has proved to be one of those very special occurrences that mark an epoch in the life of the republic. Culminating the great achievements of the Constitutional Period, it accomplished the transition from perpetuity to efficacy, from immutability to adaptation, and from heavenly to judicial sanction. Finally, it introduced an unending colloquy between the Supreme Court and the people of the United States, in which the Court continually asserts, "You live under a Constitution but the Constitution is what we say it is," and the people incessantly reply, "As long as your version of the Constitution enables us to live with pride in what we consider a free and just society, you may continue exercising this august, awesome and altogether revocable authority."[88]

These remarks are instructive in emphasizing the crucial interrelationship between judicial review and judicial self-restraint. We need only casually scan the periods during which the most severe Court curbing activity has occurred (i.e., the New Deal period, post-*Brown* decision Warren Court, etc.) to recognize that such efforts have coincided with periods during which a philosophical commitment to judicial self-restraint, even on the most abstract level, has been abandoned by the Court. Indeed, historical perspective helps us to understand the contemporary controversies about the appropriate scope of the judicial role as played out in the contemporary dialogue between the William Brennan and Edwin Meese jurisprudential camps.

Conclusion

We have attempted to demonstrate that judicial review was able to develop in America as a consequence of several distinct facets of American political thought which, while often in opposition to each other, were mutually amenable to and supportive of judicial review. This is not to say that all Americans of every persuasion welcomed the doctrine with open arms and gave it full sway. Rather, we have argued that the doctrine itself is such a multifaceted one that virtually all in America could support it because of at least one of its facets or, at worst, that a significant and vigorous opposition to the doctrine could not be mustered. Corwin has most completely captured the eclectic nature of the American experience which led to the ability of the landmark case of *Marbury v. Madison* to serve as the culmination of several distinct trends.

Upon this latent talent the problems of the times acted as incentive and stimulant, eliciting from it suggestion after suggestion which it needed but the ripe occasion to erect into institutions composing a harmonious whole . . .

1. from Massachusetts and New Hampshire came the idea of this ordered and regular procedure for making constitutions, with the result . . . of furthering the idea . . . of the legal character of the constitution.

2. from New Jersey, Connecticut, Virginia, Rhode Island and perhaps New Hampshire came the idea of judicial review, partly on the basis of the doctrine of the right of revolution and partly on the basis of the doctrine of certain principles fundamental to the Common Law that had found recognition in the State constitutions.

3. from North Carolina . . . came the idea of judicial review based squarely on the written constitution and the principle of the separation of powers.

4. from various sources came the idea that legislative power, instead of being governmental power in general, is a peculiar kind of power.

5. from various sources came the idea that judicial power exercised as it habitually was under the guiding influence of Common Law principles was naturally conservative of private rights.

6. from various sources came the idea that the judiciary must be put in a position to defend its prerogative against the legislative tendency to absorb all powers, and this idea was connected with the idea of judicial review both in the relation of means and of ends.

7. from the Congress of the Confederation came the idea that the Articles of Confederation and treatises made under them were rightfully to be regarded as part and parcel of the law of every State paramount, moreover, to conflicting acts of the State legislatures and enforceable by the State Courts.

Probably no one public man of the time shared all these ideas when the Philadelphia Convention met. But the able membership of that famous body was in a position to compare views drawn from every section of the country. Slowly, by a process of discussion and conservation, these men . . . discovered the intrinsic harmony of the ideas just passed in review; discovered, in other words, that the acceptance of the others also, that each implied a system embracing all.[89]

Perhaps Corwin has overidealized the "intrinsic harmony" of the American experience in a misplaced effort to prove that the American outcome was, somehow, "natural." Such an approach is not really necessary and is, to some extent, misleading. In examining the peculiar American phenomenon of judicial review we have chosen to emphasize its eclectic nature. Post-revolutionary America was the site of numerous conflicts which often became serious points of contention in the general and ongoing Federalist/Democratic-Republican debate.

We have argued, however, that several facets of the judicial review doctrine enabled *all* people to at least *accept*, if not actually support the power. While Jefferson clearly opposed judicial review, it seems equally clear that a Jeffersonian could, in good conscience, support the doctrine because of its natural law and limited government orientation. Staunch Federalists, on the other hand, could support the doctrine for distinctly different reasons; namely its alleged tendency to control popular majorities. Two further tendencies served to make the doctrine acceptable in the American context. First was the entire dimension of "judicial magic" whereby all aspects of legalism possessed a mystique allowing the doctrine of judicial review to appear both less dangerous and more "natural." Judges, after all, were not "creating" the law, but were simply "midwives" lacking "force" and "will." Yet despite all of this, the American experience was a particularly pragmatic one, and "judicial magic" only appears to be functional when the judiciary has adhered to narrow limits self-imposed on judicial review, the adherence to judicial self-restraint.

We have argued that in addressing the seemingly unanswerable question of whether judicial review was part of the framers' "intentions" an equally important question has been largely ignored. We have attempted to demonstrate not that judicial review was "intended," but, rather, that it is clearly consistent with several facets of American political thought and that it emerged in America, whether strictly "intended" or not, in a peculiarly amenable and ripe environment.

NOTES

This article originally appeared in Volume 71, Number 2, August-September 1987, pages 68-79. It is dedicated to Alpheus T. Mason whom I had the good fortune to serve as a Graduate Teaching Assistant a decade and a half ago. His love for and deep commitment to American constitutionalism kindled my interests and the legacy of his scholarship well informs our bicentennial celebration.

1. Hyneman, THE SUPREME COURT ON TRIAL 114 (New York: Atherton Press, 1964).
2. Dumbauld, editor, THE POLITICAL WRITING OF THOMAS JEFFERSON 147 (New York: Liberal Arts Press, 1955).
3. Corwin, THE DOCTRINE OF JUDICIAL REVIEW 9 (Princeton: Princeton University Press, 1914).
4. Curtis, LIONS UNDER THE THRONE 12 (Boston: Houghton Mifflin Co., 1947).
5. Haines, THE AMERICAN DOCTRINE OF JUDICIAL SUPREMACY 18 (New York: Macmillan Company, 1914).
6. Dumbauld, *supra* n. 2, at 107.
7. Corwin, *supra* n. 3, at 31-32.
8. *Id.* at 32.
9. Berger, CONGRESS V. THE SUPREME COURT 251 (Cambridge: Harvard University Press, 1969).
10. Carr, THE SUPREME COURT AND JUDICIAL REVIEW 45 (New York: Holt, Rinehart and Winston, 1942).
11. Berger, *supra* n. 9, at 50.
12. *Id.* at 53.
13. *Id.* at 15-16.
14. *Id.* at 15-16.
15. *Id.* at 43.
16. Corwin, *supra* n. 3, at 38.
17. Haines, *supra* n. 5, at 27.
18. Corwin, *supra* n. 3, at 18-19.
19. Berger, *supra* n. 9, at 182.
20. Corwin, COURT OVER CONSTITUTION 22 (Princeton: Princeton University Press, 1938).
21. Corwin, *supra* n. 3, at 29-30.
22. Corwin, *supra* n. 20, at 22-23.
23. Haines, *supra* n. 5, at 34.
24. Carr, *supra* n. 10, at 41-43.
25. Corwin, *supra* n. 3, at 29-31.
26. Boudin, GOVERNMENT BY JUDICIARY, volume 1, 11-12 (New York: WIlliam Goodwin, Inc., 1932).
27. Miller, THE LIFE OF THE MIND IN AMERICA 241 (New York: Harcourt, Brace, and World, Inc., 1965).
28. Haines, *supra* n. 5, at 21.
29. Corwin, *supra* n. 20, at 5.
30. Dewey, MARSHALL VERSUS JEFFERSON: THE POLITICAL BACKGROUND OF MARBURY V. MADISON 65 (New York: Alfred A. Knopf, 1970).
31. Haines, *supra* n. 5, at 23-24.
32. Miller, *supra* n. 27, at 165.
33. Haines, *supra* n. 5, at 177.
34. Levy, (ed.), JUDICIAL REVIEW AND THE SUPREME COURT 46 (New York: Harper Torchbooks, 1967).
35. Haines, *supra* n. 5, at 24.
36. Carr, *supra* n. 10, at 47.
37. Cahn, (ed.), SUPREME COURT AND SUPREME LAW 16 (New York: New York University Press, 1954).
38. *Id.* at 4.
39. Morgan, PURITAN POLITICAL MAN 101 (New York: Bobbs-Merrill Company, Inc., 1965).
40. Levy, *supra* n. 34, at 44-45.
41. *Id.* at 45.
42. Cahn, *supra* n. 37, at 2.

43. Carr, *supra* n. 10, at 48.
44. Marbury v. Madison, 1 Cranch 137 (1803).
45. Carr, *supra* n. 10, at 49.
46. Corwin, *supra* n. 3, at 37.
47. Berger, *supra* n. 9, at 72.
48. Fairfield, (ed.), THE FEDERALIST PAPERS 228 (New York: Doubleday and Company, Inc., 1961).
49. Beard, THE SUPREME COURT AND THE CONSTITUTION 95 (New York: The Macmillan Company, 1916).
50. *Id.* at 91.
51. Paul, CONSERVATIVE CRISIS AND THE RULE OF LAW 231 (Ithaca: Cornell University Press, 1960).
52. Berger, *supra* n. 9, at 8.
53. Morgan, *supra* n. 39, at 156.
54. Dumbauld, *supra* n. 2, at 222-224.
55. Morgan, *supra* n. 39, at 157.
56. Corwin, *supra* n. 3, at 59.
57. Curtis, *supra* n. 4, at 46.
58. Berger, *supra* n. 9, at 183.
59. Curtis, *supra* n. 4, at 64.
60. Morgan, *supra* n. 9, at 123.
61. *Id.* at 153.
62. Miller, *supra* n. 27, at 186.
63. Curtis, *supra* n. 4, at 53-54.
64. Miller, *supra* n. 27, at 186.
65. Curtis, *supra* n. 4, at 53-54.
66. Carr, *supra* n. 10, at 1-2.
67. Fairfield, *supra* n. 48, at 227.
68. Berger, *supra* n. 9, at 185.
69. Miller, *supra* n. 27, at 119-120.
70. *Id.* at 136.
71. Marbury v. Madison, *supra* n. 44.
72. Rostow, THE SOVEREIGN PREROGATIVE: THE SUPREME COURT AND THE QUEST FOR LAW 87 (New Haven: Yale University Press, 1962).
73. Corwin, *supra* n. 3, at 63-64.
74. *Id.* at 22.
75. Fairfield, *supra* n. 48, at 55.
76. Dumbauld, *supra* n. 2, at 148.
77. Bickel, THE LEAST DANGEROUS BRANCH 16 (New York: Bobbs-Merrill Company, 1962).
78. Rostow, *supra* n. 73, at 122-123.
79. Fairfield, *supra* n. 48, at 229.
80. Mason and Beaney, AMERICAN CONSTITUTIONAL LAW, 4th edition, 18 (Englewood Cliffs: Prentice-Hall, Inc., 1968).
81. Miller, *supra* n. 27, at 217.
82. Morgan, *supra* n. 39, at 152.
83. Haines, *supra* n. 5, at 181.
84. Curtis, *supra* n. 4, at 25.
85. Miller, *supra* n. 27, at 236.
86. Fairfield, *supra* n. 48, at 232-233.
87. Berger, *supra* n. 9, at 338-339.
88. Cahn, *supra* n. 37, at 25.
89. Corwin, *supra* n. 3, at 38-41.

Judicial review: the usurpation and democracy questions

Whatever its origins, judicial review is a fact of political life. Debate continues, however, as to whether or not it is consistent with the spirit and form of democratic government.

by Albert P. Melone and George Mace

It is emphatically the province and duty of the judicial department, to say what the law is . . .
—John Marshall in *Marbury v. Madison*

Although it may be inferred, there is no explicit mention of judicial review in the Constitution. The only "express wording" that supports that power is the oath of office, the same oath taken by other members of the national government.[1] Therefore, the justification for judicial review requires more than an inspection of the wording of the basic document. Indeed, the justification in *Marbury v. Madison* (1803)[2] rests not only upon an *interpretation* of words, but equally upon an interpretation of a much more nebulous *intent* of the entire document.

The first issue explored in this article concerns the establishment of judicial review, which has been questioned from Jefferson's time by many who insist that the Court usurped power when claiming this function. For them, there is no constitutional justification—implicit or explicit. They insist that the founding fathers never intended to invest the judiciary with such power. Thus, we will seek to answer the question best phrased by historian Charles A. Beard: "The Supreme Court—'Usurper or Grantee?' "[3]

The second part of this article concerns the matter of Court rulings which, in the final analysis, seem to be legislative mandates emanating from *lawmakers* who are not directly accountable through the electoral process. This has led some to charge

that such a power wielded by the judiciary is not consistent with the spirit and form of democratic government.

These two problems are closely linked. Those who believe judicial review is not democratic portray the judiciary, not as the unambiguous spokespersons of the Constitution, but as so many individuals who express their own personal attitudes or group interests. To them, the judiciary is little more than an outrageous oligarchy masquerading in the black robes of constitutional impartiality. The history of these issues forms the foundation for the analysis that follows.

Those interested in other issues such as the judicial capacity[4] and interpretivism[5] debates necessarily must face the fundamental questions explored in this article. If the federal judiciary may not legitimately exercise review and if that power is incompatible with democracy, then no amount of interpretation, selective use of power or its carefully considered timing may excuse its exercise.

The usurpation question

Judge John B. Gibson's 1825 dissenting opinion in the Pennsylvania Supreme Court case of *Eakin v. Raub*[6] is the classic statement addressing the usurpation of power issue. It is considered by many the most effective answer given to John Marshall's famous arguments in support of judicial review.[7] Judge Gibson weaves at least six related points.

First, he states that the ordinary and essential powers of the judiciary do not extend to the annulling of an act of the legislature.[8] In other words, the everyday duty of courts is to interpret the meaning of laws. Today, we would call this the duty of statutory interpretation; and indeed, courts spend considerable time and effort in deciding what the legislature meant when it enacted a given piece of legislation, and how the legislation should be interpreted, given the facts of the particular case or controversy before it. This task, argues Gibson, is the ordinary and essential aspect of judicial power.

Secondly, Judge Gibson argues that what is good for one co-equal branch of the government should be good for the others. He claims that it would be viewed as a usurpation of judicial power if the legislature should attempt to reverse a Supreme Court decision. Yet, it is not regarded as a usurpation of legislative power when the judiciary holds a statute unconstitutional.[9] This argument is all the more cogent in the light of twentieth century experience. Interest groups have attempted, and sometimes succeeded, in reversing controversial Supreme Court decisions by proposing the rewriting of statutes to avoid previously held unconstitutional provisions, removing appellate jurisdiction or even campaigning for constitutional amendments. Defenders of Court decisions will often appeal to a sense of deep commitment to the Court as the guardian of the Constitution.[10] Though reason may require equal regard for the authority of the legislative branch, as Gibson points out, the judiciary occupies a special status within the governmental system, unaffected by the rules of logic.

Third, Gibson argues that the concept of checks and balances does not include the idea of a judicial veto. Within the legislative branch itself, a proposal must pass through two legislative chambers. If the framers intended to impose the judiciary as an additional barrier, they would have explicitly granted to the judges the power, instead of leaving the matter in doubt.[11]

Fourth, Gibson takes up the matter of the oath, which John Marshall regarded as a high moral duty. For Gibson, the oath of office taken by judicial officers, or for that matter any government official, extends only to supporting the Constitution as far as it extends to official conduct. If one's duty does not entail excursions into the legislative realm, neither does one's oath.[12] This conclusion gives rise to a rhetorical question that we may treat as Gibson's fifth point.

Does a judge violate the Constitution when he permits an unconstitutional legislative act to stand? "No!" Gibson says. The enactment and the interpretation of a legislative act are not concurrent. In other words, the judge does not adopt unconstitutional legislation as his own simply because he interprets it. Members of the legislative branch enact legislation, not the judiciary.[13]

The sixth major point states that if the legislature enacts an unconstitutional law, the people may petition their elected representatives to repeal it. If the judiciary makes a mistake, then a constitutional amendment is needed. The former remedy is clearly preferable to the latter one, given the relatively drastic and cumbersome process of amending a constitution.[14]

The remainder of Gibson's famous dissent is an exposition of the authority of state courts under the Constitution. However, what is of lasting value is his contribution to the debate over judicial review. Interestingly, Gibson later recanted his bold view because the Pennsylvania legislature had "sanctioned the pretensions of the courts to deal freely with the acts of the legislature, and from experience of the necessity of the case."[15]

Judicial self-restraint

Forty years after Gibson's death, James B. Thayer stood before the Congress on Jurisprudence and Law Reform on August 9, 1893, to read one of the most influential papers ever delivered on the subject of judicial review.[16] After noting with favor Judge Gibson's dissent, he went on to argue for the view he had adopted early in life. If the Supreme Court exercised judicial review at all, he said, it must be with great restraint; it may declare acts void only when their constitutionality was beyond all reasonable doubt.

The Harvard law professor reviewed carefully the historical antecedents to the establishment of judicial review. He came to the skeptical conclusion: "[t]he judiciary may well reflect that if they had been regarded by the people as the chief protection against legislative violation of the constitution, they would not have been allowed . . . incidental and postponed control."[17] Yet, Thayer accepts judicial review as a legitimate judicial function, and not a per se usurpation of legislative power. What is unacceptable is the employment of judicial review in those instances in which reasonable persons may disagree. Judicial review should be reserved for those cases where there is no "reasonable doubt" that the legislature enacted an unconstitutional law.[18]

Thayer counsels for judicial self-restraint because the very independence of the judiciary may be jeopardized without it. He argues that repeated and unnecessary use of the judicial veto could excite institutional jealousy and diminish public reverence for the laws. He acknowledges that judges are part of the political process and therefore should ". . . apply methods and principles that befit their task."[19] It is this view of the Court's relationship with the other branches of government that clearly distinguishes advocates of judicial self-restraint from others—whether these be mechanistic rule-oriented absolutists on the one hand, or, on the other hand, activist judges committed to using courts to right the many wrongs abroad in the land in the manor of a superlegislature.

This famous essay is the foundation on which Justices Holmes, Brandeis and Frankfurter constructed their judicial philosophies. All three were associated with Harvard and connected with Thayer as faculty member or student. All three acknowledged the intellectual impact of Thayerism upon their own thinking. The three justices represent the most articulate spokespersons for judicial self-restraint from 1902 to 1962. While all three made unique contributions to constitutional law, reading the judicial opinions of each provides scholar and practitioner alike with the finest primer available in any form on the doctrine of judicial self-restraint. Consider the dissent from the Supreme Court's social Darwinist activist era at the turn of the century through the mid-1930s. Also reflect on the opposition to the writing of the Bill of Rights into the Constitution as a prohibition against state power through the 1950s and early 1960s and beyond. The legacy of Holmes, Brandeis and Frankfurter is unmistakable.[20]

The timelessness of the Thayer article is evident when considering contemporary criticisms of the Supreme Court. The charge that the Supreme Court has become a policy-making institution, with little regard for popular opinion and proper deference toward the legislature, is one that modern conservative ideologues, including those in the Reagan administration, have trumpeted with great resonance. Yet, the political noise directed against the Court is not limited to this age. The same arguments were directed against the Court by liberals in an earlier age who opposed the Court's tendency to strike down social and economic legislation designed to protect the masses against economic wealth and power.

Without intending undue cynicism, we must point out from a historical perspective that positions on judicial activism versus restraint often turn on whose ox is being gored. Yesterday's liberals often criticized the Court for is activism; today, it is the conservatives who condemn the Court for the same sin. Though this fact does not alter the validity, if any, of Professor Thayer's views, it nonetheless reinforces his basic underlying assumption of the Supreme Court as a political institution.

Judicial review as obligation

In the face of rising controversy surrounding the Court's activism in apparent opposition to government regulation of the economy, Associate Justice Horace H. Lurton in 1911 defended the institution against its critics.[21] Few men were more suitable for the task, whether from conviction or deed.

Justice Lurton argues that public opinion and the oath of office are not sufficient guarantees insuring that legislators will stay within constitutional boundaries when promulgating laws. Lurton proceeds from the premises first enunciated by Montesquieu in *The Spirit of the Laws* (1748). The great French scholar of the eighteenth century concluded that liberty could not be maintained without a separation of powers between the legislative, executive and judicial functions. Lurton argues that American history supports the contention that the exercise of judicial review is an obligation of the judiciary as a guarantor of liberty.[22]

Not only is early case law presented in support of judicial review, but Lurton asserts also that its practice was accepted by the people in the early years of the republic. Unfortunately, however, the enormous mass of new immigrants, "unaccustomed to democratic government," consider the judicial veto as a usurpation of legislative authority.[23] Justice Lurton then proceeds to instruct that in a government of laws there is no such thing as unlimited power. Rather, all power is delegated.

Thus, when courts exercise judicial review they are not legislating or employing uncontrolled political power; they are applying the elementary principle that ". . . the acts of an agent in excess of his authority do not bind his principal." Judges in such instances have no choice but to ". . . enforce the constitution as the law of highest obligation."[24]

There is an unstated premise in Lurton's argument. It is that law and politics are somehow separate and distinct; the judges' role is simply to find the law, not to make it. Indeed, the widespread belief that legal rules are superior to individual choice is the genesis of the phrase: a nation of laws, not of men. The ideology of legalism summarized in this phrase has as much attraction today as it did when Lurton wrote his article over three-quarters of a century ago. The search for neutral principles of law and objectivity in decision making is a recurring theme in American law. The current so-called interpretivism or intentionalism debate championed by Attorney General Edwin Meese and Robert Bork, among others, is but the latest variation on an old theme. As long as humans believe that their decisions should be based upon principles transcending self-interest and subjectivity, essays such as Lurton's will be written. Yet, how we believe we ought to behave is not always how we *in fact* behave. The confusion of a value prescription for a factual description is as common to judges as it is to ordinary mortals.

Rebutting judicial review

Justice Lurton's vigorous defense of judicial review was answered contemporaneously with an equally spirited essay. Louis Boudin, a New York labor lawyer and prominent member of the American Labor Party during the early part of this century, challenged Lurton's arguments.[25] The debate reached well beyond cloistered academic halls. The fact is the Supreme Court deployed constitutional concepts, such as substantive due process and liberty of contract, to strike down legislation designed to protect working persons. Organized labor and progressives viewed the Supreme Court at the turn of the century as an important force of reaction and opposition.

Boudin sets out to make two major points. First, he presents evidence to discredit Justice Lurton's claim that judicial review was intended by the framers of the Constitution. Second, he argues that as a matter of fact, the power of judicial review as exercised by the turn of the century Supreme Court is nothing less than revolutionary.

The author maintains that judicial review was not a recognized power at the time of the American revolution. He argues that the authority was not recognized in England, and that Lurton's reliance on the writings of Montesquieu is misplaced.

The failure of John Marshall to cite so-called existing precedents from state courts was wise because, according to Boudin, the "precedents" do not demonstrate opinion in favor of judicial review, but its very opposite.[26]

Boudin examines evidence concerning the framers' intent. He concludes that although some who gathered at Philadelphia favored judicial review, given their explicit silence on the subject, ". . . the great majority of the Framers never suspected a general power of the judiciary to control legislation could be interpreted into the new constitution."[27]

Citing Judge Gibson's dissent approvingly, Marshall's decision in *Marbury v. Madison* is characterized by Boudin in the first instance as "amazing."[28] Boudin also makes two additional points worthy of consideration. First, the *Marbury* decision related particularly to judicial power, and not to general legislation. It is one thing for the Supreme Court to defend the judicial branch against legislative encroachment; it is quite another to claim the Court is the sole and binding interpreter of the Constitution. Second, Jefferson won the immediate battle because Marbury was denied the commission he sought. Thus, the unpopular Federalist attempt to stack the judiciary with the party faithful was spoiled. The decision in *Marbury* provoked no extended public debate because it had no practical importance. The lack of a huge public outcry should therefore not be interpreted as acceptance of judicial review.[29]

If one line of reasoning fails to convince judge and jury, try another. This is true even if the two arguments proceed from different premises. This typical lawyer tactic is employed by Boudin in his "brief" against the then contemporary Supreme Court. He first makes the case that there is nothing in the pre-convention history, court precedents, intent of the framers and Supreme Court decisions to justify judicial review. Boudin then argues, in essence, that if all the arguments just presented are rejected, and one accepts the exercise of judicial review as a legitimate authority, the contemporary Court has nonetheless employed the power improperly.[30] In short, a posture of self-restraint is prescribed. Let the policy judgments of the legislatures stand, Boudin says. If the legislative branch violates the Constitution, the best protection against such abuse is the people, not the courts. At this point in the essay, Boudin reads very much like Thayer.

Boudin ends his argument with a consideration of how the Supreme Court abused its power in a number of important recent cases. Boudin argues that the Court's conservative majority substituted their personal policy views for that of legislatures. The Court's famous decisions in *Lochner v. New York* (1905), *Adair v. United States* (1908), and others are pointed to as proof that there are not "plain and simple" rules of constitutional interpretation as claimed by Justice Lurton. "On the contrary, there are now practically no rules at all,"[31] said Boudin. Once again, we are reminded of contemporary criticism. The principal difference is that since the mid-1950s, the critical voices come from the political right, instead of the political left.

The intent of the framers

Mr. Boudin's accusations and those of his fellow doubters did not pass unnoticed. A popular Columbia University professor, later to become president of both the American Historical Association and the American Political Science Association, answered the complaint.[32] Through an examination of the direct and indirect declarations of certain members of the Philadelphia Convention and the "general purpose and spirit of the federal Constitution," Charles A. Beard concludes that judicial review was not usurped; it was intended by the framers. The evidence adduced in support of his conclusion, and the assumptions underlying his research methodology, not only shed light upon the usurpation question, but also point to the many difficulties inherent in constitutional interpretation.

Beard begins his argument by conceding that the delegates to the Constitutional Convention did not consider a proposition to grant the judicial branch veto power over legislative acts. In fact, none was submitted. A council of revision was proposed that would have joined a number of judges with the executive to revise laws passed by Congress.[33] According to Beard, however, that is a different proposition from judicial review. It may be legitimately asked whether this difference is sufficiently dissimilar to sustain Beard's point. Later in the article, Beard cites the apparent support of certain delegates for the revisionary council proposition as persuasive evidence of their belief in judicial review. Logic militates against arguing on the one hand that judicial review and the revisionary

proposition were not the same; and then, on the other hand, suggesting that if a delegate favored the revisionary proposition, he probably also favored judicial review. In any event, Beard claims the "question of judicial control . . . did not come squarely before the Convention, in such form that a vote could be taken."[34]

The bulk of Beard's article is devoted to the difficult question of what the framers intended. He prefaces this research approach with the caution that any such inquiry must be incomplete because new research could uncover additional information. However, the search for intent is fraught with even greater difficulties, not the least of which are its underlying assumptions. These are succinctly outlined by Professors Walter Murphy and C. Herman Pritchett in their standard modern text.[35]

The first assumption is that future generations should be bound by the specific intentions of the framers, not the general principles that guided their actions. If the assumption is accepted, then Americans will be constitutionally mired in the eighteenth century. In this view, the Constitution must be interpreted as a set of rules that can be clearly understood as articulated by the framers. In fairness, both Beard and his intellectual antagonist, Boudin, silently accept this questionable assumption. Yet given the nature of the argument, it is reasonable for Beard to search for specific intent. It is Boudin and others who claim that, because the framers were silent on the matter of judicial review, they could not have intended to make it a part of the Constitution. Beard uses evidence of the specific intent of the individual framers to counter this point.

The second assumption underlying the search for the framers' intent is more difficult to defend. It is that the framers had a single intention. In fact, it is probable that they had many different, sometimes contradictory and even irreconcilable "intentions." Indeed, the Philadelphia Convention was not an exercise in ascertaining the "general will" or Confucian harmony. Rather, it was a matter of compromise, logrolling and negotiation about matters that do not lend themselves to simple solutions. The politics of such a setting renders the ascertainment of a solid and unified group intention difficult at best.

Beard mitigates the problem of intent by breaking the group down into its constituent parts, namely, each individual delegate. He does this by examining the debates at the Convention, public comments made after Philadelphia, congressional votes and the letters and private documents of many of the delegates.

He does not examine the views of all 55 delegates to the Philadelphia Convention. Rather, Beard first investigates the views of what he calls the leading or the most influential members of the Convention.[36] He concludes that, of these, not less than 13 believed that judicial power extended to the nullification of an act of Congress. He adds four more delegates to his total by virtue of their subsequent votes in support of the Judiciary Act of 1789.[37] Of the less influential delegates, six either expressed themselves in favor of judicial review or approved of it by virtue of their votes on the 1789 act.[38] [Beard's reference to the Judiciary Act is to that part of the law dealing with federal-state relations under the Constitution's Supremacy Clause. The argument supposes that favoring judicial review of state actions is the equivalent of support for judicial control over congressional acts. Though the two are related, one should consider whether it is reasonable to support the federalism principle without favoring third branch veto over congressional enactments. Finally, with respect to the Judiciary Act, it must be pointed out that the methodological problems inherent in ascertaining legislative intent are, in principle, similar to those met when studying constitutional intent.]

We are not persuaded that the evidence presented for each delegate's position on judicial review is clear and convincing. Beard's best case argument does not add up to even a majority of the delegates favoring judicial review. He finds that 23 were for judicial review, 5 were against review, and the views of the remaining 27 are unknown. Edward S. Corwin, whose authority ranks with that of Beard's, found only 17 in favor of judicial review.[39] Nevertheless, both scholars insist that the framers intended judicial review. It is troublesome nonetheless that as influential as the 23 or 17 delegates may have been, it requires considerable faith in their leadership abilities to conclude that all, most, or even a majority of the delegates would have voted for judicial review if the proposition were presented squarely to them.

However, as one progresses through Beard's presentation, it is discovered that numbers are not everything. Beard's fall back position is clear enough: ". . . the Constitution was not designed to be perfectly explicit on all points and to embody definitely the opinions of a majority of the Convention . . . ."[40] If this is true, then why did Beard make the case for the specific intent of as many convention delegates as he could? Beard does not rest his case with the submission of evidence on the framers' intentions. He continues the "brief" against Boudin and other named and unnamed opposing counsels by addressing the remaining usurpation charges and evidence.

Constitutions are not only framed, they are also ratified. Beard presents admittedly fragmentary evidence on this point. He offers information from the debates in 4 of 13 state ratifying conventions in support of his argument that those who ratified the Constitution favored judicial review.[41] Beard is also unimpressed by arguments that state judicial opinions do not serve as adequate precedents for judicial review.[42] Finally, Beard defends John Marshall against the charge that he created judicial review out of whole cloth. Beard points out that the concept was known within legal circles at the time of the founding; indeed, before the decision in *Marbury*, the Supreme Court had alluded to judicial review in a number of decisions.[43]

Reasonable persons may disagree on the usurpation question. It may be true, as former Chief Justice Warren Burger has stated, "[i]t is now accepted that the original assertion of the power was not judicial usurpation as Jefferson considered it."[44] However, whether that acceptance is based upon reasoned analysis or political reality is another matter altogether.

The compatibility question

Behind the usurpation of power question lurks the equally difficult issue of the compatibility of judicial review with democratic values. Democratic sensibilities are offended by nine persons voiding acts of popularly selected representatives of the people. Moreover, the judiciary is independent of the people and their elected representatives. The result is a third branch free from popular control. Is judicial review a menace to popular democracy? Alternatively, is review a way to perfect democratic government? In essence, is there any way to reconcile the practice of judicial review with democratic theory?

We first consider the arguments of Robert Yates, a leading opponent of the ratification of the proposed constitution crafted at Philadelphia. Yates,

Alexander Hamilton and John Lansing had composed the New York delegation to the Constitutional Convention. Yates and Lansing walked out on the Convention some two and one-half months before its work was completed. The two joined other Americans in making speeches, writing pamphlets, essays and letters. Collectively, they came to be called Antifederalists. The other side of the debate was represented successfully by the Federalists.

As is often the case for winners and losers, much is widely known about Federalist thought, but little is understood about Antifederalist thinking. Fundamentally, this loosely knitted group believed the great choice facing humankind was either despotism or republicanism. The latter is based on consent of the governed or self-government, and the former is insured by force. Antifederalists believed the proposed constitution granted too much power to the people's representatives without providing an effective counter check. They reasoned that privileged people would benefit from the proposed constitution at the expense of ordinary people. Unless restrictions could be placed on all three constitutional branches of the central government, they feared, the potential for despotism would become a reality. Though they lost the ratification debate, Antifederalist ideology was largely responsible for the addition of the Bill of Rights to our constitutional structure.[45]

Writing under the pseudonym of "Brutus," Robert Yates, then a judge of the New York Supreme Court, makes the case against the excesses of Article III. In the process of showing why the new government would prove destructive of political happiness, he argues that due to the nature of judicial review, members of the Court have such overwhelming power they could ". . . mould the government into almost any shape they please."[46]

For the most part, this follows from two facts. First, there was no limit to the amount of power the Court could imply from the Constitution since interpretation would not be restricted to the "letter" of the Constitution, that is, to the "words in their common acception." Thus, the Court could build through implication from nebulous "spirit" and "intent" of the document. Second, and even more to be feared, the Court was not held accountable to either the people or their representatives. As such, the Court constituted a will, independent of society, which could be "controlled" only by an appeal to the sword.[47]

Yates was one delegate to the Philadelphia Convention who had no doubt the proposed constitution contained within its meaning the power of judicial review. He finds it particularly alarming because the judges are ". . . rendered totally independent, both of the people and the legislature, both with respect to their offices and salaries. No errors they may commit can be corrected by any person above them, if any such power there be . . . ."[48]

The probable impact of the federal judiciary upon the States' rights was central to Antifederalist republican principles and concerns. Every enlargement of national power will restrict state power, Yates believed. This will happen, he said, because the necessary and proper clause of Article I, section 8, may be interpreted by the federal judiciary to permit the Congress to do ". . . which in their best judgement is best."[49] To be sure, the employment of the "elastic clause" has been a source of continuing controversy over the 200-year history of the Constitution.

Though Yates approves of judicial independence, he argues that the type of independence contained in the proposed constitution was unknown anywhere in the world, including England. Judges in both England and under the proposed constitution hold office during good behavior and possess fixed salaries. In England, Parliament may override judicial decisions but no such analogous power was contemplated for the would-be Congress of the United States.[50]

Yates' interpretation of history is important. English judges were given life tenure and salary guarantees so that the king would no longer influence them to support royal claims to the detriment of the liberties of the people. The great difference is that in the United States, there is no hereditary monarch with a vested interest in maintaining power at the expense of liberty. Government officials are elected in this country by the people and are consequently controlled by them. There is no need, according to Yates, to create uncontrolled power unless the goal is autonomy, not from a despotic king, but from the democratic tendencies of a free people.[51] Alexander Hamilton addresses this very point.

The Federalist papers

As with the Antifederalists, ratification proponents of the proposed constitution published their arguments. These appeared in New York newspapers from October 27, 1787, to August 16, 1788. Alexander Hamilton, James Madison and John Jay, writing under the name "Publius," prepared 85 short essays referred to as *The Federalist.*

The influential constitutional scholar Edward S. Corwin noted:

Hamilton's later argument in Federalist 78 and 81 seems to have been inspired by the effort of Yates, an opponent of the Constitution to inflate judicial review to the dimensions of a bugaboo, and thereby convert the case for it into an argument against the constitution.[52]

This seems all the more apparent when we look to *Federalist* 29, published in the *Daily Advertiser* on January 19, 1778, coincidently with the Brutus letters. Hamilton observed:

In reading many of the publications against the Constitution, a man is apt to imagine that he is perusing some ill-written tale or romance, which, instead of natural and aggreable images, exhibits to the mind nothing but frightful and distorted shapes—
"Gorgons, hydras, and chimeras dire"; discoloring and disfiguring whatever it represents, and transforming everything it touches into a monster.

Returning to this theme in *Federalist* 78, Hamilton wrote of his constitutional adversaries', ". . . rage for objection, which disorders their imaginations and judgments." He proposed, nevertheless, to discuss those unreasoned objections in the light of constitutional provision for the appointment and tenure of judges, the partition of authority to various courts and the relation of those courts to one another. Of all these, the major objection was ". . . the tenure by which the judges are to hold their places: this chiefly concerns their duration in office; the provisions for their support; and the precautions for their responsibility."

The crux of the matter lay in the constitutional provision for responsibility. Hamilton's argument is precisely what we would expect it not to be. Rather than showing the accountability of the judiciary to the people or how their will is not insulated from or independent of society, Hamilton instead showed a lack of direct responsibility, and why this should be celebrated and not dreaded. The reason, as Madison had observed in *Federalist* 48, is that tyranny should be feared from the legislative branch more than any other, due to our form of government. The sort of despotism most likely in a democratic republic would follow from

". . . the encroachments and oppressions of the representative body."

If it were most likely that tyranny were to stem from the branch of government most responsible to the very source of that tyranny, the people, then it would hardly seem wise to make the judiciary responsible to that tyrannical majority when its purpose is to check it. Thus, the criticism in "Brutus" is well-founded; judicial power may be used to check the will of the people's elected representatives.

It should be understood that Hamilton is reflecting in part the views of the commercial class in America. During the preceding decade (1777-1787), they experienced to their horror and detriment the practice of state legislatures giving in to the demands of the debtor classes. The excesses of the majority were at least one reason for scrapping the Articles of Confederation in favor of the Philadelphia proposal. Though clearly admitting that the judiciary may not be accountable to the elected representatives of the people, Hamilton argued there is no cause for alarm since the judiciary has ". . . neither FORCE nor WILL, but merely judgment; and must ultimately depend upon the executive arm even for the efficacy of its judgments."[53]

It can be discerned why the judiciary lacks force. Obviously, the judiciary must depend upon the executive branch for enforcement of its will. However, it is not so easy to understand why judicial will is only "judgment" and therefore not will. After all, if the judiciary is to check the legislative branch, it must have a will of its own, regardless of whether the success of that check depends upon executive cooperation. What Hamilton means is, insofar as the judiciary must depend upon the executive, the federal courts have no *meaningful will.*

The Court's will is not enforced unless it is also the will of the executive. Thus, while the Court and its determination of will remain independent of society in terms of responsibility, the application of that will is never independent since it occurs through the executive who is accountable. Though the judiciary can at times have a will independent of society, which differs from the will of the executive, it may not be applied, and thus is not to be feared.

Federalist 81 reinforces the view expressed in *Federalist* 78. Hamilton answers the charge ". . . the errors and usurpations of the Supreme

Court . . . will be uncontrollable and remediless."

First, it is argued that the powers of the federal judiciary are no different in principle from those enjoyed by the state judiciaries. The power of courts to limit legislative acts stems from the general theory of limited government, and does not follow directly from a novel authority granted to the federal bench in the proposed constitution. Second, it is not true, as some have claimed, that state legislatures or the English Parliament may correct an undesirable court decision. In this sense, the federal judiciary under the proposed constitution would be no more uncontrollable than those in Britain and the states. The final point is a reiteration of the least dangerous branch argument made in *Federalist* 78, with an additional point. Hamilton doubts whether judicial encroachment upon legislative prerogatives would ever become extensive. If, per chance, it does, the impeachment power can be employed: "[t]his alone is a complete security." Whatever might be the merits of Hamilton's first two arguments, historical experience points to the dubious quality of the last.

Neither Robert Yates nor Alexander Hamilton believed judicial review is democratic. Yates condemned it for that reason, while Hamilton applauded it as a necessary check on the majority. There is a third view. It is best expressed by former Yale Law School Dean Eugene V. Rostow. He argues judicial review is in fact democratic.[54]

Judicial review as democratic

It is not surprising that Rostow prefaces his seminal 1952 article by acknowledging widespread "uneasiness, and even guilt" about judicial review.[55] Certainly by the end of World War II the activist posture of the Supreme Court, which resulted in striking down state and federal government economic regulation during the first third of the twentieth century, was thoroughly discredited. Judicial self-restraint had become part of the liberal credo. However, by the late 1940s and early 1950s the difficult issues reaching the Supreme Court were no longer government regulation of the economy. Rather, issues such as First Amendment questions involving communist control, religious freedom, minority rights and the application of the Bill of Rights to the states through the Due Process Clause of the Fourteenth Amendment became salient. The liberal impulse is to come to the aid of the political minority and under-represented in soci-

ety. But how could the Supreme Court justify its intervention without renouncing the lessons of the past? Rostow attempts to show the way.

Rostow maintains that it is erroneous to define democracy solely in terms of people voting directly on every issue. The real task is to assure that both elected and appointed officials are ultimately responsible to the people for their acts. Moreover, Supreme Court justices are not the only governmental officers not held accountable through the electoral process. Other unelected officials such as admirals, generals and members of the independent regulatory agencies are not perceived to be acting undemocratically. Why then should Court justices be considered undemocratic?

Besides, Rostow continues,

. . . the final responsibility of the people is appropriately guaranteed by the provisions for amending the Constitution itself, and by the benign influence of time, which changes the personnel of courts. Given the possibility of constitutional amendment, there is nothing undemocratic in having responsible and independent judges act as important constitutional mediators.[56]

Article V of the Constitution, the amendment provision, requires a two-thirds and three-fourths vote depending upon the procedures employed; and thus, Rostow has not so subtly substituted simple majority rule with extraordinary majority rule. Also note that most recent U.S. presidents have usually appointed no more than two justices to the nine-member high court, thereby requiring special patience and faith in the "benign influence of time."

For the sake of argument, one may concede Rostow's point that the Supreme Court is ultimately responsible to the people. However, this proves only that our governmental system is based on popular sovereignty. It does not prove that the Supreme Court's use of judicial review to strike down acts of representative bodies is democratic.

Among the most important ideas contributed by Rostow to the judicial review debate is the notion that the Supreme Court may contribute to democracy by helping maintain a pluralistic equilibrium in society. It can mediate conflict between political institutions to insure the maintenance of rights for all citizens.[57] One way to judge how democratic institutions may be is to study what they do. That is, the substance of decisions may be at least as important as the procedures employed to make those decisions. Rostow attacks what he regards as the over-reliance upon judicial self-restraint as a failure to ensure the democratic character of U.S. society.[58]

Thus, democracy entails more than procedural majority rule; it also entails the protection of minority rights. Indeed, for Rostow, judicial review is not only compatible with democracy, it is, in fact, democratic.

Rostow would have been more correct had he written of the compatibility of the Supreme Court's exercise of judicial review with democracy, rather than "The Democratic Character of Judicial Review." Judicial review is neither democratic nor undemocratic; rather, it is anti-democratic.

Ironically, it is precisely the anti-democratic character of judicial review that imparts a major and beneficial contribution to the democratic system of which it is a part. In Aristotelian terms, judicial review contributes to our "good democracy."

The classic distinction between bad and good democracies is crucial to a justification of judicial review. To be sure, process plays a central role in any democracy. However, it is not the whole of the matter. A good democracy is directed to the interests of the whole people, including both majorities. The Supreme Court must resist the other branches or divisions of government when they act tyrannically, whether against majorities or minorities. When the Court exercises a check against a tyrannical majority it acts in an anti-democratic fashion. But it is precisely this anti-democratic feature, known as judicial review, that makes our governmental system a good democracy.[59]

Conclusion

The exercise of judicial review has often placed the court at the heart of political controversies, and this has resulted in the posing of serious questions concerning that role.

The first concerns the origins of judicial review. Many have insisted the Court usurped law-making power when claiming this function. The writings of Judge Gibson and Louis Boudin are illustrative of this viewpoint. Others, including Justice Lurton and Charles Beard, argue there is sufficient justification to support the conclusion that the Constitution framers intended judicial review and, together with other historical evidence, point to the conclusion that it is a desirable feature of our governmental system. Still others, such as James B. Thayer, accept judicial review as an authority prop-

erly possessed, but nonetheless, counsel restraint in its employment.

It is difficult to make a case one way or the other with absolute certitude. However, judicial review is a fact of political life, usurpation or not! The Supreme Court has exercised the authority and has gotten away with it. Albeit, the use of the judicial veto has from time to time in U.S. history generated serious opposition for the Court. Yet through it all, the high bench has been able to maintain its extraordinary authority, a power masterfully seized by John Marshall in *Marbury v. Madison*.

There is a second great and difficult query surrounding the exercise of judicial review; is judicial review compatible with democracy? Unlike the first question, the answer is less doubtful, though far from definitive and unqualified.

It is significant that both Robert Yates and Alexander Hamilton agreed that judicial review is inconsistent with the democratic principle that government ought to be accountable to the people. Yet, of course, they each came to different conclusions about its desirability. Yates, the Antifederalist, argued against the proposed constitution and judicial review because the Court would constitute a will independent of society. Hamilton applauds review because the Court's independence of society would serve as a safeguard against tyranny inflicted by the elected representatives of the people.

A third view is best expressed by Eugene Rostow. It is an argument positively proclaiming the democratic character of judicial review. According to this view, the judiciary is accountable to the people for its decisions. Further, judicial review must not be assessed solely in procedural terms; it also most be judged in terms of the ends it serves. Therefore, to the extent judicial review protects precious rights and liberties, it is consistent with democratic theory, and the justices of the Supreme Court should feel no guilt about its use.

There is at least one additional view. Judicial review is neither democratic nor undemocratic. Rather, it is anti-democratic. Because it is anti-democratic, it is consistent with the Aristotelian notion of a "good democracy." Therefore, we applaud judicial review as a functional tool in the service of important democratic values. While review is anti-democratic, it is nonetheless compatible with democracy; it operates to guard against threats to liberty and human happiness.

Whatever the legitimacy of its origins, judicial review may be justified in terms of democratic theory. It is also clear that many proponents of judicial supremacy find it difficult to defend. This is especially true when Court decisions seem removed from prevailing public opinion. Obviously, not all exercises of judicial review have placed the Court under severe attack. The justices themselves have attempted to protect the Court from attack through the exercise of judicial self-restraint. However, rational political calculation is not the only explanation for this behavior. No doubt, as Eugene Rostow explained, there is a sense of guilt surrounding the use of the judicial veto. It is an uneasiness that does not seem to disappear, despite repeated usage and the passing of time.

Supreme Court justices, judges of other courts, constitutional scholars, bar association representatives, members of Congress, the executive branch and others, have felt compelled to justify the Court's power. Though no responsible public figure has in recent years called for the end to judicial review, there have been forcefully presented criticisms of its uses and alleged misuses.

Contemporary conservatives such as Chief Justice William Rehnquist and Judge Robert Bork have written and spoken about the importance of exercising judicial self-restraint. Justice William Brennan and Judge Frank Johnson, who many would characterize as liberals, are representative of those arguing for the importance of an activist posture. Courts must function to articulate and protect valuable constitutional rights, so goes the refrain. President Ronald Reagan's Justice Department speaks of the Jurisprudence of Original Intention when interpreting constitutional provisions.[60] At the same time, there have been recurrent calls for Court curbing, including the introduction of legislation that would remove appellate jurisdiction from the Supreme Court to hear cases involving certain controversial issues.[61]

We believe the recurring debate about the Court's role is traceable to the fundamental question of legitimacy centering around the usurpation and compatibility issues. However, what is rarely acknowledged, and will be denied by many, is an underlying uncertainty about whether ordinary Americans can understand the intellectual justification for judicial review without coming to a conclusion that may contribute to the instability of the political system. A recently reported empirical study found that public confidence in the incumbents of the Court is related to judicial activism. The conventional wisdom that the Court skates on thin ice when it invalidates federal statutes is substantiated by the data.[62] However, confidence in particular justices of the Supreme Court is probably different from support for the Court as an institution. Empirical studies demonstrate that while specific support for Court decisions may wane from time to time, diffuse support for the Supreme Court remains relatively high and favorable.[63] It is also true that political elites have a tendency to come to the aid of the Court when direct institutional attacks are made upon its authority.[64] We do not have convincing empirical evidence linking a diminution of public confidence in Supreme Court justices or in the exercise of judicial review with a drastic decline in diffuse support. Nevertheless, it is conceivable that at some point public acquiescence may turn to intolerance, resulting in the removal of the deep reservoir of public support necessary for the Court to continue its historic role in U.S. politics.

Paradoxically, because the judicial review debate refuses to disappear, the use of that power is made more secure. Proponents and opponents of the judicial veto are compelled to carefully assess and reassess its costs against its benefits. The debate serves as a reminder to all that in a democratic society all power must be limited.

NOTES

This article originally appeared in Volume 71, Number 4, December-January 1988, pages 202-210. It is based on the authors' book, JUDICIAL REVIEW AND AMERICAN DEMOCRACY, published by Iowa State University Press.

1. *See* Judge Gibson's argument in Eakin v. Raub, 12 S.&R. 330 (Pa. 1825).

2. 5 U.S. (Cranch) 137, 2 L. Ed. 60.

3. Beard, *The Supreme Court—Usurper or Grantee?*, 27 POL. SCI. Q. 1 (1912).

4. Horwitz, THE COURTS AND SOCIAL POLICY (Washington, DC: Brookings Institution, 1977).

5. Grey, *Do We Have an Unwritten Constitution?*, 27 STAN. L. REV. 703-18 (1975); Berger, GOVERNMENT BY JUDICIARY: THE TRANSFORMATION OF THE FOURTEENTH AMENDMENT (Cambridge, MA: Harvard University Press, 1977); Ely, DEMOCRACY AND DISTRUST (Cambridge, MA: Harvard University Press, 1981); The Federalist Society, THE GREAT DEBATE: INTERPRETING OUR WRITTEN CONSTITUTION (Washington, DC: The Federalist Society, 1986).

6. 12 S.&R. at 343-81 (Pa. 1825).

7. Mason, Beaney and Stephenson, AMERICAN CONSTITUTIONAL LAW: INTRODUCTORY ESSAYS AND SELECTED CASES, 7th Ed. 50 (Englewood Cliffs, NJ: Prentice-Hall, Inc., 1983).

8. Eakin v. Raub, 12 S.&R. at 346.

9. *Id.* at 347.

10. Melone, SYSTEM SUPPORT POLITICS AND THE CONGRESSIONAL COURT OF APPEALS, 51 N.D.L. REV. 597-613 (1975); also see special issue of 69 JUDICATURE (October 1981).

11. Eakin v. Raub, 12 S.&R. at 351-52.

12. *Id.* at 352-53.

13. *Id.* at 353-54.

14. *Id.* at 354-55.

15. Mason, Beaney and Stephenson, *supra* n. 7.

16. Published as: Thayer, *The Origin and Scope of the American Doctrine of Constitutional Law*, 7 HARV. L. REV. 129-56 (1896).

17. *Id.* at 136.

18. *Id.* at 151.

19. *Id.* at 152.

20. Mendelson, SUPREME COURT STATECRAFT: THE RULE OF LAW AND MEN 5-17 (Ames, IA: Iowa State University Press, 1985).

21. Lurton, *A Government of Law Or A Government of Men?*, 193 N. AM. REV. 9-25 (1911).

22. *Id.* at 13.

23. *Id.* at 17.

24. *Id.* at 19.

25. Boudin, *Government by Judiciary*, 26 POL. SCI. Q. 238-70 (1911).

26. *Id.* at 243-47.

27. *Id.* at 248.

28. *Id.* at 253.

29. *Id.* at 254-56.

30. *Id.* at 264.

31. *Id.* at 267.

32. Beard, *supra* n. 3.

33. *Id.* at 3.

34. *Id.*

35. COURTS, JUDGES, & POLITICS, 4th Ed., 485-86 (New York: Random House, 1986).

36. Beard, *supra* n. 3, at 3-4.

37. *Id.* at 19.

38. *Id.*

39. THE DOCTRINE OF JUDICIAL REVIEW 11 (Gloucester, MA: Peter Smith, 1963).

40. Beard, *supra* n. 3, at 24.

41. *Id.* at 24-28.

42. *Id.* at 22.

43. *Id.* at 32-34.

44. Berger, *The Doctrine of Judicial Review: Mr. Marshall, Mr. Jefferson and Mr. Marbury*, in Cannon and O'Brien (eds.), VIEWS FROM THE BENCH: THE JUDICIARY AND CONSTITUTIONAL POLITICS 8 (Chatham, NJ: Chatham House, Inc., 1985).

45. Allen and Lloyds, eds., THE ESSENTIAL ANTI-FEDERALIST viii-xiv (Washington, DC: University Press of America, 1985).

46. BRUTUS XI.

47. *Id.*

48. BRUTUS XII.

49. *Id.*

50. BRUTUS XV.

51. *Id.*

52. COURT OVER CONSTITUTION 45-46 (Glouster, MA: Peter Smith, 1957).

53. FEDERALIST 78.

54. Rostow, *The Democratic Character of Judicial Review*, 66 HARV. L. REV. 193-224 (1952).

55. *Id.* at 193.

56. *Id.* at 197.

57. *Id.* at 203-10.

58. *Id.* at 210-23.

59. Mace, *The Anti-Democratic Character of Judicial Review*, 60 CAL. L. REV. 1140-49 (1972).

60. For a convenient compilation of recent speeches, see: THE GREAT DEBATE, *supra* n. 5, especially speeches by Attorney General Edwin Meese and Justice William J. Brennan, Jr.

61. *Supra* n. 10.

62. Caldeira, *Neither the Purse Nor the Sword: Dynamics of Public Confidence in the Supreme Court*, 80 AM. POL. SCI. REV. 1222 (1986).

63. Murphy and Tanenhaus, *Public Opinion and the United States Supreme Court: A Preliminary Mapping of Some Prerequisites for Court Legitimation of Regime Changes*, 2 L. & SOC'Y REV. 357-382 (1968); Murphy, Tanenhaus and Kastner, PUBLIC EVALUATIONS OF CONSTITUTIONAL COURTS: ALTERNATIVE EXPLANATIONS (Beverly Hills, CA: Sage Publications, 1973); Tanenhaus and Murphy, *Patterns of Public Support for the Supreme Court: A Panel Study*, 43 J. OF POL. 24-39 (1981).

64. Melone, *supra* n. 10.

Interpreting the Constitution:
the case for judicial restraint

Our constitutional plan was never meant to allow judges to impose their values instead of the original intent of the framers.

by J. Clifford Wallace

This year we celebrate the 200th anniversary of our Constitution. This remarkable document has structured our government and secured our liberty as we have developed from 13 fledgling colonies into a mature and strong democracy. Without doubt, the Constitution is one of the grandest political achievements of the modern world.

In spite of this marvelous record, we will celebrate our nation's charter in the midst of a hotly contested debate on the continuing role that it should have in our society. Two schools of constitutional jurisprudence are engaged in a long-running battle. Some contend that the outcome of this conflict may well determine whether the Constitution remains our vital organic document or whether it instead becomes a curious historical relic. The competing positions in this constitutional battle are often summarized by a variety of labels: judicial restraint versus judicial activism, strict construction versus loose construction, positivism versus natural law, conservative versus liberal, interpretivism versus noninterpretivism.

In large measure, these labels alone are of little assistance in analyzing a complex problem. Ultimately, what is at stake is what Constitution will govern this country. Will it be the written document drafted by the framers, ratified by the people, and passed down, with amendments, to us? Or will it be an illusive parchment upon which modern-day judges may freely engrave their own political and sociological preferences?

In this article, I intend to outline and defend a constitutional jurisprudence of judicial restraint.[1]

My primary thesis is that a key principle of judicial restraint—namely, interpretivism—is required by our constitutional plan. I will also explore how practitioners of judicial restraint should resolve the tension that can arise in our current state of constitutional law between interpretivism and a second important principle, respect for judicial precedent.

Interpretivism vs. noninterpretivism

What is the difference between "interpretivism" and "noninterpretivism"? This question is important because I believe interpretivism to be the cornerstone of a constitutional jurisprudence of judicial restraint. By "interpretivism," I mean the principle that judges, in resolving constitutional questions, should rely on the express provisions of the Constitution or upon those norms that are clearly implicit in its text.[2] Under an interpretivist approach, the original intention of the framers is the controlling guide for constitutional interpretation. This does not mean, of course, that judges may apply a constitutional provision only to situations specifically contemplated by the framers. Rather, it simply requires that when considering whether to invalidate the work of the political branches, the judges do so from a starting point fairly discoverable in the Constitution.[3] By contrast, under noninterpretive review, judges may freely rest their decisions on value judgments that admittedly are not supported by, and may even contravene, the text of the Constitution and the intent of the framers.[4]

Interpretivist review

I believe that the Constitution itself envisions and requires interpretivist review. To explore this thesis, we should first examine the Constitution as a political and historical document.

As people read the Constitution, many are struck by how procedural and technical its provisions are. Perhaps on first reading it may be something of a disappointment. In contrast to the fiery eloquence of the Declaration of Independence, the Constitution may seem dry or even dull. This difference in style, of course, reflects the very different functions of the two documents. The Declaration of Independence is an indictment of the reign of King George III. In a flamboyant tone, it is brilliantly crafted to persuade the world of the justice of our fight for independence. The Constitution, by contrast, establishes the basic set of rules for the nation. Its genius lies deeper, in its skillful design of a government structure that would best ensure liberty and democracy.

The primary mechanism by which the Constitution aims to protect liberty and democracy is the dispersion of government power. Recognizing that concentrated power poses the threat of tyranny, the framers divided authority between the states and the federal government. In addition, they created three separate and co-equal branches of the federal government in a system of checks and balances.

The framers were also aware, of course, that liberty and democracy can come into conflict. The Constitution, therefore, strikes a careful balance between democratic rule and minority rights. Its republican, representative features are designed to channel and refine cruder majoritarian impulses. In addition, the Constitution's specific individual protections, particularly in the Bill of Rights, guarantee against certain majority intrusions. Beyond these guarantees, the Constitution places its trust in the democratic process—the voice of the people expressed through their freely elected representatives.

Raoul Berger argues persuasively in *Government by Judiciary* that the Constitution "was written against a background of interpretive presuppositions that assured the Framers their design would be effectuated."[5] The importance of that statement may escape us today, when it is easy to take for granted that the Constitution is a written document. But for the framers, the fact that the Constitution was in writing was not merely incidental. They recognized that a written constitution provides the most stable basis for the rule of law, upon which liberty and justice ultimately depend.

As Thomas Jefferson observed, "Our peculiar security is in the possession of a written constitution. Let us not make it a blank paper by construction."[6] Chief Justice John Marshall, in *Marbury v. Madison*, the very case establishing the power of judicial review, emphasized the constraints imposed by the written text and the judicial duty to respect these constraints in all cases raising constitutional questions.[7]

Moreover, the framers recognized the importance of interpreting the Constitution according to their original intent. In Madison's words, if "the sense in which the Constitution was accepted and ratified by the Nation . . . be not the guide in expounding it, there can be no security for a consistent and stable government, [nor] for a faithful exercise of its powers."[8] Similarly, Jefferson as president acknowledged his duty to administer the Constitution "according to the safe and honest meaning contemplated by the plain understanding of the people at the time of its adoption—a meaning to be found in the explanations of those who advocated . . . it."[9] It seems clear, therefore, that the leading framers were interpretivists and believed that constitutional questions should be reviewed by that approach.

Next, I would like to consider whether interpretivism is necessary to effectuate the constitutional plan. The essential starting point is that the Constitution established a separation of powers to protect our freedom. Because freedom is fundamental, so too is the separation of powers. But separation of powers becomes a meaningless slogan if judges may confer constitutional status on whichever rights they happen to deem important, regardless of textual basis. In effect, under noninterpretive review, the judiciary functions as a superlegislature beyond the check of the other two branches. Noninterpretivist review also disregards the Constitution's careful allocation of most decisions to the democratic process, allowing the legislature to make decisions deemed best for society. Ultimately, noninterpretivist review reduces our written Constitution to insignificance and threatens to impose a tyranny of the judiciary.

Prudential considerations

Important prudential considerations also weigh heavily in favor of interpretivist review. The rule of law is fundamental in our society. To be effective, it cannot be tossed to and fro by each new sociological wind. Because it is rooted in written text, interpretivist review promotes the stability and predictability essential to the rule of law. By contrast, noninterpretivist review presents an infinitely variable array of possibilities. The Constitution would vary with each judge's conception of what is important. To demonstrate the wide variety of tests that could be applied, let us briefly look at the writings of legal academics who advocate noninterpretivism.

Assume each is a judge deciding the same constitutional issue. One professor seeks to "cement[] a union between the distributional patterns of the modern welfare state and the federal constitution." Another "would guarantee a whole range of nontextually based rights against government to ensure 'the dignity of full membership in society.' " A third argues that the courts should give "concrete meaning and application" to those values that "give our society an identity and inner coherence [and] its distinctive public morality." Yet another professor sees the court as having a "prophetic" role in developing moral standards in a "dialectical relationship" with Congress, from which he sees emerging a "more mature" political morality. One professor even urges that the court apply the contractarian moral theory of Professor Rawls' *A Theory of Justice* to constitutional questions.[10] One can easily see the fatal vagueness and subjectivity of this approach: each judge would apply his or her own separate and diverse personal values in interpreting the same constitutional question. Without anchor, we drift at sea.

Another prudential argument against noninterpretivism is that judges are not particularly well-suited to make judgments of broad social policy. We judges decide cases on the basis of a limited record that largely represents the efforts of the parties to the litigation. Legislators, with their committees, hearings, and more direct role in the political process, are much better equipped institutionally to decide what is best for society.

Noninterpretivist arguments

But are there arguments in favor of non-interpretivism? Let us consider several assertions commonly put forth by proponents. One argument asserts that certain constitutional provisions invite judges to import into the constitutional decision process value judgments derived from outside the Constitution. Most commonly, advocates of this view rely on the due process clause of the Fifth and Fourteenth Amendments. It is true that courts have interpreted the due process clause to authorize broad review of the substantive merits of legislation. But is that what the draftsmen had in mind? Some constitutional scholars make a strong argument that the clause, consistent with its plain language, was intended to have a limited procedural meaning.[11]

A second argument asserts that the meaning of the constitutional text and the intention of the framers cannot be ascertained with sufficient precision to guide constitutional decision making. I readily acknowledge that interpretivism will not always provide easy answers to difficult constitutional questions. The judicial role will always involve the exercise of discretion. The strength of interpretivism is that it channels and constrains this discretion in a manner consistent with the Constitution. While it does not necessarily ensure a correct result, it does exclude from consideration entire ranges of improper judicial responses.

Third, some have suggested that the Fourteenth Amendment effected such a fundamental revision in the nature of our government that the intentions of the original framers are scarcely relevant any longer. It is, of course, true that federal judges have seized upon the Fourteenth Amendment as a vehicle to restructure federal/state relations. The argument, however, is not one-sided. Berger, for example, persuasively demonstrates that the framers of the Fourteenth Amendment sought much more limited objectives.[12] In addition, one reasonable interpretation of the history of the amendment demonstrates that its framers, rather than intending an expanded role for the federal courts, meant for Congress (under section 5 of the amendment) to play the primary role in enforcing its provisions.[13] Thus, it can be argued that to the extent that the Fourteenth Amendment represented an innovation in the constitutional role of the judiciary, it was by limiting the courts' traditional role in enforcing constitutional rights and by providing added responsibility for the Congress.

Advocates of noninterpretivism also contend that we should have a "living Constitution" rather than be bound by "the dead hand of the framers." These slogans prove nothing. An interpretivist approach would not constrict government processes; on the contrary, it would ensure that issues are freely subject to the workings of the democratic process. Moreover, to the extent that the Constitution might profit from revision, the amendment process of Article V provides the only constitutional means. Judicial amendment under a noninterpretivist approach is simply an unconstitutional usurpation.

Almost certainly, the greatest support for a noninterpretive approach derives from its perceived capacity to achieve just results. Why quibble over the Constitution, after all, if judges who disregard it nevertheless "do justice"? Such a view is dangerously shortsighted and naive. In the first place, one has no cause to believe that the results of noninterpretivism will generally be "right." Individual judges have widely varying conceptions of what values are important. Noninterpretists spawned the "conservative" substantive economic due process of the 1930s as well as the "liberal" decisions of the Warren Court. There is no principled result in noninterpretivism.

But even if the judge would always be right, the process would be wrong. A benevolent judicial tyranny is nonetheless a tyranny. Our Constitution rests on the faith that democracy is intrinsically valuable. From an instrumental perspective, democracy might at times produce results that are not as desirable as platonic guardians might produce. But the democratic process—our participation in a system of self-government—has transcendental value. Moreover, one must consider the very real danger that an activist judiciary stunts the development of a responsible democracy by removing from it the duty to make difficult decisions. If we are to remain faithful to the values of democracy and liberty, we must insist that courts respect the Constitution's allocation of social decision making to the political branches.

Respect for precedent

I emphasized earlier the importance of stability to the rule of law. I return to that theme now to consider a second principle of judicial restraint: respect for precedent. Respect for precedent is a principle widely accepted, even if not always faithfully followed. It requires simply that a judge follow prior case law in deciding legal questions. Respect for precedent promotes predictability and uniformity. It constrains a judge's discretion and satisfies the reasonable expectations of the parties. Through its application, citizens can have a better understanding of what the law is and act accordingly.

Unfortunately, in the present state of constitutional law, the two principles of judicial restraint that I have outlined can come into conflict. While much of constitutional law is consistent with the principle of interpretivism, a significant portion is not. This raises the question how a practitioner of judicial restraint should act in circumstances where respecting precedent would require acceptance of law developed under a noninterpretivist approach.

The answer is easy for a judge in my position, and, indeed, for any judge below the United States Supreme Court. As a judge on the Ninth Circuit Court of Appeals, I am bound to follow Supreme Court and Ninth Circuit precedent even when I believe it to be wrong. There is a distinction, however, between following precedent and extending it. Where existing precedent does not fairly govern a legal question, the principle of interpretivism should guide a judge.

For Supreme Court justices, the issue is more complex. The Supreme Court obviously is not infallible. Throughout its history, the Court has at times rejected its own precedents. Because the Supreme Court has the ultimate judicial say on what the Constitution means, its justices have a special responsibility to ensure that they are properly expounding constitutional law as well as fostering stability and predictability.

Must Supreme Court advocates of judicial restraint passively accept the errors of activist predecessors? There is little rational basis for doing so. Periodic activist inroads could emasculate fundamental doctrines and undermine the separation of powers. Nevertheless, the values of predictability and uniformity that respect for precedent promotes demand caution in overturning precedent. In my view, a justice should consider overturning a prior decision only when the decision is clearly wrong, has significant effects, and would otherwise be difficult to remedy.

Significantly, constitutional decisions based on

a noninterpretivist approach may satisfy these three criteria. When judges confer constitutional status on their own value judgments without support in the language of the Constitution and the original intention of the framers, they commit clear error. Because constitutional errors frequently affect the institutional structure of government and the allocation of decisions to the democratic process, they are likely to have important effects. And because constitutional decisions, unlike statutory decisions, cannot be set aside through normal political channels, they will generally meet the third requirement. In sum, then, despite the prudential interests furthered by respect for precedent, advocates of judicial restraint may be justified in seeking to overturn noninterpretivist precedent.

Conclusion

It is obvious that courts employing interpretivist review cannot solve many of the social and political problems facing America, indeed, even some very important problems. The interpretivist would respond that the Constitution did not place the responsibility for solving those problems with the courts. The courts were not meant to govern the core of our political and social life—Article I gave that duty, for national issues, to the Congress. It is through our democratically elected representatives that we legitimately develop this fabric of our life. Interpretivism encourages that process. It is, therefore, closer to the constitutional plan of governance than is noninterpretivist review.

After 200 years, the Constitution is not "broke"—we need not fix it—just apply it.

NOTES

This article originally appeared in Volume 71, Number 2, August-September 1987, pages 81-84. It is adapted from an address given at Hillsdale College, Hillsdale, Michigan, on March 5, 1986.

1. I have elsewhere presented various aspects of this jurisprudence. *See, e.g.,* Wallace, *A Two Hundred Year Old Constitution in Modern Society,* 61 TEX. L. REV. 1575 (1983); Wallace, *The Jurisprudence of Judicial Restraint: A Return to the Moorings,* 50 GEO. WASH. L. REV. 1 (1981).

2. Wallace, *A Two Hundred Year Old Constitution, supra* n. 1; Ely, DEMOCRACY AND DISTRUST 1 (Cambridge, MA: Harvard University Press, 1980).

3. Ely, *supra* n. 2, at 2.

4. *See id.* at 43-72.

5. Berger, GOVERNMENT BY JUDICIARY 366 (Cambridge, MA: Harvard University Press, 1977).

6. *Id.* at 364, *quoting* Letter of Wilson Cary Nicholas (Sept. 7, 1803).

7. Marbury v. Madison, 5 U.S. (1 Cranch) 137, 176-80 (1803).

8. Berger, *supra* n. 5, at 364, *quoting* THE WRITINGS OF JAMES MADISON 191 (G. Hunt ed. 1900-1910).

9. *Id.* at 366-67, *citing* 4 Elliot, DEBATES IN THE SEVERAL STATE CONVENTIONS ON THE ADOPTION OF THE FEDERAL CONSTITUTION 446 (1836).

10. Monaghan, *Our Perfect Constitution,* 56 N.Y.U. L. REV. 353, 358-60 (1981) (summarizing theories of noninterpretivists).

11. *See, e.g.,* Berger, *supra* n. 5, at 193-220.

12. *See id.*

13. *See id.* at 220-29.

Interpreting the Constitution: the Supreme Court's proper and historic function

The Court's role, when all is said and done, is, and always has been, to create meaning for a Constitution that would otherwise be a hollow document.

by Jeffrey M. Shaman

Considerable criticism, frequently quite sharp, has recently been directed at the Supreme Court for the way it has gone about its historic function of interpreting the Constitution. In particular, Edwin Meese, the current Attorney General of the United States, has accused the Court of exceeding its lawful authority by failing to adhere strictly to the words of the Constitution and the intentions of the framers who drafted those words.[1]

The attorney general's attack upon the Court echoes a similar one made by Richard Nixon, who, campaigning for the presidency in 1968, denounced Supreme Court justices who, he claimed, twisted and bent the Constitution according to their personal predilections. If elected president, Nixon promised to appoint to the Court strict constructionists whose decisions would conform to the text of the Constitution and the intent of the framers. (Ironically, it is some of the Nixon appointees to the Court that Meese now accuses of twisting and bending the Constitution.)

I hasten to add that it is not only politicians who sing the praises of strict constructionism; there are judges and lawyers, as well as some scholars, who join the song. Among legal scholars, though, the response to strict constructionism has been overwhelmingly negative. There are legal scholars, for instance, who describe strict constructionism as a "misconceived quest,"[2] an "impossibility,"[3] and even a "fraud."[4]

Those who criticize the Court point to rulings during the tenure of Chief Justice Burger, most notably the decision in *Roe v. Wade*[5] legalizing abortion, as examples of illegitimate revision or amendment of the Constitution based upon the personal beliefs of the justices. Some years ago, similar charges were leveled at the Warren Court for its ruling requiring reapportionment along the lines of one person-one vote,[6] its decision striking down school prayer,[7] and other rulings, even including the one in *Brown v. Board of Education* outlawing school segregation.[8]

It should not be supposed, however, that strict constructionism is always on the side of conservative political values. In the 1930s it was the liberals who claimed that the Supreme Court was not strictly construing the Constitution when the justices repeatedly held that minimum wage, maximum hour, and other protective legislation violated the Fourteenth Amendment.[9] As the liberals then saw it, the conservative justices on the Court were illegitimately incorporating their personal values into the Fourteenth Amendment, which had been meant to abolish racial discrimination, not to protect the prerogatives of employers.

History lessons

The lesson of this bit of history seems to be that, whether liberal or conservative or somewhere in between, whoever has an ox that is being gored at the time has a tendency to yell "foul." Whenever the Supreme Court renders a decision that someone doesn't like, apparently it is not enough to disagree with the decision; there also has to be an accusation that the Court's decision was illegitimate, being based upon the justice's personal views and not the words of the Constitution or the intent of the framers.

We can go back much further in history than the 1930s to find the Supreme Court being accused of illegitimacy. In 1810, for instance, Thomas Jefferson condemned Chief Justice John Marshall for "twistifying" the Constitution according to his "personal biases."[10]

History also reveals something else extremely significant about the Court, which is that from its earliest days, the Court has found it necessary in interpreting the Constitution to look beyond the language of the document and the intent of the framers. In the words of Stanford Law Professor Thomas Grey, it is "a matter of unarguable historical fact" that over the years the Court has developed a large body of constitutional law that derives neither from the text of the document nor the intent of the framers.[11]

Moreover, this has been so from the court's very beginning. Consider, for example, a case entitled *Hylton v. United States*,[12] which was decided in 1796 during the term of the Court's first Chief Justice, John Jay. The *Hylton* case involved a tax ranging from $1.00 to $10.00 that had been levied by Congress on carriages. Mr. Hylton, who was in the carriage trade and owned 125 carriages, understandably was unhappy about the tax, and went to court to challenge it. He claimed that the tax violated section 2 of Article I of the Constitution, which provides that direct taxes shall be apportioned among the several states according to their populations. Hylton argued that this tax was a direct one, and therefore unconstitutional because it had not been apportioned among the states by population. This, of course, was years before the enactment of the Sixteenth Amendment in 1913, authorizing a federal income tax. Prior to that, Article I prohibited a federal income tax, but what about a tax on the use or ownership of carriages—was that the sort of "direct" tax that was only permissible under Article I if apportioned among the states by population?

The Supreme Court, with several justices filing separate opinions in the case (which was customary at that time), upheld the tax as constitutional on the ground that it was not direct, and therefore not required to be apportioned. What is most significant about the *Hylton* case is how the Court went about making its decision. As described by Professor David Currie of the University of Chicago Law School, the court in *Hylton* "paid little heed to the Constitution's words," and "policy considerations dominated all three opinions" filed by the justices.[13] In fact, each of the opinions asserted that apportioning a carriage tax among the states would be unfair, because a person in a state with fewer carriages would have to pay a higher tax. While this may or may not be unfair, the justices pointed to nothing in the Constitution itself or the intent of the framers to support their personal views of fairness. Moreover, one of the justices, Justice Patterson, went so far in his opinion as to assert that the constitutional requirement of apportioning direct taxes was "radically wrong," and therefore should not be extended to this case. In other words, he based his decision, at least in part, upon his antipathy to a constitutional provision.

While Justice Patterson went too far in that respect, he and his colleagues on the Court could hardly have made a decision in the case by looking to the text of the Constitution or the intent of the framers. The language of the document simply does not provide an answer to the constitutional issue raised by the situation in *Hylton*. The text of the document merely refers to "direct" taxes and provides no definition of what is meant by a direct tax. Furthermore, as Professor Currie points out, the records of the debates at the Constitutional Convention show that "the Framers had no clear idea of what they meant by direct taxes."[14] Thus, to fulfill their responsibility to decide the case and interpret the law, the justices found it necessary to create meaning for the Constitution.

Creating meaning

Indeed, it is often necessary for the Supreme Court to create meaning for the Constitution. This is so because the Constitution, being a document designed (in the words of John Marshall) to "endure for ages,"[15] is rife with general and abstract language. Those two great sources of liberty in the Constitution, the due process and equal protection clauses, are obviously examples of abstract constitutional language that must be invested with meaning. The Fourth Amendment uses extremely general language in prohibiting "unreasonable" searches and seizures, and the Eighth Amendment is similarly general in disallowing "cruel and unusual" punishment.

Even many of the more specific provisions of the Constitution need to be supplied with meaning that simply cannot be found within the four corners of the document. The First Amendment, for instance, states that Congress shall not abridge freedom of speech—but does that mean that the government may not regulate obscene, slanderous, or deceptive speech? The First Amendment also says that Congress shall not abridge the free exercise of religion—does that mean that the government may not prohibit polygamy or child labor when dictated by religious belief? These questions—which, by the way, all arose in actual cases—and, in fact, the vast majority of constitutional questions presented to the Supreme Court, cannot be resolved by mere linguistic analysis of the Constitution. In reality there is no choice but to look beyond the text of the document to provide meaning for the Constitution.

There are those, such as Attorney General Meese, who would hope to find meaning for the Constitution from its authors, the beloved and hallowed framers of the sacred text. By reputation, these fellows are considered saints and geniuses; in actuality, they were politicians motivated significantly by self-interest.

Theoretical drawbacks

But even if the framers do deserve the awe that they inspire, reliance on their intentions to find meaning for the Constitution still has serious theoretical drawbacks. In the first place, why should we be concerned only with the intentions of the 55 individuals who drafted the Constitution and not the intentions of the people throughout the nation who ratified it, not to mention the intentions of the succeeding generations who retain the Constitution? After all, even when finally framed, the Constitution remained a legal nullity until ratified by the people, and would be a legal nullity again if revoked by the people. The framers wrote the Constitution, but it is the people who enacted and retain the Constitution; so if anything, it is the people's intent about the document that would seem to be the relevant inquiry.

Moreover, there are considerable difficulties in discerning what in fact the framers intended. The *Journal of the Constitutional Convention*, which is the primary record of the framers' intent, is neither complete nor entirely accurate. The notes for the *Journal* were carelessly kept, and have been shown to contain several mistakes.[16]

Even when the record cannot be faulted, it is not always possible to ascertain the framers' intent. As might be expected, the framers did not express an intention about every constitutional issue that would arise after the document was drafted and adopted. No group of people, regardless of its members' ability, enjoys that sort of prescience. When the framers did address particular problems, often only a few of them spoke out. What frequently is taken to be the intent of the framers as a group turns out to be the intent of merely a few or even only one of the framers.

There are also constitutional issues about which the framers expressed conflicting intentions. A collective body of 55 individuals, the framers embraced a widely diverse and frequently inconsistent set of views. The two principal architects of the Constitution, James Madison and Alexander Hamilton, for instance, had extremely divergent political views. Madison also on occasion differed with George Washington over the meaning of the Constitution. When Washington, who had presided over the Constitutional Convention, became president, he claimed that the underlying intent of the Constitution gave him the sole authority as president to proclaim neutrality and to withhold treaty papers from Congress. Madison, who had been a leader at the Constitutional Convention, disagreed vehemently. And so, the man who would come to be known as the father of this nation and the man who would come to be known as the father of the Constitution had opposing views of what the framers intended.[17]

These examples demonstrate that it simply makes no sense to suppose that a multi-member group of human beings such as the framers shared a unitary intent about the kind of controversial political issues addressed in our Constitution. We can see, then, that, at best, the so-called framers' intent is inadequately documented, ambiguous, and inconclusive; at worst, it is nonexistent, an illusion.

Even if these insurmountable obstacles could be surmounted, there are other serious problems with trying to follow the path laid down by the framers. The framers formed their intentions in the context of a past reality and in accordance with past attitudes, both of which have changed considerably since the days when the Constitution was drafted. To transfer those intentions, fashioned as they were under past conditions and views, to contemporary situations may produce sorry consequences that even the framers would have abhorred had they been able to foresee them. Blindly following intentions formulated in response to past conditions and attitudes is not likely to be an effective means of dealing with the needs of contemporary society.

Locked to the past

Some scholars take this line of reasoning one step further by maintaining that the framers' intent is inextricably locked to the past and has no meaning at all for the present.[18] In other words, because the framers formed their intentions with reference to a reality and attitudes that no longer exist, their intentions cannot be transplanted to the present day. What the framers intended for their time is not what they may have intended for ours. Life constantly changes, and the reality and ideas that surrounded the framers are long since gone.

The futility of looking to the framers' intent to resolve modern constitutional issues can be illustrated by several cases that have arisen under the Fourth and Fifth Amendments. The Fourth Amendment prohibits unreasonable searches and seizures, and further requires that no search warrants be issued unless there is probable cause that a crime has been committed. Are bugging and other electronic surveillance devices "unreasonable searches?" May they be used by the police without a warrant based on probable cause? What about the current practice of some law enforcement agencies of using airplanes to fly over a suspect's property to take pictures with a telescopic camera—is that an "unreasonable search?" The Fifth Amendment states that no person shall be compelled to be a witness against himself. What about forcing a suspect to take a breathalyzer test, or a blood test, or to have his or her stomach pumped—do those procedures amount to self-incrimination that violates the Fifth Amendment?

Whatever you may think should be the answers to these questions, you cannot find the answers by looking to the framers' intent. The framers had no intent at all about electronic surveillance, airplanes, telescopic cameras, breathalyzer tests, or stomach pumping, for the simple reason that none of those things existed until well after the days of the framers. Not even Benjamin Franklin, for all his inventiveness, was able to foresee that in the 20th century constables would zip around in flying machines taking snapshots of criminal suspects through a telescopic lens.

Many of the difficulties in attempting to resolve constitutional issues by turning to the framers are illustrated by the school prayer cases.[19] The religious beliefs of the framers ranged from theism to atheism, and among even the more devout framers there was a wide diversity of opinion concerning the proper relationship between church and state. Moreover, as often happens when human beings ponder complex issues, the views of individual framers about church and state did not remain the same over time. As a member of Congress, James Madison, for example, once voted to approve a chaplain for the House of Representatives, but later decided that the appointment of the chaplain had been unconstitutional.[20] Insofar as school prayer specifically was concerned, the framers expressed virtually no opinion on the matter, for the simple reason that at the time public schools were extremely rare. Thus, the framers had no intention, either pro or con, about prayer in public schools.

Given the theoretical deficiencies of trying to decide constitutional questions by looking to the framers' intent, it should come as no surprise that this approach has been a failure when attempted by the Supreme Court. Scholars who have closely studied the Court's use of this approach commonly agree that it has not been a satisfactory method of constitutional decision making, because the Court ends up manipulating, revising, or even creating history under the guise of following the framers' intent.[21] The fact of the matter is that neither the framers' intent nor the words of the document are capable of providing much constitutional meaning.

Bare bones

What we are left with, then, are the bare bones of a Constitution, the meaning of which must be augmented by the justices of the Supreme Court. And that is exactly what the justices have been doing since the Court was first established. The overwhelming evidence of history shows that the meaning of the Constitution has undergone constant change and evolution at the hands of the Supreme Court. Through the continual interpretation and reinterpretation of the text of the document, the court perpetually creates new meaning for the document. Although it is formally correct that we, unlike the citizens of Great Britain, have a written Constitution, its words have been defined and redefined to the extent that for the most part we, like the citizens of Great Britain, have an unwritten Constitution, the meaning of which originates with the Supreme Court.

Strict constructionists argue that it is undemocratic for Supreme Court justices—unelected officials who are unaccountable to the populace—to create meaning for the Constitution. Of course, using the framers' intent to interpret the Constitution also is undemocratic; following the will of the 55 persons who supposedly framed the Constitution or the smaller group of them who actually participated in the framing is hardly an exercise in democracy.

When strict constructionists cry that the Court is undemocratic, they are ignoring that our government is not (and was not intended by the framers) to be a pure democracy. Rather, it is a limited or constitutional democracy. What this means is that there are constitutional limits to what the majority may do. The majority may not, for example, engage in racial discrimination, even if it votes to do so in overwhelming numbers. The majority may not abridge freedom of speech or the free exercise of religion or other constitutional rights guaranteed to every individual.

Article III of the Constitution states that there shall be a Supreme Court, and, in combination with Article II, decrees the court's independence from the electorate. By its very terms, the Constitution establishes a counter-majoritarian branch of government, the Supreme Court, in juxtaposition to the more democratic executive and legislative branches. This scheme reflects one of the guiding principles that underlies the Constitution—the principle of separate powers that check and balance one another. The Supreme Court's constitutionally mandated independence functions as a check and balance upon the more majoritarian branches of federal and state governments. It thereby provides a means of maintaining constitutional boundaries on majoritarian rule.

The role of the Supreme Court is to enforce constitutional requirements upon the majoritarian branches of government, which otherwise would be completely unbridled. As dictated by the Constitution, majority control should be the predominant feature of our government, but subject to constitutional limits.

Moreover, the Supreme Court is not quite as undemocratic as the strict constructionists sometimes like to portray it to be. While it is true that the justices who sit on the Court are appointed

rather than elected and that they may be removed from office only for improper behavior, it is also true that they are appointed by a popularly elected president, and their appointments must be confirmed by a popularly elected Senate. Turnover of the Court's personnel, which sometimes occurs frequently, enhances popular control of the Court. Additionally, the Court's constitutional rulings may be overruled by the people through constitutional amendment, which, though a difficult procedure, has been accomplished on four occasions.[22] Thus, while the Court is not directly answerable to the public, it is not entirely immune from popular control.

The ultimate authority

The people also have the ultimate authority to abolish the Supreme Court. That they have not done so during our two centuries of experience indicates popular acceptance of the Court's role. Admittedly, there are particular decisions rendered by the Court that have aroused considerable public outcry, but given the many controversial issues that the Court must decide, this is inevitable. More telling about the public attitude toward the Court is that the people have taken no action to curtail the Court's authority to interpret the Constitution. Indeed, the public has shown little, if any, inclination toward abolishing the Court or even restricting its powers. Despite Franklin Delano Roosevelt's overwhelming popularity, his "court-packing plan" was a dismal failure;[23] the proposal to establish a "Court of the Union" composed of state court justices which would have the power to overrule the Supreme Court evoked such widespread public disapproval that it was quickly abandoned;[24] the campaigns to impeach Justices Earl Warren and William O. Douglas never got off the ground;[25] and although various members of Congress often propose bills threatening to restrict the Court's jurisdiction, the full Congress always rebuffs those threats.[26] These experiences suggest that even in the face of controversial constitutional decisions, there has been abiding public consent to the role of the Supreme Court in our scheme of government.

The Court's role, when all is said and done, is to create meaning for a Constitution that otherwise would be a hollow document. It is perfectly appropriate for anyone to disagree with Supreme Court decisions, and to criticize the Court on that basis. But it is not appropriate to attack the court's decisions as illegitimate on the ground that they do not follow the framers' intent. Pretending to use the framers' intent to impugn the legitimacy of the Supreme Court is a spurious enterprise. The Court's legitimate function is, and always has been, to provide meaning for the Constitution.

NOTES

This article originally appeared in Volume 71, Number 2, August-September 1987, pages 80, 84-87, 122.

1. Address by Attorney General Edwin Meese, III, before the American Bar Association, Washington, DC (July 9, 1985); *Q and A with the Attorney General*, 81 A.B.A. J. 44 (July, 1985).

2. Brest, *The Misconceived Quest for the Original Understanding*, 60 B.U. L. REV. 204 (1980).

3. Ely, *Constitutional Interpretation: Its Allure and Impossibility*, 53 IND. L. J. 399 (1978).

4. Nowak, *Realism, Nihilism, and the Supreme Court: Do the Emperors Have Nothing But Robes?*, 22 WASHBURN L. J. 246, 257 (1983).

5. 410 U.S. 113 (1973).

6. Reynolds v. Sims, 377 U.S. 533 (1964).

7. Engle v. Vitale, 370 U.S. 421 (1962); Abington School Dist. v. Schempp, 374 U.S. 203 (1963).

8. 347 U.S. 483 (1954).

9. See, e.g., Boudin, GOVERNMENT BY JUDICIARY 433-34 (New York: W. Goodwin, 1932); Haines, THE AMERICAN DOCTRINE OF JUDICIAL SUPREMACY (Berkeley, CA: University of California Press, 1932).

10. Ford (ed.) 9 WRITINGS OF THOMAS JEFFERSON 275-76 (1902).

11. Grey, *Origins of the Unwritten Constitution: Fundamental Law in American Revolutionary Thought*, 30 STAN. L. REV. 843, 844 (1978).

12. 3 U.S. (3 Dall.) 171 (1796).

13. Currie, THE CONSTITUTION IN THE SUPREME COURT 1789-1888, 34 (Chicago: University of Chicago Press, 1985).

14. *Id.* at 36.

15. McCulloch v. Maryland, 17 U.S. (4 Wheat.) 316, 414 (1819).

16. *See*, Rohde & Spaeth, SUPREME COURT DECISION MAKING 41 (1976); 1 THE RECORDS OF THE FEDERAL CONVENTION OF 1787 xii-xiv (Farrand ed. San Francisco: W.H. Freeman, 1937).

17. Burns, THE VINEYARD OF LIBERTY 101-04 (New York: Knopf, 1982).

18. Wofford, *The Blinding Light: The Uses of History in Constitutional Interpretation*, 21 U. CHI. L. REV. 502 (1964).

19. *Supra* n. 7.

20. Stokes & Pfeffer, CHURCH AND STATE IN THE UNITED STATES 481-82 (Colorado Springs: Shepard's, 1975).

21. *See, e.g.*, tenBrock, *Uses by the United States Supreme Court of Extrinsic Aids in Constitutional Construction*, 27 CALIF. L. REV. 399, 404 (1939); Kelly, *Clio and the Court: An Illicit Love Affair*, 1965 SUP. CT. REV. 119, 122-25; Alfange, *On Judicial Policymaking and Constitutional Change: Another Look at the "Original Intent" Theory of Constitutional Interpretation*, 5 HASTINGS CONST. L. Q. 603, 617 (1978).

22. The Eleventh Amendment overruled the holding of Chisholm v. Georgia, 2 U.S. (2 Dall.) 419 (1793); the Fourteenth Amendment nullified, in part, the decision in Dred Scott v. Sandford, 60 U.S. (19 How.) 393 (1857); the Sixteenth Amendment nullified the holding of Pollock v. Farmers' Loan and Trust Co., 157 U.S. 429 (1895); the Twenty-sixth Amendment neutralized Oregon v. Mitchell, 400 U.S. 112 (1970).

23. "Not all the influence of a master politician in the prime of his popularity was quite enough to carry a program that would impair judicial review," McCloskey, THE AMERICAN SUPREME COURT 177 (Chicago: University of Chicago Press, 1960). The plan was rejected vehemently by the Senate Judiciary Committee. See SENATE COMM. ON THE JUDICIARY, REORGANIZATION OF THE FED. JUDICIARY, ADVERSE REPORT, S. Rep. No. 711, 75th Cong., 1st Sess. 23 (1937).

24. Pfeffer, THIS HONORABLE COURT 424-25 (Boston: Beacon Press, 1965).

25. Those who campaigned for Chief Justice Warren's impeachment were unable to have impeachment proceedings initiated against him. While impeachment proceedings were instituted against Justice Douglas, they never got beyond the subcommittee stage and were eventually forsaken. See SPECIAL SUBCOMM. ON H. RES. 920 OF THE HOUSE COMM. ON THE JUDICIARY, 91 Cong., 2d Sess., Final Report, Associate Justice William O. Douglas (Comm. Print 1970).

26. "In the fifteen years between 1953 and 1968, over sixty bills were introduced in Congress to eliminate the jurisdiction of the federal courts over a variety of specific subjects; none of these became law." Bator, Mishkin, Shapiro & Wechsler, HART & WECHSLER'S THE FEDERAL COURTS AND THE FEDERAL SYSTEM 360 (Mineola, NY: Foundation Press, 2d ed. 1973).

Actors in the Judicial Process

Judges: Judicial Selection Systems and Their Consequences

INTRODUCTION   Among all the actors in the American judicial process it is the judge who often emerges as the focal point, the participant at the heart of the courtroom who controls and directs an unfolding legal drama and often decides its outcome. The subject of judicial selection, how judges obtain their positions, has frequently engaged analysts because many think that the nature of selection processes has implications for the kinds of people chosen and, ultimately, for judicial decision making.

There are numerous judicial selection systems in the United States, including presidential appointment and senatorial confirmation for the three levels of the federal bench and elective, appointive and hybrid selection systems (which can incorporate elements of election, appointment and/or merit processes) throughout the American states. Making matters even more complex, in some states there are fundamentally different selection procedures for choosing judges for different levels of the judiciary. Indeed, given the reality of 50 distinct state judiciaries and a three-tiered federal judicial system, the possibilities for important nuances of difference among the judicial selection procedures in the United States is staggering. The articles in this section attempt to come to grips with alternative approaches to judicial selection while unraveling some of their consequences.

At the outset, Larry Berkson, in "Judicial selection in the United States," surveys the history and rationales for the alternative approaches to choosing judges in America. Berkson underlines that "the combination of schemes used to select judges is almost endless. Almost no two states are alike, and few employ the same method for choosing judges at all levels of the judiciary."

One of the systems outlined by Berkson, the elective system, is explored in the nominally nonpartisan context of Ohio by Marie Hojnacki and Lawrence Baum in "Choosing judicial candidates: how voters explain their decisions." While many analysts treat judicial elections as inherently unique because of the nature of the judicial office per se and the ethical constraints that are imposed on judicial campaigns, Hojnacki and Baum examine how such elections appear from the perspective of the voter. Contemplating judicial election behavior in the context of electoral behavior more generally and examining judicial elections empirically convinces Hojnacki and Baum that, "Differences in voting behavior between contests at the top of the ballot and those at lower levels result chiefly from differences in the amounts and kinds of information voters are provided." While one would predict, in instances where judicial campaigns become larger in scope and more issue-oriented in focus, that they would more closely resemble non-judicial electoral processes, the Ohio examples suggest that this is not necessarily the case. Judicial elections have a considerable distance to go before they will begin to supply voters with sufficient information to dramatically alter patterns of low voter turnout and low levels of candidate knowledge.

The most popular alternative to electing judges is the hybrid merit selection model in which nominating commissions generate a list of judicial candidates who, following appointment to a limited term, generally must run on an unopposed retention ballot through which they are either simply retained in office or defeated. Such selection systems have developed as a means of trying to balance the conflicting goals of judicial independence and accountability, and their operation has served as the subject of considerable scholarly inquiry. In "How minority judges fare in retention elections," Robert Luskin, Christopher Bratcher, Christopher Jordan, Tracy Renner and Kris Seago summarize what analysts have already learned about the retention election process. That is, you can't beat somebody with nobody and, consequently, retention elections result overwhelmingly in low turnout affirmative votes that continue judges in office. The question that Luskin and his colleagues specifically address is the degree to which this general finding holds true for retention elections that decide whether judges who belong to racial or ethnic minorities should continue in office. For the 10-year period examined, no correlation is found between a judge's minority status and the retention vote.

This finding should not, however, obscure the reality that different kinds of selection systems may, indeed, favor different kinds of people. Thus, for example, "at large" elections, in settings with broad, heterogeneous electorates, tend to minimize the chances for minority candidates who fare considerably better in small, narrowly drawn electoral districts where, in fact, they may constitute a majority of the voters. And, although minorities may fare as well as majorities in retention elections, it remains a matter of debate as to which selection system is more likely to lead to judgeships for minorities in the first instance. All of this suggests that alternative judicial selection systems and their consequences are complicated matters not easily characterized.

The final two selections in this section of readings, "Clinton's second term judiciary: picking judges under fire," by Sheldon Goldman and Elliot Slotnick, and "The voting behavior of President Clinton's judicial appointees," by Ronald Stidham, Robert Carp, and Donald Songer, turn our attention to federal judicial selection processes and their outcomes and consequences. Goldman and Slotnick examine judicial selection under Clinton, comparing and contrasting his selection processes and the judges he chose with those appointed by Presidents Carter, Reagan, and Bush. Interestingly, while a commitment to diversity, particularly as documented by the appointment of unprecedented numbers of women and blacks, was a hallmark of Clinton's selection behavior, such diversity did not necessarily translate into the appointment of ideologically extreme "liberal" judges, a point that is brought home in the empirical analysis by Stidham, Carp, and Songer. One possible explanation for Clinton's appointment of moderates is that he, himself, is a political moderate. Yet, as Goldman and Slotnick underscore, the political climate in which judicial selection takes place may influence who is chosen.

Indeed, the dynamics of judicial selection in the Clinton presidency changed dramatically when the Democrats lost control of the Senate midway through Clinton's first term and judges appointed by a president of one party had to be confirmed by a Senate controlled by the other party. In the best of times, divided government complicates judicial selection processes and, as the partisan impeachment processes played out during Clinton's second term demonstrated, the divided government context in which this president served deviated dramatically from the best of times. During Clinton's first term, unprecedented delays in confirmation processes and non-action on proffered candidates were suggestive of ongoing electoral politics as candidate and Senate majority leader Robert Dole sought to embarrass Clinton and capitalize on the judgeship issue. In Clinton's second term, judicial selection difficulties would continue for a presidency that severely embarrassed itself. It remains to be seen to what extent the "normal" and relatively smooth flow of advice and consent processes, even in the context of divided government, have been altered by the difficulties encountered by the Clinton White House.

Judicial selection in the United States: a special report

by Larry C. Berkson

Historically there has been considerable controversy about how American judges should be chosen. During the colonial era, they were selected by the king, but his intolerably wide powers over them was one of the abuses that the colonists attacked in the Declaration of Independence. After the Revolution, the states continued to select judges by appointment, but the new processes prevented the chief executive from controlling the judiciary.[1]

Gradually, however, states began to adopt popular election as a means of choosing judges. For example, as early as 1812 Georgia amended its constitution to provide that judges of inferior courts be popularly elected. In 1816, Indiana entered the Union with a constitution that provided for the election of associate judges of the circuit court. Sixteen years later, Mississippi became the first state in which all judges were popularly elected. Michigan held elections for trial judges in 1836.

By that time the appointive system had come under serious attack. People resented the fact that property owners controlled the judiciary.[2] They were determined to end this privilege of the upper class and to ensure the popular sovereignty we describe as Jacksonian Democracy.

During the next decade, there was little opposition to those who advocated popular elections. For example, in the New York Constitutional Convention of 1846 there was not even a lengthy discussion of the subject. As one writer has stated:

The debates on an elective judiciary were brief; there was apparently little need to discuss the abuses of the appointive system, or its failures, or why election would be better. A few delegates argued cogently for the retention of the old system, and indeed forecast the possible evils if the judiciary fell under political domination . . . .

But the spirit of reform carried the day.[3]

New York's adoption of an electoral system signaled the beginning of this trend. By the time of the Civil War, 24 of 34 states had established an elected judiciary with seven states adopting the system in 1850 alone.[4] As new states were admitted to the Union, all of them adopted popular election of some or all judges until the admission of Alaska in 1959.

No panacea

Within a short time, however, it became apparent that this new system was no panacea, and the need for reform again was recognized. For example, as early as 1853 delegates to the Massachusetts Constitutional Convention viewed the popular election of judges in New York as a failure and refused to adopt the system. One delegate claimed that it had "fallen hopelessly into the great cistern" and quoted an article in the *Evening Post* that illustrated that judges had become enmeshed in the "political mill."[5] By 1867, the subject was a matter of great debate in New York, and in 1873 a proposed amendment to return to the appointive system gained strong support at the general election.[6]

One of the main concerns during this period was that judges were almost invariably selected by political machines and controlled by them. Judges were often perceived as corrupt and incompetent. The notion of a judiciary uncontrolled by special interests had simply not been realized. It was in this context that the concept of nonpartisan elections began to emerge.

The idea of judicial candidates appearing on the ballot without party label was used as early as 1873 in Cook County [Chicago], Illinois. Interestingly, it was the judges themselves who decided to run on a nonpartisan ballot rather than doing so pursuant to a statute or some other authority. Elections in 1885 and 1893 were also nonpartisan (Cook County subsequently returned to partisan elections). By the turn of the century the idea of nonpartisan judicial elections had gained strength, and several states had adopted the idea. By 1927, 12 states employed the nonpartisan idea.[7]

Once again, criticism of nonpartisan elections arose almost as soon as such elections began. As early as 1908 members of the South Dakota Bar Association indicated dissatisfaction with how the idea was working in their state. By 1927, Iowa, Kansas, and Pennsylvania had already tried the plan and abandoned it.[8] The major objection was that there was still no real public choice. New candidates for judgeships were regularly selected by party leaders and thrust upon an unknowledgeable electorate, which, without the guidance of party labels, was not able to make reasoned choices.

The rise of commission plans

While others attacked nonpartisan elections, a number of well-known scholars, judges and concerned citizens began assailing all elective systems as failures. One of the most outspoken critics, Roscoe Pound, delivered a now classic address to the American Bar Association in 1906 on "The Causes of Popular Dissatisfaction with the Administration of Justice." He claimed that "putting courts into politics, and compelling judges to become politicians in many jurisdictions . . . [had] almost destroyed the traditional respect for the bench."[9]

Several years later in a speech before the Cincinnati Bar Association, William Howard Taft claimed that it was "disgraceful" to see men campaigning for the state supreme court on the ground that their decisions would have a particular class flavor. It was "so shocking, and so out of keeping with the fixedness of moral principles," he said, that it ought to be "condemned."[10]

Reformers claimed that the worst features of partisan politics could be eliminated through what they called a "merit plan" for selecting judges. The plan would expand the pool of candidates to include persons other than friends of politicians. Selectors would not consider inappropriate partisan factors such as an individual's party affiliation, party service, or friendship with an appointing executive so the most distinguished members of the bar, regardless of party, could be elevated to the bench.[11]

Origins of the plan are usually traced to Albert M. Kales, one of the founders of the American Judicature Society. Versions of his proposal were introduced in state legislatures throughout the 1930s. The American Bar Association endorsed a merit plan in 1937, and in 1940 Missouri became the first state to put one into effect. Today it is variously known as the Kales plan, Missouri plan, merit plan, or commission plan.

Almost none of the state plans is identical, but they do share common features. Most include a permanent, nonpartisan commission composed of lawyers and nonlawyers (appointed by a variety of public and private officials) who actively recruit and screen prospective candidates. The commission then forwards a list of three to five qualified individuals to the executive, who must make an appointment from the list.

Usually the judge serves a one- or two-year probationary period, after which he must run unopposed on a retention ballot. The sole question on which the electorate votes is: "Shall Judge __ be retained in office?" A judge must win a majority of the vote in order to serve a full term.

Judicial selection today

Today the combination of schemes used to select judges is almost endless. Almost no two states are alike, and few employ the same method for choosing judges at all levels of their judiciary. It is possible, however, to classify the states in two categories: those that appoint their judges and those that elect them. The two groups turn out to be fairly equal in number.

Appointment: Thirty-four states use commission plans to aid the governor in selecting judges (24 states and the District of Columbia use panels for initial selection, and 10 others use them only for midterm vacancies). Since 1980, 17 states adopted or extended their commission plan.

In four states—California, Maine, New Hampshire, and New Jersey—the governor appoints judges *without* using a nominating commission (subject to senatorial confirmation in Maine and New Jersey, and a five-member elected council in New Hampshire). In Hawaii, Louisiana, and Illinois, judges themselves appoint some of their colleagues. In Virginia, the legislature appoints all judges.

Elections: Partisan elections are held to select most or all judges in eight states and some judges in five other states. Nonpartisan elections are held to select most or all judges in 13 states and some judges in four states. Thus, 30 states choose some, most, or all of their judges by elections.

Another way to examine how judges are chosen is to group the states by the plans they use for each level in their court system. Again, the states are fairly evenly divided between those that elect and those that appoint their judges.

Supreme courts: Twenty-one states hold elections for judges on courts of last resort: 8 are partisan, and 13 are nonpartisan. In 24 states and the District of Columbia, nominating commissions help governors appoint these judges; in four states, the governor acts on his or her own. The legislature appoints court of last resort judges in Virginia.

Appellate courts: Seventeen states (out of the 39 that have intermediate appellate courts) elect judges to these courts: 7 use partisan elections, and 10 use nonpartisan elections. In 19 of the other 22 states, governors utilize nominating commissions to help appoint these judges. In California and New Jersey, the governor makes appointments without the help of a commission; in Virginia the legislature appoints appellate judges.

Trial courts: Forty-seven states have a single court of general jurisdiction, and 3 states have two or more courts of general jurisdiction (Indiana, Louisiana, Michigan).[12] Thirteen states hold partisan elections, and 17 hold nonpartisan elections to *initially* select judges for some or all general jurisdiction courts. Nineteen states and the District of Columbia use a nominating commission to aid the governor in appointing judges of some or all general jurisdiction courts. In 3 states (Maine, New Hampshire, New Jersey), the governor alone makes the choice. In California, local electors choose either gubernatorial appointment or nonpartisan election to select superior court judges. The legislature appoints these officials in Virginia.

NOTES

This article originally appeared in Volume 64, Number 4, October 1980, pages 176-193, and was updated in January 1992 and February 1999. It is condensed from a larger study, JUDICIAL SELECTION IN THE UNITED STATES: A COMPENDIUM OF PROVISIONS (Chicago: American Judicature Society, 1980).

1. Eight of the original 13 states vested the appointment power in one or both houses of legislature. Two allowed appointment by the governor and his council, and three vested appointment authority in the governor but required him to obtain consent of the council. Escovitz, JUDICIAL SELECTION AND TENURE 4 (Chicago: American Judicature Society, 1975).

2. Niles, *The Popular Election of Judges in Historical Perspective*, THE RECORD OF THE ASSOCIATION OF THE BAR OF THE CITY OF NEW YORK 523 (November, 1966).

3. *Id.* at 526.

4. Escovitz, *supra* n. 1, at 6.

5. Niles, *supra* n. 2, at 528.

6. *Id.* at 535, n. 46.

7. Aumann, *Selection, Tenure, Retirement and Compensation of Judges in Ohio*, 5 U. CIN. L. REV. 412, n. 11 (1931).

8. *Id.*

9. Pound, *The Causes of Popular Dissatisfaction With the Administration of Justice*, 20 J. AM. JUD. SOC'Y 178 (February, 1937).

10. Taft, *The Selection and Tenure of Judges*, 38 A.B.A. REP. 418 (1913).

11. Kales, UNPOPULAR GOVERNMENT IN THE UNITED STATES Chap. 17 (Chicago: University of Chicago Press, 1914). *See also* Harley, *Taking Judges Out of Politics*, in PUBLIC ADMINISTRATION AND POLITICS (Philadelphia: The American Academy of Political and Social Science, 1916); and Winters, *Judicial Selection and Tenure*, in Winters (ed.), SELECTED READINGS: JUDICIAL SELECTION AND TENURE (Chicago: American Judicature Society, 1973).

12. Courts of general jurisdiction are defined as having unlimited civil and criminal jurisdiction. In each of the four states, the initial method of selection for both courts is the same, although retention is different for the two courts in Indiana. Because judges in several states are selected by more than one method to serve on the same court, the following figures do not total to 50.

Choosing judicial candidates: how voters explain their decisions

The reasons Ohio voters have given for their choices of supreme court candidates resemble their decision making in elections for other offices. In both, they are related to the level of information supplied during campaigns.

by Marie Hojnacki and Lawrence Baum

Observers and students of judicial elections tend to treat them as unique in relation to contests for other offices. In part, this tendency reflects the widespread belief that judicial elections *ought* to be different. It also reflects, in the conduct of campaigns and the behavior of voters, enormous differences between judicial elections and elections for national office on which voting behavior research has concentrated.

The behavior of voters in judicial elections should not be viewed as unique. Rather, this behavior results from the dearth of meaningful information typically provided to voters in contests for judgeships. Thus, if voters were supplied with as much substantive information about judicial candidates as they currently receive about presidential candidates, their behavior would be similar in the two kinds of contests.

From this perspective, recent changes in the character of judicial elections are particularly interesting. While most of these contests follow the traditional pattern of limited scope and issueless content, a growing minority depart from this pattern by featuring larger-scale campaigns, greater media attention, and discussion of policy issues. But it is not clear whether these changes in the character of judicial contests have been sufficient to produce substantial changes in voters' responses to the candidates.

This article examines that issue. Specifically, it explores voting in judicial elections by looking at five contests for the Ohio Supreme Court in 1986

and 1988 that reflect recent changes in the character of judicial elections. It examines the impact of these changes by exploring the reasons that voters offer for their choices.

The character of judicial elections

Empirical evidence on voting behavior in judicial elections is limited, largely because of the limited survey research on judicial contests. But the available evidence indicates that voters typically know little about their choices in judicial contests.[1] Some studies have shown that voters leaving the polling place generally cannot recall the names of judicial candidates.[2] A survey of voters in two retention elections for the Wyoming Supreme Court indicated that most voters possessed very little information about the incumbent judges.[3] Further, analyses of aggregate voting data provide strong evidence that judicial voters rely heavily on name recognition and information provided by the ballot itself.[4] This reality was illustrated in 1990 by the victory of an unknown and non-campaigning challenger to an incumbent Washington Supreme Court justice that appeared to result almost solely from voters' reactions to the candidates' names.[5]

Voters, therefore, seem to be making their choices on different bases from those that predominate in elections to offices such as president, senator, and governor. Yet in this respect judicial voting does not seem to be very different from voting for other offices below the top levels. Although survey evidence is very limited, it appears that voters in contests for such offices typically operate in ways similar to those exhibited by judicial voters, relying heavily on what information they can glean from the ballot.[6]

Such behavior does not result from deficiencies in the people who vote in contests for offices below the top levels. If anything, these voters are likely to be better informed and more interested in politics than their fellow citizens who vote only in contests for the highest offices. Differences in voting behavior between contests at the top of the ballot and those at lower levels result chiefly from differences in the amounts and kinds of information voters are provided.[7] Given a much smaller volume of meaningful information, voters necessarily respond differently from the ways they respond to contests for governor or U.S. senator, and—even more—for president.[8] Thus, the most important distinction for students of judicial elections is not between judicial and nonjudicial contests but among contests in which voters receive different levels of substantive information.[9]

Differences in the information provided to potential voters affect their behavior in a number of respects. The most direct effect is on their participation in a contest: the more they know about the candidates, the more likely they are to vote. But information also affects the ways voters make their choices between candidates. In contests for the highest offices, especially president, voters are given a large and diverse body of information. As a result, they are able to make their choices on the basis of both "low-information cues" such as candidates' party affiliations, which require little knowledge to utilize, and "high-information cues" such as issue positions, which require greater knowledge.

In contrast, when much less information is provided, most voters can learn little about the choices, and they are forced to rely on low-information cues. Judicial elections generally follow this predominant pattern, with small-scale campaigns and minimal media attention. The information available to voters is further reduced by constraints on campaign appeals, particularly the ethical rule against discussion of policy issues by judicial candidates.[10]

Occasional contests for judgeships with high visibility and salient issues—including, in some instances, policy issues—have provided some exceptions to this pattern. Such exceptions have become more common in recent years, particularly

in the last decade, as a result of several related changes.[11]

First, policy issues are raised more often in judicial contests.[12] Sometimes candidates raise these issues explicitly. In other instances, issues arise implicitly or from sources other than the candidates. The most common issues have concerned criminal justice.[13] Because these issues are highly salient to many voters, and because most voters hold conservative views on criminal justice matters, candidates frequently make a direct or implied claim that they take a more conservative position than their opponent. (One California judge reportedly was attacked for failing to send defendants to state prison even though the judge heard no cases in which a prison sentence was possible.)[14] The death penalty has been an important issue at the appellate level, with incumbents in such states as Louisiana and North Carolina attacked for alleged unwillingness to uphold death sentences. In 1989 a candidate for the Wisconsin Supreme Court charged that his opponent had been too favorable to criminal defendants on an array of issues during her time on the court.[15]

Other issues have attained importance in some contests. One is abortion, the focus of a 1990 retention election for Florida chief justice.[16] In contests for the Texas Supreme Court, economic issues involving tort law have played a prominent role in the last decade, both as a source of funding and as a focus of campaigns themselves.[17]

Second, levels of campaign spending have increased substantially in some states, especially in supreme court contests.[18] This has been fueled in part by economic issues, which attract contributions from groups such as labor unions and the insurance industry. Groups concerned with economic issues sometimes contribute substantial amounts to judicial candidates even when these issues play only a limited role in the public campaigns.[19]

Finally, the issue content and high levels of spending in some judicial contests help induce closer media attention to these contests. It has become more common for newspapers and television news programs to give some continuing attention to judicial contests, and a few supreme court contests have been a major focus of media coverage.

These changes in judicial elections have the potential to produce changes in voter behavior. Provided with greater and more meaningful information about the candidates, voters might be able to make substantial use of high-information cues.

In at least one instance, it appears that voters did respond primarily to policy issues. In 1986, a heavily financed and publicized campaign against three justices on the California Supreme Court focused on their votes to overturn death sentences.[20] The three were defeated, and an election-day survey indicated this issue was the major reason why voters chose to remove them from office.[21] This result is all the more striking because California uses retention elections for its supreme court. There were no opposing candidates to raise and emphasize the death-penalty issue.

This set of contests may have been highly unusual, even among relatively visible judicial elections, because of the enormous amount of information provided to voters. In other contests that feature substantial publicity and policy issues, the volume of information may still be too low for voters to make much use of high-information cues. This would mean that changes in the conduct of judicial campaigns have had only a limited impact on the responses of voters. This article explores this question in the 1986 and 1988 contests for seats on the Ohio Supreme Court.

The election setting

Ohio voters chose three supreme court justices in 1986 and two in 1988. These contests were conducted under Ohio's peculiar system for selection of judges, in which a partisan primary election precedes a nonpartisan general election.

Historically, supreme court elections in Ohio featured small-scale campaigns and limited media coverage.[22] Possessing limited information, voters seemed to rely heavily on their perceptions of the candidates' party affiliations and their recognition of candidates' names in making their choices. But the achievement of a Democratic court majority in 1978 and the court's subsequent liberal trend on issues in labor and personal injury law attracted attention to the court. Further, in the early 1980s the state's mass media gave heavy coverage to conflicts between Democratic Chief Justice Frank Celebrezze and both his Republican colleagues and the state bar association. Even as a non-candidate, Celebrezze was a focus of attention in the 1984 supreme court contests, which were unusually visible by Ohio historical standards.[23]

Information on the judicial candidates and contests in 1986 and 1988 is provided in Table 1. In 1986, the seats of Celebrezze and two associate justices were up for election. The Republican party and groups representing businesses and tort defendants sought to defeat Celebrezze and win a Republican court majority. Labor unions, plaintiff-oriented groups, and the Democratic party made a major effort to reelect the chief justice and retain the Democratic majority. The result was a level of campaign spending in the chief justice contest far higher than in any prior Ohio judicial contest, a total of $2.8 million. The level of media attention was also unprecedented. Both spending and media attention were much lower in the two contests for associate justice, but the level of spending was still unusually high for Ohio Supreme Court campaigns. And there was considerable effort, especially by the Republicans, to link the three contests.

In a sense, candidates of the two parties competed to define the campaign issues. The Democrats, particularly Celebrezze, emphasized economic issues. They portrayed the court as serving

Table 1　Summary information on the electoral contests included in the survey

| Office | Candidates | | Winner | | | |
	Democrat	Republican	Name	%	Total spending	Recognition factor
1986:						
Governor	Richard Celeste*	James Rhodes	Celeste	60.6	$8.9	95.8
Senate	John Glenn*	Thomas Kindness	Glenn	62.5	$1.6	81.0
Treasurer	Mary Ellen Withrow*	Jeff Jacobs	Withrow	54.9	$2.2	61.7
Chief Justice	Frank Celebrezze*	Thomas Moyer	Moyer	53.8	$2.8	73.4
Associate Justice	Francis Sweeney	Robert Holmes*	Holmes	50.6	$0.5	46.4
Associate Justice	Herbert Brown	Joyce George	Brown	50.4	$0.3	48.0
1988:						
Senate	Howard Metzenbaum*	George Voinovich	Metzenbaum	57.0	$16.7	86.8
Associate Justice	Alice Robie Resnick	Joyce George	Resnick	53.2	$0.6	35.2
Associate Justice	A. William Sweeney*	Paul Matia	Sweeney	58.0	$0.4	35.9

Notes: Incumbents designated by asterisk. Winner's proportion is of the two-party vote. Total spending is in millions. Recognition factor is the proportion of the respondents who could recognize and rate the two candidates in the post-election period, averaged between the candidates.

the interests of working people against large institutions. The Republicans gave some attention to economic issues, but they emphasized Celebrezze's alleged improprieties[24] and the need to restore the court to a proper level of conduct. The state's news media supported the Republican definition of the issues, and all major newspapers endorsed the three Republican candidates. Celebrezze lost the election, and the parties split the associate justice contests. The Celebrezze defeat gave the court a Republican majority.

In 1988, two associate justice seats were contested. Both were held by Democrats, so a continuing Republican majority was assured. This fact, combined with Celebrezze's departure, greatly reduced interest in the judicial contests. Still, the associate justice campaigns were well funded and visible by historical standards. Ohio's labor unions gave a high priority to the contests, and other economic groups also provided candidates substantial funding. The Democratic candidates referred to economic issues in their campaigns, but these issues were less prominent parts of smaller campaigns than in 1986.

The five judicial contests exemplify the relatively large and more issue-oriented contests that have become more common in recent years. The 1986 race for chief justice featured an emphasis on policy issues that probably was unprecedented in Ohio judicial contests. Economic issues were also important in the associate justice contests in 1986 and 1988, though considerably less so than in the chief justice contest.

The scale of the campaigns and media coverage also were extraordinary, and it could be inferred that they provided more information to voters than in Ohio's past supreme court contests. This is supported by the level of voter participation in the supreme court elections, measured by the number of votes in a contest as a proportion of all people who turned out at the polls. Voter participation was calculated for the 26 contested supreme court races in the 1970s and 1980s. The chief justice contest in 1986 ranked first in participation by this measure, and each of the four associate justice contests stood at least 2 percent above the mean for the 1970-1988 period. The mean for the 1986 judicial contests was the highest in this period. The 1988 contest ranked third in this respect, slightly below 1984.

Ohio held several other contests for statewide office during these years. Included in voter surveys, along with the judicial contests, were races for governor and treasurer in 1986 and U.S. senator in both years. These contests were not homogeneous, but on average (as the data in Table 1 show) they were considerably more visible to voters than the contests for associate justice in either year. The chief justice contest stood out for its high visibility—the candidates were better known than those for treasurer. The nonjudicial contests can be used as reference points in analyzing voters' responses to the supreme court contests.

Reasons for the vote

In postelection telephone surveys in 1986 and 1988, voters were asked the reasons for their choices in each contest.[25] In most of the contests, they were given the opportunity to provide as many as three reasons. In the associate justice contests of 1988, they were allowed to cite a single reason.[26]

This question seems to be an ideal means to determine the bases for voters' choices, but it has some weaknesses. A body of research in psychology provides considerable evidence that people have a limited capacity to identify the reasons for their choices.[27] Scholars disagree about the implications of this evidence, and it is derived primarily from experimental situations that are not fully comparable with elections. This research, however, underlines the difficulties involved in retrieving and articulating the bases for a recent decision.

Nonetheless, the reasons that voters offer for their choices are useful in at least two respects. First, they are likely to provide accurate reports of some of the bases for voters' choices. If respondents cannot be expected to identify consistently the primary reasons for their decisions, those they do offer indicate some of what they knew about the candidates that they saw as relevant to their decisions.

Second, the reasons that voters offer can be compared across contests. The limitations these reasons suffer from are similar in different contests. As a result, meaningful comparisons can be made. For instance, the relative frequency of references to policy issues in two contests is a fairly good indicator of their relative importance in these contests. Thus, the nonjudicial contests in 1986 and 1988 can be employed as a kind of baseline for analysis of the supreme court contests.

In using the nonjudicial contests as a basis for

comparison, it must be kept in mind that substantially fewer respondents reported voting in the contests for associate justice than in the nonjudicial contests. In comparing contests, then, somewhat different sets of voters are compared.[28] Yet in a sense this difference is not a concern, because the important comparison is among the aggregate sets of voters who participate in each contest. It should be reiterated that while the nonjudicial contests are critical to this analysis of voters in the supreme court contests, the primary concern is with the latter.

To help in analyzing voters' reasons for their choices, individual responses were assigned to 16 categories. Such assignments were made more difficult by the ambiguity of some responses.[29] Still, it was possible to create meaningful categories and to assign responses to those categories with a fairly high degree of reliability.[30] The categories are described and illustrated in Table 2.

In the table, the categories (with one exception) are placed in three groups, based on the amount and difficulty of the information that generally would be required to offer responses in these categories. These groups are labelled "high information," "moderate information," and "low information." The high-information category includes references to ideology, issues, and links between candidates or voters and groups. The second group, more heterogeneous, includes responses that require more limited but meaningful information. An example is references to the actual or prospective performance of a candidate in office. Responses in the third group, such as references to familiarity with a candidate, generally require little real knowledge of the candidates and sometimes rest on information that can be inferred from candidates' names alone. References to the candidates' party affiliations were not placed in any group because of the ambiguity created by the nonpartisan ballot in judicial contests. Party might best be considered a moderate-information cue in these contests, depending in part on whether a candidate's name allowed inferences about party affiliation,[31] though it would qualify as a low-information cue in the nonjudicial contests.[32]

This categorization of reasons does not take into account the relative salience of different kinds of information to voters or voters' preferences concerning bases for their choices between candidates. One powerful determinant of the reasons that voters offer for their choices is likely to be what voters think are appropriate reasons. But voters can offer a particular reason for their choices only when they possess the information that allows them to make use of that reason. Thus, the distribution of reasons should vary with the volume of information provided to voters.[33]

Expectations for the analysis of voters' reasons can be derived from this article's general argument about cues for voting decisions. The use of high-information cues depends on the availability of large amounts of substantive information. Even in the relatively visible associate justice contests of

Table 2 Categories created for voters' reasons for candidate choice

	Description
High information reasons:	
Ideology	References to the general ideological stance of a candidate.
Issues	References to specific issues or to candidates' general issue positions.
Group reference	References to a candidate's support for/opposition to a social, economic, or other group, to voter's affiliation with a group, or to a candidate's receiving a group endorsement.
Moderate information reasons:	
Job skills	References to a candidate's skill, competence, or capability.
Office performance	References to a candidate's actual or prospective ability to perform in office, including references to a candidate's ability to accomplish specific tasks in office.
Continuity/change	References indicating the need for change or the desire to maintain the status quo, including incumbency.
Character	References to a candidate's honesty, trustworthiness, and fairness, as well as mentions of respect for a candidate.
Associations with other individuals	References to a candidate's affiliation with or support from individual political leaders, past and present.
Campaign	References to the conduct and quality of candidates' election campaigns as well as to information about the candidates obtained from the campaigns, including television advertisements.
Low information reasons:	
Personal characteristics	References to a candidate's background, personal attributes, or life experiences (i.e., experience not directly related to office).
Media	References to knowledge of a candidate obtained through the media (e.g., newspaper endorsements).
Personal knowledge	References to the voter's contact (direct or indirect) with a candidate, to family/acquaintance contact with a candidate, or to having heard about the candidate through contact with family/acquaintance.
Recognition/amount of information	Reference to receiving a greater quantity of information about a candidate, including name familiarity.
General impression	References to positive/negative overall impressions of a candidate or to comparative impressions of the candidates.
Contentless	References reflecting a random choice or no clear rationale for choice.
Party-related reasons:	References to candidate's partisan affiliations or to voters's agreement with or attachment to a party.

1986 and 1988, the volume of information remained fairly limited in comparison with the most visible electoral contests, so small numbers of reasons in the high-information group and a clustering in the low-information group were expected. (For the same reason, a relatively high proportion of voters providing no reasons for their choices was anticipated.)

In contrast, the contest for chief justice featured moderately high visibility. But voters still were provided with considerably less information than in contests for the highest offices. Thus there is the expectation of a greater diversity of reasons for choices between the candidates but still a tendency for voters to offer reasons in the low-information categories.

As noted earlier, the nonjudicial contests of 1986 and 1988 can be used as a baseline for analysis of voters' reasons in the judicial contests. The distributions of responses in the supreme court races can be gauged by comparing them with the distributions in other contests that ranged from very high to moderate in visibility.

The analysis will go beyond the categories and groups of categories to look more closely at the kinds of specific reasons that voters cited. In this way a fuller sense of voters' information and how they used it to make their choices can be gained.

Findings

This section begins with a general overview of the results. Table 3 shows the proportion of voters who offered a reason for their choices and the types of responses given in each of the nine contests. The patterns shown in the table can be arrayed against the expectations described earlier.

First, it was posited that as more information is made available, voters will be more likely to articulate reasons for their choices. The results in Table 3 strongly support this hypothesis insofar as it distinguishes between the low-visibility contests for associate justice and all the other races in 1986 and 1988. The mean proportion of voters who could articulate reasons in the associate justice contests was 83 percent. In the contests with greater visibility, the mean was 98 percent. This finding reinforces the impression that voters had unusually great difficulty in gaining information about the associate justice candidates.

Next is this article's primary concern: the types of reasons voters offered for candidate selection. As outlined above, it was expected that voters will be more likely to cite reasons based on high and moderate information levels in those contests where the highest levels of substantive information are available.

As Table 3 illustrates, high-information re-

Table 3   Levels of response and reasons for candidate choice as a percentage of all reasons provided in each contest

	Percent of voters providing a reason	Number of reasons provided	High-information reasons	Moderate-information reasons	Low-information reasons	Party-related reasons
High visibility contests						
Governor	99.2%	594	10.6%	30.8%	48.7%	9.8%
Senate-1986	99.2	558	8.8	36.7	38.5	16.1
Senate-1988	96.8	556	21.4	50.1	20.4	8.1
Average—high visibility contests	**98.4**	**569**	**13.6**	**39.2**	**35.9**	**11.3**
Moderate visibility non-judicial contest						
State treasurer	98.4	489	1.8	42.4	29.7	26.0
Moderate visibility judicial contest						
Chief justice	98.1	456	5.4	39.9	44.9	9.6
Low visibility contests						
Associate justice '86						
(Sweeney v. Holmes)	89.3	219	3.2	21.9	58.9	16.0
(Brown v. George)	93.0	261	3.1	18.8	61.3	16.9
Associate justice '88						
(Resnick v. George)	76.7	203	3.0	34.1	45.4	17.7
(Sweeney v. Matia)	74.7	169	8.3	30.8	45.0	16.0
Average—low visibility contests	**83.4**	**213**	**4.4**	**26.4**	**52.7**	**16.7**

Notes: Contests are categorized to reflect the amount of information they provide to voters. Reasons for candidate choice are categorized to reflect the amount of information voters would likely possess if they were to provide such a response (specific reasons included in each category are shown in Table 2). The averages shown for the high and low visibility contests reflect the mean percentage of voters who offered a response, the mean of each type of reason provided, and the mean number of reasons given in the high and low visibility contests, respectively.

sponses were uncommon in nearly all contests. In general, however, they were more prevalent in the contests for senator and governor than in other contests. Exceptions were the relative frequency of such responses in the 1988 associate justice contest between A. William Sweeney and Paul Matia and, to a lesser extent, in the contest for chief justice.

Reasons reflecting moderate knowledge of the candidates and campaigns also were typically more common in the relatively visible contests, especially in comparison with the associate justice contests of 1986. And, while responses based on low levels of information were the modal category in most contests, they were most predominant in the associate justice contests. They were also relatively frequent in the contest for chief justice.[34]

Finally, partisan rationales appear to be most common in the less-visible contests. Especially striking here is the frequency of such responses in the associate justice contests, despite the absence of candidates' party affiliations on the ballot. The relatively high proportions of party-based responses in the nonpartisan judicial contests may be due to the limited availability of other information about the candidates in these contests.

Comparison of the contests for treasurer and chief justice makes it clear that, at least by this indicator, there is no fundamental distinction between voters' responses to judicial and nonjudicial contests. Because the race for chief justice was rela-

tively visible and involved substantive issues, high-information reasons were distinctly more common in this contest. Low-information reasons also were more common in the chief justice contest, but references to party were particularly frequent in the race for treasurer. In a formally partisan race, such references require no prior information of the voter.

Overall, these findings fit reasonably well with expectations. In particular, although the Ohio Supreme Court contests were made more visible to voters than "typical" judicial contests, they appear to have provided voters with no more than a moderate volume of information on which to base their choices. This pattern is clear when voters' responses in the judicial contests are compared with those given in the more visible contests for governor and senator. While the findings for the nonjudicial contests do not paint a picture of a predominantly issue-oriented electorate, voters' responses to these contests appear to be based on richer information. With this difference in mind, attention can focus exclusively on the judicial contests, and the types of criteria voters used to select candidates for judicial office can be examined more closely.

The chief justice contest

Table 4 presents information on voters' responses to the chief justice contest in greater detail. The table shows both the percentage of rationales included in each of the 16 reason categories and the

Table 4   Reasons for selection of chief justice as a percentage of all reasons provided

	Percent of responses	Number of responses	Selected specific reasons
High info. reasons			
Ideology	0.4%	2	
Issues	2.4	11	pro-life, C (2); drug policy, C (2); hurt insurance business, M (1); county lawsuit with schools, M (1)
Group reference	2.6	12	pro-labor/union, C (6); bar association poll, M (2)
Moderate info. reasons			
Job skills	1.5	7	
Performance	11.4	52	good job/record, C (26); scandals, M (16); bar association trouble, M (1)
Continuity/change	5.7	26	
Character	8.8	40	all crooks, M (7); Celebrezze dishonest, M (5); lack of honesty, M (4); corruption, M (4)
Assocs. with others	0.0	0	
Campaign	12.5	57	bad ads/press/campaign of opponent, M (26); mudslinging (10); like t.v. ads (9)
Low info. reasons			
Personal characteristics	2.4	11	
Media	3.5	16	
Personal knowledge	3.7	17	
Recognition/amt. of info.	5.9	27	
General impressions	27.0	123	don't like opponent (54); like, general (12); not satisfied with opponent, M (11); heard bad things, M (7)
Contentless	2.4	11	
Party-related reasons	9.6	44	

Note: A specific reason followed by C or M indicates that all such responses were mentioned by Celebrezze (C) or Moyer (M) voters, exclusively. The number of voters who provided a specific response is shown in parentheses.

frequency of several specific responses mentioned by the voters that were most common or that illuminated reactions to the candidates and contests.

The data suggest that, for the most part, voters based their choices on a low to moderate level of knowledge about the candidates and campaigns. In particular, direct or indirect references to issues comprise a relatively small proportion of the rationales given for selecting the candidates in this race. In contrast, reasons that refer to the candidates' job performance, information related to their campaigns, and the candidates' party affiliations comprise a substantial proportion of the responses offered. Also, general impressions of the candidates comprise more than one-fourth of the rationales mentioned in this race.

As described above, the dominant themes of the Democratic and Republican campaigns for chief justice were quite distinct. The Republican appeal emphasized the alleged inadequacies of incumbent Chief Justice Celebrezze, while the Democratic campaign stressed the court's policy stance. Closer inspection of the specific reasons mentioned by voters for their selections of a chief justice suggests the Republican campaign message was communicated effectively to many voters, while the issue-based appeal of the Democrats met far less success.

Consider the responses categorized as pertaining to the candidate's performance. While supporters of both Celebrezze and Thomas Moyer made reference to the candidate's past or prospective job performance, all of the rationales of this type mentioned by Moyer voters refer to Celebrezze's poor performance in office. As the responses shown in Table 4 suggest, voters' selection of Moyer appears to have been based on their dissatisfaction with the "scandals" plaguing Celebrezze's administration and his "bar association troubles." In contrast, the typical performance-based reasons given by Celebrezze supporters reflect little understanding of what the incumbent had done in office. Instead, the latter include references to Celebrezze's "good record" and his "good job" in office. But both kinds of responses emphasize the importance of Celebrezze's incumbency status as a focus of voters' responses.

Awareness of the negative tone of the chief justice contest and the considerable media attention focusing on Celebrezze's activities are also apparent in the campaign-related reasons voters offered. Here, voters tend to mention the "bad ads of the opponent" or the "bad press and campaign" as their reasons for selecting Moyer. Individuals who supported Celebrezze appeared to "like his t.v. ads" but were also aware of the "mudslinging" that characterized the campaign.

Table 5   Reasons for selection of associate justice (1986) as a percentage of all reasons provided

	Percent of responses (Sweeney v. Holmes)	Number of responses	Selected specific reasons	Percent of responses (Brown v. George)	Number of responses	Selected specific reasons
High info reasons						
Ideology	0.0%	0		0.0%	0	
Issues	0.9	2		0.8	2	
Group reference	2.3	5		2.3	6	
Moderate info. reasons						
Job skills	1.8	4		2.7	7	
Performance	9.6	21	good record (9) good job (9)	6.5	17	
Continuity/change	4.1	9		1.1	3	
Character	0.9	2		0.8	2	
Assocs. with others	0.0	0		0.4	1	
Campaign	5.5	12		7.3	19	
Low info. reasons						
Personal characteristics	6.4	14		19.2	50	female (33)/male (7) too many women (2)
Media	10.0	22	read about him (10) heard/saw on t.v. (6)	8.4	22	
Personal knowledge	5.0	11		4.6	12	
Recognition/amt. of info.	9.6	21	name recognition (12) heard/know more about him (4)	10.7	28	name recognition (11) more knowledge of candidate (7)
General impressions	10.5	23	better/good man (9) heard good things (5)	10.0	26	good/better man/ woman (10) like, general (5)
Contentless	17.4	38		8.4	22	
Party-related reasons	16.0	35		16.9	44	

The number of voters who provided a specific response is shown in parentheses.

In addition, a fairly sizable number of reasons based on general impressions of the chief justice candidates suggest that voters' preferences for Moyer were based largely on his being preferred *relative* to Celebrezze. As shown in Table 4, many Moyer supporters indicated they cast their vote because they "didn't like the opponent," were "not satisfied with the opponent," or had "heard bad things" about Celebrezze. Negative reactions to Moyer were far less common for Celebrezze voters.

Only a small minority of all voters referred to the candidates' issue positions and group ties. Although the Democratic party was far more aggressive in drawing attention to issues than were the Republicans, both Celebrezze and Moyer supporters provided these types of responses. Individuals who voted for the incumbent Celebrezze cited his drug policy, his pro-life position on abortion, and, most often, his support for unions and labor. Some Moyer voters expressed dissatisfaction with Celebrezze's handling of issues. Such reasons included references to Celebrezze's having "hurt the insurance business" and his decisions in lawsuits involving school districts.

The negative character of the chief justice campaign that dominated most voters' candidate choices plus the minimal attention to the court's policy activities may help explain why the candidates' party affiliations were less important as rationales for voters' choices in this contest. Although both parties were active in all the judicial campaigns, the level of partisan involvement in the chief justice contest was the most explicit. If all else was equal, it would be anticipated that more voters knew of the candidates' party affiliations and used that information in making their choices in the chief justice contest. But all else was not equal: far more information on matters other than party was available to voters in the race for chief justice. Hence, this additional information may have become at least as important as knowledge of the candidates' party affiliations when voters were called on to provide a rationale for their vote choices.

The success of the Republican campaign focus and the Democrats' lack of success in structuring the campaign with policy issues reflect the fact that voters require more information to vote on the basis of issues than on the basis of a candidate's alleged inadequacies. Further, the media's emphasis on the Republican appeal made negative information about Celebrezze's performance more readily avail-

Table 6   Reasons for selection of associate justice (1988) as a percentage of all reasons provided

	Percent of responses (Resnick v. George)	Number of responses	Selected specific reasons	Percent of responses (Sweeney v. Matia)	Number of responses	Selected specific reasons
High info reasons						
Ideology	1.5%	3		1.8%	3	
Issues	0.5	1		1.8	3	
Group reference	1.0	2		4.7	8	union recommendation (1) keeps doctors from being sued (1)
Moderate info. reasons						
Job skills	0.5	1		1.8	3	
Performance	5.4	11		3.0	5	
Continuity/change	0.5	1		7.7	13	
Character	2.5	5		0.0	0	
Assocs. with others	2.0	4		4.7	8	
Campaign	23.2	47	campaign ads (26) campaign literature (15)	13.6	23	t.v. ads (14) seen, read good things (4)
Low info. reasons						
Personal characteristics	9.4	19	experience (11) good background (2)	1.2	2	
Media	7.9	16		11.2	19	info. in newspaper (8) heard things on t.v. (4)
Personal knowledge	5.4	11		5.9	10	
Recognition/amt. of info.	5.9	12		16.6	28	identified with name (13) familiarity with candidate (12)
General impressions	14.3	29	liked her better (9) heard all good things (4)	9.5	16	good man/best man (6) liked issues he stands for (3)
Contentless	2.5	5		0.6	1	
Party-related reasons	17.7	36		16.0	27	

The number of voters who provided a specific response is shown in parentheses.

able than information on policy issues. As a result, a judicial contest in which the potential for voting on the basis of policy issues was unusually high seemed to produce little issue voting.

The associate justice contests of 1986

Voters' responses to the 1986 associate justice contests are provided in Table 5. Most evident from these data is that, despite the relatively high levels of spending and general media attention to these contests, voters seemingly assimilated relatively little information about the candidates. The policy issues that the Democrats emphasized in the 1986 judicial contests were reflected very little in voters' responses.

In both of these contests, general impressions and recognition of the candidates appeared to be important to individuals' choices. As Table 5 illustrates, several voters in both contests reported that their choices were made because they "liked" the candidate or because the candidate was a "better man" or "better woman." Unlike the chief justice contest, the rationales offered for the choice of associate justice show little evidence that candidates were selected because of dislike or dissatisfaction with the opponent.

In addition, both of the Democratic candidates—Herbert Brown and Francis Sweeney—appear to have benefited from name recognition. Many voters mentioned that the recognition of these candidates' names or a lack of knowledge of their Republican opponents were important to their choices. Both Sweeney and Brown are well-known political names in Ohio.

In the contest between Sweeney and Robert Holmes, vague references to the candidates' abilities to perform in office (e.g., "good record," "good job") and to information obtained through the media (e.g., "heard, saw things on t.v.," "read good things") also characterized a sizable proportion of the reasons given for selecting the candidates. Reasons offered in the contest between Herbert Brown and Joyce George demonstrate the importance of cues that can be discerned from the ballot itself in small-scale campaigns: Large numbers of responses in the personal characteristics category cited gender as the basis for voters' choices.

The data also suggest that these contests were largely isolated from the chief justice contest. This isolation is surprising because the Republicans, in particular, made efforts to link the three judicial races of that year. As described earlier, the Republicans were quite successful in their attempt to structure the competition in the chief justice contest in terms of incumbent Celebrezze's alleged inadequacies. However, there is little evidence that the Republican appeal, let alone the Democrats' issue focus, carried over to the associate justice contests. And, because voters received little other information in the associate justice contests, the candidates' partisan affiliations became an important piece of information on which to base choices, despite their absence from the ballot. This pattern also distinguished these contests from the race for chief justice.

The associate justice contests of 1988

As shown in Table 6, the pattern of voters' responses to the 1988 associate justice contests is similar to that of the 1986 associate justice contests in most respects. Two differences balanced each other: While fewer voters in the 1988 contests offered low-information rationales for their choices, considerably more voters in 1988 could cite no reason.

In both contests, campaign-related rationales were prevalent. As the data in Table 6 indicate, voters typically cited television ads and campaign literature as their reasons for selecting the candidates. The reasons based on general impressions of the candidates, also common, tended to be quite vague (e.g., "liked her better," "good/better candidate," "liked issues he stands for").

In the contest between Alice Robie Resnick and Joyce George, the candidates' "experience" comprised a majority of the responses in the personal characteristics category. In the Sweeney- Matia race, as in the two 1986 associate justice contests, recognition of a well-known name (Sweeney in this instance) helped a relatively large number of voters make their choices.[35] Information that voters obtained through the media also was frequently cited as a reason for their candidate choices.

Not surprisingly, the issues that played only a small explicit part in the 1988 campaigns seemed to have little effect on the voters. Only the reasons noted in the associate justice race between Sweeney and Matia show evidence that voters' choices were based, albeit indirectly, on issues. High-information reasons were more common in this contest than in any other judicial race in 1986 or 1988 but still relatively infrequent. Most fell in the group reference category. The group-related responses were quite varied, ranging from mentions made by Sweeney voters of his union endorsement and his concern for "underdogs" to a Matia supporter's noting that Matia "tries to keep people from suing doctors."

An additional similarity between the 1986 and 1988 associate justice contests is the fairly high frequency of partisan rationales for choice. As noted earlier, this pattern lends further support to the idea that, where there is a dearth of other information, the parties' efforts to identify their candidates in a nonpartisan race provide voters with at least one piece of information on which to base their choices.

In 1988, as in 1986, one incumbent associate justice was on the ballot. But incumbency seemed to play only a limited role in the responses to Holmes in 1986 and Sweeney in 1988. Neither justice had attracted much media attention during the intracourt battles of the 1980s, and voters had little opportunity to glean much information about their performance on the bench. As a result, incumbency status was probably important primarily as a source of name recognition, and not highly important in that respect.

Conclusions

The need for caution has been emphasized in interpreting the rationales that voters offer for their choices. This should not be abandoned in drawing conclusions from this study. In particular, the limitations involved in analyzing voters' expressed reasons for their choices should be emphasized once again. Other means of probing the bases for their choices might yield somewhat different implications.[36]

Still, the findings presented here offer considerable support for the general hypothesis stated at the outset. Differences in the behavior of voters between contests for judgeships and other contests largely reflected differences in the information provided to voters rather than any unique qualities of voters' responses to judicial elections. Most important, the mix of reasons that voters offered for their choices varied chiefly with the amount of information they were given.

The results provide some evidence that recent changes in the character of contests for judgeships have had only a limited impact on the voters—

more limited than some observers have perceived. The contests for the Ohio Supreme Court in 1986 and 1988 provided far more information to voters than most judicial contests, and they had some issue content. Yet voters' responses, as reflected in the reasons they offered for their choices, largely fit the pattern that would be expected in low-information contests. The 1986 contest for chief justice was a partial exception, but it was also quite extraordinary—and unique in Ohio's political history—in the level of campaigning and media attention. Even in that contest, the policy issues that one candidate emphasized seemed to have limited impact on the voters. Thus this study suggests that the traditional pattern of voting behavior in judicial elections has remained the dominant one even in a period of bigger and more contentious campaigns.

The implications of this study are constrained not only by the limitations of the evidence but also by the specific setting in which the study took place. No state can be said to have "typical" judicial elections. This is particularly true of Ohio because of its unusual combination of a partisan primary election and a nonpartisan general election. Further, the 1986 and 1988 supreme court elections in Ohio reflected a particular set of conditions and events that influenced the conduct of the contests and the responses of voters. Confident judgments about the impact of changes in judicial contests on voters' behavior will be possible only when more extensive information is gained on judicial voters in a variety of states and settings.

NOTES

This article originally appeared in Volume 75, Number 6, April-May 1992, pages 300-309.

The authors appreciate the comments of the reviewers for *Judicature* on a previous draft of this article and Jon Krosnick's suggestions about the design of the research. The data analyzed in the article were provided by the Polimetrics Laboratory of the Department of Political Science at The Ohio State University. The research was funded by the University's Center for Labor Research.

1. *See* Sheldon and Lovrich, *Voters in Contested, Nonpartisan Judicial Elections: A Responsible Electorate or a Problematical Public?*, 36 WESTERN POL. Q. 241-256 (1983).

2. Klots, *The Selection of Judges and the Short Ballot*, 38 J. AM. JUDICATURE SOC'Y 134-140 (1955); McKnight, Schaefer, and Johnson, *Choosing judges: do the voters know what they're doing?*, 62 JUDICATURE 94-99 (1978).

3. Griffin and Horan, *Patterns of voting behavior in judicial retention elections for supreme court justices in Wyoming*, 67 JUDICATURE 68-77 (1983).

4. Dubois, *The Significance of Voting Cues in State Supreme Court*

Elections, 13 LAW & SOC'Y REV. 757-779 (1979); Dubois, *Voting Cues in Nonpartisan Trial Court Elections: A Multivariate Assessment*, 18 LAW & SOC'Y REV. 395-436 (1984).

5. Williams, *How to Get Elected Without Even Trying*, SAN FRANCISCO CHRONICLE, October 3, 1990, at A10; Bone, *Washington Primary: Judicial Politics*, 11 COMPARATIVE STATE POLITICS 45-48 (1990, #6).

6. Byrne and Pueschel, *But Who Should I Vote for For County Coroner?*, 36 J. OF POL. 778-784 (1974); Conway, *Political Participation in a Nonpartisan Local Election*, 33 PUB. OPINION Q. 578-599 (1969); Mueller, *Choosing Among 133 Candidates*, 34 PUB. OPINION Q. 395-402 (1970); Pomper, *Ethnic and Group Voting in Nonpartisan Municipal Elections*, 30 PUB. OPINION Q. 79-97 (1966); Salisbury and Black, *Class and Party in Partisan and Nonpartisan Elections: The Case of Des Moines*, 57 AM. POL. SCI. REV. 584-592 (1963).

7. *See* Sheldon and Lovrich, *Knowledge and judicial voting: the Oregon and Washington experience*, 67 JUDICATURE 235 (1983).

8. On the relationship between information and the vote across types of contests and more generally, see Converse, *Information Flow and the Stability of Partisan Attitudes*, 26 PUB. OPINION Q. 578-599 (1962); Hinckley, Hofstetter, and Kessel, *Information and the Vote: A Comparative Election Study*, 2 AM. POL. Q. 131-158 (1974); Wright, ELECTORAL CHOICE IN AMERICA (Chapel Hill: Institute for Research in Social Science, University of North Carolina, 1974); Macaluso, *Political Information, Party Identification and Voting Defection*, 41 PUB. OPINION Q. 255-260 (1977); Shaffer, *Voting in Four Elective Offices: A Comparative Analysis*, 10 AM. POL. Q. 5-30 (1982); Palfrey and Poole, *The Relationship Between Information, Ideology, and Voting Behavior*, 31 AM. J. OF POL. SCI. 511-530 (1987); and Moon, *What You Use Depends on What You Have: Information Effects on the Determinants of Electoral Choice*, 18 AM. POL. Q. 3-24 (1990).

9. This is not to say that no differences exist between judicial and nonjudicial contests in campaigns and voting behavior. The ethical constraint on the use of policy issues in judicial contests has some impact; see note 10, *infra*. Further, it is likely that voters begin with different perspectives and expectations about different kinds of offices. Some evidence of differences in expectations is provided by Sheldon and Lovrich, *supra* n. 7. But it is expected that the impact of such differences is overwhelmed by the impact of vast differences in the information provided to voters.

10. American Bar Association, MODEL CODE OF PROFESSIONAL RESPONSIBILITY AND CODE OF JUDICIAL CONDUCT, AS AMENDED AUGUST 1980, at 69 (Chicago: American Bar Association, 1982). This rule helps to create a constraint that is unique to judicial elections, yet its impact should not be exaggerated. For one thing, judicial candidates sometimes evade or directly violate the rule. More important, candidates for nonjudicial offices below the top levels have difficulty in communicating policy issues to voters, even when they seek to do so.

11. Mathias, ELECTING JUSTICE: A HANDBOOK OF JUDICIAL ELECTION REFORMS (Chicago: American Judicature Society, 1990); McFadden, ELECTING JUSTICE: THE LAW AND ETHICS OF JUDICIAL ELECTION CAMPAIGNS (Chicago: American Judicature Society, 1990); Schotland, *Elective Judges' Campaign Financing: Are State Judges' Robes the Emperor's Clothes of American Democracy?*, 2 J. OF L. & POL. 57-167 (1985).

12. Watson, *The Run for the Robes*, GOVERNING, July 1991, at 49-52; Mathias, *supra* n. 11, at 31-33.

13. Hall, *Constituent Influence in State Supreme Courts: Conceptual Notes and a Case Study*, 49 J. OF POL. 1117-1124 (1987); Press, *A Vote on the Quality of Mercy*, NEWSWEEK, November 3, 1986, at 63, 65; Taylor, *Texas Court Gets More Election Attention*, NATIONAL L. J., October 8, 1990, at 16.

14. Mathias, *supra* n. 11, at 31.

15. Jones, *Ideology and Judicial Elections in Wisconsin*, 10 COM-

PARATIVE STATE POL. 6 (1989, #4).

16. Resnick, *This Court's a Backwater No More*, NATIONAL L. J., May 28, 1990, at 1, 30; and *State's Chief Justice Keeps His Seat*, MIAMI HERALD, Nov. 7, 1990, at 17A.

17. Applebome, *Rubber Stamp is Gone in Texas Judicial Election*, NEW YORK TIMES, October 21, 1988, at B7; Jackson and Riddlesperger, *Money and politics in judicial elections: the 1988 election of the chief justice of the Texas Supreme Court*, 74 JUDICATURE 184-189 (1991).

18. Schotland, *supra* n. 11; Mathias, *supra* n. 11, at 43-44; McFadden, *supra* n. 11, at 25-27.

19. *See* GOP Makes Its Pitch to Business, Doctors, RALEIGH NEWS AND OBSERVER, October 11, 1986, at A1, A11; and Uelman, *Shopping for Judges, California Style*, LOS ANGELES TIMES, September 30, 1986, at 2:5.

20. Wold and Culver, *The defeat of the California justices: the campaign, the electorate, and the issue of judicial accountability*, 70 JUDICATURE 348-355 (1987).

21. *The Field Exit Poll*, SAN FRANCISCO CHRONICLE, November 5, 1986, at 1B.

22. For background on the court and its elections, see Barber, *Judicial Politics in Ohio*, in Lieberman, ed., GOVERNMENT AND POLITICS OF OHIO 89-133 (Lanham, Md.: University Press of America, 1984), Tarr and Porter, STATE SUPREME COURTS IN STATE AND NATION 124-183 (New Haven: Yale University Press, 1988), and Baum, *Voters' Information in Judicial Elections: The 1986 Contests for the Ohio Supreme Court*, 77 KY. L. J. 645-670 (1988-89).

23. The change in the character of Ohio's supreme court contests is indicated by the level of voter participation in those contests, as measured by the number of votes cast for the supreme court as a proportion of all the people who turn out at the polls. (This is the same measure used in the text below for the 1986 and 1988 contests.) For 1970-76 (excluding two uncontested seats), the mean was 73.7 percent; for 1978-82, it was 75.6 percent; for 1984-88, it was 81.2 percent.

24. These allegations involved several matters, including Celebrezze's exploration of a gubernatorial candidacy in 1982, his conflictual relations with the state bar association, and his use of his administrative powers as chief justice. See Tarr and Porter, *supra* n. 22, at 132-36. Late in the campaign, the state's newspapers devoted a good deal of space to charges that the chief justice had taken campaign contributions from two labor union locals allegedly influenced by organized crime; the initial story was Webb, *Mob-Linked Groups Donate to Chief Justice*, CLEVELAND PLAIN DEALER, Oct. 12, 1986, at 1-A, 6-A.

25. These surveys were conducted by the Polimetrics Laboratory of the Department of Political Science at The Ohio State University. Respondents were interviewed by telephone within the month following the election. Approximately 800 respondents were interviewed in 1986, 650 in 1988. In each of the 1986 contests, the "reasons" question was worded as follows: "What would you say was the main reason for your choice of [candidate]?" (Probes for additional reasons followed.) In the 1988 Senate contest, the wording was: "What were the main reasons for your choice?" In the 1988 contests for associate justice, the wording was: "What was the main reason for your choice?"

26. This difference potentially reduces the comparability between those two contests and the seven others. To minimize this problem while retaining full information on voters' reasons, we analyzed reasons primarily by the proportion falling into different categories rather than by the proportion of respondents citing each category.

27. The primary source of the argument for skepticism in interpreting respondents' explanations for their behavior is Nisbett and Wilson, *Telling More Than We Can Know: Verbal Reports on Mental Processes*, 84 PSYCHOLOGICAL REV. 231-259 (1977). See also Nisbett and Bellows, *Verbal Reports About Causal Influ-*

ences on Social Judgments: Private Access Versus Public Theories, 35 J. OF PERSONALITY AND SOC. PSYCHOLOGY 613-624 (1977); and Wilson and Nisbett, *The Accuracy of Verbal Reports About the Effects of Stimuli on Evaluations and Behavior*, 41 SOC. PSYCHOLOGY 118-131 (1978). Sources that question this point of view to some degree include Smith and Miller, *Limits on Perception of Cognitive Processes: A Reply to Nisbett and Wilson*, 85 PSYCHOLOGICAL REV. 355-362 (1978); Kraut and Lewis, *Person Perception and Self-Awareness: Knowledge of Influences on One's Own Judgments*, 42 J. OF PERSONALITY AND SOC. PSYCHOLOGY 448-460 (1982); and Ericsson and Simon, PROTOCOL ANALYSIS: VERBAL REPORTS AS DATA (Cambridge, Mass.: MIT Press, 1984).

28. The reduced number of voters who make choices for lower-level offices is referred to as "rolloff." Among Ohio voters the rolloff from the governor's race to the contest for chief justice in 1986 was negligible; for the associate justice contests in 1986 and 1988, the rolloff from the highest office varied from 15 to 20 percent. Respondents reported slightly higher levels of rolloff, but a considerable proportion of the respondents who reported voting in the associate justice contests could not recall their choices in those contests. Such recall failures would seem endemic to contests for lower-level offices; for a similar phenomenon, see Adamany and Shelley, *Encore! The Forgetful Voter*, 44 PUB. OPINION Q. 234 (1980). Since only those respondents who reported their choices could be asked about the reasons for their choices, the "effective rolloff" among respondents was high, from 36 to 50 percent in the associate justice contests.

The possibility that voters who could not recall their choices were less informed than those who could was probed by comparing these two sets of voters in 1986; there were meaningful differences between the two groups according to two of the four measures of the information used. Thus, the samples of voters in the associate justice contest may well be biased toward higher knowledge of the contests. This bias would tend to produce underestimates rather than overestimates of differences among contests, thereby reducing somewhat the concern about its effects on the results.

29. This ambiguity merits some discussion. Where voters offered brief, summary rationales for their choices, in some instances there undoubtedly were more detailed and substantive bases underlying that general language. Further, interviewers may have abbreviated their transcriptions of responses and thus eliminated some detail. These sources of ambiguity underline the value of comparing patterns of responses across contests, where they are largely held constant.

30. No formal reliability tests were performed. Two coders assigned specific reasons to categories, and disagreements were resolved through discussion.

31. Celebrezze and Sweeney both have Democratic connotations because several Democratic politicians have had those names; Brown is a well-known Ohio political name that has no clear partisan connotation. The other names of judicial candidates in 1986 and 1988 lack such substantial political histories in the state.

32. To reproduce the conditions under which respondents cast their votes, they were given the candidates' party affiliations in the nonjudicial contests when asked to recall their vote. For the same reason, those affiliations were not provided for the judicial candidates.

33. Of course, different voters will actually gain different amounts of information from what is provided to them. Because this study's concern is with differences among contests, differences among voters will not be analyzed in the body of the article. But the reasons offered by voters with higher and lower levels of information, as estimated by the interviewers, were compared. Not surprisingly, the better informed voters were more likely to offer what have been characterized as high-information reasons. But such reasons were relatively rare even for the better informed voters. In the four contests for associate justice, an average of 6.2 percent of the better informed voters cited high-information reasons, as against 2.4 percent for other voters.

34. The relative frequency of low-information reasons in the race for governor is striking in light of the high level of information available to voters. It is likely that some voters summarized their evaluations of the candidates in statements that did not reflect anything like the full range of information they possessed. This finding underlines the need for caution in interpreting the reasons that voters provide.

35. The Sweeney who ran in 1986 and the Sweeney who ran in 1988 were different people, though most voters probably knew too little to make such a distinction.

36. The analysis of differences between union members and other voters in the same elections, for instance, yielded stronger evidence that economic groups and economic issues influenced voting decisions. Hojnacki and Baum, *"New-Style" Judicial Campaigns and the Voters: Economic Issues and Union Members in Ohio*, W. POL. Q. (forthcoming).

How minority judges fare in retention elections

A study of nearly every judicial retention election in the United States from 1980 to 1990 shows no correlation between whether a judge is black or Hispanic and the percentage of affirmative votes the judge received.

by Robert C. Luskin, Christopher N. Bratcher, Christopher G. Jordan, Tracy K. Renner, and Kris S. Seago

Over the past decade or so, a relatively new criterion has increasingly flavored the long-contentious issues of judicial selection. Understandably dissatisfied with the relatively small proportion of judges who are black or Hispanic, many in the legal community, not to mention many black and Hispanic organizations, have urged the importance of a more racially representative bench.

One feature of many elective systems that has probably contributed to this underrepresentation is the election of judges at-large from relatively large constituencies, in which blacks and Hispanics are rarely if ever majorities. Certainly states with systems like this enrobe blacks and Hispanics at disproportionately low frequencies. In Texas as of 1991, for example, blacks and Hispanics accounted for roughly one-third of the state's population but only 45 of the state's 396 district court judges and only 3 of its 80 appellate court judges.

Such at-large elections are apparently on their way out. In *Thornburg v. Gingles*,[1] the U.S. Supreme Court ruled that at-large elections may violate Section 2 of the Voting Rights Act of 1982, which prohibits electoral practices under which the "members of a class of citizens protected by the VRA . . . have less opportunity than other members of the electorate to participate in the political process and to elect representatives of their choice." Now, in *Chisom v. Roemer*[2] and *Houston Lawyers v. Texas Attorney General*,[3] the Court has added that judges are "representatives" in the sense of Sec-

tion 2 and directed the lower courts to consider the merits of challenges brought against at-large judicial elections in a number of mostly southern states in that light.[4]

Already, some of these and other states are scrambling to revise their judicial selection systems. No doubt the simplest solution would be to split the at-large constituencies into smaller, single-member districts, while continuing to use partisan elections. If the legislature accepts the February 1992 recommendations of a gubernatorial task force, New York, for one, will follow this path.[5] Given the geographical concentration of minority populations, smaller districts, unless very artfully drawn, can be expected to include a much larger proportion of "majority-minority" districts, whose predominantly black or Hispanic populations are likely to install black or Hispanic judges.

Yet this solution may not be universally leapt at. Many white politicians and lawyers may be reluctant to surrender a larger share of office and power. Much of the white public may distrust the impartiality, competence, or integrity of judges chosen by majority-minority electorates. Legislators may fear that judges elected from more racially homogeneous constituencies will tend to be less sensitive to the minorities within their districts.

Apart from pure appointment, the most obvious alternative is the widely used merit selection system, or Missouri Plan, which couples initial appointmemt with either one-time or periodic review by means of noncompetitive, nonpartisan elections. Though still subject to court approval, the June 1992 agreement between Georgia Governor Zell Miller and the plaintiffs in a lawsuit challenging the state's judicial selection procedures involves a shift from partisan elections to merit selection.[6]

The aim of merit selection, in addition to making for more competent judges, is to insulate them from political pressures. By precisely the same token, however, it leaves them freer to ignore popular notions of justice. Historically, moreover, it has done rather poorly at turning up minority judges,[7] and though as an essentially appointive system, it would seem to escape the Voting Rights Act, it may well meet opposition on these grounds.

Yet a third possibility would be to cross single-member district elections as the means of selection with at-large retention elections as the means of review. The partisan, single-member district phase of this cycle would provide an opportunity for predominantly black or Hispanic districts to elect black or Hispanic judges, while the at-large retention phase would allow the larger jurisdiction some check on the choices made by the smaller districts within it. Illinois has recently adopted such a system for Cook County, and the Texas legislature has considered similar legislation.[8]

One way or another, then, it seems likely that many states will be considering solutions involving retention elections. But how well do retention elections serve the new goal of judicial representativeness? Are black or Hispanic judges more likely than their white colleagues to be turned out of office? We know from election statistics that sitting judges tend to roll up huge margins of approval and that the vast majority are always retained.[9] We do not know, however, whether minority judges are less likely to be retained, whether they secure fewer votes when they stand for retention, or whether they have been opposed for retention on racial grounds.

This article reports on a small corner of a much larger project. We have gathered a substantial body of data—election returns, other aspects of the state's selection system, the judge's race and gender, and constituency characteristics—for every judicial retention election in the United States between 1980 and 1990, and we expect at some later point to be reporting on a more multivariate consideration of the factors that make for retention or rejection. For the present, however, this article offers statistical impressions of the prospects of minority judges in retention elections.

Retention elections in principle

The principle of retention elections is simple. The ballot poses some version of the question, "Shall Judge X be continued in office," with voters asked to vote simply "yes" or "no." If the judge receives a sufficient proportion (usually a simple majority) of "yes" votes, he or she is retained; if not, he or she is dismissed.

This idea had its origins in the merit selection plan of Albert Kales. In Kales's original scheme, judges would be nominated by a judicial council, chosen by the state's elected chief justice, and periodically confirmed in office by noncompetitive elections, known today as retention elections.[10] The object was to recruit the ablest, most knowledgeable, and fairest-minded candidates and to afford them the near-certainty of lifetime tenure, with the independence that that allows, while still providing some measure of popular control.[11]

The Kales plan had an immediate and obvious appeal to many in the legal community, and it has now been adopted, in one form or another, by 22 states and the District of Columbia.[12] The paradigmatic and hence eponymous version has turned out to be Missouri's, which provides for gubernatorial appointments from among candidates selected by a nominating committee, followed by a one-time retention election as part of the first general election falling at least one year after the appointment. If retained, the judge then serves a full term.

Thanks largely to the diffusion of merit selection, judicial retention elections have also been widely instituted. In all, 20 states now have them,[13] although with details that vary from from state to state.[14] One dimension of that variation is in the courts for which retention elections are used. Kansas and Pennsylvania use them for nearly all courts (municipal and traffic courts excepted). California and Maryland use retention elections at the appellate level, but competitive elections for trial court judgeships. Indiana and Missouri permit merit selection with retention elections at all levels, but allow individual jurisdictions to decide whether to use the merit plan.

Another dimension is the length of the "probationary" term preceding a judge's first retention election, which ranges from the first biennial election following 30 days of service to up to three years.[15] The most common setup provides for a first retention election in the first general election following the judge's first full year of service. Subsequent terms range from 4 to 12 years, with 14 of the 20 states opting for six years.

Then, too, there is the question of what proportion of the vote is necessary. In every state but Illinois, a bare majority suffices. In Illinois, however, judges must receive 60 percent of the votes cast. This higher hurdle makes some difference, as we shall see.

But probably the most important variation is in the method of initial selection. Seventeen of the 20 states have adopted retention elections as part of the Missouri Plan. The remaining three, however, couple their retention elections with other selection procedures. In California, judges are appointed by the governor without the advice of any formal nominating committee. In Illinois and Pennsylvania, judges stand for retention after winning an initial partisan election.[16]

Retention elections in practice

The most striking thing about retention elections in practice is the near-certainty of retention. A recent study of retention elections in 10 states over a 20-year period found that in only 22, or 1.2 percent, of nearly 1,900 elections was the sitting judge defeated; nearly 99 percent were returned to office.[17] As one Arizona judge put it, a sitting judge could do anything "short of committing incest at high noon at Central and Van Buren" and still be retained.[18]

Consistent with that, retention elections produce very high percentages of "yes" votes; Hall and Aspin found a mean affirmative vote of 77.2 percent. In only 45, or 2.7 percent, of the 1,864 elections they surveyed was the affirmative vote less than 60 percent.[19] Though incumbents are re-elected at high rates in many other contested elections—for Congress, most notably—the percentages of the vote for sitting judges in retention elections far exceed those for incumbents in contested elections for other down-ballot offices.

A second striking feature is low turnout. Few people actually vote, even in comparison with other down-ballot elections. The "rolloff" from the top of the ballot to judicial retention elections on the same ballot averages 36.2 percent.[20]

Both high retention rates and vote margins and

low turnout are rooted in public ignorance and apathy.[21] People typically know little or nothing about the judges on whose retention they are being called upon to vote. In surveys of Wyoming voters, more than half the respondents confessed they had "no information" concerning the judges on whose retention they had voted.[22] Only 4.8 percent claimed to have cast their votes on the basis of "a great deal" of information. Very few voters are aware of bar ratings, despite their being widely reported.[23]

Given this level of ignorance, votes for or against retention are generally blank yea- or nay-saying. The nay-saying may be a trifle less blank—those voting against can more often give substantive reasons—but even these latter commonly look like rationalization. In one election, for example, many voters claimed to have voted against a judge because he had been on the bench too long, even though the judge in question was just finishing his probationary term and was running for retention for the first time.[24] From this perspective, the reason judges are almost always retained is that habitual yea-sayers outnumber habitual naysayers.[25]

More fundamentally, this syndrome owes much to the fact that retention elections are both down-ballot and nonpartisan. The most powerful cue used by voters to distinguish between candidates is party label, which conveys a good deal about the candidates' policy orientations. Party labels are especially important in down-ballot races, where voters almost never know anything about the candidates, except at most whether they are incumbents or challengers and their party affiliation. Retention elections, devoid of partisan cues, force most voters to make a decision on which they have no basis for judgment. Small wonder, then, that most abstain, and most of the rest vote blind.[26]

Minority representation

A number of studies have considered the relationship between judicial selection method and the proportions of judges who are black or Hispanic. On the whole, they suggest that the normal or routine method by which a state fills judgeships—not counting the filling of vacancies from resignations, deaths, and retirements—has little impact on the racial distribution of trial court judges.[27]

On the other hand, Graham finds that what might be called the real system of judicial selection—including the method by which the state fills vacancies from resignations, deaths, and retirements—does have a considerable impact on the selection of black judges.[28] Specifically, she finds that judges chosen by either the Missouri Plan or elections (whether partisan or not) are less likely to be black than judges chosen by either gubernatorial or legislative appointment (outside the merit system).

Two qualifications are worth noting, however: First, elections would probably look better, as Graham speculates, if they were more often held within single-member districts rather than at-large. And, second, the underrepresentation of blacks in merit systems undoubtedly stems from the nomination process—the commissions are generally dominated by white males[29]—rather than from retention elections.

This preliminary report examines biases in rates of and votes for retention. The data consist of returns from virtually all retention elections in the United States between 1980 and 1990.[30] The large number of elections involved (presently over 2,600) should permit a fair degree of confidence in the results despite the infrequency with which sitting judges are defeated.[31]

Tables 1 and 2 give the proportions of black,

Table 1   Percentage of judges retained by race, 1980-1990

Race	Judges retained	Percentage retained	Judges rejected	Total number of judges
District courts				
White	1,861	98.47	29	1,890
Black	70	98.59	1	71
Hispanic	35	97.22	1	36
Total	1,966	98.45	31	1,997
Appellate courts				
White	456	100	0	456
Black	16	100	0	16
Hispanic	8	100	0	8
Total	480	100	0	480
Supreme courts				
White	156	98.73	2	158
Black	3	100	0	3
Hispanic	2	66.67	1	3
Total	161	98.17	3	164
All courts				
White	2,473	98.76	31	2,504
Black	89	98.89	1	90
Hispanic	45	95.74	2	47
Total	2,607	98.71	34	2,641

Table 2   Average percentage of "yes" votes received by judges in retention elections, 1980-1990

Race	Percentage of "yes" votes received	Standard deviation	Number of judges
District courts			
White	75.27	7.99	1,890
Black	72.95	6.15	71
Hispanic	72.97	7.32	36
Total	75.09	7.91	1,997
Appellate courts			
White	71.76	6.7	456
Black	73.72	7.83	16
Hispanic	70.75	7.5	8
Total	71.8	6.74	480
Supreme courts			
White	72.6	7.93	158
Black	62.59	8.28	3
Hispanic	53.99	15.07	3
Total	72.08	8.5	164
All courts			
White	74.43	7.89	2,504
Black	72.74	6 .73	90
Hispanic	71.38	9	47
Total	74.33	7.89	2,641

Hispanic, and white incumbents winning retention and the mean proportions of the vote they received. Of the 2,641 retention elections examined, only 34, or 1.3 percent, were rejections; in 98.7 percent of the cases, the judge was retained. The retention rates vary only slightly by court level: 98.5 percent of the district court judges were retained, as were 98.2 percent of the supreme court judges and 100 percent of the apellate court judges. Furthermore, 18 of the 34 judges who were not retained were from Illinois, with its 60 percent threshold for retention.

The variation by race is not much greater. Overall, 98.8 percent of the white judges, 98.9 percent of the black judges, and 95.7 percent of the Hispanic judges were retained. These figures suggest Hispanic judges may be at a very slight disadvantage as compared with their black and white colleagues. Perhaps the reason lies in the ident-

ifiability of Hispanics by surname.[32]

It would be a mistake to make too much of this Hispanic disadavantage, however. In the first place, Hispanics (and blacks) are undoubtedly disadvantaged in other elections as well, and the 3 percent Hispanic disadvantage in retention elections is probably smaller than in most or all other elections. Second, the retention rates are extraordinarily high for all groups.

Another relevent question is how retention rates for minority judges vary across court levels. Are black or Hispanic district court judges more or less likely to be retained than black or Hispanic appellate or supreme court judges? On the surface, the evidence suggests that Hispanic supreme court judges may be particularly disadvantaged, winning only 67 percent of the time as compared to 100 percent and 97 percent retention rates for Hispanic appellate and district court judges, respec-

Table 3   Judges not retained, 1980-1990*

State	Judge	Race	Sex	Court	Year	Percent voting to retain
California	Rose Bird	W	F	Supreme	1986	33.8
	Cruz Reynoso	H	M	Supreme	1986	39.8
	Joseph Grodin	W	M	Supreme	1986	43.4
Colorado	Robert Sanderson	W	M	District	1982	40.6
	Robert Wilson	W	M	District	1986	36.5
	Paul Keohane	W	M	District	1988	48.8
Illinois	David Babb	W	M	Circuit	1980	43.6**
	John DeLaurenti	W	M	Circuit	1980	59.1**
	Victor Mosele	W	M	Circuit	1980	53.8**
	Jose Vasquez	H	M	Circuit	1982	56.3**
	Lawrence Passarella	W	M	Circuit	1986	57.4**
	Allen Rosin	W	M	Circuit	1986	55.8**
	Frank Salerno	W	M	Circuit	1986	56.1**
	Arthur Cieslik	W	M	Circuit	1988	55.5**
	Keith Campbell	W	M	Circuit	1990	54.4**
	Lehman Krause	W	M	Circuit	1990	57.6**
	Robert Mackey	W	M	Circuit	1990	51.8**
	Angelo Mistretta	W	M	Circuit	1990	56.8**
	Gerald Murphy	W	M	Circuit	1990	54.8**
	Vernon Plummer	W	M	Circuit	1990	58.9**
	David Shields	W	M	Circuit	1990	51.7**
	Pasquale Sorrentino	W	M	Circuit	1990	56.3**
	Lucia Thomas	B	F	Circuit	1990	56.0**
	John Tully	W	M	Circuit	1990	51.1**
Kansas	R.E. Miller	W	M	District	1980	25.3
Montana	Alfred B. Coate	W	M	District	1988	44.2
Nebraska	Francis Kneifl	W	M	District	1984	25.8
Pennsylvania	William Potter	W	M	Com.Pleas	1981	16.3
	A. Thomas Wilson	W	M	Com.Pleas	1983	24.0
	Bernard Snyder	W	M	Com.Pleas	1985	47.8
	Peter Krehel	W	M	Com.Pleas	1985	44.9
	Harold Fink	W	M	Com.Pleas	1987	25.9
	Bruce Brumbaugh	W	M	Com.Pleas	1989	41.5
Wyoming	Paul Liamos	W	M	District	1984	43.4

* This table includes every state supreme court, appellate, and state trial court judge defeated for retention in this period. Excluded are juvenile, probate, and other courts of lower jurisdiction.

** Illinois requires 60% approval for retention

tively. This estimate is unreliable, however, based as it is on only three cases. As Graham[33] and others have pointed out, the overwhelming majority of minority judges preside over courts of lower jurisdiction.

White judges also appear to attract slightly higher percentages of the vote, indicating a slightly greater margin of safety. White judges collected an average of 74.5 percent affirmative votes compared to 72.7 percent for blacks and 71.4 percent for Hispanics. These differences were large only in supreme court elections, where white judges averaged almost 10 percent more votes than black judges and almost 20 percent more votes than Hispanic ones, but these latter percentages, based on only three black and three Hispanic judges, are again unreliable. It is also worth noting that only one minority supreme court judge was actually rejected during the 1980-1990 period. The difference between white and black district court judges is statistically significant (p < .05), but slight. And again, the comparable differences for other sorts of elections are probably greater, and the percentages of the vote received by judges in all three groups are extremely high.

In sum, these preliminary results show that both white and minority judges benefit from extraordinarily high retention rates. Differences of roughly 2 percent do exist between the percentages of the vote received by white and minority judges, and in a closely contested election, 2 percent may make the difference between winning and losing. But the overwhelming facts about retention elections are that very few are close and that very few incumbents lose.

Reasons for ouster

To get another angle on this question, we have taken a closer look at the stories of the 34 judges in our sample who were defeated between 1980 and 1990. These judges, their race and gender, and the percentage of the vote they received are listed in Table 3. We have tried, from both written accounts and conversations with such local informants as reporters, professors, and politicians, to get a sense of the reasons these judges were defeated, and particularly of the extent to which the three minority judges who lost were dragged down by their minority group membership.

At base, the reasons lay with the judges. Some made decisions considered egregious (mostly sen-

tences considered absurdly lenient). Some behaved in ways seen as inappropriate, offensive, or bizarre. Some processed cases at a snail's pace. Some were visibly partial. Some ran their courtrooms sloppily. A few, notably the three California Supreme Court justices defeated in 1986, were ideologically out of step with their constituency. Some antagonized the bar, the press, or the political establishment. Some were investigated, indicted, or convicted on criminal charges.

As a result, most aroused unusually strong and credible opposition. Most received negative ratings from their local bar associations or from the state government committees (in Alaska, Colorado, and Utah) that evaluate judges standing for retention and publish the results. Most were editorially opposed by the local press.

The reader will have noticed that nothing has been said of the losing judges' race or ethnicity. Only three of the losing judges were black (Lucia Thomas of Illinois) or Hispanic (Cruz Reynoso of California and Jose Vasquez of Illinois), and by and large their race or ethnicity does not seem to have contributed much to their losses. But let us look more closely still:

Vasquez. An Illinois Circuit Court judge rejected in 1982, Vasquez was accused of directing defendants to hire and sometimes to sign over their bond money to a private attorney he favored. He also refused to try violent juveniles as adults, even in the case of a 16 year old accused of raping and committing a deviate sexual assault on a 79-year-old woman. He was rated "not qualified" by the Illinois State Bar Association and was opposed by the local press, including the *Chicago Tribune.* There was no overt speculation, much less evidence, that Vasquez was handicapped with the electorate by his ethnicity, and the other factors just cited are certainly sufficient to account for his defeat.

Reynoso. Like his colleagues on the California Supreme Court, Rose Bird and Joseph Grodin, Reynoso was widely perceived as too "liberal," chiefly meaning opposed to the death penalty. Reynoso had voted to reverse 46 of 47 of the capital sentences that came before him. Bar association polls and newspaper editorials were mixed, but included some negative recommendations. Along with Bird and Grodin, he was strongly opposed by Governor George Deukmejian, and some $10 milllion was spent in the campaign to defeat the three.[34] Although, in this case, some observers did speculate that his Hispanic surname cost him votes, Reynoso himself discounted these concerns. He lost by a larger margin than Grodin, but by a smaller one than Bird, and his reluctance to see the death penalty implemented seems an amply sufficient explanation for his loss.

Thomas. Like Vasquez a judge of the Illinois Circuit Court, Thomas refused to appear before the screening committees of any of the three major bar associations and consequently received "not recommended" ratings from two of the three.[35] Two white judges who made the same choice at the same time received the same ratings.[36] Thomas was also perceived by many in the legal community as deficient in legal ability. But the key factor seems to have been the opposition of the bulk of the organized bar, based on her refusal to participate in the judicial screening process.

In none of these cases, then, is there more than the faintest suspicion of the judge's race having played any part in his or her defeat. In each case, other factors seem responsible.[37]

Conclusion

It takes an awful lot for a sitting judge to lose a retention election, and so far as we can see this is roughly as true of black and Hispanic as of white judges. Hispanic judges may be rejected at slightly higher rates than their black or white colleagues, but even they are retained 96 percent of the time. The handful of black and Hispanic judges who have lost retention elections over the past decade, moreover, seem to have done so for other reasons.[38] There is no convincing evidence, in any of these elections, that the judge's race or ethnicity played any significant part in his or her loss.

Perhaps this is the silver lining of the ignorance and apathy in which these elections are enveloped. The most bigoted voters also tend to be the least politically involved. In disproportionate numbers, therefore, they stay home or vote only in up-ballot contests. Those who do vote have little way of knowing which judges are black. Accordingly, the more obscure the election, the less the impediment to minority candiates, all other things being equal.

Although merit selection systems, within which retention elections have most often been found, have historically depressed minority representation vis-à-vis purely appointive systems, their bias seems to have lain in the nominating rather than the retention process, and they have actually done bet-

ter than partisan elections on this score. It does seem unlikely, even with the recent emergence of minority representation as a criterion with which nominating commissions will have to reckon, that the many states now looking for an alternative to at-large partisan elections will secure greater minority representation by merit selection than by partisan elections within smaller and more racially homogeneous constituencies, but the probable shortfall, again, would occur in the nominating process.

As far as retention elections themselves are concerned, the verdict seems clear: The prospect of more judicial retention elections, per se, offers minorities little to fear.

NOTES

This article originally appeared in Volume 77, Number 6, May-June 1994, pages 316-321.

This research was funded by the Texas Legislative Council, to which the authors are grateful. The authors also thank the anonymous reviewers and the editor for suggestions and Kate Sampson and Susan Carbon for helpful information and advice.

1. 478 U.S. 30 (1986).

2. 501 U.S. 380 (1991).

3. 501 U.S. 419 (1991).

4. The states are Alabama, Arkansa, Florida, Georgia, Louisiana, Mississippi, Illinois, Ohio, and Texas. New York's system of electing judges by counties is now under challenge as well. New Mexico settled a suit without altering its method of judicial selection.

5. Sack, *Panel Faults Method of Electing Justices*, N.Y. Times, February 12, 1992, at A-17.

6. *See* Smothers, *Panel Challenges Method of Picking New York Justices*, N.Y. Times, June 19, 1992 at A-18; Curriden, *The Legal Hurdles*, Atlanta Constitution, November 29, 1992 at G-3.

7. *See* Graham, *Judicial recruitment and racial diversity on state courts: an overview*, 74 JUDICATURE 29-34 (1990); *But see* Fund for Modern Courts, Inc., THE SUCCESS OF WOMEN AND MINORITIES IN ACHIEVING JUDICIAL OFFICE: THE SELECTION PROCESS (1985).

8. Legislation considered in Texas in 1991 would have had judges chosen initially by partisan elections in single-member districts, but then subjected them to at-large retention elections after a fixed term. If retained, they would have served a second term, then faced partisan reelection within their single-member districts again. If reelected, they would have served another term, then faced another at-large retention election, and so on.

9. *See* Carbon, *Judicial retention elections: are they serving their intended purpose?*, 64 JUDICATURE 210-233 (1980); Carbon and Berkson, RETENTION ELECTIONS IN THE UNITED STATES (Chicago: American Judicature Society, 1980); Hall and Aspin, *What twenty years of judicial retention elections have told us*, 70 JUDICATURE 340 (1987).

10. *See* Kales, UNPOPULAR GOVERNMENT IN THE UNITED STATES, ch. 17 (Chicago: University of Chicago Press, 1914).

11. Most of Kales's supporters were wary of retention elections, apparently preferring life appointment for meritorious judges. *See* Carbon, *supra* n. 9, at 215.

12. Another 10 states use merit selection procedures to fill midterm vacancies.

13. They are Alaska, Arizona, California, Colorado, Florida, Georgia, Idaho, Illinois, Indiana, Iowa, Kansas, Maryland, Missouri, Montana, Nebraska, Oklahoma, Pennsylvania, Tennessee, Utah, and Wyoming.

14. For detailed descriptions of judicial selection provisions by state, see Warrick, JUDICIAL SELECTION IN THE UNITED STATES: A COMPENDIUM OF PROVISIONS (Chicago: American Judicature Society, 2d ed., 1993).

15. California, however, has no distinct probationary term. Once appointed, a judge serves the full 12 year term before being put on the retention ballot (although those appointed to fill interim vacancies must face retention at the end of the term of the judge they replace).

16. This dissociation of retention elections from merit selection is at odds with the merit plan's original objectives, which were to recruit highly qualified judges and to insulate them from political pressures. Kales and his colleagues distrusted competitive elections as a means of judicial selection and would undoubtedly have been loath to grant near-certain life tenure to judges chosen in this fashion. In the same spirit, Cohn argues that the mating of competitive partisan elections with noncompetitive retention elections represents an "incongruous joinder of two undesirable elements," providing life tenure to many individuals who may not have deserved selection in the first place. To a lesser extent, the same objection, from the standpoint of a merit selection supporter, applies to systems that couple retention elections with unconstrained gubernatorial appointment. *See* Cohn, TO JUDGE WITH JUSTICE: HISTORY AND POLITICS OF ILLINOIS JUDICIAL REFORM 148 (Urbana: University of Illinois Press, 1973).

17. Hall and Aspin, *supra* n. 9.

18. Quoted in Jenkins, *Retention elections: who wins when no one loses?*, 61 JUDICATURE 79, 80 (1977).

19. Hall and Aspin, *supra* n. 9; *See also* Griffin and Horan, *Judicial Retention Election Decisions: a Search for Correlates*, 19 SOC. SCI. J. 29-34 (1982); and Scheb, *Is anyone listening? assessing influence on merit retention elections in Florida*, 67 JUDICATURE 112-119 (1983).

20. Smaller districts exhibit lesser roll-off, as do elections in which the incumbent has received large doses of negative publicity. *See* Hall and Aspin, *supra* n. 9.

21. *See* Griffin and Horan, *supra* n. 19, at 29-34.

22. Griffin and Horan, *Patterns of voting behavior in judicial retention elections for supreme court justices in Wyoming*, 67 JUDICATURE 69-77 (1983).

23. Griffin and Horan, *Merit retention elections: what influences the voters*, 63 JUDICATURE 78 (1979).

24. *Id.*

25. Consistent with this interpretation is Hall and Aspin's hypothesis that retention votes are partly a function of political trust, unconnected with judicial performance. As the extent to which American citizens trust officeholders has declined, the proportion of votes cast for retention in judicial retention elections has also declined. *See* Hall and Aspin, *supra* n. 9.

26. Dubois, FROM BALLET TO BENCH: JUDICIAL ELECTIONS AND THE QUEST FOR ACCOUNTABILITY (Austin: University of Texas Press, 1980).

27. *See* Dubois, *The Influence of Selection System and Region on the Characteristics of a Trial Court Bench: The Case of California*, 8 JUST. SYS. J. 64-66 (1983); Alozie, *Distribution of Women and Minority Judges: The Effects of Judicial Selection Methods*, 71 SOC. SCI. Q. 315-325 (1990).

28. Graham writes of "formal" versus "informal" selection methods, terminology we avoid. The methods by which midterm vacancies are filled are just as prescribed by law—just as formal—as those by which judges are more routinely chosen. Graham, *Do Judicial Selection Systems Matter? A Study of Black*

Representation on State Courts, 18 AM. POL. Q. 316-336 (1990).

29. *See* Dunn, *Judicial Elections and the Missouri Plan*, in Ulmer, ed., COURTS, LAW, AND JUDICIAL PROCESSES (New York: Free Press, 1981). A Missouri Bar committee has proposed that the governor give more attention to the appointment of women and minorities as lay members of the nominating commission. *See* Alozie, *supra* n. 27; Arizona, Florida, and Minnesota now require that their nominating commissions be demographically diverse.

30. Missing are the Alaska returns from 1980 and 1984, Kansas returns from 1982 and 1990, Maryland returns from 1990, and Utah returns from 1988. In addition to filling these lacunae subsequent reports will include cases from 1978.

31. It should also be emphasized, since the numbers of black and Hispanic judges are fairly small, that the data (already) include virtually every black or Hispanic district, appellate, or supreme court judge who stood for retention in this period. The small numbers make the estimates a bit less reliable than one might wish, but it is presently impossible to do better. This is all the evidence there is.

32. Alozie, *supra* n. 27.

33. *Supra* n. 28.

34. Clifford, *Bird Calls Opposition's Attack 'Mean Spirited'*, L.A. Times, November 6, 1986, at A-3.

35. The Chicago Bar Association and Chicago Council of Lawyers. The exception was the Cook County Bar Association, a minority bar association that did endorse Thomas.

36. As well as from the Cook County Bar Association.

37. For more detail on these cases (and those of the white judges who lost), see Luskin et al., "At-large Judicial Retention Elections and the Retention of Minority Judges," manuscript. (Austin: Department of Government, University of Texas at Austin, 1991).

38. With some variation, these results closely parallel those of other case studies of judicial retention elections. See Carbon, *supra* n. 9, at 221-233.

Clinton's second term judiciary: picking judges under fire

In the face of a hostile political environment, moderation, compromise, and accommodation were paramount in making judicial appointments.

By Sheldon Goldman and Elliot Slotnick

The Clinton presidency, whether fairly or unfairly, is indelibly marked by the sex scandal that threatened to topple Bill Clinton from office during the first half of his second term. The unrelenting pursuit of the president by Independent Counsel Kenneth Starr and his staff, culminating in the referral to the House of Representatives alleging the commission of impeachable offenses (all of which were tied to the sex scandal) made for an extraordinary operating climate. Although buoyed by favorable public opinion ratings even after lurid detail after lurid detail was leaked or released to the media, the administration nevertheless appeared at times to be paralyzed and demoralized. Congress continued to be controlled by a hostile Republican majority capitalizing on the president's troubles. Within this political environment, President Clinton and his administration chose men and women to staff the nation's courts.

This article examines judicial selection and the persons ultimately confirmed for the federal bench during the first half of Clinton's second term.[1] It draws heavily on interviews with key participants and observers of judicial selection and on inferences from the statistical record. Data on the backgrounds of judges came from the questionnaires all judicial nominees complete and submit to the Senate Judiciary Committee, supplemented by data collected from standard biographical sources,[2] the appointee's home-state newspapers, boards of election, professional colleagues, and responses from Clinton appointees.

The selection process

During the first half of Clinton's second term, judicial selection continued much as it did during the first term, but at the White House greater personnel resources were invested to help accelerate the pace. At the Justice Department, Eleanor D. Acheson continued as head of the Office of Policy Development (OPD). Investigating the professional qualifications of potential judicial nominees and coordinating the evaluative process were among her office's tasks.

The evaluative process begins when the White House counsel's office sends the names of prospective nominees to OPD.[3] Each is assigned to an OPD lawyer or a lawyer from another division temporarily assigned to OPD to be in charge of the vetting process for a specific individual. The vettor will already have received copies of the extensive questionnaires that the potential nominee has completed (for the administration, the ABA, the FBI, and the Senate Judiciary Committee; the latter three are not sent to the respective institutions until the nomination is on track or has been made). The questionnaires provide investigative leads, for example, judges before whom the potential nominee appeared, opposing counsel, co-counsel, and if the candidate is a judge, other judges on the candidate's bench. The vettor will review all published opinions if the candidate is or was a judge, any writings, including law review articles, and any newspaper stories about the candidate.

Once the paper trail stage of the process is nearing completion, and assuming that nothing has emerged that the administration or senate might view as disqualifying, the vettor conducts an extensive one to two hour telephone interview with the candidate. The vettor reviews the answers to the questionnaires, discusses any discrepancies between the candidate's written responses and information that turned up from the vettor's investigation, and any possible issue that might affect the candidacy. Assuming the telephone interview goes well, the vettor will make calls to a wide variety of individuals, typically including the chief judges of the federal district and appeals courts in which the individual is a candidate, state and federal judges before whom the candidate has appeared, state judicial colleagues if the candidate is on the state bench, the U.S. attorney for the candidate's district, the local prosecutor, the public defender, local bar association leaders, opposing counsel, co-counsel, and partners/associates if the candidate has worked in a law firm.

Within OPD there is a judicial nomination working group that meets regularly and during which vettors present their reports and the group discusses individual candidacies—in some instances suggestions are made as to additional people that should be contacted. The working group also decides whether to proceed to the next stage—the personal interview. If the decision is made to invite the candidate to visit the Justice Department, he or she is interviewed by Eleanor D. Acheson, her deputy who handles selection, the individual who vetted the candidate, and at least one additional staff member. Furthermore, officials from the White House counsel's office are invited to the interviews and often come, particularly if there are any doubts about a candidate who has been strongly pushed by the home state senators.

Assuming that the in-person interview goes well, the candidate is told to submit the ABA questionnaire to the ABA. The candidate's FBI form, previously submitted by the candidate to OPD, is sent to the FBI for a full field investigation and report. The ABA and FBI investigations normally take four to six weeks. The ABA Standing Committee on Federal Judiciary sends a letter conveying the rating of the candidate—well qualified, qualified, or not qualified, and the FBI sends its full background report. These materials are read by Acheson, her deputy, and other staff members cleared to examine FBI materials. An OPD memorandum on the

candidate goes to the attorney general, who informally may have previously been told of the candidacy and any potential problems.

Every Thursday, except when other matters require a postponement, the joint White House-Justice Department committee (known as the Judicial Selection Group) meets in the office of the White House counsel, who serves as chair. That committee examines the material on each candidate and makes a decision whether or not to recommend to the president for nomination. The membership of this high level group includes, in addition to the White House counsel, the deputy White House counsel, presidential assistant Bruce R. Lindsey, chief of staff John Podesta, a representative from the vice-president's office, a representative from the first lady's office, three or four members of the White House counsel's staff who work on judges, and from the Justice Department the assistant attorney general for the Office of Policy Development and her deputy.

For district court positions the Justice Department generally evaluates one candidate per slot at a time. But for appeals courts positions more than one candidate may be evaluated for a specific slot, and sometimes a memorandum is prepared on an individual without the candidate's knowledge, although in such instances the administration by roundabout methods will have determined that the individual would be interested in a judgeship.

During the first half of Clinton's second term, the Senate of the 105th Congress confirmed 79 of the 94 district court nominees (84 percent) and 19 of the 28 appeals court nominees (67.9 percent). A look at the confirmation process during the 105th Congress places these figures in a broader political context.

The confirmation process

Efforts to analyze the confirmation process for nominees to the federal bench, save perhaps for those limited instances in which Supreme Court vacancies are being filled, are hampered by the difficulty of devising methods to recognize "success." Clearly, success cannot be measured by outcomes on the Senate floor because it is the rarest of circumstances when a lower federal court judicial appointment will result in defeat as a consequence of a confirmation vote. Indeed, such a happenstance has not occurred during the Clinton presidency. Rather, presidential success and, more to the point, presidential difficulties, may best be assessed by criteria such as the extent of delay in confirmation processes (both at the committee and floor stages), the extent to which floor debate and divided roll call votes are held on nominees, and, ultimately, the failure to gain votes on nominees who have been sent forward by the Judiciary Committee. On these and other measures it remains clear that confirmation processes were far from "business as usual," although the fabric of confirmation politics in the 105th Congress demonstrates some improvement from the situation that prevailed through much of the 104th Congress.[4]

Indeed, combining Clinton's district and appeals court appointments for the 103rd Congress reveals that almost 90 percent of the nominations received in the Senate and 100 percent of those reported out of committee resulted in confirmation in the Democratically controlled Senate. In the Republican controlled 104th Congress the administration had to contend with a conservative Republican Senator (Orrin Hatch) chairing the Judiciary Committee and, also, for most of the legislative session, a Republican presidential candidate (Bob Dole) who served as Senate Majority Leader in a setting where there was much to be gained, or so it seemed, in embarrassing the president on the judgeship front by raising questions about and delaying the confirmation of his nominees. In that setting, slightly more than 70 percent of all nominations received resulted in confirmation, while 6.4 percent of those reported favorably out of committee were not confirmed.

The environment facing Bill Clinton in the 105th Congress, the first half of his second term, did not, on the surface, appear to be much more hospitable. The Senate was still controlled by the Republicans, Orrin Hatch still chaired the critical Judiciary Committee, and now ultra-conservative Senator Trent Lott of Mississippi was the Senate's majority leader and appeared poised to continue the unprecedented slowdown in the confirmation process that characterized the 104th Congress.

Despite this confirmation context, the numbers suggest that the administration fared "better" in the 105th Congress (albeit not as well as it had in the 103rd Congress before the establishment of divided government). Thus, about 80 percent of the nominations received in the 105th Congress resulted in confirmation and there was a decline to about 3 percent in the total number of nomina-

tions reported favorably out of the Judiciary Committee, but on which no vote was scheduled or held on the Senate floor.

A number of factors help to explain the administration's greater success in 1998 than in the previous two years. These include improvements in the administration's own handling of judicial selection matters, the role of Chief Justice William Rehnquist in drawing attention to the untenable state of affairs in appointment processes and, in the final analysis, widespread and hostile reaction to the hubris displayed by the conservative right and, in particular, a number of conservative senators who had been largely responsible for the gridlock of 1996-1997.

According to a lobbyist who is an active participant in the judicial selection arena, "One thing that the Clinton administration has done better now than two years ago is in funneling judges to the Senate. In '96 and '97 when there was so much gridlock, some of that had to be attributed to the slow pace of producing nominees." Several of the sources for this article, including those in the administration itself, indicated that to rectify the slow pace of nominations some structural changes were made with more activity centered in the White House.

In particular, the judicial appointments issue was one that resonated with Charles Ruff, the White House counsel and John Podesta, the president's chief of staff, two players who were not central figures in judicial selection politics in the last two years of Clinton's first term. In addition, Mark Childress, a congressional aide with a great deal of legislative experience who had previously worked for Senator Ted Kennedy, was brought into the White House's legislative operation to work on all confirmation processes, including those involving judgeships.

An administration official in the White House counsel's office observed that the restructuring that led to Childress' entry into the process was beneficial because, "we can have one person sort of watching and having some clout on the Hill with both judicial and nonjudicial nominations. This is a much more efficient system." Assistant Attorney General Acheson agreed that broad beneficial consequences resulted from the restructuring that occurred:

I think we kind of reassessed how we were doing our

own work, not just here and at the White House separately, but how we were working together. What had been, I think, a really connected, communicating, crack organization until the mid-part of 1997 kind of struggled...for a bunch of reasons but we dealt with that. We addressed those problems and got them fixed so that we were, throughout 1998...able to move people much faster.

Greater dispatch in making nominations, as an aide to Acheson commented, had a beneficial effect simply because it drew attention away from the administration to the behavior of the Judiciary Committee and, in particular, its chair, Orrin Hatch. "As Hatch has said a bunch of times, 'I'm a good senator, but not so good that I can vote a nomination out of committee that I don't have.'" Senior Democrats on his committee, especially Patrick Leahy of Vermont, added to the continual pressure to move forward.

A second reason that was widely cited for the administration's increased success in 1998 was the critical role played by Chief Justice Rehnquist who, in his State of the Judiciary Address, called attention to the appointments crisis and, while not completely "taking sides," pointed his finger primarily at the Senate as the major "problem."[5] As one source in the White House counsel's office put it:

When in '97 we were at a stage where there was a lot of partisan bickering, the nominations process was not moving as quickly as we had hoped, and the confirmation process was certainly gridlocked...In his year end report he [the chief justice] drew attention to the situation and said, 'We can't maintain the quality of justice if this situation isn't rectified,' and both sides listened. And, so, he really jump started that and deserves the credit.

Assistant Attorney General Acheson noted that the chief justice's remarks

totally galvanized Senator Hatch. I think he felt wrongly criticized and very upset by the criticism of the Chief Justice and had a period of some reaction to it. But he very quickly...decided, as was exactly the right decision, that the best way to put all of this behind us was to at least move the process.

We have characterized the third factor that played in the administration's favor as the "hubris" displayed by its ideological opponents in judicial selection politics. As one observer stated in an interview, "there was overreaching in trying to lower the bar on what a judicial activist judge was, and that fell flat on its face." Noting particularly the opposition that conservatives raised to circuit nominee Margaret McKeown and to district judge candidates Margaret Morrow and Ann Aiken, Nan Aron of the Alliance for Justice commented that they "clearly were candidates with exemplary records. And to pick on them, they were women, they had very full backgrounds in the law, excellent, distinguished credentials, and I think they [the opponents] kind of showed their hand solely opposing them for political [reasons]."

From the administration's perspective, as Eleanor Acheson underscored, "the time delay has been, particularly in 1996 and 1997, really horrific.... I wouldn't even call them delays. It was just a complete, almost destruction of the system."

Viewed most broadly, Acheson characterized 1996-1997 as "a real effort to...penalize...the federal judiciary institutionally." While aimed partly at the administration, "it was as much about the judges" and, "it's [as much] a feature of largely Republican judges or judges appointed by Republican presidents and their actions [as] it was about Clinton and who he was picking to appoint." Perhaps ironically, the gridlock of the latter half of Clinton's first term may have been a proximate cause of the increased activity in the first half of his second term. As Acheson described the "good aspects" of the slowdown,

We had a lot of nominations building up.... As slow as you, yourself, may be...your nominations pile up. They don't go anywhere so you've got a lot pending and if you start adding to them at a pretty fair clip, which is what we were able to do last year, and really build up a lot of momentum...it puts a lot of pressure. The Committee can't get into, 'Well look, we've had hearings, but we've done all the viable people,' which is what Hatch was saying. We didn't agree with that because we thought everybody we sent up there was viable and continue to think so. But it makes it much harder to say when you've got 20 and then 30 and then 40 nominees and more.

In the final analysis, Acheson concluded that the effort to block judicial appointments by attacking judges and the judiciary writ large failed. "I'm just guessing now, but I think there was a sort of vitriol kind of spent. I think people got sick of, 'Let's yell at the judges' [which] really sort of peaked in '96 and spilled over into '97 a little bit...."

And attacking the judiciary began to garner its own enemies along the way. As Acheson noted, local Bars got tremendously and rightfully infuriated over what happened, and I mean that from the point of view of the practicing Bar and the courts themselves.... [T]hey went, not just respectfully but, after a while in an infuriated way to their senators and their members of Congress in many cases and said, "Look, enough is enough. This is stupid."

While the foregoing analysis has underscored that the administration did "better" in seating federal judges in the 105th Congress than it had in the 104th, it remains the case that this characterization does not always ring true and, indeed, that the situation in our current divided governmental setting remains far from ideal from the perspective of the pace of the confirmation process. Indeed, if undue delay was the hallmark of confirmation processes in the latter half of Clinton's first term in office, the situation did not improve appreciably and, arguably, was even worse in some respects in the first half of Clinton's second term.

This can be seen, for example, in the profiles of Judiciary Committee processes for district judgeship nominees in the past four congresses. Thus, in the unified government characterized by the 103rd Congress, with Clinton enjoying a Democratic majority in the Senate, the average number of days from the time a nomination was received on the Hill to the date of a hearing was 58.8. By way of contrast, when George Bush faced the Democratic 102nd Congress that average was 92.1 days and in the 104th Congress, Clinton's first with a Republican majority, the average was 76.2 days. In the Republican 105th Congress, that average swelled dramatically to 160.6 days. In addition, the 105th Congress also displayed the highest average number of days between the holding of a hearing to the reporting of a nomination out of committee.

Parallel and, indeed, even starker findings emerge in viewing committee processes for circuit judgeship nominees. Thus, for the 102nd, 103rd, and 104th congresses, the average number of days between the receipt of a nomination in the Senate and the holding of a hearing on the nominee ranged between 77.4 and 80.8. In the 105th Congress in 1997-1998, that figure mushroomed to 230.9 days!

The data also suggest that, first, Robert Dole and, then, Trent Lott, played important roles in dramatically slowing down the pace of final floor action on judicial nominees. Thus, for example, at the district court level, the Senate in the Democratic 102nd Congress confirmed George Bush's nominees on an average of 3.2 days after the nomination was reported out of committee. That figure was 4.3 days in the Democratic 103rd Congress enjoyed by Bill Clinton. Clinton's nominees, however, have had a considerably more difficult time in the past four years of divided government, when the average time to confirmation after being reported favorably out of committee was 35.3 days in the 104th Congress and 38.4 days in the 105th.

At the circuit level, George Bush's nominees were confirmed in an average of 14.4 days after being reported out of committee in the Democratic 102nd Congress and Bill Clinton's appointees were confirmed in an average of a mere 8.7 days after being reported out to the Democratic Senate in the 103rd Congress. Clinton has not fared as well in divided government with an average of 39.5 days until floor action in the 104th Congress and an average of 42.4 days in the 105th. It is impossible to escape the conclusion that the Republican leadership in the Senate was engaged in a protracted effort to delay decision making on judicial appointments whether or not the appointee was, ultimately, confirmable. Clearly, if there was a "crisis" in the appointments process in the Clinton presidency it was a crisis of unprecedented delay at both the committee and floor stages and not, in an absolute sense, inaction on the judgeship front.

District court appointees

The backgrounds of Clinton's district court appointees are presented in three tables. Table 1 compares the 79 judges confirmed during the 105th Congress to the 169 confirmed during Clinton's first term by the 103rd and 104th Congresses.[6] Table 2 focuses on appointees from the 105th Congress and compares the 32 nontraditional (women and minorities) to the 47 traditional (white male) appointees. Also keep in mind that by the end of the 105th Congress seven nontraditional and four traditional nominees went unconfirmed. Table 3 presents the composite portrait of Clinton's appointees through his first six years in office compared to the appointees of his three immediate predecessors.

Occupation. As seen in Table 1, Clinton's second term appointees differ from those of the first

Table 1 Clinton's first term U.S. district court appointees compared to his second term appointees (confirmed in 1997-1998)

	First term appointees		Second term appointees	
	%	(N)	%	(N)
Occupation				
Politics/government	10.7%	(18)	11.4%	(9)
Judiciary	44.4%	(75)	51.9%	(41)
Large law firm				
100+ members	8.3%	(14)	3.8%	(3)
50-99	5.3%	(9)	5.1%	(4)
25-49	3.6%	(6)	3.8%	(3)
Moderate size firm				
10-24 members	8.3%	(14)	7.6%	(6)
5-9	8.3%	(14)	5.1%	(4)
Small firm				
2-4	5.3%	(9)	5.1%	(4)
solo	2.4%	(4)	5.1%	(4)
Professor of law	2.4%	(4)	—	
Other	1.2%	(2)	1.3%	(1)
Experience				
Judicial	49.7%	(84)	54.4%	(43)
Prosecutorial	37.9%	(64)	46.8%	(37)
Neither	31.4%	(53)	26.6%	(21)
Undergraduate education				
Public	44.4%	(75)	41.8%	(33)
Private	40.8%	(69)	45.6%	(36)
Ivy League	14.8%	(25)	12.7%	(10)
Law school education				
Public	42.6%	(72)	38.0%	(30)
Private	37.3%	(63)	44.3%	(35)
Ivy League	20.1%	(34)	17.7%	(14)
Gender				
Male	69.8%	(118)	76.0%	(60)
Female	30.2%	(51)	24.0%	(19)
Ethnicity/race				
White	72.2%	(122)	77.2%	(61)
African American	19.5%	(33)	17.7%	(14)
Hispanic	6.5%	(11)	2.5%	(2)
Asian	1.2%	(2)	2.5%	(2)
Native American	0.6%	(1)	—	
Percentage white male	47.3%	(80)	59.5%	(47)
ABA rating				
Well Qualified	63.9%	(108)	45.6%	(36)
Qualified	34.3%	(58)	54.4%	(43)
Not Qualified	1.8%	(3)	—	
Political identification				
Democrat	89.9%	(152)	87.3%	(69)
Republican	3.0%	(5)	8.9%	(7)
Other	0.6%	(1)	—	
None	6.5%	(11)	3.8%	(3)
Past party activism	53.9%	(91)	49.4%	(39)
Net worth				
Less than $200,000	17.2%	(29)	11.4%	(9)
$200-499,999	22.5%	(38)	24.1%	(19)
$500-999,999	28.4%	(48)	25.3%	(20)
$1+ million	32.0%	(54)	39.2%	(31)
Average age at nomination	48.7		50.0	
Total number of appointees	169		79	

Table 2 Clinton's nontraditional appointees compared to his traditional appointees to the federal district courts, 1997-1998

	Nontraditional appointees		Traditional appointees	
	%	(N)	%	(N)
Occupation				
Politics/government	18.8%	(6)	6.4%	(3)
Judiciary	59.4%	(19)	46.8%	(22)
Large law firm				
100+ members	3.1%	(1)	4.3%	(2)
50-99	6.2%	(2)	4.3%	(2)
25-49	—		6.4%	(3)
Moderate size firm				
10-24 members	6.2%	(2)	8.5%	(4)
5-9	3.1%	(1)	6.4%	(3)
Small firm				
2-4	—		8.5%	(4)
solo	—		8.5%	(4)
Professor of law	—		—	
Other	3.1%	(1)	—	
Experience				
Judicial	62.5%	(20)	48.9%	(23)
Prosecutorial	59.4%	(19)	38.3%	(18)
Neither	15.6%	(5)	34.0%	(16)
Undergraduate education				
Public	43.8%	(14)	40.4%	(19)
Private	50.0%	(16)	42.6%	(20)
Ivy League	6.2%	(2)	17.0%	(8)
Law school education				
Public	28.1%	(9)	44.7%	(21)
Private	56.3%	(18)	36.2%	(17)
Ivy League	15.6%	(5)	19.1%	(9)
Gender				
Male	40.6%	(13)	100.0%	(47)
Female	59.4%	(19)	—	
Ethnicity/race				
White	43.8%	(14)	100.0%	(47)
African American	43.8%	(14)	—	
Hispanic	6.2%	(2)	—	
Asian	6.2%	(2)	—	
ABA rating				
Well Qualified	43.8%	(14)	46.8%	(22)
Qualified	56.2%	(18)	53.2%	(25)
Political identification				
Democrat	93.8%	(30)	82.9%	(39)
Republican	3.1%	(1)	12.8%	(6)
None	3.1%	(1)	4.3%	(2)
Past party activism	34.4%	(11)	59.6%	(28)
Net worth				
Less than $200,000	15.6%	(5)	8.5%	(4)
$200-499,999	28.1%	(9)	21.3%	(10)
$500-999,999	25.0%	(8)	25.5%	(12)
$1+ million	31.2%	(10)	44.7%	(21)
Average age at nomination	47.4		51.7	
Total number of appointees	32		47	

term in some noteworthy respects. More than half came to the federal district court bench from other judgeships, a larger proportion than for the first term appointees. Also there were proportionately fewer second term appointees who came from the superfirms (law firms with 100 or more members) and no one who came from the law schools.

Table 2 makes it evident that the surge in appointees who came from other judgeships can largely be attributed to the nontraditional appointees—three out of five of whom came with such a judicial background. Indeed, more than three fourths of the nontraditional appointees were public employees as compared to slightly more than half the traditional appointees. About 18 percent of the nontraditional appointees were in the private practice of law as compared to about 32 percent of traditional appointees. These findings are consistent with previous findings that the public sector has provided women and minorities with more opportunities for professional advancement

Table 3 U.S. district court appointees compared by administration

	Clinton %	(N)	Bush %	(N)	Reagan %	(N)	Carter %	(N)
Occupation								
Politics/government	10.9%	(27)	10.8%	(16)	13.4%	(39)	5.0%	(10)
Judiciary	46.8%	(116)	41.9%	(62)	36.9%	(107)	44.6%	(90)
Large law firm								
100+ members	6.9%	(17)	10.8%	(16)	6.2%	(18)	2.0%	(4)
50-99	5.2%	(13)	7.4%	(11)	4.8%	(14)	5.9%	(12)
25-49	3.6%	(9)	7.4%	(11)	6.9%	(20)	5.9%	(12)
Moderate size firm								
10-24 members	8.1%	(20)	8.8%	(13)	10.0%	(29)	9.4%	(19)
5-9	7.3%	(18)	6.1%	(9)	9.0%	(26)	10.4%	(21)
Small firm								
2-4	5.2%	(13)	3.4%	(5)	7.2%	(21)	10.9%	(22)
solo	3.2%	(8)	1.4%	(2)	2.8%	(8)	2.5%	(5)
Professor of law	1.6%	(4)	0.7%	(1)	2.1%	(6)	3.0%	(6)
Other	1.2%	(3)	1.4%	(2)	0.7%	(2)	0.5%	(1)
Experience								
Judicial	51.2%	(127)	46.6%	(69)	46.2%	(134)	54.0%	(109)
Prosecutorial	40.7%	(101)	39.2%	(58)	44.1%	(128)	38.1%	(77)
Neither	29.8%	(74)	31.8%	(47)	28.6%	(83)	30.7%	(62)
Undergraduate education								
Public	43.6%	(108)	44.6%	(66)	36.6%	(106)	56.4%	(114)
Private	42.3%	(105)	41.2%	(61)	49.7%	(144)	33.7%	(68)
Ivy League	14.1%	(35)	14.2%	(21)	13.8%	(40)	9.9%	(20)
Law school education								
Public	41.1%	(102)	52.7%	(78)	42.4%	(123)	50.5%	(102)
Private	39.5%	(98)	33.1%	(49)	45.9%	(133)	32.7%	(66)
Ivy League	19.4%	(48)	14.2%	(21)	11.7%	(34)	16.8%	(34)
Gender								
Male	71.8%	(178)	80.4%	(119)	91.7%	(266)	85.6%	(173)
Female	28.2%	(70)	19.6%	(29)	8.3%	(24)	14.4%	(29)
Ethnicity/race								
White	73.8%	(183)	89.2%	(132)	92.4%	(268)	78.7%	(159)
African American	19.0%	(47)	6.8%	(10)	2.1%	(6)	13.9%	(28)
Hispanic	5.2%	(13)	4.0%	(6)	4.8%	(14)	6.9%	(14)
Asian	1.6%	(4)	—		0.7%	(2)	0.5%	(1)
Native American	0.4%	(1)	—		—		—	
Percentage white male	51.2%	(127)	73.0%	(108)	84.8%	(246)	68.3%	(138)
ABA rating								
Exceptionally well qualified/well qualified	58.1%	(144)	57.4%	(85)	53.5%	(155)	51.0%	(103)
Qualified	40.7%	(101)	42.6%	(63)	46.6%	(135)	47.5%	(96)
Not Qualified	1.2%	(3)	—		—		1.5%	(3)
Political identification								
Democrat	89.1%	(221)	5.4%	(8)	4.8%	(14)	90.6%	(183)
Republican	4.8%	(12)	88.5%	(131)	91.7%	(266)	4.5%	(9)
Other	0.4%	(1)	—		—		—	
None	5.7%	(14)	6.1%	(9)	3.4%	(10)	5.0%	(10)
Past party activism	52.4%	(130)	60.8%	(90)	59.0%	(171)	60.9%	(123)
Net worth								
Less than $200,000	15.3%	(38)	10.1%	(15)	17.6%	(51)	35.8%*	(53)
$200-499,999	23.0%	(57)	31.1%	(46)	37.6%	(109)	41.2%	(61)
$500-999,999	27.4%	(68)	26.4%	(39)	21.7%	(63)	18.9%	(28)
$1+ million	34.3%	(85)	32.4%	(48)	23.1%	(67)	4.0%	(6)
Average age at nomination	49.1		48.1		48.7		49.6	
Total number of appointees	248		148		290		202	

* These figures are for appointees confirmed by the 96th Congress for all but six Carter district court appointees (for whom no data were available).

Sources: for Carter and Reagan appointees—Goldman, PICKING FEDERAL JUDGES: LOWER COURT SELECTION FROM ROOSEVELT THROUGH REAGAN (New Haven: Yale University Press, 1997) pp. 348-350; for Bush appointees—Goldman, *Bush's judicial legacy: the final imprint*, 76 JUDICATURE 287 (1993).

than the private sector.

The composite figures in Table 3 show the Clinton appointees with the highest proportion of the four presidential cohorts of appointees coming from the judiciary, with the Carter, Bush, and Reagan appointees following in that order. That is also, not coincidentally, the order of the highest to lowest proportion of nontraditional appointees. The substantial numbers of appointees from all four administrations coming to district judgeships from another judicial post point towards the trend of a career judiciary, one that is even more evident with the figures for the appeals courts, as we shall see. And the most startling example of a career judiciary is the United States Supreme Court which consists, with the exception of the chief justice, of justices who came from a lower court judgeship. The tendency toward a career judiciary is a byproduct of judicial selection processes that are concerned with judicial philosophy and temperament that administrations believe can best be discerned from judicial track records.

During the first term, more than one fourth of those who came from the judiciary were U.S. magistrates (or in some instances U.S. bankruptcy judges). But during the second term only about 10 percent of those who came from the judiciary were in federal judicial posts (three U.S. magistrates and one bankruptcy judge). Eighty percent of the first term U.S. magistrates or bankruptcy judges were nontraditional; in the second term all four were nontraditional. U.S. magistrate positions, and to a much lesser extent bankruptcy court positions, remain a source of recruitment to the federal district court bench, especially for women and minorities.

The U.S. attorney's office accounted for few Clinton appointees (only four of the second term appointees). As seen in Table 3, Clinton's proportion of superfirm appointees was less than Bush's but greater than Reagan's and Carter's. Law school faculties accounted for an insignificant proportion of appointees, all from the first term (and 3 of the 4 confirmed by the Democratic Senate of the 103rd Congress). Divided government appears to have been inhospitable to legal scholars with a paper trail of law review articles whose point of view might prove controversial.

Experience. Table 1 shows that the second term appointees, as compared to the first term, had more judicial and prosecutorial experience. And Table 2 suggests that the nontraditional appointees were largely responsible for this surge. Indeed, only about 1 in 7 nontraditional appointees had neither judicial nor prosecutorial experience as compared to about 1 in 3 traditional appointees. In Table 3 we see that in terms of all of Clinton's district court appointees more than half had judicial experience (only Carter's appointees had more) and about 2 in 5 had prosecutorial experience (only Reagan's appointees had more).

Continuing the trend begun with the Carter appointees, there was a higher proportion with judicial experience than with prosecutorial experience, another finding consistent with the trend toward a career judiciary. Overall about 3 in 10 appointees of all four administrations had neither judicial nor prosecutorial experience.

Education. Table 1 suggests few differences be-tween the educational backgrounds of the first and second term appointees. The second term appointees have more private undergraduate and law school and less Ivy League educational backgrounds. Table 2, however, shows traditional appointees with a higher proportion of Ivy League training, both undergraduate and law school. Overall, however, as Table 3 shows, close to 1 in 5 Clinton appointees graduated from an Ivy League law school. If we add to these schools such prestigious law schools as Berkeley, Chicago, Duke, Georgetown, Michigan, New York University, Northwestern, Stanford, Texas, Vanderbilt, and Virginia, the proportion of Clinton appointees with a prestige legal education rises to about 39 percent (34 percent of Bush's appointees graduated from such prestige law schools).

Gender and ethnicity. Of all four administrations, Clinton's appointed the largest proportions of women and African Americans, achieving historic highs in numbers and proportions. Close to 3 out of 10 Clinton appointees were women and close to 1 out of 5 were African American. In six years Clinton has named 70 women to the federal district bench. By contrast, in the 12 years of the Reagan and Bush presidencies 53 women were named. In six years Clinton has named 47 African Americans. In the 12 years of the Reagan and Bush administrations only 16 were named. The proportion of Asian Americans appointed by Clinton, however, was exceedingly small and the proportion of Native Americans almost non-existent. The proportion of Hispanics fell during Clinton's second term and overall Carter had a better record of appointing Hispanics than Clinton. In Clinton's six years only 13 Hispanics were appointed. During the 12 years of Reagan-Bush 20 were named to the district bench.

During the first term about 53 percent of Clinton's district court appointees were nontraditional; that fell to 40 percent during the second term. Had all nominees been confirmed, the second term proportion would have risen to about 43 percent, still a decline from the first term but nevertheless precedent-making proportions.[7] It is likely that these figures reflect a somewhat more cautious approach to selection, taking into account the fact that the Senate was controlled by Republicans. Alternatively, one can argue that the falling proportion of nontraditional appointees reflects the reality that white males still constitute the large majority of the legal profession. Even though white males can be expected to dominate the judiciary in proportions and numbers for the foreseeable future (See "Nontraditional judges in active service," page 83), Clinton's record of diversifying the federal bench will surely be one of his most significant legacies.

ABA ratings. Table 3 shows that six years worth of Clinton appointees yielded the highest proportion of all four administrations receiving the top ratings from the Standing Committee on Federal Judiciary of the American Bar Association. There were three appointees rated Not Qualified, all from Clinton's first two years in office.

The composite figures for Clinton's appointees, however, obscures a stark fact emerging from Table 1—the proportion of second term appointees with the highest rating was markedly lower than that for the first term appointees. And as Table 2 suggests that was as true for the traditional as it was for the nontraditional appointees. Indeed, comparing the traditional appointees from the first term we found that almost 3 in 4 had the highest ABA rating. But for the first half of the second term, the proportion with the highest rating fell below half (from 73.8 percent to 46.8 percent).

We can only speculate as to the reason. It could be that this was related to the announcement in February 1997 by the chair of the Senate Judiciary Committee, Orrin Hatch, which was the culmination of a number of years of criticizing the ABA rating system, that ABA ratings would no longer play an official role in the committee's evaluation process.[8] Perhaps the administration no longer saw the *highest* ABA rating as improving the chances for confirmation or as a reason for favoring one candidate over another. Nevertheless the administration clearly took the ratings seriously because it did not nominate anyone rated "Not Qualified" during the 104th and 105th congresses. If the ABA ratings are considered a measure of quality, the overall quality of Clinton's second term judiciary thus far, though high, is not as high as its first term judiciary. Another possibility is that some very talented lawyers are being scared off by the prospect of interminable delays in the confirmation process, or even worse, the partisan or ideological blacklisting by some Senate Republicans.

Political party. The composite record of the Clinton appointees seen in Table 3 shows almost 9 out of 10 identified with the president's party—a

record similar to that of the three previous presidents. And Clinton's overall proportion of appointments going to Republicans was the same as the overall proportion of Reagan's appointments going to Democrats. However, the composite portrait of Clinton's appointees masks a most interesting development that is evident from Table 1—the proportion of Republicans Clinton appointed during the first half of his second term was about triple that of the first term. And as Table 2 shows all but one of the Republicans were white males. These statistics suggest that the Clinton administration, to a limited extent, felt obliged to accommodate some Republican senators, an inevitable bowing to the reality of the Republican stranglehold on the confirmation process. This was also a corrective to the almost but not quite complete absence of Republicans during the previous 104th Congress.

Yet in terms of prominent past partisan activism less than half the appointees had such backgrounds, and of these, as suggested by Table 2, it was the traditional appointees who were most active (about 3 out of 5 appointees) as compared to the nontraditional appointees (about 1 out of 3). Clearly the absence of a political background was no hindrance for the recruitment of women and minorities for the federal district bench. Overall, as presented in Table 3, the Clinton appointees' record of past partisan activism was the smallest proportion of the appointees of all four presidents.

Net worth. The second term Clinton appointees tended to be more well-to-do than the first term appointees. But as Table 2 shows, traditional appointees tended to be wealthier than nontraditional appointees. Overall, the proportion of millionaires appointed by Clinton exceeded marginally the proportion appointed by Bush. More than 1 in 3 Clinton appointees had a net worth of at least $1 million. In contrast, fewer than 1 in 20 Carter appointees were millionaires. Even taking into account inflation, the Clinton appointees appear to have been more drawn from the well-to-do than Carter's appointees. However, the figures also show that almost 2 in 5 Clinton appointees had a net worth less than $500,000 and could not be considered wealthy.

Age. The average age of the second term appointees thus far is greater than that for the first term appointees. By gender and race, Clinton's second term nontraditional appointees were on average more than four years younger than the traditional appointees.[9] Overall, the Clinton appointees' average age was older than the Bush and Reagan appointees but about a half year younger on average than the Carter appointees. The proportion of second term appointees under the age of 45 was only about 16 percent; the figure for the first term was only 24 percent, the smallest proportions of all four administrations.[10] Age clearly does not appear to have been a consideration in Clinton's appointments.

Appeals court appointees

At first blush, it would appear that President Clinton was relatively successful in seating appeals court nominees in the first half of his second term. Table 4 (which compares Clinton's first term appointees with those made during the first half of his second term) documents that, while Clinton appointed 29 circuit judges during his entire first term in office, he has already appointed 19 during the first half of his second term. One must be cautious, however, in making an assessment of "relative" success based on those numbers alone. For one thing, the 19 appointments during 1997-1998 are quite on par with those made by Clinton during 1993-1994 (18), his first two years in office, a period during which the administration was heavily criticized for being unduly slow in processing its nominations. Further, the 29 circuit judges appointed during the first term can be considered a relatively low number compared to recent presidencies that is reflective of the few appointments (11) made during the 104th Congress, which corresponded to the second half of Clinton's first term. Indeed, in the second year of the 104th Congress, the Republican controlled Senate did not confirm any of the 7 appeals court nominations submitted.

It is in this context that the 19 appointments during the first half of Clinton's second term can be considered, in a sense, as a return to "normalcy," with the president able to seat some of the very judges he was unable to have confirmed in the final year of his first term. Further, it should be pointed out that despite the greater number of appointments in 1997-1998, when compared with the previous two years, as we enter the final two years of the Clinton presidency about 10 percent of the authorized appellate court seats remain vacant (see Table 8), and there were only two less

Table 4 Clinton's first term U.S. appeals court appointees compared to his second term appointees (confirmed in 1997-1998)

	First term appointees		Second term appointees	
	%	(N)	%	(N)
Occupation				
Politics/government	3.4%	(1)	5.3%	(1)
Judiciary	58.6%	(17)	52.6%	(10)
Large law firm				
100+ members	13.8%	(4)	10.5%	(2)
50-99	—		5.3%	(1)
25-49	3.4%	(1)	5.3%	(1)
Moderate size firm				
10-24 members	3.4%	(1)	15.8%	(3)
5-9	6.9%	(2)	—	
Professor	10.3%	(3)	5.3%	(1)
Experience				
Judicial	69.0%	(20)	52.6%	(10)
Prosecutorial	37.9%	(11)	31.6%	(6)
Neither	20.7%	(6)	36.8%	(7)
Undergraduate education				
Public	51.7%	(15)	36.8%	(7)
Private	27.6%	(8)	42.1%	(8)
Ivy League	20.7%	(6)	21.0%	(4)
Law school education				
Public	41.4%	(12)	36.8%	(7)
Private	31.0%	(9)	15.8%	(3)
Ivy League	27.6%	(8)	47.4%	(9)
Gender				
Male	69.0%	(20)	63.2%	(12)
Female	31.0%	(9)	36.8%	(7)
Ethnicity/race				
White	72.4%	(21)	84.2%	(16)
African American	13.8%	(4)	5.3%	(1)
Hispanic	10.3%	(3)	10.5%	(2)
Asian	3.4%	(1)	—	
Percentage white male	44.8%	(13)	57.9%	(11)
ABA rating				
Well Qualified	82.8%	(24)	68.4%	(13)
Qualified	17.2%	(5)	31.6%	(6)
Political identification				
Democrat	86.2%	(25)	84.2%	(16)
Republican	3.4%	(1)	10.5%	(2)
None	10.3%	(3)	5.3%	(1)
Past party activism	48.3%	(14)	68.4%	(13)
Net worth				
Less than $200,000	6.9%	(2)	5.3%	(1)
$200-499,999	10.3%	(3)	15.8%	(3)
$500-999,999	44.8%	(13)	10.5%	(2)
$1+ million	37.9%	(11)	68.4%	(13)
Total number of appointees	29		19	
Average age at nomination	51.3		51.1	

vacant circuit court seats at the beginning of 1999 (16) than there had been at the end of Clinton's first term in office two years earlier.

Finally, one must also recognize that successfully appointing federal judges, particularly those at the circuit court level, will be increasingly difficult for a lame duck (and wounded) post-impeachment Clinton presidency entering a presidential election year. Thus, when the final count is in on Clinton's second term appointees, it may be that it will not far surpass (or, perhaps, even reach) the level of the 29 appointees confirmed during his first term in office.

Table 5   Clinton's nontraditional appointees compared to his traditional appointees to the federal appeals courts, 1997-1998

	Nontraditional appointees		Traditional appointees	
	%	(N)	%	(N)
Occupation				
Politics/government	—		9.1%	(1)
Judiciary	75.0%	(6)	36.4%	(4)
Large law firm				
100+ members	12.5%	(1)	9.1%	(1)
50-99	—		9.1%	(1)
25-49	12.5%	(1)	—	
Moderate size firm				
10-24 members	—		27.3%	(3)
5-9	—		—	
Small firm				
2-4	—		—	
solo	—		—	
Professor of law	—		9.1%	(1)
Other	—		—	
Experience				
Judicial	75.0%	(6)	36.4%	(4)
Prosecutorial	12.5%	(1)	45.5%	(5)
Neither	25.0%	(2)	45.5%	(5)
Undergraduate education				
Public	50.0%	(4)	27.3%	(3)
Private	25.0%	(2)	54.6%	(6)
Ivy League	25.0%	(2)	18.2%	(2)
Law school education				
Public	25.0%	(2)	45.5%	(5)
Private	37.5%	(3)	—	
Ivy League	37.5%	(3)	54.6%	(6)
Gender				
Male	12.5%	(1)	100.0%	(11)
Female	87.5%	(7)	—	
Ethnicity/race				
White	62.5%	(5)	100.0%	(11)
African American	12.5%	(1)	—	
Hispanic	25.0%	(2)	—	
Asian	—		—	
Native American	—		—	
ABA rating				
Well Qualified	75.0%	(6)	63.6%	(7)
Qualified	25.0%	(2)	36.4%	(4)
Not Qualified	—		—	
Political identification				
Democrat	87.5%	(7)	81.8%	(9)
Republican	—		18.2%	(2)
None	12.5%	(1)	—	
Past party activism	75.0%	(6)	63.6%	(7)
Net worth				
Under $200,000	12.5%	(1)	—	
$200-499,999	—		27.3%	(3)
$500-999,999	12.5%	(1)	9.1%	(1)
$1+ million	75.0%	(6)	63.6%	(7)
Average age at nomination	47.9		53.4	
Total number of appointees	8		11	

Comparisons between Clinton's first term circuit appointees and those made during the last two years (as documented in Table 4) must be made with caution because of the small numbers involved. The same holds for Table 5, which compares the 8 nontraditional appointees from 1997-1998 with the 11 white males appointed during this period. Table 6 offers an overall assessment of all of the appeals court nominees appointed by Clinton compared with those of Presidents Bush, Reagan, and Carter.

Occupation and experience. As shown in Table 4, the majority of Clinton's appointees during his first term, as well as (a slightly smaller majority) during the first half of his second term, came to the circuit bench from other positions in the judiciary. Seven were promoted from the federal district bench, including four elevations of Clinton appointees, two elevations of Bush appointees, and one elevation of a Reagan appointee. In addition there was what we believe to be an unprecedented elevation of a U.S. magistrate judge to an appeals court.

The gap between Clinton's first term appointees and those made during the first half of his second term widens considerably when the totality of judicial experience is considered. Thus, nearly 7 out of 10 appellate judges appointed by Clinton in his first term as compared to approximately half of those he appointed in 1997-1998 have had prior experience as a judge. Further, inasmuch as Clinton has appointed relatively fewer appellate judges with prosecutorial experience in the past two years, when compared to his first term, a much greater proportion of the more recent appointees (more than 1 in 3) have neither judicial nor prosecutorial experience when compared to his first term appointees, only 1 of 5 of whom lacked such a background.

In this regard, Table 6 documents that the more recent Clinton appointees more closely resemble those of the previous presidential administrations than they do those made during Clinton's first term. Further, as was the case during his first term in office, Table 5 documents that Clinton's nontraditional appointees were disproportionately drawn from a candidate pool of sitting judges when compared with the traditional white male nominees, and the differences are even more graphic in 1997-1998 than they were in Clinton's first term.

Comparing six years' worth of Clinton appointees to those of the previous three administrations, as done in Table 6, indicates that more than 3 out of 5 appeals court appointees had judicial experience (about the same proportion as that of the Bush and Reagan appointees) and that the Clinton appointees had the highest proportion of those with prosecutorial experience. Only about 1 in 4 Clinton appointees had neither judicial nor prosecutorial experience, the lowest proportion of all four administrations.

Table 6 U.S. appeals court appointees compared by administration

	Clinton %	(N)	Bush %	(N)	Reagan %	(N)	Carter %	(N)
Occupation								
Politics/government	4.2%	(2)	10.8%	(4)	6.4%	(5)	5.4%	(3)
Judiciary	56.3%	(27)	59.5%	(22)	55.1%	(43)	46.4%	(26)
Large law firm								
100+ members	12.5%	(6)	8.1%	(3)	5.1%	(4)	1.8%	(1)
50-99	2.1%	(1)	8.1%	(3)	2.6%	(2)	5.4%	(3)
25-49	4.2%	(2)	—		6.4%	(5)	3.6%	(2)
Moderate size firm								
10-24 members	8.3%	(4)	8.1%	(3)	3.9%	(3)	14.3%	(8)
5-9	4.2%	(2)	2.7%	(1)	5.1%	(4)	1.8%	(1)
Small firm								
2-4	—		—		1.3%	(1)	3.6%	(2)
solo	—		—		—		1.8%	(1)
Professor	8.3%	(4)	2.7%	(1)	12.8%	(10)	14.3%	(8)
Other	—		—		1.3%	(1)	1.8%	(1)
Experience								
Judicial	62.5%	(30)	62.2%	(23)	60.3%	(47)	53.6%	(30)
Prosecutorial	35.4%	(17)	29.7%	(11)	28.2%	(22)	32.1%	(18)
Neither	27.1%	(13)	32.4%	(12)	34.6%	(27)	39.3%	(22)
Undergraduate education								
Public	45.8%	(22)	29.7%	(11)	24.4%	(19)	30.4%	(17)
Private	33.3%	(16)	59.5%	(22)	51.3%	(40)	51.8%	(29)
Ivy League	20.8%	(10)	10.8%	(4)	24.4%	(19)	17.9%	(10)
Law school education								
Public	39.6%	(19)	29.7%	(11)	41.0%	(32)	39.3%	(22)
Private	25.0%	(12)	40.5%	(15)	35.9%	(28)	19.6%	(11)
Ivy League	35.4%	(17)	29.7%	(11)	23.1%	(18)	41.1%	(23)
Gender								
Male	66.7%	(32)	81.1%	(30)	94.9%	(74)	80.4%	(45)
Female	33.3%	(16)	18.9%	(7)	5.1%	(4)	19.6%	(11)
Ethnicity/race								
White	77.1%	(37)	89.2%	(33)	97.4%	(76)	78.6%	(44)
African American	10.4%	(5)	5.4%	(2)	1.3%	(1)	16.1%	(9)
Hispanic	10.4%	(5)	5.4%	(2)	1.3%	(1)	3.6%	(2)
Asian	2.1%	(1)	—		—		1.8%	(1)
Percentage white male	50.0%	(24)	70.3%	(26)	92.3%	(72)	60.7%	(34)
ABA rating								
Exceptionally well qualified/well qualified	77.1%	(37)	64.9%	(24)	59.0%	(46)	75.0%	(42)
Qualified	22.9%	(11)	35.1%	(13)	41.0%	(32)	25.0%	(14)
Political identification								
Democrat	85.4%	(41)	5.4%	(2)			82.1%	(46)
Republican	6.3%	(3)	89.2%	(33)	96.2%	(75)	7.1%	(4)
Other	—		—		1.3%	(1)	—	
None	8.3%	(4)	5.4%	(2)	2.6%	(2)	10.7%	(6)
Past party activism	56.3%	(27)	70.3%	(26)	65.4%	(51)	73.2%	(41)
Net worth								
Less than $200,000	6.3%	(3)	5.4%	(2)	15.6%*	(12)	33.3%**	(13)
$200-499,999	12.5%	(6)	29.7%	(11)	32.5%	(25)	38.5%	(15)
$500-999,999	31.3%	(15)	21.6%	(8)	33.8%	(26)	17.9%	(7)
$1+ million	50.0%	(24)	43.2%	(16)	18.2%	(14)	10.3%	(4)
Total number of appointees	48		37		78		56	
Average age at nomination	51.2		48.7		50.0		51.8	

*Net worth was unavailable for one appointee.

**Net worth only for Carter appointees confirmed by the 96th Congress with the exception of five appointees for whom net worth was unavailable.

Sources: for Carter and Reagan appointees—Goldman, PICKING FEDERAL JUDGES: LOWER COURT SELECTION FROM ROOSEVELT THROUGH REAGAN (New Haven: Yale University Press, 1997) pp. 354-356; for Bush appointees—Goldman, *Bush's judicial legacy: the final imprint*, 76 JUDICATURE 287 (1993).

Table 6 also shows that the Clinton appointees had the largest proportion of those coming to the bench from large law firms and the next to the smallest proportion of those coming from a law school professorship. As for the latter findings, considering the long travail of former Berkeley professor William Fletcher, the only law professor confirmed during the 105th Congress, it may be understandable why the Clinton administration has tended to shy away from academics—or vice versa.

Education. Table 6 reveals that, unlike during Clinton's first term when the majority of his appeals court appointees received their undergraduate education in public institutions, nearly 2 out of 3 of his nominees during the first half of his second term received their college education in private settings.

While there has been a slight drop in the past two years in the proportion of the more recent Clinton appointees who attended public law schools when compared to his first term in office, a more substantial difference can be found in the increased proportion (nearly 1 out of 2) of Clinton's appointees during his second term who received Ivy League law school training. If prestigious non-Ivy law schools (such as Chicago, Georgetown, Michigan, New York University, Texas, Vanderbilt, and Virginia) are included, about 68 percent of the second term appointees were trained in the nation's top law schools. When the first term Clinton appointees are added to the mix the proportion with an elite law school education is about 58 percent (in contrast to the 45 percent for the Bush and Reagan appointees). Of the 17 Clinton appointees with an Ivy League law school education, 9 were Harvard trained, 7 were Yale educated, and 1 graduated from Columbia.

Gender and ethnicity. At the end of Clinton's first term he had appointed the largest proportion of nontraditional appeals court judges, that is, those who were not white males (55.2 percent), than any president in American history. The proportion of nontraditional appointees has decreased substantially to 42.1 percent thus far in Clinton's second term, but even this figure surpasses that of Jimmy Carter (39.3 percent). With his appointment of 7 women to the appeals courts in the past two years, Clinton has now appointed a greater number of women to the circuit bench (16) than did Carter (11), and well more than presidents Bush and Reagan collectively (11) during their 12 years in office.

The overall decline in the proportion of nontraditional appointees midway through Clinton's second term is attributable to the fact that only one African American judge has been seated on the circuit bench during the past two years, while 4 were appointed during Clinton's first term. Thus, Clinton continues to lag behind Carter in both the number and proportion of African Americans who have been appointed to the appellate bench.

Perhaps symbolic of the Clinton administration's difficulties in appointing even greater numbers of African Americans to the appeals courts has been the plight of James A. Beaty Jr., a federal district court judge from North Carolina first appointed by Clinton in 1994. An attempt was made to elevate Beaty to the Fourth Circuit in December, 1995 during the president's first term. Beaty would have become the first African American to sit on the Fourth circuit bench. Indeed, even his nomination was a historic first. No action was taken on the nomination, however, and, at the end of the 104th Congress it lapsed and was returned to the White House. Clinton renominated Beaty on January 7, 1997. Once again, no hearing was held in the Republican controlled Senate during the 105th Congress and, once again, it was returned to the White House. Thus, despite the fact that Beaty's candidacy received the ABA's highest rating, the Fourth circuit remained (along with the First, Seventh, and Tenth circuits) courts on which no African American has sat as a permanent member. The total impact of Clinton's appointments on the diversification of the federal bench is seen in "Nontraditional judges in active service," page 83.

ABA ratings. As seen in Table 6, President Clinton's appointees, in the aggregate, enjoy the highest ABA ratings among the past four presidents. Indeed, remarkably, more than 3 out of 4 of the Clinton judges received the highest rating, a record approached only by Jimmy Carter's appointees. Table 4 underscores, however, that Clinton's record is bolstered by the evaluations of his first term appointees, with nearly 1 out of 3 of the second term judges receiving the lower rating of "Qualified." Interestingly and somewhat surprisingly, given the different results for Clinton's first term appointees as well as those for earlier presidencies, the nontraditional appointees in Clinton's second term have earned higher ABA ratings than their white male counterparts.

Political party. During Clinton's first term only one Republican was seated on the circuit bench, a record of partisanship only surpassed by Ronald Reagan, who didn't appoint a single Democrat to the appeals courts during his eight years in office. With the appointment of two Republican judges thus far in his second term, however, Clinton's record, as seen in Table 6, now resembles that of presidents Bush and Carter.

While Table 6 also documents that Clinton's appointees, in the aggregate, have a lesser record of past party activism than the judges appointed by presidents Bush, Reagan, and Carter, those differences dissipate when one focuses exclusively on Clinton's second term appointees who, on this dimension, very much resemble the appointees of the previous three administrations. Fewer than 1 in 10 Clinton appointees do not identify with a political party, a figure that resembles the Carter pattern but not the pattern of the Bush and Reagan judges.

Net worth. Half of the Clinton appointees are millionaires, a display of aggregate wealth unapproached by the appellate court appointees of the past three administrations, as seen in Table 6. Clinton's record in this regard is primarily the result of his second term appointees, more than 2 out of 3 of whom are millionaires. Interestingly, this pattern of wealth among the second term appointees is even more highly pronounced among the nontraditional judges, 3 out of 4 of whom are millionaires. However, it should also be pointed out that 1 in 5 second term appointees were of more modest means, with a net worth less than $500,000.

Age. The average age of Clinton's appointees, in the aggregate, is 51.2, two and one-half years older than Bush's appointees and more than a year older than those appointed by Reagan. On average, the Carter appointees were slightly more than one-half year older than Clinton's judges. As was the case in Clinton's first term, the average age of the nontraditional appointees was younger, indeed, a robust five and one-half years younger, than his second term white male appointees. About 19 percent of Clinton's appointees were under 45 as compared to one-fourth of the Bush and Reagan appointees. There is no indication that age has been a consideration in the Clinton administration's selection process.

At the outset of this analysis of Clinton's appeals court nominees it was stressed that the findings should be viewed with caution because of the relatively small numbers involved when comparing Clinton's first term appointments with those made midway through his second term. Still, in viewing the data, one is hard pressed not to notice that the profile of the second term appointees has changed. For one, a greater proportion of appointments have gone to white males at the expense of nontraditional candidates. The judges who have been appointed in the second term have been wealthier and, to a greater extent than in the first term, they have enjoyed Ivy League law school training. In several respects, they more resemble the appointees of the previous three administrations than they do Clinton's first term appointees. In the context

of the appointment difficulties Clinton faced in the second half of his first term, it is difficult to escape the conclusion that the administration is appointing or, perhaps more to the point, the Republican controlled Senate is disposed to confirming candidates with more "traditional" legal and social profiles.

The road ahead

As of May 1, 1999, the Clinton administration had sent 37 nominations for lifetime appointments to courts of general jurisdiction to the U.S. Senate of the 106th Congress. Only two confirmations, both resubmissions, took place of nominations not acted upon by the 105th Congress. Ten other resubmissions and 25 new nominations showed no sign of movement. Although the Senate majority leader and the Senate minority leader reached an agreement in February whereby the majority leader would no longer honor secret holds on nominations,[11] a new obstacle emerged that appeared responsible for the frozen state of the confirmation process.

The new obstacle was Senator Orrin Hatch's insistence that conservative Republican Ted Stewart be named to the federal district bench in Utah. Stewart, who within the state has some Democratic support, is opposed by Democrats and environmentalists. His lack of courtroom experience and questions about his judicial temperament have made this an even more difficult candidacy for the administration to evaluate. The dilemma for the administration has been that Hatch will not schedule hearings on judicial nominations unless Stewart is nominated.[12] If the administration names Stewart it would expect that the judiciary committee would hold hearings and vote Clinton's nominees either up or down. As of this writing it is uncertain as to the resolution of this conflict that threatens to end the president's ability to appoint judges in his remaining two years in office.

There is great irony in the difficulties the Clinton administration has had in appointing judges. As one prominent liberal lobbyist, who has labored in the judicial selection domain for many years, contended, in 1998,

...[T]he White House [chose] candidates with the utmost care for one purpose: to avoid any kind of public debate whatsoever. It still [didn't] deter people like [Alabama Senator] Jeff Sessions from stepping up and raising objections, but the fact is that this administration has now written its template of its nominee. And it's probably someone from a big law firm, someone who's rich, someone, probably, that's got some prosecutorial experience, someone who's…admired by the Bar, but has very little public interest background…. [T]he administration has really looked for the most moderate candidates to send up. Hillary Clinton wouldn't get a judgeship today because of her legal services background.

With some poetic license this observation may come close to the profile of the Clinton appointees (although a judicial background rather than big law firm background is more accurate). If indeed the administration tends toward nominating moderates and the Republican leadership ends its stalling tactics, we can expect a number of confirmations at least until the summer of 2000. However, it is unlikely that Clinton will be able to appoint an additional 30 appeals court judges to match Reagan's record, though it is possible that Clinton may match Reagan's record of 290 district court appointments.

At the end of the day for the Clinton administration's appointments, many will be quick to praise the administration for its impact on advancing the development of a career judiciary, paying great heed to diversifying the fabric of the federal bench, particularly with regard to appointing women and African Americans, and for pursuing these ends with high quality appointments that earn the praise of the organized Bar.

While not denying Clinton's accomplishment of making the federal bench more representative of the American people while also meeting high standards of professional quality, there remain those in the president's Democratic constituency who, having witnessed the manner in which Presidents Reagan and Bush aggressively pursued a conservative policy agenda through their judicial appointments, view the Clinton years as a lost opportunity. Moderation, compromise, and accommodation have been paramount in the administration's appointment behavior, the critical rhetoric of conservative Republicans notwithstanding. The Clinton record in this regard may not be without consequences in terms of judicial decision making and this will constitute the crucial impact of Clinton's appointments. Whatever that impact may be on the course of the administration of justice, it is clear beyond all doubt that President Bill Clinton's judiciary will be an important component of his legacy.

NOTES

This article originally appeared in Volume 82, Number 6, May-June 1999.

Sheldon Goldman wishes to thank the Law and Social Science program of the National Science Foundation (NSF grant SBR-9810838) which helped support the gathering of data for the 1998 Clinton appointees. The authors thank Matthew D. Saronson for his help in gathering data on many of the Clinton appointees confirmed during the 103rd Congress and Julie-Anne Seeds for her excellent work in transcribing the interviews. They also appreciate the help of the dedicated staff of Senator Orrin G. Hatch at the Senate Judiciary Committee and the staffs of several other senators who serve on the committee. They thank administration officials Eleanor D. Acheson, Sheila Joy, Paul Morris, and Sara Wilson, as well as Lee Lieberman, Irene Emsellem, Nan Aron, and Stephen Klein for their generous assistance. They are grateful to the many Clinton appointees who answered queries. Errors of fact and interpretation are their joint responsibility alone.

1. For a survey of Clinton's first term, see Goldman, *Judicial selection under Clinton: a midterm examination*, 78 JUDICATURE 276 (1995); and Goldman and Slotnick, *Clinton's first term judiciary: many bridges to cross*, 80 JUDICATURE 254 (1997).

2. See THE AMERICAN BENCH (9th edition), WHO'S WHO (national and regional editions), MARTINDALE-HUBBELL LAW DIRECTORY, and THE JUDICIAL STAFF DIRECTORY.

3. Description of the evaluation process is based on interviews with Paul Morris, Eleanor D. Acheson, and Sara Wilson in December, 1998.

4. In general, see Slotnick and Goldman, *Congress and the Courts: A Case of Casting*, in Weisberg and Patterson (eds.), GREAT THEATER: THE AMERICAN CONGRESS IN ACTION 197-224 (New York: Cambridge University Press, 1998), and Goldman, *The Judicial Confirmation Crisis and the Clinton Presidency*, 28 PRESIDENTIAL STUDIES Q. 838 (1998).

5. Cushman, *Senate Imperiling Judicial System, Chief Justice Says*, New York Times, January 1, 1998, at 1.

6. Note that the Senate of the 103rd Congress, controlled by the Democrats, confirmed 107 individuals. The Senate of the 104th Congress, controlled by the Republicans, confirmed 62.

7. There were 11 district court nominations that the Senate allowed to die at the end of the 105th Congress. Four were white males, 3 were African American males, 1 was an Asian American male, 2 were white females, and 1 was an Hispanic female.

8. *See* Torry, *Putting the Magnifying Glass on the Evaluators*, Washington Post, March 17, 1997, at F7.

9. The average age of the white women appointed by Clinton to the district courts was 48.3; black women 47.3; and African American men 46.3. There was one Asian American man and one Asian American woman as well as one Hispanic man and one Hispanic woman appointed. Their ages are averaged in with the figure for nontraditional appointees.

10. During Bush's last two years in office the proportion of appointees under the age of 45 was 44 percent. During Reagan's second term, the proportion of appointees under the age of 45 was 37 percent.

11. "Senate Leaders End Secret 'Holds,'" Associated Press dispatch, March 5, 1999 in Daily Hampshire Gazette, March 5, 1999, at C8.

12. *See* McCann, *Can Politics, Lack of Courtroom Experience Derail Ted Stewarts Federal Judgeship?*, Salt Lake Tribune, March 28, 1999, at A1 and Carney, *Clinton's Deals with GOP on Judgeships Stir Discontent Among Democrats*, 57 CQ WEEKLY, 845 (April 10, 1999).

Nontraditional judges in active service

Table 7 dramatically shows the tremendous impact of the Clinton administration in diversifying the federal bench by race and gender. When all three court levels are considered, in every category the numbers and proportions increased. Overall, there was a 55 percent increase in nontraditional judges in active service from the day Clinton was first elected. The largest increase on the district bench in absolute numbers was the number of women (54). (Keep in mind that Clinton appointed 70 women to the district bench but the net increase of 54 takes into account those who left active service during Clinton's first six years or were elevated to the appeals bench). In proportions, the largest increase (excluding the one Native American appointed) was for African Americans (with women close behind). The proportion of Hispanics, however, actually slightly decreased because more left active service than were replaced by Clinton.

On the appeals courts there were significant net increases in the proportion (and numbers) of women and Hispanics, with a much more modest increase of African Americans and no net increase for Asian Americans. On the Supreme Court, Ruth Bader Ginsburg's appointment doubled the number of women.

About 3 out of 10 judges on the federal bench in the beginning of 1999 were nontraditional, an increase from about 1 in 5 when Clinton took office. White males, nevertheless, are the large majority on the federal courts, accounting for about 70 percent of the federal judiciary. Despite

Table 7   Proportion of nontraditional lifetime judges in active service on courts of general jurisdiction—November 3, 1992 and January 1, 1999

	1992 %	(N)	1999 %	(N)	% increase
U.S. district courts					
Women	10.5%*	(68)	18.9%*	(122)	79.4%
African American	5.3%	(34)	10.7%	(69)	102.9%
Hispanic	4.5%	(29)	4.3%	(28)	(-3.4%)
Asian	0.6%	(4)	0.8%	(5)	25.0%
Native American	0.0%	(0)	0.2%	(1)	NA
Total nontraditional	19.1%	(123)	30.5%	(197)	60.2%
U.S. courts of appeals					
Women	13.2%**	(22)	19.8%**	(33)	50.0%
African American	5.4%	(9)	6.0%	(10)	11.1%
Hispanic	2.4%	(4)	4.8%	(8)	100.0%
Asian	0.6%	(1)	0.6%	(1)	0.0%
Total nontraditional	21.0%	(35)	28.7%	(48)	37.1%
U.S. Supreme Court					
Women	11.1%***	(1)	22.2%***	(2)	100.0%
African American	11.1%	(1)	11.1%	(1)	0.0%
Total nontraditional	22.2%	(2)	33.3%	(3)	50.0%
All three court levels					
Women	11.1%	(91)	19.1%	(157)	72.5%
African American	5.4%	(44)	9.7%	(80)	81.8%
Hispanic	4.0%	(33)	4.4%	(36)	9.1%
Asian	0.6%	(5)	0.7%	(6)	20.0%
Native American	0.0%	(0)	0.1%	(1)	NA
Total nontraditional	19.5%	(160)	30.2%	(248)	55.0%

The total does not double count those who were classified in more than one category.

*Out of 645 authorized lifetime positions on the U.S. district courts.

**Out of 167 authorized lifetime positions on the numbered circuits and the U.S. Court of Appeals for the District of Columbia Circuit, all courts of general jurisdiction.

***Out of nine authorized positions on the U.S. Supreme Court.

the historic numbers and proportions of nontraditional judges sitting on the federal bench today, white males can be expected to remain the large majority well into the next century.

—Sheldon Goldman
and Elliot Slotnick

Make-up of the federal bench

Midway into his second term, President Clinton's appointees occupied nearly 4 out of every 10 (37.5 percent) allocated federal district judgeship seats. While Clinton has appointed a plurality of federal district judges, the combined appointees from the 12 year tenure of presidents Bush and Reagan still account for nearly half (47.3 percent) of the active district court bench seats. When the remaining active appointees of presidents Kennedy, Johnson, Nixon, Ford, and Carter are taken into account, virtually half (49.5 percent) of all allocated federal district judgeships have been appointed by Republicans, 44.7 percent have been appointed by Democrats, and 38 of the authorized district court seats (5.9 percent) remained vacant. Assuming even a modest success rate in seating federal district court judges in the last two years of the Clinton presidency, the relative partisan balance displayed here should move even closer.

On the appeals courts, where Clinton has met with much greater resistance to his nominees, Clinton appointees occupied slightly more than 1 out of 4 (27.5 percent) allocated circuit judgeships. Again, Bush and Reagan appointees still dominated the appeals courts, occupying nearly half (48.5 percent) of the authorized seats. Democratic presidents, all told, have filled 4 out of 10 (40.8 percent) appeals court judgeships, while Republican presidents have seated nearly 5 out of 10 (49.7 percent) federal appellate judges. About 1 in 10 appeals court seats (9.6 percent) remained vacant at the beginning of 1999.

The relative partisan balance displayed on the two levels of the lower federal bench, with Republicans holding a much more clear cut advantage in appeals court judgeships, is still evident when the judges in senior service on January 1, 1999 are also considered. Thus, the appointments of Democratic presidents accounted for 48.2 percent of the senior judges on the district courts, while the appointees of Republican presidents accounted for a slight majority (51.8 percent) of such senior judges. The Republican appointed majority (58.2 percent) is somewhat more pronounced at the circuit court level where Democratic presidents have appointed only 41.8 percent of the appeals court judges on senior status.

—Sheldon Goldman
and Elliot Slotnick

Table 8   Make-up of federal bench by appointing president, January 1, 1999 (lifetime positions on lower courts of general jurisdiction).

	District courts Active		Senior		Courts of appeals Active		Senior	
	%	(N)	%	(N)	%	(N)	%	(N)
Clinton	37.5%	(242)	—		27.5%	(46)	—	
Bush	21.4%	(138)	—		19.8%	(33)	2.5%	(2)
Reagan	25.9%	(167)	21.7%	(67)	28.7%	(48)	22.8%	(18)
Carter	6.8%	(44)	30.7%	(95)	12.0%	(20)	27.8%	(22)
Ford	0.7%	(5)	6.8%	(21)	0.6%	(1)	8.9%	(7)
Nixon	1.4%	(9)	20.7%	(64)	0.6%	(1)	20.3%	(16)
Johnson	0.2%	(1)	12.3%	(38)	0.6%	(1)	13.9%	(11)
Kennedy	0.2%	(1)	4.2%	(13)	0.6%	(1)	—	
Eisenhower	—		2.6%	(8)	—		3.8%	(3)
Truman	—		1.0%	(3)	—		—	
Vacancies	5.9%	(38)	—		9.6%	(16)	—	
TOTALS	100.0%	(645)	100.0%	(309)	100.0%	(167)	100.0%	(79)

The voting behavior of President Clinton's judicial appointees

President Clinton sought ideologically moderate judges. Not surprisingly, the decisions of his appointees overall also have been moderate.

by Ronald Stidham, Robert A. Carp, and Donald R. Songer

Until now, information about the voting behavior of U.S. district and circuit judges appointed by President Bill Clinton has been largely anecdotal. A significant reason for this is the substantial time between a president's election and when his judicial appointees' decisions begin appearing in print in sufficient numbers to be subject to empirical analysis.

Even near the end of Clinton's four-year term, the number of his appointees' published decisions is rather modest. Still, it is sufficiently large to begin making meaningful generalizations about the decisional patterns of the women and men Clinton has placed on the U.S. district courts and courts of appeals. We can also speculate about the impact of Clinton's appointees on the ideological content and direction of the U.S. judiciary as a whole.

The data on trial court decisions during the 1992-96 period were drawn from a larger study of 55,000 opinions published in the *Federal Supplement* by more than 1,500 judges from 1933 to 1996.[1] Only those cases that fit easily into one of 27 case types and contained a clear underlying liberal-conservative dimension were used. They included cases such as state and federal habeas corpus pleas, labor-management disputes, questions involving the right to privacy, and environmental protection cases, among others. Excluded were cases involving patents, admiralty disputes, and land condemnation hearings. The number of cases not selected was about the same as the number included.

The data on the voting patterns of circuit court judges appointed by Presidents Nixon through Clinton are from a random sample of 1,000 decisions drawn from the *Federal Reporter* from 1994 and 1995. Different time frames for the district and circuit court analyses were used because there is not a large enough body of votes by Clinton circuit court appointees prior to 1994 to make a meaningful analysis worthwhile.

Not included in the data were the votes of district court judges sitting on appellate panels. Only one case involved an en banc panel. The coding scheme used for the votes of circuit court judges followed the model for content and liberal-conservative direction of district court decisions.

Expectations

There are four general criteria by which one might evaluate or predict a president's success in securing a judicial cohort whose decisions mirror his ideological and policy values.[2] They are: (1) the level of the president's commitment to making ideologically based appointments; (2) the number of vacancies he is able to fill; (3) the extent of the president's political clout; and (4) the judicial climate into which the new judges enter.

In order to have a significant impact on the orientation of the federal courts, a president must have a strong and consistent policy of nominating judges who reflect his ideological values. Not all presidents have ranked ideology that highly in their judicial selection criteria. For instance, President Harry Truman's primary concern when appointing judges was to select individuals who were loyal to him in the 1948 presidential campaign. Truman had been deserted by the Dixiecrats who supported Strom Thurmond and by the Progressive Party supporters who backed Henry Wallace. Truman, therefore, was much more concerned with loyalty than with ideology when it came time to fill seats on the federal bench. An examination of Truman's judicial cohort reveals a mixed bag of liberals and conservatives.

Dwight Eisenhower provides another interesting example. An almost apolitical man for whom ideology counted little, experience and solid common sense ranked high on Eisenhower's selection requirements. As a consequence, his judicial cohort, like Truman's, lacked a clear-cut ideological bent.

Clinton's ideological orientation and commitment are clearly not as liberal as those of many of his predecessors, and on several occasions he has stated that he will probably go down in history as the most conservative Democrat to occupy the White House this century. He has frequently referred to himself as a "new Democrat" and has tried to distance himself from the more liberal image that characterized the Democratic party for many years. It is fair to say, then, that Clinton's general ideological orientation is one of more moderate liberalism.

During the 1992 presidential campaign, Clinton pledged to appoint to the bench "men and women of unquestioned intellect, judicial temperament, broad experience and a demonstrated concern for, and commitment to, the individual rights protected by our Constitution, including the right to privacy."[3] He also criticized George Bush for appointing insufficient numbers of women and minority judges. All this suggests that Clinton has had a commitment to appointing judges who are more reflective of the racial and gender composition of American society and who are ideologically moderate to modestly liberal. One veteran court observer noted that "Clinton's Supreme Court choices, Ruth Bader Ginsburg and Stephen Breyer, are moderates, and so are most of his lower court appointees."[4] Assistant Attorney General Eleanor Dean Acheson, who oversees judicial selection in the Clinton administration, says that "the administration rejects candidates with ideological agendas and stresses diversity without sacrificing quality."[5] Indeed, Clinton has appointed a higher percentage of women and racial minorities to the bench than any of his predecessors.[6]

Clinton began his presidency with some 100 vacancies left over from the Bush administration. In addition to leftover vacancies a president can generally expect about 50 judgeships to open up annually as a result of deaths, retirements, and moves to senior status. Some presidents, such as Jimmy Carter, may also benefit from the creation of new judgeships by Congress.

A key factor to be considered in assessing Clinton's impact on the federal judiciary is whether he will be re-elected to a second term. If that happens, his appointees will dominate the federal courts. According to a recent account, given that 50 district judges are eligible for senior status, and another 132 are slated to become eligible for such status in the next five years, a re-elected Clinton "could wind up naming well more than 300 of the 649 district judges, perhaps even a majority."[7]

A third criterion to be considered regarding a president's capacity to make an imprint on the federal judiciary is whether he possesses the political influence to obtain Senate confirmation of his ideologically based appointments. Clinton's clout has waxed and waned during his years in the White House, but for most of his term he was very successful in securing judicial confirmations. Not only did Clinton work with a Democratic-controlled Senate during the first half of his term, he earned a reputation for avoiding confirmation battles.[8] Assistant Attorney General Acheson recently said, "We've steered clear of a few people who might have been fabulous judges but who would have provoked a fight that we were likely to lose."[9]

The final criterion affecting the president's potential to make a major impact on the judiciary is the environment into which appointees to the bench enter. When Clinton began his presidency, three-fourths of the bench consisted of conservative judges appointed by his Republican predecessors. As one observer put it, "Not since election day 1952, after 20 years of Roosevelt and Truman appointees, was the federal bench so imbalanced politically and philosophically."[10] This means that the Clinton appointees must feel their way slowly and articulate their moderately liberal values only in those relatively close cases where their decisions do not risk being overturned by conservative appellate panels.

Voting behavior

We now turn to the empirical data on judicial decisions at both the district and circuit court levels. First, the Clinton judges' decisions overall are compared with those of other presidential appointees at the trial and appellate levels. Then, the same comparison is made by focusing more precisely on cases involving criminal justice, civil rights and liberties, and labor and economic regulation.

Table 1 updates our continuing research that has mapped the effect of appointing presidents on the decisions of the district judges they appoint.[11] Across time the raw numbers continue to show something meaningful about the centers of gravity of the two major parties. For example, when the liberalism scores of Democratic appointees in recent decades are compared with those of Republican appointees, it is clear that the president's party makes a differ-ence in the way decisions are made by the judges they appoint. The appointees of Democratic presidents have clearly been more liberal in their decision making than judges chosen by Republicans.

Yet there are problems associated with placing too much emphasis on these precise numbers. For one thing, the case mixture has varied greatly over time as the precise types of cases finding their way into the courts has changed. Also, definitions of "liberalism" and "conservatism" have varied to some degree over the years. Still, the indices do provide some insight into differences in the impact of the appointing president.

The data in Table 1, examining the appointees of Presidents Nixon through Clinton, indicate that Carter's judicial cohort is clearly the most liberal. Reagan's appointees are the most conservative. As one might expect, Clinton's district court appointees overall are less liberal than Carter's, but more liberal than judges appointed by any of the Republican presidents.

Table 2 shows much more precisely where the Clinton cohort parts company with that of other recent presidents. On matters of criminal justice the Clinton judges are the second most liberal group, behind only Carter's appointees. Not unexpectedly, the Reagan, Bush, and Nixon cohorts are the most conservative on matters of criminal justice.

In civil rights and civil liberties cases the Carter jurists, with a liberal score of 52 percent, far outdistance all the other cohorts. The Clinton cohort's liberal score of 39 percent is identical with that of the Ford appointees and six points higher than the Reagan and Bush judges, who have identical liberal scores of 33 percent.

In cases involving labor and economic regulation the Clinton and Carter judicial appointees are most liberal with identical scores of 62 percent. However, Table 2 reveals that the liberalism scores of all the cohorts are rather high in this case category. Even the Reagan and Bush judges are at the 50 percent mark in labor and economic regulation cases.

A possible explanation for the high percentage of liberal decisions in this case category is that increasing numbers of women have been appointed to the bench in recent years. Limited research has found that on some narrow but key issues women on the bench decide cases differently from their male colleagues. One recent study of the voting behavior of judges on the U.S. courts of appeals, for instance, found no significant differences between male and female judges in obscenity or search and seizure cases, but did find that female jurists were significantly more liberal than their male counterparts in employment discrimination cases.[12] This may be at play in the district courts as well, since more than half of the labor and economic regulation cases deal with some type of worker, an underdog, who is claiming denial of a critical benefit, often his or her job.

At the circuit court level, according to Table 3, the votes cast by judges overall reveals almost the same pattern as district court cases. The liberalism scores of the Clinton appointees are second only to those of Carter's, while the appointees of

Table 1 Liberal U.S. district court decisions overall, 1992-96

Appointing president	%	N
Richard Nixon	39	8,680
Gerald Ford	44	2,069
Jimmy Carter	53	8,860
Ronald Reagan	36	7,047
George Bush	37	639
Bill Clinton	48	332

Table 2 Liberal district court decisions for three categories of cases, 1992-96

Appointing president	Criminal justice		Civil rights and liberties		Labor and economic regulation	
	%	N	%	N	%	N
Richard Nixon	30	227	37	293	48	215
Gerald Ford	32	76	39	133	55	136
Jimmy Carter	38	656	52	1,224	62	965
Ronald Reagan	23	1,143	33	1,841	49	1,435
George Bush	29	101	33	162	51	142
Bill Clinton	34	47	39	174	62	111

Table 3 Liberal circuit court decisions overall, 1994-95

Appointing president	%	N
Richard Nixon	30	125
Gerald Ford	29	95
Jimmy Carter	43	502
Ronald Reagan	32	982
George Bush	30	510
Bill Clinton	36	113

Table 4 Liberal circuit court decisions for three categories of cases, 1994-95

Appointing president	Criminal justice		Civil rights and liberties		Labor and economic regulation	
	%	N	%	N	%	N
Richard Nixon	26	66	29	34	44	25
Gerald Ford	20	55	35	20	50	20
Jimmy Carter	40	278	42	111	54	113
Ronald Reagan	26	533	32	238	50	211
George Bush	22	267	33	129	47	114
Bill Clinton	31	65	41	32	50	16

Republican presidents are more conservative. Table 4 presents a breakdown by the three broad case categories. An analysis of votes cast by judges on appellate court panels in criminal justice cases again reveals the same pattern.

In cases involving civil rights and liberties issues the votes of Clinton and Carter appointees are almost identical in terms of liberalism, with scores of 41 and 42 percent respectively. A comparison of Tables 2 and 4 reveals that Clinton's circuit court appointees are a bit more liberal in civil rights and liberties cases than his district court appointees. However, we caution against hasty conclusions since we are only talking about 32 votes by Clinton judges at the appellate court level.

In labor and economic regulation cases there is once again the problem of a small number of votes by the Clinton appeals court judges. The data include only 16 votes by the Clinton cohort. The 50 percent liberalism score of his appointees ties them for second place with the Ford and Reagan cohorts. Once again, the Carter appointees lead the way with a liberalism score of 54 percent. There is a large difference between the Clinton appointees at the district and circuit court levels, a finding that might be explored in future studies.

*****

This is the first study of what the data indicate about the degree of liberal or conservative ideology of the decisional behavior of Clinton's appointees to the lower federal courts. While studies have focused on Clinton's accomplishments in diversifying the federal bench and the decisional behavior of his two Supreme Court appointees, there has been little study of the Clinton appointees at the trial and intermediate appellate levels.

The basic conclusion to be drawn from this exploratory study is that the Clinton appointees, at this point, exhibit moderate decisional tendencies. This comes as no surprise, given the earlier-discussed model for assessing a president's chances for success in affecting judicial decision making. At any rate, the 1996 presidential election will be an important one not only for Bill Clinton, but for the federal judiciary as well.

NOTES

This article originally appeared in Volume 80, Number 1, July-August 1996, pages 16-20.

1. For a discussion of what types of cases are and are not published in the SUPPLEMENT, and also for a discussion of the methodological merits for using it as a basis for studying federal district court opinions, see Carp et. al. *The voting behavior of judges appointed by President Bush*, 76 JUDICATURE 298, 299 (1993).

2. Stidham, Carp, and Rowland, *Patterns of Presidential Influence on the Federal District Courts: An Analysis of the Appointment Process*, 14 PRESIDENTIAL STUDIES Q. 548-560 (1984).

3. Clinton, *Judiciary Suffers Racial, Sexual Lack of Balance*, Nat'l L.J., Nov. 2, 1992, at 15.

4. Gest, *Disorder in the Courts?*, U.S. NEWS AND WORLD REPORT, February 12, 1996, at 40.

5. Quoted in *id.*

6. Goldman, *Judicial selection under Clinton: a midterm examination*, 78 JUDICATURE 276 (1995).

7. Eastland, *If Clinton Wins, Here's What the Courts Will Look Like*, Wall Street Journal, Feb. 28, 1996, at A-21.

8. *See, e.g.*, Eastland, *id.*, Gest, *supra* n. 4.

9. Quoted in Gest, *supra*, n. 4.

10. Goldman, *Bush's judicial legacy: the final imprint*, 76 JUDICATURE 282 (1993).

11. *See, e.g.*, Carp and Rowland, POLICYMAKING AND POLITICS IN THE FEDERAL DISTRICT COURTS (Knoxville, University of Tennessee Press, 1983); Carp and Stidham, JUDICIAL PROCESS IN AMERICA 3rd ed. (Washington, D.C.: Congressional Quarterly Press, 1996).

12. Davis, Haire, and Songer, *Voting behavior and gender on the U.S. courts of appeals*, 77 JUDICATURE 276 (1995).

Actors in the Judicial Process
Magistrates, Clerks, and Judicial Support Staff

INTRODUCTION

While a great deal has been written about judges and their role in judicial politics, such is not the case regarding other functionaries such as U.S. magistrate judges, law clerks, and other judicial support personnel such as centralized research staff, the subjects of the articles in this section of readings. U.S. magistrate judges are critically important yet largely invisible actors in the federal judiciary. In "From U.S. magistrates to U.S. magistrate judges: developments affecting the federal district courts' lower tier of judicial officers," Christopher Smith documents the expansion in tasks taken on by U.S. magistrate judges from the time that the position was established in 1968 through the formal recognition of the broadened scope of the office's authority signalled by the position's name change in 1990. With the exception of trying and sentencing felony cases, U.S. magistrate judges now can do pretty much what federal district judges do. Still, the magistrate judge's job can vary a good deal depending upon the district in which he or she serves. Smith provides a typology that underscores that the U.S. magistrate judge may be characterized primarily as an additional judge in the district, a team player, or a specialist. As Smith notes, "the specific mix of tasks assigned to magistrate judges within each district depends upon a variety of factors, including district judges' views on magistrate judges "proper judicial role and the nature of the caseload pressures."

In "Law clerks: their roles and relationships with their judges," David Crump explores the benefits and liabilities of the necessary clerking system in the judicial process. The article underlines the considerable diversity in what clerks do, and examines their potential for influence in judicial decision making. Crump's analysis pays heed to arguments that are suggestive of clerks wielding too much power as well as to those that suggest clerks play a positive role in the fostering of change and innovation in judicial decision making.

If magistrate judges and law clerks are relatively "invisible" actors who play critical roles in judicial processes and their outcomes, it is important to recognize that one can delve even more deeply in the judicial system to locate another level of even less publicly-prominent players, such as centralized research staff, whose role in providing support for judges undergoes less scrutiny yet may be equally controversial. Such centralized staff are used in some courts to screen cases, provide research, and make recommendations, tasks that have become necessary because of overwhelming caseloads. The justification for utilizing such staff is, of course, that they can help alleviate delay while also facilitating judicial efficiency. The concern raised by the utilization of such staff is, however, that the judge is no longer the decision maker per se but, rather, the validator of decisions that have been made elsewhere.

In the final articles in this section, Mary Lou Stow and Harold Spaeth explore the issue, "Centralized research staff: is there a monster in the judicial closet?," a question that is answered in the negative by David Brown (a former research attorney) in, "Facing the monster in the judicial closet: rebutting a presumption of sloth." In their empirical study, Stow and Spaeth find that appeals judges in Michigan almost always agreed in their decisions with the recommendations made by their prehearing staffs. While there are several reasons why such agreement might occur, one concern raised by the finding is that such agreement may, at least in part, be the consequence of judges relying too much on the reports that have been prepared for them and not giving cases the full judicial attention they warrant. Brown's response suggests that Stow and Spaeth place too much credence on stereotypes. He argues that judges probably agree with staff recommendations so much simply because the vast majority of cases are "easy" ones with only one possible outcome. In this model, central staffs emerge as "an excellent tool to use in separating the wheat from the chaff."

From U.S. magistrates to U.S. magistrate judges: developments affecting the federal district courts' lower tier of judicial officers

With their new title and increased opportunities to educate the bar about the breadth of their judicial authority, magistrate judges are poised to fulfill the potential their supporters have envisioned for broad, flexible contributions to case-processing responsibilities.

by Christopher E. Smith

Congress created the office of U.S. magistrate in 1968 to provide additional case-processing resources for the federal district courts. In December 1990, the title for the office was changed to "U.S. magistrate judge" as part of the Judicial Improvements Act.[1] Full-time magistrate judges are appointed by district court judges for renewable eight-year terms and part-timers are appointed for renewable four-year terms.[2] Because they do not possess the attributes of Article III judges (i.e., presidential appointment, senate confirmation, and protected tenure), magistrate judges are considered "adjuncts" of the federal courts who perform tasks delegated by the district judges.

Initially, the magistrates' authority was primarily confined to the limited tasks performed by the old U.S. commissioners, lay judicial officers who handled warrants, arraignments, and petty offenses from 1793 until they were replaced by the newly-created magistrates after 1968.[3] Congress subsequently amended the Magistrates Act in 1976 and 1979 to authorize magistrates to assist district judges with a broad spectrum of tasks, including the supervision of complete civil trials with the consent of litigants.[4] After the 1979 Act, magistrates could perform virtually any task undertaken by district judges except for trying and sentencing felony defendants.[5] By June 1990, the 323 full-time and 153 part-time magistrates were such an integral component of the federal district courts that they were responsible for completing 450,565 tasks, including 4,220 civil and criminal evidentiary hearings, 45,201 civil pretrial conferences, and 1,008 complete civil trials.[6] Article III judges acknowledged that magistrates "contribute significantly to the administration of justice in the United States and are an integral part of the Federal judicial system"[7] by including the magistrates' interests in arguments presented to Congress concerning the need for higher salaries for judicial officers.[8]

Because these subordinate judicial officers were intended to be utilized flexibly according to the needs of each district court, the precise judicial roles performed by magistrate judges vary from district to district. For example, one 1985 study of magistrates' roles found that they could be classified as performing three model roles: "Additional Judge," supervising complete civil cases and otherwise sharing caseload responsibilities with district judges; "Team Player," handling motion hearings, conferences, and other tasks to prepare cases for trial before district judges; and "Specialist," primarily processing Social Security disability appeals and prisoner petitions for the district judges.[10] The specific mix of tasks assigned to magistrate judges within each district depends upon a variety of factors, including district judges' views on magistrate judges' proper judicial role and the nature of the caseload pressures.[10] Because the tasks performed by magistrate judges vary, their roles within each district court are susceptible to change as court reforms, changing caseload compositions, and other factors affect the demands on federal courts and the district courts' case-processing capabilities. This article will discuss how recent developments affecting the federal courts are likely to shape the tasks and roles performed by the district courts' lower tier of judicial officers.

A new title and enhanced status

The magistrate judges' original title, "magistrate," was a source of unhappiness for many of the lower-tier judicial officers. District courts throughout the country received authorization to appoint magistrates in the early 1970s. Because neither district judges nor practicing attorneys knew how these new judicial officers, with their vaguely defined authority, ought to be regarded, many judges simply used magistrates as if they were merely permanent law clerks. Practicing attorneys followed suit by failing to treat magistrates with the deference and respect they would normally accord to a recognized judicial officer.[11] As a result, many magistrates believed their effectiveness was hampered because lawyers did not understand that they were indeed authoritative judicial officers. For example, a lawyer interviewed for one study said that "when a [district] judge tells you to do something, you jump. But when a magistrate tells you to do something, well, you do it, but it's not the same."[12]

"Magistrate" is a respected title in the British legal system, but in the United States it is merely a generic term for judicial officer. Because many state court systems employ the title "magistrate" for low-level lay officials, practicing attorneys often confused the authoritative federal judicial officers with the relatively inconsequential lay "justices of the peace" who bear the title "magistrate" in many states. The potential confusion that the title could cause was recognized when the new federal judicial office was created and the Judicial Conference of the United States subsequently discussed the issue in a report to Congress:

Those who would prefer a change in title state that the term "magistrate" has traditionally referred to a low-level local official who performs a narrow range of functions in criminal cases, i.e., a justice of the peace. They

point out that this traditional association of the term is inaccurate when applied to the full-time United States magistrates. They also note that many state magistrates are not well regarded and some have been prosecuted for wrongdoing.[13]

The title "magistrate" contributed to many practical problems when lawyers did not accord the subordinate judicial officers with appropriate deference and respect. If lawyers do not "jump" when instructed to take a specific action by a magistrate, then magistrates must waste time in the aftermath of motion hearings and discovery conferences trying to ensure that attorneys comply with the magistrates' orders. District judges could always force compliance by reiterating the magistrates' orders, but such redundant actions diminish the advantages for saving the judicial system's resources that Congress sought to attain by making magistrates authoritative judicial officers.[14] In addition, because magistrates' authority to preside over civil trials depends upon the consent of litigants,[15] the failure of attorneys to recognize magistrates' status and authority as judicial officers can reduce the likelihood that litigants will consent to magistrates' jurisdiction and thereby hinder the implementation of this mechanism to reduce district judges' civil caseload burdens. The magistrates' title may be an important component of attorneys' willingness to recommend the consent trial option to their clients:

Some magistrates view the title "judge" not only as an entitlement [for themselves as authoritative federal judicial officers], but as a functional necessity if they are to perform effectively when presiding over trials.... Many litigants may automatically prefer to have their cases heard by someone bearing the title of "judge." As a result, magistrates lose opportunities to gain visibility and build their reputations as judicial officers, and the potential flexibility and judicial economy of the magistrate system are diminished.[16]

In order to combat the confusion over magistrates' title, district judges in some districts addressed the magistrates as "judge" and instructed attorneys to do the same. This action reinforced the magistrates' status as judicial officers in those districts, but it exacerbated morale problems among magistrates in other districts who desired similar recognition but were forbidden by their supervising district judges from using the title "judge."[17]

As a result of the title change contained in the

Judicial Improvements Act, the magistrate judges can expect to be more readily addressed as "judge." The new title and form of address will help educate attorneys and litigants about the magistrate judges' status as authoritative judicial officers within the federal courts. This should enhance the magistrate judges' contributions to effective case processing within the district courts by encouraging full cooperation and compliance from attorneys and by increasing the visibility and credibility of the litigants' option to consent to have civil cases tried before magistrate judges.

In 1979, when Congress considered the legislation that authorized magistrates to oversee consent trials, two members of Congress complained that "[f]rom the standpoint of appearance, procedure, and function, an impartial observer will not be able to tell the difference between a magistrate and an Article III judge."[18] In the context in which they raised this concern as part of the debate about the proper authority of non-Article III judicial officers, this was a significant issue to consider. But is this question as compelling today? Now that Congress has explicitly endorsed magistrate judges as "federal judicial officers,"[19] federal appellate court decisions have accepted the constitutionality of magistrates' authority,[20] and magistrates have supervised civil trials for more than a decade, does it matter whether an outsider observer, be it a litigant or an attorney, knows the precise difference between a magistrate judge and an Article III district judge?

There may be legitimate, principled reasons to reopen the debate about the appropriate scope of non-Article III judges' authority.[21] However, because legislative and judicial policy makers have endorsed broad authority for magistrate judges, there is strong reason to give magistrate judges the title and status necessary for maximizing their contributions to the work of the district courts. Magistrate judges are different than Article III district judges in regard to their scope of authority and the delegation of tasks.[22] The title change contained in the Judicial Improvements Act merely indicates that when magistrate judges serve as the presiding judicial officers for matters pending before the district courts, the litigants and attorneys should be made well aware that the magistrate judges are indeed authoritative judicial decision makers who are to be accorded appropriate deference and respect.

Consent trial authority

Recent court reform initiatives threatened the magistrates' status and authority within the federal courts. One of the recommendations made in 1989 by the Brookings Institution's task force on civil justice reform[23] was aimed directly at the broad exercise of authority by magistrates: "Procedural Recommendation 11: Ensure in each district's plan that magistrates do not perform tasks best performed by the judiciary." The phrase "tasks best performed by the judiciary" seemed to imply that district judges rather than magistrates should preside over civil trials.

The task force report served as the basis for legislative proposals by Senator Joseph Biden, the chairman of the Senate Judiciary Committee. Biden's court reform bill, entitled "The Civil Justice Reform Act," contained, among other things, provisions requiring mandatory discovery/case management conferences and monitoring conferences for complex litigation that would both be "presided over by a judge and not a magistrate."[24] Such mandatory conferences would be designed to force district judges to become involved in case management for each civil case and would consequently reduce the likelihood that entire civil cases would be referred to magistrates by the consent of the litigants. In proposing his court reform legislation, Senator Biden made it quite clear that he did not think that magistrates could manage civil litigation effectively.[25]

Ultimately, Biden's "Civil Justice Reform" bill was scrapped in favor of "The Judicial Improvements Act of 1990," which was developed through negotiations between the Senate Judiciary Committee and the Judicial Conference of the United States.[26] In regard to authority of magistrates,[27] the legislation enacted by Congress followed the recommendation of the Federal Courts Study Committee's 1990 report to encourage more consent trials before magistrates. The Federal Courts Study Committee urged that "Congress...allow district judges and magistrates to remind the parties [in civil litigation] of the possibilities of consent to civil trials before magistrates."[28] The statutory change affecting magistrates' consent trial authority suited the interests of both district judges and magistrates by, respectively, maintaining district judges' discretion and autonomy with regard to case management[29] and encouraging the referral of more complete civil trials to the newly retitled magistrate judges.

The Judicial Improvements Act encourages civil consent trials by now permitting district judges and magistrate judges to inform litigants directly about their option of consenting to a trial before a magistrate judge: "[E]ither the district court judge or the magistrate may again advise the parties of the availability of the magistrate, but in so doing, shall also advise the parties that they are free to withhold consent without adverse substantive consequences."[30] The involvement of judicial officers in informing litigants about the consent option represents a significant change from previous statutory language that made clerks of court exclusively responsible for communications about the consent option and precluded any involvement by judges or magistrates.[31] When Congress officially authorized magistrates to preside over complete civil trials with the consent of litigants in 1979,[32] the statute precluded involvement by judicial officers and emphasized the voluntariness of litigants' consent in order to avoid the possibility that judicial officers might pressure litigants to consent.[33]

Magistrate judges in many districts should enjoy increased opportunities to oversee complete civil cases as a result of the statutory change. Some districts had failed to implement regular procedures for educating litigants and their attorneys about the consent option through notices from the clerk of court. Litigants often remained uninformed about their options because the court personnel with whom they came into the most frequent, direct contact through pretrial conferences and hearings, namely the district judges and magistrates, were forbidden from discussing the magistrates' consent authority.[34] Now judicial officers will be able to remind parties about the consent option throughout the stages of civil litigation. Under the previous system, some districts that had routinized the notice process informed litigants about the consent option only at the outset of litigation.[35] If litigants did not understand the scope of magistrates' authority, they would be reluctant to consider immediately consenting to an unfamiliar process under the authority of an unfamiliar judicial officer.[36] Because the parties may not recognize the desirability of consenting to a magistrate judge's jurisdiction for a firm and expedited trial date until after the initiation of discovery and pretrial conferences, the new procedure will provide the opportunity for useful reminders to litigants when judicial officers perceive that such a referral might be beneficial.

Pressure to consent

Although the new procedure will increase the flexible utilization of magistrate judges and increase their status and authority in some districts, the involvement of judicial officers in informing litigants about the consent option also entails risks. The original statutory provision concerning notice to parties precluded the participation of judicial officers because they might coerce litigants into consenting. Congress was aware of the possibility, for example, that district judges might be "tempted to force disfavored cases into disposition before magistrates by intimations of lengthy delays manufactured in district court if the parties exercise their right to stay in that court."[37] Subsequent research revealed that this was a genuine risk that, in fact, came to fruition in some districts despite the statutory prohibition on communications from judicial officers to litigants concerning consent. A Federal Judicial Center study found that:

There was a clear consensus among the [California lawyers] interviewed that when a judge raises the question of consent to a magistrate—for whatever reason—lawyers feel that they have little choice but to go along with the suggestion. Attorneys consistently reported feeling some pressure to consent, particularly in a "smaller" case; when interviewees were asked to describe the reasons for consent, the overriding one given was that the judge had suggested it.[38]

Another study found examples of district judges engaging in precisely the behavior that Congress feared, namely pressuring litigants to consent to the referral of disfavored cases to magistrates.[39]

Because the statutory revisions from the Judicial Improvements Act now invite judicial officers to communicate with litigants about the consent option, there are even greater risks that parties will be or will feel pressured to waive their right to have their case heard before an Article III judge. Such actions by judges are not likely to be challenged by attorneys: "Lawyers are not likely to admit publicly that they were weak in the face of improper conduct. They also [may] think twice about directly challenging the ethical conduct of a judge sitting in a court that provides a basis for their legal practice and livelihood."[40] Moreover, even if the issue of coercion is raised, it would be difficult to prove to an appellate court that a district judge had improper motives or undertook improper actions. Judges' coercive actions identified in one study "were essentially immune from external scrutiny because scheduling trial dates and refusing to grant continuances (two of the most frequently-manipulated mechanisms to pressure litigants) are part of a judge's prerogatives. Thus, the coercive actions were cloaked in the impenetrable discretionary authority of judges."[41] Because the new notice provision invites the participation of judicial officers, district judges and magistrate judges must become much more self-conscious about their own motives and the possible coercive consequences of their communications with litigants concerning the consent option.

Task assignments

Current developments affecting the federal courts are certain to affect magistrate judges' task assignments, although it is uncertain precisely how those assignments will be affected. Although the changes affecting the subordinate judicial officers' title and consent trial authority should encourage increased references of complete civil cases to the magistrate judges, other factors may impede an increase in trials before magistrate judges.

The Judicial Improvements Act requires each district court to develop and implement a "civil justice expense and delay reduction plan."[42] In the course of examining mechanisms for effective case management and cost-effective discovery, districts may create new procedures that actually limit the exercise of magistrate judges' authority. For example, expense and delay reduction plans may make magistrate judges exclusively responsible for oversight of discovery, pretrial conferences, and other preliminary matters. Thus formalizing the subordinate judicial officers' roles as "trial preparers" rather than as "autonomous judges" presiding over civil consent trials.[43] Because district judges exert significant control over the magistrates' roles through their authority to appoint and reappoint the subordinate judicial officers and through their power over the delegation of tasks,[44] Article III judges will continue to have substantial influence over the definition of magistrate judges' roles within each district court. If the judges within a district believe that magistrate judges should exercise limited authority, the expense and delay reduction plans are likely to reflect that preference.

The precise tasks assigned to magistrate judges

within a district depend not only upon the district judges' conceptualizations of the proper role for their judicial subordinates, but also upon the caseload composition within the district.[45] If magistrate judges work within a district containing large prisons, they may become "specialists" in prisoner petitions. Similarly, in districts that receive especially large numbers of Social Security disability appeals, the magistrate judges' working lives may be absorbed by the process of reviewing administrative law judges' findings in such cases. Although some districts utilize alternative mechanisms (e.g., staff attorneys, pro se law clerks, district judges' law clerks) for processing prisoner and Social Security cases, these two particular categories of cases have a significant impact upon workloads of magistrate judges in many districts.[46]

How are the federal courts currently being affected by these categories of cases? In regard to Social Security disability appeals, the federal district courts have experienced a steady decline in such cases. Disability cases peaked in 1984 at 24,215[47] in the aftermath of the Reagan administration's attempt to remove summarily 336,000 beneficiaries from that Social Security program.[48] By contrast, in 1990 there were only 5,212 of such cases filed in the federal district courts.[49] Thus, unless a magistrate judge serves a district that is especially affected by disability cases, these Social Security cases are becoming less burdensome and therefore are having fewer limiting effects upon magistrate judges' availability for other tasks, such as consent trials.

In regard to prisoners' petitions, the burden upon the federal courts has continued to grow. There were only 29,303 prisoners' petitions filed in the district courts in 1982[50] but that number grew to 42,630 in 1990.[51] After handling only 11,578 prisoner matters in 1980, the magistrate judges' burden peaked at 27,002 in 1987 and then dropped back to a consistent plateau just below 21,000 in 1989 and 1990.[52] Because prisoners' filings in the federal courts have shown steady annual increases throughout the 1980s, the recent reduction in the magistrate judges' burden must indicate that district judges are employing alternative mechanisms for processing such cases, such as pro se clerks[53] or their own law clerks. Although the burden upon the magistrate judges generally has, for the moment, stabilized, the tremendous increases in the number of people imprisoned throughout the United States make it likely that the number of prisoners' petitions will increase as well. There were only 329,821 people in prison in 1980, but that number leaped to 771,243 in 1990 as the result of aggressive prosecutions and stiffer sentences for narcotics and other offenses.[54]

Although rising prison populations make it appear likely that magistrate judges will continue to have some portion of their working lives absorbed by prisoners' petitions, other developments may reduce the number of such petitions in the federal courts. The Supreme Court has taken the initiative to create new rules for habeas corpus petitions that have the effect of precluding multiple petitions, enforcing procedural bars, and otherwise limiting prisoners' access to the federal courts.[55] Other potential exclusionary mechanisms have been discussed in justices' opinions[56] and may be on the horizon for implementation in future decisions. In addition, President Bush and Congress are working on legislative proposals that would, if passed, place additional limitations upon prisoners' opportunities to file habeas corpus petitions in the federal courts.[57] Although habeas corpus petitions typically constitute only 25 to 30 percent of the prisoners' petitions filed in federal court, they have constituted 40 percent of the magistrate judges' prisoner tasks in recent years.[58] The current developments aimed at reducing the number of habeas corpus petitions may reduce the magistrate judges' burden or, alternatively, district judges may simply assign their judicial subordinates more prisoner civil rights cases, which typically comprise more than 60 percent of the prisoner filings.[59]

Effect of felony prosecutions

Magistrate judges' workload is being affected by the increase in federal felony prosecutions, especially for narcotics offenses. Increases in felony prosecutions tie up the district judges because "speedy trial" requirements make criminal cases move to the head of the docket queue. Because magistrate judges cannot conduct trials and sentence offenders in felony cases, an increase in felony prosecutions should make litigants more inclined to consent to civil trials before magistrate judges, as district judges' time becomes increasingly absorbed by felony cases. By consenting to a trial before a magistrate judge, litigants in civil cases can obtain an early and firm trial date. They may

also be able to choose which magistrate judge will preside over the trial if the district court's case-processing procedures utilize references to multiple available magistrate judges. Although the increases in felony prosecutions may lead to more civil case responsibilities for magistrate judges, the subordinate judicial officers also have their time absorbed in assisting the felony work of district judges: "Magistrates handled 313 percent more detention hearings in 1990 than in 1985, 111 percent more search warrants, 45 percent more preliminary examinations, 44 percent more arrest warrants, and 38 percent more arraignments."[60]

As with other developments affecting the federal courts, the magistrate judges' task assignments are affected by increases in criminal prosecutions, but it is not clear that such changes will necessarily lead to broader, more flexible utilization of the subordinate judicial officers. For example, although the magistrate judges' responsibilities for preliminary criminal matters increased in conjunction with the increasing criminal caseload in the district courts, the number of civil consent cases for magistrate judges was virtually the same in 1990 as it was in 1986 (4,958 to 4,960).[61] Although the increase in felony cases during the late 1980s did not consistently escalate the number of civil consent cases for magistrate judges, the new statutory notice provisions permitting judicial officers to inform and remind litigants about the consent option may generate such an increase in the future. The number of civil consent trials before magistrate judges is most likely to rise if district judges continue to be preoccupied with felony cases and if those judges evince a concomitant willingness to refer complete civil cases to their judicial subordinates.

Conclusion

Recent and ongoing developments in the federal courts will shape the status, authority, and workload of the U.S. magistrate judges. With their new title and increased opportunities to educate the bar about the breadth of their judicial authority, especially their ability to supervise civil consent trials, magistrate judges are poised to fulfill the potential that their supporters have envisioned for broad, flexible contributions to the case-processing responsibilities within each district court.

Although the subordinate judicial officers received a vote of confidence from Congress in the passage of the supportive Judicial Improvements Act instead of Senator Biden's limiting Civil Justice Reform bill, it remains to be seen whether the magistrate judges will be able to exercise the full range of judicial tasks authorized by statute and desired by many of the incumbent judicial officers themselves.[62] Because the precise tasks assigned to magistrate judges are still significantly influenced by the preferences of the district judges with whom they work and by the nature of their individual districts' caseloads, the recent efforts to enhance magistrate judges' status, authority, and usefulness within the federal courts may, in fact, have little effect upon the subordinate judicial officers' contributions to the court system. The Judicial Improvements Act and continuing docket pressures have set the stage for broader, more innovative use of magistrate judges, but the actual implementation of reforms is dependent on the district judges' willingness to delegate important responsibilities to their judicial subordinates.

NOTES

This article originally appeared in Volume 75, Number 4, December-January 1992, pages 210-215.

1. References to the lower-tier judicial officers concerning their status and authority prior to December 1990 will use the previous title "magistrate" rather than the new title "magistrate judge."

2. *See* Smith, *Who are the U.S. magistrates?*, 71 JUDICATURE 143 (1987); Smith, *Merit Selection Committees and the Politics of Appointing United States Magistrates*, 12 JUST. SYS. J. 210 (1987).

3. *See* Spaniol, *The Federal Magistrates Act: History and Development*, 1974 ARIZ. L. REV. 566; Peterson, *The Federal Magistrates Act: A New Dimension in the Implementation of Justice*, 56 IOWA L. REV. 62 (1970).

4. *See* McCabe, *The Federal Magistrates Act of 1979*, 16 HARV. J. LEGIS. 343 (1979).

5. *See, e.g.*, Gomez v. United States, 109 S. Ct. 2237 (1989) (magistrates not authorized to supervise the selection of jurors in felony criminal cases).

6. Administrative Office of the U.S. Courts, ANNUAL REPORT OF THE DIRECTOR OF THE ADMINISTRATIVE OFFICE OF THE U.S. COURTS 25 (1990). Because these figures are drawn from individual magistrate judges' reports concerning their own activities and the categories of activities are not precisely defined (e.g. different activities may be classified as separate "civil pretrial conferences" by different magistrate judges), case-processing statistics provide only a rough picture of magistrate judges' responsibilities. Although the statistics from the Administrative Office cannot provide precise information on the magistrate judges' accomplishments, the figures demonstrate substantial contributions to the work of the district courts by the lower tier of judicial officers.

7. Committee on the Judicial Branch of the Judicial Conference of the United States, SIMPLE FAIRNESS: THE CASE FOR EQUITABLE COMPENSATION OF THE NATION'S JUDGES 81-82 (1988).

8. *See*, Smith, *Federal Judicial Salaries: A Critical Appraisal*, 62 TEMPLE L. REV. 849 (1988).

9. *See* Seron, THE ROLES OF MAGISTRATES: NINE CASE STUDIES (Washington, D.C.: Federal Judicial Center, 1985); Seron, *Magistrates and the work of the federal courts: a new division of labor*, 69 JUDICATURE 353 (1986).

10. *See* Smith, UNITED STATES MAGISTRATES IN THE FEDERAL COURTS: SUBORDINATE JUDGES 115-146 (New York: Praeger, 1990).

11. Smith, *The Development of a Judicial Office: United States Magistrates and the Struggle for Status*, 14 J. LEGAL PROF. 175, 184-185 (1989).

12. Smith, *supra* n. 10, at 135.

13. THE FEDERAL MAGISTRATES SYSTEM: REPORT TO THE CONGRESS BY THE JUDICIAL CONFERENCE OF THE UNITED STATES 62 (1981).

14. Many magistrates can cite examples of incidents in which the judicial officers wasted time reinforcing to attorneys the idea that magistrates are indeed authoritative federal judicial officers: "In some instances, it is very obvious to the magistrate that the attorney regards the magistrate as being of lesser importance. The magistrate may be forced to marshal resources in order to maintain his or her desired judicial role. For example, in a...case in which an attorney attempted to go over the magistrate's head in order to get a conference rescheduled, it was clear that the attorney never would have attempted such a maneuver if the district judge were presiding over the conference. After an attorney approached a judge about rescheduling, there would be nothing that the attorney could do but comply with the judge's orders. [In this] example, the magistrate hurried to contact the judge to ensure that the judge upheld the magistrate's decision. Thus the magistrate, because of the relatively new judicial office and uncertainty about [the] appropriate status and role for the magistrate position, must often actively seek to maintain proper behavior and respect on the part of attorneys." Smith, *supra* n. 10, at 135.

15. "Upon the consent of the parties, a full-time United States magistrate or a part-time United States magistrate who serves as a full-time judicial officer may conduct any or all proceedings in a jury or nonjury civil matter and order entry of judgment in the case, when specially designated to exercise such jurisdiction by the district court or courts he serves." 28 U.S.C. sec. 636(c)(1).

16. Smith, *supra* n. 11, at 181-82.

17. *Id.* at 180-184.

18. H.R. REP. NO. 1364, 95th Cong., 2d Sess. (1978) at 37 (statement of Reps. Drinan and Kindness).

19. The "definition" section of the Judicial Improvements Act clearly endorsed the magistrate judges' status as judicial officers: "As used in this chapter, the term 'judicial officer' means a United States district court judge *or a United States magistrate*" (emphasis supplied). 28 U.S.C. sec. 482 (1990).

20. *See, e.g.*, Pacemaker Diagnostic Clinic of America, Inc. v. Instromedix, Inc., 725 F.2d 537 (9th Cir. 1984) (*en banc*), *cert. denied*, 469 U.S. 824 (1984).

21. *See* Resnik, *The Mythic Meaning of Article III Courts*, 56 U. COLO. L. REV. 581 (1985).

22. For example, district judges control the delegation of tasks to magistrate judges and, unless the parties have consented to a magistrate judge's authority, magistrate judges merely make recommendations to district judges concerning dispositive motions.

23. *See* Litan, *Speeding up civil justice*, 73 JUDICATURE 162 (1989).

24. The relevant provisions proposed: "A requirement that...a mandatory discovery/case management conference, presided over by a judge and not a magistrate, be held in all cases within 45 days following the first responsive pleading" (S. 2027, 101st Cong., 2d Sess. sec. 471(b)(3) (1990)); and "[F]or cases assigned to the track designated for complex litigation, calendar a series of monitoring conferences, presided over by a judge and not a magistrate, for the purpose of ex-

tending stipulations, refining the formulation of issues and focusing and pacing discovery" (*Id.* at sec. 471(b)(3)(I)).

25. Biden's statement introducing his court reform legislation expressed doubts about the magistrates' effectiveness: "The [pretrial] conference may lose some of its significance in the minds of the attorneys if presided over by a magistrate, since the unfortunate fact is that many attorneys seem to be far more willing to take frivolous positions before a magistrate.... [M]agistrates may themselves be more reluctant than judges to frame the contours of litigation, limit discovery, establish a date-certain briefing schedule and address the full panoply of discovery/case management conference issues." 136 Cong. Rec. S414 (daily ed. Jan. 25, 1990) (statement of Sen. Biden).

26. Some aspects of the negotiation process between the judiciary and Congress apparently angered members of the Senate Judiciary Committee: "The [Senate Judiciary] [C]ommittee complied with the request of the Judicial Conference to work with one body [i.e., a four-judge task force appointed by Chief Justice William Rehnquist], only to have the [Judicial] Conference seemingly defer to another body [i.e., the Conference's Committee on Judicial Improvements which rejected the negotiated legislative proposal]—which had no role whatsoever in the discussions and negotiations—at the point of decision. Such actions only serve to undermine the cooperative relationship between Congress and the judicial branch that our citizens rightly expect and deserve." S. 416, 101st Cong., 2d Sess. (1990) at 5.

27. To counteract Senator Biden's perception that magistrates are ineffective because lawyers do not respect their authority, district judges argued that magistrates can be very capable and authoritative, especially in districts in which judges permit them to perform a broad range of tasks: "[Magistrates] have informed me that it is a rare occasion indeed, that any attorney ever takes a frivolous position when appearing before them. If that should occur in some districts, I suspect that it is more of a reflection of how the magistrates are perceived by the Article III judges, and what duties or powers those judges have permitted the magistrates to perform. If that suspicion is true, one way to address the concerns of the [Brookings Institution's] Task Force is to leave the matter of who presides at the conference to the discretion of the district court adopting its plan." Enslen, *Prepared Statement of the Hon. Richard Enslen, U.S. District Court for the Western District of Michigan, Presented in Testimony Before the Senate Judiciary Committee During Consideration of S.2027, The Civil Justice Reform Act of 1990* (Mar. 6, 1990) at 45.

28. REPORT OF THE FEDERAL COURTS STUDY COMMITTEE 79 (Apr. 2, 1990).

29. The district judges had argued to Congress that "the proposed diminution of the role of magistrates would hamper the proposed legislation's underlying purpose of improving case-processing efficiency." Robinson, *Prepared Statement of the Hon. Aubrey E. Robinson, Jr., Chief Judge, U.S. District Court for the District of Columbia, Presented in Testimony Before the Senate Judiciary Committee During Consideration of S. 2027, The Civil Justice Reform Act of 1990* (Mar. 6, 1990) at 4.

30. 28 U.S.C. sec. 636(c)(2) (1991).

31. "[T]he clerk of court shall, at the time the action is filed, notify the parties of their right to consent to the exercise of such jurisdiction. The decision of the parties shall be communicated to the clerk of court. Thereafter, neither the district judge nor the magistrate shall attempt to persuade or induce any party to consent to reference of any civil matter to a magistrate." 28 U.S.C. sec. 626(c)(2) (1982).

32. At least 36 district courts referred civil cases to magistrates for trial before Congress explicitly endorsed this practice with the 1979 Act. H.R. REP. NO. 1364, *supra* n. 18, at 4.

33. *See* Smith, *Assessing the Consequences of Judicial Innovation: U.S. Magistrates' Trials and Related Tribulations,* 23 WAKE FOREST L. Rev. 455, 474-476 (1988).

34. *See* Smith, *supra* n. 10, at 85-87.

35. One former magistrate described the old statutory notice provision as "unworkable on its face" because the notice was frequently attached to the summons and "such boilerplate is commonly ignored." Sinclair, PRACTICE BEFORE FEDERAL MAGISTRATES sec. 2303 (New York: Matthew Bender, 1987).

36. In the districts in which magistrates were used as "Additional Judges," the practicing bar became familiar with the individual magistrates and knowledgeable about their authority. Thus there was greater willingness to consent. *See* Seron, THE ROLES OF MAGISTRATES, *supra* n. 9, at 38-39.

37. H.R. REP. No. 1364, *supra* n. 18, at 14.

38. Seron, THE ROLES OF MAGISTRATES, *supra* n. 9, at 61-62.

39. Smith, *supra* n. 10, at 103-104.

40. *Id.* at 180.

41. *Id.*

42. 28 U.S.C. sec. 471 (1991).

43. For a detailed typology of eight possible model roles for magistrates, *see* Smith, *supra* n. 10, at 127-132.

44. *Id.* at 115-119; *see* Seron, *The Professional Project of Parajudges: The Case of the U.S. Magistrates,* 22 LAW & SOC'Y REV. 557 (1988).

45. Smith, *supra* n. 10, at 140-141.

46. *See* Seron, THE ROLES OF MAGISTRATES, *supra* n. 9, at 83-92.

47. Administrative Office of the U.S. Courts, ANNUAL REPORT OF THE DIRECTOR OF THE ADMINISTRATIVE OFFICE OF THE U.S. COURTS 180 (1986).

48. *See* Mezey, NO LONGER DISABLED: THE FEDERAL COURTS AND THE POLITICS OF SOCIAL SECURITY DISABILITY (New York: Greenwood, 1988).

49. Administrative Office, *supra* n. 6, at 138.

50. Administrative Office, *supra* n. 47, at 179.

51. Administrative Office, *supra* n. 6, at 138.

52. *Id.*

53. *See* Zeigler & Hermann, *The Invisible Litigant: An Inside View of Pro Se Actions in the Federal Courts,* 47 N.Y.U. L. REV. 157 (1972).

54. Cohen, *Prisoners in 1990,* BUREAU OF JUSTICE STATISTICS BULLETIN 1 (May 1991). Increases in prisoner filings are not purely a function of increases in prison populations. *See* Thomas, Keeler & Harris, *Issues and Misconceptions in Prisoner Litigation: A Critical View,* 24 CRIMINOLOGY 775 (1986).

55. *See, e.g.,* McCleskey v. Zant, 111 S.Ct. 2841 (1991) (failure to raise claim in initial habeas corpus petition in federal courts barred subsequent petition concerning claim); Coleman v. Thompson, 111 S.Ct. 2546 (1991) (procedural default under state court rules barred raising claim in subsequent federal court habeas corpus petition).

56. In a concurring opinion in *Duckworth v. Eagan,* 109 S. Ct. 2875 (1989). Justice O'Connor argued that the Supreme Court should emulate its decision in *Stone v. Powell,* 428 U.S. 465 (1976), which precludes federal court consideration of habeas corpus "exclusionary rule" claims that have been previously raised in state courts, by similarly precluding federal court review of *Miranda* claims.

57. *See* Diemer, *Blood for blood: Senate focuses upon fighting crime,* CLEVELAND PLAIN DEALER, June 30, 1991, at 15-A.

58. Administrative Office, *supra* n. 6, at 25, 140.

59. *Id.*

60. *Id.* at 24.

61. *Id.* at 25.

62. *See* Smith, *supra* n. 10, at 69-75, 182-187.

Law clerks: their roles and relationships with their judges

Although nearly everyone agrees that law clerks are necessary, there is considerable disagreement as to what their role should be.

by David Crump

To some people, law clerks are part of a long and noble tradition. To a few others, they are 25-year-old Svengalis influencing the judicial process toward views inculcated into them by a phalanx of activist law professors.

In any event, nearly everyone views law clerks as necessary. Justice John Paul Stevens has said that the Supreme Court is "too busy to decide whether there [is] anything we could do about the problem of being too busy."[1] And United States District Court Judge Norman Black, whose docket is roughly double the national average and who has managed, through hard work, only to hold down the amount of its annual increase, says simply: "I couldn't function without them."[2]

For the law clerk, the experience is likely to be a high point in his or her legal career. "It was wonderful," says Sal Levatino, a former law clerk to a federal district judge in Austin, Texas. "It really ought to be at the end of your career, rather than at the beginning."[3] In fact, law clerks speak of " law clerk letdown" when they begin practicing law. The clerkship represented a "pure" experience with the law, constantly exciting—and without the risk of failure.[4]

In contrast, the practice of law itself involves clients with unrealistic expectations, cases or transaction that don't turn very fast, and work that is more often tedious than exciting. To the law clerk's surprise, the possibilities of missing time deadlines, failing to get evidence admitted, or making any one of a variety of similar mistakes aren't something that happens to lesser practitioners. They are very real dangers for the inexperienced—such as

a lawyer fresh from a judicial clerkship.

The clerk's duties

The functions of law clerks vary tremendously. A few judges use them as research assistants only. For other judges they may perform a screening function: summarizing the contents of papers filed by the parties in the manner of an honest broker. Still others—and these are clearly the majority—use law clerks as preliminary drafters of opinions or orders. The amount of direction supplied to a clerk drafting an opinion varies enormously from judge to judge.

In a trial court, as Judge Black points out, more than 90 percent of cases are typically settled.[5] A federal district judge may well find that he can use his clerks most effectively in motion practice, because prompt, simple rulings on motions make the cases settle faster, more cheaply, and more fairly. A typical district judge may assign each of his clerks half the docket by odd and even numbers, having them coordinate with the district clerk's office to study each motion as soon as possible after its submission date.[6]

Screening of each motion for complexity and for the need for a hearing is the typical first step. As the judge considers each motion, informal discussion with the law clerk—or a memorandum prepared by the clerk, probably with a recommendation—highlights the issues (the practice varies). The judge may then orally outline the chosen disposition and discuss the general content of the order or memorandum the clerk is to prepare. If the motion does require a hearing or a conference, the assigned law clerk is likely to be made responsible for coordinating with the district clerk's office to see that it is properly scheduled. At trial, a law clerk's functions may range from assistance in charge preparation to on-the-spot research on evidence questions. And if an opinion results, the first draft will probably be written by the law clerk.

In appellate courts, law clerks' time is often largely occupied in preparing pre-argument memoranda and writing initial drafts of opinions. In courts of last resort with discretionary review, clerks often have significant (some would say, excessive) functions in deciding which cases will be heard.

The influence of clerks

There is no question among former law clerks now practicing law that the decision of their own cases can be influenced or even determined by the judgments of law clerks. Should a lawyer use different tactics if he is trying a case before a trial judge with a full complement of clerks? Former Supreme Court clerk John O'Neill says that if the judge relies heavily on his clerks, "It's important to appeal to *their* imagination."[7] In that endeavor, says O'Neill, "You'd make more academic and policy arguments."[8] Before a judge without clerks, the lawyer might do well to put more emphasis on explaining the case law. Former state appellate law clerk Rob Johnson says, "You'd play to the sympathies of the person who's really" going to report on the case.[9] Following his law school training, the law clerk may be more likely than the judge to see the case as controlled by social policy.

But Mike Kuhn,[10] a former Fifth Circuit clerk, disagrees. "There are too many variables," he says. "I don't think I'd stress public policy just because the judge has law clerks; the clerk himself might be more interested in *stare decisis*." Besides, he points out, it's risky to "play to the clerks" when the judge is still the one who makes the final decision.[11]

But whether the law clerk performs a research function, a screening or "filtering" function, or a drafting or recommending function, the judgment factor is there. And even though the judge "is the judge," and remains so, the judgment of the law clerk is frequently an ingredient in the decision.

To some observers, this "leavening effect" is a positive thing. "In our ideal form," writes John B. Oakley, a former law clerk to a judge of the Supreme Court of California, "the law clerk is meant to fiddle with the law, to advocate innovation, to introduce to its inner sanctums the views of those outside."[12] Oakley's work, *Law Clerks and the Judicial Process* (co-authored with Robert S. Thompson), is the most comprehensive recent work on the subject. The law clerk "gives the law needed capacity for change,"[13] Oakley and Thompson write. "[T]he fabric of the law has been woven from the warp of the judiciary and the woof of their law clerks."[14] This metaphor depicts the judge as the lengthwise thread (or warp) in the weave of the law and the clerk as its crosswise thread (or woof). If there are to be "passing variations in texture and elasticity," says Oakley and Thompson, "they must be woven into the fabric by means of the woof."[15] And in what they correctly acknowledge is a very bad pun, Oakley and Thompson argue that the law clerk should be "a fiddler in the woof."[16]

In a written opinion, the Fifth Circuit has provided some support for this model. "The association with law clerks is also valuable to the judge; in addition to relieving him of many clerical and administrative chores, law clerks may serve as sounding boards for new ideas, often affording a different perspective . . . .," said the court in *Fredonia Broadcasting Corporation v. RCA Corporation*.[17] Judge Frank M. Coffin, in his book *The Ways of a Judge*, adds that law clerks "bring to chambers their recent exposure to excellent professors in demanding schools of law from all parts of the country. They are questioning, articulate, idealistic." As a result, they "provide the judge with a continuing seminar that cannot fail to keep his mind open and his mental juices flowing."[18]

Oakley and Thompson point out that the historical ideal of the law clerk fits the warp-and-woof metaphor too.[19] Felix Frankfurter was given to lengthy substantive discussions with his law clerks, in which "[a]nger, scorn, sarcasm, [and] humor buttressed straightforward argument."[20] The law clerk was placed "on an equal footing" with the judge in the "ecstasy of combat."[21]

Oakley and Thompson recognize that the judge must make the final decisions. But this result, they argue, will flow from "the judge's natural resistance to the influence of a young and fleeting law clerk."[22] In fact, Oakley and Thompson conclude, a greater problem may be that the judge's thinking wins out merely because of his position and tenure. For that reason, they say, the law clerk will have a proper incentive to "fight the judge for every inch of fair ground."[23]

A different view

But to others, this "ideal" is not so attractive. They point out that the law clerk is not appointed by the president, is not confirmed by the Senate, and has not been qualified under the Constitution to perform judicial functions.

Oakley and Thompson's statement that law clerks are innovators who fiddle with the law and provide it with capacity for change is hotly disputed by most former law clerks interviewed for this article. "That's so naive," says O'Neill.[24] He points out that most activist judges do not need the intervention of law clerks to make them into innovators. "What about Mr. Justice Douglas?" he asks. "The function of the law clerk ought to be to find what the law is," he says. "And a lawyer who's practiced a long time [*i.e.*, the judge] ought to make the policy decisions."[25]

Rob Johnson, who was the single clerk for a state appellate court with three judges back in the days when "I'm not sure we even had an electric typewriter," is more blunt. "I don't like the idea of wild-eyed 24- and 25-year-olds, who come right out of law school, tinkering with the law in a way that might affect my life," he says.[26] And Judge Black (who teaches in law school himself) disagrees with the notion that a judge's chambers are "an ivory tower" that needs a recently graduated lawyer to provide "a pipeline to reality."[27] Judge Black has a simple answer to the model of the law clerk as "innovator:" "I've seen the argument made," he says. "I've never seen it put into effect."[28]

In addition to the law clerk's lack of constitutional authority, there are at least two other reasons for opposing a decision-making role. One is the effect of the law clerk's education. Harvard law student Alexander Troy describes his first year torts class (which, it is to be hoped, was atypical) as "a desultory survey of economics, epistemology and social psychology, but the professor also found time to address the issue of the limits of a court's power in a democratic society."[29] That issue, according to Troy, was resolved by the professor's conclusion that "[j]udicial decisions are substantively indistinguishable from legislative ones." Thus the "inference left for students to draw is that there is little a court cannot do."[30] Many judges may feel a

need to counteract the pronouncements of some of Troy's professors who, he says, were critical of judicial restraint as a general principle.[31]

The merit of this view is not really the issue; the point is that, for the judge himself, presidential appointment and Senate hearings—or election, in a state system—provide an acceptable filtering process as well as a reminder of the separation of powers. But as Rob Johnson says: "A law clerk, all he's done is get good grades in law school."[32]

The second reason against the law clerk as decisionmaker is experience, both in law and in life. Law clerks are less likely to have had mortgages—or children whom they must decide to send to either public or private school. "They don't see the tugs and pulls; they don't see the results down at the end of the line," says Johnson.[33] He points out that "school cases just look different when you haven't got school-age kids and neither do any of your close friends. So does freedom of speech when you don't have a home that might have an x-rated movie across from it."[34] What is more, a 25-year-old may not realize that such experiences are likely to mature his outlook. The "fiddler in the woof" viewpoint might regard this inexperience as a net plus, characterizing it as a fresh approach; a less positive view would see the lack of self-knowledge as a negative factor.

And in the law itself, lack of experience is likely to reflect itself in harmful naivete. The difficulty of preserving error for appeal, of maintaining a trial schedule, and even of presenting the bodies of one's witnesses physically at the trial may be unknown to law clerks. The proposition that an error-free criminal trial is unusual may be differently perceived by those who have seen trials firsthand and those who have seen them only in law school casebooks, through what Mr. Justice Fortas once called the "remote knothole" of appellate decisions.[35]

As Levatino puts it, even the law clerk's job itself is "somewhat deceptive."[36] As a law clerk, one might draft an opinion in a case presented by attorneys, "And you say, 'hey, this is easy.' " But "it's harder to have clients come into your office and dump something on your desk and ask if there's something you can do, when you can't even tell if it's a securities case, or a labor matter, or what." As a result, says Levatino, "If I went back now, 13 years later, I'd have a whole lot more empathy for the attorneys."[37]

The difference between the "fiddler and innovator" argument, and the opposing view (as expressed by Johnson) that the law clerk's job "is to do what he's told to," can easily be exaggerated.[38] Most law clerks acknowledge that delegation by judges to clerks of the task of writing a first draft of an opinion is common. If the judge handles the delegation properly, and deals adequately with the result, the judge remains the decisionmaker.

And former Fifth Circuit law clerk Michael Kuhn, although not himself in favor of judicial activism, defends the law clerk's prerogative. "A law clerk has a right and a duty to express his views," he says. "If you think your judge has missed a point, if he's off base, it's your job to say, 'Judge, you're deciding this case as though it were a rule-of-reason case and it's not; it's a per se violation.' "[39] Other law clerks give examples of occasions, in fact, in which law clerks have restrained judicial activism (or even prevented unfortunate displays of anger by judges with hair-trigger tempers).

The other side of the coin, says Kuhn, is that the law clerk "shouldn't be offended if his recommendation isn't adopted." If the judge replies, "I don't care; I think the rule of reason is the better way to decide this case," Kuhn concludes that the law clerk ought to draft a good, sound opinion—"using the rule of reason, as the judge said."[40]

Using law clerks well

Since law clerks are here to stay, the real question concerns the way a judge ought to go about using them. Lawyers and law clerks have a variety of opinions on the subject.

The number of law clerks. Each United States Supreme Court justice presides over a law firm of four clerks. Each federal court of appeals judge has three, and California's chief justice has an astounding 14 (although many of their duties are performed for the court as a whole or for other justices).

The suspicion arises that a plethora of law clerks dilutes the judge's ability to make the important decisions. Former district court clerk Tom Houghton thinks even a lawyer who is a good manager "can't personally supervise more than three or four associates."[41] And if he is not a good manager, he may supervise one law clerk poorly. With numbers like 14, intermediate managers are required, says Houghton. In such a situation, asks Johnson, "Does the judge write any opinions at

all? It sounds as though they wouldn't have time. They'd be reading reams of paper from their law clerks."[42]

But busy judges without adequate assistance from clerks draw criticism too. As Levatino says, a conscientious judge working alone in a complex case "may not even have time to read all of the briefs."[43]

Length of opinions. One consequence of the number of law clerks is an opinion explosion. United States Supreme Court Reports have gone from 2133 pages in the 1960 October Term to 4269 in the 1983 Term, not so much because of workload as because of the length of individual opinions. "When the opinions start looking like law review articles, you know you're in trouble," says one former law clerk.

The result is an increase in complexity—a proliferation of conflicting opinions—all without the benefit of the consistency and certainty that are the apparent aim. While it is desirable that judges express the reasons for their decisions as a means of encouraging rational decision making, there is little utility in a district court summary judgment opinion that contains a treatise on Rule 56. Former trial court clerk Levatino says flatly, "most trial level cases don't require opinions."[44] Findings and conclusions would be preferable from a functional standpoint. And Houghton points out that the great appellate judges of the past—Hand, Cardozo and Holmes—wrote long opinions when it was necessary, "but most of their opinions are a page and a half in the reporter system."[45]

The types of opinions law clerks may produce is also a matter of concern. Dan Peterson, a former law clerk on the Iowa Supreme Court, suspects that law clerks left to their own devices might draft "opinions that are full of global statements that you don't need to support the holding and don't apply as globally as they're written." These statements "muddle things in the next case and have to be distinguished."[46] A judge's experience, Peterson thinks, would help him avoid that sort of writing and eliminate it from a law clerk's preliminary draft.

Discretionary review. In courts of last resort or other courts with discretionary review, there is heavy reliance on law clerks in the selection of cases for decision. For example, it is an open secret (reported in the newspapers) that at least six Supreme Court justices rely on one designated law clerk to summarize each certiorari petition. "I do not even look at the papers in over 80 percent of the cases that are filed," Justice Stevens has publicly stated.[47]

Former Supreme Court clerk O'Neill points out that when law clerks perform such a task, "they may reflect values learned in law school, not over a career." Hence the problems they may find significant are "the ones they've been taught about, not the great practical ones that you'd identify over 10 years of practice."[48] Issues that O'Neill calls "interstitial"—crucial issues in energy, finance, or similar areas that determine the fate of the nation just as surely as do constitutional questions—may not commend themselves to a law clerk's imagination simply because they are not the subject of any law school course.[49]

It is probably inevitable that discretionary review will prompt heavy reliance on clerks, because the task is tedious. The supreme courts of Texas and California also rely heavily upon law clerk involvement. Anonymously poring over reams of dross to discover one case for review is obviously less satisfying than crafting a signed opinion, and a judge may not regard it as the most productive use of his time.

But because they are more experienced lawyers, with longer memories for recurring issues, judges can provide a corrective to the syndrome of selection by law school course content. The judge can do so by express direction to his clerk, by discussions exposing "law clerk's bias" to the law clerk himself, or by a final review in which the judge consciously tries to counteract the fact that he is, to a degree, the prisoner of his law clerk's education.

Guidance, supervision, and orientation. A good many law clerks learn about office policies of the judge through trial and error. A few judges have had success in the use of office manuals or memoranda explaining the job to new arrivals. Given the planned turnover of clerks, such a practice might be a good management tool. In a district court, identification of various procedures (different kinds of motions, jury charge preparation, etc.) and the approach the judge uses on each would shorten the learning curve—and not incidentally, would help the judge to promulgate his own decisions. In appellate courts, a written explanation of standards for the court's summary docket, methodology in handling motions, and like matters would be just as helpful.

There is, in fact, a "Law Clerk Handbook," published by the Federal Judicial Center; certain states have published similar aids. Ranging from the general to the specific, the Handbook covers such topics as the history of law clerks (the tradition was begun at the Supreme Court by Justice Horace Gray in 1882 and continued by his successor, Oliver Wendell Holmes) to telephone etiquette ("If the judge is . . . unavailable, you should inquire, 'May I take a message?' ").[50] Its coverage of procedure, drafting tips, and organization appears quite useful. It is necessarily general, and its usefulness would be enhanced if individual judges rewrote it to reflect their own practices (having their law clerks, of course, do the drafting!).

There are early limits to the usefulness of this idea; many practices in a court are "not suitable for a memorandum," as former district court clerk Tom Houghton puts it.[51] "What it takes is treatment of the clerk the way a senior lawyer uses an associate," with individual day-to-day attention recognizing that the law clerk needs supervision.[52]

Another suggestion is that law schools might provide courses in their curricula for future law clerks. For example, a one-hour course based upon the "Law Clerk Handbook" (and other materials) is under active consideration at the South Texas College of Law, which in 1985 supplied more clerks to the Texas Supreme Court than any other school. There is some question, however, whether it is feasible thus to prepare clerks for such diverse environments as federal trial courts and state appellate courts—and for an infinite variety of individual judges' preferences. Furthermore, some academics doubt that a law school's resources should be expended in a way that will guide so few students for such a brief period in their careers. Still, the proposal is worth trying because of its possible public benefits. An alternative suggestion of a national orientation program, perhaps conducted by the Federal Judicial Center, might offer some benefits, but they are not likely to justify the costs.

Management styles. Many former clerks are skeptical of proposals for periodic staff meetings, believing them to be ineffective in a small office handling highly individualized problems. But if the office handles a large volume of matters—a district court with a large backlog, for example, or a court of last resort that has a considerable discretionary docket—staff meetings in which the status of each case is reviewed may make dispositions more efficient. Similarly, if the judge has more than three or four law clerks, staff meetings may be necessary to reinforce the policies the judge wants followed.

Both judges and clerks seem to regard a one-on-one relationship as preferable. A "committee" or "intermediate manager" approach may be necessary in a larger office, however, and the trial of a larger case may require the services of more than one clerk. In normal operations, most judges and clerks view direct supervision of the clerk by the judge as more efficient. It also seems clear that this management style is best for reasons unrelated to efficiency: it maximizes control of actual decision making by the judge, and it avoids the dilution of his personal responsibility for each case.

Confidentiality and the appearance of propriety. Most law clerks probably recognize that public identification of the law clerk as a decisionmaker is undesirable. Most probably come to the task with an appreciation that what they see and hear is privileged. "I'm their client," says Judge Black. "They're my lawyers."[53] The "Law Clerk Handbook" is explicit and eloquent on the subject: "If judges wish to publish their jurisprudential, economic or social views, they know how to do so."[54]

But unfortunately, the available evidence indicates that understanding of these concepts is neither innate nor universal among law clerks. Furthermore, says Houghton, "the judge needs to emphasize that the need for circumspection goes on after the clerkship is over." "*The Brethren*[55] is inexcusable," he says.[56] Such disclosures come about because law clerks "sometimes come out of clerkships with bloated heads" and with a need to expand upon their roles in major decisions.[57] (It might be added that if one has doubt that the maturity of law clerks is a real concern, one might consider *The Brethren*—and the hemorrhage of confidential disclosures it reflects—a strong piece of evidence to that effect.)

One trial lawyer tells a related story that is equally disconcerting. While interviewing a prospective new associate, he mentioned a case he had recently tried. "Oh," said the interviewee, "That was John Smith's case." John Smith (a fictitious name) was the judge's law clerk; he had drafted the opinion. The interviewee, a former clerk himself, was apparently unaware that such disclosures do not serve the judge who trusted his circumspection. To the trial lawyer (who, of course, thought it was *his* case), it meant a more jaundiced view of the court. This was especially so since John Smith hadn't been in the courtroom when the case was orally argued, leaving the lawyer to conclude that, if the case was indeed "John Smith's," his arguments were not heard.

The subject is difficult, because courts are a part of the government. And a blanket prohibition upon law clerks talking to reporters would be inappropriate, for the same reason that it would be inappropriate to impose a gag upon personnel in other governmental offices. The important issue is one of confidentiality and deference to the judge.

A personal relationship

There is another side to the law clerk issue. Judges benefit personally from relationships with their law clerks, and not just because they need clerks' research skills. The job of a judge, strictly defined, is solitary and remote. If we are to attract good judges, perhaps we must consider the need that lawyers and judges have in common with most of the human race: the need for a collegial atmosphere, in which one's work is shared with other people.

For the best of the profession—the sort of lawyers we would like to attract to the judiciary—the job doesn't pay well in comparison to private practice. And as Judge Black points out, "Making decisions is hard work."[58] For that reason, Judge Black points out, emotional and mental maturity in a law clerk applicant is a primary qualification; there's "nothing to assure you," as he puts it, "that a person with a 98.5 grade average will be a good law clerk."[59]

The old adage holds that a federal judge is just a lawyer who knows a senator. But as far as almost every law clerk is concerned, *his* judge is extraordinary. Talking to Judge Black, one senses immediately that the affection is usually mutual—and that relationships with law clerks can sometimes go a long way toward filling the compensation gap. As Judge Coffin puts it, "[T]he pleasure of their company is one of a judge's most refreshing fringe benefits."[60]

NOTES

This article originally appeared in Volume 69, Number 4, December-January 1986, pages 236-240.

1. Middleton, *High Court's Case Load too Heavy: Three Justices*, 68 A.B.A. J. 1201 (October, 1982).

2. Interview with Judge Norman Black, United States Dis-

trict Court, in Houston, Texas (December 1, 1982).

3. Telephone interview with Sal Levantino, former law clerk (October 21, 1982).

4. *Id.*

5. Interview Black, *supra* n. 2.

6. *Id.*

7. Interview with John O'Neill, former law clerk, in Houston, Texas (October 21, 1982).

8. *Id.*

9. Interview with Rob Johnson, former law clerk, in Houston, Texas (October 21, 1982).

10. Interview with Mike Kuhn, former law clerk, in Houston, Texas (October 21, 1982).

11. *Id.*

12. Oakley and Thompson, Law Clerks and the Judicial Process 138 (Berkeley, CA: University of California Press, 1980).

13. *Id.*

14. *Id.*

15. *Id.*

16. *Id.*

17. Fredonia Broadcasting Corp. v. RCA Corp., 569 F.2d 251, 255-256 (5th Cir. 1978).

18. Coffin, The Ways of a Judge 72 (Boston: Houghton Mifflin Co., 1980).

19. Oakley and Thompson, *supra* n. 12, at 138.

20. Sacks, *Felix Frankfurter*, in 3 The Justices of the United States Supreme Court 1789-1969, 2403-2404 (New York: Chelsea House in association with Bowker Company, 1969).

21. *Id.*

22. Oakley and Thompson, *supra* n. 12, at 38.

23. *Id.*

24. Interview O'Neill, *supra* n. 7.

25. *Id.*

26. Interview Johnson, *supra* n. 9.

27. Interview Black, *supra* n. 2.

28. *Id.*

29. Troy, *Learning the Law at Harvard*, Wall St. J., August 6, 1982, at 14 col. 2.

30. *Id.*

31. *Id.* at col. 3.

32. Interview Johnson, *supra* n. 9.

33. *Id.*

34. *Id.*

35. Time Inc. v. Hill, 385 U.S. 374 (1967).

36. Interview Levatino, *supra* n. 3.

37. *Id.*

38. Interview Johnson, *supra* n. 9.

39. Interview Kuhn, *supra* n. 10.

40. *Id.*

41. Interview with Tom Houghton, former law clerk, in Houston, Texas (October 27, 1982).

42. Interview Johnson, *supra* n. 9.

43. Interview Levatino, *supra* n. 3.

44. *Id.*

45. Interview Houghton, *supra* n. 41.

46. Interview with Dan Peterson, former law clerk, in Houston, Texas (October 21, 1982).

47. Middleton, *supra* n. 1, at 1201.

48. Interview O'Neill, *supra* n. 7.

49. *Id.*

50. Dileo and Rubin, Law Clerk Handbook: A Handbook for Federal District and Appellate Court Law Clerks (Washington, D.C.: Federal Judicial Center, 1977).

51. Interview Houghton, *supra* n. 41.

52. *Id.*

53. Interview Black, *supra* n. 2.

54. Dileo and Rubin, *supra* n. 50.

55. Woodward and Armstrong, The Brethren: Inside the Supreme Court (New York: Simon and Schuster, 1979).

56. Interview Houghton, *supra* n. 41.

57. *Id.*

58. Interview Black, *supra* n. 2.

59. *Id.*

60. Coffin, *supra* n. 18, at 71.

Centralized research staff: is there a monster in the judicial closet?

A recent study in the Michigan Court of Appeals found a high level of agreement between central staff recommendations and judges' decisions. Are the overworked judges simply deferring to staff, as critics of centralized research staffs have predicted, or are there other explanations?

by Mary Lou Stow and Harold J. Spaeth

Faced with exploding dockets in the late 1960s and early 1970s, many state and federal appellate courts responded by centralizing research staff.[1] Such staff were used for case screening, research, and recommendation, with each court finding its own "best" mix of these functions.[2]

While any tendency toward delegation of judicial duties seemed troublesome, courts had few, if any, alternatives. The need to somehow enhance productivity was evident, and additional "elbow" clerks did not prove effective. (An "elbow" clerk is one who is employed by and works for a single judge, not for the court or any division of it).[3] A central team of attorneys, serving the court as a whole, emerged as the optimal fix.[4] Doubts and fears were quickly voiced but dismissed in the names of necessity and efficiency.

Attorneys are suspicious of any procedure that could conceivably result in judicial decisions by nonjudges. They want their cases decided by the judge and not by an anonymous clerk in the backroom. They want the judge to review the record and read the briefs and make all decisions concerning the case on appeal. If the judge cannot rely on a staff, however, the press of time may prevent him from giving sufficient attention to important parts of the record on appeal.[5]

Supporters pointed to the reduction or elimination of delay in those courts utilizing centralized research staff.[6] As an additional comfort, proponents assured skeptics that research staff served to assist judges, and no more.

The prehearing system endeavors to avoid delegation of authority to nonjudicial staff personnel. The basic element of the system, the prehearing report, is only a preliminary research tool to aid a panel of judges in arriving at its decision. Suggestion by a prehearing attorney...is simply a recommendation having no judicial force. The decision-making responsibility rests with, and is carried out by, a three-member panel of judges. None of the research staff has any power of decision.[7]

Meador acknowledged the sacred nature of the judges' commission yet felt that, realistically, "a sharing of the judicial work, with ultimate control in the judge, is accepted as a legitimate means of enabling the judiciary to perform its task of deciding cases."[8]

But how sure are we that the compromise has been worthwhile? Dockets have continued to expand, so that even the most productive courts are experiencing backlog and long delays. For example, the Michigan Court of Appeals has consistently ranked first among the nation's appellate courts in the number of filings per judge. It has also ranked among the top three such courts in the number of dispositions per judge. This court, in 1988, saw 8,559 filings. This meant 476 filings per judge, and a backlog of 1,717 cases at the end of that year. (The court has defined "backlog" as those cases that are awaiting submission to a panel of judges.) By 1990, total filings had grown to 13,083, with new filings per judge reaching 545. In addition, by the end of 1990, backlogged cases had more than doubled, to 3,853.[9] Given such prodigious increases, there is no insurance that the judges treat staff "recommendations" as such in all cases. In other words, there is no guarantee that the decision in a given case really is made by a three-judge panel, after careful review. In fact, the reverse may be true: judges may hurriedly accept staff recommendations, transforming a staff attorney's case evaluation into the decision of the court.

Our study, then, focuses on this question: Who really makes the decision: the judges, or the centralized staff? Clearly, the answer is important to the administration of justice. Though the scope of our study is much too narrow to provide a definitive answer, even for Michigan, it is the first systematic, empirical consideration of this question.[10] We focus on the Michigan Court of Appeals, analyzing a random sample of 603 cases submitted during the years 1989 and 1990, which for the most part were decided in 1990 or 1991.

Background

Michigan's use of centralized research staff is not completely replicated by other jurisdictions that use such staff. Suffice it to say that small differences in the structure exist among users of centralized personnel, and that large differences in judicial reliance on that staff may, or may not, exist. The findings presented here pertain only to the Michigan system. Their applicability to other states or to the federal courts will obviously require separate analysis.

The Michigan Court of Appeals was established in 1965, and began using centralized research staff three years later.[11] In the years since, such staff have become an integral part of the court. The early 1970s saw a ratio of one central staff person and two "elbow" clerks for each judge. Approximately six additional research attorneys, called "commissioners," were employed to make recommendations in cases of discretionary review. (We explain their functions more fully below.) At that time, there were nine judges. Since then, the Michigan legislature has authorized a total of 15 additional judgeships, and the ratio has shifted as well, so that there are now two central staffers and only one personal clerk for each of 24 judges. The number of commissioners stands at seven.[12]

The Michigan Court of Appeals has jurisdiction over all final judgments or interlocutory matters from circuit courts within the state, as well as re-

view of the decisions of administrative agencies and other tribunals as established by Michigan law.[13] Cases are decided by randomly selected, rotating panels of three judges. In addition to 24 elected court of appeals judges, the court employs retired supreme court justices and court of appeals judges on a visiting basis. Until the summer of 1991, oral arguments were allowed in all appeals on final review, if parties to the case requested them and complied with court rules.[14] Now cases may be decided without oral argument "if the judges determine that arguments would not help them decide the merits, if the issue had recently been resolved or if the appeal is frivolous."[15]

Research staff

There are two types of research staff, prehearing staff and commissioners, differentiated by function and permanency. Prehearing staff are almost exclusively recent graduates of top national law schools, who stay with the court approximately two years, and perform research and analysis on cases for final review by a panel. More specifically, the prehearing attorney reads the briefs and examines the record in a given case. He or she looks at the issues raised by parties in light of applicable statutes and case law, and may raise additional issues if he or she deems it appropriate. The prehearing attorney then prepares what is termed a "report," an "evaluation," or a "recommendation," the length of which ranges from 3 to 30 pages. This document summarizes the issues on appeal, the arguments in party briefs, and the facts of the record, with reference points to the respective documents. The attorney provides an analysis of relevant law, and makes suggestions as to outcome and opinion type (i.e., whether the case warrants an authored opinion; or should be decided per curiam, or via a memorandum opinion).[16]

Commissioners are permanent, more seasoned staff attorneys.[17] They make recommendations on discretionary appeals, motions, complaints, and writs. The bulk of their work involves requests for review of cases that do not have an appeal of right, or are "applications for leave."[18] As such, they do not fully summarize and evaluate the facts or merits of cases. Rather, their task pertains to the threshold consideration of whether or not the court should agree to review a case in full.[19] Unlike the prehearing attorneys whose recommendations address the outcome of the case, the commissioners' recommendations do not affect case outcome unless they advise the panel to deny review.

Skeptics and critics of the use of centralized research attorneys have focused mainly on the prehearing staff. Less attention has been afforded commissioners, or staff that perform like functions.

In Michigan, review as of right exists only within a specified number of days following a final order in a circuit court, recorder's court, or any other tribunal from which appeal of right has been established by law.[20] All interlocutory matters, agency or tribunal rulings, judgments of circuit or recorder's courts on appeal from any other court, and appeals that may have been taken by right but have not been timely filed, require a grant of review from the court of appeals.[21]

The commissioners review all such applications for leave to appeal, and provide the panel of judges with recommendations. Recommendations might be to grant or deny review, to dismiss the application, or various peremptory actions. These recommendations are made in an evaluation or report similar to the prehearing attorney's, and they are the product of similar research and analysis. In addition, the commissioner prepares an order that reflects his or her recommended decision and attaches the drafted order to the report.

Traditional fears

Any use of staff by judges creates some risk of overdelegation.[22] The shift from personal law clerks to the use of a more bureaucratic, detached research team has led to

a legitimate concern that the judges on the Court of Appeals may be delegating responsibility to an "invisible" unaccountable bureaucracy.... Michigan's shift from traditional notions of appellate justice...tends to create an incentive for overworked judges to rely unduly on non-judicial personnel.[23]

The use of staff to determine the relevant facts and issues in a case, with specific suggestions for disposition, represents a marked departure from the role of the traditional elbow clerk. As Cameron points out, "the central staff is more important in preparing the information that will be considered by the court in reaching a decision, while the law clerk is more important in justifying that decision after it is made."[24] At the same time, the personal supervision that judges provided under old systems has been lost.

...the [elbow clerk] works exclusively for a single judge in whatever way the judge wishes to use him; the job is highly personal. The [staff attorney] has no special relationship to any individual judge but rather works for the court or a panel within it as a collective unit; the staff responsibility is institutional.[25]

With central staff, a very large group of nonjudicial employees is supervised and monitored by an administrator, the research director. This research director is an experienced attorney who is charged with supervision of the central staff, yet he is no closer to being a judge than are any of the staff. Hamburger observes that

The problem with the Michigan system is that the prehearing reports reflect a significant extension of judicial decision-making responsibilities to nonjudicial personnel.... This problem is exacerbated if the attorneys performing the work are not directly supervised by the judge, as in the Michigan system.[26]

By relieving judges of some of their duties, any type of research attorney will necessarily exercise some judicial responsibility. A centralized, institutional staff removes responsibility further still from each individual judge. Reliance by the courts on such staff is therefore more problematic than judicial use of more traditional, personal clerks.

If an appellate court places too much work into the hands of staff when the judges are overburdened with cases, there is a high risk that the deliberative process will become unduly truncated. The likelihood grows that each judge will not be digesting the record, the pertinent legal authorities, and the arguments of counsel, independently reasoning his way to a decision. Paradoxically, the amount of assistance given to judges increases the threat of erosion of their judicial responsibility.[27]

Unfortunately, it is difficult to determine the extent to which these types of fears are being realized. Judges are reluctant to discuss their reliance on staff, and are not likely to criticize their own practices in the use of that staff. As Meador points out "Certainly a judge would be reluctant to acknowledge that utilization of staff work had diminished the quality of his court's adjudications."[28] When judges do address the matter, they typically do so defensively. For example, U.S. Circuit Judge Ruggero J. Aldisert claims it is an "absolute necessity that the judge read the briefs himself. I do in every case. This is an article of faith."[29] Therefore, to gain insight into judicial dependence on the centralized research staff, we undertake a comparison of staff recommendations with the judges' final decisions.[30]

Looking into the closet

We analyzed a random sample of cases disposed of by the Michigan Court of Appeals. Submission dates ranged from 1989 to early 1991, but the majority were submitted to panels in 1990. These cases are undifferentiated, and they have not been separated according to the issues they contain or the staff person and panel involved. A comparison was made, in each case, between the recommended result (staff) and the actual result (judges). "Agreement" occurred in those cases where the panel adopted exactly the outcome recommended. Instances where the panel peremptorily reversed instead of granting review as suggested, for example, were not tallied as agreement. Where recommendations and/or final decisions had several aspects, we counted the case as agreement only if it pertained to disposition. In civil cases, if the staff and the panel agreed on the prevailing party, we tallied the case as agreement, whether or not there was disagreement over relief. Similarly, if both agreed about conviction in criminal cases, we counted the case as agreement even though disagreement may have occurred on resentencing. This does not mean that we ignored instances of disagreement (or agreement) that concerned relief or sanctions. Appeals often concern only relief or sentencing, and in such cases disagreement (or agreement) was tallied only for those specific issues. By examining the prehearing report and the opinion in cases with mixed outcomes, we could determine whether the panel followed or deviated from the recommendations made.

Sample sizes were increased several times, and we found that the levels of agreement were nearly identical, regardless of the incremental number of cases examined. In addition, we identified each sampled case as civil or criminal, and further found that the ratio of criminal to civil cases remained almost exactly the same as the size of the sample increased. This ratio was 32.6 percent criminal, 67.4 percent civil, in a final sample of 307 prehearing reports. It was 32.8 percent criminal, 67.2 percent civil, in our final sample of 296 commissioners' reports. The similarity of the ratios for both types of recommendations examined does not prove the representativeness of the samples, but it is worth noting. Certain cases were necessarily ex-

cluded, the most important being those in which persons accused of crime pled guilty. Very few appeals from guilty pleas are evaluated by prehearing attorneys, as staff will prepare reports for such cases only when a judge requests it.[31] Also excluded, from both prehearing and commissioner recommendations, were cases dismissed by the clerk's office for lack of jurisdiction, frivolity, and noncompliance with court rules. These matters are typically disposed of before reaching the research staff.[32]

We consider first the extent of agreement between the recommendations of prehearing staff and final dispositions. We identified two types of agreement in the 307 cases in our prehearing sample: opinion type and outcome. While agreement on outcome is obviously of much greater significance, it is worth noting that the recommended opinion type plays an important role. It serves as a screening mechanism, signalling to judges how much time should be spent on a case. As Lesinski and Stockmeyer point out: "While no appeal is given summary treatment, and every case is fully examined, the ultimate treatment each case receives is affected by knowledge of what it involves, and the category attached to the case [opinion type] determines how it is processed."[33]

Such recommendations are of three kinds, with the "full-blown," or authored and published, opinion demanding the most attention. Such cases are considered by staff to be of some jurisprudential import, or to raise issues lacking any definitive case law.[34] Other opinion types include the per curiam, which is a rarely published statement of reasoning that typically runs two to three pages in length, and the memorandum, which amounts to little more than an order disposing of the case and citing authorities. Agreement on the type of opinion a case deserved was found in 224 cases, or 73 percent of the sample. As might be expected, it was more likely that the prehearing attorney believed the case he or she was reviewing deserved full-blown treatment than it was for the panel of judges to think so. In fact, there was no instance of an agreed outcome in the sample where staff recommended a per curiam or memorandum opinion and the panel chose an authored opinion. In only a few cases did the panel publish a per curiam where unpublished had been recommended. Far more frequent were instances of recommended per curiam opinions that the panel shortened to memoranda. The most frequent disagreement over

Figure 1   Prehearing agreement

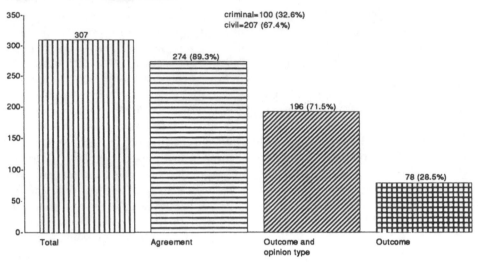

The 274 instances of agreement were composed of 196 cases (71.5%) where agreement occurred on the outcome *and* the opinion type. The remaining 78 cases (28.5%) displayed agreement on only the final outcome, and differed in opinion type.

It is important to realize that disagreement on opinion type does not amount to more than a different *presentation* of the same result. The outcome of the case is not affected substantially by this decision.

opinion type occurred when the staff attorney recommended an authored, published opinion, but the panel opted for an unpublished per curiam or memorandum decision.

More specifically, in 307 sampled cases, authored opinions were recommended in 17 percent, with the panels choosing this option in 7 percent. Per curiam opinions were recommended in 81 percent, while the panels so opted in 83 percent. Memorandums were recommended in 2 percent, and used in 10 percent. Clearly, the judges tend toward a more concise form of disposal than the staff does, although per curiams are by far the most frequent choice of both.

This finding occasions no surprise. Pride of authorship, as reflected in the reports that the prehearing attorneys prepare, should cause the staff to value their work more highly than the panel of judges that considers it, causing them to recommend a more formal opinion than the panel deems appropriate.

Agreement on the actual disposition of the case was higher than agreement on opinion type, occurring in 274 of the cases examined.[35] Of these 274, we found agreement in both opinion type and outcome in 196 cases (71.5 percent). In 78 cases, the judges differed on the opinion type chosen, but agreed with the staff person's recommended result. The two categories combined produced

agreement in 89.3 percent of the cases in the sample.[36] (See Figure 1)

The modal disposition recommended was to affirm. Fully 78.2 percent of sampled cases contained such a recommendation, while 79.5 percent produced this outcome. There was no appreciable difference here between criminal and civil cases. Recommendations to affirm criminal cases occurred 77 percent of the time, with actual affirmations at 76 percent. In civil cases, affirmation recommendations reached 78.7 percent, and actually occurred in 81.2 percent.[37]

Commissioners' recommendations were even greater predictors of the panels' decision. Here, 296 cases were sampled. The judges adhered to these recommendations in 284, or 95.9 percent, of these cases.[38] (See Figure 2)

In most cases, the court denied review. Denial or dismissal of the application was recommended in 71.6 percent of all cases examined, and occurred in 70.9 percent. A breakdown of these figures reveals that denial or dismissal was recommended in 73.2 percent of criminal cases, and occurred in 75.3 percent. In civil cases, recommendations of denial or dismissal were found in 70.9 percent, while civil applications actually were denied or dismissed 68.8 percent of the time. Here the panels showed a slight tendency to deny criminal applications more often than commissioners recommended. Conversely, when the judges disagreed with recommendations in civil matters, they tended to grant applications the commissioners would have denied.

Conclusions

The scope of our analysis does not warrant definitive conclusions about the Michigan Court of Appeals' reliance on central staff. However, it does

Figure 2   Commissioner agreement

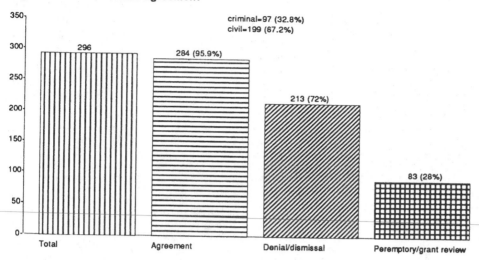

Of 296 sampled cases, only 12 (4%) displayed decisions regarding review that differed from those recommended by a commissioner.

Of the total, recommended decisions involved denial and dismissals (72%); and peremptory action or the granting of review (28%).

show high levels of agreement between staff recommendations and the judges' decisions, strongly suggesting that the judges rely almost entirely on staff recommendations to reach their decisions. Most surprising is the level of agreement on discretionary matters. The judges seemed to rely most on staff (commissioners, specifically) when deciding whether or not to grant full review. One possible explanation for this is that commissioners are tenured staff, and experience very low turnover. Prehearing staff, on the other hand, are generally freshly graduated from law school, and usually remain with the court no more than two years.

Turnover can intensify administrative problems, but it avoids the more subtle adverse effects of institutionalism.... After a year of two, some prehearing attorneys develop what we call 'second-year syndrome,' a malaise manifested by delusions of infallibility. Once a prehearing attorney starts taking more interest in defending his conclusion than in objectively discussing the alternatives, it's time for him to seek other employment.[39]

Whatever the reason for higher correspondence in recommendations regarding discretionary review, the high level of agreement in both categories is disturbing. It is far from conclusive, however. Agreement may merely reflect high-caliber attorneys who almost always please the panels with a careful, objective, and thorough analysis of each case. Even after full review of party briefs and the record, judges may find little reason to deviate from the staff recommendation. Alternatively, but less plausibly, most appeals may be so "open and shut," in the sense that no other outcome is credible, that both the staff and the judges are exactly right. It is also possible that judges, provided with a ready-made decision and analysis for each case, and haunted by an ever-growing docket are rarely able to bless cases with more than perfunctory review.[40] Or it may very well be that the actual situation reflects a combination of these possibilities.

Another possibility warrants mention here: that agreement between staff and panels may result because the staff successfully internalize the panels' preferences. This explanation lacks credibility for several reasons. Although the staff undoubtedly attempt to second-guess panels, their composition of but three out of 24 eligibles makes the task nigh impossible. An attorney is not likely to internalize the preferences of 24 judges, especially in the brief tenure of prehearing staff. Even assuming that such internalization were possible, the staffer would need to mix and match the judicial minds into an outcome equally well suited to each of the three involved, a task few judges manage among themselves even in face-to-face discussions.[41] Moreover, the staff attorneys continually address different combinations of three judges, having no consistent interaction with even one judge. When initially filed, cases are assigned to rotating panels of judges on a random basis. Prehearing staff are assigned cases in a random manner also, when the parties' pleadings are complete. The time span between these two events varies a great deal from case to case, and there is no matching of staff to panels. While the commissioners and the prehearing staff know which judges will sit on the panel for whom they write, it is doubtful that a report tailored to the personal preferences of the panel results. Having a number of recommendations to draft, a staff attorney will be preparing reports for several panels of different composition at the same time. It is more likely that the research attorney seeks a general understanding of the court as a whole, becoming aware of some individual preferences over time, but never successfully internalizing any of the judges' viewpoints.

At any rate, further research is needed to determine precisely what the Michigan court's closet contains. Extended analysis might include the issues in sampled cases, panel composition, and the "track records," so to speak, of individual staff attorneys. The impact of oral argument on levels of agreement may now be an especially relevant question for Michigan given the recent restriction on such argument.[42] Or analysis might focus on the impact of staff on the quality of decisions.[43] Additionally, only through comparison of our findings with those of other jurisdictions can the levels of agreement found in Michigan be considered in broadest perspective.

Judges must decide the cases that come before them. They must not serve a function that amounts only to review and approval of staff decisions.[44]

Experience over the last decade has suggested that numerous aspects of judicial work can be delegated to either law clerks or staff attorneys as long as the judges continue to employ their own thought processes to reach their own conclusions. The appropriate line is difficult to draw and it is even more difficult to enforce. *Ultimately, everything depends on each judge's good faith and conscientious devotion to the judicial task.*[45]

With the Michigan Court of Appeals displaying such high levels of agreement between central research staff and outcomes, the basic question is simply this: Do we trust our judges? If we hope to base our notions of justice on something more substantial than faith in their integrity and devotion to duty, we must pull this mysterious "monster" out of its closet, and have a better look at it.

NOTES

This article originally appeared in Volume 75, Number 4, December-January 1992, pages 216-221.

The authors wish to acknowledge the support provided by the Michigan State University College of Social Science, and especially the co-operation of the Michigan Court of Appeals, Lansing Office. They thank the reviewers for their insightful and judicious comments.

1. The National Center for State Courts sponsored an Appellate Justice Project, in which a Michigan model was adopted and implemented in four states: Illinois, Nebraska, New Jersey, and Virginia. The experience of courts in these states is the focus of Meador, APPELLATE COURTS: STAFF AND PROCESS IN THE CRISIS OF VOLUME (St. Paul, MN: West, 1974). The state courts of California, Missouri, and New York have also employed central staff since the late 1970s. All federal circuits except the First were using central research staff in some capacity by 1974. *Id.* at Appendix F.

The definitive work on law clerks generally, including staff attorneys, is Oakley and Thompson, LAW CLERKS AND THE JUDICIAL PROCESS (Berkeley: U. of California Press, 1980).

2. Meador, *supra* n. 1, at 11, makes a sharp distinction between the functions of screening and research/recommendation. He identifies the federal courts as mainly using staff for screening purposes, whereas Michigan's staff concentrates on research/recommendation for every case, while California staff screens cases and then researches and evaluates only those that pass through the screen. On screening, see Oakley and Thompson, *Screening, Delegation, and the Values of Appeal: An Appraisal of the Ninth Circuit's Screening Docket During the Browning Years,* in Hellman, ed. RESTRUCTURING JUSTICE: THE INNOVATIONS OF THE NINTH CIRCUIT AND THE FUTURE OF THE FEDERAL COURTS (Ithaca, NY: Cornell U. Press, 1990); Oakley, *The Screening of Appeals: The Ninth Circuit's Experience in the Eighties and Innovations for the Nineties,* 1991 B.Y.U.L. REV. 859 (1991). Oakley and Thompson explore in detail the relationship between the general problem of undue delegation and the specific problem of staff control of the information on which decisions are based in *From Information to Opinion in Appellate Courts: How Funny Things Happen on the Way Through the Forum,* 1986 ARIZ. ST. L. J. 1 (1986).

3. Hamburger, *Improving Appellate Justice by Sending Prehearing Reports to Counsel,* 65 MICH. BAR J. 1016 (1986); Cameron, *The Central Staff: A New Solution to an Old Problem,* 23 UCLA L. REV. 465, 476 (1976).

4. Lesinski and Stockmeyer, *Prehearing Research and Screening in the Michigan Court of Appeals: One Court's Method for Increasing Judicial Productivity,* 26 VANDERBILT L. REV. 1211, 1223-1224, 1239-1240 (1973). Cameron, *supra* n. 3, at 466, 479. Meador, *supra* n. 1, at 9.

5. Cameron, *supra* n. 3, at 476.

6. Lesinski and Stockmeyer, *supra* n. 4, at 1227: "Concern that prehearing research procedures dehumanize the judicial process or result in production line justice is unwarranted. A case backlog hanging over the head of a judge and his law clerk is not an incentive to a detached, unhurried examination of an individual party's rights. The prehearing system…serves to avoid the inconvenience and agony caused by case backlogs that suspend parties' rights for disturbingly long intervals."

7. *Id.*

8. *Supra* n. 1, at 126. Also see 128.

9. Data compiled by the Michigan Court of Appeals, Lansing Clerk's Office, and reported in Danhof, *Impact of Drug Appeals on the Appellate Court: Prioritization of Michigan's Drug Strategy,* testimony presented to the Department of Corrections, Office of Criminal Justice of the State of Michigan, February, 1991.

10. Meador, *supra* n. 1, does present some data, but they are not systematic. Nor does he report how they were gathered. He concentrates instead on the time that elapsed between case stages after staff had been centralized—in other words, on a study of efficiency and productivity, not quality.

11. Lesinski and Stockmeyer, *supra* n. 4, at 1226.

12. Judges were added in 1969, 1975, and 1989. Information regarding the ratio of staff to judges was obtained from *id.,* and in conversation with Carl Gromek, research director of the Michigan Court of Appeals.

13. Michigan Court Rule 7.203.

14. Oral arguments are not entertained for the disposition of applications for leave to appeal.

15. Freedman, *Appeals court moves to reduce caseload*, DETROIT NEWS, July 16, 1991, at 1B.

16. Lesinski and Stockmeyer, *supra* n. 4, at 1216; Hamburger, *supra* n. 3, at 1016-1017. We explain below the significance of opinion type recommendations.

17. Conversation with Carl Gromek; Lesinski and Stockmeyer, *supra* n. 4, at 1238; Hamburger, *supra* n. 3, at 1016.

18. Commissioner recommendations on motions, complaints, and writs will not be considered here, as writs and complaints are considerably fewer than applications for leave to appeal, and motions are of lesser significance.

19. Once the decision whether or not to grant review has been made, the case moves on to a member of the prehearing staff. Here a recommendation will be made as to the *merits* of the case. In our tabulation below, applications for leave to appeal that were granted (see Figure 2) were passed on to the prehearing staff. Because of the currency of our data, we could not track these cases for ultimate outcome due to the delay a case incurs in reaching the panel for decision. Granted applications that we examined were either undergoing prehearing evaluation, or had only recently been submitted to panels, with no decision yet filed.

20. Michigan Court Rule 7.203(A).

21. Michigan Court Rule 7.203(B).

22. Schroeder, *Judicial Administration and Invisible Justice*, 11 U. MICH. J. OF L. REFORM 322, 330 (1978).

23. Hamburger, *supra* n. 3, at 1017.

24. Cameron, *supra* n. 3, at 469.

25. *Id.* at 468.

26. Hamburger, *supra* n. 3, at 1018. Also see Lesinski and Stockmeyer, *supra* n. 4, at 1215.

27. Meador, *An Appellate Court Dilemma and a Solution Through Subject Matter Organization*, 16 U. MICH. J. OF L. REFORM 471, 472-473 (1983).

28. *Supra* n. 1, at 110.

29. Aldisert, *Appellate Justice*, 11 U. MICH. J. OF L. REFORM 317, 320 (1978). But cf. Hamburger, *supra* n. 3, at 1018 and the references cited there.

30. "An indicator of whether the judicial authority remains intact might be the extent to which the court accepts or rejects its staff attorneys' recommendations." Meador, *supra* n. 1, at 130; see also 11.

31. Conversation with Carl Gromek.

32. According to data compiled by the Michigan Court of Appeals, Lansing Clerk's Office, approximately 35 percent of total filings for 1990 were dismissed before reaching the research staff. Such dismissals may result from a clerk's order, a panel's order at the clerk's request, or a panel's order because a party failed to comply with court rules (approximately, 25.5 percent in 1990, which was a drastic increase over previous years; e.g., 16 and 13 percent in 1987 and 1989). Lesinski and Stockmeyer, *supra* n. 4, discuss dismissals by the clerk at 1217. A stipulation between parties to dismiss may also keep a filing from the research staff or judges (approximately 13.2 percent in 1990, which was also an increase from previous years—11 and 8 percent in 1987 and 1989).

33. *Supra* n. 4, at 1218.

34. *Id.*

35. All sampled prehearing reports contained a recommendation of some sort. "No recommendation" does not appear to be an option for the staff. We encountered no such instances in our sampling. Even when comparing prior decisions that conflict, the staff attorney comes to some resolution of the conflict that suggests an outcome the judges could elect.

36. Michigan's levels of agreement may actually be relatively low. Meador reports, but does not document, 97 per-

cent agreement on final dispositions in New Jersey in 1974. *Supra* n. 1, at 130-131.

37. One interesting aspect of these findings is that a very slight tendency appeared for the panels to disagree in favor of appellants in criminal matters, and to disagree against appellants in civil cases. This is curious inasmuch as the opposite pattern emerged in applications for leave to appeal, discussed below.

38. Here, our level of agreement exceeds that reported by Meador. He states that Virginia's judges accepted recommendations regarding petitions of review 88 percent of the time. *Supra* n. 1, at 12.

39. Lesinski and Stockmeyer, *supra* n. 4, at 1221.

40. "If he is provided with a staff recommendation, he is provided with an opportunity to abdicate his judicial function." Meador, *supra* n. 1, at 129.

41. As compared to elbow clerks, who seek to internalize only one judge and prepare reports geared mainly toward one set of preferences.

42. See the discussion at notes 14 and 15 above. Since oral argument follows the formulation of a prehearing recommendation and occurs face to face with the panel, it may cause the judges to give some issues more thorough consideration, to consider issues not raised by staff in the prehearing report, or both. We expect that the absence of oral argument will increase levels of agreement with prehearing staff recommendations because the judges have less information on which to base their decisions.

43. Meador avoided this question because he deemed it too difficult to evaluate. *Supra* n. 1, at 107. He did suggest that the reactions of the supreme court of the state to staff-processed cases from the intermediate appellate court might be an appropriate measure. *Id.* at 108.

44. *Id.* at 129.

45. Cameron, *supra* n. 3, at 472. Italics added. *See also* Meador's statement: "Ultimately...we depend on the integrity of the judge and his faithfulness to his judicial responsibilities. *Supra* n. 1, at 135.

Facing the monster in the judicial closet: rebutting a presumption of sloth

Appellate courts face a press of cases, many of which are mundane, easily resolved, and not worth a judge's time. Central staffs simply help separate the wheat from the chaff.

by David J. Brown

In their article on Michigan's Court of Appeals central research staff,[1] law student Mary Lou Stow and political science professor Harold J. Spaeth present the stereotypic picture of intermediate appellate court judges: overworked, facing ever-increasing dockets and backlogs, struggling to balance the needs of justice and society against the rights and needs of individuals. Stow and Spaeth use this image to suggest Michigan Court of Appeals judges are so overworked that they are looking for, and taking, alternative routes to deciding their own cases. Specifically, the authors compare the recommendations in central research staff memos with the findings of Michigan Court of Appeals panels to conclude these harried judges "may hurriedly accept staff recommendations, transforming a staff attorney's case evaluation into the decision of the court."[2]

There is a myth about the role of intermediate appellate judges and the power they wield. These mythical judges have the power of unfettered discretion to weigh, review, reject, or affirm any trial court decision, merely on whim and an arcane rule of law or two. In Kansas, and I suspect in Michigan, this myth has no relation to reality. The judges on the Kansas Court of Appeals are indeed overburdened, but they are rarely called on to do anything more than routine. After reading Stow and Spaeth's article, I reviewed 53 of my own memoranda, prepared while I served on the central re-

search staff for the Kansas Court of Appeals.[3] I was surprised to discover the court adopted my case-by-case recommendations about as often as Stow and Spaeth found the Michigan court adopted its central staff recommendations. I was not startled, however, when I determined the judges agreed with me most often simply because they had no choice—there was only one answer possible.

There are times when it helps to look past the stereotypes. There is no question that courts in America—be they city, state, or federal—are overburdened. America has a passion for litigation. The crush has hit intermediate appellate courts as well, and many of these courts have turned to central research staffs to help separate the legal wheat from the chaff.[4] But to understand what is happening in intermediate appellate courts, it is important to understand what intermediate appellate courts do and the role they play in the administration of justice.

Workhorses

Intermediate appellate courts are the workhorses of the appellate court process. If there is any doubt about this, all that is necessary is to consider the numbers. For example, in fiscal year 1991, the Kansas Supreme Court disposed of 291 cases, while the Kansas Court of Appeals disposed of 1,278 cases.[5] It is important to understand that the intermediate appellate courts are the workhorses of the appellate system because they handle the crush of appeals, correcting error by applying rules of law and periodically determining issues of law.[6] As Justice Benjamin Kaplan, retired associate justice of the Supreme Judicial Court of Massachusetts, explained:

When the intermediate courts are set up it is on the plain understanding about where the run-of-the-mine or donkey work is to fall. The point is variously expressed, but the general sense is that the job of an intermediate court is to take on the mass of appeals that involve merely claimed errors of the trial courts in applying the settled legal rules, while the supreme court, picking up a smallish number of appeals selected in one way or another as being more exotic, is by its decisions to mold, develop, and change the law to satisfy emerging social needs and keep the law in tip-top, up-to-date working order.[7]

Indeed, the major justification for creating most states' intermediate courts has been to relieve the respective supreme courts from the drudgery of handling routine cases.[8] In Kansas, the justification offered for creating a court of appeals in 1977 was that:

Creation of an intermediate appellate court will permit the separation of the review for correction of error function, to be assigned to the intermediate court, from the development and interpretation of law function which should remain in the supreme court.[9]

Further,

The removal of routine appeals from the supreme court docket will allow the supreme court time for more deliberative and mature consideration of cases having significance as precedent.[10]

The result of this dichotomy is that judges on intermediate appellate panels "are confronted with a high volume of relatively straightforward cases and a smaller volume of more complicated ones."[11] When Judge J. Edward Lumbard wrote on this issue in relation to federal appellate courts in 1968, he noted:

Most appellate judges would agree that the result in about seventy-five percent of appeals is clearly foreseeable after argument, regardless of which judges sit on those cases .... The courts of appeals thus spend the bulk of their time on only twenty-five percent of the appeals they hear."[12]

A number of studies have been done on this issue and at least one researcher has found that issues confronted by state intermediate appellate judges are so mundane that jurists are bored, to the point that some retire from the bench earlier than they had planned when they were appointed.[13]

Exploding the myth

It is time to explode the myth of midlevel appellate court judges with the power to do as they choose. Intermediate-level courts hear predominantly routine, boring matters by legislative fiat. And, as they do so, they are not free to use their own judgment in a majority of cases. As one scholar explains:

Appellate judges operate in a world not of their own making: they review cases that have already been decided. In performing that review, they are constrained by rules—standards of review—that often require substantial deference to the lower court's decision.[14]

Another scholar has defined the role of standards of review in appellate decision making as setting "the height of the hurdles over which an appellant must leap in order to prevail on appeal."[15] Unfortunately, the role left for intermediate appellate judges is often just to see if an appellant has jumped high enough to clear the hurdle. If the answer is yes, appellant wins. If the answer is no, appellant loses. Thus, intermediate courts are left to struggle not with questions of justice but with dispositive questions of substantial competent evidence, abuse of discretion, failure to preserve an issue for appeal, harmless error, and other variations on this theme. As the late Justice Benjamin N. Cardozo lamented in 1921: "Of the cases that come before the court in which I sit, a majority, I think, could not, with semblance of reason, be decided in any way but one. The law and its application are plain."[16] In 1924, Cardozo estimated that 90 percent, and maybe more, of the cases heard are "predetermined—predetermined in the sense that they are predestined—their fate preestablished by inevitable laws that follow them from birth to death. The range of free activity [for judges] is relatively small."[17]

Examining the findings

This brings us to the findings of Stow and Spaeth. In their study of 307 Michigan Court of Appeals cases, they found the judicial outcome agreed with central staff research attorneys' prehearing recommendations in 274 cases for a correlation of 89.3 percent.[18] They explain this high correlation by surmising that judges are simply relying on the work of their clerks. They do suggest, but at the same time reject, the possibility that research staffs do such a thorough job that disagreement is unlikely or that "most appeals may be so 'open and shut,' in the sense that no other outcome is credible, that both the staff and the judges are exactly right."[19] Given the role of appellate courts, the routine nature of the cases they hear, and the limitations of standards of review, the more appropriate response might be surprise that the court disagreed with the research staff as often as it did.

In their review of cases, Stow and Spaeth did not address the kinds of issues raised on appeal, nor the standards of review the court of appeals was required to apply. Thus, their baseline analysis omits any consideration of the process judges followed in deciding the cases involved. If there is indeed only one correct answer in a case, judges should not be criticized for reaching that result just because a preliminary review also reached that result. Researchers on this kind of question must determine the nature of the questions presented to intermediate courts before jumping to conclusions about the results reached by those courts.

Analyzing cases in Kansas

In my analysis of cases, I tried to get past this end-result focus. Of course, I looked at the end results, too, but my goal was to determine what kinds of issues our court was asked to resolve, rather than to focus on how often the court agreed with me. To do that, I reviewed all the issues raised on appeal in each of 53 cases. I attempted to determine whether those issues would be governed by dispositive standards of review,[20] or whether they involved questions of law that would allow the appellate court to conduct a de novo review. Further, when questions of law were raised, I attempted to determine whether there were appellate court precedents that would, in effect, remove the reviewing panel's power to decide an issue for itself. Finally, when the court disagreed with my recommendations, I reviewed the resulting opinions to determine the nature of the disagreement. To count a decision as an agreement, it had to match my recommendation. For example, if I recommended a case be affirmed in part and reversed in part, and the court simply affirmed, I counted that as the court not agreeing with me.

My study was not scientific. I do not maintain that the cases assigned to me were in any way a random sample of the cases before the court, or that my results are empirically sound. My decisions about counting and labeling issues were subjective and arbitrary. My review was limited in that I did not review opinions to make certain that when judges reached the conclusion I recommended, they reached the conclusion based on my rationale. I also did not make an issue-by-issue comparison to see if judges agreed with me issue by issue. Rather, I considered only the bottom-line result. Only when my final recommendation was not adopted by the court did I review an opinion to determine the basis for the disagreement. Nevertheless, the results provide a solid basis for discussion and a starting point for other researchers who wish to study the appellate court decision-making process.

Of 53 cases studied, 30 involved only issues governed by various dispositive standards of review. This means that in 56.6 percent of the cases, the appellate judges had to give considerable deference to the trial court's ruling and had no issues on which they were free to ignore other judges' thoughts. Of the remaining 23 cases in which questions of law were raised, 9 were directly controlled either by court of appeals or supreme court precedent. In other words, in 9 cases, or about 17 percent of the total studied, the judicial panels had to give complete deference to another appellate court's opinion. Thus, in about 73.5 percent of the cases, court of appeals judges were forced to give deference to the actions and rulings of other judges. In other words, judges were only free to make de novo determinations in 14 cases, or about 26.5 percent of the total cases studied.

This case-by-case analysis is, in itself, misleading when trying to determine the appellate court judges' responsibilities. Appellants raised 121 issues in the 53 cases I reviewed. Of the 121 issues, 31, or 24.8 percent, were issues of law. Of these 31 issues of law, 11 were governed by appellate court precedent. Thus, the appellate judges had to defer to the judgment of other courts when considering 101 of 121 issues, or 83.5 percent of the issues raised.

My recommendations were not followed in only 5 cases. The judges, therefore, agreed with my recommendations in 94.3 percent of the cases. Nevertheless, all of the disagreements were in cases that involved questions of law. Indeed, all the disagreements were on specific questions of law. When the judges were free to make up their own minds and apply a de novo standard of review, they agreed with me in 9 cases out of 14, or 64.3 percent of the time.

Important concerns

The concerns Stow and Spaeth express about judicial independence are important. Judicial opinions should reflect judicial thinking, and judges should not blindly accept the legal work of research attorneys. But there are other important concerns that should be addressed. Why are our intermediate appellate courts spending so much time addressing routine cases? If any competent legally trained person can review the cases before an intermediate appellate court and determine the outcome, and the outcome will be the same no matter who reviews those files, why must the cases be considered by a three-member judicial panel? If the standards of review make any result other than affirmance unlikely, why are appeals filed?[21] Isn't it possible that the valid, critical concerns of worthy appellants get lost in the shuffle? Why are we wasting the time of our most respected and learned jurists with cases whose fates have been predetermined?

These questions are not novel. Cardozo's comments make it clear scholars and jurists have debated them for decades. But Stow and Spaeth are naive in thinking central research staffs are the monsters in the judicial closet. They insult judges by suggesting the judiciary is too harried, or too lazy, to write its own opinions. The problem is that appellate panels face a press of cases—many of which, at best, are mundane, easily resolved, not worth one judge's time, let alone three, and at worst, are frivolous and should never have been appealed. Central staffs are an excellent tool to use in separating the wheat from the chaff. The question that must be resolved is why we keep sending the chaff to our appellate judges expecting them to make bread.

NOTES

This article originally appeared in Volume 75, Number 6, April-May 1992, pages 291-293.

The opinions expressed in this article are those of the author alone and do not represent the opinions of the Kansas Court of Appeals, the Kansas Court of Appeals central research staff, or any single judge or attorney associated with the Kansas Court of Appeals or its central research staff.

The author wishes to thank Kansas Court of Appeals Chief

Judge Mary Beck Briscoe, Kansas Court of Appeals Judge Jerry Elliott, and Kansas Appellate Courts Clerk Carol Gilliam Green for their assistance, suggestions, comments, and criticisms during preparation of early drafts of this article.

1. Stow and Spaeth, *Centralized research staff: is there a monster in the judicial closet?*, 75 JUDICATURE 216 (1992).

2. *Id.* at 217. Also see 220-221.

3. The study included all prehearing memoranda prepared for cases that were decided while I served on the Central Research Staff for the Kansas Court of Appeals. I did not consider any prehearing memoranda for cases I reviewed, but which were decided after I began working for Court of Appeals Chief Judge Mary Beck Briscoe.

There are 9 research attorneys on the Kansas Court of Appeals central research staff. In addition, the 10 judges on the court of appeals hire their own research attorneys. All research attorneys, be they "elbow clerks" or on central staff, are hired to serve for one or two years. After the court's dockets have been set, the director of central research assigns cases for review to all research attorneys. Elbow clerks review files and prepare memoranda that go directly to judges. Central research staff, however, review files and prepare memoranda that are reviewed by the staff director and then distributed to the appropriate judges. Generally, each case is heard by a three-judge panel. While oral argument is not heard in all cases, prehearing memoranda are nevertheless prepared in those cases.

4. *See, e.g.,* Oakley, *The Screening of Appeals: The Ninth Circuit's Experience in the Eighties and Innovations for the Nineties,* 1991 B.Y.U.L. REV. 859 (1991); Thompson and Oakley, *From Information to Opinion in Appellate Courts: How Funny Things Happen on the Way Through the Forum,* 1986 ARIZ. ST. L.J., 1 (1986); Lesinski and Stockmeyer, *Prehearing Research and Screening in the Michigan Court of Appeals: One Court's Method for Increasing Judicial Productivity,* 26 VAND. L. REV. 1211 (1973).

5. Annual Report of the Courts of Kansas 1990-91 Fiscal Year, Office of Judicial Administration. It is important to understand the numbers do not mean the Kansas Supreme Court decided 291 cases, or that the court of appeals decided 1,278 cases. The numbers simply reflect the number of cases the courts handled and disposed of by opinion, dismissal, or transfer.

6. *See* Hopkins, *The Role of an Intermediate Appellate Court,* 41 BROOKLYN L. REV. 459 (1975).

7. Kaplan, *Do Intermediate Appellate Courts Have a Lawmaking Function?,* 70 MASS. L. REV. 10 (1985).

8. Flango and Blair, *Creating an intermediate appellate court: does it reduce the caseload of a state's highest court?,* 64 JUDICATURE 75, 76 (1980).

9. Report of the Kansas Judicial Study Advisory Committee, *Recommendations for Improving the Kansas Judicial System,* 13 WASHBURN L. J. 271, 350 (1974).

10. *Id.*

11. Chapper and Hanson, *Taking the Delay Out of Criminal Appeals,* 27 JUDGES J. 7, 44 (Winter 1988).

12. Lumbard, *Current Problems of the Federal Courts of Appeals,* 54 CORNELL L. REV. 29, 36 (1968).

13. Wold, *Going through the motions: the monotony of appellate court decision making,* 62 JUDICATURE 58, 64-65 (1978).

14. Sward, *Appellate Review of Judicial Fact-Finding,* 40 KAN. L. REV. 1 (1991).

15. Hofer, *Standards of Review—Looking Beyond the Labels,* 74 MARQ. L. REV. 231, 232 (1991).

16. Cardozo, THE NATURE OF THE JUDICIAL PROCESS 164 (1921). Cardozo refers to the New York Court of Appeals, New York's highest court.

17. Cardozo, THE GROWTH OF THE LAW 60 (1924).

18. *Supra* n. 2, at 220. Stow and Spaeth also studied the

correlation between central staff recommendations about type of opinion to be produced and the Michigan court's actual opinion issued. Since the Kansas central research staff makes no recommendations about type of opinion to be issued, I have not addressed that issue.

19. *Supra* n. 2, at 220.

20. Issues raised and considered as definitively determinable under various standards of review included: abuse of discretion; questions of substantial competent evidence; sufficiency of the evidence; failure to object or create a record sufficient for appellate review; harmless error; failure to brief an issue; failure to meet a burden of proof, and collateral estoppel.

21. In fiscal year 1990-1991, the Kansas Court of Appeals issued 922 opinions; of those 628, or 68.1 percent, were affirmances. Annual Report of the Courts of Kansas, 1990-1991 Fiscal Year, *supra* n. 5.

Actors in the Judicial Process
Lawyers and Legal Practices

INTRODUCTION
The role of lawyers in the American judicial process has been romanticized and glamorized through accounts of the exploits, both real and fictional, of the Daniel Websters, Clarence Darrows, and Perry Masons of courtrooms past and present. At this writing, yet another television series that focuses on the legal profession, "The Practice," is among the most highly rated shows on the air. Naturally, the actual pursuit of the profession of law entails many tasks, roles, and job possibilities that would be quite foreign to our folklore's most famous litigators. Indeed, a great many lawyers never try a case and many never see the inside of a courtroom. The articles in this section address several facets of the legal profession and the diverse types of practice it may entail.

We begin with Arlin Adams' broad brushstroke essay, "The legal profession: a critical evaluation." Adams' critique of the contemporary practice of law is an important one that raises fundamental questions regarding the profession's commitment to pursuing its mission in the wake of the great "professional metamorphosis" of the past decades. Adams documents important changes in the law as well as fundamental changes in lawyering that have caused problems for the judicial process and "the disappearance of the individual legal personality." He feels that professionalism has given way to commercialism and that those civic values lawyers historically possessed while serving as the nation's "secular ministry" have eroded. Adams' sobering account ends with a call for lawyers to reassert the values of service to the community, legal craftsmanship, and professional devotion that he associates with earlier generations of his colleagues.

Nathan Posner focuses on finer details when he raises the question, "Truth, justice and the client's interest: can the lawyer serve all three?" Posner explores many ethical dilemmas faced by advocates whose clients' personal interests may conflict with the ideals of truth and justice that the lawyer must also serve, Posner is "convinced that our adversary system in its present form endorses various techniques that at best avoid the truth and at worst make a mockery of 'justice.'"

While Posner's essay focuses, in some senses, on the "justice" function of the legal practitioner, Herbert Kritzer's empirical analysis of

"Contingency fee lawyers as gatekeepers in the civil justice system" explores the systemic realities in one broad area of the law that are the consequences of attorneys' decisions whether or not to take on a case in the first place. Through a survey of practitioners in Wisconsin, Kritzer documents that the conventional wisdom of "ambulance chasing" civil litigators is belied by the day-to-day reality of attorneys turning down at least as many potential plaintiff cases as they accept. Most often, the decision to not take on a client flows from the weak basis for a viable case. Motivated by economic self-interest, Kritzer argues that, "In a sense, the lawyer is making decisions about which cases to include in his or her portfolio of risks." At the same time, however, such "rational" decision making by attorneys serves the system's interest in avoiding immobilizing case overload.

The legal profession: a critical evaluation

The legal profession and the practice of law have undergone a drastic transformation in recent years, and the changes have not been for the better. Members of the profession must regain a sense of their individual legal personality and faith in the ultimate mission of their calling.

by Arlin M. Adams

All professions, especially one as central to American life as the legal profession, should undergo a continuing process of examination and self-evaluation. Any group that does not engage in such an exercise loses much that makes it a profession: a shared set of principles and customs that transcend self-interest and speak to the essential nature of the particular calling or trade.

There are greater reasons beyond periodic examination, however, that make this topic most compelling. In recent years, the legal profession has undergone fundamental changes that threaten to sever it from its traditional moorings. A qualitative revolution has occurred within the legal community to the extent that the practice which existed 40 years ago is hardly recognizable today.

No calling has occupied a more important and undeviating role in the emergence and development of American society. The practice of law, almost by definition, should establish and promote the common good and bring forth the advancement and betterment of society. As a profession, however, we have departed from the practice as it has been envisioned from the early days of the Republic. This dramatic change has strong overtones for the future. Although many authors have chronicled the recent transition of the legal profession, few are willing to argue that these developments have evolved for the betterment of society.

The sources causing the changes in the legal profession are both external and internal. The external pressures arise from great movements in the body of substantive law and in the types of services that lawyers are now required to perform. The changes in what constitute the practice of law, in turn, have transformed who constitutes the practitioners of law. From an internal standpoint, the profession has undergone as drastic a transformation as the substantive law that governs us. I shall attempt to address these two antecedents of professional metamorphosis.

Changes in the law

Just a few decades ago the rules governing society were almost entirely of the common law variety. Under the common law system, the recognized doctrines of law originated from historic precedent and were gradually forged by lawyers and judges as society advanced and matured. In recent years, however, the proliferation of statutory and regulatory law has relegated the common law to a far less prominent position.

The common law system was designed to adjudicate disputes between two relatively equal parties according to well-established principles. The former common law practitioner drew on diverse and traditional doctrines regarding the relationship between government and property, whereas the modern day practice consists primarily of various statutory, regulatory, and administrative specialties. A great share of litigation today entails large and complicated breach of contract suits, complex real estate transactions, intricate corporate matters, and financial maneuvering in the international capital markets. The substance and function of the types of matters the law addresses has shifted from the small scale of the common law to the large scope of a practice dominated by extensive financial concerns.

The second source of change in the law is the burgeoning areas of practice relating to government. The rise of the administrative state—the so-called headless fourth branch of government—has been sweeping. The establishment of quasi-judicial authorities and agencies, such as the Federal Communications Commission, the Occupational Safety and Health Administration, and the Environmental Protection Agency, has accelerated continuously since World War II, and shows little sign of abating. The number of federal agencies alone has increased from 20 to well over 70, many with narrow, sometimes overlapping purposes.

Furthermore, in the coming months additional federal bodies governing the closing of industrial facilities and merger-and-acquisition transactions undoubtedly will be established. The proliferation of federal administrative agencies has been matched by a parallel expansion of state and local bodies. As expected, a government of greater size and scope has necessarily increased the share of legal work devoted to relatively novel, specialized administrative areas.

A third and perhaps most significant development in the law in the past few decades is the emergence of several new forms of legal actions. The number of class action suits and other types of multiparty litigation has grown substantially. This phenomenon has led to the introduction of "public" issues into the private litigation setting. Public issues are generally defined as those involving societal concerns and numerous parties, and are thus arguably more appropriate for legislative consideration. In contrast, private controversies are those amenable to judicial resolution between two discrete parties.

The distinction between public and private issues serves as a point of comparison between the past and the present era. Matters that once were clearly within the realm of public affairs now routinely appear before courts. There has been a clear departure in the perceived role of the judiciary. Litigation encompassing environmental and public health issues, products liability, industrial and nuclear safety, civil rights, and other litigation involving nontraditional plaintiffs is a relatively new development, which reflects this departure.

Much of the expansion in public interest litigation can be attributed to the characteristics of our latter-day economy. Mass producers of consumer goods, environmental polluters, and other large industrial aggregations now possess the ability to affect or injure large classes of citizens. Whether the radical innovations in the conduct of judicial affairs are a reflection of a change in the prevailing notions of the law or of greater economic forces, however, is not the issue at hand. The question whether law is a product of economic determinism or whether law shapes the path of economic change is a subject worthy of its own discrete forum.

In either event, the effect of these innovations on the profession is undeniable. The characteristic of gradualism—the belief that law originated from natural truths and was fashioned, through time, to accommodate newly developing human relationships—was the foundation of our common law history. Around this basic orientation, ethical norms and mores developed that fostered the evolution of the common law. Taken as a whole these practices emerged into a philosophy of legal professionalism. This concept of gradual change through reasoned treatment, however, is subjugated, or at least strained, in a legal climate of rapid and drastic transformation.

Changes in lawyering

The decline in professionalism as it relates to the law has occurred, at least in part, because of a diminution in the defining element of gradualism. Change in the law necessarily causes change in the profession. The great emphasis in today's practice on large transactional matters at the expense of individual client service particularly tends to undermine the values that define professionalism. The results of this transformation are readily apparent in how the typical law practice has changed.

A few year ago, single practitioners and small groups of lawyers dominated the practice. A firm with 20 attorneys was considered large. Today, firms with over 200 lawyers are not unusual, and a partnership of 20 is generally limited to handling small matters. In 1975, there were only four firms with over 200 lawyers in the United States, and they were viewed with great skepticism. In contrast, a recent survey reported well over 150 firms with more than 200 attorneys and there is far less reservation about the wisdom of the large firm as a legal institution. Indeed, last year, one of these firms celebrated the hiring of its 1,000th lawyer.

The advent of megafirms has substantially altered law practice. It is not unusual now to have firms with offices throughout the nation and even in major cities abroad. Moreover, a firm in Philadelphia attempting to hire students from Harvard, Yale, or Stanford will likely have to bid against firms from New York, Los Angeles, Chicago, and Denver. Thus, the marketplace for legal services and the marketplace for attorneys has grown national, sometimes international, in scope.

The small-town practitioner with intimate ties only to his local community is becoming a vanishing figure. Industry analysts predict that the growth in firm size will continue and will lead to a shakeout where the giant conglomerates will be the principal survivors. Indeed, proposals have been made in many state bars that would allow non-lawyers to own and control law firms so that they may operate more like business corporations. If this trend continues, there may be no place left for the individual practitioner or the small group of practitioners.

The expansion in the large, institutionalized practice has been made possible, I believe, by three developments in the way lawyers are trained and work. Taken as a whole, these elements—the new labor economies of the practice—constitute the changing internal climate of the profession.

The first development is the proliferation of law schools and lawyers. The number of lawyers in the United States has doubled since 1970 and is now well over 700,000, far and away the most lawyers for any nation in the world. The students fueling this expanding army are being trained at a growing number of law schools and in larger entering classes. The elite schools such as Harvard, Yale, and Pennsylvania have attempted to maintain the same number of students. Other law schools, however, especially state university law schools, have greatly expanded their enrollments.

A second factor allowing the progression of larger and larger firms is the fees for services that these firms now charge. This development is especially pertinent to the transactional nature of the practice. Forty years ago, the cost and time spent on legal services were a negligible part of business decisions. Today, the consideration of legal fees is a major factor in many of these transactions.

The rise of large legal fees has had other sig-

nificant effects. Many have read about the $75,000 starting salaries and $10,000 bonuses given to graduating students, but even these numbers do not reflect the magnitude of the factor of money in large firm practice. *The American Lawyer*, a publication devoted to glamorizing big firms, now publishes annual financial data on such firms. Recent figures show firms realizing over $1,000,000 per year in revenues per lawyer; $1,000,000 in profit per partner; and one New York firm approaching $300,000,000 in total revenues.[1] Under headlines that blare: "Generating Revenue: The Key to The Bottom Line,"[2] the editors assure that faltering local economies will not affect business,[3] and warn that excessive pro bono work may lower a firm's profitability.[4]

Concentration on profit-maximization provides less and less time for lawyers to spend on public and professional activities. Obligations to the community and to the profession are subordinated when constant attention must be given to monetary aspects. Consequently, these vital elements undergirding the ideal of the principled, public-minded practitioner of old are victims of the recent preoccupation with fees, firm profits, and inordinate salaries.

The third element permitting the growth of large institutional firms is the level of specialization now required in the legal profession. At one time a lawyer may have dealt with a number of different types of matters in any particular period. Today's young attorneys, however, are required to specialize almost immediately. Sizable firms generally are organized into departments practicing one type of law. Differentiation of the legal labor force is essential to sustain these large organizations. The necessity to develop "instant expertise" is particularly troublesome, I believe, as it is inconsistent with the traditional vision of legal practice as a diverse and liberal endeavor. Excessive specialization inevitably detracts from the rich and full legacy of the profession.

The strained judicial process

With a clearer understanding of what the changing legal environment encompasses, we can now focus on its implications for the historic mission of the practitioner in our society. It is appropriate to ask what effect the confluence of these pressures has had on the judicial system that attempts to adjust to them. The structure of our system of courts and judges was shaped, essentially, for the common law practice of yesteryear. Consequently, just like any other infrastructure designed to accommodate traffic, be it an interstate highway or a shopping mall, the addition of greater and greater amounts of traffic creates a strain and hinders the ability of the system to function efficiently.

The exponential growth in litigation in recent years has imposed such a tension on our legal infrastructure. The number of lawsuits filed in both state and federal courts is unprecedented. Heavier caseloads and the growing percentage of complex multiparty actions create a burden that courts are not institutionally equipped to handle. As a result, the level of procedural excess and abuse of pretrial procedures has risen as well. That our judicial system, which is charged in large part with the development of substantive law and the efficient administration of justice, must now endure a constant state of procedural impasse is without precedent and is a poor reflection on the state of the profession. A pivotal role of an advocate in our adversarial system is the public duty to advance the edification of the courts and to assist in their efficient administration. Abuse of the discovery process and dilatory tactics abridge this duty and diminish yet another public aspect of the profession.

The political response to the judicial crisis caused by the changing legal atmosphere has been primarily to add more judges to an already overburdened system. Thus, in 1945 there were 100 federal judges; today there are more than 700. To a lesser extent, the response has been to hire court administrators and to install high-tech equipment. The emergence of court administrators, whose jobs are primarily to facilitate the operation of the courts, is illustrative of the continuing need simply to keep traffic moving. The question then arises as to what effect a constant preoccupation with the quantity of judicial output has on the qualitative aspects of that product.

The destruction and replacement of historic doctrines of the law, I believe, is at least a partial result. The introduction of public issues into a judicial setting and increased use of class action methodologies are directly attributable to and symptomatic of justice dispensed in wholesale fashion. In a larger sense, the role of judges in this type of environment has changed. The gradualism and intellectual spirit of the common law, where the judge performed the passive roles of preserving legal doctrine and pursuing thoughtful objectivity, are often lost in today's courtrooms.

In recent years, there has been a robust debate within the legal community as to whether judges should follow a path of judicial activism or restraint. In many ways, this debate embraces a non-issue. The distinction between active and passive interpretation is, I believe, tenuous and better given to philosophical consideration. It is significant, however, that such a debate even exists. Whether a judge should engage in aggressive intervention in disputes departs from the ideal of the neutral and objective arbitrator. Nonetheless, many judges are now known for their predisposition to engage in activism by creating new causes of action rather than the traditional qualities of consistent thoughtful deliberation. This new emphasis in the judicial process is a direct function of what is perceived as the changing legal profession.

Disappearance of legal personality

A second, more noteworthy, consequence of the shift in the profession is the disappearance of what may be characterized as the individual legal personality. Just as increased traffic flow means that one is unlikely to be acquainted with the person driving the automobile next to yours, the increased traffic within the profession creates its own type of anonymity. Legal relationships, whether lawyer-client or among lawyers, have become far less personal in the past few decades. Practice in a large law firm has a tendency to mechanize the relationship between counsel.

At one time, admission into the bar meant passage into a sort of egalitarian fraternity. The large law firm of today, however, imposes both explicit and implicit hierarchical arrangements among its attorneys. Under these circumstances, professional alienation can flourish. A lawyer who is required, even before graduation, to focus on a specialty can easily view himself more as a technician and less as a servant of the profession itself and its role in the larger community. Since practice in a sizable firm necessarily involves large, institutionalized clients, the real sense of inclusion and obligation to the broader community is often lost.

The idea that a lawyer's day-to-day experience can be so divorced from actual contact or knowledge of his or her clients was virtually unknown just a few short years ago. Yet an attorney working for a substantial institutional client can have very little, if any, relationship with his client on a personal basis. Deprived of this type of gratifying professional satisfaction, more and more attorneys must find an external reason, whether individual enjoyment or money, to gain a sense of purpose.

Although there are numerous and diverse opportunities for an attorney to obtain satisfaction through public interest or pro bono work, those relationships too have taken on a distinct institutional flavor. Large organized programs are now required to provide pro bono services. It is most unfortunate that a graduating law student, because of the demands of time and money, has so little opportunity to secure a personal sense of reward by using his or her skills to assist an indigent individual.

Perhaps even more significant than the mechanism of lawyer-client relations is the loss of personal community among lawyers themselves. It is not unusual, in fact it is quite likely, that lawyers in a typical firm are practically strangers. This fact alone is not startling because any large organization, be it a university, a hospital, or a bank, must be operated on an impersonal, organizational level. The case of the large, urban law firm is particularly disturbing, however, because of what must be subordinated to organizational structure.

The collegiality and democratic spirit that once governed relations within a firm have been replaced by bureaucratic forms of control and frequently a somewhat oppressive "up-or-out" mentality. The sense of individual legal personality is sacrificed to the concept of firm identity. Moreover, the sense of professionalism and professional identity among lawyers is often replaced by the commercial exigencies of large firm competition.

Lawyers have historically provided a wellspring of governmental and political leadership to the nation. The common law was an incomparable incubator for developing the qualities and dedication that we ascribe to sound, progressive, and energetic civil leadership. Scholarship, broad vision, and equanimity—elements that marked a successful common law practitioner—also defined the hallmarks of a dedicated public servant.

The disappearance of the individual legal personality threatens to disrupt the profession's important role in preparing public servants. I question whether apprenticeship in a large firm today can be a measure of the training that the common law practice provided. Can the specialized, institutional experience of a large firm become the equivalent of development through individual common law practice in the selection of our next generation of governors, judges, mayors, and other officials? These questions should be quite high in the pantheon of considerations for the continuing mission of our profession as large legal entities capture the most promising legal talent available.

Regrettably, the answers to these questions appear to be in the negative. The large firms of today are simply not producing this type of leadership. Last year, of the nearly 11,000 students graduating from the top law schools, only 243 chose to begin their careers in some type of public interest work.[5] Plucked directly from school and dropped into well-paying positions that demand enormous commitments of time and energy, it is not surprising that these young attorneys might view public service as secondary and unrewarding.

The law firms themselves, however, must also share responsibility for not contributing to the leadership of their communities. As a young attorney, I was encouraged to enter public life by the senior partner of my firm as an opportunity to serve the public. Today, the structural and financial necessities of maintaining a large firm create pressures that, in turn, deter young lawyers from entering public service. Within the business mindset of large firms, it simply is not profitable to lend talent to the community at large.

Commercialization of law and practice

The third, and perhaps most pervasive, manifestation of the change in the legal climate is the decline of professionalism and its replacement with commercialism. If one general theme could encompass the many changes in our legal environment, it would be the adoption of the mores and manners of the marketplace at the expense of expressions of professional affiliation. One might legitimately ask: "What is wrong with this?" After all, lawyering is like any other calling; young people still choose to go into law primarily for monetary reasons and, more often than not, are rewarded for that choice. I suppose that one would be hardpressed to persuade the general public, whether on a street corner in New York City or Davenport, Iowa, that what the practice of law is all about is not money. But the real danger lies when those within the profession are convinced that what it is all about is material success.

The profession occupies a key role in a democratically organized society. Americans tend to divide the dimensions of public life into two general spheres. One half is the business or economic realm. An economy based on capitalism and the institution of private property is the source of this culture. Economic freedom, efficiency, and material reward are its basic values. The other half of what constitutes our public affairs is the political or civil culture. The highest virtues here are political freedom, equality, and justice. Its institutional foundations are the free-functioning political process and the unbiased administration of justice.

Each culture or set of values must be allowed to flourish; that is what, to a considerable extent, constitutes the genius of the American polity. Furthermore, it is important that neither should grow to dominate the other. A correct balance between the influences of our civil government and the business marketplace is the perpetual challenge of democracy. Given this challenge, it is the proper role of the lawyer to stabilize the social equilibrium of the forces and counterforces of a dynamic society. The law is an affirmation or expression of the structure of our government and our consensual beliefs. Lawyers must operate as its vigilant defenders. Just as the true entrepreneur may be viewed as the paradigm of the business culture, each lawyer should represent the epitome of the values and virtues of the civic culture.

When the legal profession adopts too many of the commercial aspects of business, the civic values that lawyers should represent are in danger of being eroded. It is for this reason that mourning the decline in professionalism is not merely an exercise in sentimentality. We must not permit the practice of law to become just another white-collar industry. Nor must we permit lawyers to be viewed as economic units of production and their work product to be seen as "widgets." Such a mercantilistic vision would be tantamount to an admission that our civic heritage is quantifiable and can be exchanged, and that what was once self-evident and inalienable is no longer so.

Yet, evidence of this development can be found in several respects. The one that is perhaps most representative, and coincidentally the one I personally find quite troubling, although probably necessary, is the timesheets that lawyers are required to have nearby throughout the working day.

Aside from being a continuous distraction, these instruments are a repeated reminder that everything a lawyer does can and should be quantified for payment. In large cities, some firms have begun billing based on one-twelfth of an hour. That means that every action that a lawyer performs, whether opening mail or answering a short telephone call, will be recorded and billed to the client.

The commercialization of the profession, however, runs far deeper than timesheets or expense accounts. The decline in professionalism has deprived an entire generation of practitioners of suitable role models. At the risk of sounding nostalgic, I believe that the profession has lost its grasp of the big picture and of the aspects and aspirations of the higher calling of this secular ministry.

Lawyers that are perceived as most successful today, or at least the ones gaining the most remuneration, are those who specialize in merger and acquisition work. This development is particularly illustrative of the overall commercialization of practice, in that elaborate takeover schemes in large part involve the reorganization of interests while adding little value to society. Seldom in these complex, money-changing arrangements is there room for consideration of the public interest or societal consequences. The ideal of the lawyer as vindicator of the rights vested in our civic culture is lost. Just as the inventor of the hula hoop or bikini once gained the greatest reward in the business culture, the lawyer specializing in junk bonds is the new example of success in the legal firmament.

Nor is commercialization of the civic culture lost on the general public. One astute social observer remarked recently that members of our society are no longer referred to as "citizens" but instead are simply grouped into the class known as "consumers." When the philosophy of every free person possessing an equal franchise in our democratic society is lost, and citizens are best recognized for their position in the macroeconomy, our civic heritage has been seriously compromised.

Just as we might despair over the loss of the true entrepreneur in society, the decline of professionalism in legal practice should invite equal consternation. The public perception of the profession is now gained more through avenues such as *The People's Court, L.A. Law,* or television and telephone book ads for attorneys, rather than from the practice of the profession. What could be more discouraging than a generation of individuals receiving their understanding of their civic rights and obligations through these vistas?

Equally distressing is the prospect of members of the profession *affirmatively accepting* this commercialized vision of themselves. Law schools, which should be the bulwark of the loftiest ideals of the profession, are frequently more hospitable to various hucksters or personalities of law rather than to the great role models of yesteryear. It is a melancholy commentary that the inventor of a heart valve frequently will labor in obscurity while the promoter of some new patent medicine, whether a baldness cure or weight loss miracle, will gain immediate attention and riches. But the decline in the professionalism of the legal practice and the rise of the poor substitute of commercial manners, is an equally regrettable indictment of our society. When the giants of legal history are relegated to the back of the classroom or the rear of a bar association meeting, it is important to consider who is moving to the front.

Conclusion

We must be on guard to assure that my assessment of the state of our profession is not merely the product of an affection for days past. In this regard, I am reminded that in 1905, Louis Brandeis, later a Supreme Court Justice, remarked that the profession at that time caused him much concern. He was alarmed at the progressive encroachment of material influences on the great and beloved principles of the law. A year later, Roscoe Pound, soon to be Dean of Harvard Law School, in a seminal address entitled "Causes of Popular Dissatisfaction with the Administration of Justice," criticized the prevailing legal institutions as not being able to serve a nation on the verge of realizing its destiny. Pound noted the absence of any encompassing "Philosophy of the Law" that would allow the profession to guide the nation through the challenges of the new century.

Even if what I have said thus far can be attributed to generational politics, and I concede that the thrust of my comments parallels to some extent those of Brandeis and Pound, there still remains the constant necessity to reexamine the ideals and premises of the profession. Even if we are not in the last days of the principled practice of law, the current developments, as I have sought to describe them, deserve careful attention. The quest

for Pound's "Philosophy of the Law" must continue if our profession is to lead society once again into the potentials of a new century that soon will be upon us.

Assuming that the state of the practice deserves the scrutiny of both the legal and non-legal communities, it is customary for the commentator to point out the obvious but unchosen answer. If there exists such an answer or path to be pursued, however, it will not be found in these remarks. The most compelling reason for this is simply that I am not in possession of any such remedy.

If there is an answer to the renewal of the professional ethic in the legal community, I do not believe it will come from any technical adjustment in the rules. The dramatic forces at work in the profession, both internally and externally, will not recede through administrative tinkering. That type of technocratic answer does not exist and, even if we could discover it, it recalls a solution more representative of the business culture. There simply is no quick antidote to materialism.

Rather, if a reassertion of professional faith is to occur, it must arise from a reaffirmation of our civic heritage. Members of the profession, the lawyers and the judges, must again possess a sense of their individual legal personality and faith in the ultimate mission of their calling. Additional bar programs or law school requirements may help, but by themselves they will not recapture the passion and dedication of elapsed faith. The role of the lawyer has not changed. The members of the profession must be willing to reassume it, and to do so with necessary vigor.

On the occasion of the 200th anniversary of our Constitution, I outlined the aspects of what I view as the unchanged role of the practitioner.[6] These basic qualities, I submit, merit reiteration. The first is service to the community. Lawyers must again recognize that they have been entrusted with a great privilege, and that obligations to the community go with that privilege. Attorneys have occupied a singular role in service to our society from the framing of our Constitution to the Civil Rights Movement. Members of the profession must once again accept the responsibility of formulating theories and rules to allow the various elements of the public to expand the ability of a nation to serve its citizens. Any enduring philosophy regarding legal practice must be rooted in the belief that lawyers receive their license and are empowered by the greater society, and must therefore labor to insure its progress. The idea of the practice of law as a completely private exercise of private ends is contrary to this conviction.

A second characteristic is dedication to what Justice Holmes called the "craftsmanship" of lawyering. There must be a renewed sense of pride in the work that lawyers do, not merely for its value in the marketplace, but for its historic function of vindicating the rights of citizens.

The third characteristic is devotion to the profession itself. The changing face of the law demands that lawyers reassert their professional ties and responsibilities. Members of the bar have traditionally recognized the importance of supporting their bar associations and continuing an active role in legal education. Profit must not become our dominant ethic. Nor must profit become the primary engine for professional change. A renewal in the faith of professionalism must originate from within and reverse our troubling path. Only when such a new direction is pursued will good sense and professional virtue prevail.

Despite the sobering tone of my remarks, I am not completely discouraged. Although many of us have halting doubts about recent developments in the profession, I believe it can still fulfill what is highest in the yearnings of the human spirit. Our history has been replete with inspiring figures: John Marshall, Oliver Wendell Holmes, Benjamin Cardozo, and Learned Hand, to name a few. Each can serve as a beacon.

As Judge Hand eloquently put it in addressing the conflict that is normal in a pluralistic society:

For it is always dawn. Day breaks forever, and above the eastern horizon the sun is now about to peep. Full light of day? No, perhaps not ever. But yet it grows lighter, and the paths that were frequently so blind will, if one watches sharply enough, become hourly plainer. We shall learn to walk straighter. Yes, it is always dawn.[7]

NOTES

This article originally appeared in Volume 74, Number 2, August-September 1990, pages 77-83. It was adapted from DICKINSON LAW REVIEW Vol. 93, No. 4, Summer 1989, copyright 1989 by Dickinson School of Law and was originally delivered as the Tresolini Lecture at Lehigh University on November 10, 1988.

1. *The Am Law 100 Report*, THE AMERICAN LAWYER, July/August, 1988.

2. *Id.* at 34

3. *Id.* at 58.

4. *Id.* at 20.

5. Kaplan, *Out of 11,000, 243 Went into Public Interest*, NAT'L L.J., Aug. 8, 1988, at 1, col. 1.

6. Adams, Remarks at the "We the People 200" Convocation with the Supreme Court Justices at the Arch Street Friends Society (Oct. 2, 1987).

7. Hand, THE SPIRIT OF LIBERTY: PAPERS AND ADDRESSES OF LEARNED HAND 101 (I. Dillard, 3d ed., 1974).

Truth, justice, and the client's interest: Can the lawyer serve all three?

by Nathan L. Posner

Our changing society confronts the lawyer with a serious problem: can there be a truly rational administration of justice unless *all* relevant facts are accurately determined? The lawyer usually satisfies himself with the belief that the adversary system is the proper and best means for dispensing justice. I would like to adopt such a philosophy, but I am convinced that our adversary system in its present form endorses various techniques that at best avoid the truth and at worst make a mockery of "justice." Adversary procedures must be amended and altered if we seek a better determination of where the truth lies in any issue.

A lawyer's traditional obligation is to seek justice and truth. This duty must be invulnerable to attack, because the lawyer is an officer of the court and a pillar of the system of the administration of justice. A lawyer has a professional obligation to seek the truth in every instance.

The adversary system reveals one of its major weaknesses when a skillful, well-prepared lawyer opposes an incompetent or unprepared lawyer. It is questionable whether the system enhances the cause of justice in such a case, and whether the verdict is a dispensation of justice or merely the product of competence versus incompetence. On occasion, the effect of incompetence is minimized because of the safeguards provided by the judge and jury in their respective functions of determining the law and finding the facts. Therefore, some may argue, after proper instructions from the court concerning the weight of the evidence and its credibility, the verdict rendered must be fair and proper. Nevertheless, the administration of justice in such instances has been hampered, and the adversary system has impeded rather than aided our democratic approach to the administration of justice.

Much has been written concerning lawyers' ethics in the adversary system. Some suggest that the lawyer's devotion to the success of the client's cause regardless of means and expedience overrules the requirement of decency and the search for truth. Such zealous advocates hold that the lawyer, because of his confidential relationship with the client, may not disclose the truth, and, even when the lawyer has learned the truth from sources other than the client, may not bring it to the knowledge of the authorities because it might adversely affect the client.

More to the point, despite expressly contrary prohibitions contained in the Code of Professional Responsibility,[1] some theorists argue that when the client or a witness commits perjury in the offering of testimony, the lawyer may not protest, withdraw from the case, or in any other fashion divulge the fact that perjury has been committed. I cannot agree that zealous advocacy embraces the ignoring of obvious perjury. Such behavior is equivalent to subornation.

No one would suggest that, in a case in which the life or personal liberty of one accused of a crime is at stake, there should be any diminution of the many safeguards provided by the Constitution and Rules of Criminal Procedure. The constitutional rights of a defendant charged with crime must be resistant to all attacks, and it is the duty of the lawyer to protect those rights. It is because of this principle of law that all those who advocate the lawyer's obligation to effect the cause of the client, regardless of truth and justice, feel justified in maintaining their obligation as paramount.

But let us for the moment dismiss from our minds the criminal law and the constitutional privileges of criminal defendants and view the matter of ethics and the adversary system in the context of the civil courts. There, weighty considerations of constitutional rights, which concern the members of the criminal bar who champion the client's cause above all else, are less important. In the civil courts it is largely monetary benefits and property rights that are at stake.

Even in the criminal adversary system, there has been recognition of the principle of full disclosure; the prosecutor's primary duty is to seek justice rather than simply to win cases and achieve convictions. Accordingly, he or she should attempt[2] during the course of his investigation to ferret out *all* relevant evidence even if it detracts from his case or tends to exonerate the defendant; and, at trial, should disclose *all* relevant evidence, again without regard to which side evidence favors. It is also presently recognized that the lawyer representing the government in a civil adversary proceeding should seek justice by developing a full and fair record, and should not use the power of the government and the procedural rules to harass opposing parties.[3]

Why should this responsibility not be extended to all lawyers engaged in the trial of civil cases? Such a duty would complement the existing admonition to all lawyers in all types of cases[4] to disclose to the tribunal all law applicable to the litigation, including the existence of precedents or statutes adverse to the legal positions of their clients. Once the facts and the law have been presented in this manner, the lawyers are free to zealously advocate the inferences and conclusions to be drawn from them in a light most favorable to their clients, and may challenge the applicability or the soundness of any unfavorable law. The likelihood of a truly just result is much greater under this system than under a system of trial by concealment, half-truth and subterfuge.

No one is prepared to venture an opinion concerning what perjury or subornation is committed in a typical civil case. However, it is sure that exaggerations and half-truths abound. A few examples should serve to highlight the problem.

• The adversary system is stultified when a lawyer suggests that a witness avoid certain statements because they might influence a jury against the cause of the client. I consider a lawyer in violation of his oath when he dares suggest to a witness prior to trial: "If the facts in this case are what I have been led to believe, then the proper answer to this question should be . . . ."

• I question the ethics of a lawyer who, during the preparation of a tort case, reads to the client various decisions of the appellate courts dealing with distances and car lengths, emphasizing that the appellate courts affirmed a finding of contributory negligence where the distance between the two cars was less than the certain quoted number of yards, and that therefore recovery was denied. He then asks the client, "And how many yards away were you when you first saw the other car?" Conceding that the lawyer may be properly disturbed with certain arbitrary rules that would preclude recovery to the client, has he the right to make suggestions that will give the right of recovery to his client based on "induced" testimony? Is he seeking justice and truth, or is he seeking to win the case for his client no matter what?

• Then there is a theory known as "selective ignorance." This refers to the lawyer who tells the client during their first meeting, "Don't say anything that will hurt your case." Not having been told, the lawyer can proceed with the case as he sees it on the information supplied to him after the warning. This lawyer does not recognize his responsibility to society, and does not serve the cause for which he became a lawyer. He is merely trying to justify his conduct by his rationalization of "service to the client," which unfortunately, in most instances, involves substantial fees.

Similar problems arise with respect to documentary evidence. A letter or memorandum that was never received by one party and which purports to confirm an oral agreement made by him, which in fact was never made, will appear as evidence in his opponent's case. Conversely, some clients have heeded the "message" conveyed by their lawyer when he suggests at the outset that "all those old accounting records, which you are not legally required to keep and which would be helpful evidence to your adversary, must take up a lot of filing space. Many businesses like yours dispose of their outdated records so that they can use their filing space for more current material."

• Finally, I do not believe it is ethical for a lawyer to seek delay in a matter because of the client's inability to make payment on a judgment that will be secured unless a defense is interposed.[5] There have been instances where rules have been used against parties, and technicalities raised in pleadings, in order that more time could be accorded the defendant before the inevitable judgment would be entered against him. When a lawyer is aware that there is no defense to an action, and that his sole obligation to the client's cause is to "buy" time, he is breaching the Code of Professional Responsibility. The "justice" that he seeks is one-sided and brings prejudice to others involved.

Other areas of the civil practice removed from the trial of cases have readily adopted and followed the suggested higher standards of full disclosure. For example, a lawyer representing a corporation that desires to sell its securities to the public must be certain that all relevant facts are fully and accurately represented in the documents filed with the Securities and Exchange Commission, including the prospectus that is to be distributed to the investing public in connection with the offer and sale of the securities.

Such a lawyer may not merely accept the client's description of the facts but must make his own independent investigation, using due diligence to assure himself that the client's records support the factual representations being made, that the various assets of the client are fully and accurately described in the documents, and that all financial information is correct and not misleading. If the lawyer finds a mistake, an omission of a fact, or an adverse fact, he must insist that the client make the appropriate disclosure.

These same principles are applicable to the lawyer retained to prepare the periodic reports required to be filed by public companies. Some even contend that such a lawyer, should he fail to convince the client to make the necessary full disclosure, has the obligation to report the client's failure to the appropriate regulatory agency. In the practice of decedents' estates and trusts as well, the lawyer's responsibility to disclose all assets subject to tax has long been recognized and unquestioned. Should the civil litigation system settle for lower standards?

A true lawyer must realize that he is an administrator of justice as well as an advocate on behalf of his client. Each lawyer must know and seek to inform those who are training to become lawyers of the positive responsibility on the part of every member of the profession to nurture and encourage justice and truth. The accomplishment of that goal transcends the obligation of advocacy.

NOTES

This article originally appeared in Volume 60, Number 3, October 1976, pages 111-113.

1. DR 7-102. See also EC 7-6 and EC 7-26.
2. EC 7-13.
3. EC 7-14.
4. EC 7-23.
5. *See* EC 7-4, EC 7-9, and DR 7-102 A(1) and (2).

Contingency fee lawyers as gatekeepers in the civil justice system

A recent study indicates contingency fee lawyers generally turn down at least as many cases as they accept, most often because potential clients do not have a basis for their case.

by Herbert M. Kritzer

Lawyers, particularly contingency fee lawyers, are gate-keepers who control the flow of civil cases into the courts. Although they can exercise this gatekeeping role in ways that either encourage or discourage potential litigants, the popular image of lawyers is that they stir up trouble. In *A Nation Under Lawyers*, Mary Ann Glendon argues that this should not be the case; she quotes an observation attributed to Elihu Root: "About half of the practice of the decent lawyer consists in telling would-be clients that they are damned fools and should stop."[1] Glendon implies that today lawyers are more interested in encouraging clients to sue than in being the "decent lawyers" of yesteryear.

This image is particularly associated with contingency fee lawyers. This is not surprising because of the apparent logic of the contingency fee: the lawyers get a cut of whatever they recover, and without cases there is no cut to get. Various interests—physicians, accountants, auto executives, chemical companies—blame contingency fee lawyers for much of what they view as crises arising from the liability system. Undoubtedly, there are lawyers who push the edge of the liability frontier, or who engage in practices pejoratively referred to as ambulance chasing. However, the day-to-day reality of most contingency fee legal practices is very different. While virtually every contingency fee practitioner wants to find highly lucrative cases, such cases are relatively rare. Many cases presented to lawyers are not winnable, or they do not offer a prospect of even a moderately acceptable fee. The

contingency fee practitioner seeks cases that offer a high probability of providing at least an acceptable return, hoping to find some fraction of cases that present the opportunity to generate a significant fee.

Thus, while lawyers may encourage or seek out cases, the contingency logic suggests that contingency fee lawyers should reject a large number of potential cases. Lawyers evaluate cases in terms of the risks involved and the potential returns associated with those risks. An attorney will reject cases that do not satisfy some risk/return criteria. Thus, contingency fee lawyers resemble portfolio managers, choosing to "invest" (their time) in risky cases hoping to obtain adequate or better returns.

Most of the above is speculative, and there is little published information that provides systematic insights into case-screening practices. Occasional articles in the legal press describe case-screening practices of top-end law firms[2] and prescriptive articles in periodicals targeted to the legal profession discuss what should be considered in screening cases.[3] However, there is only one, 25-year-old published study, and it focuses solely on medical malpractice.[4]

A recent survey of contingency fee practitioners in Wisconsin provides the first systematic data on case-screening patterns and practices. A total of 511 Wisconsin attorneys whose practices involve contingency fee work responded (about 48 percent). The survey covered a variety of aspects of contingency fee work, with one section focusing on the screening of potential cases. This survey is part of a larger project (see "The Wisconsin contingency fee study," page 137).

Screening cases

As shown in Table 1, among the 455 survey respondents who provided usable data, the number of potential clients contacting the respondents or their firms ranged from 1 to 5,000. (The number of clients accepted ranged from 0 to 600.) Seven respondents reported more than 1,000 contacts; an average of about 20 contacts (or more) a week, or four per day. At the other extreme, almost half reported about two or fewer contacts per month (25 or less over the year).

One problem with the figures is that some lawyers (about 10 percent of the 455 respondents) work in firms where case screening is handled on a firm-wide basis while other lawyers handle screening on an individual basis either in a firm or as solo practitioners. Preliminary analyses indicated that the general pattern in the results is the same re-

gardless of whether the "firm-level" screeners are included or excluded. Consequently, because the analysis considers individual characteristics as control variables, much of the following discussion focuses only on those lawyers in firms where individual lawyers are responsible for screening cases. Looking only at those respondents, the range of contacts is from 1 to 2,500; aggregating across all of these respondents, there were 40,518 contacts.

Selectivity

Overall, lawyers reported accepting cases from a mean of 46 percent (median 45 percent) of the potential clients who contacted them. Aggregating across the 455 lawyers, the lawyers accepted 16,519 (of 53,584) cases for an acceptance rate of 31 percent. Eliminating the seven respondents reporting 1,000 or more contacts, the mean acceptance rate is 47 percent (median 48 percent). These firms had contacts from 36,884 potential clients; they accepted 15,224 (41 percent).

Table 1   Case volume

| Number of contacts | All respondents | | | | Individual screeners | | | |
| | Number of respondents | | Total number of contacts | | Number of respondents | | Total number of contacts | |
	%	n	%	n	%	n	%	n
1-10	23%	106	1%	683	21%	87	1%	571
11-25	24	109	3	2,058	25	99	5	1,874
26-75	24	111	8	5,195	26	103	12	4,815
76-200	18	80	18	11,207	18	72	23	9,477
201-1000	9	42	30	19,131	9	37	39	15,781
over 1000	2	7	40	25,300	1	4	20	8,000
All	100%	455	100%	53,584	100%	402	100%	40,518

Table 2   Acceptance rates by case volume

| Number of contacts | Number of respondents | All respondents | | | |
		Mean percent accepted	Total number of contacts	Total number of cases accepted	Percent of total cases accepted
1-10	106	47%	683	319	47%
11-25	109	50	2,058	1,008	49
26-75	111	52	5,195	2,674	51
76-200	80	39	11,207	4,199	37
201-1000	42	37	19,131	7,116	38
over 1000	7	10	25,300	1,295	8
All	455	46	53,584	16,519	31

| Number of contacts | Number of respondents | Individual screeners | | | |
		Mean percent accepted	Total number of contacts	Total number of cases accepted	Percent of total cases accepted
1-10	87	48%	571	265	46%
11-25	99	50	1,874	921	49
26-75	103	51	4,815	2,440	51
76-200	72	38	9,477	3,804	40
201-1000	37	36	15,781	5,991	38
over 1000	4	12	8,000	855	11
All	402	46	40,518	14,276	35

As shown in Table 2, there appears to be a fairly clear link between volume and selectivity. For those lawyers or firms receiving about 1½ or fewer contacts per week, the acceptance rate tends to be on the order of 50 percent; for those with more than 1½ and up to about 20 contacts per week (1,000 cases per year), the acceptance rate is a little under 40 percent; for the very high volume practices with more than 20 contacts per week, the acceptance rate drops off sharply to less than 10 percent. Table 2 also eliminates those respondents who work in firms that screen at the firm level. Other than reducing the number of higher volume respondents, the general pattern is essentially the same.

There are many variables that might influence acceptance rates: gender, experience, specialized nature of practice or firm, and size of community. Because these might be correlated with contact volume, which the analysis above shows is clearly related to acceptance rate, volume was controlled for using two categories: low (75 or fewer contacts over the year) and medium (76 to 1,000 contacts). Eliminating the respondents in firms where screening is a firm-level function (which is necessary to look at any types of attorney characteristics), there are only four high volume (over 1,000 cases per year) respondents; the characteristics of those four respondents is reported in the right column of Table 3.

Table 3 shows acceptance rates controlling for 10 different variables one might expect to be related to how selective lawyers are in accepting cases. Of the 20 comparisons in the table (10 comparisons done separately for low and medium volume

Table 3   Acceptance rates by practice and lawyer factors

	Low contact volume Mean percent	Overall percent	n	Medium contact volume Mean percent	Overall percent	n	High contact volume
Gender							
Male	*50%*	50%	245	40%	39%	89	all male
Female	*42*	40	35	34	36	18	
Type of practice							
Personal injury plaintiffs	*55*	54	52	41	39	79	all personal injury plaintiffs
Personal injury defense	*45*	42	63	—	—	3	
Other litigation	*45*	48	88	35	46	13	
General practice	*54*	52	78	32	30	9	
% of income from contingency fees							
0-19%	*44*	42	116	—	—	(4)	all 90-100%
20-49%	*52*	49	94	34	43	12	
50-89%	*54*	55	58	40	38	34	
90-100%	*60*	55	20	43	39	57	
Firm specializes in plaintiffs work?							
Yes	53	54	54	40	40	64	all in plaintiff
No	49	48	213	40	36	36	specialist firms
Medical malpractice cases							
10% or more	47	50	29	*28*	27	25	all less than 10%
less than 10%	50	50	260	*42*	42	84	
Products cases							
10% or more	51	47	36	45	48	26	all less than 10%
less than 10%	49	50	253	37	36	83	
Nonpersonal injury contingency fee work							
50% or more	*41*	46	50	31	50	7	all 10% or less
11-49%	*51*	51	60	44	45	17	
10% or less	*50*	51	136	37	36	69	
Position in firm							
Solo	50	50	49	45	41	18	
Partner/owner	50	50	183	40	41	73	
Nonpartner	46	47	50	30	27	16	
City size							
Milwaukee	50	49	86	35	34	35	all Milwaukee
100,000 & up	45	48	54	33	36	22	
50,000-99,999	49	49	62	42	39	27	
under 50,000	53	53	79	44	43	22	
Years of experience							
10 or less	*45*	43	73	42	37	26	2, 10 or less
11 or 20	*47*	46	117	36	35	46	2, 11-20
21 or more	*56*	59	96	41	42	36	

Note: Bold italics indicate differences statistically significant at .05 level or better.

practices), only six achieve statistical significance. Five are for the low volume lawyers:

- Women lawyers are more selective than men.
- Lawyers with more than 20 years experience are less selective than those with 20 or fewer years of experience.
- Lawyers describing their practice as primarily personal injury plaintiffs or general practice are less selective than are those who do primarily personal injury defense or other types of litigation.
- Lawyers whose contingency fee caseload is predominantly (50 percent or more) personal injury are less selective than those whose contingency fee caseloads are not dominated by personal injury cases.
- Selectivity decreases as the lawyer's dependence (in terms of income) on contingency fee work goes up.

The only statistically significant difference among the medium volume lawyers is that those whose caseloads involve 10 percent or more medical malpractice work are more selective than are those with little or no medical malpractice work. The absence of statistically significant patterns for medium volume respondents probably reflects the smaller number of such respondents compared to the low volume respondents; the directional patterns for some of the variables mentioned above were similar for medium volume lawyers even though the differences did not achieve statistical significance.

The only discernible pattern in Table 3 is what appears to be an inverse relationship between selectivity and dependence on contingency fee (particularly personal injury) work: selectivity decreases as dependence on contingency fee cases increases. That is, lawyers who have substantial work that is not contingency fee based are able to be more selective in the cases that they accept. For these lawyers, the question is why take contingency fee cases that will be less lucrative than hourly fee work? One lawyer put it bluntly when he said, "I'm in contingency fee cases to beat my hourly rate."

What the table does not show is that at least some of those who are most dependent upon such work are among the most selective in which cases they take. At the extreme is the lawyer who reported that his/her firm had 5,000 contacts per year but accepted only 200 cases (an acceptance rate of 4 percent). However, most lawyers with substantial dependence upon contingency fee cases are not able to be as selective as either those lawyers or firms who "cherry pick" among potential cases or those who combine contingency fee work with hourly fee work.[5]

The most striking aspects of Table 3 are the relative lack of variation (taking into account the volume variable) and the absence of any identifiable group that accepts "most" of the cases that are screened. In fact, almost no categories accept substantially more than 50 percent of the cases screened, and the highest acceptance rate is only 60 percent. Simply stated, contingency fee lawyers generally turn down at least as many cases as they accept, and often turn down considerably more than they accept.

Table 4 When cases are declined

	All cases	All cases without high volume	Low volume	Medium volume	High volume
	Mean percentages				
After first phone call	51%		49%	55%	
Client did not appear for first appointment	7		7	5	
After first appointment	30		33	21	
After additional investigation	15		15	13	
	Aggregate percentages				
After first phone call	65%	59%	53%	60%	83%
Client did not appear for first appointment	5	5	7	5	5
After first appointment	18	22	29	21	6
After additional investigation	11	13	14	13	6

Declining cases

Typically, the first contact between lawyer and client comes in a phone call. This first call is extremely important because, on average, lawyers declined about half of all eventually declined cases based on this initial contact (see Table 4). Looking at aggregate numbers of cases declined (i.e., adding up all of the cases declined), the rate of decline based on initial telephone contacts increases as call volume goes up (see Table 4), with the low volume lawyers declining 53 percent of the total declined after the first phone conversation, medium volume 60 percent, and high volume 83 percent. Lawyers drop about 5 percent of the declined cases after a potential client fails to keep a first appointment. Most of the rest of the cases declined were declined after the first in-person meeting. Thus, lawyers make relatively quick decisions on most potential contingency fee cases.

Respondents were asked whether there was a minimum damage figure for each of three types of cases: auto accidents, medical malpractice, and products liability. Most (94 percent) provided a response for auto accidents, but only 43 percent stated that there was a minimum for such cases (the median minimum was $5,000). Substantially fewer responded regarding medical malpractice (61 percent) or products liability (69 percent), reflecting that many lawyers did not handle these kinds of cases. Of those who did respond, a higher percentage reported a minimum damage figure: 61 percent for medical malpractice (median

$100,000) and 60 percent for products liability (median $75,000).

Lawyers were also asked what percentage of cases declined were due to lack of liability, low damages or inadequate fee potential, both lack of liability and low damages, falling outside the area of the lawyer's practice, and other reasons. Not surprisingly, lack of liability and inadequate damages (singly or together) are the dominant reasons for declining cases, accounting for about 80 percent of the declined cases. Table 5 shows the aggregated figures for all lawyers, for all lawyers omitting the four high case volume lawyers, low volume lawyers, and medium volume lawyers. Lack of liability alone accounts for the largest proportion of cases declined, particularly for those lawyers with a higher volume of contacts from potential clients. Excluding the high volume lawyers (who are not shown as a separate column in Table 5 because there are only four such respondents),[6] only about a quarter of the declined cases were due solely to low damages.

The right cases?

One question this analysis cannot answer is whether lawyers turn away too many or too few cases, or whether they turn away the right cases. Many have lamented the supposed growth in "litigiousness" among the American population, but it is not necessarily self-evident that Americans are too eager to seek compensation when under our law compensation is due. We might return to Elihu Root's

Table 5   Reasons for declining cases

	All cases	All cases without high volume	Low volume	Medium volume
	Aggregate percentages			
Lack of liability	48%	40%	35%	41%
Inadequate damages	18	23	24	23
Both lack of liability and inadequate damages	13	17	21	16
Outside lawyer's area of practice	11	10	11	10
Other reasons	10	10	10	11
	Mean percentages			
Lack of liability	36%	35%	33%	41%
Inadequate damages	20	21	20	22
Both lack of liability and inadequate damages	20	20	22	16
Outside lawyer's area of practice	9	9	9	9
Other reasons	11	11	11	11

injunction, "about half of the practice of the decent lawyer consists in telling would-be clients that they are damned fools and should stop," as one possible measure. If we take "half of the practice," to refer to the proportion of potential cases accepted, then most contingency fee lawyers achieve this measure of decency.

While the survey data do show variations among lawyers in selectiveness, they do not provide direct information on variations among types of cases. Observations, however, make it clear that lawyers are more selective in some types of cases than in others. To some degree this reflects the simple fact that injury victims are more knowledgeable about whether they are entitled to compensation for some types of injuries (auto accidents) than for others (slip and falls, medical malpractice, etc.). During a month observing in a law office in the middle of a Wisconsin winter, there were several significant snow falls and a number of calls from persons who had slipped on snow or ice. Most of these cases were turned away simply because Wisconsin law allows property owners time to remove snow or ice from sidewalks before they become liable for injuries from falls.

Medical malpractice is one of the areas most talked about as needing reform to provide relief to medical providers from increasing law suits. During three months of observation in three different law practices, lawyers dealt with contacts from 14 potential medical malpractice clients; only one of which resulted in a retainer being signed, and it did not involve the potential malpractice aspects of the case. Lawyers are extremely cautious in accepting medical malpractice cases, and the lawyers observed spent a lot of time explaining to potential clients why their negative medical outcome did not constitute malpractice, or the difficulty in establishing that it did arise from malpractice, or that even if it was malpractice, the ultimate medical outcome was probably not affected by the error (and the interim consequences did not give rise to damages that made pursuing the matter financially attractive).

For example, one potential client had a surgical procedure to correct a swallowing problem that involved insertion of an instrument down his esophagus. During the procedure the esophagus was injured necessitating surgery through the chest. The potential client was upset because he

The Wisconsin contingency fee study

To remedy the lack of good contemporary data on screening of potential clients, and the more general dearth of systematic information on contingency fee legal practice, I undertook a multifaceted study of contingency fee practice focusing on lawyers in Wisconsin. This study, funded by the National Science Foundation, involved three separate data collection components.

The first was a mail survey of Wisconsin contingency fee practitioners based on the State Bar of Wisconsin's Litigation Section mailing list. A total of 511 useable questionnaires were returned; a 48 percent response rate. Most of the information in this article draws upon the survey data.

The second aspect of the data collection involved full time observation of lawyers at work. I spent approximately one month in each of three different contingent fee practices. In each practice, my formal status was that of a paralegal, and in each practice I provided some assistance with

research and other activities. The practices were chosen to reflect different types of settings: Two specialized in contingency fee cases, one relatively high volume and one low volume; the third was a mixed trial or court practice in which contingency fee work constituted about 20 percent of the lawyer's work. The specific practices were chosen based on a combination of personal contacts and suggestions by persons knowledgeable about local practitioners.

The third part of the data collection consisted of semi-structured interviews with approximately 50 contingency fee practitioners, insurance defense counsel, and current or retired insurance adjusters. The plaintiffs' lawyers were chosen by selecting from directories and yellow page listings. Defense counsel or firms were identified by the plaintiffs' lawyers, and insurance adjusters were identified by defense counsel.

—Herbert Kritzer

had been in substantial pain in the recovery room and there was a delay in realizing the problem with the esophagus, and the recovery from the more major surgery was several months longer than it would have been from the simpler procedure.

As it turned out, a torn esophagus was a known risk of the simpler procedure (and the client had been warned of that risk as indicated by a signed informed consent). Furthermore, there was a significant chance that a more invasive procedure (through the chest) would have been needed even without the injury to the esophagus because the simpler procedure was substantially less than 100 percent effective. In this case, the lawyer explained to the potential client that the physician who conducted the original procedure probably had not committed medical malpractice (even if the recovery room staff had been slow to realize that there

was a problem), and that there would be questions about damages because the final result was very good (i.e., the original problem had been corrected) and there were no residual problems from the chest surgery.

One of the standard laments of proponents of change is that lawyers pursue too many cases that prove to be unfounded, particularly medical malpractice cases. Is this the result of poor screening decisions, or is there another explanation? Michael Saks has nicely laid out the dilemma that arises in assessing case selection in medical malpractice litigation.[7] Injuries during medical treatment are common, but only a very small fraction of those injuries is attributable to negligence. The injured persons are not very good at determining whether their injuries are due to negligence, and so large numbers of persons whose injuries are not due to

---

Other forms of gatekeeping

In addition to lawyers, there are other potential gatekeeping mechanisms. One would be to ban the contingency fee and require that potential litigants be prepared to bear the cost of seeking recompense for injury or other losses. This shifts the risk from the lawyer to the potential litigant. In some countries where contingency fees are prohibited, systems of legal insurance shift the risk.[1] Such a system would disadvantage those at the bottom of the economic ladder because "legal expense insurance" would probably be one of those "extras" that would be the first item to be cut from a tight budget.

Another way of gatekeeping, which also focuses on the incentive structure/risk preferences of the potential litigant, is fee shifting, where the loser of a lawsuit is required to pay the winner's costs. This system serves to disadvantage the middle class, which has to choose between foregoing compensation or putting at risk other resources (e.g., savings); those at the bottom of the economic ladder are essentially "judgment proof" and have nothing to lose through fee shifting.[2]

Interestingly, in 1995 England, which had both a ban on contingency fees and a fee shifting regime, relaxed the former by permitting a variant the government preferred to call "conditional

fees."[3] At that same time the Law Society (the professional organization of solicitors) came forth with an insurance scheme to ameliorate the problems created by fee shifting (i.e., the client can be insured against the risks of the fee shifting rule). The result is gatekeeping may be shifting from incentives focused on the potential litigant to incentives focused on the solicitor. It is too early to know what impact this has had, or will have, on the English court system.

—Herbert M. Kritzer

---

1. This is perhaps most developed in Germany; see Blankenburg, *Changes in Political Regimes and Continuity of the Rule of Law in Germany,* in Jacob, Blankenburg, Kritzer, Provine, and Sanders, COURTS, LAW & POLITICS IN COMPARATIVE PERSPECTIVE 298 (New Haven: Yale University Press, 1996).

2. See the recent study of fee shifting in Alaska (the one state that has a blanket fee-shifting rule, although limited), Di Pietro, *The English Rule at Work in Alaska,* 80 JUDICATURE 88 (1996). A similar pattern was reported when Florida briefly imposed a fee shifting rule in medical malpractice cases; see Snyder and Hughes, *The English Rule for Allocating Legal Costs: Evidence Confronts Theory,* 6 J. L. ECON., AND ORGANIZATION 345 at 356 (1990).

3. The American contingency fee is a commission system that takes on the contingency element through the fact that 33 percent of nothing is nothing. The English conditional fee system allows the solicitor to add a bonus to his or her usual fee (of up to 100 percent), but this fee is not a direct function of the amount recovered; see Kritzer, *Courts, Justice, and Politics in England,* in Jacob, et al., *supra* n. 1, at 136.

negligence are likely to seek legal counsel. Let us assume the following:

- 100,000 persons experience injuries during medical treatment;
- 1,000 (1 percent) of these were injured due to negligence and the injuries of the other 99,000 were not due to negligence;
- 500 (half) of those injured due to negligence seek legal counsel as do 10 percent (9,900) of whose injuries were not a result of negligence;
- the lawyers make the correct decision in 90 percent of the cases;
- this means that 450 (90 percent of 500) of the cases accepted did involve negligence and 990 (10 percent of 990) did not.

The bottom line is that even though those who actually experienced medical negligence are much more likely to seek legal counsel than those who were not so injured (50 percent versus 10 percent), and lawyers make the correct decision 90 percent of the time, more than two-thirds of the cases pursued did not involve negligence. By these figures, around 1 percent of injuries not arising from medical negligence leads to legal claims, a percentage which is about the same as the rate of negligence among medical injuries.[8]

*****

This research makes it clear that contingency fee lawyers do operate as gatekeepers: they turn away substantial numbers of potential clients, most often because those potential clients simply do not have a basis for pursuing the case. The contingency fee structure means that lawyers carry out this function in large part as an exercise in economic self-interest. That is, lawyers try to choose cases they believe will yield fees at least equal to what they could earn from either nonhourly fee cases or from other contingency fee cases. In a sense, the lawyer is making decisions about which cases to include in his or her portfolio of risks. The lawyer knows that some cases will fail to yield a fee sufficient to compensate for expenses while other cases will yield a profit that will at least offset the "unsuccessful" cases,[9] and hopefully yield a profit across the entire portfolio. Some lawyers explicitly include in their portfolios a mix of hourly and contingency fee cases on the expectation that the former will cover the overhead and the latter will produce the profits; others have a mix of cases

simply because that is the nature of the clientele they are able to attract.

NOTES

This article originally appeared in Volume 81, Number 1, July-August 1997, pages 22-29.

The original version of this paper was prepared for presentation at 1996 Annual Meeting of the American Political Science Association, San Francisco, California. A short version of the analysis presented here appeared as *Holding Back the Floodtide: The Role of Contingent Fee Lawyers*, 70 WISCONSIN LAWYER 10. The research reported here is supported by National Science Foundation Grant No. SBR-9510976. Research assistance was provided by J. Mitchell Pickerill.

1. Glendon, A NATION UNDER LAWYERS: HOW THE CRISIS IN THE LEGAL PROFESSION IS TRANSFORMING AMERICAN SOCIETY 37, 75 (Cambridge: Harvard University Press, 1994).

2. Crane, *Lawyers Don't Take Every Case*, NATIONAL LAW JOURNAL (January 25, 1988), at 1, 34.

3. *See, for example*, Trine and Luvera, *Pros and Cons of Accepting a Case*, 16 TRIAL 16 (May, 1994).

4. Dietz, Baird, and Berul, *The Medical Malpractice Legal System*, in APPENDIX: REPORT OF THE SECRETARY'S COMMISSION ON MEDICAL MALPRACTICE (Washington: Department of Health, Education and Welfare, 1973 [DHEW Publication No. (OS) 73-89]), pp. 95-101. This study found that, overall, attorneys accepted only about one in eight potential medical malpractice clients who contacted them

5. One minor pattern is the difference between male and female attorneys, with females accepting a lower percentage of cases. Additional analyses indicated that this was probably not simply a result of women working in practice settings where the percent of cases accepted was lower. Why women tend to accept a lower percentage of cases than do men is not clear.

6. These four lawyers report declining a total of 7,145 cases, 68 percent solely on liability grounds, 7 percent due to low damages, 5 percent due to a combination of low damages and lack of liability, 12 percent because they were outside the lawyers' areas of practice, and 8 percent for other reasons).

7. Saks, *Do We Really Know Anything About the Behavior of the Tort Litigation System—and Why Not?*, 140 U. PA. L. REV. 1147 at 1193-1196 (1992); the numbers used here differ somewhat from those used by Saks, but the pattern is the same (although the numbers Saks uses produce an even more extreme result).

8. *Id.* at 1196, n150.

9. A case may be unsuccessful if no recovery is obtained, if an unexpectedly small recovery is obtained, or if the costs of obtaining the recovery (i.e., the amount of lawyer time) are much higher than expected. For more on these various risks see Kritzer, "Rhetoric and Reality...Uses and Abuses...Contingencies and Certainties: The American Contingent Fee in Operation," DPRP Working Paper, Institute for Legal Studies, University of Wisconsin, 1996.

Actors in the Judicial Process
Interest Groups

INTRODUCTION   Unlike the legislative process where a governmental institution may address a problem simply as a matter of choice, courts are responsive bodies and can only deal with cases brought before them by actual litigants. On the surface, litigation often appears to be an effort to redress individual concerns. It is important to recognize, however, that litigation can have significant policy consequences for society extending far beyond the importance of a case for individual litigants. Indeed, the judicial process can be the most efficient means by which interest groups pursue their preferred policy ends, either through the filing of an amicus curiae brief or, alternatively, by making the larger commitment of sponsoring a "test case." While we do not know a great deal about individual litigants in a systematic way (except, perhaps, for our knowledge about criminal defendants brought to court by the government against their will), we continue to learn much about the role of interest groups in the judicial process. This section of readings examines several facets of group participation in the American judiciary.

In "Civil rights litigation by organizations: constraints and choices," Stephen Wasby examines the real-world operation of "planned" litigation in which a group attempts to pursue societal change through the courts. Wasby's specific focus is on the NAACP's efforts in the civil rights arena, and he demonstrates convincingly that much group behavior regarding litigation is not conducive to tight organizational control. Rather, litigation seeking social change "is often reflexive and far from completely planned with many constraints...many detours along the road to organizational goals, and much flexibility of action by both the litigating organizations and individual staff attorneys."

Perhaps the most graphic single example of interest group participation in Supreme Court litigation occurred in *Webster v. Reproductive Health Services* (1989), a case dealing with state legislation regulating abortions that was perceived by many analysts as the instrument through which the Court might overturn *Roe v. Wade* (1973), the seminal precedent enhancing freedom of choice. We offer two selections that focus on the *Webster* case. Susan Behuniak's article,

"Friendly fire: amici curiae and *Webster v. Reproductive Health Services*," offers a detailed study of group participation in *Webster*. Behuniak's analysis examines who filed amicus briefs and what arguments were raised. It also explores the impact of briefs on the justices' diverse opinions by amicus participants and the possible reasons for differences in behavior between groups on the pro-life and pro-choice sides of the case.

In a related article with a somewhat different focus, Jack Rossotti, Laura Natelson, and Raymond Tatalovich utilize content analysis to explore, "Nonlegal advice: the amicus briefs in *Webster v. Reproductive Health Services*." Their study documents that the amicus briefs themselves rely on many sources of arguments beyond legal ones. Perhaps not surprisingly, when the justices cited amici in their opinions, the briefs they chose to utilize were not those that focused primarily on legal issues per se. Indeed, as the authors note, "It makes perfect sense that a justice would look to his or her own knowledge of case law or rely upon clerks to research legal precedents.... But to do an extensive search of cognate disciplines as wide-ranging as medicine, theology, history, and psychology is beyond the capacity of any judge, and it was this need for substantive knowledge and third-party representation that gave rise to the use of amicus briefs." It is in this sense that interest groups and the briefs that they author can be credited with broadening the scope and, in the process, the public policy focus of litigation before the Court.

Civil rights litigation by organizations: constraints and choices

Litigation for social change is far from completely planned. Numerous external and internal factors affect both the planning and execution of a campaign.

by Stephen L. Wasby

Organized groups have long made use of the courts in their efforts to produce—or retard—social change. Despite claims that "social policy" litigation, which courts are said to lack the capacity to handle,[1] is new, such litigation has long taken place. In the 1930s, for example, conservative groups went to court to challenge New Deal legislation. In terms of litigation systematically brought by interest groups—a litigation "campaign" or "planned" litigation—the efforts to overturn school segregation, resulting in *Brown v. Board of Education*,[2] are most likely to come to mind. These efforts by the NAACP Legal Defense Fund (LDF) have become the model for planned litigation, followed both by those seeking civil rights for other segments of society, for example, women, and those litigating outside the civil rights field, such as environmental groups like the Sierra Club and the Natural Resources Defense Council.[3] The growth of public interest law firms, both liberal and conservative, indicates the use of the model across the political spectrum.[4]

Not all litigation aimed at producing social change is "planned" litigation or takes the form of litigation campaigns. Nor are all test cases instances of planned litigation. For example, it was only recently that the American Civil Liberties Union (ACLU), which we associate with test case litigation, began to undertake systematic litigation in particular areas of the law through "projects" staffed by particular attorneys, instead of litigating primarily against "targets of opportunity."[5]

Mounting a litigation campaign is no easy task. It requires attention not only to strategy in par-ticular cases but also to larger strategy, including choosing areas of law in which to litigate, choosing cases within those areas of law, and developing the resources necessary to undertake the litigation.

Planning any individual case, such as a large antitrust case, a class action toxic injury case or a drug case like the DES litigation, poses many problems for the lawyers involved. Yet when an organization, such as a civil rights group like LDF, contemplates undertaking a litigation "campaign" in a particular area of the law,[6] matters become even more difficult: the organization must worry not simply about individual cases but about a number of them.

In an effort to cast more light on "planned" litigation, particularly in the area of civil rights, this article explores some aspects of civil rights litigation undertaken by interest groups and the lawyers associated with them, emphasizing cases on school desegregation, employment discrimination (primarily cases under Title VII of the Civil Rights Act of 1964), and housing discrimination. After a look at some possible effects of litigation campaigns on the work of courts, we turn our attention to lawyers' perspectives on the role of interest groups in planned litigation, with particular attention to organizations' choices of areas of law in which to litigate and of cases to pursue, and to the internal dynamics of those cases. Then we will examine relations between staff attorneys and "cooperating" attorneys and interorganizational relationships affecting litigation.

Primary attention is paid to the work of the National Association for the Advancement of Colored People (NAACP) and the NAACP Legal Defense and Educational Fund, Inc. (LDF) from the late 1960s through the early 1980s. This period was chosen because it was an "age of complexity" for race relations interest group litigators. The environment in which the litigators functioned became increasingly complex; in addition to having to attend to judicial rulings, they had to focus on statutes and implementing regulations as well. Moreover, pubic opinion concerning civil rights became more conservative than it had been in the early and mid-1960s. Congress also became less supportive of civil rights, as did the executive branch, in the transitions both from the Johnson to Nixon presidencies and later, from the Carter to Reagan administrations.

Litigation itself became more complex; school cases were no longer a matter of attacking segregation statutes but required considerable resources both to prove violations and then to develop and implement remedies or involved challenges to "second-generation" discrimination within schools. In employment discrimination, the most blatant forms of discrimination had been replaced by more subtle forms, varying from industry to industry, which also required considerable resources to demonstrate.

This article is based primarily on interviews with more than 40 attorneys who are or were associated with the NAACP, the LDF, or other active organizational participants in race relations litigation (e.g., the Lawyers Committee for Civil Rights Under Law, the National Committee Against Discrimination in Housing, the Center for National Policy Review, and the Center for Law and Education). Among those interviewed were the senior attorneys for these organizations; several lawyers closely involved in organizations' litigation planning, although they did not serve as staff attorneys; and many "cooperating attorneys" in major race relations cases. The cooperating attorneys include some who were expert in a particular type of litigation such as school desegregation, some who tried cases across the country, and others involved in cases in their own states and communities.

The interviews, based primarily on open-ended questions, were structured but allowed respondents to discuss matters they thought especially salient. Among matters covered were organizations' choices of areas of law in which to litigate, choices of particular cases, organizations' use of cooperating attorneys, relations between litigating organizations, and the effect and importance of factors that might affect the litigation in which the respondents or their organization had been involved. Aspects of the particular cases in which the cooperating attorneys had been involved were explored in interviews with these individuals.

Litigation campaigns and the courts

Although interest groups attempt to use the courts to achieve social change, such litigation does not *necessarily* add significantly to the courts' work. Particularly when precedent is an organization's goal, a litigation campaign may involve bringing a number of cases so that the organization has several appropriate cases reach the appellate courts in the appropriate sequence, with allowance being made for some cases being settled and some "washing out" for other reasons. Nonetheless, the number of cases may be no greater than if individual plaintiffs asserted their rights in separate cases. Whether or not a litigation campaign was under way to achieve school desegregation, suits would have had to be filed against many school districts, and many Title VII lawsuits would have been necessary to resolve complaints of employment discrimination even if the LDF had not decided to proceed systematically.[7]

Without the efforts of the NAACP and the LDF, fewer school desegregation or employment discrimination cases would have been brought, but that is primarily because those organizations provided resources—staff attorneys, cooperating attorneys, and expenses—not otherwise available to many prospective plaintiffs. It is thus the interest groups' efforts and injection of resources, not that these efforts took the form of planned litigation, that may have produced more cases for the courts, just as governmental actions with respect to schools, or action by private entities concerning employment, often prompted the litigation.

Litigation campaigns may in a way have *reduced* the number of cases with which the courts had to contend because class action suits combining many claims were major vehicles in the LDF Title VII campaign. Without the class action suits, there might have been more individual plaintiffs' suits. As it was, there were many of those, brought by attorneys using materials made available by organizational litigators. The class action suits, however, were more complex and thus took more time to litigate, just as northern school desegregation suits involved significant problems of proof. Civil rights litigation often took the form of "public law" cases—polycentric controversies involving multiple parties and entailing detailed and continuing relief, and thus requiring prolonged involvement by the judge hearing the case[8]—or "structural lawsuits" with "an array of competing interests and perspectives organized around a number of issues and a single decisional agency, the judge."[9]

The growing complexity of cases can affect case outcomes in a number of ways. Litigators' needs for substantial resources may mean that they may not be able to pursue some complaints or that some complaints once commenced must be abandoned. Principal civil rights litigating organizations concentrating only on the "big," potentially precedent-setting cases have fewer resources to devote to "small," individual-plaintiff cases, which must be pursued, if at all, by local counsel. Judicial standards, requiring proof of intent to discriminate, not merely of disparate effects,[10] not only require civil rights lawyers to put on a more elaborate case but also make it less likely that civil rights plaintiffs will prevail.

The courts have themselves contributed to the complexity of civil rights litigation—and thus to their own workload. One way is through the just-noted requirement of proof of intent to discriminate. Courts also affect litigation in other ways, for example, by their receptivity to certain arguments and, because of groups' need for financial resources for civil rights litigation, their willingness to grant attorneys fees under the Civil Rights Attorneys Fees Awards Act of 1976. The Supreme Court's willingness to grant review to cases in certain areas of the law and its disinclination to hear cases in other areas affect litigators' pursuit of cases to that level. For example, the Court's not having previously granted certiorari in restrictive covenant cases made the NAACP pay particular attention to framing cases so that the Court would grant review[11] and the Court's unwillingness to hear claims of discrimination in public housing and urban renewal cases "depressed the market" for such cases.[12]

The Court's procedural rulings, such as those on the standing of parties to sue, have important effects as well: *Warth v. Seldin*[13] is said to have had a devastating effect on the campaign against exclusionary zoning. And of course the Court's substan-

tive rulings are crucial. An example is the decision in *San Antonio School District v. Rodriguez*,[14] which shut off federal court challenges to the property tax basis for financing public education. That case led civil rights lawyers to redirect their efforts to state courts, an indication of the effect of judicial decisions on litigators' choice of federal or state forum. The abortive campaign to reform the welfare system through litigation provides another example.[15] Although the Court issued favorable rulings in benefit termination cases on due process grounds,[16] when it handed down adverse rulings on benefit levels[17] the campaign came to an end.

Planned litigation

To write about litigators' perspectives on "planned litigation" is to assume that such litigation exists.[18] We must, however, be careful not to assume that all litigation to which some attach the label "planned" is thoroughly or fully planned, with litigators in control of the areas of law in which they focus their efforts, of particular cases, or of sequence of cases. To use the term is to say, at the least, that some make efforts at planned litigation; it is not to say how thorough or successful those efforts are.

If the conventional wisdom is that civil rights litigation of the 1940s and early 1950s consisted of planned, organized campaigns to produce social change, the picture presented here of the more recent period is quite different. Even in the litigation leading to *Brown v. Board of Education*, we get a picture rather different from Kluger's portrayal in *Simple Justice*, which Mark Tushnet has properly criticized as being one of "essentially unproblematic success."[19] Instead, there was "a tremendous amount of matter extraneous to policy which determined whether a case was brought in one state rather than another or one place rather than another," and policy was made primarily "around Thurgood Marshall's desk," with a "lot of improvisation."[20]

Recent civil rights litigation certainly contains elements of planning, and much of the litigation is undertaken systematically. However, much about that litigation is problematic, in part because it is quite complex and much is unplanned, so that to a considerable degree even principal civil rights lawyers do not fully control it. Particularly in point is the observation by a major civil rights litigator, "The vagaries of litigation are such that if you bring a case solely to go the Supreme Court, there are 100 ways not to get there, and if you try to play cute in order to stay away, you end up there."

Nor do all those who have participated in "planned litigation" share a view of the activity as derived from a blueprint. Litigation, said one lawyer, is a "responsive posture" inhibiting one from doing anything. Litigation provided "some room for maneuver," but was "not a strategic tool." Civil rights lawyers—lawyers with definite goals, working for organizations which have clear statements of purpose—frequently volunteered comments about the unplanned nature of their enterprise and unhesitatingly stressed the difficulties of keeping litigation strategy under control. In particular, one must keep in mind one litigator's acerbic comment, "Retrospective analyses that discern grand (and not so grand) strategies are often piffle. Many initiatives are impromptu." Furthermore, in general "the nature of the business prevents it from being a grand design:" "Whatever gets done, gets done, rather than by design."

Control of litigation

At the heart of planned litigation is *control*.[21] This includes the ability to "influence the development and sequence of cases," so that lawyers can "produce cases which presented the issues they wanted decided, where and when they wanted them,"[22] something "far from automatic and not subject to tight control."[23] Among the many matters not subject to control are, in the words of one LDF lawyer, "the chance occurrences of any lawsuit, the defection of the plaintiffs or capitulation of defendants, disagreement among counsel, unanticipated precedents, and the effect of public sentiment and political currents on adjudication."[24] Litigators might be able to exercise control at the level of the individual case and might also be able to choose areas of law in which to litigate and to establish priorities among those areas. Within any area of law, however, there is a less tidy picture; lawyers' ability to control the flow of cases and thus to choose cases decreases because there are more problems "whenever you clutter the landscape with litigation." Many decisions are made *inductively* (or responsively), a result of pressure, circumstance, and the flow of cases to litigators, rather than *deductively*, following logically from certain established criteria.

That an organization does more than respond

idiosyncratically to cases cannot be taken for granted. Even when organizations bring test cases—the quintessence of planned litigation—they may not have done so as a result of broad litigation planning. Instead they may have responded to "fortuitous events." Even where an organization has undertaken a planned litigation campaign, such as LDF's Title VII litigation, some cases have been taken reflexively, in response to client and membership pressure. Thus even when an organization does attempt to plan litigation, its activities may not result from strategy. Although an organization may be capable of developing "offensive" strategies, "circumstances control." Thus it has been difficult for the NAACP "to control priorities and time expenditures," making it "reflective and responsive to events and developments." If at times it seemed "as if there was a grand strategy applied from New York, the opposite was true:" matters "arose in the countryside" and then moved to the national level. Moreover, when there is a plan, flexibility—essential to success—will result in departures from it. The speed with which cases arise may also make it difficult for litigators to control litigation.

Strategy sessions can be an important element of "planning" in planned litigation.[25] However, observers believe that efforts to get lawyers together to plan strategy have seldom produced "grand strategizing;" they produce "petty strategizing if anything." When six people were brought together in a hotel room to plan, "not much came out of any of that type of activity," because what results from "sitting around" is "too abstract" for use in actual situations. Even where strategy has been planned, the presence of a larger number of litigators increases the likelihood that "another actor will enter the fray and set matters back several years." Indeed, "too many people are doing too many things for planned litigation to be more than a myth. If you are going to bring up cases A, B, C, and D, before you can, 12 others bring it up." That forces you to "move when you can where you can," with litigation more like "secret warfare."

Choosing areas of law

If planning involves choice, what do we find about interest group litigators' choices?[26] The choice of particular areas of law in which to focus litigation activities is a crucial part of planned litigation. Certain areas in which organizations litigate, for example, Title VII and capital punishment by LDF, are chosen with some care, with constraints imposed mostly by limited resources. School desegregation, the "most programmatically developed" area of NAACP litigation, has been that organization's primary litigation focus, taking up "90 percent of the conscious effort" in litigation. The NAACP has also been active in the fight against employment discrimination, but that area of law did not receive the same attention by the group's legal department. Indeed, as a result of a request from the NAACP's labor director, highly involved for many years in battling job discrimination, the LDF did the "biggest piece" of the NAACP cases; the lack of NAACP resources meant the organization had to "funnel" many Title VII cases to the LDF, with "the strategy [being] LDF strategy."

Litigation in some other areas of the law evolves because many cases on a topic come to an organization, such as the sit-in and demonstration cases of the early 1960s.[27] Other areas are said "simply [to] arise naturally." To the extent staff attorneys can "free-wheel" and pursue cases that fall outside the organization's basic litigation agenda, its litigation focus will become more diffuse.

Among the elements entering into the choice of areas of law for attention is an organizational one; the NAACP "had to consider that other organizations were considering some issues." The branches' "significant input" is an important intra-organizational fact, with the size and strength of a branch a relevant factor. Resolutions by the board of directors are also relevant, but board votes don't translate directly into litigation campaigns because of the "interplay" between board votes and the views of the general counsel, who has considerable autonomy to pursue his own interests, subject to his having to deal with the organization's own "bureaucratic" problems and having to serve as NAACP's house counsel. Staff lawyers play an important role, "orchestrating, certainly in tactical matters," and their views predominate, particularly when NAACP branches do not have lawyers among their officers. As with any litigating organization, resources are a crucial matter, indeed a "primary consideration" in NAACP's choice of areas of law.

The mid-1960s enactment of new civil rights statutes provided a "natural dividing line" in LDF's litigation efforts. Its focused litigation campaign, the most significant of private efforts to enforce Title VII, came about in part because job discrimination was an issue with substantial, immediate, and visible economic ramifications for minorities. This indicates that pressures on a nonmembership "public interest law firm" like LDF may be similar to those on the membership-based NAACP. Pressure may not be felt directly by LDF, but it is felt through clients coming to cooperating attorneys, from whom LDF gets most of its cases. Indeed, although neither the LDF nor the NAACP preferred having "ad hoc" cases, both had some. "Given the nature of the [NAACP] organization," that is, its membership base, the NAACP did "have to have some ad hoc cases" and has had more than has LDF.

Funding—particularly foundation funding—has been said to particularly influence the areas in which LDF has litigated. LDF has also been thought quite persuasive in getting foundations to support what LDF wanted to do. In short, LDF "solicits for specific issues," and "to the extent the funds are earmarked, [LDF staff] play a part in the earmarking."

Choosing cases

Once cases are channeled to an organization, decisions must be made as to which ones to pursue. Choosing areas of law and choosing cases are closely related. Decisions about the former help channel certain types of cases to the litigators. At least equally important, and reinforcement for the "inductive" or responsive view of "planned" litigation, is that decisions about areas of law in which to concentrate are influenced by the flow of cases to an organization. This makes how cases come to a litigating organization quite important. With cooperating attorneys the primary source of cases, organizational control of litigation planning may be reduced unless cooperating attorneys' choices are influenced by national organizational criteria. Nor do litigating organizations enter all cases from the beginning, which would facilitate control; they may become involved in some cases already initiated by others—sometimes defensively to prevent "bad" precedent or avoid rulings not in line with organizational strategy. This is a clear indication of the limits on organizations' ability to plan their litigation and control implementation of their strategy.

Lawyers associated with civil rights groups identify a variety of criteria used to select cases, but there is no clear consensus on the criteria used;

moreover, constraints and organizational politics affect attempts to apply the criteria. NAACP decisions to take cases were based on several factors, including the significance of the case (those with broad impact were preferred) and the importance of the branch that initiated a case.

The NAACP took some cases because people in a particular community "had started to do the right thing" and one "had to help them." The NAACP also took cases because governments took actions that were "affronts [that] had to be challenged," giving the organization "no choice" but to get involved even if the cases did not fit with litigation strategy. However, the NAACP preferred not to fund a case unless the organization and its lawyers controlled the case and the case was "consistent with organizational policy." Particularly when a case had already been started, the NAACP would enter it only if it could "exercise significant direction" over the case. The view is "that general counsel and the New York staff will control litigation in which the organization is involved." Thus "if a branch went off with inconsistent litigation, or hadn't precleared the case, there would be hell to pay."

A number of observers felt, however, that case selection did not function according to prescribed procedures or on the basis of criteria related to litigation strategy. Indeed, the process by which cases came to NAACP has been called "helter-skelter," with the NAACP having "no sense of direction" and "jumping into cases without an idea of the factors or what the costs will be." At times the NAACP got involved in cases because its attorneys focused on the particular case rather than on the "larger picture." Some staff lawyers did not consider themselves "social engineers" and thus were not firm believers in planned litigation for social change. Not able to "tell what the effects of precedent will be," they focused on racial problems in individual cases. And because the organization was "relatively flexible internally as to lawyers' choices," at times it was up to the individual lawyer to decide whether to take a case.

The received tradition about LDF's planned litigation would lead one to expect case selection to be governed by a highly developed set of regularly applied criteria. Instead, LDF was criticized by lawyers associated with it for not having done more to "institutionalize" its process for deciding which cases to take and for not developing criteria for the purpose. Moreover, the process for choosing cases was "not organized, it's organic." "Greater organizational sophistication," a result of experience and organizational growth, did mean, however, "an ability to deal with the brush fires" with which the organization had to contend.

Once brought to LDF's attention, a case was evaluated to determine its "strength" in terms of cost, the quality of the cooperating attorney, "other cases doing the same thing," the state of the law, and "the likelihood of winning." LDF's criteria seemed better developed in Title VII litigation, perhaps because of the focused litigation campaign within that area of the law, leading to special attention in choosing the industries and geographical areas in which to focus litigation. In general, however, lawyers' views were that at LDF "you assess cases as they come to you," with a focus on "how to get the job done in the case."

Thus "LDF didn't make policy in the abstract; it made it through cases." The situation was "not the National Security Council with a weekly sitting-down." Instead, "by sitting in the doctor's office, you get a view of the world." There was attention to issues, "but on a day-to-day basis, you pick the best cases." One reason was that the importance of a case was not always clear when the case was initiated. More than one case had to be picked because "cases drop out for any number of reasons," including settlements offered "which you can't refuse"—although in addition to recommending taking the settlement, the lawyer "might also point out that we took the case to develop the law." In short, there was no "unified legal theory in the civil tradition" from which LDF operated; LDF took "individual cases, from which legal theory was deduced."

LDF made an "enormous commitment to initiating cases" but, while "we prefer to be in from the beginning," LDF entered other cases, particularly if it could play no other role or a cooperating attorney had handled the case, because it was "good at putting cases on the record." LDF would also enter a case after its initiation if the case was seen to have a potentially significant precedential effect. Although there are "obvious problems if you'd not had a part in planning and developing a case," some of these cases were actually viewed favorably because developments in the case provided more information than LDF would otherwise have at the case-selection stage, giving the organization a clearer picture of what it might be facing.

Case dynamics

The internal dynamics of cases also affect—and can frustrate—attempts to plan litigation. Day-to-day litigation matters often get in the way of litigation planning; lawyers "don't plan that far ahead; they deal with immediate issues." For example, lawyers are "concerned with the violation" in school cases and are "not planning ahead to the remedy stage."[28] Decisions from the Supreme Court coming in mid-litigation—likely because of the extended nature of planned civil rights litigation—can undermine the theory at the heart of a litigant's case. The effects of the Supreme Court's ruling on the welfare litigation campaign were noted previously, as were the effects of the Court's adverse ruling on standing to challenge exclusionary zoning.[29]

Although, to be successful, litigators must be responsive to changes in judicial doctrine, momentum or inertia, the *absence* of dynamics also limits planning in litigation by hindering groups from responding to changes in their environment. For example, Derrick Bell has argued that lawyers have persisted in seeking racially balanced schools despite changes in judicial outlook, "reverses in the school desegregation campaign," and "membership demands for more attention to quality education."[30] Continuing success in litigation, like the Warren Court's expansion of civil rights, is quite likely to kindle a spirit propelling a group to continue litigation and thus to limit shifts in litigation strategy. Apart from success, however, many lawyers believe in the "myth of rights," the idea that litigation can produce positive statements of rights as well as the implementation of those rights. The hold of this myth helps explain why lawyers continued to turn to the courts in pursuit of their clients' rights, even when earlier "ground-breaking" rulings had not been implemented.[31]

Closely related is the fact that victorious litigants do not wish to give up, or be seen as giving up, what they had pressed hard to achieve; altering legal theories in mid-litigation may be thought to be particularly inappropriate. Success thus reinforces what has been called lawyers' general conservatism in planned litigation. "People tend to repeat lessons from the past; lawyers trying to win a case will use what's worked." Moreover, the pace

of litigation makes litigation "not a process giving one time to think," further limiting one's ability to respond to changes in one's legal environment.

The presence of other litigators, who may get to the appellate courts first—and "on a worse record"—also serves to press litigators to continue to take cases to those appellate courts even when favorable rulings are not expected. (There are, of course, other reasons, such as the belief that perhaps a limited victory might be obtained or "damage control" achieved.) This helps explain why the talk by civil rights and civil liberties lawyers of avoiding the Burger Court was not matched by a significant decrease in "going to the High Court." After all, said one lawyer, "It's the only Supreme Court we've got." Moreover, in cases where lower court rulings have favored civil rights claims, a conservative high tribunal will be more likely to accept appeals from defeated defendants—extremely evident in recent criminal procedure cases—thus removing from the hands of civil rights litigators the choice not to pursue the case further.

Cooperating attorneys

The prescribed method by which an organization obtains cases may indicate a relatively highly centralized relationship between the organization and cooperating attorneys;[32] this is particularly the case if one looks at the formal process by which cases are supposed to come to the NAACP. However, use of cooperating attorneys means decentralization of the organization's work. An important aspect of that decentralization is whether and to what extent an organization's local units and their goals, as well as the goals of cooperating attorneys, are guided by the goals of the organization at the national level.[33]

One way to assure that cooperating attorneys act within the scope of national policy is to transmit that policy to the local level; providing assistance to the cooperating attorneys also helps achieve this goal.[34] Otherwise, decentralization can cut against a group's national strategy and local membership pressure can dominate determination of the cases to which cooperating attorneys give greatest attention. This is particularly likely when local affiliates initiate cases[35] or when lawyers act independently.[36] At times, national staff attorneys may be "lead counsel" only nominally, with local lawyers handling much of the case and planning much of the strategy and tactics. Lawyers who share a national organization's "world view" may be allowed to "fine-tune or even make major changes in litigation," and may be allowed to run the case instead of being given marching orders. However, with cases becoming more complex, local attorneys are more likely to need assistance, thus binding them more closely to the national organization.

Attorneys' roles

The processes by which cases come to national litigating organizations, and the ways in which the organizations involve cooperating attorneys in their work, serve to define cooperating attorneys' varying roles. In some situations, national staff attorneys handle all trial work, with the cooperating attorney playing a clearly "subordinate role," gathering information and filing papers, serving as required local counsel, and acting principally as liaison between national staff lawyers and the local community. In short, cooperating attorneys may seem like little more than "water carriers" for the staff attorneys, although such a role may be assumed without complaint, particularly when local counsel have their own practices to attend to and realize they can't "carry" a major case.

In another role relationship, an organization's national staff lawyers develop new theories of litigation, with cooperating attorneys applying those theories. In still other situations, cooperating attorneys, who may have generated the cases themselves, serve as "lead counsel." Having greater familiarity with state court rules, local attorneys may be used for state cases, with staff attorneys handling federal litigation.

Roles are also affected by the *availability* of cooperating attorneys to pursue cases. Here race enters the picture. The use of white counsel rather than black counsel in cases brought by the NAACP or LDF is a question of long standing, although black lawyers have long handled civil rights cases. In cases originated locally, especially in the South, one occasionally found an especially courageous white lawyer or a local black lawyer who needed even more courage. The question of who was preferred by the national organizations was complicated when local black attorneys took the initiative in bringing test cases and adopted a position the national NAACP would have preferred not be pursued.[37] In the South, NAACP branch cases were often undertaken by white attorneys, who also "bore the principal burden of the national office's

legal activity." White attorneys also handled many Northern cases because the law practices of many Northern black attorneys were not focused on civil rights and constitutional law, making "their usefulness to the . . . NAACP . . . limited."[38]

One thus found the predominant use of prestigious—and often conservative—white lawyers until the 1930s, which marked "a decisive turning point" toward greater use of black attorneys as a result of "pressure . . . from a small but growing elite of brilliant young Negroes educated in ivy league law schools" in the mid-1920s[39] and the National Bar Association's criticism of civil rights organizations for not using black attorneys. However, even when lawyers like Charles Houston and William Hastie were brought into NAACP cases,[40] there was not an adequate pool of black attorneys—nor of cooperating attorneys of any race—to handle Southern cases. This led to programs to prepare civil rights lawyers. The LDF's intern program is the best known and has been a notable success: Julius Chambers, the newly-named director-counsel of LDF, was one of LDF's first two interns, and other Southern attorneys who are "graduates" of that program are now judges. The number of available cooperating attorneys, both in solo practice and in large prestigious law firms, "recruited" by the Lawyers Committee for Civil Rights Under Law (LCCRUL), also increased because of the possibility of attorneys' fees, which provide an incentive for large law firms to handle civil rights cases.

Attorneys' views

How does the staff attorney-cooperating attorney relationship look to the attorneys? Lawyers associated with LDF suggest that there has been little change in recent years in LDF's use of cooperating attorneys, although the intern program "expanded the base" of those with whom the organization could work. The organization found itself, because of its work in poverty law and the campaign against the death penalty, in contact with attorneys with whom it had not been previously involved, altering the "relatively small and ethnically homogeneous group" with which LDF had worked. Those changes affected LDF staff attorneys' relations with cooperating attorneys.

Overall relations between staff and cooperating attorneys are "remarkably cooperative and supportive," with "remarkably little competition" between the two sets of lawyers. They work well together in part because they have a "recognized common enemy" and a common purpose. The skills of each are recognized by the other, with relationships adjusted to be appropriate to attorneys' backgrounds and case issues. When a cooperating attorney is experienced, staff might be able to help simply by providing briefs developed for other cases, which the cooperating attorney would know how to use; indeed, the staff attorneys prefer to work with those who do much work but only "need support and help."

Staff attorneys don't appreciate it when a cooperating attorney "tries to dump all the work on the staff." Indeed, they try to "keep to a minimum" cases handled solely by staff, although in some categories (e.g., Title VII for LDF), and particularly in new areas of the law, staff attorneys may do "virtually all the work." It should also be remembered that they wish to leave their own mark on a case, which can lead to a situation in which cooperating attorneys feel they are not being allowed to do very much.

Staff attorneys acknowledge the value of having cooperating attorneys who know the community from which a case comes; the cooperating attorneys "tend to know local people and problems better, and are not regarded as outsiders;" they understand the judges and the local courthouse. They may well provide a balance to the idealism and naivete of the young staff lawyers. They can also help those lawyers from New York City obtain the trust of local clients, and can provide a buffer between the organization and its clients so that client contact does not eat up a great deal of staff attorney time.

One should note that there are differences between organizations in the relations between staff and cooperating attorneys. NAACP's posture toward local attorneys seems more directive than is true at LDF, which may not need to exert pressure because cooperating attorneys who have been through the LDF internship program are well socialized in LDF values and procedures. NAACP does not appear to hesitate to assign lead counsel from outside the community, justifying this practice as being done to "protect local lawyers from pressure." The NAACP may also remove local counsel from a case if there is disagreement on how the case should be handled. NAACP staff attorneys shrug off "negative publicity" from such intervention, but there is some criticism of NAACP's willingness to engage in such "strong-arm" tactics.

Interorganizational relations

Litigation is affected by the number of litigating groups. In recent years, more groups have been litigating, and, as a result, intergroup relations have become more confused. Prior to *Brown v. Board of Education*, there really was only one national civil rights litigating entity: the NAACP and LDF were functionally one organization, but now the two are fully separate and indeed have been involved in litigation against each other. There are also many other civil rights litigating units in crucial, if less central, roles. Proliferation of litigators has led to a loss of control by any single litigator and thus has decreased the ability to pursue a concerted strategy.[41] Further dispersion has been produced by the feeling of some that instead of "total coordination," a "decentralized, multi-faceted approach" was preferable.

Dispersion and competition *and* convergence and cooperation characterize intergroup relations affecting litigation. Cooperation between groups is most likely to take the form of information exchange, which is important for control of cases as well as for more efficient resource allocation; such cooperation is likely to continue despite friction between organizations. At times more than information exchange occurs. Sessions are held among litigating groups, organizational representatives, and other attorneys to discuss issues and plan litigation,[42] and there are efforts to enlist other groups as companion plaintiffs or as amicus curiae participants in litigation.

In the latter situation, groups do make efforts to coordinate their briefs. Despite difficulties, civil rights lawyers on the whole felt—perhaps because of their frequent interactions—that coordination was not particularly difficult and that they were successful in achieving it. An attorney for a group contemplating filing an amicus brief in another group's case might "feed arguments" to the sponsoring group's attorney for those briefs; indeed, potential amici may help regular counsel develop their principal arguments. Likewise, attorneys for the parties would indicate to attorneys for groups contemplating filing an amicus brief "the general direction of their briefs." This would not, however, be a matter of "orchestrating" the other organization's amicus participation; a staff lawyer simply "would try to make them assist his case." Such attempts at coordination were not always appreciated, however, and there was a "problem of having to send a brief around" to everyone. As one lawyer put it, "writing briefs by committee doesn't work very well," leading the organization to allow others to join its brief but without attempting to coordinate with other groups.

In general, groups did not want to be associated with another organization through amicus participation unless they had input into the brief. This effort to "try to have some substantive input" was fairly general. That didn't mean civil rights litigators were always stand-offish about amicus participation even when concerned about protecting their own reputation: "It's to one's advantage to work with" some groups, said one lawyer, because "there are first-rate lawyers" working with those groups. Nonetheless, "ecumenical amicus briefs" (where everyone signed on) were generally to be avoided and a number of lawyers quoted former federal judge Marvin Frankel: "If you want to file a petition, go to Congress."

Although "some civil rights lawyers are . . . ideologically opposed to national coordination," as can be seen from the looseness of the "campaign" against exclusionary zoning,[43] a partial convergence of perspectives develops among lawyers in the generally small and relatively cohesive "civil rights bar." This convergence leads members of this "civil rights bar" to assist each other regardless of their organizations' formal positions. The civil rights bar is thus part of the "glue" that serves to hold the pieces of civil rights litigation together at both the national and local levels. Cooperation here is also more likely than in litigation that has a "commercialized purpose" because the civil rights lawyers "shared a real enemy" and "shared a conception of that enemy." This allows them to work together even when their organizational superiors are at odds, an instance of captains doing more talking to each other than the commanders-in-chief.

We also find dispersion and competition. That groups interested in a particular area of the law have similar views does not necessarily mean that they will participate conjointly in activity; instead they may decide to go separate ways as long as one of their number is stating their basic position on a particular case. This differentiation—or "comparative advantage"—allows each group to focus its efforts most effectively; some groups will concentrate on certain subjects or activities while others focus their efforts elsewhere *because* of the former's efforts. For example, at the national level, LDF did not initially direct its resources to the campaign against exclusionary zoning because other national groups already were investing their efforts there.[44] The local level also provides instances of division of labor. For example, in Mississippi, the LDF handled school desegregation cases while the Lawyers Committee for Civil Rights Under Law undertook criminal defense work, and the Lawyers Constitutional Defense Committee dealt with both criminal defense work and police and prison brutality matters.[45]

Division of labor is less likely to be the result of explicit agreement than to be implicit, to be more a matter of "we saw what they were doing" and of groups "trying to stay out of each other's way" than of explicitly "carving up the territory." This can be seen in a number of areas of race relations law. One is school desegregation, where the LDF focused on the South and the NAACP dealt with the North—in part because they used divergent theories on which to base their cases, and in part because LDF made a "tactical choice as to where to get mileage" and felt it could do so in Southern and border states rather than in Northern cases which others, particularly the NAACP, were litigating.

Examination of these instances suggests that the litigation pie is not neatly and completely divided as a result of intergroup interaction. However, clear patterns develop, thus decreasing the considerable "potential for legal chaos" possible when a number of groups are litigating issues in a major area of the law; the picture is *not* one of "fragmentation." Because of the LDF's litigating predominance, NAACP's major involvement, and the regular presence of specialized litigating entities, there is some "order and stability" with respect to the areas of law in which litigation is carried out.[46]

Conclusion

Perhaps the most important generalization to be drawn from recent interest group civil rights litigation is that much of it is responsive and reflexive, and not subject to organizational control. Thus organizational litigators definitely do not dominate the domain in which they seek to operate.

Litigators make clear that each of the major civil rights litigation organizations have intentionally focused their energies in certain areas of the law, and each also has other designated interests, such as welfare for LDF a decade ago and voting rights for both NAACP and LDF more recently; criminal justice concerns have come to occupy a major place in race relations litigation as a result of LDF and NAACP efforts. NAACP and LDF have differed in the degree to which they focused their efforts and mounted resources for concentrated litigation "campaigns." However, not even for LDF, whose work is the "model" for "planned litigation for social change," were all areas of law in which the organization became involved subjects of litigation campaigns.

Among principal factors affecting organizational attention to specific areas of law have been resources, including the availability of foundation money, and the views of staff lawyers, also a major element in determining which cases to pursue. The goal of eliminating discrimination and concern for the well-being of minorities help explain why both the membership-based NAACP and the non-membership LDF focus on employment discrimination and, more recently, on the administration of criminal justice. In addition to such overlap, there also has been an implicit division of labor, leading the two groups to emphasize differing subjects or different geographical areas within a subject. This serves to spread overall litigation resources further than if the choices of the two organizations converged fully and thus duplicated each other.

Litigators' perspectives on organizations' choices of cases indicate rather clearly that the process of choosing cases has been far more diffuse than the term "planned litigation" might suggest, with case-selection decisions inductive and much affected by the flow of cases, rather than being deduced from a firm application of previously selected criteria. Litigating organizations' legal staffs, which operate in a flexible and "noninstitutionalized" way, seem to play a larger role in choice of cases than do organizational processes on "the books."

Some selection criteria are noted by most litigators, and seem likely to be taken into account in many cases. However, identification of other criteria seems largely a post hoc process. There is also agreement that criteria are not applied systematically or uniformly, in part because events require that certain cases be pursued, with civil rights litigators entering cases even when control, identified as crucial to planned litigation for social change, is not likely. Cooperating attorneys serve as the principal source of cases for litigators, with organizations taking the experience, credibility and competence of cooperating attorneys into account in choosing cases. LDF's socialization of cooperating attorneys has facilitated organizational control of cases, and has meant that LDF's case selection is not as likely as NAACP's to be diffuse.

Not surprisingly, we have found some differences in perspectives about civil rights litigation. The world looks somewhat different from a staff position at an organization's national headquarters than it does to a cooperating attorney in the field. However, there is probably more diversity of perspectives *among* cooperating attorneys than *between* them on the one hand and staff attorneys on the other. This is largely the result of the varying roles played by cooperating attorneys. Some of the divergence of perspectives noted here is organizationally-based; NAACP lawyers and LDF attorneys tend to see the world of race relations somewhat differently. However, in the larger view of things, differences in perspectives among principal litigating organizations and other lawyers laboring in the civil rights vineyard are limited. There are also similarities in perspectives stemming from litigating experience and the cohesiveness resulting from the presence of a "civil rights bar" sharing commitment to a particular goal. Litigation for social change, then, is often reflexive and far from completely planned, with many constraints on the planning of litigation campaigns, many detours along the road to organizational goals, and much flexibility of action by both the litigating organizations and individual staff attorneys.

NOTES

This article originally appeared in Volume 68, Numbers 9-10, April-May 1985, pages 337-352.

I wish to express particular appreciation to Dr. Hubert Locke, Director, William O. Douglas Institute, for prompting the study from which this article is taken. For research support I am indebted to the Institute, the Johnson Research Fund of American Philosophical Society, and the Office of Research and the Graduate School of Public Affairs, State University of New York at Albany. I also wish to thank colleagues who have contributed useful comments at various stages of this process and two anonymous reviewers for this journal and David Richert, its editor, for their observations.

This article is dedicated to the memory of the late Clement Vose, who died in January, 1985. His presence and work stimulated the study of interest group litigation.

1. Horowitz, THE COURTS AND SOCIAL POLICY (Washington, D.C.: The Brookings Institution, 1977). *But see* Wasby, *Arrogation of power or accountability: "judicial imperialism" revisited*, 65 JUDICATURE 209 (1981).

2. 347 U.S. 483 (1954); Kluger, SIMPLE JUSTICE: THE HISTORY OF BROWN V. BOARD OF EDUCATION AND BLACK AMERICA'S STRUGGLE FOR EQUALITY (New York: Alfred Knopf, 1976). *See also* Vose, CAUCASIANS ONLY: THE SUPREME COURT, THE NAACP AND THE RESTRICTIVE COVENANT CASES (Berkeley: University of California Press, 1959).

3. O'Connor, WOMEN'S ORGANIZATIONS' USE OF THE COURTS (Lexington, MA: Lexington Books, 1980); Melnick, REGULATION AND THE COURTS: THE CASE OF THE CLEAN AIR ACT (Washington, D.C.: The Brookings Institution, 1983).

4. *See* Weisbrod et al., PUBLIC INTEREST LAW: AN ECONOMIC AND INSTITUTIONAL ANALYSIS (Berkeley: University of California Press, 1978); O'Connor and Epstein, *The Rise of Conservative Interest Group Litigation*, 45 J. OF POL. 479 (1983).

5. Scheingold, THE POLITICS OF RIGHTS: LAWYERS, PUBLIC POLICY, AND POLITICAL CHANGE 5 (New Haven: Yale University Press, 1974). *See also* Rabin, *Lawyers for Social Change: Perspectives on Public Interest Law*, 28 STAN. L. REV. 207, at 221 (1976).

6. Belton, *A Comparative Review of Public and Private Enforcement of Title VII and the Civil Rights Act of 1964*, 31 VAND. L. REV.905 (1978); Meltsner, CRUEL AND UNUSUAL: THE SUPREME COURT AND CAPITAL PUNISHMENT (New York: Random House, 1973).

7. Belton, *supra* n. 6.

8. Chayes, *The Role of the Judge in Public Law Litigation*, 89 HARV. L. REV. 1281, at 1284 (1976).

9. Fiss, *The Social and Political Foundations of Adjudication*, 6 LAW AND HUM. BEHAV. 121 at 123 (1982); *see also* Fiss, *Foreword: The Forms of Justice*, 93 HARV. L. REV. 1 (1979).

10. *See* City of Mobile v. Bolden, 446 U.S. 55 (1980) (Sec. 2 of Voting Rights Act); Washington v. Davis, 426 U.S. 299 (1976) (employment cases under 14th Amendment).

11. Vose, *supra* n. 2, at 155-158.

12. Wasby, D'Amato, and Metrailer, DESEGREGATION FROM BROWN TO ALEXANDER: AN EXPLORATION OF SUPREME COURT STRATEGIES 228-235 (Carbondale, IL: Southern Illinois University Press, 1977); Ulmer, *The Longitudinal Behavior of Hugo L. Black: Parabolic Support for Civil Liberties, 1937-1971*, 1 FLA. ST. U. L. REV. 131, at 149 (1973).

13. 422 U.S. 490 (1975).

14. 411 U.S. 1 (1973).

15. *See* Greenberg, "Litigation for Social Change: Methods, Limits and Role in Democracy" (Cardozo Lecture), Association of the Bar of the City of New York (1973).

16. Goldberg v. Kelly, 397 U.S. 254 (1970) and Wheeler v. Montgomery, 397 U.S. 280 (1970).

17. For example, Dandridge v. Williams, 397 U.S. 471 (1970).

18. This and the following sections are based on Wasby, *How Planned is "Planned Litigation"?*, 1984 A. B. F. RES. J. 83.

19. Tushnet, "Organizational Structure and Legal Strategy: The NAACP's Campaign Against Segregated Education, 1929-1950," unpublished ms. (1980), at I-1 to I-2.

20. Material which appears in quotation marks without attribution is drawn from interviews conducted by the author.

21. *See* O'Connor, *supra* n. 3, at 87-88, 144-145.

22. Greenberg, *supra* n. 15, at 20.

23. *Id.*

24. Belton, *supra* n. 6, at 943.

25. *See* Sorauf, THE WALL OF SEPARATION: THE CONSTITUTIONAL POLITICS OF CHURCH AND STATE 84 (Princeton, NJ: Princeton

University Press, 1976); Vose, *supra* n. 2, at 58, 151; and Meltsner, *supra* n. 6, at 114, 238-239.

26. This section draws on Wasby, "The Multi-Faceted Elephant: Litigator Perspectives on Planned Litigation for Social Change," paper presented to Law & Society Association, Denver, Colorado, June 1983.

27. Grossman, *A Model for Judicial Policy Analysis: The Supreme Court and the Sit-In Cases*, in Grossman and Tanenhaus, eds., FRONTIERS OF JUDICIAL RESEARCH (New York: John Wiley, 1969).

28. Leubsdorf, *Completing the Desegregation Remedy*, 57 B.U.L. REV. 34, at 94 (1977).

29. *See* Danielson, THE POLITICS OF EXCLUSION 168 (New York: Columbia University Press, 1976).

30. Bell, *Serving Two Masters: Integration Ideals and Client Interests in School Desegregation Litigation*, 85 YALE L. J. 470, at 428, 487, 492 (1976).

31. Scheingold, *supra* n. 5, at 5, 95, 151, 197.

32. This section and the next two draw on Wasby, "Some Horizontal and Vertical Dynamics of Civil Rights Litigation: Litigator Perspectives," paper presented to Southern Political Science Association, Birmingham, Alabama, November 1983.

33. *See* Vose, CONSTITUTOINAL CHANGE: AMENDMENT POLITICS AND SUPREME COURT LITIGATION SINCE 1900, 321 (Lexington, MA: Lexington Books, 1972).

34. Casper, LAWYERS BEFORE THE WARREN COURT: CIVIL LIBERTIES AND CIVIL RIGHTS, 1957-66, 142-143 (Urbana: University of Illinois Press, 1972).

35. Orfield, MUST WE BUS? SEGREGATED SCHOOLS AND NATIONAL POLICY 371 (Washington, D.C.: The Brookings Institution, 1978); Rabin, *supra* n. 5, at 212-213 (1976).

36. For examples, see Vose, *supra* n. 2, at 157; Vose, *supra* n. 33, at 315.

37. See Vose, *supra* n. 33, at 315.

38. Meier and Rudwick, *Attorneys Black and White: A Case Study of Race Relations Within the NAACP*, 62 J. OF AM. HIST. 913, 915-916 (1976).

39. *Id.* at 930, 933.

40. Note that "the first case in which the NAACP had employed exclusively black counsel before the U.S. Supreme Court" was Hillins v. Oklahoma, 295 U.S. 394 (1935), in which an Oklahoma black man had been sentenced to death for rape. McNeil, GROUNDWORK: CHARLES HAMILTON HOUSTON AND THE STRUGGLE FOR CIVIL RIGHTS 121-122 (Philadelphia: University of Pennsylvania Press, 1983).

41. O'Connor, *supra* n. 3, at 145.

42. *See* n. 25, *supra*.

43. Orfield, *supra* n. 34, at 372; Shields and Spector, *Opening Up the Suburbs: Notes on a Movement for Social Change*, 2 YALE REV. OF L. AND SOCIAL ORDER 300 (1972).

44. Shields and Spector, *supra* n. 43.

45. *See* Heck and Stewart, *Ensuring Access to Justice: the Role of Interest Group Lawyers in the 60s Campaign for Civil Rights*, 66 JUDICATURE 84 (1982); Stewart and Heck, *The Day-to-Day Activities of Interest Group Lawyers*, 64 SOC. SCI. Q. 173 (1983).

46. For intergroup relations in church-state litigation, see Sorauf, *supra* n. 25, at 81.

Friendly fire: amici curiae and *Webster v. Reproductive Health Services*

With Roe v. Wade *in the balance, the unprecedented 78 amicus briefs filed in* Webster *played an important role in helping to inform and shape the Court's debate over abortion.*

by Susan M. Behuniak

The unprecedented number of amicus curiae briefs filed in *Webster v. Reproductive Health Services*[1] signaled not only the intensity of the abortion battle, but also the extent of interest group politics before the United States Supreme Court. If the response of 57 amicus briefs to *Regents of the University of California v. Bakke*[2] was unusual, the response to Webster was extraordinary. A total of 78 amicus briefs were filed; 46 on behalf of the appellants and 32 on behalf of the appellees. With over 400 organizations signing on as cosponsors, and thousands of individuals joining as signatories, *Webster*, though not a typical case, demonstrates the importance of interest group politics before the Court.

With the 1988 appointment of Justice Anthony Kennedy to fill the vacancy left by Justice Lewis Powell, a reversal of *Roe v. Wade*[3] was possible. Court watchers tallied a 4-1-4 line-up. Expected to support Roe were Justices Harry Blackmun, William Brennan, Thurgood Marshall and John Paul Stevens. The original dissenters in *Roe*, Justices William Rehnquist and Byron White were expected to be joined by Justices Antonin Scalia and Kennedy. With Justice Sandra Day O'Connor viewed as the swing vote, *Roe* was now subject to a 5-4 reversal. When the Court agreed to hear *Webster* during its 1988 term, the time was ripe for a major abortion decision. Such anticipation led to the unprecedented number of amicus briefs.

At issue in *Webster* was a Missouri statute which contained: (1) a preamble stating that "the life of each human being begins at conception,"[4] (2) sections restricting public facilities and employees from performing or assisting in an abortion (except to save the mother's life), (3) sections prohibiting the use of public funds, employees or hospitals from encouraging or counseling a woman to have an abortion (again, with the maternal life preservation exception), and (4) sections requiring that when a physician believes a woman to be 20 or more weeks pregnant, viability will be tested by performance of "such medical examinations and tests as are necessary to make a finding of the gestational age, weight, and lung maturity of the unborn child."[5]

Because of the number of briefs filed and the fact that all the briefs were spawned by the same constitutional issue, the *Webster* amicus briefs offer a unique opportunity to study this particular form of interest group litigation and to examine how the public debate over abortion is carried out in a legal arena. In focusing on these amicus briefs, several questions will frame the study: who submitted the briefs, what was argued in the briefs, and what impact did the briefs have on the outcome of the case? These questions are asked with two goals in mind. First, what do the amicus briefs demonstrate regarding this type of interest group activity? Second, what do the amicus briefs reveal concerning the nature of the two movements involved in the struggle over abortion rights?[6]

Table 1 46 briefs in support of appellants

First sponsors of amicus briefs	Total sponsors
1. Agudeth Israel of America	1
2. Alabama Lawyers for Unborn Children, Inc.	1
3. Edward Allen	1
4. American Academy of Medical Ethics	1
5. American Assoc. of Pro-Life Obst. and Gynecol. and The American Assoc. of Pro-Life Pediatricians	2
6. American Collegians for Life, Inc. and Catholic League for Religious & Civil Rights	2
7. American Family Association, Inc.	1
8. American Life League, Inc.	1
9. Association for Public Justice and The Value of Life Committee, Inc.	2
10. Attorneys General of Louisiana, Arizona, Idaho, Pennsylvania, and Wisconsin	1
11. Birthright, Inc.	1
12. Catholic Health Association of the US	1
13. Catholic Lawyers Guild of the Archdiocese of Boston, Inc.	1
14. Catholics United for Life, et al. (10)	11
15. Center for Judicial Studies and Certain Members of Congress (56)	2
16. Certain American State Legislators (over 250)	1
17. Certain Members of the General Assembly of PA (69)	1
18. Christian Advocates Serving Evangelism	1
19. Covenant House and Good Counsel, Inc.	2
20. Doctors for Life, et al. (4)	5
21. Feminists for Life of America, et al. (4)	5
22. Focus on Family and Family Research Council of America	2
23. Free Speech Advocates	1
24. Holy Orthodox Church	1
25. Human Life International	1
26. International Right to Life Federation	1
27. Larry Joyce	1
28. Knights of Columbus	1
29. Lutheran Church-Missouri Synod, et al. (2)	3
30. James Joseph Lynch, Jr.	1
31. Paul Marx	1
32. 127 Members of the Missouri General Assembly	1
33. Missouri Catholic Conference	1
34. Bernard Nathanson, M.D.	1
35. National Legal Foundation	1
36. National Right to Life Committee	1
37. New England Christian Action Council, Inc.	1
38. Right to Life Advocates, Inc.	1
39. Right to Life League of Southern California, Inc.	1
40. Rutherford Institute, et al. (18)	19
41. Hon. Christopher H. Smith, et al. (9 Senators, 44 Representatives)	1
42. Southern Center for Law and Ethics	1
43. Southwest Life and Law Center, Inc.	1
44. United States	1
45. US Catholic Conference	1
46. Austin Vaughn and Crusade for Life, Inc.	1
Totals: 85 organizations + 5 single individuals =	90

Table 2 32 briefs in support of appellees

First sponsors of amicus briefs	Total sponsors
1. American Civil Liberties Union, et al. (5)	6
2. 281 American Historians	1
3. American Jewish Congress, et al. (35)	36
4. American Library Assoc. and Freedom to Read Foundation	2
5. American Medical Assoc., et al. (7)	8
6. American Nurses Assoc. and The Nurses' Assoc. of the Amer. College of Obstet. and Gynec.	2
7. American Public Health Assoc., et al. (8 & inds.)	9
8. American Psychological Assoc.	1
9. Americans for Democratic Action, et al. (4)	5
10. Americans United for Separation of Church and State	1
11. Assoc. of Reproductive Health Professionals, et al. (7 & inds.)	8
12. Attorneys General of California, Colorado, Massachusetts, New York, Texas, and Vermont	1
13. Bioethicists for Privacy	1
14. California National Org. for Women, et al. (2 & inds.)	3
15. Canadian Women's Orgs. (4)	4
16. Catholics for a Free Choice, et al. (3 & inds.)	4
17. Center for Population Options, et al. (3)	4
18. Certain Members of the Congress of the US (25 Senators, 115 Representatives)	1
19. Committees on Civil Rights, Medicine & Law, Sex & Law of the Assoc. of the Bar of the City of New York, et al. (6)	7
20. 167 Distinguished Scientists and Physicians Including 11 Nobel Laureates	1
21. Group of American Law Professors	1
22. International Women's Health Organizations (22)	22
23. National Assoc. of Public Hospitals	1
24. National Assoc. of Women Lawyers and National Conference of Women's Bar Associates	2
25. National Coalition Against Domestic Violence	1
26. National Council of Negro Women, Inc., et al. (114 & inds.)	115
27. National Family Planning and Reproductive Health Assoc.	1
28. National Organization for Women	1
29. 77 Organizations Committed to Women's Equality	77
30. Population-Environmental Balance, et al. (6)	7
31. 608 State Legislators from 32 States	1
32. Women Who Have Had Abortions (2887) and Friends (627)	1
Totals:	335

Who filed?

Table 1 provides a list of the names of the first group or individual listed as a sponsor hereinafter called "first sponsors" for each of the amicus briefs filed on behalf of the appellants, and Table 2 lists the first sponsors of those filed on behalf of the appellees.[7] When there are two organizations jointly filing a brief, both names are listed. When there are more than two organizations, only the first sponsor is named followed by "et al." (indicating that there are other filers), followed by a number enclosed in parentheses to indicate how many. If the individuals who signed a brief were not united under an organizational title (either permanent or ad hoc), the abbreviation "ind." also appears within the parentheses. At the right of both tables is the total number of organizational sponsors for each brief.

Coalition Building. Tables 1 and 2 show that 85 organizations filed on behalf of appellants, while 335 filed on behalf of appellees. The percentage of briefs with a single sponsor was 76 percent for the appellants and 44 percent for the appellees. The number of appellants' sponsors per brief ranged from 1 to 19 (the high being the 19 branches of the Rutherford Institute), while the number of the appellees' filers per brief ranged from 1 to 115 (the high being the brief submitted by the National Council of Negro Women and 114 others). Using rough averages, appellants had 2 sponsors per brief, while appellees had 10 sponsors per brief. What these numbers suggest is that the two sides differed concerning the value of coalition building.

Clearly, the appellees acted as if the number of sponsors was more important than the number of briefs filed, while the appellants favored the strategy of filing the most briefs (46 to 32). This raises the question of which is a more effective strategy, to file as many individual briefs as possible or to gather a larger total number of cosponsoring organizations? Caldeira and Wright have observed that there "is a general absence of large coalitions of groups on individual briefs," and that this implies that those who make the decision about filing the amicus believe "it is the number of briefs, not the number of organizations listed on each brief, that impresses the justices."[8]

So why did the appellees appear to reject this general belief? There are several possible explanations: (1) the desire to save money, (2) the belief that the justices are susceptible to the democratic principle that the majority should rule, (3) the fact that only a finite number of arguments can be made, (4) a difference between multi-issue interest groups and single-issue interest groups concerning the need to file independently, and (5) adoption of a strategy that valued impact of the collection over the number of briefs filed.

First, while the amicus brief offers groups that are limited in time and resources the access to influence litigation without assuming the financial and time burdens required of a full-fledged party,[9] there is no question that even the filing of an amicus makes demands upon the organization. In Caldeira and Wright's study of the amicus briefs filed during the Court's 1982 term, the cost of preparing and filing a brief ranged from $500 to $50,000 with a mean slightly above $8,000.[10] For some groups, the cost of filing an amicus is prohibitive. Caldeira and Wright note, "The litigation budgets of most organizations are quite modest, and most do not have sufficient in-house manpower and legal expertise to prepare briefs on their own."[11] Many of the appellees' cosponsoring groups would appear to fit this profile. For them, cosponsorship allowed participation in the *Webster* case without the financial hardship involved in preparing an individual brief.

Second, the appellees seemed to act on the democratic belief that the justices would be swayed by the numbers associated with the abortion rights position. Indeed, several of their briefs resembled petitions as they included lists of individuals as sig-

natories.[12] Collectively, the appellees' briefs signaled to the Court that their position has the support of the majority of the population and that a reversal of *Roe* would place the Court in the uncomfortable position of fighting against the mainstream. However, reliance on the democratic argument also poses risks. Justices may take offense at being pressured to defer to majority rule.[13] Another risk of assembling petition briefs is that coalition building may work to limit the number of arguments presented to the Court by decreasing the number of amicus briefs.

The appellees, however, seemed to minimize both risks. While the democratic argument was implicit in the number of sponsors and signatories, this claim was not explicitly made by the appellees. Instead, appellees let the numbers speak for themselves, thereby avoiding reliance on the democratic argument while at the same time signaling to the Court in a not-so-subtle way where the majority of the population stood on the issue. The second risk was overcome by the filing of a significant number of briefs. While 14 less than the number submitted by the appellants, 32 briefs is by any measure a considerable number. Therefore, the appellees' coalitions did not come at the price of sacrificing the number of arguments presented. In sum, the appellees' strategy of garnering the support of several hundred cosponsors was intended to add weight to the already numerous briefs.

A third explanation of the appellees' coalition building is that since there is a finite number of legal arguments to be made on any issue, too many briefs lead to repetition and perhaps even work to irritate the justices. In light of charges that amicus briefs are a waste of time, "repetitious at best and emotional explosions at worst,"[14] and that a large number would increase the already heavy burden on the justices, the appellees may have opted to limit the number of briefs even though they knew that the appellants would file more.

Fourth, an examination of multi-issue interest groups versus single-issue interest groups may explain the different values appellants and appellees attributed to coalition building. Appellees' base of support was largely multi-issue interest groups while single-issue interest groups were more prevalent among the amici of the appellants. [This fact will be discussed in greater detail below.] Multi-issue interest groups enjoy more of a choice in de-

Table 3 First sponsors categorized

	Appellants*	Totals	Appellees**	Totals
Individual	3, 27, 30, 31, 34	5		0
Citizen groups	1, 6, 7, 8, 9, 11, 14, 21, 22, 24, 25, 26, 28, 29, 33, 36, 37, 38, 39, 45, 46	21	1, 3, 7, 9, 10, 14, 15, 16, 17, 22, 26, 28, 29, 30, 32	15
Professional	2, 4, 5, 13, 20	5	2, 5, 6, 8, 11, 13, 19, 20, 21, 24	10
Public interest law	15, 18, 23, 35, 40, 42, 43	7		0
Government	10, 16, 17, 32, 41, 44	6	12, 18, 31	3
Peak organizations	12	1	4, 23, 25, 27	4
Other	19	1		0
		46		32

* Numbers refer to sponsors in Table 1.
** Numbers refer to sponsors in Table 2.

termining whether or not to file an amicus brief than do single-issue interest groups. "The broader a group's political interests, the less intense its attachment to a particular interest . . . . Focus is crucial to intensity."[15] Single-issue interest groups must react when there is a direct threat to their membership's interests. Within this context, the appellants' pro-life organizations were compelled to file independent briefs. In contrast, the multi-issue interest groups of the appellees could meet internal demands through coalitional activity rather than as independent sponsors.

Finally, the appellees' amici were organized according to a strategy that favored impact over the number of briefs. Kathryn Kolbert, who worked on behalf of the American Civil Liberties Union and Planned Parenthood Federation to coordinate all of the amicus briefs, attempted to discourage duplication among the briefs and to encourage coalition building among amici with similar interests.[16] It was believed that overlapping arguments would work to "dilute the overall impact of the collection,"[17] so groups who shared interests were encouraged to form a coalition. Coalitions were organized so that each argued points most appropriate to their interests and expertise. This contrasted with appellants who appeared to strive for a large number of briefs at the expense of repetition. For example, attorney Robert L. Sassone filed six separate briefs on behalf of clients with very similar interests rather than one brief with six sponsors.[18]

Diversity. An attempt was also made to look closer at the groups who filed in order to determine the level of diversity among the first sponsors of the 78 briefs. Seven of the 14 membership categories developed by Caldeira and Wright were used to distinguish the groups: individuals, citizen-based interest groups, professional organizations (where members share the same occupation), public interest law firms or research groups, government sponsors, peak organizations (an organization consisting of groups), and other.[19] Table 3 lists the seven categories and refers to each first sponsor according to the number assigned to it in Tables 1 and 2. Table 4 compares the percentage of briefs filed by groups of each of the seven categories.

Study of Table 4 reveals that both appellants and appellees drew the most support from briefs filed by citizen-based groups, 45.7 percent and 46.8 percent, respectively. Of all seven categories employed, the citizen-based groups category contains the most diversity in ideology, membership numbers, prestige, goals, and resources. For instance, The American Civil Liberties Union, Population-Environmental Balance, American Life League, and Agudeth Israel of America are all classified as citizen-based groups.

Next in order of frequency for the appellants were briefs filed by: public interest law firms (15.2 percent), government sponsors (13 percent), professional groups and individuals (both with 10.9 percent), then peak organizations, and other (both with 2.2 percent). Appellees had no briefs filed by individuals, public interest law firms or other. After the citizen-based groups, the order of frequency were briefs filed by: professional groups (31.3 percent), peak organizations (12.5 percent), and government sponsors (9.4 percent).

One drawback of the seven divisions is that they hide three types of groups relevant to the abortion controversy—the religious groups associated with the pro-life position, the feminist groups aligned with the pro-choice cause, and the single-issue interest groups present in both movements.[20] To remedy this problem, Table 5 was constructed to identify these three types of groups. While these three categories are not mutually exclusive, they

Table 4 First sponsors percentages

	Appellants	Appellees	Totals
Individual	5 (10.9%)	0 (0%)	6.4%
Citizen groups	21 (45.7%)	15 (46.9%)	46.2
Professional	5 (10.9%)	10 (31.3%)	19.2
Public interest law	7 (15.2%)	0 (0%)	9
Government	6 (13.0%)	3 (9.4%)	11.5
Peak organizations	1 (2.2%)	4 (12.5%)	6.4
Other	1 (2.2%)	0 (0%)	1.3
	46 (100.1%)*	32 (100.1%)*	78 (100.0%)

* Figure over 100% due to rounding.

reveal some interesting trends concerning the nature of the groups who participated as amici on both sides of *Webster*.

Table 5 confirms some expectations concerning the role feminist and religious groups play in each movement. The appellants drew great support from religiously oriented groups (16 sponsors), but also drew support from one feminist sponsor (Feminists for Life). There were nine feminist sponsors for the appellee side, but also two from religious groups. Altogether, these 28 religious and feminist sponsors account for only about 36 percent of the amicus briefs filed. Clearly, the abortion issue was of great concern to organizations whose memberships did not fit either description.

Indeed, as Table 5 reveals, single-issue interest groups played an important role in this case. In order to study the abortion issue here, a single-issue interest group is defined as an organization that is formed to advocate a position on the abortion rights question. While it is admittedly arguable whether a pro-life group has an agenda that is broader than the abortion issue, or whether NOW is more a single-issue than a multi-issue interest group, an initial appraisal of the groups indicates that about 70 percent of the first sponsors on behalf of the appellants were single-issue interest groups, while about 40 percent of the appellees' first sponsors were single-issue interest groups. When these single-issue interest groups are compared, it becomes evident that there was a difference in the nature of the permanency of the groups. Appellants drew support from permanent single-issue organizations, while appellees' single-issue organizations tended to be ad hoc groups of professional individuals or peak organizations.

Some tentative conclusions can be drawn from this information concerning the nature of the two movements. Overall, the appellants' amici appear to be more singular in purpose. The public inter-

est law firms, the individuals, the governmental coalitions, and even the professional groups were united in that most were specifically formed either to oppose abortion rights or already had religious tenets supportive of such a political posture. With the exception of the government coalitions, these were permanent groups. In contrast, the appellees relied heavily on the support of professional groups with multiple interests, five of which were ad hoc organizations formed in order to file a brief. These observations suggest that the appellants had a more single-mindedly committed and more permanent group of amici, while the appellees relied on the support of amici who joined together temporarily and who distributed their resources over a range of issues. The question of whether diversity or homogeneity translated into unity will be examined below.

In sum, the question of who filed these 78 briefs has revealed differences in coalition building and a diversity of interests among the sponsoring groups. It is expected that these organizations employed an assortment of strategies as well as provided the Court with a variety of information. The next question to be examined, therefore, is what was argued in the briefs. Did the diversity among the sponsors translate into a richness of resources for the Court?

What was argued?

Both Webster and the Reproductive Health Services had to launch an offensive campaign while maintaining a defensive posture. The appellants had to defend the Missouri statute while attacking the legal doctrines set down in *Roe*. The appellees guarded *Roe* as precedent while they took aim at the restrictive law. The strategies of the sides and the roles left to the amicus briefs are best informed by an examination of the party briefs. The party briefs carry the burden of presenting the legal arguments for the litigants and, therefore, form a good basis for comparison of the two sides as well as the 78 amicus briefs.

The appellants' brief first summarized the case and then opened its argument by attacking *Roe*, criticizing the "viability" dividing point as arbitrary and calling for the Court to overrule *Roe*. This offensive took only four pages. The rest of the party brief, approximately 28 pages, was a point-by-point defense of the Missouri law. In contrast, the appellees' brief, which omitted a reconstruction

Table 5 Special interests of first sponsors

Totals	Appellants*	Totals	Appellees**	Totals
Feminist	21	1/46	14, 15, 22, 24, 25, 26, 28, 29, 32	9/32
Religious	1, 6, 7, 9, 12, 13, 14, 18, 22, 24, 28, 29, 33, 37, 45, 46	16/46	3, 16	2/32
Single-issue	2, 3, 4, 5, 6, 7, 8, 9, 10, 11, 14, 16, 17, 20, 21, 22, 23, 25, 26, 27, 30, 31, 32, 34, 36, 37, 38, 39, 40, 41, 43, 46	32/46	2, 12, 13, 15, 16, 18, 20, 21, 22, 27, 29, 31, 32	13/32

* Numbers refer to sponsors in Table 1.
** Numbers refer to sponsors in Table 2.

of the case, began by defending *Roe* as a fundamental constitutional right and supporting the viability concept as both legally and medically sound. This defense occupied 17 pages. The next 32 pages challenged the Missouri law section by section. For both sides, then, *Roe* was of primary concern. It was only once this precedent was either challenged or defended that a discussion of the state law could begin.

Arguments. Turning to the amicus briefs and referring to the "List of amici arguments," pages 202-203, it can be seen that when the major arguments for the amici are compared, a point and counterpoint pattern emerges. There were six main points of contention concerning *Roe*: (1) fetal vs. women's rights, (2) if a constitutional basis for a right to abortion exists, (3) whether the trimester scheme is of utility, (4) how abortion fits within the context of American history and tradition, (5) the applicability of the doctrine of *stare decisis*, and (6) the consequences of overturning or following *Roe* as precedent. There were also six main disputes regarding the Missouri statute: (1) whether the state had the power to restrict abortion through its democratic process, or whether the Court must act to prevent the violation of constitutional rights, (2) the rational basis test vs. strict scrutiny as the appropriate standard of review, (3) if the statute's preamble was prefatory or of substance, (4) the constitutionality (or mootness) of the ban on funding abortion counseling, (5) the constitutionality of the ban on abortions in public facilities, and (6) the constitutionality of the viability tests requirement.

Amid the noise of these debated issues, silence is also instructive. Some of the arguments presented by the amici were not present in the party briefs. Referring again to the "List of arguments," a "*" sign indicates those arguments that were employed by both the party brief and at least one amicus. Therefore, absent from the appellants'

party brief were arguments that: fetuses are constitutionally protected persons; abortion has harmful effects on women and on society; the law would not involve criminal prosecutions; and the states are better suited than the courts to decide such a politically charged issue. On the appellee side, there was a greater overlap between the party and amicus briefs. Only two major points made by amici were not present in the party brief: the freedom of religion argument and an examination of the consequences of a *Roe* reversal. The latter, nonlegal point constituted an important focus for many of the appellee amicus briefs.

Strategies. The differences between party and amicus argumentation suggest that appellants and appellees adopted different strategies. Once again the 4-1-4 Court configuration must be appreciated. Litigants had to hold together their four-person coalition while vying for O'Connor's vote. The two sides divided the workload in different ways. O'Connor appears to be the main target of the appellants' party brief while appellees seem to make a bid for her vote through the filing of amicus briefs which focus on her central concerns.

The appellants' party brief is striking in its avoidance of any "pro-life" rhetoric or argumentation. It carefully sidesteps any discussion of the rights of the "preborn," the sacredness of human life, or the uncertain basis for the right to privacy (discussing it in terms of a liberty interest instead). The party brief challenges Roe in terms that would most appeal to O'Connor. It questions the textual, historical, and doctrinal basis of *Roe* and challenges the trimester approach by citing O'Connor's dissent in *Akron v. Akron Center for Reproductive Health*.[21] The brief also argues that should the Court uphold *Roe*, then it should apply the "undue burden" test (favored by O'Connor) to uphold the Missouri regulations. This moderate approach, then, appears to be crafted for O'Connor. However, this strategy was not universally applied as some of the amici did include language and claims from the pro-life movement.[22] The more controversial arguments on behalf of fetal rights and a ban on abortion were voiced not by the parties but by the amici. It was the amici who urged Rehnquist, White, Scalia, and Kennedy to go further than the party brief suggested and to make abortions illegal by recognizing constitutionally protected fetal rights.

The division of labor helps to explain why the appellant briefs, sponsored by organizations more homogeneous than those of the appellees, had more conflicts, inconsistencies, and contradictions. One trouble undoubtedly arose from the fact that the party brief appeared willing to "give" on two important points within the abortion debate. First, it did not call for a total ban on abortion, instead arguing that should the Court overturn *Roe*, the law should once again allow the states to determine abortion policy (presumably either way). Second, it did not assert that a fetus is a constitutionally protected person. Since these were concessions that not all the 46 amici could accept, why would the parties risk such conflict? Again, the answer seems to be the effort to capture O'Connor's vote while hoping that the arguments presented by the amici might persuade all five justices to recognize

---

List of amici arguments

Roe: offense and defense

Issue 1: Rights

Appellants: The preborn are constitutionally protected persons under the 14th Amendment. This fact is supported by scientific data which shows that life begins at conception. The Court has erred before in denying personhood to blacks and American Indians.

*Appellees: Medical evidence is not clear when life begins. Constitutional rights are only bestowed upon live birth. Therefore, there is no comparison between the history of slaves and Indians, and the rights of fetuses. To rule otherwise will threaten not only abortion, but birth control methods as well.

Issue 2: The Constitution

Appellants: *Roe* lacks a sound constitutional basis. The right to privacy was a judicial construct, and there is no constitutional right to abortion.

*Appellees: The constitutional right to privacy is fundamental and includes the right to abortion. This right is supported by the 14th's liberty guarantee as well as the concept of equality.

Issue 3: The Trimester Scheme

*Appellants: *Roe's* trimester scheme is arbitrary, incoherent, and unworkable. Due to medical technology, the viability point shifts and is too uncertain to serve as a marker for dividing the second from the third trimester.

*Appellees: Viability is a reliable cutoff point between the second and third trimesters. Medical technology has not caused the point to shift.

Issue 4: History

*Appellants: A right must be supported by the nation's history and tradition. Abortion conflicts with the American tradition in that it was restricted by the states throughout most of American history.

*Appellees: American history demonstrates an acceptance of abortion until the 1820s. Then, restrictions were for the sake of the mother's health, not to protect the fetus.

Issue 5: Stare Decisis

*Appellants: Because *Roe* is a Court created error, *stare decisis* should not stand in the Court's way in overruling this precedent.

*Appellees: *Stare decisis* requires adherence to the *Roe* precedent.

Issue 6: Consequences

Appellants: Overturning *Roe* will not lead to criminal prosecutions. It will, however, end the exploitation of women at the hands of abortionists and will prevent women from the harmful physical and emotional effects of having had an abortion.

Appellees: Overturning *Roe* will have dire consequences for women's rights, with a disproportionate impact on the lives of the poor, teenagers, and women of color. Ending abortion rights would be a violation of the 13th Amendment's prohibition on servitude. Legalized abortion is safe, and there is no evidence of harmful psychological impact. Illegal abortions will force women to obtain abortions from backalley butchers. A reversal of *Roe* has international consequences for population control.

The Missouri Statute: offense and defense

Issue 1: States' Rights vs. Constitutional Rights

*Appellants: The states are the appropriate forum for resolving political issues. The majority

fetal rights.

In contrast, the appellees appeared to assign the amici the task of capturing O'Connor's vote. There were at least two routes to her. One was to challenge O'Connor to use her test of whether the abortion restrictions in question posed an "undue burden" on women exercising their constitutional right.[23] The amicus briefs presented her with technical information regarding the dire impact of a *Roe* reversal. In fact, the brief from the National Council of Negro Women, citing the disproportionate impact on women of color, the poor, and the young, was crafted especially for O'Connor and

her test.[24] A second strategy was to challenge her statement in *Akron* that *Roe* is "on a collision course with itself."[25] O'Connor had used scientific sources to conclude that the point of "viability" would shift forward as medical technology improved. The Brief by 167 Scientists and Physicians not only refuted her argument, but included the signatures of some of the authors on whom she had relied in *Akron*.[26]

What may seem surprising is that the more diverse appellee side produced the more internally consistent argument. This can be explained in two ways. First, the parties and all the amici were aware

should rule in these issues, not the undemocratic Court. The states retain powers under the 9th and 10th Amendments to protect their citizens from harm.

*Appellees: When rights are violated, the Court has a duty to step in and void the offending state law. Rights are not subject to majority rule. The state of Missouri's law violates the constitutionally protected rights of privacy, speech [and religion— amici only].

Issue 2: Standard of Review

*Appellants: The Court should use the rational basis test in evaluating the Missouri law. This level of scrutiny is appropriate since no fundamental right is at stake and in order to protect the state's rights.

*Appellees: Strict scrutiny is required in evaluating this statute since it threatens fundamental rights. Rights cannot be balanced, they must be protected.

Issue 3: The Preamble

*Appellants: The preamble should be allowed to stand since it is a prefatory statement without legal effect.

*Appellees: The preamble should be struck down since it contradicts *Roe*, violates the Missouri Constitution, and will be used as a guide to interpreting the statute.

Issue 4: Ban on Funding Abortion Counseling

*Appellants: This section does not obstruct privacy rights. Neither is it vague nor a violation of the 1st Amendment. There is no obligation to subsidize constitutional rights.

*Appellees: There is no longer a case or con-

troversy regarding the public funds provision. The state has not contested the District Court's ruling declaring these restrictions unconstitutional. If there is a case or controversy, then the provision is unconstitutional.

Issue 5: Ban on Abortions in Public Facilities

*Appellants: This restriction does not constitute an undue burden on the woman in obtaining an abortion. The Court held in *Poelker v. Doe* (1977) that a public hospital is not obliged to provide abortion services.

*Appellees: This provision goes beyond the restrictions upheld in *Poelker* as it bans the performance of abortions in public hospitals even when no public funds or public employees are involved. It therefore unconstitutionally interferes with wholly private medical treatment.

Issue 6: Viability Testing

*Appellants: The state has a compelling interest in determining viability in order to exert its power to protect fetal life. The *Colautti v. Franklin* (1979) precedent does not apply here since not one but three factors are used to determine viability. The law does not require that all three tests be performed, but that the physician performs such tests as are necessary to make the viability determination.

*Appellees: Under any standard of review, the viability testing is unconstitutional. The required tests are expensive and dangerous and of little use in determining viability until the 28th week. The law should be read to indicate that the three tests are required in order to make specific findings regarding viability.

of how the Court had already chipped away at the right to abortion. All understood that there was no room for concessions without jeopardizing the right itself. Second, this consistency was yet another payoff of organization and coalition building. Kathryn Kolbert, the coordinator of the briefs, helped groups identify what was at issue in *Webster* and how they could best contribute to the case.[27] What emerged was a collection of evidence startling in its singularity of purpose.

Roles. While it is difficult to accurately assess the roles adopted by each interest group, the amici do appear to serve three general purposes.[28] First, there are the endorsement briefs that either repeat the party's position or offer a variation. These briefs may recount all the party's arguments or may center and expand on one point alone. Second are the technical briefs that offer the Court specialized knowledge that is predominantly nonlegalistic in nature. Third are the risk takers. These briefs range from those who undertake an unconventional legal argument to those who shun the legal elements of the case in favor of an emotional appeal. Among the *Webster* briefs, all three types of briefs were present on each side. Some examples illustrate the different roles and strategies that amici can assume.

The endorsement briefs allow interest groups to throw their prestige behind a party. While these briefs are often repetitive, Barker argues that "this very repetition reflects the 'group combat' flavor of the briefs."[29] This was true with the briefs on behalf of appellants filed by the United States, National Right to Life Association, and the Center for Judicial Studies and on behalf of appellees filed by Members of Congress, NOW, and 77 Organizations Committed to Women's Equality. These briefs presented legal arguments already present in the party briefs, although they usually focused on one element and expanded on it.

The technical briefs concentrated on providing information concerning history and medical science. Many focused on the questions of whether abortion is a part of the American social tradition, how the medical and social sciences contribute to our understanding of fetal life, and what impact legal versus illegal abortion has on women. For the appellants, the Association for Public Justice and Certain American State Legislators argued against abortion being an acceptable part of American society. Briefs filed by the American Association of Pro-life Obstetricians and Gynecologists, Doc-

tors for Life, Paul Marx, and Bernard Nathanson argued that the "preborn" are persons. For the appellees, refutations of these arguments were offered by 281 American Historians, the American Medical Association, 167 Distinguished Scientists, and the Association of Reproductive Health Professionals. The National Council of Negro Women (with 114 other groups) offered both statistical and anecdotal information illustrating the disproportionately severe impact that a reversal of *Roe* would have on poor women and women of color.

The risk takers offered the most unusual arguments. On the appellants' side, the Free Speech Advocates took a confrontational approach, arguing that the abortion cases were "shams" and that the Court "has grown to accept fawning over all its errors."[30] James Joseph Lynch, Jr. contradicted the party brief's assurance that preambles are without legal effect by asserting that the fetus is protected by the reference to "posterity" made in the United States Constitution's preamble. Agudeth Israel also challenged the party line by insisting that the Missouri preamble be struck down as a violation of religious freedom. American Collegians adopted an argument sometimes used by abortion rights advocates that the Ninth and Tenth Amendments are substantive in that they reserve rights that are not listed in the Constitution's text to the states and citizens. Birthright admitted that its brief contained "very little legal precedent," and instead relied on "logic, common sense, reasoning, intelligence, and conclusions in accord with what is best for all the people of this nation."[31]

The risk takers on behalf of the appellees argued that there was a right to be free from government imposed harm to health (American Public Health Association), that a denial of abortion rights would violate the equal protection clause (National Coalition against Domestic Violence), and that religious freedom demanded that women be free to choose (Catholics for a Free Choice). An emotional appeal made by Women Who Have Had Abortions took the form of a petition-like brief containing letters of testimony.

This survey of the three types of amici suggests that certain types of groups tend to gravitate to a specific amicus role. The most obvious connection is that between professional organizations and technical briefs. A professional organization has the knowledge and expertise necessary to provide the Court with information outside of the legal

Table 6 Briefs cited by the justices

	Majority			Minority		
	Rehnquist	O'Connor	Scalia	Blackmun	Stevens	Total
Appellants' brief	4	—	—	—	2	6
Agudeth Israel	—	—	—	—	1	1
American Assoc. of Pro-Life Obstetricians	—	3	—	—	—	3
Holy Orthodox Church	—	—	—	—	2	2
Lutheran Church	—	—	—	—	2	2
Missouri Catholic Conference	—	—	—	—	1	1
United States	1	—	—	2	—	3
subtotals	5	3	—	2	8	18
Appellees' brief	5	3	—	—	—	8
American Medical Association	—	2	—	2	—	4
Americans United for Separation of Church & State	—	—	—	—	2	2
Association of Reproductive Health Professionals	—	1	—	1	4	6
Catholics for a Free Choice	—	—	—	—	2	2
Group of American Law Profs.	—	—	—	1	—	1
National Association of Public Hospitals	—	1	—	1	—	2
subtotals	5	7	—	5	8	25
total amici alone	1	7	—	7	14	29
total briefs	10	10	—	7	16	43

realm. There also seems to be a relationship between single-issue interest groups and the role of risk taker. Since these groups enjoy a unified constituency that is devoted to promoting a particular issue, these groups may have more freedom in speaking from a perspective outside the mainstream. They can assume a challenging voice without losing their constituents. The endorsement briefs are sponsored by a variety of groups, but tend to gain the support of multi-issue interest groups. These groups tend to have less of a stake in the interest at issue, and they have to hold together a diversified constituency. Multi-issue interest groups can satisfy organizational demands by merely endorsing the party brief.

This analysis would explain why the appellants had more amici act as risk takers while the appellees had more amici submit technical briefs. Since single-issue interest groups were more prevalent among appellants' amici, it could be expected that appellants would have more amici who assumed the role of risk taker. In contrast, since professional organizations were three-to-one behind the appellees, it was predictable that this side would submit more technical briefs.

Together these three types of briefs offered the Court not only an abundance of information concerning abortion, but a sense of the urgency and complexity of this political issue as well. The Court saw briefs which towed the party line, others which offered specialized information, and still others that challenged the Court to break new legal ground. While many perspectives were present, the next question is how many were heard?

What impact?

While the main purpose of an amicus brief is to persuade the Court to rule on behalf of a particular litigant, the impact of amici is not limited to this result alone. Interest groups may also claim success if the Court adopts the language or perspective of the brief, or if the litigant's argument is strengthened by the endorsement of the amicus.[32] In filing an amicus, an interest group may gain publicity, an opportunity to refine and articulate its position, and experience in the judicial system.[33] Such third-party involvement also allows groups to feel as though they have participated in the decisional process.[34] Some of the impact of amici may not be apparent until future cases emerge which reflect the information, argument, or concerns of the earlier amici.

Impact is of course most readily identifiable in terms of the winners and losers of a case. However, such an approach is obviously limited for a case like *Webster* where the Court lineup was 4-1-4 from the start. With this in mind, the discussion here will also include a content analysis of which briefs were cited by the justices in the decision, and a study of how some of the arguments made by the amici seemed to sway certain justices.

In a 5-4 vote with two concurrences and two dissenting opinions, the *Webster* decision upheld the sections restricting public employees and facilities from performing or assisting in abortions, and the sections requiring viability testing. While the Court did not rule on the constitutionality of the statute's preamble, it declared the counseling section moot. In the course of deciding these issues, the Court also began to dismantle the principles of *Roe*, the trimester scheme in particular. Chief Justice William Rehnquist, with Justices Byron White and Anthony Kennedy, attacked the "rigid trimester analysis" as inconsistent with the Constitution.[35] He argued, "We do not see why the State's interest in protecting human life should come into existence only at the point of viability . . . ."[36] Justice Antonin Scalia concurred stating that Rehnquist's argument would effectively overrule *Roe*, but that he would do so more explicitly.[37] Justice Sandra Day O'Connor agreed with the constitutionality of the Missouri statute, but not with the need to unravel *Roe*. She relied instead on *Roe* and its progeny to uphold the Missouri law.[38] The four dissenting justices, Harry Blackmun, William Brennan, Thurgood Marshall, and John Paul Stevens, would have used *Roe* to void the Missouri statute.

Therefore, when speaking strictly in terms of win versus lose, the appellants emerged as the victors in this case. The Missouri law was upheld, the Court signaled its willingness to uphold restrictive state abortion policies, and four justices indicated a willingness to overturn *Roe*. Within these terms, appellees could claim only that *Roe* survived—for now. Yet, measuring impact in this way assumes that the win is due to arguments set forth by amici. It also ignores the fact that amici on the losing side have impact as well. Therefore, it is important to consider as well two other indicators: the amici cited by the Court, and evidence that the Court accepted arguments advanced only by the amici.

The counting of citations demonstrates that the justices considered the arguments set forth by the amici.[39] This is not to say, of course, that the only briefs which had impact were the ones cited, but the data is useful as a "blunt indicator" of how the Court used the briefs.[40] Table 6 presents the results of counting each direct reference to a brief made by one of the five justices who wrote an opinion in the *Webster* case. References to the appellants' party briefs totaled six while the appellees' party briefs were cited eight times. Excluding party briefs, amicus briefs were cited 29 times. Twelve different amicus briefs, six from each side, were cited at least once. Appellants' amici were cited 12 times while appellees' amici were cited 17 times. The amicus briefs cited tended to be those that contained either religious arguments or which provided technical information on medicine or on the law. Besides the direct references to the am-

icus briefs, Justices Blackmun and Stevens together cited seven different published articles: three which were largely scientific, two commenting on religious issues, one on the impact of illegal abortions, and one on the law.

Rehnquist, writing for the majority, cited the appellants' brief four times and the appellees' brief five times. The only amicus to which he referred was that of the United States. In O'Connor's concurring opinion, she cited the appellees' brief three times, and referred to the four amicus briefs containing medical and scientific information, again indicating her struggle with the viability issue. Scalia's concurrence made no direct references to briefs or outside sources. The dissents of Justices Blackmun and Stevens did not cite the party briefs of either side. These justices referred instead to the amicus briefs for a total of 29 citations. As with O'Connor, most of Blackmun's references came from the technical medical briefs. In contrast, Stevens cited mostly the religiously oriented briefs.

Yet, briefs can be cited and then rejected. Did the briefs have any real influence on the justices in constructing their decision? It is suggested that the answer is yes. Consider again the role of the amici. The appellants' amici seemed to urge their coalition of four justices to overturn *Roe*. The appellees' amici appeared to focus on convincing O'Connor to cast the fifth vote to protect Roe. The amici on both sides enjoyed some success.

The victory enjoyed by the appellants was not of the parties' making alone. The Court went further than the parties had urged, surging ahead on the path marked by the appellants' amici. When the Court accepts an argument that was advanced only by an amicus brief, it is an indication of influence.[41] Again, the party brief had devoted only four pages to challenging *Roe* and the viability point. It was instead the amici who supplied both the technical and legal information which subverted the *Roe* trimester scheme.

There are signs that the appellees' amici had influence as well. Again, their target was O'Connor and the two routes to her were to have her apply her "undue burden" test to strike down the Missouri statute, and to have her retreat from her criticism of *Roe's* trimester scheme. While the amici were unsuccessful concerning the first point, there are signs that they made some progress concerning the second.

It is not what O'Connor's *Webster* opinion says but what it does not say that is important.[42] Considering her *Akron* dissent in which she argued that the trimester approach was "completely unworkable"[43] and on a "collision course with itself,"[44] and that she adhered to this position three years later in *Thornburgh v. American College of Obstetricians and Gynecologists*,[45] it is curious that in *Webster*— a case that brings the viability issue to the forefront and causes four other justices to voice concerns that the trimester framework is indeed unworkable—O'Connor remarks only that she continues to regard the trimester approach as "problematic."[46] She cites her *Akron* dissent not to repudiate the trimester scheme, but to illustrate how to apply the "undue burden" test. If indeed O'Connor is retreating from her *Akron* critique, the appellees' amici may be responsible for planting the seed of doubt in her mind.

Conclusion

The 78 *Webster* amici produced an uncomparable collection of information on the abortion rights issue. While *Webster* is certainly not a typical case, nor was the response of interest groups usual, it does serve to magnify the amicus curiae role. Interest groups can lobby the Court concerning an issue even as politicized as abortion if they enter the Court through the open door extended to amici. In working to present their arguments before the Court, the pro-life and pro-choice movements also revealed something about themselves. The briefs reflected the composition of their constituencies, their legal strategies, and their core values. The study of amici, then, is not only instructive for court watching but for monitoring interest group politics as well.

The writing and organization of 78 briefs was a monumental undertaking, but it was not a wasted effort. It appears that the amici on both sides made inroads with the Court. The briefs were not only read; they also had impact. Their arguments and information helped to shape the terms of the Court debate. Whether the justices refuted the briefs, modified an argument because of them, or accepted and integrated their points, the amici mattered. Through the presentation of the briefs, the battle over abortion rights was waged before the Court. It is no surprise, then, that in the midst of this friendly fire, some of the justices were struck.

NOTES

This article originally appeared in Volume 74, Number 5, February-March 1991, pages 261-270.

I would like to thank Lee Epstein and Gregory Caldeira for sharing their research and ideas, and the anonymous reviewer who provided a list of insightful comments. Special thanks to Catherine Bell Fleming of the National Abortion Rights Action League for providing me with all the appellees' amicus briefs.

An earlier version of this article was presented at the Annual Meeting of the Northeastern Political Science Association, Philadelphia, PA, November 9-11, 1989.

1. 492 U.S. __; 109 S.Ct. 3040 (1989).

2. 438 U.S. 265 (1978).

3. 410 U.S. 113 (1973).

4. 109 S.Ct. 3040, 3041 (1989).

5. *Id.*, at 3047.

6. While I have framed the controversy in terms of abortion rights, throughout this article I refer to the two movements as "pro-life" and "pro-choice." While these labels cloud the actual legal issue, they represent not only how the popular media refer to the movements but also how the movements refer to themselves.

7. While focusing on the first sponsor may not accurately reflect the organization that assumed the bulk of the legal work, it usually illustrates the character and role of the brief. For example, although the Center for Constitutional Rights constructed the brief for which the National Council of Negro Women appears as the first sponsor, the NCNW is representative of the nature of the brief since it speaks of the impact that restrictive abortion policy will have on women of color.

8. Caldeira and Wright, *Amici Curiae Before the Supreme Court: Who Participates, When and How Much?*, Forthcoming 18 J. POL. (1990).

9. O'Connor and Epstein, *Amicus Curiae Participation in U.S. Supreme Court Litigation: An Appraisal of Hakman's 'Folklore'*, 16 LAW & SOC'Y REV. 313 (1981-82).

10. Caldeira and Wright, "Why Organized Interests Participate as Amici Curiae in the U.S. Supreme Court," paper presented at the 1989 Annual Meeting of the American Political Science Association, Atlanta, Georgia, page 11.

11. *Id.*

12. *See*, Brief for Women Who Have Had Abortions (2887 signatures and 627 signatures of friends); Brief for 608 State Legislators from 32 States; Brief for Group of American Law Professors (885 signatures); 281 American Historians; Brief for 167 Distinguished Scientists and Physicians; Brief for Certain Members of the Congress of the United States; Brief for Catholics for a Free Choice; Brief for Bioethicists for Privacy.

13. In fact, Justice Scalia's *Webster* opinion did object to the belief of interest groups that unelected and life-tenured justices should weigh popular opinion. *See*, Scalia's dissent at 3065-66.

14. Harper and Etherington, *Lobbyists Before the Court*, 101 U. PA L. REV. 1172 (1953).

15. Kobylka, *A Court-Created Contest for Group Litigation: Libertarian Groups and Obscenity*, 49 J. POL. 1073 (1987).

16. Telephone interview with Kathryn Kolbert, attorney-consultant to the ACLU Reproductive Freedom Project, November 30, 1990; Kolbert, *Webster v. Reproductive Health Services: Reproductive Freedom Hanging by a Thread*, 11 WOMEN'S RIGHTS L. REP. 153, 156 (1989).

17. Kolbert, *supra* n. 16, at 157.

18. Brief for Edward Allen, Brief for Human Life International, Brief for Paul Marx, Brief for Bernard Nathanson, Brief for Right to Life League of Southern California, and Brief for Austin Vaughn and Crusade for Life, Inc.

19. Caldeira and Wright, *supra* n. 5.

20. Alternative typologies were considered and rejected. Dividing the groups according to their purpose (governmental, religious, advocate, and multi-interest) did not provide enough detail to gain a sense of the diversity among the groups. More substantive divisions, such as religious, medical, feminist, and academic, did not provide mutually exclusive categories. An ideological divide of liberal versus conservative would essentially divide the amici into the already existing appellant versus appellee lineup. *See*, O'Connor and Epstein, *The Rise of Conservative Interest Group Litigation*, 45 J. POL. 479-489 (1983). O'Neill's typology of oligarchic, democratic, and managerial groups was designed more to study the structures of the groups themselves than the nature of Court politics. *See* O'Neill, BAKKE AND THE POLITICS OF EQUALITY: FRIENDS AND FOES IN THE CLASSROOM OF LITIGATION (Middletown, CT: Wesleyan University Press, 1985). Bradley and Gardner's underdog versus upperdog distinction provides only two divisions and appears to be designed for studying diverse cases over a period of time. *See*, Bradley and Gardner, *Underdogs, Upperdogs and the Use of the Amicus Brief: Trends and Explanations*, 10 JUST. SYS. J. 78-96, (1985).

21. 462 U.S. 416, 452 (1983).

22. *See*, Brief for Alabama Lawyers for Unborn Children, Inc.; Brief for Edward Allen; Brief for Attorneys General from Five States; Brief for Catholics United for Life; Brief for Alan Ernest; Brief for Free Speech Advocates; Brief for The Holy Orthodox Church; Brief for Human Life International; Brief for International Right to Life Federation; Brief for Larry Joyce; Brief for the Knights of Columbus; Brief for James Joseph Lynch, Jr.; Brief for Paul Marx; Brief for Bernard Nathanson; Brief for the Right to Life League of Southern California; Brief for the Southwest Life and Law Center, Inc.; Brief for Austin Vaughn and Crusade for Life, Inc.

23. *See*, Akron, *supra* n. 21, at 453.

24. Kolbert, *supra* n. 16.

25. Akron, *supra* n. 21, at 458.

26. Kolbert, *supra* n. 16.

27. *Id.*

28. Krislov, *The Amicus Brief: From Friendship to Advocacy*, 72 YALE L. J. 694-721, (1963).

29. Barker, *Third Parties in Litigation: A Systemic View of the Judicial Function*, 29 J. POL. 62, (1967).

30. Brief for Free Speech Advocates, at 6, 23.

31. Brief for Birthright, at 17.

32. O'Connor, WOMEN'S ORGANIZATIONS' USE OF THE COURTS 146 (Lexington, MA: Lexington Books, 1980).

33. *Id.*

34. Krislov, *supra* n. 28, at 721.

35. Webster, *supra* n. 1, at 3056.

36. *Id.* at 3057.

37. *Id.* at 3064.

38. *Id.* at 3060.

39. Angell, *The Amicus Curiae: American Development of English Institutions*, 16 INT'L & COMP. L. Q. 1036-1044 (1967).

40. O'Connor and Epstein, *Court Rules and Workload: A Case Study of Rules Governing Amicus Curiae Participation*, 8 JUS. SYS. J. 43 (1983).

41. Angell, *supra* n. 39, at 1036.

42. This point was brought to my attention by Kathryn Kolbert; interview, *supra* n. 16.

43. Akron, *supra* n. 21, at 454.

44. *Id.* at 458.

45. 476 U.S. 747, at 814 (1986).

46. Webster, *supra* n. 1, at 3063.

Nonlegal advice: The amicus briefs in *Webster v. Reproductive Health Services*

Although justices rely on their own knowledge of case law and legal precedent, they are likely to accept and incorporate the views of amici on nonlegal issues.

by Jack E. Rossotti, Laura Natelson, and Raymond Tatalovich

During the past decade the study of group litigation has increased substantially, but researchers "have not fully explored the kinds of tactics groups use to influence judicial decisions once they decide to sponsor a case or participate as amicus curiae."[1]

What is needed are answers to questions such as:

• Do amici seek to influence judicial decision-making through the use of one-sided nonlegal information?

• Do amici rely more heavily on nonlegal than legal information?

• Is the information supplied by amici most one-sided when it is from nonlegal sources?

• Do amici manipulate legal precedent to strategically promote their ideological agenda?

• Are Supreme Court justices more likely to accept and incorporate the views of amici on nonlegal rather than legal sources?

Previous research on amicus activity has focused on the *legal* strategies by interest groups at various stages and levels of the judicial process, the frequency of group litigation and the coalition-building process among interests, and the issues that encourage groups to file amicus briefs. But quantitative methods have not been applied to studying how amici utilize *nonlegal* information to influence judicial decision making. For example, previous scholarship on the briefs filed in *Webster v. Reproductive Health Services* relied on textual or qualitative examination,[2] not content analysis.

Webster, decided in 1989, provides a particularly useful case study of amici activity since it prompted the largest number of amicus briefs ever submitted in a single case before the Supreme Court.[3] Unlike the prior record in *Regents of the University of California v. Bakke,*[4] the 1978 case involving affirmative action, the range of interests in *Webster* was much larger.[5] *Webster* also was a defining moment for pro-choice groups as the prospects of an adverse Supreme Court decision prompted an outpouring of amici among women's advocacy organizations. *Webster* was widely perceived in lay and legal publications[6] as having the potential to reverse or fundamentally redirect *Roe v. Wade,* the 1973 case that established the precedent of a woman's constitutional right to an abortion during the pre-viability stage of a pregnancy. The outcome of *Webster,* moreover, was uniformly judged by feminist legal scholars as opening the door to further state regulations and undercutting a woman's right to abortion.[7]

Methodology

All sources to legal and nonlegal authorities and the frequency of citations to those sources in the 78 amicus curiae briefs filed in *Webster* were grouped into four broad categories—legal, medical, religious, and other (such as historical). This permitted drawing conclusions about the use of legal and nonlegal sources by the amici.

In addition, the three most important abortion decisions prior to *Webster*—*Roe, City of Akron v. Akron Center for Reproductive Health, Inc.,* (1983), and *Thornburgh v. American College of Obstetricians and Gynecologists* (1986)—were used to illustrate how the amici offered one-sided interpretations of those precedents to influence the Court. Citations to *Roe, Akron,* or *Thornburgh* were classified as to whether they referenced the majority, concurring, or dissenting opinions and then, for each citation, its ideological direction: pro-regulation, anti-regulation, or neutral (meaning the source was used for informational purposes or indicated no ideological position). Finally, to examine whether the arguments of amici influenced any of the five written opinions in *Webster,* all direct references to the amicus briefs were categorized based on whether the justice agreed with, modified, or rejected the argument put forth by the amici.

Sources cited

Nearly all (92 percent) of the sources cited by the 78 amici in *Webster* were used only by pro-life or pro-choice advocates, not both, meaning that they were selectively chosen to defend a particular viewpoint. (See Table 1.) The remaining 8 percent of sources were used by both sides. However, these two-sided references accounted for 43 percent of the total citations. The 247 sources used by both parties cited an average of 14 times each. For three categories of legal references (cases, statutes, other), barely more (11 percent) two-sided references were used. But 97 percent of non-legal references (medical, religious, other) were one-sided.

The distribution of nonlegal citations is even more skewed. Only 1 percent of the cites to nonlegal authorities were made by both pro-life and pro-choice amici. Activists who lobby the Supreme Court are more likely to make distinct arguments based on nonlegal evidence than where legal sources are involved. These patterns showing one-sided use of information, especially for nonlegal sources, indicate that amici do seek to influence judicial decision making through the use of one-sided nonlegal information and that the information is most one-sided with respect to nonlegal sources.

While each side almost never used the same references to nonlegal research to bolster its argument, one-sided sources to legal cases equaled 43 percent for pro-life amici and 42 percent for pro-choice amici, while the 15 percent of legal cases referenced by both sides accounted for 66 percent of all citations to case law. But *Roe, Akron,* and *Thornburgh* together accounted for 25 percent of all cites to legal cases and 37 percent of two-sided citations to case law. Thus one must differentiate

Table 1   Sources cited in the *Webster* amicus briefs (Total number of citations in parenthesis)

	By pro-life only	By pro-choice only	By both sides
Legal cases	535 (782)	528 (587)	184 (2,664)
Legal statutes	223 (322)	98 (236)	18 (344)
Other legal	232 (606)	131 (178)	12 (144)
Medical sources	224 (293)	397 (776)	22 (172)
Religious sources	50 (68)	31 (47)	2 (5)
Other sources	231 (366)	216 (254)	9 (79)
Totals	1,495 (2,473)	1,401 (2,078)	247 (3,408)

between abortion case law and other kinds of cases. Of 17 abortion cases from 1973 through 1988 only eight were referenced by the 78 amici, but all eight were two-sided references by pro-life and pro-choice amici. If all citations to those eight cases are tabulated, they would represent 47 percent (or 1,243) of the total 2,664 two-sided citations to legal cases.

In sum, there were six times as many one-sided references to non-abortion cases by pro-life (535) and pro-choice (528) amici as there were two-sided references to non-abortion case law. Thus, one-sided references to non-abortion case law were idiosyncratic insofar as those cases did not draw upon abortion precedents but rather were used to establish a link between some medical, scientific, or religious knowledge and other constitutional issues relevant to the abortion controversy (such as church-state separation).

Medical and religious arguments held particular sway, as indicated in the number of sources involving those topics. Only 22 (3 percent) of the medical sources were referred to by both sides, and there was even less overlap on religious sources (2 percent).

Since nearly one-half of the two-sided citations to case law involved abortion cases, we need to unravel how those precedents were manipulated by the amici to promote their unique arguments. Composite statistics were derived to show how often the pro-life and pro-choice amici referred to the majority and concurring opinions in *Roe, Akron,* and *Thornburgh* or the dissenting opinions that took issue with that jurisprudence. The patterns for the amici confirm suspicions that the antagonists did not rely upon the precedents from the majority opinions to argue the same legal position in *Webster.*

To a degree the competing amici chose selectively because 26 percent of the pro-life citations were to the dissenting opinions in the three abortion cases whereas pro-choice amici would hardly look for support from those justices who opposed *Roe, Akron,* and *Thornburgh.* Thus only 9 percent of the pro-choice citations were to the dissents. But what was not anticipated is that amici who oppose each other would rely heavily on the majority opinions in *Roe, Akron,* and *Thornburgh.* Pro-life amici cited the majority opinions 488 times (72 percent of the total), and pro-choice amici cited the majority opinions 266 times (85 percent of the total). This pattern suggests that precedent may mean something less than stare decisis for those who are opposed to *Roe.*

None of the pro-choice citations to the majority opinions in *Roe, Akron,* or *Thornburgh* were used to argue that states can promulgate regulations on abortion, and there were very few "neutral" usages of precedent by pro-choice amici. A total of 95 percent of the pro-choice cites to those abortion cases affirmed their precedents as disallowing any state regulations on a woman's right to an abortion. Similarly, none of the pro-life citations to *Roe, Akron,* or *Thornburgh* made an argument against state regulation of abortion and, again, their briefs had very few neutral references to those cases. As a whole, 98 percent of the pro-life cites were used to justify controls by state government on abortions. Clearly, amici do manipulate legal precedent to strategically promote their ideological agenda.

How influential?

The fifth research question posed at the outset asked to what degree sources referenced by the amici were influential with the justices in writing their opinions. The opinions by Rehnquist, O'Connor, Blackmun, and Stevens contained 29 citations to amicus briefs, and Scalia cited no amicus briefs in his concurring opinion. The content of the amicus brief was compared with the argument made in the opinion to determine if that justice accepted, modified, or rejected the amicus view. The analysis found that justices usually cite amici for nonlegal information and that those cites are often incorporated into their opinions.

Of the 29 citations to amicus briefs, only two referenced legal issues, 18 cited medical arguments, and nine were citations to religious sources. Overall 16 of the references were accepted by the justices. The information in eight were modified

by the opinions, and five arguments referenced in the written opinions were rejected outright.

Of the 10 references to pro-life briefs, Rehnquist rejected the legal argument advanced by the United States as amicus, and Blackmun offered a modified interpretation of another point in the same brief. O'Connor accepted the medical arguments made by three other pro-life amici, and Stevens modified three religious claims and rejected two religious arguments by pro-life amici. Thus Blackmun and Stevens, who dissented in *Webster,* never incorporated the arguments of pro-life amici in their opinions, whereas O'Connor's concurrence accepted pro-life arguments in three instances.

There were 19 references by mainly liberal justices to pro-choice briefs. However, O'Connor twice rejected the medical arguments of pro-choice amici and modified the interpretation of two other pro-choice medical briefs. Blackmun agreed with all six of his references to pro-choice medical briefs as did Stevens in five instances. Stevens also modified the religious arguments from two pro-choice amici.

Implications

It makes perfect sense that a justice would look to his or her own knowledge of case law or rely upon clerks to research legal precedents. This analysis shows that the ideological bent of each justice extends to his or her manipulation of precedent when writing opinions. But to do an extensive search of cognate disciplines as wide-ranging as medicine, theology, history, and psychology is beyond the capacity of any judge, and it was this need for substantive knowledge and third-party representation that gave rise to the use of amicus briefs.

All five of the research questions posed at the outset can be answered in the affirmative. First, the amici did supply one-sided nonlegal information, and the pro-life and pro-choice amici generally did not use the same nonlegal sources. Second, amici relied more heavily on nonlegal sources and non-abortion cases as compared to purely abortion case law, which illustrates how both sides pick and choose to support their own viewpoint. Third, nonlegal information was much more one-sided than were the legal sources simply because both sides had to give some attention to the precedential cases on abortion. Fourth, even though both sides may have referenced the same abortion precedents, each side tried to manipulate those precedents by selectively citing arguments that bolstered only the pro-life or the pro-choice position. Fifth, while there were only 29 direct references to the amicus briefs in the five *Webster* opinions, all but two referenced nonlegal sources rather than the case law, and the arguments in 16 were wholly accepted by the justices.

It was obvious that pro-choice amici would accept nothing less than a reaffirmation of the validity of *Roe, Akron,* and *Thornburgh*. There was some tendency for justices in the majority in *Webster* to cite pro-life briefs in crafting their opinions and for dissenting justices to cite pro-choice briefs. The much more important finding is that precedent was binding only on pro-choice amici, who defended the right of abortion, while every cite to precedent in *Roe, Akron,* and *Thornburgh* by pro-life amici were efforts to discredit stare decisis. Thus what at first glance appeared to be a situation where precedent might constrain judicial decision making ultimately was shown to be a technique by the amici to advance their policy goals. It was also apparent that the justices in *Webster* made the most direct use of amicus briefs primarily for the nonlegal information they provided, but the nonlegal sources were shown to be far more one-sided than the legal authorities.

It is alleged that judges are unlike other kinds of political actors because their actions are constrained by the force of precedent and stare decisis. Adherence to the settled law is one of the canons of jurisprudence, but analysts have begun to evaluate the legal model against a behavioral (ideological) model as predictors of judicial decisions.[8] A recent critique of legal precedent hypothesized that "liberal Courts should overrule conservative precedents, and conservative Courts those that are liberal."[9] They do, and this research explains how interest groups fashion their use of amicus briefs to achieve those kind of ideological results. Amici are not interested in compromise or a balanced presentation of the facts. As partisans in a political battle to influence the Court, the amici manipulate the use of nonlegal sources as well as references to legal precedent to achieve a victory.

NOTES

This article originally appeared in Volume 81, Number 3, November-December 1997, pages 118-121.

1. Epstein, *Courts and Interest Groups*, in Gates and Johnson, eds., THE AMERICAN COURTS: A CRITICAL ASSESSMENT 336-337, 349 (Washington, DC: CQ Press, 1991).

2. *The* Webster Amicus Curiae *Briefs: Perspectives on the Abortion Controversy and the Role of the Supreme Court*, 15 AM. J. L. & MED. 153-243 (1989); Woliver, "Lobbying the Supreme Court: Coalitions of Abortion Interests and the Webster Decision," Paper Delivered, Annual Meeting, Southern Political Science Association (1991); Colker, *Feminist Litigation: An Oxymoron?—A Study of the Briefs Filed in William L. Webster v. Reproductive Health Services*, 13 HARV. L. J. 137 (1990).

3. Behuniak-Long, *Friendly Fire: Amici Curiae and Webster v. Reproductive Health Services*, 74 JUDICATURE 261-270 (1991).

4. O'Neill, BAKKE AND THE POLITICS OF EQUALITY: FRIENDS AND FOES IN THE CLASSROOM OF LITIGATION (Middletown, CT: Wesleyan University Press, 1985).

5. Tatalovich and Daynes, *The Lowi Paradigm, Moral Conflict, and Coalition-Building: Pro-Choice versus Pro-Life*, 13 WOMEN & POL. 39-66 (1993).

6. *See, e.g., Abortion on the Ropes*, TIME, December 5, 1988, at 58; Reidinger, *Will Roe v. Wade be Overruled?*, 66 ABA J. 66, 68-70 (1988).

7. Mezey, IN PURSUIT OF EQUALITY: WOMEN, PUBLIC POLICY, AND THE FEDERAL COURTS 262 (New York: St. Martin's Press, 1992); Baer, *What We Know As Women: A New Look at Roe v. Wade*, 2 NWSA J. 558-582 (1990); Binion, *Webster v. Reproductive Health Services: Devaluing the Right to Choose*, 11 WOMEN & POL. 41-59 (1991).

8. George and Epstein, *On the Nature of Supreme Court Decision Making*, 86 AM. POL. SCI. REV. 323-337 (1992).

9. Brenner and Spaeth, STARE INDECISIS: THE ALTERATION OF PRECEDENT ON THE SUPREME COURT, 1946-1992, 110-111 (New York: Cambridge University Press, 1995).

Actors in the Judicial Process
Juries

INTRODUCTION   Juries have been at once the most romanticized and most vilified actors in the American judicial process. They are, at times, credited with being the public's guarantor of fairness and equity in court, but they are also sometimes heavily criticized for reaching arbitrary decisions that do not reflect the dictates of the law. Both extremes probably accurately tap the behavior of some juries some of the time. It is also important to note that jury trials are a rarity since most legal problems are resolved by settlement prior to trial or by a "bench trial" in which a judge renders the verdict. Nevertheless, dramatic jury trials remain the mythical view of judicial processes held by most Americans, and their potential use in most trial settings does render them important actors warranting our consideration. Unfortunately, scholarly attention to juries has been limited by lack of direct access to jury deliberations and the inherent difficulties of conducting jury research based on simulation and post-hoc interviewing techniques.

Peter Sperlich's article "...And then there were six: the decline of the American jury" portrays the decline in the usage of juries and the changes in their nature brought about by a series of Supreme Court holdings that allowed for reductions in jury size and less than unanimous verdicts. Sperlich argues that the Court's rulings were ill-considered and endanger the very rights juries were fashioned to protect.

When the focus turns to concerns about jury behavior, some research has suggested that the demographic characteristics of jurors may be related to the decisions that they reach. If identifiable juror characteristics are related to specific juror dispositions, it then becomes possible and desirable for attorneys to try to structure juries to produce favorable results. The "state of the art" regarding this possibility is explored by Shari Seidman Diamond in "Scientific jury selection: what social scientists know and do not know." Diamond's argument is a sobering one for critics who contend that with enough money and social science know-how congenial outcomes from jury trials can be assured. She cautions that anyone considering the use of a consultant to help develop a desired juror profile "needs to be a vigilant and critical consumer of the services that are offered."

As noted above, in the absence of access to direct observation of juror behavior, post-hoc interviews of jurors has emerged as a method for gaining an empirical handle on the decision-making processes of juries. Such an approach, focusing narrowly on one specific type of jury decision making, is utilized by William Bowers in, "The capital jury: is it tilted toward death?" Bowers' disturbing documentation of the deliberative process in death penalty cases suggests that jurors often have their minds made up about the punishment to be meted out in the sentencing stage of a trial proceeding at the same time that they are still engaged in an initial determination of a defendant's guilt or innocence. Further, Bowers suggests, capital jurors tend to misunderstand the sentencing guidelines that they have been given and, more often than not, fail to take personal responsibility for the designation of a defendant's punishment. Indeed, "8 of 10 jurors assign foremost responsibility to the defendant or to the law."

The next to last selection in this section, written by Susan Brenner, tackles a topic right out of today's newspaper headlines by asking the question, "Is the grand jury worth keeping?" Brenner offers the reader a detailed accounting of the intended purpose of grand juries and, in the end, she concludes that significant reforms are needed to ensure that such purposes are met. In particular, Brenner is concerned (as were many analysts of Kenneth Starr's role in investigating the Clinton presidency) that there is too much prosecutorial dominance and discretion in contemporary grand jury proceedings. To combat this tendency, Brenner suggests that grand juries should be given their own attorneys who would represent their unique interests. According to Brenner, "the counsel would act as a buffer between the grand juries and prosecutors and between the jurors and the targets of their inquiries." Such an approach, already operative in some state settings, would help to ensure that grand jury processes are perceived to be "fair" in their operation and in the decisions that they reach. Gerald Lefcourt, in "Curbing abuse of the grand jury," offers several additional suggestions for reform, many of which are also operative in some state judicial systems.

...And then there were six: the decline of the American jury

In the last 10 years, the Supreme Court has allowed states to reduce the jury's size and abolish the unanimous verdict. But the Court generally ignored social science evidence that shows the importance of both these factors to the jury in performing its traditional role.

by Peter W. Sperlich

The 1970s may well be remembered as the decade in which we almost lost the jury. The institution of *trial by jury* came to this continent as part of the general transfer of the English legal system to the colonies. For nearly 400 years, Americans have regarded the common law trial jury as one of the bulwarks of their liberty, and for nearly 400 years, there was no essential disagreement that trial by jury meant a body of 12 deciding unanimously.

No institution is without critics, of course. In recent years, a number of judges adopted the position that the jury was no longer needed, that judges could be entrusted with the liberties of the people, and that, in any case, the jury was an inefficient and expensive instrument of dispute resolution, one that no longer could be afforded.[1] Nevertheless, the American jury seemed secure, particularly because the U.S. Supreme Court always was one of the common law jury's strong supporters. As late as 1968, the Court extended the Sixth Amendment right to trial by jury to defendants accused of serious crimes in state courts.[2]

But then came *Williams v. Florida*[3] in 1970. *Williams* was the first act in what turned out to be a major reorientation of the Court's approach to the trial jury. The *Williams* ruling, permitting state criminal juries of six, came unexpected and sent a shock through the legal and scholarly community. Given the open-ended nature of the ruling (six was not necessarily to be the lower limit), the very

survival of the jury seemed in doubt. Had the Court begun to side with the abolitionist minority? Was this the beginning of the end of lay participation in the American judicial process? Hans Zeisel, an observer not given to panic, expressed these concerns in the very title of his *Williams* review: "...And Then There Were None."[4]

The title of this article is somewhat less despairing, reflecting two recent decisions (*Ballew* and *Burch, infra*), which indicate that the American jury will survive the 1970s. But the jury that has survived is not the jury of 10 years ago. Except for some state experimentations, the American criminal and civil trial jury at that time was the jury at common law, 12 persons deciding unanimously. As the decade ends, juries of 12 are no longer required in federal civil trials or in state criminal trials. Majority verdicts have been held to be constitutionally adequate in state criminal trials. Majority verdicts in federal criminal trials have been averted (so far) by the vote of a single justice.

What the future will bring we cannot know. But it is clear that what remains of the American jury at the end of the decade is less than firmly planted. It is possible that American developments will replicate English legal history, leading to an almost complete abrogation of trial by jury.[5] It is also possible that the worst is over. The vigorous defense of the jury that followed *Williams* and the other jury-diminishing decisions may have persuaded the Court of the error of the *Williams* approach.

I. The revolution in jury law

The U.S. Supreme Court changed the American trial jury in a sequence of six cases, spanning the full decade from 1970 to 1979. The first four served to diminish the jury: *Williams v. Florida, Johnson v. Louisiana,*[6] *Apodaca v. Oregon,*[7] and *Colgrove v. Battin.*[8] The last two indicate the current limits of jury diminution: *Ballew v. Georgia*[9] and *Burch v. Louisiana.*[10]

In *Williams*, the Supreme Court ruled that the U.S. Constitution does not require a jury of 12, and that a state may use a jury of six in criminal trials even when the sentence is as severe as life imprisonment. The decision applied only to state criminal juries, but the opinion of Justice White clearly signaled what was to come: "In sweeping language, the Court removed the constitutional obstacles to decreasing the size of federal and state juries in both civil and criminal cases."[11]

Federal judges quickly took the hint. In 1972, a year before *Colgrove*, a majority of the federal district courts already had adopted six-person civil juries. *Colgrove* legitimated this change. The Court formally ruled that the U.S. Constitution does not require 12-person civil juries, and that six-person federal civil juries are constitutionally adequate. *Johnson* and *Apodaca*, finally, produced the ruling that majority verdicts are constitutionally permissible in state criminal trials.[12]

The four cases amounted to no less than a revolution in American jury law.[13] But not only was this revolution unexpected, it also was uncompelled. There were no irresistible forces of legal or societal development to which the justices were forced to pay homage. Indeed, to achieve the goal of smaller and nonunanimous juries, the Court had to do considerable violence to legal history and empirical evidence. Not surprisingly, it reaped sharp criticism in the scholarly community.[14] Support for the decisions came largely from the same judges who had advocated jury slicing all along.[15]

The casualties of *Williams*

Williams signaled the transformation of the American trial jury and established the pattern of judicial reasoning in support of the change. The reasoning, as noted, left much to be desired, and three specific areas were short-changed: history, the American constitutional tradition, and empirical evidence.

History suffered the first blow. For nearly seven centuries, the common law jury of England and, thus, of the United States, had been a body of 12. It is not known how that size became standardized at 12 in 14th-century England; perhaps the number could equally well have been 11 or 13. It is not likely that the number could just as well have been five, or six, or seven.

The Court, however, took the position that unless it could discover a rational justification in history for the number 12, then that number could be regarded as an accident. As could have been predicted, no such justification was to be found. The Court concluded that the number 12 "appears to have been a historical accident, unrelated to the great purposes which gave rise to the jury in the first place."[16]

At least three objections must be raised to the Court's historical scholarship. The first is epistemological: the failure to discover a reason is not proof of its nonexistence. The second regards the conversion of quantitative into qualitative changes: as noted, the choice between 12 and 11 may not be of much consequence, but a change from 12 to six involves fundamental differences. The third objection involves objectivity of analysis and validity of inference: the Court only looked for reasons *for* removing the requirement of 12; it did not look for reasons *against* such a removal.[17]

The second blow was struck against an American constitutional tradition. While the Court had not explicitly ruled that the American trial jury was a body of 12 deciding unanimously, all the Court's statements and dicta had supported this position.[18] Firm tradition and invariate interpretations, however, had little power to protect the jury. The Court decided to treat the issue of jury size as open and unresolved, asking in leading language whether "this accidental feature of the jury has been immutably codified into our Constitution."[19] The answer, of course, was *no*. The Court revealed that all its prior interpretations were in error because they had assumed "that if a given feature existed in a jury at common law in 1789, then it was necessarily preserved in the Constitution."[20]

The third casualty of *Williams* was empirical evidence. The Court took the position that the six-person criminal jury would satisfy the requirements of the Sixth Amendment of "trial by an impartial jury" if it could be shown to be *functionally equivalent* to a 12-person jury: "The relevant inquiry, as we see it, must be the function that the particular feature [size] performs and its relations to the purposes of the jury trial."[21] The purpose of the jury trial "is to prevent oppression by the Government," and its essential feature is the "interposition between the accused and his accuser of the common-sense judgment of a group of laymen, and . . . the community participation and shared responsibility that results from that group's determination of guilt or innocence."[22] The Court examined the evidence and came to the conclusion that "[t]he performance of this role is not a function of the particular number of the body that makes up the jury . . . . And, certainly the reliability of the jury as a factfinder hardly seems likely to be a function of its size."[23] As will be seen, the facts do *not* support these conclusions.

Other jury-size cases

Colgrove v. Battin is the second jury-size case, legitimating the six-person civil jury in the federal courts. In substance and style, *Colgrove* was pure *Williams*. Historical, constitutional, and empirical reasoning was flawed. *Colgrove* was particularly difficult to justify on constitutional grounds since the Seventh Amendment (in contrast to the Sixth Amendment in *Williams*) explicitly refers to the common law.

The Court overcame this obstacle by announcing that the size of the common law jury was not part of the real "substance" of the common law right of trial by jury, but was a "mere matter of form or procedure."[24] What remained, as in *Williams*, was the question of functional equivalence, "whether jury performance is a function of jury size."[25] The Court inspected the evidence and ruled that performance is not a function of size. Unfortunately, once again the facts fail to support the conclusion, as we will see later.

Ballew v. Georgia,[26] the third jury-size case, was a decision of the greatest importance. It was the first indication that the diminution of the jury had come to a halt. The Court decided that Georgia's criminal trial jury of five was constitutionally inadequate, that state criminal juries must consist of at least six. *Ballew* also was the first indication that the vigorous scholarly defense of the jury, mounted in the post-*Williams* years, had met with some success.

As will be seen below, the success was far from complete. The Court still did not refrain from using empirical evidence in questionable ways. But

there were signs of a new spirit. The Court concluded "that the purpose and functioning of the jury in a criminal trial is seriously impaired, and to a constitutional degree, by a reduction in size below six members."[27] And Justice Blackmun was explicit that the empirical studies play a major role in the development of this conclusion:

But the assembled data raise substantial doubt about the reliability and appropriate representation of panels smaller than six. Because of the fundamental importance of the jury trial to the American system of criminal justice, any further reduction that promotes inaccurate and possibly biased decisionmaking, that causes untoward differences in verdicts, and that prevents juries from truly representing their communities, attains constitutional significance.[28]

The decision-rule cases

Johnson v. Louisiana and *Apodaca v. Oregon* were decided on the same day, May 22, 1972; both belong to the set of four cases that diminished the American trial jury.[29] *Johnson* permitted a 9/12 and *Apodaca* a 10/12 majority verdict in state criminal trials. *Johnson* and *Apodaca* moved along similar tracks as *Williams* and *Colgrove*. Once more, the keystone was the assertion of functional equivalence:

Our inquiry must focus upon the function served by the jury . . . As we said in *Duncan*, the purpose of trial by jury is to prevent oppression by the Government . . . In terms of this function we perceive no difference between juries required to act unanimously and those permitted to convict or acquit by votes of 10 to two or 11 to one.[30]

For this claim the Court offered no evidence at all.[31] Instead, it was satisfied to rely upon its "longstanding perceptions about jury behavior."[32] The Court did not reveal how these "perceptions" were gathered, or what kind of systematic comparisons were made between unanimous and majority-verdict juries. Nor did the Court dispute the fact that jury deliberations are secret and not easily perceived. It is unlikely that the "longstanding perceptions" are more than an exercise of judicial creativity, throwing a cloak over the uncomfortable sight of an empirical issue having been decided without reference to empirical evidence.[33]

After *Johnson* and *Apodaca* joined *Williams* and *Colgrove*, a deep and widespread concern developed for the jury's future. No end was in sight to reductions in size (*Ballew* was not decided until 1978). And combinations of smaller size and majority rule could be expected to be legitimated next. *Burch v. Louisiana*, as *Ballew*, halted the diminution of the jury this year. The Court decided in *Burch* that "conviction by a nonunanimous six-member jury in a state criminal trial for a nonpetty offense deprives the accused of his constitutional right to trial by jury."[34]

It remains to be seen, of course, whether such combinations as 6/7 or 5/8 will be found constitutionally inadequate. At least the worst fears have been set aside by *Burch*. In the foreseeable future the American trial jury will not be a body of three, deciding with a majority of two. As in the other decision-rule cases, it should be noted, the Court offered no empirical evidence for its ruling on the functional equivalence issue in *Burch*.

II. 'Functional equivalence' of juries

The major issue that emerges from the six jury decisions is the functional equivalence or nonequivalence of juries of different size and decision rules. The issue is closely related to the general question of the use of scientific evidence in the legal process. (See Sperlich, "Social science evidence in the courts: reaching beyond the adversary process," 63 *Judicature* 280 (1980)). Of course, important questions also can be raised about the Court's treatment of legal history and constitutional law. However, since the Court decides what the Constitution requires and what has been "immutably codified into our Constitution," little is to be gained by disputing with the Court about such matters as "the intent of the framers."

The U.S. Supreme Court, however, is not the highest authority on matters of fact. The case facts (adjudicative facts) must be determined by the trier of the facts, the trial judge or the trial jury. Wisely, the appellate courts have adopted a bearing of great restraint regarding case facts and generally refuse to second-guess the trier of the facts. Such well-placed restraint, unfortunately, has been less common in respect to the social facts relevant to the case in question.[35]

There is a tendency to rely on common sense and personal experience, and to take "judicial notice" of "common knowledge" rather than to obtain the required information from the appropriate expert sources, the relevant scientific disciplines. Untrained in scientific methods and isolated from the world of scientific investigations, judges seem to come quite easily to the view that judicial horse-sense is a more dependable guide to valid knowledge than scientific expertise.

Common knowledge and judicial intuition are notoriously unreliable paths to empirical fact. More often than not they lead into blind alleys and embarrassing retreats. Just as theological wisdom and common observation could not, in the long run, prevail against the expertise of scientific astronomers, so judicial wisdom and common sense could not prevail against scientific expertise in ballistics.[36] The Court reasonably can maintain its interpretation of the Constitution against the views of other constitutional experts. The Court cannot maintain its own view of social facts and scientific principles against the testimony of the experts from the relevant sciences—at least it cannot do so without being seen as willful and incompetent.[37]

In the jury decisions of the 1970s it was indeed appropriate for the justices to determine upon which principle the rulings should be based, i.e., functional equivalence. It was not appropriate, however, for the justices to assume the role of competent determiners of the facts of equivalence or nonequivalence. It is disturbing when justices decide issues of social fact by relying upon their "longstanding perceptions about jury behavior." Nor will it do for justices to complain about "reliance on numerology,"[38] when after years of erroneous determination of the facts, reliable scientific investigations finally are being used.[39]

At this time in history, of course, and perhaps for a long time to come, there are many questions to which the sciences, particularly the social sciences, cannot give unequivocal answers. Not all details have been filled out in the studies of jury behavior.[40] There is much that is not known about just how different juries differ. This much, however, is well-established: Juries of different sizes and decision rules are *not* functionally equivalent. The protections offered by smaller and majority-rule juries are not the same as those offered by the traditional common law jury—12 persons deciding unanimously.

As noted earlier, *Johnson, Apodaca*, and *Burch* decided on the equivalence/nonequivalence of different decision rules *without any reference* to empirical evidence, relying instead on mysterious "longstanding judicial perceptions." *Williams, Colgrove*, and *Ballew*, the jury size cases, do refer to empirical evidence. The relevance and validity of that evidence, thus, can be examined.

L' evidence

Relevance and validity of evidence

Given the path-setting nature of the *Williams* decision and the continuing dominance of the *Williams* doctrine (6=12), it is of considerable interest
to see how the claim of functional equivalence was
established. The Court cited six "experiments" to
support its contentions.[41] This was the substance
of the evidence: (1) an unsupported claim that "it
could be argued that there would be no differences"; (2) the unsupported statement of a judge
that he found five-person juries quite satisfactory;
(3) an unsupported report that one court clerk
and three attorneys had said that they could not
detect any difference in the verdicts of 12- and six-
person juries as these had been used on an experimental basis in a Massachusetts court; (4) another
report of the same opinions as recounted in the
previous item; (5) a notice, without any evaluation,
that a court has experimented with a six-person
jury in a civil negligence case; (6) a judge's
thoughts on the economic advantages of smaller
juries.[42]

Williams' notion of "empirical evidence" was of
embarrassing incompetence,[43] and the reviews did
not spare the Court. Zeisel concluded that the six
items were "scant evidence by any standards," and
pointed out how and where better evidence could
have been obtained.[44] Saks noted that the scholarship displayed in *Williams* would not win a passing
grade in high school.[45] Walbert chided the Court
for its errors of interpretation and for its failure to
make use of available competent evidence.[46] And
Wick charged that "[t]he willingness of the Court
to be persuaded by such flimsy evidence lays bare
its lack of concern for the institution of jury trial."[47]
Williams did not demonstrate that juries of six and
of 12 are functionally equivalent. By its own chosen standard, the Court had rendered a constitutionally invalid decision.[48] The error still awaits correction.

It may appear difficult to do worse than *Williams.* Yet *Colgrove*, the next jury-size decision, in
some ways did worse indeed. The Court showed
itself supremely scornful of the scholarly criticisms
and suggestions that had followed *Williams.* Not
only did the Court not change its general approach
to empirical evidence, it even returned for support to some of the *Williams* items, the inadequacy
of which had clearly been demonstrated.[49]

The Court refused to show doubt regarding
Williams. To the contrary, it practically taunted its
critics. There was the bold restatement of the false
claim that the *Williams* decision rested on actual
jury "studies." And there was the pointed comment that the critical literature generated by *Williams* was "nonpersuasive." Said the *Colgrove* court:

We had no difficulty reaching the conclusion in *Williams* that a jury of six would guarantee an accused the
trial by jury secured by Art. III and the Sixth Amendment. Significantly, our determination that there was
'no discernible difference between the results reached
by the two different-sized juries' . . . drew largely upon
the results of studies of the operations of juries of six in
civil cases. Since then, much has been written about the
six-member jury, but nothing that persuades us to depart from the conclusion reached in *Williams.*[50]

The flaws in *Colgrove*

In addition to resurrecting the deficient items of
Williams, *Colgrove* sought to present new support
for the functional equivalence assertion, reporting that "four very recent studies have provided
convincing empirical evidence of the correctness
of the *Williams* conclusion."[51] Far from providing
"convincing empirical evidence," however, the
new items were entirely incapable to support the
Court's contentions. The flaws can be stated
briefly:[52]

• One situation permitted attorneys to choose
a jury of 12 rather than six. The choices of the
larger jury did not occur at random but reflected
the nature and complexity of the case.

• The second new item also reported a procedure in which the litigants had a choice between
six- and 12-person juries. The choices, again, were
not random.

• The next study used a before-and-after design
to take advantage of a recent change from 12- to
six-person juries. Other changes, however, occurred at the same time (mediation board, discovery of insurance). None of these three items permitted valid comparisons of the behavior and verdicts of larger and smaller juries.

• The final study used videotaped mock trials
with student subjects. The study contained serious
errors, such as a wholly one-sided case presentation and faulty computations.[53]

Again, there were many critical reviews. Zeisel
and Diamond wrote that *Colgrove*'s handling of
evidence presented a "disconcerting picture,"[54]
and suggested that it was one of the cases where
the intent of references to empirical evidence is

not to shed light on the facts, but "merely to ornament an already determined result."[55] Regarding the functional equivalence assertions, Zeisel wrote elsewhere that "[w]ith all due respect to the judges who composed the majority of the Court in these cases—on this point they were simply wrong. The Court's so-called evidence proved nothing of the sort."[56] Referring to *Colgrove*'s "convincing empirical evidence," Wick wrote that "[t]he only conviction which emerges from examination of these four studies is that the majority of the Court was predisposed to be convinced."[57]

The *Williams-Johnson-Apodaca-Colgrove* sequence of opinions furnishes one of the more depressing sets of readings to emerge from the pens of U.S. Supreme Court justices. One aspect is technical: the uncritical and incompetent treatment of empirical evidence. The other is substantive: the continuous slicing away at the traditional common law jury and, thus, the continuing reduction in the protective function of trial by jury. The second was worrisome all the more because of strong signs that the Court would legitimate trial juries even smaller than six,[58] and majorities even smaller than *Johnson*'s nine-to-three division.[59] Indeed, there was reason to be concerned that the two methods of jury reduction would be legitimated in a combined format.[60]

Partial remedies

Eight years after *Williams* and five years after *Colgrove* the Court decided *Ballew v. Georgia* and at least partially remedied the inadequacies of the earlier cases. As *Williams* is the milestone marking the beginning of the decline of the American jury, so *Ballew* may well be the milestone marking the on-set of recovery.[61] The *Ballew* Court ruled[62] that Georgia's criminal jury of five was constitutionally inadequate because it did not meet the Court's test of functional equivalence.

For the first time in the jury decisions of the 1970s, the Court correctly used empirical evidence to establish a social fact: deliberative bodies of five and of 12 are *not* equivalent. Criminal juries of five do not offer the same protection to the accused as those of 12. The irony of *Ballew* is that the evidence used to deny five just as much condemns six. The scientific investigations cited in *Ballew* were designed to test the *Williams* doctrine of 6=12. The findings exposed the error of that doctrine. Yet *Ballew* includes an explicit affirmation of *Williams*.[63]

Ballew, thus, is only a partial redress for the Court's past failings.

Justice Blackmun noted many functional inequalities between larger and smaller juries. He arranged them in five major groups:

(1) **Effectiveness of group deliberation.** The quality of group performance and group productivity is higher in larger groups.[64] Reduction in the size of the group leads to impaired fact-finding and common-sense application. Members of smaller groups are less likely to contribute to the solution of the problem, and (collectively) are less likely to overcome the biases of their members.[65]

(2) **Accuracy, consistency, and reliability of deliberation results.** Smaller panels produce a larger proportion of conviction errors, i.e., convicting innocent persons. (Increases in panel size increase the opposite error: not convicting guilty persons.)[66] Smaller panels show more verdict inconsistency and produce less reliable decisions.[67]

(3) **Detriment to the defense.** The functional difference between smaller and larger panels is not neutral in criminal trials. Smaller panels are detrimental to the defense. The number of hung juries is substantially reduced with smaller panels, largely because of less support for the juror holding the minority viewpoint.[68]

(4) **Community participation and representativeness.** Smaller panels reduce the representativeness of the jury and allow less participation of the minority groups in the community.[69]

(5) **Substantial effects of small differences.** Some studies have found that larger and smaller juries would produce different verdicts in only a relatively small proportion of the cases, e.g., 14 percent. These small percentages, however, mask a very large number of cases. Furthermore, it is precisely in those cases of disagreement, when the evidence is not clear-cut, that the jury system is of greatest value. A similar point applies to the small percentage differences often found between jury verdicts and judge verdicts. Aggregate comparisons mask the true extent of differences. Case-by-case comparisons show higher rates of disagreement.[70]

Having noted all these differences, Justice Blackmun wrote that these studies "lead us to conclude that the purpose and functioning of the jury in a criminal trial is seriously impaired, and to a constitutional degree, by a reduction in size to below six members."[71]

It is ironic that one of the best listings of evidence to refute the *Williams* doctrine should be found in a decision that explicitly affirms that doctrine.[72] The assembly of empirical evidence in *Ballew* is particularly impressive[73] when it is recognized that the litigants brought to the attention of the Court only a small part.[74] Additional literature, however, could have been drawn upon.

Saari, for example, has pointed out that from some perspectives six is not even one-half of 12. One of the crucial issues in the jury-size controversy is the interaction of the jurors. The evidence is that both quality and quantity differ. Saari points to the interesting fact that juries of 12 have 261,624 potential relational patterns, but juries of six only have 301 (about 1/10 of 1 percent).[75] Missing from *Ballew* are references to the extensive work of Gelfand and Solomon,[76] Grofman,[77] Buckhout,[78] and Snortum et al.,[79] as well as to the partially unpublished but well-known study of Padawer-Singer & Barton.[80] A recent review of the jury literature by Davis et al. also would have been a useful addition.[81] It is important to emphasize, however, that the inclusion of these items would not have changed any of the findings of *Ballew* regarding the functional non-equivalence of five- and 12-person juries, though, again, the real message was the non-equivalence of six and 12.

A halt to jury reduction

Burch v. Louisiana is the final case in this decade's sequence of jury decisions. *Burch* stands in the same relationship to *Johnson* and *Apodaca* as *Ballew* to *Williams* and *Colgrove*. *Burch* ruled that conviction by a nonunanimous six-person jury for a nonpetty offense violates the right to trial by jury as guaranteed by the Sixth and Fourteenth Amendments.[82] While *Burch* resembled *Ballew* in putting a halt to the further diminution of the American trial jury, it greatly differs from *Ballew* in its treatment of evidence.

Burch makes no reference to empirical evidence,[83] except for an allusion to the "reasons that led us in *Ballew* to decide that use of a five-member jury threatened the fairness of the proceeding and the proper role of the jury."[84] Justice Rehnquist, the author of the *Burch* opinion, had associated himself with the Powell complaint about *Ballew*'s "reliance on numerology" (*cf* note 38 *supra*), seemingly having less use for science as a source of social facts than Justice Blackmun.

In addition to references to *Ballew* (but no anal-

ysis of the *Ballew* evidence for its relevance to *Burch*), Justice Rehnquist sought to support the *Burch* decision by taking note of current practice:

We are buttressed in this view by the current jury practices of the several States. It appears that of those States that utilize six-member juries in trials of nonpetty offenses, only two, including Louisiana, also allow nonunanimous verdicts. We think that this near uniform judgment of the Nation provides a useful guide in delimiting the line between those jury practices that are constitutionally permissible and those that are not.[85]

Justice Rehnquist also found it profitable to resurrect and reaffirm once more the functional equivalence error of the *Williams* court "that a jury of 12 was neither more reliable as a factfinder, more advantageous to the defendant, nor more representative of the variety of viewpoints in the community than a jury of six."[86]

What Justice Rehnquist failed to do was to examine relevant and competent evidence. The Court's self-chosen test in all of the jury cases is that of the functional equivalence of different juries. The question of functional equivalence is an empirical question. It can be answered only by the examination of empirical evidence. It cannot be answered by an audit of current court practices. Nor can the question of the functional equivalence of different decision rules be answered by referring to the Court's reasoning in the jury-size cases, particularly given the less than competent treatment of evidence in these cases.

The reasoning of *Burch* is sorely deficient. Nevertheless, the decision is welcome to those who have an interest in preserving trial by jury in the courts of this nation. As *Ballew* before it, *Burch* creates an important obstacle against the additional diminution of the jury.

III. Hidden agendas?

It has been argued that the Court's use of empirical evidence is "real," if occasionally faulty. But the view that the Court also refers to empirical evidence to ornament and to camouflage has considerable prevalence.[87] Short of judicial disclosure, there seems to be no clear way to verify such propositions, and judicial denial may not convince everyone.

The matter must be approached with care. We do not need another conspiracy theory. Yet, the problem cannot be ignored.[88] The conclusion that the Court ornaments and camouflages is almost inescapable when confronted with "evidence" of the nature and quality used in *Williams* to justify a jury of six.[89] The jury cases and their context suggest the possible existence of four hidden agendas: jury cost, court delay, judicial power, and law and order.

Jury cost

Five of the six jury cases are silent on the issue of jury cost, and *Ballew* rejects Georgia's argument of an overriding state interest in "savings in court time and in financial costs."[90] Yet the jury reduction literature[91] of recent decades has placed such strong emphasis on the savings to be realized by smaller juries that it is difficult to dismiss the thought altogether that the Court may have wanted to reduce the cost of justice as well as to permit jury diversity in deciding these cases. The thought is particularly hard to dismiss because *Williams* justified the six-person jury by relying, *inter alia*, on Judge Phillips' article, which is a purely economic argument for reduction,[92] and because of Chief Justice Burger's remarkable media and lecture circuit activism in the cause of court reform, more than once linking economic considerations and jury size.[93]

The jury reform/reduction literature almost without exception presents expected financial savings as a justification for reducing the size of the jury. The savings are said to occur for several reasons, including the claims that: (a) fewer panelists are required for the jury venire,[94] (b) less time is needed for the voir dire of the prospective jurors,[95] (c) less time is required for courtroom proceedings,[96] (d) jury deliberation time is shorter,[97] (e) juror fees and expenses are reduced.[98] Some of the assertions, especially (a) and (e) are quite plausible; the others are more questionable.[99] There actually appears to be rather little saving in voir dire time and trial proceedings, and, thus, in judicial time and court cost.[100]

Juror fees probably are the item in which the largest savings can be achieved by reducing the size of the trial jury. Since juror fees are notoriously low,[101] however, and since juror fees consitute a miniscule part of a court's budget,[102] the actual amount is not all that large. Even the figures presented by proponents are not particularly impressive. Bogue and Fritz write:

> Minnehaha County [spent] $27,164.50 for juror fees in 1971. There are an estimated 95,000 people living in Minnehaha County. Divide $27,164.50 into 95,000 people and it will be ascertained that it cost [sic] each person in Minnehaha County about 35¢ plus for the cost of trial by jury.[103]

This, it should be noted, is an argument *for* reducing the jury to six members. If the six-person jury saves about half the amount, it means that each resident of Minnehaha County could enjoy the full benefits and protections of the common law jury for about 18¢ extra per year.

Judge Devitt offers a nationwide figure:

> The saving in jury expenses if the six-man rule were in effect nation-wide is impressive. In fiscal year 1970, 3,371 civil jury trials were conducted in the federal court system. These cases took 10,701 trial days and, with twelve-person juries, a total of 128,512 juror days. If this figure is cut in half and multiplied by $25, the approximate saving effected by employing a jury of six, rather than twelve, could exceed $1,600,000.[104]

Assuming even a cost of $2 million, given a population of about 200 million, the saving per person per year is about *one cent*. Zeisel and Diamond have estimated a saving of $4 million annually if all federal juries consisted of six rather than 12 persons (as the civil juries now largely do). This still works out to only two cents of savings per person per year.[105]

Savings of $4 million must also be seen in the context of other expenditures, such as annual outlays of $631 million for golf equipment.[106] While, of course, no one argues in favor of waste in the judicial system, the cost of the traditional common law jury seems bearable.[107] But if savings must be achieved, there are other court reforms we can undertake, such as the elimination of the continuous presence of a newspaper-reading bailiff in all non-jury civil and in many non-jury criminal trials, and a more efficient administration of the jury system itself.[108]

Delay

This is not a topic in any of the six jury cases either. Yet there are some grounds for suspecting that this issue may also have been on the Court's mind. The chief justice has frequently spoken about the need to eliminate delay and has clearly linked the use of the jury to the existence of trial delay.[109] And the jury-reduction literature is just as emphatic that delay can be cured by jury reform,[110] as it is on the point that much money can be saved. Particularly the civil jury is seen as cause of delay. Judge Devitt, for example, writes:

I think it is fair to say that the backlog of cases in the federal courts, particularly in the metropolitan centers, is caused largely by the number of civil jury trials required by the Seventh Amendment.[111]

This type of analysis tends to be based more on wishful thinking than on fact. Inferences often are drawn from judge/jury comparisons, without full recognition of the differences in the types of cases that are submitted to bench and to jury trials. Courts without juries, it should be noted, also experience substantial delay. "The New York Court of Claims, dealing with cases against the State of New York, is almost two years behind on its calendar, yet does not use the jury system."[112]

It has been pointed out that delay is caused by some administrative practices of the courts, and that much of the delay can be cured by the addition of rather small increments in judicial worktime or judicial position.[113] While delay in court can damage the cause of justice and should indeed be cured, smaller juries, majority juries, and reduced use of jury trials do not seem to be the cure. What little *systematic* analysis exists does not identify trial by jury as the cause of delay.[114]

Judicial power

The jury reduction literature contains some interesting hints about the desirability of increasing the power of the judges. American legal history can be read as a struggle between judge and jury, between the professional and the lay element. It is evident that professional judges are in ascendance. The power of the jury to decide on the law has largely been taken away, at least as a matter of right.[115] In effect, juries still have the power to set aside laws that are perceived to be unjust (in general or in application to the case at hand). But when they exercise this power, they are regarded as "runaway" or "lawless."[116]

The argument for smaller juries sometimes is stated in the terms that this will make the court more "businesslike."[117] Often the language is stronger. Gleisser, for example, argues that the trial judge should be the "master of his own courtroom," and that he should be "free to comment in any way he wishes on the evidence," including "which witnesses are to be believed."[118] In juris-

dictions where this is not currently permissible, what can this mean but a greater judicial influence on the fact decision of the jury?[119] It should be noted, however, that studies show that the majority of trial judges favors trial by jury, even in civil trials.[120] It cannot be guessed, of course, whether the Court saw increased judicial power as one of the benefits of smaller juries and resulting reductions in the use of juries.[121]

Law-and-order

The smaller criminal jury works to the disadvantage of the defendant.[122] This fact, not acknowledged by the Court until *Ballew*, and even then applied only to the five-person issue, underlies the speculation that an increase in the rate of criminal convictions was one of the hidden agendas of the jury cases.

The 1960s saw a strong public concern with law-and-order. It was a strong factor in the election of President Nixon, and, as political pundits say, the Court follows the election returns. More importantly, the Nixon appointees to the Court were selected to at least some degree because of their position on the law-and-order issue.[123] While presidents tend to have little luck in appointing justices who will carry forward the judicial philosophy that made them attractive, it cannot be denied that the Burger Court has produced some fairly "Nixonian" rulings in respect to such matters as freedom of the press, search and seizure, admission of evidence, self-incrimination, and right to counsel.[124] Some of these decisions point in the same direction as the smaller and the majority jury: an increase in the rate of criminal convictions, reflecting a general climate of punitiveness. Zeisel has raised the issue in this way:

One wonders what is behind this new zeal for cutting into the jury. The ostensible argument is reducing costs and delay.... There is obviously more to this concerted drive at this point in time.

Unconsciously, perhaps, the motives are likely to be similar to those that went into the rewriting of the military code of procedure; not only more efficiency, but also less tolerance toward a dissenting minority.[125]

And again Zeisel:

One must see the reduction of the jury size in civil cases in the federal courts as but one move in a major attack on the jury system that began in the 'law-and-order days,' when it was thought that the jury, as we have known it since the founding of the Republic, might stand in the way of law enforcement.[126]

Speculating about hidden agendas, unstated reasons, and concealed motivations is to skate on thin ice. While some inferences may be plausible, little can be proven, yet the matter cannot be avoided. The true reasons and motivations producing the Court's decisions are among the most important facts of judicial policy analysis, constitutional law, and the planning of litigation. When, as in the jury cases, the Court's cited evidence does not support the decisions, and when the Court persists in affirming demonstrably false doctrines, speculation about hidden agendas inescapably will emerge.

IV. A role for ordinary citizens

The Declaration of Independence (1776) set forth a series of complaints against the King to justify the revolution. One of the key complaints was "For depriving us in many cases, of the benefits of Trial by jury." It can be argued that the Court's jury decisions of this decade have caused a similar deprivation. In the Virginia Ratification Convention the Wythe Committee declared that "the ancient trial by jury is one of the greatest securities to the rights of the people, and is to remain sacred and inviolable."[127] And until *Williams*, essentially, it did. It does no longer. The evidence is clear: six does not equal 12, and 75 percent does not equal 100 percent.

How will the Court decide future jury cases? *Ballew* and *Burch* indicate that the worst may be over. Yet majority verdicts for the federal criminal jury were avoided by only a single vote, and it remains undetermined what type of majority rule for less-than-12-person state criminal juries will be legitimated. *Ballew* and *Burch* are no cause for leaving the ramparts. Trial by jury is likely to survive only through vigorous efforts on its behalf.

It is unclear what combination of reasons and motivations produced *Williams* and the subsequent decisions. To the degree that empirical evidence played an important role—however mistakenly used—extraordinary scholarly efforts will be required to provide the Court with social facts, to educate the Court in the use of scientific findings, and to help the legal profession in developing new institutions and processes by which the flow of scientific evidence to the Court can be improved, while preserving principles of procedural fair-

ness.[128]

To the degree that hidden agendas were instrumental in the decisions, scholarly and political efforts will be required. The Court needs more information about just how much (how little) time and money will be saved by smaller juries and non-unanimous decisions. In addition, however, the political process will have to carry the message to the Court that the jury shall not be destroyed to save pennies or to increase the rate of criminal convictions, and that the people will not trust the professional judges with their liberties,[129] but that ordinary citizens shall retain their role in the American judicial process.

The task of preventing any further decline of trial by jury does not appear hopeless. Indeed, over time it may even be possible to persuade the Court to acknowledge the error of the functional equivalence doctrine and to reverse itself. Stare decisis is not the only principle in law. There is no *final word*, even from the U.S. Supreme Court.

NOTES

This article originally appeared in Volume 63, Number 6, December-January 1980, pages 262-279.

I am indebted to William Zinn for criticism of the first draft, to Karin Carmin and Coronet Galloway for finding some of the economic data, and to the Institute of Governmental Studies of the University of California for various forms of assistance and typing of the manuscript.

1. "When the Declaration of Independence was adopted and the Constitution drafted, we had every reason to be concerned about citizen-juror protection from King George's judges. But King George is long gone, and so are his judges. We have our own now, and they are competent, experienced, fair, and well qualified to decide law and fact issues in civil cases." Devitt, *Federal Civil Jury Trials Should be Abolished*, 60 A.B.A. J. 570, 572 (1974).

For a sampling of judicial criticism of the jury, from the mid-1950s to the mid-1970s, *see*: Augelli, *Six-Member Juries in Civil Actions in the Federal Judicial System*, 3 SETON HALL L. REV. 281 (1972), Lumbard, *Let the Jury Be—But Modified*, 7 TRIAL 17 (Nov.-Dec. 1971), Tamm, *A Proposal for Five-Member Civil Juries in the Federal Courts*, 50 A.B.A. J. 162 (1964), Thompson, *Six Will Do*, 10 TRIAL 12 (Nov.-Dec. 1974), and Wiehl, *The Six Man Jury*, 4 GONZAGA L. REV. 35 (1968).

Summaries of criticisms can be found in: Comment, *With Love in Their Hearts but Reform on Their Minds: How Trial Judges View the Civil Jury*, 4 COLUM. J. L. SOC. PROBL. 178 (1968), James, CRISIS IN THE COURTS 193-199 (New York: David McKay, rev. ed., 1971), and Powell, *Reducing the Size of Juries*, 5 U. MICH. J. L. REF. 87 (1971). The most comprehensive attack on the jury system still is Frank, COURTS ON TRIAL (Princeton: Princeton University Press, 1949).

Views supportive of the traditional common law jury can be found in: Avakian, *Trial by Jury: Is It Worth the Ordeal?*, 2 LITIGATION 8 (Winter 1976), Baum, *The Six-Man Jury—The Cross Section Aborted*, 12 JUDGE'S J. 12 (1973), Hogan, *Some Thoughts on Juries in Civil Cases*, 50 A.B.A. J. 752 (1964), Kalven, *The Dignity of the Civil Jury*, 50 VA. L. REV. 1055 (1964), Nunnelly,

When a Trial by Jury?, in Winters, THE JURY 25 (Chicago: American Judicature Society, 1971), Summers, *Some Merits of Civil Jury Trials*, 39 TUL. L. REV. 3 (1964), and Zeisel, *The Jury and Court Delay*, 328 ANNALS 46 (March 1960).

2. Duncan v. Louisiana, 391 U.S. 145 (1968). The Court extended the Sixth Amendment right of trial by jury in criminal cases to the states by way of the Fourteenth Amendment.

3. 399 U.S. 78 (1970).

4. Zeisel, *. . . And Then There Were None: The Diminution of the Federal Jury*, 38 U. CHI. L. REV. 710 (1971).

5. Trial by jury has fared better in the U.S. than in the home country. Beginning in 1854, England reduced the use of the civil jury in a series of steps from complete usage (in non-equity cases) to about 2 percent of current cases. The use of the criminal jury also has been greatly reduced (employed in less than 10 percent of current cases). The grand jury (an endangered American institution not discussed in this essay) was abolished in England in 1933.

For discussions of English jury abolition and diminution *see*: Abraham, THE JUDICIAL PROCESS 245 (New York: Oxford University Press, third ed., 1975), Clark, THE GRAND JURY 104 (New York: Quadrangle, 1972), Devlin, TRIAL BY JURY 129-133 (London: Stevens and Sous, 1966), Ehrmann, COMPARATIVE LEGAL CULTURES 97-100 (Englewood Cliffs: Prentice Hall, 1976), and Zander, *The Jury in England: Decline and Fall?*, in Annual Chief Justice Earl Warren Conference on Advocacy in the United States, THE AMERICAN JURY SYSTEM 29-34 (Cambridge, MA: American Trial Lawyers Foundation, 1977).

6. 406 U.S. 356 (1972).

7. 406 U.S. 404 (1972).

8. 413 U.S. 149 (1973).

9. 435 U.S. 223 (1978).

10. 47 L.W. 4393 (1979).

11. Zeisel, *supra* n. 4, at 712.

12. The legitimation of majority verdicts in federal criminal trials was averted by a single vote. Justice Powell interpreted the Sixth Amendment to require unanimous jury verdicts. He was unwilling, however, to extend this requirement to the states through the Fourteenth Amendment.

13. The discussion of the cases must be brief. For a more detailed treatment, *see*: Sperlich, *Trial by Jury: It May Have a Future*, SUPREME COURT REVIEW 191, 195-209, 218-222 (1979).

14. For some of the major criticisms, *see*, for *Williams*: Beiser and Varrin, *Six-Member Juries in the Federal Court*, 58 JUDICATURE 424 (1975), Stevens, *Defendant's Right to a Jury Trial: Is Six Enough?*, 59 KY. L. J. 996 (1971), Walbert, *The Effect of Jury Size on the Probability of Conviction*, 22 CASE W. RES. L. REV. 529 (1971), Zeisel, *The Waning of the American Jury*, 58 A.B.A. J. 367 (1972), and Zeisel, *supra* n. 4.

For *Colgrove*: Diamond, *A Jury Experiment Reanalyzed*, 7 U. MICH. J. L. REF. 520 (1973), and Zeisel and Diamond, *Convincing Empirical Evidence on the Six Member Jury*, 41 U. CHI. L. REV. 281 (1974).

For *Williams* and *Colgrove*: Lempert, *Uncovering "Nondiscernible" Differences: Empirical Research and the Jury-Size Cases*, 73 MICH. L. REV. 643 (1975), Saks, *Ignorance of Science Is No Excuse*, 10 TRIAL 18 (Nov.-Dec. 1974), and Wick, *The Half-Filled Jury Box: Is Half Loaf Better Than None?*, 2 LITIGATION 11 (Winter 1976).

For *Johnson* and *Apodaca*: Buckhout, *Unanimous vs Majority Verdicts in Jury Deliberations*, 4 SOC. ACTION & THE L. 15 (Sept. 1977).

For *Williams, Johnson*, and *Apodaca*: Padawer-Singer, *Justice or Judgments?*, in Annual Chief Justice Earl Warren Conference on Advocacy in the United States, THE AMERICAN JURY SYSTEM, *supra* n. 5, at 45, Padawer-Singer and Barton, "Interim Report: Experimental Study of Decision-Making in the 12- Versus 6-Man Jury Under Unanimous Versus Non-Unanimous Deci-

sions," Columbia University, Bureau of Applied Social Research (1975), and Saks, JURY VERDICTS: THE ROLE OF GROUP SIZE AND SOCIAL DECISION RULE (New York: Lexington, 1977).

For all four cases: Buckhout et al., JURY VERDICTS: COMPARISON OF SIX VS. 12 PERSON JURIES AND UNANIMOUS VS. MAJORITY DECISION RULE IN A MURDER TRIAL, Report No. CR-12 (New York: Center for Responsive Psychology, 1977).

15. *Cf. supra* n. 1.

16. 399 U.S. at 89-90.

17. *Cf.* Stevens, *supra* n. 14, at 1000-1001, and Zeisel, *supra* n. 4, at 712.

18. The leading statements are found in Thompson v. Utah, 170 U.S. 343 (1898), Maxwell v. Dow, 176 U.S. 581 (1900), Rasmussen v. United States, 197 U.S. 516 (1905), Patton v. United States, 281 U.S. 276 (1930), and Capital Traction Co. v. Hof, 174 U.S. 1 (1899), a civil action.

19. 399 U.S. at 90.

20. *Id.* at 92-93.

21. *Id.* at 99-100.

22. *Id.* at 100.

23. *Id.* at 100-101.

24. 413 U.S. at 156.

25. *Id.* at 157.

26. The facts of *Ballew* can be stated briefly. (A more detailed discussion is found in Sperlich, *supra* n. 13, at 191-193.) The petitioner, Claude Davis Ballew, manager of a movie theatre, was convicted by a jury of five on a two-count misdemeanor charge for knowingly exhibiting obscene materials. In various motions and appeals, Ballew raised a number of issues regarding the constitutionality of his trial and conviction. The U.S. Supreme Court decided the case entirely on the issue of the constitutional adequacy of a state criminal jury of five. The other issues were not reached.

27. 435 U.S. at 239.

28. *Id.*

29. It may seem at first glance that a change in decision rule does not as such constitute a case of jury diminution. But a 12 person ten-to-two jury is equivalent to a ten-person jury. "The important element to observe is that the abandonment of the unanimity rule is but another way of reducing the size of the jury. But it is reduction with a vengeance, for a majority verdict is far more effective in nullifying the potency of minority viewpoints than is the out-right reduction of a jury to a size equivalent to the majority that is allowed to agree on a verdict." Zeisel, *supra* n. 4, at 772.

30. 406 U.S. at 410-411.

31. Justice White, nevertheless, did not shrink from complaining that the petitioner (Johnson) did not provide empirical evidence to support the claim that jury deliberations are not the same under unanimity and majority rule. The matter is particularly astonishing since by this complaint Justice White shifts the burden of proof from the State of Louisiana, seeking to change a constitutional tradition, to the petitioner, pleading for his customary rights. *Cf.* 406 U.S. at 362.

32. *Id.*

33. Some, of course, would argue that empirical evidence had rather little to do with the decision on the functional equivalency issue in the four cases that diminished the trial jury. The notion is prevalent that the Court used empirical evidence not so much to reach decisions, but to dress them up after they have been made. *Cf.* Zeisel and Diamond speaking of decisions "merely ornamented by the 'facts'," *supra* n. 14, at 281.

34. 47 L.W. at 4394.

35. Legal scholars and judges have not yet agreed on a standard terminology to refer to various types of facts and evidence. "Legislative facts," "social facts," "situation sense," and other terms are used in a variety of meanings. *Cf.* Davis, 2 ADMINIS-

TRATIVE LAW TREATISE 353 (St. Paul, MN: West, 1958), and Louisell and Mueller, 1 FEDERAL EVIDENCE 395 (San Francisco: Bancroft-Whitney, 1977), as well as Horowitz, THE COURTS AND SOCIAL POLICY 274-284 (Washington, DC: Brookings Institute, 1977), Marvell, APPELLATE COURTS AND LAWYERS 149-153 (Westport, MA: Greenwood Press, 1978), and Rosen, THE SUPREME COURT AND SOCIAL SCIENCE 53-54 (Urbana: University of Illinois Press, 1972).

In this essay, *case fact* refers to the question: did this apple fall from the defendant's tree and hit the plaintiff on the head? *Social fact* is used to refer to relevant scientific principles, i.e., the law of gravity: do apples normally move up, down, or sideways when breaking off the stem?

36. Even a "hard" science, such as ballistics, has not been immune from judicial know-it-all. In People v. Berkman, 307 Ill. 492, 501, 139 N.E. 91, 94 (1923), "the court characterized offered testimony concerning ballistics as 'preposterous,' a denunciation tacitly withdrawn only seven years later in People v. Fisher, 340 Ill. 216, 172 N.E. 743 (1930)." Strong, *Questions Affecting the Admissibility of Scientific Evidence*, 1970 U. ILL. L. FORUM 1, 10, note 31 (1970).

37. Courts, of course, are put into a most difficult position when experts disagree. The problematic nature of psychiatric testimony readily comes to mind. Disagreement among competent scientific studies was not, however, the cause of the Court's inept handling of social fact issues in the jury decisions.

38. 435 U.S. at 246. Opinion of Justice Powell, joined by Justices Burger and Rehnquist.

39. Nor is it particularly gracious to refer to the investigations of the academic experts on jury behavior as "merely . . . [the] findings of persons interested in the jury system." *Id.*

40. To a large extent, the lack of knowledge about jurors and juries is due to the non-cooperation of the courts. To a smaller degree it is due to congressional opposition. *Cf.* Sperlich, *supra* n. 13, at 201, note 38.

41. 399 U.S. at 101, note 48.

42. For a detailed review of the six items, *see* Zeisel, *supra* n. 4, at 714-715.

43. The Court not only relied on incompetent items, but misinterpreted the evidence presented in competent studies. Zeisel was forced to complain that "[i]n *Williams* the Court cites the studies conducted in connection with THE AMERICAN JURY to support its proposition that 'jurors in the minority on the first ballot are likely to be influenced by the proportional size of the majority aligned against them.' It is only fair to point out that the findings were quite different." *Id.* at 719.

44. *Id.* at 715. In the circumstance, "scant evidence" is a mild rebuke. As Lempert has pointed out: "Zeisel is gentle with the Court; he never emphasizes the majority's extreme disingenuousness in citing these reports as experiments and in relying on them as evidence . . ." Lempert, *supra* n. 14, at 645.

45. Saks, *Ignorance* . . . , *supra* n. 14, at 18.

46. Walbert, *supra* n. 14, at 535.

47. Wick, *supra* n. 14, at 14.

48. "The test laid down in *Williams* indicates that the reduced jury is unconstitutional if the smaller size impairs its performance. Consequently, a correct application of the Court's test would hold that a jury of six persons is unconstitutional." Walbert, *supra* n. 14, at 554.

49. In his review of *Williams*, Zeisel noted the spurious nature of the first of the six items, the Court's reference to Judge Wiehl's comments on the six-person jury: "Judge Wiehl approvingly cites Joiner's CIVIL JUSTICE AND THE JURY, in which Joiner somewhat disingenuously states that 'it could easily be argued that a six-man jury would deliberate equally as well as one of

twelve.' Since Joiner had no evidence for his conclusion, Judge Wiehl also does not have any." (*Supra* n. 4, at 714) The *Colgrove* Court was well aware of Zeisel's criticism. (413 U.S. at 159, note 15) Nevertheless, Joiner's opinion is included in the list of items offered by *Colgrove* in support of the functional equivalence assertion. (*Id.*)

50. 413 U.S. at 158-159.

51. *Id.* at 159, note 15.

52. For detailed discussions, *see* Zeisel & Diamond, *supra* n. 14, at 282-290, and Diamond, *supra* n. 14.

53. It must be acknowledged that some of the flaws contained in the four studies were not immediately obvious and required a certain amount of methodological understanding for their detection. This, however, does not permit the inference that the justices were victimized by inadequate science. First, the Court has consistently failed to take notice of deficiencies in the evidence that were well within the competence of the justices to discover (e.g., that an unsupported opinion that there would be no differences cannot validate a claim that there are none).

Second, the degree of methological expertise required to spot the inadequacies of the *Williams* and *Colgrove* items actually was very modest (*Cf.* Saks, *Ignorance* . . . , *supra* n. 14, at 20, and Zeisel & Diamond, *supra* n. 14, at 292).

Third, the Court had the ability to call for advice on specific technical questions, without having to return the case to the trial courts. Fourth, reading the Court's opinions raises substantial doubt that the "empirical evidence" actually decided these cases. The suspicion is not easily dismissed that the empirical references served "merely to ornament an already determined result" (Zeisel & Diamond, *supra* n. 14, at 281).

54. Zeisel & Diamond, *supra* n. 14, at 290.

55. *Id.* at 281.

56. Zeisel, *Twelve is Just*, 10 TRIAL 13 (Nov.-Dec. 1974).

57. Wick, *supra* n. 14, at 14.

58. *Williams* included this sentence: "We have no occasion in this case to determine what minimum number can still constitute a 'jury,' but we do not doubt that six is above the minimum." (399 U.S. at 91, note 28) As the State of Georgia would correctly but unsuccessfully argue in *Ballew*, if six is above the minimum, five cannot be below it, given that juries cannot consist of five and one-half persons.

59. This possibility was considered by Justice Blackmun in his concurring opinion to *Johnson*, writing that "a system employing a 7-5 standard, rather than a 9-3 or 75 percent minimum, would afford me great difficulty." (406 U.S. at 366).

60. Reducing the proportion of jurors required to convict decreases the effective size of the jury. Indeed, it may be a more severe reduction in jury size than a direct decrease in the number of jurors. *Cf.* Zeisel, *supra* n. 29.

61. If not signaling recovery, *Ballew* (and *Burch*) indicate at least that there is a limit to the Court's favorable view of state experimentation with the trial jury.

62. It is of interest to note that *Ballew* does not have a majority opinion. Justice Blackmun's opinion for the Court was joined by Justice Stevens. Justices Blackmun, Powell, Rehnquist, Stevens, White, and the chief justice concurred in the judgment. Justices Brennan, Marshall, and Stewart concurred in the holding, but disagreed that the petitioner should be subjected to a new trial.

63. 435 U.S. at 239.

64. The relationships reported here do not have infinite linear extensions, of course. The quality of performance is not likely to be greater in a group of 2,000 than in a group of six. The smaller/larger comparisons in this context refer only to the 6/12 or 5/12 contrast.

65. 435 U.S. at 232-234. The findings were secured by ref-

erences to Kelley & Thibaut, *Group Problem Solving* in 4 Lindsey & Aronson, HANDBOOK OF SOCIAL PSYCHOLOGY 29 (Reading, MA: Addison-Wesley, 2d ed., 1969); Lempert, *supra* n. 14; Saks, JURY VERDICTS, *supra* n. 14; and, by way of Lempert, Barnlund, *A Comparative Study of Individual, Majority, and Group Judgment*, 58 J. AB. & SOC. PSYCH. 55 (1959), Faust, *Group versus Individual Problem-Solving*, 59 J. AB. & SOC. PSYCH. 68 (1959), and Thomas & Fink, *Effects of Group Size*, 60 PSYCH. BULL. 371 (1963).

66. Justice Blackmun's analysis of the empirical materials, *as it regards the five person issue*, stands in marked contrast to the treatment of "evidence" in the earlier decisions. The specific items are fair selections from the relevant literature, though a number of items could usefully have been added (*Cf. infra*).

The treatment of the selected items is competent, if not without weaknesses. The most important error occurs in the treatment of Nagel & Neef's modeling effort, which seems to have been regarded as an inductive-empirical study, without adequate attention to the dependence of the conclusions on the highly speculative assumptions made by the model. The justice relied on Nagel & Neef for the inference that the optimal jury size was between six and eight. (435 U.S. at 234) It can equally well be concluded from the model that the ideal jury size is 23. *See* Sperlich, *supra* n. 13, at 216, note 107.

67. 435 U.S. at 234-235. The findings were secured by references to Friedman, *Trial by Jury*, 27 AM. STAT. 21 (1972); Lempert, *supra* n. 14; Nagel & Neef, *Deductive Modeling to Determine an Optimum of Jury Size and Fraction Required to Convict*, 1975 WASH. U.L.Q. 933 (1975); Saks, JURY VERDICTS, *supra* n. 14; Walbert (Note), *supra* n. 14; and, by way of Nagel & Neef, Kalven & Zeisel, THE AMERICAN JURY (Boston: Little, Brown, 1966).

68. 435 U.S. at 236. The findings were secured by reference to Lempert, *supra* n. 14; Zeisel, *supra* n. 4; and, by way of Lempert, Asch, *Effects of Group Pressure upon the Modification and Distortion of Judgments*, in Cartwright & Zander, GROUP DYNAMICS 189 (New York: Row, Peterson, 2d ed., 1960).

69. 435 U.S. at 236-237. The findings were secured by references to Lempert, *supra* n. 14; and Saks, JURY VERDICTS, *supra* n. 14.

70. 435 U.S. at 237-239. The findings were secured by references to Diamond, *supra* n. 14; Kalven & Zeisel, *supra* n. 67; Lempert, *supra* n. 14; Nagel & Neef, *supra* n. 67; Saks, *Ignorance . . .*, *supra* n. 14; Saks, JURY VERDICTS, *supra* n. 14; Walbert (Note), *supra* n. 14; and Zeisel & Diamond, *supra* n. 14.

71. 435 U.S. at 239.

72. Justice Blackmun's opinion becomes tortured when it affirms that six equals 12, while denying that five equals 12, all of this based on evidence that does not even consider the issue five, but clearly demonstrates the falsity of 6=12. It is inconceivable that the justice was oblivious to the situation. One might speculate that the explanation lies in the political realities of Supreme Court decision making, i.e., that the votes to strike down *five* were available only at the price of affirming *six*.

73. In addition to the items referred to in the preceding paragraph, Justice Blackmun took note of a number of other studies. *See* 435 U.S. at 231, note 10.

74. The State of Georgia was satisfied to dig out one of Judge Tamm's articles of questionable relevance: *The Five-Man Civil Jury: A Proposed Constitutional Amendment*, 51 GEO. L.J. 120 (1962). The attorneys for the petitioner utilized a total of six items. *Cf.* Sperlich, *supra* n. 13, at 217, note 111.

75. Saari, *The Criminal Jury Faces Future Shock*, 57 JUDICATURE 12, 14 (June-July 1973).

76. For example, Gelfand, *A Statistical Case for the 12-Member Jury*, 13 TRIAL 41 (Feb. 1977), and Gelfand & Solomon, *Analyzing the Decision-Making Process of the American Jury*, 70 J. AM.

STAT. ASSOC. 305 (1975).

77. For example, Grofman, *Jury Decision-Making Models*, in Nagel, MODELING THE CRIMINAL JUSTICE SYSTEM 191 (Beverly Hills, CA: Sage, 1977).

78. For example, Buckhout, "The U.S. Supreme Court vs. Social Science: The Jury" (unpublished manuscript, 1977), as well as the many items published in SOCIAL ACTION & THE LAW.

79. Snortum et al., *The Impact of an Aggressive Juror in Six-and Twelve-Member Juries*, 3 CRIM. JUSTICE & BEHAV. 255 (1976).

80. Padawer-Singer & Barton, "Interim Report," *supra* n. 14.

81. Davis et al., *The Empirical Study of Decision Processes in Juries: A Critical Review*, in Tapp & Levine, LAW, JUSTICE, AND THE INDIVIDUAL IN SOCIETY 326 (New York: Holt, Rinehart and Winston, 1977).

82. 47 L.W. at 4393.

83. Many of the items cited in *Ballew*, as well as almost all of those suggested as additions in the preceding paragraph, offer evidence on the decision-rule issue. For purposes of *Burch*, it would also have been useful to direct attention to the work of Nemeth; for example, *Interactions Between Jurors as a Function of Majority vs. Unanimity Decision Rules*, 7 J. APPL. SOC. PSYCH. 38 (1977).

The various decision-rule studies lead to the same conclusion: different decision rules are not functionally equivalent. They also show quite clearly that unanimity differs not only from *Burch's* 5/6 majority rule, but also from the fractions of *Johnson* and *Apodaca*. Not critically reviewing empirical evidence, Justice Rehnquist, of course, had no opportunity to doubt the wisdom of the earlier two decisions.

84. 47 L.W. at 4395.

85. *Id.*

86. *Id.* at 4394, note 7.

87. *Cf. supra* n. 33. *See also* Horowitz, *supra* n. 35, at 279, Lempert, personal communication, as quote by Grofman, *supra* n. 77, at 6, Lochner, *Some Limits on the Application of Social Science Research in the Legal Process*, 197 L. & SOC. ORDER 815, 835-836 (1973), and Rosenblum, *A Place for Social Science Along the Judiciary's Constitutional Law Frontier*, 66 NW. U.L. REV. 459 (1971). The notion also has adherents that judicial camouflaging extends far beyond the use of references to empirical evidence. "The judicial process is overwhelmingly a means of rationalizing preferred ends." Levy, AGAINST THE LAW 36 (New York: Harper and Row, 1974).

88. False information has consequences. If the real basis of a decision is not known, parties cannot effectively respond to it, which undermines the adversary process. Camouflage also is likely to mislead constitutional scholarship, lead counsel into faulty argument, and create erroneous expectations among litigants.

89. *Cf.* pp. 240-241 *supra*.

90. 435 U.S. at 243.

91. *Cf. supra* n. 1.

92. Phillips, *A Jury of Six in All Cases*, 30 CONN. BAR J. 354 (1956).

93. As examples, *see* Burger, *Report on the State of the Federal Judiciary*, 6 SUFFOLK U.L. REV. 776, 781 (1972), and *Interview with Chief Justice Warren E. Burger*, 69 U.S. NEWS & WORLD REPORT (Dec. 14, 1970) at 32, 39.

94. Augelli, *supra* n. 1, at 292, Tamm, *supra* n. 74, at 134, Thompson, *supra* n. 1, at 14, Wiehl, *supra* n. 1, at 292, and Institute of Judicial Administration, A COMPARISON OF SIX- AND TWELVE-MEMBER CIVIL JURIES IN THE NEW JERSEY SUPERIOR AND COUNTY COURTS 19 (New York: 1972).

95. Augelli, *supra* n. 1, at 291-292, Comment, *With Love . . .*, *supra* n. 1, at 192, Institute of Judicial Administration, *supra* n. 94, at 27-28, 33-34, Phillips, *supra* n. 92, at 356, Powell, *supra* n. 1, at 96-97, Tamm, *supra* n. 74, at 131-132, Thompson, *supra* n.

1, at 14, and Wiehl, *supra* n. 1, at 40.

96. Augelli, *supra* n. 1, at 292, Institute of Judicial Administration, *supra* n. 94, at 24-26, Phillips, *supra* n. 92, at 356-357, Powell, *supra* n. 1, at 97, Tamm, *supra* n. 74, at 132, Thompson, *supra* n. 1, at 14, Wiehgl, *supra* n. 1, at 40, Bogue and Fritz, *The Six-Man Jury*, 17 S.D. L. Rev. 285, 288 (1972), and Devitt, *The Six-Man Jury in the Federal Courts*, 53 F.R.D. 273, 275 (1971).

97. Augelli, *supra* n. 1, at 292, Comment, *With Love . . .*, *supra* n. 1, at 192, Devitt, *supra* n. 96, at 276, Institute for Judicial Administration, *supra* n. 94, at 28-32, Phillips, *supra* n. 92, at 357, Powell, *supra* n. 1, at 97, 101, Tamm, *supra* n. 74, at 132, Thompson, *supra* n. 1, at 14, and Wiehl, *supra* n. 1, at 40.

98. Augelli, *supra* n. 1, at 291, Bogue & Fritz, *supra* n. 96, at 288-289, Devitt, *supra* n. 96, at 276-277, Phillips, *supra* n. 92, at 357-358, Powell, *supra* n. 1, at 98, Tamm, *supra* n. 74, at 133, Thompson, *supra* n. 1, at 14, and Zimmerman, *Evaluating the Six Member Jury*, 36 Soc. Science 45, 46 (1961).

99. Some of the claims are amusing, showing a rather desperate desire to justify smaller juries by appealing to thrift and fiscal responsibility. One learns, for example, that fewer jurors can move in and out of the jury box in a shorter time than a larger number. Devitt, *supra* n. 96, at 275, and Phillips, *supra* n. 92, at 357. One also learns that smaller juries can do with smaller jury boxes and smaller jury rooms. Thompson, *supra* n. 1, at 14.

It is astonishing to see that judges are capable of arguing that in deciding the fate of the jury we should take into account the few seconds saved in the movement of the jurors, and the few square feet of courtroom space saved by a smaller jury box. Besides, most American courtrooms serve a variety of trials, some of which will still require juries of 12, so that the larger jury box has to be preserved. Furthermore, most existing jury rooms are so small to begin with, that cutting them in half to create two smaller rooms would have juries deliberate in spaces resembling cells or closets.

100. For studies and discussions, *see* Baum, *supra* n. 1, at 128, Padawer-Singer, *supra* n. 14, at 50, Zeisel, *supra* n. 4, at 771-772, Zeisel, *supra* n. 56, at 13-15, Zeisel & Diamond, *supra* n. 14, at 294, Bloomstein, Verdict: The Jury System 128 (New York: Dodd, Mead, 1972), Broeder, *The University of Chicago Jury Project*, 38 Nebraska L. Rev. 744, 747 (1959), Pabst, *Statistical Studies of the Costs of Six-Man Versus Twelve-Man Juries*, 14 William & Mary L. Rev. 326 (1972), and Pabst, *What Do Six-Member Juries Really Save?*, 57 Judicature 6 (1973).

101. Daily juror fees range from zero to about $20, and some courts pay a fee only when a juror actually serves on a jury, not when he waits to be chosen. For an overview of fees paid, *see* Pabst & Munsterman, *The Economic Hardship of Jury Duty*, 58 Judicature 495 (1975).

102. For example, the total 1975-76 budget of New York City was $12.3 billion, of which $200 million, or 1.6 percent, was allocated to the city's courts. Juror fees can be estimated to have been $2 million, that is, less than one-tenth of one percent of the total city budget, one percent of the budget of the city courts, and approximately 25¢ per resident, per year. Looking at a state, juror fees constituted one-tenth of one percent of the Connecticut budget for 1976-77. Annual Chief Justice Earl Warren Conference on Advocacy, The American Jury System, *supra* n. 5, at 8-9.

103. Bogue & Fritz, *supra* n. 96, at 289.

104. Devitt, *Six-Member Civil Juries Gain Backing*, 57 A.B.A. J. 1111, 1112 (1971).

105. Zeisel & Diamond, *supra* n. 14, at 294.

106. Multi-million dollar savings become less impressive when it is remembered that this country spends millions of dollars each year on such products as pet rocks, animal jewelry, and white walls for tires, as well as about $156 million for nail polish, $500 million for recreational outboard motors, $2 billion for movie tickets, $17 billion for tobacco products, and uncounted billions for alcoholic beverages, drugs and gambling.

107. With the "Spirit of Proposition 13" in the country, it is particularly important to examine the relative cost of the jury system, and the actual savings that could be realized by reducing or even abolishing the trial jury. A candidate, looking for issues, might even run for president by opposing "the waste of the jury system."

108. Substantial savings, for example, can be gained by eliminating the wasteful practice of calling much larger numbers of jurors than needed to court each day. *See* Pabst, *An End to Juror Waiting*, 55 Judicature 277 (1972), and Note, *D.C. Court Achieves Jury Economies*, 43 Judicature 171 (1960).

109. *See, for example*, Burger, *Report . . .*, *supra* n. 93, at 781.

110. Comment, *With Love . . .*, *supra* n. 1, at 180, 189, Lumbard, *supra* n. 1, at 15, Phillips, *supra* n. 92, at 354 *et seq.*, Tamm, *supra* n. 74, at 120 *et seq.*, Thompson, *supra* n. 1, at 12, Wiehl, *supra* n. 1, at 35 *et seq.*, Bullivant, *Abolition of Jury Trial in Civil Cases*, 5 Oregon L. Rev. 185, 192 (1926), Gleisser, Juries and Justice 203, 205 (New York: Barnes, 1968), Kaufman, *Harbingers of Jury Reform*, 58 A.B.A. J. 695 (1972); *see also* three articles reprinted in Winters, The Jury: Selected Readings (Chicago: American Judicature Society, 1971): Desmond, *Juries in Civil Cases—Yes or No?*, 17-19, Kronzer & O'Quinn, *Let's Return to Majority Rule in Civil Jury Cases*, 71-73, and Landis, *Jury Trials and the Delay of Justice*, 20-21.

111. Devitt, *supra* n. 1, at 570.

112. Bloomstein, *supra* n. 100, at 128. Appellate courts function without juries, it should further be noted, but experience delay.

113. *See* Zeisel, Kalven & Buchholz, Delay in Court 83-86 (Boston: Little, Brown, 1959), Kalven, *supra* n. 1, at 1058-1061, Zeisel, *supra* n. 4, at 711, Pabst, *Statistical Studies . . .*, *supra* n. 100, at 330, and Flynn, *Public Preference for the Jury*, 32 N.Y. State Bar Bull. 103, 108-109 (1960).

114. In a recent study of urban criminal courts, Levin found that delay has a variety of sources, including the *benefit* of delay to some of the parties: One of the "most striking counterintuitive findings is that, in the five criminal courts analyzed, delay did not seem to be an external phenomenon thrust upon unwilling participants. Rather, it was primarily associated with the voluntary behavior of the judges, defense attorneys, and prosecutors as they pursued their own interests. This differs from the conventional causal explanations that stress the delays caused by large caseloads thrust upon mismanaged, inefficient courts," Levin, Urban Politics and the Criminal Courts 3 (Chicago: University of Chicago Press, 1977).

115. "In American legal theory, jury power was enormous and subject to few controls. There was a maxim of law that the jury was judge both of law and of fact in criminal cases. This idea was particularly strong in the first, Revolutionary generation, when memories of royal injustice were fresh . . . . But the rule came under savage attack from some judges and other authorities," Friedman, A History of American Law 251 (New York: Simon and Schuster, 1973). Broeder speaks of the process of the "judicial emasculation" of the jury. *The Functions of the Jury: Facts or Fictions?* 21 U. Chi. L. Rev. 386, 403 (1954).

116. For discussions of current jury practice regarding law decisions, *see* Jacobsohn, *The Right to Disagree: Judges, Juries and the Administration of Criminal Justice in Maryland*, 1974 Wash. U.L.Q. 571 (1976), Jacobsohn, *Citizen Participation in Policy-Making: The Role of the Jury*, 39 J. of Politics 73 (1977), Kadish & Kadish, Discretion to Disobey: A Study of Lawful Departures from Legal Rules, especially 46-66 (Stanford: Stanford University Press, 1973), and Scheflin, *Jury Nullification: The Right to Say No*, 45 So. Cal. L. Rev. 168 (1972).

117. Phillips, *supra* n. 92, at 357.

118. Gleisser, *supra* n. 110, at 309-310. Gleisser also believes that "the judges themselves would be performing a valued service to their courts if they would encourage the waiving of juries altogether . . ." *Id.* at 310.

119. Judge Lumbard, for one, wants to speed up trials, reduce the use of the jury, and give the trial judge greater control. Regarding voir dire, he advocates that all examinations of the jurors should be conducted by the judge, and writes in a singularly revealing phrase: "It should be enough that counsel be *permitted to suggest* questions to the judge." Lumbard, *supra* n. 1, at 17; emphasis added.

120. The majority of attorneys seems to favor the larger jury. The public, particularly former jurors, strongly favors trial by jury. For data regarding the views of the various groups, *see* Association of Trial Lawyers of America, *Judges and the Jury: A Distillation of a Survey*, in Annual Chief Justice Earl Warren Conference on Advocacy in the United States, THE AMERICAN JURY SYSTEM, *supra* n. 5, at 97-99, Comment, *With Love . . .*, *supra* n. 1, at 183-194, Flynn, *supra* n. 113, at 103-104, Institute of Judicial Administration, *supra* n. 94, at 5, 9-14 *et seq.*, Kalven, *supra* n. 1, at 1072-1074, and Joiner, CIVIL JUSTICE AND THE JURY, 201-205 (Englewood Cliffs: Prentice-Hall, 1962).

121. As Zeisel has pointed out: "If the jury size is reduced from twelve to six, [the lawyer's perception] of the approximate balance between jury and bench trial will be disturbed. Henceforth, the 'gamble' with a jury will be significantly greater than the 'gamble' with a judge and, as a result, more lawyers might waive their right to a jury, perhaps a consequence not unexpected by those who initiated the reform." Zeisel, *supra* n. 1, at 719.

122. *Cf.* p. 273 *supra*.

123. Levy, *supra* n. 87, at 12-36, 43-60.

124. *Id.*, especially Chapters 2-4.

125. Zeisel, *supra* n. 14, at 370.

126. Zeisel, *supra* n. 56, at 15.

127. Berger, GOVERNMENT BY JUDICIARY 399 (Cambridge, MA: Harvard University Press, 1977).

128. See, *Social science evidence in the courts: reaching beyond the adversary process*, 63 JUDICATURE 280 (Dec/Jan 1980) for a systematic examination of these matters.

129. *Cf. supra* n. 1.

Scientific jury selection: what social scientists know and do not know

The effects of scientific jury selection are modest at best. Social science consultants offer the most valuable aid when they help attorneys develop trial presentations that are clear and convincing.

by Shari Seidman Diamond

A jury is rarely unanimous when it takes its first vote,[1] but its final verdict is generally the decision initially favored by a majority of the jurors.[2] If the voir dire in a close case replaces only a few jurors who would favor one side with jurors who will favor the opposing side, jury selection can be critical. A voir dire that shifts the distribution of jurors to create a new majority can dramatically affect the probability of a favorable verdict.

The evidence presented at trial cannot account for initial disagreements among jurors: all jurors are exposed to the same evidence. The differences in juror reaction must stem from pre-existing differences among the jurors that affect juror responses to the evidence.[3] If 'scientific jury selection' (SJS) can help identify attributes of unfriendly jurors in advance, the attorney can exercise peremptory challenges to remove those jurors during voir dire. The prospect is enticing: what litigator faced with the uncertainties of trial would not appreciate a little assistance?

Before 1970, attorneys had to rely solely on their personal and trial experience with people and on their knowledge of their cases to develop voir dire questions and weed out unsympathetic jurors. The expert advice available from various trial specialists offered conflicting guidance.[4] A survey of litigators showed similarly inconsistent philosophies in jury selection.[5] Against this background of inconsistency, social scientists have offered their assistance, claiming a scientific basis for the advice they offer.

SJS began when the Berrigan brothers, two antiwar activist priests, were put on trial for conspiring to kidnap then Secretary of State Henry Kissinger. Sociologist Jay Schulman and his colleagues assisted the defense in selecting the jury that hung 10 to 2 for acquittal. In the early days of SJS, the method was used largely in political criminal cases that involved substantial publicity. Prospective jurors in those cases often had strong preconceived notions about the defendants or the alleged offense. More recently, an active consulting industry has applied SJS to a wide variety of criminal and civil actions.

Methods of SJS

A primary research method used in SJS is a telephone survey in which members of the public who would be eligible to serve as jurors are asked three sets of questions. One set asks for the respondent's background characteristics (age, sex, occupation, prior jury service, prior experience as an accident victim if the case involves personal injury, etc.). The attorneys will be able to obtain this same information on each prospective juror during the voir dire.

The second set of questions on the survey may or may not be asked during voir dire. This set measures beliefs and attitudes that are likely to be associated with a favorable or unfavorable trial verdict (a dislike of oil companies or of the particular oil company which is the defendant; for a malpractice case, the belief that doctors generally do what is best for their patients).

The third set of questions directly attempts to assess which side the respondent would favor in the trial. A brief description of the case is read and the respondent is asked to vote as if on a jury deciding the case.

The jury consultant then analyzes the responses to the survey to determine which juror characteristics correlate with favorable attitudes and verdict preferences, and which attitudes and beliefs correlate with verdict preferences. This information is used to create juror profiles to guide jury selection.

Researchers may also develop selection profiles by testing respondents at research facilities. Respondents are shown opening statements or full mock trials. When they are brought into a testing facility respondents can be exposed to a better approximation of what the trial will actually involve and can be questioned more extensively than when they are tested in a telephone survey. To the extent that the simulation accurately portrays the crucial elements of the trial as it will unfold, the verdict preferences in the simulation will more accurately reflect juror reactions to the trial than the preferences expressed in the telephone survey.

The disadvantage of tests in a research facility is that a telephone survey can test a much larger and more representative sample at a much lower cost per respondent. One large jury consulting firm uses a facility for mock trials in a north suburb of Chicago. Respondents cannot easily get to the location without a car and, not surprisingly, inner city residents who appear on the jury rolls do not appear at this facility. While facilities for mock trials can be more carefully chosen, representativeness is easier to obtain in a telephone survey because more potential respondents are willing to answer a few questions over the phone than attend a testing facility. Because each method has disadvantages, SJS often relies on a combination of telephone surveys and mock trials.

The primary test of any jury selection technique is whether it can predict, based on information available before challenges must be exercised, how jurors will react to the evidence presented at trial. For SJS there is an additional test: assuming that SJS does have some predictive power, under what conditions does the 'scientific' method outperform the more intuitive method of jury selection traditionally used by the trial attorney?

There is significant disagreement in the legal and scientific communities about the answers to both of these questions. In this article, I analyze the evidence for and against the claims made for SJS. After concluding that the approach can have a modest effect at best and that it can *decrease* as well as *increase* the probability of a favorable verdict, I outline some methods the trial attorney can use to test the value of the advice a consultant offers in a particular case. Finally, I suggest that the emphasis on SJS as the key social science tool in trial preparation is misplaced. The primary determinant of the jury's outcome is the evidence, and social science consultants offer the most valuable aid when they help the attorney to develop a trial presentation that is clear and convincing.

Effect of SJS

The consultants who offer selection advice are quick to point to cases in which the winning side used SJS techniques. While such victories are not unusual, no one has yet produced convincing evidence that advice on jury selection made the difference. The demands of the courtroom preclude a full controlled test of the technique in the courtroom setting. In the ideal test of SJS, a series of cases would be tried before multiple juries, some 'scientifically' selected and others traditionally chosen. A comparison of the verdicts rendered by the two types of juries would test the value of the method.[6] This direct test of SJS has not yet been done.

The early pioneers in SJS conducted some indirect tests. Schulman and his colleagues[7] interviewed jurors who were excused during voir dire or jury eligible community members who did not go through jury selection at all. They compared the verdict preferences of these potential jurors with those given by the jury that decided the case, that is, a jury selected with the help of SJS. The flaw in such tests is that only the real jurors have sat through the case and heard all of the evidence—those excused or never called have not. As nearly every study of jury decisionmaking indicates, the evidence presented at trial is the primary determinant of a jury verdict.[8] Accordingly, verdicts of the actual jury and the excused or never called jurors may differ, not because of the selection strategy, but because they are responses to different evidence.

In an interesting attempt to conduct a controlled test of the effects of SJS, Horowitz trained law students in either SJS or the traditional clinical approach to jury selection.[9] The law students then used the assigned technique to conduct a voir dire. Those trained to use SJS were given data from a survey of prospective jurors to guide their jury selection.

All of the prospective jurors, whether chosen or rejected, listened to the case and indicated their preferred verdicts. Horowitz then evaluated how well each method performed by examining the verdict preferences of the jurors selected by each method. On two of the four cases, the law students who used SJS made more accurate choices than those who used the traditional approach; on one case the students using the traditional approach were more accurate and on the remaining case there was no difference.

These results suggest that superior performance by SJS occurs in some, but not all, cases. The results, however, may not generalize beyond law student-attorneys. It is not clear whether the SJS method used in these cases fully replicated the range of questions used by other SJS practitioners; it is certainly clear that the law students lacked the training and experience of many trial attorneys.

SJS uses juror characteristics to predict verdict preferences and thus inform selection choices. Accordingly, a test of the foundations of SJS is the extent to which juror characteristics which predict juror verdicts can be identified. In one such study, Saks measured 461 Ohio jurors on 27 attitudes and background characteristics.[10] His respondents then watched a videotaped burglary trial and deliberated to a verdict. The best predictor of juror verdict preferences was whether a juror believed that crime was mainly the product of "bad people" or "bad social condition."[11] That question accounted for a modest 9 percent of the variance in verdict preferences.[12] Only three other predictors improved the prediction—and together the four predictors accounted for less than 13 percent of the variance in juror verdict preferences.

Penrod tested 367 Massachusetts jurors on 21 attitude and background characteristics and then had them indicate verdict preferences in three criminal cases and one civil case.[13] One predictor accounted for 7 percent of the variance in verdict preferences on the rape case: jurors who favored conviction were more likely to agree that there should be evidence of physical resistance before a defendant is convicted of rape. The best predictors were able to account for about 14 percent of the variance on the murder case, 16 percent on the rape, under 10 percent on the negligence case and under 5 percent on the robbery. Juror verdict preferences on one case did not predict verdict preferences on any of the other three cases and the best predictors of verdict were not the same across the four cases.

Hastie et al. showed 828 jurors the videotaped reenactment of a real murder trial.[14] Four of the 12 background characteristics of the jurors were significant predictors of verdict preferences; they accounted for 3.2 percent of the variance in verdicts. A sub-sample of 269 jurors was tested on a number of additional background characteristics and attitudes. With these additional predictors, Hastie et al. were able to explain 11 percent of the variance in juror verdicts.

In an effort to predict juror verdicts in real trials, Moran and Comfort mailed questionnaires to jurors who just completed jury service.[15] They obtained responses from 319 jurors who reported what their verdict preferences had been when they began deliberating as jurors, answered questions on 11 background characteristics and filled out 13 opinion/personality scales. Two of the personality measures explained 11 percent of the variation in verdict preferences for female jurors; no other variable increased the accuracy of the prediction. For males, only one measure was a significant predictor of verdict preference and it explained 6 percent.

Other studies have shown similar or lower correlations between predictors and verdict preferences.[16] While each of the studies reviewed here suffers from some limitations, the pattern of results is consistent. The most important implication of this research is that claims for predicting juror responses to trial evidence should be modest indeed. The studies reviewed here report an ability to account for up to 15 percent of the variation in juror verdict preferences.

It is, of course, possible that more powerful attitudinal measures can be developed, but there is good reason to be skeptical about the potential of SJS to improve selection decisions substantially. Assuming that more powerful attitudinal measures are available or can be developed, the measures will be valuable for jury selection only if they can be administered in court. The courtroom version of an attitude scale is a crude cousin to the sensitive measure that shows predictive power in the preparatory research. A reliable measure of attitude is generally composed of a set of questions which each respondent answers independently. In the courtroom, judges will not ask or permit attorneys to ask each potential juror the 17 questions that form the measure of empathy.[17] Even if jurors are questioned individually, they are exposed to the responses of other jurors to those same questions and their answers may be affected by those earlier responses. Moreover, courts do not permit voir dire questions unless they appear logically relevant to the case. For example, while juror support for the death penalty is consistently associated with a greater willingness to convict,[18] the question can only be asked in capital cases. Attorneys who use the results of SJS in the courtroom must thus decide which jurors to excuse based on abbreviated tests of attitudes distorted by the public arena in which they are expressed.

The national trend is toward a limited voir dire, often conducted almost entirely by the judge.[19] Under these conditions, the predictors from SJS that will be available to the attorney during jury selection will be confined to background characteristics that appear to offer limited predictive power. Even if the judge agrees to ask some of the additional questions proposed by the attorneys, the judge may change the wording so that they lose all predictive power.[20]

A second implication of the research on jury selection is that there is no profile of the good defense (or prosecution or plaintiff) juror that can be used across cases. Characteristics that emerge as predictors on one case do not show the same pattern on another case. Jurors who are most favorable to the defense in one trial will not necessarily make the best defense jurors in another trial. This is not particularly surprising. Psychologists have spent years trying to predict behavior and the results have revealed only modest levels of consistency across situations.[21] The jury consultant who provides a profile of the good defense juror suitable for all cases and applicable to all communities is offering the most blatant voodoo voir dire advice.

Finally, research on jury selection indicates that the survey efforts of SJS will not improve the accuracy of jury selection in every case. In some cases,

a jury consultant may even be less accurate than the trial attorney operating without consultant advice. Statistical prediction is usually, but not always, more accurate than clinical prediction.[22] The trial attorney knows the evidence in the case, both on the client's and on the opposition's side, better than does the consultant. In addition, the attorney operating in a familiar court may be able to use the incidental information that emerges during voir dire (e.g., the strike at a local business where a prospective juror is employed). The attorney can eliminate some hostile jurors without expert advice.[23] Accordingly, the attorney should accept advice from a survey formula for jury selection only when provided with hard evidence that the advice offers the genuine prospect of improved prediction.

Testing the consultant's advice

Consultants using SJS typically test the predictive power of a large battery of juror beliefs, attitudes and background characteristics that the consultants, the parties, and the attorneys think may be related to verdict preferences: publications read, frequency of watching the news, age, gender, number of children, occupation, marital status, income, prior jury service, attitudes toward big corporations, etc. Each of these possible predictors is compared with the juror's preferred verdict.[24] The juror characteristics that are statistically significant predictors of preferred verdicts are then included in the juror profile that will be used during jury selection.

As an example, a jury survey done in preparation for a personal injury case includes 40 potential predictors. The consultant analyzes the results of the survey and reports that males are significantly more likely to favor a verdict for the plaintiff than females; respondents who think that people generally get what they deserve are significantly more likely to favor the defense. Both relationships are significant at the traditional .05 probability level.[25] No other characteristics are significant predictors.

Any use of these results in selecting a jury would be like basing predictions on patterns in a roulette wheel. A relationship is statistically significant at the traditional .05 level if there is one chance in 20 that the result would occur in the absence of any relationship between the predictor and the verdict preference. Thus, if all 40 predictors were totally unrelated to verdict preferences, 1 in 20 or 2 of those predictors would show a significant relationship to verdict preference.[26]

Such explorations for relationships are often referred to as "fishing." They may disclose unexpected relationships between juror characteristics and verdict preferences; they may also turn up "relationships" that are simply due to chance and which will not exist when they are applied to the next set of jurors—the ones at trial. Fortunately, there are several ways to test before trial how likely it is that a relationship revealed in the survey is due to chance.[27]

First, if the number of significant predictors exceeds the number expected by chance, then the most powerful of these are likely to reflect reliable relationships.[28] Thus, if gender, age, and attitude toward oil companies are the three predictors out of 40 that are significant, it is likely that only one of the three is a dependable predictor. A consultant can easily produce the probability levels and effect sizes associated with each predictor to assess which predictor deserves attention.

Second, reliable prediction models should be reproducible on new samples. A consultant should be prepared to demonstrate that the prediction model produced from one half of the respondents in a survey can explain responses by the remaining respondents to the survey, or a new set of respondents if more than one survey is conducted. A statistical model that is based on the vagaries of sample selection or other chance elements will not produce robust results that explain the behavior or a new set of respondents. In one test of the reliability of a selection model, Baker[29] tested 18 potential predictors to produce a model with four predictors that explained 11 percent of the variance on a measure of conviction. When tested on a new sample of respondents, respondents that the model predicted would be pro-conviction did not have higher conviction scores than those the model predicted would be anti-conviction. The model was a complete failure.

Finally, when mock juries or focus groups are held after the survey results are in, it is possible to test the consultant's model prospectively and compare it with the attorney's prediction.[30] A mock trial exposes simulated jurors to opening statements or abbreviated trial enactments. The jurors answer background questions before the mock trial takes place. They also fill out questionnaires during and after the evidence is presented. After the fact, it often seems obvious why particular jurors turned out to be pro-plaintiff or pro-defendant; the key is whether those predictions can be made before the juror's verdict preference is known. The attorney who plans to use the advice of a consultant can arrange a test in which both attorney and consultant make predictions about the likely responses of prospective jurors. If attorney and consultant use the juror background questionnaires to predict juror verdicts and the survey results do not guide the consultant to more favorable jurors, the attorney should seriously question the value of the consultant's advice in jury selection.[31]

The other role for social science

Some jury consultants are well aware of the weakness of much of their selection advice. Yet prospective clients are often eager to believe that consultants can reduce the uncertain prospect of a hostile jury and consultants are naturally reluctant to reject a friendly marketing opportunity. The result is that the client gets selection advice. In addition, however, the consultant may in the process provide other services that substantially enhance the client's position at trial. These include support for a motion for change of venue or expansive voir dire, and assistance in identifying arguments jurors will and will not find persuasive.

Change of venue. When, because of pretrial publicity or the identity of one of the parties, prospective jurors in the community may have strong preconceived notions about the facts of the case or deeply held biases towards one of the parties, a party may seek a change of venue. Evidence in the form of a community survey is one standard way to demonstrate the extent of community knowledge about the case and the prospects of a biased jury pool. It is crucial that the consultant used to conduct such a survey be able to testify competently that appropriate random sampling techniques were used to identify respondents for the survey, and that the responses were verified according to the usual survey standards.[32]

Even if the court denies a motion for a change of venue, evidence of potential prejudice may persuade the court to expand the questioning of prospective jurors during the voir dire, may convince the court that individual as opposed to group questioning is appropriate and may increase the willingness of the court to grant challenges for cause when a juror gives some sign of predisposition in the case.

Clarity and persuasiveness of the evidence. The focus on SJS neglects the key determinant of trial outcomes: the evidence. In studies that have measured the contributions of juror characteristics and trial testimony to jury verdicts, the trial testimony dominates. For example, Visher[33] studied the judgments of defendant guilt by 340 jurors in actual trials for sexual assault. She was able to explain nearly half the variation in the juror's judgments: evidence factors accounted for 34 percent of the variance, victim and defendant characteristics accounted for an additional 8 percent, and jurors' characteristics and attitudes accounted for only 2 percent.[34]

The litigator has limited control over the potential evidence in a case, but litigation can involve massive amounts of potential evidence. No jury can absorb every piece of evidence that could be, or even is, presented at trial. The litigator must decide how to distill the mass of information and organize it in a framework that will be maximally intelligible and convincing. The structure provided in opening statements helps the jury organize the evidence and guides the jury's thinking during the trial.[35]

Experienced trial attorneys are skilled communicators, but they cannot see the themes of the dispute through the eyes of the juror. A pretrial test of juror reactions to the facts of the case and arguments that both sides are expected to make can provide a crucial warning that the message is unclear, that the theme initially selected is not plausible, that jurors will be bothered or unconvinced by parts of the message or that jurors are troubled by missing information that could be supplied.

By comparing the reactions of jurors to various versions of the opening statement, the consultant can help the attorney to construct the clearest and most persuasive statement of the client's position. For example, damages in the form of a firm's lost profits may be computed by showing past earnings and extrapolating into the future or by providing data on the profits of another comparable firm. A trial simulation compares jurors' reactions to the two damage models in order to determine which damage model should be emphasized at trial, and whether the presentation of both models undermines or increases the credibility of the damage estimate. Similar questions about issues like the

ordering of witnesses and the best way to present statistical data can be explored before trial.

The consultant provides this feedback by selecting lay respondents representative of those who will serve as jurors in the trial, running the focus groups or trial simulations and designing appropriate questions and questionnaires to measure juror reactions. The consultant may also help prepare opening statements and trial presentation materials, ensuring in particular that the opposition's case is powerfully presented. The attorneys can watch the simulated juries as they deliberate or the focus groups as they are questioned, or they may get transcripts or videos of the juror's discussions and reports on their questionnaire responses.[36] Whether formal or informal, these "dry runs" are nearly always instructive for the attorneys. After all, aside from verdicts and an occasional question to the jurors after a verdict comes in, few attorneys have had the opportunity to get direct feedback on their courtroom attempts to persuade.

Conclusions

Attorneys are professional critics of evidence. Why then are they willing to accept the advice of consultants on jury selection so uncritically? For most attorneys, the jury is the unknown element in the trial process. The jury trial takes place precisely because the parties do not agree what the jury's verdict will be. And, unlike the judge, a jury has no reputation before the trial begins and has made no previous rulings in the case. Silent throughout the trial, the jury has the last word.[37]

The attorney preparing to select a jury at the beginning of a trial thus confronts an uncertain outcome. The active attorney, attempting to achieve control, culls his or her store of knowledge for useful counsel, some of it based on experience and logic, and some of it based on folklore, superstition, and magic.[38] Scientific magic in the form of SJS may reduce dysfunctional stress or simply appease a client who wants to be assured that every available tool has been used to prepare for trial. Significant harm is unlikely and there may be some improvement in the use of challenges if the attorney does not simply turn the decisionmaking responsibility over to the consultant or forget that evidence, far more than jury selection, determines trial outcomes.

If the effects of SJS are generally modest at best,

what promise does the method offer for jury selection, apart from its value as a placebo to build
litigant and attorney confidence? It is likely that
SJS can in some cases affect the proportion of jurors who favor a particular verdict, just as in some
cases the peremptory challenges exercised by attorneys can make a difference.[39] The difficulty is
that we currently have no reliable way to identify
which cases will be amenable to SJS, so that at this
point we cannot be sure when the effort will justify the expense.[40] When enormous sums of money
are at risk so that even a small increase in the probability of one more favorable juror represents a
major achievement, a cost-benefit analysis may justify the investment in SJS despite the uncertainty.
In most other cases, the uncertainty suggests a
challenge for jury consultants: to demonstrate
when and how their techniques are predictive.
Until such documentation is provided, the attorney who considers hiring such a consultant needs
to be a vigilant and critical consumer of the services that are offered.

NOTES

This article originally appeared in Volume 73, Number 4,
December-January 1990, pages 178-183.

I am indebted to many people, for I have watched the development and practice of scientific jury selection as an academic psychologist, practicing attorney, and consultant.
Among those who shared their views with me along the way
(but are in no way responsible for mine) are Geraldine M.
Alexis, Philip J. Crihfield, Reid Hastie, Richard Lempert, Henry
L. Mason III, Thomas Munsterman, Arthur Patterson, Zick
Rubin and Sarah Tanford. I am grateful for their insights and
suggestions.

1. Kalven and Zeisel, THE AMERICAN JURY (Boston: Little
Brown, 1966).

2. *Id.*; Zeisel and Diamond, *The Effect of Peremptory Challenges
on Jury and Verdict: An Experiment in a Federal District Court*, 30
STAN. L. REV. 491 (1978); also see Davis, *Group Decision and Procedural Justice* in Fishbein (ed.) PROGRESS IN SOCIAL PSYCHOLOGY,
VOL. 1 (Hillsdale, NJ: Erlbaum, 1980); Penrod and Hastie,
Models of Jury Decision Making: A Critical Review, 86 PSY BULL.
462 (1979).

3. Diamond and Zeisel, *Jury Behavior* in ENCYCLOPEDIA OF
CRIME AND JUSTICE (New York: Macmillan, 1983).

4. *E.g.*, Darrow (*Attorney for the Defense* May ESQUIRE MAGA-
ZINE) counseled defense attorneys to avoid women jurors, while
Katz (*The Twelve Man Jury*, 42 TRIAL 39 (1969-70)) considered
women to be favorable defense jurors unless the defendant
was a woman.

5. Kallen, *Peremptory Challenges Based upon Juror Background—
A Rational Use?*, 13 TRIAL LAWYER'S GUIDE 37 (1969).

6. This research design was approximated in a test of the
accuracy of traditional attorney jury selection (Diamond and
Zeisel, *A Courtroom Experiment on Jury Selection and Decision-
Making*, 1 PERSONALITY AND SOC. PSY. BULL. 276 (1974); Zeisel
and Diamond, *supra* n. 2). In that study, the jurors excused by
either side were retained to form a separate jury that stayed
through the case and deliberated to a verdict. The results in-

dicated that, using traditional selection methods, defense attorneys in some cases increased their odds of winning as a
result of their choices during voir dire.

7. Schulman et al., *Recipe for a Jury*, PSYCHOLOGY TODAY 37
(June 1973); Kairys et al., THE JURY SYSTEM: NEW METHODS FOR
REDUCING JURY PREJUDICE (Philadelphia: National Jury Project,
1975).

8. E.g., Lafree et al., *Jurors' Responses to Victims' Behavior and
Legal Issues in Sexual Assault Trials*, 32 SOC. PROB. 389 (1985).

9. Horowitz, *Juror Selection: A Comparison of Two Methods in
Several Criminal Cases*, 10 J. APP. PSY. 86 (1980).

10. Saks, JURY VERDICTS: THE ROLE OF GROUP SIZE AND SOCIAL
DECISION RULE (Lexington, MA: Lexington, 1977).

11. Interestingly, people who believed that crime was primarily the product of bad social conditions were *more* likely to
regard the defendant as guilty.

12. When jurors differ in their verdict preferences, the
measure of that variability is referred to as 'variance'. If a juror characteristic or belief can help to predict jurors' verdict
preferences, it is said to explain part of the variance. The more
powerful the predictor or set of predictors, the higher the
proportion of the variance explained and the more accurate
the prediction. Explained variation in principle can be as low
as 0 or as high as 100 percent.

13. Penrod, "Study of Attorney and 'Scientific' Jury Selection Models." Unpublished Doctoral Dissertation, Harvard
University (1980).

14. Hastie et al., INSIDE THE JURY (Cambridge, MA: Harvard
University Press, 1983).

15. Moran and Comfort, *Scientific Juror Selection: Sex as a
Moderator of Demographic and Personality Predictors of Impaneled
Felony Juror Behavior*, 43 J. PERS. SOC. PSY. 1052 (1982).

16. E.g., Simon, THE JURY AND THE DEFENSE OF INSANITY (Boston: Little Brown, 1967); Berg and Vidmar, *Authoritarianism
and Recall of Evidence about Criminal Behavior*, 9 J. OF RESEARCH IN
PERSONALITY 147 (1975); Buckhout et al., *Discretion in Jury Selection* in Abt and Stuart (eds.) SOCIAL PSYCHOLOGY AND DISCRETION-
ARY LAW (New York: Van Nostrand Reinhold, 1979); Bridgeman
and Marlowe, *Jury Decisionmaking: An Empirical Study Based on
Actual Felony Trial*, 64 J. OF APPLIED PSY. 91 (1979); Mills and
Bohannon, *Juror characteristics: to what extent are they related to
jury verdict?*, 64 JUDICATURE 23 (1980).

17. Moran and Comfort, *supra* n. 15.

18. *See, e.g.*, Cowan et al., *The Effects of Death Qualification on
Jurors' Predisposition to Convict and on the Quality of Deliberation*,
8 LAW & HUM. BEHAV. 53 (1984).

19. Berman and Shapard, *The Voir Dire Examination: Juror
Challenges and Adversary Advocacy* in Sales (ed.) PERSPECTIVES IN
LAW AND PSYCHOLOGY, VOL. 2: THE TRIAL PROCESS (New York: Ple-
num, 1981); Van Dyke, JURY SELECTION PROCEDURES (Cambridge,
MA: Ballinger, 1977). Some evidence indicates that jurors are
less candid about their attitudes when a judge conducts the
voir dire than when the attorneys conduct the voir dire (Jones,
*Judge-Versus Attorney-Conducted Voir Dire: An Empirical Investiga-
tion of Juror Candor*, 11 LAW & HUM. BEHAV. 131 (1987). As a
result, the trend toward judge-conducted voir dire should reduce the reliable information available to counsel during jury
selection.

20. Some courts permit the parties to submit questions that
the jurors answer in writing before selection begins. This procedure of course standardizes the questions and permits parallel analysis of the survey and the responses to the court questionnaire.

21. Mischel, PERSONALITY AND ASSESSMENT (New York: Wiley,
1968).

22. Meehl, *When Shall We Use Our Heads Instead of the Formula?*, 4 J. OF COUNSELING PSY. 268 (1957); Kleinmuntz, *Why We
Still Use Our Heads Instead of Formulas: Toward an Integrative*

Approach, PSYCHOLOGICAL BULLETIN. Human judges make systematic errors when they gather and combine information to make prediction (Dawes, *A Case Study of Graduate Admissions: Application of Three Principles of Human Decision Making*, 26 AM. PSYCHOLOGIST 180 (1971)); Dawes, *The Robust Beauty of Improper Linear Models in Decision Making*, 34 AM. PSYCHOLOGIST 571 (1979)), but even this imperfect decisionmaking can be superior to a computer model if the model omits predictors that the human decisionmaker can use.

23. Diamond and Zeisel, *supra* n. 6; Zeisel and Diamond, *supra* n. 2.

24. A proxy for the verdict preferences may be a factor score that summarizes a series of responses to questions that are expected to indicate which side the juror is likely to favor.

25. Scientific research generally accepts a difference between two groups on some measure (e.g., the verdict preferences of males versus females) as real if a difference as big as that shown in the research would occur less than five chances in a hundred if there was no real difference between the two groups on that measure.

26. The same problem arises when multiple predictors are simultaneously tested in a multiple regression analysis and no adjustment is made in the explained variance or R^2. The probability of 'discovering' relationships due to chance is even greater when AID (automatic interaction detector) is used to test combinations of predictors (Berk et al., *The Vagaries and Vulgarities of Scientific Jury Selection: A Methodological Evaluation*, 1 EVALUATION Q. 143 (1977)). Moreover, unless sample sizes far exceed the usual 300-500 respondents typically tested in jury selection surveys, predictions about the behavior of jurors based on combinations of characteristics (e.g., female physicians) will be highly unreliable.

27. One of the reviewers suggested that no consultant would agree to cooperate with the tests proposed in this section. Markets and clients, however, determine what suppliers are willing to provide.

28. Berk et al., *supra* n. 26.

29. Baker, "Conviction Proneness as a Predictor of Sworn Jury Decisions." Unpublished Doctoral Dissertation, C.U.N.Y. (1984).

30. To adequately conduct such a test it is necessary to have a sufficient number of jurors participate in the mock trial. Even when SJS assists in selection, it only improves the odds. As a result, SJS may not appear to cause any increment in predictability in a test with a small sample, while in a large sample a genuine improvement could be detected.

31. It may be desirable to conduct a simulated voir dire before the trial simulation, but such an elaborate approach is costly in both attorney and juror time.

32. *See* National Jury Project, JURYWORK: SYSTEMATIC TECHNIQUES (New York: Clark Boardman, 1986), Chapter 7, for a good discussion of motions for change of venue.

33. Visher, *Juror Decision Making: The Importance of Evidence*, 11 LAW & HUM. BEHAV. 1 (1987).

34. *See* Saks & Hastie, SOCIAL PSYCHOLOGY IN COURT (New York: Van Nostrand Reinhold, 1978), chapter 3, for a review of research that demonstrates the dominant effect of evidence on jury verdicts.

35. Wrightsman and his colleagues have studied the way that the timing and content of opening statements can affect verdict preferences (Pyszczynski & Wrightman, *The Effects of Opening Statements on Mock Jurors' Verdicts in a Simulated Criminal Trial*, 11 J. OF APPLIED SOC. PSY. 301 (1981); Wells, Wrightsman & Miene, *The Timing of the Defense Opening Statement: Don't Wait Until the Evidence is in*, 15 J. OF APPLIED SOC. PSY. 758 (1985)). They suggest that an opening statement sets up a thematic framework that guides jurors in their processing and interpretation of subsequent testimony and evidence.

36. With little or no assistance from a consultant, an attorney can also obtain a low cost, informal reading on prospective juror reaction. Consultants generally sub-contract to field services in the city where the trial is to take place. The field service obtains respondents who are eligible for jury service according to the specifications of the consultant. Attorneys who, for example, want to try out an opening statement before a jury-eligible audience can use these same field services to obtain respondents. It may, however, be useful to use the services of a consultant to probe juror reactions.

37. The exception is that rare case in which the jury's verdict is so inconsistent with the evidence that the court sets it aside.

38. Saks, *Blaming the Jury*, 75 GEO. L. J. 693 (1986).

39. Diamond and Zeisel, *supra* n. 6; Zeisel and Diamond, *supra* n. 2.

40. Two requirements appear to be an opportunity for extensive voir dire and subject matter about which prospective jurors have substantial experience or strong opinions.

The capital jury: is it tilted toward death?

Preliminary findings from the Capital Jury Project indicate that jurors make life and death punishment decisions early in the trial, misunderstand sentencing guidelines, and often deny their responsibility for the punishment given to a defendant.

by William J. Bowers

How the capital jury should make the grave life or death sentencing decision has been the subject of two decades of capital jurisprudence. The U.S. Supreme Court's dissatisfaction with what the plurality found to be the "arbitrary," "capricious," and "standardless" manner in which the decision to impose the death penalty was being made, as articulated in *Furman v. Georgia*,[1] brought the use of capital punishment to a halt in 1972. And it was the efforts of states to reform the capital sentencing process by guiding jurors' exercise of sentencing discretion that revived the death penalty and has become the focus of vastly expanding capital jurisprudence since *Furman*.

Whether the capital sentencing process has been sufficiently purged of arbitrariness by these reforms is a nagging constitutional question.[2] The chief challenge has been that the imposition of the death penalty remains arbitrary in one very specific respect: racial bias. Evidence of racial disparities, especially race-of-victim bias, was brought to the Court in *McCleskey v. Kemp*.[3]

The Court, in *McCleskey*, acknowledged the presence of victim based racial disparities in sentencing outcomes, but it held 5-4 that these statistical disparities did not, in themselves, impeach the sentencing of capital jurors. Disparate sentencing outcomes were no substitute, the Court said, for knowing how individual jurors focus their collective judgment in particular cases. The Court implied that it would be necessary to look inside the "black box" of jury decision making to address the issue of arbitrariness—that knowing what comes out of the black box is no substitute for knowing what goes on inside the box.

This is what the Capital Jury Project (CJP) is doing—looking inside the black box of capital sentencing. It has taken the Court's view in *McCleskey* of what would be needed to demonstrate arbitrariness as a guide, finding out what real jurors do in actual cases to decide whether defendants should live or die. In each of 14 participating states,[4] Capital Jury Project investigators attempt to interview four randomly selected jurors from each of 20-30 full capital trials that had both guilt and sentencing phases. The trials are chosen to provide equal numbers with life and death verdicts; preference is generally given to more recent trials.

In 3-4 hour interviews, CJP investigators ask a common core of questions in all states, and additional questions tailored to the particular concerns of investigators in their own states. In the development and pretesting of the interview instrument, it was found that jurors often provided rich, detailed narrative accounts of their decision making, in addition to their briefer responses to structured questions. To capture this richness and detail, with jurors' permission (granted by four out of five), the interviews are tape recorded. Some of the findings of the Capital Jury Project to date are reported below.[5]

Premature decision making

What jurors tell researchers about their thinking and deliberations during the guilt stage of the trial indicates that many began taking a stand on what the defendant's punishment should be well before they were exposed to the statutory guidelines for making this decision. In response to the question "After the jury found [defendant's name] guilty of capital murder but before you heard any evidence or testimony about what the punishment should be, did you then think [defendant's name] should be given…a death sentence, a life sentence, [or were you] undecided?" virtually half of the jurors said that they thought they knew what the punishment should be before the sentencing stage of the trial began, and those for death outnumbered those for life by 3-2. A follow-up question to the jurors who thought they knew what the punishment should be at this point asked, "How strongly did you think so?" Of all jurors, more than 3 out of 10 said they were "absolutely convinced" of what the punishment should be and nearly 2 in 10 were at least "pretty sure."

Why are so many jurors absolutely convinced or at least pretty sure what the punishment should be even before the sentencing stage? One possibility is that they talk about what the punishment should be when they are supposed to be deliberating on guilt. When asked, *"How much did the discussion among the jurors [during guilt deliberations] focus on…jurors' feelings about the right punishment?"* half of the jurors said "a great deal" and almost two thirds said at least "a fair amount."

On the assumption that discussion of the "right punishment," might not necessarily mean that considerations of punishment actually figured in the guilt decision, jurors were asked a more pointed question specifically about the death penalty as a consideration in the jury's guilt decision. It read, *"In deciding guilt, did jurors talk about whether or not the defendant would, or should, get the death penalty?"* Four out of 10 jurors conceded that in deciding guilt the jury explicitly discussed whether the defendant would or should be sentenced to death.

Thus, some who said the jury discussed the "right punishment" a great deal during guilt deliberations did not mean to say that they talked specifically about the death penalty or that such discussion actually figured in their guilt decision. But more notable is the fact that so many jurors claimed that in deciding guilt they talked about whether the death penalty would or should be the defendant's punishment.

Misunderstanding guidelines

CJP investigators for North and South Carolina have found that jurors misunderstand how the capital sentencing decision should be made; which factors can and cannot be considered, what level

of proof is needed, and what degree of concurrence is required for aggravating and mitigating factors. And, they do so in a way that leads them to improperly accept aggravating and improperly reject mitigating considerations. The bias is especially pronounced for mitigating factors.[6] The North Carolina investigators also examined how jurors understood the procedure for weighing aggravating against mitigating factors and for deciding what the punishment should be. "[I]t is disturbing that roughly one-fourth of the jurors felt that death was mandatory when it was not and approximately one-half of the jurors failed to appreciate those situations which mandated life."[7]

More fundamental to capital sentencing than which factors can be considered, what level of proof is needed, whether unanimity is required, or how the weighing of factors must be conducted and interpreted, is the prohibition against having a "mandatory" death sentence; that is, requiring jurors to impose a death sentence without considering mitigation.[8] Hence, no state "requires" the death penalty simply or solely upon the finding of a particular aggravating factor.[9]

To test jurors' understanding of this basic principle, they were asked, "After hearing the judge's [sentencing] instructions, did you believe that the law required you to impose a death sentence if the evidence proved" that the defendant's "conduct was heinous, vile or depraved," or if it proved that the defendant "would be dangerous in the future?" Four out of 10 capital jurors wrongly believed that they were "required" to impose the death penalty if they found that the crime was heinous, vile, or depraved, and nearly as many mistakenly thought the death penalty was "required" if they found that the defendant would be dangerous in the future.

In every aspect of sentencing guidelines CJP investigators have so far examined, then, there is a "tilt toward death" in jurors' understanding. Some of this may be a "carryover" of the rules for decision making from the guilt to the sentencing phase of the trial. But some of it may reflect a tendency among jurors to hear sentencing instructions in a way that justifies or reinforces decisions that many have already made. One question bears on this latter point, *"Would you say the judge's sentencing instructions to the jury…simply provided a framework for the decision most jurors had already made?"* Three out of four jurors said "yes."

Alternative punishment

The most common question jurors ask judges during sentencing deliberations, according to an analysis of Georgia capital trial transcripts, is how long would the defendant actually spend in prison if not given the death penalty.[10] Judges usually respond that the law prohibits them from answering this question; soon thereafter, the jurors typically return a death sentence.[11]

With the data now available from more than 800 jurors in 11 states the CJP has further documented jurors' considerable ignorance and consistent underestimation of the death penalty alternative, and the connection between their erroneous perceptions of the alternative and their decisions to impose the death penalty. When asked, "How long did you think someone not given the death penalty for a capital murder in this state usually spends in prison?" in only 2 of 11 states are most estimates within a 10-year interval, and in all seven states where interviewing is now complete a majority of the jurors who give an estimate believe such offenders usually get out of prison even before the law makes them eligible for parole. What is more, jurors most mistaken about the death penalty alternative are the ones most apt to vote for the death penalty in all seven states where the CJP data collection has been completed.

The evidence from juror interviews thus indicates that it is not simply whether or not, but *how soon*, jurors think the defendant will get out of prison that influences their final punishment decision. Since life without parole is the alternative to the death penalty in only a small fraction of cases, to inform jurors only when it is the alternative, as provided by *Simmons v. South Carolina*, does relatively little to remedy the arbitrariness introduced by the widespread ignorance and consistent underestimation of the alternative punishment.[12]

What about the other limitation in *Simmons*, namely, that future dangerousness be advanced as a reason for the death penalty before the defendant may have the jurors know what the alternative punishment really is? This issue was addressed by examining whether jurors' perceptions of the alternative punishment are associated with their sentencing decisions only when the defendant's possible dangerousness is an issue, or, as well, when dangerousness is not a factor.

As expected, jurors' perceptions of the alternative punishment are a strong predictor of a final

vote for the death penalty when the prosecutor argues that the defendant would be dangerous in the future, when jurors believe the evidence proves this to be true, and when jurors are concerned in their sentencing deliberations about the possibility that the defendant will return to society someday. But, there is also a statistically reliable association between jurors' perceptions of the alternative punishment and their likelihood of voting for the death penalty, when these respective indications of dangerousness are not present. That is to say, the decision to impose the death penalty is definitely a function of what the alternative punishment is thought to be even when dangerousness is not an issue. Hence, the application of *Simmons* only to cases of alleged dangerousness, like its application only when the alternative is life without parole, makes it a very minor corrective to a major problem in the exercise of capital discretion.

Further analysis reveals that: (1) it is early in sentencing deliberations (at the first vote on punishment) that underestimating the alternative is most strongly associated with favoring death as punishment; and (2) it is among those who were undecided about what the punishment should be before sentencing deliberations began that underestimating the alternative is especially apt to yield a vote for death on the first jury ballot. The data thus indicate that it is primarily at the point when jurors sit down to deliberate about what the punishment should be that their typically mistaken underestimates of the death penalty alternative come into play.

Denying responsibility

It is an "intolerable danger" for jurors to believe that "the responsibility for any ultimate determination of death will rest with others," the Supreme Court said in *Caldwell v. Mississippi*.[13] Yet, as Robert Weisberg has argued,[14] sentencing guidelines, by appearing to provide jurors with an authoritative formula that yields the "correct" or "required" punishment, may actually diminish their sense of responsibility for the awful punishment they may be called upon to impose.

To see where capital jurors place foremost responsibility for the defendant's punishment, jurors were asked to rank five options from "most" through "least" responsible for the defendant's punishment. The five options, together with the percent saying each option was "most responsible," are:[15]

47.2 the defendant because his/her conduct is what actually determined the punishment

34.0 the law that states what punishment applies

9.1 the jury that votes for the sentence

6.0 the individual juror since the jury's decision depends on the vote of each juror

3.8 the judge who imposes the sentence

Eight of 10 jurors assign foremost responsibility to the defendant or to the law. While the defendant is more often seen as "most responsible," for the punishment, the law more consistently outranks the defendant in responsibility for the punishment.[16] By contrast, jurors overwhelmingly deny that they individually or as a group are primarily responsible for the defendant's punishment. Altogether, only 3 in 20 said that the jurors as a group or individually were the most responsible. The jury ranked third, the individual juror fourth, and the judge fifth in punishment responsibility.[17]

The *Caldwell* Court speculated that when jurors minimize the importance of their role, "[O]ne can easily imagine that in a case in which the jury is divided on the proper sentence, the presence of appellate review could effectively be used as an argument for why those jurors who are reluctant to invoke the death sentence should nevertheless give in."[18] One question bears on this issue. It asked jurors whether during their sentencing deliberations they thought responsibility for deciding what the defendant's punishment should be was shared with trial or appellate judges or was strictly the jury's. Two of three jurors think of themselves as sharing responsibility with trial or appellate judges in states where the jury's decision is binding on the trial judge, and nearly all do so in states where the trial judge can override the jury's sentencing decision.

The data also show that jurors who see the punishment decision as shared with judicial authorities were more likely to vote for death than those who take sole responsibility for the decision. Moreover, this greater readiness to vote for death among those who see the decision as shared comes at or near the end of sentencing deliberations, as the *Caldwell* Court surmised. Thus, it is between their first and final vote on the defendant's punishment that jurors who feel the decision is shared or passed on to judicial authorities as compared to those who accept sole responsibility for the decision were es-

pecially likely to cross over from life to death, especially unlikely to cross over from death to life, and far more likely than others to move from undecided to death than to life. In other words, as jurors move closer to the final life or death decision, those who deny full or strict responsibility for the defendant's punishment are more apt to impose the death penalty, indeed are more apt to move from being for life or undecided to a death vote.

Most capital jurors disclaim primary or sole responsibility for the awesome life or death decision they must make. They want the cover of law for their decision, although they often make their decision before learning what the law says they should consider, often misunderstand what the law requires of them after being told by the judge, and often do not know what the alternative punishment actually is because the law prohibits the judge from telling them. Yet, most jurors still want to see the law as more responsible than they themselves for the defendant's punishment. Significantly, this tendency to deny full responsibility for the defendant's punishment appears to make it easier for jurors to vote for death.[19] Joseph Hoffmann's examination of Indiana jurors' narrative accounts of their sentencing decisions documents the importance to jurors of "higher authority" for guidance in the momentous life or death decision, not infrequently includ-ing "divine guidance"—hardly what the Supreme Court had in mind as "guided discretion."[20]

*****

The findings at this still early stage of research present a picture of capital sentencing afflicted with a "tilt toward death." It will take longer to learn just how decisions are being made, what dynamics are at work, and what model or models of decision making best fit the way jurors think and act in making their life or death decisions. As the work proceeds, it should become clearer in what ways and to what extent the operation of modern capital statutes do and do not conform to constitutional requirements. The inevitable questions will be, just how arbitrary can the system be and still remain constitutionally acceptable, and how much impropriety of what kinds by how many jurors can the Constitution tolerate—especially in light of the constitutionally mandated higher standard of care and reliability for capital cases?[21]

NOTES

This article originally appeared in Volume 79, Number 5, March-April 1996, pages 220-223.

This research has been supported by grant NSF SES-9013252. The author thanks the members of the Capital Jury Project who helped bring together this partial overview of the work to date, and expresses appreciation to Patricia Igo for her able assistance.

1. 408 U.S. 238 (1972) (per curiam).

2. *See* Justice Harry Blackmun's dissent in the denial of cert. in *Callins v. Collins*, 114 S.Ct 1127 (1994).

3. 481 U.S. 279 (1987). The empirical evidence on which the *McCleskey* challenge was based is reported in Baldus et al., EQUAL JUSTICE AND THE DEATH PENALTY: A LEGAL AND EMPIRICAL ANALYSIS (Boston: Northeastern University Press, 1990).

4. States have been chosen to represent the principal forms of guided discretion capital statutes, and to ensure regional diversification of the sample. *See* Bowers, *The Capital Jury Project: Rationale, Design, and Preview of Early Findings*, 70 IND. L.J. 1043 (1995) for a discussion of the state sample selection criteria and a listing of the participating states.

5. Previously published CJP research appears in the *Indiana Law Journal* 1995 CJP symposium issue, and other sources including: Bienen, *Helping Jurors Out: Post-Verdict Debriefing for Jurors in Emotionally Disturbing Trials*, 68 IND. L.J. 1333 (1993); Bowers, *Capital Punishment and Contemporary Values: People's Misgivings and the Court's Misperceptions*, 27 LAW & SOC'Y REV. 157 (1993); Eisenberg and Wells, *Deadly Confusion: Juror Instructions in Capital Cases*, 79 CORNELL L.J. 1, 4 (1993); and Hoffmann, *How American Juries Decide Death Penalty Cases: The Capital Jury Project* in Bedau, ed., THE DEATH PENALTY IN AMERICA: CURRENT CONTROVERSIES (forthcoming, 1997).

6. Luginbuhl and Howe, *Discretion in Capital Sentencing Instructions: Guided or Misguided?*, 70 IND. L.J. 1161, 1170 (1995).

7. *Id.* at 1173.

8. Woodson v. North Carolina, 428 U.S. 280 (1976).

9. Oregon and Texas make the defendant's possible future dangerousness a prominent aggravating factor in the punishment decision, though not to the exclusion of mitigating considerations, see Penry v. Lynaugh, 492 U.S. 302 (1989).

10. Lane, *Is There Life Without Parole?: A Capital Defendant's Right to a Meaningful Alternative Sentence*, 26 LOY. L.A. L. REV. 327 (1993); also see, Paduano and Stafford-Smith, *Deathly Errors: Juror Misperceptions Concerning Parole in the Imposition of the Death Penalty*, 18 COLUM. HUM. RTS. L. REV. 211 (1987).

11. Lane, *id.* at 338ff.

12. In *Simmons v. South Carolina*, 114 S.Ct. 2187, 2193 (1994) the Supreme Court ruled that a capital defendant was entitled to have the jury know what the alternative to the death penalty would actually be under two conditions: (1) when the alternative was a life sentence with no chance of parole, and (2) when the prosecution argued that the defendant's possible danger to society was a reason for imposing the death penalty.

13. 472 U.S. 320 (1985) at 333.

14. *Deregulating Death*, 1983 SUP. CT. REV. 305, at 343. Weisberg posits that sentencing instructions give no real guidance, but have the appearance of legal rules. He argues that these pseudo-instructions dilute the jury's sense of responsibility, rather than guide discretion.

15. The following percentages are based on the responses of the 729 jurors who ranked all five options, so that the ranks sum to 15. The percentages add to 100.1 percent because of rounding error.

16. *See* Bowers, *supra* n. 4, Table 10 for the full distribution of jurors' responsibility rankings of these five agents in 7 of the 11 states examined here.

17. In three states (Alabama Florida and Indiana) that permit the judge to override the jury's sentencing decision, the judge ranks third, the jury fourth, and individual jurors fifth in responsibility for the defendant's punishment. *See* Bowers *supra* n. 4, at note 233 and accompanying text.

18. *Supra* n. 13.

19. Weisberg, *supra* n. 14, at 391, draws a parallel between capital jurors and Stanley Milgram's experimental subjects who were willing to impose painful shocks so long as they could remain convinced that it was the experimenter not they themselves who were responsible for the suffering. *See* Milgram, OBEDIENCE TO AUTHORITY: AN EXPERIMENTAL VIEW 132-134 (New York: Harper & Row, 1974).

20. Hoffman, *Where's the Buck?—Juror Misperception of Sentencing Responsibility in Death Penalty Cases*, 70 IND. L.J. 1137 (1995).

21. Woodson, *supra* n. 8, at 305.

Is the grand jury worth keeping?

The grand jury plays a critical role in law enforcement, but reforms are needed to restore its intended purposes.

by Susan W. Brenner

Independent Counsel Kenneth Starr's investigation of alleged crimes surrounding President Clinton's relationship with a White House intern has focused a great deal of popular attention on the grand jury as an institution. Unlike the petit, or trial, jury, the grand jury operates in secret and ignores principles such as the Fourth Amendment's exclusionary rule, *Miranda* rights, and the Federal Rules of Evidence.

To the grand jury's proponents, these are essential characteristics of an institution that plays a critical role in law enforcement. To its critics, these and other aspects of the grand jury make it an instrument of oppression, a modern-day Star Chamber. Defenders of the status quo are correct in maintaining that grand juries cannot, and should not, be bound by many of the strictures imposed on courts and law enforcement officers. However, prosecutors do have too much control over grand jury proceedings.

What can be done to reduce the prosecutor's dominance and restore the grand jury to its intended purposes? A review of the functions of a grand jury and the relationship between a grand jury, a court, and a prosecutor is helpful to provide some answers.

An inquisitorial body

In some states grand juries handle civil matters, but for the most part they concentrate on criminal activity. The federal system and most of the states use them to bring charges for serious crimes, the felonies for which one can be incarcerated a year or more. Grand juries do this by hearing evidence presented by prosecutors and then reviewing a set of charges—an indictment—a prosecutor drafts and submits to them. The prosecutor asks the grand jurors to vote for the indictment. To do so, the jurors have to find that the evidence they heard establishes probable cause to believe the charges in the indictment are true. If a majority of the jurors find there is probable cause and vote for an indictment, it is "returned" and a criminal case is initiated against those named as defendants. If a majority does not vote for an indictment, no case results.

As part of this process, grand juries investigate. The investigations can be wide-ranging, because a grand jury (according to the Supreme Court in a 1950 case, *U.S. v. Morton Salt Co.*) "can investigate merely on suspicion that the law is being violated, or even just because it wants assurance that it is not." In approving the breadth of these inquiries, the Supreme Court in a 1919 case, *Blair v. U.S.*, described the grand jury as "a grand inquest, a body with powers of investigation and inquisition, the scope of whose inquiries is not...limited...by questions of propriety or forecasts of the probable result of the investigation, or by doubts whether any particular individual will be found properly subject to an accusation of crime." Practically speaking, therefore, a grand jury can investigate whomever and whatever it will, and those from whom a grand jury seeks information will almost certainly be unable to resist its demands.

These demands take the form of subpoenas that require the recipient either to testify before a grand jury or to provide the grand jury with documents or other evidence. Prosecutors obtain blank subpoenas from the court clerk's office and issue them to anyone who may have evidence relevant to an investigation. The recipient of such a subpoena may not want to comply with its demands, but if she ignores it she will be held in contempt of court and jailed, because the subpoena is an order from the court.

Consider one infamous example involving President Clinton's former business partner Susan McDougal. When she was subpoenaed by a Whitewater grand jury in 1996 and refused to testify, she was incarcerated for civil contempt and held for almost two years, until the grand jury's term was about to expire, which meant it would be dissolved and prosecutors would have had to start over with a new grand jury. Prosecutors could then have subpoenaed her before a new grand jury. If she still refused to testify, she would have been held in contempt and incarcerated until she spoke or until that grand jury's term ended. (Instead, they chose to indict her for criminal contempt and for obstruction of justice, both charges being based on her refusal to testify.) Since federal grand juries sit for up to three years, this is an unnerving prospect, one that usually convinces recalcitrant witnesses to cooperate with the grand jury. There are no records showing how many grand jury witnesses are serving sentences for contempt or how long recalcitrant witnesses generally serve, but in one state case a witness spent more than seven years in jail for refusing to testify after being subpoenaed.

Relevance-related objections to trial subpoenas are not usually successful in the grand jury context. In a 1991 case, *U.S. v. R. Enterprises, Inc.*, the Supreme Court held that the trial standard of relevance does not apply to grand jury subpoenas because, unlike trials, grand jury investigations do not focus on a set of issues defined by an indictment or by the complaint in a civil case. The Court explained that since grand juries investigate to ascertain whether charges should be brought, it is impossible to put limits on the scope of their inquiries. The justices held that grand jury subpoenas are presumed to seek relevant information and that when a subpoena recipient raises a relevance challenge, the challenge must be denied unless the court finds there "is no reasonable possibility that the category of material the Government seeks will produce information relevant to the general subject of the grand jury's investigation."

This can give rise to the appearance of unfairness, especially when a subpoena for documents is involved. For instance, a few years ago a modest midwestern trucking company received a sub-

poena that ordered the company to provide the grand jury with all records it had generated or received during the preceding 15 years. When company officials began the process of complying with the subpoena, they realized doing so would require them to locate, collate, and transport more than a million pages of documents that would have to be copied if the company were to retain a set of these essential records.

Like many who have found themselves in this position, the officials were appalled when they realized that the effort and expense of complying with the subpoena would cripple their ability to operate the business. They moved to quash the subpoena, arguing that it must seek irrelevant information because it was inconceivable the entire universe of documents sought could pertain to an inquiry within the grand jury's purview. Since the motion was filed after the Supreme Court decided *R. Enterprises*, the trucking company lost. The Court found the company had not shown there was "no reasonable possibility" that the records sought by the subpoena would "produce information relevant to the general subject of the grand jury's investigation."

It may seem odd, and even unfair, that grand juries are given such latitude, but this is at once necessary and reasonable. Those who criticize the *R. Enterprises* decision tend to misunderstand the nature of a grand jury, to think of it as a court. It is not a court; it is an investigative body whose inquiries are more analogous to those of the police than they are to those of the judiciary. When the police investigate a crime, they operate according to broad notions of relevance, in that they seek information that can be used to identify the precise contours of the crime and those who perpetrated it.

Like a grand jury, the police want to solve a crime and charge the perpetrators. Often, when the police or a grand jury begin an investigation, they believe a crime may have been committed but know very little about the specifics of the offense; they must be able to explore any avenue that can produce evidence about the crime which originally came to their attention and about any satellite offenses of which they may originally have been unaware. It would be as difficult, and as unreasonable, to limit the scope of a grand jury's inquiry as it would be to enforce relevance limitations on police investigations.

Privilege

However, grand juries are not perfect analogues of the police. Grand juries defer to the notion of privilege, while police do not. Privilege usually arises at trial; trial witnesses can claim evidentiary privileges to avoid testifying. While grand juries generally ignore the rules of evidence, they honor privileges. The federal system and most states implement the privileges that arose at common law. These include the attorney-client privilege, the marital privileges, the doctor-patient privilege, and the clergy-penitent privilege. Many jurisdictions add a reporter's privilege and executive privilege, and a few recognize a parent-child privilege. If someone subpoenaed to testify before a grand jury invokes a privilege recognized by the jurisdiction in which the grand jury sits, the grand jury must respect the privilege and cannot require the witness to answer questions on any issue it protects.

The availability of these privileges gives grand jury witnesses an advantage over police suspects, but they are disadvantaged in another respect. To understand why, it is necessary to begin with the different categories into which grand jury witnesses fall. Since grand juries investigate to ascertain whether criminal charges should be brought, those subpoenaed can occupy an uneasy state, somewhere between witness and suspect. Many of them are summoned simply as sources of information, as "fact witnesses." If they are forthcoming with the grand jury and do not perjure themselves or try to conceal evidence of criminal activity, their testimony will end their involvement with the investigation. But others who receive subpoenas are "subjects" or "targets" of the investigation. "Targets" are analogous to police suspects; the grand jury believes they committed crimes and is trying to gather the evidence it needs to charge them. "Subjects" exist in a gray area between witness and target—the grand jury believes they may have been involved in the crimes being investigated, but has not yet focused its energies on trying to charge them.

Suspects brought to a police station for interrogation are protected by *Miranda*. The police must warn a suspect that *Miranda* gives him the right to remain silent and the right to an attorney. Unlike suspects, grand jury witnesses are not protected by *Miranda*, not even when they are a subject or target of the investigation. In a 1976 case, *U.S. v. Mandujano*, the Supreme Court held that *Miranda* is limited to police interrogations because the rights it defined were designed to prevent the police from using physical intimidation to elicit confessions. The Court explained that since neither grand jurors nor the prosecutors with whom they work are likely to use physical violence against a witness, there is no need to apply *Miranda* to grand jury inquiries.

Before *Miranda* was decided, suspects cited the Fifth Amendment's privilege against self-incrimination as their reason for not cooperating with police interrogators. Grand juries honor this privilege, but it is harder to claim the privilege than it is to invoke *Miranda*, and the privilege offers less protection. A suspect can invoke *Miranda* rights at will. If a suspect invokes the right to silence, the police cannot ask him any questions. If a suspect invokes the right to counsel, the police must give him an attorney and cannot ask him any questions unless his attorney agrees and is present.

A grand jury witness, on the other hand, cannot claim the privilege against self-incrimination unless she shows that the grand jury wants (1) to compel her (2) to give testimony (3) that can be used to convict her of a crime. If a witness tries to claim the privilege, the prosecutor can challenge her claim, asking the court supervising the grand jury to decide if she has met all three requirements. The subpoena acts as compulsion, since she must do what it requires or be incarcerated for contempt, but the other requirements can be problematic. A witness cannot, for instance, claim the privilege and refuse to give samples of her handwriting or blood because both are physical evidence, not testimony, and physical evidence is not protected. And a witness cannot claim the privilege because testifying would embarrass her or would incriminate someone she cares for. She can only claim it if testifying would yield information that can be used to convict her of a crime.

If the court finds the witness cannot claim the privilege, it will order her to testify or be held in contempt. If she agrees to testify, she will enter the grand jury room alone, unaccompanied by an attorney. In most jurisdictions, a witness's attorney (if she has one) stays outside the grand jury room, and the witness is given a "reasonable opportunity" to go outside and confer with him during questioning. In practice, this opportunity is very limited.

Unlike suspects, witnesses are in a perilous situation. Suspects can cut off questioning whenever they want by invoking their rights to silence or to an attorney. But for witnesses, even a valid claim of privilege does not stop prosecutors from asking questions, and a skilled prosecutor can use ostensibly innocuous questions in an effort to trick a witness into inadvertently making incriminating statements. Once she does so, she has waived the privilege on that issue, and the prosecutor can explore the topic with further questions.

While this may seem unfair, it is consistent with the constitutional rules that govern police interrogations. *Miranda* is not one of them. According to the *Mandujano* Court, *Miranda* did not reflect constitutional requirements; it merely established prophylactic rules designed to deter specific police tactics. Consequently, the only constitutional standards governing interrogations are the Sixth Amendment's right to counsel, the due process voluntariness test, and the Fifth Amendment privilege.

The Sixth Amendment only applies when someone has been indicted. Since grand jury investigations precede indictments, they generally do not implicate this right to counsel. The due process test bars the government from using physical violence or extreme psychological ploys to extort a confession, but it lets interrogators trick people into confessing. Neither grand jurors nor the prosecutors assisting them use violence or psychological ploys to break down witnesses. If a prosecutor tricks a witness into making incriminating statements by asking seemingly innocuous questions, that does not violate the due process voluntariness standard. And since grand juries enforce the Fifth Amendment privilege, their treatment of witnesses is constitutionally unimpeachable.

Immunity

Aside from tricking witnesses into waiving the privilege, prosecutors can deprive them of it. If a witness shows she can claim the Fifth Amendment privilege, a prosecutor can prevent her from doing so by giving her immunity, the government's promise to a witness that it will not use what she says before the grand jury, or any evidence it finds as a result of what she says, to prosecute her for a crime. The Supreme Court has held that this kind of immunity is constitutional because it puts the witness in the same position she would have been in had she not testified. A witness can also try to

persuade the prosecutor to give her another kind of immunity, one in which the government promises not to prosecute her if she testifies before the grand jury. This kind of immunity is also constitutional, since it puts the witness in an even better position than she would have been in had she not testified.

Immunity can be a bargain for some witnesses. Often, though, witnesses do not want immunity and try desperately to avoid it; some even go so far as to persist in claiming the privilege after they have been immunized and can no longer do so. Witnesses resist immunity for various reasons, one being the fear of retaliation. Someone who was involved, say, in organized drug activity may be told that if he accepts immunity and testifies against the leaders of that organization, his family will be killed. On hearing this, the witness will try to avoid immunity. He may petition the court for relief, reporting the threats. This will not prevent his being forced to cooperate; courts have held that the possibility of retaliation cannot interfere with an immunized witness' duty to testify, as any other result would simply encourage witness intimidation.

As this overview illustrates, grand juries exercise an extraordinary amount of power in a context that is seldom held up to public scrutiny. Why are grand juries given such power, and what can be done to prevent abuse of power?

A constitutional fixture

The grand jury is often characterized as a sword and a shield: As the Sixth Circuit ruled in a 1977 case, *U.S. v. Doss*, the grand jury "wields the sword of accusation against persons who the grand jurors have probable cause to believe are involved in criminal activity, and shields the innocent against oppressive prosecution." This characterization implies that the grand jury somehow stands apart from other branches of government, and that implication was the focus of a recent Supreme Court opinion.

For centuries, grand juries were considered part of the court system, presumably because of the close working relationship between courts and grand juries. While grand juries were regarded as an arm of the courts, federal judges readily exercised a measure of control over grand jury proceedings, citing their inherent supervisory power over the administration of federal criminal justice as the basis for doing so.

In 1992, the Supreme Court repudiated this view in *U.S. v. Williams.* The issue was whether federal courts could use their supervisory power to require prosecutors to present to the grand jury evidence pointing against indictment. The Court held that they cannot, that federal courts do not possess broad supervisory authority over grand jury proceedings because the grand jury "is an institution separate from the courts, over whose functioning the courts do not preside." The Court pointed out that while the grand jury is mentioned in the Fifth Amendment, it was not included in the "body of the Constitution" and, therefore, "has not been textually assigned...to any of the branches described in the first three Articles." It explained that "the whole theory of [the grand jury's] function is that it belongs to no branch of the institutional Government, serving as a kind of buffer or referee between the Government and the people."

The *Williams* holding was a departure from earlier decisions in which the Court (for instance in 1959's *Brown v. U.S.*) had described the grand jury as "an appendage of the court." Despite what the Court ruled in *Williams*, an excellent case can be made that the grand jury is part of the judicial branch, if only because of its dependence on the courts. A court decides when a grand jury should be convened and issues an order to that effect. Upon receiving this order, the clerk's office uses the same procedure it employs for petit jurors to summon a panel of prospective grand jurors from whom the members of the new grand jury are chosen. The court swears in the grand jurors and charges them, and they meet in a room located in the courthouse and guarded by courthouse security personnel. As discussed earlier, the grand jury relies on the court's subpoena power to obtain testimony and other evidence. And, of course, without the court, the grand jury could not exist. Outside the common law movement, grand juries do not convene themselves, just as petit juries do not convene themselves.

Most states regard the grand jury as a component of the judicial branch. *Williams* creates an anomaly in which the federal grand jury is in effect a fourth branch of government, while in most (if not all) states it is part of the court system. *Williams*'s characterization of the grand jury also produces another anomaly: The federal system includes two juries—the petit jury and the grand jury. In most (if not all) states, both are considered part of the court system, just as both were traditionally considered part of the federal court system. Under *Williams*, the federal grand jury becomes an institution unto itself, while the petit jury presumably remains part of the judicial system. Unlike the grand jury, which is not referred to in the body of the Constitution, the petit jury is mentioned in Article III, which requires that all criminal charges be tried by jury. Since Article III established the federal judiciary, it seems to follow that the petit jury is part of the federal court system.

Anomalies aside, why does it matter whether the grand jury is considered part of the judicial branch or an independent entity? The answer is that the grand jury's status is very important insofar as it determines whether any outside agency can exert a measure of control over a grand jury's activities. The grand jury is a powerful institution. As such, it has the potential to wreak a fair amount of havoc, especially when it acts as a "sword." For example, as Richard Younger explained in his 1963 book, *The People's Panel: The Grand Jury in the United States 1634-1941,* early in this nation's history a grand jury overreacted and indicted a congressman for criticizing the federal government. Recently, a California county grand jury nearly brought local government to a halt when it returned "rogue indictments" against eight top county officials, and a Texas county grand jury's investigation of a former mayor seriously damaged his reputation even though it turned up no evidence of wrongdoing.

Under *Williams*, courts cannot head off these misguided enthusiasms. The Supreme Court ruled that because the grand jury is a separate institution, courts cannot intervene unless a grand jury is violating a specific statute or rule of law. Since grand juries operate relatively unimpeded by statutes or other rules of law, this leaves the courts relatively powerless.

Prosecutorial dominance

On one level, the courts' powerlessness is probably of little moment given prosecutors' ascendance over grand jurors. For the most part, grand juries operate under the de facto control of a prosecutor who initiates and directs an investigation. One source of a prosecutor's control is the relationship he or she cultivates with a grand jury. Prosecutors try to develop a rapport with grand jurors, which is usually easy because prosecutors are the only people the jurors see consistently. Once established, this rapport becomes an informal control mechanism that ensures the jurors will accede to a prosecutor's wishes. In this sense, grand jurors become the prosecutor's cheering section. Or, as former New York Court of Appeals Judge Sol Wachtler famously put it, a good prosecutor can get a grand jury to "indict a ham sandwich." This dominance is exacerbated by the prosecutor's legal expertise. Grand jurors rely on prosecutors to interpret the law and put the facts they uncover into a legal context. Even if grand jurors for some reason do not identify with the prosecutor, their ignorance of the law makes it very difficult to challenge a prosecutor's conduct of an investigation or wish to indict.

The extent to which prosecutors dominate grand jury proceedings is both good and bad. Prosecutorial control is good in that it channels the grand jury's awesome power into areas of legitimate law enforcement concern and minimizes, if it does not eliminate, the possibility that a grand jury will begin inquiring into matters that should be out of bounds for legal or policy reasons. The expansive, capricious inquiries of common law grand juries that suited the small, rural communities from which they emerged would introduce an unpredictable and disruptive element into modern law enforcement.

To understand why this is true, one needs only to consider the Clinton-Lewinsky investigation to imagine the specter of a runaway federal grand jury that, infatuated with its own publicity, pursues ever more outrageous inquiries to its own detriment and to the ruin of many of those on whom it focuses its attentions. Of course, while prosecutors' influence may keep grand juries in line, it does nothing to keep prosecutors themselves from exploiting the grand jury, which many are accusing Independent Counsel Starr of doing. In several post-*Williams* decisions, federal judges lament their inability to stop prosecutors from engaging in conduct that, while it may not explicitly violate federal law, is clearly abusive.

Unfortunately, prosecutorial control effectively nullifies the role grand jurors are supposed to play in the investigating and indicting processes. Having grand jurors become a prosecutor's cheering section may not interfere with their ability to act as the sword of justice, but it certainly does not encourage them to shield individuals from unwarranted investigations and accusations. A grand jury should second-guess the prosecutor's decisions. The whole purpose of the grand jury is to have the jurors act as the voice of the community, injecting a lay perspective, a ration of common sense, into the law enforcement process.

In the 1930s, for instance, a New York grand jury did something that would be improbable in the 1990s. It rejected the efforts of Tammany Hall prosecutors who wanted to limit its inquiries into racketeering and corruption. The grand jurors barred the prosecutors from appearing before them and embarked on their own investigation, which resulted in the indictment and convictions of 73 racketeers. It is highly unlikely this could happen today: One attorney interviewed for a recent *Chicago Tribune* article described the modern grand jury as "23 people in a room taking up oxygen and having lunch," and it is not uncommon for witnesses to report having seen grand jurors sleeping or reading newspapers during their testimony. The relationship prosecutors develop with grand jurors and the complexity of the law combine to overwhelm the jurors and mute the voice of the community.

A proposal

"The principal value of a grand jury…consists in the independence of the jurors." That was the conclusion reached by the judge in a federal court case, *U.S. v. Watkins*, in 1829. What can be done to restore that independence recognized as necessary so long ago?

A number of possibilities have been suggested, but one offers the best hope of restoring the grand jury to what it once was, and was intended to be. The greatest threat to a grand jury's ability to exercise independent judgment comes from the influence prosecutors exert over the grand jurors. It follows that reducing a prosecutor's influence over grand jurors should enhance a grand jury's independence. The obvious way to do this is to bar prosecutors from grand jury proceedings, leaving the jurors to act on their own, but this brings it own risks.

The solution is to give grand juries their own attorney. In 1978, Hawaii began providing grand juries with their own counsel. The purpose was to increase the independence of grand juries by minimizing a prosecutor's influence over grand jurors.

Grand jury counsel, appointed by the state's chief justice, serve one year terms and are available to provide legal advice throughout a grand jury's proceedings. Grand jury counsel serve along with prosecutors, who bring matters warranting investigation to a grand jury's attention, provide it with evidence, and submit proposed indictments for its review.

Other jurisdictions would do well to follow Hawaii's lead. The court impaneling a grand jury could appoint its grand jury's counsel when it swears the jurors in. To avoid biases resulting from serving an extended tenure as grand jury counsel, each counsel should be appointed to serve for a limited period. This period could be linked to the grand jury's term or set generically, such as Hawaii's one-year term. Giving each grand jury its own counsel would produce a close working relationship between the two without creating the unhealthy dependence that currently results from prosecutor-grand jury relationships. Unlike a prosecutor, who serves as both advocate and legal adviser, the grand jury counsel would act solely as a legal adviser, one with no stake in the outcome.

The counsel would act as a buffer between the grand jurors and prosecutors and between the jurors and the targets of their inquiries. He or she could advise the jurors on the advisability of hearing exculpatory evidence or of subpoenaing additional evidence beyond that presented by the prosecutor. Since the counsel is impartial, he or she would be more likely to recommend that the jurors take these steps. This would let them hear a more balanced presentation, which would itself increase the objectivity of their decision making.

Grand jury counsel could also facilitate the jurors' consideration of illegally obtained evidence. The Fourth Amendment's exclusionary rule does not apply to grand jury proceedings, the Supreme Court having held that the prohibition on illegal search and seizure is adequately protected by preventing illegally obtained evidence from being used at trial. A grand jury's counsel could advise them on the ramifications of basing their decision to indict on evidence that was seized in violation of the Fourth Amendment. The jurors could weigh this information in deciding whether such charges are warranted. Aside from enhancing the accuracy and objectivity of the jurors' decision making, this step reduces the perception that grand juries implicitly approve lawless police behavior by basing their decisions on the fruits of such conduct.

Along with enhancing a grand jury's independence, the grand jury counsel could intervene to prevent grand jurors from abusing their authority. Grand jury counsel cannot be given the power to veto grand juror decisions. This would substitute his or her opinions for those of the grand jury and effectively transform the "voice of the community" into a one-person grand jury. Counsel would have to exert control informally, in the same way prosecutors currently control grand jury proceedings. That is, counsel would develop a close relationship with grand jurors, one in which the jurors relied on their counsel and accepted his or her advice. Once this relationship was established, it should help the counsel persuade grand jurors not to embark on unfounded, ill-advised inquiries.

Conversely, counsel could assist a grand jury that wants to initiate a legitimate investigation of matters that have not been presented to it by a prosecutor. In many states, grand juries are statutorily authorized to initiate investigations based on their own knowledge of community affairs, without waiting for a prosecutor to request such an investigation. Counsel would help grand jurors decide when such an inquiry was, and was not, appropriate. This would revive the independence found in the racket-busting New York grand jury while avoiding the abuses of unfettered grand jury discretion.

Giving the grand jury its own counsel does not run afoul of the Supreme Court's characterization of the grand jury's unique institutional status. Prosecutors play two roles before a grand jury—advocate and legal adviser. By creating the position of grand jury counsel, a jurisdiction simply divides the prosecutor's responsibilities among two people, thus freeing the prosecutor from the inherent conflict of interest involved in wearing two hats, that of advocate and that of disinterested legal adviser. Unlike federal courts' pre-*Williams* efforts to use their supervisory powers to shape the course of grand jury proceedings, this simply reallocates the performance of duties that have been an integral part of the grand jury since it emerged in 12th-century England.

NOTE

This article originally appeared in Volume 81, Number 5, March-April 1998, pages 190-199.

Curbing abuse of the grand jury

by Gerald B. Lefcourt

The grand jury is an institution embodied in our common law traditions of due process. When it emerged in England in the 12th century, it may have been as much a tool to further the powers of the crown as it was a protective shield between citizen and crown. Yet when the American colonists brought the grand jury to this country, it was clearly viewed as a citizen's body, to protect them from the whims of royal governors and English tyranny. It was according to this colonial conception of the institution—as a means of protecting citizens—that the founders enshrined the right to grand jury indictment in the Constitution.

But, far from the concept of the founders, the federal grand jury is no longer a shield to protect citizens from being arbitrarily charged. Due to the Supreme Court's regrettable 5-4 decision in *U.S. v. Williams* in 1992, just about everything the independent counsel has been criticized for will stand as long as a defendant charged by his grand jury is later given a fair trial. No judge or magistrate can check the independent prosecutor's unbridled, grand inquisitor powers, nor those of any other federal prosecutor. And, as we know well, federal prosecutors do this sort of thing all the time.

Correcting abuses

Only Congress can reverse the steady erosion of grand jury independence. It can start on reform by considering the following proposals:

• A federal prosecutor should not be allowed to intentionally withhold clearly exculpatory information from the grand jury. Without this duty, the grand jury is simply a tool to be manipulated by a prosecutor seeking an indictment. To ensure that this duty is real, courts must be given the power to review grand jury minutes and dismiss indictments (without prejudice) that result from procedures where this duty is violated.

• A federal prosecutor should not be allowed to intentionally use illegally seized information to secure an indictment. If federal agents and prosecutors know they can use such information, they will hardly be discouraged from engaging in illegal practices. The federal code recognizes as much in its electronic surveillance sections: 18 U.S.C. 2515 prohibits illegally "intercepted" information from being used before a grand jury. This rule should apply to all evidence acquired by confession or search.

• A target of a grand jury should be able to approach the foreperson in writing, to offer information to the grand jury. Again, this is to ensure that the grand jury receives all the relevant information it needs to make an informed decision. Note that there is no requirement that the foreperson accept the proffered information. This simply ensures that he or she is made aware of its existence, and afforded the choice as to whether it is relevant and helpful to the important work of the grand jurors in deciding the fate of their fellow citizens.

• All witnesses called before a grand jury should be given a *Miranda*-type warning by the prosecutor before being questioned. Prosecutors routinely tell witnesses they are not "targets" to get them to answer questions without counsel before the grand jury, only to indict them later, after they have helplessly incriminated themselves. The problem can be addressed by requiring the brief issuance to grand jury witnesses of a *Miranda*-type warning. This is only fair.

Complex and important legal issues face any grand jury witness. The experience is especially daunting for the typical lay witness. An appearance before the grand jury may subject an individual to the grave danger of self-incrimination or imprisonment for contempt.

• Witnesses called before the grand jury should be allowed to have counsel present. Currently, when a federal prosecutor places a citizen under oath before a grand jury, the person cannot have counsel in attendance. This is both unfair and inefficient.

Without counsel's presence, the witness is at a decided disadvantage. Inherent pressures and accompanying nervousness associated with appearing before a grand jury can make it difficult for any witness, especially the average lay witness, to remember counsel's instructions relative to each question from the prosecutor. A witness must make quick judgments that even a seasoned lawyer would find difficult. She is forced to make judgments, even while testifying, that will legally bind and potentially incriminate her, or subject her to a perjury charge. Her testimony can also be used at a later trial to impeach her. The witness who wants to consult with counsel is unrealistically expected to go through a disruptive drill in the midst of questioning—asking permission to leave, getting up, going outside the room, repeating to her attorney (from memory) the prosecutor's question, remembering her attorney's advice, and then returning to the room. The process could be repeated numerous times. This routine hurts the witness by annoying grand jurors and raising inevitable speculation in their minds as to the purpose of the consultation.

• All subpoenas for witnesses called before a grand jury should be issued at least 72 hours before the date of appearance, not including weekends and holidays, unless good cause is shown for an exception. This would prohibit the all-too-frequent ambushing of witnesses by prosecutors, who serve "forthwith" subpoenas at the 11th hour. They often do so simply to gain an undue advantage over an unprepared (and most likely uncounseled) witness.

• Witnesses should have the right to receive a transcript (at their own expense) of their grand jury testimony. Federal Rule of Criminal Procedure 6 does not apply an obligation of secrecy to witnesses who appear before the grand jury. Thus, there is no reason they should not be allowed access to their own statements before the grand jury, as transcribed. Since the government may well seek to use these statements against the witness, this is only fair.

• Grand jurors should be given meaningful jury instructions, on the record. Grand jurors cannot exercise their historic powers of independence without meaningful instructions regarding their duties and powers, including the power to reject, as well as accept, the prosecutor's request for charges. Grand jurors, additionally, are entitled to receive instructions regarding the elements of the charges they are to consider. All instructions, as well as any statements made to grand jurors by prosecutors regarding the charges or the people who are being investigated, must be on the record so that courts, upon a proper showing by the parties, are able to properly supervise the fairness and integrity of the grand jury process.

Toward reform

Many of these proposals are law in some states such as New York, which has dutifully considered the matter. There, an indictment cannot be based on inadmissible or incompetent testimony such as hearsay evidence or on illegally obtained evidence. Evidence in the prosecutor's possession that substantially indicates a suspect may be innocent must be presented to the grand jury. A defendant on notice of the grand jury investigation has an absolute right to testify before the panel if he or she chooses. Most important, the court has the power to inspect minutes from the grand jury, and to dismiss any charges against a citizen if the grand jury evidence is actually insufficient. The judge can even reduce the charges to a lesser offense.

These are essential checks and balances for the grand jury process. In the aggregate, they can prevent prosecutorial abuse of individuals whether they are targets or witnesses. And they can help to secure institutional credibility and citizen confidence in the grand jury, and indeed, the criminal justice process itself. These rights and safeguards, which have enabled the grand jury system to work effectively and fairly in New York, enjoy the broad support of prosecutors and defense attorneys alike.

Only when reforms such as these are in place will grand juries be liberated from their captivity by prosecutors. When that happens, grand juries can resume serving their important historic role as a neutral, apolitical buffer between the government and the citizenry.

NOTE

This article originally appeared in Volume 81, Number 5, March-April 1998, pages 196-197. It is an edited version of an article that originally appeared in *The Champion*, April 1998.

The American Judiciary and the Politics of Representation

INTRODUCTION   Unlike legislatures, courts are not generally thought of as "representative" institutions. Nevertheless, most judges do "represent" well-defined geographical constituencies and many are, indeed, elected. To the degree that judges in a given judicial system carry unequal workloads or "service" different numbers of people, we may legitimately raise a concern about judicial "malapportionment." The issue of representation and the judiciary is a multifaceted one, and the articles in this section explore this issue in its diversity.

One major concern involving representation and American courts centers on the applicability of the 1964 Voting Rights Act to allegations of racial discrimination in numerous state judicial selection settings. Our readings begin with companion pieces on "The Voting Rights Act and judicial elections litigation." Robert McDuff offers the plaintiff's perspective based on his experiences representing black voters, while Ronald Weber outlines the defendant's position based on his experience as an expert witness for Louisiana. For McDuff, the judiciary remains a segregated institution where important improvements can be brought about through rigorous enforcement of the Voting Rights Act. Weber counters by summarizing the major points put forward by the states, starting with the fundamental argument that the Voting Rights Act does not apply to judicial elections and ranging through less radical positions which, nevertheless, maximize state prerogatives while creating difficulties for the plaintiffs.

For the moment, the debate between McDuff and Weber has been "settled" by a 1991 Supreme Court ruling in which the Voting Rights Act was held to be applicable to the judicial elections at issue in Texas and Louisiana. The scope and full implications of the ruling will, undoubtedly, continue to unfold in ongoing litigation. It should be noted that the Court specifically excluded appointive systems from its holding. Further, the Court's decision applying the Voting Rights Act to judicial elections was based on statutory interpretation. Consequently, future congressional action could alter the Court's ruling if legislators are unhappy with the justices' reading of congressional intent in the Voting Rights Act.

The complexity of the representational facets of Supreme Court behavior is explored in Thomas Marshall's study, "The Supreme Court and the grass roots: whom does the Court represent best?" Marshall's analysis attempts to link public opinion data to 110 actual Supreme Court decisions during the Warren, Burger, and Rehnquist Courts in an effort to assess which of four competing representational models the Court's work output most closely follows. That is, does judicial decision making reflect the will of numerical majorities, unpopular minorities, politically and economically advantaged elites, or the attitudes of those in the polity who share the justices' partisan leanings? Many readers will, undoubtedly, be surprised that Marshall's analysis leads to the conclusion that, "The modern Supreme Court has been relatively evenhanded in representing different social and demographic group attitudes." The article attempts to both explain this finding while exploring its implications and consequences.

The next two selections , "Voting behavior and gender on the U.S. courts of appeals," by Sue Davis, Susan Haire, and Donald Songer, and Jennifer Segal's study of, "The decision making of Clinton's nontraditional judicial appointees," attempt to assess the degree to which judicial decisions reflect the gender or race of the decision-making judges. Thus, Davis, Haire, and Songer focus on the dictates of feminist legal theory and, in particular, the work of psychologist Carol Gilligan to frame the question, "How might the alleged different perspective of women manifest itself in judging?" In two of the three legal areas examined, gender based differences are, indeed, found in case outcomes. Thus, women were more likely than men to favor claimants in employment discrimination cases and defendants in search and seizure cases. No significant gender-based differences were found, however, in decisions regarding obscenity. Given their mixed results, the authors are appropriately cautious in discussing their findings. Segal's analysis, utilizing a paired-judge research strategy to examine the decisions of judges who varied on gender or race but who were otherwise similarly situated, also offers results that are suggestive yet mixed.

The final piece in this section leaves the empirical question of the representational nature of judicial decision making behind and, instead, focuses on some normative and policy concerns regarding representation and the judiciary. Sheldon Goldman's "Should there be affirmative action for the judiciary?" is an advocacy piece written during a time when considerable controversy existed over the Carter administration's efforts to increase the number of women, blacks, and other minorities on the federal bench. Goldman considers the litany of criticism leveled at affirmative action in judicial recruitment and offers his arguments for why none offer compelling indictments. In many respects, the concerns over affirmative action and judicial representation highlighted in Goldman's thoughtful and provocative essay remain with us today.

The Voting Rights Act and judicial elections litigation: the plaintiffs' perspective

by Robert McDuff

When a lawsuit was filed in federal court in Mississippi in 1984 challenging at-large voting for state court judges, only one of the state's 100 trial court judges was black. In July 1989, five black judges were sworn into office as the result of special court-ordered elections from revised districts and voting systems, and it is possible more will be elected during the regular 1990 elections.

When a similar suit was filed in federal court in Louisiana in 1986, only six black citizens sat among the 233 judges of the state district courts, courts of appeal, and supreme court. This past July 5, the Louisiana legislature responded to a federal court order mandating changes by creating majority black voter registration districts covering 49 of those judgeships.

These are the first fruits of the proliferation of cases challenging the dilution of minority voting strength in judicial elections in a number of states around the country. Once the dust settles from all of the litigation, several state judiciaries will likely be much more racially integrated than now.

It has been a long time coming. The courts in this country are almost completely the enclave of white judges. Although the nation's population is over 18 percent black and Hispanic according to the 1980 census, and is expected to be even higher under the 1990 count, less than 4 percent of the judges are black and just over 1 percent are Hispanic.[1]

This article is about the litigation over judicial election systems and its importance in desegregating state court judiciaries. It is written from my perspective as an attorney for black voters in the first two cases to go to trial, the challenge involving state trial judges in Mississippi[2] and the case dealing with state trial and appellate judges in Louisiana.[3]

Application of the Act

For nearly two decades now, minority citizens have challenged at-large elections for state legislative seats, city and county governing boards, and school boards under legal principles that prevent unfair dilution of minority voting strength. Many of the challenges have been successful, resulting in major increases in the number of black and Hispanic public officials in this country. But it is only recently that judgeships have become the target of similar lawsuits.

The question has been raised whether Section 2 of the federal Voting Rights Act, which is the primary basis for dilution lawsuits, even applies to the election of judges. Some of the states that have been sued say that the Act applies only to those public officials whose functions include representing the political interests of their constituents in specific policy decisions. Since judges are not supposed to "represent" the substantive political interests of the voters, goes the argument, the racial power-sharing principles behind the Voting Rights Act should not apply to judicial elections.

The fact that judges are not supposed to "represent" the substantive political concerns of the voters is irrelevant. The judicial districting litigation does not hinge on a theory that minority citizens should have greater political access to judges in order to affect particular judicial decisions. Instead, it is grounded in the notion that the process of electing judges—of choosing those who will sit on the bench—should be free of racial discrimination, and that minority voters should have a meaningful say in the choice just as white voters do.

The federal courts have resolved the dispute by holding that Section 2 does apply to judicial elections. The leading decision is *Chisom v. Edwards*,[4] where the United States Court of Appeals for the Fifth Circuit said this:

Where racial discrimination exists, it is not confined to elections for legislative and executive officials; in such instance, it extends throughout the entire electoral spectrum. Minorities may not be prevented from using Section 2 in their efforts to combat racial discrimination in the election of state judges; a contrary result would prohibit minorities from achieving an effective voice in choosing those individuals society elects to administer and interpret the law.[5]

The nature of the problem

Given that Section 2 applies, the next question is how to determine whether specific judicial districts violate Section 2. An answer to that question requires an understanding of the way at-large elections tend to discriminate against minority voters.

The major problem being challenged in the judicial districting litigation is the widespread use of at-large voting in multimember districts with a majority of white voters.[6] The Supreme Court noted in the recent voting rights case of *Thornburg v. Gingles*[7] that "multimember districts and at-large voting schemes may 'operate to minimize or cancel out the voting strength of racial [minorities in] the voting population.'"[8] The problem stems from the winner-take-all feature of at-large voting in multimember districts. Since every voter casts a ballot for each seat, white voters who constitute a majority in a district can control all of the seats in that district.

This becomes a particularly acute problem in light of the unfortunate and well-documented tendency of white voters in this country rarely to vote for minority candidates. For instance, between 1978 and 1987, black candidates ran against white candidates for judgeships in Louisiana on 54 different occasions, and in none of those elections did a majority, or even a plurality, of the white voters support a black candidate.[9] When that type of bloc voting is combined with the winner-take-all feature of at-large elections in districts with a majority of whites casting ballots, it is extremely difficult for minority candidates to be elected.

By contrast, changes can be made in the system to open it up so that minority voters have the power to elect candidates of their choice. For example, many at-large districts can be subdivided into smaller election districts, some of which would have black or Hispanic voting majorities. Instead of being virtually shut out from the opportunity to se-

lect judges, as in the at-large setting, minority voters would have sufficient voting power to choose some of the judges just as white voters choose judges. The practical result of this would be more minority judges, inasmuch as minority voters generally support minority candidates in the same way white voters usually vote for white candidates.

All of these factors come into play when courts are deciding whether particular at-large election districts transgress Section 2, which specifically prohibits election systems that cause minority voters to have less opportunity than white voters to elect candidates of their choice. The court have held that at-large elections are discriminatory, and Section 2 is violated, where (1) minority voters generally support minority candidates, (2) white voters generally support white candidates, with the result that minority candidates are usually defeated, and (3) an alternative system can be created by which minority voters could better elect candidates of their choice.[10] Although other factors are relevant, those are generally the core of a Section 2 violation.[11] This is true of judicial election cases as well as of legislative election cases, inasmuch as the analytical tools used to uncover discrimination in one are just as useful for detecting discrimination in the other.[12]

Designing the remedy

Once liability in particular districts has been found, the need arises to implement a remedy, a new system which cures the prior racial discrimination.

Probably the best remedial concept in most situations is that of dividing existing at-large districts into smaller subdistricts for the election of judges, with some of the subdistricts containing black or Hispanic majorities sufficient to elect candidates of choice. Indeed, subdistricts have been adopted as a remedial response in the only two cases to reach the remedial stage thus far. The subdistrict concept is discussed momentarily, as are two other systems which offer the potential to cure unlawful dilution—limited voting and cumulative voting. But first, it is important to set to rest the erroneous notion that Section 2 violations can be remedied easily by switching from elective to appointive systems.

The case against appointment

After liability was found in Louisiana for most trial and appellate court districts, the federal court gave the Louisiana legislature an opportunity to come up with a remedial proposal. Proponents of appointive judgeships attempted to persuade the legislature to change to an appointive system. The effort failed, but a similar push is underway in Texas, where Section 2 litigation is pending over existing at-large election districts.

However, appointive systems are not likely to be acceptable as a remedy for Section 2 violations in judicial elections. First of all, there is something rather sinister about taking away the power to vote for judges at the very time litigation under the Voting Rights Act promises that minority citizens will finally have their fair share of that power. States that find elective systems quite satisfactory during the years and decades when white voters control nearly all of the judicial seats ordinarily should not junk elections once it looks as though minority voters will elect judges to some of the seats as well. That kind of timing may well lead to disapproval by the federal courts of any change to appointment, or to objection by the U.S. Department of Justice in those states where the Justice Department's approval of voting changes is required under Section 5 of the Voting Rights Act.

Indeed, there are historical parallels. For instance, in 1966, just as black voters were becoming registered in Mississippi by virtue of the 1965 passage of the Voting Rights Act, the state legislature changed the method of choosing county school superintendents in a number of majority black counties from election to appointment. The Justice Department refused to approve the change under Section 5, concluding that it had the purpose and effect of diluting black voting strength.[13] A change to appointment of judges in the wake of voting rights litigation could well meet a similar fate.

Also, in a sense, appointive systems would not satisfy the key objective of Section 2 of the Voting Rights Act, which is to increase the opportunity of minority voters to elect candidates of their choice, be those candidates black, Hispanic, or white. It so happens that minority voters generally cast their ballots for minority candidates, and if a remedy increases the opportunity of minority voters to elect candidates of choice, it likely will increase the number of minority judges. But whatever candidates are chosen, the goal of the Voting Rights Act is to assure minorities a fair share of the power to choose those candidates, and that goal is not met when elective power is taken away altogether and placed in the hands of an appointing authority such as the governor.

Even if the objective were conceived simply as increasing the number of minority judges—rather than giving minority voters a greater voice in the selection of judges—an appointive system in no way guarantees a fair number of minority judges. It depends entirely upon the discretion of the person or persons making the appointments. When a violation of the Voting Rights Act is found by a federal court, an effective remedy must be ensured by the court and not left to the discretion of a single state official.

The same uncertainties apply even where the governor's choices are limited to a list of names submitted by a nominating commission. It might help the situation to draw majority black and Hispanic nomination districts, with a requirement that the nominating commissions reflect the racial composition of the districts. Even then, however, several variables could prevent the appointment of a reasonable number of minority judges.

For all of these reasons, the efficacy of appointive systems as a Section 2 remedy is questionable. This is not to say, as a matter of general principle, that elective systems are better than appointive systems. It is only to say that a switch to an appointive system at the very time minority citizens are gaining, through voting rights litigation, a meaningful opportunity to elect some of the judges may not remedy any voting rights violations in a state's judicial election scheme. Years down the road, after a fair election system has been instituted and a state's judiciary is well integrated, it might make more sense to move to appointment of judges.

Election subdistricts

One of the best methods for remedying voting rights violations arising from multimember judicial election districts will be to divide those multimember districts into smaller subdistricts, with some having black or Hispanic voting majorities sufficient to elect candidates of choice. That is what has happened in the first two cases to proceed to the remedy stage, *Martin v. Mabus* in Mississippi and *Clark v. Roemer* in Louisiana.[14]

After the federal court in *Martin* found a violation of Section 2 in eight multimember judicial districts, no remedial action was taken by the Mississippi legislature, so the judge had to fashion the remedy. He carved the eight districts into single-member subdistricts, with judges being elected from the subdistricts yet continuing to serve the original district, and with case assignment among the judges allowed to proceed as before. No subdistrict residency requirement was imposed, and candidates were able to run from any subdistrict within their original district.[15] The plaintiffs had suggested, and were pleased with, the subdistrict concept, but contended that some of the court's subdistricts were not drawn in a way that would give black voters a fair shot at electing candidates of choice, particularly in the rural Mississippi Delta. Nevertheless, they agreed to a compromise with the state by which neither side would appeal, and court-ordered special elections went forward in the spring and summer of this year. More black trial judges were elected than ever before in Mississippi, although not as many as would have been elected under the plaintiffs' proposed subdistricts.

Meanwhile, in *Clark*, the Louisiana legislature heeded the call to devise a remedy after the federal court struck down most of the districts used to elect district and appellate court judges in the state. The new plan, passed on July 5, adopted subdistricts, many with substantial black majorities. The demographics required that some of the pre-existing districts be divided into single-member subdistricts in order to achieve sufficient black majorities, while others were divided into multimember subdistricts somewhat smaller than the original districts. Like the plan adopted by the federal court in Mississippi, the Louisiana legislature's proposal retains district-wide jurisdiction for judges elected from subdistricts, with case assignment to proceed as before, and imposes no subdistrict residency requirement. The Louisiana redistricting is linked to a state constitutional amendment which will be considered by the state's voters on October 7, 1989, and which also must be precleared by the U.S. attorney general under Section 5 of the Voting Rights Act and approved by the federal court hearing the Clark case before implementation.

Objections

A handful of objections have been raised to the subdistrict concept. Examined closely, they are meritless. Some say, for example, that it is improper to elect judges from districts that are not coterminous with the judges' geographic jurisdiction. However, no jurisprudential or constitutional principle prevents that. Indeed, it is done in several states, and repeatedly has been held to comply with the federal Constitution.[16]

Another objection to the subdistrict system is that citizens would not have an opportunity to vote on all judges who may end up hearing cases involving those citizens. Yet no right exists for litigants to vote on the particular judges who may hear their cases. As it is now, citizens are often in court in civil or criminal cases in jurisdictions where they do not live or vote, yet none has ever been able to challenge a judge's authority because the citizen had no opportunity to vote for that judge.

Some have raised the specter of corruption in the sense that judges may favor litigants from their own subdistrict over litigants from another subdistrict. If that is a problem, it is a problem as well under existing election systems inasmuch as judges frequently hear cases involving one litigant from the local judicial district and another from outside the district. Yet that has never been considered a disqualifying feature, and no one has demonstrated that any state's judiciary is rife with home-team favoritism. And no evidence exists to show that judges elected from subdistricts will be any less honest or diligent than those chosen under the current systems.

It has been suggested that subdistricts will intolerably exacerbate political pressures on judges because they would be smaller and contain fewer voters than the existing districts. This ignores the fact that most decisions made by state court judges have little political effect—they are important to the litigants and no others. To the extent that state judges do face, from time to time, controversial decisions whose outcome may sway the electorate, those decisions are usually of such notoriety that they would be as well-known, and would have as much political effect, in the pre-existing larger district as in the smaller subdistrict. Finally, even if some slight difference did exist in the political pressure coming from a subdistrict as opposed to a district election, judges are already expected to withstand that type of pressure, and such a slight difference is worth the price in order to cleanse the judicial election process of unlawful discrimination.

Limited and cumulative voting

Where the demographics make it difficult to create subdistricts with sufficiently high black or Hispanic percentages, or where other considerations suggest that subdistricts are not the way to go, other possible remedies include limited voting and cumulative voting. Briefly, the systems work this way.[17]

Under limited voting, voters have fewer votes than there are seats up for election, with the exact ratio being dependent upon the racial demographics of the district. All candidates continue to run at-large, but in a pool, and the highest number of vote getters equivalent to the number of open seats win the election. By keeping the number of ballots lower than the number of seats, limited voting minimizes the ability of white voters to sweep all of the seats and allows minority voters to concentrate their ballots behind minority candidates.

Cumulative voting is similar, except each voter has a like number of votes as there are contested seats, and each voter may cast all votes for a single candidate, or split the votes among a number of candidates. For instance, if four seats are up, a voter may cast four votes for a candidate, or three for one candidate and one for another, or one vote for each of four candidates, or any other combination. This system is much more complicated than subdistricts or limited voting, and requires a greater degree of political organization. But, it allows minority voters to concentrate their voting strength behind minority candidates and makes it unlikely that white ballots will be cast in such a way as to take all seats.

Both of these systems have been used in some jurisdictions to elect officials of local governments, with limited voting the more common of the two. They are also occasionally being adopted as remedies in local government voting rights cases.[18]

Conclusion

America's judiciary is fairly well segregated. Although that is not going to change overnight, the application of the Voting Rights Act to judicial elections will make some important inroads in several states. If the Act is applied vigorously, and strong remedies are implemented when violations are found, changes will come, and the changes will be for the better.

NOTES

This article originally appeared in Volume 73, Number 2, August-September 1989, pages 82-85.

1. The latest comprehensive statistics covering the state courts are from the 1985 publication of the Fund for Modern Courts, Inc., entitled *The Success of Women and Minorities In Achieving Judicial Office.*

2. Martin v. Allain, 658 F.Supp. 1183 (S.D. Miss. 1987) (on liability); Martin v. Mabus, 700 F.Supp. 327 (S.D. Miss. 1988) (on remedy).

3. Clark v. Edwards, No. 86-435-A (M.D. La., unpublished opinions of August 15, 1988, and August 31, 1988).

4. 839 F.2d 1056 (5th Cir.), *cert. denied,* __ U.S. __ (1988).

5. *Id.* at 1065. *See also,* Mallory v. Eyrich, 839 F.2d 275 (6th Cir. 1988) (also holding that Section 2 applies to judicial elections).

6. In addition to contesting the use of at-large voting in particular districts, some of the lawsuits also complain about the actual drawing of lines between districts, contending that the lines fragment minority voting populations in a way that unfairly minimizes the number of majority black or Hispanic districts. In such lawsuits, the complaint is not only with the use of at-large voting within given districts, but also the placement of the lines which create the districts in the first place.

7. 478 U.S. 30 (1986).

8. *Id.* at 47, *quoting* Burns v. Richardson, 384 U.S. 73, 88 (1966).

9. The analysis of those 54 elections is documented by Professor Richard Engstrom, *When blacks run for judge: racial divisions in the candidate preferences of Louisiana voters,* 73 JUDICATURE 87 (August-September 1989).

10. Thornburg v. Gingles, 478 U.S. 30 (1986); Citizens For A Better Gretna v. City of Gretna, 834 F.2d 496 (5th Cir. 1987), *cert. denied,* __ U.S. __ (1989).

11. Thornburg v. Gingles, 478 U.S. at 48-49, n. 15, 50-51.

12. Martin v. Allain, 658 F.Supp. at 1204; Clark v. Edwards, unpublished opinion of August 15, 1988, at 38-39, and unpublished order of August 31, 1988, at 3-4; Rangel v. Mattox, No. B-88-053 (S.D. Tex., opinion of July 28, 1989), at 17-18, 20.

13. Section 5 objection letter of the Mississippi attorney general from the assistant attorney general, Civil Rights Division, U.S. Department of Justice, May 21, 1969, p. 2. *See also,* Allen v. Board of Elections, 393 U.S. 544, 570 (1969) (holding that any change from election to appointment of public officers in a covered jurisdiction must be precleared under Section 5 of the Voting Rights Act).

14. The cases originally were entitled Martin v. Allain and Clark v. Edwards, but by the time the cases reached the remedy stage, the names of the new governors were inserted as defendants, and the cases are now known as *Martin v. Mabus* and *Clark v. Roemer.*

15. Martin v. Mabus, 700 F.Supp. 327 (S.D. Miss. 1988).

16. For instance, supreme court justices in a number of states, including Louisiana and Mississippi, are elected from a portion of the state, yet hear cases from throughout the state. The same is true with some intermediate appellate court judges, whose jurisdiction is larger than their electoral district. On the trial court level, the non-record justice court judges in Mississippi (formerly justices of the peace) are elected from single-member districts within the county but have countywide jurisdiction. Certain city judges in New York City come from districts within the city but have citywide jurisdiction. Many trial judges from North Carolina are elected from areas different from their normal territorial jurisdiction, being chosen in statewide balloting but generally serving smaller districts, and until recently many trial judges in Georgia were chosen the same way. Systems such as these have been held to comply with the federal Constitution even though the jurisdiction of the judges is not geographically coterminous with their election districts. *See* Cox v. Katz, 241 N.E.2d 747 (Ct. App. N.Y. 1968), *affirming* 293 N.Y.S.2d 829 (App. Div. 1968), *cert. denied,* 394 U.S. 919 (1968); Stokes v. Fortson, 234 F.Supp. 575 (N.D. Ga. 1964) (three-judge court); Holshouser v. Scott, 335 F.Supp. 928 (M.D.N.C. 1971) (three-judge court), *summarily affirmed,*

409 U.S. 807 (1972).

17. For a fuller discussion, *see, e.g.*, Karlan, *Maps and Misreadings: The Role of Geographic Compactness in Racial Vote Dilution Litigation*, 24 HARV. C.R.C.L. 173, 223-236 (1989); Still, *Alternatives to Single Member Districts* in Davidson, ed., MINORITY VOTE DILUTION 253 (1984).

18. Karlan, *supra* n. 17, at 227-230, 233-235.

The Voting Rights Act and judicial elections litigation: the defendant states' perspective

by Ronald E. Weber

The electoral systems for selecting state judges are now under challenge in about 10 states by plaintiffs who allege that those systems dilute the opportunity of minority voters to elect judicial candidates of choice and hence, those systems violate Section 2 of the U.S. Voting Rights Act as amended in 1982. To date, the defendant states have employed a variety of approaches and defenses in trying to rebut the challenges of the plaintiffs. I will summarize the major approaches and defenses taken by the defendant states in responding to these voting rights suits.

The inapplicability of Section 2 of the Voting Rights Act to judicial elections

In the initial stage of each case, the state defendants have sought to show that Section 2 of the Voting Rights Act does not apply to judicial elections. They argue that judges are not "representatives" within the meaning of the word as used in Section 2 and that the U.S. Congress did not intend for Section 2 to apply to the judiciary. They further argue that since the U.S. Supreme Court has held that judicial districting plans are not subject to "one-person, one-vote" challenges under the Fourteenth Amendment to the U.S. Constitution because judges do not perform governmental functions, the Voting Rights Act adopted to carry out the Fourteenth Amendment does not apply to judicial elections. To date, all circuit and trial courts which have addressed this question have held that Section 2 does apply to judicial elections.[1]

Applicability of Section 2 requires use of "One-Person, One-Vote" criterion in proving violations

Once it is decided that Section 2 does apply to judicial elections, it is then the position of state defendants that the federal courts must employ the "one-person, one-vote" criterion in assessing whether or not judicial electoral systems are in violation of Section 2. State defendants argue that the plaintiffs must prove that the minority group is sufficiently large and geographically compact to be a majority in a single-member district. This argument suggests that a Section 2 claim cannot be proven by creating illustrative single-member districts that violate the "one-person, one-vote" criterion.

Judicial roles and judicial elections are sufficiently unique that the federal courts must exercise caution in applying the Voting Rights Act to judicial elections

The state defendants also argue that the judicial functions and roles are sufficiently different from those of the legislature and executive to warrant caution by the federal courts in applying the Voting Rights Act to the judiciary. They argue that elites and voters view the judiciary differently from other governmental institutions and hence bring different criteria to bear when making voting decisions in judicial elections. State defendants suggest that this point is borne out by evidence about the uniqueness of judicial elections. Studies of judicial elections show that, compared to elections for legislative and administrative offices, they are quite different. Judicial elections are distinguished by lower levels of turnout and voter roll-off, less competition and greater reliance by the voters on factors such as incumbency, previous judicial experience, and party affiliation in making choices among competing candidates. Thus, state defendants contend that the federal courts need to be cautious in reaching conclusions about voter polarization and dilution in judicial elections based on what they have learned before about elections for legislative and administrative offices.

The minority group must be sufficiently large and geographically compact to be a voter majority in an ungerrymandered single-member district

The state defendants contend that plaintiffs must prove clearly that the minority group is sufficiently large and geographically compact to be a voter majority in an ungerrymandered single-member judicial election district. This is a threshold requirement in Section 2 voting rights cases and if it is not met, the state defendants argue that the federal courts must dismiss the case. A simple population majority is not enough to prove the claim; instead, the plaintiffs must use voting age population or voter registration data to meet this threshold requirement.[2] Furthermore, because the minority group must be geographically compact, racially gerrymandered illustrative single-member districts cannot be employed to meet this test.

The methodologies and data used to estimate the turnout and voting preferences of racial groups must be valid and reliable

State defendants argue that estimates of turnout and voting preferences of racial groups in judicial elections are valid and reliable only under special circumstances. The analyses conducted by plaintiffs' experts should be given credibility by the courts when the analyses meet all the following tests: a) a sufficient number of cases, b) variation on both dependent and independent variables, c) contemporaneousness of election returns with the data on the racial composition of the voting age population, d) comparability of the geographical units (usually precincts) in the analysis, e) proper procedures to verify the data and f) a properly functioning statistical analysis program. Plaintiffs' experts bear the burden of showing that their analyses meet these criteria.

Racially polarized voting in judicial elections must be shown by analyzing all elections for judicial office

The state defendants also contend that it is inappropriate for plaintiffs to try to prove the presence of racially polarized voting by examining only those elections in which minority candidates have participated. In the absence of judicial elections with minority candidate participation, plaintiffs employ

elections for nonjudicial offices with minority candidate participation as substitutes for the judicial elections. State defendants' position is that elections for nonjudicial offices cannot be used to prove racially polarized voting for judicial offices. Instead, they argue that only recent judicial elections must be analyzed and that the analyses should not be limited to the subset of elections with minority candidates.

Vote dilution in judicial elections must be shown by proving that the majority bloc votes regularly in judicial elections to prevent the choices of minority bloc voters from being elected

State defendants also argue that the presence of racially polarized voting in judicial elections does not necessarily mean that vote dilution is occurring in those elections. It is their position that vote dilution occurs only when the majority bloc votes regularly to prevent the election of candidates supported by minority bloc voters. This regularity must include all elections for judicial office and not just those in which minority candidates have participated.

The failure of minority bloc supported candidates to win judicial elections may be accounted for by factors other than the race of the candidates

State defendants further contend that the federal courts must look into alternative explanations to explain why minority bloc supported candidates fail to win judicial elections. Whereas plaintiffs allege that it is the race of the candidates that provides the explanation for minority supported candidate failure, state defendants suggest that other factors may apply. Political party affiliation, incumbency, previous judicial experience, campaign spending, and voter mobilization efforts often will explain the lack of success by minority supported judicial candidates.

Remedies in judicial election voting rights cases may include the retention of multijudge election subdistricts, staggered terms, and place election systems

State defendants finally claim that the single-member election subdistrict remedy may not always be the best solution to vote dilution by at-large judicial election systems. They argue that multimember election subdistricts should be adopted if at all possible when the minority population is sufficiently large. They also suggest that staggered term and place election systems can be used when the election subdistricts are sufficiently homogeneous so those systems will not have the effect of acting as anti-single shot voting impediments to voting participation.

NOTES

This article originally appeared in Volume 73, Number 2, August-September 1989, pages 85-86, 118.

1. Martin v. Allain, 658 F.Supp. 1183 (S.D. Miss. 1987); Chisom v. Edwards, 839 F.2d 1056 (5th Cir. 1988); Mallory v. Eyrich, 839 F.2d 275 (6th Cir. 1988); Clark v. Edwards, No. 86-435-A (M.D. La., unpublished opinion of August 15, 1988); SCLC v. Siegelman, No. 88-D-0462-N (N.D. Ala., unpublished opinion of June 7, 1989).

2. Houston v. Haley, 869 F.2d 807 (5th Cir. 1989); Westwego Citizens for Better Government v. City of Westwego, 872 F.2d 1201 (5th Cir. 1989).

The Supreme Court and the grass roots: whom does the Court represent best?

Evidence from nationwide polls during the Warren, Burger, and Rehnquist Courts suggests that the modern Supreme Court's rulings have represented the attitudes of major demographic and social groups at similar rates. This evenhanded pattern of representation contributes to the Court's reputation as a neutral arbiter.

by Thomas R. Marshall

Whether the U.S. Supreme Court represents some groups better than others has long been a question of interest to judicial scholars, journalists, and litigants. Typically, the Court's representation of social or demographic groups has been measured in one of two ways. First, researchers may examine the justices' rulings, dicta, or voting patterns for evidence of sympathy toward group claims. Second, some researchers have computed which interest group litigants have the best win-loss records before the Court, and whether interest group litigants fare better, or worse, over time.[1]

Analyzing the Court's voting patterns and doctrines or counting interest group litigants' successes and failures, however, does not directly indicate how well the Court's rulings represent grass-roots group attitudes. A recent example may help demonstrate the differences among Court doctrine, interest group claims, and grass-roots group attitudes.

In *Johnson v. Transportation Agency of Santa Clara* (1987), a divided Court held, 6-3, that employers could take sex and race into account in promotion decisions and give an advantage to women or racial minorities in promotions to "traditionally segregated job categories."[2] The *Johnson* ruling was widely cited as a victory for women and minority employees; several women's and civil rights interest groups had submitted amicus curiae briefs in support of the Court's eventual ruling.[3] A nationwide Gallup Poll, however, reported that while a 57 percent to 35 percent majority of nonwhites favored the ruling, a 59 percent to 32 percent majority of women opposed it. Many other such examples can be found of apparent conflicts between interest group amicus positions, oral argument, or Court dicta versus grass-roots group poll attitudes.[4]

As *Johnson* illustrates, an alternative approach to answering the question—whom does the Supreme Court represent best?—is to rely on actual attitudes of social or demographic groups, as measured by scientific, nationwide public opinion polls. Here, a "grass-roots" demographic or social group does not refer to dues-paying members of organized interest groups. Instead, it refers to the reported attitudes of poll samples of specific demographic groups, such as men, women, Catholics, Protestants, upper-, middle-, or lower-income groups, and so forth.

Pollsters frequently write poll items to tap issues in Supreme Court disputes. Major nationwide polls also routinely report, or at least archive, poll results not only nationwide, but also for major demographic groups. As a result, it is often possible to determine which groups' attitudes a Supreme Court ruling actually represents—according to available public opinion poll results.[5]

Representing groups' claims

In a legal or electoral sense, the Supreme Court does not clearly "represent" social or demographic groups at all. The justices sit for life terms (with good behavior), without any popular election. Few Supreme Court seats are any longer informally "reserved" for a member of a religious, regional, social, or demographic group. The "black" seat of Justices Thurgood Marshall and Clarence Thomas and the "woman's" seat occupied by Justice Sandra Day O'Connor, now remain the clearest concessions to group representation. Several justices currently supervise federal circuits from which they geographically hailed,[6] although the practice of geographically balancing appointments according to circuits apparently died out well before the Warren Court.

Although most Supreme Court justices may not legally, informally, or electorally "represent" specific social or demographic groups, the Court may nonetheless agree with some groups' attitudes more frequently than it agrees with others. For example, in the *Johnson* ruling the Supreme Court agreed with (thus, represented) a majority of non-whites, but disagreed with a majority of 21 other group attitudes reported in a Gallup Poll. In this sense, the Supreme Court "represents" a group when the Court's ruling agrees with a majority (or at least a plurality) of a group's reported attitudes as measured in a scientific, nationwide poll. The Supreme Court fails to represent a group if it disagrees with a majority (or plurality) of a group's attitudes.

Four widely cited theories exist in the judicial literature, each suggesting that the Supreme Court will represent the attitudes of some demographic or socioeconomic groups better than others. These theories are reviewed briefly below, then tested with available poll data.

As the available poll data since the early 1950s indicates, none of the four theories of Supreme Court representation is completely correct. In part, each errs because modern American public opinion only occasionally has been deeply polarized. In part, each theory also errs because even where group attitudes have been polarized, the modern Supreme Court has been relatively evenhanded in its rulings.

Four theories

The first and perhaps oldest theory suggests the Supreme Court will best represent numerically large, economically and politically dominant majorities. Robert Dahl's much-debated 1957 essay popularized the argument that the Supreme Court

is essentially a majoritarian institution, which best represents prevailing political majorities.[7] Except during brief political realignment periods, Supreme Court rulings will typically represent the views of national and legislative majorities. Deaths, retirements, and new appointments ensure that the Supreme Court is seldom long out-of-line with a public opinion majority.

To be sure, majoritarian theories of judicial representation seldom examine actual poll results, largely because scientific public opinion polls were not available until the 1930s, and poll items tapping Court rulings were seldom written until the 1950s.[8] Majoritarian theories of Supreme Court representation, however, might predict that the Supreme Court would best represent groups that comprise numerical majorities and that have also been socially, economically, and politically dominant—for example, Protestants, whites, men, middle-aged or older Americans, and middle- or upper-income Americans.[9]

By contrast, a second theory holds that the Court is—or at least should be—especially responsive to small, unpopular, or politically impotent minorities who have little other effective access to the political arena. Several accounts have criticized the majoritarian theory and have argued that both the Warren and Burger Courts were often sympathetic to minority claims on civil rights, civil liberties, and political dissent.[10] This countermajoritarian theory of representation also has been argued frequently as a normative theory on behalf of blacks and other racial minorities, women, small religious sects, prisoners, gays and lesbians, children of unwed parents, aliens, and the poor.[11]

Testing this second theory poses several methodological problems. Many minority groups—for example, the Amish or Jehovah's Witnesses—are so few in number that nationwide poll samples of 1,000 or 1,500 cannot reliably measure group members' attitudes. In other instances pollsters do not separately identify minorities—for example, homosexuals or noncitizens. Modern polling techniques usually undercount some minorities—such as the poor, transients, prisoners, or non-English speakers. Even for relatively numerous minority groups—such as blacks, Hispanics, or Jews—measurement errors may be relatively high.[12] Further, only a handful of Supreme Court rulings each term addresses issues of special interest to unpopular or numerically small minorities, and some of these disputes are not of sufficiently general interest to elicit a nationwide poll item.

These methodological problems notwithstanding, major nationwide polls routinely identify several different minority groups' attitudes on poll items. The countermajoritarian theory might predict that the Supreme Court would best represent the attitudes of racial minorities (blacks), religious minorities (Catholics), politically impotent groups (the young, or low income, or less-well-educated Americans), or women—at least on issues of key interest to these groups. These groups are typically underrepresented in top public or private leadership positions,[13] and all (except women) comprise clear numerical minorities in American society.

A third theory also predicts that the Supreme Court will best represent the attitudes of numerically small groups—but in this case, politically and economically advantaged elites. Supreme Court justices, like other policy makers, may respond to the best organized, best financed, most often elected, and most articulate interests in American society.[14] High-status elites may also be more successful in elective politics, and the norm of judicial deference may lead the Court to uphold elite-inspired laws and policies enacted elsewhere. In addition, Supreme Court justices themselves typically come from relatively advantaged backgrounds and enjoy high levels of education and high incomes. As a result, the justices may sense and share elite values.[15] Elite theories predict that the Supreme Court will best represent upper-income and well-educated Americans.[16]

The fourth and final theory argues that the justices best reflect attitudes of their own political party identifiers. A considerable literature documents that federal judges, including Supreme Court justices, sometimes differ significantly in their voting patterns according to their political party ties.[17] This literature does not tie the judges' voting patterns directly into grass-roots Republican and Democrat identifiers' attitudes. Yet one might hypothesize that the justices would best represent their own party identifiers' preferences. As a result, when the Court has a majority of Republican justices, the Court will best represent Republican identifiers' preferences. Conversely, when the Court has a majority of Democratic justices, the Court will best represent Democratic identifiers' preferences.

Data and methodology

Each of these four theories of representation yields different predictions about which group attitudes the Supreme Court will best represent. At present there is no research that indicates which theory is most accurate. These theories, however, can be tested by using breakdowns from available nationwide public opinion polls. Major polling organizations such as Gallup, Harris, the Times-Mirror, CBS/*New York Times*, or the *Los Angeles Times* polls frequently include poll items to measure attitudes toward pending, or recently announced, Supreme Court rulings, at least on prominent controversies. During the Warren, Burger, and Rehnquist Courts (1953-54 through 1990-91 terms) some 110 major nationwide poll items could be matched closely with the substantive issues raised in a Supreme Court ruling.[18]

Nationwide polls do not simply report the poll results for the entire nationwide sample. Pollsters also routinely report (or at least archive) results broken down by standard demographic categories. As a result, for poll items that address these 110 Supreme Court rulings, it is also possible to examine the attitudes of 22 social or demographic groups: by sex (male, female); education (college, high school, less than high school); region (East, Midwest, South, West); income (high, medium, low); religion (Protestant, Catholic); age (under 30, 30 to 64, 65 and older); race (black, white); and party identification (Republican, Democrat, Independent).[19]

When a poll item could be closely matched, in substance, with a Supreme Court ruling, that ruling was classified as either "consistent," "inconsistent," or "unclear"—both for nationwide public opinion and also for each of the 22 social and demographic groups described above. This procedure permits an empirical test of how often the modern Court has agreed with major American social groups, and which groups' grass-roots attitudes the Court best represents.

Three simple examples may help clarify this classification. A Supreme Court ruling was classified as "consistent" if it agreed with a public opinion majority or plurality, either nationwide or for a reported group. In *South Dakota v. Dole* (1987), for example, a 64 percent to 23 percent nationwide poll majority favored withholding federal highway funds from states that did not raise their drinking age to 21—a view consistent with the Supreme Court's ruling. Further, majorities of all 22 groups agreed with the Supreme Court's ruling, with majorities in favor ranging from 55 percent (among Independents) to 72 percent (among Republicans).[20]

By contrast, a 63 percent to 29 percent nationwide poll majority disagreed with the "inconsistent" *Johnson v. Transportation Agency of Santa Clara County* (1987) ruling to allow the promotion of women or minorities over men or whites to achieve better balance in the workforce. Majorities of all 22 groups disapproved of the Court's ruling—with the sole exception of blacks, among whom a 56 percent to 34 percent majority approved of the Court ruling.[21]

Public opinion was divided more closely on a few "unclear" decisions where the polls were divided closely within the .05-level margin of error, or where contradictory poll results appeared. In *Kassel v. Consolidated Freightways Corp.* (1981), for example, 45 percent favored and 43 percent opposed a state law prohibiting tandem trailers on interstate highways. Because the close poll margin fell within the 95 percent confidence level margin of error, the Kassel ruling was classified as "unclear." In this instance the Kassel ruling was classified as consistent with 4 groups, inconsistent with 11 groups, and unclear for the remaining 7 groups.[22]

Results

Table 1 reports the percentage of Warren, Burger, and Rehnquist Court rulings that were consistent with nationwide polls, and also the percentage of these rulings that were consistent with attitudes of the 22 social and demographic groups reported here. Tables 1 through 5 exclude the few instances of "unclear" poll-to-ruling matches, where poll results were evenly divided or where contradictory poll results appeared.

Overall, 53 percent of the 110 decisions were classified as consistent with nationwide polls, another 37 percent were inconsistent, and 10 percent were unclear. If the unclear decisions are excluded, as in Table 1, then 59 percent of the remaining rulings were consistent with nationwide public opinion polls, and the remaining 41 percent were inconsistent.

Of greater interest here are the results for each of the 22 social or demographic groups. Table 1

Table 1 Percentage of Supreme Court decisions that represent group attitudes, 1953/54-1990/91 terms

	Percent consistent	Percent consistent, reweighted
Nationwide public opinion	59%	58%
By education:		
College	59	61
High school	59	58
Less than high school	54	54
By race:		
Black	63	63
White	58	57
By region:		
East	60	62
South	53	51
Midwest	64	62
West	58	58
By income:		
High	59	60
Medium	59	57
Low	57	56
By religion:		
Protestant	59	57
Catholic	57	58
By sex:		
Male	62	61
Female	55	56
By age:		
Young	63	64
Middle-aged	58	58
Older	52	52
By party identification:		
Republican	57	55
Democrat	63	61
Independent	61	63

Note: Table 1 excludes instances of evenly divided or contradictory poll results. None of the results in Tables 1 through 5 are statistically significant except as noted: *(.05 level), **(.01 level). To obtain the percentage of inconsistent decisions, subtract the percent consistent from 100 percent.

reports the percentage of consistent decisions in two ways. The first column reports the overall results; the second column reports results for a reweighted sample to correct for sampling biases over time and across caseload.[23]

Results in Table 1 indicate that the modern Supreme Court has represented all 22 groups' attitudes about equally often. For each of the 22, about three-fifths of the Court's rulings were consistent with group attitudes. The range between the best- and least-well-represented group was only about 11 percent (for the unweighted sample) to 13 percent (for the reweighted sample).

Given the relatively small number of Court rulings that could be matched with identifiable polls, these results should be interpreted cautiously. Table 1 results, however, indicate that there is no strong evidence that the modern Court has significantly better represented some groups than others during this period. Overall, the results in

Table 2 Representation of grass-roots Republicans and Democrats, by partisan makeup of the Supreme Court

Partisan majority on the Court were:	Percent of rulings consistent with:	
	Grass-roots Republicans	Grass-roots Democrats
Majority Republican	63	66
Majority Democrat	49	58

Note: Percentages indicate the majority of Court rulings that agreed with the indicated group's attitudes during each time period. For neither time period were the reported differences statistically significant at the .1-level.

Table 1 offer little support for any of the first three theories of Supreme Court representation reviewed above.

Table 2 breaks down the results for party affiliation for two time periods—first, for Court terms when there was a majority of Republican justices on the Court, and second, for Court terms when there was a majority of Democratic justices on the Court.[24] Table 2 offers little support for the theory of partisan representation, since the Court's representation of party identifiers did not significantly differ depending on the partisan makeup of the Court itself. Grass-roots Democrats were marginally better represented by the Court than were grass-roots Republicans, regardless of whether there were a majority of Democratic or Republican justices on the Court, but the differences were not large.

Why has the modern Supreme Court represented all 22 groups' attitudes nearly equally often? A large part of the answer lies in the structure of modern American public opinion. As the examples in Table 3 indicate, only rarely do majorities of comparison groups (e.g., blacks versus whites) hold opposing views on Supreme Court controversies.[25] In the extreme instance, majorities (or pluralities) of blacks disagreed with majorities (or pluralities) of whites in 17 percent of the 110 rulings examined here. Yet in the remaining 83 percent of these 110 rulings, majorities (or pluralities) of both blacks and whites held similar attitudes, and the Supreme Court's rulings simultaneously represented both groups' attitudes equally well.

As Table 3 further indicates, most groups disagreed with their comparison group less often than did blacks and whites. Majorities (or pluralities) of men and women disagreed very rarely—in only 8 (7 percent) of the 110 rulings examined here. Majorities (or pluralities) of Democrats and Republicans disagreed in only 6 (5 percent) of the 110 rulings. In short, the typical Supreme Court case has not been one in which group attitudes were sharply polarized.

Further, in most Supreme Court decisions, public opinion is also relatively one-sided. In two-thirds (67 percent) of the 110 rulings examined here, the overall margin between poll item responses was greater than 20 percent.[26] In few instances—only 16 (15 percent) of the 110 rulings—was nationwide public opinion closely divided, with a poll margin between responses of less than 10 percent.[27] Where nationwide public opinion is very one-sided—as is so frequently the case for Supreme Court controversies—few instances of conflicting majorities between comparison groups will occur.

The modern Supreme Court's relatively even-handed pattern of representation may also result, in part, from characteristics of the Court itself—particularly the shifting nature of majority coalitions and lack of clear ideological direction that has characterized the modern Supreme Court during much of this time period.[28] Ad hoc doctrinal decisions, shifting majorities, and the lack of an overreaching philosophy during much of the Burger and early Rehnquist Courts, coupled with

Table 3 Percentage of Supreme Court decisions in which comparison groups disagree and Supreme Court representation in these decisions

Groups compared	% of decisions in which groups disagree	Supreme Court decision favors (group) where groups disagree
Whites versus blacks	17%	Whites (47%); blacks (53%)
East versus South	14*	East (77%); South (23%)
College versus less than high school	14	College (62%), less than high school (38%)
Young versus old	14*	Young (77%), old (23%)
High versus low income	13	High (67%), low income (33%)
Protestant versus Catholic	8	Protestant (43%), Catholic (57%)
Male versus female	7*	Male (86%), Female (14%)
Republican versus Democrat	5	Republican (20%), Democrat (80%)
Republican versus Independent	6	Republican (33%, Independent (67%)
Democrat versus Independent	4	Independent (50%), Democrat (50%)

Note: None of the comparison groups omitted from Table 3 produced statistically significant differences.

Table 4　Supreme Court representation of group attitudes for selected groups and issues

Issue and number of decisions	Supreme Court agreement with group attitudes in these cases:
Racial (19)	Whites (63%); blacks (89%)
Religious (5)	Protestants (40%); Catholics (40%)
Privacy, gender (19)	Men (53%); Women (44%)
Business, economic (18)	High Income (61%); medium (47%); low (50%)
Free speech, dissent (11)	College-educated (56%); high school (40%); less than high school (40%)
Party-related (55)	Republicans (61%); Democrats (61%); Independents (60%)

a large number of nonunanimous, closely divided votes, may contribute to the Court's pattern of representing different social and demographic groups at roughly similar rates.

Table 3 also reports which group attitudes the Supreme Court represented for those rulings in which comparison groups (e.g., blacks versus whites) disagreed. These results may offer a good test of Court representation because they consider only the instances where there was actually a disagreement in group attitudes. Here, the Court's ruling would represent one group, but not the comparison group.[29] In these instances, the majoritarian theory would predict that the Court's ruling would represent the more numerous and influential group, but the countermajoritarian theory would predict that the Court's ruling would represent the smaller or politically impotent group.

Polarized group attitudes most often occurred on racial, sex and gender, and crime and punishment issues. Other issues, such as economic issues, seldom led to polarized group attitudes. For example, blacks and whites disagreed on 19 rulings— among them, 7 racial issues, 6 crime and punishment issues, and 3 sex and gender-related issues. Easterners and Southerners disagreed on 15 rulings—among them, 8 racial issues, 1 crime and punishment issue, and 3 sex and gender-related issues. Young and old Americans disagreed on 15 rulings—among them, 4 racial issues, 5 crime and punishment issues, and 3 sex and gender-related issues.

In most instances, the Court remained relatively evenhanded in its decision making. In rulings where majorities (or pluralities) of blacks and whites disagreed, the Supreme Court's rulings agreed with black attitudes in 9 of 17 instances, but agreed with white attitudes in 8 of 17 instances. In only three instances did the modern Court sig-

nificantly more often prefer one group to its comparison group. The Court more often represented Eastern (versus Southern) attitudes, younger (versus older) attitudes, and male (versus female) attitudes. These mixed and seldom significant results provide little support for any of the four theories of representation reviewed earlier.

Table 4 reexamines the data differently, by reporting only a subset of decisions involving specific issues of special importance to comparison groups. For example, 19 of the 110 rulings involve racial issues. In 17 (89 percent) of these 19 rulings the Court agreed with black majorities (or pluralities), while in 12 (63 percent) of these 19 rulings the Court agreed with white majorities (or pluralities).

These results again provide little support for any of the theories of representation reviewed earlier. The modern Court has sometimes more often (blacks), but sometimes less often (women, low income groups) represented attitudes of less influential groups. On other instances (as for grassroots Republicans or Democrats) there was no clear pattern.[30] Overall, the evidence as to which groups the Court best represents is mixed and inconclusive; none of the results reported in Table 4 reach statistical significance.

Finally, Table 5 examines the modern Court's pattern of representation of group attitudes by two frequently arising issues: fundamental freedoms and economic decisions. Fundamental freedoms rulings include all disputes over Bill of Rights or Fourteenth Amendment claims, while economic rulings involve employment, taxation, or business regulation disputes.

The differences reported in Table 5 are slight and do not achieve statistical significance. Again they provide little consistent support for any of the four theories. Upper-status group elites (high education, high income) are marginally better represented, especially on economic issues, and males are marginally better represented than females. But some low-status or politically impotent groups (the young, blacks) are also marginally better represented than their comparison groups. Overall, these slight and statistically insignificant results provide little consistent support for any of the four theories of representation.

Table 5 also examines the Court's representation of group attitudes over time. Two time periods are reported. The first comprises the Warren

Table 5 Supreme Court representation of groups, by Court term and type of issue involved

	By issue		By term	
	Fundamental freedoms	Economic decisions	1953/54–1975/76	1976/77–1988/89
Nationwide:	57%	54%	58%	59%
By education:				
College	57	60	63	56
High school	56	53	56	62
Less than high school	53	47	50	62
By race:				
Black	61	64	68	55
White	57	50	54	62
By region:				
East	61	64	64	57
South	51	44	43	63
Midwest	63	57	60	65
West	57	53	59	58
By income:				
High	58	61	60	60
Medium	57	47	55	62
Low	54	50	52	62
By religion:				
Protestant	58	50	52	64
Catholic	57	50	59	58
By sex:				
Male	60	60	58	64
Female	54	44	56	56
By age:				
Young	60	67	66	59
Middle-aged	56	56	57	60
Older	52	40	50	55
By party:				
Republican	56	53	50	63
Democrat	63	50	59	66
Independent	60	60	64	60

Court and early Burger Court from the 1953–54 term through the 1975–76 term—until with Justice Stevens's appointment, the five Nixon-Ford appointees formed a Court majority. The second period spans the remaining Burger and Rehnquist Courts, from the 1976–77 through the 1988–89 terms. Again, the evidence fails to support any of the theories. In neither the earlier nor the later periods did the Court statistically significantly better represent a group than its comparison group. Even the over-time decline in support for black attitudes does not achieve statistical significance.

Discussion

The modern Supreme Court has been relatively evenhanded in representing different social and demographic group attitudes. Since the early 1950s the Court has not significantly better represented dominant majorities, nor unpopular and politically impotent minorities, nor elite groups from which most of the justices themselves come, nor grass-roots Republican or Democratic Party identifiers. Very little support appeared for any of four theories of representation frequently found in the judicial literature.

Why has the modern Supreme Court repre-

sented different group attitudes and values in such an evenhanded manner? Two explanations stand out. First, in most Supreme Court controversies, group attitudes are not sharply polarized. As a result, few rulings require the Court to "referee" disputes that pit demographic or social groups against one another.

Even when group attitudes do differ, the modern Court has been relatively evenhanded in deciding between group attitudes. This may result largely from a second reason. The closely balanced ideological coalitions on the modern Court, coupled with ad hoc and shifting doctrinal values during much of this time period, may help create a pattern in which, over time, the Court's rulings have not consistently represented some group's attitudes at the expense of others.

This pattern of evenhanded representation of group attitudes over time may also help explain why the modern Court has enjoyed relatively favorable approval ratings, compared with Congress or the executive branch. Over the last one-third century the Court has "satisfied" American public opinion majorities or pluralities in about three-fifths of its rulings where a clear poll majority actually existed. Further, the Court's rulings have represented most social, economic, and demographic groups at very similar rates.

A Court that satisfies most groups in most rulings and that also satisfies different and sometimes competing groups at roughly similar rates may well come to enjoy an image of a neutral arbitrator, above the routine political fray. In this sense the modern Court's evenhanded representation of group attitudes may in part contribute to one element of "mythic" beliefs—that the Court is a fair, neutral, and evenhanded arbiter of social conflict.[31]

NOTES

This article originally appeared in Volume 76, Number 1, June-July 1992, pages 22-28.

1. For recent examples of this approach, see Epstein and Hadley, *On the Treatment of Political Parties in the U.S. Supreme Court, 1900-1986*, 72 J. OF POL. 413 (1990); Wheeler, et. al., *Do the "Haves" Come Out Ahead?*, 21 LAW & SOC'Y REV. 403 (1987); and George and Epstein, *Women's rights litigation in the 1980s: more of the same?*, 74 JUDICATURE 314 (1991).

2. Johnson v. Transportation Agency of Santa Clara County, 480 U.S. 616 (1987), at 626-640.

3. See, e.g., *Supreme Court, 6-3, Extends Preferences In Employment for Women and Minorities*, NEW YORK TIMES, March 26, 1987, at 1. The NOW Legal Defense and Education Fund, the Lawyers' Committee for Civil Rights Under Law, and the Equal Opportunity Advisory Council, among others, submitted amici briefs in support of the Court majority's position.

4. "The U.S. Supreme Court recently ruled that employers may sometimes favor women and members of minorities over better qualified men and whites in hiring and promoting to achieve better balance in their work forces. Do you approve or disapprove of this decision?" (Gallup, April 10-13, 1987 and June 24-26, 1988).

At least 17 instances appeared among these 110 cases where inconsistencies could be identified between grass-roots group attitudes and the legal positions of organized interest groups or public officials that might be thought to represent these groups. These 17 instances included religious, labor, women, black, state attorney generals, and U.S. solicitor general positions. A complete list of these apparent inconsistencies between grass-roots attitudes and interest group or public official positions is available, upon request, from the author.

5. Random sampling polling replaced quota sampling methods by the 1950s. The poll items here are not a random sample of all Supreme Court cases, and inferential statistics reported herein should be interpreted cautiously. However, reweighting cases for sampling biases over time or between types of cases did not significantly affect the results reported below; see results in Table 1. A listing of cases may be found in Marshall, PUBLIC OPINION AND THE SUPREME COURT 194-201 (Boston: Unwin Hyman, 1989), and *Public opinion and the Rehnquist Court*, 74 JUDICATURE 232 (1991). The poll items here overwhelmingly relied on dichotomous, forced-choice responses (e.g., "agree" versus "disagree"); only four poll items used a filter question. If rulings were omitted for poll items where only a poll plurality existed, the conclusions reported below would not change.

6. During the 1991/92 term, for example, Justices Souter, Stevens, Blackmun, O'Connor, and White supervised circuits from which they had geographically come to the Court.

7. Dahl, *Decisionmaking In a Democracy: The Supreme Court as National Policymaker*, 6 J. OF PUB. L. 279 (1957). For criticisms of Dahl's essay, see *infra*, nn. 10 and 14.

8. For exceptions, see Barnum, *The Supreme Court and Public Opinion: Judicial Decision Making in the post-New Deal Period*, 47 J. OF POL. 652 (1985); Marshall, *supra* n. 5; and Casper, THE POLITICS OF CIVIL LIBERTIES (New York: Harper and Row, 1972).

9. The majoritarian theory may also frequently be found in normative arguments that the Court should defer to political majorities to prevent noncompliance or defiance of Court rulings; see, e.g., Cox, THE ROLE OF THE SUPREME COURT IN AMERICAN GOVERNMENT (New York: Oxford University Press, 1979); and Kurland, POLITICS, THE CONSTITUTION, AND THE WARREN COURT (Chicago: University of Chicago Press, 1970). Other authors argue that the Court should defer to popular majorities to heighten the people's sense of political responsibility; see, e.g., Thayer, *The Origin and Scope of the American Doctrine of Constitutional Law*, 7 HARV. L. REV. 129 (1893); and Bickel, THE LEAST DANGEROUS BRANCH: THE SUPREME COURT AT THE BAR OF POLITICS (New Haven: Yale University Press, 1986). Others argue that deference to popular majorities will avoid sanctions against the Court itself; see Choper, JUDICIAL REVIEW AND THE NATIONAL POLITICAL PROCESS 139-162 (Chicago: University of Chicago Press, 1980).

In fact, men do not actually comprise a major- ity of adult Americans, but they have typically so dominated public and private offices that they are usually considered as a dominant majority.

10. *See, e.g.*, Abraham, FREEDOM AND THE COURT: CIVIL RIGHTS AND LIBERTIES IN THE UNITED STATES (New York: Oxford University Press, 1982); Cox, *supra* n. 9; Choper, *supra* n. 9, and *The Burger Court: Misperceptions Regarding Judicial Restraint and Insensitivity to Individual Rights*, 30 SYRACUSE L. REV. 767 (1979); Cortner, THE SUPREME COURT AND THE SECOND BILL OF RIGHTS (Madison, Wis: University of Wisconsin Press, 1981); Casper, *The Supreme Court and National Policy Making*, 70 AM. POL. SCI. REV. 50 (1976); and Shapiro, *The Supreme Court from Warren to Burger*, in King, ed., THE NEW AMERICAN POLITICAL SYSTEM (Washington, DC: American Enterprise Institute, 1979).

11. Ely, DEMOCRACY AND DISTRUST: A THEORY OF JUDICIAL REVIEW (Cambridge, Mass: Harvard University Press, 1980); and Richards, *Sexual Autonomy and the Constitutional Right to Privacy*, 30 HASTINGS L. J. 122 (1979); Choper, *supra* n. 9, at 79-122.

12. Bradburn and Sudman, POLLS AND SURVEYS 111, 132 (San Francisco: Jossey-Bass, 1988); and Thornberry and Massey, *Trends in U.S. Telephone Coverage Across Time and Subgroups*, in Groves, et. al, eds., TELEPHONE SURVEY METHODOLOGY 27-36 (New York: John Wiley & Sons, 1988).

13. Ornstein, VITAL STATISTICS ON CONGRESS, 1984-85 (Washington, DC: American Enterprise Institute, 1984).

14. Devine, THE ATTENTIVE PUBLIC: POLYARCHIAL DEMOCRACY (Chicago: Rand-McNally, 1970); and Domhoff, WHO RULES AMERICA? (Englewood Cliffs, NJ: Prentice-Hall, 1967).

15. Spaeth, SUPREME COURT POLICY MAKING 109-118 (San Francisco: W.H. Freeman, 1979); Abraham, JUSTICES AND PRESIDENTS: A POLITICAL HISTORY OF APPOINTMENTS TO THE SUPREME COURT (New York: Oxford, 1985); Friedman and Israel, THE JUSTICES OF THE UNITED STATES SUPREME COURT, 1789-1969 (New York: Chelsea, 1969); and Schmidhauser, THE SUPREME COURT (New York: Holt, Rinehart, and Winston, 1960).

16. Elite theories have more often been applied historically to earlier Court periods, especially the late 1800s and early 1900s, and to individual justice's biographies; see, e.g., Abraham, *supra* n. 7 at 291-293. *See also* Schmidhauser, *The Judges of the Supreme Court: A Collective Portrait*, 3 MIDWEST J. OF POL. SCI. 1 (1959).

17. The literature on the impact of political parties on judicial behavior is extensive; see, e.g., Goldman, *Voting Behavior on the United States Courts of Appeals Revisited*, 69 AM. POL. SCI.

Rev. 491 (1975); and Tate, *Personal Attribute Models of the Voting Behavior of the U.S. Supreme Court Justices*, 75 Am. Pol. Sci. Rev. 355 (1981).

18. For a listing of the issues and poll matches, see *supra* n. 5.

19. The Gallup Poll routinely reports nationwide results broken down by major social and demographic groups. Breakdowns by groups for the Harris Poll may be obtained from the University of North Carolina, Chapel Hill, NC, and for other network and newspaper polls, from the Roper Center, University of Connecticut, Storrs, Ct. The .05-level error margins were applied to nationwide poll results to classify rulings as consistent, inconsistent, or unclear. When applied to smaller numerical groups, such as blacks or Catholics, this may lead to .1-level error margins.

20. "In 1984 a law was passed requiring all states to raise their legal drinking age to 21 or face reductions in Federal highway funds. At present, nine states and the District of Columbia permit legal drinking under age 21. Would you favor or oppose having the Federal government start withholding funds from these states if they fail to raise their drinking age to 21 by October first?" (Gallup, June 9-16, 1987).

21. *Supra* n. 4.

22. "Would you favor or oppose a law in this state that would prohibit tandem truck rigs—that is, large trucks with two trailers attached—on major interstate highways?" (Gallup, April 29-May 2, 1983).

23. Cases were reweighted to the figures reported in O'Brien, Storm Center 205 (New York: W.W. Norton, 1986). The 110 rulings were also tested to see if different levels of representation occurred, depending on whether the poll items were taken before, versus after the ruling was announced. However, pre- versus post-ruling differences results were not significant at the .05 level.

24. Terms during which there were five (or more) Democrat justices include 1953/54-1956/57 and 1962/63-1974/75. Terms for which there were five (or more) Republican justices include 1975/76-1990/91. The 1957/58-1961/62 terms were excluded from this analysis since the justices were evenly divided between the two parties, with one self-described Independent justice (Frankfurter).

25. For evidence that these patterns occur frequently, see Erikson, et al., American Public Opinion 169-207 (New York: MacMillan, 1988).

26. Examples of one-sided poll results include South Dakota v. Dole (1987) and Johnson v. Transportation Agency of Santa Clara County (1987), at *supra* n. 4, 20, and 21.

27. An example of a more narrowly-divided poll result includes Kassel v. Consolidated Freightways Corp. (1981), *supra* n. 22.

28. *See, e.g.*, Shapiro, *supra* n. 10; Blasi, The Burger Court: The Counterrevolution That Wasn't 217 (New Haven: Yale University Press, 1983); and O'Brien, *supra* n. 23, at 262-275.

29. For the argument that representation is best measured by situations in which conflict occurs, see Dahl, *The Concept of Power*, 2 Behavioral Sci. 201 (1957), and A Preface To Democratic Theory 63-67 (Chicago: University of Chicago Press, 1956).

30. In Table 4, the "partisan" category includes issues where differences between Republicans and Democrats were most often found since the early 1950s. These include racial, foreign policy, business and labor, social welfare, and lifestyle issues. *See* Sorauf and Beck, Party Politics In America 141-158 (Glenview, IL: Scott, Foresman, 1988); and Gitelson, Conway, and Fiegert, American Political Parties: Stability and Change 138-144 (Boston: Houghton Mifflin, 1984).

31. Casey, *The Supreme Court and Myth: An Empirical Investigation*, 8 Law & Soc'y Rev. 385 (1974); Bass, *The Constitution as Symbol*, 8 Am. Pol. Q. 237 (1980); and Frank, Law and the Modern Mind (New York: Brentano, 1930).

Voting behavior and gender on the U.S. courts of appeals

The votes of women circuit court judges in employment discrimination and search and seizure cases differ from those of their male counterparts.

by Sue Davis, Susan Haire, and Donald R. Songer

Not long ago, women judges were too scarce to study in any meaningful way. Only two women had served on the federal appellate bench when President Jimmy Carter reformed the judicial selection process in 1977.[1] Subsequently, 11 women were appointed to the U.S. courts of appeals during Carter's term. Ronald Reagan appointed four women to the intermediate appellate judiciary, and George Bush appointed seven. Thus, a minimally sufficient number of women of various political persuasions now hold positions on the courts of appeals to make it feasible to study their decision making. This analysis of voting behavior on the U.S. courts of appeals attempts to reveal whether voting patterns of women judges differ from those of their male colleagues.

Although feminist scholarship encompasses a variety of perspectives,[2] much of feminist legal theory argues that the presence of significant numbers of women as professionals in the legal system will have a profound impact on the law. Some feminist scholars argue that women lawyers and judges will bring a different perspective to the law, employ a different set of methods, and seek different results from prevailing legal tradition.

The work of psychologist Carol Gilligan[3] provides a source of feminist legal theory as well as empirical support for its claims. Gilligan discovered differences in the ways men and women understand themselves and their environment and the way they resolve moral problems. She found that men tend to define themselves through separation, measure themselves against an abstract ideal of perfection, equate adulthood with autonomy and individual achievement, and conceive morality in ladder-like hierarchical terms. In contrast, women often define themselves through connection with others and activities of care, and they perceive morality in terms of an interconnected web. While women tend to perceive moral conflicts as a problem of care and responsibility in relationships, men tend to emphasize rights and rules.

Gilligan by no means claimed to make generalizations about men and women. Rather, she argued that since the traditional theory of human psychological development was based on studies of male subjects only, that theory invariably found that women failed to develop on measurement scales. Gilligan showed how an alternative perspective emerged when researchers included women in their studies and when they discarded frameworks constructed with only men in mind. Her "different voice" refers not to a voice that differs from men, but one that differs from traditional theory. Gilligan also pointed out that most people in her studies (an average of 65 percent across six studies) represented both voices in defining moral problems. Still, there was a strong tendency to focus on one voice or the other. About 70 percent of those who used both orientations focused on one. Only 3 men from a total of 60 demonstrated a focus on care. Among the women, about 60 percent focused on care.[4]

Gilligan's findings parallel the assertion of many feminist legal scholars that because the law has been so thoroughly infused with the male perspective, an approach to legal decision making that is based on separation, rights, and abstract rules has come to represent the "correct" legal method. Any departure is viewed as illegitimate and is judged to fall outside the framework of law. Thus, the female perspective is excluded. As one writer explained, "It takes no sophistication . . . to recognize that American law is predominantly a system of the ladder, by the ladder, and for the ladder."[5] Gilligan's work combined with much of feminist jurisprudence provide the foundation for a theory that the presence of women judges has tremendous potential for significantly changing the law.

Gender difference and judging

How might the alleged different perspective of women manifest itself in judging? Generally, the traditional legal approach could be expected to focus on individual rights, freedom from interference, procedural fairness, and concern for correctly applying appropriate legal rules. In contrast, the "different voice" would speak about connection, care, response, substantive fairness, communitarian values, and context.

Drawing on Gilligan's work, Suzanna Sherry identified characteristics of a feminine jurisprudence—one that emphasizes connection (in contrast to autonomy), context (as opposed to fixed rules), and responsibility (in contrast to rights).[6] Sherry analyzed the decision making of Justice Sandra Day O'Connor and concluded that it did, in fact, manifest such concerns. Her analysis of O'Connor's opinions in cases where the rights in question belonged to individuals as members of communities rather than as autonomous units revealed a different perspective from her male colleagues. Sherry argued that O'Connor has not been as willing as the other conservative justices to permit violations of the right to full membership in the community. Likewise, Sherry found that O'Connor has tended to support individual rights only when they involve community membership. Sherry also discovered a contextual approach in O'Connor's decision making and a tendency to reject rigid rules.

Social scientists have begun to explore the behavior of women decision makers. Their work, however, has produced mixed results. For example, an examination of interest group ratings of members of Congress suggested that women were more liberal than men, particularly in the areas of social welfare and defense spending.[7] In contrast, studies of the views of political party elites[8] and civil servants[9] failed to reveal significant differences based on the sex of the decision maker. Another study found that women state legislators in California were no more liberal than their male counterparts,[10] while another found women legislators in 12 other states to be only slightly more likely than men to give higher priority to women's issues than to business and commerce.[11]

Similarly, studies of judicial behavior have provided some support for the contention that women will bring a different perspective and decision-making pattern to the bench. For example, an examination of the votes of judges on four state supreme courts found that four of the five women voted on women's issues in a way that placed them at the liberal extreme of their courts.[12] Analyzing the behavior of federal district judges, another study revealed that in cases involving criminal procedure and women's policy issues, there were no significant differences between men and women judges. But for personal liberties and minority policy issues, the differences between male and female judges were statistically significant: male judges were 1.5 times more likely than female judges to support the liberal position. These results also indicated that female judges were significantly more likely than their male counterparts to defer to positions taken by government.[13] On the other hand, recent research on the voting behavior of women judges on the federal appellate courts has revealed only slight differences between men and women.[14]

Methods

The federal intermediate appellate judiciary was chosen as the subject of this study for several reasons. The U.S. courts of appeals play a vital role in interpreting federal law, enforcing norms, and creating public policy.[15] Because the Supreme Court can review only a limited number of cases from the lower federal courts, the decisions of the courts of appeals are final in an overwhelming majority of cases.[16] Studies also have shown that the appellate courts have substantial decision-making discretion.[17]

Voting behavior was analyzed in three areas: employment discrimination, criminal procedural rights (search and seizure), and obscenity. Gilligan's studies and feminist legal theory would suggest that women judges can be expected to vote differently from their male colleagues in ways that

Table 1   The women on the U.S. courts of appeals, 1979-1992

Name	Circuit	Appointing president	Date of appointment
Amalya Kearse	2	Carter	6/21/79
Carol Los Mansmann	3	Reagan	4/4/85
*Jane Roth	3	Bush	6/27/91
Dolores Sloviter	3	Carter	6/21/79
*Karen J. Williams	4	Bush	2/27/92
Edith Jones	5	Reagan	4/4/85
Carolyn Dineen King	5	Carter	7/13/79
*Alice M. Batchelder	6	Bush	11/27/91
Cornelia Kennedy	6	Carter	9/26/79
*Ilana D. Rovner	7	Bush	8/12/92
Betty Fletcher	9	Carter	9/27/79
Cynthia Holcolm Hall	9	Reagan	10/4/84
Dorothy Nelson	9	Carter	12/20/79
*Pamela Ann Rymer	9	Bush	5/22/89
Mary Schroeder	9	Carter	9/26/79
Stephanie Seymour	10	Carter	11/2/79
Deanell Reece Tacha	10	Reagan	12/16/85
Phyllis Kravitch	11	Carter	3/23/79
*Susan H. Black	11	Bush	8/11/92
Ruth Bader Ginsburg	D.C.	Carter	6/18/80
*Karen LeCraft Henderson	D.C.	Bush	7/11/90
Patricia Wald	D.C.	Carter	7/26/79

*Excluded from the analysis

Sources: WANT'S FEDERAL-STATE COURT DIRECTORY, 1992 edition (Washington, D.C.: Want Publishing Co., 1991); Wildman, FEDERAL JUDGES AND JUSTICES: A CURRENT LISTING OF NOMINATIONS, CONFIRMATIONS, ELEVATIONS, RESIGNATIONS, RETIREMENTS, 102nd Congress, rev. September 1992 (Littleton, Co.: Fred B. Rothman and Company, 1992).

Table 2   Gender differences in judges' voting in employment discrimination cases

Gender	Liberal	Conservative	% for plaintiff
Female	40	23	63.5%
Male	210	246	46.1

n=519, chi square=6.74, P<.01

reflect a tendency to emphasize interdependent rights—the right to full membership in a community—rather than rights against the community. When communitarian values and individual rights conflict, women judges would be expected to support the former.

The votes of all judges on the U.S. courts of appeals, including those on senior status, from the District of Columbia Circuit and the 11 numbered circuits from 1981 to 1990 were analyzed.[18] Table 1 lists all women who have served on these courts. The analysis of obscenity cases was based on all opinions published in the *Federal Reporter* during this period. Those opinions contained 239 votes suitable for analysis. Since there were more than 3,000 published opinions for both search and seizure and employment discrimination cases, samples of each of these case types were drawn.[19] The samples contained 1,283 votes in search and seizure cases and 519 votes from the employment discrimination cases. The samples included the votes of 9 female and 122 male judges in obscenity cases, 15 females and 237 males in search and sei-

zure cases, and 16 females and 188 males in employment discrimination cases. No judge cast more than 2.4 percent of the votes in any one area.

For employment discrimination cases, votes were categorized as follows: (1) "conservative," supporting either the defendant's position or, in cases where a male challenged an affirmative action plan, the plaintiff's position; and (2) "liberal," supporting the plaintiff's charge of discrimination in all other cases. For search and seizure decisions, votes holding that a challenged search was unreasonable or that challenged evidence could not be used were classified liberal, and votes upholding a search or allowing the use of challenged evidence were classified conservative. For obscenity cases, votes were categorized as either supporting or opposing a restriction on the use and dissemination of the materials in question. A simple cross-tabulation of votes by the sex of the judge for each of the three types of cases was conducted. Cross-tabulations for each type of case controlling for party of appointing president and region were also performed. These variables have been found to be associated with voting patterns.[20]

Results

The analysis revealed statistically significant differences between men and women judges in two of the three areas examined. The employment discrimination cases revealed that women, more often than their male colleagues, supported claimants (Table 2). More than 63 percent of the votes cast by women judges supported the plaintiff's claim of discrimination. In contrast, male judges supported the plaintiff 46 percent of the time.[21] For search and seizure cases, women judges were more likely than their male colleagues to support the claims of criminal defendants (Table 3). In the obscenity cases, there were no significant differences in the behavior of male and female judges (Table 4).

Addition of a control for party of appointing president produced the following results (Table 5). Differences persisted in employment discrimination cases as women judges appointed by a Democratic president (all by Jimmy Carter) supported the plaintiff's claim at a level of 68 percent, whereas the men appointed by Democrats (including but not limited to Carter) supported the plaintiff's claim at a level of 54.3 percent. The analysis revealed no statistically significant differences in votes of judges appointed by Republican presidents in employment discrimination cases.

In search and seizure cases, once the control for the appointing president's party was added, there were no statistically significant differences in the votes of male and female judges. In obscenity cases, the addition of this control supported the initial finding that there were no significant differences.

With the addition of the control for region, statistically significant differences remained in the voting behavior of women and men judges in employment discrimination cases (Table 6).

In search and seizure cases, the analysis revealed no significant differences in the voting behavior of male and female judges in the South and elsewhere. In obscenity cases, the controls for region did not alter the results—there were no statistically significant differences in the votes of males and females.

To further explore the gender differences in employment discrimination cases, a cross-tabulation with controls for both party and region was conducted. Table 7 displays the results of a comparison of votes by Southern males and Southern females appointed by a Democratic president, suggesting that the differences are attributable to the sex of the judge rather than region or party of appointing president.

Discussion

Overall, the results of this analysis provide some support for the thesis that women judges bring a different perspective to the bench. Employment discrimination may be viewed as a problem of exclusion, as members of certain groups are precluded from participating as full members of the community. Thus, women judges' support for plaintiffs may reflect a concern for the right to such membership. The rights of criminal defendants may be conceived as involving claims against the community, but such a generalization may not hold for all cases. Support of some claims could result in harm to innocent people and to the community, while support of other claims may recognize the need to preserve relationships. If concerns of connection and community underlie women's votes, those votes would vary depending on the facts of each case. Consequently, they would manifest no pattern distinguishable from their male colleagues. In the context of obscenity, explicit sexual materials may be viewed not only as a source of the oppression of women but also as detrimental to the moral quality of the community. The analysis, however, failed to produce any evidence that such concerns provide the basis for women's votes in obscenity cases.

Although the results in two of the three areas examined are consistent with the proposition that women judges bring a different perspective to their decision making, drawing conclusions is problematic. Women may support plaintiffs in employment discrimination cases because they identify with members of subordinate groups rather than because of a particular concern for relationships or the right to full membership in a community. Also, the absence of difference between women's and men's votes in search and seizure cases may not reflect women judges' support for community and relationships. Instead, it may simply be a manifestation of a method of resolving claims involving individual rights that does not differ from that of their male counterparts.

The analysis of employment discrimination

Table 3   Gender differences in judges' voting in search and seizure cases

Gender	Liberal	Conservative	% liberal
Female	22	102	17.7%
Male	126	1,033	10.9

n=1283, chi square=5.18, P<.05

Table 4   Gender differences in judges' voting in obscenity cases

Gender	For suppression	Against suppression	% against suppression
Female	9	4	30.8%
Male	156	70	30.9

n=239, chi square=0.01, P>.10

Table 5   Gender differences in Democratic and Republican judges' voting in employment discrimination cases

Democratic

Gender	Liberal	Conservative	% for plaintiff
Female	34	16	68.0%
Male	107	90	54.3

n=247, chi square=3.05, P<.08

Republican

Gender	Liberal	Conservative	% for plaintiff
Female	6	7	46.2%
Male	103	156	39.8

n=272, chi square=0.21, P>.10

Table 6   Gender differences in Southern and non-Southern judges' voting in employment discrimination cases

Southern

Gender	Liberal	Conservative	% for plaintiff
Female	30	10	75.0%
Male	122	158	43.6

n=320, chi square=13.86, P<.001

Non-Southern

Gender	Liberal	Conservative	% for plaintiff
Female	9	10	47.4%
Male	85	77	52.4

n=181, chi square=0.18, P>.10

Table 7   Gender differences in Southern Democratic judges' voting in employment discrimination cases

Gender	Liberal	Conservative	% for plaintiff
Female	27	6	81.8%
Male	58	53	52.2

n=144, chi square=9.19, P<.002

cases is consistent with the thesis that women judges are more concerned than their male colleagues with relationships and inclusion than with personal autonomy and individual rights. Yet the analysis revealed no such difference in decisions involving obscenity—an area that commonly raises concerns associated with the community's moral health. How might these results be explained?

First, it is possible that the psychological and legal theories of difference are simply wrong—that women's purported tendency to approach and resolve moral and legal problems differently from men does not exist.[22] As noted, women may tend to support the claimant in employment discrimination cases simply because they are likely to have experienced such discrimination directly, or have encountered gender-related obstacles in their professional lives, or feel a close affinity with those who have.

Second, while it is possible that a different voice exists, it might not reveal itself readily in analyses of voting behavior. Additional research is needed before any conclusions can be drawn regarding the extent to which, if at all, women judges differ from their male colleagues. Although Sherry[23] found that Justice O'Connor's opinions differed from the male conservatives on the Supreme Court, a recent analysis of opinions of judges on the U.S. Court of Appeals for the Ninth Circuit concluded that while women judges sometimes spoke in a different voice, men judges did as well.[24]

Third, it is possible that differences between men and women judges are neutralized by the very nature of law and legal processes. For example, to succeed in law school and subsequently in the legal profession, an individual—male or female—must master the tools of legal reasoning and adopt the norms of the profession. In Gilligan's framework, those tools are distinguished by their male character: legal reasoning is rule-based and abstract, and American law is thoroughly grounded in a political theory of individualism. Thus, any propensity to emphasize context, caring, and community would be discouraged and subverted by the constraints imposed by legal education, the legal profession, and the process of judicial socialization. Moreover, because they are still relatively new and constitute a small minority on the federal bench, women judges are likely to be particularly conscious of the importance of maintaining their reputations as neutral decision makers—that is, "good judges." In short, the constraints of the judicial process may well overcome differences based on the sex of the judge.

Fourth, a generational phenomenon may mask any possible gender differences. Women currently serving on the federal courts attended law school and pursued careers in an environment thoroughly controlled by men, in which any hint of a differ-ent approach would most likely have been considered evidence of women's lack of capacity to acquire legal skills and understand the law. Therefore, women judges who have been socialized into and have succeeded in the male world are unlikely to manifest the differences attributed to women by feminist theory.

Finally, it is possible that differences between men and women in judicial decision making are obscured by a selection process designed to produce judges—male or female—whose views are compatible with those of their appointing president. The Reagan administration took great care to fill vacancies on the federal bench with individuals who clearly endorsed the president's political agenda.[25] And while Carter clearly gave his nominating commissions an affirmative action mandate, he was also careful to nominate only women who shared his basic values and approach to judging. Virtually all the women on the courts of appeals have been selected by presidents who were extraordinarily successful in selecting judges whose policy preferences were compatible with their own.

The findings presented here certainly do not preclude the possibility that women will transform the law in ways that many feminist legal scholars predict. It is unlikely, however, that any evidence of women's unique voice will emerge until women are trained and socialized in an environment that welcomes diversity in values and approaches to decision making.

Feminist jurisprudence and women judges are both new to the legal process, and the study of women judges has barely begun. Only future research examining the career patterns and socialization of women judges, as well as their voting behavior and opinions, will make it possible to assess the nature and extent of women's impact on the legal system.

NOTES

This article originally appeared in Volume 77, Number 3, November-December 1993, pages 129-133.

1. *See* Berkson and Carbon, THE UNITED STATES CIRCUIT JUDGE NOMINATING COMMISSION: ITS MEMBERS, PROCEDURES AND CANDIDATES (Chicago: American Judicature Society, 1980); Martin, *Women on the federal bench: a comparative profile,* 65 JUDICATURE 307-313 (1982) and *Gender and judicial selection: a comparison of the Reagan and Carter administrations,* 71 JUDICATURE 136-142 (1987); Cook, *Women as Judges,* in WOMEN IN THE JUDICIAL PROCESS (Washington, D.C.: The American Political Science Association, 1988).

2. *See, e.g.,* Goldstein, *Can This Marriage Be Saved? Feminist*

Public Policy and Feminist Jurisprudence, in Goldstein, ed., FEMINIST JURISPRUDENCE: THE DIFFERENCE DEBATE (Savage, Md.: Rowman and Littlefield, 1992); Sunstein, *Feminism and Legal Theory*, 101 HARV. L. REV. 826-848 (1988).

3. Gilligan, IN A DIFFERENT VOICE: PSYCHOLOGICAL THEORY AND WOMEN'S DEVELOPMENT (Cambridge, MA: Harvard University Press, 1982).

4. Marcus, Spiegelman, DuBois, Dunlap, Gilligan, MacKinnon, and Menkel-Meadow, *The 1984 James McCormick Mitchell Lecture. Feminist Discourse, Moral Values and the Law—A Conversation*, 34 BUFFALO L. REV. 47-49 (1985).

5. Karst, *Woman's Constitution*, 1984 DUKE L. J. 463 (1984).

6. Sherry, *Civic Virtue and the Feminine Voice in Constitutional Adjudication*, 72 VA. L. REV. 543-615 (1986).

7. Leader, *The Policy Impact of Elected Women Officials*, in Cooper and Maisels, eds. THE IMPACT OF THE ELECTORAL PROCESS (Beverly Hills: Sage Publications, 1977). A factor analysis of congressional voting from 1961 to 1975 led Kathleen Frankovic to similar conclusions. *Sex and Voting in the U.S. House of Representatives*, 5 AM. POL. Q. 315-331 (1977). Additionally, Freida Gehlen found more support among female members of Congress for both the Civil Rights Act of 1964 and the Equal Rights Amendment. *Women Members of Congress: A Distinctive Role* in Githens and Prestage, eds., A PORTRAIT OF MARGINALITY (New York: McKay, 1977). Susan Welch, who analyzed conservative coalition scores, found that women were more likely than men to cast liberal votes, but that the differences had decreased over time. *Are Women More Liberal Than Men in the U.S. Congress?*, 10 LEG. STUDIES Q. 125-34 (1985).

8. Constantini and Craik, *Women as Politicians: The Social Background, Personality and Careers of Female Party Leaders*, 28 J. SOC. ISSUES 217-36 (1972)

9. Thompson, *Civil Servants and the Deprived: Sociopolitical and Occupational Explanations of Attitudes Towards Minority Hiring*, 22 AM. J. POL. SCI. 325-47 (1978).

10. Thomas, "The Effects of Race and Gender on Constituency Service." Presented at the Annual Meeting of the American Political Science Association, August 1987.

11. Thomas and Welch, *Women Legislators: Legislative Styles and Policy Priorities*, 44 W. POL. Q. 445-56 (1991).

12. Allen and Wall, "The Behavior of Women State Supreme Court Justices: An Update." Unpublished manuscript, 1990; *The Behavior of Women State Supreme Court Justices: Are They Tokens or Outsiders?*, 12 JUST. SYS. J. 232-244 (1987). In contrast, two studies of the sentencing patterns of urban trial court judges revealed no significant differences between males and females. Kritzer and Uhlman, *Sisterhood in the Courtroom: Sex of Judge and Defendant in Criminal Case Disposition*, 14 SOC. SCI. Q., 77-88 (1977); Gruhl, Spohn, and Welch, *Women as Policy Makers: The Case of Trial Judges*, 25 AM. J. POL. SCI. 308-322 (1981).

13. Walker and Barrow, *The Diversification of the Federal Bench: Policy and Process Ramifications*. 47 J. POL. 596-617 (1985). In still another study, Gerald S. Gryski, Eleanor C. Main, and William Dixon found only a weak and statistically insignificant relationship between the presence of a female judge and state high court decision making in sex discrimination cases. *Models of State High Court Decision Making in Sex Discrimination Cases*, 48 J. POL. 143-155 (1986).

14. *See, e.g.* Davis, *The Impact of President Carter's Judicial Selection Reforms: A Voting Analysis of the United States Courts of Appeals*, 14 AM. POL. Q. 320-344 (1986); Gottschall, *Carter's Judicial Appointments: The Influence of Affirmative Action and Merit Selection in Voting on the U.S. Courts of Appeals*, 67 JUDICATURE 165-173 (1983).

15. *See* Howard, COURTS OF APPEALS IN THE FEDERAL JUDICIAL SYSTEM: A STUDY OF THE SECOND, FIFTH, AND DISTRICT OF COLUMBIA CIRCUITS (Princeton, N.J.: Princeton University Press, 1981);

Songer, *The Circuit Courts of Appeals*, in Gates and Johnson, THE AMERICAN COURTS: A CRITICAL ASSESSMENT 35-59 (Washington, D.C.: Congressional Quarterly Press, 1991).

16. *See* Davis and Songer, *The Changing Role of the United States Courts of Appeals: The Flow of Litigation Revisited*, 13 JUST. SYS. J. 323-340 (1988-89).

17. See the work cited by Songer, *supra* n. 15, at 41-46.

18. The number of female judges remains so low that in cases in which they participate, the panel usually consists of two males and one female. In the sample, there was never more than one female judge in an obscenity case, there were four search and seizure cases with two women on the panel, and five panels in employment discrimination cases with two female judges.

19. The Westlaw electronic data base identified the universe of cases in which decisions were published in the FEDERAL REPORTER. A random sample of 200 decisions was selected for each case type. This sample was supplemented to guarantee that there would be a sufficient number of votes by women by identifying the universe of cases in which each woman judge participated and randomly selecting three additional cases from the universe of participations of each woman.

20. *See, e.g.*, Tate, *Personal Attribute Models of Voting Behavior of U.S. Supreme Court Justices: Liberalism in Civil Liberties and Economics Decisions, 1946-1978*, 75 AM. POL. SCI. REV. 355-67 (1981); Goldman, *Voting Behavior on the United States Courts of Appeals Revisited*, 69 AM. POL. SCI. REV. 491-506 (1975); Songer and Davis, *The Impact of Party and Region on Voting Decisions in the United States Courts of Appeals, 1955-1986*, 43 W. POL. Q. 317 (1990).

21. In a preliminary report of the present study, based on incomplete data (a paper presented at the 1991 meeting of the Midwest Political Science Association), no significant differences were found based on gender in the analysis of employment discrimination cases which controlled for case facts and partisan effects in a logistic regression model. When that logit model on the complete sample was re-run, however, the differences were significant and of approximately the same magnitude as those reported here.

22. *See, e.g.*, Epstein, DECEPTIVE DISTINCTIONS: SEX, GENDER, AND THE SOCIAL ORDER (New Haven, Ct.: Yale University Press and New York: Russell Sage Foundation, 1988) reviewing criticisms of Gilligan's work.

23. *Supra* n. 6.

24. Davis, *Do Women Judges Speak in 'A Different Voice'? Carol Gilligan, Feminist Legal Theory and the Ninth Circuit*, WISC. WOMEN'S L. J. (December 1993, forthcoming)

25. *See, e.g.*, Goldman, *Reagan's judicial legacy: completing the puzzle and summing up*, 72 JUDICATURE 318-330; Schwartz, PACKING THE COURTS: THE CONSERVATIVE CAMPAIGN TO REWRITE THE CONSTITUTION (New York: Charles Scribner's Sons, 1988).

The decision making of Clinton's nontraditional judicial appointees

by Jennifer A. Segal

Historically, the federal bench has been largely white and male. How-ever, beginning with Jimmy Carter, and continuing with Bill Clinton, earnest attempts have been made to populate the federal bench with less traditional judges. Carter appointed 37 blacks and 56 women to the U.S. district and circuit courts during his single term. Clinton appointed 37 blacks and 60 women during his first term.

Carter and Clinton clearly made explicit attempts to represent, at least symbolically, these two groups of Americans. These nontraditional appointments also illustrate, implicitly if not explicitly, intentions to influence judicial decision making. As President Carter stated in a 1980 speech:

...whenever I appoint a black judge or Hispanic judge or even a woman judge, I know that they not only have committed in their own hearts a vision of what this nation ought to be but a special knowledge of the effects of past discrimination that are still there as a means to prevent equality of opportunity."[1]

The extent to which women and blacks act on their particular "vision" and "special knowledge" has been the focus of research, but it is still not clear whether judges actually do make different decisions because of their gender and race. The research on which this note is based examined the decision making of President Clinton's nontraditional appointees to the federal district courts.

Twenty-four judges who varied on gender or race were paired. Several additional variables were also controlled for, including the appointing president and judicial district. Each of the 8 pairs in the gender analysis consisted of a male and female judge of the same race who did not vary on the other variables; each of the 10 pairs in the race analysis consisted of a white and black judge of the same gender who did not vary on the other variables. Decisions published in the *Federal Supplement* through July 1996, categorized by issue (individual liberties, criminal rights, federal economic regulation, female-specific, black-specific, and other minority issues), were analyzed.

Results

The data suggest that black judges are significantly more supportive of issues relating to blacks and the black community than white judges. Black judges supported black's claims in 50 percent of their decisions, whereas white judges did so in only 10 percent. Additionally, black judges were more supportive of women's claims (in 9 of 15 cases) than their white colleagues (in 5 of 14 cases). No meaningful racial difference was found with regard to criminal rights, federal economic regulation, and personal liberties issues.

The gender analysis also revealed a representative role by Clinton's female judges. Half of the decisions written by women supported the black or minority position (in 17 of 34 cases) whereas less than a third of the decisions authored by men did so (8 of 28 cases). Interestingly, there was no significant gender difference in cases involving women's issues.

The explanation of these gender results is unclear. On the one hand, the data correspond to the expectation that women on the bench are more likely to represent the interests of the disadvantaged in society. On the other hand, it is somewhat surprising to find that the only gender difference arose with regard to *non*female minority issues. Beyond the potential difficulty of the small number of cases (24) involved in the women's issue category, one explanation may be related to the legal and political socialization of female judges that does not differentiate men and women as it once did. Data not reported here suggest there is essentially no gender difference among Clinton's appointees included in the gender analysis in either legal education or occupation prior to appointment. These similarities suggest that the women may not have, in the context of their roles on the bench, particularly different views on women's issues than their male counterparts. And these female judges (indeed, male judges as well) who have come of age when increasingly more women are members of the legal profession may not perceive women as a disadvantaged group.

Finally, it should be noted that the race and gender differences reported here do not mean that blacks and women *always* decide in favor of the disadvantaged party. In fact, in each of the two analyses, 50 percent of the nontraditional judges opposed the minority position. Apparently, then, decisions delivered from representatives on the bench are not purely the product of visceral responses to particular litigants and their interests. This should be encouraging for those on either side of the debate about affirmative action and the federal judiciary.

NOTES

This article originally appeared in Volume 80, Number 6, May-June 1997, page 279.

The original version of this article was presented at the American Political Science Association meetings, August 31-September 1, 1996, San Francisco. The author thanks the members of the panel, Elliot Slotnick and Brad Canon, for their constructive comments and Scott Peters for his contribution to the data collection. More detailed information about the data and methods is available from the author.

1. Davis, BLACKS IN THE FEDERAL JUDICIARY 21 (Bristol, Indiana: Wyndham Hall Press, 1989)

Should there be affirmative action for the judiciary?

Special efforts to find qualified women and minorities for the federal bench are not incompatible with merit selection because they ensure that we choose the "best" judges from among all possible candidates.

by Sheldon Goldman

The Carter administration jolted the legal community with its outspoken and widely publicized affirmative action policy of placing women and ethnic minorities on the federal bench. Many of the arguments raised against the implementation of affirmative action programs elsewhere are now being heard with regard to the judiciary along with arguments attuned to the special status of the federal bench. But after considering the nature of the administration's efforts and successes in implementing judicial affirmative action, I have concluded that the legal profession ought to applaud President Carter and Attorney General Bell.

As I see it, six major objections can be raised against an affirmative action approach to federal judicial selection. Each, I believe, can be persuasively answered. I would like to discuss these objections briefly and the rejoinders I find convincing.

1. The dangers of classifying people. Affirmative action inevitably leads government agencies to define race, critics argue, and it leads government officials to make judgments about racial characteristics. Is an individual with one black grandparent or great-grandparent (say, Homer Plessy) to be classified as black? What about someone with one black parent who was raised by white foster parents? Is an American-born individual with an American father and Mexican mother Hispanic? The argument, essentially, is that it is dangerous for government to make any racial classifications. Such activities stir memories of the racial laws of Nazi Germany and run counter to the value Americans have traditionally placed on treating individuals on the basis of their personal qualities and not their racial attributes.

Response: While many (including myself) are uncomfortable with government concern with race/ethnicity, I believe there is a crucial and fundamental distinction between America's official racial consciousness for purposes of affirmative action and the racial classifications of totalitarian regimes. America's purpose is to aid definable classes of persons who have historically suffered from official discrimination. Racial classifications in Nazi Germany were, of course, for ghastly purposes, and in more contemporary totalitarian societies ethnic designations on identity cards and other records form the basis for official discrimination.

The federal judiciary has been and still is an overwhelmingly white, male institution, for many reasons. America's long-standing racism and sexism, for example, have historically limited opportunities in the judiciary for women, blacks, and Hispanics. It does not seem unreasonable to make special efforts to recruit from these groupings of Americans for federal judgeships. Deliberate considerations of race and sex should not be given negative connotations so long as the government demonstrates positive, anti-racist, anti-sexist motives and purposes.

2. The threat of reverse discrimination. The real result of affirmative action, opponents argue, is reverse discrimination. Government selects a group or groups of persons for favored treatment, thereby putting all others at a disadvantage. This is reminiscent of George Orwell's *Animal Farm* where all animals are equal but some are more equal than others. On an individual basis this produces reverse discrimination; individuals are ruled out of consideration *because* they are the "wrong" race or sex. Furthermore, when it comes to judicial selection, those women, blacks, and Hispanics who are favored for judgeships are frequently from the same social class and similar backgrounds as competing white males, and their careers have not necessarily suffered from discrimination. Why then should they have an advantage?

Response: I cannot be persuaded that affirmative action is reverse discrimination—at least when the objective is *not* to give minorities a majority hold. I have not seen evidence that any affirmative action program of any kind in the United States has seriously threatened the majority status of white males in government, industry, the professions, or academia. Certainly the type of affirmative action that the Carter Administration is promoting for the judiciary in no way threatens the overwhelming majority status of white males.

Although the administration's efforts thus far to place women, blacks, and Hispanics on the federal bench have been spectacular when compared with the record of previous administrations, taken alone the results of the Carter administration's affirmative action policy are actually very modest. About 12 percent of the Carter nominees have been black, and about the same proportion have been women.[1] In terms of the entire federal bench, the proportions of blacks and women are exceedingly small and for Hispanics almost non-existent.

At the individual level, the charge of reverse discrimination potentially can be more troublesome, as it was in the *Bakke* case. But we do not have to be concerned with this since judicial selection traditionally has involved numerous variables. The addition of racial/ethnic and sexual considerations is in no way inconsistent with the host of other considerations that have been involved in judicial selection, including geography, party affiliation, party activity, sponsorship by senators and other key politicians, professional connections, ideological or policy outlook, and so on. Race/ethnicity and sex are today politically relevant variables and they have been added to other political

type variables in a selection process that historically has been political.

3. The error of focusing on group affiliation. No matter how worthy an objective it may be, critics say, affirmative action is inconsistent with the professional goal of merit selection, which many judicial reformers and the Carter administration itself espouse. How can one accept the principle that only the best qualified should be given judgeships and then decree that women, blacks, and Hispanics are to be given special preference? Merit selection emphasizes individual qualities; affirmative action stresses group affiliation.

Response: It does a disservice to women, blacks, and Hispanics to suggest that they do not ordinarily possess as strong a set of professional credentials as white males do, but I will not dwell on this obvious rejoinder. What I find persuasive is the fact that, based on my own extensive research and that of others,[2] we never had, we do not now have, and we probably never will have a judicial selection method based solely on professional merits. The professional credentials of candidates do play a part in judicial selection, but rarely have they been the determining factor. Of course, it is important to have qualified persons sitting on the bench, and there is no question in my mind that Attorney General Bell, under affirmative action, is recommending to the president only persons with the professional credentials essential to perform the job.

Ironically, affirmative action may provide a more potent push towards merit selection than anything else that has ever been done. By searching for well qualified women, blacks, and Hispanics, the administration and Democratic senators are downplaying party activity and political connections. This breaks with the past judges-as-patronage syndrome that historically characterized much of judicial selection.

Let me add for the record that the administration's so-called merit selection of appeals judges is not merit selection in fact. As recent issues of *Judicature* have shown,[3] mostly Democrats (including large numbers of Carter loyalists) have chosen mostly other Democrats for placement on the lists given the president. Other Democrats then lobby the Democratic president as to which Democrats to choose.

However, the selection process has become more open in large part due to institution of merit commissions and the affirmative action push. It is highly unrealistic to expect a civil service type merit approach to judicial selection ever to be established. Even assuming that an effective merit selection process could be instituted, I would have to be persuaded that the sorts of people chosen were better suited for the bench than the sorts of people chosen through our traditional political processes.

4. The need for government neutrality, not favoritism. Affirmative action is a remedy to right a proven constitutional wrong, critics emphasize. Even if it could be proven that racism and sexism served to exclude blacks, women, and Hispanics from the judiciary, that would not justify affirmative action in choosing the highest officials of the federal government. It would only justify efforts to ensure that these groups were no longer deliberately excluded.

Blacks prevented from voting were eventually protected by federal legislation and action to enable them to exercise the franchise, but they were not given the right to elect so many black congressmen or black state representatives. Women given the right to vote in 1920 were not given the right to have a specific number of women in high elective or appointive office. Isn't it sufficient that the judicial selection process be non-discriminatory? Isn't affirmative action inappropriate here?

Remedy: The racial and sexual make-up of the judiciary, past and present, speaks for itself. It is clear that all-pervasive societal attitudes toward women, blacks, Hispanics, and indeed other groups such as Asian-Americans and American Indians severely limited their opportunities in the law and that they were, in fact, routinely and systematically excluded from federal judgeships. Justice Department officials and senators were not necessarily themselves racist or sexist. It is simply that within the framework of political reality and racist and sexist belief systems in the larger society, appointments of women, blacks, and some other ethnic groups were impossible.

But leaving aside the difficult questions of proof, and, indeed, whether constitutional wrongs were committed in the past, it can be argued that government can serve as a teacher by setting a good example and structuring situations in which learning and personal growth can occur. Clearly, the widespread racist and sexist attitudes of the past and the discrimination so widely practiced were

moral, if not constitutional, wrongs. We should seize this opportunity to correct them.

By seeking out and appointing to federal judgeships a visible number of qualified women and minorities, government is teaching the nation that racial and sexual stereotypes are invalid. Government is also teaching young women, young blacks, and young Hispanics that it no longer recognizes as political reality the racial and sexual biases of the past, and that individual accomplishment and achievement are more important than race and sex.

Yes, it is ironic that affirmative action that recognizes race and sex is necessary in order to hasten the time when race and sex will be irrelevant, and when racism and sexism are virtually non-existent. Perhaps most importantly, by voluntarily undertaking affirmative action, the government is practicing what it preaches (although, make no mistake about it, the Carter administration is responding to its own political needs and commitments). We ought to welcome any diminution of government hypocrisy.

5. The problem of quotas. Affirmative action in practice results in a quota system, opponents contend, and quotas are dysfunctional for the workings of American institutions. Quotas based on group affiliation and not individual merit can work grave hardship on well-qualified individuals who are in excess of their group's quota, and, in general, quotas tend to promote mediocrity. Quotas can exclude superior qualified persons who have the wrong sex, race, religion, or ethnic affiliation; they can include not only the marginally qualified, but even unqualified persons. Affirmative action is the first step on the road to the balkanization of America, and the courts—our prized palladiums of justice—should be the last place where this concept is imposed.

Response: Affirmative action programs have existed for close to a decade, and I am not persuaded that the parade of horrors suggested above has even begun to come about. I see no movement within the United States for each ethnic or religious grouping to claim a quota of public or private jobs. Most Americans accept individual merit as the proper basis for school admissions and employment opportunities.

Although the distinction may be fuzzy, I do see a difference between affirmative action and a quota system. Affirmative action does not have a rigid numerical goal; it retains flexibility yet is a good faith effort to widen the recruitment net, indeed to vigorously recruit, and pay particular attention to women and disadvantaged racial/ethnic groups. Affirmative action also means selecting the individual from the previously discriminated-against group when all else is approximately equal.

I have not heard or read the word "quota" in connection with the Carter administration's affirmative action objectives for judicial selection. I would oppose the use of a quota system as unnecessarily rigid and singularly inappropriate for the judiciary, but this is not at issue. The Carter administration itself, as I understand it, is making strenuous efforts to recruit, or have selection commissions and senators recruit, qualified women, blacks, and Hispanic candidates. The administration, as I also understand it, is quite concerned with the qualifications of minority and women candidates.

If the politics of federal judicial selection today makes it unlikely that incompetent white males will go on the bench, the politics of affirmative action requires that only competent minorities and women be appointed. The surest way to sabotage affirmative action is to link it with incompetency. The Carter Administration's record of minority and women appointments thus far has been excellent and there is every reason to believe that the concern with credentials of minority and women candidates will continue to yield well-qualified judges.

6. An inappropriate program for the judiciary. No matter what the merits of affirmative action may be for other spheres of American life, critics insist, it is highly inappropriate for the judicial branch. Even though merit may not actually be the sole criterion for judicial selection, it is recognized as ideally the basis for choosing judges, and leading professional groups have been working to make progress towards that goal. But if a criterion other than individual merit gains legitimacy, it becomes all the more difficult to assign to oblivion the "extraneous" political considerations that have traditionally "polluted" the process. And it becomes more difficult to win support for a partisan-free merit selection process.

Part of the justification for merit selection is that a federal judge must be highly skilled since the federal courts are the fastest legal tracks in town. We need the best people for the job; would we se-

lect a surgeon to perform a highly complex and delicate operation on any basis other than the best person available? Why should we do less with the judiciary? We need the best people on the bench regardless of race, sex or national origin. In the words of the president, "Why not the best?"

Response: This is a slippery argument to counter. To be sure, there must be highly competent judges to service the trial and appellate courts of the nation. Official recognition of race and sex does appear at first blush to detract from the goal of a non-discriminatory process for obtaining the best qualified persons to serve. But a closer look at the job of federal judges should make it clear that our judges have always been involved in the major political controversies of the day. As Tocqueville so perceptively observed over 140 yeas ago, "Scarcely any political question arises in the United States that is not resolved, sooner or later, into a judicial question."[4]

Today, racial and sexual discrimination are major legal issues before the courts. A judge who is a member of a racial minority or a woman cannot help but bring to the bench a certain sensitivity—indeed, certain qualities of the heart and mind—that may be particularly helpful in dealing with these issues. This is not to say that white judges are necessarily insensitive to issues of racial discrimination or that male judges cannot cope with issues of sexual discrimination. But the presence on the bench in visible numbers of well qualified judges drawn from the minorities and women cannot help but add a new dimension of justice to our courts in most instances.

These judges cannot help but educate their colleagues by the example they set, by the creation of precedents, and by informal as well as formal interchange. They are likely the "best" people to fill certain of the vacancies and new judgeships.

Yes, we ought to aspire to obtaining the "best" people for our judiciary—but the "best" bench may be one composed of persons of all races and both sexes with diverse backgrounds and experiences and not necessarily only those who were editors of the Harvard and Yale law reviews. It is difficult to define—much less find—the "best." Despite occasional mistakes, the current selection process with its political sensitivity has served the nation well. But affirmative action of the sort advocated and being practiced by the Carter Administration should strengthen the federal bench. And perhaps most significantly, it may be that by searching for the best possible women and minority candidates, a precedent will be established for emphasizing the individual professional merits of all candidates for judgeships, regardless of race and sex.

NOTES

This article originally appeared in Volume 62, Number 10, May 1979, pages 488-494.

1. Goldman, *A profile of Carter's judicial nominees*, 62 JUDICATURE 246 (November 1978).

2. *See* the text and citations in Goldman and Jahnige, THE FEDERAL COURTS AS A POLITICAL SYSTEM 47-78 (New York: Harper & Row, 1976, 2nd ed.).

3. Carbon, *The U.S. Circuit Judge Nominating Commission: a comparison of two of its panels*, 62 JUDICATURE 233 at 236 (November 1978); Slotnick, *What panelists are saying about the circuit judge nominating commission*, 62 JUDICATURE 320 (February 1979).

4. de Tocqueville, DEMOCRACY IN AMERICA 290 (New York: Random House, Vintage Books edition, vol. 1, 1945).

Trial Courts: Civil and Criminal Justice Processes

INTRODUCTION

Trial courts are tribunals of first instance in the American judiciary, the forum in which civil and criminal justice matters are initially heard. In most instances, the trial court is also the arena in which legal matters are definitively resolved either through pretrial negotiated settlements or actual trial proceedings. The articles in this section consider several aspects of the operation of American trial courts.

"Critical issues in the courtroom: exploring a hypothetical case" calls our attention to criminal court proceedings. Panel participants (including judges, prosecutors, defense attorneys, and academicians) discuss a wide range of concerns including setting bail, plea bargaining, jail crowding, and alternatives to incarceration.

Alissa Worden's study of "Policy making by prosecutors: the uses of discretion in regulating plea bargaining," starts with the recognition that different prosecutors have different plea bargaining policies and explores a number of variables that are putatively related to the decisions prosecutors make. Based on a survey of 27 Georgia prosecutors, Worden documents that their values and motives are complex and varied. Prosecutorial decisions regarding plea bargaining flow from a brew that includes the personal values of the prosecutor, the resource and caseload constraints under which the prosecutor labors, constraints imposed by the courthouse environment where the prosecutor is just one actor among many, and the local community's needs and expectations. Prosecutors, "as politicians and administrators must reconcile their policy choices with organizational and political constraints and obligations."

Michael Tonry's essay, "Twenty years of sentencing reform: steps forward, steps backward," explores the enormous changes that have occurred in sentencing policies since 1970 as well as the ambiguous consequences such changes have wrought for American justice. Clearly, the biggest alterations in sentencing policies during the past three decades center on efforts to promulgate sentencing guidelines and mandatory sentences in lieu of indeterminate sentences. While such changes may have worked to reduce racial and gender biases in sentencing, they raise the alternative concern of "unacceptable risks of injustice because they make it impossible to take account of important differences among defendants." Tonry's discussion draws an important distinction between federal sentencing reform and the changes that have occurred in the states where implementation of new policies has, generally, been more successful.

In "'Three strikes and you're out,': are repeat offender laws having their anticipated effects?," John Clark, James Austin, and D. Alan Henry explore one of the most popular sentencing reforms implemented in many jurisdictions in recent years. The authors note, "The purpose of these laws is simple: offenders convicted repeatedly of serious offenses should be removed from society for long periods of time, in many cases for life." The Washington and California models of such "three strikes" policies are examined closely, as are the variations of these two prototypes in other states. The difficulty of assessing the impact of such laws is underscored because, "'Three strikes and you're out' can mean dramatically different things in different states. A review of the provisions of all the states that have enacted this type of legislation reveals differences in how a 'strike' is defined, how many strikes are required to be 'out' and what it means to be 'out.'" Clark, Austin and Henry conclude that most of the publicly prominent three-strike laws will have minimal effects. Because most such laws have been targeted at violent criminals, they will have little impact on people already serving lengthy sentences.

It is difficult to discuss issues such as incarceration, prosecutorial discretion, sentencing, and three-strike laws without attention turning, at some point, to the relationship between race and outcomes in the criminal justice system. Norval Morris's "Race and crime: what evidence is there that race influences results in the criminal justice system?" examines this question. His data support the argument that the criminal justice process discriminates against blacks at multiple stages, including arrest, conviction, and punishment. Morris considers remedies for the problems highlighted and concludes, "The whole law and order movement...is, in operation though not in intent, anti-black and anti-underclass—not in plan, not in design, not in intent, but in operation."

The final selection, by Steven Flanders, diverts our gaze from criminal justice to address "The unanswered question: the impact of the Civil Justice Reform Act of 1990." The act, which required the "development and implementation of a civil justice expense and delay reduction plan" in every federal judicial district has not, according to Flanders, come close to meeting its goal nor should it have been expected to. "The fanfare with which the original draft legislation was introduced, and the need to magnify the importance of later versions in order to secure passage...seem to have forced everyone into hyperbole at every stage." Despite all of the rhetoric that surrounded the act's passage, Flanders contends that it was, in reality, little more than an extension of existing practices aimed at fostering speedier civil trial processing.

Critical issues in the courtroom: exploring a hypothetical case

Editor's note: One of the highlights of the "Presiding in Criminal Court," the First National Judicial State of the Art Conference, was a session in which Professor Charles Nesson of Harvard Law School led a panel of judges, prosecutors, defense attorneys, and other court and justice system personnel in a spirited exchange about several hypothetical criminal court cases.

The participants wrestled with a wide range of issues, including setting bail, predicting dangerousness of the defendant, plea bargaining, victim input into both the charging and sentencing decisions, jail crowding and alternatives to incarceration, drug testing, and AIDS. Although no definitive answers emerged, the session stimulated much thinking and debate.

Presented here is an edited version of that session.

Professor Charles Nesson: You know Vernon Jones to be the reverend of Zion Baptist Church for 15 or 20 years and he is being arraigned in front of you and when the charges are read, they're very serious. It's rape, attempted rape, and assault.

Judge Daffron, you are going to have to set bail. That's the first order of business. Tell me how you are going to proceed.

Judge John Daffron: The consideration would be the danger to the community, the likelihood that the accused would appear for future proceedings, and if he, in fact, is an established member of the community. On the point of his likelihood to appear, it seems he would be very likely to have bail set and be able to post bond in spite of the fact that the offenses are very serious.

Nesson: Do you want to know any details about the offenses?

Daffron: I would ask the prosecutor or the police officer the facts of the offenses and try to make some determination of the strength of the case, the potential danger to the community, and the effect on the victim.

Nesson: Here is apparently what happened. Mr. Jones has been molesting young women right in his office at the Zion Baptist Church. He apparently has been making a practice of picking out young, impressionable women who were deeply religious, having sex with them in his office and

The participants on the panel

Facilitator: Charles Nesson, professor, Harvard Law School.

Panelists: Rusty Burress, U.S. probation officer, U.S. Sentencing Commission; Thomas Coughlin III, commissioner, New York State Department of Correctional Services; John Daffron, judge, Circuit Court, Chesterfield, Virginia; Mercedes Deiz, judge, Circuit Court, Portland, Oregon; Larry Dye, president, National Association of Ex-Offenders; Lucy Friedman, executive director, Victim Services Agency, New York, New York; Stephen Goldsmith,

prosecutor, Marion County, Indianapolis, Indiana; Donald Lumpkins, attorney, Washington, D.C.; Robert Murphy, chief justice, Court of Appeals, Annapolis, Maryland; Thomas O'Toole, presiding criminal court judge, Superior Court of Maricopa County, Phoenix, Arizona; A. Charles Peruto, attorney, Philadelphia, Pennsylvania; Ricardo M. Urbina, presiding judge, Family Division, Superior Court of the District of Columbia; Frances Washington, probation officer, Superior Court of the District of Columbia.

then following it up with the strictest, scariest direction to them not to disclose to anyone or God will punish them and their mothers. By the way, there are people taking notes out there like mad. Suddenly you see a scurry in the back of the courtroom with people running out and court reporters starting to filter in.

Daffron: If there is a probability that other charges may be placed or that other people were at risk, then it seems to me that it swings toward pretrial confinement.

Nesson: What do you mean it swings towards pretrial confinement? What are you actually going to do now?

Daffron: If these are all the facts, I'm going to lock him up.

Nesson: You're going to lock him up period? No bail, no bond, no nothing?

Daffron: Place him in confinement. I would set a bail. It would be commensurate with what I think the risk is and so far, from what I've heard, there is a significant risk to others.

Nesson: Judge O'Toole, are you right along with him here?

Judge Thomas O'Toole: I just want to make sure that if he is going to be released, the community is assured he is going to abide by the conditions of the release and I would make my decision according to those factors.

Nesson: You don't have any problems at all using the dangerousness of this fellow as the criterion on which you are making the judgment?

Daffron: If there is not a significant risk to the community or individual people, then there should be a moderate amount applied that would be designed to assure his appearances at the proceeding. When you add in the factor of potential risk as it has been presented so far, it comes across as a matter that requires pretrial detention.

Nesson: How are those reporters in the back of the room affecting you?

Daffron: It sounds pompous, but I don't really think I'd be particularly concerned with the fact that it's going to be a news item.

Nesson: Do you want that news item to be "Judge Daffron Releases Jones"?

Daffron: No, I'd rather it say, "Judge Daffron Makes Wise Decision."

Nesson: And it's sounding wiser and wiser to you, at least for the moment, to lock this guy up?

Daffron: From what I've heard so far, yes. My leaning is to confinement.

Nesson: Mr. Peruto, you represent this fellow. Now what do you think you could do for him?

A. Charles Peruto: Well, in the first place, I need a couple of facts that would make me think he's a hell of a man.

Nesson: We should let our audience know that you have in front of you a little sheet that gives some minor details on this fellow. It's got his name and his date of birth (he's 52 years old), his address (Rocky Peak), and telephone number. He was divorced seven years ago and he's employed. It also includes the date of the offense, the charges, possible penalties, and his employment history. His employment history is basically fairly impressive; it amounts to that he's been a minister here for 20 years.

Peruto: In the first place, I'd argue that he's been removed from his position where this was alleged to have occurred and therefore the likelihood of recurrence is remote. I would point out that he has a splendid record. I'm going to say to the judge that there are alternatives. I have to recognize that rape is a very frightening thing in the community, at least to half of the community, and that the judge is in a ticklish position. I also have to recognize that I'm not going to get very far persuading the judge to release this man on a bail that he can make because I've got to understand that he's going to be incurring the wrath of the press. So I think I would start thinking about alternatives, such as daily calling-in, but confined to his own home. In other words, present a program for a man who otherwise had had a splendid record and obviously has been disturbed in some fashion and promise to present him for psychiatric examination; present a program of reporting to the court with regard to any evidence of propensities along the lines of the charges that he faces and suggest alternatives to prison.

Nesson: Ms. Washington, should this fellow be locked up right now or not?

Frances Washington: Yes, he should. He's one of the most trusted members of the community. He molested children, little girls who are probably taught to trust him, and he violated that trust. He inflicted physical and long-lasting psychological damage to these children. He should go to jail. I would not release him back to the community, not to call in. He could be molesting more children while he's calling in. Calling in doesn't have anything to do with this.

Nesson: Judge Murphy, do you have any problem with this reaction? We've got a guy who's got roots in the community that are solid as a rock. He's going to show up on the day of trial and yet the reaction from all of these folks is, "Hey, that's not what counts. What counts is, 'Is he dangerous?' " Is that what counts?

Chief Justice Robert Murphy: I think the fear of those who are opposed to pretrial detention to some extent may be justified by what we're hearing here. I share defense counsel's view on this entirely. He starts with the presumption of innocence. He's probably going to say, "I was in Chicago when all this happened." But this man, based on what I have before me, does not seem to be a candidate for pretrial detention. I don't know how much space you have in the Rocky Peak jail detention center, but I'd save it for someone who's got a track record of dangerousness.

Washington: If this man was a drifter, a drunk, a drug addict, or a burglar who had a history of appearing in court for every hearing, he would still be held with or without bond. I believe that the minister's about to get away with rape because he is "somebody" in the community. Granted, we don't know that he's guilty and I've already found him guilty, but you have to look out for your children and you have an obligation to look out for other people's children.

Nesson: What does the presumption of innocence mean to you?

Washington: That you're innocent until found guilty. But mind you, I work with juveniles and 90 percent of the juveniles who are caught did what they were accused of doing and that is just the way it is.

Judge Mercedes Deiz: What we are hearing from the probation officer is clearly what we are all concerned about at this conference. The arraigning judge must make a decision as to whether the individual should be released, recognizing the tremendously terrible crime that he is charged with. I have to somehow push that out of my mind and get input from defense counsel and the attorney who is representing this minister. We're lucky enough in my area to have a closed-street supervision outfit and so if the closed-street supervision people will take this man under their regular supervision pending the time of trial then, based upon everything I'm hearing from defense coun-

sel and the district attorney, I think I would release him.

Nesson: Respond to Ms. Washington. She says, "Listen, the presumption of innocence is a very important part of our trial procedure, but let's not set it up as something totally realistic. I've worked day to day for years in the system and I know that 90 percent of the people that come into the system as arrestees are guilty. If I have to presume that they are innocent, you're asking me to take a totally unrealistic view of the world. And certainly a view of the world that the constituency out there and the reporters scribbling on their pads aren't going to take." What do you say to her?

Deiz: Thank God for the jury system because they listen. The jurors listen to that instruction and literally apply it and recognize that the defendant has to be proven guilty beyond a reasonable doubt on every material aspect of the case. Too often, the DAs goof and forget some material aspect of the case and some guy gets off who is just as guilty and horrible a human being as Ms. Washington is concerned about. But the guy gets off because we have a system that says the person has to be proven guilty.

Judge Ricardo Urbina: You haven't given us the law of the jurisdiction, but I think the judge has to bite the bullet on a case like this. The information you've given us makes it rather clear that there are alternatives to locking this person up before trial. He is presumed innocent and there's any number of reasons that explains the allegations that have been made. It's a heinous crime that he's charged with, but the fact of the matter is that there is a presumption of innocence and that's what the court is required to act on. If there is some danger to the community, there's a number of things the court can do to try to insulate the community from being harmed. The first factor in my mind is going to be whether or not he's going to return to court. The second would be trying to set up some system to assure me, as the judge, the court or the system in the community that they can rest at ease, even based on these allegations about him.

Nesson: Ms. Washington's got a system. Her system to put the people in that church at ease is to lock him up, and that is very reassuring. And in fact all the rest of this stuff, about keeping him at home and checking in with the probation officer once a week, is not very reassuring.

Urbina: I think it's the judge's job to identify the

issue and to deal with it directly. It's not the judge's job to make the community feel comfortable with that decision. The judge has got the law to rely on and often that's what the judge has to do—make a decision that's going to make the community uncomfortable.

Lucy Friedman: I think that in this case the judge's job is not to make the community feel comfortable in general terms but to deal with the specifics of this case. From the victim's perspective, this is a troubling case because although we want to presume innocence, we clearly don't want to have this man take advantage and continue doing what he's been doing. I hope the reporters are out there because the more publicity about this case, the better. If he were then released with some kind of supervision, the community would be protected because people would be aware of what he has been accused of doing.

Nesson: Judge Daffron, after considering this very difficult problem, winds up making the judgment that he's going to set a fairly high bond of $150,000. After bond is set, there's quite a bit of action out there in the community. There's a lot of people raising money in support of this fellow to pay off his bond. And you, Mr. Peruto, kind of like the political support that he's getting. You figure you'll have him out in awhile and I want you to think about talking to Mr. Goldsmith about pleading this one out. Mr. Goldsmith, you're willing to talk with him?

Plea bargaining

Stephen Goldsmith: Yes, I think so.

Peruto: I would talk about plea bargaining in the sense of assault and point out that there was no serious injury because I haven't heard anything like that, and that this man obviously has mental difficulty, which I can assure him will be taken care of. Now I would have had him thoroughly examined by people whom I hired that knew how to examine people. You'll always find psychiatrists who you can interest in the efficacy of the problem.

Nesson: You're gonna hire these psychiatrists and you're then going to write the script for them?

Peruto: Absolutely, with all due honesty.

Nesson: Let's assume I'm your psychiatrist. What are your interests in this examination, Mr. Peruto?

Peruto: I want you to examine my client because obviously he has some aberration of mind which has caused this. He's been divorced seven years.

He's been very, very morose and he's been very, very depressed. I think it's worked on him to such a point where it's caused him to be a little bit, well, a little careless. He's misinterpreted the smiles of these young ladies. I think that once you've examined him, you'll agree that this man is not dangerous, but really in dire need of medical attention.

Nesson: Mr. Goldsmith, is this somebody you're gonna press hard with?

Goldsmith: This is a difficult case for the prosecutor, in fact, an unusual case, because the dynamics are against the prosecution. The church has rallied and they're convinced of the man's innocence. It's not a case the prosecutor particularly wishes to test. At the same time, we know there are multiple counts, whether you call them child molesting or rapes. We've gotten your psychiatric report saying he's not a pedophile; he's really a sick person.

The issue is whether this is an aberrational event and he can be treated. We ought to take into consideration whether he is in fact a pedophile who will continue to molest children if he's out. I would say to his attorney, we will not bring the other 16 counts if you will pick one of these counts for which we want a guilty plea. Leave sentencing open to the judge.

Nesson: And what's that going to mean if you take the plea to one count?

Goldsmith: We would require some sort of prison term to be determined by the court.

Nesson: It's going to be up to the judge to sentence?

Goldsmith: I'm assuming that either there's a mandatory imprisonment period or the prosecution requires some imprisonment to be determined by the court.

Nesson: All right, so let me see if I've got this straight. It depends a little bit for you on what the law is in the jurisdiction.

Goldsmith: What the judge's discretion is under the law.

Nesson: If the judge has no discretion, then you are in a total position of power, aren't you? You are going to decide whether this guy does time or not? On the other hand, if the judge has discretion, you have a good deal less power? And you'd respond to that by saying I'm gonna be much less willing to bargain away charges?

Goldsmith: We're trying to get him to plead to something and what I'm giving up is my requirement he goes for a fixed period of time. We're going to kind of roll the dice. He's gonna put his psychiatrist on before the judge; I get a guilty plea out of it. So long as the guy goes to prison, that's good for the state.

Nesson: All right, now here's the situation in the jurisdiction. The judge has discretion. He could put this fellow on probation. That's possible. And the law in your jurisdiction is that you can't sentence-bargain. You can charge-bargain; you can't sentence-bargain. You go in front of the judge; he pleads guilty; it's up to the judge to sentence. Now, where does that leave you?

Goldsmith: The reason we have a lot less with which to deal is because the sentence ranges from the three counts that have been provided to us are 20-40 years for rape, 15-35 for attempted rape and 8-20 for aggravated assault. If there's no realistic chance the man's ever going to get more than eight years, there's not much advantage for the state to go to trial at all on the top two charges because we know the judges are way to the left of prosecutors and it's going to come down to the minimum sentence. So we say plead guilty to one of the counts, 8-20 years, and we'll forgive the other two counts.

If the judge has a full range of discretion on sentencing, which essentially in this case is 0-40 years, we want a guilty plea which will allow the court—after it hears from you and the probation department, thank goodness, and the other psychiatrist—to come in with a range of penalty that's appropriate. Or we say, "Plead guilty to the 8-20, that's the lowest one, you reduce your risk of going to prison for 40 years, and then let the judge decide."

Nesson: Mr. Goldsmith, is this the discussion between you and Mr. Peruto that's taking place down in your office?

Goldsmith: Right.

Nesson: What happens if Mrs. Robinson wants to be present? She's Darlene's mother. Darlene was the victim of charge number one. Ms. Washington, would you be Mrs. Robinson for me? Talk to Ms. Washington here and discourage her.

Goldsmith: We think, Mrs. Robinson, that if this man is found guilty, the sentence is going to be six or eight years, and there is a chance it could go higher. We could go to trial with your 12-year-old daughter and the chances of an increased sentence are a little bit greater. We can try to get a guilty plea and not put her through it. I'd like your per-

mission to offer a guilty as charged to the count of 8-20 years.

Washington: I don't want my 12 year old to be subjected to a trial after what she has been subjected to by this man. I want him to serve 16 years, not eight, because when he is released, I want my child to be grown, through college, maybe even out of the area and hopefully over this.

Goldsmith: Well, I'm going to have a settlement discussion with his attorney. I'll offer him 15-35 years. I think it would be easier if you weren't there. If he rejects it, then I'll come back to you and talk to you about whether your daughter wants to go through it. But one thing I want you to understand is even if we do go through this trial, the judge could still give the range of sentence that could go all the way down to zero. We can't guarantee a sentence to you, but I'll take your proposal to the defense attorney.

Nesson: You're letting her run your office?

Goldsmith: In this case, the mom has a major say in whether to put her daughter, the victim, through the trial for what could come out of it, much more so than in a robbery or other case that doesn't put her child victim on the stand.

Nesson: Mr. Peruto, what are you going to do about this?

Peruto: Well, I would point out to the district attorney that even with eight years, the man will be 60 so I don't know where she's coming off with the protection of her own child. I would talk to Mr. Goldsmith about things such as considerations of track record. For example, if he has tried cases against me before that he thought were winners and wound up losers, I would say that one of the bits of input has to do with the possibility of success at the trial. I would point out to him that although he gets great sympathetic appeal from the fact that the child is 12, he also has a child that is not going to be able to withstand the kind of cross-examination that I would put the child through. I would suggest that he speak again to Mrs. Robinson and let her know these things and that it might result in serious damage to the child, far greater than the risk she would fear after his release in eight years. It might cause irreparable harm to her. I would throw in all of these things and I would suggest to him that if he wants a plea from me to the extent he wants a plea on the higher charge of rape and leave it to the judge, I could not accept that because he's only passing the buck. I am all too familiar with judges saying, "Well, he's already gotten his break on the reduction of the number of counts," and the judge is on the hot seat because now it's not a question of presumption of innocence. You have a guilty person before you and he's gonna face the press and we all know the way the press came down on that one judge who made that unfortunate comment, "She'll get over it." No judge is going to give him eight years or less than eight years on a plea to the rape charge. It must be the kind of bargain where we have a cap on the sentence; otherwise, I would have to tell my client, "You're a fool—you may as well face a thousand charges than one which exposes you to 95 years total because you can't trust the judge." You gotta put yourself in that judge's position. We just cannot deal under those circumstances on anything higher than the assault charge.

Nesson: What I hear you saying to me, Mr. Peruto, is if you can't make a firm deal that at least caps the sentence, you don't want any deal at all.

Peruto: That's right. I would point out to the DA that I've got my doctors who are going to testify, I've got the great number of parishioners that are going to come in for him; it's going to be a real donnybrook. I'm just going to have to tell my own client you're shooting crap if you come in on a rape plea because then you're defenseless and you're putting the judge in the position that I've previously described and I would advise him to go for broke.

Nesson: Judge O'Toole, should the law permit the prosecutor and defense to make a firm deal on the amount of the sentence? Must it be the law that the prosecution and the defense can make a firm deal on the amount of the sentence?

O'Toole: The answer to that is no, because the judge has to impose sentence and if he has no discretion in accepting or rejecting the deal, they're passing the buck to him whether it's a bad deal. The judge gets the buck from the community so to speak, and they don't suffer from it.

Nesson: Judge Urbina? Do you understand the problem? How should it be?

Urbina: I don't like the idea of having the defense and prosecution dictate what the sentence should be in the case. The judge, as more or less of a neutral person in the situation, has oversight of what's going on and has insight into what should ultimately be appropriate as a sentence. Both the prosecution and defense are coming at the prob-

lem with a particular point of view in mind and they've reached a point where they've compromised. I don't think that compromise should really involve the judge.

Nesson: Judge Murphy, how should it be?

Murphy: To a large extent, judges know their prosecutors and their defense counsel and, to some extent, will pay deference to their judgment. They certainly don't have all of the facts before them, but by no means or measure can a trial judge be bound by a bad deal on his judgment. As a practical matter on the plea bargaining process, the bargainers know their judge and I think they ride on the philosophy that what they agree to will in fact be accepted, but they can never be totally assured.

Nesson: What would happen in this case if we were to live in a world with no plea bargaining, no sentence-bargaining, no charge-bargaining?

Murphy: It's a cruel, cruel world and a very unrealistic one. Obviously, the court system would probably break itself very, very shortly if you didn't have the plea-bargaining process.

Goldsmith: It's an unrealistic world that doesn't allow those people closest to the case to negotiate an outcome based on the dynamics of the evidence, the dynamics of the community, and the importance of the charge.

Nesson: So as far as you're concerned, it's part of the prosecutor's job to negotiate outcomes?

Goldsmith: Absolutely.

Nesson: And God help the defense—if they didn't have that to do, what else would they offer their clients?

Goldsmith: Well, I think we arrive together at a decision that more than anything takes the evidence and predicts the judge.

The sentence

Nesson: All right. Let's predict the judge here. Judge O'Toole, just looking for a reaction. What are you going to sentence this man to?

O'Toole: Well, he's gonna go to prison, it's just a question of how long. It's a very serious crime and apparently we have mitigating factors and aggravating factors.

Nesson: He's a distinguished member of the civil liberties movement, civil rights movement, and a pillar in the Baptist Church. Tremendous support from his congregation.

O'Toole: That isn't at the top of my list of priorities for determining sentence.

Nesson: And he's sick.

O'Toole: Is that a factor to consider? That also works the other way because if he's sick, who's to know whether he's going to recover? I would perhaps have a psychiatric examination conducted by a court-appointed expert and you also have the expert input from the probation department. Included in the expert input would be statements of the victims and interested parties. All these players come in line on a sentence.

Mrs. Robinson rings a loud bell when she talks about the concerns of her daughter. I would want to know the impact on the victim. I'd also want to be satisfied as to the length of incarceration this man would serve under the particular sentence. I'd want to know the guidelines for release and what type of parole supervision he's going to have. The man's 52 years old, perhaps it's somewhat pragmatic but I'd want to see him incarcerated until he's 60 and put parole on him. I'd propose a sentence that considers not only punishment and deterrence but community safety and also the interests of the defendant. This is a very serious ongoing pattern of conduct, evident not only by this particular charge, but if I understand the facts, this has been occurring with other young females in the parish.

Nesson: You're going to find out about that during sentencing?

O'Toole: I would think so.

Nesson: Commissioner Coughlin, can you use this man? You've got him now and you've got him for a minimum of eight years. What are you going to do with him?

Thomas Coughlin: Put him to work. I would probably use whatever skills I could get out of him. Not in terms of ministerial skills, but I'd imagine he could read and write pretty good and we'd probably put him in some setting within the prison system where we could use those skills.

Fact pattern

Nesson: All right now, let me introduce you to another character. Judge Thomas O'Toole, you're in the arraignment session and in comes a young man, 19 years old, by the name of James Michael O'Reilly.

He's been charged with armed robbery, assault and battery with a dangerous weapon, unauthorized use and possession with intent to distribute. Jimmy and the co-defendant, who's a 23 year old, much bigger fellow, apparently entered a 7-Eleven convenience store the night before, and Turner, the co-defendant, had a weapon in his hand. They stuck the place up and Jimmy removed $234 from the cash register, and at that point the woman behind the counter apparently made some quick move, and Turner shot and wounded her. She's in the hospital now, in serious condition. They fled, got into a Ford 4x4, took off and the cops stopped the truck, arrested the two, and there they are before you. Now you are going to set bail for Jimmy. What are you going to do?

O'Toole: He's not going to get out. Looking at the additional information, it doesn't look like he has any substantial means of living. He's single, living with his parents, unemployed. Any bail—reasonable, substantial bail—is going to keep him in jail in fact.

Nesson: So that's what you're gong to do? You're going to keep him in jail? And you're going to do it on the basis that he's a danger to the community?

O'Toole: He's likely to violate the conditions to release if he gets out. He's got an active police record. He's 19 and he's got an active police record . . . juvenile . . . six or seven arrests.

Nesson: So you don't have any problem looking at his juvenile record? None of this business about, "Hey, we seal the record at the point when he's become an adult and we don't look at it after that"?

O'Toole: That's correct.

Nesson: Judge Deiz, does it bother you that he's monkeying around in the juvenile record, making his judgments on the basis of that?

Deiz: I don't look at the juvenile record on whether or not to set bail or whether or not you release a person on personal recognizance because we can't; it's not permitted by statute. However, if someone was looking at it at the time of sentencing, I would like to see this kind of record and I have always wanted to see it, no matter what the charge, in order to assess whether or not an individual should be released. In the practical point of view, the fact that the young man or young woman did something when they were 17 and now that they are 19 is very relevant to how I'm going to assess whether or not they are a good risk to be out pending trial. But I can't have that information.

Nesson: Judge O'Toole, when they arrest this fellow, they tested him for drugs and he comes up dirty. He's apparently high on PCP at the time. How does that affect your judgment?

O'Toole: That obviously would be a factor to consider as to whether that is one of the motives for his committing the offense. Whether it's an indicator of his likelihood to violate conditions of release, I don't know.

Nesson: Mr. Lumpkin, you're representing this fellow. What significance do you think that test is going to have?

Donald Lumpkin: I think the drug test would be negative and as a defense attorney, I have basically two jobs. One is to put my client in the best light. Sometimes it's total darkness. So then I look to my client's best interest. I think it's terribly important which judge I'm going before and I think that a young man, 19 years of age, certainly has some hope. I think with the record before me, he falls within the Youth Act in the District of Columbia.

Nesson: We've got a fellow that's charged as I described and a juvenile record that includes: truancy; another truancy; destruction of property for which he got fined; possession of marijuana, dismissed; possession of marijuana with intent to distribute, for which he was committed to a youth home for six months; petty larceny, for which he's on probation; and a previous adult incident, possession of cocaine, which was not pressed.

Lumpkin: In the District of Columbia, he's still a youth—anyone under 22 years of age. I think this is terribly crucial in this particular case and looking at Mr. O'Reilly's best interest, I would recommend that he undergo detention for 60 days with an intensive psychiatric evaluation. I think it's terribly important that this young man enter a structured environment. I do not wash my hands thinking there isn't hope and I'd certainly ask the judge to give immense weight to the fact that he is only 19. In a properly structured environment, I think there is hope and if there isn't hope, then there's no point even trying.

Nesson: I'm interested in drug testing here. Once he shows up dirty, what does that have to do with anything?

Lumpkin: It shows a couple of things. It shows that we're dealing with a very troubled young man, but it also shows that we're dealing with not such an exceptional person. Thousands and thousands of people, certainly in the District of Columbia, have shown up dirty with PCP. This is not to justify, I'm simply saying that it's not such an exception. It's something to be concerned about, but I would

not use him as the single example. Yes he's drugged, it's a matter of great concern, but so are thousands of others.

Nesson: Let me come from a different perspective. Mr. Dye, do you have any problem with this jurisdiction testing everybody that comes through for drugs?

Larry Dye: I do have objections to jurisdictions doing drug tests.

Nesson: Mr. Lumpkin says they're accurate and Judge O'Toole says that's valuable information.

Dye: And there are cases where it is not accurate. There are cases where the drug company doing their testing has made errors. There have been errors made in all kinds of testing so, consequently, I would raise that as a question because potentially you have people who have not used drugs that would turn up dirty.

I'm an offender coming in and when I've been tested, I want my attorney to challenge that test because this jurisdiction has the law that states you're going to take a test. So I'm going to want my attorney to be able to challenge that.

Pretrial release conditions

Nesson: Judge Daffron, we go forward with Jimmy and we put some bail on him and he's been in the can now for some 35 days waiting trial. Let's say he's able to make the bail and it comes up to you now. What kind of pretrial release conditions are you gong to put on him, when you got this drug test and he was dirty when it came in? Are you going to use that test in the context of imposing conditions on him?

Daffron: I'm going to require that he be free from drugs or alcohol. As a condition of bond, he will subject himself to announced and unannounced screenings.

Nesson: Announced and unannounced screenings? How are we going to work the announced screenings?

Daffron: Tell him to come in at a given time.

Nesson: Tell him to come in at a given time and he's going to see Mr. Burress? Mr. Burress, explain it all to me.

Rusty Burress: Essentially they are probably going to put this person in some type of drug program where he will be giving urine samples and then we will have him either reporting to us or we will go out to his home or place of employment, confirm he is still in the community and we'll take urine samples from him at that time.

Nesson: How do you feel about this one? You're going to go to Jimmy's home and you're going to say, "All right, Jimmy, let's go to the bathroom together."

Burress: Yes, I am. It's not a most enjoyable part of the job, but that's one of the regular things you do and particularly if that's the condition of his bond. If he's on the street by remaining drug-free, that's the only way to check it.

Nesson: What happens if he misses an appointment? What's going to happen?

Burress: We'd notify the court. Actually, before we notify the court, we'd probably go out and check on the individual to see if the individual was at home, what reason they had for not coming in, probably take a urine sample at that time just to see if he's reverted to drug use and probably make some judgment as to whether it warranted reporting based upon what this person had told us. If we can't locate them, of course, or if their reason doesn't appear to be a valid one then we'd report it to the court.

Nesson: And suppose he comes in and he tests dirty, what happens?

Burress: We'd report that to the court immediately and then see if the court had any further directions, additional programming.

Nesson: All right, Judge Daffron, you just get a report from Mr. Burress that Jimmy has come up dirty on one of his drug tests three weeks after release?

Daffron: He would be back in court for determination of whether his bond should be revoked.

Nesson: And are you going to revoke his bond?

Daffron: I would say the odds are probable.

Nesson: By the way, I didn't tell you that it isn't in Rocky Peak. This is in a jurisdiction where the jail is chock-a-block full. It's so far over capacity that federal judges have been breathing down the necks of various local administrators and here's Jimmy and he's dirty on his PCP test. You're going to put him back in?

Daffron: He is there until I let him out. This would be a case, it seems to me, for a reasonable bond that Jimmy could make and if he wants to play by the rules of the game he stays out. If he can't, I'm not absolutely convinced right now that he would go back, but I think that the probability is that he will.

Nesson: Mr. Coughlin, just be a jail administra-

tor for me right now, will you? Your jail is just popping at the seams. Do you have any way of letting Judge Daffron know that he really shouldn't be plugging in kids you really don't need just because they come up dirty on their urine test?

Coughlin: Well, if the judge would read the morning newspapers everyday, he'd see all the reasons in the world for not just bringing a guy back for something minor. However, I personally have an opinion on this. You give a guy a bite of the apple, you put him on bail and he gets out and he comes back dirty. Well that's enough to bring him back in; in my opinion, it shouldn't be the judge's concern whether or not there's room in the jail. That's my concern. That's the executive's concern.

Nesson: Well, it sounds like what should happen is the executive should raise some money and build some new jails, but out in the real world that's pretty tough to make happen.

Coughlin: That's the problem we have with politics. The mayors and the governors around this country don't want to make the hard choice and I'm convinced that they have to make that hard choice.

Nesson: So convinced that you'd be prepared to say it's just not the judge's business to concern themselves with that problem at all?

Coughlin: It's been my experience that they don't concern themselves with that problem and I've been doing this long enough to know. I've talked to judges saying, "It's not your business. You do what you do and I'll do what I do and you use your resources and I'll use my resources." Anything less than that and the system starts to fall apart and you have federal judges stepping in to release people. The top 37 guys on the list are out the door tomorrow. That's not the way it should work.

Nesson: All right, now let me come back to you, Judge Daffron. If you follow the structure, you're going to put a release condition on this kid with respect to drug use and you're going to be under a system where if he's dirty, he's back in the can.

Daffron: Not absolutely, but that would be a likelihood. I don't think it's a bright line rule. You use PCP or heroin or cocaine, you are back in jail and pretrial confinement—the probabilities are certainly higher with that use than it may be with the use of alcohol, marijuana.

Nesson: All right, Mr. Burress, the real rules, aren't they, are that if I use beer or marijuana, I'm not going to get yanked off the street, am I?

Burress: If that's what this judge's criterion is, then that probably is the rule, but I would not tell the defendant that.

Nesson: By the way, if that's the real rule would you bother reporting marijuana use to the judge?

Burress: Yeah, but I probably wouldn't go through a formal procedure. I'd probably just advise the court of this situation and see if the court wanted us to take any action at that time.

Nesson: Let's see it happen. Advise him, advise him.

Burress: Judge, I've been seeing this Jimmy O'Reilly on a regular basis. He's begun working. He's going to the drug program in general. They have been taking urine samples from him. However, the urine sample we took this week turned up positive for marijuana use. He seems to be basically staying close to the home and at employment. No indications of any other type of activity. The drug program feels that he seems to be making some progress and seems to be trying to profit from attending those sessions. At this point, I think it probably would warrant giving him another shot.

Daffron: Intensify the supervision and leave him on the street.

Nesson: That's it. So you just bought yourself a little more work. Intensify the supervision and when you intensify it, you find out he's smoking marijuana more and more. Are you going to go back again? You're a glutton for punishment, aren't you?

Burress: To some degree, yes sir. Because you do create work for yourself when you report these violations. That's just part of what you do. I could turn a blind eye to the thing, not report it and it would reduce the amount of work but that's not what the function is.

Plea bargaining

Nesson: Mr. Goldsmith, I want Mr. Lumpkin to talk to you for a minute. We want to see if we can deal this one out. We did very well with Vernon. I want to see whether we can deal Jimmy. What do you think just on what you know?

Goldsmith: I just think this conversation is kind of outrageous—a few minor crimes, you're out on bail, no big deal. I'm predisposed against that because he's got a longer history.

Nesson: Mr. Lumpkin?

Lumpkin: If my client is spaced out on drugs, I would explain to him fully he has the responsibil-ity to get off. If he needs help, we'll try to get him help. I cannot see people walking around the city on PCP. If it comes to walking around the city or being in jail, they're safer in jail because then they are not going out to bring harm to society or the community.

I'll tell you an interesting case I had. I had one client who was running down the street in the nude, yelling "liberty for all" on PCP and got shot by a sting gun and was taken to St. Elizabeth's. I talked to five attorneys in Washington, asking if I should speak to the judge regarding this matter out of the best interest for my client. Absolutely not, they told me. I went to the judge and talked to him. I am not doing any client a favor by not giving him help on drugs.

Nesson: Mr. Peruto, you agree with Mr. Lumpkin here?

Peruto: I am in great pain because I agree with Mr. Goldsmith. You know, the guy that knows more about the condition of the full jail is Jimmy; he knows more about that than anybody. I'm also sick of the judges who say that we have to release people from jail. If they were really concerned with these terribly overcrowded conditions, they would enjoin a man close to the executive to force him to build more institutions. I don't like a judge who says to a guy, "If you use (drugs) while you're out on this bail against my order, you will be recommitted" and then he doesn't recommit, because that promise is the surest way of keeping them in line. If you promise you're going to put them back, put them back. I would have to say to my own client, "Fellow, you're carrying the keys to the jail with you. You got the keys in one pocket and you can put the joint in the other pocket. Don't come crying to me if you're going to smoke the joint." I just don't see my role as defense counsel in the preservation of the presumption of innocence to extend itself to where I'm going to do otherwise in this position.

I think that one of the major causes of crime is the kind of thing you're talking about. I think the system is known much, much better by the offender than it is by the people who administer the system. I think that the newspapers have a lot to do with it. I think we have a bunch of chicken-lily livered people who are in the system who react to newspapers and are scared off by executives for fear of raising taxes and therefore their political party is being defeated.

Nesson: This case looked pretty bad for Jimmy when we first heard about it but there are some details that kind of go his way. There were two witnesses in the 7-Eleven who said in their interviews that Turner was clearly the shooter. Turner seemed to be directing Jimmy during the robbery, telling him what to do and when Turner shot, Jimmy was extremely upset about it and yelled at Turner that he shouldn't have done it. He didn't want anything to do with that shooting and he immediately ran out of the place and hopped into the truck. In fact, when the officers caught up with them, Jimmy stopped the truck and Tuner was yelling, "Why did you stop the truck?" and Jimmy was completely peaceful after that. So it begins to look like maybe Jimmy's not the hardest guy in the world. Could you use that with Mr. Goldsmith?

Lumpkin: Certainly. I see Jimmy as probably a very troubled young man, probably with very poor guidelines, not really having any type of structured environment. What is so frustrating as a defense attorney is representing the best interest of my client and all I have to deal with is incarceration.

Nesson: Mr. Goldsmith, let me make it a little richer. Mr. Lumpkin does a kind of psychiatric look at Jimmy and they find out he's a kid with some learning disabilities, bad self-image on account of it and got himself into some drugs, but really doesn't seem to be such a bad kid. Are you going to hit a point where you're ready to say this kid doesn't have to go away?

Goldsmith: Not for this charge, maybe in 1985 when he stole a leather jacket from the department store but not with the armed robbery with a sawed-off shotgun. We're dealing with how much time, not whether he does time.

Nesson: Suppose he convinces you, in fact, Turner was dragging him along on this one? Still no?

Goldsmith: That's an important factor in reducing the length of the sentence, not in reducing it to zero. Too serious a crime, too long a history. If it's a regular good time two-for-one situation, we'd offer him eight years which means he does four, he testifies and does drug counseling and testing after release from the prison.

Nesson: And what about Mrs. Woods, the lady behind the counter who got shot, now out of the hospital in a wheel chair? Do you consult with her on this one? Ms. Friedman, what do you say if you were representing Mrs. Woods here?

Lucy Friedman: Well, I'd first wish that someone had notified us when Jimmy made bail. I would have liked to have known because my client was getting phone calls from people hanging up. I mean we don't know who it was. It might have been Jimmy, Jimmy's family, it may have been the other guy. So in addition to being injured, perhaps permanently for life, she's been terrified because she's been afraid to go out and got no notice from the courts about what's happening in the case. Then Jimmy went back into jail, we didn't know why.

Nesson: Judge O'Toole, the case comes in front of you for sentence and there is a plea. Clearly the understanding of Jimmy and his lawyer is that he's going to get a maximum of four years but you're under a guideline system that says, armed robbery, dangerous weapon, minimum eight. Will you go along with the plea bargain?

O'Toole: The plea agreement with the prosecutor is before me and it says he's going to get a maximum of four years. He's obviously not pleading armed robbery to the facts; he's pleading to a less serious offense. I probably would get background information. I prefer not accepting the plea until I read the pre-sentence report. If I didn't like the information, I would reject it. I'd like to have more input from the victim as to what she believes regarding the plea bargain. I'd take the plea, but I wouldn't accept it until I had that information. At the time of sentencing, I'd decide whether or not to accept or reject it.

Sentencing

Nesson: Judge Murphy, here's the situation—your state's adopted sentencing guidelines. Lo and behold, here comes this case in front of you and it's below the guidelines.

Murphy: It's a judgment call. We have hundreds of Jimmys coming into the system every day and they go on a scale of 10 down to 1. There may be a lot to be said for him. If you're a defense lawyer, his juvenile record is really unremarkable.

Deiz: You've made a decision in this case. You're saying that because Jimmy had a troubled childhood and maybe he wasn't of the strongest character with a learning disability, that allowed you to give him a sentence half of what the minimum was.

Murphy: That's what guidelines are all about. You can go above or below. You can get a fellow who looks worse than Jimmy. That sawed-off shotgun is a real loser, although this is a first offense. A sawed-off shotgun just sets off bells in trial judges and if you change the facts a little bit you could go above it.

Nesson: Judge O'Toole, you've got all this information about how Jimmy really was importuned by Turner in this thing and seems to have been dragged along and resisted at every step. He really looks like a salvageable kid in some ways. Tell you something else about Jimmy. He's a small kid. He's about 5'5", long blonde hair, real pretty kid. Does that bother you in sentencing him?

O'Toole: Well it bothers me, but I'm not going to make any decision on the length of incarceration or whether I incarcerate him based upon a likelihood that he may be sexually assaulted in prison.

Nesson: Mr. Coughlin, tell me about your prison system. Have you tested for AIDS in your system?

Coughlin: No, we haven't tested for AIDS, because I wouldn't know what to do if I found someone who tested positive and displayed clinical symptoms of the disease.

Nesson: Here you got Jimmy coming up to your prison and you look at him and you say, "Now there is a pretty kid and I just know what's going to happen to that kid." And your attitude is, "I just don't want to know what the AIDS situation is in my prison."

Coughlin: If you have 42,000 people in prison and a large number, let's say 60 or 70 percent, have been involved with narcotics use, you're going to have a significant number of people within that prison system who could very well test positive for the virus, not being ill now, but testing positive for the virus. The numbers range anywhere from 20 percent, depending upon whether the researcher wanted to get his name in the paper, to as high as 80 percent. If I get a person to test positive, say he shows up at sick call with three or four symptoms and we do the test and we find it positive, we treat him as a medical case. If, however, the guy has a positive test but is not ill, I don't know what to do with him. Do I keep him locked up? Do I start a special prison for him? If I have a prison full of guys who test positive for AIDS, the next step is to lock them all in a cell and not let them out because they're all nasty people; they're going to be doing things to each other, and pretty soon the whole prison will have the actual disease. So, no, I won't test for AIDS unless there's some clinical indication that the person has it.

Nesson: Now, you're not in any doubt about your ability to test for AIDS, that is, there's no legal impediment to your doing this, is there?

Coughlin: No, there's not. We take blood samples when they come into the prison, but we don't run it through the particular screen for the AIDS virus because no one has told me what I'm going to do with the man when I find out that he's got AIDS or been exposed to the AIDS virus. In this whole issue of being exposed to the AIDS virus, nobody has come up with the solid number on conversion—nobody. In the research that we have done—we've had AIDS in our prison system since 1981 and now we've got the largest number in the country today—we have not had a single case of AIDS being contracted within the prison, not a single case. I'll tell you how we know. We have people who have come to prison, gotten sick and have died of AIDS within six months of coming to prison. You don't die from AIDS within six months, that's how we know. The period of development stretches anywhere from six to seven years before the AIDS virus becomes active enough to kill you. If you've been in prison six months and you die from AIDS or AIDS-related complex issues, it's obvious from medical research that you haven't contracted AIDS within the prison system.

Nesson: All right, Mr. Lumpkin, let's now wind the clock back a moment to the point where you're appearing in front of Judge O'Toole on behalf of Jimmy and you know that Judge O'Toole has got it in his mind that he's going to send Jimmy away for a little bit. Maybe not a long time. He's really kind of wobbly because really this kid doesn't look like he's that bad, maybe salvageable, and he knows that sending him away is extremely serious. Now, do you make an argument to Judge O'Toole based on the AIDS problem?

Lumpkin: I would like to address one issue before getting into that one. I would like to say that studies have shown that blacks and Hispanics generally do die within six to seven months. It is the white gay population that will not die until about two years. And the reason—we're speaking about drug users whose immune system is so low as compared to the white population which is very high among gay males.

Nesson: What you're saying is that generally speaking the gay white population is healthier in terms of the immune system than the narcotic-using population?

Lumpkin: Exactly. Their immune system is much better than the Hispanic or black male who has been using drugs and has no immunity whatsoever, virtually, and they die much, much sooner from the date of diagnosis.

Nesson: All right, so now come back to my question. Do you want to say something to Judge O'Toole about what Jimmy's prognosis is, going off to the prison that Mr. Coughlin runs?

Lumpkin: I would have no problem addressing this issue in the least, but I'm afraid the judge would come back to me and say, "Mr. Lumpkin, that is not my problem as a judge."

O'Toole: I think it's a legitimate concern, especially when the Department of Corrections or the Bureau of Prisons have decided not to test or sample blood of inmates coming in but, as I understand, the hypothetical isn't so much what his blood condition is when he goes in, it's what it's going to be after he's been there for awhile.

Given the role that I've got in determining a sentence, I could not base any decision on length of incarceration on the possibility that we go to prison and do some testing and this boy's going to be sexually assaulted. I would recommend to the department of corrections that he be placed so that his safety is preserved as much as possible. And I think if he gets to the prison system and he's got a problem, hopefully he's going to be able to file a petition of writ of habeas corpus or something like that.

Daffron: My reaction at the moment on the facts is that Jimmy would go to prison. It seems to me that if there is not a mandatory, minimum period of confinement, that this case may well lend itself to some alternative other than confinement to the penitentiary. For example, it may be a jurisdiction that has a type of youthful offender law that provides confinement but not in the general prison population or adult prison population. But, assuming that doesn't exist, I see a hard time.

Nesson: No, we're perfectly happy to assume we've got house arrest in this state. We could put a little cuff on Jimmy's pants or around his ankle and have him check in once a day though the telephone. We can have intensive probation . . . . Mr. Burress, he's got nothing much to do, now that he's been relieved of all his marijuana work. He can go out on a once-a-day basis and check in on Jimmy to make sure he's staying in the house.

Daffron: Is the first determination either confinement in the penitentiary or something else, or is there an institutional confinement that may be less than the adult prison population? That would make a significant difference to me.

The hardest one is it's either/or, that if there is confinement, he's going to be placed in spite of a classification system within a correctional system in confinement with other adult fellows, and so he is significantly at great risk there. It would be a significant matter whether or not to place this defendant in prison because of the great risk of assault that needs determination without the other facts that I'm waiting for you to give me. I think probably that this defendant, regrettably, would be confined in prison and about the limit of the judge's intervention would be perhaps a letter that we sometimes write to corrections or classifications expressing concern because of evidence presented.

Nesson: What do you do when you get one of those letters, Mr. Coughlin?

Coughlin: Well, we pay pretty close attention. There are a number of options that we have in the prison system to deal with people like this. There are programs within the system. This kid, depending upon what was the final charge—whether it was armed robbery or whether it was less than armed robbery—we would probably put this individual into our shock incarceration program.

You take a young kid who's 19 years old with an on-going juvenile record and this is his first big-time run-in, then you make the assumption the kid is salvageable somehow and you put him into a program designed to test that salvageability, an intensive six-month program, narcotics counseling, disciplined regimen and maybe after six months you can turn somebody out who's not going to come back.

Goldsmith: That's not my deal.

Coughlin: But you don't make that deal.

Goldsmith: Oh no, we made a deal.

Coughlin: It's not yours to determine, it's mine. We're in my statutes.

Nesson: Once you put it in his hands, he says where the kid resides, right? And, if you want it in the maximum security, that's your choice and if you want it in the half-way house, that's your choice.

Let me just change this problem a little bit. Judge Deiz, same kid, Jimmy, in front of you. He's still pretty, but this time things are a little different. Mr. Burress has been talking to Jimmy quite a bit and in fact Mr. Burress has included in the sentence report that he thinks Jimmy makes a little money on the side by being a male prostitute. And, we've come up with information that Jimmy tests positive for AIDS. I want to know if that changes the way you think. Are you going to send Jimmy off to this prison where he's cute, he's available, and he's possibly lethal?

Deiz: All of us in this work know that fashioning appropriate sentences is the most difficult task for all trial judges, and what I've gotten since I'm down here in Phoenix is this new curve of AIDS. This man is now going to the penitentiary because he is involved in drugs and I'm satisfied with the correlation between drugs and continuing criminal activity so, therefore, it isn't so much that he's salvageable as a person that I would put him in an alternative placement in the community, but he would go. The problem now is what you've just thrown at me—how do I get this wonderful commissioner here to really give credence to the strong recommendation that I make that this fellow be followed and somehow kept away from the prison population so that he doesn't spread AIDS. If I'm sending that very kind of potential weapon into your penitentiary knowing about it, I'm not dumping it on you to say that I don't know what to do. I can't understand why you don't know what to do.

Coughlin: Of course I know what to do. If the fact pattern has changed now and you have a male prostitute who tests positive for the AIDS virus, well, that's whole different set of circumstances. I know exactly what to do with this person.

Nesson: Let me do it this way, Mr. Coughlin. This AIDS problem is the big one that's kind of looming over the horizon at everybody and it does kind of wind up with you in the end. The system funnels it towards you and gives it to you in a nice, confined situation where you've got the toughest problems to deal with. Talk to that situation, would you. What are we going to do with this problem?

Coughlin: If he is a male prostitute, tests positive for AIDS, gets convicted, gets sentenced, and comes to prison, the prison system knows what to do with a person like that. Now we have mechanisms within the system that permit us to isolate people like that with equal administrative segregation. I can assure you, he would probably wind up in an administrative protective custody unit very quickly and would stay there until we got some indication of how he was behaving. If his behavior in that administrative protection unit was success-ful for a period of time, we might try him out in limited contact with the general population where he would go out with everybody knowing that he is a male prostitute and that he tests positive for AIDS. But he's not going to get into the general population until myself or the warden is satisfied that he can handle it and the system can handle him.

Nesson: You'll turn him loose in the general population and you're going to let everybody know that he tests positive?

Coughlin: You said that this AIDS problem is booming on the horizon? At least for my prison system we are beyond the horizon already. Now I'm being very frank with you. We have dealt with the problem of AIDS since 1981. I think we know how to do it. Remember before we dealt with AIDS, we dealt with a lot of other infectious diseases within a congregated institution and it can be done in a very reasonable way. I have never, in my experience, seen an AIDS patient beat up by other inmates. I have never known an AIDS patient to be murdered by other inmates. Usually other inmates want to stay very far away. Inmates constantly ask, "What can I do? I don't have AIDS and I don't want to catch AIDS." I say the best thing you can do is to "look at the guy living in the cell next to you and say that he's got AIDS and therefore, I'm not going to share a needle with him nor am I going to kiss him." It may sound very simple and it might sound very basic but that's how not to catch AIDS in prison. Prisoners, by and large, are not dumb people and they don't want to catch AIDS and they pay attention to these very simple rules.

Nesson: Ladies and gentlemen on the panel, thank you very much for participating with me.

NOTE

This transcript originally appeared in Volume 72, Number 1, June-July 1988, pages 12-22.

Policy making by prosecutors: the uses of discretion in regulating plea bargaining

The values and motives of prosecutors are complex and varied. As administrators and politicians, they must reconcile their policy choices with organizational and political constraints and obligations.

by Alissa Worden

Although court observers agree that the prosecutor plays an important role in shaping local legal culture, most research on prosecutors has examined only legal and strategic considerations in charging and other case-processing decisions,[1] and has largely overlooked chief prosecutors' administrative and political uses of discretion in making policies that structure their assistants' day-to-day decisions. Office policies are an important means of standardizing staff behavior and of developing an institutional role within the courthouse community; and there are few formal constraints on prosecutors' discretion in setting policy. Therefore, policy decisions may offer clues to prosecutors' efforts to dominate or adapt to their courthouse colleagues and their political environments.

This article examines prosecutors in their roles as policymakers, focusing on office policies concerning one important feature of criminal adjudication, plea bargaining. The findings offer some support for political and organizational explanations of policy choices: prosecutors' plea bargaining policies represent responsiveness to community crime problems as well as adaptations to the level of workgroup cooperation and conflict in their courthouses. However, plea policies are also associated with prosecutors' personal beliefs about the conflicting values of due process and crime control. These findings are significant because they offer insight into a complex set of motivations behind prosecutors' administrative and political decisions, and thereby illustrate the importance of

more systematic study of prosecutors' policy choices.

The uses of discretion

Studies of prosecutors' policies have been more illustrative than definitive. Many examine only one or a small number of jurisdictions, so they are primarily useful for generating, but not for testing, hypotheses about the causes and consequences of policies.[2] Most research on criminal courts has been conducted in urban areas, and therefore variation on theoretically interesting characteristics, such as organizational size, cannot be observed or measured.[3] Moreover, many researchers have focused on practices or patterns of decisions rather than on formal or even informal policies.[4] Finally, research on prosecutors has been handicapped by overly simplified conceptions of prosecutorial motivations, such as the assumption that all prosecutors strive to maximize convictions or to impose maximally harsh sentences, despite the fact that interviews and observation have revealed considerable variation in prosecutors' values and beliefs, incentives, and role orientations.[5] In sum, there have been few systematic attempts to account for how and why prosecutors fashion the rules that govern their staffs' behavior.

One of the most important processes that chief prosecutors can regulate is plea bargaining. All court actors have incentives to negotiate dispositions rather than take cases to trial. Trials are slow and unpredictable, they require prodigious investment of resources for preparation, and they produce one winner and one loser, with no room for compromise. From the point of view of a prosecutor, negotiated guilty pleas offer certain (and virtually irreversible) convictions in return for a commodity, leniency, of which prosecutors have a potentially unlimited supply. It is reasonable to assume that chief prosecutors who attempt to restrict plea bargaining do so in order to counteract these pervasive incentives to negotiate dispositions.

But why do some prosecutors attempt to regulate plea bargaining through formal and informal policies, while others do not? The most common explanation is that restrictive plea bargaining policies represent efforts to crack down on crime by refusing to offer lenient sentences. For example, in one of the jurisdictions he studied, Roy Flemming found that restrictive policies were part of a package of internal office reforms aimed at stiffening sentences and establishing a stronger anti-crime image in the courthouse and the community.[6] But this is only one of several plausible explanations. Plea bargaining policies might be shaped by the personal values of prosecutors, and by organizational opportunities and limitations, as well as by environmental constraints.

Attitudes

Although some theoretical work on prosecutorial decision making has been premised on the assumption that prosecutors uniformly pursue the objectives of maximizing convictions and maximizing sentence severity,[7] the empirical observations of other court researchers challenge this assumption. David Neubauer, for example, studied one Midwestern prosecutor who insulated his staff from community and law enforcement pressures in order to establish policies and practices consistent with his own view of the proper role of the prosecutor in the criminal justice system.[8] Prosecutors' beliefs, Neubauer suggested, lead them to become either crime fighters, deploying resources to maximize the number of wrongdoers convicted, or officers of the court, responsible for ensuring due process even as they argue the state's case. Likewise, Lief Carter observed that prosecutors in a California office varied not only in how much satisfaction they sought (and derived) from the interpersonal aspects of their jobs, but also in whether they placed stronger emphasis on controlling crime or on maintaining high standards of due

process.[9]

As Herbert Packer observed more than 20 years ago, although controlling crime and protecting defendants' rights are not theoretically incompatible values, in practice they often conflict.[10] For the purpose of understanding prosecutors' policy choices, this tradeoff may be particularly important. While some critics claim that plea bargaining results in overly lenient sentences, many court actors and observers recognize that plea bargaining is not only a means of conserving scarce resources, but also a way of ensuring conviction and punishment in cases involving evidentiary problems or reluctant witnesses. Critics on the other side of the plea bargaining debate agree with this observation, but object for precisely that reason: plea bargaining is a means of ensuring (perhaps through coercion) the self-conviction of defendants while avoiding the rigorous standards of due process and proof imposed during trials.

It is reasonable to hypothesize that the policy choices of court actors, like those of other politicians, are influenced by personal beliefs, and that the "essential policy choices for judges and prosecutors entail an accommodation of crime control and due process values."[11] Thus, prosecutors who emphasize the court's crime-control mission may be more willing to tolerate practices that compromise due process standards in order to increase convictions, and to implicitly encourage plea bargaining by placing no restrictions on negotiated dispositions. Prosecutors who balance their commitment to crime control with concern about due process may be more likely to restrict or regulate plea bargaining.

Resources and caseload constraints

As administrators, prosecutors must find ways of managing caseloads by efficiently processing cases within the constraints of staff and resources. If, as some have argued, growing caseloads and the increasing costs of trial are responsible for the pervasiveness of plea bargaining,[12] then one might infer that courts with the heaviest caseloads (or, more accurately, the largest ratio of cases to resources) must resort to plea bargaining most frequently.[13]

Of course, case pressure may be felt differently in different sectors of a courthouse. That a jurisdiction has too few judges, courtrooms, or public defenders to keep up with dockets need not imply that the prosecutor's staff feels equally burdened (indeed, such a differential burden might work to the prosecutor's advantage). Therefore, an examination of the effects of caseload on prosecutors' plea bargaining policies must focus on prosecutorial rather than courthouse resources and caseloads.[14] It is hypothesized that where prosecutors operate under conditions of scarce resources, they can ill afford to adopt restrictive policies that may prolong negotiations or, worse yet, encourage defendants to take their chances on trial. Slack resources may be a necessary (albeit not sufficient) condition for the adoption of restrictive plea bargaining practices.

Courthouse constraints

Restrictive plea bargaining policies may also represent pragmatic adaptations to the degree of cooperation and competition evidenced by other actors involved in the sentencing process. One of a prosecutor's most important advantages in plea negotiations is control over sentencing. While prosecutors can implicitly constrain the range of sentence severity through their charging decisions, of even greater value is the opportunity to recommend specific sentences following pleas and convictions. In many courts the sentence recommendation is the means by which a prosecutor communicates the terms of a plea agreement to a judge, so prosecutors who enjoy the cooperation of judges in sentencing have greater credibility and flexibility in plea negotiations.

Judges vary, however, in the extent to which they delegate their sentencing discretion to prosecutors, and not all passively acquiesce to prosecutors' recommendations. In many jurisdictions probation officers conduct pre-sentence investigations (PSIs) for all convicted defendants, and the reports submitted to judges typically include specific sentence recommendations. While these recommendations are not binding, they comprise an important cue for some judges. Unlike judges, defense lawyers, and law enforcement officials, probation officers have little incentive to develop reciprocity relationships with prosecutors, and therefore little incentive to incorporate prosecutorial preferences into their recommendations.[15] Judicial deference to PSI recommendations reduces prosecutors' ability to negotiate with confidence, a point not lost upon defense attorneys and their clients. Where judges are attentive to PSI recommendations, prosecutors' credibility in sentence bargaining is diminished.

Prosecutors' influence over sentencing varies directly, therefore, with the level of judicial receptivity to prosecutors' recommendations, and inversely with the level of judicial receptivity to probation office recommendations. Neither factor is within the control of prosecutors; rather, the degree of judicial cooperation and the presence of competition from probation officers are environmental constraints to which prosecutors must adapt. Prosecutors who find that judges routinely disregard their staffs' recommendations or frequently acquiesce to PSI recommendations may decide that there is little to lose, and perhaps something to gain, by a no-plea policy.

These circumstances appeared to explain the no-plea policy maintained by the district attorney in one of the jurisdictions included in this study. Interviews with a judge, several assistant prosecutors, and the public defender, supplemented by courtroom observations, revealed that although the prosecutor's staff routinely recommended stiff sentences upon entries of guilty pleas, judges routinely disregarded those recommendations in favor of those included in PSI reports. The assistant prosecutors explained that their chief's extremely restrictive plea bargaining policy was the result rather than the cause of judges' apparent indifference to their recommendations. Having learned early in his career that local judges saw the probation office as the legitimate source of sentencing advice, and frustrated in his efforts to establish credibility with the defense bar, the district attorney made the most of his predicament by realizing the political benefits of a widely publicized no-plea policy. This anecdotal evidence suggests a pair of hypotheses: where prosecutors' recommendations are seldom heeded by judges, and where PSI reports are routinely incorporated into sentencing decisions, chief prosecutors are more likely to impose restrictions on plea bargaining.

Community needs and expectations

Prosecutors' policies may be influenced not only by characteristics of the immediate courthouse environment, but by the perceived needs and expectations of the community as well. To an even greater extent than judges, prosecutors are local politicians. Their elections are more likely to be contested, and contested over matters of job performance, than are those of judges; and the job of a prosecutor, in the eyes of the public, is fighting crime. One way of demonstrating determination to "crack down" on crime is to refuse to negotiate with defendants, a policy that may be adopted for its symbolic value (as was the case with the district attorney discussed above), or for its expected impact on sentencing. However, because restrictive policies entail costs, in terms of efficiency and perhaps goodwill among court actors, such policies are worth implementing only when persecutors feel they are badly needed or that the public will observe and appreciate them. These conditions are most likely to prevail in communities with serious crime problems, communities whose citizens (and media) may be particularly attentive to officials' efforts to combat crime.

Of course, there are other ways of conceiving of prosecutorial responsiveness to the public. Many observers have noted the importance of conviction rate as a measure of individual and collective performance.[16] Conviction rates constitute simplistic but easily advertised indicators of success since they appear to measure prosecutors' ability to win cases. Guilty pleas are the easiest kind of conviction to obtain, of course, so a strong emphasis on maintaining a high conviction rate may be inversely related to policies that restrict or regulate plea bargaining; prosecutors concerned about maintaining high conviction rates may be less inclined to adopt policies that restrict their staff's ability to secure convictions.

Data and analysis

Data were gathered from several sources in the Georgia Superior Courts, the courts of original jurisdiction for felony prosecutions. Georgia is an appropriate site for this study for several reasons. Georgia's court system is representative of many states' systems in that its judges have stable assignments and considerable discretion in sentencing, and its prosecutors are elected to office for four-year terms and operate under few statutory restrictions on their discretion, including discretion to make plea bargains. Moreover, Georgia is economically, culturally, and politically diverse.[17]

Data for constructing the dependent and independent variables were drawn from surveys of all district attorneys, assistant district attorneys, and judges in the superior courts in the summer of 1986. The survey included items on court staffing and organization, perceptions of local adjudication practices and policies, and attitudes toward crime and criminal justice policy. The response rates on the surveys for judges, district attorneys, and assistant district attorneys were 69 percent, 60 percent, and 61 percent, respectively.[18] Data on circuit crime rates and caseload were compiled from archival sources. Complete data were available for 27 of the 45 circuits.

The dependent variable measures the presence of policies restricting plea bargaining. Jurisdictions in which district attorneys formally or informally restricted their assistants' discretion in plea bargaining were identified through prosecutors' responses to a question about the presence of formal or informal policies restricting or prohibiting plea bargaining. Despite the general nature of the question, there was complete agreement among prosecutors and their assistants within every circuit about whether or not such restrictions existed, suggesting that even informal policies are clearly communicated to office personnel.[19] These responses were used to create a dichotomous variable that distinguishes between circuits with no plea bargaining restrictions, and those with some form of restrictive policies. In 14 of the 27 jurisdictions district attorneys impose some limits on plea bargaining discretion.

A simple measure of district attorneys' attitudes about the function of the courts was derived from responses to an item that asked them to indicate, on a six-point scale anchored by the values of crime control (1) and due process (6), their placement of the proper function of the criminal courts. As one might expect, district attorneys as a group clustered closer to the crime-control end of the scale than did defense lawyers, judges, or assistant prosecutors. However, district attorneys are by no means unanimously committed to a crime-control orientation at the expense of due process concerns; the mean score was 2.8, and scores ranged from 1 to 6.

Measures of judges' receptivity to prosecutors' sentence recommendations, and of receptivity to the recommendations of probation officers,[20] as well as measures of the importance of high conviction rates within prosecutors' offices,[21] were derived from responses to survey items.[22] A measure of office caseload was constructed from the ratio of felony court filings to the number of attorneys working in the office. The magnitude of a circuit's crime problem was measured as the per capita rate of serious personal and property crimes reported

Table 1 Discriminant analysis of prosecutors' plea bargaining policies

Eigenvalue	.697*
Canonical correlation	.641
Group centroids:	
Restrictive plea policies	.834
Absence of restrictive policies	-.774
Function coefficients:	
Ratio of cases to staff	.165
Judges' receptivity to prosecutors' recommendations	-.459
Judges' receptivity to probation recommendations	.372
Crime rate	.637
Concern with maintaining high conviction rate	.560
Attitude toward crime control/due process tradeoff	.778

n=27
*significant at the .07 level

during the year preceding the survey.

Table 1 presents the results of a discriminant analysis of plea bargaining policy. Discriminant analysis estimates the effects of independent variables on a nominal or categorical dependent variable by deriving from the independent variables a function or set of functions that maximize discrimination among the groups defined by the dependent variable. The functions are generated such that separation between the groups is maximized, and discriminant scores for cases within each group are similar; group centroids are the points in multidimensional space that represent the mean values on the independent variables for cases within each of the categories defined by the dependent variable. The variables in the model discriminate moderately well between the two categories of the dependent variable, correctly classifying 81 percent of the cases, an improvement of 29 percent over the percentage that would be correctly classified by chance.

The functions can be interpreted through examination of the discriminant function coefficients (weights attached to the independent variables that describe their contributions to the function); interpretation of these coefficients is analogous to interpretation of the coefficients produced by ordinary least squares regression. Hence, variables that are positively associated with the function are positively associated with restrictive plea policies, and variables that are negatively associated with the function are negatively associated with restrictive plea policies. The magnitude of the coeffi-

cients indicates the relative strength of their contributions to the function.[23]

This analysis suggests that preferences between the conflicting values of crime control and due process, and the seriousness of crime problems, have important effects on the way prosecutors run their offices. Contrary to conventional wisdom that restrictive plea policies are manifestations of strong crime-control attitudes, the relationship between prosecutors' attitudes and plea bargaining policy indicates the opposite: greater emphasis on due process protections is strongly and positively associated with the restrictive rules. However, the relationship between plea policy and actual crime rate supports the hypothesis that restrictive rules are associated with serious crime problems.[24]

Of course, plea bargain restrictions may represent sincere efforts to battle serious crime problems, or symbolic reassurance to fearful citizens that such battles are being fought (or both). The data permit only a tentative exploration of these competing interpretations. The survey included two items regarding perceptions of crime: first, a question that asked chief prosecutors to evaluate the seriousness of their circuits' crime problems, compared with that of other areas in the state (less serious than average, about average, more serious than average, very serious); and second, a question that asked how they thought residents of their

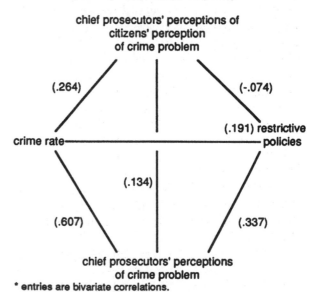

Figure 1
Crime rate, prosecutors perceptions, public perceptions, and policy*

chief prosecutors' perceptions of citizens' perception of crime problem

(.264)   (-.074)

(.191) restrictive

crime rate —————————————— policies

(.134)

(.607)   (.337)

chief prosecutors' perceptions of crime problem

* entries are bivariate correlations.

circuits perceived the local crime problem (same response set). The bivariate correlations among these variables, actual crime rate, and plea bargaining restrictions are presented in Figure 1. These relationships suggest that prosecutors do not believe that citizens accurately gauge the relative seriousness of their communities' crime problems, nor do they allow citizens' perceptions to affect their policy decisions; however, their own perceptions *are* relatively accurate, and they are correlated with policy choices. This offers some support for the interpretation that restrictive plea policies are reactions to actual crime problems, rather than symbolic responses to high levels of public fear. This interpretation is consistent with other research that suggests that the relationships between crime levels, fear of victimization, and decision patterns are weak.[25]

Prosecutors who emphasize the importance of maintaining high conviction rates are more, rather than less, likely to impose restrictions on plea bargaining, contrary to the hypothesized relationship. One possible explanation for this finding is that the observed relationship is spurious, in that plea bargaining restrictions and monitoring of conviction rates might both be manifestations of a close supervisory style, one that tightly constrains assistant prosecutors' professional discretion. However, the data offer no evidence for this explanation. Survey items on closeness of supervision, percent of district attorney's time spent in administrative tasks (rather than on litigation or public relations), and task technology (horizontal or vertical prosecution) were related to each other in predictable ways, but were related neither to emphasis on conviction rate nor to plea policies.[26]

However, these findings offer some support for an explanation of restrictive policies as adaptations to courthouse environments. As predicted, restrictive plea policies are associated with low levels of judicial receptivity to prosecutors' sentence recommendations, and they are associated with high levels of judicial receptivity to PSI recommendations. Finally, case pressure appears to have almost no effect on plea bargaining policies. This suggests that district attorneys do not relax the degree of discretion granted to assistants as a means of coping with heavy caseloads. It also highlights the importance of controlling for other factors when estimating the effects of resource constraints on policy decisions.

Discussion and conclusions

This analysis reinforces the observations of others that the values and motivations of prosecutors are not uniformly oriented toward controlling crime, and that furthermore, these values are reflected in the policies that govern prosecutors' offices.[27] The findings also indicate that high crime rates prompt restrictive policies, and suggest that prosecutors react to genuine crime problems, rather than to constituency perceptions. Furthermore, restrictive policies are associated with courthouse environments that give prosecutors few opportunities to gain the upper hand in plea negotiations through control of sentencing decisions; and while these observed associations are not strong, they are substantively significant. However, when the effects of potentially confounding factors are statistically controlled, caseload appears to have a negligible effect on plea bargaining policy. This does not mean, of course, that case pressure has no effect on plea bargaining rates; but these data offer no evidence that prosecutors' *policies* are constrained by resource limitations.

Of course, these findings must be interpreted carefully. The analysis is based on only 27 prosecutors from a single state. While the research design adopted here permits more systematic examination of hypotheses than can be achieved through case studies, the empirical results are more suggestive than conclusive. All the same, the findings are sufficiently provocative to justify recommendations for further study of prosecutorial policy making; they offer support for some predictions generated by previous research, but cast doubt upon others. More generally, these findings have implications for theoretical models of criminal adjudication, for our understanding of the values and role conceptions of prosecutors, and for future research on the structure and organization of prosecutors' offices.

Empirical work on criminal adjudication, departing from traditional judge-centered models of decision making, has increasingly stressed the importance of understanding personal relationships among court actors,[28] as well as formal and informal constraints imposed by actors' sponsoring organizations.[29] The results of this study offer further support for a growing consensus that courts should be studied as networks of interdependent organizations and actors, characterized by varying rather than uniform levels of cooperation and conflict.[30] The analysis presented here exploits this theoretical framework, examining chief prosecutors who, as administrators and politicians, must reconcile their policy choices with organizational and political constraints and obligations. These findings illustrate the significance of judicial co-operation, and suggest that by refusing to passively acquiesce to plea-bargained sentences (and perhaps by taking cues for sentencing decisions from an independent organization, the probation office), judges can potentially destabilize the system of bargained justice that characterizes prosecutor-dominated courthouses.

This analysis also offers some insight into the relationships between prosecutors' beliefs and behavior. Prosecutors, like law enforcement officials, are frequently stereotyped as punitive individuals motivated to maximize the number of criminals caught, convicted, and punished; but this unidimensional portrait does not square with empirical research that portrays the values and motives of prosecutors, like those of law enforcement officers, as complex and varied.[31] The strong relationship between appreciation for due process and restrictive plea bargaining policies suggests that, contrary to conventional wisdom, regulation of plea practices stems from a preference for adjudication processes that are not compromised by the temptation and coercion inherent in plea bargaining.

This apparently counter-intuitive relationship makes more sense, of course, if one remembers that an appreciation for due process protections does not preclude a preference for severe sentencing (indeed, a preference for harsh punishments is logically consistent with a desire to take every precaution to ensure that innocent defendants are not convicted)—or in other words, willingness to sacrifice due process protections in order to gain convictions may be accompanied by willingness to tolerate more lenient punishments if more offenders can thereby be punished. A strong crime-control orientation may manifest itself in practical efforts to maximize convictions, efforts which include permitting plea bargaining. This finding invites further research into the seldom-examined dimensions of prosecutors' value systems, and into prosecutors' uses of discretion in achieving desired policy objectives.

Finally, this study departs from most research on prosecutors by focusing on an important but often overlooked subject, policy decisions, and by modeling these decisions as expressions of fundamentally political choices. This analysis suggests that we should not only study prosecutors as lawyers, engaged in a series of individual case decisions, but we should also examine them as politicians, obliged to develop decision rules for their staff to follow. There are few formal constraints on prosecutors' discretion in making management decisions about recruitment and retention of personnel, resource allocation, division of labor, and case-processing practices, and therefore these decisions are open to the influence of courthouse and community politics, as well as personal values. This study only begins to explore the factors that influence these choices.

NOTES

This article originally appeared in Volume 73, Number 6, April-May 1990, pages 335-340.

The author gratefully acknowledges the research support of the American Judicature Society, the Earhart Foundation, and the Graduate School of the University of North Carolina; the assistance of Theresa Lynn Humphrey; and the advice of Robert E. Worden. The opinions and conclusions expressed in this paper are, of course, the sole responsibility of the author.

1. Albonetti, *Prosecutorial discretion: the effects of uncertainty,* 21 LAW & SOC'Y REV. 291 (1987); Gilboy, *Prosecutors' discretionary use of the grand jury to initiate or to reinitiate prosecution,* 9 AM. B. FOUND. RES. J. 1 (1984); Adams, *The effects of evidentiary factors on charge reduction,* 11 J. OF CRIM. JUST. 525 (1983); Mellon et al., *The prosecutor constrained by his environment: a new look at discretionary justice in the United States,* 72 J. OF CRIM. L. AND CRIMINOLOGY 52 (1981). Most of this research has concluded that screening and charging decisions are determined primarily by legally relevant and tactical considerations, such as strength of evidence and likelihood of conviction. However, other findings suggest that extra-legal factors, such as race and victim characteristics, influence these decisions. See Radelet and Pierce, *Race and prosecutorial discretion in homicide cases,* 10 LAW & SOC'Y REV. 587 (1985); Pruitt and Wilson, *A longitudinal study of the effect of race on sentencing,* 17 LAW & SOC'Y REV. 613 (1983); Stanko, *The impact of victim assessment on prosecutors' screening decisions: the case of the New York County District Attorney's Office,* 16 LAW & SOC'Y REV. 225 (1981-82); Myers and Hagan, *Private and public trouble: Prosecutors and the allocation of court resources,* 26 SOC. PROB. 439 (1979).

2. Cole, *The decision to prosecute,* 4 LAW & SOC'Y REV. 331 (1970); Carter, THE LIMITS OF ORDER (Lexington, MA: Lexington Books, 1974); Neubauer, *After the arrest: the charging decision in Prairie City,* 8 LAW & SOC'Y REV. 495 (1974).

3. Church, *Examining local legal culture,* 10 AM. B. FOUND. RES. J. 449 (1985); Eisenstein and Jacob, FELONY JUSTICE: AN ORGANIZATIONAL ANALYSIS OF CRIMINAL COURTS (Boston: Little Brown, 1977).

4. Scheingold and Gressett, *Policy, politics, and the criminal courts,* 12 AM. B. FOUND. RES. J. 461 (1987); Glick and Pruet, *Crime, public opinion, and trial courts: an analysis of sentencing policy,* 2 JUST. Q. 319 (1985); Jones, *Prosecutors and the disposition of criminal cases: an analysis of plea bargaining rates,* 69 J. of CRIM. L. AND CRIMINOLOGY 402 (1978).

5. Carter, *supra* n. 2; Neubauer, *supra* n. 2; Mellon et al., *supra* n. 1; Flemming, "The political styles and organizational strategies of American prosecutors: examples from nine courthouse communities," paper presented at the annual meeting of the Midwest Political Science Association, Chicago (1989).

6. Fleming, *id.*

7. Landes, *An economic analysis of the courts*, 14 J. OF L. AND ECON. 61 (1971); Weimer, *Vertical prosecution and career criminal bureaus; how many and who?*, 8 J. OF CRIM. JUST. 369 (1980); Reinganum, *Plea bargaining and prosecutorial discretion*, 78 AM. ECON. REV. 713 (1988).

8. Neubauer, *supra* n. 2.

9. Carter, *supra* n. 2.

10. Packer, THE LIMITS OF THE CRIMINAL SANCTION (Stanford: Stanford University Press, 1988).

11. Scheingold and Gressett, *supra* n. 4, at 466.

12. Alschuler, *Plea bargaining and its history*, 13 LAW & SOC'Y REV. 211 (1979); Friedman, *Plea bargaining in historical perspective*, 13 LAW & SOC'Y REV. 247 (1979).

13. Feeley, *The effects of heavy caseloads*, in Goldman and Sarat, editors, AMERICAN COURT SYSTEMS (San Francisco: W.H. Freeman, 1978).

14. It is also important to distinguish between plea bargaining policies and plea practices. One would expect to find that case pressure is more strongly associated with plea bargaining rates than with plea bargaining policies.

15. Kingnorth and Rizzo, *Decision making in the criminal courts: continuities and discontinuities*, 17 CRIMINOLOGY 3 (1979).

16. Alschuler, *The prosecutor's role in plea bargaining*, 26 U. CHI. L. REV. 50 (1968); Eisenstein and Jacob, *supra* n. 3; Myers and Hagan, *supra* n. 1.

17. Many of the most populous circuits in Georgia sharply contradict the stereotype of the rural, poverty-ridden, populist, and racially tense state. The metropolitan area of Atlanta alone comprises seven of the state's judicial circuits, several of which are solidly white, Republican, and economically but not socially conservative. Evidence of the state's political diversity can be found in the wide range of candidates who have successfully run for national office, a list that includes Newt Gingrich, Wyche Fowler, Sam Nunn, and Jimmy Carter. Moreover, the popular image of local politics in the South, which includes closely knit networks of long-time residents, holds only in some of the state's jurisdictions; 40 percent of the state's district attorneys, and 60 percent of the assistant district attorneys, were not born in Georgia.

18. This response rate compares favorably with those achieved by other scholars employing mail surveys; see Vetri, *Guilty plea bargaining; compromise by prosecutors to secure guilty pleas*, 112 U. PENN. L. REV. 865 (1964); Jones, *supra* n. 4; Flango et al., *The concept of judicial role: a methodological note*, 19 AM. J. OF POL. SCI. 277 (1978); Ryan and Alfini, *Trial judges' participation in plea bargaining: an empirical perspective*, 13 LAW & SOC'Y REV. 479 (1979); Meeker et al., *Perceptions about the poor, their legal needs, and legal services*, 9 LAW & POL. 143 (1987); Scheb, *State appellate judges' attitudes toward judicial merit selection and retention: results of a national survey*, 72 JUDICATURE 170 (1988); Hagan et al., *Class structure and legal practice: inequality and mobility among Toronto lawyers*, 22 LAW & SOC'Y REV. 9 (1988). The survey was sent to 127 judges, 45 prosecutors, and 124 assistant prosecutors, all identified through legal directories and court publications.

19. The validity of this measure is further established by the responses of defense attorneys to a similar survey question: lawyers in all circuits fully corroborate the reports of prosecutors.

20. Judges' receptivity to prosecutors' sentence recommendations is the product of responses to two items (and of judges' mean responses in multijudge circuits). The first question asked judges how often prosecutors in their courts made sentence recommendations and the second asked judges how often they accepted sentence recommendations when they were made. Both variables were coded as follows: 1=less than half the time; 2=about half the time; 3=most of the time; 4=always. Neither of these items would be a valid measure by itself, since the frequency with which prosecutors offer recommendations may be depressed in circuits where judges routinely disregard them. Judges' receptivity to probation officer recommendations was coded in a similar fashion.

21. All prosecutors were asked how important maintaining a high conviction rate was in their offices—not very important (=1), somewhat important (=2), or very important (=3). Prosecutors and their assistants tended to be in agreement on this item, and the variable for importance of office conviction rate is the mean value of DAs' and ADAs' intracircuit responses on this item.

22. While the operationalizations rely on perceptions of actors to measure practices and customs, actors' perceptions are sometimes the most reliable source of information not available in case files or through direct observation; see, for example, Nardulli et al., THE TENOR OF JUSTICE: CRIMINAL COURTS AND THE GUILTY PLEA PROCESS (Urbana: University of Illinois Press, 1988); Church, EXAMINING LOCAL LEGAL CULTURE: PRACTITIONER ATTITUDES IN FOUR CRIMINAL COURTS (Washington, D.C.: National Institute of Justice, 1982). Moreover, by averaging the responses of actors with potentially different customs (for the judicial receptivity variables), one gains a closer approximation of the situation confronted by the several prosecutors whose circuits contained more than one judgeship.

23. *See* Klecka, DISCRIMINANT ANALYSIS (Beverly Hills: Sage, 1980).

24. Furthermore, it is important to note that prosecutors' values on the crime control-due process scale are not associated with crime rates; the correlation between these variables is neither statistically nor substantively significant. The absence of a relationship between these two variables suggests (although certainly does not establish) that prosecutors' attitudes about the court's function are not shaped by the objective conditions in which they find themselves.

25. *See* Glick and Pruet, *supra* n. 4; Blumstein and Cohen, *Sentencing of convicted offenders: an analysis of the public's view*, 14 LAW & SOC'Y REV. 223 (1980). In this analysis, when the prosecutors' perception variable is substituted for crime rate in the discriminant analysis, the coefficients for all variables remain unchanged; the perception variable has a slightly larger coefficient than does crime rate, and the eigenvalue is slightly larger (1.06). The overall explanatory power of the model is not significantly increased.

26. An index measure of supervisory style was constructed from these related measures and was originally included in the analysis. This measure had no substantively significant effect on plea bargain policy, and its presence did not affect the coefficients for other variables included in the model. Since the index was not hypothesized to be *causally* related to plea bargaining policy, and because it had no effect when included as a control variable, it was dropped from the analysis presented here.

27. Fleming, *supra* n. 5; Scheingold and Gressett, *supra* n. 4; Neubauer, *supra* n. 2; Carter, *supra* n. 2.

28. Maynard, *The structure of discourse in misdemeanor plea bargaining*, 18 LAW & SOC'Y REV. 75 (1984); Nardulli et al., *Criminal courts and bureaucratic justice: concessions and consensus in the guilty plea process*, 76 J. OF CRIM. L. AND CRIMINOLOGY 1103 (1985).

29. Eisenstein et al., THE CONTOURS OF JUSTICE: COMMUNITIES AND THEIR COURTS (Boston: Little Brown, 1987); Myers and Talario, THE SOCIAL CONTEXTS OF CRIMINAL SENTENCING (New York: Springer-Erlag, 1987); Church, *supra* n. 3; Feeley and

Lazerson, *Policy-prosecutor relationships: an interorganizational perspective*, in Boyum and Mather, editors, EMPIRICAL THEORIES ABOUT COURTS (New York: Longman, 1983).

30. For additional documentation of the persistence of an adversarial culture under conditions that are typically thought to foster cooperation and compromise, see McIntyre, THE PUBLIC DEFENDER: THE PRACTICE OF LAW IN THE SHADOWS OF REPUTE (Chicago: University of Chicago Press, 1987).

31. Carter, *supra* n. 2; Neubauer, *supra* n. 2; see also Brown, WORKING THE STREET: POLICE DISCRETION AND THE DILEMMAS OF REFORM (New York: Russell Sage Foundation, 1981); Muir, POLICE: STREETCORNER POLITICIANS (Chicago: University of Chicago Press, 1977).

Twenty years of sentencing reform: steps forward, steps backward

by Michael Tonry

If a time machine were to transport a group of state and federal judges from 1970 to a national conference on sentencing in 1995, most would be astonished by a quarter century's changes. Many, perhaps all, would be disapproving.

Their astonishment would result from the number and enormity of the changes they would learn about. Sentencing, as they knew it, had not changed significantly for many years.[1] In 1970, every American state and the federal government had indeterminate sentencing systems, in which lawmakers enacted and amended the criminal code and set maximum penalties. A few jurisdictions had minimum penalties, which many judges disliked. These penalties generally required one- or two-year minimums except for murder, which carried a mandatory life sentence in some jurisdictions.

Subject only to statutory maximums and the occasional minimums, judges had the authority to sentence convicted defendants either to probation (and under what conditions) or to prison (and for what maximum term). Parole boards decided when prisoners were released. Usually, prisoners became eligible for release after serving a third of the maximum sentence, but they could be held until the maximum term expired. Prison managers typically were allowed to reduce sentences by awarding time off for good behavior.

In 1995, the time-traveling judges would learn that since the mid-1970s, the federal system and many states had rejected indeterminate sentencing and repealed much of its apparatus, often on tough-on-crime political grounds. More than 20 jurisdictions had adopted sentencing guidelines to limit judicial discretion, more than 15 had eliminated parole release, 20 had adopted parole guide-lines, most had narrowed time off for good behavior, and all had enacted mandatory minimum sentence legislation, which often included 10-, 20-, or 30-year minimum terms and life without possibility of parole.[2] Most recently, the judges would learn, Congress in 1994 authorized billions of federal dollars to states that abolish parole release, establish guidelines to constrain judicial sentencing discretion, and require abolition or narrowing of time off for good behavior.

There can be little doubt that the time-traveling judges would disapprove much of what they would find. Partly this can be attributed to parochialism. Human beings tend to prefer the familiar over the new and what we know over what we don't. Because the broad outlines of indeterminate sentencing had been the same everywhere since 1930, few judges at work in 1970 would have had experience working in any other system.

Some of their objections would, however, concern matters of principle and conceptions of justice that transcend parochialism. Rigid sentencing laws, including mandatory penalties, they would insist, create unacceptable risks of injustice because they make it impossible to take account of important differences among defendants. Laws that specify penalties for particular cases are unwise, they would argue, because legislators are far likelier than judges to be influenced by short-term emotions and concern for political advantage. Limits on judicial discretion are unsound, they would urge, because they shift discretion into the hands of prosecutors who will exercise it less judiciously than judges.

We can predict that these arguments would be made because many judges from the early 1970s to today have opposed sentencing reforms in these terms, and many judges (and nonjudges) still do. There is, however, one 1970s argument that is seldom heard today—that there is no need for substantial changes in sentencing because there is no convincing evidence that indeterminate sentencing was afflicted by unwarranted sentencing disparities or racial and gender bias. These arguments are seldom heard because the weight of the research evidence has become clear. Unwarranted disparities, explicable more in terms of the judge's personality, beliefs, and background than the offender's crime or criminal history, have repeatedly been demonstrated.[3] So has substantial gender disparity in indeterminate sentencing—in favor of women.[4] The evidence is unclear on the causes of racial disparities, but their existence is well-documented.[5]

State versus federal reforms

The overall impression the time-traveling judges would take back with them would probably be shaped by whether they learn first about federal or state sentencing reforms. If they were to study the changes brought about by the federal Sentencing Reform Act of 1984, they would return to 1970 determined to fight the first signs of the sentencing reform movement. But if they were to study the experiences of states like Delaware, Minnesota, Pennsylvania, Oregon, and Washington, they would be likely to go back apprehensive but with an understanding that meliorable injustices did exist under indeterminate sentencing that can be mitigated without creating larger injustices in their place.

For the time-traveling judges to be able to understand contemporary sentencing issues, they would need a briefing on developments since 1970. Here is what they would learn: Sentencing became a focus of criminal justice reform efforts in the mid-1970s, influenced by several contemporaneous developments. First, civil rights activists, concerned by what they perceived to be racial bias in sentencing and correctional administration, called for controls on the discretion of judges and other officials.[6] Second, research reviews by social scientists reported that little systematic empirical evidence showed that corrections programs successfully reduced recidivism, which undermined the rehabilitative foundation on which indeterminate sentencing stood.[7] Third, proceduralists throughout the legal system—who had been working to make le-

gal processes fairer and decision makers more accountable—argued that sentencing too should be subject to rules and review procedures.[8] And finally, political conservatives, concerned about a specter of "lenient judges," supported sentencing reforms as a way to set and enforce harsher sentencing standards.[9]

Most of these influences shaped an influential book, *Criminal Sentences: Law without Order*, by then-U.S. district judge Marvin Frankel.[10] On fairness grounds, he decried the absence of standards for the sentences federal judges set and the related absence of meaningful opportunities for sentence appeals. As a solution, Judge Frankel proposed creation of a specialized administrative agency, called a sentencing commission, that would develop guidelines for judges to use in making sentencing decisions. The guidelines would be presumptively applicable, and their application would be subject to appeal by aggrieved parties.

Judge Frankel's proposals were based partly on the concerns that influenced sentencing reform generally, but they were also shaped by appreciation of the institutional properties of administrative agencies and legislatures. Over time, agencies such as Judge Frankel's proposed commission develop specialized expertise that legislatures cannot match. Moreover, because commissioners are typically appointed for fixed terms and are ordinarily outside day-to-day political battles, such agencies can be somewhat insulated from emotionalism and short-term political pressures.

Judge Frankel's sentencing commission proposal became the most widely adopted vehicle for sentencing reform. In the 1970s, several states—most notably Minnesota and Pennsylvania—created sentencing commissions. Several others—including California, Illinois, and Indiana—replaced indeterminate sentencing with statutory determinate sentencing schemes, in which criminal codes specified specific prison terms for particular crimes.

The comparative merits of sentencing commissions soon became clear. Evaluations in Minnesota and Pennsylvania (and later in Oregon and Washington) showed that use of sentencing guidelines reduced disparities generally and lessened racial and gender disparities in particular. (Since the effect was to increase sentences for women, some might see this as a mixed blessing.)[11] In addition, many judges in those states came to favor guidelines for two reasons—guidelines provided a starting point for considering sentences, and judges recognized that guidelines reduced disparities. By contrast, the statutory determinate sentencing systems were shown to have had no significant effects on sentencing processes or outcomes.[12]

More importantly, experience confirmed Judge Frankel's ideas about administrative agencies. For instance, Minnesota's commission tied sentencing policy to available prison resources and managed to hold the prison population within capacity throughout the 1980s, while most states experienced record increases. Commissions in Oregon and Kansas and, for a time, Washington also helped insulate sentencing policy from political pressure. But in states like California, where fine-grained sentencing policies were left in legislative hands, statutory sentencing provisions were amended upwards nearly every year, and the prison population increased by 400 percent between 1980 and 1994.[13]

Success and disaster

By 1995, the success of Judge Frankel's innovation was clear. Twenty-two states have created commissions, guidelines are in effect in 17 of these states, and new commissions are at work in the other five.[14] No state adopted a statutory determinate sentencing scheme after the mid-1980s, and some that had, like Colorado, diluted its effects by reintroducing parole release.[15]

Because the federal commission had the prior experiences of the states to draw on, ample resources, and the capacity to recruit staff from throughout the country, all of the auguries would have predicted that the U.S. Sentencing Commission would build on the state experiences and produce the most successful guidelines system to date.

The Sentencing Reform Act of 1984 abolished parole release prospectively and directed the newly created sentencing commission to develop guidelines for federal sentencing. Few outside the federal commission would disagree that the federal guidelines have been a disaster. The highly detailed guidelines divide crimes into 43 different categories, and the rules governing their application are highly mechanistic. The commission has forbidden judges to take account in sentencing of many factors—such as the effect of the sentence on the defendant or his family, or the defendant's mental health or drug or alcohol dependence, or a severely deprived background or victimization by

sexual abuse—that many judges believe to be ethically relevant to sentencing. The guidelines are based not on the offense of which the defendant was convicted, but his "actual offense behavior" including alleged crimes of which he was acquitted or never charged. The guidelines allow virtually no role for non-imprisonment sentences.[16]

For all these reasons, the federal guidelines are deeply disliked by most federal judges and lawyers who practice in federal courts, and they are widely circumvented.[17] In addition, a majority of federal judges surveyed in 1991 said they believe sentencing disparities were as bad or worse under the guidelines as before their adoption.[18] Even commission-sponsored research demonstrates that prosecutors and judges disingenuously circumvent the guidelines in a third of cases,[19] while the true rate is probably higher.

Staff of newly created state commissions report that negative stereotypes created by the federal guidelines have been a major obstacle to their work. Commissions in Texas, Ohio, and North Carolina recently adopted resolutions repudiating the federal guidelines as a model for any policies they might later develop. Both the North Carolina commission and the American Bar Association's sentencing standards project (which proposed that states create sentencing commissions) avoided use of the word "guidelines" because of the negative connotations associated with the federal guidelines.[20]

No one factor can explain why the federal guidelines have been so much less successful than state guidelines. Some judges use words like arrogant and hostile to describe the commission's attitude to the federal judiciary. Some observers argue that the failure was in management: With all of its resources, a better-managed commission that consulted more widely and made efforts to learn from the state experiences could have done better. Others note that only two of the initial commissioners had ever imposed a sentence (one of them 30 years earlier), and three were full-time academics. Still others point out that a number of the initial commissioners were long known to be aspirants for higher judicial office and suggest that the guidelines were an effort to show that the commission's policies were consonant with the views of influential congressional conservatives.

No doubt there is truth in all these explanations. The primary explanation, however, is a structural

one: The federal sentencing commission legislation was formulated and agreed on in one political era, in which Judge Frankel's ideas and goals
were widely shared. However, they were implemented in a different political era, in which
Judge Frankel's ideas had little weight.

The first commission legislation, introduced in
Congress in 1974, was a direct outgrowth of a Yale
Law School seminar that attempted to convert
Judge Frankel's general proposal into proposed
legislation.[21] After reintroduction in successive
Congresses as a stand-alone bill, the proposal was
folded into then-pending federal criminal code
bills. By 1979, Senators Edward Kennedy and Strom
Thurmond, the ranking Democratic and Republican members of the Senate Judiciary Committee
(who succeeded one another as chairs), agreed to
support the legislation, which the Senate went on
to approve overwhelmingly. Although the House
of Representatives did not act that year, the Senate agreement held. The bill including the sentencing commission sections repeatedly thereafter passed both the Senate Judiciary Committee
and the full Senate by wide margins.

Eventually, the proposed criminal code was
abandoned as unpassable, but the less controversial commission sections became part of an omnibus crime bill enacted in 1984. Unfortunately,
when this good-government, rationalistic proposal,
initially intended to make sentencing fairer and
to distance sentencing policy from politics, took
effect, the government in power did not hold those
goals.[22]

The crime-control policies of the Reagan administration in 1985, when the commissioners were
appointed, were oriented more toward toughness
than fairness. It should not therefore be a surprise
that many of the commissioners who were appointed did not share Judge Frankel's belief that
sentencing policy should be, to the extent possible,
insulated from partisan politics. Instead, influential commissioners demonstrated that they too
were tough on crime and had little sympathy for
"lenient" judges.[23] (This stereotype of judges is
odd, since a large percentage of federal district
judges by 1987, when the guidelines took effect,
were Reagan appointees—as today are a large percentage of the guidelines' fiercest critics).

Mixed results

So the picture the time-traveling judges would see

is mixed—federal guidelines that at least match
their worst preconceptions of what would happen
if indeterminate sentencing were abandoned, and
state guidelines that turned out much better than
they would have predicted.

This issue of *Judicature* could serve as a briefing
document for the judges from 1970. It demonstrates there is merit in most of their concerns and
that some good has been achieved in the shift from
indeterminate to determinate sentencing. Richard
Frase's article summarizes developments in the
states and provides information on guidelines activities in more than 20 jurisdictions. Marc Miller's
article demonstrates that the eight-year-old federal
sentencing guidelines remain deeply disliked and
offers suggestions for reform.

An article by Kevin and Curtis Reitz describes
the American Bar Association's effort in its sentencing standards project to learn from the combined state and federal experiences and to offer
guidance to states that have not yet overhauled
their sentencing laws. David Boerner's article
traces the evolution of policy and practice concerning prosecutorial powers under guidelines, and
concludes, with Frase, that there have been both
gains and losses. Saul Pilchen discusses the effects
of the "organizational guidelines," a version of the
federal guidelines that applies to sentences for corporations and other collective entities. Finally, a
transcript of an American Judicature Society panel
discussion offers the insights of state and federal
judges and academics regarding sentencing guidelines.

The conclusion the time-traveling judges would
most likely take back is that the judiciary itself must
listen to complaints about sentencing and work to
address them. Otherwise, other agencies of government will, with results ranging from tolerable
to awful.

NOTES

This article originally appeared in Volume 78, Number 4,
January-February 1995, pages 169-172.

This article is drawn from the author's book, SENTENCING
MATTERS, to be published by Oxford University Press later this
year.

1. Blumstein, Cohen, Martin, and Tonry, eds. RESEARCH ON
SENTENCING: THE SEARCH FOR REFORM, 2 vols. (Washington, D.C.:
National Academy Press, 1983), chap. 3.

2. Tonry, *Sentencing Commissions and Their Guidelines*, in
Tonry, ed., CRIME AND JUSTICE: A REVIEW OF RESEARCH, vol. 17,
(Chicago: University of Chicago Press, 1993).

3. *Supra* n. 1, at chap. 2.

4. Knapp, THE IMPACT OF THE MINNESOTA SENTENCING GUIDE-

LINES: THREE YEAR EVALUATION (St. Paul: Minnesota Sentencing Guidelines Commission, 1984).

5. Tonry, MALIGN NEGLECT: RACE, CRIME, AND PUNISHMENT IN AMERICA (New York: Oxford University Press, 1995).

6. American Friends Service Committee, STRUGGLE FOR JUSTICE: A REPORT ON CRIME AND PUNISHMENT IN AMERICA (New York: Hill & Wang, 1971).

7. Lipton, Martinson, and Wilks. THE EFFECTIVENESS OF CORRECTIONAL TREATMENT: A SURVEY OF TREATMENT EVALUATION STUDIES (New York: Praeger, 1975).

8. Davis, DISCRETIONARY JUSTICE: A PRELIMINARY INQUIRY (Baton Rouge: Louisiana State University Press, 1969).

9. Messinger and Johnson, *California's Determinate Sentencing Laws,* in DETERMINATE SENTENCING: REFORM OR REGRESSION (Washington, D.C.: U.S. Government Printing Office, 1978).

10. Frankel, CRIMINAL SENTENCES: LAW WITHOUT ORDER (New York: Hill & Wang, 1972).

11. *Supra* n. 2.

12. *Supra* n. 1.

13. Zimring and Hawkins, INCAPACITATION: PENAL CONFINEMENT AND THE RESTRAINT OF CRIME (New York: Oxford University Press, 1995).

14. *See* Frase, *Sentencing guidelines in the states: still going strong,* 78 JUDICATURE 173 (1995).

15. Wesson, *Sentencing Reform in Colorado: Many Changes, Little Progress,* 4 OVERCROWDED TIMES 14-17, 20 (1993).

16. U.S. Sentencing Commission, SENTENCING COMMISSION GUIDELINES MANUAL (St. Paul, Minn.: West Publishing, 1994).

17. U.S. SENTENCING COMMISSION, THE FEDERAL SENTENCING GUIDELINES: A REPORT ON THE OPERATION OF THE GUIDELINES SYSTEM AND SHORT-TERM IMPACTS ON DISPARITY IN SENTENCING, USE OF INCARCERATION, AND PROSECUTORIAL DISCRETION AND PLEA BARGAINING (Washington, D.C.: U.S. Sentencing Commission, 1991).

18. *Id.*

19. Nagel and Schulhofer, *A Tale of Three Cities: An Empirical Study of Charging and Bargaining Practices under the Federal Sentencing Guidelines,* 66 S. CAL. L. REV. 501-566 (1992).

20. Orland and Reitz, *Epilogue: A Gathering of State Sentencing Commissions,* 64 COL. L. REV. 837-845 (1993); Reitz and Reitz, *Building a sentencing reform agenda: the ABA's new sentencing standards,* 78 JUDICATURE 189 (1995).

21. O'Donnell, Curtis and Churgin, TOWARD A JUST AND EFFECTIVE SENTENCING SYSTEM (New York: Praeger, 1977).

22. Stith and Koh, *The Politics of Sentencing Reform: The Legislative History of the Federal Sentencing Guidelines,* 28 WAKE FOREST L.REV. 223-290 (1993).

23. *Id.*

'Three strikes and you're out': Are repeat offender laws having their anticipated effects?

by John Clark, James Austin, and D. Alan Henry

In recent years, a great deal of legislation has been passed at both the state and federal levels increasing penalties for criminal offenses, particularly violent crimes. These actions have come in response to public concerns about crime, and the belief that many serious offenders are released from prison too soon. Many such laws have come under the general label of "three strikes and you're out." The purpose of these laws is simple: offenders convicted repeatedly of serious offenses should be removed from society for long periods of time, in many cases for life.

For many years, most states have had provisions in their laws for enhanced sentencing for repeat offenders. Yet between 1993 and 1995, 24 states and the federal government enacted new laws using the "three strikes" moniker, with similarly labeled bills introduced in a number of other states.

Washington and California were the first states during this period to implement three-strikes laws. (South Dakota, which has had similar legislation since 1877, is one of several states that have had such laws on the books for many years.) As the proposals in Washington and California were being debated, concerns were raised about how they would affect the criminal justice system. It was argued that defendants facing very lengthy mandatory sentences would be more likely to demand trials, slowing down the processing of cases and adding to the problems of court delay and jail crowding—in effect creating an unfunded mandate for counties and cities. A longer-term concern was that as more and more offenders began serving more lengthy terms of incarceration, prison overcrowding, already at crisis levels in many states,

would also grow worse.

Have any of these concerns materialized?

Two models

Differing provisions. Even though the Washington and California laws were enacted within months of one another using the same "three strikes and you're out" rallying cry and include many of the same offenses as strikes, they are very different. The Washington law, which took effect in December 1993 through a voter initiative that passed by a 3-1 margin, requires a life term in prison without the possibility of parole for a person convicted for the third time of any of a number of statutorily-listed "most serious offenses."

The California law, signed by the governor in March 1994 and later ratified by voters in a state referendum, differs from Washington's law in three important ways. First, in Washington, all three strikes must be for felonies specifically listed in the legislation. Under the California law, only the first two convictions need be from the state's list of "strikeable" offenses—any subsequent felony can count as the third strike. Second, the California law contains a two-strike feature in which people convicted of any felony who have one prior conviction for a strikeable offense are to be sentenced to twice the term they would otherwise receive. Third, the sanctions for a third strike differ. Unlike in Washington, a "third striker" has at least the possibility of eventually being released in California, albeit after serving a minimum imprisonment of 25 years. (The Washington law does contain a provision retaining the governor's authority to grant a pardon or clemency, but it also recommends that no person sentenced under this law to life in prison without parole be granted clemency until the offender has reached 60 years of age and is judged to be no longer a threat to society.)

Impact on local courts and jails. Because of these differences, when the three-strike laws were initially implemented in Washington and California, it was projected there would be a much greater impact on the local criminal justice system in California than in Washington, due to the much broader scope of the California law. It was predicted that California courts would become overwhelmed as defendants facing enhanced penalties would demand jury trials. The added time to process cases through trial, and the reluctance to release before trial defendants who were facing long prison terms, would cause jail populations to explode as the number of admissions and length of stay in jail would grow.

Early evidence from California indicated these predictions were proving correct. For example, a 1995 review of 12,600 two- and three-strike cases from Los Angeles showed that two-strike cases remained pending in court 16 percent longer and three-strike cases 41 percent longer than nonstrike cases. In addition, the Countywide Criminal Justice Coordination Committee found that strike cases were three times more likely to go to trial than nonstrike felonies, and four times more likely than the same type of case before the law took effect. This led to a 25 percent increase in jury trials and a rise in the proportion of the jail population held in pretrial status from 59 percent before the law was enacted to 70 percent. Furthermore, a report published in 1995 by the State Sheriffs' Association showed the pretrial detainee population to be growing statewide, from 51 percent of the average daily population before three strikes to 61 percent by January 1995.

However, at least some counties in the state are learning to absorb the increases brought about by the law. A Center for Urban Analysis survey of eight counties with populations of more than 1 million identified several counties that have been successful in disposing of two- and three-strike cases early in the process. Also, under a new pilot delay reduction program in one of Los Angeles County's Superior Court districts, implemented as a result of the added burdens the three-strikes law imposed on the court, the pending caseload of criminal cases has been reduced by nearly half.

In addition, the most recent data from the Los Angeles sheriff's department suggests that the pace of strike cases coming into that system may be slowing. The number of two-strike cases filed by the Los Angeles district attorney from 1995 to 1996 declined by 15 percent. Likewise, there was a 28 percent decline between the two periods in the number of third-strike cases filed. However, the sheriff's department reports that it is too early to say whether these findings indicate a trend, and if there is any possible cause.

Impact on state prison systems. The impact of these laws on state corrections has not been as severe as projected in either Washington or California. Planners in Washington had expected that each year between 40 and 75 people would fall under three-strike provisions. Even this low projection has not been met. In a 3 $\frac{1}{2}$ year period after the law took effect in December 1993, only 85 offenders—as compared to the 120-225 that had been projected—had been admitted to the Washington prison system under its three-strikes law, according to the state Department of Corrections.

A similar overestimate has been made on the California law's impact on its prison system. As of December 31, 1996, 26,000 offenders had been admitted to the California Department of Corrections for either a two- or three-strikes sentence. Of this number, nearly 90 percent were sentenced under the two-strikes provision. Although the sheer number of cases affected by the law is significantly higher than for any other state, the numbers are not as great as originally projected. Consequently, the department recently lowered its 5-year projection by nearly 40,000 inmates, principally because there have not been as many two-strikes admissions as expected and because judges have modified their sentencing practices for the two-strikes cases. The Department of Corrections had incorrectly estimated that judges would choose longer sentences within the ranges provided by the law.

One recent development that might further reduce inmate projections is a 1996 California Supreme Court ruling, *People v. Superior Court (Romero)*, that allows judicial discretion in applying the law. This ruling may further limit the use of the statute and create a major logjam of appeals for the now nearly 20,000 inmates sentenced under the law who may be eligible for resentencing.

Variations among states

"Three strikes and you're out" can mean dramatically different things in different states. A review of the provisions of all the states that have enacted this type of legislation reveals differences in how a "strike" is defined, how many strikes are required to be "out," and what it means to be "out."

"Strike zone" defined. In keeping with the baseball analogy, the strike zone—what constitutes a strike and under what conditions—varies from state to state. There are some constants—violent felonies such as murder, rape, robbery, arson, aggravated assault, and carjacking are typically included as strike offenses in such legislation. But states have included other charges, such as:

- In Indiana—the sale of drugs.
- In Louisiana—any drug offense punishable by imprisonment for more than five years.
- In California—the sale of drugs to minors.
- In Florida—escape.
- In Washington—treason.
- In South Carolina—embezzlement and bribery.

At least two states define strikeable offenses based on the prior charge and the sentence imposed. Maryland and Tennessee both require that a sentence of incarceration must have been imposed in order for listed offenses to qualify as strikes.

Some states have even defined different levels of strikeable offenses. For example, in Georgia, a second conviction for a defined violent felony mandates a sentence of life without parole, while a fourth felony conviction of any kind requires that the maximum sentence allowable for the charge be imposed.

Number of strikes for an "out." There are also variations in the number of strikes needed to be "out." In South Carolina, a person convicted a second time for any of a list of "most serious offenses" is sentenced to life without parole. There is no third strike.

Three strikes are required to be "out" in 20 states, but seven of them—Arkansas, California, Connecticut, Kansas, Pennsylvania, Montana, and Tennessee—also have enhanced sentences for two strikes in their laws, depending on the offense.

What it means to be "out." Finally, states differ as to what sanction will be imposed when sufficient strikes have accumulated. A mandatory life sentence with no possibility of parole is imposed when

"out" in Georgia, Indiana, Louisiana, Maryland, Montana, New Jersey, North Carolina, South Carolina, Tennessee, Virginia, Washington, and Wisconsin. In three states, parole is possible after an offender is out, but only after a significant period of incarceration. In New Mexico, such offenders are not eligible for parole until after serving 30 years, while those in Colorado must serve 40 years before parole can be considered. In California, a minimum of 25 years must be served before parole eligibility.

Most three-strikes laws involve minimum mandatory sentences. Four states—Connecticut, Kansas, Arkansas, and Nevada—have recently enacted laws enhancing the possible penalties for multiple convictions for specified serious felonies, leaving the actual sentence to the discretion of the court.

In Connecticut, judges can sentence an offender to life in prison for the third conviction for any of a group of serious felonies, and to 40 years in prison for the second such conviction. In Kansas, legislatively enacted sentencing guidelines provide a range based on the offense and the offender's prior record from which the judge is to choose in sentencing. A recent amendment allows judges to double the sentences on the guidelines for offenders convicted for the second and third time for certain listed violent felonies.

In Arkansas, a judge may choose either a mandatory sentence short of life imprisonment for a second or third strikeable offense, or a life sentence. Similar provisions exist in the Nevada law, which gives the judge the option on a third strike conviction of imposing a life sentence without parole, a life sentence with parole possible after 10 years, or a 25-year sentence with parole possible after 10 years.

Five states—Florida, North Dakota, Pennsylvania, Utah, and Vermont—provide ranges of sentences for repeat offenders that can extend up to life when certain violent offenses are involved.

Pre-existing provisions

To accurately describe the impact of three strike-type laws on a state's justice and corrections systems, one must first consider how each state was equipped to respond to repeat violent offenders *prior to* the enactment of three strikes. Did the new legislation successfully close a loophole in the state's criminal sanctioning authority as hoped, or was the new law in effect targeting a population already covered by existing laws?

As it turns out, all but one of the 24 three-strikes states provided for enhanced penalties for repeat offenders before the passage of the latest three-strike legislation. (Kansas is the only exception.) In Louisiana, Maryland, South Carolina, and Tennessee, the mandatory penalty for a person found to be a repeat violent offender—life in prison without the possibility of parole—already existed and remained unchanged, but the definition of such an offender was expanded under the new legislation.

Preexisting law in Louisiana mandated life in prison without parole for the third conviction for certain violent and drug felonies. It also required life imprisonment with no parole for any fourth or subsequent felony conviction if at least two of the felonies were among the listed violent or drug offenses. The three-strikes provisions were not changed, but the four-strikes provisions now require a sentence of life without parole if any of the four felonies are on the list of violent or drug felonies.

South Carolina, which since 1976 had a law mandating life imprisonment without parole upon the third conviction for a violent felony, simply reduced the number of such convictions needed to two.

Tennessee likewise had a preexisting three-strikes law with a penalty of life imprisonment without parole. Amendments to this law in 1994 and 1995 expanded the number of charges that qualify for a three-strikes sentence and added a new two-strikes category for the most serious violent offenses.

Maryland added carjacking and armed carjacking to a preexisting law that mandates a term of life in prison without parole on the fourth conviction for a listed crime of violence, if separate prison terms have been served for the first three such convictions.

The definition of a repeat offender was expanded in Vermont and North Dakota, with the penalties remaining the same. In Vermont, which had allowed a court to sentence an offender convicted for the fourth time for *any* felony to up to life in prison, a new law allows for a life sentence upon the third conviction for a listed violent offense while retaining the fourth conviction provision for any felony. Under pre-existing law, an offender in North Dakota would receive an enhanced

sentence upon the second conviction for Class A or B offenses. The new law expands that statute to include Class C offenders.

In at least one state the definition of a repeat violent offender remained essentially the same (third conviction for a violent offense), but the punishment was enhanced. Virginia moved from providing no parole eligibility for those convicted of three separate violent felonies, regardless of the sentence, to mandating life sentences with no parole eligibility for this group.

Several states supplemented existing habitual offender laws that targeted repeat offenses for *any* felony with new laws that focused on violent felonies. For instance, preexisting Colorado law requires a tripling of the presumptive sentence for people convicted for the third time within a 10-year period of any Class 1, 2, 3, 4, or 5 felony. The new three-strikes law, which mandates a life sentence with no parole eligibility for 40 years for a third conviction for a violent offense, does not contain the 10-year time period of the preexisting law.

In some states, the changes involved both expanding the definitions of repeat violent offenders and enhancing the sentences. For instance, preexisting Pennsylvania law mandated an extended prison term of five years for the second or subsequent conviction for certain specified crimes of violence. The new law expanded the list of violent offenses and amended the extended mandatory minimum prison term from five to 10 years.

Other states had had habitual offender laws that allowed for enhanced sentences, but such sentences were not mandatory. For instance, previous Florida law allowed the court to sentence habitual violent felony offenders to extended prison terms, including up to life in certain instances. The recent law created a new category of "violent career criminal," which establishes mandatory sentences ranging from 10 to 15 years for a third-degree felony, 30 to 40 years for a second-degree felony, and life imprisonment for a first-degree felony. And until New Jersey enacted a law in 1995 mandating life in prison without parole for a third conviction for certain violent offenses, it was left to the discretion of the sentencing judge to determine if the third conviction for a first-, second-, or third-degree felony merited an extended term of imprisonment.

Since many of the new strikes laws target offenders who already would have received lengthy prison terms under existing repeat offender statutes, it is not likely that these laws will have a significant impact on the courts, jails, or prison systems in those states. However, even though the actual number of cases in these states is expected to be small, it is too early to determine more specifically the impact because the laws have not been in place very long, and serious cases, by their nature, take longer to reach disposition.

Conclusion

"Three strikes and you're out" as a typology for criminal justice sanctioning is not easily defined. No common definitions exist for the terms "three," "strike," or "out" across the states. However, certain factors are associated with all of the three-strikes laws passed in the 24 states. The first is the authorization—or in some instances, mandate—for longer periods of incarceration for those convicted of violent crimes. Other similarities include the following:

• Except for Kansas, all of the states that enacted strikes laws had preexisting statutes that targeted repeat violent offenders; the breadth of those earlier statutes will largely determine the effect of the new laws in each state.

• All of the statutes either increase the period of incarceration for violent crime, expand the number of crimes that are included in the violent crime category, or both. In some instances the period of incarceration has simply been changed from a range available to the sentencing judge for a particular crime to a fixed, mandated number of years.

• In the majority of states, the new legislation has reduced judicial sentencing discretion. This appears to continue the recent trend of legislatures imposing more discrete limitations on judges' decisions, as evidenced by the expansion of mandatory minimum sentence legislation and sentencing guidelines.

The rapid expansion of three-strikes laws, regardless of how they are defined, reflects the perception that existing laws did not adequately protect public safety in their application or outcome, that exceptional incidents had occurred that the new laws would address, or that the intent of current laws was being frustrated by other factors, such as prison crowding. It is unclear whether these perceptions were accurate and what impact the new laws will have.

Early evidence, however, suggests that most of these laws will have minimal effects on their respective state prison systems. States have drafted these laws so that they would be applied to only the most violent repeat offenders. In most states, these offenders were already receiving lengthy prison terms under existing statutes. Only broadly defined two-strikes provisions such as California's have the potential to radically alter existing sentencing practices. Even in that state, judicial interpretations of the law—recently supported by a state supreme court decision—as well as prosecutorial discretion in how the law is applied may blunt the anticipated increases.

Follow-up research will continue to track in detail the effect of three-strikes laws on each stage of the criminal justice process (including bail setting, detention, time to trial, type of trial, plea negotiations, and the jail and prison population levels, as well as the budget ramifications of any changes that have taken place. The following questions need to be addressed to learn more about this sentencing reform effort and its impact:

• Is there a measurable effect on crime in any of the states where such a law was passed? Do these trends differ from states that have not adopted such laws?

• What factors differentiate states that have not adopted three strikes legislation from those that have?

• To what extent are the laws modified by practice or new legislation?

• To what extent are there variations in the application of the laws, both between and within the courts and counties?

• To what extent does the differential application of the law affect inmate behavior within the prison and jail systems?

• What features of two- and three-strikes laws are associated with compliance (or lack of compliance) with the laws' provisions by prosecutors and judges?

• What impact have these sentencing reforms had on public perceptions of the criminal justice system and its ability to incapacitate dangerous offenders?

• Based on the early experiences of California and Washington state, what lessons can be learned about projecting the effect of sentencing reforms on the courts, corrections, and crime?

NOTES

This article originally appeared in Volume 81, Number 4, January-February 1998, pages 144-149.

This article is adapted from Clark, Austin, and Henry, *Three Strikes and You're Out: A Review of State Legislation*, NIJ RESEARCH IN BRIEF, September 1997. The project was supported by contract 95-IJ-CX-0026 awarded to the National Council on Crime and Delinquency by the National Institute of Justice. Findings and conclusions are those of the authors and do not represent the official position or policies of the U.S. Department of Justice.

Race and crime: what evidence is there that race influences results in the criminal justice system?

by Norval Morris

I would like to talk about a topic that I find important, yet not much talked about. There is a problem in discussing this topic, and indeed many topics; nowadays, you can't finish framing the question before someone is giving you the answer. That disease is particularly prevalent among my colleagues who study economics and law combined, but I find it increasingly infects lawyers generally and even those people who are referred to as intelligent laymen. As a result, I have turned to fiction. The advantage of fiction is that you can be transported from contemporary society with its knee-jerk reactions to every serious problem; in fiction, you can at least have some hope of framing the question before you get the answer.

Come with me and escape the necessity to avoid talking seriously and quietly about blacks and crime in America. With a teletransporter, we can go to another country and another time to see what conclusions we can draw about that country; what facts we know and what conclusions we might be able to draw from those facts. I've done a lot of work over the years in trying to gather those facts about that country. So let me tell you about that country—not the United States—though it bears a striking resemblance to it. So, "Beam us up, Scottie."

In proportion to the distribution of blacks and whites in that society, let me give you five facts: First, for every one white male in prison, more than seven blacks are in prison. That discrepancy has grown larger, not smaller, over the last 30 years. In 1933, blacks made up less than a quarter of the prison population; now they are nearly a half. Second, although on this "fact" there is some slight doubt, of every 12 black males in their 20s, 1 in

every 12 is in prison or jail. That's a fantastic figure. (The Bureau of Justice Statistics says it's not quite that bad, that it's 1 in 15, but I think they are wrong.) The third fact: Of all black babies born in that distant society today, 1 in 30 will die a victim of intentional or non-negligent homicide. Among black males and females, ages 15 to 44, the leading cause of death is homicide.

Let me give you the fourth fact—a little more encouraging about race and crime and a bit more complicated—a fact that has not been publicized much; blacks are not more likely than whites to be persistent offenders. The return to prison rates differ very little, if at all, between blacks and whites of those in prison, first time, second time, etc. The differential in prison populations between blacks and whites is accounted for by the patterns of first-time criminality within each racial group, rather than by any difference in the patterns of continuing criminality. So the great difference is the function of the percentage of those who commit first-time crimes, not of any unique persistence in crime. That is not an unimportant point.

There is a current belief among people in my trade, interested in sentencing reform, that sentencing should be based in part on incapacitation, on taking high-rate offenders out of circulation, and that we should prolong and adjust sentences according to the threat that the individual prisoner presents. We are good at increasing sentences, but not so good at the reduction. Because blacks are not disproportionately likely to be persistent criminals, sentencing policies that target persistent offenders will not further disadvantage them.

The final, fifth fact about this strange country

that I ask you to survey today is that in recent years an increasing number of blacks have moved into the middle class from the underclass, leaving the destroyed inner-city neighborhoods with their astronomical crime rates to those left behind. The crime and delinquency rates of incarceration, and rates of arrest and of victimization of those who move away from these slums, are indistinguishable from whites of the same social class. So much for genetic explanations! That doesn't mean that all human behavior doesn't have a genetic trace, it's all a question of degrees of influence, but that the genes of the blacks play a large part in crime is balderdash.

Professional vs. citizen obligations

So, crime in this country we are visiting, just as in the United States, comes from intense pockets of criminality to be found in the destroyed neighborhoods of the inner-city. Street crime is overwhelmingly intra-racial; it is not inter-racial. On average, the profiles of the criminals and the victim are very similar. In Chicago in the 1970s, for example, 98 percent of black homicides were committed by other blacks with their ages and social circumstances tending to match. For black males, that mystical country to which we've transported ourselves may not be the land of the free, but it is certainly the home of the brave!

The overwhelming question is this: "Are these racial skewings, in that country, in large part a product of social prejudice, discrimination conscious or unconscious, among the police, the prosecutors, the courts and the correctional agencies of that country, or are they a product of other forces over which those agents of the criminal justice system have little professional control? It's not an unimportant question. Max Weber made the nice distinction between one's obligation professionally and one's obligation as a citizen. If there is substantial racial discriminatory skewing within our system, then the obligations on us as lawyers to do something about it is a very obvious professional duty. If the criminal justice system is less to blame, being merely a barometer of a serious social problem, there may be citizen obligations of high order but they don't happen to be professional obligations.

It's no good going to the legal scholars of this country to answer this question—they don't deal with it, they don't write about it, and they don't discuss it publicly. The first serious legal work on this question seems to me to have been published very recently—on May 19, 1988. The *Harvard Law Review* published a 200-hundred page developments in the law piece in that issue which, if this topic interests you, you really should read. It's a very well done piece, looking at race in the criminal process. They actually reach rather more extreme conclusions than I will be offering.

Crime reports

So far I have been looking at prison rates in that far country; the ultimate question of discrimination, of course, is whether blacks are imprisoned unfairly in relation to the amount of crime they commit. If you look at the uniform crime reports and the national crime surveys, but particularly the uniform crime reports concerning crimes that are divided into index crimes and other crimes (index crimes are the more serious felonies including homicide, robbery, rape and aggravated assault; others are less serious crimes); the arrest ratio of blacks to whites for index crimes is about 3.6 to 1; for other crimes the ratio is about 2 to 1. But, of course, the prison differential is about 7 to 1. I tried to break those data down into particular crimes and I tried to find a crime in which whites outnumbered blacks proportionately. I thought embezzlement would be right, but it isn't so; I'm afraid the blacks are 2.3 times as frequently arrested as the whites for embezzlement. I couldn't understand that and then I thought about what embezzlement was—it's often a very small purloining of money by a person in a relatively low position of economic trust. The only crime where there was a clear crime report differential adverse to whites was drunk driving, where whites are 1.46 times as likely to be involved in drunk driving as blacks.

There are undoubtedly crimes that whites commit more than blacks, such as insider trading, security fraud, and environmental pollution, but arrest rates don't tell us very much at all about those overwhelmingly white crimes. Many crimes aren't reported to the police and most of those that are reported don't result in arrest. In the inner city, where crimes are highest, a much lower proportion of street crime is reported to the police than is reported in more privileged areas. What we need to know in answer to the question we are addressing is whether there is racial discrimination within the justice system in the differential rates of black and white involvement in crime, as distinct from arrest for crime.

National crime surveys give us some insight into this. There is in every instance some increment of black adversity in the processes that follow commission and arrest for crimes, but nothing like the 7 to 1 differential that is to be found in prison. The starkest prejudice in our system is to be found in the death penalty. Forty-two percent of the occupants of death row are black and the evidence that racial stereotypes influence the death penalty is powerful. The frequency of exercise of prosecutorial discretion in Georgia adverse to blacks is extraordinary. In matched cases, the prosecutors sought the death penalty in 70 percent of the cases where there was a black killer and a white victim. The same prosecutor sought it in 15 percent of the cases when there was a white killer and a black victim, holding constant the gravity of the crime and 200 other matching factors.

To my astonishment, the Supreme Court managed to look at that differential of between 70 percent and 15 percent and concluded that it does not rise to the level of being constitutionally objectionable—the McCleskey case is simply a miscarriage of justice, irreconcilable with the rest of the jurisprudence of racial discrimination. It's a scandal and will be seen as such, I'm convinced.

Prejudice in the system

What is one left with? One is left with a situation where some areas seem clear of prejudice within our system and others where the prejudice does not seem to be easily measured, but there is some.

Let me pose four questions arising from this overview of the data and give brief answers to them. Does the criminal justice system discriminate unfairly against blacks at arrest, convictions, and at punishment? Is the death penalty applied unfairly to black killers and yet insufficiently to protect black victims? Do the police disproportionately use deadly force against suspected black felons? If there is injustice in all this, what are the remedies? Justice Harry Blackmun put the point beautifully, and it's an important point: "In order to get beyond racism, we must first take account of race, there is no other way. In order to treat some persons equally, we must treat them differently." Nobody can look responsibly at these data and not agree with that approach.

Well, does the criminal justice system discriminate against blacks in arrest, conviction, and at punishment? The *Harvard Law Review* suggests quite strongly that it does. What I would conclude is that there is a fairly strong case of more vulnerability of the black in relation to the police and prosecution and in plea bargaining, and at the punishment stage. The studies of Dean Alfred Blumstein of Carnegie-Mellon and of Joan Petersilia of the RAND Corporation conclude that about 80 percent of the black over-representation in prison can be explained by differential involvement in crime and about 20 percent by subsequent racially discriminatory processes.

That's probably fair. I think it is as much knowledge as we have. So the answer to the first question is: there appears to be measurable skewing on account of race in the criminal justice system but that skewing is not nearly as dramatic as the figures of differential imprisonment would suggest. That is not at all to say that racial discrimination within the criminal justice system is unimportant; it certainly is important. What is suggested is only that it is relatively less important than other discriminatory pressures.

Now, the second question: is the death penalty applied unfairly to blacks who kill? I won't re-hash the cases and studies on this since I do not think that there is much doubt that the answer to that question is "yes." Why is that important?—after all, capital punishment is largely symbolic. It has no effect on the crime rate generally and it seems to be reasonably well established that it doesn't have much effect on any rates of homicide or attempted homicide, so, why worry? Because it is a centrally important symbol.

Now suppose I am wrong about the death penalty, suppose it is an effective deterrent. Suppose that, as some proponents of that punishment implausibly argue, for every one execution seven or eight lives of potential victims are saved. If that is so, then the *McCleskey* case exhibits something worse than what I've said. If you believe in capital punishment then you must conclude that we are failing to protect black victims—you must, there is no way out of it. So, whatever you believe about capital punishment, whether you approve of it or reject it, the discriminatory effect is profound.

So to question three: Do the police disproportionately use deadly force against black felons? This is an important question because it leads to racial tensions and sometimes to racial riots. Police shoot at about 3,600 people in this country each year. Of these 3,600, about 600 are killed, about 1,200 are wounded and about 1,800 are missed entirely. (Anyone who knows anything about handguns knows that is fairly accurate shooting; the handgun, except at close quarters, is a very inaccurate weapon.)

Police officers in New Orleans are 10 times more likely to kill criminal suspects than police officers in Newark. New Orleans and Newark are both high crime rate areas. The general pattern is typical; Chicago is also fairly typical—70 percent of the civilians struck by police bullets in the five years that we collected data were black. An additional 20 percent were white and 10 percent Hispanic. Philadelphia, Los Angeles, New York have similar figures. The general pattern in most cities where these things have been studied is that minorities being shot by the police are approximately proportional to rates of minorities in street crime, but like earlier figures there is a slight added increment and all you can conclude is the data support what common observation and folk tales make very clear—there is an element of racial prejudice in police shooting at minorities. The *Harvard Law Review* goes much farther than that, but I am content to assert the lesser proposition.

Remedies

Now to the final question. If what I have said about that country we are visiting is true, what are the remedies? First, police can do a lot more to protect the rights of potential victims in a non-discriminatory manner. Some police forces are beginning to do so. The key is to break from the tyranny of the 911-reporting system which disrupts the proper allocation of police resources. Police resources are allocated in the United States by the telephone. There has to be a movement to community-based policing. Black communities have to be mobilized to collaborate with the police. The police have to stop seeing the city's high crime areas as if they were hostile territories. There are people in those areas greatly in need of protection. They can be mobilized and they can be helped. Mini-police stations can be created in inner-city ghettos. It's been demonstrated, it does work. It gives those who have to live there a sense of diminution of fear if not of a diminution of crime.

We need more resourceful police leadership.

This hasn't happened much but is happening in a small way. There is a core of younger able administrators coming forward in the police, but there remains a lack of effective leadership in the city police forces. Cities focus on the number of officers in the field and on the budgets, but both are largely irrelevant. They overlook inefficiency and the poor mobilization of resources. There are very many police officers in jobs that could be better done by civilians. We have to change the structure of policing to better protect minorities. There is nothing new in what I've said but the political effort of achieving change when there are no votes in it is challenging.

We have to do better to weed out discrimination in prosecution, plea bargaining and sentencing. The sentencing guideline system has as its greatest virtue the promise of a vehicle which can reduce the current demonstrable adversity to blacks in sentencing.

Changes in the criminal justice system won't do much about the problem of blacks in crime in America. The criminal justice system is a necessary, but limited, system. We've rarely been able to demonstrate any changes in crime rates by making marginal or even relatively substantial changes in policing or in correctional practice. We have got to make these changes because it is the proper thing to do; it's proper to try to diminish unjustified discrimination. But it's not going to make a big difference to the overall crime problem.

Thoughtful scholars now argue that black crime is the symptom, not the disease. The disease, says University of Chicago sociologist William Julius Wilson, the most thoughtful person writing in this field on this problem, is the increasing social isolation of an increasingly concentrated black underclass. University of Chicago political scientist Gary Orfield's study of the schools in Chicago indicates that the problems of the black underclass in the school system of Chicago has grown worse. In family situations today in America, 20 percent of all children are born to unwed mothers. Unwed mothers account for 15 percent of all white births, 60 percent of black births. In Illinois, 64 of each 100 births of black mothers are out of wedlock. I'm not making moralistic propositions, I am speaking of the problems of people being locked in, unable to escape from an inner city underclass. All I've done is underscore an excruciatingly difficult and worsening situation.

To try to sum up, if you look as closely as you can at these data, the bottom line conclusion is: Yes, there is measurable racial discrimination in our police practices, in our prosecutorial practices, in our plea bargaining practices, and in our sentencing, but the bulk of discrimination generating crime lies elsewhere.

I had written a conclusion but a couple of critics I shared these ideas with tell me that I shouldn't say it, since it might be offensive to some. So I have decided not to say it. But, just for your information, the rejected conclusion was: The whole law-and-order movement that we have heard so much about is, in operation though not in intent, antiblack and anti-underclass—not in plan, not in desire, not in intent, but in operation.

NOTE

This article originally appeared in Volume 72, Number 2, August-September 1988, pages 111-113.

The unanswered question: The impact of the Civil Justice Reform Act of 1990

*Research on the effects of the Civil Justice Reform Act of 1990
tells little about how to mitigate excessive cost or delay.*

by Steven Flanders

Based on premises that were mistaken or at least exaggerated, the Civil Justice Reform Act of 1990 incorporated a research strategy that was inherently flawed. Changes in judicial practice resulting from the federal legislation could be no more than marginal and thereby unlikely to have dramatic effects. But the sponsors and proponents of the act generated an overheated atmosphere that included the most massive and best-endowed research project the federal judiciary has ever seen. So potent a combination of grand intentions and poor prospects was sure to generate hype and exaggeration.

Senator Joseph Biden of Delaware, then-chair of the Senate Judiciary Committee, introduced what became the Civil Justice Reform Act following decades of steady efforts by policy bodies, judges, and lawyers to realize the promise of Rule 1, Federal Rules of Civil Procedure: "...to secure the just, speedy, and inexpensive determination of every action." At least since the late 1950s, federal judges had been telling each other that the way to counter the ills of uncontrolled litigation was for judges to assert control early and sustain it. Nationwide training programs were founded on this principle, and these were incorporated into the training effort of the Federal Judicial Center following its establishment in 1967. Most recently, Civil Rule 16 had been modified in 1983, following a lengthy and searching process, to embody an explicit and mandated managerial role for the district judge in each civil case (unless excluded categorically).

Had the Civil Justice Reform Act mandated

something truly radical, the American people might have had a plausible expectation that the new law would result in big changes, for good or ill. Let us imagine, for example, that the act had cut away most or all discovery rights, and specified an early trial date roughly on the pattern of the Speedy Trial Act of 1974 as to criminal cases. Fortunately, nothing more radical than mandatory "tracking" was ever even considered. But in deciding only to require every U.S. district court to consider doing a bit more of what it was doing already, and requiring a massive research effort to see what difference this would make, Congress imposed a recipe for confusion.

Indeed, confusion resulted, notwithstanding a good deal of intelligent and energetic research effort. The Rand Corporation Institute for Civil Justice undertook the largest quantitative study of federal civil dockets ever attempted, as well as massive surveys of attorneys and other participants at a total price tag that approached $5 million.[1] The Federal Judicial Center did a separate study of statutory "demonstration" districts.[2] But at the core of most of the findings specially highlighted by the Rand researchers is a significant methodological error or question that draws their results out of the realm of causation, rendering them mere hypotheses, and not even the most plausible ones available.

Old wine, old bottles

The most notable new element of the act was the requirement of "development and implementation of a civil justice expense and delay reduction plan" in every district. Even this was not as novel as some seem to believe, as the Speedy Trial Act of 1974 contained a more aggressive requirement to bring together the major institutional players in criminal proceedings and make them work together. But no one had ever required all courts to focus institutionally on the civil docket, gather data, and set explicit policy.

As to content, the act required each court to consider for inclusion in its plan six "principles" and six "techniques" for litigation management and cost and delay reduction. These are well summarized by James Kakalik in his *Judicature* account of the Rand study as falling into "four basic categories: differential case management, early active judicial management, judicial management of discovery, and referral of appropriate cases to nonbinding alternative dispute resolution."

The most casual scan of 40-year-old volumes of *Federal Rules Decisions* will reveal that the principles and techniques pressed by the act for controlling federal litigation have been the subject of lively discussion for a long time. And it is not only the judges who have been discussing this among themselves. Serious scholarly and quantitative work goes back to the 1920s, and was influential in initial adoption of the Federal Rules of Civil Procedure in 1938. Research on these matters was a major need discussed at the hearings leading to creation of the Federal Judicial Center, and these issues were central to its early research agenda.

U.S. district judges have vast discretion and, somewhat paradoxically, are at the same time constrained by vast and conflicting pressures and demands. Their highly diverse dockets of 400-500 new cases each year per judge include civil and criminal matters in hundreds of distinct case types. Congress has imposed statutory scheduling preferences for many. Depending on the year one examines, few or none of the different kinds of cases exceed 10 percent of all judicial activity, and most of the well-known and important ones are in the 1 percent to 3 percent range. The latter include all the criminal case types (though drug offenses are divided several ways; taken together, these do generally exceed 10 percent), and diversity/product liability and the separate asbestos category, securities, patents, prisoner civil rights, prisoner habeas corpus, insurance, motor vehicle personal injury, antitrust, social security reviews, and so on. The only types of cases that have sometimes been more dominant were "other" contract cases under diversity jurisdiction and employment cases under the civil rights laws, and "other" civil rights cases.

As Congress walked into the buzzing confusion of conflicting priorities in diverse jurisdictions across and beyond a continent, the most plausible basis for the Civil Justice Reform Act of 1990 would have run along the following lines, though I have never seen the matter articulated quite this way:

Congress has determined that the federal civil justice system is in crisis. Federal civil cases cost far too much, take far too long, and impose other excessive burdens also, notwithstanding recent improvements. Congress thereby requires every court and every judge to reorder priorities, notwithstanding other priorities Congress has imposed from time to time by statute, the Speedy Trial Act of 1974 notable among them. Every court and every judge shall find an effective way to sharply increase judicial management and/or the use of alternative dispute resolution techniques, in every civil case. Congress will provide resources to help them do so.

Looked at in this way, the act was a rather conservative but not implausible response to what Congress had determined to be a crisis. What *was* implausible was the research hypothesis upon which much of the act rested: that through the vast jumble of activities and participants represented by everything the federal courts do, involving millions of participants in hundreds of thousands of cases each year in hundreds of diverse categories, for all district judges to increase as much as they possibly could their managerial control over civil cases would have effects so compelling that gross docket measures would reveal them. Such effects, or effects on litigation costs, would have to overcome all the considerable "noise" in the system and all the intervening and overlapping factors that might mask any effect.

Solutions and new problems

The act's research strategy was to compare 10 "pilot" with 10 "comparison" districts selected by the U.S. Judicial Conference. True to sound research principles, the districts had no option whether to participate or not. Separately evaluated in a study by the Federal Judicial Center was an additional group of six demonstration programs in five districts. Kakalik asserts that "the pilot and comparison districts, which are comparable and represent the full range of districts in the United States, encompass about one-third of all federal judges and one-third of all case filings." Unfortunately, we know much less about the demonstration districts than about the pilot and comparison districts because the comprehensive data collection effort did not extend to them.

For what probably were good and sufficient reasons, the Rand researchers seem to have concluded that the statutory scheme was unworkable in comparing two groups of 10 districts with one another as a whole. They do say, in *Judicature* and elsewhere, that the pilot and comparison districts turned out pretty much alike as to the dependent variables addressed. Instead, they mobilized their incomparable data base in a rather novel fashion: their most important and highlighted results rest on a cross-jurisdictional comparison drawn from the 12,000 sampled cases, which are divided into "early judicial management cases" and the others.

It didn't take much for a case to be placed in the category of cases that were managed. Any docket entry that reflected a preliminary conference, or the setting of a schedule, or reference to ADR, or setting a trial date, among other possibilities sufficed. From the "case-level" analysis comparing these with the cases that the court didn't touch at all flows most of the assertions of causality that Kakalik highlighted in *Judicature* and that the Rand Institute for Civil Justice presented in its press releases and in reports of testimony before Congress. Headed in *Judicature* as "Effects of case management" these include:

- "The case-level analysis clearly showed that early judicial management significantly reduced time to disposition…

- "However, the study also found that early judicial management significantly increases the direct cost of litigation, thereby debunking the myth that cutting time to disposition necessarily cuts costs."

- "Shortening the median time to discovery cutoff from six to four months
    - reduces time to disposition by $1\frac{1}{2}$ months (about 10 percent);
    - reduces lawyer work time by 17 hours (about 25 percent);
    - does not change lawyer satisfaction or views of fairness."

Two comments are in order concerning these extremely strong assertions of causality. First, it is notable that the corresponding passages in the full reports are far more cautious; the brief summaries in *Judicature* and elsewhere are the only places where statements of this character can be located. Consider the following prominent and significant passage from the main report, titled *An Evaluation of Judicial Case Management Under the Civil Justice Reform Act*:

Given the observational nature of our data, one should not treat our statistical results as exact estimates of causal effect. For instance, if we find that using a particular case management procedure predicts a 60-day reduction in time to disposition in our sample of cases, this should not be interpreted to mean that if all judges were to use that particular procedure in every case, we would find exactly a 60-day reduction in time to disposition. Rather, our statistical analyses summarize the differences observed in our sample of cases. We have made every effort to ensure that our estimates clearly represent effects in our observed data, but since the pilot program did not randomly assign case management procedures to cases using an experimental design, we cannot say definitively that our observed effects correspond to causal effects among the studied cases and districts. Thus, interpretation of our statistical results should take place only in the context of an understanding of how the judicial system functions in practice.

Intrinsically different?

Having noted the uncertainty of this connection, an alternative hypothesis that may be more plausible than at least some of the claims of causality based on the case-level data can be advanced. In reaching across jurisdictions through their considerable number-crunching apparatus to identify cases that evidenced one or more episodes of "early" judicial management, in 180 days, the Rand researchers may have succeeded mostly in identifying a population of cases that was intrinsically different at the outset from the population of not-managed cases. This is a population, it is worth noting, from which low-management case types had already been excluded, such as prisoner petitions and bankruptcy appeals.

My strong conjecture is that most of the early management cases were managed because they presented management issues, and would to almost anyone, regardless of the case management approach employed. Similarly, I imagine that most of the non-managed cases were rather straightforward, and were not managed either because of a case-based determination to that effect, or because this was done implicitly—a courtroom deputy clerk or other responsible person scanned them and didn't get around to them in the press of business because something about them gave them a low priority or made them seem unpromising. In short, the "early management" cases may have differed from the non-managed cases intrinsically, and from the outset, and did not become different because different case management practices were applied to them.

It would be interesting to know much more about the managed and non-managed cases. If most of the determinations not to manage were based on such factors as the identity of the lawyers and prior experience with them, further analysis would not be very illuminating. But it seems likely that the two populations differed dramatically according to such variables as the amount at stake (always a good indicator, for good reasons as well as bad, of the amount of lawyering that is in prospect), the number of disputes, legal and factual, the number of parties, the likelihood that some party has a stake that goes beyond the confines of the particular case (sometimes repeat players fight hard in small cases in order to try to forestall an unfavorable pattern), and so on. Fortunately the data base is readily available to other researchers. Exploring these additional hypotheses could keep platoons of researchers occupied for years.

The causality problem goes beyond the one issue of what conclusions to draw from differences between the two populations in the case-level data. Notwithstanding their own cautions as quoted above, the Rand authors peppered even the full report with findings of statistical association that are transmogrified into conclusions of the form that A causes B. And almost all conclusions and policy recommendations are presented in this incautious way, especially in the various summaries and press releases Rand has issued, not to mention the Kakalik article in *Judicature* that is the prime focus here. To convert statements of statistical association into declarations as to cause requires considerable underpinning in theory and in related quantitative findings, usually from prior research. To claim causality requires, in short, an inferential leap. Neither the full Rand reports nor the short ones provide much of the necessary foundation for this.

Pufferies

The fanfare with which the original draft legislation was introduced, and the need to magnify the importance of later versions in order to secure passage in the face of significant opposition, seem to have forced everyone into hyperbole at every stage. The original task force of the independent Brookings Institution, whose 1989 report gave rise to the act, opened by stating, "The United States has long been admired *throughout the world* (emphasis added) for its sophisticated and well-developed system of civil justice…"; yet suddenly this group of wise heads that should have known better achieved a "consensus" not only "…that the system is not working very well…" but that it is so beset by high transaction costs and related ills that something truly radical was needed. As already suggested, however, the changes proposed were actually no more than marginal extensions of existing practice. Nothing in the Brookings report or any of its successors could possibly have addressed the ills of a system in crisis and restored it to its rightful place of world wide preeminence.

Overheated rhetoric is hard to resist or suppress, once begun. Consider the following from Kakalik's article in *Judicature*:

• "The act also broke new ground in calling on every federal district court to establish an advisory group of court users…." As noted earlier, this provision was anticipated by the planning groups required in the Speedy Trial Act. Those groups, however, were far more muscular: the specific requirement was that each court get together with the U.S. attorney, investigative agencies, and representatives of the defense bar and find a way to comply with the will of Congress.

• "Expectations were high that the implementation of [CJRA] principles would have substantial effects." One wonders who thought this and why, especially in light of the steady and well-documented improvement in recent decades in federal court civil disposition times in the face of large increases in caseload, both absolutely and in relation to the number of judges. The point should have been that the relevant publics of the federal courts, notwithstanding these improvements, demanded dramatic reductions in the cost of federal litigation and its duration.

What have we gained?

The greatest benefit from all of this may be a component that seems to have been mentioned only in passing in the various reports. The project generated a remarkable data base that will be very useful to future inquiries that are not subject to the grinding time constraints the statute imposed on this research. In combination with the national data base created a decade earlier by University of Wisconsin researchers under the Civil Litigation Research Project contract with the Department of Justice, the Rand effort puts the legal community in a better position than ever before to learn about controlling the cost of litigation, among other important matters.

Another substantial benefit comes from a more modest research effort, the Federal Judicial Center's evaluation of the "demonstration" districts. Though the data are more limited and the conclusions rest on attorneys' perceptions, the study suggests that such case management practices as initial differentiation for tracking have benefits both as to disposition time and to litigation cost. Unexpected is the finding that a more rigid case management system seemed beneficial to lawyers and to judges alike because it was more predictable.

Unhappily, this review of the Civil Justice Reform Act experience must conclude on a tiresome and familiar note: a call for more research. The "unanswered question" here is not unanswerable in principle, only in the setting of the act. It may be that the data base the Rand researchers created can be teased so as to provide more solid answers. And the Wisconsin data base, which includes state as well as federal data from all over the United States, may help too. But all these data are old and getting older. If renewed recycling efforts are to be of any policy value, they should begin soon.

NOTES

This article originally appeared in Volume 82, Number 2, September-October 1998, pages 55-56, 91-92.

1. Kakalik, *Just, speedy and inexpensive? Judicial case management under the Civil Justice Reform Act*, 80 JUDICATURE 184 (1997) summarizes briefly the three comprehensive project reports Rand published in 1996.

2. Stienstra, et al, REPORT TO THE JUDICIAL CONFERENCE COMMITTEE ON COURT ADMINISTRATION AND CASE MANAGEMENT: A STUDY OF THE FIVE DEMONSTRATION PROGRAMS ESTABLISHED UNDER THE CIVIL JUSTICE REFORM ACT OF 1990, (Washington, D.C.: Federal Judicial Center, January 24, 1997).

Appellate Court Processes
Access and Docketing Decisions

INTRODUCTION

The lawyer who advises his or her client that, "We will fight this case all the way up to the Supreme Court," is usually guilty of overstatement. For one thing, cases ultimately heard by the Supreme Court must implicate a question of federal law. More to the point, as a practical matter only a handful of the cases initiated in the American judicial system ultimately seek Supreme Court review. Further, the Court exercises virtually complete discretion in composing its appellate docket and more than 90 percent of the cases seeking Supreme Court review are denied that appellate opportunity.

It is exceedingly unlikely that any one case will be heard by the Supreme Court. At the same time, however, the litigious nature of American society dictates that even if the percentage of cases seeking Supreme Court review is small, and the proportion granted such review even smaller, the numbers remain great enough to raise the possibility of a workload crisis of substantial magnitude for the Court. Indeed, petitions for review (certiorari petitions) have increased geometrically during the past half century. Consequently, concerns about the Court's workload and what to do about it have become primary issues for contemplation in the American judicial system.

This section broadly examines how the Supreme Court determines its docket as well as many suggested reforms for dealing with the Court's workload. It is important to keep in mind that the Court's role as a policy maker is largely a reflection of the types of cases that it hears. Consequently, reforms that touch upon the accessibility of the Court to cases seeking review may have substantial implications for the Court's policy-making role.

In "Deciding what to decide: how the Supreme Court sets its agenda," D. Marie Provine utilizes a valuable data source, Justice Harold Burton's docket books, to explore how the Court exercises its discretionary docketing jurisdiction. Unlike earlier work, which focused on the collective institutional outcomes of certiorari voting, Provine's data allowed her to focus on the behavior of individual justices as they voted for and against granting certiorari. Provine's work suggests that the justices' conceptions of the Court's proper role have great implications for their case-selection votes. In the time period studied, a broad consensus existed on the Court's role and, consequently, the expression of the policy preferences and political attitudes of individual justices did not appear to be widespread in certiorari voting. In other time frames, however, such as cases seeking review of the constitutionality of the Vietnam War in the 1960s and 1970s and those dealing with capital punishment throughout the 1980s, greater divisiveness existed over the Court's role and, therefore, we would expect considerably more contentious certiorari voting than Provine found. Her article remains quite instructive in highlighting the wide variety of concerns that may enter into certiorari decision making.

Justice John Paul Stevens' offering of "Some thoughts on judicial restraint" was first delivered as an address to the American Judicature Society. In it, he proposed the establishment of a new federal court that would have the authority to decide which cases the Supreme Court would decide on the merits. Such a court, in Stevens' view, would alleviate the Supreme Court's caseload crisis, which he feels has been responsible for the unwise proliferation of per curiam opinions and the increased dismissing of writs of certiorari as improvidently granted. While it is now widely known that most Supreme Court justices rely heavily on their clerks in the certiorari process and that they participate in a certiorari "pool" with their colleagues, Stevens' 1982 public admission that, "I do not even look at the papers in over 80 percent of the cases that are filed" was quite startling.

Justice William Brennan's 1982 address, "Some thoughts on the Supreme Court's workload," takes issue with Justice Stevens' call for a new tier in the federal judiciary. Indeed, Brennan asserts, the proposal for a new tribunal would violate the Constitution's provision calling for "one Supreme Court" and it could only be established by amending the Constitution. Brennan rejects Stevens' basic premise that the Court's decisions have been compromised by the pressures of an inflated docket. To reduce the Court's workload, Brennan recommends the exercise of greater care in identifying certworthy cases and congressional removal of virtually all of the Court's mandatory appellate jurisdiction, a reform that has largely taken place. He also alludes to various reforms in lower court processes that could alleviate some Supreme Court problems. Brennan argues that the Court's case-screening function gets easier for a justice the more it is done and he directly confronts Stevens' confession of delegation. "...[M]y view that the screening function is second to none in importance is reflected in my practice of performing the screening function myself." Admittedly, however, no justice on the Court today would likely make that statement.

In "Caseload, conflicts, and decisional capacity: does the Supreme Court need help?," Arthur Hellman closely examines one particular reform proposal, the creation of an Intercircuit Tribunal of the United States Courts of Appeals. Such a tribunal, unlike the reform most focused on by Stevens and Brennan, which dealt with a court that would screen cases for Supreme Court review, would decide cases referred to it by the Supreme Court. Hellman opposes such a plan, finding it both unnecessary to reduce the Court's workload and unlikely to achieve its stated goal of fostering uniformity in the law. The article highlights the disagreement that exists over the Court's workload problem, even among the justices, regarding its nature and appropriate solutions. Hellman's thoughtful analysis suggests that the workload problem may be a more complex one than first meets the eye. He concludes, "There is simply not enough evidence that the Supreme Court's limited capacity for authoritative decision making has significantly frustrated society's need for uniformity and predictability in the law. Moreover, too little attention has been paid to the possible adverse consequences of creating a new court."

David O'Brien's study of "The Rehnquist Court's shrinking plenary docket" examines the expansion and contraction of the Supreme Court's output through the Burger and Rehnquist Court eras. While O'Brien agrees that both external factors (such as a diminishing number of statutes that induce litigation and expand the Court's discretionary jurisdiction) and internal factors (such as personnel changes) have played a role in the contemporary Court's reduced propensity to hear cases, the major cause of the reduced workload has clearly been the replacement of grant-prone justices on the Court by those with a more constrained vision of the judicial role.

The final selection in this section, Judge Roger Miner's assertion that "Federal court reform should start at the top," takes a bit of an alternative tack in considering the issue of judicial overload. In his view, it is the federal judiciary writ large and not the Supreme Court that is overburdened. The reasons for this dilemma, according to Miner, lie at the doorstep of both Congress and the Court. For his part, Miner would like to see Congress pull back from the proliferation of statutes, particularly in the criminal domain, that expand the range of potential federal causes of action. With regard to the Supreme Court, Miner calls for the acceptance of a greater number of cases in which there is interpretive conflict among the circuits and, in addition, he issues a plea for new-found clarity in the development of case law. Interestingly, in Judge Miner's provocative essay, the prospect is raised of a reduced workload in the federal judiciary that is brought about, in part, because of an increased caseload for the Supreme Court. Clearly, the issues addressed in this section are complex ones that will continue to be the subject of considerable debate and calls for reform for the foreseeable future.

Deciding what to decide: how the Supreme Court sets its agenda

Justices generally agree about what cases to review largely because they share a concept of the proper business of the Court.

by D. Marie Provine

Since the passage of the 1925 Judiciary Act, the U.S. Supreme Court has enjoyed broad discretion to decide which cases it will resolve on their merits. As dockets have grown more crowded in recent decades, this discretion has become an increasingly significant feature of the Court's institutional power. Currently, for example, the justices refuse review to more than 90 percent of the cases which come before them, which amounts to approximately 3,500 cases denied review per term.[1] Clearly the criteria the justices use to set their agenda should be of considerable interest to students of the Supreme Court.

Research on the Court, however, remains fixed almost exclusively upon the cases to which the justices have granted review.[2] One explanation for the paucity of research on case selection is lack of data. The Court issues no opinions and releases no votes in denying or granting review. Traditionally, the only exceptions to complete secrecy in case selection have been occasional published dissents from denials of review, sporadic citations of reasons for granting review in opinions on the merits, general statements by justices and their law clerks on the case selection process, and the broadly-stated criteria of the Supreme Court Rules.[3]

Scholars interested in analyzing case selection criteria with statistical tools had only the bare facts of grants and denials to work with until 1965, when the papers of Justice Harold H. Burton became available. Burton's papers, on file at the Library of Congress, include complete docket books recording the case selection votes of each justice for the 13 terms that Burton sat on the Court (1945-

1957). These are the only complete records of case selection votes that are currently available for any period since the advent of discretionary review.

The Burton data make it possible to analyze case selection and its relationship to the more familiar work of the Supreme Court on the merits. Such an analysis suggests that the justices' conceptions of the proper role of the Court have a major impact on their votes to select cases for review. Consensus about the Court's role appears to have channeled and limited the expression of individual policy preferences and political attitudes in review decisions during the Burton period. Even when the justices disagreed in assessing review worthiness, role perceptions seemed to be significant to their decisions. The only case selection records currently available thus suggest that, in agenda setting, judicial sensitivity to the appropriate business of the Court is crucial.

I. Theories of case selection

The case selection process, because of its secrecy, provides the justices with a special opportunity for favoring certain litigants or side-stepping volatile cases, possibilities that have been noted by scholars.[4] Alexander Bickel, for example, suggested that Supreme Court justices should assess the political implications of the merits of cases and use case selection to limit "the occasions of the Court's interventions" in the political process.[5]

Schubert's certiorari game

Theories of how case selection actually proceeds may also take account of the opportunities for politically motivated behavior that the secrecy of the process provides. In the earliest and most provocative analysis, Glendon Schubert used game theory to explore the possibility that in Federal Employers' Liability Act (FELA) cases, a subgroup of justices manipulated others on the Court to gain the outcomes it preferred on the merits.[6] Such manipulation could occur because, by tradition, only four affirmative votes are needed to review, while five are ordinarily necessary to win on the merits. A minority could thus force a reluctant majority to consider minority-selected cases on the merits.

Schubert postulated that the "certiorari bloc," which varied in size and membership over the years, consistently attempted to maximize the number of Supreme Court judgments favorable to worker claims. The object of the bloc was to encourage the lower courts to look more favorably upon worker petitions. To achieve this objective, the bloc would vote against review in all cases brought by railroads, because in those cases the injured worker had been successful below. For worker petitions, the bloc's strategy was to vote for review only when a majority of the whole Court could be expected to reverse on the merits.

Black and Douglas were long-standing members of the "certiorari bloc." Murphy, Rutledge, Clark, Warren, and Brennan were also members during all or almost all of their shorter terms of office. Frankfurter represented an opposing player in the certiorari game. Others on the Court were uncommitted "pawns" to be "coopted" in the conflict between the two sides.

Schubert found that the "certiorari bloc" was not always successful in implementing its goal of achieving a judicial gloss on the FELA most favorable to workers. Its failures to win reversals in as many worker petitions as it might have stemmed in part from its failure to follow what Schubert conceived to be its optimal or "pure" strategy: to vote for review only when the worker won at trial and lost for the first time on appeal.

Schubert's theory is not seriously damaged by the failure of the "certiorari bloc" to adhere to its optimal strategy. Whether or not the justices behaved rationally at all times, the implications of the hypothesis are profound: the behavior of at least some members of the Court in certain cases can be understood in the language of power politics. Schubert's argument, in other words, was that

certain members of the Court, desiring to control the Court's decision making to effectuate preferred policies, made use of the opportunity for subgroup manipulation of the majority afforded by the so-called Rule of Four.

Schubert's analysis cannot be dismissed as a theory of Supreme Court decision making simply because of the limited subject matter it considers. Though the Court received, on the average, fewer than 10 worker-brought FELA cases per term in the period Schubert studied (1942-1960), these cases appear to have been a source of sharp disagreement among the justices. Opinions on the merits in FELA cases reveal deep divisions among the justices about the propriety of plenary, or on-the-merits, review. FELA litigation was, in fact, the most likely locus for outcome-oriented case selection voting on the Supreme Court of that era.

Testing Schubert's theory

The theory of voting behavior Schubert offers is open to criticism, however, on grounds that it does not fit actual voting patterns in FELA cases. Schubert based his research on the pattern of grants and denials in these cases, the only information available when he wrote. The Burton docket books make it possible to check the accuracy of Schubert's suppositions about case selection voting against actual votes.

Burton's records indicate that the "certiorari bloc" Schubert identified did not always vote in the pro-worker direction Schubert hypothesized. Members of the "certiorari bloc," for example, occasionally voted *against* the worker in favor of hearing railroad petitioners. Although no member of the Court did this often, alleged bloc members cast four of the seven pro-railroad votes in the period. The "certiorari bloc" also varied considerably in its support of worker cases; Brennan, for example, voted for only one-third of the cases he should have supported unequivocally. Furthermore, in five cases, the negative vote of one bloc member prevented the review on the merits that the rest of the bloc desired, and in five other cases that did gain review on the merits, the votes of non-bloc members neutralized a negative vote from a bloc member.[7]

Most importantly, the overall voting pattern in worker-brought cases does not match the pattern a theory of power-oriented voting would predict. Schubert's hypothesis implies that certiorari votes in FELA cases should tend to clump around zero and four votes for review. Only during the three-term period when the "certiorari bloc" had a fifth member should five vote grants be common. A consistent pattern of five or more votes would indicate that the bloc had more members than Schubert hypothesized, and frequent instances of fewer than four votes would indicate that conscious manipulation of case selection was absent.[8]

When the worker cases are subdivided by the number of votes they received, however, it is clear that a tight-knit power bloc was not operating during the Burton period. Table 1 indicates the actual pattern in these cases. As this table shows, there were 52 instances in which one, two, three, five, or six votes were cast for review in FELA cases, far too many to suggest the operation of a "certiorari bloc." Table 1 also shows that some justices almost invariably opposed review in FELA cases. Their on-the-merits opinions indicate that Justices Frankfurter, Harlan, and Burton were the members of the Court who consistently opposed review.

Cue theory

Other theories of case selection decision making conceptualize judicial motivation much differently than Schubert did. In an often-cited article, Tanenhaus, Schick, Muraskin, and Rosen hypothesized that Supreme Court justices are concerned with reducing their workload, rather than with competing to get their policy preferences incorporated into decisions on the merits, as Schubert presumed.[9] The authors theorized that the justices cut down case-processing time by summarily eliminating much of the caseload from careful consideration. According to this hypothesis, they use a set of agreed-upon cues to differentiate cases that might be worthy of review from those they know they did not want to hear.

Like Schubert, Tanenhaus and his colleagues wrote before the release of the Burton papers, so they had only the pattern of grants and denials with which to work. Nevertheless, they established an ingenious test of their hypothesis that the Court uses cues to reduce its workload. Relying on the statements of Chief Justice Hughes and others that between 40 percent and 60 percent of the petitions filed were clearly without merit, the authors hypothesized that this percentage of the cases contained no cues and was not examined beyond the initial search for cues. The rest of the petitions,

Table 1　The distribution of votes for review in worker-brought F.E.L.A. cases and overall, 1945-57

Number of votes for review	F.E.L.A.	Overall (appell. dkt.)
1	7 (10%)	762 (24%)
2	12 (17%)	635 (20%)
3	9 (13%)	381 (12%)
4	16 (23%)	317 (10%)
5	16 (23%)	190 (6%)
6	8 (11%)	159 (5%)
7	1 (1%)	159 (5%)
8	0 —	127 (4%)
9	1 (1%)	417 (14%)
	Total=70	Total=3147

which did contain one or more cues, constituted the pool from which cases were selected. Because only 5 percent to 17 percent of the docket as a whole was reviewed on the merits in the period under analysis, the authors concluded that the grant rate for the pool of cases containing cues must be between 25 percent and 43 percent.

The authors named three cues the Court used to select cases for careful scrutiny, and to eliminate summarily the remaining (cueless) 40 percent to 60 percent of the caseload:

- the presence of the United States as petitioner;
- the existence of a civil liberties issue;
- disagreement among the lower courts.

Testing cue theory

The accuracy of cue theory can be assessed by examining the fate of cue-containing cases during the Burton period, which matches almost exactly the 1947-1958 period Tanenhaus examined. Burton's papers permit a test of cue theory because his records reveal that a significant proportion of cases were eliminated with only cursory analysis, while the remainder were given more careful attention. The separation was accomplished by special listing, an administrative convenience devised by Chief Justice Hughes before Burton joined the Court.

The practice while Burton sat on the Court was for the chief justice and his staff to prepare a special list, or dead list, of cases deemed unworthy of conference time. The list circulated among the justices each week, and unless one of them put a special-listed case up for conference consideration, it was denied review automatically. Burton filed each week's special lists, and he kept a record of any changes justices requested. These records show that such alterations were rare.

Table 2 Disposition of cases containing Tanenhaus cues, 1947-57

Disposition of petitions cases	U.S. petn'r.	Tanenhaus cues Dissen. below	Civ. libs. issue	All other appellate
Special listed	1%	27%	16%	45%
In conference:				
Denied unan.	8%	23%	22%	21%
Denied nonu.	25%	25%	26%	18%
Gr'ntd nonu.	41%	16%	21%	12%
Gr'ntd unan.	25%	9%	15%	5%
Total cases:	554	131*	629	6323

*Includes data only for 1947 Term.

Table 2 indicates the percentage of cue-containing cases that were put on the special list, and the number of votes attracted by those cases with and without cues that survived special listing. As this table shows, cases with cues were significantly more likely to get case selection votes than others on the Appellate Docket. Clearly the cues, especially the U.S. as petitioner, are related to the concerns the justices have in selecting cases for review on the merits. This is not surprising, since Tanenhaus settled upon the cues by examining the statements of Supreme Court justices and others about the types of cases of particular interest to the Court.[10]

Were the authors simply suggesting that some types of cases have a better chance of getting votes for review than others, the Burton data would tend to substantiate the hypothesis. Cue theory, however, purports to explain how the justices reduce the mass of petitions they receive to a more manageable number without actually considering the argument each petitioner makes for review on the merits. As the authors describe the process:

The presence of any one of these cues would warn a justice that a petition deserved scrutiny. If no cue were present, on the other hand, a justice could safely discard a petition without further expenditure of time and energy.[11]

If the cues actually served this short-circuiting purpose, cases containing cues should not appear on the special lists. Yet as Table 2 shows, in all three categories, some cue-containing cases are special listed.

Not a mechanical process

This pattern of voting suggests that the case characteristics that Tanenhaus deemed cues may be significant to the justices in case selection decisions, but that the decision-making process is not as mechanical as the authors suggest. Of course, something differentiates special-listed cases from those

discussed in conference. The memos Burton's clerks wrote for him on each case and the case selection voting patterns suggest that cases with jurisdictional defects, inadequate records, and no clearly presented issues were the most likely to be special listed.[12]

No easily identifiable case characteristics are invariably associated with special listing, however. This suggests that neither the justices nor the clerks rely on a fixed set of cues to separate cases into those worthy of scrutiny and those to be discarded summarily. With the assistance law clerks provide in digesting cases and writing memos, there is little reason to expect Supreme Court justices need such an abbreviated preliminary screening procedure.

It is more likely that the justices reduce the time they spend in evaluating petitions by relying on the clerks' memos. The justices may then reach a decision by engaging in a weighing process in which a few characteristics of cases—including probably the Tanenhaus cues—encourage at least some of the justices to vote for review, while many other characteristics act like demerits, preventing review in the absence of strong reasons in favor. The special-listed cases are those which contain one or more demerits and no countervailing considerations in favor of review.

The pattern of voting in U.S.-brought cases supports this interpretation. Because of the solicitor general's careful screening,[13] these cases seldom contain characteristics strongly discouraging review, so the Court seldom puts them on the special lists. In fact, as Table 2 indicates, U.S. cases are sufficiently impressive that in the Burton period they usually received at least one justice's vote for review. The evidence does not suggest, however, that the justices initially separate U.S. cases from the rest in an attempt to save reading time.

The attitudinal hypothesis

Another approach for understanding how the

Court selects cases for plenary review emphasizes judicial predispositions towards litigants and policies. Sidney Ulmer has actively promoted this perspective, using the Burton papers to test his attitudinal conception of the case selection process.[14]

One of Ulmer's principal findings has been that a justice's votes to review and his later votes on the merits are strongly related to each other.[15] Ulmer was able to show, for example, that for eight of the 11 justices whose votes he examined, a justice's vote to review helped to predict his vote on the merits.[16] Votes to review were associated with votes to reverse on the merits, a pattern which Ulmer explained in terms of judicial attitudes:

Theories of cognitive dissonance and attitudinal stability would lead one to expect some consistency in decisional direction if the factors underlying both decisions are identical or similar. Moreover, if the judge is conditioned to respond in a particular way to the stimulus (S) presented by a case on the first trial (t_1), the conditioned relationship may be reinforced by the mere act of response.[17]

Similarly, in a study limited to cases brought by state and federal prisoners, Ulmer hypothesized that a justice's underlying attitude towards institutional authority explained consistency at both stages of decision.[18]

Recently Ulmer has gone further, arguing that the justices sometimes try to disguise the extent to which they are influenced by their attitudes towards litigants in case selection. According to this hypothesis, when a justice suspects he cannot win review on the merits, he suppresses his ever present desire to vote for the underdog or the upperdog. In so doing, the justices defer to, but do not assimilate, the norm of impartiality in judicial decision making.[19]

Ulmer's emphasis on judicial attitudes in his analysis of case selection raises a question familiar to students of judicial behavior: are broad, pre-existing attitudes toward litigants and the policy issues in which they are entangled the sole or primary determinant of the votes of judges? Or do judges internalize norms that significantly limit the expression of personal preferences in their decisions? This much-debated question is, of course, central to traditional justifications for judicial power in a democracy. It is especially relevant in the context of case selection where, because of the secrecy of the process, external restraints on judicial judgment are absent.[20]

Cross pressures in case selection

While case selection is insulated from the public scrutiny that characterizes decisions on the merits, it is, of course, subject to strictures the justices place on themselves. The Court has consistently articulated one such self-imposed rule: that the justices decide whether a case should be reviewed not on the basis of their agreement or disagreement with the outcome between the parties in the lower court, but on the basis of their assessment of the intrinsic importance of the issues in controversy. A denial of review, therefore, does not mean that the Court agrees with the outcome of the case in the lower court, and a denial carries no significance as a legal precedent. As Frankfurter explained:

It simply means that fewer than four members of the Court deemed it desirable to review a decision of the lower court as a matter "of sound judicial discretion."[21]

The procedure the Court uses to select cases for plenary review, however, ensures that each justice will be well-acquainted with the arguments for relief from the lower court judgment when he decides whether to vote for review. The parties incorporate their views of the proper resolution of the case into their briefs for and against review.[22]

The Burton papers suggest that law clerks respond to these arguments and may even feel competent to pass on the merits at this stage in the proceedings. Burton's clerks typically suggested what they believed to be the correct outcome of the underlying dispute in their memos to the justice. The case selection process thus provides the justices with an easy opportunity to vote for review on the basis of their agreement or disagreement with the lower court result.

Ulmer's finding that votes to review and votes to reverse were correlated suggests that the justices *do* let their assessment of the merits of cases influence their review decisions. This finding does not necessarily mean, however, that the justices simply vote according to their attitudes towards certain types of litigants or policies at each stage of decision. The justices could just as well be responding to litigants in case selection, and later in votes on the merits, in light of general principles that determine the availability of judicial relief.

Ulmer's finding thus suggests two questions for further analysis: whether case selection and voting on the merits are, as a practical matter, indistinguishable; and, to the extent that they are, whether motivation can be persuasively explained in attitudinal terms.

II. An overview of voting patterns

If case selection is functionally equivalent to decision making on the merits, most case selection decisions should be nonunanimous, as most decisions on the merits are. Also, individual decisions to grant review should correlate highly with votes to reverse the lower court on the merits, and votes to reverse should be rare when a justice did not vote for review. Finally, the frequency with which a justice votes for review should be directly related to the level of his overall dissatisfaction with lower court results.

If attitudes towards litigants explain why individual case selection votes correspond with votes in fully considered cases, then the justices generally presumed to be the most politically liberal and the most conservative should seldom vote to review the same case. On the Court as a whole, disagreement among the justices should be parallel at both stages of decision, and this pattern should be consistent with the liberal-conservative spectrum we see in on-the-merits voting.

With the Burton records, we can determine whether or not these patterns existed during a significant portion of the modern Court's history. Analysis of case selection votes can thus contribute to our understanding of the relative significance of role constraints and attitude in judicial decision making.

Unanimity in case selection

Contrary to what one would expect if judicial views of the merits alone determined review decisions, the prevailing pattern in case selection is unanimity. During the Burton period, 82 percent of case selection decisions were unanimous: 79 percent were unanimous denials of review and 3 percent were unanimous grants.[23] Available evidence indicates that the level of unanimity in case selection has remained high since the Burton era.[24] This numerical evidence alone suggests that case selection decisions are not functionally equivalent to decisions on the merits, and that some norm or norms guide the justices in deciding whether to vote for review.

Analysis of the types of cases decided unanimously during the Burton period suggests that the

Table 3   Unanimity in favor of review by case type, 1947-57

Case type	N	% granted review unanimously
U.S. petitioner	554	25%
Civil rights/liberties claims	630	14%
Labor claims	593	15%
Federalism issues	578	11%
All criminal petitioners	8572	0%
All other cases not noted above	4311	2%

justices shared a conception of the work appropriate to the Court that overshadowed policy preferences and sympathies for certain litigants. Evidence of this is that the types of cases usually presumed to tap judicial attitudes most directly were the very types most often denied review unanimously: the petitions of prisoners and suits by business interests seeking relief from government regulation.

This pattern of unanimity in presumably ideologically charged cases cannot be attributed to an unusual period of ideological uniformity on the Supreme Court. The Court's membership in this period included civil libertarians like Black and Douglas as well as nonlibertarians like Reed and Vinson. Yet all of them were in agreement that most of these cases should not be reviewed. In other words, all of the justices seem to have been convinced that certain types of cases were not important enough to review, even if they touched the private sympathies of individual justices.

A review of memos written by Justice Burton's law clerks suggests that this consensus has both procedural and subject-matter aspects. As noted earlier, cases with defective records from below or other weaknesses unrelated to the substance of their claims tended to be denied review unanimously, usually by special listing. Likewise, certain subject matters almost never got votes for review. Contract disputes, common law issues, and real property litigation were prime candidates for unanimous exclusion. Sixty percent of these cases were special listed.[25]

Unanimity in favor of review

The types of cases in which the justices were most often unanimous in favor of review also suggest the importance of shared views about the proper business of the Court. During the Burton period, as Table 3 indicates, the justices tended to be unanimous in four types of cases which are related to basic areas of responsibility for the court of last resort in a federal system.

Table 4 The relationship between votes to review and votes to reverse, 1947-57

(Nonunanimous cases)

Justice	Percent of votes to reverse in cases he voted to review*	Percent of votes to reverse in cases he voted against**	Difference between the two columns
Whittaker	93	43	50
Rutledge	85	37	48
Black	80	36	44
Minton	64	25	39
Warren	76	42	34
Vinson	61	31	29
Douglas	75	46	29
Jackson	62	34	28
Frankfurter	67	39	27
Brennan	79	52	27
Reed	58	31	27
Clark	62	35	27
Harlan	62	41	21
Murphy	74	57	17
Burton	56	39	17

*N=100 or more for all except Whittaker (27 votes to reverse in 29 cases favoring review).

**N=100 or more for all except Murphy, Rutledge, Brennan, and Whittaker where instances range from 20 to 50.

• U.S. petitions and labor claims which are similar in frequently raising issues concerning the proper scope of federal law-making authority.

• Civil rights and liberties petitions which usually claimed federal constitutional rights against asserted state and local authority.

• Federalism cases, which require the Court to adjust competing jurisdictional claims among governmental and quasi-governmental authorities and which are clearly a central function for the court of last resort in a federal system.

Differences among the justices

When the justices of the Burton era disagreed in case selection, they differed considerably in the extent to which their votes to review paralleled their final votes on the merits, and they differed dramatically in the frequency with which they voted to review. These two measures of differences among the justices appear to be independent of each other.

The association between voting to review and to reverse already noted by Ulmer is evident in Table 4, which ranks the justices according to their tendency to vote for review and then vote to reverse on the merits. As the table shows, although the justices differed in the extent to which considerations favoring review and reversal paralleled each other, all of the justices were more likely to vote to reverse a case they voted to review than one they did not vote to review.

Were the justices considering simply the desired outcome of the dispute in case selection, however, the differences between the two columns in Table 4 would be much closer to 100 percent. Nor can the failure of these differences to approximate 100 percent plausibly be attributed to the effect of mistaken assessments of the merits at the case selection stage. The inadequacy of transposing the plenary decision to the case selection stage is particularly evident for the justices at the bottom of the table, for whom the relationship between case selection votes and votes for reversal is weakest.

It seems more likely that judicial beliefs concerning the proper work of the Supreme Court explain the imperfect correlations between votes to review and votes to reverse. A justice's failure to vote for reversal in every case he voted to review can be attributed to his belief that the subject was too important to pass over for reasons unrelated to the correctness of the outcome below. Likewise, a justice's vote to reverse a case he voted against reviewing can be attributed to the view that the case was wrongly decided below, but not important enough to review.

Considered in this light, departures from merits-consciousness in nonunanimous votes are consistent with the preponderance of unanimity in case selection: both depend on judicial conceptions of the proper role of the Court which limit the expression of individual sympathies and preferences in case selection votes.

Frequency of votes for review

The significance of role perceptions in case selection decisions is also evident when the Burton period justices are compared according to the frequency with which they voted for review. As Table

Table 5   Differences in the propensity to vote for review, 1947-57

(Each justice's votes for review//total opportunities to vote for review in pool of cases receiving at least one favorable vote; expressed as percentages)

Justice	1947-48	1949-52	1953-54	1955	1956	1957	Overall	Rank
Murphy	59	—	—	—	—	—	59	1
Douglas	53	61	61	55	59	54	58	2
Black	43	56	54	57	58	54	53	3
Rutledge	49	—	—	—	—	—	49	3
Brennan	—	—	—	—	42	44	43	5
Warren	—	—	31	43	54	38	40	6
Reed	28	38	31	30	—	—	33	7
Harlan	—	—	—	31	36	31	32	8
Jackson	22	30	31	—	—	—	27	9
Burton	22	33	23	29	30	23	27	10
Frankfurter	23	29	26	24	33	28	27	11
Clark	—	25	26	28	32	25	26	12
Vinson	—	21	—	—	—	—	25	13
Whittaker	—	—	—	—	—	21	21	14
Minton	—	10	10	18	—	—	13	15

5 shows, the justices differed greatly in the frequency with which they voted for review. (This table segments the Burton period into natural courts defined by periodic shifts in the membership of the Court.)

Certain justices during the Burton period consistently voted more often for review than their colleagues. The justices often divided into groups on this issue, with 20 percentage points or more separating them in some natural courts. Black and Douglas were the long-standing members of the review-prone group, while Frankfurter and Burton were mainstays of the review-conservative group.

The remaining justices who voted in more than one segment of time also showed consistency in their propensity to vote for review. Generally, when a justice's percentage of votes for review did drop or rise from one natural court to the next, other carryover justices changed in the same direction. The rank order of the justices thus remained fairly constant over the entire period.

Changes in the membership of the Court also did not disrupt voting propensities, even when they affected how a majority of the Court could be expected to vote on the merits. This suggests that those who voted often for review did so with little regard for probable outcome on the merits, and even without regard to marshalling enough votes to gain review. The review-prone justices, in other words, appear to have been unconcerned with the impact of their case selection votes in specific cases.

This pattern raises the question of whether the review-prone justices voted most often for review because they were more dissatisfied with lower court outcomes than the rest of the Court. Such an explanation must assume that, for the more

review-prone justices at least, votes to review are motivated primarily by disagreement with lower court outcomes.

Yet the ranking of the justices in Table 4, which estimates the relative tendency to vote to review in order to reverse, does not correlate with the ranking of the justices in their tendency to vote for review (Table 5). The two justices who voted most often for review, for example, were not especially likely to equate case selection and plenary decision making, while the two least review-prone justices were among the most likely to vote the merits in case selection.

In short, the tendency to vote often for review appears to be independent of the tendency to make disagreement with the lower court outcome the primary criterion of review-worthiness. Thus, while disagreement with lower court outcomes almost certainly influences the justices to vote for review, this variable can not by itself account for differences in the tendency to vote for review.

Propensity to vote for review

It seems likely that differences in the frequency with which individual justices voted for review are related to differences in the disposition of the justices to exercise Supreme Court power. Clearly the structure of case selection requires the justices to consider the proper scope of Supreme Court activity in voting for or against review. The identity of the most review-prone and the most review-conservative justices during the Burton period also suggests the relevance of such a concern.

Pritchett's discussion of differences among the justices in plenary decision making is particularly useful in showing this connection. Even though

Table 6 Justices' propensities to vote for review by case type, 1947-57

(Justice's votes for review/total opportunities to vote for review in pool of cases receiving at least one favorable vote; in percentages)

Justices ranked by overall tendency Federalism to vote to review	Criminal rights claims	Civil rights & liberties claims	U.S. claims	cases
Murphy	77	78	76	61
Douglas	73	76	42	50
Black	67	75	47	39
Rutledge	67	63	60	42
Brennan	68	56	62	56
Warren	42	44	57	34
Reed	23	21	69	27
Harlan	32	38	62	49
Jackson	27	29	33	48
Burton	21	22	54	43
Frankfurter	43	36	21	41
Clark	30	20	53	34
Vinson	12	14	52	47
Whittaker	10	28	23	48
Minton	9	7	35	20
Range:	68	71	41	41
Standard deviations:	26.1	22.9	15.6	10.3

Pritchett restricted his analysis to civil rights and liberties cases, his explanation for voting differences is broad, and it seems applicable to Supreme Court decision making generally.

Those men whom Pritchett labeled "libertarian activists" in *Civil Liberties and the Vinson Court* were the most review-prone justices who sat during the entire Burton period.[26] Pritchett's "less libertarians" are among the least review-prone justices. Frankfurter, Pritchett's lone example of libertarian restraint, is somewhere near the middle in case selection, as he is in Pritchett's typology.

Pritchett described the libertarian activist as the judge whose sympathies are aroused by the underdogs in our society and for whom "the result is the test of a decision."[27] A believer in libertarian restraint, on the other hand, emphasizes the process of judicial decision making and the nondemocratic basis of judicial power. For Pritchett, a justice's activism or restraint is a function of the interaction of two variables: his sympathies towards underdogs and "the conception which the justice holds of his judicial role and the obligations imposed on him by his judicial function."[28]

Information about the frequency with which the justices vote for review is consistent with this two-dimensional interpretation of judicial motivation. Sympathy for underdogs and an expansive interpretation of the availability of Court-fashioned relief seemed to play a part in explaining voting frequency.

As Table 6 shows, review-prone justices tended

to be willing to go further than their brethren in voting to hear criminal and civil rights and liberties claims. These were the types of cases that raised new arguments for rights not yet established in precedent or legislation, and they occasioned the greatest disagreement among the justices over review-worthiness. In more established areas of litigation, represented here by U.S.-brought and federalism cases, the review-prone justices were relatively less likely to favor review, although, overall, they still tended to be more likely to vote for review than their colleagues.

The Court's proper workload

Differing convictions among the justices about the workload appropriate to the Court, a question central to the role it should perform, also appear to have been crucial. This is particularly evident when differences in voting frequencies are examined in detail. Table 7 provides such a close-up view of the voting history of the four justices who sat together throughout the Burton period: Douglas, Black, Frankfurter, and, of course, Burton. Douglas and Black, as Table 5 showed, were review prone, while Burton and Frankfurter were not.

Table 7 shows that, had two other justices consistently voted with them, Black and Douglas would have engaged the Court in several times as many cases as either Frankfurter or Burton. The willingness of Black and Douglas to involve the Court in this number of plenary decisions suggests that they placed little value on time-consuming methods of

Table 7   A comparison of the voting propensities of the four justices who sat together on the Court, 1947-57

(In numbers of votes for review, nonunanimous cases)

| | Number of justices voting with justice in left column | | | | | | |
	0	1	2	3	4	5	6 or 7
Burton	47	78	88	95	94	220	
Frankfurter	27	92	109	103	83	81	219
Douglas	243	353	237	186	139	117	216
Black	221	326	198	187	128	107	195

decision making. These men exhibited in their case selection behavior a willingness to reach decisions quickly and to justify them without ado, characteristics that are also evident in their behavior on the merits.

Table 7 also shows that Black and Douglas participated in many more four-, five-, and six-vote grants than either Burton or Frankfurter. Only when seven or eight votes were cast were Burton and Frankfurter slightly more likely to have voted for review than Black or Douglas. This pattern indicates that Black and Douglas must have voted for review in many cases without paying much attention to the ideological similarities and differences with their colleagues that were usually in evidence in published decisions. Black and Douglas thus appear to differ from Burton and Frankfurter less in the types of cases they voted to hear than in the numbers they felt competent to decide on the merits.

In the weekly case selection conferences, the contrast between the two approaches must have been continually apparent and frequently irritating. To review-conservative justices like Frankfurter, the more review-prone justices must have seemed insensitive about the workload they were willing to impose on the Court. To the review-prone justices, those who seldom voted for review must sometimes have seemed callous about the plights of petitioners and the development of legal rights.

Conclusion

This analysis suggests that Supreme Court justices during the Burton period shared a powerful conception of the role of their institution, which appears to have sharply limited the level of disagreement that could otherwise have been anticipated in case selection voting. Consensus on the norms of judicial behavior also appears to have discouraged these justices either from combining forces

to achieve the results they preferred on the merits or from voting individually in a way that would indicate routine calculation of probable outcomes in the case selection process.

The voting patterns examined here thus suggest that role conceptions serve both a limiting and a liberating function. Judicial conceptions of appropriate behavior help to limit the expression of judicial predispositions towards litigants in voting. Yet role conceptions also operate to free the justices from ideological isolation, permitting them to vote routinely with ideologically dissimilar justices.

The evidence here also suggests that role conceptions can also be a source of disagreement in case selection. The considerable differences among the Burton-period justices in their willingness to vote for review appear to be at least partly attributable to variation in conceptions of the Court's role.

The self-imposed limits of role conceptions, it is important to note, are essentially the only limits upon judicial discretion in case selection. Because of the secrecy of the process, case selection exceeds even plenary decision making in the scope it provides for the exercise of unfettered judicial judgment. The Taft period justices campaigned hard for this broad authority, and until recently, Supreme Court justices were unanimous in their efforts to maximize their agenda-setting power.[29]

Disagreement among the current justices has finally made Court-controlled case selection a public issue, however.[30] The question for policymakers is whether the Court should be permitted to maintain complete control in setting its agenda, limited only by the conceptions the justices hold of the proper way to perform this function.

For students of judicial decision making, the significance of role conceptions in case selection has additional implications. The explanatory power of the concept in this context suggests that role perceptions deserve more attention in analyses of Supreme Court decision making on the merits. Differences in role conceptions have, of course, been the focus of some research,[31] but the phenomenon of consensus among justices has received too little attention.

Preoccupation with voting differences among the justices gives a misleading impression of judicial motivation. Differences in judicial attitudes and role conceptions tend to receive lopsided attention, while the influence of shared norms derived from legal and professional socialization tends to be ignored. This makes it difficult to determine the extent to which judicial decision making parallels political decision making in other contexts. A more accurate picture will emerge only when political scientists acknowledge that the work of Supreme Court justices includes more than nonunanimous decisions on the merits.

NOTES

This article originally appeared in Volume 64, Number 7, February 1981, pages 320-333. It was adapted from the author's book, CASE SELECTION IN THE UNITED STATES SUPREME COURT (Chicago: University of Chicago Press, 1980).

1. *See* ANNUAL REPORT, DIRECTOR OF THE ADMINISTRATIVE OFFICE OF U.S. COURTS. For a brief review of caseload growth, *see* the Federal Judicial Center, REPORT OF THE STUDY GROUP OF THE CASELOAD OF THE SUPREME COURT (Washington, D.C.: Administrative Office of U.S. Courts, 1972).

2. Ulmer, *Selecting Cases for Supreme Court Review: An Underdog Model*, 72 AM. POL. SCI. REV. 902 (1978).

3. The high degree of secrecy the Court has sought to maintain about all its work prior to the release of final decisions was made evident recently by the flurry of interest which greeted *The Brethren*, a journalistic expose of decision making on the Burger Court. Woodward and Armstrong, THE BRETHREN: INSIDE THE SUPREME COURT (New York: Simon and Schuster, 1979).

4. Earp, *Sovereign Immunity in the Supreme Court*, 16 AM. J. OF INT'L L. 903 (1976); and Hanus, *Denial of Certiorari and Supreme Court Policy-Making*, 17 AM. U. L. REV. (1967).

5. Bickel, THE LEAST DANGEROUS BRANCH 128 (Indianapolis: Bobbs-Merrill, 1962).

6. Schubert, QUANTITATIVE ANALYSIS OF JUDICIAL BEHAVIOR (New York: Free Press, 1959); and Schubert, *Policy Without Law: An Extension of the Certiorari Game*, 14 STAN. L. REV. 284 (1962).

7. Provine, CASE SELECTION IN THE UNITED STATES SUPREME COURT 168-169 (Chicago: University of Chicago Press, 1980).

8. Bloc members intent upon persuading the uncommitted members of the Court to vote for workers on the merits would be ill-advised to throw away votes on losing cases because such behavior would expose the true extent of their proworker bias. Of course, occasional instances of three votes would be understandable as mistakes, but even these should be rare.

9. Tanenhaus, Schick, Muraskin, and Rosen, *The Supreme Court's Certiorari Jurisdiction: Cue Theory*, in Schubert (ed.), JUDICIAL DECISION-MAKING (New York: Free Press, 1963).

10. *Id.* at 122-125.

11. *Id.* at 118.

12. These were some of the considerations Tanenhaus hypothesized to control the review decision *after* the initial search for cues has occurred. *Id.* at 118.

13. Brigman, "The Office of the Solicitor General of the United States," doctoral dissertation, University of North Carolina, 1966.

14. Ulmer was the first, and for a considerable time, the only scholar to mine the Burton papers for evidence of what Supreme Court justices consider in case selection.

15. Ulmer, *The Decision to Grant Certiorari as an Indicator to Decision 'On the Merits,'* 4 POLITY 429 (1972); and Ulmer, *Supreme Court Justices as Strict and Not-So-Strict Constructionists: Some Implications*, 8 LAW & SOC'Y REV. 13 (1973).

16. Ulmer, *The Decision . . . , supra* n. 15.

17. *Id.*

18. Ulmer, *Supreme Court Justices . . . , supra* n. 15.

19. Ulmer, *supra* n. 2.

20. Of course, assessments of the relative significance of role perceptions are necessarily tentative because available evidence is indirect, and the concepts of role and attitude are too amorphous to operationalize very satisfactorily. *See* Howard, *Role Perceptions and Behavior in Three U.S. Courts of Appeals*, 39 J. OF POL. 916 (1977); and Gibson, *Judges' Role Orientations, Attitudes, and Decisions*, 72 AM. POL. SCI. REV. 911 (1978).

21. Frankfurter, opinion explaining denial of review in State v. Baltimore Radio Show, 338 U.S. 912 (1950).

22. Prettyman, *Opposing Certiorari in the U.S. Supreme Court*, 61 VA. L. REV. 197 (1975).

23. Provine, *supra* n. 7, at 32

24. Brennan, *Justice Brennan Calls National Court of Appeals Proposal 'Fundamentally Unnecessary and Ill-Advised,'* 59 A.B.A. J. 835 (1973).

25. Provine, *supra* n. 7.

26. Pritchett, CIVIL LIBERTIES AND THE VINSON COURT (Chicago: University of Chicago Press, 1954).

27. *Id.* at 198.

28. *Id.* at 191.

29. Provine, *supra* n. 7, at 10-12 and 72-73.

30. Commission on Revision of the Federal Court Appellate System, STRUCTURE AND INTERNAL PROCEDURES: RECOMMENDATIONS FOR CHANGE (Washington, D.C.: U.S. Government Printing Office, 1975; and REPORT OF THE STUDY GROUP ON THE CASELOAD OF THE SUPREME COURT (Washington, D.C.: Administrative Office of U.S. Courts, 1972).

31. For other research on differences in role conceptions, *see* Pritchett, *supra* n. 26; Grossman, *Role-Playing and the Analysis of Judicial Behavior: The Case of Mr. Justice Frankfurter*, 11 J. OF PUB. L. 285 (1962); and *Dissenting Blocs on the Warren Court: A Study in Judicial Role Behavior*, 30 J. OF POL. 1068 (1968); Howard, *Role Perceptions and Behavior in Three U.S. Courts of Appeals*, 39 J. OF POL. 916 (1977); and Gibson, *supra* n. 20.

Some thoughts on judicial restraint

by John Paul Stevens
As delivered to the annual meeting and banquet of the
American Judicature Society, August 6, 1982[1]

During my exceptionally long tenure as the junior justice on the Supreme Court of the United States, I was frequently asked to compare the work on that Court with the work on the Court of Appeals for the Seventh Circuit on which I sat for five years. My answer to that question always made the point that I was much more conscious of the similarities between the two courts than of their differences.

During my brief tenure as one of the eight senior justices on the Court, I have frequently been asked to compare the work on an integrated court with the work on a segregated court. My answer to that question has usually made the point that although every retirement and every new appointment produces a different Court than its predecessor, the similarities between the Court on which Justice Stewart sat, and the Court on which Justice O'Connor sits, far outweigh their differences.

My belief that the common characteristics of the work of judges in a free society are far more significant than their differences has persuaded me that it may be worthwhile to share with you some of my concerns about the way the Supreme Court is presently discharging one of its judicial responsibilities. A frank discussion of our problems may identify some pitfalls that all of us should try to avoid and may uncover some possible solutions that merit further study.

The Supreme Court is now processing more litigation than ever before. The Court is granting more petitions for certiorari; litigants whose petitions are granted next fall may have to wait a full year before their cases are argued.[2] The Court is issuing more pages of written material; opinions for the Court are longer and more numerous, and

separate opinions are becoming the norm instead of the exception. The Court is deciding more cases on the merits without the benefit of full briefing and argument, using the currently fashionable technique of explaining its reasons in a "per curiam" opinion—a document generally written for the Court by an anonymous member of its ever increasing administrative staff.[3]

More and more frequently, after a case has been fully argued, the Court finds it appropriate to dismiss the writ of certiorari without making any decision on the merits because it belatedly learns that certiorari was improvidently granted.[4] As is true in so many courts throughout the country, the heavy flow of litigation is having a more serious impact on the administration of justice than is generally recognized.

Some of the consequences of this increased flow are predictable and have already begun to manifest themselves. The problem of delay—which is not yet serious—in a few years will be a matter of national concern. Of even greater importance, however, is what may happen within the Court itself. For when a court is overworked, the judges inevitably will concentrate their principal attention on the most important business at hand. Matters of secondary importance tend to be put to one side for further study or to be delegated to staff assistants for special consideration. Two examples illustrate this point.

At the beginning of our last term, after the Court had processed the list of certiorari petitions that had been filed during the summer recess—if my memory serves me correctly there were about a thousand cases on that list—we agreed that it was essential that we confront the question whether the Court should either support legislation that would increase the appellate capacity of the federal judicial system or try to develop new internal procedures that would ameliorate the impact of the case volume on our own work. As the term developed, however, and we became more and more deeply involved in the merits of a series of difficult cases, our initial recognition of the overriding importance of evaluating our own workload problems—and the desirability of scheduling conferences devoted exclusively to that subject matter—gradually dissipated and no such conference was ever held. We were too busy to decide whether there was anything we could do about the problem of being too busy.

Reviewing approximately 100 certiorari petitions each week and deciding which to grant and which to deny is important work. But it is less important work than studying and actually deciding the merits of cases that have already been accepted for review and writing opinions explaining those decisions. Because there simply is not enough time available to do the more important work with the care it requires and also to read all the certiorari petitions that are filed, I have found it necessary to delegate a great deal of responsibility in the review of certiorari petitions to my law clerks. They examine them all and select a small minority that they believe I should read myself. As a result, I do not even look at the papers in over 80 percent of the cases that are filed.

I cannot describe the practice of any of my colleagues, but when I compare the quality of their collective efforts at managing the certiorari docket with the high quality of their work on argued cases, I readily conclude that they also must be treating the processing of certiorari petitions as a form of second-class work. My observation of that process during the past seven terms has convinced me that the Court does a poor job of exercising its discretionary power over certiorari petitions. Because we are too busy to give the certiorari docket the attention it deserves, we grant many more cases than we should, thereby making our management problem even more unmanageable.

At this point I should make clear that I am expressing only my own opinion—an opinion that perhaps none of my colleagues may share. Indeed, some of them believe we should be taking many more cases and that our overflow should be decided by a newly created National Court of Appeals.

Under that view, the aggregate lawmaking capacity of the federal judiciary would be enlarged. There would be a significant increase in the number of federal adjudications binding on courts throughout the nation. Moreover, under that view, the management functions performed by the Supreme Court would require a relatively greater portion of the justices' total time. For the justices would not only decide what cases are important enough to justify decision on the merits at a national level, but they would also decide which of the two courts with nationwide jurisdiction should hear those cases. In other words, they would be managing the docket of two courts instead of just one.

The increased national capacity would also make it more difficult for us to resist the temptation to review every case in which we believe the court below has committed an error. Like a new four-lane highway that temporarily relieves traffic congestion, a new national court would also attract greater and greater traffic volumes and create unforeseen traffic problems. In my opinion, it would be unfortunate if the function of the Supreme Court of the United States should become one of primarily—or even largely—correcting errors committed by other courts. It is far better to allow the state supreme courts and federal courts of appeals to have the final say on almost all litigation than to embark on the hopeless task of attempting to correct every judicial error that can be found.

In my opinion, the Court and the nation would be better served by re-examining the doctrine of judicial restraint and by applying its teachings to the problems that confront us. The doctrine of judicial restraint is often misunderstood. It is not a doctrine that relates to the merits of judicial decisions; it is a doctrine that focuses on the process of making judicial decisions. It is a doctrine that teaches judges to ask themselves whether, and if so when, they should decide the merits of questions that litigants press upon them.

It is not a doctrine that denies the judiciary any lawmaking power—our common law heritage and the repeated need to add new stitches in the open fabric of our statutory and constitutional law foreclose the suggestion that judges never make law. But the doctrine of judicial restraint, as explained for example in Justice Brandeis' separate opinion in *Ashwander v. Tennessee Valley Authority*,[5] teaches judges to avoid *unnecessary* lawmaking. When it is necessary to announce a new proposition of law in order to decide an actual case or controversy between adversary litigants, a court has a duty to exercise its lawmaking power. But when no such necessity is present, in my opinion there is an equally strong duty to avoid unnecessary lawmaking.

The fact that the court is granting a larger number of certiorari petitions than ever before raises the question whether it is engaging in unnecessary lawmaking. The answer to that question is suggested by a few examples of the way the Court has exercised its discretionary jurisdiction in recent years. For both in deciding when to review novel questions and in deciding what questions need review, the Court often exhibits an unfortunate lack of judicial restraint.

Thus, the various opinions in our recent case involving a school library plainly disclose that the Court granted certiorari at an interlocutory stage of a case in which further proceedings in the trial court would either have clarified the constitutional issue or perhaps have mooted the entire case.[6] Similar considerations in the case involving a court clerk's claim of immunity prompted the Court to dismiss the writ as improvidently granted.[7] The Court's *timing* in these cases demonstrates that patience is both a virtue and a characteristic of judgment that judges sometimes forget.

In other cases, the Court has displayed a surprising unwillingness to allow other courts to make the final decision in cases that are binding in only a limited geographical area and in which no conflict exists. Thus, in *Watt v. Alaska*, apart from the possibility that error had been committed, there was no reason for our Court to involve itself in a dispute between the State of Alaska and one of its counties over the division of mineral leasing revenues that could only arise in the Ninth Circuit.[8]

In *Oregon v. Kennedy*, the Court elected to review a misapplication of double jeopardy doctrine by the Oregon Court of Appeals even though the particular facts of the case may never be duplicated in other litigation.[9] The fact that the new double jeopardy doctrine pronounced in the opinion of five of my colleagues was totally unnecessary to decide that case adds emphasis to the lack of necessity for granting certiorari at all. Moreover, despite that pronouncement, the Oregon court remained free to reinstate its prior judgment by un-

ambiguously relying on Oregon, rather than federal, law to support its holding.

In *South Dakota v. Opperman*, the state supreme court followed that precise course, thereby proving that our Court had unnecessarily taken jurisdiction of a case in which deference to the state court's judgments would have been appropriate in the first instance.[10] The decision to review (and to reverse summarily without argument) a novel holding by a California intermediate appellate court concerning the burden of proof in an obscenity trial,[11] or an equally novel holding by the Pennsylvania Supreme Court concerning a police officer's order commanding the driver of a vehicle to get out of his car after a traffic violation,[12] are examples of the many cases in which the Court has been unwilling to allow a state court to provide one of its residents more protection than the federal Constitution requires, even though the state decision affected only a limited territory and did not create a conflict with any other decision on a question of federal law, and even though the state court had the power to reinstate its original judgment by relying on state law.[13] A willingness to allow the decisions of other courts to stand until it is *necessary* to review them is not a characteristic of this Court when it believes that error may have been committed.

The Court's lack of judicial restraint is perhaps best illustrated by the procedure it followed in the *Snepp* case.[14] A former CIA agent filed a petition for certiorari seeking review of a Fourth Circuit decision holding that his publication of a book about Viet Nam violated his secrecy agreement with the CIA;[15] he contended that his contract was unenforceable because it abridged his right to free speech. The government opposed his petition and also filed a conditional cross-petition, praying that *if* the Court should grant Snepp's petition, it should also consider whether the remedy ordered by the lower court was adequate.

The Court denied Snepp's petition, but nevertheless granted the cross-petition and, without hearing arguments on the merits, issued a per curiam opinion ordering a constructive trust to be imposed on all of the book's earnings, even though there was neither a statutory nor contractual basis for that novel remedy. Since the government had not even asked the Court to review the remedy issue unless it granted Snepp's petition, it is undeniable that the Court's exercise of law-making power in that case was totally unnecessary.

If you think the *Snepp* case is unique in the revelatory light it casts on the Court's present approach to the doctrine of judicial restraint, I suggest that you read the Court's per curiam opinion in the *McCluskey* case, decided on the last day of this term, in which the Court exercised its majestic power to reinstate the suspension of a high school student who had consumed too much alcohol.[16]

You may think I have wandered away from a discussion of problems created by the mounting tide of litigation that is threatening to engulf our Court. My purpose in discussing the doctrine of judicial restraint, however, is relevant for two quite different reasons. First, it lends support to a possible solution to the problem that I favor; second, it explains why judges who do not share my respect for the doctrine will surely oppose that solution.

Instead of creating a new court to decide more cases on the merits, thereby increasing the aggregate judicial power that the Supreme Court may exercise, I favor the creation of a new court to which the Supreme Court would surrender some of its present power—specifically, the power to decide what cases the Supreme Court should decide on the merits. In essence, this is the proposal that was made by the committee headed by Professor Paul Freund several years ago[17] with one critical difference. I would allow that court to decide—not merely to recommend—that a certiorari petition should be granted or denied. Let me just briefly explain why I believe the creation of a new court with that power would significantly improve the administration of justice.

First, and of greatest importance, I believe an independent tribunal that did not have responsibility for deciding the merits of any case would do a far better job of selecting those relatively few cases that should be decided by the Supreme Court of the United States. As I have already suggested, I think the present Court does a poor job of performing that task. It grants too many cases and far too often we are guilty of voting to grant simply because we believe error has been committed rather than because the question presented is both sufficiently important for decision on a national level and also ripe for decision when action is taken on the certiorari petition. I recognize that a different court might make similar mistakes, but reflection has persuaded me that such a court would

be more likely to develop a jurisprudence of its own that properly focused on the factors—other than possible error—that should determine whether or not a certiorari petition should be granted.

Second, if I am correct in my belief that such a court would grant fewer petitions, this Court would be required to decide fewer cases on the merits. Even if that assumption is not correct, if the vast flood of paper and the small army of administrative personnel associated with the processing of our certiorari docket could be entirely removed from the Supreme Court, the time available to the justices for doing their most important work would be dramatically increased.[18] The threat to the quality of that work that is now posed by the flood of certiorari petitions would be entirely removed.

Finally, if the new court were granted the power to control our docket, I believe capable judges would regard membership on that court as worthy of their talent. When the original Freund Committee proposal was made, my initial reaction to it was the same as that of other circuit judges with whom I was serving—it seemed to offer us the opportunity to become law clerks instead of judges. But an important reason for that reaction was the fact that the proposed court was not expected to exercise any real power—it would have done no more than perform a preliminary screening function for the Supreme Court without the actual power of decision.

If the Supreme Court surrendered that power to the new court, the status of that court would indeed be significant. I am firmly convinced that a proper performance of the function of selecting the cases for the Supreme Cout's docket would be rewarding judicial work, requiring a scholarly understanding of new developments in the law and of our democratic institutions that only our ablest judges possess.

Those who question the wisdom of allowing the Supreme Court to relinquish control over its own docket, and who favor the creation of a new National Court of Appeals to decide cases that are referred to it by our Court, rely heavily on the perceived need to enlarge our capacity to resolve conflicts among the circuits. Let me therefore say a word about that asserted need. Again the doctrine of judicial restraint sheds light on the problem.

Putting to one side my own view that the number of unresolved conflicts is exaggerated, I would like to suggest, first, that the existence of differing rules of law in different sections of our great country is not always an intolerable evil and, second, that there are decision makers other than judges who could perform the task of resolving conflicts on questions of statutory construction. As Justice O'Connor noted in her eloquent dissent in the *FERC* case,[19] the fact that many rules of law differ from state to state is at times one of the virtues of our federal system. It would be better, of course, if federal law could be applied uniformly in all federal courts, but experience with conflicting interpretations of federal rules may help to illuminate an issue before it is finally resolved and thus may play a constructive role in the law-making process. The doctrine of judicial restraint teaches us that patience in the judicial resolution of conflicts may sometimes produce the most desirable result.

The doctrine of judicial restraint also raises the question whether the conflict resolution task need always be performed by judges. If the conflict is on a question of constitutional law, it must be resolved by the Supreme Court. But if, as is more frequently the case, the conflict is over the meaning of an ambiguous statutory provision, it may be both more efficient and more appropriate to allow Congress to make the necessary choice between the alternative interpretations of the legislative intent.

If the conflicts problem is—or should become—sufficiently important to justify the creation of an entirely new federal appellate court, I would suppose that the problem would also justify the creation of a standing committee of the Congress to identify conflicts that need resolution and to draft bills to resolve them one way or the other. If the source of the conflict is ambiguity resulting from an omission in a statute, it would seem to make good sense to assign Congress the task of performing the necessary corrective law making.[20]

At the outset, I suggested that a discussion of problems I perceive in our Court might be useful to other judges because the similarities among courts outweigh their differences. Before I close, let me therefore explain why I hope my comments may be relevant to the problems that arise in other courts. First, I would urge you to identify your problems and to discuss them openly and frankly. Disagreements with other judges is a characteristic of our profession that implies no disrespect and no lack of faith in the inherent strength of our insti-

tution. We must begin to talk about our problems before we can solve them.

Second, when you are considering possible changes in your procedures—as well as when you are deciding particular cases—keep in mind the teachings of the doctrine of judicial restraint. Consider whether, when, and how the special talent of judges—the thoughtful application of impartial judgment—should play a role in the decision-making process. And finally, I must note that although my remarks have indicated that proper management of a docket requires a court to treat some cases as having a greater importance or priority than others, distinctions that are made for administrative reasons are not applicable to the decisional process itself.

With regard to our primary responsibility, I would urge you to heed the advice of a truly great judge. In an interview a few weeks ago Justice Potter Stewart was asked if there was some opinion of which he was particularly proud. This was his answer:

I worked hard on every opinion. I think they were all satisfactory. I think it's very important for a judge—any judge, anywhere—to remember that every case is the most important case in the world for the people involved in that case, and not to think of a case as a second-class case or a third-class case or an unimportant case. It behooves the judge or justice to apply himself fully to every case and to give it conscientious consideration.

Justice Stewart's example, as well as his written word, is a great teacher.

NOTES

This article originally appeared in Volume 66, Number 5, November 1982, pages 177-183.

1. I wrote these remarks while away from my office and library. Thus, a few of my impressions about our docket have not been borne out by further research. Instead of rewriting the text, I have added a few documentary explanatory footnotes.

2. Of course, cases selected for review under the Court's certiorari jurisdiction are not the only source of backlog. This past year the Court exercised its discretion to grant more petitions for certiorari than ever before, but it also was required to note probable jurisdiction in 25 percent more cases than in any prior year.

3. This sentence needs elaboration in two ways. First, as a factual matter, I was mistaken. When I say "per curiam," I have in mind an unsigned opinion that decides a case on the merits without argument and does not merely remand for reconsideration in light of a recently decided case. The number of per curiams has oscillated over the past 20 years, and this past term's total of 20 was not unusually large. I should probably have stressed a more disturbing statistic—the number of divisive per curiams, those from which three or more justices dis-

sent. The past term produced 10 divisive per curiams, whereas six prior terms I have examined (1951-52, 1961-62, 1965-66, 1971-72, 1976-77, 1980-81) have produced at most four.

Second, my choice of the phrase "ever increasing administrative staff" was unfortunate. I intended the term "staff" to include the justices' personal law clerks as well as other court employees.

4. Here my memory of this past term failed me. In fact, our dismissal of only two petitions for certiorari as improvidently granted was less than our annual average. The fact that this is a recurring phenomenon, however, provides added support for my central thesis.

5. 297 US. 288, 341-356 (1936).

6. Board of Education, Island Trees Union Free School Dist. No. 26 v. Pico, 102 S. Ct. 2799 (1982).

7. Finley v. Murray, 102 S. Ct. 1703 (1982).

8. 451 U.S. 259 (1981).

9. 50 U.S.L.W. 4544 (May 24, 1982).

10. 428 U.S. 364 (1976); *on remand,* 247 N.W.2d 673 (S.D. 1976). *See also* Idaho Dep't of Employment v. Smith, 434 U.S. 100 (1977), *on remand,* Smith v. Department of Employment, 100 Idaho 520, 602 P.2d 18 (1979) (state ct. originally finds that state statute violates federal equal protection clause; after reversal, state ct. construes statute to be inapplicable to facts of the case).

11. Cooper v. Mitchell Brothers' Santa Ana Theater, 102 S. Ct. 172 (1981).

12. Pennsylvania v. Mimms, 434 U.S. 106 (1977).

13. *See also* Washington v. Chrisman, 50 U.S.L.W. 4133 (Jan. 13, 1982) (state supreme court held that a police officer violated the Fourth Amendment when, after stopping a student, asking for identification, and accompanying the student back to his room, he entered the room uninvited and without a warrant; U.S. S. Ct. reversed); Minnesota v. Clover Leaf Creamery Co., 449 U.S. 456 (1981) (state supreme court struck down a statute that banned the retail sale of milk in plastic nonreturnable nonrefillable containers, but permitted such sale in other nonreturnable nonrefillable containers such as paperboard cartons; U.S. S. Ct. reversed); Arkansas v. Sanders, 442 U.S. 753 (1979) (state supreme court held that police violated the Fourth Amendment by making a warrantless search of luggage located in an automobile they had lawfully stopped; U.S. S. Ct. affirmed); County Board of Arlington County, Virginia v. Richards, 434 U.S. 5 (1977) (state supreme court struck down a county zoning ordinance prohibiting automobile commuters from parking in designated residential neighborhoods; U.S. S. Ct. reversed).

14. 444 U.S. 507 (1980).

15. 595 F.2d 926 (4th Cir. 1979).

16. Board of Education of Rogers, Ark. v. McCluskey, 50 U.S.L.W. 3998.25 (July 2, 1982).

17. The Freund Committee said: "We recommend creation of a National Court of Appeals which would screen all petitions for review now filed in the Supreme Court . . . . The great majority, it is to be expected, would be finally denied by that [new] court. Several hundred would be certified annually to the Supreme Court for further screening and choice of cases to be heard and adjudicated there." Federal Judicial Center, REPORT OF THE STUDY GROUP OF THE CASELOAD OF THE SUPREME COURT 18 (Washington, D.C., 1972).

18. Perhaps "dramatically increased" overstates the significance of saving approximately one day each week for work on argued cases instead of certiorari petitions. The more important saving would, I believe, result from the selection of a smaller number of cases for plenary review.

19. Federal Energy Regulatory Comm'n v. Mississippi, 102 S. Ct. 2126, 2145 (1982).

20. In using the word "assign," I do not mean to suggest that the Supreme Court should seek to certify issues of statutory construction to a legislative committee. Rather, I am suggesting that the policymaking branch of the federal government might assign itself that task and an overburdened Court might do well to consider denying certiorari if a case raises only an issue of statutory or regulatory construction—an issue that could be resolved by another branch of the federal government.

Some thoughts on the Supreme Court's workload

by William J. Brennan Jr.
As delivered at the Third Circuit Judicial Conference, September 9, 1982,
Philadelphia, Pennsylvania.

You doubtless have read of the concern expressed at the ABA and AJS meetings in San Francisco by Justices White and Stevens that the Supreme Court confronts a calendar crisis so severe as to threaten the Court's ability effectively to discharge its vital responsibility. Justice Powell also addressed the problem but in the broader context of proposals designed to lessen the burdens of the entire federal court system. I should like in these brief remarks to address the problems of the Supreme Court calendar.

First, what is the problem? Justice White identified it:

During last term we granted review in 210 cases, which is 26 more than the term before and 56 more than two terms ago (and I may say parenthetically the largest number of grants in one term during my 26 terms on the Court). Apparently there were just too many petitions for certiorari that we could not conscientiously deny. Our docket is now full through February, next term, and will be completely full (only the March and April sessions remain to be filled) by the end of November if grants next term proceed at the same rate as they did last term.

Of course this means that we shall not be current in our work; cases will be ready for argument and we shall not be ready for them. This is something new and disturbing . . . The [problem thus is] not that the Court [is] not hearing all the cases that it [has] the capacity to hear but that it [does] not have the capacity to review all those cases that the system contemplated would be reviewed at the Supreme Court level.

Justice White asked, "Can or does the Court hear all the cases that must be reviewed and authoritatively decided if the federal law is to survive in the form contemplated by the Constitution?"

For now, I think I'd say yes, it does.

It is true, as Justice White said, "that there is a finite limit on the number of cases that the Court can hear and decide with opinion in any one term." For more than 15 of my 26 terms, starting in 1956, the Court averaged about 100 opinions per term plus a few per curiams in argued cases. But since the 1970 term that number has inexorably crept up, first to the high 120, then to the 130s, and last term to 141 signed plus nine per curiam.

That didn't set any record—the 1975 term produced 151 opinions, 138 signed, and 13 per curiam. And since we schedule 160 hours of argument from October through April, it is clear that 150 is the maximum. Of course we could add another month of arguments and theoretically turn out 20 more opinions. But I suggest that the Court, as Justice White says, "should not be expected to produce more than 150 opinions per term in argued cases, including per curiam opinions in such case." There is a limit to human endurance, and with the ever increasing complexity of many of the cases that the Court is reviewing in this modern day, the number 150 taxes that endurance to its limits.

I suppose the solution to the question whether the number of grants can be kept under control and the calendar made manageable without rejection of cases that should be heard and decided depends (a) on what the Court can do for itself to avoid granting cases that should not be granted and (b) on what the Congress and the courts of appeals can do to minimize the necessity for granting review of some cases.

What can we do for ourselves? I must admit frankly that we too often take cases that present no necessity for announcement of a new proposition of law but where we believe only that the court below has committed error. But ever since the Congress enacted the Judges Bill of 1925, the Supreme Court has not been expected to take on the function of primarily—or even largely—correcting errors committed by other courts. As Justice White reminded us, in 1925 Congress was presented with the proposition that after decision in a trial court and after at least one review in federal or state appellate court, further appeal to the Supreme Court should be permitted only where issues of federal law important to the country were involved, or where further review was essential to resolve conflicts between lower courts on questions of federal constitutional or statutory law, which, by definition was to be equally and uniformly applicable in all parts of the country. "Absent these qualifications, one trial and one appellate review were enough."

It was this history that prompted Justice Stevens to remark, "It is far better to allow the state supreme courts and federal courts of appeals to have the final say on almost all litigation than to embark on the hopeless task of attempting to correct every judicial error that can be found."

And, too, we have made mistakes in granting certiorari at an interlocutory stage of a case when allowing the case to proceed to its final disposition below might produce a result that makes it unnecessary to address an important and difficult constitutional question. Last term's school library case is a paradigm example. It presented the question of whether schools boards were in any wise restrained by the First Amendment in the removal of books from a school library. The district judge held not and granted the school board summary judgment. The Second Circuit reversed on the ground that the case presented a genuine issue of fact as to the school board's motivation and therefore the case should be tried. Obviously, further proceedings in the trial court would either have clarified the constitutional issue or perhaps have mooted the entire case. Yet the Court took the case at the interlocutory stage, disposed of it by an affirmance of the remand for trial, and filed eight separate opinions without producing one that commanded the votes of a majority. Surely we should discipline ourselves to be more faithful to the *Ashwander* principle not to address constitutional issues if there is a way properly to avoid doing so.

Congress could afford the Court substantial assistance by repealing to the maximum extent possible the Court's mandatory appellate jurisdiction and shifting those cases to the discretionary certiorari docket. A bill to this end is pending in the Congress and every member of the Court devoutly hopes it will be adopted. Cases on appeal consume a disproportionate amount of the limited time available for oral argument. That's because time and again a justice who would conscientiously deny review of an issue presented on certiorari cannot conscientiously say that when presented on appeal the issue is insubstantial, the test on appeal. Policy considerations that gave rise to the distinction between review by appeal and review by writ of certiorari have long since lost their force, and abandonment of our appellate jurisdiction (leaving a writ of certiorari as the only means of obtaining Supreme Court review) is simply recognition of reality.

Can we perhaps decide more cases on the merits by denying ourselves the benefit of full briefing and oral argument? There is sentiment among some of my colleagues to do so. Because I wholeheartedly agree with Justice Stevens that "oral argument is a vital component of the appellate process," and have too often witnessed colleagues, who favored summary affirmance at the cert stage, change their minds after oral argument—and because I think further that the Court's favorable image in the eyes of both bar and public rests so heavily on oral audience before us—I have continuously protested against summary dispositions, unless at least all of us believe that the judgment below flatly rejects the controlling authority of one of our decisions. If the losing side commands the agreement of a single justice, it seems to me he's entitled to an opportunity orally to persuade others of us.

One of the Court's important functions of course is the resolution of conflicts in statutory construction or constitutional principles decided by the courts of appeals; a major segment of each term's docket is provided by such cases. Both Justice White and Justice Stevens offered some provocative suggestions for reducing the burden of such cases. "If the resolution of conflicting decisions is at the root of the problem," said Justice White, there is the option of creating new courts of appeal that would hear appeals from district courts countrywide in certain kinds of cases.

For example, the Court of Appeals for the Federal Circuit, created by the merger of the Court of Customs and Patent Appeals and the Court of Claims, will hear all appeals from district courts in cases arising under the patent laws. Another court that hears all appeals from cases arising under specified statutes is the Emergency Court of Appeals. Courts like these, of course, bypass the regular court of appeals, but they eliminate the possibility of conflicts that normally would have to be heard in the Supreme Court.

That surely is a suggestion worth exploring. It does not foreclose Supreme Court review but removes conflict as the reason for review. No constitutional impediment occurs to me, although doubtless policy considerations might be a reason for congressional opposition.

Justice White offered still another and novel idea for reflection: "That is," he said, "to require a court of appeals to go *en banc* before differing with another court of appeals and to make the first *en banc* decision the nationwide rule." I expect that the court of appeals and district court judges here today might want to mull that one over a bit.

Justice Stevens' contribution is equally imaginative and innovative. If, he says, "as is more frequently the case, the conflict is over the meaning of an ambiguous statutory provision it may be more efficient and more appropriate to allow Congress to make the necessary choice between the alternative interpretations of the legislative intent." This could be accomplished, he suggests, by

the creation of a standing committee of the Congress to identify conflicts that need resolution and to draft bills to resolve them one way or the other. If the source of the conflict is ambiguity resulting from an omission in a statute, it would seem to make good sense to assign Congress the task of performing the necessary corrective law making.

The problem I see with this suggestion is that it overlooks the role of compromise in the legislative process, compromise that often accounts for the studied ambiguity of legislative language, deliberately adopted to let the courts put a gloss on the words that the legislators could not agree upon. If the legislators could not avoid the ambiguity in originally enacting the law it might be no different if they attempted to resolve the conflict.

Justice Stevens also asked whether in any event conflicts of interpretation were necessarily a bad

thing. He said,

the existence of different rules of law in different sections of our great country is not always an intolerable evil . . . it would be better, of course, if federal law could be applied uniformly in all federal courts, but experience with conflicting interpretations of federal law may help to illuminate an issue before it is finally resolved and thus may play a constructive role in the law making process. The doctrine of judicial restraint teaches us that patience in the judicial resolution of conflicts may sometime produce the most desirable result.

I think there is already in place, and has been ever since I joined the Court, a policy of letting tolerable conflicts go unaddressed until more than two courts of appeals have considered a question. Indeed, Justice White has filed opinions in recent terms chiding his colleagues for being too tolerant of conflicts. I confess for myself that I doubt there is much more we can do along those lines.

But suppose, as the Commission on Federal Appellate Revision concluded a few years ago, that these various efforts failed to achieve a manageable calendar and "that at some point the percentage of cases accorded review will have dipped below the minimum necessary for effective monitoring of the nation's courts on issues of federal statutory and constitutional law"—what then? Justice White thought, "There are surely obvious alternatives, particularly if more fundamental structural changes are thought necessary to remedy the problem. Rather than one Supreme Court," he said, "there might be two, one for statutory issues and one for constitutional cases; or one for criminal and one for civil cases." That proposition of course would require a constitutional amendment, but in any event, I cannot see any crisis confronting us that would require so drastic a wrench of our constitutional structure.

Then there is the revival of the proposal originally made a decade ago by the distinguished Freund Commission to create a National Court of Appeals. As Justice White noted, the essence of that proposal was this:

all certioraris and appeals would come to the Court as they do now. The Court would select cases for its own docket as it does now, but if there were other cases deserving of review that it could not hear, it would have the authority to refer those cases to a so-called national court of appeals . . . that court's decisions would be subject to certiorari review, but it was thought that only rarely would certiorari be granted in those cases . . . .

Justice White acknowledged that a bill is now pending in Congress to create such a court but says, "I see no great flurry of activity around it."

Justice Stevens opposes the suggestion of transferring cases for decision by the proposed national court of appeals, but he also opposes the suggestion that that court assist the Supreme Court in selecting the cases that will be set for oral argument and plenary review. This would be done by that court screening out seven-eighths of the cases filed in our Court, leaving us to choose from some 400 to 500 cases the 150 or so that would be heard and decided. Instead of that system, Justice Stevens, in his words,

favors the creation of a new court to which the Supreme Court would surrender some of its present power, specifically the power to decide what cases the Supreme Court should decide on the merits [Unlike the Freund Committee proposal] I would allow that court to decide—not merely to recommend—that a certiorari petition should be granted or denied,

and that court's decision to deny would not be reviewable.

I completely disagree with my respected and distinguished colleague. I dissented from the form in which the Freund Committee made the proposal and feel even more strongly that adoption of Justice Stevens' proposal would destroy the role of the Supreme Court as the framers envisaged it.

Justice Stevens believes that the screening function "is less important work than studying and actually deciding the merits of cases that have already been accepted for review and writing opinions explaining those decisions." Apart from the fact that the plan would clearly violate the constitutional provision establishing "one Supreme Court," and therefore require a constitutional amendment, I reject Justice Stevens' fundamental premise that consideration given to the cases actually decided on the merits is compromised by the pressures of processing the inflated docket of petitions and appeals.

I don't have time to demonstrate here why that premise is unsupportable. Suffice it for present purposes that my view that the screening function is second to none in importance is reflected in my practice of performing the screening function myself. I make an exception only during the summer recess when the initial screening of petitions is invaluable training for next term's new law clerks.

For my own part, I find that I don't need a great deal of time to perform the screening function—certainly not an amount of time that compromises my ability to attend to decisions of argued cases. I should emphasize that the longer one works at the screening function, the less onerous and time-consuming it becomes. Unquestionably the equalizer is experience, and for experience there can be no substitute, not even a second court.

If the screening function were to be farmed out to another court, some enormous values of the Supreme Court decisional process would be lost. Under the present system, a single justice may set a case for discussion at conference, and in many instances that justice succeeds in persuading three or more of his colleagues that the case is worthy of plenary review. Thus the existing procedure provides a forum in which the particular interests or sensitivities of individual justices may be expressed, and therefore has a flexibility that is essential to the effective functioning not only of the screening process but also of the decisional process which is an inseparable part.

Similarly, the artificial construction of the Supreme Court's docket by others than the members of the Court would seriously undermine the important impact dissents from denials of review frequently have had upon the development of the law. Such dissents often herald the appearance on the horizon of possible re-examination of what may seem to the judges of another court doing the screening work to be an established and unimpeachable principle. Indeed, a series of dissents from denials of review played a crucial role in the Court's reevaluation of the reapportionment question, and the question of the applicability of the Fourth Amendment to electronic searches. This history of the role of such dissents on the right to counsel in criminal cases and the application of the Bill of Rights to the states surely is too fresh in mind to ignore.

Moreover, the assumption that the judges of a national court of appeals could accurately select the "most review-worthy" cases wholly ignores the inherently subjective nature of the screening process. The thousands upon thousands of cases docketed each term simply cannot be placed in a computer that will instantaneously identify those that I or any one of my colleagues would agree are "most review-worthy." A question that is "substantial" for me may be wholly insubstantial to some, perhaps all, of my colleagues. As Chief Justice

Warren said:

The delegation of the screening process to the National Court of Appeals would mean that the certiorari "feel" of the rotating panels of that Court would begin to play a vital role in the ordering of our legal priorities and control of the Supreme Court docket. More than that, this lower court "feel" would be divorced from any intimate understanding of the concerns and interests and philosophies of the Supreme Court Justices; and that "feel" could reflect none of the other intangible actors and trends within the Supreme Court that often play a role in the certiorari process.

I repeat that a fundamental premise of Justice Stevens' proposal is that the screening function plays only a minor and separable part in the exercise of the Court's fundamental responsibilities. I think that premise is clearly, indeed dangerously, wrong. In my experience over more than a quarter century, the screening process has been, and is today, inextricably linked to the fulfillment of the Court's essential duties and is vital to the effective performance of the Court's unique mission "to define the rights guaranteed by the Constitution, to assure the uniformity of federal law, and to maintain the constitutional distribution of powers in our federal union."

The choice of issues for decision largely determines the image that the American people have of their Supreme Court. The Court's calendar mirrors the ever-changing concerns of this society with every more powerful and smothering government. The calendar is therefore the indispensable source for keeping the Court abreast of these concerns. Our Constitution is a living document and the Court often becomes aware of the necessity for reconsideration of its interpretation only because filed cases reveal the need for new and previously unanticipated applications of constitutional principles. To adopt Justice Stevens' proposal to limit the Court's consideration to a mere handful of the cases selected by others would obviously result in isolating the Court from many nuances and trends of legal change throughout the land.

The point is that the evolution of constitutional doctrine is not merely a matter of hearing arguments and writing opinions in cases granted review. The screening function is an inseparable part of the whole responsibility; to turn over that task to a national court of appeals is to rent a seamless web. And how traumatic and difficult must be the screening task of the judges of a court of appeals required to do major Supreme Court work without being afforded even the slightest glimpse of the whole picture of a justice's function.

It is not only that constitutional principles evolve over long periods and that one must know the history of each before he feels competent to grapple with their application in new contexts never envisioned by the framers. It is also that he must acquire an understanding of the extraordinarily complex factors that enter into the distribution of judicial power between state and federal courts and other problems of "Our Federalism." The screening function is an indispensable and inseparable part of the entire process and it cannot be withdrawn from the Court without grave risk of impairing the very core of the Court's unique and extraordinary functions.

You may rightly ask me then, what would you do to bring about the shrinking of the size of the calendar to manageable numbers? First, I would urge greater care by the Court in the selection of cases for review. Second, I would urge repeal by Congress of virtually all the Court's mandatory appeal jurisdiction. Third, I would urge an immediate study of the feasibility of Justice White's suggestion of creating new courts of appeals that would hear appeals from district courts countrywide in certain kinds of cases, thus obviating conflicts. Fourth, I would urge an immediate study of Justice White's other suggestion for minimizing conflicts—to require a court of appeals to go *en banc* before differing with another court of appeals and make the first *en banc* decision the nationwide rule.

But I would most emphatically reject all proposals for the creation of a national court of appeals, or any other court, to which would be assigned the task of doing the Court's work, whether decisional or screening. Adoption of that proposal would sow the seeds of destruction of the Court's standing as we know it. For remember, Justice Brandeis ascribed the great prestige of the Court with the American public to a single factor, "Because we do our own work."

NOTE

This article originally appeared in Volume 66, Number 6, December-January 1983, pages 230-235.

Caseload, conflicts, and decisional capacity: does the Supreme Court need help?

Examining the Court's work, and workload, suggests we should give more thought to the need for—and structure of—the proposed Intercircuit Tribunal.

by Arthur D. Hellman

Congress is now giving serious consideration to legislation that would effect the most far-reaching change in the structure of the federal judicial system since the creation of intermediate appellate courts nearly a century ago. Bills introduced by Senator Dole and Congressman Kastenmeier, with the apparent support of Chief Justice Burger, would create an "Intercircuit Tribunal of the United States Courts of Appeals" that would hear and decide cases referred to it by the Supreme Court. Unless overruled or modified by the Supreme Court, decisions of the Tribunal would constitute binding precedents in all other federal courts and, with respect to federal issues, in state courts as well.[1]

Proponents argue that creation of the new court is necessary for two reasons: "to relieve the dramatically increased workload of the Supreme Court" and to "provide desperately needed additional decisional capacity for the resolution of disputes where nationwide uniformity is needed."[2] Curiously, although the problems perceived by the sponsors originate in conditions that can hardly be expected to disappear as the years go by, the bills now in committee would create only a temporary court composed of circuit judges who would sit on the Intercircuit Tribunal in ad hoc panels while continuing to serve on their own courts.

The premises underlying this proposal raise fundamental questions about the role of the Supreme Court in the American legal system and the extent to which one tribunal of nine justices can fulfill that role. In this article, I shall address those questions. I conclude that notwithstanding its impressive sponsorship, the legislation should not be enacted, at least in its present form. To the extent that it seeks to reduce the workload of the justices, it is unnecessary. To the extent that it seeks to promote uniformity in the law, it rests on assumptions that have not been proved; but even if those assumptions are correct, creation of a temporary tribunal would do little to foster uniformity, while it would have undesirable consequences for the Supreme Court's performance of the tasks it would not delegate.

One preliminary observation is in order. During the past year, eight of the nine sitting justices have expressed concern about the Court's caseload and the management of its docket. This has led some observers to conclude that the justices agree that the caseload problem has reached crisis proportions and requires immediate legislative reform. However, the more important fact is that the diagnoses offered by the members of the Court are quite different and to some extent contradictory.

Justices White and Rehnquist think that limited decisional capacity is causing the Court to deny review in some cases that require resolution at the national level; Justice Stevens thinks that the Court grants review in more cases than are necessary. Chief Justice Burger finds a plenary docket of 150 cases a term—the current figure—to be so burdensome as to threaten a breakdown of the system; but in the eyes of Justice Rehnquist, it is well within the limits of the tolerable. The chief justice predicts an increase in summary reversals, especially in criminal cases; Justices Brennan, Marshall, and Stevens think that the summary reversal is overused even today. Justices Powell and O'Connor have spoken only in general terms about the Supreme Court's workload; their principal concern has been the proliferation of litigation in the lower federal courts.

This diversity of views provides a poor basis indeed for immediate structural reform. On the contrary, it only emphasizes the need for careful analysis of the Court's functions and practices before any legislation is enacted.

The workload of the justices

In considering whether the justices are overworked, it is necessary to look separately at the two tasks they perform: selecting the cases they will decide, and deciding them. Attention must also be given to the effect of the obligatory jurisdiction on the Court's workload.

Screening cases for plenary review

With the possible exception of Justice Stevens, no member of the present Court has asserted that the process of screening cases for plenary review has become unmanageable.[3] Nor would such an assertion be persuasive. Admittedly, the number of cases to be examined is much greater than it was two decades ago—4,417 in the 1981 term. But a caseload of that size does not impose nearly the burden that it would, for example, at the court of appeals level.

From Taft onward, the justices have emphasized that the function of the Supreme Court is not to correct errors in the lower courts, but to "secur[e] harmony of decision and the appropriate settlement of questions of general importance."[4] Thus, except for the cases that come to the Court on appeal—less than 5 percent of the total—the purpose of screening is not to determine whether there was error, or even probable error, in the court below. Rather, the Court considers whether the case presents an issue of "wide public importance or governmental interest."[5] Making that determination will usually take very little time, compared with assessing the probable correctness of the decision below.

More important, the vast majority of applications clearly do not meet the standard for "certworthiness" that the justices have articulated. A few years ago, Justice Brennan revealed that 70 percent of the cases were so obviously unworthy of review that not even one justice requested that they be discussed at the Court's conference.[6] More recently, Chief Justice Burger—who has been in the forefront of those arguing that the Court is overburdened—has said that two-thirds of the new filings are not only unworthy of review but "utterly frivolous."[7]

Perusal of the case summaries in *United States Law Week* confirms these perceptions. In one case after another, the party seeking review asserts only that the lower court abused its discretion or erred in applying well-established rules to particular facts. And those are the paid cases. Almost half of all applications for review are filed by indigent litigants, nearly all of whom are criminal defendants who have nothing to lose by filing petitions whether or not they present an issue appropriate for the Supreme Court.[8]

Deciding cases and writing opinions

The screening process thus constitutes a relatively small part of the justices' total workload. The more time-consuming task is that of reaching decisions and writing opinions in the 140 to 150 cases that do receive plenary consideration each term. Yet is is far from clear that a calendar of that size truly imposes an intolerable burden on the justices.

Under current conditions, each justice is required to write 15 or 16 majority opinions a term—barely two for each month that the Court is in session. Some of the cases will involve intractable social and political issues warranting extended reflection and research, but not all fit this description. In particular, by the time the Court resolves a statutory issue, the competing arguments should have been thoroughly ventilated in the lower courts and the law reviews, and the justices should be able to reach a decision and write their opinions with a minimum of agonizing.

This is not to deprecate the amount of time and effort required for the process of reaching and justifying decisions in the cases on the plenary docket. After all, the justices not only have their own opinions to write; they should also be giving careful scrutiny to the drafts prepared by their colleagues. And if caseload pressures become too great, review of other justices' opinions is likely to be the first casualty, thus reducing the opportunities for clarifying the language, sharpening the reasoning, or otherwise improving the final product through collegial consultation.

This analysis suggests that whether or not the workload has begun to overwhelm the justices, creation of a new court might still be desirable on a different theory: that the Supreme Court could then reduce the number of cases that receive plenary consideration and thus be able to produce opinions of higher quality—however one might measure that elusive goal. Indeed, that was a major theme of Chief Justice Burger's speech in New Orleans calling for creation of an intercircuit panel similar to the one contemplated by the pending legislation.

It might seem intuitively obvious that the justices would write better opinions if they had more time. Nevertheless, the available evidence indicates that the matter is not that simple. In the middle and late 1950s the Court was hearing fewer cases than at any other time in this century; but that was also the era when eminent scholars filled the law reviews with devastating criticism of the Court's craftsmanship. Not everyone agreed with those criticisms, but the history provides little comfort for those who see a smaller docket as leading to wiser adjudications or more illuminating opinions. More recently, the abortion decisions of 1973 were handed down only after an extended process of research, reflection, and deliberation; yet those opinions too have been subjected to vehement criticism, even by scholars who sympathize with the results.

In any event, before we can reach any conclusions about the burdens imposed by the plenary docket, we must consider the actions of the justices themselves. If the members of the present Court are truly overworked, they are behaving in some very strange ways. Consider:

• Separate expressions of views have proliferated in recent years to an extent never before known. In the 1981 term alone the justices issued more than 175 separate opinions.[9] It is understandable, and indeed desirable, that a justice would write separately when he or she cannot support the result or rationale of the majority opinion. But more than 20 of these separate opinions were written by justices who had already joined the opinion of the majority. In addition, there were half a dozen dissenting opinions by justices who had already joined another dissent. Strangest of all, there was one case in which the author of the majority opinion also wrote a separate opinion reversing the court below on a second ground, and another case

in which two opinions were joined by different majorities of justices.[10]

• In recent terms, a major component of the plenary docket has consisted of criminal cases in which the lower courts had upheld the defendant's constitutional claims. In some of the cases, a state court had arguably rested its judgment on adequate and independent nonfederal grounds.[11] Other decisions appeared to involve little more than the application of established rules to a particular set of facts.[12] While a Supreme Court ruling would add something to the body of nationally binding precedents, the contribution would be marginal enough that an overburdened Court could deny review without concern that it would be missing an opportunity to significantly clarify the law.

• In other cases where lower courts have accepted a litigant's federal constitutional claim, the Court has reversed without hearing oral argument. These reversals have been accompanied by per curiam opinions, a few of which approach the length of many signed opinions.[13] Here, too, some of the cases have involved only the application of established rules to particular facts.[14] For the most part, nothing in the per curiam opinions has suggested that the particular situations are recurring ones, or that the decisions below reflect oft-repeated errors or a consistent disregard of the governing law.[15] Thus consideration on the merits could not be justified either from the standpoint of the Court's lawmaking functions or as a necessary exercise of its supervisory power.

• In the current term the Court ordered reargument on an important issue that had neither been litigated in the court below nor raised in the petition for review. As the dissenting justices pointed out, these circumstances make more work for the Court in deciding the case.[16]

Effect of obligatory jurisdiction

Assessment of the "workload problem" also requires attention to the fact that the Court today does not have an entirely free hand in selecting the cases it will decide. When a case comes to it on appeal rather than by certiorari, the Court has no choice but to decide the merits. The Court need not—and usually does not—give the case plenary consideration or write an opinion, but it cannot avoid the duty of determining whether the lower court committed error. In recent terms, about half of the cases decided on the merits have been appeals.

It might be thought that because most of the appeal cases are disposed of by summary orders without opinion, abolition of the obligatory jurisdiction would not significantly lighten the Supreme Court's workload. Study of the Court's practices, however, indicates that the continuing flow of appeal cases imposes at least three kinds of burdens on the justices.

First, the obligation to decide the merits of a case sometimes leads the Court to grant plenary consideration to appeals that would have been denied review if they had come up by certiorari. As the justices have pointed out, "[t]here is no necessary correlation between the difficulty of the legal questions in a case and its public importance."[17] As a result, the Court often feels obliged to call for full briefing and oral argument in appeal cases that are too difficult to decide summarily but not important enough to warrant review by certiorari standards. In the 1981 term, fully one out of every four cases on the plenary docket came to the Court on appeal. While many of the cases were worthy of review by certiorari standards, some—probably 10 or more—were not.[18]

Second, even if the issue presented by an appeal is one that the Supreme Court would ultimately want to decide, the particular case may raise it prematurely or in a setting inappropriate for a definitive resolution. Either circumstance makes the Court's job harder. If the issue has not yet been thoroughly ventilated in the lower courts, the process of reaching a decision and writing an opinion will be more difficult because the Supreme Court will be deprived of the benefits of "percolation." If the case is not an appropriate vehicle, not only will the opinion be harder to write, but the decision may not settle the issues, so that they will come back in somewhat different form and require additional consideration.

Finally, the obligatory jurisdiction adds to the Court's burdens even in the cases that receive summary treatment. Whatever the practice may have been before the Court announced that summary dispositions are decisions on the merits,[19] the Court today must give every appeal a degree of attention and thought that need not be accorded a certiorari petition. After all, if certiorari is denied improvidently, the issue remains open in all other jurisdictions, and if the question is truly worthy of review, it will return in another case. But if the Court improvidently affirms a case on appeal, the effect is to establish a nationally binding precedent and to discourage if not preclude further litigation of the issue.[20] Thus the justices must examine each jurisdictional statement with at least enough care to assure themselves that affirmance will not settle a question that they prefer to leave open.[21]

☆ ☆ ☆

Two conclusions emerge from this analysis. First, the Court's workload has not yet reached anything resembling crisis proportions. Second, before implementing structural change, Congress should take the uncontroversial and long-overdue step of eliminating the remaining elements of the obligatory jurisdiction.[22] Once that is done, we will have the opportunity to see how the Court manages its docket on a wholly discretionary basis. If, after a few years, the workload is shown to be truly burdensome, there will be no alternative to structural reform; but Congress, the bar, and the public will have had that much more time to consider the merits of various possible solutions.

The problem of disuniformity

To say that the Court's workload does not justify creation of a new tribunal is not to say that the justices could reasonably be expected to increase the number of cases that receive plenary consideration, and indeed no one takes that view. Thus the stronger argument for structural change rests on the assertion that "additional decisional capacity" is needed to secure uniformity and consistency in federal law.

To evaluate this claim, it is necessary to answer four questions. First, to what extent is there disuniformity in the law today as a result of the limited number of cases the Supreme Court can decide on the merits? Second, how has the lack of "appellate capacity" affected those who must conform their conduct to federal precedents—judges deciding cases in the lower courts, lawyers advising clients, and citizens carrying out their everyday activities? Third, how effective would the proposed new court be in reducing the existing uncertainty? Finally, how would the availability of the reference option affect the Supreme Court's performance of the work it would not delegate?

Unresolved intercircuit conflicts

In introducing the bill to create an Intercircuit

Tribunal, Senator Dole asserted that the proposed court would "provide desperately needed additional decisional capacity for the resolution of disputes where nationwide uniformity is needed, many of which are now left unresolved because the Supreme Court cannot make room on its docket." In a similar vein, Congressman Kastenmeier stated that hundreds of petitions from the courts of appeals are denied review even though some "identify serious conflicts between circuits." The clear implication is that the Supreme Court is denying review in such a large number of conflict cases, with such a substantial impact on consistency in the law, that the need for additional decisional capacity has reached the point of desperation.

But where is the evidence? Where is a list of 50 cases in which the Supreme Court, during a recent term, has denied review despite the presence of a conflict? Where are 30 unreviewed conflicts? Where are 20? One searches in vain for any such compilation, either in the record of the hearings on similar legislation held in 1981 and 1982 or in the statements submitted on the Senate bill this spring.[23]

Within the Court, the most persistent advocate of the view that intercircuit conflicts remain unresolved because the Court "cannot make room on its docket" has been Justice White. A casual reader of the weekly order lists might get the impression that Justice White has identified a substantial number of cases in which the Court has denied review despite the presence of a conflict. But careful counting reveals that in the 1981 term Justice White published only 12 opinions dissenting from the denial of review on that ground. Two involved the same issue; two others involved issues that are scheduled to be considered in the 1982 term. And study of all unreviewed cases in the 1980 term in which Justice White filed a dissenting notation of any kind yields no more than 15 in which the decision below appeared to conflict with the ruling of another appellate court.[24]

On the basis of the available evidence, then, it cannot be said that the number of conflicts presented to the Supreme Court has, to any substantial degree, outstripped the Court's capacity to resolve them. At first blush, this may seem rather surprising. After all, during the last few decades Congress has substantially added to the body of federal statutes that require interpretation; the number of circuits has been enlarged; and the volume of appellate litigation has grown enormously.

But these developments do not necessarily bring about a proportionate increase in the number of conflicts. For one thing, the courts of appeals generally attempt to avoid intercircuit disagreements if they can conscientiously do so.[25] More important, as new issues arise, old ones become settled (through the accumulation of precedents)[26] or irrelevant (through developments in the law or in the activity being regulated).[27] Finally, as will be discussed more fully below, there are many issues that for one reason or another are just not likely to give rise to conflicting decisions. Thus, even though the United States Code may occupy an ever-larger space on the shelf, the number of questions on which the courts of appeals will actually differ may remain relatively stable.

Potential conflicts

Up to this point I have focused on unresolved intercircuit conflicts as a measure of the adequacy of the national appellate capacity. But the more thoughtful supporters of the proposed new court argue that the desirability of obtaining a definitive resolution of a particular issue does not depend on the existence of an actual conflict. They point out that for those who must regulate their activities in accordance with federal precedents, the presence or absence of a conflict is almost irrelevant; the crucial question is whether there is an issue that is doubtful enough that the possibility of conflict exists. If conflict is possible, uncertainty is inevitable. And, as Professor Meador has suggested, "uncertainty about the ultimate meaning to be given statutory provisions can make the work of lawyers and administrators difficult and more costly to citizens and to government."[28]

Yet even when these considerations are taken into account, it does not necessarily follow that the focus on unresolved conflicts has been misdirected. At the least, the further we move away from an actual conflict, the less likely it becomes that a given case warrants a decision by the Supreme Court, and the more likely it is that the Court would deny review even apart from caseload pressures. There are two reasons why this is so.

First, the particular explanation for the absence of a conflict may suggest that a decision by the Court is unlikely to make a significant contribution to uniformity in the law. For example, if there

are no other cases on point, the reason may be
that the precise problem arises very seldom; if so,
no other court is likely to confront the issue in the
future. If there are several decisions, all reaching
the same result, that may be because the answer is
obvious, and any reasonable lawyer would confi-
dently predict that future courts will follow in the
same path.[29]

Finally, and perhaps most important, if there
are multiple decisions that look in somewhat different directions without actually conflicting, the
reason may be that the underlying factual contexts
are so numerous, and the relevant legal considerations so varied, that no one decision—or six—
could be "definitive." In short, a Supreme Court
decision is most likely to make a significant contribution to uniformity in the law when the issue it
addresses is both discrete and recurring as well as
doubtful. Issues of that kind are probably the exception rather than the rule in a common law system.[30]

But even if an issue is discrete and recurring,
the justices will often be well advised, from the
standpoint of reaching sound decisions, to wait for
an actual conflict before addressing it. A contrary
voice—whether or not it is ultimately persuasive—
can illuminate a problem in a way that a series of
generally harmonious opinions will not. Sometimes the nonconforming decision will reveal flaws
in the reasoning of the courts that considered the
question initially.[31] At other times the
unpersuasiveness of the later decision will provide
reassurance that the first cases reached the correct result after all.[32] In either situation, the Court
benefits from the judicial system's analogue to the
adversary process—though with the additional and
crucial element that the opposing perspectives
come from two or more disinterested courts, each
of which must justify its position through reasoning that will have the force of law. Moreover, by
looking at the various decisions applying the competing rules, the Court can get a sense of how each
works in practice and thus be in a better position
to make an informed choice between them.

Some lawyers appear to assume that the desirability of speedy resolution and the probable gain
from additional "percolation" are independent
values that compete with and must be weighed
against one another. But this is not necessarily so.
The certainty that is supposed to come from speedy
resolution may prove illusory if a premature deci-

sion raises more questions than it answers. At best
the Court will forthrightly modify the view it took
before the additional considerations were brought
to its attention. At worst the Court will retain the
rule but hedge it about with so many qualifications
and subrules that the law is more confused than it
was before. It is no accident that justices with widely
differing views of the Court's proper role in the
American system of government have lauded the
values of percolation in both constitutional and
statutory cases.[33]

Uncertainty and interstitial lawmaking

Those who argue that an Intercircuit Tribunal is
needed to bring about uniformity and consistency
in federal law bear the burden of showing that the
Supreme Court's limited capacity for decision
making has resulted in disuniformity and inconsistency on a large scale. They have not met that
burden. But this failure of proof is not necessarily
dispositive on the question of whether some sort
of auxiliary court should be created. The Supreme
Court may be able to resolve all ripe intercircuit
conflicts. What it cannot do, to any substantial extent, is engage in interstitial lawmaking—the task
of interpreting and elaborating upon its landmark
precedents. But the essence of a common law system is that "no case can have a meaning by itself,"[34]
and that legal rules have meaning only as they are
applied in a series of cases. From that standpoint,
advocates of the new court would be quite correct
in arguing that one Court of nine justices can do
at best an incomplete job of declaring the law.

The difficulty is that the common law process
need not take place within a single court. The job
of filling in the interstices of the Supreme Court's
landmark rulings will be carried on in the federal
courts of appeals and state appellate courts in any
event. How much difference does it make that the
United States Supreme Court can make only a limited contribution to the process?

Even on its own terms, that question may be
unanswerable. But it is made even more problematic by the fact that the lack of a squarely controlling Supreme Court precedent is only one of the
sources of uncertainty and unpredictability in the
law. For example, the legal consequences of a particular transaction may depend on a well-settled
rule that gives the factfinder wide discretion to
reach different or even inconsistent results that will
not be disturbed on appeal.[35] Administrative agen-

cies not only have wide leeway in determining the "facts" upon which legal obligations will be based;[36] they may also modify or even reverse the governing rules without running afoul of appellate courts' willingness to defer to "expertise" or the lessons of experience.[37] Within a single agency or appellate court, different panels may view a given transaction quite differently while applying the same articulated rule of law.[38] Even when the Supreme Court addresses a recurring issue, its opinion may be so ambiguous as to leave the question little more settled than it was before.[39] Finally, life is too varied to accommodate itself to a necessarily finite number of precedents. Inevitably, there will be situations that do not fall within any existing rule; perhaps more commonly, situations will arise that are arguably governed by more than one rule, each of which may point to a different result.

These sources of uncertainty are magnified by the operation of the adversary system. In structuring a transaction or considering litigation, a lawyer must make an informed guess about the probable responses of the other parties. Those responses in turn will depend on such variables as wealth, aversion to risk, transaction costs, and familiarity with the law.

Taking these and other considerations into account, Professor Anthony D'Amato has recently argued that legal certainty actually decreases over time, and that "[r]ules and principles of law become more and more uncertain in content and in application because legal systems are biased in favor of unraveling those rules and principles."[40] One need not accept this extreme position to recognize that there are numerous forces that produce uncertainty in the law, and that these forces will continue to have a powerful effect even if the number of nationally binding decisions is increased from 150 to 200 or even to 300.[41] And as long as it cannot be said that actual intercircuit conflicts are going unresolved to any substantial extent, there is a real question whether a larger number of interstitial decisions by a national tribunal would contribute more than marginally to certainty and predictability in the law. At the least, Congress should wait for more evidence before creating a new structure to issue those decisions.[42]

Uniformity and the proposed court

If the evidence showed that the Supreme Court's limited capacity for definitive adjudication consti-tuted a significant impediment to the achievement of uniformity in federal law, could the proposed Intercircuit Tribunal be expected to solve or mitigate the problem? There is good reason to believe that it could not.

The legislation now under consideration contemplates a court of 27 judges who would hear and decide cases in randomly composed panels of five. This is exactly the system that has led lawyers to complain of inconsistency and unpredictability in the decisions of the large circuits.[43] Nor is this surprising. A court that sits in small panels selected by lot from among a much larger number of judges can hardly develop any kind of institutional approach or recognized set of policies. The lack of continuity in the proposed Intercircuit Tribunal would thus make it difficult if not impossible to achieve the predictability and stability in the law that the design is intended to create.

Recognizing the force of these arguments, several witnesses at the Senate hearings have urged that the new court be composed of a smaller number of judges—seven or nine—who would always sit en banc. That would certainly be an improvement over S. 645 as it now stands, but it would leave untouched the more fundamental flaw in the proposed structure: its reliance on a system of ad hoc case referrals prompted by the need to resolve or perhaps forestall an intercircuit conflict. That approach assumes that cases presenting actual or incipient conflicts typically involve self-contained issues that can be shunted off for resolution by a separate court with little or no effect on the development of the law generally.

But federal law is not a body of distinct rules that operate in isolation from one another. Even a narrow, relatively technical question of statutory construction may depend on the application of doctrines such as the "plain meaning" rule, the weight to be given to an agency's interpretation of the statute it administers, or the significance to be accorded the views of a Congress subsequent to the one that enacted the law. By the same token, lower courts confronted with widely divergent statutory questions will look to the entire corpus of Supreme Court opinions for guidance on these matters.[44] At a simpler level, unclear or ambiguous language in one clause or section often must be interpreted in the light of other provisions of the legislation or with a gloss furnished by the language or law of related statutory schemes.[45] In either situation, the result is to broaden the range of precedents that must be taken into account when any of the various issues are litigated.

If a new tribunal were to issue nationally binding decisions in a selection of cases having nothing in common except the fortuity of an intercircuit conflict, the lower courts would be required to harmonize dual lines of authority in a way that might create more uncertainty rather than less. And the more deeply the new court moves into interstitial lawmaking, the greater the likelihood that its decisions will have arguable relevance for superficially unrelated kinds of litigation.[46] On the other hand, if the new court's docket is confined to square conflicts on narrow issues, the available evidence suggests that there would be very little for the Tribunal to do.

Is there any escape from this dilemma? One possible approach would be to have categorical rather than ad hoc referrals. That is, instead of asking the new court to decide a collection of unrelated cases involving actual or potential conflicts, the Supreme Court would announce in advance, preferably through some kind of rulemaking process, that the new court would be given primary responsibility for overseeing the development of the law in particular areas of federal regulation. Thereafter, all cases in those areas would be referred unless the justices found good reason not to do so. The Intercircuit Tribunal would grant or deny review in accordance with what it perceived the needs of the national law to be.

This arrangement would permit a substantial amount of interstitial lawmaking to be carried on at the national level in those areas of the law that the Supreme Court chose to commit to the new tribunal. And while the Supreme Court would be empowered to review the Tribunal's decisions by writ of certiorari, the assumption must be that review would almost never be granted; otherwise the whole system would be pointless. Thus the new court would provide all of the precedential guidance that otherwise would have to come from the Supreme Court, but in limited areas of the law.

What I have described is, in essence, the approach proposed several years ago by Dean Paul Carrington and other members of the Advisory Council for Appellate Justice.[47] On the surface, at least, it would involve a more radical restructuring than the bills now under consideration. But it would be more consistent with the traditions of the common-law lawmaking process; would minimize (though not avoid entirely) the development of inconsistent lines of authority applicable to the same cases; and would permit the performance of a task that clearly cannot be performed by the Supreme Court alone. Whether this kind of reform is necessary is another question; I am not yet convinced that it is.

Risks for the Supreme Court

In giving qualified support to Chief Justice Burger's proposal for a tribunal very much like the one contemplated by the pending legislation, Professor Daniel Meador suggested that creation of the new court "would involve little expense [and] carry virtually no risk of harm to the system or to anyone's interest."[48] I fear that this view is unduly optimistic.

I do not refer to fiscal costs or to the possible effect on the morale of courts of appeals judges who are not chosen for the new tribunal. What concerns me, rather, is the effect of creating the Intercircuit Tribunal on the Supreme Court's performance of the responsibilities it would not delegate. In particular, I foresee two undesirable consequences. First, the case selection process would become more complex and perhaps more divisive. Second, the Supreme Court would tend to become, even more than it is today, a court of constitutional adjudication—a result that would pose risks both for the decisional process within the Court and for public acceptance of the Court's role.

The case selection process

The current legislation contemplates that the Supreme Court would select the docket of the new court. For reasons I have set forth elsewhere, that is the only acceptable approach.[49] But there is no blinking the fact that it would entail additional work for the justices.

Admittedly, when seven members of the present Court gave their views on the Hruska Commission's proposal for a National Court of Appeals with reference jurisdiction, none of them—even those who opposed the idea—appeared troubled by the prospect of having to select the new court's docket. But I cannot help wondering whether they fully thought through the implications of this arrangement.

Today, the justices have only three ways of handling the cases that are brought to them for review: they can grant plenary consideration; they can decide the case summarily; or they can deny review altogether. Reference jurisdiction would add a fourth option.[50] It does not take an expert in small-group theory to hypothesize that to expand the number of choices available to a nine-person committee in a large number of decisions would substantially increase the potential for dissension and even deadlock. In particular, the justices are unlikely to share the same view of the appropriate role of the Intercircuit Tribunal in the development of federal law; and even if they do, they will probably differ in the weight that they give to "percolation," both generally and in particular cases.

No doubt the Court could devise procedures or standards that would enable it to handle potentially divisive situations, but it is hard to avoid the conclusion that the availability of an ad hoc reference option would complicate the selection process and thus add to the justices' burdens.[51] A categorical reference system would probably operate more smoothly; to what extent would depend on the nature of the categories used.

Risks of delegating statutory issues

In any event, the more serious cost of creating an Intercircuit Tribunal lies in its effect on the Supreme Court's decisional work. What kinds of cases would the Supreme Court refer to the new court? Surely it would not refer cases involving issues of civil rights or other questions of constitutional law. Almost inevitably, decisions in these cases implicate large questions of social policy or turn on deep-seated ethical judgments about the competing claims of liberty and authority. As a consequence, it is highly unlikely that the justices would be willing to share their jurisdiction with another court, whatever its composition.

Moreover, it is on constitutional issues that differences in language, approach, or emphasis are most likely to convey conflicting messages to litigants and lower courts. For example, Fourth Amendment jurisprudence is confusing enough today with only one Court handing down nationally-binding decisions; to have a separate tribunal participate in the process would invite even greater disarray.[52]

Thus the Court is likely to refer only petitions raising narrow or technical questions of statutory construction. A few such referrals would do no harm, but the temptation would be great to refer all or most cases of this kind. The effect would be to restrict the Court's work largely to great issues of civil rights law, federalism, and the interpretation of statutes such as the Sherman Act or the National Labor Relations Act, which have almost the breadth of a constitutional provision. Indeed, it is quite possible that with a new tribunal to resolve some of the narrow statutory issues that today must be heard by the Supreme Court, the justices would take a larger number of constitutional cases for the purpose of correcting possible error.

For some commentators, a de facto division of the Court's work into constitutional and nonconstitutional issues, with the latter diverted to a new tribunal, would be a welcome solution to the caseload problem. Others will see it as but another step in a process that is already far advanced; in recent terms, only one-third of the Court's plenary decisions have involved pure issues of statutory construction, divorced from constitutional concerns. In my view, however, to move further in that direction would entail grave consequences both for the way in which the Court goes about its work and for the way in which that work is perceived by the citizenry.

Internally, the Court would lose an important source of self-discipline. As Justice Rehnquist has pointed out, "[t]o the extent that the Court must deal with statutory and other nonconstitutional questions, in which the permissible limits of adjudication are narrower, the . . . Court is kept on its toes and pressed to remain a classical court rather than a branch of government largely freed from the necessity for giving closely reasoned explanations for what it does."[53] Statutory cases serve another internal function as well: they remind the justices that the Constitution is not the only source of values and that the decisions of the representative branches of government are entitled to respect.

Routine statutory issues may also play an important role in preserving collegiality within the Court. Voting blocs that persist across a wide range of constitutional issues often tend to break up when less earth-shaking questions of statutory interpretation are presented.[54] The existence of cases in which the Court finds itself unified—or divided along unexpected lines—serves to moderate the tensions that are likely to build up in cases involving the Bill of Rights, the Fourteenth Amendment, and the division of powers between state and federal governments.[55] Conversely, the loss of routine statutory issues might well serve to intensify and make more bitter the divisions that do exist among the justices.[56]

For the Court to cut itself off from narrow statutory questions would pose even greater dangers for the way in which the Court's work is perceived by legislators and other citizens. In a democratic society, the legitimacy of judicial review depends in no small part on a shared recognition that the Court nullifies decisions by the representative branches of government not because it is empowered to second-guess the wisdom or appropriateness of majoritarian determinations, but only, in Justice Harlan's words, "because [it is] a court of law . . . charged with the responsibility of adjudicating cases or controversies according to the law of the land and because the law applicable to any such dispute necessarily includes the Federal Constitution."[57]

The more the Court devotes itself to constitutional adjudication, and the less attention it gives to statutory questions of a more conventionally "legal" kind, the easier it is to lose sight of the underpinnings of the Court's role, and the more difficult it will be to defend the Court's intervention. And because constitutional decision making necessarily involves a large element of policy choice on matters not addressed by the text or contemplated by the framers, it is all the more important that the public be reminded at frequent intervals that the Court does, after all, decide questions of law.

It is true that a conscientious Supreme Court could minimize these dangers by keeping 30 to 40 relatively routine statutory cases for itself each term. Yet the more the Court attempts to retain a representative sample of statutory issues, the greater the danger that the two courts will develop parallel lines of authority that are arguably applicable to the same cases. Here again, categorical reference would reduce, through perhaps not entirely eliminate, the problem.

Some empirical evidence

Inevitably, debate over the desirability of creating an auxiliary court involves a large degree of speculation. We must first make predictions about how the Supreme Court would manage its docket if it had the option of referring cases to the new tribu-nal, and then, on the basis of those predictions, gauge the probable effects on the Court and on uniformity in the law. The latter inquiry must be almost entirely hypothetical, but as to the former there is one bit of evidence that may provide some clues.

By examining the Court's published order lists, we can identify those cases that, under the present system, came within one vote of the four required for plenary review. The inference can be drawn—though it is far from compelling—that these are the cases that would have been adjudicated at the national level if the Intercircuit Tribunal had been in existence. That is, if the total national decisional capacity had been enlarged through the availability of the reference option, these are the cases that would most likely have received either four votes for review by the Supreme Court or five votes for reference to the new tribunal.

Study of the order lists in the four terms 1977 through 1980 reveals that there were 119 cases in which three justices voted to grant certiorari or note probable jurisdiction but could not persuade a fourth justice to join them; thus, under the Rule of Four, review was denied.[58] The overwhelming majority were civil rights cases, and the largest portion of these involved issues of criminal law and procedure.[59] Only 27 cases in all four terms dealt with questions of federalism, general federal law, or jurisdiction and procedure outside the context of civil rights.

These findings lend at least some support to the views expressed in the preceding pages. They confirm the justices' strong, indeed overriding, interest in constitutional issues. We already know that the Court cannot expand the number of cases that receive plenary consideration, and that some statutory cases reach the plenary docket only because the Court feels obliged to resolve an intercircuit conflict.[60] Putting these facts together, it is quite plausible to suppose that if the reference option had been available, at least some of the three-vote constitutional cases would have received a fourth vote for consideration within the Court, while an equal number of statutory cases would have been routed to the Intercircuit Tribunal. The effect would have been to bring the Court one step closer to having a purely constitutional docket without necessarily increasing the number of nationally binding precedents on statutory issues, where the need for additional guidance exists if it exists anywhere.

Admittedly, these data are far from definitive. For one thing, there may well be cases in which three justices voted at the Court's conference to grant plenary review, but one or more of them chose not to make their position public. More important, the availability of the reference option would itself change the justices' voting behavior in ways we cannot fully anticipate. Nevertheless, at the present time we have no better evidence as to what would happen if the national decisional capacity were to be expanded in the manner proposed by the pending legislation. And that evidence is not reassuring.

Nor is reassurance provided by anything the justices have said. On the contrary, statements by one member of the Court tend to confirm the hypothesis advanced here. In his speech to the American Bar Association, Chief Justice Burger predicted that "if there is not prompt action to give relief [to the Supreme Court], there will be a large increase in summary dispositions, particularly in . . . criminal cases when the lower courts have either misread or ignored our controlling holdings."[61] Presumably the Court would not allow these judgments to stand if the new tribunal were created; instead, it would give them plenary consideration. And if the pattern of recent years were to continue, these would be largely cases in which the lower court had accepted the defendant's constitutional claim.[62]

It would be wrong to read too much into the Chief Justice's comments, but they do suggest a line of inquiry that Congress ought to pursue. There would be no point in creating the Intercircuit Tribunal—or any auxiliary court—unless the members of the Supreme Court were in substantial agreement both as to the need for the new structure and on the use to which it would be put. Thus, at some point in the national debate, the justices will have to speak out. Would it not be desirable to ask them to tell us quite specifically how they would use the reference option—perhaps even to identify the cases that would be sent to the new court?

There would be no need for the justices to submit agreed-on case lists to Congress. Rather, they could provide the information in a series of individual or joint opinions dissenting from—or concurring in—the denial of plenary review. Opinions and notations of this kind are already part of the Court's regular practice; the added burden of specifying the cases that particular justices would send to the new court would be minimal. And only on the basis of such a record can Congress and the public make informed judgments about how the reference option would work and what its consequences would be.[63]

Designing a structure

Further research may well show that there are indeed more cases deserving resolution at the national level than one Supreme Court can comfortably handle. The task then will be to design a structure that will enlarge the national decisional capacity without compromising the values that have given the federal judicial system the stature it has today.

I have already argued that a rotating panel system is unlikely to foster uniformity and certainty in the law. Assuming that that problem can be avoided by having a court of seven or nine judges who would always sit en banc, two questions remain to be addressed. First, how should the judges of the new court be selected? Second, should the tribunal be established on a temporary or on a permanent basis?

Selection of the judges

Under the bill now pending in the Senate, the members of the Intercircuit Tribunal would be designated by the circuit councils of the various circuits. There are several difficulties with this approach. To begin with, it is anomalous at best to decentralize the process of selecting judges for a national court. The incongruity is particularly striking in view of the 1980 legislation that gave the circuits wide leeway in deciding how many judges would serve on the councils and how they would be chosen.

More than a lack of symmetry is at stake. Ordinarily, when new judges are selected for a court, the appointing authority considers, among other factors, the composition of the court apart from the positions to be filled. That kind of coordination would be impossible if the members of the Tribunal were chosen in separate proceedings in the various circuits.[64] Indeed, there is surely some irony in creating a court to promote uniformity, but having the judges selected by 13 separate groups of individuals, each employing its own standards and procedures.

Vesting the appointment power in the circuit councils also runs a substantial risk of fostering dissension and politicization among the judges. To avoid those consequences, many if not all of the circuits are likely to adopt some sort of lottery system for choosing the members of the new tribunal. In this they would be following the procedure used by the Ninth Circuit Court of Appeals to select its "limited en banc" panels. But whatever the merits of that system for declaring the law of the circuit, it would introduce a jarring element of arbitrariness, both in appearance and in reality, if a group of judges selected at random were to be given the power to establish the law of the nation.

For all of these reasons, it would be unwise to have the members of the auxiliary court chosen within the various circuits. How, then, might they be selected? Some proposals have vested the appointment power in the Supreme Court as a whole; others, in the chief justice alone. However, neither system is desirable. The former would not only add to the burdens of the justices; it would also provide a fertile ground for tension and dissension within the Supreme Court. The latter would give far too much power to one individual.

It is one thing to authorize the chief justice to designate judges for specialized tribunals such as the Temporary Emergency Court of Appeals or the Judicial Panel on Multidistrict Litigation. It is quite another to allow him to select the individuals who will be establishing nationally-binding precedents on a wide variety of recurring issues, subject only to occasional review by the Supreme Court.

Indeed, a more fundamental point is at stake. Recent events have reminded us of the inherent tension between majoritarian power and an independent judiciary. To allow judges—any judges— to select the members of an important court would upset the delicate balance that has been worked out over the years. By eliminating the role of the Senate and the president at the appointment stage, such an arrangement would severely weaken the majoritarian check that makes it possible for a democratic society to accept the exercise of vast lawmaking powers by judges who, once appointed, are not responsive to the political process.

It is no answer to say that because the new court would be dealing only with statutory issues, Congress could always overrule its decisions. Even if the court has misinterpreted the legislative will, forces such as inertia, deadlock, or the pressure of other business will often make it impossible to amend a statute. Nor is it adequate that the members of the panel, as circuit judges, will have previously been nominated and confirmed through the Article III process. Appointments to the circuit bench are generally treated as regional appointments; often they are the prerogative of a single senator. While the quality of the judges has been very high, the candidates simply do not receive the kind of national scrutiny that could be anticipated for appointments to what would be, in effect, an auxiliary Supreme Court.

I conclude, therefore, that the new tribunal should be constituted in the same way as all existing general-function federal courts: its judges should be appointed by the president with the consent of the Senate. That, indeed, was the recommendation of the Hruska Commission, which reached its conclusion after carefully weighing the alternatives. As already noted, however, the legislation now before Congress takes a different approach: the new court would be composed of sitting circuit judges who would be designated to serve for limited periods of time.

Proponents of this system place great emphasis on how little it would cost. And at a time when both political parties are struggling to reduce government spending, there is an obvious attraction in the prospect of increasing the national decisional capacity without creating any new judgeships. However, in the context of a federal budget that now exceeds $800 billion, the amount of money that would be required for an auxiliary court barely rises above the level of the trivial. In fiscal 1983 the budget for the Supreme Court came to about $15 million—less than was authorized for the maintenance, care, and operation of the House office buildings. If disuniformity is truly rampant in federal law, interfering on a large scale with the efficient planning of transactions and the speedy resolution of disputes, the cost of a new national court, smaller and less prestigious than the Supreme Court, would be a small price to pay to set things right.

In any event, it would be shortsighted to consider only fiscal costs. Even now, Congress is considering a recommendation by the Judicial Conference of the United States that 24 new judgeships be created in the courts of appeals to meet the demands imposed by current caseloads. Those caseloads are not likely to diminish in the years to come. Obviously, judges who are deciding cases at the national level can handle correspondingly fewer cases in their own circuits. Something would have to give: either circuit backlogs would grow, or decisional processes would be further truncated. Whatever the outcome, the system and its users incur costs, albeit not ones that would be reflected in the federal budget.

The preference for the designation approach also rests on the feeling that it would be politically unacceptable to give a single president the opportunity to appoint the entire initial membership of the new court. However, as long as at least one house is controlled by a party other than the president's, it should be possible, at the time of establishing the court, to reach an informal understanding that would require diversity and bipartisanship in the first group of appointments.

Last—and emphatically least—the designation approach may be seen as a way of mollifying the feelings of circuit judges who would otherwise perceive the new tribunal as eroding the prestige of their own courts. But if the new court is created on the basis of convincing evidence that the present system is not working, it is unlikely that circuit judges would feel more than a twinge of regret at the passing of the old order. In any event, if the lack of national appellate capacity has reached the point of desperation, the judges' sensitivities surely should not be allowed to stand in the way of necessary reform.

Temporary or permanent?

The legislation now before Congress differs from the Hruska Commission's proposal in a second important respect: it would create only a "temporary" tribunal that would automatically go out of existence if Congress did not re-authorize it. The concerns underlying this approach are certainly understandable. The proponents seek to mute the instinctive opposition of the bar and the judiciary to the creation of additional structures within the judicial system. And what could be more reassuring than to provide that unless the new court has proved its worth, it will simply disappear into oblivion? But notwithstanding its surface appeal, I think that a "sunset" provision would be unwise.

To begin with, it is important to remember that Congress can abolish even a "permanent" court. That is precisely what happened with the Commerce Court: three years after it was created, Congress put an end to its existence, and thereafter the judges continued to serve on other Article III courts.

Of course, it must be conceded that the new court is much less likely to suffer this fate if abolition rather than re-authorization requires affirmative action by Congress. And in any event, proponents of the sunset provision will ask, what's wrong with an experiment? What harm can there be in giving the new court a trial run so that advocates and doubters alike can see how it will actually work?

I see three major drawbacks to the "experimental" approach. First, in the words of the Hruska Commission, a new court "would be significantly handicapped . . . if its decisions lacked the authority and credibility of an independent tribunal, the position of which was secured by a permanent charter."[65] Why so? The court would be exercising the power of review over judges who previously had to answer only to the United States Supreme Court. To make matters worse, under a system of reference jurisdiction the panel would be in the anomalous situation of not being able to enforce its precedents without the intervention of another tribunal. If by law the new court were scheduled to go out of existence on a specified day a few years in the future, the authority of its decisions would be rendered even more precarious. In contrast, if the new court were designed to be permanent, both judges and lawyers would have a much stronger motivation to treat it as a fait accompli and respect its judgments.

Second, a sunset provision would make the new court much more vulnerable to the combined effect of various human weaknesses. Making the tribunal only "temporary" reduces the incentive for its creators to build a solid record showing that the present system is inadequate. The weaker the evidence of need, the more likely it is that lower-court judges will resent the new court as an unjustifiable addition to the hierarchy that reduces the authority of their own decisions. And the more widespread that perception, the greater the difficulty the tribunal will have in securing understanding and absorption of its precedents.

Finally, notwithstanding what I have just said, "temporary" structures have a way of becoming permanent. That fate is particularly likely to befall the proposed new court because it will be impossible to know after five or even seven years whether it is achieving its purpose of reducing something as intangible as disuniformity in the law. Thus, unless the tribunal has proved an utter disaster, Congress is likely to extend its life. And given the pressure of other business, there will be neither time nor inclination to rethink any of the particulars. Unfortunately, a structure that is created for the short term is not likely to be satisfactory in the long run, nor is it likely to receive the same degree of care in its design. But that initial structure is the one that is likely to endure.

Thus, if Congress is convinced that the Supreme Court cannot provide all of the nationally-binding precedents that the legal system needs, it should establish a seven-judge court without a termination date.[66] The legislation could provide for a study commission that would come into existence six years after the new court begins operations, and that would be required, three years later, to make recommendations to Congress and the president as to whether the court should be continued. If the evidence shows that the court is not needed or is working badly, Congress would abolish it and designate the judges to sit on the circuit and district courts.

Finally, if political realities compel the inclusion of a sunset provision, the new court should be given an initial lifespan of 10 years rather than five. Without at least that much time, evaluation would be little more than guesswork. Of greater importance, the limited lifespan need not and should not preclude Congress from providing for appointment of the judges by the president with the consent of the Senate. If, after 10 years, the court is not reestablished, the judges will be able to provide useful service elsewhere in the federal judicial system.

Conclusion

Arguments that the Supreme Court is overworked, or that it cannot resolve all of the issues that deserve resolution at the national level, comport easily with our intuitions. We are a litigious nation of 235 million people, and in an era when the scope and complexity of federal law have expanded far beyond what was contemplated by the framers, it almost strains credulity to suggest that one Court of nine justices does *not* need help in performing the functions assigned to it in our system of government.

Yet all would agree that changes in the structure of the federal judicial system should not be based on intuitions, but on convincing evidence

that existing arrangements are not working. Legislation to eliminate the remaining vestiges of the Supreme Court's obligatory jurisdiction meets that test, and should be enacted without further delay. The same cannot be said of proposals to create an auxiliary tribunal to assist the Court in deciding cases. There is simply not enough evidence that the Supreme Court's limited capacity for authoritative decision making has significantly frustrated society's need for uniformity and predictability in the law. Moreover, too little attention has been paid to the possible adverse consequences of creating a new court.

The want of evidence is not less tolerable if the new court is established with a "sunset" provision. Indeed, the saddest aspect of the current drive for a "temporary" tribunal is that the experimental label can all too easily become a substitute for careful analysis of the need for the new court and the structure that would best satisfy it. And if that analysis is not undertaken before the tribunal is first created, it is unlikely ever to be attempted at a time when it can make a difference. Moreover, the shaky empirical foundation would itself increase the difficulty the new court will have in maintaining the authority of its precedents.

In the end, judgments about the need for an Intercircuit Tribunal or something similar to it may depend as much on one's perception of how legal rules operate as on the results of empirical studies. Thus, if it were shown that actual intercircuit conflicts were going unresolved on a large scale, the case for structural reform would be quite strong; but even then there would still be room for "arguments about how essential it is . . . that . . . particular question[s] be taken up and authoritatively settled at the highest judicial level."[67] And the more meager the numbers, or the larger the proportion that are no more than "sideswipes," the easier it will be to maintain that inaction by the Supreme Court pales into insignificance in the light of other sources of uncertainty in the law.

Nevertheless, it is a necessary first step to find out what the Supreme Court is not doing and how its limited capacity for decision making actually affects people's ability to plan and litigate efficiently. To forgo this inquiry is to run the risk of pursuing mischievous "solutions" to problems that exist only in the mind of the beholder.

NOTES

This article originally appeared in Volume 67, Number 1, June-July 1983, pages 28-48.

1. The Senate bill is S. 645, 98th Cong., 1st Sess. §§601-07 (1983); *see* 129 CONG. REC. S1947-48 (daily ed. Mar. 1, 1983) (remarks of Sen. Dole). The House bill is H.R. 1970, 98th Cong., 1st Sess. (1983); *see* 129 CONG. REC. H1 192-93 (daily ed. Mar. 15, 1983) (remarks of Cong. Kastenmeier). Congressman Kastenmeier stated that Chief Justice Burger, as an individual, had "expressed support" for his proposal, and indeed the chief justice had endorsed a very similar suggestion in his midyear report to the American Bar Association. *See* Burger, *Annual Report on the State of the Judiciary*, 69 A.B.A. J. 442 (1983). In this article, I shall focus primarily on the Senate bill, which has already been the subject of hearings.

2. *See* 129 CONG. REC. at S1947-48 (remarks of Sen. Dole).

3. Although Justice Stevens has argued that the Court is "too busy to give the certiorari docket the attention it deserves," his real complaint is not that the selection process imposes a great burden, but rather that his colleagues are too free in granting review of cases that he believes need not be heard by the Supreme Court. *See* Stevens, *Some thoughts on judicial restraint*, 66 JUDICATURE 177, 179 & *passim* (1982).

4. Address of Chief Justice Hughes at the American Law Institute Meeting, quoted in 20 A.B.A. J. 341, 341 (1934). Whether the justices always adhere to this principle is of course another question—one that cannot be pursued here.

5. *Supreme Court Jurisdiction Act of 1978: Hearings on S. 3100 Before the Subcomm. on Improvements in Judicial Machinery of the Senate Judiciary Comm.*, 95th Cong., 2d Sess. 40 (1978) (letter signed by all nine sitting justices) [hereinafter cited as *Supreme Court Jurisdiction Hearings*].

6. Brennan, *The National Court of Appeals: Another Dissent*, 40 U. CHI. L. REV. 473, 477-478 (1973).

7. *Chief Justice Burger's Challenge to Congress*, U.S. NEWS & WORLD REPORT, Feb. 14, 1983, at 38, 40 [hereinafter cited as Burger interview].

8. Although the total number of cases on the docket has little significance as a measure of the justices' workload, the figures have been cited so often that two points about them deserve mention here. First, the rate of increase in the overall caseload has declined dramatically from what it was in the 1960s. In the decade preceding the Freund Study Group's report in 1972, the growth rate averaged just under 7 percent a year. Over the past decade the rate has been only about 2 percent. Thus, even in the 1981 term, which brought the largest number of new cases in the Court's history, the total was only 21 percent greater than it was in the 1971 term. In contrast, filings in the federal courts of appeals nearly doubled over the same period. Second, for whatever it is worth, new filings have fallen off in the 1982 term. At this writing it appears that the number of cases docketed will be about 200 under what it was in the 1981 term.

9. This figure does not include concurring and dissenting opinions less than a page in length.

10. *See* Logan v. Zimmerman Brush Co., 455 U.S. 422 (1982); Mills v. Habluetzel, 456 U.S. 91 (1982).

It may be suggested that the proliferation of separate opinions, far from signifying that the justices are not truly overburdened, actually reinforces the conclusion that they are. The premise would be that the pressures of caseload make it impossible for the justices to hammer out consensus opinions, so that the only alternative is the separate expression of views. But the available evidence does not support this premise. For example, Professor Dennis Hutchinson's study of the Court's decisional practices under Chief Justice Vinson points out that when the Court "was able or willing to debate issues internally at great length, . . . it frequently produced multiple opinions and judgments with no majority opinion." Hutchinson, *Felix Frankfurter and the Business of the Supreme Court, O.T. 1946-O.T. 1961*, 1980 SUP. CT. REV. 143, 208-209. More recently, former Justice Potter Stewart, when asked shortly after his retirement whether he had any regrets about his tenure on the Court, expressed the wish that he had had more time to write his own dissenting opinions instead of joining dissents that "were written not exactly the way I would have written them." *Interview With Justice Potter Stewart*, THIRD BRANCH, Jan. 1982, at 1, 9.

In short, there can be no doubt that the members of the Court have a strong desire to make known their individual views in the cases before them. The evidence suggests that with a smaller plenary docket the justices would satisfy this desire more often, rather than spend the extra time working with the authoring justice to produce a single opinion that embodied the majority's collective wisdom.

11. *See, e.g.*, Oregon v. Kennedy, 102 S. Ct. 2083, 2092 n. 1 (1982) (Stevens, J., concurring in the judgment); People v. Long, 413 Mich. 461, __, 320 N.W.2d 866, 870 (1982), cert. granted, 103 S. Ct. 205 (1982).

12. *See, e.g.*, Marshall v. Lonberger, 103 S. Ct. 843 (1983); State v. Bradshaw, 54 Or. App. 949, 636 P.2d 1011 (1981), cert. granted, 103 S. Ct. 292 (1982).

13. *See, e.g.*, Harris v. Rivera, 454 U.S. 339 (1981); Jago v. Van Curen, 454 U.S. 14 (1981).

14. *See, e.g.*, Anderson v. Harless, 103 S. Ct. 276 (1982); Board of Educ. v. McCluskey, 102 S. Ct. 3469 (1982). Justice Stevens believes that most of the recent summary reversals fit this description. See *id.*, 102 S. Ct. at 3473 & n. 4 (Stevens, J., dissenting).

15. Cf. Bauman v. United States, 557 F.2d 650 (9th Cir. 1977) (standards for mandamus).

16. Illinois v. Gates, 103 S. Ct. 436 (1982) (Stevens, J., dissenting).

17. *Supreme Court Jurisdiction Hearings*, *supra* n. 5, at 40.

18. *See, e.g.*, Blum v. Bacon, 102 S. Ct. 2355 (1982); Rodriguez v. Popular Democratic Party, 102 S. Ct. 2194 (1982); Greene v. Lindsay, 102 S. Ct. 1874 (1982). In three other appeal cases, the Court unanimously reversed decisions by single district judges holding federal statutes unconstitutional. If the obligatory jurisdiction had been abolished, these cases would have gone to the courts of appeals, which in all likelihood would have upheld the statutes. In that posture it is questionable whether the cases would have merited Supreme Court review.

19. Hicks v. Miranda, 422 U.S. 332 (1975). *See* Hellman, *The Business of the Supreme Court Under the Judiciary Act of 1925: The Plenary Docket in the 1970s*, 91 HARV. L. REV. 1709, 1722-1723 (1978).

20. *See* Sidle v. Majors, 429 U.S. 945, 949-950 (1976) (Brennan, J., dissenting from denial of certiorari). Here and elsewhere I shall refer to dismissals for want of a substantial federal question as affirmances; certainly they are in effect. *See* Hellman, *supra* n. 19, at 1722 n. 57.

21. The obligatory jurisdiction also imposes another kind of burden: that of determining whether cases have properly been brought as appeals. Particularly in cases from state courts, the scope of the appeal jurisdiction depends on rules that are not always easy to apply. In the 1980 term, 80 state-court appeals were decided summarily on the merits; 47 others were found to have been improperly brought as appeals. Determining which cases fell into each category took time and effort that would not have been necessary if the obligatory jurisdiction had been abolished.

22. I recognize that the legislation would not eliminate every vestige of the obligatory jurisdiction, but the remaining

fragments would be of such small moment, from the standpoint of workload, that for the sake of convenience I use the term without qualification.

23. The two most comprehensive empirical studies, both conducted nearly a decade ago, came to very different conclusions. Compare COMMISSION ON REVISION OF THE FEDERAL COURT APPELLATE SYSTEM, STRUCTURE AND INTERNAL PROCEDURES: RECOMMENDATIONS FOR CHANGE 93-109 (1975) [hereinafter cited as Hruska Commission Report], with Casper & Posner, THE WORKLOAD OF THE SUPREME COURT 87-92 (Chicago: American Bar Foundation, 1976).

24. There were only five cases in which a dissent by Justice White explicitly adverted to the existence of a conflict. Another dozen or so cases involved recurring issues, and in perhaps half of those there appears to have been a conflict of some sort.

25. *See, e.g.,* Nygaard v. Peter Pan Seafoods, Inc., 701 F.2d 77, 80 (9th Cir. 1983); Aldens, Inc. v. Miller, 610 F.2d 538, 541 (8th Cir. 1979), cert. denied, 446 U.S. 919 (1980).

26. *See, e.g.,* Copper Liquor, Inc. v. Adolph Coors Co., 701 F.2d 542 (5th Cir. 1983) (en banc court overrules case that created intercircuit conflict); United States v. Adamson, 700 F.2d 953, 956-965 (5th Cir. 1983) (en banc court, overruling prior decisions, adopts rule followed in eight other circuits that had considered the question).

27. *See, e.g.,* United States v. Gelb, 700 F.2d 875 (2d Cir. 1983) (circuits divided on scope of 1970 legislation; 1982 law eliminated ambiguity).

28. Meador, *A Comment on the Chief Justice's Proposals,* 69 A.B.A. J. 448, 449 (1983).

29. I put to one side the very serious problems raised by the federal government's practice of relitigating an issue without seeking certiorari even after its position has been rejected in several circuits. In this situation a Supreme Court decision would certainly make a significant contribution to uniformity in the law, but because of the government's litigation policy the Court does not get a chance to address the issue. *See, e.g.,* May Dep't Stores Co. v. Williamson, 549 F.2d 1147, 1149-1150 (8th Cir. 1977) (Lay, J., concurring). It is true that the solicitor general, in deciding whether to seek review, probably takes into account the fact that the Court can hear only a limited number of cases; on the other hand, these issues do seem to reach the Court eventually. Compare Hruska Commission Report, *supra* n. 23, at 133-143, with NLRB v. Enterprise Ass'n of Steam Pipefitters, 429 U.S. 507 (1977), and Bayside Enterprises, Inc. v. NLRB, 429 U.S. 298 (1977). Thus it is not clear whether the problem (apart from government intransigence) is truly one of inadequate decisional capacity or is more a matter of timing.

30. Thus it is somewhat ironic that United States v. Cartwright, 411 U.S. 546 (1973), has so often been cited as exemplifying the kind of question that should be settled at the earliest possible time without necessarily waiting for an intercircuit conflict. Perhaps it is, but the issue presented by that case—whether mutual funds shares in a decedent's estate are to be valued, for federal tax purposes, at the "bid" or the "asked" price—is of a kind that is relatively rare in the law: there are no shades of gray, but only black and white; and once the issue is decided in one case, that ruling will immediately resolve, without further inquiry, all disputes of a similar nature. Compare, e.g., Florida v. Royer, 103 S. Ct. 1319, 1329 (1983) (plurality opinion); Hillsboro Nat'l. Bank v. Commissioner, 103 S. Ct. 1134, 1144 (1983), discussed *infra* n. 39.

31. *See, e.g.,* Illinois v. Abbott & Assocs., 103 S. Ct. 1356 (1983) (Court unanimously affirms decision that rejected holdings by first two circuits to address issue); Bayside Enterprises, Inc. v. NLRB, 429 U.S. 298 (1977) (same); Otte v. United States, 419 U.S. 43 (1974) (Court unanimously affirms deci-

sion rejecting both of the two alternate positions taken by the circuits that initially addressed the issue).

32. *See, e.g.,* Coffy v. Republic Steel Corp., 447 U.S. 191 (1980) (Court unanimously reverses decision that declined to follow earlier holdings by two other circuits).

33. *See, e.g.,* Colorado Springs Amusements, Ltd. v. Rizzo, 428 U.S. 913, 917-918 (1976) (Brennan, J., dissenting from denial of certiorari); Maryland v. Baltimore Radio Show, Inc., 338 U.S. 912, 918 (1950) (opinion of Frankfurter, J., respecting the denial of certiorari); Burger interview, *supra* n. 7, at 39. It is particularly important to note that in the justices' eyes the value of the process is not limited to constitutional cases. *See, e.g.,* E. I. du Pont de Nemours & Co. v. Train, 430 U.S. 112, 135 n. 26 (1977): "This litigation exemplifies the wisdom of allowing difficult issues to mature through full consideration by the courts of appeals. By eliminating the many subsidiary, but still troubling, arguments raised by industry, these courts have vastly simplified our task, as well as having underscored the reasonableness of the agency view."

34. Llewellyn, THE BRAMBLE BUSH 48 (Dobbs Ferry, New York: Oceana, 1951).

35. *See, e.g.,* Pullman-Standard v. Swint, 102 S. Ct. 1781, 1788-1791 (1982); Commissioner v. Duberstein, 363 U.S. 278, 287-291 (1960).

36. *See, e.g.,* Herman Bros., Inc. v. NLRB, 658 F.2d 201, 209 (3rd Cir. 1981).

37. *See, e.g.,* NLRB v. J. Weingarten, Inc., 420 U.S. 251, 265-267 (1975); Permian Basin Area Rate Cases, 390 U.S. 747, 784 (1968); Texaco, Inc. v. NLRB, 700 F.2d 1039, 1042-1043 (5th Cir. 1983); Melrose-Wakefield Hospital Ass'n v. NLRB, 615 F.2d 563, 567 (1st Cir. 1980).

38. *See, e.g.,* Friendly, *Adverting the Flood by Lessening the Flow,* 59 CORNELL L. REV. 634, 655 (1974).

39. For example, in Hillsboro Nat'l. Bank v. Commissioner, 103 S. Ct. 1134, 1144-1145 (1983), the taxpayers and the government proposed competing formulations of the tax benefit rule. The Court rejected both formulations and concluded instead that the rule "must be applied on a case-by-case basis."

40. D'Amato, *Legal Uncertainty,* 71 CALIF. L. REV. 1, 1 (1983).

41. Chief Justice Burger envisaged a temporary panel that would decide about 50 cases a year. A full-time, seven-judge National Court of Appeals could probably be expected to hand down about 150 decisions annually.

42. Much has been made of the fact that in the 1981 term, for the first time in recent history, the Court granted review in more cases than it could hear in a single term. However, even putting aside the question whether all of the cases truly deserved consideration at the national level, the significance of this development should not be overstated. In the preceding term—1980—the Court had granted review in so few cases that it was unable to fill its argument calendar for the April session. (The figures for the 1977 through 1979 terms were also below the level of the 1971-1976 period.) The justices may well have responded by moving somewhat too far toward the other extreme. In the current term the number of cases granted review has again decreased. In any event, it would be shortsighted to place great reliance on year-to-year fluctuations in the number of cases heard rather than trying to assess the needs of the national law.

43. *See* Hellman, *Legal Problems of Dividing a State Between Federal Judicial Circuits,* 122 PA. L. REV. 1188, 1208-1209 (1974) (citing lawyers' statements).

44. *See, e.g.,* Mid-Louisiana Gas Co. v. FERC, 664 F.2d 530, 534-535 (5th Cir. 1981) (in assessing degree of deference due to agency order under Natural Gas Policy Act, court cites cases involving, inter alia, securities regulation, welfare, and truth in lending), cert. granted, 103 S. Ct. 49 (1982); Montana Wil-

derness Ass'n v. United States Forest Service, 655 F.2d 951, 957 (9th Cir. 1981) (in construing Alaska Lands Act, court relies on Supreme Court decision interpreting Freedom of Information Act), cert. denied, 455 U.S. 989 (1982); Leist v. Simplot, 638 F.2d 283, 319, 327 (2d Cir. 1980) (majority and dissent differ on implications to be drawn from Supreme Court decision interpreting different statute), aff'd, 102 S. Ct. 1825 (1982).

45. *See, e.g.*, United States v. Stauffer Chemical Co., 684 F.2d 1174, 1187-1188 (6th Cir. 1982) (Clean Air Act and Clean Water Act), cert. granted, 51 U.S.L.W. 3756 (U.S. Apr. 18, 1983).

46. *Compare, e.g.*, Coffy v. Republic Steel Corp., 447 U.S. 191 (1980) (resolving conflict in interpretation of Vietnam Era Veterans' Readjustment Assistance Act; decision has been cited almost exclusively in cases involving veterans' reemployment rights), with Vermont Yankee Nuclear Power Corp. v. Natural Resources Defense Council, Inc., 435 U.S. 519 (1978) (reaffirming and applying precedents on scope of review of agency action; decision cited in wide variety of administrative law cases).

47. *See* Carrington, Meador & Rosenberg, JUSTICE ON APPEAL 215-216 (St. Paul: West, 1976); Hufstedler, *Courtship and Other Legal Arts*, 60 A.B.A. J. 545, 547 (1974).

48. Meador, *supra* n. 28, at 449.

49. Hellman, *How Not to Help the Supreme Court*, 69 A.B.A. J. 750 (1983).

50. In fact, the pending legislation would actually add two new options: referring the case with directions to decide it, or referring the case and giving the new court discretion whether to decide it.

51. Some of the potential complications could be avoided if cases could be referred to the new tribunal only on the affirmative vote of six justices, rather than the five contemplated by the current Senate bill.

52. For this reason, not only disarray but chaos would likely result if the Intercircuit Tribunal (or any other auxiliary court) were given direct jurisdiction to review state-court judgments resting on federal law, as some have suggested. Under a system of reference jurisdiction, the Supreme Court at least has the ability to limit the issues the new court would address; if direct appeals were permitted, the only safeguard against inconsistency would be Supreme Court review of the new court's decisions—an additional burden that would defeat one of the purposes of the enterprise.

53. Rehnquist, *Whither the Courts*, 60 A.B.A. J. 787, 790 (1974). Dean Terrance Sandalow of the University of Michigan Law School has expressed similar concerns. *See* 2 Commission on Revision of the Federal Court Appellate System, Hearings Second Phase 739-740 (1975).

54. For example, in the 1981 term, Chief Justice Burger and Justice Brennan invariably took opposing positions when the Court divided 5-4 on civil rights issues, but they found themselves on the same side in two cases where matters of general federal law were resolved by 5-4 votes.

55. In the 1981 term, the Court was unanimous in only 25 percent of the civil rights cases decided on the merits, but in the general federal law segment of the docket the figure was 40 percent.

56. I am indebted to Professor David L. Shapiro for bringing this point to my attention.

57. Mackey v. United States, 401 U.S. 667, 678 (1971) (Harlan, J., concurring and dissenting).

58. This figure excludes cases in which Justices Brennan, Stewart, and Marshall would have reversed obscenity convictions, along with a few cases in which the dissenting justices would have vacated the judgment below for reconsideration in light of an intervening Supreme Court decision or other development.

Of the 119 cases, 28 came before the Court on appeal, thus the dissents might well have rested on an unwillingness to affirm rulings of dubious correctness, rather than a belief that the cases warranted consideration by the Supreme Court. This interpretation is supported by the fact that in 15 of the appeal cases, one of the three votes for plenary consideration came from Justice Stevens, who takes a very narrow view of the Court's certiorari function and never notes his dissent from the denial of discretionary review.

59. In two-thirds of the cases in which the lower court had rejected a civil rights claim, Justices Brennan and Marshall provided two of the three votes for review. In two-thirds of the cases upholding the claim, Chief Justice Burger and Justice Rehnquist were among the three dissenters.

60. *See* Hruska Commission Report, *supra* n. 23, at 182 (letter from Justice White).

61. Burger, *supra* n. 1, at 455.

62. *See also* Massachusetts v. Podgurski, 103 S. Ct. 1167 (1983) (Burger, C.J., dissenting from denial of certiorari): "In my view, only the finite limitations of the Court's time preclude our granting review of this case. I would grant certiorari and summarily reverse the judgment of the Supreme Judicial Court of Massachusetts [upholding the defendant's Fourth Amendment claim]." *See also* Stevens, *supra* n. 3, at 179-180.

63. The need for this information is underscored by consideration of the differing views expressed by Chief Justice Burger and Justice Rehnquist. Both have endorsed the idea of an intercircuit tribunal, and both envision sending 35 to 50 cases a year to the new court. However, the chief justice would use the reference option to reduce the Supreme Court's own docket to about 100 cases a year, while Justice Rehnquist would retain the present level of 150. Since a plenary docket of 100 cases would be just about filled by the civil rights and federalism caseloads of recent years, the chief justice's approach would almost certainly bring about the results hypothesized in the text: a Supreme Court devoted almost entirely to constitutional litigation, and little if any increase in the number of nationally binding decisions on statutory issues. Justice Rehnquist's approach might or might not have those consequences; that would depend on how many constitutional cases were heard by the Supreme Court in the place of statutory cases sent to the new tribunal. What the full Court would do, we do not know. But of the 55 cases in which Justice Rehnquist dissented from the denial of plenary review in the 1977-1980 terms, 41 involved constitutional issues.

64. For example, as Professor A. Leo Levin pointed out in his statement to a Senate subcommittee, it would probably be a good idea to have some senior judges on the new court, but it would not be desirable if all of the members of the court had senior status. Under the system contemplated by the pending legislation it would be impossible to assure an appropriate balance.

65. Hruska Commission Report, *supra* n. 23, at 31.

66. Seven is preferable to nine because it distinguishes the new tribunal from the Supreme Court, and because a smaller number of judges can work together more easily. Certainly no showing has been made that the volume of work destined for the court would require more than seven full-time judges.

67. *National Court of Appeals Act: Hearings Before the Subcomm. on Improvements in Judicial Machinery of the Senate Comm. on the Judiciary*, 94th Cong., 2d Sess. 190-191 (1976) (statement of Prof. Rosenberg).

The Rehnquist Court's shrinking plenary docket

Changes in the Supreme Court's composition and case selection process help explain why only about 1 percent of the cases on the docket now receive plenary consideration.

by David M. O'Brien

The "incredibly shrinking" plenary docket of the Supreme Court has drawn considerable attention. In the 1995 and 1996 terms, the Court heard only 75 hours of oral arguments and decided just 90 cases by written opinions each term, half the number of a decade ago. Moreover, the total docket has grown rather steadily, reaching more than 8,000 cases in the 1994 term before falling slightly to 7,602 cases in the 1996 term. Yet, since William H. Rehnquist became chief justice in 1986, fewer and fewer cases have been granted annually. Barely 1 percent of the cases now on the docket receive plenary consideration.

Even some justices are "amazed"[1] by the trend. Prior to arriving at the Court in 1990, Justice David H. Souter noticed the number had "come down significantly from the historical highs," which reached 184 decisions in the 1981 and 1983 terms. On the high bench, he found there had not been a conscious decision to reduce the number. "It had in fact just happened."

Justice Souter also considered possible explanations. All were factors external to the Court. Presidential vetoes of legislation by Ronald Reagan and George Bush, according to Justice Souter, may have resulted in "a diminishing supply of new statutes...that cried out for some immediate and speedy" interpretation. As for the rights of the accused, he observed that the Fourth Amendment's "basic standards...are products of the 60s and the 70s and the 80s." Finally, he speculated that, after 12 years of Republican judicial appointments, the

Rehnquist Court had found less disagreement with the lower federal courts because of "a diminished level of philosophical division within the federal courts from which so much of the conflicting opinions tend to arise."

Other external factors may also have played a part. Notably, the Court's discretionary jurisdiction was expanded with the 1988 Act to Improve the Administration of Justice. Virtually all non-discretionary appellate jurisdiction was eliminated. Afterwards the plenary docket did decline. But, as Figure 1 shows, the docket started declining before that.[2]

Factors internal to the Court were undoubtedly decisive. Specifically, fluctuations in the plenary docket register changes in the Court's composition and case selection process. The data and analysis presented here shows that certain members of the Burger Court were predisposed to grant cases review, and thereby inflated the plenary docket in the 1970s and early 1980s. The plenary docket jumped in the 1971 term to more than 170 cases, remaining in that range for the rest of the decade. Beginning in the 1981 term, the docket reached its height of more than 180 cases per term. Following the retirements of Chief Justice Warren E. Burger at the end of the 1985 term and Justice Lewis F. Powell Jr. at the end of the 1986 term, however, the plenary docket gradually declined and then fell more sharply following other retirements in the early 1990s.

The increase in the number of granted cases in

the 1970s and early 1980s also appears directly related to changes in the Court's operation made early in Chief Justice Burger's tenure. One important change he persuaded the others to make was in the oral argument calendar. Prior to 1970, attorneys in cases granted oral argument were each given one hour to present arguments. In 1970, the time allotted each side was reduced to 30 minutes. Instead of hearing 12 cases during a two week oral argument session, the justices went to hearing 12 cases in three days. Accordingly, the number of orally argued cases rose from 144 to 151 to 177 during the 1969, 1970, and 1971 terms.

Join-3 votes

Besides increasing the space on the oral argument calendar came another change—a change in the justices' voting practice in granting cases. In the early 1970s Chief Justice Burger and some other justices began casting "join-3" votes rather than simply voting to grant or deny petitions for certiorari. Because earlier in this century the Court adopted the informal "Rule of Four"—namely, that at least four justices must agree that a case merits review—a join-3 vote is a vote to provide a fourth vote if others vote to grant review, but is otherwise considered as voting to deny. The introduction of join-3 votes, arguably, contributed to the Court's taking more cases by lowering the threshold for granting review established by the Rule of Four.

In response to Congress's expansion of the Court's discretionary jurisdiction with the Judiciary Act of 1925, the Rule of Four was adopted in order to ensure important cases would still be granted. At first exceptions were made, but by Earl Warren's chief justiceship (1953-1969), the Rule of Four was firmly in place; his docket books record no join-3 votes.

Although the Rule of Four operates in only a fraction of the cases on the total docket, the percentage of cases granted on that basis is not insignificant. In 1982, Justice John Paul Stevens concluded that between 20 to 30 percent of the plenary docket was typically granted on only four votes and that those "are significant percentages."[3] He did so after reviewing Justice Harold Burton's docket books and determining that during 1946-47 about 25 percent of the cases granted had the support of no more than four justices. Based on his docket books, he reported that no more than

four votes resulted in granting between 23 and 30 percent of the cases in the 1979-81 terms. A review of Justice Thurgood Marshall's docket book for the 1990 term reveals, likewise, that 22 percent of the granted cases had only four votes.

In 1982, Justice Stevens thus proposed adopting a "Rule of Five." He did so as an alternative to Chief Justice Burger's proposal for the creation of a national appellate tribunal as a solution to the Court's workload problems. Abandoning the Rule of Four, Justice Stevens pointed out, would eliminate as much as a quarter of the cases granted review.

In retrospect, Justice Stevens's diagnosis of the Court's workload problem was right on the mark: the justices simply voted to grant too many cases. But at the time, he did not mention that other justices cast join-3 votes. Nonetheless, he had clearly identified the main cause of the Court's workload problem: the Rule of Four no longer imposed the kind of self-restraint it previously had. The propensity of some justices to cast join-3 votes lowered the threshold imposed by the Rule of Four for granting cases, thereby inflating plenary docket.

While the origin of join-3 votes remains unclear, such votes were not recorded prior to Burger's chief justiceship. Justice Harry A. Blackmun, who came aboard in 1970, recalls neither who began the practice nor any "definite discussion about the use of the vote." Neither does Chief Justice Rehnquist have a clear recollection of the origin of such votes. Whatever their origin, join-3 votes were established by the time Justice Stevens joined the Court in 1975. One possible explanation is that in leading conferences Chief Justice Burger began voting to join three, and other justices did the same. Within a few years, join-3 votes became almost routine. After the oral argument calendar was changed, Chief Justice Burger may have felt pressures to fill an expanded plenary docket. In addition, he may have done so because his discussion of cases was often vague and unclear.

Still, two other factors may bear on the casting of join-3 votes. First, following Justice Blackmun's appointment, Justices Powell and Rehnquist joined the Court in 1971. They came aboard with no prior judicial experience, though Rehnquist clerked for Justice Robert H. Jackson in 1952-53. They arrived after the oral argument calendar was expanded and Chief Justice Burger had already made the rising caseload a major concern. In 1971 he per-

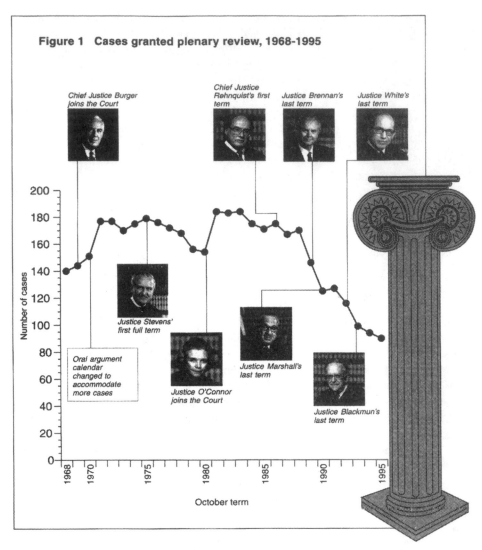

Figure 1   Cases granted plenary review, 1968-1995

Chief Justice Burger joins the Court

Chief Justice Rehnquist's first term

Justice Brennan's last term

Justice White's last term

Justice Stevens' first full term

Oral argument calendar changed to accommodate more cases

Justice O'Connor joins the Court

Justice Marshall's last term

Justice Blackmun's last term

Number of cases

October term

cases would be discussed at conference. During the chief justiceship of Harlan Fiske Stone (1941-46), his law clerks' memos on unpaid cases circulated to each justice. That remained the practice until Chief Justice Burger claimed that his chambers could no longer carry that burden. Hence, the creation of the "cert pool."

Noting votes and dissents

The creation of the cert pool provoked controversy within the Court. The four most senior and liberal justices— William O. Douglas, Potter Stewart, William J. Brennan Jr., and Thurgood Marshall— refused to join. Justice Douglas, in particular, adamantly opposed on the grounds that petitions would receive inadequate attention from the justices. During the 1972 term, as

suaded Harvard Law School professor Paul Freund to head a study group on the Court's workload problems. The increasing size of the total docket and the declining percentage of cases given plenary review caused concerns about the Court's supervisory capacity and may have inclined some justices to vote to grant review.

Second, in response to the "caseload crisis" in 1972, at Justice Powell's suggestion, a majority of the justices agreed to pool their law clerks and to have them write memos on incoming petitions for certiorari and appeals. Traditionally, each justice received the briefs in all cases. However, beginning with Chief Justice William Howard Taft (1921-30), the justices deferred to the chief justice and his law clerks on which unpaid (in forma pauperis)

senior associate, he began systematically noting his votes to grant petitions and his dissents from denial of review. Notably, his dissents from denial increased almost threefold from the 1969 term to the 1973 term.[4] Few justices followed his practice. One who did was Justice Byron White, who in 1973 also began noting his votes to grant cases and dissents from denial. As Figure 2 shows, he did so throughout the rest of his career. He also wrote longer dissents from the denial of cases in which he identified a conflict among federal circuit courts or between state supreme court rulings. Not surprisingly, his notations increased as the plenary docket shrank.

What Figure 2 does not reveal is no less important. In the first three terms, 1973 to 1975, in which

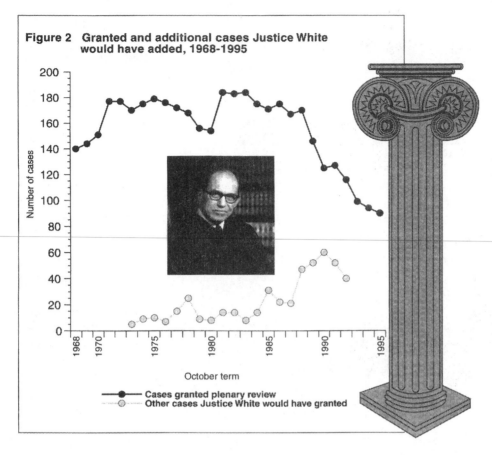

Figure 2 Granted and additional cases Justice White would have added, 1968-1995

Number of cases

October term

● Cases granted plenary review
○ Other cases Justice White would have granted

the practice of casting such votes became accepted. Furthermore, as Figure 3 shows, some justices cast an extraordinary share of such votes, whereas others rarely did. In the 1980s, Justice Blackmun led in join-3 votes. By comparison, Justice Stevens never cast such a vote. Other justices fell somewhere between. Figure 3 is based on data from Justice Marshall's bench memos, recording votes on cases granted during the 1979 to 1990 terms.[5] There are 1,556 memos on cases in which oral arguments were heard, and of those, join-3 votes were cast in 408 (26 percent).

More specifically, 192 cases (12 percent)

Justice White noted votes to grant cert, he was joined in 18 out of 24 cases by two other justices. The percentage remained high throughout the decade: during the 1976-80 tcrms, 22 percent (183 out of the 818 cases denied) had dissents joined by three justices. Justices Brennan and Marshall often dissented together, but Justices Stewart, White, Powell, and Blackmun tended to join dissents from denial as well.

The practice of noting votes to grant and dissents from denials is strategic, particularly when joined by other justices. In this way, especially by circulating drafts of proposed dissents, justices may persuade others to reconsider votes to grant cases otherwise denied. In short, the practice of noting votes to grant and dissenting from the denial of cert encouraged or reinforced the practice of casting join-3 votes. In other words, Chief Justice Burger and others may have voted to join-3 in anticipation of such notations and dissents from denial of review.

Regardless of the exact origin of join-3 votes,

were placed on the plenary docket on the basis of less than four votes to grant plus one or more join-3 votes; some were granted on the basis of only two votes to grant and two or more join-3 votes. Notably, Justice Blackmun cast join-3 votes in 55 percent of the cases granted on less than four firm votes to grant. Justice Sandra Day O'Connor followed with 21.8 percent, Chief Justice Burger in 12.5 percent, and Justice White in 11.4 percent. Justices Powell and Rehnquist each cast 8.8 percent. The point is that had these justices not cast Join-3 votes and the Rule of Four held, the plenary docket would have been reduced by 12 percent and, possibly, as much as 26 percent.

The shrinking docket

The key to the Rehnquist Court's shrinking docket in the 1990s, therefore, may be found in the Burger Court's responses to its rising caseload. Besides enlarging the plenary docket by changing the oral argument calandar, the Burger Court no longer strictly adhered to the Rule of Four, thereby

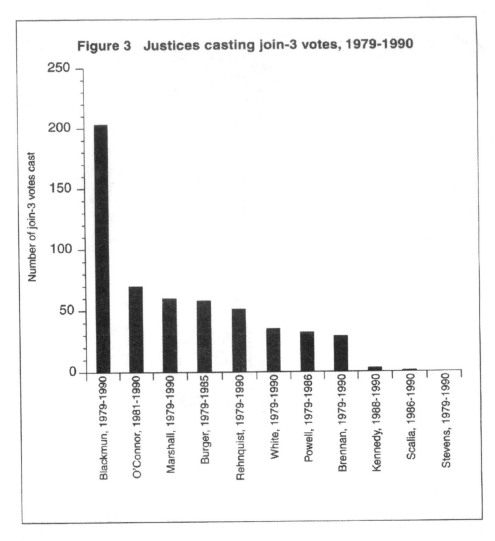

Figure 3   Justices casting join-3 votes, 1979-1990

at the end of the 1992 and 1993 terms. In sum, the inflation and contraction in the plenary docket registered changes in the Court's composition and its case selection process.

The cert pool's impact

Yet, some Court-watchers hypothesize that the cert pool remains the primary factor and an independent variable explaining the shrinking plenary docket. For instance, Kenneth W. Starr, a former clerk for Chief Justice Burger, complained that the cert pool exerts too much influence and that important cases are now passed over.[6]

Concerns about the cert pool have grown because, with the exception of Justice Stevens, every jus-

sacrificing some control over what and how much to decide. After an initial increase in the early 1970s, the number of cases annually decided rose again following the 1981 appointment of Justice O'Connor, who cast a fair number of join-3 votes, less than Justice Blackmun but more than the others. With several justices casting join-3 votes, by the early 1980s the numbers granted reached their historical highs. Following the retirements of Chief Justice Burger and Justice Powell, the plenary docket began to shrink. Neither Justice Antonin Scalia nor Justice Anthony Kennedy is as inclined as those two former justices to vote to join 3. The decline continued after the retirements of Justices Brennan and Marshall at the end of the 1989 and 1990 terms, respectively, and then fell further after the retirements of Justices White and Blackmun

tice appointed during the last two decades joined the pool. However, several problems arise with hypothesizing that the increasing number of justices belonging to the pool produces less scrutiny of cert petitions and results in granting fewer cases.

On the one hand, the justices not participating in the cert pool differ in their attention to petitions. Justice Douglas quickly perused them, while Justice Brennan tried to review each but generally relied on his clerks' memos. Justice Stevens relies entirely on his clerks' screening and does "not even look at the papers in over 80 percent of the cases that are filed." In short, there is no evidence that justices not in the cert pool give more attention to petitions than those in the pool. In other words, independent review need not guarantee searching review. So, too, those in the cert pool undoubt-

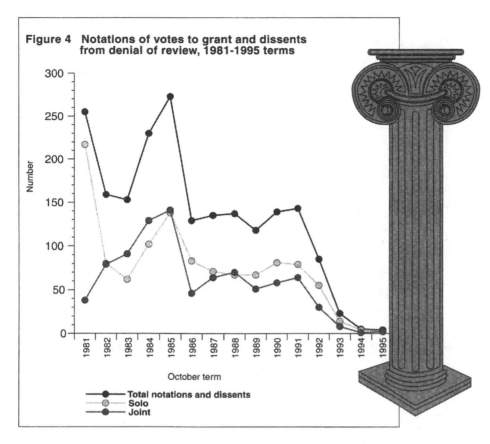

Figure 4 Notations of votes to grant and dissents from denial of review, 1981-1995 terms

October term

— Total notations and dissents
— Solo
— Joint

cert pool, like Justices Blackmun and Powell, may have been inclined to vote to join 3 in deference to the senior justices not in the pool and due to concerns about the Court's declining supervisory capacity. Second, cert pool memos flag cases alleging intercircuit conflicts. Given concerns about declining supervisory capacity, pool memos may have inclined some justices, especially Chief Justice Burger and Justice White, to vote to grant those cases, as well as moved the latter to file dissents from denials in them.

Conversely, though, the increase in the size of the cert pool may have contributed to the decline in the plenary docket. With more justices belonging to the cert pool, and assuming greater attention is given to petitions by the justices' chambers, the cert pool process may highlight circuit conflicts, which after further scrutiny are deemed "tolerable" or in need of "percolation." Hence, cases in which particularly Justice White would vote to grant were more frequently denied, resulting in a diminished docket.

In short, it is unclear that the cert pool either determines the amount of scrutiny given petitions or was the underlying factor in increasing, and subsequently decreasing, the size of the plenary docket. Whether in or out of the cert pool, justices differ in their scrutiny of petitions and cert memos. Although measuring the extent of their independent review appears impossible, one indication remains their published notes to grant and dissents from denial. While not an entirely satisfactory gauge, because some justices oppose the practice of publicizing such votes, notations of votes to grant and dissents from denial provide a measure for the theory that the changes in the ple-

edly vary in the amount of time and attention they give to cert memos and petitions. At the beginning of his service, for instance, Justice Scalia found it necessary to read only the memos on cases the justices agreed to carry over for another conference discussion.

On the other hand, the chambers of justices participating in the cert pool might actually give more attention to case selection. Although only one pool memo on each case circulates among the eight chambers, most of the justices in the pool assign at least one of their clerks to review, even draft supplementary memos to, those coming from the cert pool. The cert pool process thus might result in petitions receiving greater attention. If so, ironically, the cert pool could have contributed to increasing the size of the plenary docket in two ways.

First, in the 1970s and early 1980s the justices opposed to the cert pool, and concerned about important cases being overlooked, may have given greater scrutiny to petitions as well as more often voted to grant cases. Justices participating in the

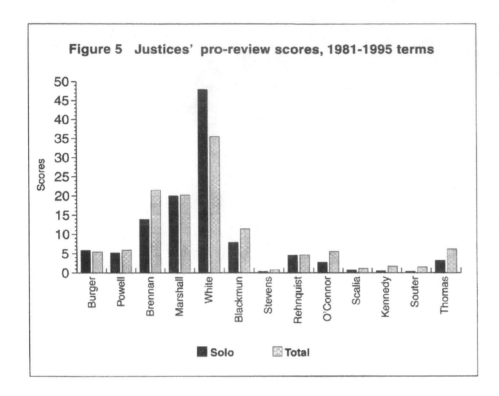

Figure 5   Justices' pro-review scores, 1981-1995 terms

■ Solo   ▨ Total

clined to grant review and tried to persuade others to vote to grant by casting join-3 votes as well as by circulating notes of votes to grant review and dissents from denial. The number of notations of votes to grant and dissents from denial provides a measure of the justices' pro-review dispositions, at least in the 1980s; in the 1990s fewer justices issue them and do so in far smaller numbers.

Figure 5 assigns pro-review scores to justices serving during the 1981 to 1995 terms. Two scores are assigned: one for their solo notations and dis-

Declining notations

nary docket dovetail with those in the Court's composition and voting practices.

As seen in Figure 4,[7] the number of notations of votes to grant and dissents from denial of review tracks the decline in the plenary docket shown in Figure 1. In the 1981 term, when the plenary docket reached its zenith, there were 255 notations of votes to grant additional cases and dissents from denial. Five terms later in 1986, Rehnquist's first as chief justice, the number fell to 129. By the 1994 and 1995 terms there were less than 10 in those combined terms.

As with the diminishing plenary docket, the number of notations of votes to grant and dissents from denial declined in three stages: first, following Chief Justice Burger's retirement and Rehnquist's elevation to the center chair; second, after Justices Brennan and Marshall retired; and, third, following the retirements of Justices White and Blackmun.

The data underscore that members of the Burger Court were far more disposed to grant cases than those on the Rehnquist Court in the early and mid-1990s. Certain justices were especially in-

sents, and another for their total contribution of such issuances, which includes both their solo notes to grant or dissent from denials, as well as those they joined or were joined by one or more other justices. The scores are based on dividing their number of such notations for each term they were on the bench by the total number issued during those periods, and then multiplying by 100. Justice White, for example, served during 12 of those 15 terms. During that time, he issued 532 solo notes to grant and dissents from denial, and there was a total of 1,102 such notations during that period. Thus, he has a 48.2 solo pro-review score for voting to grant cases beyond the number already granted plenary consideration.

Figure 5 reveals considerable variation among the justices. Justice White filed more solo notations of votes to grant and dissents from denial than any other justice. By contrast, Justice Blackmun, who held the record on join-3 votes, more frequently joined other justices in noting votes to grant or dissents from denials than he did in filing his own.

The pro-review scores further confirm the theory that the inflation in the plenary docket during the Burger Court years and its contraction with the Rehnquist Court reflects changes in the composition of the bench and the justices' voting practices. Given the high pro-review scores of the four justices—Brennan, Marshall, White, and Blackmun—who retired in the early 1990s, the steep decline in the plenary docket should come as no surprise.

*****

It is, perhaps, unremarkable to conclude that the inflation and subsequent contraction of the plenary docket registers changes in the composition of the high bench and the justices' voting practices in case selection. The justices, not their clerks nor external forces, ultimately determine what and how much to decide. Nonetheless, the analysis here confirms the observations of Justices Souter and Stevens. The diminished plenary docket, as Justice Souter put it, "in fact just happened," due specifically to changes in the Court's composition and operation. And as Justice Stevens pointed out, the Court's "workload problem" in the 1970s and 1980s arose precisely because the justices failed to exercise self-restraint in case selection. We are left, then, with an irony of history: While recognized for his interest in judicial administration, Chief Justice Burger failed to appreciate that the Court's "workload problem" was one of its own making.

NOTES

This article originally appeared in Volume 81, Number 2, September-October 1997, pages 58-65.

1. Justice David H. Souter, quoted by Shannon Duffy, *Inside the Highest Court: Souter Describes Justices' Relationship, Caseload Trend*, Pennsylvania Law Weekly (April 17, 1995) at 11. All subsequent quotes from Justice Souter are from this article.

2. The analysis and data presented here is more fully developed by the author in *Join-3 Votes, the Rule of Four, the Cert. Pool, and the Supreme Court's Shrinking Plenary Docket*, 13 J. L. & POL. (forthcoming 1997).

3. Justice John Paul Stevens, *The Life Span of A Judge-Made Rule*, 58 N.Y. U. L. REV. 1, 17 (1983).

4. *See* Feeney, *Conflicts Involving Federal Law: A Review of Cases Presented to the Supreme Court*, in STRUCTURE AND INTERNAL PROCEDURES: RECOMMENDATIONS FOR CHANGE 112-113 (Washington, D.C.: Commission on Revision of the Federal Court Appellate System, 1975).

5. Thurgood Marshall Papers, Boxes 239, 240, 260, 261, 281, 305, 306, 329, 330, 352, 353, 375, 376, 398, 399, 427, 452, 453, 483, 513, 514, (Manuscripts Room, Library of Congress). Note that some of the bench memos for cases heard during each term were missing, particularly for the 1987 term in which there are memos for only about one third of the cases granted oral argument.

6. Starr, *Supreme Court Needs A Management Revolt*, Wall Street Journal, Oct. 13, 1993, at A23, and *Trival Pursuits at the Supreme Court*, Wall Street Journal, Oct. 6, 1993, at A17.

7. This figure is based on notations of votes to grant review and dissents from the denial of petitions published in the U.S. Reports from the 1981 to 1995 terms. Both notations of votes to either grant or dissents from denial and opinions dissenting from the denial of review were counted.. Excluded were opinions cooncurring in or respecting the denial of review and dissents from denials of requests for stays of execution and other motions. Also excluded are dissents filed by Justices Brennan, Marshall, and Blackmun in death penalty cases unless the dissent provided an explanation for voting to grant other than simply stating their opposition to capital punishment. In the 1980s, Justices Brennan and Marshall had the Court's computer system programmed to print automatically all of their dissents from the denial of certiorari when a capital punishment case was denied review. As a result, each term they filed hundreds of such dissents and including them here would have skewed the data. Justice Blackmun, likewise, adopted their practice in his last term after concluding that the imposition of capital punishment was unconstitutional and announcing his opposition in a dissent from denial of review in *Callins v. Collins*, 114 S.Ct. 1127 (1994).

Federal court reform should start at the top

An increase in the number of cases decided by the Supreme Court and changes in its decision-making process would help ease the caseload of the lower federal courts, an appellate judge suggests.

by Roger J. Miner

There can be little doubt that the federal courts are confronting a caseload crunch of mammoth proportions. How could it be otherwise, with more and more attorneys filing more and more lawsuits as the result of more and more causes of action created by Congress? Let's look at the numbers. In 1981, approximately 180,000 civil cases were filed in the U.S. district courts.[1] In 1991, the number was nearly 208,000.[2] In 1981, approximately 31,000 criminal cases were filed in the district courts, and in 1991 the figure was about 46,000.[3] During the same decade, Congress authorized increases in district judgeships from 516 to 649.[4] The circuit courts of appeals had 132 authorized judgeships and about 26,000 filings in 1981.[5] By 1991, filings had increased by roughly 16,000 cases to 42,000, but there were only 35 more judgeships than there were in 1981.[6]

In the 100 years since the U.S. courts of appeals were formed, authorized judgeships in the Second Circuit have gone from 3 to 13, an increase of 433 percent.[7] During the same period, however, filings in the circuit have gone from 196 to 4,165, an increase of more than 2,000 percent![8] As filings increase, without any corresponding increase in the number of judges, each judge must handle more cases, and the median disposition time for each case necessarily becomes longer.

If the mission of the lower federal courts is to provide for the just, speedy, and inexpensive determination of every dispute brought before them, their present overburdened condition calls into question their ability to perform the mission. There are two options. The first is to continue the present course, with the expectation of incremen-

tal increases in the caseload and with expansion of the judiciary continually lagging behind need. The other option is reform, including changes in such areas as court structure, procedural rules, case management techniques, the decisional process, subject matter jurisdiction, and methods of alternate dispute resolution. It seems clear that the time for reform is at hand.[9]

Reforms

Three years ago, the Federal Courts Study Committee, created by Congress to assess the developing crisis and to make appropriate recommendations, rendered its final report. In the report, the committee noted the existence of "mounting public and professional concern with the federal courts' congestion, delay, expense, and expansion."[10] The committee did not recommend any increase in the number of judges, although that would seem to be a logical place to start. A lively debate is now in progress between those who believe that there should be a "cap" on the number of federal judges and those who think expansion is in order, with excellent arguments on both sides.[11] However that question may be resolved, the fact is that in recent years the president and Senate have had a great deal of difficulty in filling current vacancies. At this moment, there are 106 unfilled slots in the district courts and 20 unfilled slots in the courts of appeals.[12]

In 1975, the Hruska Commission proposed the establishment of a National Court of Appeals, a new court to be interposed between the Supreme Court and the regional courts of appeals.[13] It would receive cases on reference from the Supreme Court and by transfer from the regional courts. The study committee rejected the idea of a national intermediate appellate court but did present five structural change possibilities for further inquiry and discussion: A single unified National Court of Appeals operating through regional divisions; a four-tier system, with the first appellate tier consisting of 25 to 30 regional appellate divisions hearing appeals of right from the district courts and the second-tier appellate court taking cases on a discretionary basis from the first; national appeals courts structured according to subject matter, as in the federal circuit; a single, centrally organized court of appeals; and consolidation of existing courts into five jumbo circuits.[14] All these proposals have their unique problems, as the study committee indicated.[15]

There are those who see merit in giving the courts of appeals discretion as to what cases they will accept.[16] My chief judge, Jon Newman, has a different approach. He favors a system of discretionary access to federal courts at both the trial and appellate levels in order to reallocate jurisdiction between state and federal courts.[17] Under his proposal, discretion as to access would be vested in the federal courts and would be exercised for individual cases and designated categories.[18] Proposals have been made to modify or severely curtail diversity jursidiction,[19] to replace with a workers' compensation scheme the statutes allowing injured railroad workers and seamen to sue in federal courts,[20] and to establish a special court to adjudicate claims under the Social Security Act.[21]

Other suggestions for reform have included a small claims procedure for certain federal tort claims,[22] the creation of an Article III appellate division of the United States Tax Court with exclusive jurisdiction over federal income, estate, and gift tax cases,[23] a requirement for exhaustion of state administrative remedies prior to the commencement of prisoners' civil rights suits,[24] and mandatory use of alternative dispute resolution mechanisms.[25]

The federal judiciary, with the assistance of the Federal Judicial Center, long has experimented with case management techniques. The authority of judges to take hold of a case in its earliest stages and to keep the case under close supervision, with established deadlines, has proved to be essential to the achievement of maximum efficiency in court operations. Despite the fact that the lower federal courts are running as fast as they can and have been refining management techniques and administrative procedures over the years, Congress enacted the Civil Justice Reform Act in 1990.[26] The act requires each district court in the nation to create an expense and delay reduction plan. Just what the courts needed at a time when they are understaffed and underfunded: a congressional requirement to micromanage the courts and to reinvent the wheel. What a waste!

Congress's responsibility

It is Congress, of course, that is responsible for all this mess in the first place. Justice Sandra Day O'Connor once referred to the "underdeveloped capacity [of Congress] for self-restraint."[27] Nowhere is the lack of self-restraint more evident than in the federal criminal laws. I have been writing and speaking about the federalization of crimes for more than a decade, but nobody seems to listen. There are about 3,000 separate provisions scattered throughout the U.S. Code criminalizing various forms of conduct. Do you know that it is a federal offense to reproduce the image of Woodsy Owl[28] and Smokey the Bear?[29] To impersonate a 4-H Club member?[30] To transport water hyacinths in interstate commerce?[31] To bring false teeth into a state without the permission of a local dentist?[32]

Every time Congress meets, more state crimes are made federal crimes in response to the problems of the moment. Last year it was car jacking.[33] This year it looks like it will be domestic violence,[34] a quintessential state crime. Is it any wonder that the number of assistant U.S. attorneys has increased two-and-one-half fold since 1980?[35] If the number of Article III judges had increased at that rate, we would have 1,620 judges instead of the 816 we now have.

Criminal statutes have not alone been responsible for the increase in business in the federal courts. Congress continues to create new sources of civil litigation as well. Last year, Congress established a civil cause of action providing for the recovery of damages from any individual who engages in torture or killing under color of the law of any foreign nation.[36] It appears that any victim of state terrorism may sue here if there is no remedy in the place where the conduct occurred.[37] And there is a 10-year statute of limitations.[38] Congress has decided to turn loose on world terrorism the mightiest force it could think of—lawyers pursuing civil litigation. That ought to strike fear into their hearts! In passing that legislation, Congress had no idea how many suits the new statute would spawn or what impact it would have on the federal judicial system.

Such is the way with all congressional legislation. When I was a member of the Judicial Conference Committee on Federal-State Jurisdiction, I participated in the preparation of a checklist for Congress to consider in reviewing proposed legislation.[39] The checklist was designed to identify technical and interpretive problems, duplicative and unnecessary legislation, and the general impact of legislation on the courts. The checklist has, I fear, come to naught.

The Supreme Court's role

One of the major reasons for the inundation of the federal district and circuit courts is the uncertainty of the law. The Scriptures ask this question: "If the trumpet give an uncertain sound, who shall prepare himself to the battle?"[40] My answer is: "Every lawyer worth his salt." If the law is not settled, there is every incentive to litigate.

In our judicial system, only one body can resolve uncertainty—the U.S. Supreme Court. Yet the Court seldom takes the trumpet to its lips, and when it does, the sound often is very weak. I respectfully suggest that, at the Supreme Court level, an increase in the number of cases decided and some changes in the decision-making process itself would go far toward alleviating the caseload problems of the lower federal courts. Federal court reform should start at the top.

The Supreme Court is lumbering into the 21st century at the leisurely pace of the 19th century, seemingly oblivious to the needs of the federal judicial system. The trial and appeals courts are overwhelmed by caseload growth, but the Supreme Court actually is deciding fewer cases each year. This year, 116 cases were decided, 127 the year before, and 125 the year before that.[41] Back in the 1980s, the figure reached as high as 151.[42] The Court certainly is trimming its docket in the face of an explosive growth of cases in the lower courts.

This makes no sense. We need to get the Supreme Court up to speed. The interesting part of it is that the shrinkage has come as the Court has gained more and more control over its docket, culminating in the 1988 legislation that effectively eliminated the Court's mandatory appellate juris-

diction.[43] As most lawyers know, the only way to get there on appeal now is by cert. And the justices are not granting enough cert petitions. For one thing, more cases should be taken in order to settle the law where circuit courts of appeals are in conflict.

Intercircuit conflicts

In the Judicial Improvements Act of 1990, Congress directed the Federal Judicial Center to undertake a study of the problems created by intercircuit conflicts, including economic costs, forum shopping among circuits, unfairness to litigants, and non-acquiescence by federal agencies.[44] The study has not yet been completed, but preliminary reports indicate that the number of conflicts has been greater than originally thought.[45] Justice Byron White, who recently retired, has been in the vanguard of those who believe that the Supreme Court should do more to resolve intercircuit conflicts. He frequently dissented from the denial of cert, pointing out the conflicts and urging his colleagues to resolve them. His dissents include language such as this:

One of the Court's duties is to do its best to see that the federal law is not being applied differently in the various circuits around the country. The Court is surely not doing its best when it denies certiorari in this case, which presents an issue on which the Courts of Appeals are recurringly at odds.[46]

and this:

I agree with petitioner and the Government that the outcome of a federal criminal prosecution should not depend upon the circuit in which the case is tried.[47]

and this:

Because a uniform rule should be announced by this Court on this important and recurring issue, I would grant the petition.[48]

Clearly, allowing circuit conflicts to continue generates litigation, because the law remains unsettled, and attorneys take their cases to the forum most favorable. Where the Supreme Court has not spoken on an issue, but some circuits have resolved the question in one way and some in another, litigation is encouraged in those circuits that have not yet spoken. Clients doing business nationally may have their conduct regulated one way in one place and another way in another and continue to challenge unfavorable precedent. Government agencies, charged with the administration of national law in a uniform way, follow policies of non-acquiescence, refusing to accept the views of a circuit that rejects the agency position.

Aside from the fact that fairness is lost and justice is not seen to be done, the lower courts become clogged with cases that would not be brought if the law was clearly stated. The Supreme Court is the only place where the conflicts can be resolved, and the resolution must be accomplished more frequently and in greater numbers of cases. And I think that a greater number of important issues that have not yet festered into intercircuit conflicts should be identified and decided by the Supreme Court in an effort to head off the inevitable clogging of the pipeline that comes from unsettled questions of law. Included in the issues that need to be resolved are thorny questions of statutory interpretation.

An uncertain trumpet

As a frequent consumer of Supreme Court services, I often am a confused victim of the Supreme Court's uncertain trumpet. For example, in 1990 the Supreme Court decided *Grady v. Corbin*[49] in a 5-4 opinion by Justice William Brennan. The case involved the double jeopardy clause of the Fifth Amendment and changed the rule established in 1932 in *Blockburger v. United States*.[50] According to *Blockburger*, whether you can be prosecuted for the same criminal act under two different criminal statutes requires a determination whether one statute requires proof of a fact that the other does not. *Grady* established a new gloss on the old rule. I was one of a three-member panel of my court to which fell a case requiring an interpretation of *Grady*. Each member of the panel wrote a separate opinion,[51] so disparate were our views of what the Supreme Court had said. It is bad enough to interpret unclear statutes, but it is even worse to interpret some Supreme Court decisions.

In 1992, the Supreme Court modified *Grady* somewhat in *United States v. Felix*,[52] in which it noted our difficulties in deciding the case in the Second Circuit, which it then remanded for consideration in light of *Felix*. We subsequently wrote a new decision in which we all concurred.[53] A little over a month ago, in a case called *United States v. Dixon*,[54] the Supreme Court overruled the *Grady* decision (I think) and returned to the *Blockburger* rule. I say "I think," because five separate opinions were

filed in the most recent case. The double jeopardy trumpet continues to emit an uncertain sound.

One author has referred to "the Justices' muddy, footnote-filled expository prose."[55] Far be it from me to accept such a characterization. I do note that the members of the Court have some difficulty agreeing on things. In *Brecht v. Abrahamson*,[56] a habeas corpus case decided this term, the following line-up, not especially unusual, was given: "Rehnquist, C.J., delivered the opinion of the Court, in which Stevens, Scalia, Kennedy, and Thomas, JJ., joined. Stevens, J., filed a concurring opinion. White, J., filed a dissenting opinion, in which Blackmun, J., joined, and in which Souter, J., joined except for the footnote and Part III. Blackmun, O'Connor, and Souter, JJ., filed dissenting opinions."[57]

All those 5-4 and plurality opinions serve only to engender hope among lawyers and a resolve to continue litigating. Maybe there will be a switch in votes. Maybe a new member will join the Court. Maybe some new, persuasive reasoning will be advanced by the bar. Without certainty in the law, litigation proliferates. An attorney would not serve his or her client well if he or she did not litigate issues left open. Forgotten is this admonition of Justice Louis Brandeis: "It is usually more important that a rule of law be settled, than that it be settled right."[58]

Several other cases decided this term do not fully resolve the questions presented. In *TXO Production Corp. v. Alliance Resources Corp.*,[59] the vote was 6-3 to uphold an award of punitive damages, but the reasoning was all over the lot and no one opinion attracted a five-vote majority. The qualifications of expert witnesses were left to the discretion of the district judges in *Daubert v. Merrell Dow Pharmaceuticals*,[60] but little guidance was given as to how that discretion should be exercised. And, despite the strong language about gerrymandering used in *Shaw v. Reno*[61] (another 5-4 decision), acceptable methods of drawing congressional district boundary lines are still very much up in the air.

Thus do cases proliferate in the lower federal courts for failure of the Supreme Court to resolve intercircuit conflicts, to identify and decide important procedural and substantive issues before they ripen into intercircuit conflicts, and to provide clear, crisp, and certain opinions for the guidance of the lower courts, the bar, and the American citizenry. As I see it, a greater volume of cases fully decided at the Supreme Court level as well as more brevity and clarity in the Court's opinions would do much to relieve the congestion in the lower courts.

Proposals for reform

To achieve these ends, I propose consideration of the following possibilities:

• More attention by the individual members of the Court should be paid to cert petitions in an effort to identify the most important conflicts and issues for review. There is some basis for the belief that the present cert pool of law clerks from the various chambers is not the most effective way of handling these matters.[62] More cert petitions should be granted.

• The newest justice has stressed the importance of collegiality, which sometimes includes the need to submerge one's views in unimportant matters for the good of the institution and of the consumers of its products.[63] Let us hope that Justice Ruth Bader Ginsburg is able to persuade her colleagues of the importance of one voice. Too often is heard the cacophony of what appears to be nine separate courts.

• Each Supreme Court opinion need not read as if it were the History of the World, Part I. If brevity is a virtue for judges of other courts and for lawyers, it should also be a virtue for justices of the Supreme Court. The necessary increase in production can also be achieved through per curiam opinions and summary orders. Many an intercircuit conflict could be resolved by a brief opinion adopting the decision of one of the circuits that considered the issue.

• The effort to increase production in the Supreme Court might be assisted by cutting the summer recess from three months to two.[64] That lengthy recess really is a relic of the 18th century, and I know of no justice who must return to the farm at harvest time.

• There is a statutory provision allowing certification of questions of law to the Supreme Court by the courts of appeals.[65] This provision has fallen into disuse, but should be revived, even though the Supreme Court has the right to reject the matter certified.

• The Court should be alert to the availability of its Rule 11, which allows it to grant cert before judgment in the court of appeals. This allows the Court to take up an important case without delay, as it did in *Mistretta v. United States.*[66] In that case, it was important to deal with the constitutionality of the Sentencing Reform Act of 1984[67] quickly, since some district courts throughout the nation were sentencing under the new act, and some were sentencing under the old law.

• Some mandatory appellate jurisdiction might be restored in an effort to increase the Court's production. The erosion of mandatory jurisdiction over the years has been gradual,[68] and the end result seems to be fewer cases decided. Perhaps cases that involve the declaration of unconstitutionality of federal statutes would be a good place to start with mandated appeals.

• The Supreme Court certainly could address more issues if it divided itself into panels to hear cases of a more routine nature. Three panels of three judges each can decide more cases more efficiently and faster than can an en banc panel of nine.[69] Hearings by the full Court could be reserved for cases in which a panel is in disagreement or for important constitutional issues.

• The number of Supreme Court justices is fixed by Congress.[70] Despite the explosion in federal litigation, the number of justices has been fixed at nine since 1869.[71] Before that, the number varied between 5 and 10.[72] There is nothing sacrosanct about the number nine. In light of the potential business that the Court should be addressing, an addition of at least three seems to be warranted. The rejected proposal of Franklin D. Roosevelt to increase the number of justices was known as a Court-packing plan and was highly political in nature. What is called for now is a Court-expanding plan to take care of additional work.

• I suppose there is no way to mandate the issuance of clear and thoughtful opinions in one voice by the Supreme Court. But the observations of one justice on the subject of clarity of opinions is most illuminating. The *New York Times* recently published a photograph of Justice White and, in a caption underneath the picture, noted his retirement after 31 years of service.[73] The caption continued: "He said that he intended to sit on Federal appeals courts during his retirement, and that he hoped that the Supreme Court's opinions would be clear and easy to follow."[74]

I hope that Justice White comes to sit in the Second Circuit as Justice Thurgood Marshall did after his retirement.[75] I hope that I have the opportunity to sit with him and to join him in applying Supreme Court precedent. We will then see if his subtle message to his former colleagues got through. We both can hope, can't we?

NOTES

This article originally appeared in Volume 77, Number 2, September-October 1993, pages 104-108.

This article is adapted from Judge Miner's speech at the American Judicature Society-National Conference of Bar Presidents joint luncheon, August 7, 1993, in New York.

1. Annual Report of the Director of the Administrative Office of the United States Courts 86 (1991).

2. *Id.*

3. *Id.* at 90.

4. *Id.*

5. *Id.* at 81.

6. *Id.*

7. Miner, *Planning for the Second Century of the Second Circuit Court of Appeals: The Report of the Federal Courts Study Committee,* 65 St. John's L. Rev. 673, 677 (1991).

8. *Id.*; United States Courts for the Second Circuit: Second Circuit Report 1992, at 4.

9. "At times in our system the way in which courts perform their function becomes as important as what they do in the result." United States v. United Mine Workers of Am., 330 U.S. 258, 363 (1947) (Rutledge, J., dissenting).

10. Report of the Federal Courts Study Committee 3 (1990).

11. *See, e.g.,* Bermant et al., Imposing a Moratorium on the Number of Federal Judges: Analysis of Arguments and Implications (Federal Judicial Center, 1993); Newman, *1,000 judges—the limit for an effective federal judiciary,* 76 Judicature 187 (1993); Williams, *Solutions to federal judicial gridlock,* 76 Judicature 185 (1993); Sloviter, *The Judiciary Needs Judicious Growth,* Nat'l L.J., June 28, 1993, at 17.

12. *Judicial Boxscore,* The Third Branch (Administrative Office of the United States Courts, Washington, D.C.), July 1993, at 11.

13. *See* Commission on Revision of the Federal Court Appellate System, *Structure and Internal Procedures: Recommendations for Change, reprinted in* 67 F.R.D. 195, 236-241 (1975); *see also* Wallace, *The Nature and Extent of Intercircuit Conflicts: A Solution Needed for a Mountain or a Molehill?,* 71 Cal. L. Rev. 913 (1983) (criticizing the Hruska Report).

14. *See Study Committee Report, supra* n. 10, at 117-123.

15. *See id.*

16. *See, e.g.,* Shapiro, *Jurisdiction and Discretion,* 60 N.Y.U. L. Rev. 543 (1985).

17. *See* Newman, *Restructuring Federal Jurisdiction: Proposals to Preserve the Federal Judicial System,* 56 U. Chi. L. Rev. 761, 770-776 (1989).

18. *Id.*

19. *See, e.g.,* Sloviter, *Diversity jurisdiction through the lens of federalism,* 76 Judicature 90 (1992); *Study Committee Report, supra* n. 10, at 38; Miner, *supra* n. 7, at 717 n. 288 (citing sources).

20. *See Study Committee Report, supra* n. 10, at 62-63.

21. *See id.* at 55-59.

22. *See id.* at 81.

23. *See id.* at 69.

24. *See id.* at 48-50.

25. *See id.* at 83-85.

26. Pub. L. No. 101-650, tit. I, 104 Stat. 5089 (1990) (codified at 28 U.S.C. §§471-482 (Supp. 1993)).

27. Garcia v. San Antonio Metropolitan Transit Auth., 469 U.S. 528, 588 (1985) (O'Connor, J., dissenting).

28. *See* 18 U.S.C. §711a (1988).

29. *See id.* §711.

30. *See id.* §916.

31. *See id.* §46.

32. *See id.* §1821.

33. *See* Anti-Car Theft Act of 1992, Pub. L. No. 102-519, §101, 106 Stat. 3384, 3384 (codified at 18 U.S.C. §2119 (Supp. 1993)).

34. *See* H.R. 1133, 103d Cong., 1st Sess. (1993); H.R. 688, 103d Cong., 1st Sess. (1993); S. 11, 103d Cong., 1st Sess. (1993); S. 6, 103d Cong., 1st Sess. (1993).

35. *See* Novack, *How About a Little Restructuring?,* Forbes, Mar. 15, 1993, at 91.

36. *See* Torture Victim Protection Act of 1991, Pub. L. No. 102-256, 106 Stat. 73 (codified at 28 U.S.C. §1350 (Supp. 1993)).

37. *See id.* §2(b), 106 Stat. at 73.

38. *See id.* §2(c), 106 Stat. at 73.

39. *See* Miner, *supra* n. 7, at 722-723.

40. I Corinthians 14:8.

41. These statistics were provided by the Office of the Solicitor General (on file with author).

42. Greenhouse, *Lightening Scales of Justice: High Court Trims Its Docket,* N.Y. Times, Mar. 7, 1992, at A1; *see* Greenhouse, *Case of the Shrinking Docket: Justices Spurn New Appeals,* N.Y. Times, Nov. 28, 1989, at A1; *see also* Strauss, *One Hundred Fifty Cases Per Year: Some Implications of the Supreme Court's Limited Resources for Judicial Review of Agency Action,* 87 Colum. L. Rev. 1093, 1100 (1987) (suggesting that Court's docket cannot accommodate more than 150 cases per term).

43. *See* Act of June 27, 1988, Pub. L. No. 100-352, 102 Stat. 662.

44. *See* Judicial Improvements Act of 1990, Pub. L. No. 101-650, §302, 104 Stat. 5089, 5097.

45. *See* Hellman, Unresolved Intercircuit Conflicts: The Nature and Scope of the Problem (Federal Judicial Center, 1991).

46. Taylor v. United States, 112 S. Ct. 2982, 2982 (1992) (White, J., dissenting) (circuit split over whether indictments against defendants should be dismissed after state officials technically violate the Interstate Agreement on Detainers).

47. Tomala v. United States, 112 S. Ct. 1997, 1998 (1992) (White, J., dissenting) (circuit split regarding "whether the weight of uningestible waste material should be included in calculating the weight of a 'mixture or substance' containing a detectable amount of a controlled substance for purposes of [U.S.S.G.] §2D1.1").

48. Carroll v. Consolidated Rail Corp., 112 S. Ct. 916, 916 (1992) (White, J., dissenting) (circuit split over whether the Federal Employers' Liability Act "creates a cause of action for emotional injury brought about by acts that lack any physical contact or threat of physical contact").

49. 495 U.S. 508 (1990).

50. 284 U.S. 299 (1932).

51. *See* United States v. Calderone, 917 F.2d 717, 718-722 (2d Cir. 1990) (Pratt, J.), *vacated,* 112 S. Ct. 1657 (1992); *id.* at 722-726 (Newman, J., concurring); *id.* at 726-729 (Miner, J., dissenting).

52. 112 S. Ct. 1377 (1992).

53. *See* United States v. Calderone, 982 F.2d 42 (2d Cir. 1992).

54. 61 U.S.L.W. 4835 (U.S. June 28, 1993).

55. Hirsch, *Book Review,* 61 Geo. Wash. L. Rev. 858, 859 (1993) (reviewing Goldstein, The Intelligible Constitution: The Supreme Court's Obligation to Maintain the Constitution as Something We the People Can Understand (1992)).

56. 113 S. Ct. 1710 (1993).

57. *Id.* at 1713.

58. Di Santo v. Pennsylvania, 273 U.S. 34, 42 (1927)

(Brandeis, J., dissenting).

59. 61 U.S.L.W. 4766 (U.S. June 25, 1993).

60. 61 U.S.L.W. 4805 (U.S. June 28, 1993).

61. 61 U.S.L.W. 4818 (U.S. June 28, 1993).

62. *See* Gest, *The Court: Deciding Less, Writing More*, U.S. NEWS & WORLD REPORT, June 28, 1993, at 24, 26.

63. *See* Lewis, *The Supreme Court; Ginsburg Affirms Right of a Woman to Have an Abortion*, N.Y. TIMES, July 22, 1993, at A1.

64. See *Promoting public understanding of the Supreme Court*, 76 JUDICATURE 4 (1992).

65. *See* 28 U.S.C. §1254(2) (1988); *see also* Sup. Ct. R. 19 (procedure for certifying a question).

66. 488 U.S. 361 (1989).

67. Pub. L. No. 98-473, 98 Stat. 1988 (codified at 18 U.S.C. §§3551 *et seq.* (1988)).

68. *See* Surrency, HISTORY OF THE FEDERAL COURTS 254-255 (1987).

69. *See* Stern, *Remedies for appellate overloads: the ultimate solution*, 72 JUDICATURE 103, 106-108 (1988).

70. U.S. Const. art. III., §1.

71. *See generally* Frankfurter & Landis, THE BUSINESS OF THE SUPREME COURT: A STUDY IN THE FEDERAL JUDICIAL SYSTEM (1927); Surrency, *supra* n. 68.

72. *See* Act of Sept. 24, 1789, ch. 20, §1, 1 Stat. 72, 73 (six justices); Act of Feb. 13, 1801, ch. 4, §3, 2 Stat. 89, 89 (repealed 1802) (five justices); Act of Feb. 24, 1807, ch. 16, §5, 2 Stat. 420, 421 (seven justices); Act of Mar. 3, 1837, ch. 34, §1, 5 Stat. 176, 176 (nine justices); Act of Mar. 3, 1863, ch. 100, §1, 12 Stat. 794, 794 (ten justices); Act of July 23, 1866, ch. 210, §1, 14 Stat. 209, 209 (seven justices); Act of Apr. 10, 1869, ch. 22, §1, 16 Stat. 44, 44 (nine justices).

73. *See* N.Y. TIMES, June 29, 1993, at A11.

74. *Id.*

75. N.Y.L.J., Jan. 15, 1992, at 1.

Appellate Court Processes
Internal Court Processes and Decisions on the Merits

INTRODUCTION

Many of the efforts of social scientists studying appellate courts have focused on judicial decision making. In particular, scholars have utilized several theoretical perspectives in an effort to understand why judges decide cases the way they do. At times, academic research has even resulted in the successful prediction of outcomes in pending cases. Among the concerns researchers have focused on to understand judicial behavior have been factors such as the social background characteristics of judges, their ideological preferences, their interrelationships in a collegial appellate court setting, their judicial philosophies, their concerns about the "proper" judicial role and, moving beyond factors intrinsic to the individual judge, the fact patterns present in cases before the court.

While these concerns are not exhaustive of the variables that can enter into a judge's decisional equation, and while none of them acting alone are likely to be the exclusive basis for judges deciding cases the way that they do, social science research has demonstrated clearly that such factors do matter and that judicial decisions do not emanate solely from the law itself. The articles in this section all focus on some facet of decision-making processes or the decisional patterns of appellate courts and shed some light on how such courts reach decisions on the merits in cases before them.

Stephen Wasby's "The functions and importance of appellate oral argument," utilizes data from interviews with lawyers and judges to explore this underexamined area of the judicial process. While examining oral argument in an intermediate appellate court setting, the Ninth Circuit, Wasby's observations have clear relevance for all appellate courts, including the U.S. Supreme Court. The article examines two alternative perspectives on the value of oral argument. On one end of the spectrum some contend that oral argumentation facilitates the development of information and clarification of issues and helps focus case proceedings. Face-to-face contact among the actors in the judicial process also provides real and symbolic benefits. Others contend, however, that oral argument is often unnecessary and exacerbates delay in an already overloaded system. Wasby finds a degree of truth in both perspectives as well as an inherent tension between them. "On the one hand is the desire to maintain a practice that is not merely an 'amenity' but is also thought to have considerable importance for both appellate judges and appellate lawyers. On the other hand is a feeling of the need to adjust to substantial appellate caseloads by recognizing that different types of cases can be treated differently."

When a decision is reached by the Supreme Court, the chief justice, if in the majority, exercises the power of designating the majority opinion author for the case. Analysts have long noted that, in the exercise of this authority, chief justices have considerable ability to structure the reasoning that is used to justify and explain a case outcome. The chief may, at times, decide to author an opinion himself, assign the case to an ideological ally or, in closely divided cases, follow a strategy aimed at holding the Court's tenuous majority together. In the exercise of his authority, the chief must also be concerned about the maintenance of equitable workloads among the justices and both collective and individual satisfaction with the assignments that have been made. Historically, justices who wished to dissent from the Court's rulings generally did so as an individual act. While they might be joined by one or more of their colleagues, the decision to pen a dissent was an exclusively personal one. That such is no longer the case is well documented in Beverly Blair Cook's study of "Justice Brennan and the institutionalization of dissent assignment."

Cook's fascinating analysis begins with a historical discussion of dissent on the Supreme Court and documents the central role played by Justice William Brennan in fostering an institutional role with significant power potential for the Court's senior associate justice in the minority. Through delving into the private papers of justices, Cook illuminates the internal workings of the Supreme Court and highlights its strategically laden environment where "minority opinion solidarity [becomes] a strong tool with which to threaten the majority." More broadly, Cook concludes that the now-routine reality of dissent assignments as well as the propensity for solo dissenters to author opinions explaining their stance both underscore that the norm of consensus that once characterized the Court has been trumped by the institution's openly competitive environment.

The institutional role and importance of "The spirit of dissent," is also the focus of the piece by J. Louis Campbell III. Here, dissent is described as being analogous to civil disobedience and characterized as "institutional disobedience" that offers protest and seeks systemic change. At bottom, dissents are seen as "sources of energy and cogency in the law." Examples of now-famous dissenting opinions and their impact are offered throughout Campbell's analysis.

While Cook and Campbell focus, in part, on evolving norms for dissent behavior on the Supreme Court, Christopher Banks' examination of "The Supreme Court and precedent: an analysis of natural courts and reversal trends," looks at adherence to stare decisis, a fundamental norm that dictates that courts should, whenever possible, decide cases by following established precedent. Banks writes in the context of substantial criticism that has been leveled at the contemporary Court for allegedly violating the stare decisis norm. He makes an important distinction between statutory and constitutional interpretation and finds that the pattern of reversal on the Rehnquist Court is not significantly different from earlier tribunals. Indeed, Banks argues, departure from adherence to precedent generally characterizes periods of protracted personnel change on the Court, and we have often witnessed periods of jurisprudential transition such as the one that marked the early Rehnquist Court. Ultimately, Banks sees such periods of interpretive flux as salutary. "The clarion call that precedent is no longer viable has more ring than substance. It is largely a hollow cry, because it fails to take into account that constitutional law inexorably changes with an evolving society or the Court's composition. In this perspective, the transitory periods that account for short-term upheavals of law are more beneficial than harmful for constitutional law and the Court."

In "Justice Frankfurter and Justice Reed: friendship and lobbying on the Court," Bradley Canon, Kimberly Greenfield, and Jason Fleming utilize private correspondence and interview data to take the reader behind the Court's closed doors to offer a detailed case study of how the collegial relationships among justices may include substantial efforts to influence one's behavior on the bench. In this instance, Justice Felix Frankfurter, who sought to be the Court's intellectual leader, is portrayed in his relentless attempts to influence Justice Stanley Reed's votes and the content of his opinions. Interestingly, despite all of the evidence the authors present of Frankfurter's overbearing pursuit of Reed, considered to be a swing justice on a highly divided Court, "Reed possessed sufficient independence to become neither a devotee of Frankfurter nor a victim of too much manipulation." Further, as the authors also point out, one should not, necessarily, view the Frankfurter-Reed relationship as evidence of a judiciary run awry. "The ideal of a collegial court...envisions decisions and opinions stemming from discussions among the justices instead of, as Justice John M. Harlan put it, 'a tally of individual votes.' "

The articles in this section of readings discussed so far have, in one fashion or another, made reference to the "special" roles on the Court that might be occupied by its chief justice, a senior associate justice in opposition to the chief, and a justice who perceived himself to be the Court's intellectual leader. Conventional wisdom has dictated that another "special" place on the Court has been occupied by its least-senior members who have been posited to succumb to a "freshman effect." According to the conventional wisdom, freshmen jurists generally take a centrist position on the Court and do not ally with any existing ideological extremes. In addition, freshmen judges are alleged to carry a lighter and less consequential workload than their colleagues on the Court in terms of their opinion-writing responsibilities. Empirical analyses of both dictates of the supposed freshman effect have raised serious questions as to its existence. In "Freshman opinion writing on the U.S. Supreme Court, 1921-1991," Terry Bowen and John Scheb II utilize an extensive data set to demonstrate definitively that freshmen jurists are assigned cases as frequently as their more senior colleagues and, further, that the cases they are assigned are as "difficult" as those assigned to the rest of the Court. At least as far as the question of opinion writing is concerned, "the freshman effect posited...as part of the conventional wisdom regarding the Court simply does not exist."

The substantive decisions of the Supreme Court and attempts to explain its decisional trends are the subjects of the last three articles in this section. In their study of "Rehnquist Court disposition of lower court decisions: affirmation, not reversal," Jeffrey Segal and Harold Spaeth call into question, at least for a brief and early time period of the Rehnquist Court, another conventional wisdom about judicial behavior. Thus, whereas analysts have generally found that the Supreme Court follows an "error correction" strategy with "a decided propensity to accept for review cases that it intends to reverse," the early Rehnquist Court, "abruptly and sharply discontinued the reversal practice of its predecessor Courts." Segal and Spaeth ponder several possible reasons for their finding including the Rehnquist Court's propensity to review cases in which there was conflict in the lower courts and to accept and affirm an unusually large number of "congenial" conservative decisions. The authors recognize that there is a good deal that their study does not address and they are appropriately cautious in their conclusions.

Christopher Smith and Thomas Hensley's effort at "Assessing the conservatism of the Rehnquist Court," labors in the same vineyard as Segal and Spaeth and also demonstrates the complexity of efforts to understand judicial decision making and the difficulties of even making "simple" judgments about the ideological direction of a Court's decisions. When viewed by the numbers alone, Smith and Hensley demonstrate the counterintuitive finding that the early Rehnquist Court was no more conservative than the Burger Court before it. Numbers, however, (in this instance, the percentage of conservative decisions) may only tell a part of the story. For one, it may be the case that the Supreme Court, at times, found itself in the position of having to rein in lower court judges who had simply gone "too far" in applying and extending conservative holdings, thereby giving the misleading impression that the Supreme Court favored a "liberal" ruling. Similarly, the Rehnquist Court, like all courts, found itself addressing issues that were somewhat different than those of its predecessor and, further, the reasoning that was utilized to justify seemingly liberal decisions would often be more conservative than first meets the eye. The authors conclude their analysis on the cautionary note that, "Conclusions about the Rehnquist Court's relative liberalism cannot rest on quantitative measures alone...[a]ccurate and complete conclusions about the Supreme Court must draw from both empirical techniques and case analysis in order to detect how issues are changing and how the justices manifest disagreements even when they agree on case outcomes."

The broadest view of judicial decision-making dynamics offered in the articles included in this section is found in Leslie Goldstein and Diana Stech's article, "Explaining transformations in Supreme Court policy," an effort that is made here in the context of the history of women's rights litigation before the Court over a 30-year period. This rich analysis demonstrates the role that the Court can play in shaping the national and, indeed, its own future agenda in a policy domain. Court decisions are shown to influence the kinds of arguments that are subsequently brought before it and, in a similar vein, the Court's ongoing dialogue that its decisions initiate with state and federal legislators as well as with interest groups has enormous implications for the unfolding of critical public policy.

The articles in this section of readings underline the considerable diversity in subject matter and methodology that characterizes social scientific research on internal court processes and decisions on the merits. Indeed, the questions asked in this domain and the manner in which they are addressed are subject only to the limits of the resources and imagination of the analyst. Eclectic and interesting research efforts in the area of judicial decision making promises to remain a staple in future writing on the subject of judicial politics.

The functions and importance of appellate oral argument: some views of lawyers and federal judges

Although some critics have proposed curtailing or eliminating oral argument in certain cases, both judges and lawyers believe it plays a vital role in the appellate process, a recent survey shows.

by Stephen L. Wasby

One of the most traditional and important elements of deciding cases on appeal is oral argument, an element of advocacy older than written briefs in this country. Briefs originally were not required in appeals, and oral argument continued without time limits even when briefs were submitted. Eventually briefs did begin to displace argument: the Supreme Court first waived oral argument when written arguments were submitted, then mandated briefs prior to argument, and finally both reserved argument for the most important cases and reduced the time granted each party.[1]

Curtailment of oral argument in other appellate courts, partly the result of caseload pressure, has attracted continued attention. Various sources have warned that eliminating oral argument in all cases would harm the appellate process.[2] Most recently, the Devitt Committee (the Committee to Consider Standards for Admission to Practice in the Federal Courts of the Judicial Conference of the United States) brought further attention to legal advocacy at both trial and appellate levels. The "substantially divided" committee, however, made no recommendations concerning appellate advocacy because it found "the problems presented . . . not sufficiently serious to call for the recommending of remedies"[3]—at least by comparison with trial advocacy, to which the committee devoted the bulk of its attention. Despite the Devitt

Committee's view, appellate advocacy remains of considerable importance.

Recent literature shows tension between two divergent tendencies: to retain an essential practice, part of the "procedural amenities" through which courts are "seen to be obeying and enforcing the law,"[4] and to curtail its use in some types of cases to facilitate its retention in others, where it is thought more useful.[5] This article looks at the opinions of the two groups most immediately concerned with appellate argument: lawyers and judges. It is based on interviews with circuit and district judges in the Ninth U.S. Circuit Court of Appeals and with attorneys who had argued before that court.[6]

All the circuit judges and most of the district judges, in their careers as lawyers, had argued appellate cases, but only a few had done so extensively. The experience of the surveyed lawyers is disproportionate to that of most lawyers because not many lawyers engage frequently in appellate work and still fewer argue appellate cases. Two of the attorneys had argued more than 200 state and federal appellate cases each, two others had argued more than 100, and two more had argued between 50 and 100. The least experienced attorneys, by contrast, had argued fewer than 20.

Half the circuit judges said their views of oral argument had changed since their days as practicing lawyers, also true of most of the district judges responding; the other half of the circuit judges said their views had not changed. Those whose views had changed used to feel that as lawyers they could help judges or could "guide the judges" with their knowledge and that "there was something I could add."[7] Now, observed one, he had found as a judge that a "strong minority" of cases was so deficient in merit that "if John Davis argued, it wouldn't make a difference." Other judges now realized that the court's caseload prevented oral argument in every case. Moreover, one noted, judges' preparation—consistently high, unlike the situation in some state appellate courts—made argument less useful, as did the short time allowed for it.

Almost two-thirds of the lawyers had changed their views of appellate argument from prior to participating in it; most now saw it as less important. They found that "brilliance" had little effect on the court, that argument was not "the highly persuasive medium for the judges" they had thought it would be, and that the judges asked fewer questions than they had anticipated. Indeed, some said that at times argument seemed superfluous. This did not, however, stem from any dissatisfaction with the Ninth Circuit. On the whole, the lawyers were satisfied with oral argument in that court—"by and large, an agreeable court to argue to," "prepared," and "open," with the judges asking "intelligent questions."

In the remainder of this article, we examine first whether appellate oral argument is thought more important for judges or for lawyers. Then we turn to discuss ways in which oral argument helps judges and attorneys and the functions oral argument is thought to perform. We follow this by a look at whether judges and lawyers believe oral argument significant or determinative, as well as the types of cases in which oral argument is thought to be most and least helpful. We draw on Ninth Circuit interviews and on comments from other studies, particularly Federal Judicial Center surveys of judges and of attorneys in the Second, Fifth, and Sixth Circuits.[8]

How oral argument helps

"A great many appellate judges . . . strongly believe that the arguments are a major help," Marvell has noted.[9] The chief judges of the U.S. courts of appeals, responding to Judge Myron Bright's queries, generally found oral argument valuable—"sometimes when least expected," according to First Cir-

cuit Judge Frank Coffin,[10] but generally "only in some cases." Screening out cases thought not worthy of argument, the practice in most circuits, has made argument valuable more often when it takes place. Some feel, however, that when judges have long thought about a problem, oral argument is not likely to add much to the resolution of a case.

Both circuit and district judges and lawyers in the Ninth Circuit were almost unanimous in finding appellate oral argument helpful. An interesting difference does occur, however, between judges' and lawyers' opinions on whether argument is more important for lawyers or judges or is equally important for both. Roughly half the circuit judges felt oral argument equally important for both groups; the other half was divided between those who thought it more important for judges and those who thought it more important for lawyers.[11] However, *no* lawyers believed oral argument more important for themselves, except perhaps as a way of impressing clients; two-thirds said it was equally important for the two groups, with the remainder finding it more important for the judges. The lawyers' position may be explained by a circuit judge's observation that "at the appellate stage, the case is no longer the lawyer's but the court's."

A retired state supreme court justice has written that the functions of oral argument are, in descending important:

(1) to persuade judges, (2) to focus on one important matter only, (3) to reiterate most major points in the brief, (4) to clarify facts, (5) to counter opposition's arguments, (6) to appeal to "justice," "right," and "fairness," (7) to legitimate the legal process by a public confrontation of issues, (8) to urge judges to read (or reread) briefs, (9) to prepare judges for conference deliberations, (10) to force judges to communicate with each other.[12]

Ninth Circuit judges and attorneys differed in the emphasis each group placed on ways that appellate argument helped.[13] Judges found principally that argument helped them clarify matters and focus on important issues, with the opportunity to communicate with lawyers and ask questions only slightly less important. Judges also suggested that oral argument provided information and aided in disposing of cases. Least frequently noted was argument's assistance in increasing the visibility of the court.

For attorneys, clarification and an opportunity for communication with judges were mentioned more than other functions of argument for the judges, with neither function predominant. Attorneys gave far less attention to providing information, assisting in disposition of cases, giving judges an opportunity to ask questions, and helping to save judges' time.

Judges' and lawyers' comments on argument's functions for lawyers also revealed differences. Most frequently mentioned by judges were argument's functions of assisting lawyers in clarifying matters, persuading judges, and generally in communicating with the judges. Least frequently noted were providing information to judges, answering judges' questions, and making the lawyer's case more visible.

Lawyers spoke about the usefulness of argument for themselves in persuading and prodding judges. They also gave considerable weight to argument's help in clarifying issues. Lawyers also found of moderate importance that oral argument helped them learn about judges. Least frequently mentioned as a function of appellate argument for lawyers were the opportunities to answer questions or to help facilitate disposition of cases.

Assisting the judge

Public relations. There is a "public relations" reason for oral argument—so that lawyers and their clients will feel that their cases have been heard. As one judge observed, lawyers need the satisfaction of knowing they have presented their cases well. The other side of this "P.R." coin is that oral argument assists in legitimating the court's judicial function.[14] The Federal Judicial Center's lawyer survey showed that slightly more than half the lawyers in each circuit studied agreed that "when a litigant is denied the right to have his lawyer argue his appeal, the litigant will feel that he has not had his day in court."[15] Submission of briefs is not thought sufficient to assure lawyers and litigants that judges have focused on the case, because one could not be sure the briefs were read.

As Marvell notes, the "public relations function" of contact between attorneys and judges during argument "is especially important when attorneys suspect that not all judges read the briefs or that the court's staff plays a major role in the decision process."[16] An observer of the First Circuit adds that "by demonstrating the openness and

the balanced presentation of all material issues in an individual case, the court assures the public that each action is being given their personal and undivided attention in order to reach a reasoned solution."[17] The Hruska Commission echoed this perspective in pointing out that oral argument "assures the litigant that his case has been given consideration by those charged with deciding it."[18]

Communication. Oral argument is valuable for "establish[ing] a human connection between bench and bar" because it is the only face-to-face communication between attorneys and judges during a case's appellate course. As a Ninth Circuit judge noted, argument assists lawyers by "help[ing] the judges to know who the attorneys are" as well as giving lawyers "a notion of the orientation of the court" and the way it is thinking.

The crucial role of the judge-attorney communication has often been stressed. According to the late Third Circuit Judge William Hastie, "The oral argument is the court's one chance to invite counsel to meet head on what seemed to be the strongest opposing contentions."[19] In the Federal Judicial Center survey, there was extremely high agreement among lawyers that "oral argument permits the attorney to address himself to those issues which the judges believe are crucial to the case."[20]

In addition to the above considerations, the process and "mechanics" of conducting argument help Ninth Circuit judges, particularly because argument comes after a judge has read the briefs. The judge thus hears counsel "against the generalized background of the case." Some judges found this particularly so when a lawyer is "a better talker than a writer"—and some judges simply hear better than they read, as one judge commented. (Oral argument also allows judges to criticize an incompetent lawyer without having to reduce the criticism to writing.)

A less-well-noted aspect of oral argument is communication *among* judges. Questions ostensibly directed to an attorney may be intended for a judicial colleague, to sway that judge or at least to warn of the need to face certain issues.[21] As one lawyer noted, judges "may use the attorney's mouth to convince his colleagues." Appellate argument thus provides judges an "opportunity to respond to each other's questions" and to communicate the "key points of a case" to other members of the panel. If this is effective, at argument's conclusion judges "will have an excellent idea of the key points of a case" and of a problem's "soft underbelly" as well as a sense of other judges' views. Concessions may be more important to judges when a lawyer makes them than if they heard the same argument from a colleague during their collective consideration of the case in conference.

Questions. Central to communication during appellate argument are the judges' questions. Ninth Circuit judges emphasized the opportunity that oral argument provides for exploring doubts they had about the record and "items not entirely clear." A lawyer's response may emphasize a point differently from the emphasis conveyed by the briefs. As a result, "Sometimes we can't understand until we ask questions." (Ninety percent of attorneys in the Federal Judicial Center survey agreed that "by asking questions of counsel, the judges are better able to avoid erroneous interpretations of the facts or issues in the case.")[22]

Questions also allow judges to test attorneys' positions, particularly to see whether the lawyer can help the judge "decide the case his way easily." A lawyer unable to answer effectively will not carry the court. In a complex case, an attorney's responses may provide a judge with necessary "reinforcement" for tentatively adopted positions.

Ninth Circuit attorneys found it easier to argue to judges who asked more questions. They disliked "passive judges," "who stare at you or over your head" or "just smile or go to sleep." Indeed, one lawyer said he didn't object to a judge "disposed against him" if the judge asked questions. The lawyers were, however, concerned about the quality as well as about the frequency of questions; judges who merely "interrogated" were not appreciated, but lawyers generally preferred "tough" or "perceptive" questions.

Despite lawyers' general preference for judges who asked (good) questions, some lawyers felt that judges' questioning cut into the time needed to argue their cases. This is like the conflict Marvell found: several attorneys he interviewed "said they liked questions; yet they complained that the questions cut into their allotted time so much that they had to abandon some of the points they had wished to emphasize."[23]

Information, clarification, and focus

Questioning allows judges to obtain information and to clarify elements of a case. Appellate argument brings to their attention matters not evident in the briefs or not available earlier.[24] Finding out about matters the last brief left unresolved is of some importance when much time has elapsed between filing of the last brief and oral argument. Information conveyed to the judges through argument includes factual and procedural items as well as new legal arguments. Argument is particularly likely to provide judges new information when a lawyer " 'lays back' and doesn't put everything in the briefs." Argument also allows judges to "learn where new cases would go if unleashed in this case" as well as to learn about the "practical effect" unique cases might have.

Oral argument "allows the judges . . . to clear up any doubts that the court might have about the case or the lawyer's approach to it," observes Eighth Circuit Judge Myron Bright;[25] many Ninth Circuit judges agreed that clarification was a salient function of appellate argument. Clarification occurs not only when briefs are "ambiguous" or even poor, but also when they are of high quality, especially in extremely complex cases.

Argument can lead to clarification when it prompts judges to return to the record, but a lawyer can also "straighten out" a judge at argument before the judge engages in such research. Clarification involves the correction of errors, but it also includes "cast[ing] new light" on important aspects of cases that are vague in the briefs when the court requires the lawyer to clarify his position through a "good, logical analysis of the briefs" during argument.

Part of clarification is a focus on issues. Several federal judges have testified to argument's importance in this regard.[26] At least a majority of judges surveyed by the Federal Judicial Center favored oral argument in part because it "focuses the court's attention on the issues [and] provides the needed impetus to get the 'tough' thinking done efficiently."[27] The late Judge Frederick Hamley of the Ninth Circuit commented that judges found argument helpful because of its "tendency to narrow and pinpoint the question to be decided and the points of law to be reviewed," with "the exact point of disagreement which must be resolved" emerging during argument.[28] The Ninth Circuit judges interviewed concurred. They noted argument's function of narrowing issues, allowing judges to "determine what counsel thinks most salient," and permitting worthless arguments to be swept away.

Disposition. Both clarification and focus assist with disposition of a case; focus is essential before the court can bring a case to resolution. The argument process assists in this regard by setting some issues aside as peripheral, so that the judges can deal with the key issues more directly and quickly. By sharpening judges' thinking, argument provides an "opportunity to formulate a judgment." Even if argument does not itself speed disposition, judges' preparation for it does so.[29]

Improving assistance to judges. Before appellate argument takes place, judges must engage in some communication, among themselves and with the attorneys who are to present argument, if argument is to be most helpful both to the court and the attorneys. A preargument conference of the judges can serve this purpose; it can result in questions to be asked to help guide argument in ways that will assist the judges without the attorney having to cover ground of little (or less) interest to them.

More helpful would be communication before the argument session, where judges could indicate points from the briefs on which they wished lawyers to concentrate, those they wished developed further, and questions they wanted answered. Of course, judges need not pose all their questions prior to argument. They could, however, provide some guidance while reserving further questions for argument itself. Judges often object to such suggestions either because their heavy caseload makes it difficult to consider briefs or the record in advance or because they feel it interferes with the adversary process. Yet argument would be more useful for the judges even if attorneys received questions—perhaps developed from staff attorneys' bench memoranda—only a couple of days before argument.

A further and more extreme suggestion is to hold argument *after* the judges have written and circulated a tentative opinion. Marvell made such a suggestion because of his concern about "the lack of communication back and forth between counsel and the court to iron out exactly what points interest the court so that the counsel can give information the court needs."[30] A natural objection is that judges' views would tend to become frozen. However, if judges could keep their opinions tentative, such a procedure would certainly communicate to attorneys the issues the judges wanted addressed. To be effective, however,

the procedure does require judges to put "a good deal of work into a case early, in time to tell counsel of their concerns and to give counsel a chance to prepare answers."[31]

Assisting the lawyers

Communication. Judges, we have noted, find that appellate argument assists them in establishing communication with lawyers. Lawyers find it similarly helpful in establishing communication with judges. Argument provides a lawyer "the opportunity to discourse with the court, and to argue and discuss with the court, or share ideas," as well as to get "points firmly lodged in the judicial mind."[32] For Ninth Circuit attorneys, appellate argument "allows face-to-face contact between an attorney and the court," thus permitting a lawyer "to grapple with a mind which has already come to grips with the problem" in a case and work through problems bothering the judges.

Appellate argument also allows indirect communication of certain messages. If an attorney tells judges at argument that the attorney's client is present, judges, who appreciate such candor, "understand that some of the things he says are for the benefit of the client, who came to hear them said." An important part of what is communicated at appellate argument is information. This includes "background details," material not covered in briefs, and information about cases decided since the briefs were filed. (Argument may also serve to warn lawyers that they should file supplemental briefs to provide more information on specific points.)

Lawyers also use appellate argument to persuade judges. One senior circuit judge observed that it is the "forcefulness, preparation, and dedication" of particular lawyers that made argument helpful. Part of persuasion for the lawyers was catching the judges' attention or "stimulat[ing] their minds into active thought processes." Another part was to "challenge the judges' concept of a case" and to make them "re-examine their positions."

Clarification and focus. Clarification is a particular significant function of oral argument for attorneys, just as it is for judges. Argument is "enormously beneficial in illuminating . . . precisely what the issues are as counsel sees them."[33] In addition, argument can "cure factual misapprehensions and legal misconceptions," "the two areas than can be met only by oral argument."[34]

Also involved in clarification is the "opportunity to explain seeming contradictions, inconsistencies, or weaknesses in the client's position." When argument allows a lawyer to sense the court's problems with a case, the lawyer can "develop a new theory" to help resolve them. As roughly three-fifths of the attorneys surveyed by the Federal Judicial Center responded, oral argument "allows counsel to gauge the feelings of the judges and to couch his arguments accordingly."[35]

The most crucial element involved in focusing a case at argument is the direct emphasis that can be placed on the most important issues in the case: the lawyer can provide "the crystallized oral statement of the 'gut issue.' "[36] Focusing may entail discarding certain issues as well as stressing others. When flaws in a lawyer's position are revealed at argument, the court does not have to deal with those matters. A lawyer may also use argument to "signal . . . that one or more points in his brief are not well taken"; the judges, realizing that the points were included "to satisfy his client," can then "apply more attention to what he says about his important points" and the lawyer also gains "a little extra credit for his candor."

Oral argument's importance

Relative importance and significance. A large majority of both Ninth Circuit judges and lawyers felt oral argument not of equal importance in all cases. Moreover, no Ninth Circuit appellate judge and only two district judges believed that all cases required the same amount of argument time. Their position is like that of judges surveyed by the Federal Judicial Center, who stressed "varied sets of criteria" for determining appropriate time length for argument and indicated "that a case-by-case method is mandatory with an examination of issue complexity and nature of record and briefs as a starting point."[37]

Ninth Circuit judges felt that complex cases— those with either legal or factual complexity or cases with multiple issues or multiple-defendant criminal cases—required more extended argument. However, they noted only a few specific areas of law in which longer argument was thought necessary, although antitrust, patent, and securities were mentioned by several judges.

Asked to estimate the proportion of cases where appellate argument was "significant," Ninth Circuit judges gave opinions ranging from 5 percent to 85 percent. However, only five judges gave estimates of over 10 percent. Several judges commented specifically that argument was helpful in greater proportions of cases if criminal cases were excluded, because so many of those cases were thought not to raise important issues. Several judges, however, were especially sensitive about eliminating oral argument in criminal appeals; they thought retaining it necessary for the appearance of justice. All the circuit judges and most district judges responding also thought oral argument "determinative"[38] in at least some cases, but, as expected, the proportion of cases in which argument was thought determinative was much smaller than the proportion in which it was considered significant; most estimated the proportion of cases to be "relatively small" or "minimal."

Where most helpful? In what types of cases is appellate argument thought most helpful? In the Federal Judicial Center study, a majority of circuit judges thought oral argument "essential" in "cases that involve matters of great public interest despite the absence of substantial legal issues" and in only one other category—cases involving the constitutionality of a state statute or state action. By contrast, in civil appeals based on sufficiency of the evidence, only 9 percent thought argument essential.[39]

In the present study, Ninth Circuit judges defined helpfulness in terms of both legal subject-matter and case characteristics. All but a couple of the judges stressed that appellate oral argument helped most in government regulation cases, particularly those involving new statutes or new administrative agencies. *No* judge found appellate argument more helpful in criminal appeals. Ninth Circuit lawyers primarily found appellate argument most helpful when cases were complex or novel. They cited "novel or undeveloped legal issues," "issues of first impression," or "changing fields of law," as well as "sensitive, complicated, political issues" where a lawyer's views tended to differ from prevailing judicial sentiment or where a lawyer was trying to move the law in a new direction.

Lawyers form the Second, Fifth, and Sixth Circuits considered oral argument essential in "cases which involve matters of great public interest (despite the absence of substantial legal issues) [and] cases involving the constitutionality of a state statute or a state action."[40] Half of the Sixth Circuit lawyers and a clear majority of those from the Second Circuit also thought oral argument essential in direct criminal appeals.[41] Generally, lawyers were more likely than judges to find appellate argument essential than were judges, although "the essentiality of oral argument varies from case-type to case-type for [both] judges and lawyers, with order of preference almost the same from the perspective of bench and bar."[42]

Where least helpful? Ninth Circuit judges tended to find argument least helpful in cases where the circuit had controlling precedent. Resolution of such cases was "largely mechanical." Otherwise, they found argument least helpful in "frivolous cases" or "factual, run-of-the-mill" cases. Not surprising in view of their other comments, argument commonly was felt least helpful in criminal cases. The lawyers also suggested that argument was least helpful in cases where briefs were short and the issue simple (a simple fact pattern), particularly if the law were "static." However, in a comment counter to the typical views, one attorney found oral argument not helpful "when the lawyer was trying to overturn old legal principles and establish new rules of law." Such matters, he believed, were best argued in the briefs.[43]

Some judges said oral argument was not needed when briefs are adequate and "address the issues and are cogent" or when judges and lawyers agree as to what the principal argument is. Thus, ironically, for these judges, good briefing makes argument of less help. Others thought a lawyer might make his point better orally when briefs were poor, but some colleagues felt poor briefs usually meant poor argument.

Most judges, however, focused on lawyers' deficiencies at argument; lawyers agreed that deficiencies in attorney skills detracted from oral argument. (Some attorneys also suggested that certain characteristics of judges interfere with the effectiveness of argument, for example, when judges were "not inclined to listen" or were "impatient," appearing to "have made up their minds." Only one circuit judge blamed judges—when they preempt argument time—for detracting from argument.)

Judges thought that in a number of cases lawyers' argument was of little help because the lawyers were "not well prepared," not "up to" argument, or were "not good on their feet when asked questions." Lawyers agree that "boring, incompe-

tent presentations" by lawyers can cause damage. Just as important is that lawyers not "take too rigid a position" or adopt a stance they know is not valid—something that will produce a loss of credibility.

Judges noted and lawyers also frequently mentioned as less than helpful situations in which attorneys read their presentations or "simply repeated the briefs." Recitation of facts not woven into the law were also thought not helpful. Lawyers who made speeches, engaged in fancy rhetoric, or made "impassioned jury pleas to an appellate judge" were also thought ineffective. However, comments about the need for a "just result" in a case are thought appropriate if they are related to the law—not made in isolation from the law.

Attorneys may not make most effective use of appellate argument because relatively few of them have tried appellate cases. Still fewer have handled appeals in the federal courts. The skills of a trial lawyer and an appellate attorney can differ markedly, and attorney specialization decreases the likelihood that an individual attorney will possess both. Ability to make an effective jury argument is not the same as being able to focus succinctly on often rapid-fire questions from a "hot" bench of three appellate judges, well-prepared from having read the briefs.

A Federal Judicial Center survey of lawyer competence casts some light on types of lawyers judges think least effective in appellate argument. A majority "believe there is a serious problem among lawyers employed by state or local governments," but less than 10 percent thought such a problem existed among "public or community defenders, Justice Department lawyers other than those in U.S. attorneys' offices and on strike forces, and private practitioners representing corporate clients in civil cases."[44] Age, size of a lawyer's office, previous courtroom experience, and a lawyer's educational background were all found not to be related to judges' ratings.

Curtailing and eliminating oral argument

The Hruska Commission stated in 1975 that "to mandate oral argument in every case would clearly be unwarranted." The Commission also thought it inappropriate to ignore "risks to the process of appellate adjudication inherent in too-ready a denial of the opportunity to present a litigant's case."[45] At about the same time, the Advisory Council on Appellate Justice recommended that "oral argument should be allowed in most cases" but also conceded "it may be curtailed or eliminated in certain instances."[46] The American Bar Association's position was most direct. In 1974, the ABA's House of Delegates opposed "the rules of certain United States courts of appeals which drastically curtail or entirely eliminate oral argument in a substantial proportion of non-frivolous appeals . . ."[47]

Federal Judicial Center surveys show agreement between judges and lawyers on limiting oral argument but definite disagreement on situations in which it might be eliminated. *All* circuit judges found it acceptable to limit argument to 15-20 minutes per side and over 98 percent of the lawyers agreed.[48] Continuing their agreement, both judges and lawyers were less willing to limit oral argument to 15-20 minutes per side and to deny argument completely when the reason was "avoidance of extreme delay" than they were to do so either when an appeal was close to "frivolous" or where clear issues could be decided by circuit precedent.

Moreover, "approximately 90 percent of the judges recognized occasions when elimination of oral argument is an acceptable procedure." Eighty-eight percent of the circuit judges agreed that denying oral argument was "ever acceptable." However, the percentages of lawyers agreeing with such a proposition ranged from 84 percent (Fifth Circuit) to only 67 percent (Second Circuit).[49]

Roughly 95 percent of judges were willing either to limit or eliminate oral argument in frivolous cases, and similarly high percentages were willing to do so in cases governed by precedent. When the reason was to avoid extreme delay, the proportions declined (86 percent for limiting argument, only 62 percent for denying it).[50] Lawyers showed a similar pattern of differences between cases types, with ranking parallel to the judges'. By comparison with the judges, however, proportionately far more lawyers objected to eliminating argument than were willing to accede to time limitations.

Lawyers' objections to time limits on argument can be seen in the Hruska Commission testimony of Moses Lasky, "dean" of Ninth Circuit appellate attorneys. Lasky argued against any "official limitation on the time for arguments." Arguments, he felt, should take as much time as necessary for the judges "to squeeze all the values out of it that they can get out." Endless argument would not be the result, said Lasky, citing the comment attributed to Abe Lincoln: "When asked how long should a man's legs be, he replied, 'Long enough to reach the ground.'" Some arguments would take no longer than 15 minutes, while some might profitably extend for hours.[51]

A clear majority of judges in the Federal Judicial Center survey saw oral argument as dispensable in two types of cases: prisoner petitions seeking alteration of prison conditions, and collateral attacks on federal and state convictions. Almost half the judges also thought oral argument could be eliminated in sufficiency-of-evidence cases. However, only 7 percent of circuit judges thought that courts court dispense with argument in "cases which involve matters of great public interest despite the absence of substantial legal issues."[52]

Not surprisingly, a greater proportion of judges than attorneys thought oral argument was dispensable for each type of case.[53] In no case category did a majority of attorneys agree that oral argument was dispensable, although the proportion reached 30 percent for challenges to prison conditions and diversity-of-citizenship cases raising only state law questions.[54] Furthermore, faced with limitations on traditional procedures, including argument, lawyers were less willing to accept limitations—"to the extent that they accept [them] at all"—for "administrative reasons" than for "substantive legal reasons."[55]

All Ninth Circuit circuit and district judges interviewed believed that oral argument could be eliminated in some cases. Four of 12 circuit judges thought, however, that eliminating oral argument would not "assist the court in completing its business." Despite the repeated concerns about the need to allow argument in criminal cases for the sake of the appearance of justice, criminal cases were most frequently mentioned as the type where argument could be eliminated. However, some judges distinguished between direct criminal appeals, in which they were reluctant to eliminate argument, and habeas corpus cases, where they would do so, particularly in pro se appeals.

At least some judges found some civil cases—particularly simple ones—to require "no oral argument," especially if all members of a panel agreed that all problems were already presented in the briefs. Even if a case contained more than one issue, argument might not be necessary if all issues were simple. Some judges also did not find argument helpful in administrative agency cases, where their task was a limited review of the record. Similarly, argument was not thought to aid the judges in agency cases involving the "abuse of discretion" standard.

Only a bare majority of Ninth Circuit attorneys agreed that the court could dispense with argument in even some cases. Other than an occasional mention of criminal cases and a suggestion of cases involving ineffective counsel or misjoinder of offenses, lawyers seldom mentioned specific subject-matter areas for eliminating oral argument. They instead focused on cases where "it is perfectly obvious how it would go," and noted as well cases that had been dispositively handled by the circuit, particularly if the briefs indicated agreement on the issues.

Oral argument versus written opinion

Reduction or elimination of oral argument is only one way of reducing appellate court workloads. Both judges and lawyers in the Federal Judicial Center surveys were more willing to accept limitations on oral argument than to approve limitations on written opinions. However, judges, faced with a choice between argument and full written opinions, clearly preferred retaining argument and making greater use of memorandum opinions or "reasoned oral disposition" in most categories of cases. A majority of judges also agreed on the importance of issuing at least memoranda, so the courts "do not give the appearance to litigants of acting arbitrarily." However, only one-third of the circuit judges thought that "the absence of a reasoned disposition" would provide "no guidance to . . . district judges or the bar in future cases."[56] Conversely, in terms of the courts' legitimacy, "nearly half the circuit judges agreed that in the absence of a reasoned disposition, members of the bar may infer that the court has acted arbitrarily, yet little more than a quarter of the district judges concurred."[57]

Fifty-six percent of attorneys from the Second Circuit preferred oral argument and memorandum opinions or reasoned oral disposition rather than full opinion and limited or no oral argument, a preference consistent with practice in their circuit. Attorneys from the Fifth and Sixth Circuits had the reverse preference.[58] Ninth Circuit attor-

neys in the present study were closely divided in their preferences.[59] Among those preferring oral argument, one attorney found "bad results without it" but thought written opinions were "needed for development of the law." The value of a written opinion, said another attorney, was the "proper check" placed on "the court's superficiality and discretion"; an opinion forced the court to express its views in ways "credible to the bar."

Willingness to accept delay in order to obtain certain practices is a measure of support for those practices. A "large proportion" of judges surveyed by the Federal Judicial Center felt that retaining both argument and written opinions was worth waiting longer than the current time to disposition. Judges were, however, "more concerned about avoiding extreme delay" than were attorneys.[60] Lawyers also wanted both argument and written opinions even if more time would be consumed in the process.

Indeed, "the speed with which opinions are rendered is a matter of relatively low priority" for the attorneys; few felt that eliminating argument or limiting opinions is "the most acceptable way to avoid long delays in the court's calendar when the docket becomes crowded."[61] In no category of cases were more than one-fifth of the attorneys willing to give up both oral argument and written opinions to reduce time to disposition. Conversely, slightly over three-fourths would accept longer disposition times to obtain traditional practices.[62]

Conclusion

Although trial advocacy has received more attention than appellate argument in recent years, the latter also is significant and deserves attention. Efforts by both federal and state appellate courts to "streamline" proceedings require an understanding of the functions appellate oral argument is expected to perform. Lawyers need a better grasp of judges' views concerning the types of cases for which reduced oral argument or elimination of argument is considered appropriate and vice versa. The view of Ninth Circuit judges and lawyers and data from Federal Judicial Center surveys should make clear that the range of opinions about appellate argument is wide. It should also be clear that appellate oral argument is expected, by both attorneys and judges, to serve multiple functions.

Beneath all these views runs a recurrent theme of tension between perspectives, a tension that shows little sign of abating. On the one hand is the desire to maintain a practice that is not merely an "amenity" but is also thought to have considerable importance for both appellate judges and appellate lawyers. On the other hand is a feeling of the need to adjust to substantial appellate caseloads by recognizing that different types of cases can be treated differently. Despite "inroads" some feel have been made in appellate argument, neither element in the tension has ousted the other, and appellate argument is in no danger of being extinguished as a significant part of appellate practice.

NOTES

This article originally appeared in Volume 65, Number 7, February 1982, pages 340-353. It is drawn from a more extensive report, Wasby, *Oral Argument in the Ninth Circuit: The View from Bench and Bar*, 11 GOLDEN GATE L. REV. 21 (1981). Financial assistance for the research came from the Office of Research and Projects, Southern Illinois University at Carbondale, and from the Penrose Fund of the American Philosophical Society.

1. *See generally* Wasby, D'Amato and Mertrailer, *The Function of Oral Argument in the U.S. Supreme Court*, 62 Q. J. SPEECH 410, particularly at 412 (1976).

2. *See* Commission on Revision of the Federal Court Appellate System, STRUCTURE AND INTERNAL PROCEDURES: RECOMMENDATIONS FOR CHANGE 106, 107 (1975).

3. Judicial Conference of the United States, Committee to Consider Standards for Admission to Practice in the Federal Courts, Report and Tentative Recommendations 30-31 (1978).

4. Carrington, *Ceremony and Realism: Demise of Appellate Procedure*, 66 A.B.A. J. 860 (1980).

5. Godbold, *Improvements in Appellate Procedure: Better Use of Available Facilities*, 66 A.B.A. J. 863 (1980).

6. In the spring of 1977, all but one of 11 active-duty circuit judges and five of the seven senior circuit judges were interviewed as were a dozen district judges, primarily from California and Oregon, chosen from those who had sat frequently on the appellate court "by designation." To provide some comparison with the judges' responses and a different perspective, 13 San Francisco lawyers (all those contacted) were also interviewed, and responses to mail questionnaires were obtained from six Los Angeles lawyers (roughly one-third of those contacted). All the lawyers had argued more than one case before the Ninth Circuit in the previous year. Lawyers and judges were, for the most part, asked parallel questions.

7. Material appearing in quotation marks without attribution is drawn from the author's interviews.

8. Goldman, ATTITUDES OF UNITED STATES JUDGES TOWARD LIMITATION OF ORAL ARGUMENT AND OPINION-WRITING IN THE UNITED STATES COURTS OF APPEALS (Washington, D.C.: Federal Judicial Center, 1975); Drury, Goodman, and Stevenson, ATTORNEY ATTITUDES TOWARD LIMITATION OF ORAL ARGUMENT AND WRITTEN OPINION IN THREE U.S. COURTS OF APPEALS (Washington, D.C.: Bureau of Social Science Research, 1974).

9. Marvell, APPELLATE COURTS AND LAWYERS: INFORMATION GATHERING IN THE ADVERSARY SYSTEM 75 (Westport, CT: Greenwood Press, 1978).

10. Bright, *The Changing Nature of the Federal Appeals Process in the 1970s: A Challenge to the Bar*, 65 F.R.D. 496, 505 n. 8 (1975).

11. Both one senior district judge and two lawyers thought argument equally unimportant for both lawyers and judges.

12. Weaver, quoted in Sheldon and Weaver, POLITICIANS, JUDGES, AND THE PEOPLE: A STUDY IN CITIZENS' PARTICIPATION 86 (Westport, CT: Greenwood Press, 1980).

13. In discussing oral argument's functions as viewed from the Ninth Circuit, we draw primarily on judges' comments about why oral argument is helpful to them, and on lawyers' responses as to why they find argument helpful. Although a high proportion of lawyers found oral argument more important for judges than for themselves, they made few specific comments as to how it helped the judges. Perhaps they simply found reasons why oral argument was helpful to judges to be the complement of reasons why it assisted lawyers.

14. *See* Wasby et al., *supra* n. 1, at 418.

15. Drury, *supra* n. 8, at 306 n. 13.

16. Marvell, *supra* n. 9, at 306 n. 13.

17. Corey, *Some Aspects of Oral Argument in the United States Court of Appeals for the First Circuit*, 21 BOSTON B. J. 21, 32 (1977).

18. STRUCTURE AND INTERNAL PROCEDURES, *supra* n. 2, at 106.

19. Quoted in Maris, *In the Matter of Oral Argument*, 1 PRACTICAL LAWYER (1955), quoted in Commission on Revision of Federal Appellate System, FIRST PHASE: HEARINGS 67 (Washington, D.C.: 1973).

20. Drury, *supra* n. 8, at 38 (Table 26).

21. *See* Wasby et al., *supra* n. 1, at 418; Wasby, *Communication Within the Ninth Circuit Court of Appeals*, 8 GOLDEN GATE L. REV. 1, 5 (1977).

22. Drury, *supra* n. 8, at 38 (Table 26).

23. Marvell, *supra* n. 9, at 79.

24. However, less than half the attorneys in federal appellate practice surveyed by the Federal Judicial Center felt oral argument the *only* way to inform judges effectively of facts and issues in a case. Drury, *supra* n. 8, at 38 (Table 26).

25. Bright, *supra* n. 10, at 506.

26. See Commission, 2 HEARINGS: SECOND PHASE 1974-1975, 408, 826 (Washington, D.C.: 1975).

27. Sutcliffe, addendum to Goldman, *supra* n. 8, at 2 (1975).

28. Quoted at FIRST PHASE, *supra* n. 19, at 777.

29. For examination of judges' preparation for argument, *see* Wasby, *Oral Argument in the Ninth Circuit: The View from Bench and Bar*, 11 GOLDEN GATE L. REV. 21, 74-78 (1981).

30. Marvell, *supra* n. 9, at 247.

31. *Id.* at 248.

32. FIRST PHASE, *supra* n. 19, at 66, 322.

33. 1 SECOND PHASE, *supra* n. 26, at 350.

34. FIRST PHASE, *supra* n. 19, at 804.

35. Drury, *supra* n. 8, at 38 (Table 26).

36. FIRST PHASE, *supra* n. 19, at 794.

37. Sutcliffe, *supra* n. 27, at 1.

38. Like "significant," "determinative" was not further defined when the question was asked. When a judge inquired as to its meaning, the interviewer said he was interested in cases in which oral argument made the judge change his mind or made the essential difference in the case.

39. Goldman, *supra* n. 8, at 8 (Table V). The only other categories where substantial proportions of circuit judges found oral argument essential were direct criminal appeals (38 percent) and en banc cases previously heard by a panel (35 percent). For the views of Ninth Circuit judges on the latter, *see* Wasby, *supra* n. 9, at 69-71.

40. Drury, *supra* n. 8, at 22.

41. Intercircuit differences in responses could be explained in part by intercircuit differences in argument practices. Goldman, *supra* n. 8, at 20-21. The Second Circuit had oral argument in every case, but decided a number of cases from the bench without opinion: the Fifth Circuit made "extensive use of truncated procedures," *id.* at 3, with "no oral argument" in a high percentage of cases; and the Sixth Circuit, by con-

trast, had retained a relatively traditional oral argument arrangement.

42. *Id.* at 8-10.

43. *See also* comments by Hruska Commission Executive Director A. Leo Levin, FIRST PHASE, *supra* n. 19, at 503-504.

44. Partridge and Bermant, THE QUALITY OF ADVOCACY IN THE FEDERAL COURTS 25 (Washington, D.C.: Federal Judicial Center, 1978).

45. STRUCTURE AND INTERNAL PROCEDURE, *supra* n. 2, at 107.

46. Advisory Council on Appellate Justice, Recommendations, summarized in 7 THIRD BRANCH (November 1975).

47. *See* 60 A.B.A. J. 1214 (1974).

48. Goldman, *supra* n. 8, at 13 (Table III).

49. *Id.* at 5; *id.* at 13 (Table III); Drury, *supra* n. 8, at 19 (Table 13).

50. Goldman, *supra* n. 8, at 7a (Table IV).

51. FIRST PHASE, *supra* n. 19, at 932.

52. Goldman, *supra* n. 8, at 11 (Table IV).

53. Drury, *supra* n. 8, at 16; Goldman, *supra* n. 8, at 12.

54. Drury, *supra* n. 8, at 24 (Table 16). The difference among the three circuits were less severe for judgments about dispensability of argument than for judgments that argument was essential. However, "in the Second and Sixth Circuits, where oral argument is generally allowed, the idea that oral argument should always be accorded unless the appeal is frivolous received the greatest support." *Id.* at 47.

55. *Id.* at 19.

56. Goldman, *supra* n. 8, at 12, 17 (Table IX).

57. *Id.* at 20 (Table XII).

58. Drury, *supra* n. 8, at 26 (Table 17).

59. The judges were not asked about their preference between oral argument and full written opinions.

60. Goldman, *supra* n. 8, at 7, 14.

61. Drury, *supra* n. 8, at 32, 34.

62. *Id.* at 33 (Table 22) and 34 (Table 24). *See also id.* at 35-36 (Table 25), indicating the median number of months attorneys perceive required to obtain a final disposition and median number of months they are willing to wait to have both oral argument and written opinion.

Justice Brennan and the institutionalization of dissent assignment

The formal assignment of dissenting opinions is a recent but now firmly established practice for which Justice William Brennan was largely responsible.

by Beverly Blair Cook

While the practice of assigning U.S. Supreme Court majority opinions dates back to the Marshall Court, the practice of assigning dissenting opinions is a recent development. Textbooks on the Supreme Court make no reference to dissent assignment by the senior justice in the minority. A 1988 article on dissenting opinions indicated that authorship was voluntary, and that "no one formally assigns such opinions."[1] The first published reference to the practice was in 1987, when Chief Justice William Rehnquist explained that the "senior justice among those who disagreed with the result reached by the majority at conference usually undertakes to assign the preparation of the dissenting opinion...."[2]

Institutionalization of the assignment of dissenting opinions required the recognition of dissent as a legitimate option. In early years, public disagreement violated a Court norm, and special opinions were seldom joined. Because justices often dissented or concurred without written explanation, opinion assignment was not an issue. Not until the regular appearance of written opinions joined by a bloc of justices did ad hoc arrangements for dissent writing prove inefficient.

Today, a dissent unaccompanied by reasoning is rare. To the extent that routine behaviors exemplify norms, a Court norm requiring a written opinion to support a dissent now exists: assignment of dissenting opinions is by the senior justice in the minority. Responsibility for the firm establishment of this practice belongs to Justice William Brennan Jr., who stated his duty clearly in a 1979 memo to Justice Lewis Powell: "I am undertaking to appor-

tion the dissents in which I am senior."[3]

Traditional practices

Assignment procedures on the Court have become formal and institutionalized, not on the basis of written rules, but through usage. Other informal "rules" of Supreme Court decision making that have become fixed include the rule of four to grant certiorari, the rule of unanimity to bring closure to any Court matter, and the rule of seniority for leadership. The new practice of dissent assignment imitates the established practice of majority opinion assignment.

Guidelines for Court opinion assignment developed over time include assignment by the senior justice in the majority, distribution of the workload among the justices, circulation of draft opinions to every member of the conference, negotiation of the final product through a series of revised drafts, and public identification of the opinion writer (except for per curiams). Surviving today of early opinion practices are the single Court opinion, the public announcement of per curiam decisions by the chief justice, and control over most assignments by the chief (by suiting his votes to the conference majority).

Dissent assignment was not an issue on the early courts because public disagreement by dissent or concurrence, with or without opinion, was considered deviant behavior. Justices referred to the "misfortune" of bringing their differences over law and policy to public attention, a rhetoric repeated with less sincerity into this century.[4] In the first Marshall period, conflict did arise in minor cases, but beginning in the 1812 term, strong differences were openly expressed. Before the end of the Marshall era, the publication of a few opinions by dissenting blocs signalled the breakdown of the solidarity norm.[5]

There was no need to assign dissents as long as each justice simply noted disagreement or wrote separately. When two or more justices agreed on the reasoning behind the minority preference, they could exercise one or a combination of three options: write a separate opinion, jointly write one opinion, or join another's writing.

Separate opinions were the rule if justices did not circulate drafts in timely fashion to give their colleagues opportunity to join. The notation of dissent was a work-saving but uninformative practice, employed with less frequency over the Court's history. But the increasing workload of Court opinion writing, from more than 100 per term after the Civil War to more than 200 between 1875 and 1925, increased the justices' incentive to avoid individual writing.

The second option, joint writing, was an intermediate step between separate writing and joining an opinion written by a like-minded justice. Joint writing was inefficient but useful to signal the strong commitment of the signers to their result and doctrine.

The third option was efficient and also carried a message of unity but required some method for selecting the writer, informing the bloc members, and circulating the draft. The practical utility of an opinion assignment practice for dissents became evident in the mid-19th century when multiple opinions and open disagreement became common.[6]

In the absence of such a standard operating procedure, justices lacked accurate and timely information on the intentions of colleagues in the conference minority. A justice who is weakly committed to the minority position and unwilling to invest time in writing might drift to the majority. But assured of an opportunity to support another's labor, such justices could delay their final votes until the dissent draft appeared.

Justice William O. Douglas's response to a circulated majority opinion was typical of the attitude of a justice not highly motivated to write a dissent. He joined an opinion by Justice Stanley Reed in the 1942 term with this warning: "...I will stay quiet and acquiesce, unless perchance some Brother

with lots of time on his hands decides to write."[7] Justice Robert Jackson revealed the same viewpoint in the 1947 term, writing to Justice Hugo Black: "Unless someone writes a dissent I will keep still." Justice John Marshall Harlan's attitude as expressed in a 1957 memo was typical of the justice who did not desire to use his own resources to develop an opinion. He wrote to Douglas: "Do you intend to write something in No. 89? If so, I shall hold up my return on Bill Brennan's opinion, awaiting yours." At the end of the 1971 term, Douglas sent a note to Lewis Powell: "...I voted the other way. But I acquiesce in your opinion subject to reexamination if anyone writes in dissent."

Prior to the Burger era, justices who felt obligated to provide some reasoning for their disagreement with the Court would at times urge a like-minded colleague to do the writing. Justice Louis Brandeis persistently pressed Justice Oliver Wendell Holmes to write for both of them.[8] Following Brandeis's pattern, Justice Felix Frankfurter in the 1950s exchanged memos pressing Justices Douglas, Harold Burton, and Brennan to write dissents.[9] Such behavior was informal and collegial.

The simple but effective practice of giving notice of intent to write a dissent to the assigned majority opinion writer, with copies to the conference members, developed over time. No doubt the earliest mode of communication, in the days of the boardinghouse conferences, was informal and oral. When the justices were scattered on circuit or in separate home studies, and without the technology for producing multiple copies of memos, some would remain unaware of a member's intent to dissent. Moreover, there was no opportunity to join a dissent when the author kept his plan to himself or delayed writing and publication until after the majority opinion appeared in print. By contrast, typical of the modern period are Brennan's terse memos during the 1950s: "Please be advised that I plan to write a dissent in No. 27..." and "I shall, in due course, undertake the writing of a dissent in the above case."

Precursors

When did the senior justice in a dissenting bloc first take responsibility for opinion assignment? It is reasonable to suppose that a chief justice, when in the minority, made the first dissent assignment. Because the chief, when in the majority, routinely chooses Court opinion authors, it would seem natural to adopt the same practice when in dissent. Prompt selection of the dissent author increases efficiency, since in modern times no decision is announced until the conference has ascertained that every special opinion is ready, and every justice is satisfied with the finality of his or her choice.

Chief justices, however, have few opportunities to make dissent assignments because they avoid membership in the minority unless driven by strong principle. Of the cases where any dissent was registered, Chief Justices Marshall and William Howard Taft joined the minority in less than 10 percent of the cases; Roger Taney, Morrison Waite, Edward White, and Charles Evans Hughes did so in less than 15 percent; Melville Fuller, Fred Vinson, and Earl Warren in less than 20 percent; and Salmon Chase, Harlan Fiske Stone, Warren Burger, and William Rehnquist in less than 30 percent of the cases.[10]

A chief seldom in the minority would have little motivation to streamline the assignment process. When in dissent, Vinson evidently made no effort to produce a rationale; he waited until someone else wrote and then joined or simply noted his dissenting vote.[11] Recent chiefs, who have found themselves in dissent more often, have felt more pressure for efficiency. Burger, with his special concern for court management, probably facilitated the new practice.

Dissent assignment practice was not institutionalized before the Burger era. Prior to the 1970s, justices in dissent tried to reduce their workloads through informal consultation and agreement on a writer. On the Stone Court, Black, the senior liberal justice, evidently chose the dissent writer in some cases.[12] On the Vinson Court, there was still no formal assignment process; the dissenters conferred informally to choose a writer or simply wrote separately.[13]

In the Vinson and Warren eras, Frankfurter took steps toward institutionalization by pushing for a single dissent and assigning writers. In the 1950 term, he urged Vinson, Black, and Douglas to find a formula for their minority position and promised to join them. During the 1953 term, Burton drafted a dissent in response to an oral invitation by Frankfurter and Jackson. Frankfurter reported to Reed in the 1955 term that "Harold has been good enough to undertake to write for the dissent-

ers."

The first written memo of assignment was found in papers from the 1956 term; Frankfurter cleared it with the other senior dissenters and then invited newcomer Brennan to write for the bloc: "Harold and John agree with me in asking you to write for us in dissent in *LaBuy*. I hope you will." Brennan responded, "Delighted to! Thanks very much." Most invitations, however, continued to be oral.

The justices followed no standard operating procedure in the 1950s and 1960s. Dissenters often had to wait for a volunteer to write. In the 1956 term, Douglas sent a memo to the author of the Court opinion: "...I will acquiesce in it unless someone else writes in dissent. If anyone does write in dissent I will reconsider...."[14] In 1963 Douglas switched his conference vote to the majority side and then revoked it when a dissent draft reached his desk. He wrote to Justice Potter Stewart, "...now that the dissent has come around, I have decided to adhere to my original view and to join it."

In the later Warren period, some justices openly admitted their cooperative efforts to conserve individual resources. Brennan explained in 1963 that the "dissenters agree among themselves who shall write the dissenting opinion."[15] This collegial consultation apparently operated sporadically and was a middle stage between voluntarism and senior responsibility for assignment. In the absence of a fair distribution of dissent assignments by a senior, the volunteers or recruits rationed their efforts. The effect of this informal system was to discourage dissents; the effect of the new formal practice has been to encourage the writing of a single dissent.

Indirect evidence

Indirect evidence suggests that the dissent assignment practice developed during the Burger period when the increasing number of close votes made minority opinion solidarity a strong tool with which to threaten the majority. From the Hughes through Rehnquist eras, the number of decisions per term with minimal majorities trended upward: from 5.8 percent in 1933, 12.5 percent in 1943, 10.7 percent in 1953, 12.2 percent in 1963, 21.9 percent in 1973, to 19 percent in 1983.[16] The sudden increase in close decisions in 1973 matches the period when the senior dissenter took responsibility for assignments.

From Hughes through Warren, success in holding a four-member coalition behind a single dissent decreased: from 89 percent under Hughes, 77 percent under Stone, 57 percent under Vinson, to 49 percent under Warren.[17] The trend reversed in the Burger period, with 63 percent of the 5-4 decisions producing an opinion signed by all four dissenters. On the Rehnquist Court (1986-1992 terms), the ratio of successful coalitions to opportunities increased again to 69 percent.

Another measure of minority coalition unity is the change in the ratio of dissenting opinions to dissenting votes. If each justice wrote separately to explain a dissenting vote, the ratio would be 1:1.[18] On the Warren Court, there was a dissenting opinion for every 1.7 dissenting votes, on the Burger Court for every 2.0 votes, and on the Rehnquist Court (1986-1990 terms) for every 2.3 votes. One explanation for these changes is that the new practice of dissent assignment contributed to holding the coalition together.

The abrupt end of the practice of notation (dissenting without opinion) at the beginning of the Burger period was another indicator of change in the assignment practice. On the Hughes Court, the average number of dissents without opinion per term was 10.5, on the Stone Court, 15, and on the Vinson Court, 26. The average dropped to 11.5 on the Warren Court. On the Burger Court, evident from the first (1969) term, the practice almost disappeared with an average per term of only 1.5. On the Rehnquist Court (1986-1990 terms), the average dropped to less than one per term.

One can speculate that under the new assignment practice where an opinion is prepared for every minority, justices acquiesce to dissenting opinions that do not entirely satisfy them, just as earlier they acquiesced to Court opinions. The sharp reduction in dissents by notation signals a new norm requiring an explanation for every vote rejecting the majority disposition.[19]

Additional encouragement for the open expression of dissent was implicit in a change that appeared to be purely administrative. Through the Warren period, a justice could convey an impression of agreement with the majority without going on record, since the official reporter did not list the names of joiners of the opinion. The official reports named the authors of Court opinions (except for per curiams) and special opinions and named the joiners of special opinions but not of Court opinions. The attentive reader of a Supreme Court reporter could thus reconstruct the composition of the majority in the announced decision only by assumption.

Early in the 1971 term, Chief Justice Burger expanded the duties of the court reporter to include the writing of a syllabus specifying each justice's vote in a case. Burger's format for the official reports offered a modest response to the contemporary movement for open meetings, providing explicit information about each justice's final vote without giving access to conference deliberations. For the first time, every justice was publicly accountable for every vote. This change helped press the justices toward the rationalization of dissent writing.

Direct evidence

In the two transitional terms of the Burger Court while Black continued as senior justice, the archives offer no evidence of routine or written dissent assignments. In his first term as senior justice in 1971, Douglas made some written dissent assignments but did not cover all cases. He believed it appropriate to consult first with his senior colleagues in dissent. In the 1972 term, Brennan began to spur his senior to take responsibility for assigning the dissenting opinions. He offered suggestions for dissent assignments after looking at the chief's periodic assignment sheets for Court opinions.

As Douglas's disabilities increased, Brennan employed his diplomatic talents to assist the senior justice in distributing dissents. Throughout the 1973 term, Brennan indicated to Douglas that every dissent was to be assigned. He wrote, "…I note that from the very first October Argument List there is one dissent that hasn't been assigned by you…," and "I've been looking at the assignment list with the view to possible dissents." Douglas's law clerks embellished Brennan's lists of unassigned cases, providing the names of justices available to write, adding information on current chambers' work on each case, and attaching the chief's assignment sheet to show who would be writing the Court opinion.

In the 1974 term, Brennan persisted in reminding Douglas of his duty: "I've been going over the assignment sheet anticipating that there will be dissents to be written." But even as he took the initiative to suggest assignments, Brennan took care to leave the authority with his senior. He indicated that he was simply serving as expediter, using phrases such as: "I'll be happy to take that if you want me to"; "...I think you can do a better job than either of us"; and "I have taken the liberty of asking Thurgood to take on the dissent."

Despite his disinterest in routine duties, Douglas proposed to Burger in 1972 the reinstatement of an old policy that emphasized the importance of dissenting opinions:

I have been planning to bring to the attention of the Conference, for discussion, a practice which was in vogue when I took my seat under Hughes and which has been more or less in vogue since that time, although some regimes have not observed it as faithfully as others. Stone, for example, meticulously observed it. Vinson, and to an extent Warren, did not. I refer to the policy that whenever an opinion for the Court is circulated that the dissenters drop everything else and prepare their dissents. It is, I think, a good practice as it enables the case to come to a rather rapid focus.

Burger did not renew the policy Douglas described, but Chief Justice Rehnquist did take such an initiative.

Brennan's role

Brennan's "enormous influence on the Court and the enduring legacy of his opinions" have been noted.[20] His leadership, before and after Douglas's retirement, in the institutionalization of dissent assignment must also be recognized. When senior justice in the minority, Brennan made an opinion assignment in every case, even when unsure that he would remain with the minority. His law clerks kept for him a running record of opinion assignments, circulations, and vote changes. Immediately after conference, he sometimes made an oral request of a justice, particularly one who was not closely aligned with the liberal bloc, and followed up with a written notification. By sending a memo describing his distribution of the dissent workload to each dissenting justice at the end of every oral argument period, Brennan assured colleagues of his fair and complete coverage of the assignments.

Brennan moved expeditiously to make his dissent assignments. In the 1985 term, he made them the day before or on the same day that the chief justice distributed his assignment sheet for the Court opinions. Brennan's timely actions helped hold the minority together. He favored consensus among the dissenters and tried to identify the writer who would preserve the coalition. His pur-

pose was obvious in his 1986 note to Justice Thurgood Marshall: "Please join me in your superb dissent.... It is really a great job and ought to change some votes."

The formal assignment of the dissenting opinion, like that of the majority opinion, was simply a stage in the process of resolving the case issues and did not bind the justices. Sometimes no justice wanted to author a dissent until after reading the majority's reasoning. Nor could Brennan promise that all members of the minority would sign the dissent. When Justice John Paul Stevens wrote in 1982 that "I will be delighted to try to spell out the reasons...," Powell wrote that he was not committed to Stevens's approach. Brennan was not always certain of his own posture after a close vote in conference. In the 1979 term, for instance, Brennan wrote, "I must say my vote is a little weak" and invited Blackmun to write.

Brennan did not try to bring together dissenters who offered different reasoning at conference or who were bound into a personal stare decisis. If a justice agreed on disposition but not on doctrine, he did not propose a joint dissent. Brennan's note to Douglas in the 1972 term was typical: "I assume you'll be expressing your own view...whereas I dissent there only on the search and seizure question. And as usual with me in Establishment Clause cases, I'll be writing out my own view...."

After a conference during the 1974 term, Brennan recognized that the reasoning of several dissenters differed. He wrote to Douglas: "You and I have different views...and I will be writing my own dissent in those two cases." Even when Brennan wrote separately, however, he wanted to make sure that a dissent was assigned. Justices who decided not to join after reading the proposed bloc opinion were, of course, free to write separately or switch to the majority.

Selecting authors

In selecting authors for the dissents, Brennan kept in mind two important considerations—to make a fair distribution of the workload and to give recognition to a particular justice's interests and precedential writings. In the 1976 term he wrote, "I am at the task again of trying to distribute dissents equitably." If a justice not usually in his camp, such as Powell or Rehnquist, became available, Brennan would select him. Brennan himself took a large share of the work, including some of the most interesting cases.

Brennan was continually aware of the work pressures on his colleagues. A typical letter read: "I have the feeling that you are very badly overloaded and accordingly I hesitate to ask you to take on the dissent." He noted in a close vote: "If Lewis can fit it in an already crowded schedule he'll try his hand at a dissent.... The assignment may be subject to further consideration if he's pressed for time."

Familiarity with and commitment to the issues formed the second basis for assignment. A memo to Potter Stewart in the 1977 term explained: "Actually the only reason I thought to ask you to do it was that I expect it would turn on *Florida Power* which you wrote." A similar memo to Stevens in the 1982 term asked: "As author of *Henderson v. Morgan*, John would you be willing to undertake the dissent?" If a justice had already written a draft in the prior term, he was also likely to be selected.

Some voluntarism for dissent writing still occurred but always in relation to the senior justice's lead role. Justices with a special interest in a case could volunteer to the senior. Powell wrote to Brennan in the 1979 term, "As you are the senior in dissent in this case, I write to say that I will be happy to draft a dissent for the four of us if you wish.... I merely want you to know of my availability."

The thorough institutionalization of dissent assignment by Brennan was symbolized by changes in the distribution of information on dissent writing. In each case, the senior assigner sent a memo to other justices in the conference minority announcing his choice of writer. The assignee notified the Court opinion author of intent to write (as did the volunteer in the past), and finally the senior informed the entire conference of the assignment. Beginning in the 1983 term, in the notes on his chamber's case circulation sheets, Brennan listed his specific assignment letters, instead of the traditional memos that he would "await the dissent."[21] By the 1980s, every justice had full and timely information on the distribution of both the Court and dissenting opinions.

By the end of his tenure, Burger assumed that the senior justice in dissent would make an assignment. In the 1982 term, he wrote a note to Blackmun emphasizing his responsibility: "...the dissent will be up to the 'affirms,' of which group you are 'senior.'" Although he occasionally needed a re-

minder from Brennan, Burger routinely made the dissent assignments when he was in the minority.

Brennan's contribution was to routinize the assignment of dissenting opinions and to place the authority of delegating assignments firmly in the hands of the senior justice in the minority bloc. Consultation with others was possible but no longer expected, and every justice now had full information on the writing plans of colleagues. The work pattern of the senior's chambers for distributing the dissents imitated the established pattern for distributing the majority opinions.

The post-Brennan era

For justices serving on the Rehnquist Court, dissent assignment has been standard practice. Its routine nature seems evident in the note from O'Connor to Rehnquist in 1990: "My vote at Conference was very tentative. I plan to see what Tony writes and decide whether I can join it. Is it all right with you if we defer assignment of this dissent?" Stevens, appointed in 1975, was the first justice socialized into the new practice from his first term. With Blackmun's retirement in 1994, only Rehnquist has personal experience under the less structured system of dissent writing.

The survival of a new practice depends upon its adoption by those who follow its founder. Brennan's long tenure as senior (1975-1989 terms) and his preference and ability to mediate and produce consensus gave the practice a firm foundation. Marshall assumed Brennan's role of selecting the writer of liberal dissents for one term. In fact, he followed the new practice even earlier on those rare occasions when he disagreed with both Brennan and Rehnquist. Marshall continued the policy of giving Blackmun the opportunity to respond to the conservative majority in abortion cases, and, further reinforcing the new practice, ensured that the small as well as the large minorities produced joint opinions. For each assignment period of the 1990 term, Marshall's clerks kept track of the cases requiring his dissent assignment and recommended an assignee.

The role of senior on the liberal side devolved on Blackmun in the 1991 term. Blackmun writes that he "tried to follow the Brennan practice."[22] Upon White's retirement in 1993, Blackmun took the senior seat for one term but was replaced by Stevens in the 1994 term. Despite Stevens's record as a maverick with a preference to write lone dissents even when a group dissent was available, it is probable that he is also following the Brennan practice.[23]

With six newcomers on the Rehnquist Court by the 1994 term and with the unfolding of new issues and doctrines, the critical senior in dissent may not be Stevens but O'Connor, the senior member of the centrist bloc. With talents more similar to Brennan's, she would appreciate the utility of maintaining and further institutionalizing the practice. O'Connor's political experiences in Arizona and her preference to negotiate suggest the possibility that she may make good use of Brennan's legacy when she moves into the senior position upon Stev-ens's retirement.[24]

Survival of the practice also depends on its use by the chief justice in dissent. Rehnquist has indicated that he considers dissent assignment a routine practice. In 1989 Rehnquist proposed to levy a serious penalty on justices who failed to circulate a promised dissenting opinion after the Court opinion had been available for four weeks.[25] Such a policy would reinforce the production of work-saving coalitional dissents.

Court vs. dissent assignments

The practice of assigning dissents is not identical to the practice of assigning the opinion for the Court. One of the expectations associated with opinion assignment is that the assignee automatically and graciously accepts the chief's (or senior's) directive; it is not considered fitting for the associate justice to complain or resist. Only a few excuses are legitimate: disagreement with the reasoning of the largest bloc in the majority coalition, the potentially adverse effect of the author's identity on the Court's image of impartiality, and the undermining of the writer's reputation for consistency.

In the 19th century, justices complained about, rejected, and solicited case assignments.[26] In the late 20th century, however, justices accept without question the senior's authority to distribute Court opinions, except to inform him of an ethical issue, a miscount of conference votes, or a prior promise. The assignment of a Court opinion, signed or per curiam, has become over time a mandate; the assignment sheets circulated by the chief justice constitute, in effect, work orders. By including the assignments made by seniors on the sheets, the chief thereby places his authority be-

hind them. Associate justices accept their writing jobs as the price of the Court's institutional productivity and reputation.

Dissent assignments, however, do not carry the same authority; they are couched in a language of collegiality rather than of hierarchy. Seniors address their juniors with circumspection in making dissent assignments. For example, in the 1973 term Douglas wrote to Stewart: "Would you want to undertake the dissent...?" Brennan's courtesy is evident in his request to Marshall during the 1975 term: "I know how jammed up you are going to be but John is taking on nine dissents after a discussion with me and I've got about twelve. I know you have several but can I add [two more]?"

Justices treat the letter from their senior in dissent as an invitation, not an order, and immediately respond. The assignee may not write the dissent as promptly as the senior hoped but does feel an obligation to complete the work unless he or she intends to switch sides or develop an idiosyncratic argument. If a dissenter does reject the assignment, however, the senior chooses a substitute to ensure that the case is covered.

The coalitional dissenting opinion has at least two important functions—the efficient utilization of justices' writing time and the development of a doctrine to replace the precedent. A well-crafted dissenting opinion also has the potential to force the rethinking and modification of the majority opinion, but this can occur only if the dissenting opinion appears before the opinion of the Court reaches final draft form. The assignment of the dissent by memo at the same time as the assignment for the Court has the virtue of expediting its production and increasing its leverage over the majority. For justices on the fence, the dissenter's reasoning is a resource to press for revisions in the majority opinion.

Moreover, under the new practice, the goal of the assigner is to produce a single dissent. By articulating the arguments of the minority, the opinion gives a legitimacy to its point of view that discourages defection. The strategic purpose of the solidary dissent in a close case is to win a majority. As Harlan wrote to Brennan in the 1956 term, "I hope you won't spare full dress treatment of the problem in writing for the dissenters.... I am hoping that your opinion will be so convincing as to pick up one more vote, and thus carry the day."

A powerful vehicle

Dissent assignment contributes to efficiency and offers a powerful vehicle for a four-justice bloc to present its alternative reasoning to external constituencies. Unity of viewpoint by dissenters in a close case sends a message to potential litigants about their chances of winning in the future and about the line of argument most likely to retain or to expand the coalition supporting their positions.

Politicians involved in the judicial appointment process will also be interested in any opportunity to change the direction of Court doctrine by the substitution of a new justice who shares the large minority's view for a retiring justice in the majority. Although appointment strategies do not necessarily work, the repetitive voice of a unified large minority in a series of cases on the same issue calls attention to Court disequilibrium.

Beyond its putative functions, what meaning does the new practice carry? The routinization of the practice is an indicator of the normalization and acceptance of dissensus. Although Chief Justice Marshall's strong norm of solidarity behind a single opinion for the Court, preferably announced by the chief justice, was not effectively enforced after his own era, the weaker norm encouraging consensus, except on matters of special salience to the individual, did survive at least into the Hughes Court.[27]

The behavior of justices, however, openly belied the existence of any consensual norm after 1940. Judges and commentators who persist in debating the virtue of presenting a facade of Court harmony are discussing a model, not an institutional reality. When minority justices on the Stone and later courts did overlook their disagreements to join a large majority, their motives were more relevant to their personal budgets of time and interest than to any normative philosophy of Court behavior.

Both routine assignment of the writing of a dissenting opinion when two or more justices disagree with the majority at conference and the routine production of an opinion to explain a lone dissent are unobtrusive indicators that the consensual norm has expired. Institutions do not develop standard procedures to accomplish an activity that violates its norms. Instead, the dissent assignment practice, established during the Burger era and continued into the Rehnquist period, indicates that the Court's normative structure now includes

a competitive norm. Justice John Catron claimed that disagreement on the Taney Court was "just as natural as in the Senate, and almost as common."[28] Court practice has caught up with Catron's observation. By institutionalizing the selection of its spokesperson for the minority, the Court has adopted a fundamental feature of other American political institutions.

NOTES

This article originally appeared in Volume 79, Number 1, July-August 1995, pages 17-23.

1. Brenner and Spaeth, *Ideological Position as a Variable in the Authoring of Dissenting Opinions on the Warren and Burger Courts*, 16 AM. POL. Q. 317-328, at 318, 320 (July 1988).

2. Rehnquist, THE SUPREME COURT 302 (New York: William Morrow, 1987).

3. William J. Brennan papers, Box 548, Library of Congress, to Lewis from Bill, 3/5/79. Subsequent quotations from the justice's papers are not cited, but a copy of the article with full documentation is available from the editor or from the author (e-mail: bcook@pinot.callamer.com).

4. White, THE MARSHALL COURT AND CULTURAL CHANGE, 1815-35, 187, n. 131 (New York: Macmillan, 1988). Joseph Story was probably the last justice to internalize the solidarity norm. In 1844 he was the senior justice and the only holdover of the "old Court." "He had to choose between continuous dissent and yielding in the face of his own convictions. Neither alternative seemed tolerable." Swisher, THE TANEY PERIOD, 1836-64, 233 (New York: Macmillan, 1974).

5. Justice Smith Thompson challenged Marshall's solidarity norm by writing separately in constitutional cases. He followed Oliver Ellsworth's seriatim rule for this important set of cases by producing a series of concurrences. Although the senior justices generally followed the chief's lead, justices new to the Court after Thompson arrived in 1823 were not disturbed to reveal their real policy differences in published opinions. White, *supra* n. 4, at 307, 318. Justice William Johnson explained in *Gibbons v. Ogden*, 9 Wheat. 1, 223 (1824), that it was his "duty to the public" to write out his dissent on "questions of great importance and great delicacy." In the Taney era Peter Daniel felt "constrained" to dissent in a large number of cases that stimulated his strong feelings on states' rights. Swisher, *supra* n. 4, at 69.

6. White, *supra* n. 4, at 195.

7. William O. Douglas papers, Box 77, Library of Congress, 11/13/42. *See* n. 3.

8. White, JUSTICE OLIVER WENDELL HOLMES: LAW AND THE INNER SELF 322 (New York: Oxford University Press, 1993).

9. Harold Burton papers, Box 303, Library of Congress, to Harold from FF, 5/23/57. *See* n. 3.

10. Ulmer, *Exploring the Dissent Patterns of Chief Justices: John Marshall to Warren Burger*, in Goldman and Lamb (eds.), JUDICIAL CONFLICT AND CONSENSUS 53 Table 2.1 (Lexington: The University Press of Kentucky, 1986). Burger and Rehnquist data from Spaeth, U.S. SUPREME COURT DATABASE, 1953-1993 (Ann Arbor, Mich.: ICPSR).

11. Note, *Chief Justice Vinson and His Law Clerks*, 49 Nw. U. L. REV. 26-35 (March-April 1954).

12. John P. Frank, who was Black's law clerk in the 1942 term, writes, "I have no doubt but that he assigned the dissenting opinion" but does not recall his modus operandi. Letter to author, April 28, 1995. A Black law clerk from the later 1940s also recalls his assignment of some dis-

sents. Eugene Gressman, Murphy's law clerk from 1943 to 1948, reports that Black assigned his judge to write in *Western Union v. Lenroot* (1945) for the four dissenters. Newman, Hugo Black, A Biography 335 n. * (New York: Pantheon Books, 1994).

13. *Supra* n. 11.

14. Earl Warren papers, Box 350, Library of Congress, to Chief from Bill, 2/18/57. *See* n. 3.

15. Brennan, *Inside View of the High Court*, N.Y. Times Magazine, Oct. 6, 1963.

16. Easterbrook, *Agreement Among the Justices: An Empirical Note*, 1984 Supreme Court Review 389-409, extrapolated from appendix tables, 401-9. Note that Easterbrook calculated the rate of "real" disagreement based on his interpretation of the doctrinal issue, see appendix, 397-400.

17. Figures on close cases, and on dissents without opinion, are based on the author's collection of data from the reporters for Hughes through Vinson courts and on the Spaeth data set for Warren through Rehnquist.

18. The ratio is calculated after subtracting the instances of dissent without opinion.

19. Thurgood Marshall papers, Box 536, Library of Congress, to Thurgood from HAB, 5/3/91. *See* n. 3.

20. Irons, Brennan vs. Rehnquist: the Battle for the Constitution 330 (New York: Alfred A. Knopf, 1994).

21. Prior to the 1983 term, Brennan's dissent assignments are not recorded on the circulation sheets kept in his chambers. Some are recorded for 1983 and all for 1984 and 1985.

22. Letter to author, May 19, 1995.

23. Sickels, John Paul Stevens and the Constitution 159 (The Pennsylvania State University Press, 1988).

24. Cook, *Justice Sandra Day O'Connor: Transition to a Republican Court Agenda*, in Lamb and Halpern (eds.), The Burger Court 239, 272 (Champaign: University of Illinois Press, 1991).

25. His proposed penalty was to deny new majority opinion assignments until the laggard justice produced the dissent. His memo stated that he would weigh three factors in making majority opinion assignments. Besides the late dissenting opinions, he would take account of any failure to circulate a majority opinion within four weeks after assignment or of any delay in deciding to join circulated opinions. He wrote that "it only makes sense in the assignment of additional work to give some preference to those who are 'current' with respect to past work." "Policy Regarding Assignments." Memorandum to the Conference from William H. Rehnquist, Papers of Thurgood Marshall, Box 492, Folder 7, 11/24/89.

26. Magrath, Morrison R. Waite: The Triumph of Character 261-263 (New York: The Macmillan Company, 1963).

27. Haynie, *Leadership and Consensus on the U.S. Supreme Court*, 54 J. Pol. 1158-1169 (November 1992).

28. Swisher, *supra* n. 4, at 64.

The spirit of dissent

Although there is a bias in the legal community against judicial dissent, dissenting opinions function analogously to acts of civil disobedience in bringing about needed legal and political changes.

by J. Louis Campbell III

Since the advent of collegial courts minority-view judges have used published dissents to register their objections and reservations to majority judgments.[1] This has been particularly true of the U.S. Supreme Court, where, in fact, the first reported opinion of a justice was a dissent, coming as the justices delivered their opinions *seriatim*.[2] Chief Justice Marshall, though highly regarded for his dissent in *Ogden v. Saunders*,[3] fostered a preference against dissents and secured the Court tradition of one majority opinion standing as the last word on the law.

Marshall's leadership and a rather homogeneous tribunal militated against dissents for some time.[4] Then with Marshall's death and the ascendency of Chief Justice Taney (1836), the era of dissent began. The great dissenters in the Court's history have since included some of our most illustrious justices, such as Holmes, Brandeis, and Douglas.

Notwithstanding, there remains a bias in the legal community against dissent. There seems in particular to be some question about its efficacy. Prominent legal philosopher H. L. A. Hart has written that "A supreme tribunal has the last word in saying what the law is, and when it has said it, the statement that the Court was 'wrong' has no consequence within the system: no one's rights are thereby altered."[5]

Nevertheless, statements that the Court was wrong, I propose, do have important consequences apart from direct and immediate alteration of rights and duties, and these consequences may be found within the system. Dissenting opinions function analogously to acts of civil disobedience in offering protest and securing systemic change. "Institutional disobedience" is a good term to characterize dissents and their authors. That is, in writing and publishing dissents, judges are protesting as authorities within institutional roles, analogous to civilians in non-institutional roles who physically enact their protest. Dissent can influence change in both the judicial system and the larger political milieu, and many legal professionals have provided corroborative evidence for this theory of dissent.

The roots of civil disobedience

First, what is "civil disobedience"? Civil disobedience is an appeal to controlling authorities and to the general public "to alter certain laws or policies that the minority takes to be incompatible with the fundamental principles of morality, principles to which it believes the majority is committed,"[6] according to Marshall Cohen. In self-governing communities its essence is:

... propositional, stipulative, suggestive. Discovery, harangue, advocacy are its instruments of corrective persuasion of the beliefs and desires of others ... Its central function is not directly to change the law ... by forcing new policy ... its function is to *locate* wrong, *inform* the public of such wrong, and *persuade* the electorate to reconsider.[7]

Perception, identification, criticism, persuasion—these are the mechanisms of civil disobedience as a means of social change, influence, and coordination toward a point of view. It is not purposeless, reckless, or anarchistic. On the contrary, the civil disobedient has chosen to participate in democratically sanctioned processes for democratically praiseworthy ends.

A civil disobedient person serves two such democratic ends: First, the reinforcement of the ideal of self-choice, the freedom to arrive at one's own perspective, "a fundamental condition of free government and of all moral judgment;" and second, persuasion of others to join the cause celebre.[8] The cause of the disobedient is:

concerned with improving the existing legal system. He envisions his role as therapeutic rather than destructive. He believes that the ideal of justice is being violated in some way in the existing laws . . . He therefore makes of himself a martyr, bearing witness to the truth, and hoping thereby to educate and enlighten and to move men of good will.[9]

The civilly disobedient person appeals to the democratic ethos:

[He is] a man who defies that law out of conscience or moral belief . . . If he acts out of conscience it is important to remember that he appeals to it as well . . . . It is to protest the fact that the majority has violated these principles that the disobedient undertakes his disobedience.[10]

The form of civil disobedience need not, and indeed some would argue that it must not, be violent. It is a "quiet, symbolic act . . . aimed at peaceful revision of attitude."[11] Acts that run counter to the majority can be justified as civil disobedience only when they are acts of political speech, appeals, a form of persuasion as opposed to coercion.[12]

Institutional disobedience

It is this nonviolent quality of civil disobedience that has allowed modern democracies to provide *institutional* means of protest to minorities in recognition of their prerogative to oppose majority viewpoints.[13] This type of dissension can "observe, or follow, lines of political 'due process.' "[14] In fact, contemporary scholars suggest that instead of perceiving civil disobedience as essentially contrary to the ideas of authority and obligation, "we might consider building into the very idea of authority and obligation in a democracy a conception of allowable civil disobedience."[15] Dissenting opinions, indeed, may be seen in just this kind of light, as inherent, disparate, due process "acts" allowed to system authorities on behalf of minority viewpoints, or in other words, as institutional disobedience.

Dissents are protestual, propositional, stipulative, and suggestive in appealing to the authority of conscience, with the hope of a future remedy for a present wrong. Thus they militate against monolithic solidarity in the judiciary, reflecting the innate nature and exigence of law in contemporary society as a mosaic. Dissents offer an avenue of representation for perceptions at variance with the dominant vision. They locate wrong in the majority, inform the audience of such wrong, and persuade the audience to reconsider.[16] Thus in this respect dissents function analogously to civil disobedience in our society.

Further, as the world changes so must the law. And the dissenting opinion is "one of the processes that aids that development as the law meets and solves new situations."[17] The dissent initiates and presses change in the system, again analogous to civil disobedience. Without the judicial dissent, "boulders which are fused together with time-defying cement form a wall which could some day obstruct the passage of a needed road to the City of the Realized Hope of Man."[18]

Though there may be various bases for dissent, many dissents are grounded in moral or ethical terms, just as is civil disobedience. These subsets of judicial opinion move beyond the purely legal world "by placing the imprimatur of respectable moral leadership upon controversial social or economic reforms."[19] The appeal is to conscience. Justice Douglas wrote that dissents "may salvage for tomorrow the principle that was sacrificed or forgotten today. Their discussion and propagation of the great principles of our Charter may keep the democratic ideal alive in the days of regressions, uncertainty, despair."[20]

Contesting the imprimatur of infallibility for majority opinions, dissents are foresighted.[21] Chief Justice Hughes pointed to the conscience inherent in minority opinions, regardless of specific rationale, when he wrote, "The dissent is an appeal to the brooding spirit of the law, to the intelligence of a future day . . . ."[22] Advocacy is the instrument of this corrective persuasion. Dissents are evidence that the minority view has been heard—the wrong located, the public informed and persuaded. Though the minority view has not triumphed, it has been endowed with a quality of permanence for constant review by sympathetic advocates and system authorities.

The symbolic means of protest is an area of difference between civil and institutional disobedients. Civil disobedients use acts to oppose, such as sit-ins. Judges, on the other hand, use rhetoric. This difference does not make either civil or institutional disobedience inherently more effective. Rather, it reflects a strategic awareness of which symbols, acts or words, can best facilitate protest given the different contexts.

Civil disobedients resort to action because language has failed to effectively oppose. "Mere speech may fail to produce change in many situations because it does not demand a response."[23] To elicit a response, protesters act. In the civil context, this works well as a tool of opposition.

Language and the law

It is fitting that institutionally disobedient persons oppose through rhetoric the majority encroachment of their values. Law and language are inherently related. By stressing conflict resolution through procedure, ceremony, and rhetoric, "legal institutions provide the methods both for symbolically encouraging change while preserving continuity, and for symbolically assuring stability while fostering change."[24] Specifically, it has been argued that "language is the greatest instrument of social control . . . . law is only a division of language."[25] Why is it that language has such power?

In part, the answer lies in the nature of rhetoric. "words are important as words in that they represent symbolically and artificially an order which exists nowhere in the actual daily lives of persons."[26] Words are able to represent a sense of order because they continuously interact with the human psyche. We naturally experience a need for order, for structure. This need arises out of our normal experience of life, its vastness, complexity, variety. Words organize our thoughts, feelings, responses. They are therefore able to produce a sense of satisfaction, a reduction of the psychological tension arising from our need for order in the face of massive quantities and qualities of stimuli. Language acts as a screen through which our inherent needs, particularly for order, can be filtered. This essential nature of language is of critical significance in law, and makes words appropriate tools of protesting an order imposed by the majority, and designing an alternative order.

A second reason why rhetoric is appropriate deals with its communicative advantage. Laws, as rules and guidelines, must be persuasively communicated to those for whom they will serve as frameworks, and they must be communicated in such a way that the person absorbing them understands

that they apply to a variety of situations.[27] The two main devices available for communicating are the example and rhetoric.[28]

H. L. A. Hart argues that examples are imprecise means of communication. While they may be couched in explicit or implicit "do as I do" directives, they still "may leave open ranges of possibilities, and hence of doubt, as to what is intended."[29] Walter Probert agrees that examples are too indeterminant left embedded in concrete with the actor. Others then must speculate on intent, on what will be approved, and on the extent to which one's behavior must trace that of the actor in order to rightly follow the guidelines.[30]

In contrast, language may offer a clearer, more dependable means of communicating standards. The rules are no longer embedded within the confines of a single actor. They are contained in words and language structures about which there is broad agreement as to meaning. The observer, the respondent, can know what he or she must do in the future and at what time. "He has only to recognize instances of clear verbal terms to 'subsume' particular facts under general classificatory heads and draw a simple syllogistic conclusion."[31]

The power of judicial dissent

This theory of dissent sounds rather romantic, relying on such supporting phrases as "the brooding spirit of the law," "the City of the Realized Hope of Man," and other idealized references. But beyond the romance of dissent are important, substantive, systemic effects. The primary persuasive objective of disobedience is remedy—the remedy of a perceived wrong. And the remedy has been applied successfully in numerous cases. The dissent of a Supreme Court justice avoids the civil disobedient's scorn as "mere speech" that does not demand a response, and it can "heavily influence the allocation of values among relevant competing interests . . . In broader social terms [it] may modify or enhance the legitimacy that relevant publics in the larger social system accord a decision, a policy, or a law."[32] Three major examples in the area of civil and human rights alone, where dissents eventually became the majority viewpont, add substance to the romance.[33]

In *Plessy v. Ferguson*, [34] the Supreme Court upheld the East Louisiana Railway's right to require Homer Plessy to ride in the "separate but equal" Colored" car of the train, contrary to Plessy's wish.

Justice John Marshall Harlan dissented, describing "the thin disguise of 'equal' accommodations" for what it really was, a veil of racism. Fifty-six years later, in 1952, the Court began hearing the series of cases known as *Brown v. Board of Education.*[35] And the core premise of Harlan's dissent became law—separate was no longer to be considered equal. Harlan's view of segregation as unconstitutional and a social evil became the majority position.

In 1938 Smith Belts, an unemployed farm worker on relief, was charged with armed robbery and assault. At arraignment, Belts, unable to afford a private counsel, asked Judge Forsythe to appoint an attorney for him. The judge informed him that attorneys were appointed only for indigent defendants charged with murder or rape. Declaring his innocence, Belts saw no possibility of conducting a jury trial himself, so he waived his right to trial by jury. The court found Belts guilty and handed down a prison sentence. From prison Belts sought a writ of habeas corpus, the denial of which he appealed to the Supreme Court. In *Belts v. Brady,*[36] the Court found no violation of due process. Justice Hugo Black dissented, supported by justices Douglas and Murphy, arguing for the right of counsel for the poor as a safeguard of freedom. Twenty-one years later, in *Gideon v. Wainwright,*[37] analogous circumstances saw Black's dissent become a majority position, and the right to counsel became a cornerstone in American law.

A final example from the many available is Justice Douglas' dissent in *Dennis v. United States.*[38] Here 11 persons were convicted under an extremely broad Smith Act for conspiring to organize a Communist Party and to advocate the forcible overthrow of the U.S. government. The Supreme Court upheld the conviction of the 11 with justices Black and Douglas dissenting. While Black's opinion was brief, revolving around an absolute view of the First Amendment, Douglas wrote a more detailed argument on the clear and present danger test. Six years later, after the close of the McCarthy Era, a similar case reached the Supreme Court. In *Yates v. United States,*[39] however, the Court moved largely within Douglas' preview. Douglas concurred in part and dissented in part. Notwithstanding, the guarantee of freedom of advocacy had been substantially restored.

Courts are not alone in accepting the persuasion of non-majority opinions. Legislatures frequently accept remedial measures advocated therein.[40] Justice Iredell's dissent in *Chisolm v. Georgia,*[41] became part of the Constitution as the Eleventh Amendment.[42] The Dred Scott dissenters' arguments became the foundations for the Thirteenth, Fourteenth, and Fifteenth Amendments to the Constitution.[43] Justice Story's dissent in *Cary v. Curtis*[44] was enacted into law by Congress in 36 days—before the publication of the volume containing his opinion.[45]

Judicial dissents may also influence lawyers. Advocates note not only the majority opinions and the ratio therein, but also the non-controlling, non-majority messages.[46] "Essentially retrospective, [lawyers] search for a comforting precedent, whether it be in a majority or dissenting opinion."[47] Prospectively, lawyers may draw lines of difference among majority and minority opinions and justices, and anticipate future results and alignments under changed facts.[48] Thus, judicial history has shown that non-majority opinions have "exercised a corrective and reforming influence upon the law."[49]

Dissent has potential effects outside the judicial system, as well, in a larger political context. Public allies of the ideology embodied in the dissent find image enhancement in this form of due process disobedience a positive step in resolving discord. Rehetoric from authorities with status also tends to defuse more violent acts of civil disobedience, and to calm those who must be persuaded.

Official support of one group's claim acts as a positive statement of the stature of that group's subculture .... The use of supportive rhetoric ... would allow opponents of the functioning ideology to strive for and occasionally gain official support while reducing the overt threat to the governmentally sanctioned value set.[50]

Perceptions of dissent

What the dissenter intends to do by dissenting may be identified in part by what he or she says. But another crucial element in recognizing intent is what members of the legal community believe about the dissents. What are mutual beliefs about the genre of judicial opinion labeled, "dissent"?

The metaphors used when discussing dissents are important clues to perception. More than a literary device, the metaphor represents a way of seeing, a way of believing. It symbolizes inferences the thinker has made through comparison or analogy regarding the subject.

For example, Richard Stephens, writing in the

Florida Law Review, perceived authors of dissents "acting" as advocates.[51] Here, the metaphor is "acting," and Stephens sees dissenters as engaging in physical behavior, with the implicit comparison to civil disobedients who enact their protest.

Justice Douglas conjured images of civil disobedience when he wrote:

It is the right of dissent, not the right or duty to conform, which gives dignity, worth, and individuality to man. As Carl Sandburg recently said, 'There always ought to be beatniks in a culture, hollering about the respectables.'[52]

Thus we have judicial dissenters analogyzed to non-conformity, individualistic "beatniks hollering about the respectables." Mr. Douglas' view of dissent must surely have flowed from his view of the Supreme Court's role in our cultural lives. He wrote, "The Court that *raises its hand against the mob* may be temporarily unpopular; but it soon wins the confidence of the nation. The court that fails to *stand before the mob* is not worthy of the great tradition."[53]

Significantly, there are others who share Mr. Douglas' point of view on dissent while avoiding his reputation as a maverick. Benjamin Cardozo used metaphor to characterize judicial dissent:

The voice of the majority may be that of force triumphant, content with the plaudits of the hour, and recking little of the morrow. The dissenter speaks to the future, and his voice is pitched to a key that will carry through the years. Read some of the great dissents . . . and feel after the cooling time of the better part of a century, the glow and fire of a faith that was content to bide its hour. The prophet and martyr do not see the hooting throng. Their eyes are fixed on the eternities.[54]

Again, the dissenter is painted in colors of civil disobedience.

A final example comes from prominent legal philosopher Karl Llewellyn. Though he prefers the quantity of dissents kept at a minimum, as indicated below, he nevertheless acknowledges the quality of dissent in terms familiar to civil disobedients. He writes, "the dissent, by forcing or suggesting full publicity, rides herd on the majority."[55] Thus, from scholars, attorneys, and dissenters we have seen a mutual belief about dissents. These beliefs seem to confirm the analogy of dissent as civil disobedience.

A second mutual belief that lends support to dissent as civil disobedience concerns the reception of dissents. Dissents do not have to be received as illegitimate to be versions of disobedience. On the contrary, due process is at the core of civil disobedience. And judicial dissent is the institutional due process equivalent to civil disobedience. However, acknowledgment of the disparate nature of the act or opinion, its contraction of the mainstream or authoritative will, would seem necessary to warrant the characterization, "disobedience." There is evidence of such a belief about dissent.

Though dissents have been published since the earliest cases and are common today, they remain eschewed. Justice Douglas alluded to the controversy surrounding dissents when he wrote, "All of us in recent years have heard and read many criticisms of dissenting . . . opinions. Separate opinions have often been deplored. Courts have been criticized for tolerating them."[56] Justice Edward White declared that the only purpose a dissent could serve is to weaken the Court.[57] Chief Justice Hughes deprecated "persistent expressions of opinions that do not command the agreement of the Court."[58] Philosopher Llewellyn prefers dissents to be few in number because they tend to diminish a "single way of seeing."[59]

Conclusion

The importance of judicial dissent has been debated for years. A school of thought represented by H.L.A. Hart has argued that dissents have no system-wide consequences because they do not alter rights in immediate cases. Here, I have disagreed. To the goal of system-wide change is dissent, its effects, and supporting perceptions deployed.

The conclusion that dissents are sources of energy and cogency in law is important in order to understand how and why we carry on the ideals of our system of justice. Knowledge enhances our effectiveness. The makers of dissent need not question the efficacy of their effort, and the audiences of dissent can appreciate the value of the message. They are both engaged in a significant expression of the legal process.

More generally, analysis of any function of that process can offer insight into the process itself, and ease the identification of essential characteristics. The analysis of dissent here points to the conclusion that the law is far more complex than the status of rights in immediate cases. First, law is transcendent—it lives not only within a particular set of facts and determines a particular set of rights, but also rises to a more universal plane of consciousness. It encompasses more than the present in its spread.

Second, and related to the first, law is enduring rather than ephemeral. It lives beyond the cases that animated it; it is progenerative. Its participation in the historical process into which all humans are born gives even aged or overturned law a role in contemporary dynamics. And third, law is infused with humanity, and thus is inherently concerned with symbolizing human yearnings and the persuasion of humans by means of the quintessential human process, the power of language. Dissent calls forth these characteristics of the judicial system, and helps illumine Chief Justice Hughes' perception that the dissent appeals to the "brooding spirit" of the law.

NOTES

This article originally appeared in Volume 66, Number 7, February 1983, pages 304-312.

1. Evans, *The Dissenting Opinion—Its Use and Abuse*, 3 Mo. L. Rev. 120 (1938).
2. McWhinney, *Judicial Concurrences and Dissents: A Comparative View of Opinion-Writing in Final Appellate Tribunals*, 31 Canadian B. Rev. 609-610 (1953).
3. 12 Wheat 22, 331 (1827).
4. Ganoe, *The Passing of the Old Dissent*, 21 Or. L. Rev. 286 (1942).
5. The Concept of Law 138 (New York: Oxford University Press, 1961).
6. *Civil Disobedience in a Constitutional Democracy*, Philosophic Exchange 104 (1970). "Morality" here broadly refers to that which is considered "good" or "valuable." Additional discussions may be found in Power, *Civil Disobedience as Functional Opposition*, 34 J. Pol. 37 (1972); and On Civil Disobedience in Recent American Democratic Thought, 64 Am. Pol. Sci. Rev. 35 (1970); Spitz, *Democracy and the Problem of Civil Disobedience*, 48 Am. Pol. Sci. Rev. 386 (1954).
7. Black, *The Two Faces of Civil Disobedience*, 1 Soc. Theory & Prac. 21 (1970).
8. *Id.* at 22.
9. Morano, *Civil Disobedience and Legal Responsibility*, 5 J. Value Inquiry 193 (1971).
10. Cohen, *supra* n. 6, at 99.
11. Black, *supra* n. 7, at 22.
12. Frazier, *Between Obedience and Revolution*, 1 Phil. & Pub. Aff. 316 (1972).
13. Endres, *Civil Disobedience and Modern Democracy*, 43 Thought 503 (1968).
14. Martin, *Civil Disobedience*, 80 Ethics 136 (1970).
15. *Id.*
16. "Persuade" here refers to the process of influencing, not necessarily the result.
17. Simmons, *Use and Abuse of Dissenting Opinions*, 16 La. L. Rev. 498 (1956).
18. Musmanno, *Dissenting Opinions*, 6 Kan. L. Rev. 411 (1958).
19. Davis and Reynolds, *Juridical Cripples: Plurality Opinions in the Supreme Court*, 1974 Duke L. J. 63 (1974).
21. Carter, *Dissenting Opinions*, 4 Hastings L. J. 121 (1953).

22. Hughes, as quoted in Edwards, *Dissenting Opinions of Mr. Justice Smith*, 34 U. Det. L. J. 82 (1956).
23. Frazier, *supra* n. 12, at 317.
24. Ingber, *Procedure, Ceremony and Rhetoric: The Minimization of Ideological Conflict in Deviance Control*, 56 B. U. L. Rev. 321 (1976).
25. Williams, *Language and the Law*, 62 L. Q. Rev. 71 (1945).
26. Pranger, *An Explanation for Why Final Political Authority is Necessary*, 60 Am. Pol. Sci. Rev. 996 (1966).
27. Probert, *Law Through the Looking Glass of Language and Communicative Behavior*, 20 J. Legal Educ. 51 (1968).
28. Hart, *supra* n. 5, at 121.
29. *Id.* at 220.
30. Probert, *supra* n. 27, at 51.
31. *Id.*
32. Ulmer, *Dissent Behavior and the Social Background of Supreme Court Justices*, 32 J. Pol. 581 (1970).
33. These examples, along with others, are discussed in detail in Barth, Prophets With Honor: Great Dissents and Great Dissenters in the Supreme Court (New York: Random House, 1974, 1975). For additional examples *see* Carter, *supra* n. 21; Brown, *A Dissenting Opinion of Mr. Justice Story Enacted as Law Within Thirty-Six Days*, 26 Va. L. Rev. 759 (1940); Ganoe, *supra* n. 4, at 295; Lashly and Rava, *The Supreme Court Dissents*, 28 Wash. U. L. Q. 191 (1943); Sanders, *The Role of Dissenting Opinions in Louisiana*, 23 La. L. Rev. 676 (1963); and McWhinney, *supra* n. 2, at 611.
34. 163 U.S. 537 (1896).
35. 347 U.S. 483 (1954).
36. 316 U.S. 455 (1942).
37. 372 U.S. 335 (1963).
38. 341 U.S. 494 (1951).
39. 354 U.S. 298 (1957).
40. Brown, *supra* n. 33, at 759.
41. 2 U.S. 419 (1793).
42. Carter, *supra* n. 21, at 119.
43. Musmanno, *supra* n. 18, at 140.
44. 3 Howard 236, 252 (1845).
45. Brown, *supra* n. 33, at 760. For additional examples *see* Fuld, *Voices of Dissent*, 62 Col. L. Rev. 927 (1962).
46. Freedman, *Dissenting Opinions and Justice Musmanno*, 30 Temp. L. Q. 253 (1957).
47. Sanders, *supra* n. 33, at 675.
48. Jackson, *Dissenting Opinions*, 100 Pittsburgh L. J. 3 (1952).
49. Carter, *supra* n. 21, at 118.
50. Ingber, *supra* n. 24, at 269.
51. Stephens, *Function of Concurring and Dissenting Opinions in Courts of Last Resort*, 5 U. Fla. L. Rev. 404 (1952).
52. Douglas, America Challenged 4-5 (Princeton, NJ: Princeton University Press, 1960).
53. Douglas, We The Judges 443 (Garden City, NY: Doubleday, 1956).
54. Cardozo, Law and Literature and Other Essays and Addresses 36 (New York: Harcourt, Brace & Co., 1931).
55. Llewellyn, The Common Law Tradition: Deciding Appeals 26 (Boston: Little, Brown & Co., 1960).
56. Douglas, *supra* n. 20, at 104.
57. Pollack v. Farmers Loan and Trust Co., 157 U.S. 429, 608.
58. Federal Trade Comm'n v. Beechnut Co., 257 U.S. 441, 456 (1922).
59. Llewellyn, *supra* n. 55, at 463. For a discussion of non-majority opinions as anathema to Continental European jurists, *see* Dumbauld, *Dissenting Opinions in International Adjudication*, 90 U. Pa. L. Rev. 929 (1943); *see also* Fuld, *supra* n. 45, at 924-925.

The Supreme Court and precedent: an analysis of natural courts and reversal trends

Although some critics maintain the Rehnquist Court is undermining the doctrine of stare decisis, *historically precedents have been reversed during periods in which changing majorities reassess old law in an attempt to give new life to constitutional jurisprudence.*

by Christopher P. Banks

In his last opinion as a justice of the U.S. Supreme Court, Thurgood Marshall, dissenting in *Payne v. Tennessee,*[1] sharply criticized the majority for undermining the doctrine of *stare decisis.*[2] In *Payne,* the Court overturned two cases[3] that had held that victim-impact statements were inadmissible in the sentencing phase of a capital trial. In Justice Marshall's words, "power, not reason, is the new currency of [the] Court's decision-making."[4] In large measure, the basis for his criticism was that changes in the Court's rulings and the precedential value of *stare decisis* reflected simply the dramatic changes in the Court's composition in the last few years. In Justice Marshall's view, the *Payne* majority transformed *stare decisis* into nothing more than a reflection of who was sitting on the bench at a particular time.[5] Accordingly, for Justice Marshall, *Payne* signals "an unmistakable course" for overturning precedents by a new majority on a Rehnquist Court bent on a "radical reconstruction of the rules" governing the doctrine of *stare decisis* and constitutional law.[6]

Justice Marshall is no doubt correct. More to the point, the present Rehnquist Court, like other Courts in our country's history, exhibits a pattern of decision making that threatens the value of precedents. Nor was Justice Marshall alone in criticizing the Rehnquist Court's assault on *stare decisis.*

In a recent speech, retired Justice Lewis F. Powell Jr. warned of the "threats" to the doctrine, and he admonished the Court to adhere to past law more carefully by exercising more judicial restraint.[7] To be sure, neither the justices nor Court watchers are of one mind as to the value of *stare decisis.* At least one commentator has proclaimed that *stare decisis* is "dead,"[8] while others argue that a new theory of "constitutional" or "statutory" *stare decisis* is needed because of the Rehnquist Court's propensity to overturn cases.[9]

Constitutional "flux"

In historical perspective, critics of the Rehnquist Court's view of *stare decisis*, including retired justices Marshall and Powell, are only partly correct about the significance of the Court's reconsideration of precedent and the doctrine of *stare decisis.* Historically, personnel changes on the Court have directly affected reversal trends in the short term, but their ultimate impact on the development of the rule of law is, arguably, negligible over time. Simply put, when the Supreme Court overturns past rulings, it frequently does so precisely because the Court's composition has changed, often dramatically, in a short time period. Concomitant with changes in the Court's composition is a process of reexamining precedent by those justices confronting the issues the first time. To be sure, this process may well result in a time in which constitutional law in many areas is in "flux,"[10] as new members of the Court establish their own positions on the issues of the day, and a majority coalesces on the bench.

Justice Marshall and other critics of the Rehnquist Court correctly point up the fact that the Court is more prone to reversing precedent during times in which its composition changes sharply and new majorities emerge on the high bench. But Justice Marshall and the other critics incorrectly suggest that *stare decisis* is dead or dying. Nor is the implication plausible that the Court in overturning precedents is acting illegitimately or extraordinarily.

On the contrary, the Court's overturning of precedents may be entirely expected, if not welcomed, given the process of change or "flux" that invariably occurs whenever the Court's membership changes and one "natural Court"[11] yields to another. Tables 1 through 5 indicate that historically the Court by and large has adhered to precedent. But they also show that when the Court's composition changes dramatically in relatively short time spans, periods of increased reversals of prior rulings are likely to result.

Two caveats about the tables, however, should be considered. First, the data do not illustrate reversal trends and flux patterns relating to all precedents that were implicitly overturned, as is the case when precedents are "distinguished." Thus, reasonable minds may differ on the number of re-

versals accounted for in any given period. Second, the number of decisions reversed is likely to increase over time simply because there are more available precedents to overturn as the volume of rulings increases. Yet these limitations do not diminish the conclusion that changes from one natural Court to another affect reversal trends.

Constitutional or statutory case?

Table 1 summarizes the Supreme Court's overturning of precedent throughout the Court's history. The data show the number of reversals of prior rulings within a specific Court and the extent to which those reversals have involved either constitutional or statutory cases. Although the number and percentage of reversals of precedent is significant, it is important to distinguish between the Court's reversal of constitutional versus statutory cases. As Justice Louis D. Brandeis once explained, the Court is likely to give more deference to precedent involving statutory rulings and less deference to those concerning interpretations of the Constitution because the legislature, and not the Court, should correct bad statutory rulings, whereas the Court, and not Congress, should rectify wrongly decided constitutional decisions.[12]

But as Table 1 shows, the Supreme Court mainly has adhered to the rule of law. Prior to 1930, only the Waite Court reversed more than 10 cases, and it did so over the course of 14 terms. Also, none of the pre-1930 Courts produced any meaningful percentage of reversals (all are less than 10 percent for both statutory and constitutional precedents).

Table 1   The percentage of total overturns, United States Supreme Court, by chief justice term (1789 to 1991)

Chief justice	Overturns	Number of Const.	Stat.	Percentage of Const.	Stat.	Percentage of overturns
Marshall (1801-1835)	3	0	1	0.0	0.5	2.0
Taney (1836-1864)	4	1	2	0.5	1.0	1.5
Chase (1864-1873)	4	0	3	0.0	1.5	2.0
Waite (1874-1888)	13	5	4	2.5	2.0	6.5
Fuller (1888-1910)	4	1	1	0.5	0.5	2.0
White (1910-1921)	5	2	2	1.0	1.0	2.5
Taft (1921-1930)	6	3	1	1.5	0.5	3.0
Hughes (1930-1941)	21	15	5	7.5	2.5	10.4
Stone (1941-1945)	15	9	3	4.5	1.5	7.5
Vinson (1946-1953)	13	8	3	4.0	1.5	6.5
Warren (1953-1969)	45	30	14	15.0	7.0	22.4
Burger (1969-1986)	52	36	11	18.0	5.5	25.9
Rehnquist (1986-1991)	16	11	4	5.5	2.0	8.0
Total:	201	121	54	60.5	27.0	100.2*

*The percentage of excluded cases is 12.5 percent. Cases that could not meaningfully be classified as "constitutional" or "statutory" were excluded from the analysis.
  Note: Percentages were derived by dividing the number of overturn decisions in the chief justice term at issue by the total number of overturns of the Court as a whole. For example, the Rehnquist Court overturned 16 cases: 11 "constitutional" cases and 4 "statutory" cases. Thus, for that chief justice tenure, the percentages are as follows: for constitutional cases, 5.5 percent (11/201); for statutory cases, 2.0 percent (4/201); and, for total overturns, 8.0 percent (16/201). All percentages are subject to rounding error. Since there were no overturns for the Jay (1789 to 1795), Rutledge (1795 to 1795) or Ellsworth (1796 to 1800) tenures, the results of the table begin with the Marshall Court.

Although since 1930 more precedents have fallen, the rate of reversals is not high, comparatively speaking. Out of a total of 13 Courts in which precedents were reversed, only three overturned cases in any significant number. These were the Hughes Court (21 overturns during 11 terms), the Warren Court (45 overturns during 16 terms), and the Burger Court (52 overturns during 17 terms). Table 1 shows that these three Courts were responsible for more than half (58.7 percent) of all reversals in the Supreme Court's history.

More significantly, as Table 2 reveals, the percentage of reversals for the Courts headed by Hughes (1.25 percent), Warren (2.54 percent), and Burger (2.00 percent) is quite low when considered in light of the total number of written decisions handed down during the relevant spans of their respective stewardships.[13] And, of those three Courts, none displayed less respect for statutory cases. Indeed, on balance, none of the Courts in Table 1 overturned more statutory cases than constitutional cases. Each exhibited respect for both statutory and constitutional precedent. While the percentage of constitutional reversals is higher than statutory reversals, the highest percentages occurred in the Burger (18 percent) and Warren (15 percent) Courts. As expected, then, the numbers and percentages compiled in tables 1 and 2 suggest that the Court generally adheres to the Brandeisian notion of showing more deference to statutory rulings and less to constitutional ones.

Majorities and natural Courts

Significantly, the data presented in tables 3, 4, and 5 also indicate that the issue of *when* precedent falls is often resolved by who is collectively sitting on the Court at a particular time. The tables are designed to show the relationship between natural Courts and stability of precedent—that is, whether past decisions are more subject to reversal in those times when Court membership is reconstituted through the ebb and flow of the appointment process. They also suggest that the changes of membership on the Court reflect democratic influences on the Court through the presidential election and judicial appointment processes. Accordingly, since the Court's composition is determined by whom the president picks to sit on the high bench, the rate of reversals, or constitutional "flux," is good evidence of how the Court may be held democratically accountable and brought into line with the prevailing national political coalition.

Specifically, Table 3 provides an overview of the natural Courts (in a given chief justice's term) that have produced the greatest percentage of reversals, both in terms of constitutional and statutory precedents. While the sheer volume of natural Courts occurring in a particular chief justice tenure is not entirely conclusive[14] as to whether more precedents will be overturned, Table 3 identifies the periods when particular natural Courts have been more prone to overturning cases. Table 4, on the other hand, summarizes overturns relative to significant transition periods in the Court's history. Table 4 also indicates which natural Courts have been most active in overturning cases. Finally, Table 5 shows the number of cases overturned relative to the number of cases decided during the Court's most activist periods.

When read together, the tables thus support the proposition that precedents are likely to fall during a transitional process in which changing majorities reassess old law in an attempt to give new life to constitutional jurisprudence. For instance, Table 3 specifically demonstrates which natural Courts have been responsible for overturning the highest number and percentage of cases. Table 3 indicates that the 16th natural Court of the Hughes Court reversed 28.6 percent of precedent; the fifth natural Court of the Stone Court overturned 53.3 percent of precedent; the first natural Court of the Vinson Court reversed 84.6 percent of precedent; the 13th natural Court of the Warren Court over-

Table 2   The percentage of reversals in light of total number of cases decided by full written opinion for the Hughes, Warren, and Burger Courts

Chief justice and terms	Total number of overturns	Total number of written opinions	Percentage of overturns
Hughes 1930 to 1940	21	1,686	1.25
Warren 1953 to 1968	45	1,770	2.54
Burger 1969 to 1986	52	2,598	2.00

Note: The total number of written opinions decided in the Court was compiled with data obtained from the Clerk's Office, United States Supreme Court. Percentages were derived by dividing the number of reversals into the total number of written opinions issued in the relevant period.

turned 31.1 percent of precedent; and the seventh natural Court of the Burger Court reversed 42.3 percent of precedent. While these percentages are illustrative, it is important to put them in context with the various membership changes that preceded the natural Court under examination.

With the exception of the Vinson Court,[15] each one of the natural Courts above were the product of multiple membership changes, sometimes occurring in bunches, that reconstituted the preexisting majority on the bench. These reconstitutions signaled a shift in constitutional law as the newly appointed justices reexamined precedent when deciding cases. Thus, not surprisingly, past law began to fall as the new members of the Court established their positions in newly created ideological voting blocs.

The Hughes, Warren, and Burger Courts

An analysis of the key membership changes in the Hughes, Warren, and Burger Courts provides insight on how new majorities are created that, in turn, begin a period of constitutional flux and an increasing questioning of past constitutional principles. For example, between June 2, 1937, and July 8, 1941, the Hughes Court's membership was en-

Table 3   A summary of the percentage of natural Court overturns, United States Supreme Court, 1801-1991

Natural courts Date	Total number/overturns Ovtrns.	Const.	Stat.	Percent of overturns/nat. cts. Const.	Stat.	Exc.*	Percent
Marshall 1801 to 1836 (21 NC)	3	0	1	0.0	33.0	67.0	100.0
*# of Exclusions: 2							
Taney 1836 to 1864 (25 NC)	4	1	2	25.0	50.0	25.0	100.0
* # of Exclusions: 1							
Chase 1864 to 1873 (9 NC)							
N3 07/05/67 to 01/31/70	2	0	1	0.0	25.0	25.0	50.0
N6 03/23/70 to 11/28/72	2	0	2	0.0	50.0	0.0	50.0
Total:	4	0	3	0.0	75.0	25.0	100.0
* # of Exclusions: N3, 1; N6, 0. Total: 1.							
Waite 1874 to 1888 (14 NC)							
N1 03/04/74 to 03/04/77	2	0	2	0.0	15.4	0.0	15.4
N2 03/04/77 to 12/10/77	1	0	0	0.0	0.0	7.7	7.7
N3 12/10/77 to 12/14/80	1	0	0	0.0	0.0	7.7	7.7
N5 01/05/81 to 01/24/81	1	0	1	0.0	7.7	0.0	7.7
N6 01/24/81 to 05/17/81	1	1	0	7.7	0.0	0.0	7.7
N11 04/03/82 to 05/14/87	4	1	1	7.7	7.7	15.4	30.8
N12 05/14/87 to 01/18/88	2	2	0	15.4	0.0	0.0	15.4
N14 03/23/88 to 10/08/88	1	1	0	7.7	0.0	0.0	7.7
Total:	13	5	4	38.0	31.0	31.0	100.0
* # of Exclusions: N2, 1; N3, 1; N11, 2. Total: 4.							
Fuller 1888 to 1910 (28 NC)							
N3 01/06/90 to 10/13/90	1	1	0	25.0	0.0	0.0	25.0
N6 01/22/92 to 10/10/92	1	0	0	0.0	0.0	25.0	25.0
N11 03/12/94 to 08/08/95	2	0	1	0.0	25.0	25.0	50.0
Total:	4	1	1	25.0	25.0	50.0	100.0
* # of Exclusions: N6, 1; N11, 1. Total: 2.							
White 1910 to 1921 (11 NC)							
N4 03/18/12 to 07/12/14	1	1	0	20.0	0.0	0.0	20.0
N9 06/10/16 to 10/09/16	1	0	1	0.0	20.0	0.0	20.0
N10 10/09/16 to 05/19/21	3	1	1	20.0	20.0	20.0	60.0
Total:	5	2	2	40.0	40.0	20.0	100.0
* # of Exclusions: N10, 1. Total: 1.							
Taft 1921 to 1930 (10 NC)							
N1 07/11/21 to 09/18/22	1	1	0	16.7	0.0	0.0	16.7
N6 01/02/23 to 02/19/23	1	0	1	0.0	16.7	0.0	16.7
N9 03/02/25 to 02/03/30	4	2	0	33.3	0.0	33.3	66.6
Total:	6	3	1	50.0	17.0	33.0	100.0
* # of Exclusions: N9, 2. Total: 2.							
Hughes 1930 to 1941 (18 NC)							
N3 06/02/30 to 01/12/32	2	1	1	4.8	4.8	0.0	9.6
N5 03/14/32 to 06/02/37	4	3	0	14.2	0.0	4.8	19.0
N7 08/19/37 to 01/17/38	1	1	0	4.8	0.0	0.0	4.8
N9 01/31/38 to 07/09/38	2	1	1	4.8	4.8	0.0	9.6
N12 02/13/39 to 04/17/39	2	2	0	9.5	0.0	0.0	9.5
N13 04/17/39 to 11/16/39	1	0	1	0.0	4.8	0.0	4.8
N14 11/16/39 to 02/05/40	2	1	1	4.8	4.8	0.0	9.6
N15 02/05/40 to 01/31/41	1	1	0	4.8	0.0	0.0	4.8
N16 01/31/41 to 06/30/41	6	5	1	23.8	4.8	0.0	28.6
Total:	21	15	5	71.0	24.0	5.0	100.0
* # of Exclusions: N5, 1; Total: 1.							

tirely transformed by the number of opportunities given President Franklin D. Roosevelt to appoint justices to the Supreme Court. During this period, justices Willis Van Devanter (June 2, 1937), George Sutherland (January 17, 1938), Benjamin Cardozo (July 9, 1938), Louis D. Brandeis (February 13, 1939), Pierce Butler (November 16, 1939), and James Clark McReynolds (January 31, 1941) all left the bench.[16] Their replacements—justices Hugo L. Black (August 19, 1937), Stanley F. Reed (January 31, 1938), Felix Frankfurter (January 30, 1939), William O. Douglas (April 17, 1939), Frank Murphy (February 5, 1940), and James F. Byrnes (July 8, 1941)—in the main constituted a new liberal voting bloc that stimulated a reexamination

of precedent from a solid pro-New Deal perspective.[17] Table 3 illustrates that 15 of the 21 overturns in the Hughes Court took place between the seventh and 16th natural Courts. Tables 4 and 5 chart the upward reversal trends accordingly and, not surprisingly, show that the trend continued into the Stone era up to 1943.[18]

In the Warren Court, a similar link between membership reconstitution and reversals is apparent, especially in the period from 1962 to 1968. Prior to 1962, the Court largely had been dominated by Justice Frankfurter's advocacy, which primarily promoted a doctrine of judicial restraint. After Frankfurter's retirement in 1962, however, the Court moved in a much stronger pro-civil lib-

Table 3 (continued)

Natural courts Date	Total number/overturns Ovtrns.	Const.	Stat.	Percent of overturns/nat. cts. Const.	Stat.	Exc.*	Percent
Stone 1941 to 1945 (8 NC)							
N3 07/11/41 to 10/03/42	4	3	1	20.0	6.7	0.0	26.7
N4 10/03/42 to 02/15/43	2	1	1	6.7	6.7	0.0	13.4
N5 02/15/43 to 07/31/45	8	5	0	33.3	0.0	20.0	53.3
N7 10/01/45 to 04/22/46	1	0	1	0.0	6.7	0.0	6.7
Total:	15	9	3	60.0	20.0	20.0	100.0
* # of Excluded Cases: N5, 3. Total: 3.							
Vinson 1946 to 1953 (6 NC)							
N1 06/24/46 to 07/19/49	11	6	3	46.1	23.0	15.4	84.6
N5 10/12/49 to 09/08/53	2	2	0	15.4	0.0	0.0	15.4
Total:	13	8	3	62.0	23.0	15.0	100.0
*# of Exclusions: N1, 2. Total: 2.							
Warren 1953 to 1969 (18 NC)							
N1 10/05/53 to 10/09/54	1	1	0	2.2	0.0	0.0	2.2
N2 10/09/54 to 03/28/55	1	0	1	0.0	2.2	0.0	2.2
N5 10/16/56 to 02/25/57	1	1	0	2.2	0.0	0.0	2.2
N7 03/27/57 to 10/13/58	2	2	0	4.4	0.0	0.0	4.4
N9 10/14/58 to 03/31/62	6	3	3	6.7	6.7	0.0	13.4
N13 01/10/62 to 07/25/65	14	9	4	20.0	8.9	2.2	31.1
N15 10/04/65 to 06/12/67	9	7	2	15.6	4.4	0.0	20.0
N17 10/02/67 to 05/14/69	8	4	4	8.9	8.9	0.0	17.8
N18 05/14/69 to 06/23/69	3	3	0	6.7	0.0	0.0	6.7
Total:	45	30	14	67.0	31.0	2.2	100.0
# of Exclusions: N13, 1. Total: 1.							
Burger 1969 to 1986 (9 NC)							
N1 06/23/69 to 06/09/70	2	1	1	1.9	1.9	0.0	3.8
N2 06/09/70 to 09/17/71	6	3	2	5.8	3.8	1.9	11.5
N5 01/07/72 to 11/12/75	10	7	2	13.5	3.8	1.9	19.2
N7 12/19/75 to 07/03/81	22	15	4	28.8	7.7	5.8	42.3
N9 09/15/81 to 09/26/86	12	10	2	19.2	3.8	0.0	23.0
Total:	52	36	11	69.0	21.0	10.0	100.0
* # of Exclusions: N2, 1; N5, 1; N7, 3. Total: 5.							
Rehnquist 1986 to 1991 (5 NC)							
N1 09/26/86 to 06/27/87	3	2	1	12.5	6.3	0.0	18.8
N3 02/18/88 to 07/20/90	8	5	2	31.3	12.5	6.3	50.0
N5 10/09/90 to 10/24/91	5	4	1	25.0	6.3	0.0	31.3
Total:	16	11	4	69.0	25.0	6.3	100.0
* # of Exclusions: N3, 1. Total: 1.							

Note: With the exception of the Marshall and Taney Courts, percentages were computed by dividing the number of overturn decisions by the total number of overturns in the chief justice term at issue. For example, for the fifth natural Court in the Rehnquist Court there were a total of 16 overturns. Four cases were "constitutional" and one was "statutory". Thus, the percentages were as follows: 25.0 percent were constitutional cases (4/16); 6.3 percent were statutory cases (1/16); and the total percentage for that natural Court was 31.3 percent (5/16). Due to excluded cases, the total percentages do not equal 100 percent. Consequently, the difference between 100 percent and the total sum of percentages for constitutional and statutory cases represents the percentage of excluded cases for that chief justice tenure. All percentages are subject to rounding error.

Since all of the specific dates of reversals were not available for the Marshall and Taney Courts, overturns occurring in their respective periods could not be placed into their natural Courts. Hence, the natural Court data for those Courts are not included in the analysis.

ertarian direction. Already on the Court were justices Black (1937), Douglas (1939), Earl Warren (1953), and William J. Brennan (1956). With the departure of justices Frankfurter and Charles Whittaker,[19] this liberal bloc became a solid working majority with the appointments of justices Arthur Goldberg (October 1, 1962), Abe Fortas (October 4, 1965), and Marshall (October 2, 1967).[20] Consequently, 34 of 45 precedents overturned by the Warren Court were between January 1962 and June 1969.[21]

The liberal bloc established in the Warren years gradually gave way to another reconstitution, this time on the Burger Court. Perhaps one of the more surprising results presented in Table 3 is that the Burger Court had more overturns (52) than its predecessor (45). Table 3 indicates that most (22) occurred in natural Court seven, the period from November 12, 1975, (the date of Justice Douglas's retirement) to July 3, 1981 (the date of Justice

Table 4   Summary of overturns relative to important transition periods, by natural Court, United States Supreme Court

	Natural Courts	No. of overturns	Percent
1937 to 1943 (Hughes)*			
1937	N7 08/19/37-01/17/38	1	4.8
	N9 01/31/38-07/09/38	2	9.6
1938	N12 02/13/39-04/17/39	2	9.5
	N13 04/17/39-11/16/39	1	4.8
1939	N14 11/16/39-02/05/40	2	9.6
	N15 02/05/40-01/31/41	1	4.8
1940	N16 01/31/41-06/30/41	6	28.6
*Percentages based upon 21 total overturns occurring in Hughes Court.			
(Stone)*			
1941	N3 07/11/41-10/03/42	4	26.7
1942	N4 10/03/42-02/15/43	2	13.4
	N5 02/15/43-07/31/45	3	
1943	N5 02/15/43-07/31/45	5	53.3
*Percentages based upon 15 total overturns occurring in Stone Court.			
N.B. Total overturns for NC 5: 8 (8/15 = 53.3%)			
1946 to 1948 (Vinson)*			
1946	N1 06/24/46 to 07/19/49	4	
1947	N1 06/24/46 to 07/19/49	2	
1948	N1 06/24/46 to 07/19/49	5	84.6
*Percentages based upon 13 total overturns occurring in Vinson Court.			
N.B. Total overturns for NC 1: 11 (11/13 = 84.6%)			
1962 to 1968 (Warren)*			
1962	N13 01/10/62 to 07/25/65	6	
1963	N13 01/10/62 to 07/25/65	6	
1964	N13 01/10/62 to 07/25/65	2	31.1
1965	N15 10/04/65 to 06/12/67	3	
1966	N15 10/04/65 to 06/12/67	6	20.0
1967	N17 10/02/67 to 05/14/69	7	
1968	N17 10/02/67 to 05/14/69	1	17.8
*Percentages based upon 45 total overturns occurring in Warren Court.			
N.B. Total overturns for NC 13: 14 (14/45 = 31.1%)			
Total overturns for NC 15: 9 (9/45 = 20.0%)			
Total overturns for NC 17: 8 (8/45 = 17.8%)			
1975 to 1980 (Burger)*			
1975	N7 12/19/75 to 07/03/81	9	
1976	N7 12/19/75 to 07/03/81	4	
1977	N7 12/19/75 to 07/03/81	4	
1978	N7 12/19/75 to 07/03/81	2	
1979	N7 12/19/75 to 07/03/81	2	
1980	N7 12/19/75 to 07/03/81	1	42.3
*Percentages based upon 52 total overturns occurring in Burger Court.			
1987 to 1991 (Rehnquist)*			
1987	N3 02/18/88 to 07/20/90	2	
1988	N3 02/18/88 to 07/20/90	4	
1989	N3 02/18/88 to 07/20/90	2	50.0
1990	N5 10/09/90 to 11/01/91	5	31.3
*Percentages based upon 16 total overturns occurring in Rehnquist Court.			
N.B. Total overturns for N3: 8 (8/16 = 50.0%)			
Total overturns for N5: 5 (5/16 = 31.3%)			

Note: All percentages subject to rounding error.

Potter Stewart's retirement). Also, this table demonstrates that natural Court nine was responsible for 12 reversals. Natural Court nine was created by the appointment of Justice Sandra Day O'Connor on September 15, 1981, and ended with the departure of Chief Justice Warren E. Burger on September 26, 1986.[22] Thirty-four of 52 reversals occurred between the seventh and ninth natural Courts. Interestingly, tables 3 and 4 indicate that natural Courts seven (42.3 percent) and nine (23.0 percent) reversed a total of 65.3 percent of precedent between 1975 and 1986, thus making it a fairly active Court.

The Burger Court's reconstitution is not as easy to explain in terms of constitutional flux than the one that transpired during the Hughes or Warren Court years. But it is likely that much of its reversal activity can be attributed to the departure of Justice Douglas in 1975. Two new justices ascended to the Court in 1972: justices William H. Rehnquist (January 7, 1972) and Powell (January 7, 1972). At that time, with Chief Justice Burger and Justice Harry A. Blackmun already on the bench,[23] these

conservative/moderate appointments to the Court explain the emergence of a period of flux that gradually affected the constitutional jurisprudence established during the Warren Court years. In other words, as new justices assumed the bench, precedent began to be reexamined and fall. This pattern, however, must be weighed in light of the contradictory data offered in Table 5. In this table, the reversal trend produced from natural Court seven in the Burger Court era is markedly downward when considered in light of the total number of written opinions decided during the relevant period.

All of the other Courts in Table 5 show a pattern of flux; for Burger's natural Court seven, however, only one year (1975) shows a high number of reversals (nine) and, thereafter, a steadily diminishing number of reversals. The explanation is that Justice Douglas's departure probably had an immediate, short-term effect but one that diminished with time. In many ways, Justice Douglas was an important liberal vote on many of the civil liberties cases confronting the Warren Court. Af-

Table 5   **Total number of cases overturned in relation to total number of cases decided, by term and natural courts, in most activist periods, United States Supreme Court (1789 to 1991)**

Transition periods	Nat. cts.	Ch. just.	#/ovtrns.	#/opinions*	%/ovtrns.
1937 to 1943					
1937	N7, N9	Hughes	3	152	1.97
1938	N12, N13	Hughes	3	139	2.15
1939	N14, N15	Hughes	3	137	2.19
1940	N16	Hughes	6	165	3.63
1941	N3	Stone	4	151	2.65
1942	N4, N5	Stone	5	147	3.40
1943	N5	Stone	5	130	3.85
1946 to 1948					
1946	N1	Vinson	4	142	2.82
1947	N1	Vinson	2	110	1.82
1948	N1	Vinson	5	114	4.39
1962 to 1967					
1962	N13	Warren	6	129	4.65
1963	N13	Warren	6	131	4.58
1964	N13	Warren	2	108	1.85
1965	N15	Warren	3	105	2.86
1966	N15	Warren	6	115	5.22
1967	N17	Warren	7	127	5.51
1975 to 1980					
1975	N7	Burger	9	146	6.16
1976	N7	Burger	4	145	2.76
1977	N7	Burger	4	138	2.90
1978	N7	Burger	2	137	1.46
1979	N7	Burger	2	141	1.42
1980	N7	Burger	1	132	0.76
1987 to 1991					
1987	N3	Rehnquist	2	147	1.36
1988	N3	Rehnquist	4	133	3.01
1989	N3	Rehnquist	2	129	1.55
1990	N5	Rehnquist	5	112	4.46

* The number of opinions refers to the number of full written opinions decided in the relevant term. Data was obtained from the Office of the Clerk, United States Supreme Court.

Note: All percentages are derived by dividing the number of overturns into the number of opinions for the relevant period. Percentages are subject to rounding error.

ter President Nixon's appointment of Chief Justice Burger in 1969 and Justice Douglas's retirement in 1975, three other Nixon appointees, justices Blackmun, Rehnquist, and Powell,[24] had already begun a retrenchment of the progressive civil liberties jurisprudence established during the Warren Court era.[25] Notably, since Justice Douglas was quite ill during his last few years on the Court, he was not as strong an advocate as in past years of Court service. Thus Justice Douglas's absence on the bench most likely had a short-term effect on precedent, but it dissipated with time as a new majority began to make its own mark in constitutional politics. In any event, notwithstanding the data contained in Table 5 and regardless of Justice Douglas's single importance as a liberal vote, the results in Table 3 reveal the constitutional flux during the Burger Court years from 1969 to 1986.

The Rehnquist Court

Finally, the recent appointments to the Rehnquist Court (from 1986 to 1991) bring the issue of constitutional flux again to the forefront of constitutional law. The data contained in the tables reveal a reversal trend that is consistent with the decision-making patterns established with the Hughes, Warren, and Burger Court reconstitutions. With the retirements of justices Powell (1987), Brennan (1990), and Marshall (1991), a new, more firmly ensconced conservative majority has formed with the additions of justices Anthony Kennedy (1988), David Souter (1990), and Clarence Thomas (1991). From 1987 to 1990, for example, 13 precedents fell as the new justices (with the exception of Thomas) began to reevaluate past law and define their respective ideological positions on the Court. Table 5, in particular, suggests the flux well. And, while natural Courts three and five have been the source of most of the reversals, it is submitted that the next natural Court (created by the departure of Justice Marshall and the appointment of Justice Thomas) will produce more *stare decisis* turmoil as Justice Thomas seeks to define the parameters of his constitutional philosophy as a new jurist.

Despite the critics, however, it should be recalled that the process Justice Douglas identified as "constitutional flux" is not inimical to the doctrine of *stare decisis* as a whole. The clarion call that precedent is no longer viable has more ring than substance. It is largely a hollow cry, because it fails to take into account that constitutional law inexorably changes with an evolving society or the Court's composition. In this perspective, the transitory periods that account for short-term upheavals of law are more beneficial than harmful for constitutional law and the Court.

Accordingly, the critics of *stare decisis* should heed the immortal words of Chief Justice Marshall that "we must never forget, that it is a *constitution* we are expounding."[26] Only then will they truly grasp the significance of reversal trends naturally occurring throughout the history of the U.S. Supreme Court.

NOTES

This article originally appeared in Volume 75, Number 5, February-March 1992, pages 262-268.

The author wishes to thank sincerely David O'Brien, professor of government at the University of Virginia, for his generous time, patience, and assistance in formulating and completing this article. An equal measure of gratitude is extended to Bob Campbell at the University of Virginia's Academic Consulting Center and my wife, Diane, for her endless tolerance and support. © 1992, Christopher P. Banks, Esq.

1. Payne v. Tennessee, 59 U.S.L.W. 4814 (1991).

2. "Stare Decisis et non quieta movere" means that a court should adhere to precedent and not unsettle things which are established. 20 *Am. Jur.* 2d "Courts" Sec. 183 (1965). *See also* Stevens, *The Life Span Of Judge Made Rule*, 58 N.Y.U. L. REV. 1, 1 (1982) n. 1 (stating that the above quotation means "to stand by the decision and not disturb settled points.")

3. Booth v. Maryland, 482 U.S. 496 (1987) and South Carolina v. Gathers, 490 U.S. 805 (1989).

4. Payne, *supra* n. 1, at 4823.

5. As Marshall wrote, "It takes little real detective work to discern just what has changed since this Court decided *Booth* and *Gathers*: this Court's own personnel." *Id.* at 4825. Justice Marshall also roundly criticized the Court for creating a new, more flexible standard of judicial review that suggested that certain precedents (albeit cases expressing libertarian principles) will inevitably fall: that the full protection of *stare decisis* will be afforded only to those cases involving property or contract rights and to those decisions that were not decided by a 5-4 vote.

6. *Id.* at 4826.

7. Powell, *Stare Decisis and Judicial Restraint*, 47 WASH. & LEE L. REV. 281, 287-289 (1990) (A reprint of Justice Powell's remarks given at the Association of the Bar of the City of New York on October 17, 1989, in memory of Leslie H. Arps).

8. Maltz, *Some Thoughts On The Death Of Stare Decisis In Constitutional Law*, 1980 WISC. L. REV. 467 (1980).

9. *See e.g.* Note, *Constitutional Stare Decisis*, 103 HARV. L. REV. 1344 (1990) (arguing that a doctrine of constitutional *stare decisis* should be adopted by the Supreme Court); Marshall, *'Let Congress Do It': The Case For An Absolute Rule Of Statutory Stare Decisis*, 88 U. MICH. L. REV. 177 (1989) (arguing for an "absolute" theory of interpretation relative to statutory cases).

10. Douglas, *Stare Decisis*, 49 COL. L. REV. 735, 736-737 (1949). *See generally* O'Brien, and Collins, *Power Over Precedent: The Supreme Court Today*, CHRISTIAN SCIENCE MONITOR 16 July 1991, at 19.

11. A "natural Court" is one in which the Court's membership remains stable for any given time period. When the

composition of the Court changes, a new natural Court emerges and remains constant until the next alteration. Thus, a natural Court is created whenever a justice of the Supreme Court either assumes a seat on the bench after taking oath or departs from the bench by reason of resignation, retirement, or death. Impeachment would also trigger the creation of a new natural Court, but no sitting justice has been impeached to date; therefore, for purposes of this study it is not employed as a triggering event.

In constructing the natural Courts, the following sources were consulted: Abraham, JUSTICES AND PRESIDENTS: A POLITICAL HISTORY OF APPOINTMENTS TO THE SUPREME COURT (New York: Oxford University Press, 2nd ed. 1985); O'Brien, STORM CENTER: THE SUPREME COURT IN AMERICAN POLITICS (New York: W.W. Norton & Company, 2nd ed. 1990); Abraham, THE JUDICIAL PROCESS: AN INTRODUCTORY ANALYSIS OF THE COURTS OF THE UNITED STATES, ENGLAND AND FRANCE 398-401 (New York: Oxford University, 5th ed. 1986).

In computing the number of precedents overturned, the following sources were consulted: THE CONSTITUTION OF THE UNITED STATES OF AMERICA, ANALYSIS AND INTERPRETATION, ANNOTATIONS OF CASES DECIDED BY THE SUPREME COURT OF THE UNITED STATES TO JULY 2, 1982, 2117-2127 Prepared by the Congressional Research Service, Library of Congress, (Washington, D.C.: U.S. Government Printing Office, 1987), and its 1990 Supplement, pps. 265-266; Payne v. Tennessee, *supra* n. 1.

12. In Burnett v. Coronado Oil and Gas Co., 285 U.S. 393, 406-408 (1932) (J. Brandeis dissenting), Justice Brandeis stated: "Stare decisis is usually the wise policy, because in most matters it is more important that the applicable rule of law be settled than it be settled right . . . This is commonly true even where the error is a matter of serious concern, provided correction can be had by legislation. But in cases involving the Federal Constitution, where correction through legislative action is practically impossible, this court has often overruled its previous decisions. The court bows to the lessons of experience and the force of better reasoning, recognizing that the process of trial and error, so fruitful in the physical sciences, is appropriate also in the judicial function" (citations omitted).

Implicit in Brandeis's reasoning is a recognition that the Court is the final arbiter of the Constitution, thus making the amendment process the exclusive alternative to changing the outcome of a badly decided constitutional case. Note, "Constitutional Stare Decisis", *supra* n. 9, at 180-181. Conversely, in statutory cases, the Court is more likely to adhere to prior law in order to successfully develop a consistent body of jurisprudence. Marshall, *supra* n. 9, at 181-182.

13. *See* Table 2.

14. For instance, the sheer number of natural Courts occurring within a chief justice period will not definitively prove that more precedents will fall. A good illustration of this point appears in Table 3 with the Fuller Court (1888 to 1910), where 28 natural Courts produced only 4 overturns. Likewise, the Burger Court (1969 to 1986) produced only 9 natural Courts but 52 reversals. Thus, who is on the natural Court, and not how many emerge, is the critical variable in assessing the amount of constitutional flux in any given time period.

15. The first natural Court in the Vinson Court (from June 24, 1946, to July 19, 1949) was created by the ascension of the chief justice to the Court on June 24, 1946. Although his appointment was the only membership change during that Court, the rate of reversals was still fairly high. As such, a "flux" period may result with the change of only one justice. *See* Tables 4 and 5.

16. It is noteworthy that the basis of the conservative anti-New Deal coalition—Van Devanter, Sutherland, Butler, and McReynolds (the "Four Horsemen")—all left within approximately three and a half years of each other.

17. Between June 2, 1937, and July 8, 1941, 14 new natural Courts were created, three of which were formed by the departure of Chief Justice Hughes and the elevation of Associate Justice Stone to the chief justiceship.

18. In the Stone Court, natural Courts three, four, and five were created by the arrival of Justice Robert H. Jackson (July 11, 1941) and the departure of Justice James F. Byrnes (October 3, 1942); and the arrival of Justice Wiley B. Rutledge (February 15, 1943) and the departure of Justice Owen J. Roberts (July 31, 1945). Between July 11, 1941 and July 31, 1945, 14 precedents were reversed. *See* Tables 3 and 4.

19. Justice Frankfurter retired on August 28, 1962. Justice Whittaker left the bench on March 31, 1962.

20. *See* Schwartz and Lesher, INSIDE THE WARREN COURT 199-213 (New York: Doubleday & Co., Inc., 1983); Schwartz, THE UNPUBLISHED OPINIONS OF THE WARREN COURT 3-21 (New York: Oxford University Press 1985).

21. *See* Tables 3 and 4. But, unlike the Hughes reconstitution, most precedents fell early in the term and continued in a downward trend.

22. Justices William H. Rehnquist (to chief justice) and Antonin Scalia (as associate justice) were also appointed to the bench on September 26, 1986.

23. Justice Blackmun assumed the bench on June 9, 1970; Justice John Paul Stevens took judicial oath on December 19, 1975.

24. On June 23, 1969, Chief Justice Warren E. Burger took the judicial oath of office. Justice Harry A. Blackmun took the oath on June 9, 1970; and Justice Lewis F. Powell Jr. and Justice William H. Rehnquist on January 7, 1972 (as associate justice).

25. Tribe, GOD SAVE THIS HONORABLE COURT: HOW THE CHOICE OF SUPREME COURT JUSTICES SHAPES OUR HISTORY 43, 130-131 (New York: Mentor, 1986).

26. McCulloch v. Maryland, 4 Wheaton 315, 407 (1819).

Justice Frankfurter and Justice Reed: friendship and lobbying on the Court

Despite their dissimilarities and Frankfurter's often patronizing attempts to influence Reed, the two justices had a collegial relationship not seen on the Supreme Court today.

by Bradley C. Canon, Kimberly Greenfield, and Jason S. Fleming

The question of who influences whom on the Su-preme Court has long intrigued scholars and observers. They realize that the Court's opinions reflect collegial interaction among the justices that is designed to modify or even change positions. But learning about such interaction is difficult since the Court deliberately shrouds its inner workings in secrecy. Thus, secondhand accounts, journalists' reports,[1] or mere speculation based upon the justices' personalities and intellect are relied on to figure out who influenced whom, through what tactics, and to what degree.

Scholars most often pierce the veil of secrecy by analyzing the papers of retired or deceased justices.[2] To be valuable in this respect, such papers must include candid correspondence with other justices. If there are enough such letters, it is possible to develop an understanding about influence on the Court. This article, which focuses on the efforts of Justice Felix Frankfurter to influence Justice Stanley F. Reed during their joint service on the Court (1939-57), is based primarily upon their correspondence and is supplemented by the recollections of Reed's law clerks.[3]

Frankfurter and Reed were not very similar. Frankfurter was a a Jew, born in Vienna in 1882. His parents immigrated to Manhattan's teeming Lower East Side when he was 12. He learned English as an adolescent yet graduated first in his class at Harvard Law School. As an adult before coming to the Court, Frankfurter, an intimate of Justice Louis Brandeis, led an urbane life, one centering on Boston academic circles and the intellectual rigors of Harvard Law School. He wrote widely, including three scholarly books on the Supreme Court,[4] and frequently advised governors, cabinet officers and, most notably, President Franklin D. Roosevelt. In 1939, he became FDR's third appointment to the Court.

By contrast, Stanley Reed, born in 1884, grew up in Maysville, Kentucky, a small town on the Ohio River. He did not complete law school and practiced small-town law in Maysville for more than 12 years. Reed started his national career in 1929 as an attorney for the Federal Farm Board. Later he became general counsel for the newly established Reconstruction Finance Corp. In 1935 Reed was named solicitor general and defended several major New Deal programs before the Supreme Court. He was Roosevelt's second Supreme Court appointee in January 1938. Reed was as at home in the camaraderie of middle America as Frankfurter was in that of the East Coast liberal establishment.

Despite their dissimilarities, Frankfurter and Reed developed a friendship during Reed's RFC and solicitor general days. It was refreshed by regular correspondence and further blossomed during their years on the Court. The two often visited each other's offices and in good weather walked the mile and a half to and from the Court together.[5] Apparently, only Justices Hugo Black and (in the 1950s) Tom Clark shared the same degree of friendship with Reed as did Frankfurter.[6]

"Lobbying" Reed

Frankfurter was the Court's premier lobbyist during his era and probably rivaled John Marshall in this respect. He had an image of himself as the Court's intellectual leader in the tradition of Holmes and Brandeis.[7] He was forever writing or talking to his colleagues in an effort to win undecided votes, change ones already stated, soften or strengthen opinions, induce or stifle dissents, or otherwise affect the outcome and nature of a Court decision. While personality or ideological conflicts limited his efforts with some justices such as William O. Douglas, Frankfurter directed his efforts at justices such as Harold Burton, Robert Jackson, and Clark, as well as Reed. In the late 1940s, Reed was perceived as the swing vote on an ideologically divided Court, thus making Frankfurter's efforts to woo Reed even more crucial.[8]

Frankfurter wrote Reed 253 letters or notes during their 17 years on the Court.[9] This is almost half (47 percent) of the total correspondence Reed received from every justice during this period. This graphically illustrates how often Frankfurter "lobbied" Reed. No other justice even approached Frankfurter's efforts. Chief Justice Harlan F. Stone and Justice Wiley Rutledge each wrote Reed an average of 7 times per term, compared to Frankfurter's 15 times. Some colleagues rarely wrote Reed. Black, for example, did so at a rate of only 1 time per term.[10] However, the flow of correspondence was asymmetrical: only 18 percent of Reed's outgoing correspondence was directed to Frankfurter. In fact, Reed wrote Stone more often per term than he did Frankfurter and wrote Burton only slightly less often. Reed's letters to Frankfurter were less intimate than those he received from him, but they contained occasional regard or humor.

Frankfurter supplemented his written efforts to lobby Reed with frequent visits to his chambers. As one clerk put it:

[Frankfurter] would frequently try to persuade Reed to his point of view.... Sometimes we [would] all end up in a three way conversation or discussion or argument...in Reed's office with Frankfurter very vigorously espousing his views and sometimes pontificating, always showing his erudition.[11]

A clerk from the late 1940s recalled:

Reed was sort of a centrist on the Court; he was fair game for judges from both sides to try to get him over to their side to make up a majority. And therefore he was importuned frequently by them to join them. Frankfurter did this a lot. Frankfurter loved argument and discussion.... He would frequently try to persuade Reed to his point of view.[12]

There are, of course, no records of how often other justices came to Reed's chambers, but interviews with the clerks leave the clear impression that Frankfurter was far and away the most frequent visitor.

In addition to direct persuasion, Frankfurter was, in one clerk's words, "forever trying to seduce Reed's law clerks in the expectation that they would help seduce Stanley Reed. [But] Frankfurter's efforts in that direction were transparent and Reed had a good time in watching them."[13] Another clerk reported,

Justice Frankfurter was quite fond of using Justice Reed's law clerks as an avenue to the justice's opinions. Frankfurter was quite likely to walk into our [the clerks'] chambers and discuss issues with us that he never talked to the Justice about.[14]

Substantive efforts

Opportunities for Frankfurter to try to influence Reed's positions or the substance of his opinions abounded. The Court's non-unanimous decisions rose sharply after 1940, exceeding 50 percent by the 1943 term, and the justices' willingness to write concurring opinions increased to more than 25 percent of the cases by the late 1940s.[15] While there were few fundamental differences between Frankfurter and Reed, their votes diverged about 40 percent of the time in dissensual decisions.[16] Frankfurter, considerably more ideologically and doctrinally oriented than Reed, often tried to persuade or instruct Reed, particularly—in keeping with his image as heir to Holmes and Brandeis—with regard to judicial restraint.

While both Reed and Frankfurter believed generally in judicial restraint and had few ideological differences, they had divergent perspectives in two areas. One was police behavior, particularly search and seizure cases.[17] With amusing insight, Reed once explained his differences with Frankfurter in this area.

Do you know why Felix and I decide these search and seizure cases differently?... Well, when Felix was a young Jewish boy growing up in Vienna, there could be a knock at the door in the night. It could be a policeman coming to take him away. When I was a young boy, I grew up in Maysville, Ky. I had a white pony and I used to ride

[him] down the main street…and as I passed the main intersection, there was a policeman there and he would stop traffic for me. And as I passed, he would pat me on my golden curls. And when Felix thinks of a policeman, he thinks of a knock on the door in the night, and when I think of a policeman, I think of the man stopping traffic for me and patting me on my curls.[18]

The other area was freedom of speech and the press. Reed subscribed to the "preferred position" doctrine elevating these guarantees above others. He did not apply the doctrine anywhere near as broadly as did Hugo Black, William O. Douglas, Wiley Rutledge, and Frank Murphy, and commentators never touted Reed as a champion of First Amendment claims, but Reed was sympathetic to its application in certain situations.[19] Frankfurter adamantly opposed the preferred position argument and favored a "balancing" approach to the First Amendment. In several First Amendment cases Frankfurter urged Reed to give more weight to other factors and in *Ullman v. U.S.* (1956) he lectured Reed directly and forcefully against the preferred position approach, but to no avail.[20]

While Justice Douglas once said that Frankfurter "never missed a chance to line up a vote,"[21] the Reed papers show only four instances when Frankfurter sought Reed's vote directly. Two were on the merits and two were strategic, the latter asking that Reed, who was silently subscribing to a liberal bloc majority opinion, write an opinion concurring in the result but withholding approval of the liberal rationale.[22] Reed rejected all the requests.

Nor did Frankfurter try much to shape Reed's opinions through explicit threats of concurrences or dissents if his suggestions were not incorporated. Justices sometimes resort to this tactic, and Frankfurter used it with some of his brethren.[23] But the correspondence shows Frankfurter putting the matter to Reed in such overt terms only three times, with Reed acceding once.[24]

Much more often Frankfurter tried to persuade Reed to make changes in opinions. This persuasion could take several forms. He often made straightforward arguments that the development of Reed's position was illogical and needed substantial rewriting (the outline of which Frankfurter would suggest) or that it was at odds with important precedents or legal doctrines. He often cautioned Reed against obiter dicta, particularly when he feared that the unnecessary writing might well haunt the Court in future cases. An illustrative case

is *Regan v. New York* (1955), involving a police officer who as a condition of remaining one had to waive testimonial immunity in a grand jury appearance. Frankfurter advised Reed to excise a discussion of matters such as what constituted a valid waiver and to stick to settling *Regan* on grounds that the guarantee against compelled self-incrimination was not incorporated into the Fourteenth Amendment. He told Reed:

You have heard my song before and I am afraid you will hear it as long as we are on the Court together, but nothing but mischief comes from talk that a case does not call for, especially when constitutional issues are involved.[25]

Reed, however, kept such discussion in the opinion and Frankfurter concurred separately.

Frankfurter sometimes tried convincing his colleague by invoking the giants of the legal profession in his behalf, most often Holmes and Brandeis. A good example occurred in *U.S. v. Line Material Co.* (1948), an anti-trust case. Frankfurter first tried to to dissuade Reed from upholding a broad interpretation of the act.

All the 'liberals' threw their hats in the air when Brandeis castigated the then majority for assuming to exercise the power of a 'super-legislature'. It would shock Holmes and Brandeis out of their boots to learn that the beauty of the Sherman Law is its vast vagueness, whereby five members of this Court are able to decide what is good or bad for 'the economy' of this country. Yes, I know I am again invoking the names of Holmes and Brandeis. I am unashamed to be reverent to the great.[26]

A few weeks later Frankfurter urged Reed to suppress his *Line Material* opinion.

Some of the best writings, by far, both of Holmes and Brandeis were circulated but unpublished opinions…. I suspect they no more liked committing intellectual infanticide than do you or I. But they did it frequently during their service on the Court, because it advanced the best interests of the Court and of the Law. Reflecting on the examples of Holmes and Brandeis emboldens me to suggest that the circumstances in which we find outselves in the *Line* case may make it equally wise for you to subject your opinion in that case to intellectual infanticide.[27]

Reed, however, was not dissuaded and never seemed particularly impressed on those occasions when Frankfurter referred to one or both of the memorable duo.

The same was true when other greats were brought to bear. In a disagreement over a question about federal equity power, Frankfurter told Reed, "My understanding of equitable principles was derived from James Barr Ames, who, I suspect, was the deepest student this country ever produced on that subject."[28]

Scholars have remarked upon Frankfurter's frequent use of flattery in persuading his colleagues, and Reed was often an object of this tactic.[29] For example, one effort to get Reed to reduce his reliance on a set of precedents Frankfurter disliked began, "…I know enough to appreciate how deft your job. Therefore I am even more unhappy than I am on ordinary occasions to touch your opinion."[30] In another, he said:

You have done not only a very faithful and careful but so helpful a piece of work…that I dislike to bother you further with a suggestion which may merely resolve itself to a preferential way of putting a thing. And yet words are the very stuff of our business and inextricably determine substance…[31]

Flattery occasionally worked, largely depending upon how much change Frankfurter wanted.

When other tactics seemed inappropriate, Frankfurter might try to get Reed to see the facts differently. These efforts could result in an exchange of several letters. In *McNabb v. U.S.* (1943) where the Court first held that due process required the arraignment of federal prisoners within a few hours of arrest, Frankfurter sent Reed two long letters emphasizing the delay in arraignment and McNabb's meantime interrogation in isolation; he cited the uncontroverted facts in trial record.[32] Reed nonetheless put a different gloss on the case and dissented solo.

Criminal cases were a prime area for factual disputes between the two, but they could occur in other areas too. In *Poulos v. New Hampshire* (1953), a Jehovah's Witness case, Frankfurter in a three-week series of memos to Reed argued that Poulos had not made a First Amendment challenge in the state courts to a city ordinance requiring a permit prior to using a public park for a religious meeting. Reed was unpersuaded: "it seems to me clear from the motions and the facts…that Poulos made an attack in New Hampshire and here on the constitutional validity of this ordinance."[33]

Their longest exchange came in *Williams v. North Carolina* (1945), holding that other states could challenge the validity of their own citizens' six weeks Nevada domicile for purposes of obtaining

a divorce. Thirteen letters went back and forth in five weeks. The arguments mixed law and fact and eventually Reed reluctantly came around to Frankfurter's viewpoint.[34]

Frankfurter's success

Reed could be quite stubborn, sometimes illogically so. Frankfurter recorded the following conversation with him about a case where Reed sided with Black against Frankfurter.

After I circulated my concurring opinion…Reed, J. phoned and said 'I am very glad you wrote what you did, because you put in words what I tried inadequately to express to Black to indicate my dissatisfaction with his opinion.'
FF: 'But I understand you are going with him.'
Reed: 'That's right.'
FF: 'In other words, you are going with Black because he is not expressing your views, and you're not going with me because I *am* [sic] expressing your views.'
Reed: 'That's a funny but fair way of stating the situation.'[35]

Because Reed dug in his heels at times, the professor sometimes bluntly expressed his frustration. "Either I have written to no point or you have read to no point," he wrote Reed in one case. "I could not believe that…you could support Bill's [Douglas] concoction in *Screws [v. U.S.]*, that you could give adherence to something that has not the support of your mind nor the comfort of your conscience," he said in an early civil rights prosecution. "You are incorrigible in your desire to make law like mathematics," he sighed in an administrative law case.[36]

Sometimes Frankfurter gave up before he began. In a case centering on racial discrimination in grand juries, Frankfurter started to write Reed but ended up writing a concurrence. He told Reed that "it would be a hopeless enterprise and an utter waste of your time for me to ask you to, in effect, revamp your opinion along [my suggested] lines."[37]

But sometimes Frankfurter was successful in persuading Reed to alter an opinion substantially. This was especially likely in Reed's early years when he was more hesitant and cautious in writing majority opinions. *Smith v. Allwright* (1944), which struck down Texas's whites only Democratic primary, is an important and illustrative example.[38] Reed relied heavily upon *U.S. v. Classic* (1941), which held that Congress had power under the Fifteenth

Amendment to regulate primary elections. His first draft worked around a 1935 case, *Grovey v. Townsend*, that upheld the whites only primary. Frankfurter strongly believed that *Grovey* should be unequivocally overruled. He wrote Reed:

You are of the opinion that the South can be gently eased into acceptance of our decision in *Allwright* if only we are not too explicit. My own prophecy is precisely the opposite—that no matter with what tissue paper covering the blow [when it] is administered, it will be felt, and by appearing to screen it an added grievance will be aroused…. We are absolutely turning an about face [in] that *Allwright* is a square and unmitigatory overruling of *Grovey*,… not a thing is before us now that was not before the Court in *Grovey* [and] no intervening event of legal or practical significance has happened except a change in the membership of this Court.[39]

Here Reed listened to Frankfurter and decided to risk angering the South. The final opinion had four sentences not contained in the first draft, ending with "*Grovey v. Townsend* is overruled."[40]

Similarly, in *Viex v. Sixth Ward Building and Loan Assn.* (1940) Reed wrote an opinion rejecting a contract clause challenge to a Depression-era statute designed to protect the solvency of a state's savings and loan banks by making withdrawals more difficult. Doing this was problematical because Reed had to distinguish *Viex*'s outcome from two earlier precedents where the Court had applied the contract clause to somewhat analogous situations. Frankfurter told him:

"since [these two] cases are decisions that we really wouldn't decide that way if we had the deciding of them, I think we ought to carry as little of their baggage as possible. And so I have ventured to put to you a softened rephrasing of what you said about [them]."[41]

In the published opinion, Reed followed Frankfurter's suggestions almost verbatim. Reed also adopted some Frankfurter themes in rejecting a convicted murderer's double jeopardy claim when Louisiana's electric chair malfunctioned in the first attempt to execute him. Frankfurter wrote back, "Thank you for the changes you have made. I am confident that history will approve of them."[42]

Reed's editor

When Frankfurter could not or had no desire to convince Reed to change the tenor of his opinion, he would nevertheless suggest numerous changes in his colleague's drafts. It did not matter whether Frankfurter was subscribing to Reed's opinion. As

he once told Reed, "[T]o some of my brethren I feel free to make suggestions even as to opinions in which I do not join."[43] Frankfurter made similar suggestions to several other colleagues, particularly Harold Burton and Owen Roberts. But Reed, who did not delegate much opinion writing to his clerks, was a slow and sometimes awkward writer and was particularly receptive to Frankfurter's help.[44] It is fair to say that Frankfurter served as the primary editor for many a Reed opinion.

Some Frankfurter suggestions were aimed at strengthening Reed's arguments. For example, when Reed circulated a draft that responded to Douglas's dissenting point by saying, "We see no reason why…," Frankfurter told him that it was "no answer to an argument, if there is anything in it, to say there is nothing in it…. if you are going to refer to Bill's argument, you ought to say a little something." Frankfurter then wrote a paragraph-long suggestion on how to "properly" answer the argument. When Reed incorporated much of the paragraph, Frankfurter scribbled on Reed's circulation, "Thank you. Yes! -FF"[45]

In *Champlin Refining Co. v. U.S.* (1946), a pipeline regulation statutory question in which Frankfurter was joining Reed in dissent, Frankfurter enclosed a substitute paragraph for Reed's concluding one, explained why it would better answer the majority opinion, and then told his colleague, "So be a nice boy." The very next day Frankfurter suggested to Reed that if "you insist on keeping in the last sentence of the next to last paragraph, it ought to be phrased more clearly in some such way as the following:…."[46] Reed adopted Frankfurter's language almost verbatim.

When Frankfurter wanted something excised, he could edit through sarcasm. A Reed sentence in a draft of *Breard v. City of Alexandria* (1951), upholding the constitutionality of an anti-canvassing law as applied to magazine subscription salesmen, read: "True liberty is indivisible." Frankfurter scrawled back, "Really, really,… How about 'true security is indivisible?'"[47] Later in the draft, Reed wrote, "[F]ortunately, subscribers may be secured [in other ways]." Frankfurter again took exception:

Why 'fortunately'? If you mean that it is fortunate for our country that *Time, Life*, etc., can sweep in subscriptions, then it is a pronouncement that this Court has no business to make…. I can assure you that I am not the only one who does not regard *Time* and *Life* as a blessing for the country, but, on the contrary, deems them among the most powerful forces of miseducation and debasement.[48]

Reed eliminated the objectionable phrases.

Another example: In a copyright case Reed wrote, "Sacrificial days devoted to such creative activities deserve rewards commensurate with the services rendered." In big letters in the margin, Frankfurter observed, "Gawd! A ditchdigger also spends sacrificial days."[49]

In fact, Frankfurter was the Supreme Court's "Mr. Language Person" and Reed his main pupil. By his own admission, Frankfurter was a "pernickety" teacher. His letters and marginal comments were studded with spelling, vocabulary, and grammatical corrections, sometimes at considerable length. He wrote two pages to Reed on the correct usage of "cf.," explained the difference between "presupposition" and "preposition" and between "jurisdiction" and "justiciable," and told him when to use ellipses and when to use brackets in an opinion.[50] Even when Frankfurter was willing to tolerate a grammatical slip-up, he let Reed know about it: "OK. Even with the split infinitive!" he said of one Reed draft.[51]

Patronizing friendship

Frankfurter viewed most of his brethren as lesser intellects. He particularly thought Chief Justices Harlan Fiske Stone and Fred Vinson and Justices Owen Roberts, Frank Murphy, Harold Burton, and Sherman Minton were not strong minds.[52] He also included Reed in this class. In candid letters to Judge Learned Hand, he dismissed Reed as "largely vegetable" and the "least judicial as well as the stupidist" justice.[53] Nonetheless, Frankfurter saw Reed as an oft-time ally, a vote or opinion capable of being won over, and maintained his strong friendship with him.

Even so, Frankfurter was often and obviously patronizing toward Reed. He frequently instructed Reed about legal matters in conversations or long letters. A clerk described Frankfurter's behavior during one of his visits to Reed's office: "It really wasn't a conversation so much as a lecture. And Frankfurter literally dressed Reed down…. He was treating Justice Reed almost like a student…."[54]

Some Frankfurter letters were mini-lectures (slightly softened by flattery) in the sense that they treated Reed as someone unlearned in an area of law or legal history. Reed received the first such letter only a few months after Frankfurter came to the Court. It involved a tax case and is excerpted here for style and tone:

> Judges depart from wisdom…due to a lack of rigorous realization that even the best of judges are poorly equipped to be shapers of tax policies and that too free use of the power of invalidation inevitably is in effect policy-making. Saying yes to a tax measure has not terribly serious consequences, at the very worst. There are always legislative remedies if the thing hurts too much. But saying no is full of potential danger way beyond the immediate exercise of the taxing power under review. I happen to know that this Court came pretty close to throwing out William J. Bryan's notions of bank deposit guaranty legislation. What a heavy price we would have had to pay if the poor formulation of that idea had been invalidated instead of sustained in *Noble State Bank v. Haskill*. Take, for instance, the whole relatively recent history on "double" taxation. How wise in the retrospect Holmes' attitude of abstention appears, beginning with his dissent in the *Union Refrigerator Case* and culminating in *Blackstone v. Miller*. Compare the contradictory movement culminating in *Farmers Loan and Trust Co v. Minnesota* and then consider the painful and partial return to the original line….[55]

A half dozen or so such letters lectured Reed each term, falling off somewhat during their last years on the Court. Frankfurter would instruct him on such broad legal questions as when to exercise judicial review, the wisdom of judicial restraint, the canons of statutory construction, the nature of concurrent jurisdiction, and on constitutional questions such as the scope of the commerce clause, the "proper" approach to interpreting the freedom of speech and press guaranties, and the need for restraints on the police. In one commerce clause case, Frankfurter referred Reed to his recent book on that clause, and a few days later he asked Reed whether he had read it yet.[56]

Sometimes a frustrated Frankfurter would simply denigrate a Reed draft opinion like a top sergeant might chew out a poorly performing private. He did not pull his punches. The best example is *Higgins v. C.I.R.* (1941), a tax case in which Frankfurter told Reed that were he still a professor, "I would feel obliged to tear [your opinion] to tatters [because it] lacks even the intellectual forthrightness in which judges can safely indulge." He then suggested the removal of some "disfiguring warts" that "I should like to have done to make me as happy as an otherwise miserable opinion could."[57]

Responding to Reed's draft in *Uverges v. Pennsylvania* (1949), a right to counsel case, Frankfurter excoriated him for treating opinions of the Court and dissents with equal weight. He ended by telling Reed, "[This] is merely the froth of my feeling about your *Uverges* opinion. In due course you will have a full blast."[58] Of another Reed draft he said, "If I did not have...a cast iron stomach, your attitude toward Congressional legislation would give me ulcers."[59] A note responding to another Reed draft began "Good God! Truly a shoestring opinion!!!"[60] A case's disposition did not necessarily end the matter. Once, after publication of a Reed opinion for the Court, Frankfurter forwarded him an anonymous criticism of it, saying of the writer: "You know him well and respect him greatly."[61]

Despite being patronized and almost openly taken for a dullard, Reed was better able to tolerate Frankfurter's behavior than were most of his colleagues. He did not have a large ego and genuinely respected Frankfurter's legal intellect. He once said of Frankfurter, "[H]e knows so much he antagonizes, but he is good."[62]

Reed was open to persuasion, but he was his own man. Several Reed law clerks relate amusing anecdotes illustrating their justice's patience with Frankfurter. Once when Frankfurter came into Reed's office to discuss a case with him, the clerk recounted:

Reed just sat there quietly, nodding his head very politely, and [when] Frankfurter was satisfied with himself he wheeled out, going out like a little bird.... Reed turned to us and said, 'What a wonderful disquisition. What a marvelous analysis. What a brilliant mind. Don't you envy that capability? If only he had some common sense!'[63]

Another described a Reed reaction thusly:

Felix would be jumping around like a hummingbird [with] this great smiling...benign figure watching [and] listening with a kind of bemused tolerant smile. At the end of which, he would say, 'Thank you very much, Felix. I appreciate your spending time with me.'[64]

Genuine friendship

By all appearances, the two justices kept a warm friendship despite Frankfurter's open patronizing and his limited success in shaping Reed's positions or opinions. One manifestation of this was Frankfurter's willingness to share with Reed his contempt of their colleagues on the Court's lib-

eral wing. Frankfurter's sarcastic references to them ranged from the simple "Black and Co." to "the great civil libertarians" through "those who profess to be [the Bill of Rights'] special guardians and true interpreters" and on to "the guardians of the great writ."[65] He especially zeroed in on Hugo Black and what Frankfurter saw as his stubborn preconceptions. In one case he wrote Reed:

I put it to you: do you think that any amount of relevant or irrelevant discussion could shake Hugo loose from his conclusion?...You might as well ask him to climb a greased telephone-pole as to change his conclusion by [what you are writing].[66]

In *Adamson v. California* (1947), which featured the famous debate between Black and Frankfurter about whether the Fourteenth Amendment's due process clause incorporated the entire Bill of Rights, Frankfurter advised Reed (who was writing the opinion) against compromise:

There are statesmen, whom Neville Chamberlain best illustrates, who seem to think that the way to conciliate enemies is to lose friends. That odd notion has not been wholly unreflected even in the work of this Court. No matter what you wrote in rejecting the claim that there was a denial of due process in the *Adamson* case, because of the disregard of immunity from self-crimination, you could not win the support of Black and Co."[67]

Another time Frankfurter told Reed, "[Your] opinion is impregnable to the assault by the projectiles of the Black-Douglas fountain pen! F.F."[68] When a Black draft misquoted the Constitution's religious test clause so that it appeared to bar such tests for state office as well as national ones, Frankfurter remarked sarcastically, "I suppose the printer is to blame for that."[69] Murphy also came in for a swipe or two. "You would no more eat Murphy's tripe today than you would be seen naked at DuPont Circle at high noon tomorrow," Frankfurter told Reed.[70] Reed was not so denigrating of the liberal justices, although he did once tell Frankfurter that Chief Justice Vinson was "just like me only less educated."[71]

Also revealing of their friendship is the degree to which they were teasing or playful in discussing cases. Frankfurter especially enjoyed this. For example, when Reed's draft dissent in *Pennsylvania v. Nelson* (1956), which struck down state anti-subversion laws on grounds of federal preemption, referred approvingly to Reed's majority opinion in

Cloverleaf Butter Co. v. Patterson (1942), Frankfurter sent him a copy of the relevant part of *Cloverleaf* with a hand-written comment: "Dear dear dear: I thought that as you grew in understanding you had repented of that reprehensible decision; the inalienable right to sell rancid butter to the poor."[72] Once, after several letters about a case did not move Reed, Frankfurter sent the next letter on just a regular sheet of paper. "The upshot of my correspondences with you is that I shall cease the wasteful use of my fine Seribuer-made Cambridge Stationery."[73]

In an Indian claims case, Frankfurter, with Reed's sometime adherence to Justice Stone's famous Footnote Four philosophy in mind, wrote:

"Since Indians are not among the disadvantaged as to whom your 'zeal for the underdog weights your judicial judgment,' I can agree with you on an analysis of your opinion and not have to reconsider everything from the beginning."[74]

"It would be a pleasure to expose the difficulties of your views on the merits, but we lack jurisdiction here," Frankfurter responded to a Reed argument.[75] "You will comfort Chiang," he teased when Reed dissented from a Frankfurter ruling against the Nationalist Chinese government.[76] Frankfurter even sent Reed "groaners." When a 1947 Reed dissent relied on Reed's majority opinion in *Miles v. Illinois Central RR* (1942), Frankfurter wrote playfully, "Must you compound *Miles* of error!"[77]

Reed returned his colleague's humor. After receiving several letters of Frankfurter's philosophical analyses of freedom of speech in *Dennis v. U.S.* (1951), which upheld the constitutionality of the Smith Act, Reed responded with the salutation "Dear Plato."[78] Even in their prolonged dispute in *Poulos v. New Hampshire* noted earlier, Reed could be teasing. When Frankfurter gave Reed a draft of a memo to the conference charging Reed with indifference to the case record and asked, "Should I circulate?" Reed replied in the margin, "One more circulation from you and I am bound to win." Frankfurter fired back in the other margin, "Of course, you mean you can't win on the merits."[79]

Indeed, with Frankfurter's devotion to precision and purity of language in mind, Reed went out of his way to find unusual words to insert in his draft opinions just to get a rise out of the former professor. In one case Reed wrote about the "metal of

the road" and Frankfurter crossed it out and inserted "middle." But Reed knew what he was about and, citing the *Oxford English Dictionary*, pointed out that metal was an archaic usage for middle. "Metal" remained in the opinion.[80] Another time he sprang the word "autocephalous" on his colleagues with Frankfurter responding, "I'm glad I'm not without the power of anagnorisis with regard to this."[81]

A full relationship

Clearly Frankfurter and Reed were good friends who shared considerable intimacy in their work. But it was not a friendship based on equal regard. Frankfurter saw himself as the teacher, the transmitter of legal logic and tradition, and Reed as the not-too-bright pupil, at best a follower but more likely a stubborn and intermittant ally. Reed's weak ego and his admiration for his colleague's intellect made him potentially receptive to Frankfurter's suggestions, despite their often patronizing and sarcastic tone. However, although Frankfurter lobbied Reed frequently both in person and in writing, Reed possessed sufficient independence to become neither a devotee of Frankfurter nor a victim of too much manipulation.

Frankfurter's ability to persuade Reed varied by situation. In general, Reed, while bemusedly tolerant, was not likely to heed Frankfurter's urgings on major points and sometimes rejected minor suggestions as well. He never succumbed to Frankfurter's occasional direct request for a change of position and only seldom, despite repeated attempts, was Reed persuaded to make significant substantive changes in his opinions. Reed could be adamant in shaping an opinion to the way he saw the legal issue, although *Smith v. Allwright* shows that at times he could be persuaded to make important changes. He was, however, often open to Frankfurter's suggestions about giving an opinion greater clarity, felicity, or force. In fact, good writing did not come easily to Reed, and he more often than not gratefully accepted his colleague's services as his editor. In this sense, Frankfurter certainly had an influence in shaping Reed's opinions.

What the correspondence does not contain is also noteworthy. There are virtually no instances of Frankfurter threatening Reed with a pointed dissent or concurrence if an opinion was not altered or supressed. Frankfurter was certainly manipulative, but he did not engage in "hard ball" negotiation with his friend.

From a modern perspective, a striking thing about the Frankfurter-Reed relationship is its fullness. In this day and age when the Court is described by Justice Lewis Powell as "nine small, independent law firms" or composed of justices who in Justice Byron White's words "stay at arm's length" from one another,[82] it is refreshing to recall a relationship between justices that in fact contained real aspects of collegiality. The idea of a collegial court, of course, envisions decisions and opinions stemming from discussions among the justices instead of, as Justice John M. Harlan put it, "a tally of individual votes."[83] Perhaps Frankfurter and Reed's collegiality reflects a more intimate era on the Court, when each justice had just one law clerk and a secretary until 1948. Or perhaps it reflects the right mesh of personalities in Frankfurter and Reed. Or both.

NOTES

This article originally appeared in Volume 78, Number 5, March-April 1995, pages 224-231.

An earlier version of this article was presented at the annual meeting of the Western Political Science Association in Albuquerque, N.M., in March 1994. The authors acknowledge the research help of Terri Ann Smith.

1. *See, e.g.*, Woodward and Armstrong, THE BRETHREN (New York: Simon and Schuster, 1979).

2. *See, e.g.*, Mason, HARLAN FISKE STONE: PILLAR OF THE LAW (New York: Viking Press, 1956), Howard, *On the Fluidity of Judicial Choice*, 62 AM. POL. SCI. REV. 43-56 (1968), Ulmer, *Earl Warren and the Brown Decision*, 33 J. POL. 689-702 (1971).

3. Justice Reed's papers are at the University of Kentucky's King Memorial Library. Justice Frankfurter's papers at the Library of Congress and the Harvard Law School Library were also used, but they contain little correspondence with Reed that is not also in the Reed papers and they do not contain Frankfurter's marginal comments on Reed's opinions or many of Frankfurter's handwritten notes. Consequently, most correspondence citations are to box numbers and case files in the Reed papers. Oral interviews with Justice Reed's law clerks were conducted by the University of Kentucky Library around 1980, and transcripts are available there. All interview citations are to transcript pages.

4. Frankfurter and Landis, THE BUSINESS OF THE SUPREME COURT: A STUDY IN THE FEDERAL JUDICIAL SYSTEM (New York: Macmillan, 1927); Frankfurter, THE COMMERCE POWER UNDER MARSHALL, TANEY AND WAITE (Chapel Hill, N.C.: University of North Carolina Press, 1937); Frankfurter, MR. JUSTICE HOLMES AND THE SUPREME COURT (Cambridge: Harvard University Press, 1938).

5. F. Aley Allan interview (1946 term) 8, 17; Robert von Mehren interview (1947 term) 11-12; Joseph Barbash interview (1949 term) 16; George D. Mickum interview (1953 term) 14, 24; Roderick Hills interview (1955 term) 37; Arthur L. Rosett interview (immediate post-retirement clerk) 29, 33.

6. Edwin M. Zimmerman interview (1950 term) 7; Hills interview, *id.* at 28-29; Rosett interview, *id.* at 33.

7. Hirsch, THE ENIGMA OF FELIX FRANKFURTER 159 (New York: Basic Books, 1981).

8. Note, *Mr. Justice Reed—Swing Man or Not?*, 1 STAN. L. REV. 714-729 (1949). *See also* Pritchett, CIVIL LIBERTIES AND THE VINSON COURT 17-18 (Chicago: University of Chicago Press, 1954). Black, Douglas, Murphy, and Rutledge composed the liberal bloc and Vinson, Frankfurter, Jackson, and Burton the conservative bloc. Despite this perception, statistical analysis of those terms shows Reed voting with the liberal bloc only slightly more often than the other conservatives. *See* Schubert, THE JUDICIAL MIND 50-52 (Evanston, Ill.: Northwestern University Press, 1965). In 1949 when Clark and Minton came to the Court following the deaths of Murphy and Rutledge, Reed's vote became less pivotal.

9. The counts reflect correspondence housed at the UK Library. We know of a few letters to or from Reed that are not in the UK collection, so the numbers are not absolute. Our count includes all letters, memos, and handwritten notes sent to or by Reed. This includes letters, etc., addressed to more than one but fewer than five justices (18 items). Simple join letters (e.g., "Dear Stanley: I join your opinion in *Allwright.* Sincerely, Wiley"), comments in the margins of a draft opinion, or the very occasional letters unrelated to Supreme Court business were not counted.

10. These figures are skewed to some extent because of different forms of communication among the justices. For instance, Black sometimes wrote long comments in the margins or on the backs of galley opinions while Rutledge wrote brief comments about draft opinions in short but formal letters.

11. Mac Asbill Jr. interview (1948 term) 6.

12. *Id. See also* David Schwartz interview (1942 Term) 11, von Mehren interview 12, and Barbash interview 22-23, both *supra* n. 5.

13. Zimmerman interview, *supra* n. 6, at 5. O'Brien (STORM CENTER, 3rd ed. 169-170 (New York: Norton, 1993)) notes Frankfurter's frequent lobbying of other justices' clerks.

14. Hills interview, *supra* n. 5. *See also* Mickum interview, *supra* n. 5, and Asbill interview, *supra* n. 11.

15. Walker, Epstein, and Dixon, *On the Mysterious Demise of Consensual Norms on the Supreme Court*, 50 J. POL. 361, 363-364 (1988).

16. Pritchett, THE ROOSEVELT COURT 38-44 (New York: Macmillan, 1948) and Pritchett, *supra* n. 8, at ch. 9.

17. Reed voted for criminal defendants about 20 percent of the time while Frankfurter voted for them about 55 percent of the time, and the gap was even wider in search and seizure cases. *See* Schubert, QUANTITATIVE ANALYSIS OF JUDICIAL BEHAVIOR 87, 347 (New York: The Free Press, 1959). *See also* Frankfurter's three letters to Reed in *McNabb v. U.S.*, 318 U.S. 332 (1943), Box 74 (Feb. 24, Feb. 26, and Mar. 3, 1942). In this and subsequent notes, all references are to letters from Frankfurter to Reed unless otherwise noted.

18. Bayless Manning interview (1949 term) 14. Apparently Reed was fond of making this point. Zimmerman, *supra* n. 6, at 6, and Barbash, *supra* n. 5, at 18-19, also remember Reed making this comparison.

19. Pritchett, *supra* n. 16, at 131, shows Reed considerably more supportive of freedom of speech and press claims in the early 1940s. Pritchett, *supra* n. 8, at 190, shows Reed more supportive of such claims against state intrusion than Frankfurter, but considerably less supportive against federal intrusion. Certainly Reed was not perceived as a civil libertarian justice, but his majority opinion in *Poulos v. New Hampshire*, 345 U.S. 395 (1953), and his concurring statement in *Ullman v. U.S.* 350 U.S. 422 (1956), demonstrated support for the "preferred position" approach. O'Brien, JUSTICE REED AND THE FIRST AMENDMENT, ch. 12 (Washington, D.C.: Georgetown University Press, 1958), argues that Reed was sympathetic to such claims.

20. *Id.*, Box 176 (Feb. 7, 1956; SR reply, Mar. 8, 1956).

21. Douglas, THE COURT YEARS 173 (New York: Random House, 1980). Frankfurter leveled the same accusation against Douglas and Black, calling their maneuvering for votes "crafty." Hirsh, *supra* n. 7, at 182.

22. On the merits: Jersey Central Power and Light Co. v. FPC, 319 U.S. 61 (1943), Box 76 (Mar. 10. 1943), and Bay Ridge Operating Co. v. Aaron, 334 U.S. 446 (1948), Box 111 (Mar. 24, 1948). Strategic: Bridges v. California, 314 U.S. 252 (1941), Box 171 (Dec. 3, 1941), and U.S. v. Line Materials Co., 333 U.S. 287 (1948), Box 106 (Dec. 9, 1947). Frankfurter once wrote Reed, "If by this time you do not know how foreign it is to my purpose to angle for votes, nothing I can say would persuade you of it," regarding Black Diamond SS. Co. v. Robert Stewart & Sons, 336 U.S. 386 (1949), Box 173 (Jan. 31, 1949).

Another example of Frankfurter's (successful) maneuvering is *Winters v. New York*, 333 U.S. 507 (1948). Frankfurter and Chief Justice Vinson were dissenting, but he persuaded Vinson to vote with the liberal majority so that Vinson could assign the opinion to Reed who Frankfurter believed (and lobbied) would strike down a law banning books or magazines depicting excessive crime or violence on grounds of vagueness rather than on First Amendment grounds. *See* Lash, FROM THE DIARIES OF FELIX FRANKFURTER 307 (New York: Norton, 1975).

23. *See* Murphy, ELEMENTS OF JUDICIAL STRATEGY 54-68 (Chicago: University of Chicago Press, 1964) for a description of such tactics. Hirsh, *supra* n. 7, at 179 and 190, discusses Frankfurter's use of such threats.

24. Reed withdrew an objectionable phrase in *Gray v. Powell*, 314 U.S. 402 (1942), Box 68 (Dec. 2, 1941), and remained firm in *Poulos v. New Hampshire*, *supra* n. 19, Box 151 (Apr. 20, 1953), where Frankfurter then wrote a lengthy concurrence. Frankfurter sent a draft dissent to Reed in *Fleming v. Rhodes*, 331 U.S. 100 (1947), Box 101 (Apr. 26, 1947). Although Reed did not budge, Frankfurter later withdrew it (but did cast a dissenting vote).

25. 349 U.S. 58 (1955), Box 160 (Jan. 24, 1955)

26. *Supra* n. 22, Box 106 (Nov. 25, 1947). Several of the justices resented Frankfurter's "hero worship" of Holmes and Brandeis. *See* Schwartz, SUPER CHIEF: EARL WARREN AND HIS SUPREME COURT 42 (New York University Press, 1983).

27. Box 106 (Dec. 9, 1947).

28. S.R.A. Inc. v. Minnesota, 327 U.S. 558 (1946), Box 92 (Mar. 20, 1946). Ames was dean of the Harvard Law School at the turn of the century.

29. Hirsch, *supra* n. 7, at 142-144 and 160. O'Brien, *supra* n. 13, at 319.

30. Viex v. Sixth Ward Bldg. and Loan Assn., 310 U.S. 32 (1940), Box 61 (Apr. 5, 1940).

31. Hawk v. Olson, 326 U.S. 271 (1946), Box 90 (Nov. 9, 1945).

32. *Supra* n. 17 (Feb. 24 and Feb. 26, 1943).

33. Box 151 (SR Memorandum to the Conference, Apr. 9, 1953). Writing for the majority, Reed acknowledged Poulos's First Amendment right to use the park, but upheld his conviction on grounds that the city's refusal to give a permit should have been litigated prior to the Witnesses' use of the park.

34. Williams v. North Carolina, 325 U.S. 226 (1945), Box 172 (letters between Mar. 23 and Apr. 30, 1945). This was a 6-3 decision, Frankfurter for the Court. Reed originally planned a short dissent, then shifted to a short concurrence and finally joined Frankfurter.

35. Tiller v. Atlantic Coast Line RR., 318 U.S. 54 (1943), FF papers, Harvard Law School (no date).

36. The citations are respectively: McDonald v. C.I.R., 323 U.S. 57 (1945), Box 172 (Nov. 14, 1944); Screws, 325 U.S. 91 (1945), Box 85 (no date); and Gray v. Powell, *supra* n. 24, Box 68 (no date). Ironically, *Screws* involved police brutality of the

first magnitude and Frankfurter was voting to overturn the sheriff's conviction.

37. Cassell v. Texas, 339 U.S. 282 (1950), Box 127 (Dec. 8, 1949).

38. 321 U.S. 649 (1944). Chief Justice Stone had originally assigned the opinion to Frankfurter. When Justice Jackson suggested that it would be better for a southerner to write the opinion, Stone reassigned *Allwright* to Reed. *See* Mason, *supra* n. 2, at 615-616.

39. Smith v. Allwright, *supra* n. 38, Box 80 (Mar. 15, 1944).

40. *Id.* at 665-666. After all this effort, Frankfurter did not subscribe to Reed's opinion but merely concurred in the result.

41. *Supra* n. 30, Box 61 (April 5, 1940).

42. Louisiana ex rel. Francis v. Resweber, 329 U.S. 459 (1947), Box 100 (Dec. 12, 1946).

43. Joint Anti-Fascist Refugee Committee v. McGrath, 341 U.S. 123 (1951), Box 133 (Apr. 13, 1951).

44. *See* Hirsch, *supra* n. 7, at 184, on suggestions to other justices. Frankfurter once remarked, "The trouble with Stanley is that he doesn't let his clerks do enough of the work. The trouble with Murphy is that he lets his clerks do too much of the work." Allen interview, *supra* n. 5, at 6.

45. United Public Workers v. Mitchell, 330 U.S. 75 (1947), Box 98 (Jan. 13 and 16, 1947).

46. 329 U.S. 29 (1947), Box 98 (Nov. 15 and Nov. 16, 1946).

47. Breard v. City of Alexandria, 341 U.S. 622 (1951), Box 137 (no date).

48. *Id.*, Box 137 (May 26, 1951).

49. Mazer v. Stein, 347 U.S. 201 (1954), Box 156 (no date).

50. Respectively: U.S. v. Line Material Co., *supra* n. 22, Box 106 (Mar. 5, 1948); Angel v. Bullington, 330 U.S. 183 (1947), Box 99 (no date); Thompson v. Gaskill, 315 U.S. 442 (1942), Box 171 (no date); and Jay v. Boyd, 351 U.S. 345 (1956), Box 167 (no date).

51. Higgins v. Smith, 308 U.S. 473 (1940), Box 60 (no date).

52. Hirsch, *supra* n. 7, at 136, 144, 184, and 188

189. O'Brien, *supra* n. 13, at 302.

53. Hirsch, *supra* n. 7, at 184-85. Frankfurter once described Reed to the latter's law clerk as "a man who crawls from detail to detail." Zimmerman interview, *supra* n. 6, at 6.

54. Allan interview, *supra* n. 5, at 8.

55. Ford Motor Co. v. Beauchamp, 308 U.S. 331 (1939), Box 60 (Nov. 30, 1939).

56. *Id.*, Hirsch, *supra* n. 7, at 143, reports that Reed seemed startled by this, and Frankfurter later wrote to soothe his feelings. The book is THE COMMERCE POWER..., *supra* n. 4. In their argument over the "preferred position" approach in *Ullman v. U.S.*, *supra* n. 19, Box 176 (Feb. 7, 1956), Frankfurter called Reed's attention to another of his books, MR. JUSTICE HOLMES..., *supra* n. 4.

57. Higgins v. C.I.R., 312 U.S. 212 (1941), Box 65 (Jan. 30, 1941).

58. Uverges v. Pennsylvania, 335 U.S. 447 (1949), Box 120 (Dec. 1, 1948). There is no "full blast" in the Reed papers.

59. Mastro Plastics Corp. v. NLRB, 350 U.S. 270 (1956), Box 176 (Feb. 14, 1956). Frankfurter wrote Reed several angry letters about *Mastro* even though Reed did not write the opinion. *See* Schwartz, *supra* n. 26, at 197-198.

60. Memphis Natural Gas Co. v. Stone, 335 U.S. 80 (1948), Box 110 (no date).

61. Johnson v. New York, New Haven and Hartford RR., 344 U.S. 48 (1953), Box 148 (Jan. 3, 1953).

62. Zimmerman interview, *supra* n. 6, at 7.

63. *Id.* at 6.

64. Manning interview, *supra* n. 18.

65. Respectively: Adamson v. California, 332 U.S. 46 (1947), Box 100 (Feb. 5, 1947); U.S. v. Line Material Co., *supra* n. 22,

Box 106 (Dec. 9, 1947); Winters v. New York, *supra* n. 22, Box 106 (Feb. 28, 1948); Jones v. City of Opelika, 319 U.S. 103 (1943), Box 76 (Apr. 9, 1943); and Wade v. Mayo, 334 U.S. 672 (1948), Box 108 (May 24, 1948). Lash, *supra* n. 22, at 286-87, notes a Reed-Frankfurter conversation about Black's manipulativeness.

66. Baltimore Contractors v. Bodinger, 348 U.S. 176 (1955), Box 159 (Dec. 21, 1954).

67. *Supra* n. 69, Box 100 (Feb. 5, 1947).

68. American Trucking Assn. v. U.S., 344 U.S. 298 (1953), Box 146 (Dec. 19, 1952).

69. In re Summers, 325 U.S. 561 (1945), Box 87 (May 31, 1945). Illinois refused to admit Summers to the bar because he was a conscientious objector. Black's draft quoted the clause thusly: no religious test shall ever be required as a Qualification to any Office or public Trust *in* the United States. The clause in Article VI actually reads:...any Office or public Trust *under* the United States.

70. Dec. 5, 1951. Part III, Reel 3 (FF papers, Harv. Law Sch.). Frankfurter was writing about Murphy's majority opinion (which Reed joined) in *Schneiderman v. U.S.*, 320 U.S. 118 (1943), a denaturalization case. He wrote in the context of *Dennis v. U.S.*, 341 U.S. 494 (1951), involving the conviction of Communist Party leaders under the Smith Act.

71. Lash, *supra* n. 22, at 270. This was a pejorative comment. Reed was under no illusions about his own intellectual capacity.

72. Box 165 (no date).

73. U.S. v. Felin & Co., 334 U.S. 624 (1948), Box 108 (no date).

74. Hynes v. Grimes Packing Co., 337 U.S. 86 (1949), Box 119 (Jan. 27, 1949). Two Reed clerks remarked that Reed was notably unsympathetic to Indian claims. Zimmerman, *supra* n. 6, at 8, quotes Reed as saying of Frankfurter, "he'll give this country back to the Indians." *See also* Rossett, *supra* n 5, at 25. Dissenting in *U.S. v. Alcea Band of Tillamooks*, 329 U.S. 40 (1946), at 57-59, Reed referred to the Indians as a vanquished people whose title to land was extinguished by the sword. The footnote 4 reference is to Stone's famous suggestion in *U.S. v. Carolene Products Co.*, 304 U.S. 144 (1938), that the Court might give special consideration to claims from "discrete and insular minorities."

75. Johnson v. Muelberger, 340 U.S. 581 (1951), Box 136 (Feb. 17, 1951).

76. National City Bank v. Republic of China, 348 U.S. 356 (1955), Box 159 (no date). The reference is to Chiang Kai-shek, the leader of the Nationalist forces on Taiwan.

77. Koster v. Lumbermans Mutual Casualty Co., 330 U.S. 530 (1947), Box 100 (no date).

78. Dennis v. U.S., *supra* n. 70, Box 137 (Feb. 17, 1951).

79. *Supra* n. 19, Box 151 (handwritten notes on an SR memorandum dated Apr. 9, 1953).

80. Hills interview, *supra* n. 5, at 32-34. The case was *NLRB v. Babcock and Wilcox Co.*, 351 U.S. 103 (1956), at 107.

81. Kedroff v. St. Nicholas Cathedral, 344 U.S. 94 (1952), Box 141 (no date).

82. Both quotes are from O'Brien, *supra* n. 13, at 164-165.

83. *Id.* at 165.

Freshman opinion writing on the U.S. Supreme Court, 1921-1991

New justices have been no less likely than their senior colleagues to author majority opinions or to be assigned difficult decisions, suggesting the nonexistence of a freshman effect.

by **Terry Bowen and John M. Scheb II**

Part of the conventional wisdom about the U.S. Supreme Court is the presumed existence of a freshman effect, a distinct pattern of behavior associated with newly appointed justices.[1] In his study of the freshman years of Justice Frank Murphy, Howard asserts that "a season of adjustment has been found necessary by virtually every new justice, regardless of era or of prior occupation, before he became a fully effective member of the Court."[2]

Howard attributes freshman behavior on the Supreme Court to three factors. First, the Supreme Court's enormous workload demands great discipline and sacrifice. Second, disputes before the Court tend to be "infinitely more complex than those [freshmen] have encountered before."[3] Third, the Court's internal procedures ensure a freshman effect. Junior justices "speak last and vote first during conferences, and receive relatively light assignments."[4]

Conventional wisdom, however, is not always borne out by empirical examination. Mounting evidence challenges the freshman effect posited by Howard and other scholars.[5] Despite this evidence, questions remain about certain aspects of the freshman effect.

Most empirical analyses of the freshman effect have focused on the hypothesis that freshmen justices are less likely than their senior colleagues to defend an extreme ideological position and, as a consequence, fail to join existing blocs. Generally speaking, these studies have concluded that while the freshman effect may have been prominent from 1921-1952, it has been declining since 1953.[6] Yet in the most comprehensive study to date on the topic, Bowen and Scheb found no relationship between bloc voting and freshman/senior status, even during the 1921-1952 period.[7] The debate over the freshman effect, however, is not limited to bloc voting behavior. As Howard suggested, an equally important component of the freshman experience is the expectation that junior justices will be assigned lighter workloads.

Majority opinion assignments

The manner in which majority opinions are assigned on the Supreme Court is well established. As a matter of institutional practice, the duty of assigning majority opinions falls to the chief justice. If the chief justice does not vote with the majority, the duty falls to the senior justice on the winning side. Several factors are thought to influence opinion assignment.

A number of scholars submit that the opinion assigner seeks to strengthen or maintain existing coalitions by assigning opinions to the justice whose views are thought to be closest to the minority position.[8] Although these studies provide limited empirical support for this proposition, Brenner and Spaeth found no significant relationship between assignment to the marginal justice and the maintenance of coalition strength.[9]

Other researchers speculate that opinion assignments are made in an effort to further the assigner's policy preferences. Testing this proposition for civil liberties decisions by the Warren Court, Rohde found that majority opinions were either self-assigned or were assigned to the justice whose views were nearest the opinion assigner. This pattern of opinion assignment was more pronounced in important cases and as the size of the majority increased.[10]

Interestingly, Rathjen found that Rohde's findings did not hold for the Warren Court's economics cases,[11] yet he did not discount the influence of the opinion assigner's policy preferences in the assignment decision. Instead, Rathjen suggested that Rohde's explanation was relevant among issues the Court considered most important. Less important opinion assignments were made in an attempt to balance the Court's workload. Subsequent studies have provided some evidence for this belief, finding that while Chief Justices William Howard Taft through William Rehnquist disproportionately assigned important cases, they maintained equality across the total range of cases.[12]

Experience is an additional consideration in the assignment of majority opinions. For Chief Justices Charles Evans Hughes and Harlan Fiske Stone, easing the transition of freshmen members apparently was an important consideration in awarding majority opinion assignments.[13] Hughes, for instance, believed that "the community has no more a valuable asset than an experienced judge. It takes a new judge a long time to become a complete master of the material of his Court."[14] Similarly, Stone thought that "a new judge beginning the work of the Court should be put at his ease in taking on the work until he is thoroughly familiar with it."[15] Such a consideration is not inconsequential. Attempts to ease freshmen justices into the Court's work require other justices to produce at a higher level.[16]

Although some justices might attempt to ease the transition of freshmen members by assigning lighter workloads, Slotnick's study of opinion assignments for the years 1921-1973 suggests that freshmen do not generally receive a disproportionate amount of opinion assignments. Rather, Slotnick argues that "there is no minimal assignment apprenticeship . . ."[17] Using an opinion assignment ratio (OAR) that reflects the number of opinion assignments with the number of times a justice voted in the majority, Slotnick found that

the "relatively young and relatively inexperienced justices are also the most prolific."[18]

More recent studies provide conflicting evidence regarding the assignment of majority opinions. Using the OAR, scholars have found that Justices David Souter, Antonin Scalia, and Anthony Kennedy ranked last in the number of opinions assigned to them during their initial terms.[19] Similarly, Scheb and Ailshie found that Justice Sandra Day O'Connor ranked last in the number of opinion assignments she received, at least in absolute terms.[20]

Workload considerations cannot be fully understood without giving some consideration to the difficulty or importance of the decision. As Melone suggests, "[I]t is not enough to know how many opinions a new justice has written," because important and difficult decisions "may require more legal and political skill than writing many routine ones."[21] Thus, "if new justices must craft difficult and important decisions, then it matters little that they write fewer opinions than their senior colleagues."[22] This suggests that the number of important decisions may be negatively correlated to the number of opinions assigned. Using the headlines on the cover of the advance sheets of the *United States Supreme Court Reports—Lawyers' Edition* to identify important decisions,[23] Melone found that Justice Kennedy received a fair shair of important decisions, at least by his second term. Rubin and Melone found that Justice Scalia was not as fortunate.[24] Of 14 important decisions during his initial term, Scalia was assigned none. Likewise, during his inaugural term, Justice Souter received none of the Court's important decsisions.[25] Generally speaking, these findings are consistent with Slotnick's.[26] Although his methodology differed,[27] Slotnick found that the greatest number of important opinions was written by justices in their second year.

'Difficult' decisions

A possible objection to using only "important" decisions to understand the justices' workloads is that the total range of the opinion-writing experience is diluted; that is, importance cannot necessarily be equated to difficulty. Therefore, it may be useful to develop a different measure of opinion difficulty: the margin of victory that majority opinions represent. Arguably, as the margin of victory declines, crafting a majority opinion becomes

Table 1　OAR rankings on the Supreme Court, 1921-1991, by term

1921	1922	1922-23	1924-25	1930	1931-32	1937	1937-38
Holmes	Taft	Taft	Taft	Hughes	**Cardozo**	Roberts	Roberts
Taft	Holmes	Holmes	Holmes	**Roberts**	Stone	Hughes	Stone
Brandeis	**Sutherland**	Sutherland	Brandeis	Stone	Hughes	Stone	Hughes
Clarke	Brandeis	Brandeis	**Stone**	Holmes	Roberts	Butler	**Reed**
McReynolds	McKenna	**Butler**	Butler	Sutherland	Sutherland	Brandeis	McReynolds
McKenna	McReynolds	McKenna	McReynolds	Brandeis	Butler	**Black**	Black*
Day	Van Devanter*	**Sanford**	Sutherland	Butler	Brandeis	McReynolds*	Butler*
Pitney*		McReynolds	Sanford*	McReynolds	McReynolds		
Van Devanter*		Van Devanter*	Van Devanter*	Van Devanter*	Van Devanter*		
(M=11.90)	(M=12.77)	(M=11.63)	(M=11.16)	(M=11.06)	(M=11.65)	(M=11.94)	(M=12.85)
(S=3.99)	(S=4.28)	(S=2.95)	(S=2.71)	(S=4.91)	(S=4.95)	(S=2.46)	(S=1.58)

1938-39	1939-40	1941	1942-43	1945
Douglas	Douglas	Douglas	Black	Black
Stone	Black	Stone	Stone	Douglas
Hughes	Stone	Roberts	Douglas	Stone
Frankfurter	Hughes	Black	Jackson	Rutledge
Roberts	Roberts	Frankfurter	Roberts	Murphy
Black	Reed	**Byrnes**	Reed	Reed
Reed*	**Murphy***	Murphy	Murphy	Frankfurter
		Jackson	Frankfurter*	**Burton***
		Reed*	**Rutledge**	
(M=12.86)	(M=13.04)	(M=12.48)	(M=12.25)	(M=14.81)
(S=2.02)	(S=2.45)	(S=3.75)	(S=3.24)	(S=7.16)

1946	1949	1953	1954-55	1956	1956-57	1958	1962	1965
Black	Black	Douglas	Warren	Douglas	Douglas	Douglas	Stewart	Stewart
Douglas	Jackson	Black	**Harlan**	Clark	Harlan	Harlan	**White**	Douglas
Murphy	**Minton**	**Warren**	Douglas	Frankfurter	Clark	Brennan	Clark	Black
Frankfurter	Black	Warren	Frankfurter	Harlan	Brennan	Black	**Goldberg**	White
Reed	Frankfurter	Jackson	Reed	Burton	Black	Warren	Douglas	Clark
Frankfurter	Vinson	Frankfurter	Black	**Brennan**	Brennan	Whittaker	Brennan*	**Fortas***
Clark	Harlan	Frankfurter	**Stewart**	Warren	Harlan	Clark*	Black*	Warren*
Rutledge	Reed*	Minton	Burton*		**Whittaker***			
Burton*		Burton	Minton*		Burton*			
(M=13.76)	(M=12.98)	(M=12.14)	(M=12.87)	(M=11.72)	(M=11.55)	(M=12.55)	(M=11.22)	(M=11.42)
(S=6.92)	(S=4.11)	(S=2.97)	(S=1.82)	(S=2.01)	(S=2.93)	(S=1.80)	(S=1.32)	(S=1.92)

Jackson	**Clark**	Reed
Vinson	Burton	Clark

1967-68	1969	1970	1971-72	1975-76	1981
Marshall	Douglas	Douglas	**Powell**	Brennan	Rehnquist
Black	Black	Stewart	Brennan	Marshall	White
Harlan	Stewart	Black	**Rehnquist**	Rehnquist	Marshall
Stewart	**Burger**	White	Douglas	**Stevens**	Brennan
Douglas	White	Brennan	Marshall	White	Stevens
White	Marshall	Burger	White	Stewart	Burger
Brennan	Harlan*	Marshall	Stewart	Blackmun	Powell
Warren	Brennan*	**Blackmun***	Burger	Burger	Blackmun
Fortas*		Harlan*	Blackmun*	Powell	**O'Connor***
(M=10.62)	(M=13.57)	(M=12.15)	(M=12.61)	(M=10.33)	(M=11.50)
(S=1.57)	(S=2.40)	(S=3.21)	(S=2.41)	(S=1.41)	
			(S=1.16)		

1986	1987-88	1990	1991
Marshall	Stevens	Stevens	O'Connor
Brennan	Brennan	Marshall	White
O'Connor	Marshall	O'Connor	Stevens
Powell	White	White	Scalia
Stevens	Blackmun	Rehnquist	Blackmun
Rehnquist	Rehnquist	Blackmun	Rehnquist
White	O'Connor	Kennedy	Souter
Blackmun*	**Kennedy**	Scalia	**Thomas**
Scalia*	Scalia*	**Souter***	Kennedy
(M=13.55)	(M=12.59)	(M=12.43)	(M=13.52)
(S=2.07)	(S=2.07)	(S=3.08)	(S=1.58)

Note: Justices are listed in descending order of OAR scores. Freshmen justices are **boldfaced**; M=mean; S=standard deviation; * indicates that justice's OAR is more than one standard deviation below the Court's mean.

more difficult, because the majority opinion writer strives to deal with dissenting arguments. Conversely, as the Court approaches unanimity, the crafting of the majority opinion becomes easier. This is tacitly acknowledged by the Court's tradition "that precludes any qualifying opinion in a decision involving a new justice's first opinion for the Court."[28]

If opinion difficulty correlates to experience on the Court, freshmen should be less likely to author majority opinions as the margin of victory decreases. This would be consistent with the notion that opinion assigners consider a justice's experience in assigning difficult decisions. This proposition, however, has not yet been tested. Any test of this proposition must take into account Slotnick's finding that chief justices tend to retain unanimous opinions for themselves.[29]

Although earlier studies suggest there are no significant differences between freshmen and senior justices in terms of opinion assignments, the most recent evidence suggests that justices receive lighter assignment loads in their initial terms.[30] How can these differences be explained? One possibility is the type of analysis employed. While earlier findings were based on aggregate results that might have masked individual effects, later studies based their conclusions on data from one justice. To further understand this aspect of the freshman effect, a more definitive study is required.

Hypotheses

The literature regarding majority opinion assignments suggests that opinion assigners are guided by two basic considerations. First, opinion assigners consider the ideology and policy preferences of justices they choose to write majority opinions.[31] Second, opinion assigners attempt to maintain equality in the number of opinions assigned to all justices.[32] Given the first consideration, freshmen justices who are less ideologically committed would be expected to receive significantly fewer opinion assignments. Since freshmen justices are not less ideologically committed than their senior colleagues,[33] however, the equality principle should apply to freshmen as well as senior justices.

Hypothesis 1, therefore, is that the number of majority opinions will be distributed evenly between freshmen and senior justices, at least in the aggregate. This does not discount the possibility that individual justices might indeed exhibit a freshman effect. Therefore, this article develops a criterion that can isolate cases in which the freshman effect may be present.

Even if freshmen are not assigned significantly fewer majority opinion assignments than their senior colleagues, it might nevertheless be the case that they are assigned significantly less difficult opinions.[34] Accordingly, Hypothesis 2 is that opinions by freshmen justices are significantly less difficult than those of their senior colleagues.

Methodology

Data for this research were collected using the decisions of the Supreme Court as reported in the *United States Reports*. The data consist of all plenary decisions of the Court rendered during the period beginning with the 1921 term (the first year studied by Slotnick) and ending with the 1991 term.

To test for a freshman effect in the assignment of majority opinions to new justices on the Supreme Court, the behavior of all justices was examined for the 32 terms in which there were freshmen justices on the Court.[35] A justice's freshman period was defined as his or her first term on the Court, assuming the newcomer participated in at least 70 percent of the Court's plenary decisions on the merits rendered with full opinions. In instances where a new justice did not meet this condition, the freshman period was expanded to include all plenary decisions during the Court's following term.[36] For each term, an opinion assignment ratio was determined for each justice. These scores represent the percentage of times a justice was assigned an opinion when voting with the majority.

To test for the existence of the freshman effect, freshmen and senior justices were compared in terms of the proportion of opinion assignments they received. Although no theory defining meaningful differences exists, the existence of the freshman effect is identified here in instances where a justice's assignment load is more than one standard deviation below the Court's mean.

To test the proposition that freshman opinion assignments are less difficult than senior ones, the average size of the victory margin of winning coalitions for each justice for each term was calculated. Freshmen and senior justices were then compared in terms of the consensus level, or margin of victory, underlying their majority opinions.[37] If Hypothesis 2 is correct, the consensus level would be

Table 2   OAR scores by freshman/senior status

All terms	Freshman	Senior
Mean	11.60	12.38
Std. Dev.	2.63	3.28
Number	38	238
F=1.94	Sig.=.16	

1921-1952 terms	Freshman	Senior
Mean	11.94	12.53
Std. Dev.	3.01	4.23
Number	19	106
F=.35	Sig.=.55	

1953-1991 terms	Freshman	Senior
Mean	11.26	12.26
Std. Dev.	2.22	2.26
Number	19	132
F=3.21	Sig.=.07	

Table 3   Freshman OAR thresholds

No freshman effect	1921-1952 Freshman effect
N=16 84%	N=3 16%
Taft	Murphy
Sutherland	Rutledge
Butler	Burton
Sanford	
Stone	
Roberts	
Cardozo	
Black	
Reed	
Douglas	
Frankfurter	
Byrnes	
Jackson	
Vinson	
Clark	
Minton	

No freshman effect	1953-1991 Freshman effect
N=13 68%	N=6 32%
Warren	Fortas
Harlan	Blackmun
Brennan	O'Connor
Stewart	Scalia
Goldberg	Souter
White	
Marshall	
Burger	
Powell	
Rehnquist	
Stevens	
Kennedy	
Thomas	

Overall	
N=29 76%	N=9 24%

Table 4   Consensus level underlying majority opinions by freshman/senior status (all justices)

All terms	Freshman	Senior
Mean	6.16	6.02
Std. Dev.	1.23	1.54
Number	38	238
F=.30	Sig.=.58	

1921-1952 terms	Freshman	Senior
Mean	6.81	6.98
Std. Dev.	1.17	1.40
Number	19	106
F=.23	Sig.=.63	

1953-1991 terms	Freshman	Senior
Mean	5.52	5.26
Std. Dev.0.92	1.17	
Number	19	132
F=.87	Sig.=.35	

Table 5   Consensus level underlying majority opinions by freshman/senior status (associate justices only)

All terms	Freshman	Senior
Mean	6.08	5.96
Std. Dev.	1.23	1.56
Number	34	210
F=.17	Sig.=.68	

1921-1952 terms	Freshman	Senior
Mean	6.77	6.93
Std. Dev.	1.15	1.45
Number	17	93
F=.18	Sig.=.68	

1953-1991 terms	Freshman	Senior
Mean	5.38	5.19
Std. Dev.	0.86	1.18
Number	17	117
F=.40	Sig.=.53	

significantly higher for majority opinions authored by freshmen justices. To address Slotnick's finding that chief justices retain unanimous opinions for themselves,[38] the analysis was run again, omitting chief justices.

Finally, to test the "decline of the freshman effect" hypothesis suggested in other studies, separate comparisons were run for the periods 1921-1952 and 1953-1991. Table 1 indicates those OAR rankings relevant to this inquiry.

Results and discussion

For the entire period of the study, 1921-1991, only 24 percent of the freshmen on the Court failed to meet the established threshold of opinion assignments. Overall, between 1921 and 1991, no significant difference exists between freshmen justices and their senior colleagues with respect to opinion assignments, as seen in Table 2. Notwithstanding methodological differences, this finding is consistent with Slotnick's findings for the 1921-73 period.[39]

For the period 1921-52, which includes the Hughes-Stone era, there was no greater tendency for freshmen to receive lighter opinion loads, as shown in Table 3. Given Hughes's and Stone's affinity for easing freshmen into the Court, it was suprising to find that only Justices Frank Murphy, Wiley Rutledge, and Harold Burton failed to receive workloads similar to the senior members on the Court while these two were chief justice. This does, however, provide empirical support for the argument that both Murphy[40] and Rutledge[41] were treated differently, at least initially, from their senior colleagues with respect to opinion assignments.

Likewise, the 1953-1991 period does not differ from the earlier period. Again, there is no evidence of any greater tendency of freshmen to receive fewer opinion assignments. It is noteworthy, however, that during the Warren-Burger-Rehnquist era, 32 percent of freshmen received lighter workloads (twice as many as the earlier period) than their senior colleagues. This trend has been prominent since 1981, as three of the five new appointees (O'Connor, Scalia, and Souter) received lighter workloads. This finding is consistent with more recent studies that have confirmed the existence of the freshman effect in opinion assignments.

There is also no evidence for the proposition that the opinions assigned to freshmen justices are any less difficult than those assigned to senior justices, as shown in Table 4. There is no appreciable difference between the level of consensus underlying the majority opinions authored by freshmen versus senior justices. This remains the case when chief justices are removed from the analysis (see Table 5). Therefore, even if freshmen workloads are lighter, it appararently is not related to the difficulty of the decision.

Conclusion

This study of opinion assignments on the Supreme Court during 1921-1991 terms suggests the freshman effect posited by Howard and established as part of the conventional wisdom regarding the Court simply does not exist. Newcomers are no less likely to author majority opinions, nor are they less likely to be assigned difficult opinions. A cautionary note is appropriate here. This examination of the freshman effect has been limited to the phenomenon of opinion assignments and says nothing about the legal impact or scholarly quality of those opinions. It might well be that freshmen on the Supreme Court differ from their senior colleagues in other meaningful ways. Evidently, they do not differ in terms of being assigned majority opinions.

NOTES

This article originally appeared in Volume 76, Number 5, February-March 1993, pages 239-243.

1. *See, e.g.,* Brenner, *Another Look at Freshman Indecisiveness on the Supreme Court*, 16 POLITY 320 (1983); Snyder, *The Supreme Court as a Small Group*, 32 SOC. FORCES 232 (1958).

2. Howard, MR. JUSTICE MURPHY: A POLITICAL BIOGRAPHY 237 (Princeton, N.J.: Princeton University Press, 1968).

3. *Id.*

4. *Id.*

5. *See* Bowen and Scheb, *Reassessing the 'Freshman Effect': The Voting Bloc Alignment of New Justices on the United States Supreme Court, 1921-90*, Forthcoming in POLITICAL BEHAVIOR (1993); Heck, *The Socialization of a Freshman Justice: The Early Years of Justice Brennan*, 10 PAC. L. J. 707 (1979); Heck and Hall, *Bloc Voting and the Freshman Justice Revisited*, 43 J. POL. 852 (1981); Melone, *Revisiting the freshman effect hypothesis: the first two terms of Justice Anthony Kennedy*, 74 JUDICATURE 6 (1990); Rubin and Melone, *Justice Antonin Scalia: a first year freshman effect?*, 72 JUDICATURE 98 (1988); Scheb and Ailshie, *Justice Sandra Day O'Connor and the 'freshman effect'*, 69 JUDICATURE 9 (1985).

6. *See* Heck, *supra* n. 5; Heck and Hall, *supra* n. 5; Melone, *supra* n. 5; Rubin and Melone, *supra* n. 5; Scheb and Ailshie, *supra* n. 5. *For a competing view, see* Brenner *supra*, n. 1.

7. Bowen and Scheb, *supra* n. 5.

8. *See* Danelski, *The Influence of the Chief Justice in the Decisional Process of the Supreme Court*, in Goldman and Sarat, eds., AMERICAN COURT SYSTEMS (San Francisco: Freeman, 1978); McLauchlan, *Ideology and Conflict in Supreme Court Opinion Assignments, 1946-1952*, 25 W. POL. Q. 16 (1972); Rohde, *Policy Goals, Strategic Choice, and Majority Opinion Assignments in the U.S. Supreme Court*, 16 AM. J. POL. SCI. 652 (1972); Ulmer, *The Use of Power in the Supreme Court*, 30 J. PUB. L. 49 (1970).

9. Brenner and Spaeth, *Majority Opinion Assignments and the Maintenance of the Original Coalition on the Warren Court*, 32 AM. J. POL. SCI. 72 (1988).

10. Rohde, *supra* n. 8.

11. Rathjen, *Policy Goals, Strategic Choices, and Majority Opinion Assignments in the U.S. Supreme Court: A Replication*, 18 AM. J. POL. SCI. 713 (1974).

12. Davis, *Power on the Court: Chief Justice Rehnquist's opinion assignments*, 74 JUDICATURE 66 (1990); Slotnick, *Who Speaks for the Court? Majority Opinion Assignments from Taft to Burger*, 23 AM. J. POL. SCI. 60 (1979); Spaeth, *Distributive justice: majority opinion assignments in the Burger Court*, 67 JUDICATURE 299 (1984).

13. Mason, HARLAN FISKE STONE: PILLAR OF THE LAW (New York: Viking Press, 1956); Pusey, CHARLES EVANS HUGHES, Vol. 1 (New York: Macmillan, 1951).

14. Hughes, THE SUPREME COURT OF THE UNITED STATES 74-75 (New York: Columbia University Press, 1928).

15. Mason, *supra* n. 13, at 602.

16. Mason, *supra* n. 13.

17. Slotnick, *Judicial Career Patterns and Majority Opinion Assignments on the Supreme Court*, 41 J. POL. 640, 645 (1979).

18. *Id.* at 648.

19. Johnson and Smith, *David Souter's first term on the Supreme Court: the impact of a new justice*, 74 JUDICATURE 238 (1992); Melone, *supra* n. 5; Rubin and Melone, *supra* n. 5.

20. Scheb and Ailshie, *supra* n. 5.

21. Melone, *supra* n. 5, at 8.

22. *Id.*

23. For a description of this method *see* Spaeth, *supra* n. 12.

24. Rubin and Melone, *supra* n. 5.

25. Johnson and Smith, *supra* n. 19.

26. Slotnick, *supra* n. 17.

27. Cases were identified as important if they appeared in two leading public law sourceboooks. *See* Slotnick, *supra* n. 17, at 642.

28. Abraham, THE JUDICIAL PROCESS 212, n.1 (New York: Oxford University Press, 1986).

29. Slotnick, *supra* n. 12.

30. Davis, *supra* n. 12; Slotnick, *supra* n. 12; Spaeth, *supra* n. 12.

31. Danelski, *supra* n. 8; McLauchlan, *supra* n. 8; Rohde, *supra* n. 8; Ulmer, *supra* n. 8.

32. Davis, *supra* n. 12; Slotnick, *supra* n. 12; Spaeth, *supra* n. 12.

33. Bowen and Scheb, *supra* n. 5.

34. Melone, *supra* n. 5.

35. There were 37 freshmen justices during the period of this study. Chief Justice Charles Evans Hughes was classified as a non-freshman due to his earlier service on the Court.

36. Based on Howard's study of Justice Murphy, see Howard, *supra* n. 2, it might be argued that a longer period should be examined. Assuredly, the time it takes to be assimilated into the work of the Court is an important consideration of the freshman effect. But this represents an entirely different question. Moreover, no theory has been developed that precisely describes what this period should or might be. We are, therefore, more concerned with identifying if justices, at least initially, systematically differ from their senior colleagues. Fundamental to that comparison is that each justice must hear a similar number of cases during their initiation to the Court. The 70 percent criterion employed here serves that purpose well.

37. "Margin of victory" is not to be confused with the concept of "size of winning coalition." For example, in a 6-3 decision, the margin of victory is three whereas the size of the winning coalition is six. Because this analysis includes unanimous decisions, the average margin of victory is higher than would otherwise be expected.

38. Slotnick, *supra* n. 12.

39. Slotnick, *supra* n. 17.

40. Howard, *supra* n. 2.

41. Mason, *supra* n. 13.

Rehnquist Court disposition of lower court decisions: affirmation, not reversal

The Rehnquist Court, during its first three terms, has not adhered to the "error correction" strategy of the Warren and Burger Courts. The reasons for its higher affirmation rate remain unclear.

by Jeffrey A. Segal and Harold J. Spaeth

Scholars and commentators have long observed that the U.S. Supreme Court has a decided propensity to accept for review cases that it intends to reverse.[1] This penchant has been described as "too definite to have arisen by sheer happenstance."[2] Some analysts suggest that the Court's practice of reversing lower courts reflects an "error correction strategy."[3] One can find language in the Court's opinions to support this judgment: "Because we find that the Court of Appeals erred in its construction...we reverse."[4] Others carry reversal a step further and cite it as evidence of the operation of the justices' personal policy preferences.[5] Clearly, these two positions are not incompatible.

The reason for a reversal or error-correction strategy is clear. Given a finite number of cases that can be reviewed in a given term, the Court must decide how to utilize its time, its most scarce resource. Certainly, overturning unfavorable lower court decisions has more of an impact—if nothing else than to the parties to the suit—than affirming favorable ones. Thus the Court will be more likely to hear cases with which it disagrees, other things being equal.

The purpose of this article is to investigate why the Rehnquist Court has abruptly and sharply discontinued the reversal practices of its predecessor Courts. No one has yet conducted such an inquiry. It is an important matter because it not only indicates a basic change in most, if not all, of the justices' strategies to grant and deny review, but it also suggests that marked changes are occurring in the Court's management and control of its docket.

Procedure

We begin by delineating the degree to which the Rehnquist Court's decisional behavior differs from that of the Warren and Burger Courts. We will then attempt to explain empirically why the Rehnquist Court has altered the Court's behavior in this crucial aspect of its decision making.

Our data are drawn from the preliminary version of the U.S. Supreme Court Judicial Data Base[6] and consist of all orally argued cases decided from the 1953 through the 1988 terms of the Court that are not listed on the Court's original docket. This period includes the Warren and Burger Courts and the first three terms of the Rehnquist Court. We use docket number as our unit of analysis because the Court does not necessarily dispose of all cases decided by a single opinion in the same fashion. We also count as separate cases the handful that the Data Base identifies as containing split votes, in the sense that one or more of the justices voted with the majority on one aspect or issue of the case and dissented on another. We include these to avoid making an arbitrary judgment of whether the Court affirmed or reversed the lower court's decision.

Because the Court's formal disposition of the cases it decides is not an unerring guide to affirmation or reversal, the U.S. Supreme Court Data Base specifies whether the petitioning party prevailed or not. If the petitioning party prevailed, we count the case as a reversal of the lower court. If the data base indicates that the petitioning party did not prevail, we count the case as affirmed.[7]

Analysis and findings

Table 1 specifies the frequency with which each Court upheld and reversed the court whose decision it reviewed. Although the Warren and Burger Courts do not appreciably differ, the Rehnquist Court does. The likelihood that this overall pattern occurred by chance is extremely remote (p<.0001). Breaking these data down by term (see Table 2) shows that only in the first term of the Warren Court and in the two most recent terms of the Rehnquist Court did the justices affirm as many as half their cases. Reversals peaked in the 1963 and 1964 terms at 74.7 and 76.2 percent, respectively.

Table 3 examines reversal rates by Court and issue area. The issue areas are the 13 broad categories into which the Supreme Court Data Base is divided.[8] We so divide the Court's decisions because reversal may disproportionately occur in certain areas and not in others. We examine issue areas in two ways: First, we combine the Warren and Burger Courts together and compare the resulting hybrid with the Rehnquist Court. We do so because, as we have seen, both the Warren and Burger Courts followed a reversal practice while the Rehnquist Court has not. Second, we compare the Burger Court with the Rehnquist Court. We do this because these Courts are conservative in the thrust of their decision making, unlike the Warren Court.

The second, third and fourth columns of Table 3 provide the percent of cases each Court reversed in each issue area, followed by the total number of cases heard in that area. The fifth column specifies the probability that the pattern of affirmations and reversals between the hybrid Warren/Burger Court and the Rehnquist Court occurred by chance for each of the 13 issue areas into which the data base is divided. The sixth column specifies this probability when the Burger and Rehnquist Courts are compared. In each of the asterisked areas, the Rehnquist Court affirmed a significantly larger proportion of its decisions than its predecessor Courts. As the table shows, this is especially true of civil rights and judicial power, and less so—but still significantly—of due process,

Table 1   Affirmation and reversal, by Court

	Warren	Burger	Rehnquist	Row total
Affirm	756	976	231	1963
	(35.2%)	(34.9%)	(46.0%)	(36.1%)
Reverse	1393	1818	271	3482
	(64.8%)	(65.1%)	(54.0%)	(63.9%)
Column total	2149	2794	502	5445

Table 2   Reversal rate by term

Term	Rate	Term	Rate	Term	Rate	Term	Rate
53	48.2	62	74.7	71	61.2	80	66.7
54	66.7	63	76.2	72	68.2	81	65.0
55	53.3	64	72.5	73	67.5	82	62.6
56	66.0	65	71.1	74	68.1	83	72.1
57	56.6	66	69.9	75	65.5	84	63.6
58	57.1	67	68.0	76	64.6	85	58.3
59	60.3	68	72.1	77	68.7	86	61.7
60	53.1	69	64.5	78	66.9	87	49.7
61	68.9	70	60.1	79	61.5	88	50.0

Table 3   Reversal rates by issue area

	Warren	Burger	Rehnquist	Sig.[1]	Sig.[2]
Criminal procedure	61.2 (376)	65.1 (548)	62.4 (109)	.90	.58
Civil rights	70.5 (244)	66.4 (574)	48.8 (80)	.001*	.002*
First Amendment	71.2 (177)	63.7 (237)	61.7 (47)	.58	.79
Due process	68.4 (38)	71.6 (141)	51.7 (29)	.06	.04*
Privacy	100.0 (1)	70.8 (48)	60.0 (5)	.98	.62
Attorneys	77.8 (9)	59.4 (32)	72.7 (11)	.83	.43
Unions	68.5 (149)	58.9 (129)	47.1 (17)	.25	.35
Economic activity	65.5 (559)	64.9 (504)	52.6 (78)	.03	.04*
Judicial power	63.2 (345)	64.4 (365)	44.3 (70)	.002*	.002*
Federalism	66.0 (103)	69.6 (112)	60.0 (35)	.47	.29
Interstate relations	25.0 (12)	58.8 (17)	100.0 (1)	.95	.41
Federal taxation	54.2 (131)	58.7 (75)	28.6 (14)	.09	.04*
Miscellaneous	60.0 (5)	41.7 (12)	50.0 (6)	1.00	.74

1. Significance of difference between Warren/Burger Court and Rehnquist Court.
2. Significance of difference between Burger Court and Rehnquist Court
*=statistically significant
Numbers in parentheses are the total number of cases decided by the Court in the relevant issue area.

economic activity, and federal taxation. These findings indicate that the Rehnquist Court's affirmation posture results because it reverses significantly fewer cases in these areas than the Warren and Burger Courts did.

Explanations

What accounts for this difference? One may plausibly assume that the frequency of reversal will be less in cases that are reviewed because of conflict in the courts below than in cases where the lower courts do not conflict. The Court's usual proclivity to reverse should be mitigated when the Court's reason for review is conflict below. Consider the following scenarios. In situation one, a lower court rules one way on an issue unresolved by the Supreme Court. Like the overwhelming majority of cases, it is either not appealed or denied review. The following year, a different court hears a similar case and, not bound by horizontal stare decisis, rules in the opposite direction. Now, because there is conflict below, the Supreme Court is much more likely to grant hearing. But because the order in which the lower courts decided the case is unrelated to the predispositions of the Supreme Court, the Court should be no more likely to reverse the recent case than affirm it.

In situation two, both lower courts again decide the question differently, but now they do so at the same time. While the Court could take only the case with which it disagrees, the more likely course of action is to decide both cases together.[9] Presumably, one case will be affirmed and the other reversed, thus precluding the possibility of a reversal strategy. It is thus possible that the Rehnquist Court's affirmation policy stems from hearing a higher proportion of cases in which conflict is stated to be the reason for review.

Three caveats should be noted when analysis considers conflict. First, the Court gives no reason for reviewing cases except on writ of certiorari. Of the 5,445 cases we consider, only 4,074 arose on cert. (All but a handful of the rest came on writs of appeal.) Second, the Court does not provide a reason for review in every cert case. In 1,678 such cases, the Court gave no reason. Mitigating this concern is the fact that the Rehnquist Court was much less derelict in providing reasons for review than its predecessor Courts. It gave reasons two-thirds of the time, while the Warren and Burger Courts each did so in only 57.8 percent of its cert cases. Moreover, slightly more of the Rehnquist Court's cases rose on certiorari (79.3 percent) than did those of the Warren and Burger Courts (75.5 and 73.6 percent, respectively). Also note that the frequency with which the three Courts affirmed and reversed cert and non-cert cases approximates the proportions shown for each Court in Table 1. The Warren Court reversed 65.1 percent of its cert

Table 4   Conflict stated as a reason for the Court's granting cert

	Warren	Burger	Rehnquist	Row total
No conflict	1371 (84.6%)	1599 (77.8%)	242 (60.8%)	3212 (78.8%)
Conflict	250 (15.4%)	457 (22.2%)	156 (39.2%)	863 (21.2%)

cases and 63.9 percent of those that did not arise on cert. The Burger Court's percentages are 65.4 and 64.1, respectively; while those of the Rehnquist Court are 54.8 and 51.0. Clearly then, the writ litigants use to secure review of their cases does not explain affirmation or reversal.

Third, not all authors of opinions and judgments of the Court give reasons at an equal frequency. Douglas did so in barely a third of his Warren Court assignments, while Frankfurter gave a reason in more than 92 percent of his. The variation among the Rehnquist Court justices is much less marked, however. Except for White, who gave a reason in only 41.2 percent of his assignments, and Brennan, 60 percent, the others range between Kennedy's 68.0 and Powell's 87.5.[10] With these caveats in mind, the data indicate that better than two-thirds of the cases in which the Court either gives no reason for review or provides a reason other than conflict were reversed (67.1 percent), as opposed to 53.6 percent that specify conflict as the reason for review. The differences in these proportions are highly significant.

Table 4 shows that the Rehnquist Court does in fact take a much higher percentage of cases with conflict than did either the Warren or Burger Courts. Almost 40 percent of the Rehnquist Court's cert decisions involved conflict (156 of 398), as opposed to only 22.2 percent for the Burger Court (457 of 2056) and a mere 15.4 percent for the Warren Court (250 of 1621). This, though, does not *fully* explain the Rehnquist Court's low reversal rates. While all three Courts affirm more cases involving conflict than they do those without, the Rehnquist Court affirms more frequently than the Warren and Burger Courts even after controlling for conflict (see Table 5).

Specifically, the Rehnquist Court reverses only 46.5 percent of the time in cases involving conflict, compared to 52.4 percent and 56.7 percent for the Warren and Burger Courts, respectively; the Rehnquist Court reverses 60.3 percent of the time in cases not involving conflict, compared to 67.4 percent and 67.9 percent for the Warren and

Burger Courts respectively.

When we examine conflict controlled for issue area, we see that the Rehnquist Court affirms cases with conflict at a significantly higher rate than the Warren and Burger Courts in federal tax cases (p>.04). Similarly, affirmation rates are significantly higher in no conflict cases for the Rehnquist Court in cases involving the exercise of judicial power (p>.04).[11] Accordingly, factors other than conflict or its absence account for the Rehnquist Court's significant proclivity to affirm civil rights, due process, and economic activity cases.

The result of this is as follows: if the Rehnquist Court decreased its granting of cert to cases in which conflict was present from 40 percent to 20 percent, and if its percentage of reversals within the conflict and no conflict cases stayed the same, its overall reversal rate in certiorari cases would increase from 54.9 percent to 57.5 percent. We therefore conclude that the Rehnquist Court's affirmation posture is partially explained by its acceptance of a higher percentage of cases with conflict below, but we do not know why the Rehnquist Court affirms both cases with and without conflict at a higher rate than did the Warren and Burger Courts. In an effort to explain the Rehnquist Court's higher rate of affirmations regardless of conflict, we initially compare the issues contained in the Rehnquist Court's cases with those of its predecessors and the "direction" (liberal or conservative) in which it resolved them.

Content and directionality

Table 6 presents the proportion of each Court's cases that fall into the 13 general issue areas into which the data base is divided. The table shows relatively little difference between the Rehnquist and Burger Courts except for the small "federalism" and "miscellaneous" categories. Indeed, greater differences exist in the issue areas of the cases decided by the Warren and Burger Courts, who parallel one another's reversal rates, than between the Rehnquist and Burger Courts, who do not. We therefore exclude differences in the content of the cases on the Court's docket as an explanation for greater affirmation by the Rehnquist Court.[12]

We turn to the alternative possibility, the direction of the Court's decisions, as a further explanation for affirmation. What we want to know is whether the conservative Rehnquist Court prima-

Table 5 Affirmation and reversal by Court, controlled for conflict

	Warren	Burger	Rehnquist	Row total
Conflict below				
affirmed	119	198	84	401
	(47.6%)	(43.3%)	(53.8%)	(46.5%)
reversed	131	259	72	462
	(52.4%)	(56.7%)	(46.2%)	(53.5%)
column total	250	457	156	863
No conflict below				
affirmed	447	513	96	1056
	(32.6%)	(32.1%)	(39.7%)	(32.9%)
reversed	924	1086	146	2156
	(67.4%)	(67.9%)	(60.3%)	(67.1%)
column total	1371	1599	242	3212

Table 6 Number and proportion of cases by Court, by issue area

	Warren	Burger	Rehnquist	Row total
Criminal	376	548	109	1033
procedure	(17.5%)	(19.6%)	(21.7%)	(19.0%)
Civil rights	244	574	80	898
	(11.4%)	(20.5%)	(15.9%)	(16.5%)
First Amendment	177	237	47	461
	(8.2%)	(8.5%)	(9.4%)	(8.5%)
Due process	38	141	29	208
	(1.8%)	(5.0%)	(5.8%)	(3.8%)
Privacy	1	48	5	54
	(0.0%)	(1.7%)	(1.0%)	(1.0%)
Attorneys	9	32	11	52
	(0.4%)	(1.1%)	(2.2%)	(1.0%)
Unions	149	129	17	295
	(6.9%)	(4.6%)	(3.4%)	(5.4%)
Economic activity	559	504	78	1141
	(26.0%)	(18.0%)	(15.5%)	(21.0%)
Judicial power	345	365	70	780
	(16.1%)	(13.1%)	(13.9%)	(14.3%)
Federalism	103	112	35	250
	(4.8%)	(4.0%)	(7.0%)	(4.6%)
Interstate relations	12	17	1	30
	(0.6%)	(0.6%)	(0.2%)	(0.6%)
Federal taxation	131	75	14	220
	(6.1%)	(2.7%)	(2.8%)	(4.0%)
Miscellaneous	5	12	6	23
	(0.2%)	(0.4%)	(1.2%)	(0.4%)
Column total	2149	2794	502	5445

rily affirms conservative lower court decisions. Phrased differently, are the conservative members of the Rehnquist Court so well entrenched that the additional benefit of strengthening a conservative lower court decision is well worth the rather small probability that the case will be reversed? This does not appear to be the case. Less than 41 percent of the "ideological" cases[13] heard by the Rehnquist Court were decided conservatively by the lower court, compared to almost 45 percent for the Burger Court. The Rehnquist Court affirms more than the Burger Court despite the fact that it takes a smaller percentage of conservative cases than did the Burger Court.

Under these conditions it is not surprising that

the Rehnquist Court affirmed a higher percentage of conservative lower court cases than did the Burger Court (61 percent vs. 37.5 percent) as Table 7 shows. What is surprising is that it also affirmed a higher percentage of liberal lower court cases (39 percent vs. 32.8 percent). Though the affirmation rate for conservative lower court decisions is much higher in the Rehnquist Court than in the Burger Court, the liberal affirmation rate is slightly higher too. Thus, like conflict, ideology explains part but not all of the puzzle. The Rehnquist Court is expectedly deferential to conservative lower court decisions, but it is relatively deferential to liberal lower court decisions as well. Indeed, its conservative affirmation rate is higher than the liberal affirmation rate in the Warren Court (61 percent vs. 52.2 percent), while its liberal affirmation rate (39 percent) is higher than the Warren Court's conservative affirmation rate (27.5 percent). Thus the Rehnquist Court shows more deference to both ideologically consonant and ideologically dissonant lower court decisions than either the Warren or Burger Courts.

One result of the Supreme Court's case selection strategy (preferring to hear unfavorable lower court decisions) is that by hearing so many more unfavorable cases, the Court might end up not only reversing but also affirming more lower court decisions antithetical to its overall direction than those that were congruent therewith. In fact, as shown in Table 8, a majority of each Court's affirmations was antithetical to its overall direction. At the extreme, the Warren Court took three times as many conservative lower court decisions as liberal ones. The result is that 61 percent of its affirmations were of conservative decisions. Indeed, almost two-thirds of the Warren Court's conservative decisions occurred because it affirmed the lower court. By contrast, affirmation of the lower court produced only one-third of the Burger and Rehnquist Courts' conservative decisions.

While the Rehnquist Court's affirmances come primarily from liberal lower court decisions, it is of course true that, like the Burger Court, it affirmed a higher proportion of conservative lower court decisions than liberal lower court decisions. Alternatively, the Warren Court affirmed a higher proportion of liberal lower court decisions than conservative ones even though a majority of its affirmations were of conservative decisions.

Table 7 Affirmation rates by Court controlled for lower court direction

Lower court direction	Warren	Burger	Rehnquist
Liberal	52.2%	32.3%	39.0%
Conservative	27.5%	37.5%	61.0%

Table 8 Affirmations by Court controlled for Supreme Court direction

	Warren	Burger	Rehnquist	Row total
Liberal	204	394	87	685
Conservative	319	373	78	770
% conservative	61.0	48.6	47.3	52.9

Conclusion

We have found that the Rehnquist Court, during its first three terms, has not adhered to the "error correction" strategy of the Warren and Burger Courts. This is in part because it accepts for review a significantly higher proportion of cases in which it finds a conflict in the lower courts and in part because it affirms a tremendous percentage of conservative lower court decisions. But we also found that the Rehnquist Court affirmed a higher proportion of cases than the Warren and Burger Courts after controlling for conflict and ideology. Though affirmation rates are higher in some areas than others, the Rehnquist Court's affirmation proclivities do not result from appreciable changes in the content of its docket.

Although these findings indicate a basic shift in the Court's access strategies and in the management and control of its docket, we do not know the primary reasons for its occurrence. Why is conflict below important to the Rehnquist Court but not to the Warren and Burger Courts? Do lower courts conflict more today than they did in earlier years? If so, why? Does it result from differences between the overall ideological orientation of lower court judges and that of the Supreme Court? What is there about the civil rights, due process, and business cases of the Rehnquist Court that produces disproportionate affirmation? Are the justices pursuing strategies in their certiorari voting of which we are unaware? Answers to these and other questions that bear on the dispositional change that we have identified require research methods that go behind the record provided in the *United States Reports*, methods that instead employ a "soaking and poking" approach.[14]

NOTES

This article originally appeared in Volume 74, Number 2, August-September 1990, pages 84-88.

We wish to thank Tom Phelan, Director of the Social Science Data Lab at SUNY Stony Brook, for his valuable assistance.

1. Richardson and Vines, *Review, Dissent and the Appellate Process: A Political Interpretation*, 29 J. OF POLS. 605 (1967); Baum, THE SUPREME COURT 2d ed. 97 (Washington: Congressional Quarterly, 1985); Epstein, Walker, and Dixon, *The Supreme Court and Criminal Justice Disputes: A Neo-Institutional Perspective*, 33 AM. J. OF POL. SCI. 831 (1989).

2. Schubert, QUANTITATIVE ANALYSIS OF JUDICIAL BEHAVIOR 66 (Glencoe, IL: Free Press, 1959).

3. Brenner and Krol, *Strategies in Certiorari Voting on the United States Supreme Court*, 51 J. OF POLS. 828 (1989). Also see Provine, CASE SELECTION IN THE UNITED STATES SUPREME COURT 180 (Chicago: University of Chicago Press, 1980); Palmer, *An Econometric Analysis of the United States Supreme Court's Certiorari Decisions*, 39 PUBLIC CHOICE 387 (1982); Stern, Gressman and Shapiro, SUPREME COURT PRACTICE 6th ed. 221-224 (Washington: Bureau of National Affairs, 1986).

4. Federal Trade Commission v. Grolier Inc., 462 U.S. 19 (1983), at 23.

5. Baum, *supra* n. 1; Wasby, THE SUPREME COURT IN THE FEDERAL JUDICIAL SYSTEM 3d ed. 216 (Chicago: Nelson-Hall, 1988).

6. The project has been supported by the National Science Foundation, Harold J. Spaeth, principal investigator.

7. Intercoder reliability of this variable exceeded 98 percent.

8. Criminal procedure includes the rights of persons accused of crime, plus the statutory construction of criminal laws. Civil rights, in addition to race and gender discrimination, pertains to indigents, aliens, handicapped persons, Native Americans, military personnel, juveniles, poverty law, reapportionment, and residency requirements. First Amendment excludes attorney advertising while including internal security matters. In addition to notice and hearing, due process includes the takings clause, jurisdiction over non-resident litigants, impartial decision making, and the due process rights of prisoners. Privacy pertains to abortion and the Freedom of Information Act and related statutes. Attorneys encompasses their fees and commercial speech. Unions includes disputes with management and union members, as well as Fair Labor Standards and OSHA litigation. Economic activity concerns business activities and regulation. In addition to the jurisdiction of the federal courts, judicial power includes judicial review of agency action, comity, and the Federal Rules of Evidence and of Civil and Appellate Procedure, and the Court's own non-meritorious disposition of cases it has agreed to review. Federalism concerns national supremacy, pre-emption, and federal-state ownership disputes. Interstate relations concern state boundary and non-real property disputes between states. Federal taxation concerns the Internal Revenue Code and related statutes, along with the priority of federal fiscal claims. Miscellaneous contains those cases that do not locate in one of the other categories.

9. *E.g.*, Traynor v. Turnage, 99 L Ed 2d 618 (1988).

10. The percentage for the others is: Stevens 68.2, O'Connor 68.3, Marshall 70.6, Rehnquist 74.4, Scalia 77.3, and Blackmun 85.0.

11. The Rehnquist Court affirmed 81.8 percent of the federal tax cases in which lower courts conflicted, as compared to the Warren Court's 41.0 percent and the Burger Court's 53.1 percent. In judicial power, the Rehnquist Court affirmed 55.3 percent of its no conflict cases; the Warren Court 39.7 percent, and the Burger Court 34.2 percent.

12. The Rehnquist Court has not appreciably discriminated between state and federal cases in rate of affirmation: 42.1 percent of the former and 46.5 percent of the latter. As Table 1 shows, the Rehnquist Court's overall affirmation rate is 46.0 percent.

13. These are cases dealing with criminal procedure, civil rights, the First Amendment, due process, privacy, attorneys, unions, and economics. Excluded are judicial power, federalism, interstate relations, federal taxation and miscellaneous cases.

14. See the symposium, *Strategies for judicial research: soaking and poking in the judiciary*, 73 JUDICATURE 192 (1990).

Assessing the conservatism of the Rehnquist Court

An empirical analysis of civil liberties decisions indicates that the Rehnquist Court, despite its reputation, is no more conservative than the Burger Court. But data alone do not tell the whole story.

by Christopher E. Smith and Thomas R. Hensley

Because the U.S. Supreme Court is the literal and symbolic pinnacle of the judicial system's hierarchy, it has attracted significant attention from scholars seeking to analyze decisional trends affecting law and public policy. Traditionally, scholars have analyzed the Court by dividing its history into segments that correspond with the tenures of chief justices. Although generalizations about the Court's institutional actions are most precise in studies that focus on "natural Courts" (periods during which the Court's composition remains unchanged), tradition and convenience have led scholars to examine broader eras by comparing, for example, the Hughes, Warren, and Burger Courts.[1]

Analyses of the Supreme Court's decisions under the leadership of specific chief justices produce generalizations about decisional patterns and the Court's role in the governing system. The Warren Court (1953-1969), for example, has been regarded as producing "what can only be described as a constitutional revolution, generated by a group of justices who were perhaps the most liberal in American history."[2] During the Warren era, the Supreme Court expanded the protection of individuals' civil rights and liberties by broadly interpreting the Bill of Rights, the Fourteenth Amendment, and other constitutional provisions. By contrast, the Burger Court (1969-1986) has been regarded as more conservative and less willing to exercise judicial power on behalf of individual rights. Although the Court expanded some rights

(e.g., gender equality, abortion, affirmative action) under Chief Justice Warren Burger, a leading Supreme Court specialist has maintained that "members of the Burger Court selected cases in order to cut back, if not reverse, the [liberal] direction of Warren Court policy-making."[3]

Like the Burger Court, the Rehnquist Court is regarded as significantly more conservative than the Warren Court. The infusion of conservative justices appointed by Presidents Ronald Reagan and George Bush produced, in the words of one scholar, a Supreme Court in which "the conservative bloc has become the most cohesive that it has been in half a century."[4] Since President Reagan appointed Justice Anthony Kennedy in 1988, a strong and growing conservative majority on the Rehnquist Court has had the opportunity to change the precedents and decisional patterns established during prior eras.[5] This article examines the Rehnquist Court's reputation and performance in order to assess both current understandings about the contemporary Supreme Court and the challenges facing scholars and lawyers who study it.

The Court's reputation

The Rehnquist Court has attracted significant attention from both the national news media[6] and from scholars[7] for a perceived sharp movement toward conservatism. Decisions by the Rehnquist Court significantly narrowed the established scope of individual rights regarding many controversial issues, including abortion,[8] affirmative action,[9] free exercise of religion,[10] and criminal defendant rights.[11] The Court's conservative justices have been criticized for their activist inclination to disregard the value of case precedent.[12] For example, a 1991 decision[13] permitting victim impact testimony in capital sentencing hearings directly overturned precedents that were merely two and four years old.[14] Such eagerness to overturn precedents generated veiled criticism from retired Justice Lewis Powell, a generally conservative member of the Burger Court,[15] who said that such disregard for precedent "represent[s] explicit endorsement of the idea that the Constitution is nothing more than what five justices say it is. This...undermine[s] the rule of law."[16]

Although the conservative justices have thus far reversed fewer precedents than many had predicted, "[t]he strategy of the Rehnquist Court is more often simply to reinterpret a precedent in such a way as to reverse it without explicitly saying so."[17] In rewriting the established interpretations of employment discrimination statutes,[18] for example, the Court purported to uphold prior interpretations while actually making it more difficult for discrimination victims to file successful lawsuits.[19]

The decisional patterns of both the Burger and Rehnquist Courts establish them as more conservative than the Warren Court. However, a recent scholarly analysis has interpreted the Burger Court "as a bridge spanning the Warren Court's liberalism and concern for individual rights, on the one hand, and the Rehnquist Court's conservatism on the other."[20] The Rehnquist Court's reshaping of constitutional law in profoundly different directions has given rise to the perception that the contemporary Supreme Court has ushered in a new era of conservatism and hostility to civil rights and liberties. In this sense, the Rehnquist Court has been regarded as much more conservative than the Burger Court:

The appointment of an astute, forceful, and ideological chief justice who has regularly opposed the civil-liberties orientation of the Court, the emergence of an ostensibly cohesive conservative bloc on the Court, and some initial [case decisions] from the Court itself all point in [the] direction [of a new, consistent conservatism].[21]

One news correspondent who covers the Supreme Court reinforced this assessment: "The transformed [Rehnquist] Court no longer sees itself as the special protector of individual liberties and civil rights for minorities."[22]

The Court's performance

An evaluation of empirical evidence using standard scholarly techniques raises questions about the strength and consistency of the contemporary Court's purported conservatism.[23] In order to assess the Rehnquist Court's decisional patterns, the contemporary Court's case decisions on civil rights and liberties issues, normally referred to as "civil liberties cases," have been classified as "liberal" or "conservative." The classification procedures employed are consistent with those in previous studies. According to a study employing this classification, "Liberal decisions in the area of civil liberties are pro-person accused or convicted of a crime, pro-civil liberties or civil rights claimant, pro-indigent, pro-[Native American], and anti-government in due process and privacy."[24]

As indicated by Table 1, although the Burger and Rehnquist Courts' decisions favored liberal outcomes less frequently than did those of the Warren Court, the Rehnquist Court's decisional patterns on civil liberties are not significantly more conservative than those of the Burger Court. In fact, the Supreme Court's support for liberal and conservative outcomes is nearly identical during the two eras.

Because the recent changes in the Supreme Court's composition are perceived to have made the Rehnquist Court's conservative majority increasingly powerful, the data presented in Table 2 pose a puzzling challenge to the contemporary Court's reputation for conservatism. Despite the addition of President Bush's appointees to replace liberal justices from the Warren Court era, the Supreme Court has produced higher levels of support for liberal decisions than those produced during the previous terms. For example, the Rehnquist Court's lowest level of support for liberal outcomes (36.6 percent) occurred prior to the appointments of Justices David Souter and Clarence Thomas.

As Table 3 indicates, Bush appointees Souter and Thomas were much less inclined than their predecessors to support liberal outcomes in civil liberties cases. While Justice William Brennan supported liberal outcomes in nearly 86 percent of such cases during his final term, his successor, Justice Souter, supported such outcomes in only 36

Table 1 Decisions in civil liberties cases during the Warren, Burger, and Rehnquist Court eras, 1953-1991 terms

Direction of decision	Warren era (1953-1969)		Burger era (1969-1986)		Rehnquist era (1986-June 1992)	
	%	(n)	%	(n)	%	(n)
Liberal	71.4	(728)	43.8	(698)	42.8	(195)
Conservative	28.6	(291)	56.2	(896)	57.2	(261)
Total	100.0	(1,019)	100.0	(1,594)	100.0	(456)

Table 2 Decisions in civil liberties cases during each term of the Burger and Rehnquist eras

Term	Direction of decision			
	Liberal		Conservative	
	%	(n)	%	(n)
1969-1970	59.8	(52)	40.2	(35)
1970-1971	48.8	(42)	51.2	(44)
1971-1972	58.6	(65)	41.4	(46)
1972-1973	42.2	(46)	57.8	(63)
1973-1974	46.1	(47)	53.9	(55)
1974-1975	53.8	(42)	46.2	(36)
1975-1976	36.7	(36)	63.3	(62)
1976-1977	38.4	(43)	61.6	(69)
1977-1978	48.7	(38)	51.3	(40)
1978-1979	41.2	(40)	58.8	(57)
1979-1980	46.7	(42)	53.3	(48)
1980-1981	34.2	(26)	65.8	(50)
1981-1982	41.8	(38)	58.2	(53)
1982-1983	36.8	(32)	63.2	(55)
1983-1984	33.7	(35)	66.3	(69)
1984-1985	41.4	(36)	58.6	(51)
1985-1986	37.6	(38)	62.4	(63)
1986-1987	45.3	(43)	54.7	(52)
1987-1988	48.0	(36)	52.0	(39)
1988-1989	36.8	(32)	63.2	(55)
1989-1990	36.6	(26)	63.4	(45)
1990-1991	44.3	(27)	55.7	(34)
1991-1992	46.3	(31)	53.7	(36)
Totals	43.6	(893)	56.4	(1,157)

Table 3 Support for liberal outcomes in civil liberties cases, by individual justices

Justices	1989-1990 %	1990-1991 %	1991-1992 %	Totals %
Rehnquist	12.7	25.0	31.3	22.7
Scalia	22.5	34.4	26.9	27.6
Thomas	—	—	30.0	30.0
Kennedy	22.9	40.0	47.8	36.5
O'Connor	19.7	43.3	49.3	36.9
White	28.2	45.9	38.8	37.2
Souter	—	36.4	47.8	42.6
Blackmun	60.6	78.7	65.7	67.8
Stevens	73.2	82.0	77.6	77.4
Brennan	85.9	—	—	85.9
Marshall	90.0	86.9	—	88.5

and 48 percent of cases during the following two terms. Justice Thomas's 30 percent support level for liberal outcomes was drastically different than the 90 and 87 percent levels of his predecessor, Justice Thurgood Marshall, during the preceding two terms.

Oddly enough, however, the replacement of the Court's most consistent liberals by two much more conservative justices did not lead the Court to support liberal outcomes less frequently. The Supreme Court's 1990 term was the first during which Justice Brennan, an acknowledged leader and outspoken liberal from the Warren era, was replaced by Republican appointee Justice Souter. Despite Souter's pronounced conservatizing impact on the Court's decisions, especially his decisive fifth vote favoring conservative outcomes in 11 cases that would probably have been decided differently if Brennan had remained on the Court,[25] the Court's support for liberal outcomes during the 1990 term exceeded the levels produced during the two prior terms when Brennan was present. Surprisingly, the following year when the other ultra-liberal holdover from the Warren Court era, Justice Marshall, retired and was replaced by conservative Justice Thomas, the Rehnquist Court's support for liberal outcomes in civil liberties cases approached its peak for the post-Burger era by being second only to the 1987 term.

Because of the Rehnquist Court's conservative composition and highly publicized decisions on controversial issues, the contemporary Supreme Court gained a reputation as a markedly different decision-making institution than it was under the two prior chief justices. However, the empirical evidence used in standard assessments of the Supreme Court's liberalism during specific eras presents quite a different picture. Why is the Rehnquist Court apparently less conservative than it is reputed to be? Is the Rehnquist Court, despite its controversial decisions, actually as liberal as the Burger Court? Or, alternatively, does the traditional empirical approach for analyzing the Supreme Court's decisional patterns present misleading conclusions about the Rehnquist Court?

Causes of change

Previous studies of the Supreme Court have recognized three possible causes of change in decisional patterns.[26] The most obvious and well-documented is the addition of new justices with judicial philosophies and policy preferences that differ from those of their immediate predecessors. Membership change was a "dominant force" in decision-making changes that occurred during the Warren and Burger eras,[27] and membership change is generally presumed to be the cause of the Rehnquist Court's conservatism as Reagan and Bush appointees replaced more liberal justices. According to one Supreme Court correspondent, "With the change in membership, the old [liberal] agenda has been pronounced dead."[28]

There are, however, two other potential causes of changes in decisional patterns.[29] First, continuing justices may change their voting patterns. Their experiences on the Supreme Court may lead them to change their views on specific issues or to otherwise change their approaches to judicial decision making. Second, the Court may face new kinds of issues that divide the justices between "liberal" and "conservative" outcomes in ways that differ from those measured empirically during previous terms. The nature of civil liberties issues can change over time as the Court moves from confronting an initial, stark injustice to struggling with precise remedies for intractable social problems. As described by one scholar, "A familiar example is the evolution of school segregation cases in the Supreme Court from those involving government action that directly mandated segregation to those involving more ambiguous and implicit government action."[30]

The surprising results of this study's empirical examination of the Rehnquist Court's decisional patterns raise questions about the possible impact of both changes in decision-making behavior by incumbent justices and new kinds of civil liberties issues that may be facing the Court. It is possible that either or both of these sources of change are moderating the strong conservatism that was generally presumed to stem from recent membership changes. Alternatively, the Rehnquist Court simply may not be as conservative as it is portrayed to be in news reports and scholarly articles.

Changing issues

It is difficult to know whether the Rehnquist Court's support for liberal outcomes stems from new kinds of issues being presented to the Supreme Court. As one scholar has noted, although issue change has been examined for specific kinds of cases,[31] "it is probably impossible to develop an adequate direct measure of issue change in a field as broad as civil liberties."[32]

Because issue changes are not detectable in the traditional empirical method of counting and classifying "liberal" and "conservative" decisions, simple quantitative methods alone are not adequate for comprehensive analysis of Supreme Court decisions. Scholars must necessarily rely on anecdotal evidence and case analysis to discern changes in issues presented to the Court and changes in the justices' reactions to such issues. Despite the fact that case analysis is necessarily more subjective and less systematic than empirical methods, individual case decisions must be examined in order to assess whether and to what extent the nature of issues decided by the Supreme Court have changed. Because systematic, comprehensive analysis of Supreme Court cases requires time-consuming efforts by scholars, final conclusions about possible issue changes in the Rehnquist Court's recent terms are not immediately available. In the short term, however, individual cases and anecdotal evidence provide indications that issues may be changing.

Reining in lower courts

After leading the Supreme Court in a new, more conservative direction, it appears now that the justices on the Rehnquist Court may be forced to rein in lower court judges whose decisions are too conservative. One of the primary functions of the Supreme Court is to supervise lower courts to promote uniformity in the application of constitutional doctrine. By 1992, most federal district and circuit judges were conservative Reagan and Bush appointees who were selected through "the most systematic ideological or philosophical screening of judicial candidates since the first Roosevelt administration."[33] The Reagan administration carefully evaluated potential judicial appointees to ensure they would be sufficiently conservative. The Bush administration emulated Reagan's emphasis on selecting judges who were sufficiently conservative and loyal to Republican party positions.[34] With a large body of like-minded lower court judges looking to the Supreme Court's conservative majority for guidance, the Rehnquist Court's highly publicized reputation may have encouraged increasingly conservative arguments by attorneys and decisions by judges. Thus, after changing Supreme Court precedents on many issues, the Rehnquist Court may find itself required to review conservative decisions of lower courts in order to demonstrate the limits of the justices' preferences for conservative outcomes.

Justice Sandra Day O'Connor, for example, issued an opinion warning appellate courts not to be too hasty in rejecting capital cases after it became clear that they had interpreted one of her earlier opinions as justifying their refusals to review death sentences.[35] In an Establishment Clause case during the 1991 term, Justices Antonin Scalia and Anthony Kennedy, two critics of Supreme Court decisions maintaining separation of church and state, were reported to have been "visibly troubled" when an attorney argued that the Establishment Clause, properly understood, permitted the federal government to adopt an official national religion as long as it did not coerce people to join the religion.[36] It was perhaps a case of the conservative justices seeing an attorney adopt their strident criticisms of contemporary jurisprudence and proceed to carry their ideas farther than the justices ever intended. According to one newspaper account, the justices appeared disturbed "at the prospect that [the lawyer's] vision might indeed be the logical stopping point on the journey which [the conservative justices] had embarked."[37] If the justices of the Rehnquist Court are accepting cases for review in order to place limits on conservative decisions produced by the lower courts, then, without the justices becoming more liberal themselves, these new kinds of issues would lead them to produce liberal outcomes as a means of establishing new jurisprudential boundaries.

The cases in which the Supreme Court supported liberal outcomes during the 1991 term appear to represent instances in which the Court chose to rein in lower courts and clarify its intentions. In only 6 of these 31 cases did the Supreme Court affirm a decision by an appellate court. With the exception of one case in which the Court declined to issue a writ of mandamus,[38] in the other 24 cases the Supreme Court reversed or vacated 13 decisions by federal courts of appeals and 11 decisions by state supreme courts. These cases did not simply curb the preferences of Republican-appointed judges seeking to advance conservative decisions beyond the Rehnquist Court justices' intentions. In the cases reversing or vacating federal appellate judges' decisions,[39] the Supreme Court effectively overruled decisions by 11 Democratic-appointed judges (10 Carter appointees and 1 Johnson appointee) as well as 34 Republican-appointed judges (21 Reagan appointees, 5 Ford appointees, 4 Bush appointees, 3 Nixon appointees, and 1 Eisenhower appointee).

In their efforts to avoid reversal and fulfill the perceived intentions of the Rehnquist Court, liberal and conservative appellate judges may make decisions that are "too conservative" when they incorrectly interpret or anticipate the views of the Court's conservative majority. Thus these appellate judges generate new kinds of issues that may force even the most conservative Supreme Court justice to support liberal outcomes in order to define and clarify jurisprudential boundaries.

Changing views of incumbents

Changes in the judicial behavior of incumbent justices are more readily identifiable than are changes in the nature of issues presented to the Supreme Court. Justice Harry Blackmun, for example, who joined the Supreme Court as a consistently conservative Nixon appointee, eventually became one of the most liberal justices on the Rehnquist Court (Table 3):

[Justice Blackmun] started his Supreme Court service with a rather conventional outlook toward the disadvantaged, such as welfare recipients. However, as he realized that the system he had assumed would function benignly was not doing so, he came to side more with the individual against the government, demanding that his colleagues pay heed to problems of the "real world" that he himself had not closely examined in his early opinions, and calling for greater judicial protection of those individuals....[40]

Justice Blackmun's transformation, however, is not the source of the Rehnquist Court's apparent liberalism during recent terms because he has had relatively high levels of support for liberal outcomes since the close of the Burger Court era.[41] With the exception of criminal justice decisions, Justice Blackmun has been a relatively consistent supporter of liberal outcomes in civil liberties cases throughout the Rehnquist era. Thus, if decision-making changes by individual justices have produced the Rehnquist Court's increased support for liberal outcomes during the past two terms, it must be attributable to changes by one or more of the conservative members of the Court.

During the 1991 term, liberal outcomes were produced in at least two of the Supreme Court's most controversial decisions because of unexpected changes in Justice Kennedy's views. In 1989, Kennedy joined Chief Justice William Rehnquist's opinion that criticized *Roe v. Wade*[42] and the right of choice for abortion.[43] It was widely anticipated in 1992 that, with the addition of conservative Justices Souter and Thomas, Justice Kennedy would be a member of a five- or six-member majority to overturn *Roe*. Kennedy surprised nearly everyone,[44] however, by joining Justices Souter and O'Connor in a jointly authored opinion that upheld *Roe* on behalf of a five-member majority.[45] The joint opinion emphasized the need to preserve the Court's legitimacy by respecting case precedent. According to Kennedy, O'Connor, and Souter, a reversal of the 19-year-old precedent in *Roe* would be "at the cost of both profound and unnecessary damage to the Court's legitimacy, and to the Nation's commitment to the rule of law."[46] Kennedy apparently believed that the maintenance of stability concerning a highly controversial issue was more important than vindication of his previously expressed preference for the conservative outcome of permitting states to ban abortion.

It can be argued, of course, that the 1992 abortion decision produced a conservative rather than a liberal outcome because a majority endorsed most of Pennsylvania's restrictions on the right of choice. However, the case warrants classification as a "liberal" outcome because the Court had already invited states to regulate abortion in the 1989 decision in *Webster v. Reproductive Health Services*, so the 1992 case focused most importantly on whether the right of choice initiated in *Roe* would be preserved.

Regarding the religion clauses of the First Amendment, Justice Kennedy had been a critic of Supreme Court decisions that he believed enforced too rigidly the separation of church and state. He authored a sharp opinion in 1989 that accused the liberal justices of "an unjustified hostility toward religion"[47] and of discriminating against the nation's Christian majority.[48] Kennedy was also the only justice to agree with the Rehnquist Court's two most strident conservative critics of liberal jurisprudence on religious freedom, Chief Justice Rehnquist and Justice Scalia, in all eight religion cases decided from 1988 to 1990.[49] In 1992, however, Kennedy not only deserted his conservative colleagues in a case concerning prayers at public school graduations, he actually authored the majority opinion that emphasized the need to protect high school students from government-sponsored prayer.[50] As indicated by the apparent shift on Kennedy's decisions on abortion and religious freedom,[51] changes by individual incumbent justices appear to explain some of the liberal outcomes produced recently by the Rehnquist Court.

Conclusion

Is the Rehnquist Court more liberal than people generally believe? It is difficult to reach a firm conclusion. The recent changes in the Court's composition, especially the replacement of Warren-era liberals William Brennan and Thurgood Marshall by Bush appointees David Souter and Clarence Thomas, generated predictions that the Supreme Court would be notably more conservative on civil liberties issues than in the past. However, traditional empirical techniques for counting and classifying civil liberties decisions indicate that the Rehnquist Court may be no more conservative than the Burger Court, which preserved and extended many of the liberal doctrines developed during the Warren era.[52] Because changes in personnel did not produce the Rehnquist Court's increasing and unexpectedly high levels of support for liberal outcomes during the 1990 and 1991 terms, it is possible that individual justices changed their views or that the nature of issues presented to the Supreme Court changed.

Changes in the views of Justice Kennedy (and possibly other justices) appear to account for some of the decisions contributing to the Rehnquist Court's statistical support for liberal outcomes. A strong possibility exists, however, that the Rehnquist Court's apparent liberalism also results from new kinds of issues being presented to the Supreme Court. A justice's apparent liberalism may be overstated if analysts do not consider the kinds of issues addressed by the Court and the divisions among justices who support a particular case outcome.

Chief Justice Rehnquist's performance, for example, was not as liberal as it appeared to be from the latest figures showing his support for individuals in civil liberties cases. A close examination of his decisions reveals that conservative motivations and reasoning underlie his support for individuals in a number of civil liberties cases.[53] Thus, speculative conclusions about his perceived moderation while performing the role of chief justice are probably premature.[54]

Likewise, conclusions about the Rehnquist Court's relative liberalism cannot rest on quantitative measures alone. The development of empirical techniques for measuring and monitoring the Supreme Court's performance has been extraordinarily useful for scholars seeking comprehensive, standardized assessments of the Court's actions during different historical eras. However, because Chief Justice Rehnquist and other conservatives may support individuals in specific civil liberties cases for a variety of nonliberal reasons,[55] accurate and complete conclusions about the Supreme Court must draw from both empirical techniques and case analysis in order to detect how issues are changing and how the justices manifest disagreements even when they agree on case outcomes.

NOTES

This article originally appeared in Volume 77, Number 2, September-October 1993, pages 83-89.

The authors gratefully acknowledge the contribution to this article made by data drawn from the United States Supreme Court Judicial Data Base, Harold J. Spaeth, principal investigator (ICPSR study number 9422).

1. *See* Banks, *The Supreme Court and precedent: an analysis of natural courts and reversal trends*, 75 JUDICATURE 262 (1992).

2. Walker and Epstein. THE SUPREME COURT OF THE UNITED STATES: AN INTRODUCTION 19 (1993).

3. O'Brien, STORM CENTER: THE SUPREME COURT IN AMERICAN POLITICS 196 (2d ed. 1990).

4. Goldman, CONSTITUTIONAL LAW 151 (2d ed. 1991).

5. *See* Smith. *The Supreme Court in Transition: Assessing the Legitimacy of the Leading Legal Institution*, 79 KY. L. J. 317, 335-346 (1990-91).The Rehnquist Court has also behaved differently from the Burger and Warren Courts in selecting lower court cases for hearing and in affirming selected lower court decisions. Segal and Spaeth, *Rehnquist Court disposition of lower court decisions: affirmation not reversal*, 74 JUDICATURE 88 (1990).

6. *See, e.g.,* Savage. TURNING RIGHT: THE MAKING OF THE REHNQUIST SUPREME COURT (1992); Lacayo. *Is the Court Turning Right?*, TIME, Oct. 24. 1988, at 78; McDaniel. *The Court Spins Right*, NEWSWEEK, June 26. 1989, at 16.

7. *See, e.g.,* Chemerinsky. *Forward: The Vanishing Constitution*, 103 HARV. L. REV. 43 (1989); Glennon. *Will the Real Conservatives Please Stand Up?*, 76 A.B.A. J. 49 (Aug. 1990).

8. *See, e.g.,* Webster v. Reproductive Health Services. 492 U.S. 490 (1989) and Planned Parenthood v. Casey, 112 S. Ct. 2791 (1992) (states may regulate but not ban abortion services).

9. *See, e.g.,* City of Richmond v. J.A. Croson Co., 488 U.S. 469 (1989) (local governments may not have affirmative action programs for public contracts without proof that they are remedying their own past discrimination).

10. *See, e.g.,* Employment Division of Oregon v. Smith, 494 U.S. 872 (1990) (valid government regulations take precedence over individuals' religious practices).

11. *See, e.g.,* Duckworth v. Eagan, 109 S. Ct. 2875 (1989) (police not required to give complete, precise Miranda warning to suspect).

12. *See, e.g.,* Smith, *The Supreme Court's Emerging Majority: Restraining the High Court or Transforming Its Role?*, 24 AKRON L. REV. 393 (1990).

13. Payne v. Tennessee, 111 S. Ct. 2597 (1991).

14. Booth v. Maryland. 482 U.S. 496 (1987); South Carolina v. Gathers. 490 U.S. 805 (1989).

15. Although Justice Powell gained a reputation as a moderate for his decisions affecting affirmative action and abortion, a systematic study of his decisions revealed that he was generally a dependable conservative. See Blasecki, *Justice Lewis F. Powell: Swing Voter or Staunch Conservative?*, 52 J. POL. 530 (1990).

16. Glennon, *supra* n. 7, at 51.

17. O'Brien, *supra* n. 3, at 212.

18. Wards Cove Packing Co. v. Atonio, 109 S. Ct. 2115 (1989); Patterson v. McLean Credit Union, 109 S. Ct. 2363 (1989).

19. *See* Smith. *The Supreme Court and Ethnicity*, 69 OR. L. REV. 797, 823-845 (1990).

20. Lamb and Halpern, *The Burger Court and Beyond*, in Lamb and Halpern eds., THE BURGER COURT: POLITICAL AND JUDICIAL PROFILES 446 (1991).

21. *Id.* at 455.

22. Savage, *supra* n. 6, at 453.

2S. The data for the tables that follow were taken from the U.S. Supreme Court Judicial Data Base for the 1986 through 1990 terms. See Segal and Spaeth, *Decisional trends on the Warren and Burger Courts: results from the Supreme Court Data Base Project*, 73 JUDICATURE 109 (1989). Case citations provide the unit of analysis. and all cases in which the Court issued a written opinion. including orally argued cases with signed opinions, orally argued cases with unsigned opinions, and non-orally argued cases with unsigned opinions are included. Variation exists in studies regarding which cases to include. Segal and Spaeth, for example, include only orally argued cases and use docket numbers as their unit of analysis. *Id.* at 84. Civil liberties cases are those involving criminal procedure, the First Amendment, civil rights, due process, and privacy. The Supreme Court Judicial Data Base did not cover the 1991 term of the Court, however, when this research was undertaken, and thus the authors gathered these data using the *Lawyers' Edition, United States Reports*. The coding instructions and categories employed were those in the Inter-University Consortium for Political and Social Research Codebook for the Supreme Court Judicial Data Base. Complete reliability checks were not undertaken, but the annual review of the Supreme Court's 1991 term in *The National Law Journal* was used as a check on coding.

24. Segal and Spaeth, *supra* n. 23, at 104.

25. Smith and Johnson. *Newcomer on the High Court: Justice Souter and the Supreme Court's 1990 Term*, 37 S.D. L. REV. 21, 39-43 (1991).

26. *See* Baum, *Measuring Policy Change in the U.S. Supreme Court*, 82 AM. POL. SCI. REV. 905, 906 (1988).

27. Baum, *Membership Change and Collective Voting Changes in the United States Supreme Court*, 54 J. POL. 3, 22 (1992).

28. Savage, *supra* n. 6, at 453.

29. *Supra* n. 27, at 5.

30. *Id.*

31. *See* Segal, *Measuring Change on the Supreme Court: Examining Alternative Models*, 29 AM. J. POL. SCI. 461 (1985).

32. *Supra* n. 27, at 6.

33. Goldman. *Reagan's second term judicial appointments: the battle at midway*, 70 JUDICATURE 324, 326 (1987).

34. Lewis, *Bush Travels Reagan's Course in Naming Judges*, N.Y. TIMES, Apr. 10, 1990, at A1; Goldman, *The Bush imprint on the judiciary: carrying on a tradition*, 74 JUDICATURE 294 (1991).

35. Greenhouse, *Court Denial of Appeal Prompts Unusual Action*, N.Y. TIMES, Dec. 3. 1991. at B10.

36. Greenhouse. *Justices Define Limits of Own Power*, N.Y. TIMES, Nov. 22. 1991. at A8.

37. *Id.*

38. In re Blodgett, 116 L. Ed. 2d 669 (1992).

39. The case of *Woodell v. International Brotherhood of Electrical Workers*, 116 L. Ed. 2d 449 (1992) is excluded because the court of appeals' opinion was unpublished.

40. Wasby, *Justice Harry A. Blackmun: Transformation from*

"Minnesota Twin" to Independent Voice, in Lamb and Halpern eds., THE BURGER COURT: POLITICAL AND JUDICIAL PROFILES 96 (1991).

41. Lamb and Halpern, *The Political and Historical Context of the Burger Court*, in Lamb and Halpern eds., THE BURGER COURT: *supra* n. 20, at 33.

42. 410 U.S. 113 (1973).

4S. Webster v. Reproductive Health Services, 109 S. Ct. 3040 (1989).

44. *See* Greenhouse, *High Court, 5-4, Affirms Right to Abortion But Allows Most of Pennsylvania's Limits*, N.Y. TIMES, June 30. 1992, at A1, A15.

45. Planned Parenthood v. Casey, 112 S. Ct. 2791 (1992).

46. *Id.* at 2816.

47. County of Allegheny v. A.C.L.U., 109 S. Ct. 3086, 3314 (1989) (Kennedy, J., concurring in the judgment in part and dissenting in part).

48. *Id.* at 3145 ("I am quite certain that [people] will take away a salient message from our holding in this case: the Supreme Court of the United States has concluded that the First Amendment creates classes of religions based on the relative number of adherents. Those religions enjoying the largest following must be consigned to the status of least-favored faiths so as to avoid any possible risk of offending members of minority religions.").

49. Smith and Fry, *Vigilance or Accommodation: The Changing Supreme Court and Religious Freedom*, 42 SYRACUSE L. REV. 893, 917 (1991).

50. Lee v. Weisman, 112 S. Ct. 2649 (1992).

51. It is possible that Kennedy's opinion in the graduation prayer case did not represent a change in his views because his strident accommodationist opinion concerning the establishment clause previously came in a case concerning religious displays in government buildings. Both cases concerned Establishment Clause issues but Kennedy may distinguish the degree of government involvement or the potential coerciveness in the two situations.

52. *See* Schwartz. *Introduction*, in Schwartz ed., THE BURGER YEARS: RIGHTS AND WRONGS IN THE SUPREME COURT, 1969-1986 xi-xxv (1987).

53. During the 1991 term, Chief Justice Rehnquist supported liberal outcomes in 21 civil liberties cases. Ten were unanimous decisions, three had one dissenter, five had two dissenters, and three had three dissenters. A close examination of the 21 cases reveals that the simple process of counting and classifying cases in which Rehnquist supported liberal outcomes may overstate the extent of the chief justice's liberalism. Five cases in which Rehnquist supported outcomes favoring individuals cannot reasonably be construed as endorsing liberal decisions, and in other cases Rehnquist and other conservatives disagreed with the more liberal justices' reasoning in cases in which the entire Court agreed on the outcome.

54. While Rehnquist has remained one of the justices least likely to support liberal outcomes in civil liberties cases, empirical examinations of his decisional patterns have led some scholars to speculate that he is changing his views. *See*, Goldman. CONSTITUTIONAL LAW, *supra* n. 4, at 151, 155-156.

55. *See supra* notes 53-54 and accompanying text.

Explaining transformations in Supreme Court policy

An examination of women's rights cases from 1965 to 1994 suggests that while litigation flow influences decisions, the Court's previous opinions can invite or discourage certain types of appeals and thus the direction of policy.

by Leslie Friedman Goldstein and Diana Stech

What factors shape Supreme Court policy leadership on a given topic? It is evident that the Court's interest in particular policy topics varies over time. For instance, in interviews conducted from 1976 to 1980, H.W. Perry elicited an intriguing acknowledgment from an unidentified Supreme Court justice: "The Court was ready for [*Gideon v. Wainwright*], and a third-rate lawyer from Yonkers could have won it. To a degree, the Court was ready for *Brown*—same way with one man, one vote."[1] While it is clear that the Supreme Court's attention to particular topics varies over time, the causes of this variation have received little attention.[2]

During the past three decades, a combination of judicial and legislative innovation has revolutionized women's rights in the areas of gender equity and reproductive freedom. The Supreme Court's role in this can be grouped into three slightly overlapping phases of roughly equal duration. The first, involving the constitutionalization of reproductive freedom, extended from 1965 through 1977. The second, involving the constitutionalization of gender equity, extended from 1971 through 1982. The third phase, enhancing gender equity by feminist interpretation of federal statutes, seems to have run from 1978 to at least the fall of 1993.[3]

The rise and fall of Supreme Court policy making on abortion is not particularly puzzling. It naturally takes a certain number of cases presented over a course of years for the details, various applica-

tions, and limits of a new judicial policy or doctrine to be spelled out by the Court, and such a period would normally be followed by one of stabilization. But the shift from the second phase to the third cries out for explanation. The Court issued many important expansions of gender equity by statutory interpretation from 1982 through 1993, but in that period it did not declare a single gender discriminatory statute unconstitutional.

Two models of how the Supreme Court decides to hear cases may help explain this shift in judicial policy and reveal something in general about transitions in judicial policy. The first is derived from a picture presented in many contemporary American government textbooks. Under this model, the Court is not a passive branch of government forced to wait for issues to be raised by parties outside its control. Instead, the Court is able to make policy as it chooses because, with 5,000 cases brought to it annually, a suitable vehicle is always available for justices to create a policy they have in mind. According to this model, one would find a steady flow of gender equity litigation, some based on the equal protection aspects of the Constitution, and some based on federal statutes such as the Civil Rights Act of 1964 (Title VII) and the Education Amendments of 1972 (Title IX).

An alternative model would reveal the Court as not choosing from a steady flow of litigation, but sharply constrained to shift the kinds of gender equity decisions it was handing down because the requests for cert based on the Constitution had virtually dried up while those based on statutory violations kept flowing. Although this model better fits the evidence, it does not necessarily confirm that the Court is a passive branch of government. This is because the Court's own decisions invite or discourage certain types of cases.

Patterns of judicial policy

Beginning under the chief justiceship of Earl Warren, but taking on a substantial policy significance under the chief justiceship of Warren Burger, the Supreme Court secured as a constitutional right "the right of the individual to be free of unwarranted governmental intrusion into those decisions so fundamentally affecting a person as the decision whether to bear or beget a child."[4] This phase began in earnest prior to the women's movement when the Supreme Court in 1965 declared unconstitutional a 90-year-old Connecticut law forbidding the use of contraceptive devices.[5] It reached its peak in 1973 with the famous *Roe v. Wade* and *Doe v. Bolton* decisions, which in a single day declared unconstitutional the criminal abortion statutes of 46 states.[6] It pretty much concluded by 1977, by which time the Supreme Court had delineated the basic contours of how much abortion restriction it would and would not permit. By that time, the Court had extended the right to obtain contraceptives even to children under the age of 16;[7] had indicated that husbands could not be given a veto over their wives' abortions and that it would uphold parental consent laws for abortions performed on minors as long as such laws provided the option of obtaining permission from a judge;[8] and had allowed government to refuse to fund abortions even when funding childbirth costs.[9]

These contours were slightly altered in 1992 in the *Casey* decision, in that the Supreme Court allowed states to insist that women seeking abortions be exposed to information about fetal development and adoption resources. It also allowed states to impose a 24-hour waiting period prior to abortion consent.[10] Still, the magnitude of the 1992 shift does not come close to approaching that of the 1973 innovation, and it does not significantly alter the basic contours of policy crafted in the 1965-1977 period. *Roe v. Wade* survives pretty much intact more than 20 years—and a great many abortion cases—later (with a majority of justices still committed to what they call its "essential holding"), despite three completed terms of presidents

who pledged to appoint anti-*Roe* justices and who managed to name a total of six new justices to the Court.

Thus, if one were to examine only judicial policy on abortion, one would find clear confirmation of the textbook picture of the Court able to make and then reaffirm the policies it prefers by selecting cases from a steady flow. The gender equity side of the story, however, is different.

The constitutionalization of gender equity began somewhat later. As recently as 1968 the Warren Court refused to reconsider its own 1961 rejection of that constitutionalization in the context of systematic exemption of women from jury duty.[11] In 1971, however, Chief Justice Burger led the Court in a new direction by means of a cryptic opinion.

The opinion in *Reed v. Reed*[12] purported to explain why the Court was declaring unconstitutional an Idaho law that preferred men in selecting among equally connected relatives in appointing an estate administrator for someone who died intestate. Justice Burger called this discrimination "arbitrary" and said it therefore violated the equal protection clause. In constitutional discourse, "arbitrary" was a code word for "lacking any rational connection to any legitimate governmental purpose." But the Idaho Supreme Court had pointedly argued that this law was indeed rationally designed to produce estate administrators more likely to be familiar with business affairs, and to do so quickly without a lot of bureaucratic paperwork. This was only 10 years after *Hoyt v. Florida*, where the Court found it "reasonable" to give a blanket jury duty exemption to women (on the grounds that women are "regarded as the center of home and family life"), even when this resulted in an all-male jury for the trial of a woman who murdered her husband.[13] By the standard that had governed decisions like *Hoyt*, the Idaho law favoring males in estate administration should have passed muster. The fact that it did not meant the Court was toughening the standards. Yet the Court refrained from saying so for quite awhile.

An explanation for the Court's doctrinal reticence might be found by recounting the attempted ratification of the Equal Rights Amendment. In response to a bustling women's movement, Congress by late 1970 was indicating massive support for the ERA. While the ERA specifically prohibited denying "equality of rights under the law on account of sex," the Fourteenth Amendment used only the general phrase "equal protection of the laws." The traditional reading of the latter allowed plenty of unequal treatment, as long as it had a rational basis. The ERA would do for gender discrimination what the Fourteenth Amendment had done for its historic target, race discrimination—namely, make such discrimination all but forbidden (short of the rare instance of a "compelling government interest" necessitating a particular discrimination).

By the time *Reed v. Reed* came along, the House of Representatives had voted for the ERA twice, first by a margin of 10-1 and then 20-1. One month later the Supreme Court handed down *Reed.* Four months later the Senate overwhelmingly passed the ERA. Several states ratified immediately, and the ERA looked like it was on its way to easy passage. As it turned out, eventually the ratification process stalled, even though public opinion polls in every state were showing majorities in favor. That the ERA was widely popular but politically stalled became evident by late 1976; eventually 35 states rather than the needed 38 had ratified by the 10-year deadline.

Meanwhile, many gender discrimination cases were being brought to the Supreme Court posing challenges under the Fourteenth Amendment's equal protection clause.[14] The Court at first relied on the old rational basis test but produced case results that made sense only as viewed through the lens of some stricter test. From 1971 to 1976 the justices applied this approach to declare unconstitutional not only the preference for males as estate administrators, but also to laws that gave spousal benefits to all army officers who had wives but denied such benefits for officers who had "nondependent" husbands;[15] automatically exempted all women from jury duty;[16] gave social security benefits to the surviving wives, but not husbands, of contributors who died leaving young children;[17] and established a younger age of majority for females (18) than for males (21), which provided fewer years of divorced parental support payments to daughters than to sons.[18]

Eventually, once it became clear that the ERA was both widely popular and likely to die, the Supreme Court stepped in and unofficially amended the Constitution by producing a new rule of law for gender discrimination. The Court opted for language between that of the ordinary, rational basis test and that of the compelling government

interest test applied to racial classifications. Beginning in December 1976, gender-based classifications officially had to meet the requirement of being "substantially related to" (not quite necessary for, but not merely rationally related to) an "important" (not merely a legitimate, but not quite a compelling) governmental interest.[19]

This "important governmental interest" test was then used to strike down most laws that discriminated by gender.[20] After July 1982, the Supreme Court stopped declaring instances of gender discrimination unconstitutional until 1994.

Statutory extension

The Burger Court did not stop innovating on behalf of women's rights in 1982 when it turned away from declarations of unconstitutionality on behalf of gender equity. Instead, it embraced feminist interpretations of federal laws, extending them in ways probably unanticipated by the Congresses that passed them. The law in question was usually Title VII of the 1964 Civil Rights Act, which prohibited employment practices that tend to discriminate on the basis of race, sex, national origin, or religion absent a "bona fide occupational qualification" (such as religion in the case of clergy). Sometimes the law was Title IX of the education amendments of 1972, which forbid most gender discrimination in schools that receive federal funds.

This period actually began in 1978 and arguably was triggered by Congress's reaction to a Supreme Court interpretation of Title VII handed down at the end of 1976. Employer exclusion of childbirth costs from employee health insurance benefit packages that covered all other medical disabilities, even elective plastic surgery, had been challenged as sex discrimination, with the argument that all of male workers' disabilities were covered but a woman-only disability was excluded.[21] The Supreme Court reasoned that the exclusion discriminated not between men and women but between "pregnant [persons] and non-pregnant persons." Therefore it was not sex discrimination. The congressional rebuff was swift and emphatic. In 1977 the Senate voted 75-11 for the Pregnancy Discrimination Amendment to Title VII, a bill that specifically defined employer discrimination on the basis of pregnancy as being included in the forbidden practice of sex discrimination. The bill became law by 1978.

Meanwhile, the Supreme Court promptly

started more aggressive readings of Title VII. Even before the PDA became law, but after it had passed the Senate overwhelmingly, the Supreme Court said (in patent inconsistency with its *Gilbert* reasoning, but refusing to overrule the decision) that it counted as illegal sex discrimination for employers to deny accrued seniority to workers returning after a maternity leave when the employers do not deny it to workers who take other medical disability leaves.[22] In the years to follow, even though the PDA referred specifically only to maternity benefits for employees, the Supreme Court was to extend its reach to benefits for the spouses of employees.[23]

The lesson evidently inferred by the Court— that Congress wanted aggressive readings of Title VII on sex discrimination—extended to many other arenas besides pregnancy during this period. First, despite the fact that women have longer life expectancies on average than men, the justices interpreted Title VII as forbidding sex discrimination in employee pension plans, whether by deducting bigger pension payments from female paychecks to put into the plan or by providing smaller monthly payments to female retirees.[24] Second, despite the freedom of association arguments that were posed to the contrary, Title VII's reach was extended to promotion decisions labeled as entry into a partnership, such as those that are the norm in major law and accounting firms.[25] Third, in 1986 the Supreme Court unanimously accepted the idea that sexual harassment in the workplace is included in the category "discrimination on the basis of sex...in terms or conditions of employment," which Title VII forbids.[26] Fourth, while the words of Title VII forbid the making of employment decisions such as hiring or promotion "because of [an] individual's sex [or race, etc.]" the Supreme Court ruled that affirmative action programs to diversify the employees in a traditionally segregated job category are permitted, so that it is not illegal to pick a woman over a roughly equally qualified male simply on the grounds that she is female.[27] Fifth, also in the late 1980s, the Court ruled that penalizing a female for not conforming to her stereotypical gender role in personality, demeanor, and clothing style violated Title VII's ban on sex discrimination.[28]

It is remarkable that the Burger and then the Rehnquist Courts, in the face of both expectations and general reputation to the contrary, have acted as liberal innovators on the women's rights front

via aggressive interpretations of federal statutes at least from 1978 through 1988.[29]

After a pause in judicial feminist momentum in 1989, followed by a second congressional rebuff in the 1991 Civil Rights Restoration Act, the Supreme Court, as in 1978, responded to Congress's push by again moving out ahead of Congress. In 1991, 1992, and 1993 the Court returned to its pattern of feminist extensions of civil rights statutes. In 1991 the Court ruled in *UAW v. Johnson Controls* that an employer's fear of lawsuits was not adequate (under Title VII) as a "bona fide occupational qualification" to justify eliminating all fertile women or even all pregnant women from jobs that endanger a fetus.[30] In 1992 the Court expanded the reach of Title IX of the Education Amendments of 1972. It did so contrary to the arguments of the U.S. solicitor general and to the rulings of lower courts, and it did so unanimously. The Court ruled that under Title IX individual students who felt themselves to be victims of sex discrimination (in this case, sexual harassment) could sue school boards for damages. (The Court cited a related 1986 congressional statute as offering implicit support for its position.)[31] And in the fall of 1993 the Supreme Court reaffirmed and clarified its decision concerning workplace sexual harassment. It did so in such a way as to correct circuit court rulings that had narrowed the reach of its own 1986 precedent. Employees, the Court ruled, do not have to prove they have actually suffered some measurable psychological damage in order to bring a sexual harassment complaint; employers are obligated under Title VII to maintain a workplace that is free of discriminatory intimidation or ridicule.[32]

Beginning in 1971, therefore, a mix of Warren Court holdovers and early Burger Court justices were willing to alter constitutional interpretation dramatically on behalf of women's rights. Although this has not been the case from 1982 to 1994, since 1978 the Burger and Rehnquist Courts have continued to be willing to expand women's rights by means of feminist statutory interpretation.

Explaining the shift

While there was plenty of litigation concerning abortion restrictions from 1977 to 1992, the Supreme Court's constitutional doctrine on abortion remained steady. Many political forces besides signals from the Supreme Court affect whether litigation will be brought on a given issue. And whether the litigation is brought, or even granted certiorari, does not of itself determine that judicial policy will shift.

The litigation pattern would seem to be a more central concern with respect to the Court's turning away from Constitution-grounded policy making regarding gender equity. Did the cases simply stop coming to the Supreme Court because state laws had all been reformed by 1982, leaving nothing left to challenge? Or might this shift reveal a conscious strategy of the post-1982 Burger Court and the Rehnquist Court? Are the justices choosing among available cases on the basis of a deliberate approach to the judicial role, one in which statute-based policy innovation is preferred as more in keeping with a representative democracy? In this conception, if the unelected justices "get it wrong," the elected Congress is free to tell them so. With legislative interpretation, Congress can override the Supreme Court; with constitutional interpretation, such action is not so readily available.

The litigation pattern for gender equity appeals to the Supreme Court in the 1968-1994 period reveals that requests for cert claiming constitutional violations of gender equity were relatively few in the 1968-1972 period (fluctuating between two and seven per term), as were requests for cert claiming statutory violations of gender equity in the 1968-1971 period (ranging from zero to four per term). After the 1971 term, during which the ratio of grants of cert to requests for cert on constitutional gender equity claims was an astoundingly high 3:4 (the overall ratio of grants to requests in a term is approximately 1:40), both types of gender equity cert requests rose sharply. Constitution-based cert requests in the 1973-1980 terms numbered 15 or more in seven of the eight years. Statute-based requests increased somewhat more gradually, but in the 1975, 1976, and 1977 terms numbered more than 20 per year. Beginning in the 1980 term, they have dramatically outnumbered Constitution-based requests, ranging from 28 to 9 and averaging 16.3, in the 1980 to June 1994 period. This marked predominance of statute-based gender equity requests continued uninterrupted through the 1993-1994 term.

Thus, the fact that the Supreme Court decided virtually no Constitution-based gender-equity claims after the 1982 term is largely a reflection of the fact that the cert requests were not there to be decided. As in the pre-1973 period, the number of such requests fluctuated between one and seven. But unlike the earlier cases, these 1980s and 1990s claims did not present broad questions of law. The Constitution-based claims of this latter period virtually all presented custody-related claims of unwed fathers, claims that were heavily fact-specific. These are just the sort of cases the justices routinely avoid, not as an exercise of policy preference but simply because they are not good vehicles for establishing or clarifying broad legal principles.[33] So the data do show that cert requests claiming constitutional violations of gender equity did essentially dry up after the 1981 term.

This pattern invites the conclusion that the combination of Supreme Court decisions in the 1971-1976 period and then the clear constitutional doctrine after December 1976 (the "important government interest" test of *Craig v. Boren*) served in the short term to stir up lots of litigation to clarify the contours of the doctrine and eventually pushed state and federal legislators to cleanse the statute books of gender discriminations that lacked strong justification. And the Supreme Court, still committed to a much stronger version of gender equity policy than prevailed prior to 1970, continues to hand down important policies protecting gender equity against statutory violations. It appears not that the justices have been unwilling over the past decade to base their decisions on constitutional grounds, but rather that appropriate cases requiring such reasoning have simply not come forth from litigants.

Does this finding mean that the Supreme Court really is a passive branch that must wait quietly for issues to be brought to it? Not necessarily. First, it is worth noting that the litigation dry-up, while a response to legislative change, at root is responding to the Supreme Court moves that stimulated the legislative reform.

Second, it is possible both that statutes violating gender equity were eliminated at the state level and that the late Burger Court consciously preferred statute-based to Constitution-based jurisprudence. Indeed, the drying up of Constitution-based gender-equity claims may in part reflect litigators' responsiveness to signals the Court was sending in its opinions. In other words, interest group lawyers may have stopped bringing Constitution-based appeals to the Court in the fear of losing. They may have been calculating that their chances of success were greater if they had a reinforcing statute to rely on than if they were relying simply on constitutionally mandated equal protection.

H.W. Perry documents that at least some justices consciously issue veiled "invitations" in opinions they write, indicating which future litigation they would welcome.[34] It is also likely that poential litigants read, and follow, some opinions that appear to contain messages that are the opposite of these invitations. The Court's decisions to strike down employment policies on Title VII grounds in *Dothard v. Rawlinson*[35] and *L.A. Water and Power v. Manhart*[36] may have invited more Title VII challenges. And its rejection of an equal protection clause challenge to a state civil service rule in *Personnel Administrator v. Feeney*[37] may have discouraged future Constitution-based challenges to similar policies.

In interviews with the senior author of this article, lawyers from three organizations that were involved in the 1980s in litigating for women's rights[38] said that *Feeney* and *Dothard* definitely pushed them toward litigating on statutory grounds. These lawyers also reported that they eventually stopped bringing Supreme Court cases because by 1982 all state laws of sizable impact that openly discriminated by sex had been either eliminated or upheld by the Court.

The Court's dominant role

The Supreme Court's role in interaction with litigators is dominant. The Court structures the litigation pattern by setting forth legal doctrine that indicates the kinds of claims that have a good chance of winning. It also controls that pattern by setting forth clear constitutional doctrine that causes laws to be eliminated so that they are no longer around to be litigated against. In these ways, the Supreme Court is in charge. On the other hand, the Court often chooses to respond to congressional signals, and Congress not uncommonly alters statutes in order to control judicial interpretation of them. While the pattern of cert requests naturally reflects the general political climate to a degree, it is also powerfully shaped by judicial as well as Congressional choices.

Approximately five years after the Court set forth clear constitutional doctrine in December 1976 (*Craig*) condemning all governmental gender discrimination that could not be proved "substantially related to an important governmental interest," litigation alleging such discrimination essentially stopped coming to the Supreme Court. This fact left a Court still sympathetic to gender equity with, for the most part, only statutory claims to adjudicate.

Interviews with the prominent litigating interest groups of the period revealed that this drying up of constitution-based gender equity litigation was caused by a combination of the success of such litigation and consequent elimination of statutes that explicitly discriminated on the basis of sex, and judicial doctrine interpreting the language of Title VII and of the constitutional equal protection clause, such that practices with a gender-disproportionate impact became much harder to challenge on constitutional grounds than on Title VII grounds.

Further research would determine whether these findings on the Supreme Court's role in shaping gender policy over the past three decades have a wider applicability. In this context, the Burger Court and the pre-1994 Rehnquist Court exhibited a substantial degree of deference to Congress as a co-equal branch of government, Supreme Court decisions relatively quickly produced an impressive level of reform at the state legislative level, and interest groups with litigative strategies were closely attuned to pronouncements of judicial doctrine relevant to their goals. Refinement of these suggestions might be produced by a close look at other time periods and other congressionally regulated policy sectors such as those concerning the rights of racial minorities, protection of the environment, and burdens on interstate commerce.

NOTES

This article originally appeared in Volume 79, Number 2, September-October 1995, pages 80-85.

The authors gratefully acknowledge the financial support of the University of Delaware Humanities Scholars' Program for the research on which this article is in part based.

1. Perry, DECIDING TO DECIDE 210 (Cambridge, Mass.: Harvard University Press, 1991).

2. *See* Caldeira, *The United States Supreme Court and Criminal Cases: Alternative Models of Agenda-Building*, 11 BRIT. J. OF POL. SCI. 449 (1981); and Pacelle, "The Supreme Court's Agenda and the Dynamics of Policy Evolution," paper presented at annual meeting of American Political Science Association, Aug.30-Sept. 2, 1990, San Francisco, Calif., and THE TRANSFORMATION OF THE SUPREME COURT'S AGENDA (Boulder, Colorado: Westview Press, 1991).

3. It is conceivable that the Court is at the point of a new period of innovation with the summer 1993 accession of Justice Ruth Bader Ginsburg. The decision in *J.E.B. v. T.B.* (114 S.Ct. 1419 (1994)) that declared it unconstitutional to permit the gender-based use of peremptory strikes for jury composi-

tion marked the first time in 12 years that the Supreme Court declared any gender discrimination unconstitutional. Note, however, that the Court granted cert for that case during the 1992 term, long before Justice Ginsburg was nominated.

4. Eisenstadt v. Baird, 405 U.S. 438 (1972).

5. Griswold v. Connecticut, 381 U.S. 479 (1965).

6. 410 U.S. 113; 410 U.S. 179.

7. Carey v. Pop. Services, 431 U.S. 678 (1977).

8. Planned Parenthood v. Danforth, 428 U.S. 52 (1976).

9. Beal v. Doe, 432 U.S. 438 (1977); Maher v. Roe, 432 U.S. 464 (1977); Poelker v. Doe, 432 U.S. 519 (1977).

10. Planned Parenthood of Southern Pennsylvania v. Casey, Governor of Pennsylvania, 112 S.Ct. 2791.

11. Hoyt v. Florida, 368 U.S. 57 (1961); State v. Hall, 385 U.S. 98 (1968).

12. 404 U.S. 71.

13. *Supra* n. 11.

14. For a more detailed account of the linkages between ERA politics and Supreme Court alterations of constitutional doctrine see Goldstein, *The ERA and the U.S. Supreme Court*, 1 RESEARCH IN L. AND POLICY STUD. 145 (1987).

15. Frontiero v. Richardson, 411 U.S. 677 (1973).

16. Taylor v. Louisiana, 419 U.S. 522 (1975).

17. Weinberger v. Weisenfeld, 420 U.S. 636 (1975).

18. Stanton v. Stanton, 421 U.S. 7 (1975).

19. Craig v. Boren, 429 U.S. 190.

20. Gender discriminating statutes were declared void in all of the following: Califano v. Goldfarb, 430 U.S. 199 (1977) (giving social security benefits to all surviving wives of contributors who died but only to those surviving husbands who could prove economic dependency; Orr v. Orr, 440 U.S. 268 (1979) (allowing alimony awards only to wives); Caban v. Mohammed, 441 U.S. 380 (1979) (requiring permission from all mothers and from married or divorced fathers but not from unwed fathers before their parental rights could be terminated; Califano v. Westcott, 443 U.S. 76 (1979) (giving welfare benefits to families with unemployed fathers but not to those with unemployed mothers; Wengler v. Druggists Mutual Insurance, 446 U.S. 142 (1980) (giving workers' compensation to widows but not to widowers of protected workers; Kirchberg v. Feenstra, 450 U.S. 455 (1981) (giving husbands unilateral control over all marital property; Mississippi University for Women v. Hogan, 458 U.S. 718 (1982) (allowing only women to attend a particular state nursing college). The Court did uphold some discrimination, e.g., in draft registration and in statutory rape laws.

21. G.E. v. Gilbert, 429 U.S. 125 (1976).

22. Nashville Gas v. Satty, 434 U.S. 136 (1977).

23. Newport News Shipbuilding v. EEOC, 462 U.S. 669 (1983).

24. Los Angeles Department of Water and Power v. Manhart, 435 U.S. 702 (1978); Arizona Governing Committee v. Norris, 463 U.S. 1073 (1983).

25. Hishon v. King & Spaulding, 467 U.S. 69 (1984).

26. Meritor Savings v. Vinson, 477 U.S. 57.

27. Johnson v. Transportation Agency, 480 U.S. 616 (1987). Earlier in this period the Supreme Court made the same move regarding race-based affirmative action, United Steelworkers v. Weber, 443 U.S. 193 (1979).

28. Price Waterhouse v. Hopkins, 490 U.S. 228 (1988).

29. This conclusion is based on a qualitative, political analysis of the substantive policy impact of Court decisions in this decade. For a quantitative analysis that comes to the same conclusion, see George and Epstein, *Women's rights litigation in the 1980s: more of the same?*, 74 JUDICATURE 314 (1991). The George and Epstein analysis does not notice the shift from constitution-based decisions to statute-based ones.

30. 499 U.S. 187 (1991).

31. Franklin v. Gwinnett County Schools, 503 U.S. 60 (1992). For details see Goldstein, CONTEMPORARY CASES IN WOMEN'S RIGHTS 256-257 (Madison: U. of Wisc. Press, 1994).

32. Harris v. Forklift Systems, Inc., 114 S.Ct. 367 (1993).

33. Perry, *supra* n. 1.

34. *Id.* at 212-214.

35. 433 U.S. 321 (June 1977).

36. 435 U.S. 702 (1978).

37. 442 U.S. 256 (June 1979). The combined import of *Dothard* and *Feeney* is that equal protection challenges to government policies with a gender discriminatory impact need to prove the discrimination is intentional; Title VII-based challenges do not have that burden.

38. For a close look at this litigation campaign during the 1970s, see O'Connor, WOMEN'S ORGANIZATIONS' USE OF THE COURTS (Lexington, Mass.: Lexington Books, 1980). Lawyers interviewed included Isabelle Katz Pinzler, director of the Women's Rights Project of the American Civil Liberties Union during the 1980s; Phyllis Segal and Sally Burns, two of the directors of the NOW Legal Defense and Education Fund during the 1980s; and Helen Norton of the Women's Legal Defense Fund.

The Courts and Their Publics
Public Opinion and the Media

INTRODUCTION

The judiciary is the most invisible branch of American government and the branch about which the public knows the least. Consequently, the media have a uniquely important informational role to play in this domain and, indeed, they may be the exclusive source of information about the courts for most Americans. In this section we focus on the complex of relationships among the courts, the media, and public opinion.

Perhaps the most prominent and ongoing issue regarding the courts and the media has centered on the access of photojournalists to judicial proceedings, a subject that is examined by Ruth Ann Strickland and Richter Moore Jr. in, "Cameras in state courts: a historical perspective." Strickland and Moore take the reader on a journey that considers the role of cameras in famous historical trials including, among others, the Scopes monkey trial, the case of the kidnapping of the Lindbergh baby, the Sacco and Vanzetti and Leopold-Loeb murder trials, and the trial of Lyndon Johnson's confidant, Billie Sol Estes. The authors document current practices regarding cameras in the courtroom in the American states and link these practices to prior court rulings, ABA Canons, and varied state experimentation choices. For Strickland and Moore, the impact of cameras in American courts has been salutary. "Cameras…have enhanced the public's awareness of the judicial system as a human one, dedicated to protecting and preserving individual rights to a fair trial, and at the same time, protecting and preserving the rights of society."

In "Shall we dance? The courts, the community, and the news media," a wide-ranging panel discussion of several facets of the media/court/public interface, a number of critical issues including that of cameras in courtrooms are discussed, sometimes heatedly, by a group of expert panelists. The panel members explore the degree to which the public is adequately informed about the judiciary by the media and, more broadly, the question of whether the media is, "obligated" to educate the public about our government's least visible branch.

The premise of, "'The Supreme Court decided today…,' or did it?," a study conducted by Elliot Slotnick and Jennifer Segal, is that network television newscasts are the primary source of information for the public about what the Court has done. If the newscasts get it "wrong," public misunderstanding about judicial policies is bound to follow. Slotnick and Segal content-analyze the limited news coverage in one term of Supreme Court certiorari decisions, that is, the Court's decisions about whether or not to hear cases. Remarkably, in three out of four instances where the Court declined to hear a case, the newscast misreported the Court's non-action and suggested that a decision had been made on the case's merits. Slotnick and Segal explore the implications of such woeful inaccuracy in reporting for a misinformed public.

The relationship between Supreme Court rulings and public opinion is examined much more directly by Thomas Marshall and Joseph Ignagni in "Supreme Court and public support for rights claims." In their research design, Marshall and Ignagni attempt to link public opinion on a number of rights issues with specific decisions that addressed those issues for a period spanning four decades. They find that while the Court's rights orientation was, historically, marginally more sympathetic towards rights claims than the public, these differences between judicial decisions and public opinion have eroded over time. The authors conclude that, generally, their results, "are consistent with the theory that justices sense and share widely held public attitudes."

While Marshall and Ignagni examine the relationship between specific judicial decisions and public opinion, in "Public perception of the Supreme Court in the 1990s," John Scheb II and William Lyons address the more general issue of how the public regards the Court, utilizing survey data from 1994 and 1997. Their analysis reveals a good deal of stability in attitudes about the Court and a much more positive evaluation of the High Court than of Congress. Positive assessments of the Court tend to dissipate somewhat, however, when attention is focused on some specific decisions it has rendered. Interestingly, assessments of the Court do not vary much along racial, gender, or partisan lines. Scheb and Lyons conclude that, "the Court appears to be doing a good job of holding the middle ground, where its legitimacy is likely to be maximized."

The articles in this section underscore the judiciary's institutional invisibility, the insulation of judges from the public they serve, inadequate and often misguided media coverage of the courts, and an ill-informed public when the subject turns to the judicial system. It is in this context that we close this section with Kevin Esterling's "Public outreach: the cornerstone of judicial independence." Esterling's provocative and suggestive analysis argues that, "judges' isolation from politics and society is increasingly insufficient to maintain judicial independence. Contrary to the traditional view of judicial independence, in contemporary society the ability of courts to act as *independent* decision makers depends on their involvement in local communities through various public outreach efforts."

Cameras in state courts: a historical perspective

The excesses that marked the early days of camera coverage of court proceedings no longer occur, and fears about negative consequences have been put to rest.

by Ruth Ann Strickland and Richter H. Moore Jr.

Televised trials, appellate proceedings, or both are now a reality in 47 states, and 35 allow filming of criminal trials. For years, however, the acceptance of cameras in the courtroom has been overshadowed by ambivalence. The U.S. Judicial Conference's recent rejection of camera coverage of federal court proceedings and the debates over televising O.J. Simpson's murder trial are only the latest manifestations of this ambivalence.

During the three-year experiment that began in July 1991 and is scheduled to last until the end of 1994, cameras were allowed in 6 of 94 federal district courts in civil trials only. Most judges who took part in the experiment perceived few or no effects on the participants, proceedings, court decorum, or administration of justice, and the report commissioned by the Judicial Conference recommended extension of televised trials.[1] Nevertheless, the Judicial Conference in September voted by a nearly 2-1 margin against extending the experiment or permanently allowing cameras in federal court proceedings. Judges voting not to extend coverage reportedly were concerned about the negative effects of television cameras on courtroom dignity and on jurors and witnesses.[2]

With the current media frenzy surrounding the Simpson trial, the broader context of cameras in the courtroom is easily overlooked. As Los Angeles Superior Court Judge Lance A. Ito considered blocking television access to the trial due to alleged erroneous reporting and the perceived "tabloidization" of the judicial process,[3] the intense debate over the potential effects of filming and broadcasting court proceedings in general resurfaced.[4]

Thus it is now appropriate to reexamine the historical context of electronic media coverage of state court proceedings, efforts to restrict such access, and the current use of cameras in state courts.

Historical background

The American public traditionally has supported its right to attend trials and participate in the judicial process. Trials often serve as cathartic events for the public, allowing citizens to hold wrongdoers accountable and reestablish order in the community. When the United States was less populous, predominantly rural, and more homogeneous, and the citizenry was largely self policing, the number of trials were few and the days of court were limited. People could therefore travel in a leisurely manner to the county seat to participate in the judicial process. Court days were festive days, with the trials as the center of the community's interest.[5]

Yet as the population grew and became more heterogeneous and urban, the number of trials and court days also rose. With the advent of the Industrial Revolution, the average citizen began working during most of the daylight hours. Time to attend trials became less available, but the public still wanted to know whether the perpetrator of a criminal act had been brought to justice. Consequently, a smaller group of individuals took on the responsibility for observing trials and relaying the results.[6]

As society changed, the technology for informing the public of trial proceedings shifted from word of mouth to the printed page. By the mid-

19th century, information was transmitted almost instantaneously over great distances by wire. Newspapers obtained and passed along trial results very soon after a verdict was reached. If people were too anxious to wait for the newspaper account of a particularly infamous trial, they could go to the local telegraph office and wait for results. This was the case, for instance, in the early 20th century trial of Harry Thaw for the murder of Stanford White over the affections of Evelyn Nesbit, known as "the girl in the red velvet swing." To provide nationwide coverage, a telegraph office was set up in the main hall of New York's criminal court building. According to one account, "Cables hung from the skylight in the old court's central hall like strange black vines."[7]

As other modes of communication developed, they too became tools for reporting trials. After World War I, courtroom photographs became a regular feature of newspapers, especially the tabloids. One particularly egregious example of still and newsreel camera coverage of the courts occurred in 1925 in the infamous Scopes trial in Dayton, Tennessee.[8] One of the greatest circuses in the annals of the American judicial process, the "monkey trial" focused some attention on the excesses of the news media in the 1920s.

The Scopes trial not only brought the issue of evolution to the American public, it also introduced another technological innovation in trial coverage—radio broadcasting. It was the first trial to be broadcast over radio, allowing lawyers William Jennings Bryan and Clarence Darrow to orate to large radio audiences. Judge John T. Raulston exaggerated only slightly when he stated, "My gavel will be heard around the world."[9] Telegraph wires were run into the courtroom, phone booths were installed in the corridor just outside, and newsreel cameras along with many news photographers were present in the court. The proceedings were punctuated with requests that were more apt for a movie director than an officer of the court: "Put your face a little more this way, Judge." "Come a little more forward, Mr. Darrow."[10]

Due to unruly media coverage of the murder trials of Bartolomeo Vanzetti and Nicola Sacco in 1921 and the 1924 trials of Richard Loeb and Nathan Leopold Jr. for the murder of 14-year-old Robert Franks, the American Bar Association in 1924 appointed a special committee to curb troublesome tendencies in news reporting of court-room proceedings. It was not until 1927, however, that the appellate courts, for the first time, examined the issue of cameras in the courtroom. A Maryland court convicted five Hearst newspaper editors and photographers in Baltimore of contempt of court for violating a ban on taking pictures in court during a murder trial. Although the conviction was appealed on the grounds that a judge cannot absolutely prohibit photography, the Court of Appeals of Maryland rejected this argument and upheld the contempt.[11]

Despite efforts to regulate news photography, most court officials seemed unconcerned with the new technologies in the courtroom. When questioned about cameras in court in 1933, an Oklahoma judge who allowed photography in his court stated: "The court belongs to the people. Only a few of them can get inside the courtroom and the Constitution says our trial shall be open and above board for all."[12]

Not until after the 1935 trial of Bruno Richard Hauptmann, who was charged with kidnapping and murdering the baby son of American hero Colonel Charles Lindbergh, were cameras in the courtroom and unprincipled news coverage substantially challenged. The trial was highly publicized, with approximately 700 newsmen, including 120 cameramen, present.[13] With messenger boys employed by the press running about and virtually uncontrollable photographers climbing on counsel tables for better shots, blinding witnesses with their flash bulbs, Hauptmann appealed his conviction, claiming he could not get a fair trial.[14] The New Jersey Court of Appeals held that despite some confusion, the public is entitled to reports on the court proceedings, and judges must afford reasonable access.[15]

Although the New Jersey Court of Appeals saw no major problem with the conduct of the Hauptmann trial, the ABA reconsidered the role of cameras in the courtroom due to the reported carnival-like atmosphere of the Hauptmann trial. Consequently, in 1937 it added to its Canons of Judicial Ethics Canon 35, which prohibited photographing and broadcasting of court proceedings. More recent scholars point out that cameras were a scapegoat for prejudicial behavior not only of the news media but of lawyers and other trial participants, as no proof was established of any negative effects on due process by cameras per se.[16]

Most states adopted the canon, although a few

courts continued to allow photographs in the courtroom.[17] Later, in 1952, the ABA amended Canon 35 to forbid television coverage in the court as well as photographic and broadcast coverage. Again, most states accepted the change either in whole or in part.[18]

In 1956 the Colorado Supreme Court held hearings concerning Canon 35 and concluded that the matter of cameras and radio or television instruments in the courtroom should be left solely to the discretion of the sitting judge. Justice Otto Moore, speaking for the court, held that citizens should be educated about the functioning of all branches of government and that court operations are most misunderstood by the public. He dismissed the contention that opening courtrooms to photographers and radio and television broadcasters would induce abnormal behavior, declaring that should judges or lawyers perform for the camera, society should have a chance to witness and judge such behavior as offensive. Justice Moore further argued that such behavior would be reduced if televised.[19]

In 1958 the Oklahoma Court of Criminal Appeals was asked to overturn a burglary conviction on the grounds that the defendant had been denied a fair trial because television was allowed in the courtroom and the defendant had been filmed in the presence of the jury during a break between the court proceedings. The court declared the defendant's contention was "a baseless boogey constructed out of pure conjecture."[20] In balancing the scales of competing interests, the Oklahoma court saw an inherent educational value for the public in televising trials, arguing that people could not respect a branch of government they did not understand.[21]

The *Estes* case

Texas was one of the states that ignored Canon 35 and allowed cameras in the courtroom at the discretion of the presiding judge. In 1962 Texas produced the case that served for more than a decade and a half as the basis for the argument against cameras in the courtroom.[22]

Financier Billie Sol Estes, a friend of President Lyndon B. Johnson, was charged with swindling of such proportions as to attract national notoriety. The trial judge, exercising his discretion, permitted television and photographic coverage of the pretrial hearing and the trial itself.

There was considerable disruption during the pretrial hearing, with as many as 12 camera operators taking motion and still pictures and televising the proceedings.[23]

When the trial began, all of the television cameras and newsreel photographers were restricted to a specially constructed booth at the back of the courtroom, painted to blend with the room's permanent structure. Upon conviction, Estes contended that televising and broadcasting his trial deprived him of a fair trial. Both the trial court and the Texas Court of Criminal Appeals found no denial of due process, and Estes appealed to the U.S. Supreme Court, which heard the case in 1965.[24] In a 5-4 decision, the Court reversed the conviction, although no actual prejudice to Estes was shown. The Court held that in this case the circumstances were inherently suspect, and a showing of actual prejudice was not a necessary requisite for reversal. Writing for the majority, Justice Tom Clark declared at length that the mere presence of television cameras in the courtroom had a detrimental psychological impact on jurors, witnesses, judges and the defendant. Yet he provided no empirical evidence to substantiate his point.

In his dissent, Justice Potter Stewart wrote there was no evidence to indicate that cameras had an adverse effect on court proceedings during the trial, given that there was no distractive noise or lighting problems in the courtroom. The disturbances of television, newsreel, and still photographers evident in the pretrial hearing were not experienced during the trial itself. Justice Stewart also mentioned that the judge, jury, and counsel were apparently not influenced by the presence of photographers or by television.[25]

Justice Clark, however, saw the pretrial hearing and the trial as part of a continuum, which was a determining factor in the denial of due process. Moreover, he stressed, the presence of television did not materially contribute to determining the truth. Four of the five justices joining in the majority insisted the televising of criminal trials is inherently a denial of due process. Clark, while generally agreeing, left the gate open, stating: "When the advances in these arts permit reporting...by television without their present hazards to a fair trial we will have another case."[26]

The Court spent little time with the question of whether the First Amendment granted the news media the right to broadcast from the courtroom and whether refusing broadcast coverage unfairly discriminated between the newspapers and electronic media. Yet, in response to these questions, Justice Clark left open the possibility of the Court's eventual change of the *Estes* decision. He wrote that while a free press must be allowed to perform its function in a democratic society, its exercise must be balanced against the interest of a fair judicial process.[27]

After *Estes*

Within three years of the *Estes* decision, the issue of televised trials was again before the courts. In *Gonzales v. People* (1968), the Colorado Supreme Court faced the issue of whether a single concealed television camera under the direct supervision of the judge violated the defendant's right to a fair trial. The court reiterated its earlier position that the question of cameras in courts must be left to the discretion of the trial judge. It noted that the balance of the competing interests of fair trial and free press could only be decided by independent judicial discretion on a case-by-case basis.[28]

In 1972, the ABA replaced the Canons of Judicial Ethics with the Model Code of Judicial Conduct. The prohibition against broadcasting, televising, or photographing during sessions of court remained and became Canon 3A(7) of the new code. However, it included an exception to allow for photographic or electronic recording and reproduction of court proceedings under very restricted guidelines and only for instructional purposes in educational institutions, recognizing that in proper hands, and carefully controlled, electronic or photographic coverage would not necessarily impair judicial serenity.[29]

Within just over a decade of *Estes*, and soon after the ABA's adoption of the Code of Judicial Conduct, several states began to examine the validity of the prohibitions of Canon 3A(7), which had been adopted in whole or in part by almost every state. Many states experimented with camera usage in their courts during the late 1970s.[30]

Florida's experiment

By far one of the most important early experiments with cameras in the courtroom occurred in the state of Florida. In 1975, the Post-Newsweek stations in Florida petitioned the Florida Supreme Court to eliminate its prohibition of television coverage in the courtroom. The petition as presented

was not approved, but the court authorized the televising of one civil and one criminal trial subject to court-imposed guidelines.[31] Because of difficulty in obtaining the consensus required by the guidelines, more than a year passed without any televised trials. Sensing a need for a test period of electronic media trial coverage, the Florida Supreme Court in 1977 authorized a one-year pilot program during which the electronic media were permitted to cover judicial proceedings in all of Florida's state courts without the consent of the participants.[32]

The cornerstone of the pilot program was *State v. Zamora* (1977), which involved a 15-year-old boy charged with murdering an elderly neighbor who caught him and an accomplice burglarizing her home. The trial attracted international interest because of the unusual defense—"involuntary television intoxication." The defense contended Zamora was unaware of what he was doing due to the massive amounts of crime and violence he had watched on television.[33]

Segments of the trial were televised nightly over Miami television stations, and worldwide coverage was estimated by Judge Paul Baker, the trial judge, to involve several million viewers. Judge Baker submitted a report to the Florida Supreme Court, giving his views of the impact of the television coverage.[34] The grim predictions of Justice Clark from the U.S. Supreme Court's *Estes* decision did not occur. Judge Baker reported that the television and audio equipment present during the Zamora trial produced no distracting noises or light flashes. Having spoken privately with jurors, Baker concluded that the presence of cameras caused only slight distractions but not any that interfered with jurors' consideration of testimony, arguments of counsel, or judicial instructions.[35] Judge Baker found no support for the supposition that judges would act for the camera, and he wrote that the public has a right to know how a judge conducts court business. Whether this was accomplished by spectators in the court or by television viewing made little difference, he wrote.[36]

As a result of this and other cases, the Florida Supreme Court in 1979 permanently opened the state courts to televised coverage, subject always to the authority of the presiding judge. The court observed that electronic technology had improved immeasurably since *Estes*.[37] Moreover, others noticed that camera coverage reduced physical distractions by limiting the need for on-site sketch artists and reporters.[38]

Chandler v. Florida

Justice Clark stated in *Estes*: "When the advances in these arts permit reporting by...television without their present hazards to a fair trial, we will have another case."[39] That other case, *Chandler v. Florida* (1981), grew out of the Florida experiment.

The case came to the U.S. Supreme Court as a result of the televised trial of two Miami Beach policemen charged with burglary and other related crimes. Their criminal activities were discovered by chance when an amateur radio operator, the state's principal witness, overheard and recorded conversations between the police officers over their walkie-talkie radios during the burglary. The case attracted major media attention due to the involvement of law enforcement officers and the unique circumstances surrounding the chance discovery of the crime.

The defendants objected to the televising of their trial and sought to have Florida's experimental Canon 3A(7) declared unconstitutional. When all attempts to prevent electronic coverage of the trial failed, the defendants' counsel during voir dire asked each potential juror if he or she could be fair and impartial despite the presence of television cameras in the courtroom. Each of the selected jurors responded that such coverage would not affect his or her consideration of the case. Because of television coverage, the defense moved to sequester the jury. The court refused, instructing the jurors not to watch or read anything about the case.[40]

A single television camera was present in the courtroom during the state's presentation of testimony. No camera was present when the defense presented its case. Only 2 minutes, 55 seconds of the trial were telecast, and this coverage depicted only the prosecution's side. After the jury delivered a guilty verdict on all counts, the defendants moved for a new trial, contending television coverage had denied them a fair and impartial trial— yet they presented no evidence of specific prejudice.[41]

The Florida District Court of Appeals affirmed the conviction, finding no evidence that the presence of a television camera had hampered the defendants in presenting their case or had deprived them of an impartial trial. Next, the Florida Su-

preme Court denied review on the grounds that the challenge to Canon 3A(7) was moot because of its decision in the *Post-Newsweek Stations* case.[42]

Finally, the U.S. Supreme Court accepted the case for review and eventually ruled, in a unanimous decision, that *Estes* did not prescribe a constitutional ban on still photographic, radio and television coverage in all cases and under all circumstances. The Court observed that any criminal case generating substantial publicity presented risks that the publicity could compromise the defendant's right to a fair trial. In its decision, however, the Court declared that such risks did not justify an absolute ban on news reporting and broadcast of trials.[43]

The opinion further noted that no sufficient empirical evidence was presented to establish that the mere presence of broadcasting media has an inherently adverse effect on the judicial process. The Court found that the defendant must show specific prejudice in a case. In this case, there was no effort to show that cameras in the court impaired the ability of jurors to decide the case on only the evidence before them, or that any of the participants in the trial were adversely affected by cameras and the prospect of broadcasting. Consequently, the Supreme Court held, there was no evidence the trial was compromised by television coverage.[44]

The justices also held that since the U.S. Supreme Court possesses no supervisory authority over state courts, its review authority over state court actions was confined to cases involving a possible constitutional violation. Since there was no showing of prejudice of a constitutional dimension due to the televising of trials, Florida could permit electronic media coverage of trials in its state courts. The Court concluded states must be free to experiment; only when the experiment actually infringed on a fundamental guarantee was the U.S. Supreme Court authorized to intervene.[45] The decision in *Chandler*, while not requiring states to admit television cameras to their courts, went a long way toward limiting their exclusion.

Just the year before the *Chandler* case, the U.S. Supreme Court in *Richmond Newspapers Inc. v. Virginia* (1980) specifically recognized the right of the press to attend criminal trials. The Court stated that the holding did not mean the First Amendment rights of the public and representatives of the press were absolute. A trial judge, the Court held, could impose reasonable limitations on access to a trial in the interest of the fair administration of justice.[46] In 1982, the Court reaffirmed this position in *Globe Newspaper Company v. Superior Court.* The Court held that the First Amendment afforded protection to the press and the public to attend criminal trials and that the state could not establish arbitrary exclusions without valid cause.[47]

By applying the *Richmond Newspapers* principle of open courtrooms and the *Globe* prohibition of arbitrary state exclusion from them, combined with the *Chandler* acceptance of televised trial sessions, opened the possibility that remaining state and federal rules barring or severely limiting the electronic media from the courtroom could be challenged as an infringement of First and Fourteenth Amendment rights.[48] In 1982, the ABA approved a new Canon 3A(7), replacing the 1972 prohibition on camera coverage of trials for news purposes. The new canon recommended allowing camera usage in courtrooms for news purposes at the discretion and under the supervision of the state's highest appellate court. While the canon did not endorse cameras in the courtroom, it eliminated a potential obstacle to electronic media in courts.[49]

Generally legal actions since *Chandler* have involved specific instances in which the televising of court proceedings was challenged on fair trial grounds. In almost all instances, the appellate courts have found there were no denials of due process or a fair trial.[50] After *Chandler*, states rapidly began to open their doors to television cameras on a permanent or experimental basis.

Current use

As of 1994, 47 states allow cameras in their trial or appellate courts on either a permanent or experimental basis. Thirty states allow cameras in all courts, trial and appellate, criminal and civil, on a permanent basis. Only three states—Indiana, Mississippi, and South Dakota—plus the District of Columbia do not allow cameras in any courts. Ten states did not go through an experimental stage; they simply adopted permanent guidelines from the beginning. Colorado was the first to permanently allow cameras in appellate courts, and Florida was the first to permit coverage of trial courts on a permanent basis.

There are various state-by-state restrictions on cameras in the courtroom, with the majority of states giving judges discretionary control over coverage in their courts. In most states, television may not cover certain cases, such as those involving domestic relations, juveniles, and sex crimes. Televised coverage of voir dire and of jurors is usually restricted or prohibited. Some states limit the coverage of various participants, such as witnesses who appear under subpoena or victims who object to such coverage.[51]

Fears put to rest

The experiments of states before and since *Chandler* have put to rest most of the fears expressed in *Estes.* Few today forecast doom if cameras are allowed in the halls of justice. In places such as Florida where trials on television are commonplace on a day-to-day basis, doomsday forecasts do not accurately reflect reality.[52] Although lurid trials, such as those of Lorena and John Bobbitt, raise questions about the tendency of the electronic news media to sensationalize criminal cases, many feel the public's right to know outweighs the occasional feeding frenzy. Moreover, the impact of television on the average participant in a judicial proceeding today appears inconsequential. Intense media scrutiny, however, may galvanize the courtroom work group, prompting defense attorneys to file more motions to protect their clients' rights and prompting judges to listen more closely and rule more carefully on every motion.[53]

Television has grown up, becoming more sophisticated technologically and gaining prominence as society's chief means of communication.[54] It has become an inseparable part of American society, as it not only entertains but informs. In almost every aspect of daily life, citizens come into contact with television cameras. They watch or are watched on a security monitor while entering public and private buildings. Federal and state government officials, including presidents, members of Congress, governors, and mayors, are under the watchful eye of cameras daily. State legislative sessions, city council meetings, and public hearings conducted by governmental agencies are also televised. Concerns from sexual harassment to landfill sites to zoning changes are presented by television, opening the workings of government to the average citizen.

Now the courts have come into their own with a cable television channel, Court TV, that primarily televises real trials and has prominent attorneys discuss them and major points of law. Public knowledge of the operation of the courts, distorted by television shows and movies, can be enhanced by television in the courtroom, allowing viewers to become better educated about the cumbersome as well as sensational aspects of the judicial process. Unlike other news media, gavel-to-gavel coverage limits the possibility of sensationalism. In addition, there are commentators to explain key legal concepts during trials, and legal education programming is available for those more interested in the judicial process.[55]

As predicted, televising trials has done much to remove the mystery surrounding the judicial process. From the results of previous experiments, most experts agree cameras in the courtroom have little or no influence on jury verdicts.[56] And according to one study, as viewers of a televised trial learned about court procedures and the judicial process, their confidence in the courts did not decline, even when an ordinary citizen lost to a big corporate entity.[57]

In the courtroom of the real world, as opposed to that of television and movies, the viewing public has found few ultra-polished lawyers and judges, only human beings who, like the rest of us, search for words, lose their place, and sometimes become confused. Instead of the fast pace of "L.A. Law," they see a slow-moving, mostly low-key process, with complex rules and arguments that focus on technical procedure. Cameras in the courtroom thus have enhanced the public's awareness of the judicial system as a human one, dedicated to protecting and preserving individual rights to a fair trial, and at the same time, protecting and preserving the rights of society.

The U.S. Supreme Court has recognized the right of states to allow cameras in the courtroom. The courtroom is not sacrosanct; it belongs to the people just as any other part of government does. The mystique that surrounds the judicial process is under revision. Televising judicial proceedings provides greater opportunity for more public scrutiny of court proceedings and allows the citizenry to judge for itself whether the courts are functioning well.

As criminal defense lawyer F. Lee Bailey said when asked whether televised coverage made a difference in the William Kennedy Smith rape trial, "There was no difference in the courtroom. The difference is the public gets to see what happens,

rather than what a print reporter thinks happened."[58] While some cases might require restrictions on broadcast media coverage, the advantages of such coverage of most court proceedings far outweigh the disadvantages.

NOTES

This article originally appeared in Volume 78, Number 3, November-December 1994, pages 128-135, 160.

1. Administrative Office of the Courts, THE PRELIMINARY REPORT OF THE PROCEEDINGS OF THE JUDICIAL CONFERENCE OF THE U.S. (September 27, 1994); *Conference Acts on Courtroom Cameras* 26 THE THIRD BRANCH 1 (Oct. 1994).

2. Greenhouse, *U.S. Judges Vote Down TV in Courts: 3-Year Experiment to End on Dec. 31*, N.Y. Times, Sept. 21, 1994, at A-18; Greenhouse, *Disdaining a Sound Bite, Federal Judges Banish TV*, N.Y. Times, Sept. 24, 1994, at E-4.

The Conference, however, may be having second thoughts about its rejection of cameras in federal courts. It is anticipated that at its semiannual meeting in March 1995, the Conference will approve a proposal to allow cameras in the circuit courts of appeals on a permanent basis and to revive the experimental exploration of cameras in trial courts. The "experiments may test whether judges' concerns about the misleading nature of sound bites can be allayed by requiring the broadcast of at least a minute or 90 seconds of tape at one time." *See* Greenhouse, *Federal Judges Propose Letting Cameras in Appellate Courts*, N.Y. Times, Nov. 18, 1994, at B9.

3. Judge Ito eventually ruled in favor of allowing the Simpson trial to be televised. Noble, *Simpson Judge May Restrict Coverage: Asserting Errors, He Threatens to Bar TV and Radio From Trial*, N.Y. Times, Sept. 24, 1994, at E-4; Margolick, *Judge in Simpson Trial Allows One Camera in Courtroom*, N.Y. Times, Nov. 8, 1994, at A16.

4. For recent opponents of televised coverage of courtroom proceedings, see: Thaler, THE WATCHFUL EYE: AMERICAN JUSTICE IN THE AGE OF THE TELEVISION TRIAL (Westport, Conn.: Praeger, 1994); Burleigh, *Preliminary Judgments*, 80 ABA J. 55 (1994); Dershowitz, *Court TV: Are We Being Fed a Steady Diet of Tabloid Television? Yes: Its Commercialism Hides Its Potential*, 80 ABA J. 46 (1994); Streisand, *Can He Get A Fair Trial?*, 117 U.S. NEWS & WORLD REPORT 56 (Oct. 3, 1994); Spence, *Justice: The New Commodity*, 78 ABA J. 46 (1992).

For recent supporters of televised coverage of courtroom proceedings, see: *Who's Afraid of TV Trials?*, Washington Post, Sept. 25, 1994, at C6; Mirell and Ripston, *Cameras Ensure Public Confidence*, L.A. Times, Sept. 27, 1994, at B7; Sableman, *Simpson's Fair Trial Right: Impartial, Not Ignorant, Jurors*, 23 ST. LOUIS JOURNALISM REV. 7 (July-August 1994); Quindlen, *Order in the Court*, N.Y. Times, July 13, 1994, at A19; Brill, *The Eye That Educates*, N.Y. Times, July 15, 1994, at A27; Mauro, *A Public Civics Lesson*, USA Today, Jan. 24, 1994, at A3; Boyarsky, *TV Conveys Drama—And Opens Up Courts*, L.A. Times, July 2, 1994, at A4; Libby, *Court TV: Are We Being Fed a Steady Diet of Tabloid Television: No: Tacky or Not, It Helps Bring the Law to Life*, 80 ABA J. 47 (1994) *Fair Trial vs. Free Press*, 82 THE QUILL 9 (September 1994); Barber, NEWS CAMERAS IN THE COURTROOM: A FREE PRESS-FAIR TRIAL DEBATE (Norwood, N.J.: Ablex Publishing Corp., 1987).

5. Richmond Newspapers v. Virginia, 100 S. Ct. 2814 (1980).

6. State v. Green, 395 So.2d 532, 537 (Fla. 1981).

7. Mooney, EVELYN NESBIT AND STANFORD WHITE: LOVE AND DEATH IN THE GILDED AGE (New York: William Morrow & Co., 1976).

8. Kielbowicz, *The story behind the adoption of the ban on court-*

room cameras, 63 JUDICATURE 15 (1979).

9. Ginger, SIX DAYS OR FOREVER? 103 (Boston: Beacon Press, 1958).

10. *Id.* at 96.

11. Ex parte Sturm, 136 Atl. 312 (Md. 1927).

12. *Supra* n. 8, at 17.

13. Harris, *The Appearance of Justice: Court TV, Conventional Television, and Public Understanding of the Criminal Justice System,* 35 ARIZ. L. REV. 785-827 (1993).

14. Killian, *Property of Restrictive Guidelines for Cameras in the Court,* 9 COMMUNICATIONS & THE LAW 27-43 (April 1987).

15. State v. Hauptmann, 180 Atl. 809, 827 (N.J. 1935).

16. *See, e.g., supra* n. 8.

17. Alexander, *Curious History: The ABA Code of Judicial Ethics Canon 35,* 18 MASS COMM. REV. 31-37 (Summer 1991).

18. Dyer and Hauserman, *The Electronic Coverage of the Courts: Exceptions to Exposure,* 75 GEO. L. J. 1633-1700 (1987).

19. In re Hearings Concerning Canon 35, 296 P.2d 465, (Colo. 1956).

20. Lyles v. State of Oklahoma, 330 P.2d 752 (1958).

21. Goldman and Larson, *News Cameras in the Courtroom During* State v. Solorzano: *End of* Estes *Mandate?,* 10 S.W.-NEV. L. REV. 2001-2067 (1978).

22. Estes v. Texas, 381 U.S. 532 (1965).

23. *Id.* at 536.

24. Wice, *Cameras in the Courtroom: What Next After Chandler?,* 7 J. OF CRIMINAL DEFENSE 445-458 (1981).

25. *Supra* n. 22, at 613.

26. *Id.* at 540.

27. *Id.* at 539-540.

28. Gonzales v. People, 438 P.2d 686 (Colo. 1968).

29. Goodwin, *A report on the latest rounds in the battle over cameras in the courts,* 63 JUDICATURE 74-77 (1979).

30. Lindsey, *An Assessment of the Use of Cameras in State and Federal Courts,* 18 GA. L. REV. 389-424; Graves, *Cameras in the courts: the situation today,* 63 JUDICATURE 24-27 (1979).

31. Petition of Post-Newsweek Stations, Florida, Inc., 327 So.2d 1 (Fla. 1976).

32. Petition of Post-Newsweek Stations, Florida, Inc., 347 So.2d 402 (Fla. 1977); Whisenand, *Florida's Experience with Cameras in the Courtroom,* 64 ABA J. 1860-1864 (1978).

33. Gerbner, *Trial by television: are we at the point of no return?,* 63 JUDICATURE 416-426 (1980).

34. Report of Judge Paul Baker to the Supreme Court of Florida re: The Conduct of Audio-Visual Coverage in *Florida v. Zamora* 17 (1979).

35. *Id.* at 4.

36. *Id.* at 15-16.

37. Petition of Post-Newsweek Stations, Florida, Inc., 370 So.2d 764 (Fla. 1979).

38. Kelso and Pawluc, *Focus on Cameras in the Courtroom: The Florida Experience, California Experiment, and A Pending Decision in* Chandler v. Florida, 12 PACIFIC L. J. 1, 32 (1980).

39. *Supra* n. 22, at 540.

40. Press, *Giving Cameras a Day in Court,* Newsweek, February 9, 1981, at 102.

41. Chandler v. Florida, 101 S.Ct. 802 (1981).

42. Chandler v. Florida, 376 So.2d 1157 (Fla. 1979).

43. *Supra* n. 41, at 809, 810.

44. *Id.* at 812-813.

45. *Id.* at 813-814.

46. *Supra* n. 5, at 2830.

47. Globe Newspaper Company v. Superior Court For the County of Norfolk, 102 S.Ct. 2613 (1982); Freedman, PRESS AND MEDIA ACCESS TO THE CRIMINAL COURTROOM (New York: Quorum Books, 1988).

48. Winter, *Cameras in the Courtroom: What Next After* Chandler*?,* 67 ABA J. 277-279 (1981).

49. Barber, *supra* n. 4.

50. State v. Newsome, 426 Atl.2d 68 (N.J. Super. A.D. 1980); Dieh v. Commonwealth, 384 S.E.2d 801 (Va. App. 1989); Maxwell v. State, 443 So.2d 967 (Fla. 1983); Gore v. Florida, 573 So.2d 87 (Fla. App. 1991); State v. Hovey, 742 P.2d 515 (N.M. 1987); Johnson v. C. Nix, 763 F.2d 348 (8th Cir. 1985); State ex rel. Grinnell Com. Corp. v. Love, 406 N.E.2d 809 (Ohio 1980).

51. National Center for State Courts, "Summary of TV Cameras in the State Courts," Compiled by the Information Service on August 1, 1994.

52. A compilation of successful experiments with television in state courts, which include the following, can be obtained from the National Center for State Courts: Judicial Planning Coordination Unit; Office of the State Courts Administrator, *A Sample Survey of Attitudes of Individuals Associated With Trials Involving Electronic Media and Still Photography Coverage in Selected Florida Courts Between July 5, 1977 and June 30, 1978,* Nov. 1979; Short and Associates, *Evaluation of California's Experiment With Extended Media Coverage of Courts,* Administrative Office of the Courts, Sept. 1981; *Cameras in the Courtroom—A Two-Year Review in the State of Washington* released by the Washington State Superior Court Judge's Association Committee on Courts and Community in 1978; Raker, *An Evaluation of the Experiment* (1983) examines cameras and recorders in Arizona's trial courts; Report of the Committee on Audio-Visual Coverage of Court Proceedings (New York) May 1994; Ellsworth, *Start of Year Long Experiment in R.I. Went Well, Presiding Judge Says,* Providence Journal (R.I.), Oct. 2, 1981; McCollum, *Extension Is Urged For Cameras in Court,* Hartford (Conn.) Courant, February 27, 1983; Schechet, *Supreme Court Extends Trial of News Cameras in Courtrooms,* Wichita-Eagle Beacon, Dec. 27, 1985; Sherman, *Court Cameras: A Gain,* Times-Argus (Barre, Vt.), Dec. 3, 1983.

53. Lace, *Trial by Television,* Time, Dec. 16, 1991, at 30-31; Gest, *Media Megatrials: Why They Go On and On...and On,* U.S. News and World Report, May 11, 1987, at 10.

54. Weinstein and Zimmerman, *Let the people observe their courts,* 61 JUDICATURE 165 (1977).

55. *See* Libby, *supra* n. 4 at 47; Steenland, *On Trial: Courtroom Television,* 25 TELEVISION Q. 39-43 (1992).

56. Stone and Edlin, *T.V. or Not T.V.: Televised and Photographic Coverage of Trials,* 29 MERCER L. REV. 1119-1135 (1978); Barber, *The problem of prejudice: a new approach to assessing the impact of courtroom cameras,* 66 JUDICATURE 248 (1983); Steenland, *On Trial: Courtroom Television,* 25 TELEVISION Q. 39 (Winter 1992); Kelso and Pawluc, *supra* n. 38; Martin, *Cameras in the Courtroom: A Denial of Due Process?,* 30 BAYLOR L. REV. 853 (1978); Anderson, *Trial by Press?,* 76 ABA J. 32 (Sept. 1990); also, *see supra* n. 52.

57. Raymond, *The impact of a televised trial on individuals' information and attitudes,* 75 JUDICATURE 204-209 ((1992).

58. Reske, *Cameras Controversy: Panelists Differ Over TV's Impact on Trials,* 78 ABA J. 44 (1992).

Shall we dance? The courts, the community, and the news media

An edited transcript of a panel discussion at the American Judicature Society's 1996 midyear meeting.

Recent high-visibility trials and controversial court decisions have focused intense media and public attention on the courts. The O.J. Simpson trial, pretrial events surrounding the Oklahoma City bombing, and high-profile decisions in cases involving patricide, spousal abuse, child custody, and other issues have all raised the public's consciousness about courts and the justice system.

This scrutiny brings both problems and opportunities for courts and the media. From the courts' point of view, the media may focus too much on outcomes and not enough on process, judges and court personnel struggle with the boundaries of their roles as information providers, and problems with the system may become uncomfortably visible. Reporters may be criticized for superficial or sensational coverage and suffer from lack of access to those within the courts who could or should provide them with information.

Opportunities exist, too. Courts often are described as the least visible branch of government, so accurate media coverage can improve public understanding of the role and functions of courts. Since courts' legitimacy depends on the public's willingness to abide by judicial decisions, the public's perceptions of courts and confidence in them are critical. Further, if the public becomes more informed about and interested in courts, courts can pursue more interaction with the community, and media can garner more readers and viewers.

In a conversation on mutual concerns at the 1996 American Judicature Society midyear meeting, judges, journalists, and others discussed the role of courts and the media in informing the public and enhancing public trust and confidence in

the courts. The panelists explored various aspects of the following issues and invited reaction and participation from audience members:

• Is the public getting accurate information about courts? Is it getting complete information? To what extent does media coverage affect public trust and confidence in the courts? How can courts learn more about how the public views them?

• To what extent can or should courts become involved in community and news media outreach? What kinds of information need to be conveyed? Who should speak for the courts? What are some sticking points in the relationship between courts and the news media, and how can they be resolved?

• To what extent are the media obligated to learn the language and procedures of courts? What impedes the ability of media representatives to get

---

Moderator

Thomas S. Hodson, Eslocker, Hodson, Oremus & Co., L.P.A., Athens, Ohio.

Panelists

Suzanne DelVecchio, judge, Massachusetts Superior Court.

Vincent Femia, judge, Maryland Circuit Court.

Gilbert Merritt, chief judge, U.S. Court of Appeals for the Sixth Circuit.

Lyle Denniston, Supreme Court correspondent, *Baltimore Sun.*

Fred Graham, chief anchor/managing editor, Courtroom Television Network.

Kathy L. Mays, director of judicial planning, Supreme Court of Virginia.

information, and how can those obstacles be overcome?

• What obligation, if any, do broadcasters have to explain or interpret court proceedings?

—Kathleen Sampson, director, Information and Program Services, American Judicature Society

Thomas Hodson: Over the last 20 years we have looked at the relationship between courts and the community. The National Center for State Courts did a national survey in the late 1970s about public perception of the courts, how people feel about the courts, how people get information about the courts, and how they form opinions about the courts. This was followed in the mid-1980s by a Hearst Corporation survey. Many states and citizens groups have also done surveys.

Throughout all of these surveys several things have been consistent. One is that the general public knows little to nothing about the functioning of our courts. And the second consistency is that people who do know about the courts generally feel hostile about them—either regarding their administration or the results of particular cases. In general there's an underlying hostility toward the third branch of government.

A third thing that came out of these surveys was information about how people learn about the courts, how they form their opinions—TV news, newspapers, magazines, television dramas about the courts. Most of these surveys were done in the 1980s. Since then we've added a new element, gavel-to-gavel coverage by Court TV, CNN, and others. Not only do we have the courtroom drama of the Perry Masons, the Matlocks, etc., in our living rooms, we have actual court cases on a day-to-day basis.

Lyle, assuming that it's correct that the general public knows little to nothing about the functioning of the court system, do you feel it is the news media's role to educate the public about the courts, the court's role, or both?

Lyle Denniston: In my perception it is not part of our obligation, nor do we even have an opportunity to be a public spokesperson for the courts. We are not part of the furniture of the jurisdiction, we are not here to assist the system to function. It is quite inappropriate to assume that when a reporter walks into the courthouse he or she is going to feel that his or her function is best fulfilled

by helping the court explain themselves to the public or function as the medium through which courts are understood.

We are covering the judiciary as an arm of the government. We are no more an apologist for the judiciary than one can expect reporters covering the White House to be apologists for the president or the presidency. We have to get away from the notion that the press somehow has an obligation, a duty, to be an educative medium for a complicated institution like the judiciary.

First of all, we're not competent to do that. Second, we're not interested in doing that. We are covering the news as news, and the judiciary just happens to be another arm of the government in which we have, unfortunately, transitory interest. But it's only a transitory interest, and we're not going to make it work better.

Sometimes we find that the better news stories are when the court system doesn't work very well at all. So we are as interested in seeing the errors of the judiciary as we are in its positive performance. We need to get away from the notion that the press has the right to cover the courts in order to make the courts work better. We're going to cover it the way that we want to cover it.

Vincent Femia: We don't want you educating the public about us. No disrespect, but the average reporter in our courthouse is still a little wet behind the ears, not a Lyle Denniston. It may be his or her first assignment out of school and he or she first has to be shown how to find the courthouse. Second, we really don't want the press forming in the public mind what it is we do. We in the courts are the ones who have to educate the public as to what we do, not the media.

Fred Graham: My experience through the years is that judges don't do enough to enable reporters to cover the courts fully. Judge Merritt, do you think judges do enough?

Gilbert Merritt: No, we don't do much at all. Judges, generally, are very skittish when it comes to the press. And there are a lot of reasons for that, many of which are invalid. The only way you're going to have a neophyte reporter understand what's going on is to explain it.

Suzanne DelVecchio: I would rather have Court TV cover a case of mine than have the media interpret it. When somebody from the media says, "You know he got off on a technicality," and that technicality is the Fifth Amendment, that's where the problems lie.

Hodson: How do you remedy it?

DelVecchio: Well, first of all there is a problem with having neophytes cover the system. That's already been mentioned. We now have lawyers in the press who are covering the system, and I think that helps a lot because they do explain, sometimes. I think judges should be available to the media, from time to time, to explain what we do, to talk about what we do. But I really think the media tends to distort.

Graham: With regard to journalists calling the Fifth Amendment a technicality, let's look at the current cause celebre. Federal District Judge Harold Baer in New York agreed to reconsider his decision regarding a drug bust in which the drug agents suspected someone who was using an automobile in a very high-crime drug market area. As I understand the case, the key was that when some likely looking purchasers saw officers approaching, they ran away. That was taken to be probable cause to make an arrest and open the back of the car, where a huge stash of drugs was found. Judge Baer threw the evidence out. It's not for any of us to say whether he was right on the law or not. But it's entirely possible that in the Fourth Amendment area he could have been right on the law and come to a ridiculous outcome as far as the average person is concerned. And that's what's happened here. A lot of people think it's stupid. The law is stupid. And that is a problem for journalists and for the public and for judges.

Merritt: It's stupid if you don't explain it. It's like so many things in law that are for deterrent purposes, to keep things from happening, but the outcome is unsatisfying. But when you think about the long term it makes more sense. And that's what doesn't get explained. I've never quite understood how, for 200 years, we have maintained the federal judiciary, how we have maintained a nonmajoritarian institution in a society that thinks that everybody should be elected for everything, and that their officials should reflect the public will. Yet we have done that. And there doesn't seem to be any great outcry for change. There is a grudging acceptance over a long period of time of this nonmajoritarian institution.

There is a synergistic relationship between the federal courts and the state courts and the press. The press understands, when it thinks about it, that its free speech rights have to be enforced by some-

body. And although the judiciary is not very good at it, at least that is what they're there to do. If they weren't doing it at all, they wouldn't have rights of free speech, or they would be much circumscribed. So, I think the federal courts are dependent on the press to explain to the public, to some extent, why we should maintain this nonmajoritarian institution. And the press is dependent on the federal courts to preserve, at least to some extent, the rights of free speech.

Hodson: Kathy, you work with planning in the state court system. I believe your judges are appointed in Virginia, and not elected, is that correct?

Kathy Mays: They are elected by the general assembly.

Hodson: What is the constituency of the courts? What constituencies are we talking about? And do courts even have constituencies they need to worry about?

Mays: I suppose it depends on whom you ask. Some judges would say lawyers are their biggest constituency because lawyers are the people who are in courts every day. Others would say that it's the public. Still others might say that it's the law enforcement community.

It it is fairly incredible that we haven't taken the opportunity, as an institution, to find out what the public thinks. In Virginia, when we tried to find out, there were things that just shocked us about what members of the public knew and what they did not know, and what they wanted to know and did not know.

I think the reason we haven't found out is in part because as an institution we're afraid. When we announced we were going to initiate our consumer research project, many of my judges said, "Don't you know what the answers are going to be already? Fifty percent of the people are going to happy and 50 percent of the people are going to be mad at you." But after talking with, surveying, and having telephone interviews with at least 2,700 Virginians in our first round, that's the one thing that was disproved. There were many litigants who prevailed in their cases who said, "Never again. I am never doing this again. It costs too much. You made me come five different times. You couldn't find my files. You couldn't do anything right. And I will not do it." And then there were people who did not prevail, who lost, who came out saying, "I had my day in court."

Femia: Every time you sit down to one of these press/media interactive meetings it always comes down to the same thing, how the courts feel about media coverage and what the courts' involvement should be. The title of the program this morning asks, "Shall we dance?" Folks, let me suggest a few things to you. Number one, it is no longer a question of shall we dance. These are the 1990s, and we're dancing whether we like it or not. Now this is something I generally say to judges, "You better learn the steps if you want to lead the dance." The judiciary has a duty to lead the media coverage. Beat 'em like a drum if you can. Fairly, but make them play your tune. Otherwise, they're going to play everybody else's tune.

Number two: you talk about court constituency. Judges have only one constituent—a lady who has scales in one hand and a sword in the other and a blindfold. Now, to be sure, whenever a judge makes a decision, half the people think he's right, half the people think he's wrong. And of the half that thinks he's right, half of them think he's right for the wrong reason. So you're not there to try and please the public, though a pragmatist would say, quite correctly, "Yeah, but if the public has a bad perception of you, you're not going to get pay raises, you're not going to get facilities." I agree with that, but again it is a question of backing up and saying, "OK, how do we manipulate—I use the word advisedly—manipulate the perception."

We have a judge who's all over every newspaper in Maryland right now because of some alleged dalliance in chambers. Boy does he have coverage. Yet that same judge, if he were to rule in a high-profile case, the ruling would be on page three and there would be no comment from him whatsoever about why or what happened. Usually it is either "No comment" or "My comments are in the record." There's no guidance for how the media could cover the case.

The point I'm making is this: education has to start with the judiciary. It's very hard to break down the judicial wall. Judges do not like to make public comment off the bench. They just don't like it. As a judge you get tired of everybody in the world having a crack at what you do, so why provide a gratuitous opportunity. But that reticence has to be overcome because we are no longer in the day and age where judges can just go into a closet and say we won't talk to you.

Audience member: It seems to me that the courts belong to the public and the newspapers belong to the public. Those are your customers, and those are the people you ought to be serving, whether or not you're pleasing them. But so far what I hear is a very parochial interest in your own position and your own point of view—the media, the courts and judges, and the court personnel show little concern about how they affect a betterment of a community, which is what we're really all about in the end anyway.

It seems to me as long as we're so concerned with our own point of view, and we don't ever communicate with and engage the public in the conversation, we're never going to get beyond where we are now. I read in the *Washington Post* today about a particular topic that if I wanted more information I could get it on the Internet. That tells me the media is interested in education, and I know that courts are interested in education because of the kinds of things they do, so how can you say that's not part of what you do?

Denniston: Again, I will harp on what for me is a fundamentally important factor. The many people in this country who audit the behavior of the press, think of the press, in some respects, the same way they think of the judiciary, as a public institution that is supposedly performing a public service. And a lot of people will make the argument, and they make it very sincerely and indeed with a good deal of passion, that the only reason there's a First Amendment is for you to perform a public service. Absent the proper responsibility in the performance of that public service, you're not entitled to any rights at all.

I have spent a good deal of my professional life and on forums like this trying to make the point that we just happen to be an institution that has a constitutionally guaranteed right to speak in the same way that every one of you has a right to speak. We do not have to pay for that right by fulfilling somebody's objective sense of public service. It is not a right that is going to be withdrawn from us, except by the appropriate processes of constitutional amendment. We do not have to perform in a way that will earn a Good Housekeeping seal of approval from the judiciary or indeed from our own readers. Our readers vote with their subscriptions or with their quarters in the box. And if they stop voting for us, then we go under.

We will not, in my business, improve what we do in terms of the product, the news the consuming public buys, on the basis of trying to earn our rights, or trying to earn your respect. That's not what we're about. What I do think is important to remember, and this gets away a little bit from the public's relationship with us and with the judiciary, that in this dance we have with the judiciary, the judiciary has to understand that it has no obligation to speak to us, to explain itself to us, if it has the perception that we don't know what we're doing when we're in the courthouse.

I think it's lunatic for a judge to invite a reporter in the first day the reporter is on the beat and expect the reporter to have a meaningful conversation with the judge. I would recommend to the judiciary, don't talk to a reporter until you've done some research in advance and know with some reasonable degree of certainty that the reporter knows what the judiciary is doing. And if the reporter doesn't, don't let him in chambers. You've got to let him in the courthouse, but don't let him in chambers.

That may sound like a contradiction to my former comment about public servants. But what I'm saying is that there is a dance going on here. We are going to be in the courthouse, we are going to be there covering things that we think are newsworthy, not necessarily socially significant. That's why we cover the trial bench and don't cover the appellate bench. But when we are in that courthouse there has to be an understanding that they owe us nothing and we owe them nothing. And in the combat that comes out of that kind of almost mutual indifference, or maybe even hostility, we ultimately do a pretty good job of reporting the part of the judiciary that is newsworthy. We do a very poor job of explaining the part of the judiciary that is not newsworthy.

Audience member: I regard the argument that the press has its rights in order to perform a public service as a red herring. It's quite a leap, however, to conclude that it is somehow inconsistent with the press's function to perform a public service, namely of education. You seem to think of the relationship between government and the press as adversarial, and that the only way in which the press can do its job, whatever that is, is in some sort of adversary way. I don't think it has to be that way. I don't think the press is performing as good a role as it could in this society. And I think that when the press does regard education as properly part of its provence and not just making money or

getting a Pulitzer Prize, we'll be better served as a society.

Denniston: It's a nice thing if one of the unintended consequences of quality journalism is that we educate the public now and then. But what I'm trying to stress is that I do not think of this as an obligation. Do not lay upon us a burden of justifying our rights by the quality of our performance.

And let me just throw in a little saw here that I keep moving back and forth. The judiciary of this country, at least in the federal system, now treats the broadcast media as if it had no right to be present in the courtroom because the judiciary does not trust how they will use those rights. Cameras in the court are controlled at the federal level by a bigoted, ignorant, know-nothing attitude about their opportunity to control what appears on television, and if they can't control it, they're not going to let cameras in. That's the kind of thing that is behind my comment.

Do not assume that we have an obligation to report the judiciary in the way the judiciary would like, and that if we fail in that obligation we're going to have our rights taken away from us or we're going to tell the public you should amend the Constitution and take away those rights.

Merritt: Lyle is great in provoking comment, but that is an overstatement, macho journalism. I've heard this same kind of thing from very close friends. As human beings we're not first a member of the press, or first a judge. We're first human beings who have some requirements of civility to try to empathize with others, to understand where they're coming from. I know Lyle Denniston personally to be a very civil person with whom you can reason. But when he starts on one of these programs, all you get is this macho journalistic stuff. And I know judges who feel exactly the same way about the press or even stronger. And I think both points of view are way too macho and we've got to get away from that.

Hodson: Can I have comment from a non-macho journalist? A lot of the states are now looking to put cameras into the courtroom. Others are saying that the federal courts made the right decision. How do you respond to that?

Graham: Well, I'm not going to respond to it right now because I did want to amend from the non-macho point of view what Lyle said. I would agree in some sense that there is not a responsibility to the courts or to a certain level of coverage.

But all journalists, I believe, feel there is a responsibility to themselves as professionals and as journalists, and as Judge Merritt says, as citizens, to do what they do in a responsible way.

There is a constitutional right in the First Amendment, but of course it's premised on the fact that the result will be socially beneficial coverage. When Court TV selects the cases that it's going to cover we have a mix and we have a formula. And the formula is not just necessarily where the most titillating action will be. It's so many civil cases, so many criminal cases, some appellate cases. Part of the reason for that mix is to serve some public function in informing and educating the public.

Now, as to your question about cameras in courts, earlier this week a federal judge in the Southern District of Manhattan had a hearing on a very important case in which the foster care system of the city of New York, which apparently is an abomination, was being challenged in court. There could hardly be a matter of more public interest. There's great public interest in how it is that children who are forced into foster care are allegedly not being protected. The judge did permit television into that trial.

Now, there is an institutional problem here. Judge Merritt, as we know, is the chairman of the Executive Committee of the Judicial Conference, which saw fit without very complete deliberations to rule out cameras in federal court after a successful experiment. And it seems to me that there are tensions now within the federal judiciary where some judges are looking at what the judicial conference did and saying, "It makes no sense.

We had a successful experiment. The people who evaluated the experiment of cameras in the federal court said it worked and recommended that it be continued. The majority of the judicial conference decided without much deliberation. And I don't think probably more than one or two of those 26 or 27 judges had ever presided over a trial in which there was a camera; they had no firsthand experience. They apparently paid no attention to their own study. They turned it down, and what we're seeing now is that individual members of the judiciary with individual cases that are important are saying that's wrong. The problem is that it's unclear now whether or not the judicial conference can enforce its rule.

Audience member: Last year, I took the year off from my law practice and spent it as an on-air correspondent for Entertainment Television and CBS radio covering the O.J. trial. For better or worse, I was an ersatz journalist for the year. Despite what Mr. Denniston says I struggled every day with the question, "What are my obligations here?" I don't mean my constitutional obligations, but my personal obligations to the audience. What is it I'm sifting out or emphasizing or not emphasizing? And so I'd like to cut to what for me is the chase. I'd like to ask the journalists, what are your personal standards when you cover this complex thing called the legal system? How do you decide what to emphasize? What do you do when somebody calls the Fifth Amendment a technicality? Do you talk about short-term values versus long-term values? Or do you just blow it off? And I'd like to ask the judges on the panel, what do you think about the job that the media is doing covering this? I'd like to get away from rights versus obligations and talk about practicalities.

Denniston: Let me say that your opening comments illustrate why it's a bad idea to take somebody out of law practice and put them in the journalism business. They come burdened with all of that lawyerly stuff about how they're serving the public.

But that having been said, let me say that after being in this business now for very close to 40 years, I don't wake up at night wondering how I'm going to cover the judiciary tomorrow. I've been doing it long enough that it's not simply a transitory adventure as it was for the last speaker. I am a professional journalist in the sense that I know what's news and I can tell it when I see it. You don't have to bring me into the editor's office on Monday morning and say, "Now Lyle, during the balance of this week are you going to remember that you have to cover this or that?" I go into the office on Monday morning, I check in, I start my work, and I know what's news. And I don't have to consult any muse. I certainly don't have to ask any lawyer. And, God knows, I don't ask any judge.

What is news to me is what, perhaps, transitorily fascinates the milkman in Hyattsville, Maryland, who gets up in the morning at 4 and is done with his work by about 2 in the afternoon and maybe he gets to read the *Baltimore Sun* at 2:30. He has maybe, maybe three minutes to read Lyle Denniston's work. He trusts me not to waste his time with material that is irrelevant to what fascinates him. So I find myself routinely putting myself in his seat and saying, "If I were going to read this story, what would I most want to know?" And it's not whether the process worked, but what was the outcome and why did it come out that way, in a way I can understand.

To my mind, the biggest problem we who cover the judiciary now have is the final triumph of that notion that you ought to go to law school before you cover a courthouse for a medium of communication. That is pure nonsense. You do not need to go to law school to cover a courthouse. The law teaches you respect for order. It teaches you respect for tradition. It teaches you respect for hierarchy. And every one of those values is alien to the proper practice of journalism.

Let's be very clear about this. The fact that Judge Merritt has spoken approvingly of the way I cover the judiciary is because he knows that I know what I'm doing. He knows I am a self-confident journalist who would not think of walking into a courthouse to cover it unless I was properly prepared to do so. And that does not mean I have a law degree. It means I'm properly prepared to translate what goes on there for people who don't care about the substance of the law. They buy me, not as a law review, but as a medium of immediate communication, and that's all they want from me.

Merritt: I'm troubled about the way the press covers the courts. I don't think the press ought to be supportive or not supportive. They should try, as Lyle does, to be objective. But also, it is newsworthy, it seems to me, to explain why something happens as well as that it happened. There is an element that is lacking when all you say is this happened today, this person said this, without ever trying to explain why. Why is an interesting question, and it ought to be newsworthy.

Hodson: Kathy, you're sort of in-between. You're not a judge, but you sort of act as a spokesperson for judges. What's your feeling?

Mays: We are talking a lot about some sensational cases and about big principals of law. But what we have to deal with, at least in the state courts, is the everyday citizen who comes into the courthouse. And I think it would be a really good exercise for judges to ask themselves the same question that Lyle just posed: If I had the milkman coming into our court today, what would that person need to know in order to have effective access, in order to be able to participate meaningfully?

That is what I am consumed with on a day-to-day basis. And I think if we asked ourselves that question, any of us—judges, lawyers, clerks, administrators—our courts might be run very differently. We might not use words that are always in Latin. We might not say, "Do you waive your right to counsel?" We might have a different schedule for cases. We might not have as many continuances. We might not have information pamphlets that basically tell people what we want them to know about the courts, not what they want to know about the courts. So I think it would be a very good exercise for us to ask those questions ourselves.

Audience member: Kathy Mays is starting to get to what interests me. What do judges do to communicate with the public? What can judges reasonably try to do to inform the public so they have a clue about what's going on?

Femia: The answer to your question, in general terms, is judges do nothing to communicate with the public. Egotist that I am, I have never met a microphone or camera I was not instantly in love with. So I have always been very available to the press. As a consequence I've learned to talk in sound bites. And I can get away with it. Most members of my profession cannot do that. And they see no reason why they should do that. If they're of my generation, they remember a press corps that came to the government building armed with a hunting license and a very sharp pen. They don't like them, and they don't want anything to do with them. The problem is we are now in the '90s, and it's a new world out there for judges. Whether we like it or not, in our business we have to learn to communicate.

Merritt: If Lyle is right that the press is not going to educate, judges are basically going to have to do something themselves, and the question is how. Let me just say two or three things.

First, it would be helpful if the U.S. Supreme Court would allow cameras. It would begin to explain, and people would watch, and slowly, a more informed public would come about. Second, we're going to have to rethink the question of whether we ought to have cameras in civil cases in the federal courts if we're going to communicate effectively with the public. The public now gets most of its news through television. And last, judges have got to be willing to talk to the press, to do some interviews, to try to explain how the system works and why it works. It seems to me those three things could be very helpful.

DelVecchio: Lyle's been here this morning like a criminal in a courtroom trying to admit that he's guilty and the judge saying, "No, no, you have to plead not guilty." We're all saying, you have to enter a plea of not guilty so we can go forward with the process. He's really laid it on the line as to what the press does. Courts have been relying on the press to carry our water for us, and we can't do that. But we don't have anything in place at all, in the system, to deal with the press.

Hodson: How about dealing with the public regardless of the press?

DelVecchio: We judges do it on an individual basis. How do we get to the public without the press? They are the medium that deals with the public. What do we do?

Denniston: How about through a web site?

DelVecchio: We don't even have computers.

Audience member: What troubles me is not the affirmative duty, perhaps, of the press to educate, it's the affirmative duty to not mis-educate. It has been suggested that judges not talk to that reporter who's wet behind the ears because the reporter doesn't know what he or she is talking about. But, in fact, the story then comes out even more inaccurately. If you think there's no responsibility on the part of the press to educate, isn't there at least a responsibility for accuracy? And if there can't be some education of reporters in law school, then should newspapers educate those reporters so that they don't get it wrong so often?

Denniston: Let me indulge myself in a habit that the judiciary never indulges in, which is confessing error. A good deal of the problem that a lot of our readers and listeners have with what they see and read is our fault. I will tell you, in the hierarchy of importance and prestige in the newsroom, the courthouse beat is somewhere down around fourth or fifth. In the Washington bureau of the *Baltimore Sun*, coverage of the Supreme Court is generally perceived by the hierarchy as somewhere well below politics, the presidency, and the Congress. Somewhere down there with the alphabet soup regulatory agencies is the Supreme Court, and somewhere off the charts is the lower federal judiciary. And nowhere mentioned, except in the most fleeting way, are the state judiciaries.

When was the last time that a Baltimore television station covered any decision out of a Maryland Court of Special Appeals, our intermediate court? When did Kathy last see anything in the *Richmond Times Dispatch* about the court of special appeals in Virginia? We do not regard legal news as front-rank news, so we usually assign it to a subaltern.

The Maryland Court of Appeals, which is my state's supreme court, is covered by a young man who works in a local bureau. And when he's not covering the cops, when he's not covering, let's say, the problems in the city administration of Annapolis, he waltzes over to the state courthouse and picks up the opinions and tries to write about them. Now, it won't do any good for a judge to call in that young reporter and try to explain to him what it's all about.

What has to happen is that we in the press have to begin to perceive that legal news is of great fascination to the people, that it's enormously interesting if done right and if done accurately. But it has to be understood that until we clean house ourselves, nothing the judiciary can do will improve the quality of what image is conveyed in the media.

The next question is, what can the courts do alternative to that? Can you have public education programs? Can you have a newsletter of your own? Can you have conferences? Can you have a web site? Can you communicate with people?

One thing I know as a professional journalist is that it is sometimes very difficult for me even to get a document. A judge in Alexandria recently decided a case on gays in the military, and I had to drive over to an Alexandria courthouse and pay $16 for a 32-page public document. Now why couldn't I get that on a web site somewhere? When Judge Merritt's court decides it, I can get it on a web site. It's there instantly. It's immediately available. I can do that with the Maryland Court of Appeals. But can I do it with Vince's court? No. So if you think of the public's image of the judiciary as being only what's in the print and broadcast commercial media you have given away all kinds of media outlets and assume they don't count. But in this day and age, ladies and gentlemen, most children are more computer literate than they are newspaper literate. And if I were in your side of the business I would be assuming the press is not going to do this the way we want them to do it, so let's find alternative ways. I mean, we're still going to have to let the press cover us in their kind of clumsy and bad fashion, but we've got to do something affirmatively on our own in order to get our message across.

DelVecchio: There's no funding. There's no way for us to get the message out. We don't have computers. We just converted one courthouse in Boston from direct current to alternating current. If you sat there last year it was like going to Bulgaria. You had to put your transformer in. This is what we're dealing with in the state courts. We don't have the resources of the federal court system, and we're not going to have them for a long time.

Audience member: I want to pick up on a couple of comments that have been made. A point was made about nobody talking about the responsibility to the public. I want to come to the defense of Judge Femia who talked about the obligation to Lady Justice. I think judges are fulfilling their ultimate responsibility to the public when they recognize that their primary constituent is Lady Justice. That's not to say we don't have a responsibility to communicate with the public.

In response to Judge DelVecchio, at least in California we apparently are a little bit better off than some other states. We have a judges association that organizes courses for judges on how to deal with the media. There is also a program that California judges have been involved in for a long time called "Meet Your Judges," where judges go out in the community to meet members of the public so we don't have to use the media as an intermediary.

I also want to comment on one thing that Lyle said. As a judge, I would be absolutely delighted if I saw Fred Graham or Lyle Denniston walk into my court. With Lyle, it has nothing to do with the fact that I am the daughter of a milkman. But I know that if Mr. Graham or Mr. Denniston come into my court and criticize what I've done or criticize the process, they do it from a knowledgeable standpoint.

The problem I have are those reporters you were talking about, the guy from the local bureau or whatever. Sometimes it absolutely amazes me. I have read newspaper reports of trials I have done where I have to get down to the fourth or fifth paragraph before I realize it's the trial I sat through. It strikes me that the *Baltimore Sun* or the *Los Angeles Times* or any of those newspapers would never send a reporter to cover a football game who had never seen a football game before. I can't understand why they send people to cover the courts who have no clue what's going on in the courts.

Audience member: I appreciate what Mr. Denniston said because he just let us in on a dirty secret of the media. To what extent is what you said shared by your editors and the people who send out that young reporter, and by the people who make up the paper before it goes to print?

Denniston: First of all, be a little careful about assuming that anybody but a legal reporter is going to have spent the time thinking about the scope of the coverage. In most newspapers I know of, and certainly in all broadcast outlets I know of, there is not a deep sense of the importance journalistically of the law. Law just doesn't often enough produce high-color, high-visibility events to get the attention of the press. So editors don't spend a lot of energy thinking about covering the courthouse. When they do, they will think about it in what now is the conventional habit of the print media borrowed from television media—not, let's have a good piece on the substance of law, let's have a piece about the personalities in the law.

Let me give you an example. Some years ago I wanted to do a piece about how Justice Scalia's moment had come and passed on the Supreme Court in terms of his potential for really leading the Court. I produced a 50-inch story, 40 of which were substantive information and commentary on Justice Scalia's career and 10 were about his personal life, behavior, and so on. The story was kicked back to me, and I was told to reverse the margins so that ultimately what I got in the paper was 60 percent what Scalia eats, what he drinks, what he does when he goes to an Orioles ballgame, what he says to his clerks and to his secretaries, and 40 percent was the jurisprudence of Antonin Scalia. And that was a hugely successful story in my newspaper. My editors tend to think, "Oh, Jesus, here comes Denniston with another one of his 50-inch stories about the doctrine of presidential immunity when the president has been sued by Paula Jones." What they want me to do is write about Paula Jones.

Audience member: Fred Graham cannot go with his cameras to Maryland's trial courts. But one courtroom that you can go into in Maryland and bring cameras is the court of appeals. And yet, in the federal judiciary it is exactly the opposite. If there's one appellate court where the country would have an interest in going, where Fred would want to take his cameras, it's the U.S. Supreme Court. And yet that seems to be the one where we are least likely to ever go in my lifetime. I'd like to know why that is.

Merritt: My guess is the vote in the Supreme Court is 6-3 against cameras. When you talk to members of the Court about why they feel like they do, you get a lot of different answers, but basically they want to maintain their anonymity, they don't want to become celebrities, and they don't want to have all of the security that you might need if you were a big celebrity. They also don't think that it is consistent with the law, with the purposes and functions of the Court as a restrained nonmajoritarian institution, to join in the sensational celebrity kind of orientation of American society. The other side of that argument is, doesn't the Supreme Court have some obligation to have the public understand what it does?

Femia: That's why we get the judges who say, "I don't want cameras in my courtroom. I don't have time to be bothered with people stopping me in the street, commenting on my last case." That's not, in fact, true. In fact if you diagnose and think about us from the psychological viewpoint, there's not a person among us who doesn't want to control his or her environment as totally as he or she can. It's natural. You want to control your environment. And when you're writing your thoughts you have complete and total control—until it gets to the editor, of course. But when you're on camera, you don't have any control of that aspect of your environment. And a lot of people, people who feel themselves unable to respond to criticism, such as judges, don't like the idea that they can't control how that camera over there is zeroing in right now on their nasal hairs.

Audience member: I'd like to go back to the point Fred Graham made early on about the search and seizure case in New York that got all this coverage. I was watching TV and Dateline came on with "Judge lets druggie walk" or something like that. My blood started to boil, and I started thinking that this had to be a Miranda case, or a search and seizure case. And then I got to thinking, isn't it legitimate in a democracy for the public to question the exclusionary rule? And isn't it legitimate for the public to question excessive damage awards when somebody spills coffee? And isn't it appropriate for the press to focus in on those three, four, maybe five cases, maybe 500 cases to the point of having the public respond in an appropriate way whether it's through legislation or through other legitimate democratic means?

Graham: I second everything you say. I think the law is too important to be left exclusively to the lawyers and the judges. And to the extent that the public suddenly looks at the way the Fourth Amendment and the exclusionary rule works, and says, "This is ridiculous," I think that's good and healthy for the whole system.

Audience member: I don't mean to seem elitist, but I wonder if all the talk about the connection between the courts and the public is really missing the point and that Mr. Denniston's milkman, with all due respect, isn't going to have much influence in the long run simply because we know that the level of visibility of the courts is very low and it's going to stay that way. The important relationship may be between the courts and, pardon the term, the elites, the legal profession. They're the ones who are determining, more or less, the persistence of legal rules and the persistence of institutions. From a tactical point of view, that ought to be the relationship we're concerned about.

Mays: I very much disagree. When the question, who is the court's constituency was asked, I would have liked to have said Lady Justice, but quite frankly, on a day-to-day basis, I believe that judges run into, whether it's in the halls or bar luncheons or something—they run into lawyers most of all. Judges tend to talk to lawyers more than they talk to the general public. And I think that is a real mistake.

When we surveyed the public, as I mentioned before, we found some things that were shocking. The first thing we found that was shocking was that we had 60, 70, 80 percent approval rate when we asked the question, "What is your overall impression of Virginia's courts." When we asked, "Do judges follow the law in performing their duties?" When we asked, "Did you think that the decisions were fair?" We couldn't believe it, we were shocked. We thought something was wrong, that we did it wrong. When we asked about the process, though, people just gave us all kinds of bad marks. When we asked how people were treated when they came into our courts—was there sufficient signage, getting up the stairs to participate as a juror if you're handicapped—we got terrible marks on things like that. When I'm standing in the Safeway checkout line and I hear, "I served on a jury," I back out of the line, because I know that something bad is going to be said. And I know that what they're going to say is, "Do you know that that judge let that lawyer go in last-minute motions for $3\frac{1}{2}$ hours? Don't these people realize that I have time constraints too?" I think it is absolutely incorrect simply to consider that our most important constituency is the legal profession, because we are missing it with a lot of other people.

Merritt: Among the elites the federal judiciary is most concerned about and that affect our daily life are the Congress and the president. Those groups are elites, but they reflect, more than any other thing, what the public thinks. And if the public thinks poorly of courts, and of particular doctrines, and of particular ways of doing business, the elite that reflects public opinion is going to attack that problem. We live in a democratic society, and we have to be conscious that where we get our pay and our sustenance and our power is through the democratic process.

Audience member: I think the problem is, as judges know and as lawyers know, unless a person is in a courtroom listening to all the evidence, seeing the witnesses, hearing what comes in, not hearing what doesn't come in, to come to a valid opinion about a case is difficult. To the extent the press fosters in the public the belief that one can make judgments without knowing the evidence and without knowing the law is a disservice.

I issued an opinion about two weeks ago and got called by a reporter to comment. I talked to this guy—because the case was over, there were no appeals pending—for 10 or 15 minutes over the phone. I explained why it came out the way it did. The next day, in the newspaper, there was one sentence from me, which was an inaccurate quote that explained nothing, and the article didn't either. I know why, because that was boring, that didn't sell the newspaper. That is a problem judges have with coverage.

Audience member: I think it is often illegitimate to criticize the media for not reporting the why of what's going on when very few judges ever take the time to make sure the litigants in a case understand the why. Judges need to start explaining enough about Lady Justice for the litigants to know that's who the judge is serving. Don't we need to take care of that issue first, before we start talking about why the press isn't doing its part of the job?

Chief Judge Michael M. Mihm, U.S. District Court, Central District of Illinois (audience member): I'm one of the supposedly ignorant people who didn't adequately consider the question of cameras in the federal courts before we turned it down last fall. Let me say first of all that I agree with a lot of what Mr. Denniston says. I think that's the right approach for the news media to have. I've never asked for anything more than that. But there's an interesting disagreement that appears between the print media and the video media. The print media says, "It's not our responsibility to educate the public." But you started this morning with the suggestion that somebody has to. And so, of course, if it's not the media, it has to be the courts. But the video media actually insinuated itself into the courtrooms on the idea that the main purpose for doing it was to educate the public. I think that's seriously open to question.

But the point I want to make is this. I'm sitting here listening to this discussion and I'm wondering what kind of a world is it we're creating? What sort of an assessment will we have 10 or 15 years from now about the quality of justice in this country? What is the purpose of a trial? What is the purpose of a court proceeding? The purpose of it is to do justice in an individual case. It is not the purpose of a trial, it is not the purpose of a court proceeding, to educate the public. There are other ways to do that.

The basic reason I voted against cameras in the courtroom is because I think that having cameras changes the equation of what should happen in the courtroom. It does affect the way judges act, it does affect the way juries act, it does affect the way witnesses act. And if that's the kind of justice we're headed toward, a politicized form of courtroom proceedings, then it's a sad day for this country.

Graham: Have you ever presided over a case when there was a camera in the courtroom?

Mihm: No I have not, and I hope I never do.

Graham: Well, I think that if you did, you would have a more enlightened and accurate view of what goes on. We at Court TV have now televised more than 300 trials gavel-to-gavel, so we have some experience and knowledge. And what you find is that, as we all know, the trial experience is a very vivid one for all the participants—lawyers, witnesses, and others. And immediately, even though there's a camera back there somewhere, they become so absorbed in what's going on that they forget the camera. And I just have to tell you, based on experience, it doesn't change the process.

There is more to justice, sure. Everybody wants justice to be done in every trial. But the confidence of the public that it's being done is important. People get information these days through television, and it should be in the courts.

Merritt: Just to confirm what Fred said, although we do not have broadcast cameras in our courtroom, I have an experimental courtroom where cameras are being used for recording purposes, including a monitor that sits facing the jury and the public. I am amazed how quickly people ignore the fact there's any cameras. In fact, you have to remind the lawyers, "Look, you're walking all over this courtroom, we're not getting you on the record, please." It's amazing how quickly you yourself and the people involved in the trial just absolutely ignore the cameras.

Audience member: I'm trying to get behind what the Judicial Conference did. It had to be they wanted to protect the judicial process from the political process. I don't know. And yet it seems to me that Judge Mihm's comment reached that way. The question becomes, is there a balance to be struck between an anti-majoritarian organization such as the judiciary and the political process, and have we got the balance right? How do we strike the balance between public involvement and knowledge and the need to protect the process that, as Judge Mihm says, is individual and justice-oriented in a single case?

DelVecchio: I think having the camera in the courtroom is a fabulous process because it shows a trial from beginning to end. And if there's a good judge with good lawyers, and the case is well-tried, I think it, in itself, is the best education possible for the American public. And it shows that we do our job well. It's not distilled through Lyle or anyone else. The public sees it as if they were in that courtroom watching.

Audience member: Sometimes I suspect that some of us, perhaps more of the judges, would like to read the First Amendment as requiring that news could only be reported with a quill on a piece of parchment. Today, the public gets its news from television. Television is, frankly, the most accurate reporter. You see and you hear what is happening, and it's not digested through the opinions of the headline writer. It's not digested through the ears of a reporter who may be much less responsible than the reporters on this panel. When you see some of the headlines and try to evaluate the rela-

tionship between the headline and what has actually occurred, you think you're in two different worlds. And yet we keep insisting that communication to the public is a privilege that we can shut off, that we want to have take place only as we choose to have it. The best protection is knowledge. And the best protector is accurate knowledge. And the most accurate knowledge that we have today, at least, is to see and to hear what's going on.

Merritt: If television coverage was as Court TV is, if that's what you mean by television coverage, you're exactly right. But that is not what happens. What happens most of the time is this. There is a picture of participants in the courtroom, on the stand, and a headline reader, an anchor, or a reporter tells you in 15 to 30 seconds what it means. And the picture is often used to authenticate a false or, if not false, an inaccurate statement. That is the problem. It's not Court TV. It's the problem of how it's used in this sound-bite world that we live in and oftentimes that is much less accurate than Lyle Denniston's more substantive discussion of the problem.

Denniston: Judge, when was the last time a clerk told a reporter from *USA Today*, "You may not come into my courthouse because your account is going to be too brief, or too selective?" I'm glad that Judge Mihm stood up and had the courage to try to defend the exclusion of the broadcast media, because that's a hard thing to do. But one of the things that the Judicial Conference forgot is a decision called *Richmond Newspapers v. Virginia* that says the courts are public property. And the courts are open to the public. And the only time you can tell a reporter you can't come in is when that reporter threatens to bring a riot in the courthouse. Yet when the judiciary turns to the broadcast media it says, "Your right of access depends on whether we like what you say about us."

Nobody has ever said to me, as a print reporter, "Denniston, you can't come in here unless you give 40 inches to this. You can't come in here unless you cover us gavel-to-gavel. You can't come in here unless you run the transcripts." Nobody has the guts to tell me that I can't cover a public institution because of the way I'll cover it. But, God bless them, the judiciary around this country, the judge who tried the Susan Smith case in South Carolina, the judge who's trying John Salvi in Massachusetts, they sit there on their high and mighty bench and decide that if the coverage is not what they're going to like, you can't even be in their courtroom. Judges need to understand that if television and radio people can't bring their mikes and their cameras, they're not there. They are simply not there. And there's no reason to assume that anybody is ultimately going to tolerate a judiciary that says coverage of the courts depends on the judiciary's agreement with the scope of coverage. Judges have got to get that straight. It's not their call.

Audience member: I am a psychologist who deals with judges. Taking away spectacular cases, in ordinary state trial cases the judges I talk to are very anxious when they have to deal with the press or when anything appears on television or in print about them, because it is usually not to their liking. Usually judges meet with enormous approval and sometimes even fawning behavior. They don't get anything negative up close. Then they get negative reactions through the media. The shock of those two perceptions is unbearable.

I talk to reporters, editors—visual and print— and I say "What's the story when you cover the courts. I want to know because I'm a counsellor to judges and I want to help them." And they couldn't quite answer me. I then said, "What mental set do you have when you judge what goes on page 1, or has 60 lines or 20 lines?" And we finally got it. The mental set is it has to respond to "Ain't it awful?" or, it has to say, "I can't believe it!" So the reader has to be fed the "Ain't it awful" or the "I can't believe it." That rates space. Anything else is boring.

My own lay opinion as to what can be done is bypass the media and go right to the public with all sorts of educational efforts, all sorts of appearances—deal directly with the public and try to bypass the media. The media's got its own business and will never, never care about what the courts want to convey.

NOTE

This article originally appeared in Volume 80, Number 1, July-August 1996, pages 30-42.

"The Supreme Court decided today…," or did it?

Despite evidence of the news media's ability to present the U.S. Supreme Court's actions accurately, there is a pronounced tendency for network newscasts to mischaracterize docketing decisions as decisions on the merits.

by Elliot E. Slotnick and Jennifer A. Segal

The woeful state of public knowledge about the U.S. Supreme Court and its decisions is well documented. *Lack* of information is just one component of the problematic relationship between the Court and the public. *Mis*information about the Court's actions and their consequences for public policy making is another.

Network television news is the primary source from which most people receive the bulk of their political information. How accurately do television news stories report the Supreme Court's docketing decisions? Data from the 1989-90 term reveal a pronounced tendency for newscasts to mischaracterize docketing decisions as merits holdings. This phenomenon inevitably fosters public misunderstanding of the Court's public policy-making role.

Research reveals that most adult Americans have limited knowledge about the Supreme Court.[1] More to the point, "many Americans little recognize or little remember the Court's rulings. On open-ended questions that probe for specific likes or dislikes… only about half (or fewer)…can offer an opinion on even the most prominent Supreme Court decisions."[2] Perhaps the most telling example of public ignorance is a Wisconsin study that tested respondents' recognition of whether the Court had recently rendered a decision in eight controversies, half of which the Court had actually decided and half of which it had not. A majority of the actual decisions and non-decisions were correctly identified by only 15 percent of the respondents. While only 2 percent could correctly identify all eight items, six times as many people (12 percent) got all eight items wrong.[3] More recently, while less than 10 percent of the public could name the chief justice of the United States, more than a quarter of the populace recognized Judge Wapner of "The People's Court."[4]

Docketing vs. merits decisions

Beyond the problem of limited information is the potential for even well-informed citizens to be misinformed about the Court and its activities. For instance, relatively knowledgeable citizens might recall two actions the Court took in October 1992 and paraphrase them as follows: (1) the Court allowed self-insured employers to curtail insurance coverage for expensive maladies such as AIDS and (2) the Court protected freedom of choosing abortion by overturning Guam's restrictive abortion law.

In both instances these characterizations are, at best, half truths. The Court's action in each of the cases was, in fact, to refuse to hear the case seeking a writ of certiorari or a writ of appeal. Yet incorrect labeling of the Court's actions is quite understandable given the manner in which the media covered the Court's certiorari denials. For example, coverage of these two cases by *The Columbus Dispatch* illustrates what a casual citizen might learn about what the Court had done.

In the first case, the headline announced, "Court Refuses to Outlaw Curtailing AIDS

Benefit." The article that followed, taken off the AP wire, began,

The Supreme Court *refused* yesterday to let AIDS sufferers use a federal pension-protecting law to sue when self-insured employers cut health-care benefits for the disease [emphasis added in all quoted material].[5]

Adding to the potential confusion about what the Court had actually done in this matter, the newspaper's editorial page later contained the following view (reprinted from a *Chicago Tribune* editorial):

The Supreme Court last week made far more difficult the task of those who argue that whatever solution the nation crafts for its health-care mess ought to rely more on markets than mandates.

It did so by (*affirming*) a lower court's decision that an employer may slash an employee's health insurance coverage after the worker contracts an expensive illness.

(This *decision*) further erodes the fundamental principles on which the institution of insurance is based. And it creates more momentum for great but potentially dangerous simplifications like national health insurance.[6]

In the second example from 1992, *The Columbus Dispatch* ran a front-page banner headline, "Court Again Backs Right to Abortion." The article began, "The nation's most restrictive abortion law died yesterday as the U.S. Supreme Court, for the second time in five months, *confirmed* a woman's right to abortion. Justices voted 6-3 to *reject an appeal* that would have continued the territory of Guam's almost complete ban on abortion. Lower courts had struck down the law."

Mischaracterization of Court actions such as these would not be very significant if the media were not the major source of public information about the Court or if certiorari decisions were generally tantamount to definitive decisions on the merits with widespread precedential value. But the media is and the Court's cert decisions may not be.

The dominance of the media in informing people of the Court's work has been well documented. For example, 76 percent of a Florida sample claimed that newspapers are their primary source of news about Court decisions, and 71 percent said that television plays that role.[7] As Marshall notes, "Public awareness of Supreme Court decisions depends heavily on the quality of coverage provided by the mass media."[8] According to Davis,

[The media's] role is even more salient here than in the relationship between the mass public and other political institutions due to the absence of any alternative methods of direct communication. The justices, unlike elected officials, lack other nonmedia mechanisms for interactions with this constituency such as town meetings, newsletters, and frequent campaigning. Knowledge on the part of the mass public of the activities of the Court comes exclusively from the [news media].[9]

Increasingly, the role of television in informing the public has overcome other media formats. Katsh notes that most people claim to receive all of their news from television.[10] Iyengar and Kinder have argued, "As television has moved to the center of American life, TV news has become Americans' single most important source of information about political affairs."[11]

Denying certiorari

Misreporting of the Court's decisions to deny certiorari as merits holdings is important only if such decisions are generally not equivalent to decisions on the merits. The literature is replete with persuasive arguments on both sides of the question. Technically, all that a cert denial means is that the Supreme Court, using its appellate discretion, has refused to hear a case, thereby leaving a lower court decision and the immediate holding undisturbed. This formal view of certiorari denial suggests that the Court, by not hearing the case, has given no indication of where it stands on the merits of the lower court judgment or the issues involved. Consequently, the lower court decision prevails but carries no broad legal precedential or policy significance.

Many justices and commentators have aggressively insisted that this minimalist perspective on the meaning of certiorari denials is an accurate one. Justice Felix Frankfurter argued the position most frequently and in the greatest detail. At the most general level, Frankfurter noted that "...a denial nowise implies" agreement with a lower court decision. Rather, "It simply means that fewer than four members of the Court deemed it desirable to review a decision of the lower court as a matter 'of sound judicial discretion.' "[12]

In a 1950 dissent, Frankfurter expounded on what a denial of review could signify:

[I]t seemed...to at least six members...that the issue was either not ripe enough or too moribund for adjudication; that the question had better wait for the perspective of time or that time would bury the question or, for one reason or another, it was desirable to wait and see; or that the constitutional issue was entangled with nonconstitutional issues that raised doubt whether the constitutional issue could be effectively isolated; or for various other reasons not related to the merits.[13]

On another occasion, Frankfurter simply opined that denial

means only that, for one reason or another, which is seldom disclosed, and not infrequently for conflicting reasons, which may have nothing to do with the merits and certainly may have nothing to do with any view of the merits taken by a majority of the Court, there were not four members of the Court who thought the case should be heard.[14]

In a similar vein, Justice William Rehnquist also emphasized that the decision to not hear a case may occur for many reasons, none of which necessarily implies a substantive decision. "Some members of the Court may feel that a case is wrongly decided, but lacking in general importance; others may feel that it is of general importance, but rightly decided; for either reason, a vote to deny certiorari is logically dictated."[15] Thus, it appears reasonable to conclude that "[b]ecause denials are usually not explained, there may be no way of knowing how a majority views the merits of particular cases."[16]

Nevertheless, many analysts and jurists continue to dispute this minimalist interpretation of docketing decisions, often taking as their starting point the words of Justice Robert Jackson: "Some say denial means nothing, others say it means nothing much. Realistically, the first position is untenable and the second is unintelligible....The fatal sentence that in real life writes finis to many causes cannot in legal theory be a complete blank."[17] And, as Wasby and others have noted, cases accepted for review are not randomly decided, but are reversed approximately two-thirds of the time.[18] This seemingly implies that denial generally equates with affirmance.

In addition, lawyers and even some justices themselves have been known to cite certiorari denials and to draw inferences from them. As Neubauer notes, "Some infer consideration of the merits when the Court consistently leaves undisturbed lower court decisions seemingly at variance with past Court rulings."[19] According to Chief Justice Earl Warren, "Denials can and do have a significant impact on the ordering of constitutional and legal priorities. Many potential and important developments in the law have been frustrated, at

least temporarily, by a denial of certiorari."[20]

Moreover, using logic some might find faulty, Linzer argues, "If a denial of certiorari were a purely discretionary act, largely or totally unconcerned with the merits of a particular case, it would be anomalous for justices to note their dissents."[21] It can be argued, however, that even if denial were substantively meaningless, a justice seeking a substantive decision might dissent from the Court's refusal to hear a case.

Clearly, there is no obvious or absolute answer to the question of what a certiorari denial means substantively. According to Abraham, "No matter which of these...contrasting views may be 'correct,' the effect in the eyes of the disappointed petitioner is necessarily the same: at least for the present, he or she has lost."[22] Taking a more balanced view, Goldman and Jahnige state,

At the most, a denial of certiorari may represent an approval of lower court decision-making; at the least, it is a nondecision, that is, a decision not to do anything. Because they involve the Court neither in new policy departures nor in the overt responsibility for existing policy, such nondecisions are generally perceived as not being politically salient.[23]

Abraham is certainly correct in noting that in the immediate case at hand, the Court's denial of cert means that the petitioner has "lost." This does not, however, suggest a "loss" from a broader judicial policy-making perspective. Returning to the examples from 1992, it would be difficult to characterize the Court's refusal to hear the appeal in the insurance exclusion case as definitive in any fashion. Many of the considerations outlined by Justice Frankfurter and others easily could have been applicable in this case, and the Court is likely to address the issue on its merits in the foreseeable future.

As for the Guam anti-abortion statute, it is difficult to glean any broad substantive implications, however hard the media tried, from the Court's decision to leave undisturbed a lower court's decision to overturn what was acknowledged to be the most restrictive existing anti-abortion regulation in the United States. The lower court holding and the Supreme Court's refusal to hear the appeal offer no clue about how the Court will treat less restrictive state regulatory laws.

Data analysis
Although the ultimate meaning of certiorari deni-

als is unclear, they are clearly not always tanta-mount to decisions on the merits. As a conse-quence, the mischaracterization by news stories of denials as substantive decisions is important and deserves scrutiny.

In earlier research conducted by the authors of this article, all network news stories of the Supreme Court during the 1989-90 term were examined with a primary focus on television's docket-related cov-erage.[24] The analysis used videotapes of Court-related stories compiled by the Vanderbilt Televi-sion News Archive. Several docket-related stories were coded as merits decisions but were subse-quently unable to be matched with any decisions actually rendered by the Court during the term. Coding errors in initially viewing the news stories, coupled with a longtime realization of significant misreporting of docketing decisions by television news, led to the genesis of this article.

For this analysis, all 41 network evening news stories from the Supreme Court's 1989-90 term that were about docketing decisions—whether or not they were characterized as such by the news-cast—were isolated. The stories were coded along a number of variables tapping the technical facets of the news coverage (such as story placement and length) as well as on a number of variables gaug-ing the stories' substantive content. Most impor-tantly for this analysis, the stories were coded ac-cording to the Court's actual action in the case, how the network presented the Court's action, and how definitive the Court's action actually was. Viewed most broadly, the data indicate that while the networks did a credible job when they chose to report grants of certiorari, reporting of the Court's denials of certiorari was much more prob-lematic.

Of the 41 stories examined, 13 (31.7 percent) covered the Court's granting of certiorari in seven cases. Nine of these stories (69.2 percent) reported on three cases that involved important issues: dis-crimination against women of child-bearing age in jobs involving hazardous chemicals, flag burn-ing, and abortion counseling. Each of these cases was covered by all three networks. The remaining four stories focused on four other cases, each re-ported by only one network. They involved the death penalty (for those in possession of specified amounts of cocaine), search and seizure (the es-tablishment of road blocks to catch drunk drivers), federalism (state control of the deployment of state

national guard troops), and trial rights (whether alleged child abusers have the right to face their accusers).

While these cases represent only a small pro-portion of those that were actually granted certio-rari during the 1989-90 term, such sparse cover-age was less problematic than it might seem be-cause a number of other cases that were granted cert subsequently became the subject of news sto-ries when they were in later stages of the decision-making process.[25]

The cases involving certiorari grants received very little air time and relatively low prominence. Ten of the stories were just 30 seconds or less, and 12 were presented after the first commercial break. Only two stories, both about the abortion counsel-ing case, included considerable substantive infor-mation about the litigation. Clearly, despite the im-portance of many of the issues that were the sub-ject of these cases, stories covering their cert grants were not very substantial.

Nevertheless, all 13 of these certiorari grant sto-ries reported accurately the Court's decision to ac-cept review of the case involved. In reporting the stories, language such as the Court agreed to "de-cide," "take up," "take on," make "a quick rul-ing," "review," "hear arguments," and "consider" made understanding the Court's decision to grant certiorari quite clear.

The same cannot be said, however, for the sto-ries about the Court's denials of certiorari. More than two-thirds of the 41 stories (28) about the Court's docketing decisions concerned a decision to deny cert.[26] These stories reported on 16 cases categorized broadly by four issue areas: equal pro-tection, privacy, abortion, and the First Amend-ment. The greatest number of cert denial stories (10, 35.7 percent) concerned four abortion-related cases. (These four cases involved Operation Res-cue blockades and demonstrations, the use of rack-eteering laws to sue anti-abortion groups, and the legitimacy of tax exemptions for the Roman Catho-lic Church when it has engaged in anti-abortion lobbying.)

Story characteristics

Cases involving the issue of equal protection—in-cluding gender discrimination in a Maryland coun-try club, the rights of homosexuals in the armed services, school programs for handicapped chil-dren, and an affirmative action suit by Gulf Oil employees—were the focus of six stories. Five stories involved issues of privacy, including two cases about random drug testing, one about seat belt laws, and another about cordless phones. The First Amendment was the subject of two cases covered in three stories, two about school dances in a public high school and the other about the sinking of Greenpeace's *Rainbow Warrior*. Finally, two other cases were the subjects of four stories, three about a case that sought the reevaluation of the trust fund established for the victims of the Dalkon Shield and a case about water rights in Wyoming.

Thus, these 16 instances of certiorari denials generally involved some of the most contentious political issues of the day. This is not surprising, since such issues allow for interesting, dramatic television stories and are likely to be attractive to the most television viewers. Nevertheless, and despite comprising the vast majority of the docketing decisions broadcast by the networks, these 16 certiorari denials constituted a minute proportion (well under 1 percent) of the 4,705 denials the Court made during its 1989-90 term.

As was the case regarding stories about the granting of certiorari, almost all the stories about the Court's denial of cert were quite short and placed without prominence in the broadcast. Twenty-four (85.7 percent) were 30 seconds or less in length, and 22 (78.6 percent) were shown after the newscast's first commercial break. On the other hand, most stories (25, 89.3 percent) about a denial of certiorari included at least one piece of substantive information about the case. The vast majority (23, 82.1 percent) included some case facts, and nearly half of the stories (13, 46.4 percent) identified at least one of the litigants. Other substantive information, however, was rarely given. The four stories about the Operation Rescue cases were unique in their presentation of a large amount of substantive information.[27] Overall, coverage of the Court's cert denials was quite thin, thereby compounding the fundamental problem of misreporting examined below.

Coverage of certiorari denials was divided fairly evenly among the three networks. NBC presented the most stories about cert denials (12, 42.9 percent), with CBS and ABC each airing eight. NBC reported the greatest proportion of its stories accurately (4, 33.3 percent), but it also reported the greatest number of stories inaccurately (8). CBS reported only one story accurately and seven in a misleading or incorrect fashion, while ABC reported only two correctly and six with demonstrable error. Admittedly, the numbers are very small, and it is not the intention here to gauge which network did the "best" job of covering the Court's cert denials. In the final analysis, in those rare instances where certiorari denials were reported, none of the networks did a very thorough or accurate job of reporting what the Court had done.

Indeed, inaccuracy in the newscasts' characterization of the Court's action is clearly the most important deficiency of these stories. In contrast to the stories about grants of certiorari, most of the stories about cert denials (21, 75 percent) were coded as fundamentally inaccurate or, at best, misleading, in reporting what the Court had done. In nearly half of the certiorari denial stories (13, 46.4 percent), the Court's actions were misreported as decisions on the merits rather than as denials of certiorari. In eight stories (28.6 percent), the terminology used to report the story was sufficiently ambiguous to cause some difficulty in determining whether a decision had been made or cert had been denied. After further investigation, the cases that were the subject of these ambiguous reports were determined to be cert denials. Only seven of the 28 stories about denials of certiorari (25 percent) were reported accurately.

The actual language in the stories best illustrates the manner in which the Court's actions were characterized by the three networks during their evening news programs. It is quite apparent from a number of stories that the Court's decision to deny cert can, indeed, be reported correctly. For example, Peter Jennings of ABC News was quite clear in his discussion of the Court's docketing decision in the Dalkon Shield case. "In Washington, the Supreme Court today removed the last major roadblock facing a 2½ billion dollar settlement for women injured by the Dalkon Shield....The Court *refused to hear* a challenge to the settlement which sets up a trust fund to be shared by thousands of the victims" (November 6, 1989, emphasis added in all quoted material). Tom Brokaw of NBC News used similar language when he reported the decision to deny certiorari in a case involving mandatory seat belt laws in Iowa: "...the Court *refused to hear* [the petitioner's] arguments" (December 11, 1989). In these instances, as well as others, "refused to hear" is exactly what the Court did when it denied certiorari.

There are, however, many more examples of inaccuracy by the networks. As noted above, 21 stories (75 percent) were erroneous in their portrayal of the Court's action, 13 quite obviously, and 8 somewhat more ambiguously. In each instance, the impression that viewers were likely to gain was that the Court had made a decision on the merits rather than denied certiorari.

Ambiguous language

Ambiguous language such as "refused to overturn" was used in a number of stories, including one about the ban on homosexuals in the military. As ABC's Jennings stated, "In Washington, the Supreme Court has *refused to overturn* the regulation that forbids acknowledged homosexuals from being members of the armed forces" (February 26, 1990). Brokaw used similar terminology in NBC's story on the same case.

In a story about the Dalkon Shield settlement, CBS's Dan Rather reported, "The U.S. Supreme Court *turned down* the last major challenge and cleared the way today for a 2.5 billion dollar settlement for women injured by the Dalkon Shield birth control device" (November 6, 1989.) The Court's action in a random drug testing case was also ambiguously reported when Rather stated,

The U.S. Supreme Court today *gave qualified approval* for random drug testing among government workers in sensitive jobs. The Supreme Court *turned down appeals* from Justice Department employees and civilian army counselors (January 22, 1990).

In this instance, imprecise characterization of the Court's action is linked with a substantive direction in the Court's holding, perhaps compounding the problem.

In reporting the same case, NBC's Brokaw similarly stated, "Mandatory drug laws *got another vote of confidence* today from the Supreme Court. Without comment, the Court *rejected challenges* to two testing programs for Justice Department employees with top security clearance and for the Army's civilian drug counselors" (January 22, 1990).

These examples illustrate some of the language that was conservatively characterized as ambiguous or misleading for this study. While phrases such as "turned down," "refused to overturn," "rejected challenges," and "killed a lawsuit" may appear to trained ears as indirect means of describing certiorari denials, it is more than likely that the typical viewer of the evening's news would interpret this language to mean that the Court had rendered a substantive judgement in these cases. (Indeed, even the authors of this study, as noted previously, initially miscoded the Court's action in several of these stories.) The networks failed to portray clearly and accurately the Court's actions in these stories.

Most importantly, the largest proportion of stories about the Court's denial of certiorari could not be deemed ambiguous at all. Rather, they were clearly wrong. The most frequently used words to characterize the Court's actions in these stories was "upheld" and "ruled." In reporting on the Court's decision to deny cert to the petition challenging a ban on dances in public schools, Brokaw reported, "The U.S. Supreme Court *ruled* today on an issue that most youngsters in this country say is a fundamental right: the school dance…But the Court *upheld* a ban on dances in the public schools of Purdy, Missouri, where many people are Southern Baptists who believe that dancing is sinful and satanic" (April 16, 1990).

On April 30, Brokaw stated in a story on a case of random drug testing that "…the Court *upheld* random drug testing of thousands of air traffic controllers and other Transportation Department employees in safety related jobs." Similarly, Bob Schieffer of CBS News reported on a case regarding special education programs in public schools for handicapped children: "In effect, today's *ruling* means that these schools must keep trying to find programs that will help these children" (November 27, 1989). The implica-tion of these and other stories was that the Court made a decision on the merits of the cases rather than denying them certiorari.

Perhaps the most blatant misreporting of cert denials during the 1989-90 term occurred in the stories about the demonstrations and protest activities of the anti-abortion group Operation Rescue. On May 14, 1990, both ABC and CBS reported on the Court's refusal to hear the group's assertion that blocking access to abortion clinics in Atlanta was protected by the First Amendment's guarantee of free speech. Ted Koppel of ABC introduced the story by reporting that "…before the Supreme Court [there was] *a defeat* today for the anti-abortion group Operation Rescue. The Court *said* that a claim of free speech does not give them the right to block access to abortion clinics in Atlanta, Georgia."

Bettina Gregory followed up on this story by stating, "Today the Supreme Court *said* those restrictions on Operation Rescue blockades instituted in Atlanta did not violate freedom of speech because these protestors had a history of unlawful conduct."

CBS's coverage of this case appeared even more misleading. Schieffer reported,

...the Supreme Court split 5-4 today and *upheld* a ban on anti-abortion demonstrators who tried to block entrances to Atlanta abortion clinics. The Court *rejected the demonstrator's arguments* that they were just exercising free speech.

Beyond using the words "upheld" and "rejected...arguments," which imply that the Court made a substantive decision, Schieffer's report included the outcome of a vote taken by the justices. Although it appeared that the justices had made a decision on the merits, the vote was actually taken to determine whether Operation Rescue's application for a stay on a lower court's temporary injunction should be granted. By a 5-4 vote, the application was denied.

If this was not confusing enough, a week later (May 21, 1990) each of the three networks aired stories about Operation Rescue's activities in New York. Once again, the presentation of this certiorari denial was problematic. The stories included erroneous references to the earlier Atlanta case, treating it as if a merits decision had been made. For instance, Jennings reported:

There has been a second *legal defeat* at the Supreme Court for the anti-abortion group Operation Rescue. The justices today *agreed with lower courts* which ruled the Operation Rescue pickets may not block access to abortion clinics in New York. Last week the Court made a similar *ruling* for clinics in Atlanta.

CBS's explanation of the Court's action went even further. The opening visual headline for the evening's entire newscast was, "The Supreme Court *Bans* Abortion Clinic Blockades." Rather introduced the story by reporting,

The U.S. Supreme Court *approved* new limits today on protests by anti-abortion groups. The justices *upheld* a permanent ban on demonstrators who physically try to block entrances to abortion clinics. Today's *ruling* was on a case from New York...

And, in the expansive follow-up report, Rita

Braver repeated the problematic reference to the Atlanta case when she stated, "Last week the Court voted 5-4 to allow a temporary ban against Operation Rescue to stand in Atlanta. But today's action is considered even more significant because it involves a permanent ban and can have an impact on similar cases now underway in other states."

Expanding on the implications of the case, Braver opined, "The Supreme Court action is bad news for Operation Rescue.... Abortion rights activists call it a victory for them." Confirmatory interviews were then conducted with spokespersons for the Legal Defense Fund of NOW and the Feminist Women's Health Centers.

These stories starkly illustrate the extent to which the network news programs may misreport the activities of the Court. Both cases were denied review, yet the stories about them gave the distinct impression that the Court had made decisions on the merits. This impression was further substantiated for the Atlanta case by the subsequent references in the stories about the New York case. Moreover, in addition to mischaracterizing certiorari denials as merits decisions, these examples also demonstrate that network newscasts may unjustifiably draw broad policy implications from the Court's certiorari action. Anyone viewing these stories, regardless of which newscast they were watching and how knowledgeable they were about the Court, probably would have misperceived the nature of the action the Court had taken and its implications.

Less egregious errors

Despite the frequency of misreporting revealed in the data, it might be argued that for some cases a denial of certiorari is tantamount to a decision on the merits. As noted previously, that is surely the case for the actual litigants involved. More broadly, however, there are likely to be instances where a case's policy issues are definitively resolved by a cert denial. When, for example, the issue before the Court is a very narrow one and quite fact-intensive, as in the Wyoming water rights dispute mentioned earlier, certiorari denial clearly ends the matter for all intents and purposes and may serve the same function as a merits ruling. In such a setting, misreporting the cert denial as a merits decision seems to be a less egregious media problem.

It was not the intention of this study to add to the scholarly debate regarding the meaning of certiorari denials. Indeed, it is clear that in some instances it makes good sense to talk in terms of the broad substantive implications of certiorari denials, while in other instances it does not. With that in mind, the certiorari denial news stories were coded for whether the Court's docketing action definitively resolved the underlying policy issue raised by the case. In only 4 of the 21 certiorari denial stories deemed inaccurate (19.0 percent) could the Court's refusal to hear a case be characterized as definitive. Three of the 16 certiorari denial cases were the focus of these stories: the Dalkon Shield settlement, the sinking of the *Rainbow Warrior*, and the Wyoming water rights case. In these instances, the networks' misreporting of the Court's action may not have been very consequential, since the denial of certiorari amounted, practically, to the resolution of the issue involved.

This leaves, however, an overwhelming majority (17, 81.0 percent) of inaccurate stories about the 13 other cases for which the Court's cert denial was not definitive in nature. Faulty reporting here is especially problematic since the issues involved in these cases were very controversial and would likely be raised in subsequent litigation.

Reporting such certiorari denials as if the Court had made substantive decisions on the merits was clearly avoidable. As the data amply illustrate, the networks are indeed capable of reporting cert denials accurately. Thus, it appears that there is little excuse for misreporting the Court's docketing decisions. The consequences of such misreporting can best be seen in instances where the Court ultimately makes a merits ruling that is inconsistent with earlier reporting of a cert denial on the issue involved. Most recently, a graphic example of such an occurrence from the data set emerged when the Court resolved the substantive issues in the Operation Rescue cases in favor of the anti-abortion group.[28]

An unsatisfying picture

The picture that emerges of network news coverage of Supreme Court docketing decisions is not a very satisfying one. Most striking in the findings is this fact: of the 28 stories about certiorari denials, only 7 (25 percent) accurately and unambiguously characterized the Court's refusal to hear the case. In the plurality of stories covering cert denials (13, 46.4 percent), the Court's inaction was presented as if it were a decision on the merits. Coupled with

the eight stories coded generously as "ambiguous" in their presentation of what the Court had done, a full three-fourths of the certiorari denial stories (21, 75 percent) misrepresented the Court's action. Importantly, in only four (19.0 percent) of these instances could the Court's cert denial be characterized as "definitive" in any sense. Moreover, there were a number of stories in which the network newscast included a projection of broad policy implications from the Court's action.

The data clearly indicate that coverage of the Court's docketing decisions by the network newscasts is cursory, at best. When given, however, coverage can be more accurate. Because there are examples of accurate reporting of the Court's docketing decisions—even certiorari denials—it is puzzling why the newscasts do not present docketing decisions more accurately more of the time. Some may believe that a focus on accuracy inevitably diminishes drama and induces dullness, thereby hampering a broadcast's commercial viability. Reporters, however, must first "get it right." Then they remain free to analyze, speculate about, and draw implications from a docketing decision that has been presented accurately.[29]

Media coverage of the Supreme Court has consequences for the information the citizenry possesses about what the Court has done. The public may often be constrained in its knowledge by faulty presentations or misrepresentations of the Court's behavior. This link between network newscast coverage of the Supreme Court and citizen knowledge of Court actions can be the subject of experimental testing. Using videotapes of newscast coverage, it is possible, in a future phase of this project, to examine what a subject pool learns from accurate and inaccurate newscasts about the Supreme Court's activities.

NOTES

This article originally appeared in Volume 78, Number 2, September-October 1994, pages 89-95.

1. Caldeira, *Neither the Purse Nor the Sword: Dynamics of Public Confidence in the Supreme Court*, 80 AM. POL. SCI. REV. 1211 (1986).

2. Marshall, PUBLIC OPINION AND THE SUPREME COURT 143 (Boston: Unwin Hyman, 1989).

3. Dolbeare, *The Public Views of the Supreme Court*, in Jacob, ed., LAW, POLITICS AND THE FEDERAL COURTS 194-212 (Boston: Little, Brown and Co., 1967).

4. Washington Post, June 23, 1989, at A21.

5. *Court Refuses to Outlaw Curtailing AIDS Benefit*, Columbus Dispatch, Nov. 10, 1992.

6. *Other Viewpoints*, Columbus Dispatch, Nov. 22, 1992, at

2B.

7. Berkson, The Supreme Court and its Publics 64 (Lexington: Lexington Books, D.C. Heath and Co.,1978).

8. *Supra* n. 2, at 142.

9. Davis, "The Supreme Court in the News: Covering a Political Institution," Presented at the annual meeting of the Midwest Political Science Association, Chicago, Illinois, 1993, p. 2.

10. Katsh, *Law in the Lens: An Interview with Tim O'Brien*, 5 Am. Leg. Stud. F. 31 (1980).

11. Iyengar and Kinder, News That Matters 112 (Chicago: University of Chicago Press, 1987).

12. State v. Baltimore Radio Show, 338 U.S. 912 (1950).

13. Darr v. Buford, 339 U.S. 200 (1950).

14. Brown v. Allen, 344 U.S. 443 (1953). Frankfurter's voice is not an isolated one on this issue. See, for example, the comments of Justices Jackson (Brown v. Allen, 1953), Marshall (U.S. v. Kras, 409 U.S. 434 (1973)) and Stevens (Hambasch v. U.S., 490 U.S. 1054 (1989)).

15. Huch v. U.S., 439 U.S. 1007 (1978).

16. O'Brien, Storm Center: The Supreme Court and American Politics 238-39 (New York: W.W. Norton and Company, Inc., 2d ed., 1990).

17. Brown v. Allen (1953), Jackson, J. concurring.

18. Wasby, The Supreme Court in the Federal Judicial System 215-219 (Chicago: Nelson Hall, Inc., 4th ed. 1993).

19. Neubauer, Judicial Process: Law, Courts, and Politics in the United States 382 (Pacific Grove, California: Brooks Cole Publishing, 1991).

20. *Retired Chief Justice Warren Attacks Freund Study Group's Composition and Proposal*, 59 A.B.A. J. 728 (July 1973), quoted in Wasby, *supra* n. 18, at 216.

21. Linzer, *The Meaning of Certiorari Denials*, 79 Col. L. Rev. 1255 (1979).

22. Abraham, The Judicial Process 179 (New York: Oxford University Press, 6th ed., 1993).

23. Goldman and Jahnige, The Federal Courts as a Political System 188 (New York: Harper and Row Publishers, Inc, 3rd ed., 1985).

24. Slotnick and Segal, "Television News and the Supreme Court," presented at the annual meeting of the American Political Science Association, Chicago, Illinois, 1992.

25. *See supra* n. 24.

26. Actually, two stories reported on the Court's decision to deny an application for a stay but for purposes here, given the manner in which the stories were presented, they have been included in the category of certiorari denials. In fact, Justice Kennedy's dissent in this decision to deny the stay suggested that the application was analogous to a certiorari petition. "The lower court's actions require us to treat the stay application as a petition for certiorari..." (*U.S. Reports*, p. 493, No. A-752).

27. Actually, the story about the case of disputed water rights in Wyoming was also quite thorough in its presentation of substantive information about the case. This story was anomalous in the data set, however. Focused on a rather narrowly framed case, it was one of the longest stories and only one of two feature/news stories. Because it was broadcast on a Saturday, we suspect that it was probably aired as filler for a light evening's newscast.

28. Bray, et. al. v. Alexandria Women's Health Clinic, et. al., 113 S.Ct. 753 (1993).

29. The authors are indebted to Steve Wasby for this succinct phrasing of a solution to the problem.

Supreme Court and public support for rights claims

Until the 1980s, the modern Supreme Court supported rights claims more often than did American public opinion. Today, that difference has narrowed significantly.

by Thomas R. Marshall and Joseph Ignagni

Of great concern to litigants, scholars, and civil libertarians alike is the level of support in American society for civil liberties, civil rights, and equality rights claims. Since the mid-20th century, the federal courts, especially the U.S. Supreme Court, have accepted many new rights claims, but rejected others. Many of these claims, which have been made in cases involving issues such as abortion, flag burning, and affirmative action, have been among the most controversial in American politics. Not surprisingly, such controversies have often sparked the interest of pollsters, and numerous public opinion polls have gauged public support for these rights claims. This article examines the question of who supports rights by directly comparing public opinion polls with Supreme Court decisions for a variety of rights claims that have reached the Court since the 1950s.

Perhaps the most memorable study of public support for new rights claims focused on the Cold War era of the 1940s and 1950s, when public opinion remained extremely hostile toward the free speech, free association, and employment protection rights of accused leftists.[1] In the face of this, the Supreme Court seldom supported civil liberties claims by accused leftists. Indeed, as Justices Hugo Black and William O. Douglas complained in one often-cited dissent:

Public opinion being what it is now, few will protest the conviction of these Communist petitioners. There is hope, however, that in calmer times, when present pressures, passions, and fears subside, this or some later Court will restore the First Amendment liberties to the high preferred place where they belong in a free society.[2]

The "classical tradition" of public opinion has typically assumed that public opinion during most periods is hostile toward individual rights.[3] Other literature suggests that a large share of American public opinion continues to be intolerant toward controversial or dissenting individuals or groups.[4] Taken together, this research suggests that public opinion may seldom be supportive of civil liberties, civil rights, or equality rights claims.

At the same time, several studies suggest that the federal courts have usually been more accepting than the public of rights claims. Jonathan Casper's historical study, for example, reported that the Supreme Court often struck down restrictive state laws, and occasionally even federal laws, that penalized controversial or unpopular claimants.[5] Other accounts suggest that the Warren Court strongly supported civil liberties, civil rights, or equality rights claims, even for controversial individuals or groups who had previously fared poorly in the political process.[6] The Burger Court continued to support rights claims, albeit less predictably.[7] Indeed, even the generally conservative Rehnquist Court was more tolerant toward controversial rights claims in the flag-burning controversy[8] than public opinion and state and federal laws.[9]

In short, past research suggests that while public opinion has often been hostile toward rights claims, especially in highly publicized cases or during times of crisis, the Supreme Court has been, on the whole, more tolerant. Whether these assumptions accurately describe the modern Supreme Court is examined in the remainder of this article.

Examining rights claims

To explore how often American public opinion and the Supreme Court supported new rights claims, public opinion polls were compared with Supreme Court decisions in 88 instances in which a civil liberties, civil rights, or equality claim against a restrictive federal, state, or local law or policy reached the Supreme Court between 1953 and 1992.

These 88 matches average about 2.2 rulings per term, and include every identifiable instance in which a scientific, nationwide poll item closely matched the substantive issue in a Supreme Court decision during the Warren, Burger, and Rehnquist Courts.[10] As a result, it is possible to directly examine public opinion versus Supreme Court support for rights claims across a wide variety of claims.

These 88 poll-to-decision matches tap a wide variety of civil liberties, civil liberties, and equality claims. The central issues involved racial equality,[11] abortion and gender rights,[12] political and religious dissent,[13] gay and lesbian rights,[14] labor,[15] welfare,[16] the death penalty,[17] criminal defendant rights,[18] students,[19] and commercial media claims.[20]

To be sure, these 88 poll-to-decision matches are not a purely random sample of all the Court's rights claims rulings, and they do not necessarily capture how intensely public opinion was focused on each controversy. Rather, they represent a diverse sample of the Court's high-profile decisions involving rights claims—at least in that each of these 88 decisions elicited at least one poll item.[21] As the evidence below indicates, however, reweighting the sample to correct for under- or oversampling of caseload does not change the results.

Examining the 88 controversies suggests that public opinion support for rights claims ranged from strong support for some to equally strong opposition to others. Three well-known examples illustrate this diversity. At one extreme, an 80-to-12 percent poll majority agreed with the claim in *U.S. v. U.S. District Court* (1972) that citizens should not be "spied on by any kind of electronic surveillance, except with a court order."[22]

In a few instances, available polls were closely divided. Before the *Roe v. Wade* (1973) ruling, the last available pre-decision Gallup Poll reported that 46 percent of Americans favored and 45 percent opposed "a law which would permit a woman to go to the doctor to end pregnancy at any time during the first three months."[23]

At the other extreme, large majorities of the public opposed several rights claims. The controversy over school prayer provides an example.[24] In *Engle v. Vitale* (1962) and *Abington School District v. Schempp* (1963), the Supreme Court held that officially sponsored school prayers or Bible readings violate the Constitution. These rulings disagreed with large public opinion majorities. A Gallup Poll taken shortly after the *Abington* ruling indicated that a 70-to-24 percent majority disapproved of the rulings.[25]

For each of these 88 claims, a "poll margin" was computed, measuring the percentage who favored the claim minus the percentage who opposed it. For example, for *U.S. v. U.S. District Court*, the poll margin was +68 percent (80 percent in favor of the claim, minus 12 percent opposed to the claim). For *Roe v. Wade*, the poll margin was +1 percent, well within the .05-level error margin. For *Engle v. Vitale* and *Abington v. Schempp*, the poll margin was a -46 percent, indicating strong disapproval of that claim.

Public and Court support

Overall, public opinion support for rights claims during the Warren, Burger, and Rehnquist Courts has been decidedly mixed. In slightly more than half (53 percent, or 47) of the 88 claims, public opinion opposed the claim in question. In 13 percent (or 11) of them, nationwide polls were evenly divided (within the .05 margin level of error). In the remaining 34 percent (or 30) of the 88 claims, public opinion favored the claim.

Some disputes (such as death penalty or abortion rulings) are polled more often than others.[26] To correct for this bias, the 88 poll-to-decision matches were also reweighted to correct for over- or under-sampling.[27] Results for the reweighted sample were nearly identical to the unweighted sample. For the reweighted sample, public opinion opposed 55 percent of the claims, supported 35 percent, and was evenly divided on 10 percent.

Overall, the modern Supreme Court has been marginally more supportive than public opinion. For all 88 poll-to-decision matches, the Supreme Court supported the rights claim 53 percent of the time (or 47 instances), and opposed the claim 47 percent of the time (41 instances). At first glance, then, the Supreme Court has indeed been more sympathetic to rights claims than the mass public.

The Court's record of supporting rights claims often follows public opinion. When public opinion opposed the claim, so typically did the Supreme Court, supporting less than half (40 percent) of these claims. When public opinion was either evenly divided or supported the claim, however, the Court supported 73 percent and 67 percent of these claims, respectively. Table 1 compares public opinion with Supreme Court support for rights claims.

Another way to examine public attitudes toward rights claims is to examine the poll margin. The average margin for all 88 claims was -9 percent, indicating that slightly more Americans opposed the average claim than favored it.

An average poll margin of -9 percent is quite small compared to public opinion toward earlier Cold War-era claims of accused leftists. For six of these rights claims,[28] the average poll margin was -27 percent, indicating that public opinion was very hostile. By comparison, attitudes toward the 88 rights claims during the Warren, Burger, and Rehnquist Courts were much more closely balanced. For only 22 of the 88 (or 24 percent) were attitudes as negative as for the average Cold War-era leftist dissent claim.

The poll margins varied widely according to the type of rights claim asserted. Only labor and racial rights claims received, on average, a positive poll margin, +9 percent and +2 percent, respectively. The most negative margins involved student or welfare rights, where the average margin was -24 percent and -53 percent, respectively.

The public opinion poll margin can also be compared with the vote split among the Court's justices by computing the (net) percent of justices who favored or opposed a rights claim. For example, in *Roe v. Wade*, concerning first-trimester abortions, seven justices voted for and two justices voted against the claim, yielding a "vote margin" of +56 percent (7 justices minus 2 justices, or 78 percent minus 22 percent).

In almost all types of cases, the justices gave more support to rights claims than did available public opinion polls. Overall, the poll margin was -9 percent, but the vote margin among the justices was +24 percent. Except for gay and lesbian rights, the vote margin among the justices was always more favorable toward rights claims than the poll margin was.[29]

Public opinion support versus Supreme Court

Table 1   Public opinion versus Supreme Court support for rights claims

	Public opinion		
	Opposed	Divided	Favorable
Supreme Court ruling:			
Opposed the claim	60%	27%	33%
Favored the claim	40%	73%	67%
(Number of cases)	(47)	(11)	(30)

(Chi-square significant at .05; Mantel-Hanzel significant at .02)

Table 2   Public attitudes toward rights claims during the Warren, Burger, and Rehnquist Courts

Type of claim:	Percent of times public favored the claim	Percent of times court favored the claim
Overall	34%	53%
Labor	33%	67%
Racial	47%	82%
Death penalty	38%	63%
Gay and lesbian	25%	0%
Media	33%	67%
Gender	29%	59%
Criminal (non-death)	39%	31%
Political and religious dissent	33%	100%
Student	25%	25%
Welfare	0%	40%

support for rights claims can also be compared for different types of claims. Admittedly, the number of claims per category is small, ranging from 17 for racial and women's rights claims, to only four gay and lesbian rights claims. Table 2 compares public opinion with Supreme Court support for each type of claim.

The first column in Table 2 reports the percentage of times that American public opinion clearly favored each type of rights claim. Again, welfare rights claims were the least popular: not in a single instance did public opinion support a rights claim for welfare recipients. Racial claims were the most often favored, with public opinion supporting nearly one-half of the 17 such claims.

The second column in Table 2 reports the Supreme Court's record of support for different types of claims. For most types of rights claims, the Supreme Court was more likely to support the claim than public opinion was. In only two instances (gay and lesbian rights and non-death-penalty criminal claims) were rights claims less likely to prevail at the Supreme Court than among the American public.

Public attitudes toward rights claims that reach the Supreme Court have changed surprisingly little over time. During the 1950s and 1960s, the public opposed 56 percent of the rights claims examined here, favored 28 percent, and was split on the remaining 17 percent. During the 1970s, the public opposed 49 percent of rights claims, favored 35 percent, and was evenly divided on the remaining 16 percent. During the 1980s and through 1992, the public opposed 54 percent of claims, favored 37 percent, and was split on 9 percent.

The Supreme Court's record of support for rights claims has varied much more dramatically over time, as the Court has become less willing to support rights claims.[30] Among the 88 cases, for example, the Court supported 67 percent of rights claims during the 1950s and 1960s, but only 58 percent of the claims during the 1970s. During the 1980s and 1990s, the Court supported only 37 percent of the rights claims. This pattern is opposite to the trend of American public opinion.[31] Figure 1 depicts the over-time change in support for rights claims, comparing public opinion to the Court.

Taken together, these results suggest that American public opinion has been decidedly mixed, not uniformly hostile, toward civil liberties, civil rights, or equality claims since the early 1950s. The public in nationwide polls has more often opposed than supported rights claims, but the differences should not be exaggerated. The modern Court's support for rights claims has usually exceeded public opinion support, although these differences have eroded over time.

Predicting Court support

How important is public opinion compared to other well-known predictors of Supreme Court decision making? Public opinion appears to be closely related to the modern Court's support for new rights claims, either when considered separately or when also considering other predictors of Supreme Court decision making.

Seven predictors of Supreme Court decision making were tested for the 88 claims, among them two separate measures of American public opinion. The first, the poll margin for each dispute, was described above. The poll margin is a ratio-level (percentage) variable that measures the extent to which the public in nationwide polls favors (or opposes) a specific rights claim before the Court.

A second, less direct measure of public opinion is the "national mood," a more general measure of the nation's prevailing leanings. Two accounts have estimated the national mood by tracking identically worded poll items over time.[32] Both studies

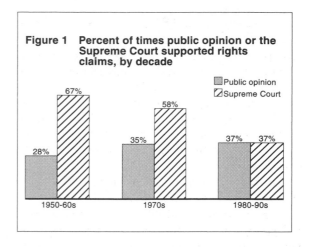

Figure 1 Percent of times public opinion or the Supreme Court supported rights claims, by decade

suggest that the national mood moved from more liberal to more conservative, and then back again, from the mid-1950s through the early 1990s.[33] Three separate versions of the national mood were tested—the current (annual) national mood, mood with a three-year lag, and mood with a five-year lag. The national mood is also a ratio-level variable.

Public opinion is not the only predictor of Supreme Court decision making. The presidential elections and judicial appointments model has also been widely used. In this model, Republican-appointed justices less often support rights claims than do Democrat-appointed justices.[34] Over time, presidential elections and judicial appointments significantly impact the Court's support for rights claims.[35] To test this model, the number of Republican-appointed justices on the Court was coded. The number of GOP-appointed justices on the Court during the 1953 through the 1991 terms ranges from a minimum of two to a maximum of eight.

Another predictor of the Supreme Court's decision making is the U.S. solicitor general's position. Many studies have reported that the solicitor general's position has great influence on the Court.[36] This variable was coded as (+1) to indicate support for the rights claim, (0) to indicate no federal position, and (-1) to indicate opposition to the claim.

A fifth predictor is whether the rights claim challenged a restrictive state law or policy. Typically, the Court gives less deference to state-level laws and policies than to federal laws.[37] This variable was coded as (1) to indicate the presence of a restrictive state-level law or policy, otherwise (0).

Table 3   Probability of a pro-claim ruling based on
public opinion and the Supreme Court's
partisan makeup

Number of GOP justices	Poll margin		
	Strongly favorable (+30%)	Evenly divided (0%)	Strongly opposed (-30%)
2	88%	85%	79%
3	81%	75%	69%
4	70%	63%	56%
5	57%	50%	43%
6	44%	37%	30%
7	32%	25%	19%
8	21%	15%	11%

A sixth predictor measures the decision's visibility. Research has shown that the Supreme Court may behave differently in highly visible cases than in less visible ones.[38] Here, a simple variable tapped whether the decision captured news coverage in the *New York Times* within two days of the decision's announcement. A (2) indicates one or more post-decision front-page news stories, (1) indicates inside news coverage only, and (0) indicates no coverage at all.[39]

Finally, to examine a possible artifact of the poll's timing, a seventh variable examined whether the poll was taken before or after the Court's decision. Most research has indicated that the Court has little, if any, ability to influence public opinion through its announced decisions.[40] If the public opinion poll was taken before the Court's decision was announced, the decision was coded (1). Post-decision polls were coded (2).

When all seven variables are combined in a joint probit model to predict whether the Court will support a rights claim (coded 1), or reject it (coded 0),[41] only three variables significantly predict the Court's support for new rights claims.[42] As the number of GOP justices increases, Court support for rights claims declines. For example, when the Court had its maximum number of Democratic appointees (either 6 or 7), the Court made pro-rights rulings 67 percent of the time. By comparison, when the Court had its minimum number of Democratic appointees (only 1 or 2), the Court ruled in favor of rights claims only 25 percent of the time.[43]

The Court also has more often supported a rights claim either when the solicitor general or public opinion supported the claim. Overall, public opinion was roughly as strong a predictor as the solicitor general's position, and nearly as strong a predictor as the Court's partisan makeup.

These results were also reexamined in a reduced model, eliminating the insignificant predictors. A three-predictor model combined only the solicitor general's position, the Court's partisan makeup, and public opinion. This model predicted decisions as well as did the full, seven-variable model,[44] and all three variables remained significant (at the .05-level).

On grounds of parsimony, however, a two-variable model stood out as the most attractive. This two-variable model included only the public opinion poll margin and the number of GOP-appointed justices.[45] Adding other variables, even the solicitor general's position, did not improve on this model's ability to predict Court decisions correctly.[46] For example, even when the solicitor general's position was added, the number of correctly predicted decisions barely improved (only to 69 percent).

In short, public opinion support for a rights claim is a significant predictor of whether the Supreme Court will accept it. Public opinion remains a strong predictor even when other, more traditional explanations of Supreme Court decision making are considered.[47]

Table 3 reports the probability that the Court will accept a rights claim, based solely on the Court's partisan makeup and public opinion toward that claim. The number of Republican-appointed justices varied between two and eight (as it did during the 1953 to 1991 terms). Public opinion is considered for three examples—when the polls strongly supported the claim (a poll margin of +30 percent), when polls were evenly divided, and when polls strongly opposed the claim (a poll margin of -30 percent).

Overall, the likelihood of a pro-rights claim ruling by the Court changes about as much when the polls change by a large margin as when the Court's partisan makeup changes by one seat. For example, with five GOP-appointed justices and evenly divided polls, the chance of a pro-claim rights ruling would be exactly 50 percent. Still with five GOP justices, but strongly favorable polls, the probability of a pro-claim ruling is 57 percent. With five GOP justices but strongly negative polls, the probability of a pro-claim ruling is only 43 percent.

Conclusions

This research points to several conclusions. First, since the mid-1950s public opinion has been quite mixed, but not uniformly hostile, toward civil liberties, civil rights, and equality rights claims. Available polls indicate that the American public clearly opposed about one-half, and clearly favored about one-third, of these claims. Public opinion may now slightly more often support rights claims than it did during the 1950s and 1960s.

Second, until the 1980s, the modern Supreme Court more often supported rights claims than did public opinion. Rights claims have usually received wider support from the justices than from the public. The Supreme Court's greater support for rights claims, however, has declined over time, and in more recent times, these differences no longer exist.

Third, public opinion is closely linked to the Supreme Court's own support for rights claims. Recent debates in judicial politics have reconsidered the question of what influences Supreme Court decision making, pointing to the judges' own values, solicitor general positions,[48] or the weight of legal arguments.[49] To those explanations may well be added public opinion. When public opinion either supports a rights claim, or when the polls are closely divided, the Court itself has overwhelmingly supported that claim. Indeed, public opinion remains closely linked to the Court's support for rights claims even when other explanations of Supreme Court decision making are also considered, such as the solicitor general's position or the Court's partisan makeup.

Exactly how this influence works remains somewhat speculative. However, these results are consistent with the theory that justices sense and share widely held public attitudes. As Chief Justice William Rehnquist once wrote:

...I was recently asked...whether the justices were able to isolate themselves from the tides of public opinion. My answer was that we are not able to do so, and it would probably be unwise to try. We read newspapers and magazines, we watch news on television, we talk to our friends about current events. No judge worthy of his salt would ever cast his vote in a particular case simply because he thought the majority of the public wanted him to vote that way, but that is quite a different thing from saying that no judge is ever influenced by the great tides of public opinion that run in a country such as ours. Judges are influenced by them....[50]

Even so, this research also suggests that public opinion is only one of several influences on the Court.[51] The Court's unusually unbalanced current partisan makeup strongly influences it against accepting rights claims, regardless of prevailing public opinion.[52] Even if both the solicitor general and the American public favor a rights claim, the probability of the current Supreme Court accepting that claim will remain quite small until the Court's composition itself changes.

Finally, this research also addresses the longstanding debate over judicial review. By far, the most commonly cited argument for this institution is that it helps protect controversial or unpopular minorities' civil liberties and rights.[53] The results here suggest that this argument should be reconsidered. True, the modern Supreme Court has been somewhat more sympathetic to rights claims than has public opinion. The difference, however, should not be overstated, and varies according to the time period considered. In recent years, the Supreme Court has not been more likely to support rights claims than public opinion. Those who advocate judicial review on the grounds that it is, in practice, countermajoritarian—that is, it defends beleaguered minorities against a hostile public opinion—might consider the evidence here.

NOTES

This article originally appeared in Volume 78, Number 3, November-December 1994, pages 146-151.

1. Murphy, THE CONSTITUTION IN CRISIS TIMES (New York: Harper & Row, 1972); Becker, COMPARATIVE JUDICIAL POLITICS 229 (Chicago: Rand McNally, 1970).

2. Dennis v. U.S. 341 U.S. 494, at 580 (1951).

3. Marshall, PUBLIC OPINION AND THE SUPREME COURT 2, 9 (Boston: Unwin Hyman, 1989).

4. For a review, see, e.g., Sullivan, Piereson, and Marcus, POLITICAL TOLERANCE AND AMERICAN DEMOCRACY (Chicago: University of Chicago Press, 1982).

5. Casper, *The Supreme Court and National Policy Making*, 70 AM. POL. SCI. REV. 50 (1976).

6. *See, e.g.*, Murphy, *supra* n. 1, at 310-457; McCloskey, THE MODERN SUPREME COURT (Cambridge, Mass.: Harvard University Press, 1972).

7. Shapiro, *The Supreme Court from Warren to Burger*, in King, ed., THE NEW AMERICAN POLITICAL SYSTEM (Washington, D.C.: American Enterprise Institute, 1979); Blasi, THE BURGER COURT: THE COUNTERREVOLUTION THAT WASN'T (New Haven: Yale University Press, 1983); Schwartz, ed., THE BURGER YEARS (New York: Viking, 1987).

8. Texas v. Johnson, 491 U.S. 397 (1989); U.S. v. Eichman, 496 U.S. 310 (1990).

9. Savage, TURNING RIGHT—THE MAKING OF THE REHNQUIST SUPREME COURT (New York: John Wiley & Sons, 1992).

10. The breakdown of poll-to-decision matches, by Court, is 19 Warren Court rulings, 56 Burger Court rulings, and 13 Rehnquist Court rulings (through 1992).

11. Racial rights claims and the issue involved include: Loving v. Virginia, 388 U.S. 1 (1967), miscegenation; Cooper v. Aaron, 358 U.S. 1 (1958), Little Rock school desegregation;

South Carolina v. Katzenbach, 383 U.S. 301 (1966), federal voting registrars; Heart of Atlanta Motel v. U.S., 379 U.S. 241 (1964), integration of public accomodations; Swann v. Charlotte Mecklenburg Board of Education, 402 U.S. 1 (1971), same-district school busing; Brown v. Board of Education of Topeka, Kansas, 354 U.S. 483 (1954), school integration, and 349 U.S. 294 (1955), speed of integration; Bob Jones University v. U.S. 461 U.S. 574 (1983), tax exemptions for segregated schools; Jones v. Mayer, 392 U.S. 409 (1968), racial discrimination in housing; Regents of the University of California v.Bakke, 428 U.S. 265 (1978), fixed racial quotas, and affirmative action without rigid quotas; Green v. New Kent Co. School Board, 391 U.S. 430 (1968), federal funds cutoff to segregated schools; Alexander v. Holmes Co. Board of Education, 396 U.S. 19 (1969), immediate public school desegregation; Griggs v. Duke Power Co., 401 U.S. 424 (1971), employment discrimination; Fullilove v. Klutznick, 448 U.S. 448 (1980), affirmative action programs in industry for minorities; Milliken v. Bradley, 418 U.S. 717 (1974), cross district school busing; and Boynton v. Virginia, 364 U.S. 454 (1960), segregation in public transportation waiting rooms. Companion cases are not listed here.

12. Harris v. McRae, 448 U.S. 297 (1980), federally funded abortions; Carey v. Population Services International, 431 U.S. 678 (1977), contraceptives for teenagers; Eisenstadt, Sheriff, v. Baird, 405 U.S. 438 (1972), contraceptives for single persons; Planned Parenthood of Central Missouri v. Danforth, 428 U.S. 52 (1976), spousal consent for a married woman's abortion; Roe v. Wade, 410 U.S. 113 (1973), first, second, and third trimester abortions; Doe v. Bolton, 410 U.S. 179 (1973), hospital abortion requirements; Bowen v. American Hospital Association, 476 U.S. 610 (1986), Baby Doe case; Johnson v. Transportation Agency of Santa Clara Co., 480 U.S. 616 (1987) affirmative action in hiring and promotions; Board of Directors of Rotary International v. Rotary Club of Duarte, 481 U.S. 537 (1987), club discrimination by sex; Webster v. Reproductive Health Services, 106 L. Ed. 2d 410 (1989), public hospital restrictions, and fetal viability tests; Planned Parenthood of Southeastern Pennsylvania v. Casey, No. 91-744 (1992), husband notification, informed consent, and 24-hour waiting rule; Rust v.Sullivan 114 L. Ed.2d 233 (1991), gag rule.

13. Abington School District v. Schempp, 374 U.S. 203, and Engle v. Vitale, 370 U.S. 421 (1962), school prayers; New York Times Co. v. U.S. and U.S. v. Washington Post, 403 U.S. 713 (1971), Pentagon Papers; Albertson v. SACB, 382 U.S. 70 (1965), registration of Communist Party members; U.S. v. U.S. District Court, 407 U.S. 297 (1972), warrantless electronic surveillance; Edwards v. Aguillard, 482 U.S. 578 (1987), creation science; Texas v. Gregory Lee Johnson, 491 U.S. 397 (1989), flag burning.

14. Gaylord v. Tacoma School District No. 10, cert denied, 434 U.S. 879 (1977), school teachers; Doe v. Commonwealth's Attorney for the City of Richmond, 425 U.S. 901 (1976), private acts; Beller v. Lehman, cert denied, 452 U.S. 905 (1981), military service; Bowers v. Hardwick, 478 U.S. 186 (1986), private acts.

15. Pipefitters Local Union 562 v. U.S., 407 U.S. 385 (1972), campaign funds; PATCO v. U.S., cert denied, 454 U.S. 1083 (1981), air traffic controllers' strike; Rogoff v. Anderson, 404 U.S. 805 (1971), public employee right to strike; NLRB v. Bildisco & Bildisco, 465 U.S. 513 (1984), bankruptcy and labor union contracts; AFSCME v. City of Muskegon, cert denied, 375 U.S. 833 (1963), public employees' right to join a labor union; United Federation of Postal Workers v. Blount, 404 U.S. 802 (1971), public employees' right to join a labor union.

16. Shapiro v. Thompson, 394 U.S. 618 (1969), waiting period for welfare recipients; Shapiro v. Doe, 396 U.S. 488 (1970), naming the father of illegitimate children for AFDC payments; Dandridge v. Williams, 397 U.S. 471 (1970), maximum welfare grants per family; Wyman v. Boddie, 402 U.S. 991 (1971), local cost-of-living AFDC adjustments; New York State Department of Social Services v. Dublino, 413 U.S. 405 (1973), work rules.

17. Coker v. Georgia, 433 U.S. 584 (1977), death penalty for rape; Woodson v. North Carolina, 428 U.S. 280 (1976), mandatory death penalty; Roberts v. Louisiana, 428 U.S. 325 (1976) and 431 U.S. 633 (1977), mandatory death penalty for killing a policeman; Gregg v. Georgia, 428 U.S. 153 (1976), death penalty for first degree murder; Moore v. Duckworth, Warden, 443 U.S. 713 (1979), insanity defense; Furman v. Georgia, 408 U.S. 238 (1972), death penalty; Wilkins v. Missouri, No. 87-6026 (1989), death penalty for teenagers; Penry v. Lynaugh, No. 87-6177 (1989), death penalty for mentally retarded.

18. Miranda v. Arizona, 384 U.S. 436 (1966), Gideon v. Wainwright, 372 U.S. 355 (1963), and Escobedo v. Illinois, 378 U.S. 478 (1964), criminal confessions; Schmerber v. California, 384 U.S. 757 (1966), blood tests for drunk driving; Delaware v. Prouse, 440 U.S. 648 (1979), random traffic spot checks; Glaser v. California, cert denied, 385 U.S. 880 (1966), possession of marijuana; New York v. Quarles, 467 U.S. 649 (1984), Nix v. Williams, 467 U.S. 431 (1984), and U.S. v. Leon, 468 U.S. 897 (1984), exclusionary rule; Smith v. Maryland, 442 U.S. 735 (1979), pen registers; Oatis v. Nelson, Warden, cert denied, 393 U.S. 1108 (1969), sale of marijuana; Chimel v. California, 395 U.S. 752 (1969), warrantless searches; Skinner v. Railway Labor Executives Assn., No. 87-1555 (1989), and National Treasury Employees Union v. Von Raab, No. 86-1879 (1989) drug testing in the workplace.

19. Ingraham v. Wright, 430 U.S. 651 (1977), corporal punishment; Stamos v. Spring Branch ISD, No. 85-1232 (1986), no-pass, no-play; New Jersey v. T.L.O., 469 U.S. 325 (1985), student searches; Goss v. Lopez, 419 U.S. 565 (1975), student suspension hearings.

20. Branzburg v. Hayes, 407 U.S. 665 (1972), reporters' confidentiality; New York Times Co. v. U.S., and Washington Post v. U.S., 403 U.S. 713 (1971), Pentagon Papers case; Zurcher v. The Stanford Daily, 436 U.S. 547 (1978), search warrants for newsroom searches; Richmond Newspapers, Inc., v. Virginia, 448 U.S. 555 (1980), attendance at criminal trials; Nebraska Press Assn. v. Stuart, 427 U.S. 539 (1976), right to print information about criminal trials; American Booksellers Assn. v. Hudnut, No. 85-1090 (1986), pronography restrictions.

21. Further, a large majority of these 88 decisions received front-page coverage in prominent newspapers. Some 72 percent of these cases received front-page post-decision coverage in the *New York Times*, while another 18 percent received coverage on an inside page.

22. Harris Poll, September 5, 1974.

23. Gallup Poll, December 8-11, 1972.

24. Weissberg, PUBLIC OPINION AND POPULAR GOVERNMENT 121-126 (Englewood Cliffs, NJ: Prentice Hall, 1976); Sorauf, THE WALL OF SEPARATION (Princeton: Princeton University Press, 1976).

25. Gallup Poll, June 21-26, 1963: "The United States Supreme Court has ruled that no state or local government may require the reading of the Lord's Prayer or Bible verses in public schools. What are your views on this? (favor or oppose)"

26. Marshall, *supra* n. 3, at 78-79.

27. The 88 cases were reweighted to reported numbers in the Spaeth database for the 1954-1989 period for comparable civil liberties, civil rights, and equality claims.

28. Trumbo v. U.S., 339 U.S. 934 (1950), cert denied; American Communications Association, C.I.O., v. Doud, 339 U.S. 382 (1950); Garner v. Board of Public Works of Los Angeles, 341 U.S. 716 (1951); Bailey v. Richardson, 341 U.S. 918 (1951);

Dennis v. U.S., 341 U.S. 494 (1951); and Weiman v. Updegraff, 344 U.S. 193 (1952).

29. The largest single difference was for welfare rights claims, where the poll margin was a very negative -53 percent, but among the justices, the vote margin was +23 percent. Gay and lesbian rights claims are the only exception to this pattern, receiving a poll margin of -6 percent, but among the justices, a less favorable vote margin of -22 percent.

30. Sheehan, Mishler, and Songer, *Ideology, Status, and the Differential Success of Direct Parties Before the Supreme Court*, 86 AM. POL. SCI. REV. 464 (1992); Lamb and Halpern, *The Burger Court and Beyond*, in Lamb and Halpern, ed., THE BURGER COURT (Urbana, Ill.: University of Illinois Press, 1991).

31. Sheehan, Mishler, and Songer, *supra* n. 30; Segal and Spaeth, THE SUPREME COURT AND THE ATTITUDINAL MODEL 244-251 (New York: Cambridge University Press, 1993).

32. Stimson, PUBLIC OPINION IN AMERICA—MOODS, CYCLES, AND SWINGS (Boulder, CO: Westview, 1992); and Smith, *Liberal and Conservative Trends in the United States Since World War II*, 54 PUBLIC OPINION Q. 479 (1990).

33. The Stimson (1992) data were used here, with updated figures through 1992, courtesy of the author.

34. Epstein and Kobylka, THE SUPREME COURT AND LEGAL CHANGE 13-21 (Chapel Hill: University of North Carolina Press, 1992), report that 11 GOP-appointed justices voted for (non-unanimous) civil liberties claims only 41 percent of the time, versus 69 percent of the time for 7 Democrat-appointed justices during this time period.

35. For recent descriptions, see Segal, *Senate Confirmation of Supreme Court Justices*, 49 J. OF POL. 998 (1987); Overby, Henschen, Walsh, and Strauss, *Courting Constituents? An Analysis of the Senate Confirmation Vote on Justice Clarence Thomas*, 86 AM. POL. SCI. REV. 997 (1992).

36. Segal and Spaeth, *supra* n. 31, at 237-239 and 313-314.

37. Wasby, THE SUPREME COURT IN THE FEDERAL JUDICIAL SYSTEM 228-267 (New York: Holt, Rinehart, and Winston, 1984); Abraham, THE JUDICIAL PROCESS 296-297 (New York: Oxford, 1980); Segal and Spaeth, *supra* n. 31, at 310-312, 320; Spaeth, *Burger Court Review of State Court Civil Liberties Decisions*, in Spaeth and Brenner, STUDIES IN U.S. SUPREME COURT BEHAVIOR (New York: Garland, 1990).

38. Marshall, *supra* n. 3, at 82-83.

39. Whether the decision was one of the three top problems in the Gallup Poll's "most important problem" was not significantly related to pro-rights outcomes; see Smith, *The Polls: America's Most Important Problems*, 49 PUBLIC OPINION Q. 264 (1985), and subsequent Gallup Polls.

40. Page, Shapiro, and Dempsey, *What Moves Public Opinion?*, 81 AM. POL. SCI. REV. 23 (1987); Marshall, *supra* n. 3; Bass and Thomas, *The Supreme Court and Policy Legitimation*, 12 AM. POL. Q. 335 (July 1984).

41. A probit equation estimates the probability of a (0,1) dichotomous outcome where the dependent and independent variable may not be related in a linear fashion. For a detailed explanation, see Aldrich and Nelson, LINEAR PROBABILITY, LOGIT, AND PROBIT MODELS (Beverly Hills, Calif.: Sage, 1984).

42. The "national mood" was not a significant predictor, either in the year-to-year version or when lagged either three or five years.

43. The differences are statistically significant at the .05 level. As Table 3 indicates, even when public opinion is quite hostile to a rights claim, the Court has a 79 percent probability of supporting that claim if there are seven Democrats on the Court. By contrast, if there are seven Republicans on the Court, the probability of supporting an equally unpopular rights claim falls to only 19 percent.

44. In this model, MLEs, standard errors and MLE/S.E., respectively, were: poll margin (.006, .004, and 1.64*); num-

ber of GOP justices (-.273, .138, and -1.97*), and solicitor general position (.394, .242, and 1.63*). The three-variable model correctly predicted 69 percent of the decisions. *Asterisked figures were significant at the .05 level.

45. In this two-predictor model, MLEs, standard errors, and MLE/S.E., respectively, were: poll margin (.007, .004, and 1.72*) and number of GOP justices (-.338, .132, and -2.56**). This model correctly predicted 68 percent of the decisions. *Asterisked figures were significant at the .05 level; ** at the .01 level.

A two-variable model with solicitor general position and the number of GOP justices was somewhat less successful—predicting only 64 percent of the decisions correctly.

46. Solicitor general position failed to significantly improve predictions over the two-variable model, in large part because the number of GOP justices was significantly correlated to solicitor general support for rights claims (r = .27). Public opinion, however, was uncorrelated with either solicitor general position or the Court's partisan makeup.

47. Public opinion is significant at the .05-level when entered alone in a probit equation (MLE = .007; S.E. = .004; MLE/SE = 1.75*; constant = .15 n.s.). *Asterisked figures were significant at the .05 level.

48. Segal and Spaeth, *supra* n. 31.

49. Epstein and Kobylka, *supra* n. 34.

50. Rehnquist, THE SUPREME COURT 98 (New York: William Morrow & Co., 1987).

51. For example, the presence of partisan unbalanced courts may counterbalance a one-sided public opinion. When the Court handed down pro-rights rulings despite strongly anti-rights polls, it typically had an above-average number of Democrats; *see, e.g.,* Abington School District v. Schempp (1963), Jones v. Mayer (1968), or Albertson v. Subversive Activities Control Board (1965). By contrast, when the Court handed down anti-rights rulings, despite strongly pro-rights polls, it typically had an above-average number of Republicans; *see, e.g.,* Penry v. Lynaugh (1989), NLRB v. Bildisco & Bildisco (1984), or Rust v. Sullivan (1991).

52. *See also* Sheehan, Mishler, and Songer, *supra* n. 30.

53. Rostow, *The Democratic Character of Judicial Review*, 66 HARV. L. REV. 195 (1952); Choper, JUDICIAL REVIEW AND THE NATIONAL POLITICAL PROCESS (Chicago: University of Chicago, 1980).

Public perception of the Supreme Court in the 1990s

The results of surveys conducted in 1994 and 1997 indicate the Court is doing a good job of finding and holding the middle ground, where its legitimacy is likely to be maximized.

by John M. Scheb II and William Lyons

Although the Supreme Court is ostensibly immune to the ebbs and flows of public opinion, most observers agree that it must enjoy a reasonable measure of public support or risk losing the legitimacy that undergirds its decisions. The question, then, is simple: How do the American people regard the Supreme Court? This question, using data from a national survey conducted during the winter of 1994, was addressed four years ago in *Judicature*.[1] A survey conducted during the fall of 1997 enables us to delve more deeply into the matter to see whether the public's perception of the Court has changed significantly and to explore further the contours of public opinion.[2]

As in 1994, respondents to the 1997 survey provided an overall rating of both the Supreme Court and Congress. Just as they did nearly four years earlier, Americans in late 1997 rendered a relatively positive assessment of the Court (see Table 1). In 1994, 45 percent said the Court's performance was "good" or "excellent." In 1997, 47 percent gave these responses. In 1994, 51 percent rated the Court's performance as "fair" or "poor." In 1997, 49 percent gave these ratings. Thus, attitudes toward the Court appear to be rather stable. If one considers the "excellent" and "good" ratings to be positive assessments of the Court and the "fair" and "poor" ratings to be negative assessments, then public attitudes toward the Court in the 1990s tilt slightly in the negative direction.

But to fairly evaluate the public's view of the Court, we need comparative data, which is why Congress was included in the surveys. Looking at the dismal ratings of Congress in both 1994 and 1997, the Court's ratings appear relatively positive. Clearly, the Court continues to fare much better in public opinion than does Congress.

As in 1994, respondents in 1997 were almost twice as likely to rate the Court's performance as 'good' or 'excellent' than they were to provide these positive ratings to Congress. By the same token, respondents in both 1994 and 1997 were more than twice as likely to rate Congress' performance as 'poor' than they were to render this most negative assessment of the Court. These data are certainly not unique; virtually all public opinion polls that compare confidence in Congress and the Court find the same phenomenon. The public continues to hold Congress in low esteem while it harbors a relatively positive view of the Court.

Court decision making

When asked about specific areas of Court decision making—civil rights, criminal justice, abortion, and school prayer—the public renders a more negative assessment (see Table 2). Not surprisingly, the percentage of "not sure" responses rises sharply when the questions become more specific and require greater attentiveness to the Court's output. Evidently, respondents who are inattentive to the Court's decisions in particular areas are more favorable to the Court generally. Only in the area of civil rights does the public's assessment of the Court's performance begin to approach its overall evaluation of the Court.

The Court's worst performance rating is on school prayer, where roughly 4 in 10 respondents in 1997 rated the Court "poor." Given the unpopularity of school prayer decisions going all the way back to the early 1960s, this is not surprising. The Court also is perceived poorly on abortion, where it has arguably tried to steer a middle course in recent years and thus has displeased people on both sides of this sharply divisive issue. On criminal justice, where the Court has been most consistently conservative over the last decade, the public's continuing fear of crime probably detracts somewhat from the public's assessment of the Court's work.

Variation in opinions

Conventional wisdom holds that the liberal activism of the Warren Court during the 1960s, especially in the criminal justice area, contributed to a decline in public confidence in the Court. When asked whether they agreed or disagreed with the statement that "The Supreme Court today is doing a better job than it did in the 1960s," half the respondents to the 1997 survey agreed, about a quarter disagreed, and about a quarter were not sure (see Table 3). Responses varied somewhat by age, with older respondents being slightly less likely to agree that the Court is doing a better job today. Not surprisingly, respondents who identified themselves as "liberals" were most likely to disagree with this proposition. Still, there appears to be a reasonable degree of consensus that the Court today, which is both more conservative and more given to judicial restraint than the Warren Court, is performing better.

How do opinions vary, if at all, across the lines that often divide Americans politically? In 1994, Democrats, Independents, and Republicans differed slightly in their overall assessments of the Court. In 1997 these differences appeared to be more pronounced, with Democrats seeming to render more favorable judgments than Republicans and Independents, but given the sample size the differences were not statistically significant (see Table 4). The Supreme Court can ill-afford to have its decisions second-guessed as expressions of partisan politics. One could well argue that given the controversial nature of its work, the Court is about as even-handedly regarded as it could hope to be. There is very little difference between the attitudes

Table 1 Performance ratings of Congress and the Supreme Court

	Congress 1994	Congress 1997	Supreme Court 1994	Supreme Court 1997
Excellent	2%	2%	4%	7%
Good	21	23	41	40
Fair	46	47	40	37
Poor	28	26	11	12
Not sure	3	2	5	4

Table 2 Supreme Court ratings in several areas of decision making, 1997

	Overall	Civil rights	Criminal justice	Abortion	School prayer
Excellent	7%	3%	4%	3%	3%
Good	40	32	28	20	19
Fair	37	36	32	30	30
Poor	12	17	25	35	41
Not sure	4	12	11	12	7

Table 3 "The Supreme Court today (1997) is doing a better job than it did in the 1960s."

	All	18-35	36-55	Over 55
Strongly disagree	4%	3%	3%	7%
Disagree	20	14	22	27
Agree	43	49	44	34
Strongly agree	7	6	8	8
Not sure	26	28	23	24

of Republicans and Democrats; about half of each group provide "excellent" or "good" ratings.

The results are rather different when ideology is considered. There is evidence in the surveys that the Court enjoys more support among liberals and moderates. In 1994 conservatives were twice as likely as moderates and liberals to render "poor" assessments of the Court. In 1997, the pattern was the same (see Table 5). Although the Court of the 1990s is clearly more conservative than the Warren Court or even the early Burger Court, conservatives probably object to the fact that many of the precedents from a more liberal era remain in effect. In the 1997 survey, conservatives rendered more negative assessments of the Court's work in the criminal justice and civil rights areas, and *much* more negative ratings in the school prayer and abortion areas.

Interestingly, no significant differences by ideology were found in the 1997 survey when support for the basic power of judicial review was measured. It is not that self-identified conservatives harbor some deep-seated populist aversion to the role and function of the Court. Rather, they seem to object to what they perceive to be the ideological tenor

Table 4 Supreme Court performance rating by party affiliation

	Democrats	1994 Independents	Republicans	Democrats	1997 Independents	Republicans
Excellent	4%	3%	4%	8%	8%	4%
Good	42	42	39	42	39	40
Fair	34	42	40	40	33	39
Poor	14	9	12	7	15	15
Not sure	5	4	5	3	5	2

Table 5 Supreme Court performance rating by ideology

	Liberals	1994 Moderates	Conservatives	Liberals	Moderates	1997 Conservatives
Excellent	4%	4%	3%	12%	7%	2%
Good	48	44	33	44	44	35
Fair	34	41	42	33	36	42
Poor	8	9	16	8	9	18
Not sure	6	3	6	3	4	3

Table 6 Supreme Court performance rating by race and gender

	Whites	1994 Non whites	Males	Females	Whites	Non whites	1997 Males	Females
Excellent	4%	2%	5%	2%	7%	6%	7%	7%
Good	41	38	40	41	41	37	41	39
Fair	40	37	40	39	36	43	35	40
Poor	10	18	11	12	13	10	14	10
Not sure	5	5	4	7	3	4	3	4

of the Court's output over the years.

There is no evidence that the Court is seen through a racially tinted lens. In 1994 nonwhites rendered more negative assessments of the Court, but the differences were not statistically significant. In 1997, there was even less evidence of racial differences in evaluations of the Court (see Table 6). There also does not appear to be a "gender gap" in the public's view of the Court. As in 1994, there were no significant gender differences in assessments of the Court in 1997 (Table 6).

Ideology and decision making

As observed in 1994, traditional views of the judicial role dictate that the ideology of the judge ought not to have an impact on that judge's decisions. Of course, numerous political scientists and legal commentators have argued that ideology is in fact a major determinant of judicial decision making. Most of the people who responded to the survey in 1994 said that the ideologies of the justices should not be a factor in Supreme Court decision making. This was generally true regardless of respondents' ideological orientations. Much the same thing was found in 1997, when 6 out of 10

respondents said that the ideologies of the justices should have no impact on the Court's decisions. Not surprisingly, moderates were more likely to take this position than either liberals or conservatives (see Table 7).

In 1994, respondents were closely divided between those who thought the Supreme Court was too liberal and those who thought it was too conservative (see Table 8). About 40 percent thought that the Court's ideological orientation was "about right." In 1997, there was a definite shift, with fewer Americans regarding the Court as "too conservative." This change seems to have taken place among those classifying themselves as liberals, 49

Table 7 "How much impact should ideology, that is whether the judges are liberals or conservatives, have on the Supreme Court's decisions?"

	All	Liberals	1997 Moderates	Conservatives
Not much	61%	53%	66%	57%
Somewhat	29	34	27	29
A lot	8	12	5	12
Not sure	2	1	2	2

Table 8 "Do you think that the current U.S. Supreme Court is too liberal, too conservative, or about right in its decisions?"

	1994				1997			
	All	Liberals	Moderates	Conservatives	All	Liberals	Moderates	Conservatives
Too liberal	26%	11%	20%	48%	28%	12%	21%	51%
About right	41	33	46	40	43	48	46	35
Too conservative	24	49	26	5	16	27	17	8
Not sure	8	8	8	7	13	13	16	6

percent of whom thought the Court was too conservative in 1994 as opposed to 27 percent in 1997. The Court may be approaching a realistically attainable "preferred position." Those of either ideological persuasion feel the Court leans too far in the other direction, while those in the middle tend to think the Court is where it should be.

*****

Both the 1994 and 1997 surveys demonstrated that the public holds the Supreme Court in substantially higher regard than the Congress, although the public's high regard for the Court appears to break down somewhat in the context of specific, controversial areas of decision making. Moreover, assessments of the Court do not appear to vary substantially across the race, gender, and party lines that often divide Americans. Thus, the Court appears to be doing a good job of finding and holding the middle ground, where its legitimacy is likely to be maximized.

NOTES

This article originally appeared in Volume 82, Number 2, September-October 1998, pages 66-69.

1. Lyons and Scheb, *Public holds U.S. Supreme Court in high regard*, 77 JUDICATURE 273 (March-April 1994).

2 The survey was conducted October 6-16, 1997 by the Social Science Research Institute at the University of Tennessee, Knoxville. 658 randomly selected adults were interviewed by telephone using a computer-assisted telephone interviewing (CATI) system. The margin of error is +/- 4 percentage points at the 95 percent confidence level. The response rate, defined as number of completed interviews as a proportion of contacts with eligible subjects, was 50.7 percent.

Public outreach: The cornerstone of judicial independence

The ability of courts to act as independent decision makers depends on maintaining public confidence through involvement in the community.

by Kevin M. Esterling

Judicial independence is an essential component of constitutional government and the separation of powers. A politically independent judiciary serves as an important check and counterweight to the political branches and majority opinion. Courts, in turn, depend on citizen support to perform their constitutional function as independent interpreters of the law. As Alexander Hamilton wrote in *The Federalist #78*, courts "have neither Force nor Will, but merely judgement." If the public does not have confidence in courts' judgment, then their legitimacy and influence as democratic institutions are endangered.

The public gets much of its information about courts secondhand, mostly from the mass media and through the political process. And courts can find themselves vulnerable to the representations these outsiders give to the public. A recent American Judicature Society survey of state and federal judges in the Midwest demonstrates the difficulties for courts in relying on third parties to represent their functioning to the public, and that these dilemmas are becoming more pronounced over time. These findings suggest that judges' isolation from politics and society is increasingly insufficient to maintain judicial independence. Contrary to the traditional view of judicial independence, in contemporary society the ability of courts to act as *independent* decision makers depends on their *involvement* in local communities through various public outreach efforts.

The traditional view is that the courts' institutional legitimacy arises from decision-making fairness, a result of political independence and due

process. This view was articulated, for example, in a 1986 article in *Justice System Journal*, which stated, "when individual judges render decisions fairly, responsively, and competently, the courts as an institution will presumably enjoy the respect and goodwill of the citizens." This view, however, overlooks the vulnerability of courts to media sensationalism, political campaigns against judges, and issue-oriented attacks on the outcomes of judicial decisions, all of which can impair citizens' willingness to accept judicial decisions.

Criticism of judicial practices is not only a First Amendment right, it also provides judges with important feedback for improving their decision making, at minimum reminding judges that they are public servants. But as legal scholar Stephen Bright notes, irresponsible critics will occasionally frame their message in a way inappropriate to courts' role. Irresponsible critics may focus on the outcome of a decision without regard for the facts or legal reasoning underlying the decision, or single out one among many decisions a judge has made over a career.

Such critical attacks on courts appear to be on the rise. Judges, however, have limited means to respond to public criticism or to clarify the reasoning or a point of law underlying a decision, principally because of ethical restrictions on judicial speech. When a judge is constrained from responding to a public critique or attack on a judicial process or decision, the public often has no countervailing information to evaluate the persuasiveness or veracity of the message. As in any exchange of ideas, the truth of a criticism is exposed only when the audience is able to weigh a response.

Because judges have a difficult time responding publicly to criticism, their isolation from society is increasingly insufficient for maintaining their courts' legitimacy. Organized public outreach efforts instead represent the best institutional response to issue-oriented attacks on judicial decisions, inaccurate or incomplete media reporting, and citizen disenchantment, frustration, or skepticism.

Public outreach programs can benefit courts in several ways. These programs help to educate citizens about courts' role in government, which may help citizens to evaluate criticism of judges as it occurs. In addition, these programs provide a means for courts to remain in touch with, and be more responsive to, the more enduring norms of fairness and justice in the local community, as well as citizens' perceptions of the effectiveness of the local administration of justice.

Conflicting perspectives

This emphasis on public outreach is related to, but often is outside of, most debates over judicial independence. For example, many observers of courts suggest that judges can promote independence by isolating themselves from politics and the community. Several judges' remarks in the AJS survey reflect this view. One judge wrote that the greatest threat to judicial independence is the "politicization of the judiciary," especially due to judicial elections at the state level. According to another judge, the high-visibility interest group campaign in 1996 against former Tennessee Supreme Court Justice Penny White "proves that retention elections are not the sole answer" to judicial independence at the state level.

In response, other commentators voice strong democratic concerns over judicial retreats to isolation since this make judges less responsive. They object to unaccountable judges deciding underlying political or policy issues as constitutional or purely legal matters. This view is reflected in the remarks from several judges in the survey who identified the greatest threat to judicial independence as the judiciary itself. One judge wrote that

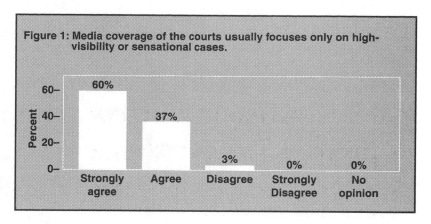

Figure 1: Media coverage of the courts usually focuses only on high-visibility or sensational cases.

the greatest threats to courts are

Judges who exceed their role as interpreters of the law and substitute their own policy views for those of our elected officials. All of the other sources of threats...are reactions to perceived judicial excesses and, unfortunately, judges too often give the media and the politicians the excuse they need to attack judges.

Another judge wrote in response to a survey question that the greatest threat to judicial independence is "Judgeitis; arrogance, unaccountability...."

These conflicting perspectives on judicial independence, focusing either on the importance of judicial autonomy or accountability, reflect an inevitable tension for courts in a democratic society. The democratic instinct demands both that government officials be responsive to citizens' preferences, and that the government not infringe on the rights of individuals irrespective of the popular opinion of the day. These two expectations appear in many ways contradictory, and courts often find themselves caught in between.

A middle ground to this debate holds that judicial public outreach programs aimed at maintaining the public's confidence in the courts can promote both independent and responsive judicial decision making. Public outreach programs promote judicial independence when they enable citizens to evaluate critical attacks on judges as they occur. These programs also promote judicial responsiveness to the extent they help judges know local social values and perceptions on the effective administration of justice.

In this vein, a plurality of the judges in the survey state that the problem of the independence of the courts lies in the level of public discourse on courts and the law in contemporary society. One judge wrote,

We are living in a time in which many people decide major issues (including who to vote for) based upon sound bites: 'soft on crime,' 'anti-teacher,' 'anti-family,' 'pro-traditional values.' Politicians and the media buy into that method of communication with the public. There is little public discussion of the legal process in judicial decision making.

The media, politicians, and interest groups at times serve to elevate public dialogue on courts and the judicial process. Judges' responses to the survey show, however, that the media and political actors do not reliably represent court processes and judicial decision making to the public. Relying exclusively on these third parties is a particular concern for courts since judges have a difficult time responding publicly to criticism. In contrast, reaching out to the public can benefit courts as institutions in many perhaps unforeseen ways.

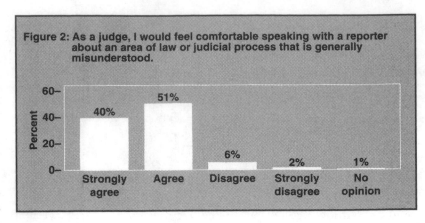

Figure 2: As a judge, I would feel comfortable speaking with a reporter about an area of law or judicial process that is generally misunderstood.

Responding to the media

Although citizens get much of their information about government from the press and other mass media, Midwest judges take a pretty dim view of how the mass media reports on courts. Ninety-seven percent of respondents to the AJS survey feel that media coverage of courts focuses on sensational or high-visibility cases. Amazingly, none of the respondents strongly disagreed with this statement or had no opinion (see Figure 1). A majority of judges who had an opinion on the matter feel that the national media's coverage of courts is not accurate, while only a bare majority feel that their local media's coverage of courts is relatively accurate.

Nearly all judges in the survey, 91 percent, indicated that they would be comfortable speaking to a reporter about an area of law or judicial process that is commonly misunderstood (exclusive of commenting on active cases) (see Figure 2). As a practical matter, however, judges are not very effective at communicating with the media. Professor Robert Drechsel, writing in *Judicature*, has shown that judges often do not have an established policy for how to approach the media. And, as Professor Doris Graber wrote in her book *Mass Media and American Politics* "Judges infrequently grant in-

terviews, almost never hold news conferences, and generally do not seek or welcome media attention, primarily because they fear their impartiality might be compromised." This judicial isolation can adversely affect even the most responsible reporting. U.S. Court of Appeals Judge Bruce Selya argues that courts "impede the development of a more responsible press by turning their backs on the media."

Responding to political actors

The political process also produces information for citizens on how courts function, through such activities as election campaigns, legislative debate, and interest group grassroots efforts. The survey results show, however, that judges perceive a considerable amount of political criticism of the judiciary. Seventy-three percent of responding judges report observing what they feel are political attacks on the judiciary in their state or jurisdiction in recent years (see Figure 3). (There is no way to know if the criticisms the respondents are reporting are in fact fair or unfair, since the survey does not explicitly define what counts as an issue-oriented or political "attack" on judges. The reader should bear in mind that some judges may feel that any public statement about their work is an "attack" on their court.) Courts need to be concerned about public criticism, irrespective of the nature or relative merits of the message, to the extent judges are unable to respond to or rebut the criticism.

More than half of the judges responding to the survey (52 percent) had themselves been publicly criticized in the past five years. Most of the first-hand criticisms that judges reported were sparked by criminal cases. Other types of cases that prompted public comment involved hot-button issues such as abortion, civil rights, death penalty, domestic violence, adoption, and relations with local Indian tribes. Some judges experienced public criticism as well for governmental process and constitutional issues, such as term limits, legislative and judicial redistricting, and religion in public life. Federal judges mention in particular labor, bankruptcy, and organized crime rulings as ones that sparked public criticism.

Ethical as well as some pragmatic concerns, however, will limit the extent to which a judge will be able to respond publicly to unfair or inaccurate criticism, or to some form of issue-oriented public attack. Of the 88 judges in the survey who had been recently and publicly criticized, only 9 percent responded to the criticism in some way. The most common reason judges gave for not responding was concern over violating the Code of Judicial Conduct or a feeling that it is not appropriate for, or is beneath the dignity of, judges to respond to criticism (40 percent mentioned this).

Other judges report that they did not respond to public criticism because they felt that the criticism did not warrant a response, that a response would have no effect, or would prolong the attack (38 percent mentioned one of these reasons). With respect to the media, one judge cautioned: "Don't argue with anyone who buys ink by the barrel"; another mentioned that "the media always gets the last word." On the effectiveness of responding to political actors, one judge wrote that politically-oriented attackers often do not "wish to understand the opinion and simply do not agree with it. They are entitled to their position." (Other reasons judges give for not responding to an attack are: no institutional mechanism for responding, respect for the democratic rights of citizens to complain about the government, or that the case was still pending.)

Few of these judges even attempted to respond to a public attack (7 out of 88), and only two of them felt that their response effectively countered the criticism. Those who did respond tried to speak directly to the attacking group to help them understand the legal reasoning behind their decisions, some wrote to the local newspaper, and one judge responded by making speeches on judicial independence to bar and citizens groups.

Very few of the judges who were publicly criticized report that others spoke on their behalf, and

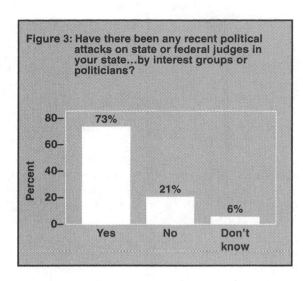

Figure 3: Have there been any recent political attacks on state or federal judges in your state...by interest groups or politicians?

most of those speaking up were attorneys. One judge gives an illustration: "I was up for retention...and two weeks before the election, a PAC of the local police union, led by one officer I had taken to task, sent out 50,000 fliers and stood on street corners with signs." In response, "friends and lawyers raised $20,000 in two days for radio spots and ads." In the survey, however, only one judge reported that a citizen spoke on his or her behalf, only one judge reported a politician doing so, and only two mentioned the media speaking in support.

A skeptical public

Unanswered public criticism of judges may diminish the public's confidence in courts. Of those judges responding in the survey that knew of issue-oriented attacks on judges, 81 percent felt that these attacks did serious harm to the public's opinion of the judiciary (see Figure 4). The vast majority of judges responding to the survey feel that citizens are not aware of ethical constraints that prohibit judges from commenting on active cases (85 percent), or of the mechanisms in place for enforcing standards of judicial conduct (84 percent).

In addition, a large majority of responding judges, 87 percent, either agree or strongly agree with the statement that they are under increasing pressure to be directly accountable to public opinion (see Figure 5). Public pressure can affect the independent decision making not only of elected state judges, but even of the life-tenured federal judiciary. Professor Gerald Rosenberg, for instance, in his 1992 *Review of Politics* article titled

"Judicial Independence and the Reality of Political Power," shows how anti-court national election campaigns historically have constrained the U.S. Supreme Court's judicial discretion. This is a concern because the role of judges in our government is to decide cases based on existing law and individual rights rather than the prevailing opinion of the day.

These statistics suggest a relatively bleak picture for courts. Judges feel that they are under pressure to be accountable to public opinion, and they perceive that public and issue-oriented criticism of judicial decisions are harming the public's confidence in courts. More and more, courts are feeling pressure from an increasingly skeptical public.

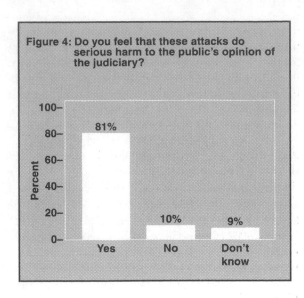

Figure 4: Do you feel that these attacks do serious harm to the public's opinion of the judiciary?

Public outreach efforts

The survey results underscore the need for courts and judges to engage in their own public outreach efforts. The vast majority of the responding judges (84 percent) feel that courts should devote more resources to public relations. One judge wrote that courts need to "educate the public concerning the functions and purposes of the judicial branch of government and how these functions and purposes differ from the legislative and executive branches."

When courts come to rely on third parties to represent their workings to the public, they have few means to respond to criticisms as they arise. When citizens better understand the role of the judicial branch, they are more likely to put criticisms in proper perspective. The earlier-mentioned article in *Justice System Journal*, for example, found that "the more attentive and knowledgeable the public becomes, the more they are able to balance the competing demands of [judicial] independence and accountability." Public outreach efforts give courts the opportunity to explain their role outside of the context of an attack on a specific decision or of a contested election, and in addition help courts remain in touch with local social values.

At the AJS Midwest Conference on State-Federal Judicial Relationships, held in the fall of 1997, judges and court staff from 13 Midwest states endorsed the need for improved public outreach efforts and issued policy recommendations for promoting an independent judiciary. Each delegation listed improved media relations and public outreach as top priorities for courts in their state, and most made public outreach the top recommendation.

Media relations. A recent Federal Judicial Center publication states that "Judicial leadership at both the state and federal level now recognize that improved public relations skills are critical for the courts to maintain a high level of public confidence." Courts are increasingly using public relations specialists, often called public information officers, to help educate reporters and editors about the courts. These officers not only respond to press inquiries, they also can develop consumer information packets and provide training for judges and court staff on how to communicate with the media. In addition, bench-bar-media committees help improve courts' relations with the media. They not only enable judges and reporters to exchange information and views outside of the context of a controversial case or disputed decision, they also give judges and reporters an opportunity to develop guidelines for covering legal matters. These committees in addition provide a forum for resolving "fair trial, free press" disputes as they arise. One of the delegations at the AJS Midwest Conference made recommendations to "establish a program of continuing legal education for the press, designate a media contact in each court (e.g. presiding or chief judge), and communicate standards of reporting on courts and the legal process to editors."

Reaching out to the public. Many court systems have established programs that directly reach out to educate the public. The Wisconsin state court system, which has a variety of public and educational outreach programs, notes in an informational brochure for the public that its efforts "are built on the notion that the courts need to work every day to strengthen their relationship with the communities they serve." Some of these programs, such as the traveling courtroom, classroom programs, and the Supreme Court's web page, seek to educate the public and provide information on how courts work. This information helps give citizens perspective when, for example, they hear criticism that focuses on the outcome rather than the substance of a particular judicial decision.

When courts reach out to the community to better involve citizens in their judicial system, they are doing more than simply educating citizens about what courts do. Public outreach efforts also give courts continuing contact with their community, and this helps them learn the community's enduring norms, standards, and perceptions of fairness. To be in contact with the community helps judges to bring a community perspective to their basic approach to decision making. Jack Weinstein, a senior federal trial judge in New York, argued in a 1994 *Judicature* article that judges should balance judicial restraints on speaking against their ethical obligations to participate in the community and to speak on judicial matters. In this spirit, one Midwest Conference delegation suggested that: "state and federal courts should take the responsibility to educate the general public about the court system, by including them in...programs, and through speaking engagements and explanatory remarks in opinions and the daily work of the courts."

Public "inreach" programs, such as volunteer programs or legislative relation programs, are a particularly effective way to bring judges and court personnel into direct contact with citizens in the community. These efforts enable judges to inform their general decision making in light of local values, and can help generate feedback that enables courts to find ways to better serve the public in their policies, procedures, and the organization of facilities. As one conference delegation wrote, "Opening a two-way communication between citizens and courts can result in a win-win situation for all. The public will perceive the courts as more accessible and courts may receive information which could cause them to re-examine and improve the way they do business."

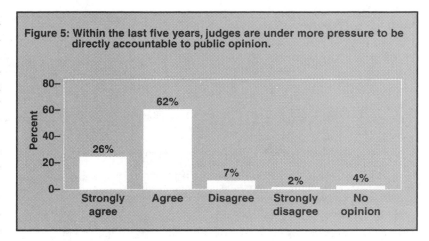

Figure 5: Within the last five years, judges are under more pressure to be directly accountable to public opinion.

Outreach and independence

The debate between judicial independence and accountability—that independence and accountability are at odds or involve a tradeoff between fairness and responsiveness—is a product of an implicit assumption that judicial independence simply follows from judicial isolation from the community. Both sides in this debate assume that independence comes at the cost of courts' responsiveness to the local community. Judges reinforce this image in interpreting the judicial speech components of the Code of Judicial Conduct to mean that judges should not speak publicly, should shun the media, and should not actively seek advice and input from lay citizens.

The apparent tension between judicial independence and accountability implies a circular institutional logic. Courts' legitimacy rests on their independence and fairness in applying law to facts, since following majority sentiment is to predetermine the outcome in individual cases. At the same time, simply asserting the importance of judicial independence in response to a specific criticism rings hollow given democratic expectations for accountability. Judicial independence itself is vulnerable to the claim that judges are "out of touch." The problem of public criticism of courts exposes this circularity—that judicial independence rests on judicial legitimacy and vice versa—and implies that courts' best institutional response is to pro-

mote both responsiveness and independence simultaneously through greater involvement in the
community, and through public education and
outreach efforts.

NOTE

This article originally appeared in Volume 82, Number 3,
November-December 1998, pages 112-118. It is based on JUDI-
CIAL INDEPENDENCE, PUBLIC CONFIDENCE IN COURTS, AND STATE-FED-
ERAL COOPERATION IN THE MIDWEST: A RESEARCH REPORT ON THE
MIDWEST REGIONAL CONFERENCE ON STATE-FEDERAL JUDICIAL RELA-
TIONSHIPS, which was published by the American Judicature
Society under a grant from the State Justice Institute (#SJI-97-
20J-E-021). The State Justice Institute bears no responsibility
for the results, analysis, or interpretations.

The Courts and Their Publics
Courts, Congress, and the Presidency

INTRODUCTION

We have already seen that the judicial recruitment process is the most public setting for the carrying out of the relationship between the courts, Congress, and the presidency. Additional perspectives on that interface are offered in the first three articles in this section of readings. It is useful to recognize, however, that there are many other matters that have importance to the courts and other institutions of American government in tandem. Thus, for example, judicial decisions based on constitutional or statutory interpretation may be the start of a continuing and heated substantive dialogue between the Court and Congress that is marked by additional legislation, public posturing by legislators and, perhaps, additional decisions by courts. In the areas of greatest controversy, Congress may even initiate measures under its constitutionally-defined jurisdictional powers to alter the nature of the cases that federal courts can hear. Matters such as these are the subject of the two final selections in this section of readings.

In "The Senate's confirmation role in Supreme Court nominations and the politics of ideology versus impartiality," Albert Melone offers a historically driven account of the confirmation process, taking the position that it is perfectly legitimate for senators to ask questions of judicial nominees that explore the nominees' ideological preferences. Such questioning, according to Melone, has considerable historical precedent and, further, was envisioned by the Constitution's framers. Melone concludes that, "In brief, senators should have a good idea about how future judges and justices will behave." Wm. Bradford Reynolds, an assistant attorney general during the Reagan years who played a central role in judicial selection processes, takes issue with and responds to Melone's analysis in "The confirmation process: too much advice and too little consent." Reynolds sees the Senate's advice and consent role as a much more constrained one than does Melone, claiming that, "The argument fashioned by Professor Melone and his like-minded academic colleagues is but an intellectual fig leaf for the senators to hide behind," a somewhat ironic comment from an individual who participated in judicial selection processes during a presidential administration most often critiqued for the utilization of an ideological litmus test in the vetting of candidates for the federal bench.

The most public manifestation of senatorial behavior regarding advice and consent, particularly in Supreme Court confirmation processes, takes place in the setting of public Senate hearings. In "Supreme Court confirmation hearings: a view from the Senate," George Watson and John Stookey offer a broad view of the functions of such hearings and stress that even those that lack great controversy warrant public interest and attention. Based on interview data and the public records of the confirmation hearings of Justice Sandra Day O'Connor, Chief Justice William Rehnquist, and Justice Antonin Scalia, the authors demonstrate that senators pursue numerous roles (evaluator, validator, partisan, educator, and advertiser) in both controversial and noncontroversial hearings, although different roles predominate in different settings. In an addendum on the Bork nomination's confirmation process, Watson and Stookey develop and illustrate a model of Senate hearings based on their degree of situational and nominee controversy that helps to "make sense" out of the outcomes of the Bork and other nomination battles.

Kenneth Kay's exploration of "Limiting federal court jurisdiction: the unforeseen impact on courts and Congress," documents the increasing tendency for members of Congress to react to their unhappiness with judicial rulings by initiating efforts to alter the Court's jurisdiction so as to remove its ability to hear future cases in the offending area of legal development. Kay contends that, too often, such action has been "an emotional response to a particular decision of the Supreme Court," rather than a considered judgment of the larger impact of withdrawing jurisdiction from the Court. For one thing, jurisdictional removal "freezes" the very decision Congress may be reacting against, possibly giving the Court the "last word." More broadly, in addition to raising vexing constitutional questions about Congress' powers, jurisdictional removal threatens judicial independence and the separation of powers. From the perspective of Congress, the public's perception of the jurisdictional weapon could make the halls of the legislature a haven for those unhappy with any and every judicial ruling. Kay concludes that ample protections exist in several facets of our governmental system that offer protection against judicial tyranny without the necessity of removing the Court's jurisdiction. It is clear, however, that for the foreseeable future, congressional power over the Court's jurisdiction will remain an important subject of controversy in any discussion of the proper scope of judicial power.

We conclude this section with an edited panel discussion, "Perspectives on court-Congress relations: the view from the Hill and the federal bench." The panelists, including experts who have made their mark in academia, on the bench, and in legislative settings, comment on and debate multiple facets of the interface between courts and legislatures.

The Senate's confirmation role in Supreme Court nominations and the politics of ideology versus impartiality

Nothing in the Constitution, historical experience, political practice, ethical norms, or statutory enactments prohibits senators from asking questions that reveal judicial nominees' views on political and ideological issues.

by Albert P. Melone

Controversy surrounds the appropriate role of the United States Senate in exercising its constitutional responsibility of advice and consent. Conservative thinkers and propagandists, right-wing politicians, and others question whether the Senate should rightly concern itself with anything more than the professional qualifications of judicial nominees. The Senate's rejection of Judge Robert Bork's nomination to the Supreme Court is touted as a particularly egregious example of the Senate exceeding its constitutional responsibility.[1] Senator Orrin Hatch of Utah termed the Bork hearing an "...ideological inquisition."[2] Iowa's Senator Charles Grassley charged that Bork's critics "...prefer judges who will act as some kind of super legislature who will give them victories in the courts when they lose in the legislature."[3] Senator Gordon Humphrey of New Hampshire said that the charges against Bork are "pure political poppycock, 99.9 percent pure, so pure it floats."[4]

Nominees are not passive targets of ideological interrogation. They often refuse to answer questions designed to illicit answers about their judicial attitudes. They do so by appealing to the often misunderstood but powerful norm of judicial impartiality. They state that if they reveal their attitudes today about a case that may come before them tomorrow as sitting jurists they will be unable to participate fairly in decision making. Disqualification and recusation is the only honorable

course in such a situation, so goes the refrain. Silence, it is believed, is a better course than failing to decide at all.[5]

It is my view that senators may reasonably inquire into and base their final decision to confirm or reject presidential choices on factors other than the nominees' personal and professional qualifications. Senators may legitimately ask nominees about their political and judicial ideology as it may manifest itself in judicial decision making. I base this conclusion upon an analysis of three related factors.

First, the constitutional framers did not intend the Senate to be a rubber stamp for presidential appointments. The advice and consent clause of the Constitution justifies an independent scrutiny of nominees by members of the Senate.

Second, the historical record reveals that from the beginning of the Republic the Senate has rejected nominees for reasons other than personal and professional qualifications. In one fashion or another, political considerations, including evaluations of the ideological soundness of nominees, influence Senate advice and consent decisions.

Finally, I will clarify the claim that nominees should not give answers to questions that may bring into question their impartiality. Nominees may conduct themselves before Senate hearing panels with honor and probity while at the same time providing vital political information. Properly understood, statutory and ethical norms do not prohibit nominees from revealing their views on the great issues of the day.

The meaning of advice and consent

The plain words of the Constitution suggest that the framers contemplated a sharing of responsibility between the executive and legislative branches. Yet a striking feature of this sharing arrangement is the placement of the appointment and confirmation functions in Article II—the executive article—not Article I—the legislative article. Section 2 of Article II provides that the president shall have the power to nominate by and with the consent of the Senate. Clearly, the president may select the persons he or she wants to nominate. The Senate may advise the chief executive on the initial selection, but it may not select particular nominees. Through its consent function, the Senate has the power to accept or reject presidential choices. Therefore, it is erroneous to conclude, as Richard Nixon once did, that the president may name whomever he pleases without senatorial checks.[6] Indeed, a literal interpretation of the Constitution does not indicate any boundaries for senatorial consent. The Constitution's plain words do not prescribe or dictate justification for confirming or rejecting nominees. Moreover, because the Constitution is a document limiting the use of power that derives its authority from the consent of the governed, and since the advice and consent provision of Article II does not impose any limit to its discretion, it is fair to conclude that the Senate may use its constitutional authority as it sees fit. It may do so for whatever reason, be it professional qualifications, personal integrity, or political and ideological considerations.

Investigating beyond literal interpretation to the framers' probable intent reinforces the shared responsibility view. However, historical evidence introduces ambiguity otherwise not present with the more simplistic literalism approach.

The records of the Philadelphia Convention reveal that the shared responsibility feature of the nomination process was the result of compromise,[7] as is the explanation for many other constitutional provisions.[8] Choices presented by the competing Virginia and New Jersey plans framed many of the debates held in Philadelphia. The original Virginia Plan, the basic proposal supported by the large states, sought to locate the appointment of judges in the two legislative chambers. On at least two occasions, however, James Madison expressed the fear that members of the more numerous branch would be ill-suited to evaluate prospective judges. He thought they might select judicial candidates for the poor reason that they were particularly talented legislators or because the aspirants had assisted ignorant legislative members in their own businesses or those of their constituents. On the other hand, the Senate, being an unelected body and therefore a more select group of persons, would be better qualified to evaluate the abilities of candidates with a higher regard for qualifications.[9] William Paterson, the author of the small state plan called the New Jersey Plan, and James Wilson argued for appointment by the executive alone.[10]

Alexander Hamilton informally suggested what finally emerged as the convention's final recommendation, and the one ultimately ratified by the states. In their initial voting, convention delegates rejected both the plan granting advice and consent to the Senate and a proposal to place the appointing authority in the president alone. Instead, what survived until the final days of the convention was a provision granting the appointing power to the Senate alone. Then, finally, in the last days of the convention, there emerged from the Committee of Eleven the present system: nomination by the president, and advice and consent of the Senate.[11]

As is often the case when attempting to identify the framers' original intention, the precise reasons for the compromise are unknown. However, James E. Gauch, the author of a recent and carefully conducted study, reasonably concludes that the framers were concerned with three related issues: the ability to evaluate potential nominee qualifications; the matter of corruption and intrigue in the nomination process; and finally the matter of small versus large state interests.[12] The import of Gauch's finding is that the framers' concerns went beyond good character and professional qualifications of future judicial office-holders. In one form or another, politics entered their thinking.

Analyzing the ratification debates adds somewhat to our total understanding of the framers' intent. But reading too much into a few paragraphs may result in overstating the case. Alexander Hamilton's *The Federalist* 66 and 76 are the authoritative source for evidence of the framers' intent as expressed during the ratification debate.[13]

Without question, Hamilton reinforces a plain meaning interpretation of the advice and consent provision. To that end, the Senate's role is properly confined to the confirmation or rejection of presidential nominees. *The Federalist* 66 reads:[14]

> There will, of course, be no exertion of choice on the part of the Senate. They may defeat one choice of the Executive and oblige him to make another; but they cannot themselves choose—they can only ratify or reject the choice of the President.

The Senate, then, is a major player in the selection drama. However, the chief executive plays a leading role because he or she is in the position of submitting the names of only those persons thought desirable. For what reason then require senatorial consent? Hamilton's answer is instructive. He writes:

> I answer, that the necessity of their concurrence would have a powerful, though, in general a silent operation. It would be an excellent check upon the spirit or favoritism in the President, and would tend greatly to prevent the appointment of unfit characters from state prejudice, from family connection, from personal attachment or from a view to popularity.[15]

Thus, at the very least, the Senate must act as a check against a president who might appoint persons of unfit character. Further, the Senate is in a position to embarrass a chief executive for such attempts. The Senate's institutional leverage will deter presidents from such conduct. Hamilton makes this point by writing:

> ...It will readily be comprehended, that a man who had himself the sole disposition of offices, would be governed much more by his private inclinations and interests than when he was bound to submit the propriety of his choice to the discussion and determination or a different and independent body....[16]

Wrong reasons

Hamilton contributes two major points to our understanding. First, he reinforces the literal understanding of the advice and consent clause; namely, the appointment power is a shared responsibility between the president and the Senate. Second, upper house concurrence is a requisite because the chief executive might otherwise appoint persons for the wrong reasons. Hamilton indicates four wrong reasons for appointment. These are: the appointment of unfit characters "from state prejudice," "from family connection," "from per-

sonal attachment," or "from a view to popularity." Do these four justifications for senatorial denial of presidential choices pertain to ideological tests for office? The probable answer is yes.

First and paramount, Hamilton's words commit senators to inquire beyond personal and professional qualifications. It requires the Senate to ascertain whether nominees are associated with the president in any of the four ways. If they are, it does not necessarily mean that the nominees are unqualified to serve. It means that the relationship between the president and the nominees bears scrutiny.

Second, each of the four points have ideological elements. In the context of the eighteenth century, "state prejudice" meant more than good will toward one's neighbors. It also signified common points of view or shared consciousness about the political order. Carolinians two centuries ago, as they do even today, had a different perspective on political events than, for example, do New Yorkers. Indeed, these differences, that are easily describable as ideological, were a source of political disagreement current at the Philadelphia Convention. Appointing persons "from family connection" and "from personal attachment" likewise have ideological dimensions. Conventional wisdom and modern social science informs us that the family is a strong socializing agent, inculcating attitudes and beliefs including those concerning politics.[17] Further, persons often choose friends who share basic values and attitudes. Finally, appointing persons "from a view to popularity" reasonably entails situations wherein presidents appoint persons meeting with popular approval. Persons with ideological views consistent with those of either elite decision-making bodies, such as the Senate or wider publics, are likely to be popular. The president may then be applauded for his outstanding choices, thereby increasing the value of his political currency.

Third, by his words Hamilton does not exclude any of the four unacceptable reasons as factors in a president's or senator's nomination or a confirmation calculation. He objects to persons named to the judiciary who have "*no other merit than...*coming from the same State...or being in some way or other personally allied to him, or of possessing the necessary insignificance and pliancy to render them the obsequious instruments of his pleasure."[18] It is perfectly acceptable, therefore, for a president to nominate an individual of personal and professional qualifications who also comes from a preferable state or region, has family connections, is well-liked by the president, and enjoys widespread popularity.

It is conceivable and probable that each of the four reasons for Senate concern contain non-ideological components. However, understood within the context of the time, Hamilton's words leave little doubt that ideology as a belief system, and as reflected in one's character, renders legitimate Senate inquiries into matters other than narrowly conceived personal and professional qualifications.

James E. Gauch suggests that Hamilton's reference to the Senate having a responsibility to explore the "propriety" of executive choices commits senators to look beyond the professional and personal qualifications of the nominees.[19] However, it is unclear to me that Hamilton uses the word "propriety" to mean anything more than a summary term for the four unacceptable reasons for solely nominating persons to the bench: cronyism, family connections, favoring one state over others, or responding to the popular will regardless of qualifications. If this is true, then the word "propriety" is a redundancy and little more than a convenient use of language.

The search for intention is an interesting exercise. Although others have come to conclusions different from the one found here, the weight of the evidence tends to justify Senate inquiries into nominees' ideology. However, the search for original intention in this case does not render other interpretations incorrect. There is no evidence that the framers explicitly debated in the eighteenth century what is today a central concern. Unless an issue is explicitly discussed and a record of that debate is available, what the framers really intended remains a matter of intellectual speculation and curiosity.

I suspect there was no full debate and discussion of the appropriate reasons for rejecting nominees, including an explicit analysis of the proper place for ideological inquiries, because it did not occur to the framers that future judges and justices would be asked to perform anything more than traditional judicial tasks. Surely the framers did not anticipate the considerable institutional authority courts now enjoy. There is considerable doubt the framers envisaged courts with the power to strike down acts of Congress: statutes and ad-

ministrative acts unrelated to the jurisdiction of the Supreme Court.[20] They could not have imagined an institution as central to the American political system as the contemporary Supreme Court has become.

However, given the framers' clear preference for checks on power, and the institutional importance played by the judiciary today, it seems reasonable that they would consider, as do many contemporary senators, the ideology of unelected and unaccountable lawmakers as appropriate objects of inquiry by a popularly elected body. Senators must respond to the constitutional facts of life as they find them. The living constitution requires the responsible evaluation of potential judicial lawmakers whose eighteenth-century counterparts enjoyed a different kind of status.

Nominee bashing: the historical record

An examination of past Senate practices reveals the considerable extent to which judicial nominees are evaluated on political and ideological grounds. Otherwise well-qualified persons are rejected for a variety of political reasons. Further, contrary to the supposition of some commentators,[21] nominations preceding the 1987 Robert Bork debacle were marked by questions and speculations concerning the ideological fitness of presidential nominees. Judge Bork's case is dramatic because the nominee himself was more than willing to enter into intellectual discourse, thereby revealing his controversial policy inclinations. The existing literature contains several different classification schemes defining the various reasons judicial nominees are rejected by the Senate. Depending upon the purpose, the adoption of one scheme over another can be important. What is pertinent to note, however, is that all the schemes point out that past nominees were evaluated on political grounds unrelated to professional qualifications.[22]

During the first decade after the adoption of the 1789 Constitution, the Senate rejected a person for reasons unrelated to professional competence. An extremely well-qualified justice of the South Carolina Supreme Court was rejected because he angered powerful Federalist politicians with his vigorous denunciation of the controversial Jay Treaty.[23] Most Federalists viewed support for the treaty as a true indicator of party loyalty, while Republicans thought the treaty an unnecessary concession to British might. The vote to reject John Rutledge was 14 to 10; it was a party vote with 13 Federalists voting against, and only three voting for confirmation. The remaining votes to confirm came from Anti-Federalists.[24] The Rutledge episode is an early example of how politicians mask their real political reasons for opposing candidates by attacking nominees' personal and professional qualifications. Historians point out that Rutledge was attacked falsely as mentally unsound, and therefore unfit for Supreme Court service. The Federalist press employed this malicious tactic rather than stating the true reason for Federalist opposition. They realized that the Jay Treaty was so unpopular that to publicly attack Rutledge for his opposition to it would cause a political backfire.[25]

There are many other examples of nominee-bashing for reasons unrelated to professional competence. The Senate defeat of President James Madison's nomination of Alexander Wolcott was due in large part to the nominee's opposition to the enforcement of embargo and intercourse acts when he was U.S. collector of customs in Connecticut. Federalist senators and the press opposed him for this reason, although, in fairness, there were authentic questions raised about Wolcott's judicial qualifications.[26] An otherwise well-qualified Grant appointee, Ebenezer R. Hoar, suffered rejection because as attorney general he championed the merit system in government. He also drew fire from radical Republicans because of his earlier opposition to the impeachment of President Andrew Johnson.[27]

Harlan Stone's 1925 appointment is the first time a nominee appeared before the Senate Judiciary Committee to explain himself. Senators questioned his qualifications because of his prosecution as attorney general of a senator for participation in an oil and land fraud deal.

There was vigorous Senate floor debate when his nomination came before the entire body; the nomination was recommitted for further consideration to the Senate Judiciary Committee. Unfortunately, transcripts of that appearance are unavailable, but a biographer describes it as an impressive performance that served to vindicate Stone's nomination.[28]

Nominees have been rejected by the Senate for local political reasons having little if anything to do with their professional ability. Senators concerning themselves with their political power bases have invoked senatorial courtesy to block confirmation of presidential nominees. The Senate's rejection of President Polk's 1845 nomination of George Woodward resulted in large part because of home state opposition. A year earlier, in 1844, senatorial courtesy was invoked and was a lesser factor in the defeat of President Tyler's nomination of Reuben H. Walworth. President Cleveland had two nominations defeated when in each case the Senate would not confirm a nominee who was opposed by the senior senator in the president's party from the nominee's state.[29] There are many more instances of its invocation for lower federal court judges, but the point is indisputable.

The twentieth century

The matter of evaluating nominees primarily on ideological grounds is better documented for the present century than for the previous one. There are at least two interrelated explanations. First, in the twentieth century the Senate has become more responsive to popular control. In a recent paper, Charles R. Epp points out that by 1913 the Seventeenth Amendment had shifted the Senate's electoral base from the state legislatures that had theretofore named senators to the popular electorate. This institutional shift in accountability may have made senators more sensitive to interest-group and grassroots awareness of judicial policy making.[30] Second, it may be that judicial ideology played a more limited and ordinarily a less-obvious role during the first century of the Republic than it does today. During the first 100 years of the Republic, only 17 acts of Congress were declared unconstitutional, but in the next 90 years the Court struck down 87 more, an increase of more than 400 percent.[31]

In the nineteenth century there were fewer controversial Supreme Court opinions. Then the full scope of the Court's real and potential ability to affect public policy was not fully understood. However, late in that century and in the first third of this century, the Court's role in policy making became a matter of considerable debate. It became clear that Supreme Court justices exercise their discretion in dramatic ways, including striking down popular congressional acts and state laws. The Court had become a bastion of conservative ideology.[32] By the mid-1960s, it became equally clear that the Court had again become a policy maker; this time, however, it was a vehicle for liberal causes, and once again, many of its decisions were unpopular.[33] In short, because the stakes are high, the judicial philosophy and ideology of potential jurists have become a subject of close scrutiny.

President Wilson's appointment of Louis Brandeis is an early twentieth-century example of how ideology has had a probable impact on the selection process. Wilson attempted to name the brilliant Brandeis as attorney general but met considerable opposition from the elitist Boston bar. When that appointment failed, Wilson pledged to name Brandeis to the next important vacancy. That position turned out to be the Supreme Court. The Brandeis appointment was put off for months as the Senate took volumes of testimony. Much of the opposition was due to the liberal crusader's so-called radical views and his sociological jurisprudence. There is also evidence of an unhealthy dose of antisemitism. But many, including William Howard Taft, were opposed to Brandeis for other reasons, including his views in support of the working classes and his alleged animosity toward big business.[34]

Ideology was a factor in 1930 with the nominations of two otherwise well-qualified persons. Charles Evans Hughes was attacked because, among other reasons, he was regarded by liberal senators as a tool of corporate power, and conservative southerners opposed him as a city slicker who stood against states' rights.[35] The Senate rejected John J. Parker on a close vote due in large measure to opposition generated by the American Federation of Labor and the National Association for the Advancement of Colored People. Parker was thought unfriendly to labor, and he was under attack, probably erroneously, as a racist. There would be no other Senate rejection of a presidential Supreme Court nominee for 40 years.[36]

New Deal opposition to the High Court was transparently ideological. There was an attempt to disguise the ideological source for the conflict by appealing to another motive. President Roosevelt presented his ill-fated Court-Packing plan as a way to relieve elderly justices from a heavy workload. This obvious attempt by the president to change the decision-making composition of the Court by increasing the number of justices was not lost even among the most casual observers. The plan failed to receive congressional approval, but not because members revered the Court and wanted to pro-

tect it from institutional attack. As Schmidhauser and Berg point out, an ideologically conservative coalition existed in Congress before FDR introduced his plan. It coalesced before and functioned after the 1937 Court-Packing congressional vote. The purpose of this coalition was to put the brakes on the New Deal.[37] Though the Court-Packing episode did not involve the confirmation of particular justices, it demonstrates that members of Congress viewed the Court in ideological terms. They did not want to give Roosevelt an opportunity to appoint to the Court a sufficient number of persons who would vote to support New Deal programs and goals. Roosevelt ultimately got his way when the Supreme Court began to uphold New Deal initiatives to save the nation's economy from ruin. The lesson is clear. Ideology has been a prominent factor in inter-branch governmental conflicts.[38]

The Warren Court Era (1952-1969) was another period in this century when the Supreme Court came under severe attack. Decisions concerning such matters as segregation, internal security, school prayer, and criminal justice precipitated hostile reaction in and out of Congress. Many of these issues remain hotly contested into the 1990s, and so does the proper role of the Supreme Court.

Warren Court opponents used the occasion of Thurgood Marshall's 1967 nomination to attack the Court's decisions. Southern senators on the Judiciary Committee, including John McClellan, Samuel Ervin, and Strom Thurmond, questioned Marshall, a former solicitor general and then federal appeals court judge, about matters other than his professional qualifications. They also grilled him on his judicial philosophy. For example, Senator McClellan said he could not vote to confirm Marshall's nomination without an answer to his question: "Do you subscribe to the philosophy that the Fifth Amendment right to assistance of counsel requires that counsel be present at a police lineup?"[39] Marshall weathered the storm by employing the now-familiar retort that a number of cases were pending before the Court and therefore he should not respond.[40]

About a year later, in 1968, Abe Fortas became the convenient target for those opposed to the Warren Court when President Lyndon Johnson attempted unsuccessfully to promote his old friend and advisor from associate to chief justice.[41] Senator Strom Thurmond vigorously attacked Fortas by harping on the ill effects of the Court's 1957 decision in *Mallory v. United States*.[42] Significantly, Fortas was not on the Court at the time that this decision was handed down. Besides ideology, Fortas was charged with judicial impropriety by informally advising the president on a variety of policy matters, and also for accepting large lecture fees during the summer of 1968. Further, the nomination of Homer Thornberry as associate justice, a Texas crony of the president, to fill the empty seat upon the elevation of Fortas, was another negative factor.[43] In the end, the president was forced to withdraw the name of the liberal jurist as chief justice when a motion to invoke cloture failed by a 14-vote margin.[44] Because the 1968 presidential election was near at hand, and since the election of a president from the other political party was thought a distinct possibility, the defeat of Fortas is an outward and visible sign of partisan and ideological politics in the modern battle over the struggle for control of the Supreme Court. Richard Nixon ran on an anti-Warren Court platform, and the selection of justices with "strict constructionist" sentiments was part of his winning strategy.[45]

In politics, what goes around comes around. Nixon's 1968 campaign invited intense scrutiny of judicial nominees who might exhibit any professional or personal weaknesses. As part of his "Southern Strategy" to gain grassroots support for the Republican Party in that region of the nation, Nixon sought to appoint to the Court southerners with a "strict constructionist" perspective. The code words fooled no one. This was not simply a matter of choosing for the Court persons who would exercise judicial self-restraint. Nixon wanted to reverse the liberal trend of the Warren Court. Then, as is the case today, arguments about the proper judicial function and role of justices in interpreting statutes and the Constitution are really debates about judicial outcomes.

Factors involving professional conduct and qualifications played important roles in the defeat of two Nixon nominees. South Carolinian Judge Clement Haynsworth was thought by organized labor and its Senate supporters to be anti-labor.[46] Floridian Judge Harold Carswell was painted as a racist. Haynsworth was ostensibly rejected for failing to recuse himself in a few cases involving personal financial gain, and Carswell was portrayed as mediocre.[47] But it is difficult to believe that the underlying causes for their rejections did not involve politics and concerns about the ideological direction of the Court.

Other Nixon and, later, Reagan appointees were subjected to ideological interrogation of one sort or another. However, the 1987 confirmation hearings on the nomination of Judge Robert Bork to the Supreme Court is the clearest case to date of the Senate concerning itself with the ideological characteristics and probable future judicial behavior of a High Court nominee. Those hearings taught Americans that questioning nominees about their judicial philosophy will not bring down the legal edifice. It is possible to probe nominees' attitudes without exacting promises or compromising judicial neutrality toward present or future litigants. In large measure, learning this lesson took place because the nominee himself wanted his views aired. Ironically, it was the ventilation of his own views that contributed directly to Judge Bork's 42-to-58 vote Senate rejection.[48] Bork felt compelled to present his views and fully answer most questions because he felt that his many published articles on constitutional subjects could be misinterpreted, and therefore, his views may be misrepresented.[49] He did so without invoking the oft-heard disarming refrain that discussion of constitutional matters may prejudice cases coming before the High Court.

Some senators conducted themselves with distinction. Senator Arlen Specter, in particular, displayed intelligence and courage in defying his president and his party. During and after the Senate hearings, the Pennsylvania Republican asserted that the Supreme Court confirmation hearings will never be the same.[50] Subsequent Senate confirmation hearings held for the nominations of Judges Kennedy and Souter were not as revealing as the Bork hearings. However, in both cases, senators attempted to probe, albeit with limited success, the nominees' fundamental values and attitudes toward judicial law-making. The hearings for both nominees were relatively brief, lasting only a few days.[51]

Available empirical research indicates that senatorial attitudes are affected by nominees. Controversial nominations stimulate the ideological proclivities of senators, thereby subjecting some nominees to negative votes. The extent to which ideology may adversely affect particular nominee confirmation chances depends upon the direction and intensity of that sentiment.[52] It is little wonder, therefore, why most nominees refrain from full disclosure of their attitudes and beliefs.

In summary, there is ample evidence supporting the working supposition that the judicial ideology of presidential nominees is a factor that senators probe when deciding whether to confirm or reject candidates. This practice did not start with Robert Bork as has been argued.[53] By the early part of this century, as the Supreme Court became a more visible policy-making institution, the matter of nominee ideology became a more salient concern.

The issue of impartiality

The oft-heard justification for failing to answer certain questions put by senators during confirmation hearings is that to do so will violate professional norms of impartiality. Nominees protest that to answer particular queries may at the very least lead to the appearance that their minds are closed on specific legal issues, and therefore, litigants may feel they cannot get a fair hearing in court. Sandra Day O'Connor and Antonin Scalia have been the least cooperative. Robert Bork was the most forthcoming, although he refused to answer some questions. Yet nominees before and after Bork have used the impartiality argument to deflect questions.[54] Their reticence has frustrated attempts by senators to obtain pertinent information useful in evaluating nominee suitability. Complicating the matter is the existence of a federal disqualification statute, and ethical standards of conduct gleaned from the American Bar Association Model Code of Judicial Conduct. However, neither constitute sufficient justification for failing to answer queries aimed at ascertaining nominees' general legal and philosophical perspectives.

Section 455 of Title 28 of the United States Code is a revision of a law first enacted in 1911. Section 24 of Title 28, U.S.C., 1940 edition, contains the amended basic law making it applicable to all justices and judges of the United States. The law was amended in 1974 and again in 1978.[55] Most of section 455 applies unambiguously to disqualifications due to personal biases arising out of private financial or fiduciary interests, previous relationships in law practice or government employment, and being a material witness in a case. Section 455(a) raises the most difficulty. It reads: "Any justice, judge, or magistrate of the United States shall dis-

qualify himself in any proceeding in which his impartiality might reasonably be questioned."

Canon 3C(1) of the Model Code of Judicial Conduct adopted by the American Bar Association in 1972 recommends a judge's disqualification when impartiality is an issue because of personal bias or prejudice toward a party involved in litigation.[56] However, Canon 4 permits judges to "...speak, write, lecture, teach, and participate..."[57] in matters impacting the legal system. Jeffrey M. Shaman, Steven Lubet, and James J. Alfini, the authors of a recent treatise on judicial ethics, point out Canon 4 applies to the broader circumstance of quasi-judicial activities where judges speak or write in settings such as public hearings. The normative proscription applies to "*any issue* and not to *pending or impending* judicial proceedings that may come before the judge."[58] The ABA's 1990 version of the Model Code opts for greater expression of opinion. Yet these or any other statutory or ethical provisions do not directly address the matter of nominees revealing their ideological viewpoint. Nor do they require justices to recuse themselves for public comments they might have made prior to their accession to the High Court.

The statutory subject matter found in 28 U.S.C. section 455 deals specifically with appropriate recusal behavior. In the main, the Model Code of Judicial Conduct focuses more broadly upon ethical conduct involving both those situations inviting recusal and those that do not. Although the Code was raised as an issue in recent nomination hearings, no one has invoked any section of it in refusing to answer questions during oral testimony. Sandra Day O'Connor did, however, refuse to answer a written question posed by then-Senator Gordon Humphrey of New Hampshire, citing the Code as the basis for her decision. In several other instances the Code was raised as an issue, but the nominees did not rely on it as a basis for refusing to answer questions.[59]

The ABA Code of Judicial Conduct was first approved in 1972, and in August, 1990, the association's House of Delegates adopted a revised one. It will take some time before the 1990 version is promulgated in the various jurisdictions. Until then, the 1972 Code remains in effect in 47 states and applies to all judges in those jurisdictions. Within the federal system, the District of Columbia and the Judicial Conference of the United States have approved the 1972 Code, applying its provisions to all judges of the United States district courts, the United States courts of appeals, the Court of Claims, the Court of Customs and Patent Appeals, the Customs Court, and to all bankruptcy judges and United States magistrates. Significantly, the Code does not apply to justices of the United States Supreme Court.[60] Technically, then, sitting justices do not fall under the Code's ethical prohibitions and mandates. This also applies to nominees who are not sitting on any bench at the time of their confirmation hearings. However, most recent nominees have been sitting federal judges, and one was a state appellate judge at the time of nomination. Since the 1972 issuance, only two nominees, William Rehnquist and Lewis Powell, have not fallen under the purview of the Code.[61]

Grounds for disqualification

William Rehnquist is the author of the only United States Supreme Court opinion on the subject of recusal.[62] His written opinion was in response to a motion for recusal by the plaintiffs in a class action suit challenging the constitutionality of a program of the federal government for surveillance of civilians. The plaintiffs in *Laird v. Tatum*, (409 U.S. 1 (1972)), wanted Associate Justice Rehnquist to recuse himself because while he was a deputy attorney general he appeared before the Senate Judiciary Committee in support of a program of civilian surveillance, and he also made comments in another public forum concerning the subject.

Although a reasonable case is made that he should have recused himself in *Laird v. Tatum*,[63] Rehnquist's memorandum in defense of his decision not to disqualify himself is instructive. Among other arguments, he points out that other justices have not disqualified themselves in cases involving points of law with which they had expressed an opinion before coming to the High Court. Justices Black, Frankfurter, Jackson, and Hughes are prime examples.[64] However, because other justices may have done the wrong thing does not make it proper for Rehnquist to do the same. Yet the fact that these distinguished jurists did not recuse themselves could mean that they reject the view that because persons don judicial robes they become intellectual and political eunuchs. For these justices, disqualification applies to the more narrow matter of bias toward the litigants, not impartiality toward the great issues of the day. Rehnquist's

major point is summarized in one eloquent paragraph. He wrote:

Since most Justices come to this bench no earlier than their middle years, it would be unusual if they had not by that time formulated at least some tentative notions which would influence them in their interpretation of the sweeping clauses of the Constitution and their interaction with one another. It would be not merely unusual, but extraordinary, if they had not at least given opinions as to constitutional issues in their previous legal careers. Proof that a Justice's mind at the time he joined the Court was a complete tabula rasa in the area of constitutional adjudication would be evidence of lack of qualification, not lack of bias.[65]

The history of the subject is also revealing. Before the establishment of the court system in the United States, English common law judges were disqualified for only the reason of financial interests. Even finding themselves sitting in cases involving relatives was not a cause for recusal. Personal bias was unacceptable grounds for disqualification.[66] The American practice was broadened by adding relationships and bias to financial interests. Not only are cases involving relatives cause for disqualification, but so are relationships with the attorney or party to the suit.[67] The 1974 amendment to 28 U.S.C:. section 455 requires disqualification of any justice or judge who "...has been of counsel, is or has been a material witness, or is so related to or connected with any party or his attorney as to render it improper, in his opinion, for him to sit on the trial, appeal, or other proceeding therein."[68]

Modern practice recognizes the possibility that past associations with colleagues in law firms or government agencies may make it difficult for judges to always behave impartially. Sitting in a case involving former clients is such a circumstance. However, it is unclear how much time should pass between serving a client as counsel and sitting on the bench in a case involving that client.

In the past, some justices did not feel restrained to occupy the bench in disputes involving former clients. This is also true for those cases where they were indirect parties, or in cases in which they personally were similarly situated at one time. Both Justices Horace Lurton and Willis Van Devanter heard cases involving former railroad clients.[69] Chief Justice John Marshall was the secretary of state who affixed the seal of the United States to the judicial commission, but failed to deliver the midnight appointment to the intended recipient,

John Marbury. Fellow Federalist John Marshall
then wrote the opinion declaring that Marbury had
a right to the commission, but then went on to
deny the remedy sought.[70] Besides the case of
Marbury v. Madison (1803), John Marshall failed
to recuse himself in *Fletcher v. Peck* (1810), a landmark decision involving the infamous Yazoo land
fraud and state confiscation that was similar to a
situation where Marshall was likewise a victim.[71]
Further, years earlier, as a congressmen from Virginia, Marshall voted to compensate those who lost
money in the Yazoo land fraud scandal.[72]

Today's standards are considerably higher. Justice Robert Jackson publicly criticized Justice Hugo
Black for participating in *Jewell Ridge Coal Corp. v.
Local No. 6167*, (325 U.S. 161, 897 (1945)). The
case was argued by Crampton Harris, who had
practiced law with Hugo Black some 19 years earlier for a brief two-year period.[73] More recently, Justice Byron White felt compelled to disqualify himself from a Denver school desegregation case. Thirteen years earlier his old law firm had once been
the bond counsel for the Denver School District.
Justice Lewis Powell disqualified himself in a 1972
case involving a court-ordered city-suburb merger
of the Richmond School District. From 1952 to
1961, he was chairman of the district's school
board.[74] Finally, unlike his questionable conduct
in *Laird v. Tatum*,[75] Justice Rehnquist's conduct in
the Watergate case, *Nixon v. United States*, (418 U.S.
683 (1974)), is beyond doubt an example of proper
recusal. Rehnquist disqualified himself in the case
because, as a United States Department of Justice
official, he worked closely with the president's men
in drafting Richard Nixon's original position on
executive privilege.

There may be a need for stronger laws requiring recusal in a variety of compromising situations.[76] Nevertheless, it is a mistake to suggest that
because candidates for judicial posts have formed
attitudes, values, and beliefs about legal and constitutional questions they should be prohibited
from rendering judgments. It is reasonable and
compelling to expect from jurists a lack of personal
favoritism, prejudice, or bias toward particular litigants coming before them. Judges can and should
be impartial toward the litigants. However, an expectation that they be neutral toward the great issues of the day is an unreasonable one. While attempting to appear more virtuous than Caesar's
wife, prospective judges and justices may fall into

twin traps. First, they may fail to perform their fundamental responsibility to decide cases once on
the bench. As members of a collegial body they
should participate in its deliberations and carry
their fair share of the workload. And second, by
not answering questions concerning their ideology, nominees withhold important political information from senators. These constitutional officeholders have a duty to discharge reasonably their
advice and consent function.

Canon 4 of the 1972 Model Code of Judicial
Conduct provides that judges may appear at "a
public hearing before an executive or legislative
body or official on matters concerning the law, the
legal system, and the administration of justice, and
he may otherwise consult with an executive or legislative body or official, but only on matters concerning the administration of justice."[77] Thus, in
the first instance there is no ethical problem giving testimony before the Senate Judiciary Committee. Why voluntarily appear if one is obliged to
remain mute? The answer, of course, is that nomi-
nee-judges may speak and exchange ideas with
those asking the questions. However, Canon 4 requires that when judges do so they do not raise
doubts about their "...capacity to decide impartially
any issue that may come before...them.[78] This creates no insurmountable problem for judicial nominees. They must make it clear that they are open
to persuasion on the legal issue, and that the facts
of particular cases vary widely and are important
in deciding whether general rules might apply. As
Professor Shaman and his colleagues rightly conclude, Canon 4 is violated only when nominees
display a clear intention to decide a forthcoming
case in a certain way without the benefit of hearing the arguments within the controlled setting of
the courtroom.[79]

The use of the word *impartiality* found in Canon
3C(1) of the 1972 Code of Judicial Conduct is also
a source of confusion. It instructs judges to disqualify themselves in proceedings where their impartiality might be reasonably questioned,[80] but it
fails to give a precise definition of the word, "impartially." However, the term cannot mean the
absence of preexisting values, attitudes, and opinions. That we know already from elementary logic.
Furthermore, subsections (a), (b), (c), and (d) of
3C(1) all relate to personal knowledge of the parties or third-party relationships. The Canon does
not reference preexisting attitudes about issues

raised in particular cases.

Canon 3A(6) is a major source of ambiguity. It counsels that a "judge should abstain from public comment about a pending or impending proceeding in any court."[81] Note that 3A(6) does not forbid general analysis and discussion of the great legal issues of the day. Rather, it applies to *pending or impending* proceedings. As legal ethics experts Shaman, Lubet, and Alfini argue, these words must mean pretrial, trial, appellate activity, and litigation poised for litigation.[82] Consequently, Canon 3A(6) applies only to comment on actual cases or controversies in law and in equity and not general issues of law and philosophy. If nominee testimony does not reach actual fact situations that involve real issues begging for a legal resolution, then the canon is inapplicable."

Months before the Senate confirmation hearings on the Judge David Souter nomination, the American Bar Association revised its Model Code of Judicial Conduct. The August 1990 revision affirms a freedom of speech approach to public comment. The ABA Standing Committee proposed a number of significant changes in the Code. Twenty-five amendments to the committee's document were proposed, but all were defeated. They sought to keep a number of prohibitions, including that dealing with public comment on pending or impending legislation.[84] Canon 3A(6) is now Canon 3B(9) in the 1990 revision and it reads: "A judge shall not, while a preceding is pending or impending in any court, make any public comment that might reasonably be expected to affect its outcome or impair its fairness or make any nonpublic comment that might substantially interfere with a fair trial or hearing.[85] The addition of the words "reasonably be expected to affect its outcome or impair its fairness" represents an important recognition that not all public comment may make it difficult for judges to render justice impartially.

There can be little doubt that under the terms of the 1990 Model Code judges may comment publicly on court decisions, provided their remarks do not influence the outcome or impair the fairness of litigation currently pending or impending. Michael Franck, a member of the ABA Standing Committee on Ethics and Professional Responsibility, reportedly said: "We ought to allow speech when it serves a legitimate purpose."[86] Further, George Kuhlman, ethics counsel for the ABA's Center for Professional Responsibility is quoted as saying: "Until a genuine conflict occurs, there's no reason to infringe the First Amendment rights a judge should have."[87] Nominee responses to questions of United States senators designed to understand ideological propensities are appropriate if constitutional responsibility and accountability are to have meaning. Consequently, those who argued in the past that the Code of Judicial Ethics constrained nominee behavior before the Senate Judiciary Committee now have even less justification to do so today.

Neither statute nor ethical norms prohibit nominees from discussing the great constitutional questions of the day with United States senators or others. There are no compelling reasons why, at the very least, nominees' general views should not be known in advance of Court service. Expressing one's view today will not make it impossible or difficult to change that view tomorrow. As the venerable Senator Sam Ervin of North Carolina argued—why should it? After carefully considering the established facts in a case, reviewing the law, reading the briefs, hearing oral arguments, and consulting with colleagues, justices may very well change their minds or at least modify their general views to fit the specific facts before the Court and the desired result.[88] In fact, judges tell us that this happens to them. Good arguments, they insist, can convince them.[89]

A positive feature of the common law tradition is its postulate that we can learn from past lessons. The law is a great laboratory wherein rules and regulations are regarded as testable propositions requiring, from time to time, re-examination. Persons who are ill-disposed to uncertainty make poor judges. Those who are not open to persuasion and do not understand the logic of fact analysis to produce welcome and unwelcome precedents misunderstand the nature of the judicial process, and therefore should not, in any event, become members of the Supreme Court. Nominees only need to avoid answering questions about identifiable cases that may be extant in the legal process system or are pending in an immediate sense. Otherwise, they have a responsibility to cooperate fully with constitutional officers to answer questions pertinent to the office they seek.

Conclusions

Senators should feel free to ask questions that may reveal judicial nominees' views on past, present, or future constitutional issues. There is no statutory or ethical justification for secrecy in such matters, save the exception of commenting on pending or impending actual cases or controversies in law and in equity, and then, only when public comment may affect the fairness or outcome of deliberations.

Despite nominee Antonin Scalia's protestations to the contrary,[90] querying nominees about their attitudes concerning past court decisions is consistent with statutory and ethical norms. There is no reason senators may not ask nominees about how they envision the future shape of the law both in general and specific terms. In brief, senators should have a good idea about how future judges and justices will behave. Yet, they should do so with the knowledge that specific facts of particular cases can impact how jurists will behave, and once on the bench the force of argument may persuade the judges and justices to change their minds.

Although asking questions about particular cases and rules of law are pertinent and possess considerable appeal, senators may also gain considerable insight into the minds and possible future behavior of nominees by employing social science knowledge more broadly. Research in political jurisprudence and judicial behavior establishes the explanatory power of inquiries into the social, economic, political, and judicial philosophies of judicial nominees.[91]

Ideology is the summary term describing the set of attitudes and values that are particularly relevant to the performance of the judicial function. The object of the inquiry is to ascertain probable nominee impact upon the policy-making output of the judiciary. Queries may center on the nominees' past political and judicial decision making, and upon their likely short- and long-term future impact upon the Court's decision making.

Existing knowledge is based on aggregate data and does not hold true in all instances. But there is solid social science evidence that values and attitudes are stable. This is particularly true of judges and justices.[92] Persons acquire attitudes toward political objects or issues through a lifetime of experience, learning, and interaction. Furthermore, attitudes direct actions. Hence, if past, present, and future situations are sufficiently similar, there is every justification to assume that persons will behave in the present and future as they did in the past. It is true that attitudes of adults can change,[93]

but it is the exception, not the rule.

Judicial nominees are usually in their middle years of life. Because they often have previous political and judicial experience, there is a record of public decision making. Lawyers as an occupational group have a propensity to write down ideas in the course of conducting their professional activities. This makes the task of gathering attitudinal information less difficult than it otherwise might be.

For instance, senators might ask former criminal prosecutors about the policy of their office toward capital punishment, sentencing policy, the exclusionary rule, or other matters that may help to establish the nominees' past and present attitude toward criminal justice matters. Did a nominee participate in political campaigns as a worker or candidate, and what were the ideological positions at stake in those campaigns? If a nominee has had a private law practice, what was the style of that practice? Did the nominee have for clients Fortune 500 corporations or did he or she devote much of his or her professional life to aiding America's poor and underrepresented?

Depending on the number, studying the published opinions of nominees with prior judicial experience may reveal consistent attitude patterns. Wherever possible and practical, Judiciary Committee staff could construct Guttman-type scales on a variety of issue dimensions to ascertain ideological consistency and relative scale position of those judges sitting in collegial settings.[94] Asking sitting judges informed questions about particularly controversial cases in which they cast votes and wrote opinions can serve to uncover not only policy views, but also nominees' conceptions of the proper judicial role.

Contrary to what some believe, however, prior judicial experience is not a good predictor of a commitment to stare decisis.[95] Finally, culling through and questioning nominees about their publications, including law review and other writings, can serve to reveal a wealth of attitudinal information. Much of the Senate Judiciary Committee's interrogation of Robert Bork centered on his prolific writings. Bork felt compelled to explain his writings, and in the process the nation was treated to a splendid constitutional law seminar. Ironically, it may be that President Bush chose David Souter as his first Supreme Court nominee because of the lack of a paper trail, and consequently, senators had one less indicator of nominee ideology.

There was a period when researchers assumed that newly appointed justices take several years before they settle into their new job. The neophytes were said to exhibit signs of bewilderment by their new duties and responsibilities. Being awed by their new surroundings they need several years to become psychologically adjusted. Attempting to ease newly appointed justices into the demands of the job, senior justices do not assign their junior colleagues an equal share of opinion writing. Finally, freshmen fail to align immediately with the Court's existing voting blocs.[96] Recent research findings, however, reject the freshmen-effect hypothesis.

Findings for the Reagan appointees indicate the period of bewilderment is short, if it exists at all. Although freshmen justices write fewer opinions during their first term on the Court, by the end of the second term they no longer write the fewest number of opinions. Even so, freshmen author important opinions during their initial terms signifying early integration into the work group. Finally, freshmen are not timid about joining preexisting voting blocs.[97]

The importance of the freshmen-effect research is that it highlights the importance of considering the near term consequences newly appointed justices may have on Supreme Court decision making. They can have an immediate impact that senators must consider seriously.

It is untrue that justices today are appointed without considering their immediate impact upon the Court. Particularly during the Reagan administration, nominees were carefully screened by the president or his advisors for their ideological commitment to a judicial agenda, including a view of the judicial function that in the contemporary context is supportive of conservative ideals. The Reagan appointees did not need time to figure out positions on the great legal and constitutional issues of the day. They were chosen for their ideological correctness. The Bush administration also carefully chose judicial nominees with ideology as a general concern.[98] Because today the U.S. Supreme Court deals mostly with matters affecting statutory and constitutional law and because a good number of constitutional law topics are controversial, it makes good political sense to discover nominee attitudes about these subjects.

In summary, senators need not ask the kinds of questions that require nominees to promise how they will vote in future cases. There is no need to do so. Nominee attitudes and values are discernible and may serve as indicators of likely future behavior. The constitutional framers contemplated an inquisitive and active role in confirming presidential appointments. The advice and consent clause of the Constitution justifies an independent scrutiny of nominees by members of the Senate. The historical record reveals that from the beginning of the new republic the Senate has rejected nominees for reasons other than personal and professional qualifications. In one fashion or another, political considerations, including evaluations of the ideological soundness of nominees, influence Senate advice and consent decisions. Properly understood, statutory and ethical norms do not prohibit nominees from revealing their views on the great issues of the day. Nominees may conduct themselves before Senate hearing panels with honor and probity while at the same time providing vital political information.

Briefly stated, nothing in the Constitution, our historical experience, our political practice, ethical norms, nor statutory enactments prohibits senators from asking judicial nominees pertinent ideological questions. Nominees owe an obligation to the nation to be forthcoming if the advice and consent provision of the Constitution is to have real meaning.

NOTES

This article originally appeared in Volume 75, Number 2, August-September 1991, pages 68-79.

The author wishes to acknowledge with deep appreciation the devoted effort of research assistants Alan Arwine, Alan Morris, and Marc George Pufong.

1. Fein, *Commentary: A Circumscribed Senate Confirmation Role*, 102 HARV. L. REV. 687 (1989); Bork, THE TEMPTING OF AMERICA: THE POLITICAL SEDUCTION OF THE LAW 298-299 (New York: Simon and Schuster, 1990); *Were the Bork Hearings Fair?* [Bork Nomination], ABA J. December, 1987, at 42-43; Carter, *The Confirmation Mess*, 101 HARV. L. REV. 1185 (1988); Ackerman, *Transformative Appointments*, 101 HARV. L. REV. 1164 (1988); Griffin, *Politics and the Supreme Court: The Case of the Bork Nomination*, 5 J. L. & POL. 551 (Spring, 1989); Curran, *Bork's Credentials Beyond Challenge: Opponents Use Political Standards*, N.Y.L. J. Sept. 23, 1987, at 2, col. 7; Kooper and Lloyd, *Judge Bork Should Be Confirmed*, N.Y.L.J. Sept. 30, 1987, at 2, col. 3; McLaughlin, *For Confirmation*, N.Y.L. J. Oct. 7, 1987, at 2, col. 3.

2. Bork, *Id.*

3. *Id.*

4. *Id.*

5. U.S. Congress, Senate, Committee on the Judiciary, *Nomination of Thurgood Marshall, of New York, to be an Associate Justice of the United States*, Ninetieth Congress, First Session, 1967, p. 9; U.S. Congress, Senate, Committee on the Judiciary, *Nomi-*

nation of William H. Rehnquist, of Arizona, and Lewis F. Powell, Jr., of Virginia, to be an Associate Justice of the Supreme Court of the United States, Ninety-Seventh Congress, First Session, 1981, p. 56; U.S. Congress, Senate, Committee on the Judiciary, *Nomination of Judge Sandra Day O'Connor of Arizona, to be an Associate Justice of the Supreme Court of the United States*, Ninety-Seventh Congress, First Session, 1981, p. 199; U.S. Congress, Senate, Committee on the Judiciary, *Nomination of Judge Antonin Scalia, to be an Associate Justice of the Supreme Court of the United States*, Ninety-Ninth Congress, Second Session, 1986, p. 33; U.S. Congress, Senate, Committee on the Judiciary, *Nomination of Anthony M. Kennedy to be an Associate Justice of the Supreme Court of the United States*, One-Hundredth Congress, First Session, 1987, p. 164.

6. Abraham, JUSTICES AND PRESIDENTS: A POLITICAL HISTORY OF APPOINTMENTS TO THE SUPREME COURT 2nd ed., 18-19 (New York: Oxford University Press, 1985).

7. Gauch, *The Intended Role of the Senate in Supreme Court Appointments*, 56 U. CHI. L. REV. 341-347 (1989).

8. Swisher, AMERICAN CONSTITUTIONAL DEVELOPMENT 28-45 (Boston: Houghton Mifflin, 1954); Kelly and Harbinson, THE AMERICAN CONSTITUTION: ITS ORIGINS AND DEVELOPMENT 114-167 (New York: Norton Press, 1955).

9. Farand (ed.), 1 THE RECORDS OF THE FEDERAL CONVENTION OF 1787, 120, 232-234 (1966).

10. Gauch, *supra* n. 7, at 341 (note 23).

11. *Id.* at 341-342.

12. *Id.* at 342-347.

13. *Id.* at 347-458; Slotnick, *Reforms in judicial selection: Will they affect the Senate's role?*, 64 JUDICATURE 62 (1980); Jilson, CONSTITUTION MAKING: CONFLICT AND CONSENSUS IN THE FEDERAL CONVENTION OF 1787, 80-81, 170-171 (New York: Agathon, 1988).

14. Hamilton, THE FEDERALIST, No. 66 at 405 (New American Library edition, 1961).

15. Hamilton, THE FEDERALIST, No. 76 at 457 (New American Library edition, 1961).

16. *Id.*

17. Jennings, GENERATIONS AND POLITICS: A PANEL STUDY OF YOUNG ADULTS AND THEIR PARENTS (Princeton, N.J.: Princeton University Press, 1981).

18. *Id.* at 458. Italics added.

19. Gauch, *supra* n. 7, at 352.

20. Melone and Mace, JUDICIAL REVIEW AND AMERICAN DEMOCRACY 120-144 (Iowa State Univ. Press, 1988).

21. Fein, *supra* n. 1 at 672; Ewing, THE JUDGES OF THE SUPREME COURT, 1789-1937 (Minneapolis: University of Minnesota Press, 1938).

22. Sulfridge, *Ideology as a Factor in Senate Consideration of Supreme Court Nominations*, 42 J. POL. 562 (1980). Slotnick, *supra* n. 13, at 63-65. *See more generally*, Chemerinsky, *Ideology, Judicial Selection and Judicial Ethics*, 2 GEO. J. LEGAL ETHICS 644-646 (1989); Abraham, *supra* n. 6, at 3-12.

23. Abraham, *supra* n. 6, at 41.

24. Gauch, *supra* n. 7, at 359-360.

25. *Id.* at 359-361.

26. Abraham, *supra* n. 6, at 41, 88.

27. *Id.* at 42.

28. Mason, HARLAN FISKE STONE: PILLAR OF THE LAW 181-200 (New York: Viking Press, 1956).

29. Abraham, *supra* n. 6, at 27-28.

30. "The Brandeis and Bork Battles: A Systematic Comparison," (Paper Delivered at the 1991 Annual Meeting of the Midwest Political Science Association, Chicago, April 18-20, 1991).

31. Witt (ed.), THE SUPREME COURT: JUSTICE AND THE LAW 168 (Washington, D.C.: Congressional Quarterly Press, 1977); and Clinton, FROM PRECEDENT TO MYTH: MARBURY V. MADISON AND THE HISTORY OF JUDICIAL REVIEW IN AMERICA 209 (Lawrence, Kan.: Uni-

versity Press of Kansas, 1989).

32. Melone and Mace, *supra* n. 20; see also, Rodell, NINE MEN: A POLITICAL HISTORY OF THE SUPREME COURT FROM 1790-1955, 187-189 (New York: Random House, 1955).

33. Melone and Mace, *Id.*

34. Abraham, *supra* n. 6, at 178-181.

35. *Id.* at 198-199.

36. *Id.* at 42-43.

37. Schmidhauser and Berg, THE SUPREME COURT AND CONGRESS: CONFLICT AND INTERACTION 1945-1968, 136-142 (New York: The Free Press, 1972).

38. The saliency of ideology is further illustrated even after FDR began to appoint justices to the Supreme Court. Hugo Black, Franklin Roosevelt's first appointee, encountered serious difficulties after his confirmation. He felt compelled to go on national radio to account for his prior membership in the Ku Klux Klan. *See*, Abraham, *supra* n. 6, at 212-213.

39. U.S. Congress, Senate, Committee on the Judiciary, *Nomination of Thurgood Marshall*, *supra* n. 5, at 14.

40. *Id.*

41. Schmidhauser and Berg, *supra* n. 37, at 111.

42. *Id.* at 129.

43. Abraham, *supra* n. 6, at 286-287.

44. Congressional Quarterly Service, *Congressional Quarterly Almanac*, vol. 24, s.v. "Nomination of Abe Fortas," at 531.

45. Funston, CONSTITUTIONAL COUNTERREVOLUTION? THE WARREN AND THE BURGER COURTS: JUDICIAL POLICY MAKING IN MODERN AMERICA (New York: Halsted Press, 1977); Blasi, THE BURGER COURT: THE COUNTER-REVOLUTION THAT WASN'T (Boston: Atlantic-Little Brown, 1986).

46. Abraham, *supra* n. 6, at 15.

47. *Id.* at 16-17; Frank, *Disqualification of Judges: In Support of The Bayh Bill*, 35 LAW & CONTEM. PROB. 52-62 (1970).

48. Congressional Quarterly Service, *The Congressional Quarterly Almanac*, vol. 43 s.v. "Bork Nomination," at 271.

49. Bork, *supra* n. 1, at 300-301.

50. Bork, *supra* n. 1, at 301; U.S. Congress, Senate, Committee on the Judiciary, *Nomination of Robert H. Bork to be Associate Justice of the Supreme Court of the United States*, One Hundredth Congress, First Session, 1987, p. 75-76; Noble, *Four Key Senators Say They Will Vote Against Bork*, NEW YORK TIMES, 2 October, 1987, at A17.

51. The Bork hearings took 12 days to complete, and the hearings totaled 6,511 pages. On the other hand, Kennedy's hearings lasted only three days and the total pages for the hearings is only 1,119. Beginning with Thurgood Marshall and extending through Kennedy, the average number of days to conduct the hearings is only 3.6. The average number of pages of hearings for those same hearings is only 577.

52. Sulfridge, *supra* n. 22, at 560; Melone, "The Senate's Confirmation Role in Supreme Court Nominations: Politics, Ideology and Impartiality (Paper Delivered at the 49th Annual Meeting of the Midwest Political Science Association, April 18-20, 1991), at 21-29.

53. Fein, *supra* n. 1.

54. Shaman, Lubet, and Alfini, JUDICIAL CONDUCT AND ETHICS 361, 362, 369 (Charlottesville, Va.: The Michie Company, 1990).

55. 28 U.S.C.S. section 455 (Law, Co-op. 1986).

56. Ross, *The Questioning of Supreme Court Nominees at Senate Confirmation Hearings: Proposals for Accommodating the Needs of the Senate and Ameliorating the Fears of Nominees*, 62 TULANE L. REV. 113 (1987); see: American Bar Association, CODE OF JUDICIAL CONDUCT 14 (Chicago: American Bar Association, 1972), [hereinafter cited as *1972 Code of Judicial Conduct*].

57. *1972 Code of Judicial Conduct*, at 18.

58. Shaman, Lubet, and Alfini, *supra* n. 54, at 372. Italics added.

59. *Id.* at 363-364, footnote 7.

60. *Id.* at 364.

61. *Id.* at 365. This includes Justice David Souter who was first an associate justice of the New Hampshire Supreme Court, and then for a short period a judge of the U.S. Court of Appeals for the First Circuit.

62. Memorandum on Motion to Recuse, Laird v. Tatum, 490 U.S. 824, 34 L. Ed. 2d 50, 93 S.Ct. 7 (1972).

63. Stempel, *Rehnquist, Recusal, and Reform*, 53 BROOKLYN L. REV. 589-667 (1987).

64. Memorandum on Motion to Recuse, Laird v. Tatum, 490 U.S. 334 L. Ed. 2d 57 (1972).

65. *Id.* at 59.

66. Frank, *Disqualification of Judges*, 56 YALE L. J. 609-612 (1947).

67. *Id.* at 615-616.

68. 28 U.S.C.S. Section 458: at 578.

69. Frank, *supra* n. 66, at 623, footnote 32.

70. Melone and Mace, *supra* n. 20, at 37-54.

71. Magrath, YAZOO: THE CASE OF FLETCHER V. PECK 73-74 (New York: W.W. Norton and Company, 1966).

72. *Id.* at 34.

73. Frank, *supra* n. 66, at 605-606, footnote 2.

74. Melone, *A Political Scientist Writes in Defense of the Brethren*, 64 JUDICATURE 142 (1980).

75. Stempel, *supra* n. 63.

76. *Id.*

77. *1972 Code of Judicial Conduct*, at 18.

78. *Id.*

79. Shaman, Lubet, and Alfini, *supra* n. 54, at 373.

80. *1972 Code of Judicial Conduct*, at 14-15.

81. *Id.* at 12.

82. Shaman, Lubet, and Alfini, *supra* n. 54, at 368.

83. *Id.* at 370-371.

84. Guccione, *ABA Adopts a New Code for Judiciary: Jurists Allowed to Comment on Court Proceedings, Now Reflects Reality*, LOS ANGELES DAILY JOURNAL, August 8, 1990, at 1, 11.

85. American Bar Association, Standing Committee on Ethics and Professional Responsibility, *Code of Judicial Conduct (1990): as submitted for consideration at the 1990 Annual Meeting of the House of Delegates of the American Bar Association* 15 (Chicago: American Bar Association, 1990). For comments of committee members see, Appendix D, at 13-14.

86. Guccione, *supra* n. 84.

87. Shoop, *ABA Revises Judicial Conduct Code*, TRIAL (Nov. 1990), at 107.

88. U.S. Congress, Senate, Committee on the Judiciary, *Nomination of Thurgood Marshall, supra* n. 5, at 13.

89. U.S. Congress, Senate, Committee on the Judiciary, *Nomination of Robert H. Bork, supra* n. 50, at 152, 153, 155, 716, 718, 720.

90. U.S. Congress, Senate, Committee on the Judiciary, *Nomination of Antonin Scalia, supra* n. 5, at 33, 37-38, 45, 58, 86.

91. Stumpf (ed.), *Whither Political Jurisprudence: A Symposium*, 36 W. POL. Q. 533-570 (1983).

92. Spaeth, *The Attitudes and Values of Supreme Court Justices*, in Ulmer (ed.) COURTS, LAW, AND JUDICIAL PROCESSES 287-388 (New York: The Free Press, Macmillan Publishing Co., 1981).

93. Melone and Jones, *Constitutional Convention Delegates and Interest Groups: A Panel Study of Elite Socialization*, 44 J. POL. 183-192 (1982).

94. Ulmer, *Scaling Judicial Cases: A Methodological Note*, 4 BEHAVIORAL SCIENTIST 31-34 (April, 1961); Schubert, THE JUDICIAL MIND (Evanston, IL: Northwestern University Press, 1965).

95. Schmidhauser, *Stare Decisis, Dissent, and the Background of the Justices of the Supreme Court of the United States*, 14 U. TORONTO L. J. 192-212 (May, 1962).

96. *See* Snyder, *The Supreme Court as a Small Group*, 36 SOC. FORCES 232 (1958); Howard, *Mr. Justice Murphy: The Freshman Years*, 18 VAND. L. REV. 473 (1965).

97. Scheb and Ailshie, *Justice Sandra Day O'Connor and the "Freshman Effect,"* 69 JUDICATURE 9 (1985); Rubin and Melone, *Justice Antonin Scalia: A First Year Freshman Effect?*, 72 JUDICATURE 98-102 (1988); Melone, *Revisiting the Freshman Effect Hypothesis: The First Two Terms of Justice Anthony Kennedy*, 74 JUDICATURE 6-13 (1990).

98. Goldman, *The Bush Imprint on the Judiciary: Carrying on a Tradition*, 74 JUDICATURE 297 (1991).

The confirmation process: too much advice and too little consent

The Senate's "advice and consent" role under the Constitution was understood by the framers in modest terms—as a guard against the president's naming a justice of "unfit" character, or one without professional "merit." Yet the Senate believes it has the authority to do "as it sees fit."

by Wm. Bradford Reynolds

Editor's note: Although Albert Melone's article, "The Senate's confirmation role in Supreme Court nominations and the politics of ideology versus impartiality," was prepared prior to the resignation of Justice Thurgood Marshall, it became quite timely with the confirmation hearings on Judge Clarence Thomas. In order to provide another perspective on the process, particularly as it might apply to Judge Thomas, *Judicature* invited Wm. Bradford Reynolds, who during his tenure as assistant attorney general in the Justice Department was involved in selecting federal judges, to prepare the following commentary.

With the announcement of Justice Thurgood Marshall's resignation from the United States Supreme Court, the stage is set once again for Senate confirmation hearings to fill a vacancy on the High Court. The president nominated an exceptionally well-qualified judge on the District of Columbia Circuit Court, Judge Clarence Thomas, to fill the seat.

Almost immediately, the political battle lines were drawn, and interest groups on both sides began their all-too-familiar refrains. Their objective, ultimately, is to convince a majority of senators to support (or oppose) Judge Thomas because he agrees (or disagrees)—or is perceived to agree (or disagree)—with a particular ideology they endorse. The fine art of confirmation by litmus test, as developed and honed during and after the confir-

mation hearings of Judge Robert Bork for the Supreme Court, seems to be here to stay.

The question of whether the Senate should rise above the fray and exercise its "advice and consent" responsibility untainted by the political haranguing of special-interest agitators is no longer seriously asked or answered. Rather, as Professor Melone's heavily footnoted article makes clear, the debate has shifted. The legitimacy of politicizing the confirmation process is no longer open for discussion. That other nominees have been mistreated over the past 200 years—even if only a relatively few—apparently justifies the crudest of tactics in the present environment. The criticism, it is argued, should not be heaped on the senators for seeking politically correct answers, but on the nominee for declining to respond (whatever his or her reason) or, in responding, failing the standard of political correctness.

I continue to be of the school that believes the Senate's "advice and consent" role under Article II, Section 2, cl. 2 of the U.S. Constitution was understood by the framers in far more modest terms. Professor Melone does an adequate job with the historical compromise that placed in the Executive the power to nominate and in the Senate a check on that power to guard against the president's naming of a justice of "unfit" character, or one without professional "merit."[1]

He stumbles badly, however, in extrapolating (albeit somewhat tentatively) from the framers' debates that the door was unwittingly opened for the Senate to inquire as well into "nominees' ideology." Nor does even that shaky premise sustain the penultimate of the professor's thesis (which we have come to expect from academic circles when the historical analysis fails to produce the desired result), to wit: it is, after all, a "living constitution," which permits the Senate essentially "to use its constitutional authority as it sees fit."

So much for original intent. Not that it makes much practical difference. The argument fashioned by Professor Melone and his like-minded academic colleagues is but an intellectual fig leaf for the senators to hide behind. Senators Biden and Specter wore it rather well to cultivate at least a public perception that their opposition to Judge Bork was reasoned, not political. Senators Heflin and Leahy were far less convincing, while Senators Kennedy and Metzenbaum cast aside all pretexts, seemingly unashamed by the public exposure of their crass political campaign that did not take the measure of the man and his credentials, but instead subjected him and the process to a most unforgiving liberal litmus test. Whether one agrees or disagrees with my view that such senatorial gracelessness mocks that body's "advice and consent" responsibility is, I would submit, quite beside the point. The reality is that Professor Melone summed things up about right: the senators will do as they damn well please in the confirmation jousting over a nominee for the High Court—even as they pretend to be more deliberative.

Thus, we can expect the inquiry to move sharply away from the topics of judicial qualifications, philosophy, and temperament—all legitimate areas to probe—and, sadly, toward an issues-oriented game of chicken, focused on decisional outcomes, not the methodology a nominee employs to get there. If abortion happens to be the political "hot button" at the time of hearings, whether the candidate is or is not pro-life becomes the litmus test for confirmation. The same holds true for "affirmative action," capital punishment, the exclusionary rule, flag burning, and a host of other issues that make up the grist of the Supreme Court's jurisprudence.

There is, of course, nothing wrong with senators seeking to determine *how* a nominee would approach and go about deciding any or all of these issues. Whether or not historical context is deemed important, what source materials are considered

authoritative, the degree of deference (if any) that attaches to Court precedents, and the analytical framework generally followed—these are all appropriate inquiries. But to go beyond methodology and insist on a statement of *what* the nominee's decision will be in any particular case makes political correctness the yardstick for confirmation, not juridical competence.

The correct stand

Refusing to answer the *what* question—except, as with Judge Bork for example, where a thoughtful response had previously been given in writings or opinions—has yet to defeat a nomination. Justice David Souter adopted what seems to me to be the unquestionably correct stand. He demonstrated his general knowledge of competing considerations, identified relevant precedents, even in some instances made reference to learned commentary bearing on the subject raised; he noted that his decision, ultimately, would turn on a careful analysis of the matters he touched upon, the briefs filed by counsel and discussions with his colleagues on the Court. That is, of course, precisely how a Supreme Court justice should approach each issue when first presented to him or her for decision. The demand in confirmation hearings for snap judgments to be offered in response to invariably poorly crafted questions (which all too frequently do not even ask what the senator *thinks* he is asking) encourages highly injudicious behavior. Resisting such pressure is properly judicious.

A case in point involves the law of privacy. Virtually all the senators—with the notable exception of Senator Hatch—have demonstrated repeatedly and emphatically in the last six Supreme Court confirmation hearings—stretching back to Justice Sandra Day O'Connor in 1982—that their grasp of the issue of constitutional privacy is untutored and inexpert. Judge Thomas, too, will soon be subjected to the ordeal of trying, politely, to answer the predictably inept inquiries from Judiciary Committee members about his views on the "law of privacy" (we all know they really mean "abortion"). He would, in my view, be well advised to give the Souter response if, as I suspect, he has not yet had occasion to sort through the constitutional complexities that attend the issue and have divided learned scholars and jurists for years. Such an answer has the virtue of avoiding the litmus test trap set by those senators intent on securing advance commitments on substantive issues—besides which, it happens to be honest.

This does not suggest that Judge Thomas need equivocate on his *personal* views in the pro-life debate *if* he has heretofore shared them publicly with others. Should the question be asked on that level, I would hope the nominee would make the point that his personal views (whatever they may be) are wholly irrelevant to his constitutional analysis; they then should have no bearing on the confirmation deliberations. Nor do I agree with Governor L. Douglas Wilder's misguided observation (later fuzzily recanted) that Judge Thomas' Catholic upbringing serves to disqualify him—any more than the same religious affiliation undid Justice Kennedy or, at the executive level, stood in the way of John F. Kennedy's bid for the presidency.

To be sure, on issues where he has been outspoken, a more intense probe of that nominee's stated positions can be expected, and properly so. Judge Thomas has not been bashful about his views on "affirmative action," for example. The Senate can properly challenge, and the nominee had better be prepared to defend. The search, however, should be not for areas of personal agreement or disagreement, but for the reasoned explanation. Judge Thomas has Supreme Court precedent and Justices William O. Douglas and Lewis Powell among the reasoned advocates on his side of the debate. His open stand against government policies that promote uneven treatment of individuals because of racial, gender, or ethnic differences—oxymoronically labelled "affirmative"—commands the respect of a majority of today's sitting justices, as well as many judges on the federal appellate and district courts. That reality predictably counts for little among the *political* opposition. Among those for whom intellectual honesty still has value, on the other hand, it is the full answer to critics who seek to miscast this nominee as a "radical thinker" or "outside the mainstream."

Bases for consent

Will Judge Thomas be confirmed? By any objective measure, he should be—overwhelmingly. The framers' nod to the Senate—to give its "advice and consent"—left to the president (and the president alone) the task of nominating. Not surprisingly, George Bush's choices for the Supreme Court are not going to be the same as Michael Dukakis'. So long as the persons proposed are of high moral character, strong legal training and experience, and in good physical health, Senate "consent" should not be withheld because conservative credentials shine through.

Fidelity to the written law and disdain for judicial improvisation is a philosophy of judging that undoubtedly dismays liberal senators weaned on a Warren Court openly disdainful of the written law and known best for judicial improvisations. Yet, it is a philosophy that returns to the legislative branch its constitutional responsibility of framing the law, to the executive branch its constitutional responsibility of administering the law, and to the judicial branch its constitutional responsibility of interpreting the law.

If such conservative thinking is all that stands in the way of confirmation by a liberal Senate—because it is regarded as not politically correct—the worst fears of what mischief could come out of Judge Bork's mishandled confirmation hearings will have been realized. The judiciary will no longer be able to lay claim to independence from the other two branches, having become captive to a highly charged and overly politicized selection process that demands from nominees advance commitments to particular policy results being pressed by a senator or favored "interest group."

The Senate Judiciary Committee's scrutiny of Judge Thomas thus bears close viewing. Not only does the future of the nominee hang in the balance, but so, too, does the very character of the Supreme Court. Regrettably, the fate of both the man and the institution will be determined with little senatorial respect for the constitutional role that assigns that body an "advice and consent" responsibility more modest than it is prepared to wield.

NOTES

This article originally appeared in Volume 75, Number 2, August-September 1991, pages 80-82.

1. *See* Hamilton, THE FEDERALIST No. 76, at 513.

Supreme Court confirmation hearings: a view from the Senate

Through the adoption of certain roles, senators pursue distinct goals throughout Supreme Court confirmation hearings, one of which includes influencing future nominations.

by George Watson and John Stookey

Editor's note. The following article was prepared prior to the nomination and subsequent defeat by the Senate of Judge Robert Bork. The authors discuss the unique nature of the Bork hearing in "The Bork hearing: rocks and roles," page 507.

With the exception of the initial announcement of a nominee's name by the president, public attention to the Supreme Court nomination process is focused mostly on the Senate confirmation hearings. They represent the most visible and formal evaluation of the nominee's suitability and qualifications. With the consideration of Justices Rehnquist and Scalia behind us and with the expectation of others to come in the not too distant future, it is a good time to examine the role of such hearings in the nomination process.

Drama or theatrics

At a common-sense level the significance of a confirmation hearing depends upon how controversial the nomination is. For example, in a relatively controversial nomination, like that of Justice Rehnquist, the hearings of the Judiciary Committee often rate as high drama in the media and are considered a significant part of the confirmation process. Conversely, the hearings in noncontroversial nominations are often dismissed as theatrics, a mere formality of going through the motions.

The conclusion that the high degree of confirmation certainty associated with a noncontroversial nominee precludes interesting and important questions about the hearing process, however, is uninformed. It is based on the limited views that these hearings are worthy of attention only if the voting is expected to be close or if a significant proportion of the legislators are playing what might be called an "evaluator role," namely, seeking information at the hearings to help them decide whether to support or oppose the nominee. From this perspective, the hearings of two of the last three nominees (O'Connor and Scalia) can be ignored as inconsequential, mere theatrical events devoid of any genuine drama or substantive value to judicial or legislative scholars. There was little doubt the decisions to confirm O'Connor or Scalia were assured before the hearings.[1] Nor are such hearings uncommon, as reflected by two scholars who noted that the hearings are "... essentially a pro-forma part of the decision process."[2]

Among the last three hearings, only the Rehnquist one provided the drama that attracts public and scholarly attention. Such interest springs primarily from the uncertainty of the outcome, which derives from a division of opinion among the senators or from an apparent indecision by senators concerning which way to vote. Because scholars have focused primarily on the outcome of hearings, their attention has been on variation in voting behavior and the factors that affect vote decision. While outcome is clearly a significant concern, we believe that a more complete understanding of the confirmation process is desirable. A perspective that helps to make sense of both controversial and noncontroversial nomination hearings is both possible and fruitful.

Such an alternative perspective focuses not on how controversial the nomination is, nor on the impact of the hearings on the outcome, but rather on the individual perceptions and goals of the senators involved. What is each senator trying to accomplish, and how does the configuration of the senators' goals change depending upon the level of controversy involved? Rather than a filter that determines whether the hearings are even worth our attention, level of controversy becomes a variable that affects the goals and behaviors of the senators involved.

Senatorial roles

The concept of legislative role has a long tradition. For example, representation roles, such as delegate and trustee, are often discussed by political scientists.[3] A delegate is a legislator who sees his role as reflecting the wishes of his or her district. On the other hand, the trustee role suggests that the legislator should rely on his or her own judgment about issues, rather than attempt to directly reflect home district opinion on each vote.

These generic types of roles are useful in explaining the behavior of a legislator in the confirmation setting, as well as other legislative decision making. For our discussion here, however, the term "role" is used as a convenient and common sense label to describe what a legislator is trying to accomplish in a given setting. We call these purposive situational roles, because they reveal the purpose or intent of the senator, and they are specific to a particular setting or situation, in this instance, a confirmation hearing. For example, in a Supreme Court confirmation hearing, a senator seeking to gather information and insight concerning the nominee in order to decide about his vote is playing the role of evaluator. The evaluator role provides the normative model of the open-minded senator who uses the hearings to gather and evaluate information in making a decision on how to vote.[4] It is the nature of virtually all nominations, however, that this role is assumed by a distinct minority of the committee membership, whether the nomination be controversial or noncontroversial. The question arises, then, what other roles are adopted by senators in these nomination hearings? If their vote is not at stake, just what *is* happening at these hearings?

Our effort to establish the various roles that senators may play during confirmation hearings, as well as the factors that affect role selection, began with the O'Connor hearings in September 1981. For this initial effort, it seemed important to gather information concerning role selection contemporaneous with the hearing itself. The narrow time frame available, however, provided an obvious problem of access to the senators. As an alternative, we suspected and confirmed that the key people to interview in the attempt to identify roles were the staff members responsible to the various senators for developing information and formulating statements and questions for the hearings.[5] Each senator assigned this responsibility to his chief staff member serving on the Judiciary Committee or, more often, on one of the Judiciary subcommittees.

While the use of staff to measure senator role conceptions may be second-best to interviewing each senator directly, it seems that little measurement error occurs. This is due to the fact that the interaction between senator and staff member actually produces an articulation of role conception as the senator directs staff members to develop an opening statement and subsequent questions that will reflect the objectives sought by the senator. In those four instances in which both senators and staff were interviewed separately, we found no difference in the role conceptions articulated by the senator and his staff member. In the O'Connor nomination, interviews were conducted with the appropriate staff members for 16 of the 18 senators.[6] One senator was not included in the analysis because of his virtual absence from the proceedings. We were unsuccessful in repeated efforts to gain interviews with staff members for another senator.

In the Rehnquist and Scalia hearings, a different approach was used. Although motivations and behaviors are best understood by talking with the senators or with the staff members responsible for developing the opening statements and questions, such opportunities for "insider information" are rare. Since one purpose of this article is to provide insight that would permit outside observers to interpret the behavior and actions of the senators, we decided to examine the Rehnquist and Scalia hearings by analyzing only the information that would be available to any careful observer, namely, normal press coverage along with the opening statements and subsequent questioning by the senators.

News accounts serve to provide an understanding of the political milieu and an assessment of the nominee's qualification, background, and ideology. They also may serve to provide some sense about senatorial reaction to the nomination. Moreover, we observed a reasonably close adherence in the O'Connor hearings between what senators and staff told us in private and the comments made in the opening statements by these senators in the confirmation hearings. These statements often provide a clue to the senators' intentions and role predispositions.

On the basis of this combination of interviews in the O'Connor hearings, along with the opening statements from all three hearings, we identified various roles that appear to characterize the intentions and goals of senators during these Senate confirmation hearings. The behaviors determined by these roles are the questions and statements made by the senators during the question-and-answer part of the hearings. A specification of these roles and examples of behaviors they engender should prove most helpful in providing insight to the significance of these Senate confirmation hearings.

The prelude to role selection

The fact that many or most senators do not play an evaluator role in Supreme Court nomination hearings is perhaps more easily understood if one realizes that the hearings represent not the first, but the fourth step of the information gathering process for the Judiciary Committee members. Moreover, senatorial role selections are affected by the political environment in which the hearings occur, as well as the personal attitudes and attributes of the senators.

The information gathering process. The first step involves the collection of information by each senator's staff once the nominee is known. Each staff member becomes an independent collector of considerable printed material concerning the nominee and the nomination, in addition to letters and calls that come into the senator's office. At the same time, staffers make telephone calls to friends and associates of the senator in the nominee's home state and elsewhere in an effort to secure overviews and evaluations of the nominee. Almost without exception, special attention

is paid to any known liabilities or problems concerning the nominee, such as past memberships in segregated clubs or suspect financial dealings. Because of some presumption by the senators in favor of the president's choice,[7] attention focuses on any negative factors that might alter that presumption. In fact, Wayne Sulfridge posits as virtually a necessary condition for opposition to a nominee "strong emotional issues which can excite the public imagination."[8]

The second step in this process is the collection of information from official sources. FBI reports on nominees, once considered provocative, are now commonplace, but access to them is strictly limited to the senator only, not his staff. The chief counsel, with cooperation from the minority counsel, is responsible for gathering information for the committee as a whole. A questionnaire submitted to the nominee gathers basic biographical information, financial data, conflict of interest statements, and responses to some general interest questions. In the cases of these three justices, questions asked their response to a short criticism of "judicial activism" and to specify actions in their professional and personal lives that demonstrated their concern for "equal justice under the law."

The third part of the pre-hearing process involves a private meeting with the nominee by each of the senators on the committee. This is an important part of the process for both the nominee and the senator. From the nominee and administration's perspective, it provides insights into the concerns of the committee members and permits a preview of questions that are likely to be put to the nominee during the formal hearings. Each senator, in turn, is able to evaluate various aspects of the nominee and check out certain reservations he may possess.

By the time of the hearings, senators have acquired and evaluated substantial information concerning the nominee. They tend to assume that the information gathered is fairly exhaustive and that the nominee's strong and weak points have been identified. Since the senators presume that any important negative information concerning the nominee will be discovered before the hearings, it is further assumed that those who will testify against the confirmation will reveal no startling new information that will alter their assessment of the nominee.

The political and personal environment. While

the information gathering process is critical to the individual decisions of senators concerning their vote, there are also many political and personal factors that structure the nature of the hearings. In turn, we may distinguish between those political factors that deal with the political situation in which the nomination occurs and those that involve the specific nominee to the Court. Among those situational variables of importance are presidential power and popularity; partisan and ideological distribution in the Senate; the president's party and ideology; the current make-up of the Court with respect to ideology, race, sex, and other dimensions; and public opinion. Characteristics of the nominee that may assume prominence are ideology, race or ethnicity, sex, religion, character, experience, and other such factors. For an individual senator, factors include, but are not limited to, his general legislative role orientation, sense of loyalty to party and president, personality, constituency consideration, and personal agenda in the Senate.

While any one or more of these factors may play a significant role in one nomination or another, there are two factors, more than any others, that serve to structure the hearings of the modern era: the presumption in favor of the president's nominee and political ideology. As articulated by Senator Simpson in the Rehnquist hearings:

President Reagan was elected by a large majority.... He has the right and the obligation to nominate qualified men and women who share the philosophy of this president.[9]

This presumption exists not from respect for the president's wisdom, although there is an assumption that some initial screening will have produced a nominee without severe moral, ethical, or legal liabilities; rather, the presumption is a recognition of his power. A president willing to "go to the wall" on an issue is a formidable opponent indeed. When that power is augmented by a compatible Senate Judiciary Committee and/or Senate, then the minority must conserve its effort for those situations in which it can appeal beyond ideology. Senator Biden's attempt to place the burden of proof on the supporters of Justice Rehnquist to the contrary,[10] Grossman and Wasby have correctly noted that

... the confirmation process has been based on the assumption that the president should be allowed to make

any reasonable choice and that the "burden of proof" as to a nominee's lack of qualifications must be sustained by the opposition.[11]

As Biden's effort demonstrates, however, such a presumption is less likely to be respected by those in ideological opposition to the nominee. There seems little doubt that the ideological match between senator and nominee serves as the primary source of a senator's disposition concerning the nomination. Where ideological congruence exists, the qualifications and background of the nominee are simply less important. The positive elements emerge as great strengths and the negative elements as relatively minor problems. However, where the ideologies of senator and nominee are in conflict, a very careful scrutiny of the qualifications and background is typically pursued by the senator. Positive elements tend to be reduced to a presumptive minimum, and negative items assume considerable prominence.

The significance of ideology on predispositions to the nominees is clearly evident in Table 1. Support for the three Reagan nominees was explicitly forthcoming from committee conservatives in their opening statements in all but four instances. In one of those four, Simpson engaged in a rambling, introspective presentation in which his support for Scalia seemed apparent, but which avoided an explicit statement of it.[12] The other three, occurring in the O'Connor nomination, actually reinforce the importance of ideological congruence rather than refute it. For senators East, Grassley, and Denton, the so-called "right-to-life" principle was a critical component of their conservative ideology. O'Connor's stand on this dimension was unclear. In other words, ideological congruence was precisely the question here. To the extent that they found her in step with them, their support would be forthcoming. On the other hand, to find her in ideological opposition on this principle would likely prompt their opposition.

Examination of the moderates and liberals on the committee confirms that those not in ideological "sync" with the nominees were more likely to withhold support. There are two exceptions. Senator DeConcini qualifies as a moderate based on his voting record, yet he explicitly supported all three nominees. His is an unusual case, however, because of his position as home state senator for both O'Connor and Rehnquist. For DeConcini,

Table 1 Political ideology and pre-hearing commitment to the nominee

Senator	Party	Ideology	O'Connor	Rehnquist	Scalia
Thurmond	Rep.	Conservative	ex. sup.	ex. sup.	ex. sup.
Mathias	Rep.	Moderate	ex. sup.	noncom.	im. sup.
Laxalt	Rep.	Conservative	ex. sup.	ex. sup.	ex. sup.
Hatch	Rep.	Conservative	ex. sup.	ex. sup.	ex. sup.
Dole	Rep.	Conservative	ex. sup.	ex. sup.	ex. sup.
Simpson	Rep.	Conservative	ex. sup.	ex. sup.	im. sup.
East	Rep.	Conservative	noncom.	n.a.	n.a.
Grassley	Rep.	Conservative	mixed	ex. sup.	ex. sup.
Denton	Rep.	Conservative	uncertain	ex. sup.	ex. sup.
Specter	Rep.	Moderate	noncom.	noncom.	im. sup.
McConnell	Rep.	Conservative	n.a.	ex. sup.	ex. sup.
Broyhill	Rep.	Conservative	n.a.	ex. sup.	ex. sup.
Biden	Dem.	Liberal	im. sup.	uncertain	noncom.
Kennedy	Dem.	Liberal	ex. sup.	ex. opp.	mixed
Metzenbaum	Dem.	Liberal	ex. sup.	uncertain	mixed
DeConcini	Dem.	Moderate	ex. sup.	ex. sup.	ex. sup.
Leahy	Dem.	Liberal	ex. sup.	uncertain	noncom.
Baucus	Dem.	Liberal	noncom.	n.a.	n.a.
Heflin	Dem.	Conservative	ex. sup.	ex. sup.	ex. sup.
Simon	Dem.	Liberal	n.a.	uncertain	im. sup.

1. The levels of commitment for the last three columns in this table use the following labels: ex. sup.—support for the nominee was stated in the senator's opening remarks: im. sup.—support for the nominee seemed apparent from the senator's positive statements, but a specific commitment of support was not given; uncertain—indecision concerning how one might vote was explicitly stated; noncom.—statement was noncommittal, containing no positive or negative statements concerning the nominee nor any statement of indecision; mixed—both positive traits and negative bases for concern were mentioned, but no explicit support nor opposition was provided; ex. opp.—opposition to rather than support for the nominee was indicated; n.a.—not applicable, the senator was not on the committee for those particular hearings.

2. Political ideology was established using the ratings of the Conservative Caucus and Americans for Democratic Action. Scores between 25 and 75 were assigned a "moderate rating" while scores of 75 and above or 25 and below were assigned the appropriate "conservative" or "liberal" label. The 1981 scores were drawn from the "Congressional Voting Scores" data file made available by the Interuniversity Consortium for Political and Social Research. The 1986 scores were assessed from the November 15th and 22nd issues of *Congressional Quarterly Weekly Report*, 1986. Of course, neither the ICPSR nor *Congressional Quarterly* bears responsibility for the interpretation of the data.

3. With pre-hearing commitment reduced to three categories—support; uncertain/mixed/noncommittal; and opposition—gamma=.80, P<.01, indicating a relationship between ideological congruence and support for the nominee.

4. Denton abstained in the Committee vote on O'Connor. All others voted "Yes." For Rehnquist, the vote was 13-5. The "No" votes came from Biden, Kennedy, Metzenbaum, Leahy and Simon. The Scalia vote was a unanimous "Yes" one.

the political milieu and his own agenda as an Arizona senator seem to have played a role in his explicit support. The other exception comes in the explicit support for O'Connor from three of the five committee liberals and implicit support from a fourth. Once again, however, the apparent exception to the importance of ideology is actually in accord with it. There is no doubt that O'Connor's status as the first female appointee to the Court overshadowed the concerns of liberals and moderates about her conservative ideology. Committee liberals could hardly place themselves in a position of opposing the first woman, especially in the absence of any considerable negative factors about her. In a real sense, liberal opposition to O'Connor was pre-empted by the liberals' own claims in support of women's rights.

The presumption of confirmation clearly worked to the benefit of nominees O'Connor and Scalia, both of whom were perceived as politically conservative nominees. In the absence of negative findings in any of the pre-hearing information, no opposition emerged. O'Connor's status as the first

female nominee overcame questions of experience and competence. Scalia, on the other hand, was unable to win over his ideological adversaries in advance of the hearings. However, the normal presumption in favor of the nominee was augmented in his case by the fact that his hearings came immediately on the heels of Justice Rehnquist's. Opposition from the liberal minority to both of these back-to-back nominations surely seemed unwise, so Justice Rehnquist was targeted as the more vulnerable of the two, precisely because of the presence of certain negative factors on which to base an opposition.[13] Thus, while Scalia failed to gain the prior support of the liberal faction, he at least avoided their opposition.

While one might consider that Justice Rehnquist had a double presumption in his favor, being a sitting justice as well as the president's choice, Justice Fortas' problems in a similar setting in 1968 demonstrate the potential difficulty with being a sitting justice. There is no doubt that Rehnquist's record of conservative judgments bothered committee liberals. While Scalia appeared to be as conservative as Rehnquist in many areas, there were simply no negative emotional issues associated with Scalia over which the ideological opposition could muster an attack. With Rehnquist, however, there seemed to be several, none of which by itself constituted a sufficient cause, but the cumulative effect of which just might. As we shall see, this ultimately laid the foundation for certain role selections by various senators.

Role types

Given the amount of pre-hearing information and the usual context of the political and personal milieu, it is hardly surprising that by the time of the hearings most senators have already made up their minds and therefore do not pursue an evaluator role. Our concern here is with what alternative roles might be played by the non-evaluators. In these three hearings, we isolated four additional distinct situationally specific roles: validator, partisan, advertiser, and educator.

Each of these roles is a function of the senator's certainty of support for or opposition to the nominee, strategic considerations in light of the senator's political agenda and personal predispositions to act in a certain way. Thus, one who is uncertain about the nominee will almost surely pursue an evaluator role. On the other hand, strategic considerations are significant for those who are certain about their votes. The hearings may be expected to be controversial by virtue of a close or uncertain voting outcome or by a conscious decision by opponents to stir up controversy over the nominee; then the likelihood of a "certain" supporter playing a partisan role to help ensure approval is much more likely. Noncontroversial nominations permit a wider choice of roles. In the absence of uncertainty, which promotes the evaluator role, and controversy, which stimulates partisan roles, senators pursue other objectives. Some of these will become manifest as we describe each of the roles in turn.

The evaluator. The evaluator role is one designed to help a senator make up his mind concerning his vote on the nominee. The archetypical evaluator is probably one who carefully evaluates the nominee's responses to all questions, listens to all the evidence, and poses carefully framed questions designed to determine the fitness of the nominee. In reality, the evaluator is more likely to be one who is uncertain or unsettled about the

nominee on some one or just a few issues. It is also likely that any such issue is pivotal, virtually a necessary condition for the senator's consent or opposition to the nomination. The pivotal nature of such an issue usually means that it is a very prominent issue or that it strikes at that senator's "core requirements" for a Supreme Court justice. The evaluator is best characterized as one who will ask serious questions of the nominee that are designed to resolve those doubts in the senator's mind. Such a role is exemplified by the opening statement of Denton to Judge O'Connor:

Your answers at this hearing . . . will determine my estimate of your position . . . . It is my earnest hope that your responses will be neither broad nor bland, because I will base my single vote on those responses.[14]

Evaluators do not appear to be all that common in confirmation hearings, because so many of the factors that affect the voting decision have already made their impact. Evaluators are often recognizable, however, because of their forthrightness in an opening statement, as with Denton above. However, alternative opening styles for an evaluator are the noncommittal approach, used by East, which often simply notes the significance of the occasion, and the mixed approach of Grassley, who both praised and expressed reservations concerning nominee O'Connor.

Since the evaluator seeks to resolve doubts of a particular nature, he typically displays a very direct style of questioning that relates to those issues deemed so pertinent. For two of the three evaluators we observed in the O'Connor hearings, the issue of abortion was clearly pivotal. East asked eight questions during the hearings, seven of which dealt specifically with abortion. Denton managed 23 questions, 17 of which dealt specifically with abortion, two of which dealt with parents' rights concerning a young daughter's abortion and three of which concerned the role of women in the military. The abortion issue presented precisely the type of strong emotional issue Sulfridge asserts as essential for opposition to a nominee.[15] Had O'Connor given responses that indicated a pro-abortion stance, there seems little doubt that opposition would have resulted.

What makes life particularly difficult for an evaluator in a Supreme Court nomination hearing is the problem of getting straightforward answers from the nominee on any particular issue.

Nominees typically are unwilling to comment on particular cases that have come before the Supreme Court or on specific issues that could conceivably come before the Court. After two dozen or so questions dealing with abortion, Denton lamented, "I do not feel I have made any progress personally in determining where you stand on the issue of abortion . . . ."[16] When asked by the chair whether another 15 minutes to question the nominee would be helpful, Denton responded, "I do not know whether another month would do, Mr. Chairman."[17]

Grassley did not pursue the same line of questioning on abortion as the other two, although his questions did support their efforts. His initial round of questions for the most part did not deal with substantive questions designed to assist his evaluation of O'Connor. Rather he attempted to surmount O'Connor's earlier evasiveness with East's questions on abortion and her refusal to comment on *Roe v. Wade* on the grounds that it was an issue that might again confront the Court.[18] The nature of his questioning reminds us that there is more to the evaluator's role than just asking substantive questions with respect to the issues of concern. There may also be "sparring time" in which the evaluator must try to elicit responses from the nominee with an acceptable degree of specificity.

The validator. The validator role is often played by a senator who has made a preliminary decision on the nominee and who wishes to use the hearings to confirm or validate that opinion. Typically, such a role involves one who is inclined to vote "yes" on the confirmation, but who remains sufficiently open-minded to change his mind in the event that some serious shortcoming or flaw in the nominee arises. Such a position was expressed by Senator Metzenbaum in his opening statement in the Scalia hearings, in which he praised the nominee's integrity but proceeded to note that he retained an "open mind on this nomination."[19]

Empirically, we observed no validators who were leaning against the confirmation in any of the three nominations, and it seems probable that an individual leaning in opposition is likely to pursue a more active role in revealing the negative aspects of the nominee's credentials, a role different from that of validator. This assumption stems from the premise of the presumption in favor of the nominee. Since those who oppose carry the burden of establishing the nominee's "unfitness," those who lean in opposition must pursue the negative traits of the nominee to establish certainty of opinion in functionally the same way a negative partisan might carry the battle.

While the evaluator seeks to resolve for himself some very fundamental concerns regarding the fitness of the nominee to serve, the validator usually has resolved such basic questions. There is no need, then, for the validator to ask questions that will reveal the position of the nominee on a fundamental issue that relates to the necessary conditions of fitness for the senator. More commonly expressed is a desire to evaluate the quality of the nominee's mind and to assess the nominee's ability to function in pressure situations. The validator's goal, in effect, is to reassure himself concerning his vote, as exemplified by Biden's "relief" when Scalia affirmed that free speech can encompass physical actions and his overall "feeling better" about Scalia at the conclusion of his questioning.[20]

An analogy to doctoral dissertation defenses comes to mind here. Just as professors engage a doctoral student in mental gymnastics, the validating senator seeks to gain insight into the mental capacities of the nominee. It is conceivable that questions posed by the doctoral committee may reveal an unanticipated weakness that leads to failure of the exam. However, the norm is that the exam is passed, just as it is also the norm that validating senators do indeed validate their prior notions concerning the nominee.

The types of questions that provide such insight will vary widely, according to the knowledge, experience, and characteristics of each individual senator, as well as the order in which the senator is permitted to question. A staff member of one junior senator noted the problem of assuring that the senator would have good questions to ask even after his 15 colleagues had preceded him. Thus, Senator Baucus' so-called "tombstone question" ("How do you want to be remembered?") is an effort to be creative, clever and, at the same time, provide some psychological insight into the nominee.

More often than not, the validator assumes a somewhat benign approach in his questioning. Just as in a dissertation defense, however, senators will not hesitate to pursue certain points where the nominee betrays a weakness. For example,

O'Connor responded inadequately on a question dealing with *Brown v. Board*, which prompted further probing by two validating senators on the Republican side.[21] Also similar to dissertation defenses in which the basic subject and approach of the dissertation is accepted, questions tend to focus on procedural matters and questions of interpretation. Among the 100 questions asked O'Connor by presumably validating senators, 85 percent dealt with legal principles and procedures as opposed to substantive policy issues like abortion or school prayer. Thus, O'Connor was quizzed on *stare decisis*, federal-state jurisdictions, federal court jurisdiction, legislative-judicial relationships, constitutional revision, and other topics of judicial relevance, but not on topics one would think sufficient to prompt a negative decision concerning the nominee.

Partisan. A partisan is one who has already decided how to vote on the nominee and uses the hearings to press the partisan view. A partisan may be either positive or negative toward the nominee. The positive partisan will use the hearings as an opportunity to assist the nominee. This is done through praise of the nominee, by posing questions that permit the nominee to look as good as possible and by defending the nominee against attacks of opponents. On the other hand, the negative partisan will use the hearings to call the fitness of the nominee into question.

Senator Thurmond provides an interesting profile of a positive partisan for the Reagan nominations and, by way of contrast, a negative partisan in the Thurgood Marshall and Abe Fortas (nomination to be chief justice) hearings. In the O'Connor, Rehnquist, and Scalia hearings, Thurmond's opening statements were supportive of the nominees. His lead-off questions to each of the justices provided them with the opportunity to confront major issues of their nominations in a relatively unthreatening way. As the initial interrogator, Thurmond was able to pose questions in a very open-ended fashion that dealt with what was perceived to be the concern of potential opponents. In this way the nominee was able to make initial statements about these issues in a nonconfrontational way. This is exemplified by the following questions to O'Connor, each of which was not followed with further probes by Thurmond, but was simply dropped after O'Connor made what appeared to be virtually a prepared statement.

. . . would you state your views on the proper role of the Supreme Court in our system of government?[22]

Would you discuss your philosophy on abortion, both personal and judicial, and explain your actions as a state senator in Arizona on certain specific matters?[23]

In more controversial nominations, the positive partisan may find it necessary to play a more vigorous role in defense of the nominee and in counter-attacking the negative partisans. In the Rehnquist hearings, Senator Hatch displayed this vigorous aspect of the positive partisan. For example, he defended Rehnquist's lone dissent in the "Bob Jones" case, arguing there were legitimately two sides to the question involved and that Rehnquist's dissent was indeed rational and not a function of racial prejudice. He presented detailed data concerning the frequency of Rehnquist's dissents to demonstrate how his tendency to dissent on his own had declined in more recent years. Even though the Scalia nomination was less controversial, Hatch pursued the positive partisan role there as well, defending certain decisions by Scalia to allay fears that he might be anti-press with respect to the First Amendment.

For negative partisans, the hope is to persuade others to oppose the nomination and to make the nominee look bad. In the Abe Fortas hearings, Thurmond also played the partisan role with cunning and vigor, but in that instance as a negative partisan. His questions were of a type that Fortas, as would have most any other nominee, refused to answer as inappropriate. However, whereas Thurmond invited O'Connor to decline to answer if she felt her answers ". . . would impinge upon (her) responsibilities as an Associate Justice of the Supreme Court . . . ,"[24] Thurmond rifled question after question at Fortas, chiding each refusal to answer with ". . . and you refuse to answer that?"[25] In the Marshall hearings, Thurmond took the nominee through questions of legal technicalities and historical occurrences that proved difficult to answer in an effort to embarrass the nominee and perhaps gain support for the opposition effort.[26]

In the Rehnquist hearings, some Democrats tried to make Rehnquist look bad with respect to certain legal, moral, and ethical questions. For example, they raised questions concerning Rehnquist's accession to restrictive housing covenants, whether he had participated in intimidating minority voters, whether he supported maintaining the "separate but equal" doctrine at the time of *Brown v. Board*, and other issues. They argued that his frequency of lone dissents placed him out of the mainstream of legal thought in the country. In the absence of a single major negative issue, the opponents tried to construct a basis for opposition on an accumulation of negative elements over a period of 32 years. In the end, their failure to rally enough opposition may have been due in part to the absence of a sufficiently strong emotional issue, and certainly in part to the fact that political liberals constituted a distinct minority of senators both on the committee and in the Senate.

Educator. Senators who have made up their minds before the hearings have the most flexibility in their role selection. Unencumbered by a need to establish information on which their decision will be based, they are free to pursue a wide range of objectives. This is particularly true in a noncontroversial nomination in which the role of partisan seems relatively unnecessary. One additional role that surfaced in the O'Connor and Scalia hearings is that of "educator." This is a broad role that may have different targets for educational improvement. Senators may wish to educate the nominee, fellow committee members, fellow senators, the president, the public, and perhaps specific population subgroups as well. The educator, then, is one who wishes to use the hearings as an opportunity to inform and perhaps influence one or more of these targets.

In the Scalia hearing, Senator Kennedy was explicit about his role as he expressed in his opening statement the ". . . hope that, as a result of these hearings . . . he (Scalia) will look with greater sensitivity on (the) critical issues . . ." of race discrimination and women's rights.[27] While it might seem futile to "educate" the nominee, more than one senator thought it worth the effort. As Metzenbaum, an educator in the O'Connor hearings told us, "You just might get her to think or rethink about points that you have made and, at some point down the line, perhaps something positive will happen." Biden also played the educator with nominee O'Connor as the target:

Would it be, in your opinion, inappropriate for you as the first and only woman at this point on the Supreme Court . . . to for example be involved in national efforts to promote the ERA?

It is your right, if it were your desire, to go out and campaign like the devil for the ERA. It is your right to go out and make speeches across the country about inequality for women, if you believe it. Don't wall yourself off.[28]

Other targets of the educator also surfaced. One Democratic senator commented privately on the need to educate the president to the fact that he should be concerned with more than pleasing conservative Republicans by his appointments, that liberal senators in both parties were concerned about and would scrutinize the views of Supreme Court nominees. Another senator commented on the opportunity provided by the hearings to raise an issue concerning legislation that he was backing and to obtain publicity for it, targeted at both senatorial colleagues and the general public. In one such instance, a senator proceeded to describe the legislation that was pending, provide his justification for the legislation, and secure the nominee's somewhat passive assent that the legislation probably posed no constitutional problems.[29]

Advertiser. Closely akin to the role of educator is that of advertiser. Like the educator, the advertiser may have a variety of targets. Behaviorally, the difference between trying to educate and simply advertise is rather obscure, at best. At this initial stage of inquiry, however, we think there is an important conceptual distinction that relates to the intentions of senators. The intent of the educator is to develop the target's mind and perhaps to persuade to some point of view, while the intent of the advertiser is to inform or publicize some point without the developmental or persuasive component. One example of advertiser behavior is the line of questioning pursued by Kennedy in the O'Connor hearing.

From your own knowledge and perception how would you characterize the level of discrimination on the basis of sex today?[30]

I wonder if you briefly would discuss your perception of the degree to which black Americans or Hispanic Americans are denied equality in our society.[31]

Such a line of questioning could come from either an educator or an advertiser. This illustrates the inappropriateness of trying to classify role type from the behavioral enactment of that role. Our interview with Kennedy's staff during the O'Connor hearing led us to conclude that he wished to use this opportunity to demonstrate his concern about what he believed to be the persistent discrimination in our society.

In still other instances, questions asked by the advertiser may not differ much from questions asked by an evaluator, to the extent that both may be reflecting concerns that are relevant to their constituents. For example, Senator Dole's question concerning O'Connor's interpretation of the term "strict constructionist" and whether or not she felt that concept described her might come from an evaluator who thought the concept was particularly pertinent. In this case, however, it came form a senator who perceived a home constituency would be reassured by the nominee's anticipated answer. He sought to advertise to his constituency that she was a "strict constructionist" and he was safeguarding the Court by making that determination. These examples suggest that, quite often, the advertising senator is also advertising himself by advertising an issue.

Conclusion

With respect to Supreme Court nomination hearings, it seems a fact of political and scholarly life that only controversial nominations offer any interest and insight regarding the confirmation process. Such a view tends to focus only on the outcome of the nomination as being significant. From that perspective, the most recent three hearings were merely theatrics. As Table 1 shows, the vast majority of senators in each of the three hearings had already made up their minds how to vote even before the hearings had begun. Table 1 reveals that those who expressed "uncertainty" concerning their votes ended up opposing the nominee in committee. On the other hand, those whose statements were best characterized as "mixed" or "noncommittal" always favored the nominee in the committee vote. If one is interested only in outcome, the hearings offered little in drama or significance.

It is our contention, however, that outcome is not the only relevant question for hearings. Senators pursue important goals in both controversial and noncontroversial nominations, as reflected by the efforts of negative partisans, educators and advertisers. Not the least of these goals is to influence the next nomination even before it is made. We do hope that our discussion of several situationally specific roles, along with an explanation of factors that foster these roles, will contribute not only to an understanding of the last three confirmation hearings, but will enhance our comprehension of future hearings—controversial or noncontroversial.

NOTES

This article originally appeared in Volume 71, Number 4, December-January 1988, pages 186-196.

1. In the O'Connor nomination, 13 of the 18 committee members made opening statements that voiced satisfaction with the nominee, while only three explicitly expressed any reservations. NOMINATION OF SANDRA DAY O'CONNOR: HEARINGS BEFORE CONGRESS, FIRST SESSION Serial No. J-97-51, 1-31, 34-36, *passim.* (Washington: U.S. Government Printing Office, 1982). For Scalia, 13 of the 18 also voiced satisfaction in opening statements, while none of the Senators expressed explicit reservations. TRANSCRIPT OF PROCEEDINGS; UNITED STATES SENATE; COMMITTEE ON THE JUDICIARY; NOMINATION OF ANTONIN SCALIA, TO BE ASSOCIATE JUSTICE OF THE SUPREME COURT 2-3, 11-64, *passim.* (Washington, DC: Miller Reporting Co., 1986).

2. Grossman and Wasby, *The Senate and Supreme Court Nominations,* 1972 DUKE L. J. 563.

3. Jewell, *Attitudinal Determinants of Legislative Behavior: The Utility of Role Analysis,* in Kornberg and Musolf, (eds.), LEGISLATURES IN DEVELOPMENTAL PERSPECTIVE 491 (Durham, NC: Duke University Press, 1970).

4. The myth of the hearings as a meeting of open-minded senators seeking information for their decisions is poignantly illustrated during the testimony of Reverand Carl McIntire in the O'Connor hearing. In providing testimony against nominee O'Connor, the Rev. McIntire finds himself addressing only the chair, Senator Thurmond. All other senators are absent. "Senator, I want to protest it. I want to protest coming down to the end of this hearing and only having you to talk to. I sat here and listened at every Senator here on the bench . . . and a majority have already said they are going to vote for her . . . ." O'CONNOR HEARINGS, *supra* n. 1, at 345.

5. The role of the staff in interacting with and preparing senators for their committee presentations is noted in Jones and Woll, THE PRIVATE WORLD OF CONGRESS 154-171 (New York: Free Press, 1979); and in Mackenzie, THE POLITICS OF PRESIDENTIAL APPOINTMENTS 182 (New York: Free Press, 1981).

6. The research design is best described as field research involving an unstructured interview, but one that consistently sought answers to a basic set of concerns, namely:
• the criteria considered important in Supreme Court nominations;
• the techniques and sources for gathering information concerning the nominee;
• the sources of efforts to influence a senator's decision regarding the confirmation;
• the importance of the nominee's gender in this particular nomination;
• the purposes or functions of the senator's questions during the hearings.

7. Grossman and Wasby, *supra* n. 2, at 588.

8. Sulfridge, *Ideology as a Factor in Senate Consideration of Supreme Court Nominations,* 42 J. OF POL. 566 (May 1980).

9. REHNQUIST HEARINGS (C-Span televised hearings, July 30, 1986).

10. In his opening statement of the Rehnquist hearings, Senator Biden, the ranking Democratic member of the committee, asserted that ". . . as the framers of the Constitution intended, the burden is upon the nominee and his proponents to make the case for confirmation of Chief Justice." REHNQUIST HEARINGS, *supra* n. 9.

11. Grossman and Wasby, *supra* n. 2, at 588.

12. SCALIA PROCEEDINGS, *supra* n. 1, at 36-40.

13. For newspaper coverage of Rehnquist, see especially, THE NEW YORK TIMES July 27, 1986, at A18, and July 29, 1986, at A14. For a report on Scalia, see THE NEW YORK TIMES, August 6, 1986, at A13.

14. O'CONNOR HEARINGS, *supra* n. 1, at 29.

15. Sulfridge, *supra* n. 8, at 566.

16. O'CONNOR HEARINGS, *supra* n. 1, at 249.

17. *Id.* at 248.

18. *Id.* at 116-118.

19. SCALIA HEARINGS, *supra* n. 1, at 29.

20. *Id.* at 118, 121.

21. O'CONNOR HEARINGS, *supra* n. 1, at 102-103, 131-132.

22. *Id.* at 60.

23. *Id.* at 60.

24. *Id.* at 132.

25. NOMINATIONS OF ABE FORTAS AND HOMER THORNBERRY; HEARINGS BEFORE THE COMMITTEE OF THE JUDICIARY, UNITED STATES SENATE, NINETIETH CONGRESS, SECOND SESSION 183-184 (Washington, DC: U.S. Government Printing Office, 1968).

26. NOMINATION OF THURGOOD MARSHALL; HEARINGS BEFORE THE COMMITTEE OF THE JUDICIARY, UNITED STATES SENATE, NINETIETH CONGRESS, FIRST SESSION 183-184 (Washington, DC: U.S. Government Printing Office, 1968).

27. SCALIA PROCEEDINGS, *supra* n. 1, at 25.

28. The written transcript deviates somewhat from Biden's actual comments as revealed by a videotape playback. We provide a quote from the videotape.

29. O'CONNOR HEARINGS, *supra* n. 1, at 153-154.

30. *Id.* at 76.

31. *Id.* at 77.

The Bork hearing: rocks and roles

From the day the president nominated Robert Bork, it was apparent this hearing would be different from those of Reagan's other three nominations. Senator Kennedy sounded immediate opposition that grew to include the five liberal Democrats pitted in a partisan battle against the five conservative Republicans[1] for the hearts and votes of the committee moderates (Specter, Deconcini, Byrd) and the conservative Democrat Heflin. As undecided decision makers, these latter four would pursue evaluator roles in an effort to make up their respective minds concerning their votes. Given the uncertainty of the outcome, no one had the luxury of pursuing the validator, educator, and advertiser roles discussed in our accompanying article.

Not only was the configuration of role playing different from the previous hearings, the level of hostility was considerably greater. Partisans on both sides hurled verbal rocks at each other, the president, various groups and individuals lobbying the hearing, and the nominee himself. These differences from previous hearings stimulated our interest in two directions. First, we wanted to see if our approach in the accompanying article could help make sense of these events. Second, we wanted to determine if a more generalized model of the role playing process could be suggested to incorporate the different hearings of the four Reagan nominees.

Hearing controversy

Clearly, what was different about the Bork hearings was their level of controversy. The O'Connor and Scalia hearings lacked any real drama. The Rehnquist elevation to chief justice had stirred some controversy because the relatively small group of Democratic liberals on the Judiciary Committee chose to play negative partisan roles. The Bork nomination added the essential defining characteristic of a controversial nomination, namely, the potential for actually defeating the nomination. For the first time among the Reagan nominees, the outcome was genuinely in doubt.

The controversy stemmed from two of the basic components that structure the nature of the hearings: the political situation at the time of the nomination and the nominee himself.[2] Three aspects of the political situation seem especially significant:

First, the partisan and ideological opposition to the nominee no longer constituted a distinct minority who faced certain defeat. The 1986 election produced a substantial Democratic majority (54 to 46) to replace the Republican majority that had considered the president's previous nominees. On the Judiciary Committee, the Republican majority of 11 members, containing 9 conservatives, was reduced to only 5 conservatives (plus the moderate Specter). On the other hand, the Democrats retained their five liberals, two moderates, and one conservative (see Table 1).

Second, the president's power had waned. Combined with the electoral resurgence of the Democratic opposition in 1986 were the facts that the president had now entered the "lame duck" period, the last two years in office, and had suffered prestige and credibility drops due to the Iran-contra hearings and other political setbacks. At the time of the Rehnquist and Scalia hearings, the president's approval rating hovered around 67 percent. When the Bork hearings took place, these ratings had dropped to about 52 percent.[3] The presumption in favor of a president's nominee, based on the president's power, was seriously eroded.

Third, the ideological balance of the Court seemed to be at stake. The retiring Justice Powell had been on the winning side of more 5 to 4 decisions than any other justice.[4] His apparently pivotal role on the Court upped the ante for this particular nomination.

In addition to the inherently controversial situation, Bork proved to be a nominee who provided several negative emotional issues around which to rally an opposition. In prior nominations, negative emotional issues more commonly involved questions of ethics, incompetence, or racism. The nomination of Bork, an academician with nearly impeccable ethical and intellectual credentials, might normally have provoked little excitement. Instead the hearings provided a rare sight in judicial nomination proceedings, a controversy stirred by emotions about legal concepts. It was Bork's own intellectual passion, as represented in a career of provocative conservative writings, that roused the opposition, which articulated concerns over the nominee's apparent lack of commitment to a variety of civil rights and liberties.

Controversy, it seems, can arise as a result of an interplay of factors that constitute the political situation or as a result of factors that relate to an individual nominee; however, these are not independent factors. Whether the nominee's sex, ethnicity, religion, or ideology are potentially controversial matters depends, in part, on the political atmosphere of the times. In turn, these factors may help structure the political situation.

In Justice O'Connor's case, gender played a major role in creating a noncontroversial nomination. In Judge Bork's case, his ideology, portrayed by opponents and even some supporters as an ardent, almost reactionary, conservatism, assured his status as a controversial nominee to liberals and eventually to moderates and southern Democratic conservatives as well. Of course, Justice Rehnquist attained a certain controversiality among liberals by virtue of his conservative record. Yet his initial nomination and his more recent elevation to chief justice did not reach the level of controversy surrounding the Bork nomination. Why?

The answer lies with those aspects of the political system and environment in which Judge Bork found himself, as highlighted by the three factors specified at the beginning of this note. In short, the situation was highly charged. Contrast this with Scalia and Rehnquist, both of whom were perceived as quite conservative nominees. Those hear-

Table 1   Political ideology and pre-hearing commitment to Judge Bork

Senator	Party	Ideology[1]	Pre-hearing commitment
Biden	Dem.	liberal	explicit opposition
Kennedy	Dem.	liberal	explicit opposition
Byrd	Dem.	moderate	uncertain
Metzenbaum	Dem.	liberal	explicit opposition
DeConcini	Dem.	moderate	uncertain
Leahy	Dem.	liberal	explicit opposition
Heflin	Dem.	conservative	uncertain
Simon	Dem.	liberal	implicit opposition
Thurmond	Rep.	conservative	explicit support
Hatch	Rep.	conservative	explicit support
Simpson	Rep.	conservative	explicit support
Grassley[2]	Rep.	moderate	explicit support
Specter	Rep.	moderate	uncertain
Humphrey	Rep.	conservative	explicit support

1. Political ideology was established by averaging the ratings of the Conservative Coalition and Americans for Democratic Action (ADA). Scores between 25 and 75 were assigned a "moderate" rating, while scores of 75 and above and 25 and below were assigned the appropriate "conservative" or "liberal" label. The ADA scores were drawn from the *Congressional Quarterly Weekly Report*, August 22, 1987, at 1968. The Conservative Coalition scores were kindly provided by the *Congressional Quarterly* research staff (Michael Amin and Andrew Taylor) and covered 23 votes in 1987 up to the August recess.

2. Senator Grassley's classification reflects a departure from previous, more conservative ratings. With scores of 30 on the ADA index and 61 on the Conservative Coalition, he remains closer to his conservative colleagues than to the other moderates. Given his initial support for Bork and his consistent conservative stance in the Reagan nominations, we have continued to characterize him in the text as one of the five conservative Republicans on the committee.

Figure 1. Interplay of situation and nominee controversy in the Reagan nominations

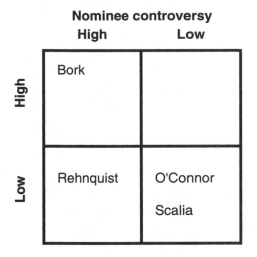

ings, however, occurred with a stronger president, prior to the next congressional election, with a more conservative dominated Republican majority in the Senate, and at a time when the ideological make-up of the Court did not rest in the balance. Conservative Scalia replaced the equally conservative Burger. Rehnquist, of course, was already on the Court.

Figure 1 models the interplay of these two areas. We place the O'Connor and Scalia nominations in the cell that denotes a relatively low level of controversy with respect to both the nominee and the situation. Rehnquist presents a controversial nominee, but in a political situation devoid of so many of the potential conflicts that beset Bork. Of course, Bork falls in the cell of high controversy for both situation and nominee, which helps to visualize why the hearings were so controversial. We shall return to this model later to discuss some implications that derive from it.

Controversy and role playing

Given the controversy surrounding the Bork nomination, we may ask whether the types of roles differed from those played in the less controversial hearings of the three previous nominees. Implicit in our article is a model of individual role selection, presented in Figure 2.

We have identified a considerable number of situational, nominee, and personal factors that affect whether or not a senator will make a decision concerning his vote by the commencement of the

hearings.[5] These factors determine the level of controversy surrounding the nomination and they affect the pre-hearing disposition of the senator's confirmation decision. The model also suggests that the level of controversy may influence a senator's pre-hearing decision status. For example, it is our perception that controversy tends to reduce the likelihood of a "somewhat certain" position. Controversy is partly generated by firmly held opposing opinions, which, in turn, induces those holding less firm opinions into one or another of the two camps.

The role adopted by a senator at the hearings will depend most directly on his pre-hearing disposition. The model asserts that those senators who are uncertain about their vote will pursue an evaluator role. They must ask questions designed to address their uncertainties. In the Bork nomination senators Specter, DeConcini, and Heflin seem to have done just that.[6] All other votes on the committee were already certain, as evidenced by pre-hearing and/or opening statements. Because the opposition carries the burden of establishing the unfitness of the nominee, they tend to adopt partisan roles in an aggressive effort to discredit the nominee. The "certain Yes" senators can pursue a variety of strategies unless the nomination is controversial. In such circumstances, they too must pursue a partisan role in an effort to combat the opposition. This clearly occurred in the Bork hearing, with the partisan efforts reaching spectacular heights (or depths) that were, in turn, deplored by both sides.

In less controversial hearings, those who still are uncertain about the nominee as the hearings begin will adopt the evaluator role. We are also likely to see the re-emergence of a few who are somewhat certain supporters, in which case the validator role will be pursued. Any opposition will play the negative partisan role.[7] The biggest change in less controversial hearings is that those whose votes are certain for confirmation are free to pursue the educator and advertiser roles, as well as a somewhat less intense positive partisan role.

Implications

The two models and the ensuing discussions have implications for assessing the character of future hearings, the individual roles that are pursued in those hearings, and even the outcome. The model of situation/nominee controversy provides one way

Figure 2. A model of individual role selection

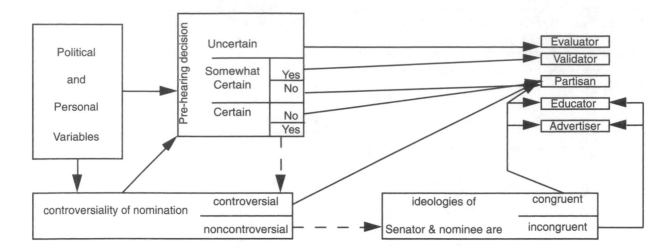

of characterizing hearings. In conjunction with the individual role selection model, one may seek the presence, absence, or predominance of certain roles in particular types of hearings. Thus, partisan and evaluator roles are most likely in instances of high situation and high nominee controversy. Conversely, in a nomination that is low on both dimensions of controversy, senators are able to play educator, advertiser, and validator roles, in addition to the evaluator and partisan ones.

In mixed nominations, where there is controversy on one dimension but not on the other, the partisan and evaluator roles are also quite likely to surface. The other roles may be played as well, but predicting their appearance depends in part on the degrees of controversy presented by the nominee or situation. We save a fuller exploration of such specification for another time.

Another interesting aspect of the situation/nominee controversy model is the implication for predicting outcome. For example, in instances of low situation and low nominee controversy, confirmation is a certainty. Where either the situation or nominee is controversial, but not both, the odds still favor confirmation, depending on the location of the nominee in that particular cell. Finally, in highly charged situations with a controversial nominee, the outcome can go either way. These implications are diagrammed in Figure 3.

An interesting aspect of this model is an implication that, had the Bork and Scalia nominations

Figure 3. Interplay of situation and nominee controversy on Committee confirmation

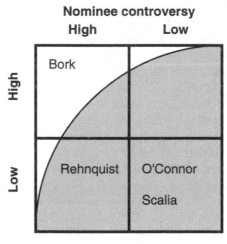

Committee recommends confirmation
Committee recommends against confirmation

been reversed in order, both would likely have gained seats on the Court. A Bork nomination in a less controversial situation should have succeeded. Scalia's noncontroversial status as an individual presumably would have produced confirmation even in a more volatile political situation.

Whether the failure of the Bork nomination serves to defuse an inherently controversial political situation remains to be seen at this writing. That seemed clearly to be the administration's strategy in pursuing the Bork nomination to a Senate vote. We think a more certain route towards confirmation is another strategy offered by the model. A simple appointment of a noncontroversial individual, even if quite conservative, can still gain confirmation to the Court.

—John Stookey and George Watson

NOTES

This article originally appeared in Volume 71, Number 4, December-January 1988, pages 194-196.

1. See note 2 in Table 1.

2. Watson and Stookey, *Supreme Court confirmation hearings: a view from the Senate*, 71 JUDICATURE 188-189 (1988).

3. As communicated to us by Richard Morin, polling editor, *Washington Post*, from data collected through the ABC/ Washington Post surveys of September 1986, and September 1987, respectively.

4. Goldman, CONSTITUTIONAL LAW: CASES AND ESSAYS 157 (New York: Harper and Row, 1987).

5. Watson and Stookey, *supra* n. 2, at 188-189.

6. Senator Byrd did not participate fully in asking questions due to his other commitments as majority leader. While he did exhibit uncertainty in his opening statement of the Bork hearing, his diminished or lack of participation in all of the Reagan nominee hearings has led us to omit him from the analysis.

7. Watson and Stookey, *supra* n. 2, at 191-192.

Limiting federal court jurisdiction: the unforeseen impact on courts *and* Congress

Limiting jurisdiction will not change past Supreme Court decisions. In fact, it will leave American rights and liberties vulnerable to the whims of future Congresses and the states.

by Kenneth R. Kay

Congressional attempts to remove the jurisdiction of the federal courts over specific controversial issues are not new or unique to the 97th Congress. In the last 25 years, there have been isolated efforts to remove the Supreme Court's jurisdiction over specific subjects in response to Court opinions.[1] However, in the last two years, the incidence of such attempts by Congress has increased dramatically.

• In April 1979, the then Democrat-controlled Senate voted 51 to 40 in favor of an amendment, offered by Senator Jesse Helms of North Carolina, to a Supreme Court jurisdiction bill.[2] The amendment would have eliminated Supreme Court and lower federal court jurisdiction over the issue of school prayer.

• This year, subcommittees of both the House and Senate judiciary committees have held hearings on the overall issue of congressional attempts to limit the federal courts, and on July 9 the Senate Separation of Powers Subcommittee favorably reported legislation that would eliminate lower federal court jurisdiction in certain abortion cases.[3]

• The Senate recently engaged in a lengthy filibuster because of an amendment to the Department of Justice authorization bill, which would limit those instances in which a federal court could issue a busing order.[4] This same issue is currently under active consideration in the Senate Judiciary Committee.[5]

• There are approximately 20 separate pieces of legislation pending in the House and the Senate that would limit the jurisdiction of the federal courts.[6]

Clearly, congressional attempts to remove federal court jurisdiction are no longer limited to isolated occurrences. Nor are the bills introduced merely to serve as vehicles for congressional hearings or to send a "message" to the courts. Rather, the jurisdiction bills are beginning to serve as the legislative centerpieces of the lobbying efforts of several constituencies. Single-interest groups that until now have failed to mobilize sufficient support for constitutional amendments have shifted their focus to court jurisdiction proposals. The issue of court jurisdiction is likely to be the battlefield on which the struggles over the nation's most controversial social issues will be fought. The court jurisdiction proposals represent a profound and substantial assault on the federal judiciary.

It is in this context that the emphasis of the current congressional dialogue is most disturbing. The focus on each piece of court jurisdiction legislation has been an emotional response to a particular decision of the Supreme Court, rather than on the substantive impact of withdrawing court jurisdiction. For example, when the full Senate voted on the Helms amendment in April 1979, the vote was perceived as a vote on school prayer. Congressional consideration of these bills continues to be in the context of school prayer, abortion, or busing, and not in the context of the role of the federal courts in the American system of government.

The constitutional debate

Equally disturbing has been the congressional pre-occupation with whether or not the proposals to withdraw court jurisdiction are constitutional. The debate, thus far, has progressed on the premise that if the Constitution gives the Congress the *authority* to do it, then the Congress *ought* to do it.

There are credible constitutional arguments on both sides. In the case of Supreme Court jurisdiction, the "exceptions clause" in Article III, Section 2, clearly gives Congress some meaningful power to withdraw jurisdiction in certain cases. This power was upheld by the Supreme Court in *McCardle*.[7] However, the Supreme Court has recognized that the power does not include the power to determine how the court shall decide cases.[8] Equally significant is the fact that the Supreme Court does not exist at the discretion of Congress, but is created by Article III of the Constitution. Therefore, the "exceptions" clause cannot be read as including in it the power to virtually eliminate the Court as a branch of government.

Congressional power to remove the jurisdiction of lower federal courts is a less complicated matter. Under Article III, Congress has the power to create the inferior federal courts and from that flows the power to reduce or eliminate their jurisdiction. However, even this power of Congress cannot be exercised in violation of other provisions of the Constitution.

For example, Congress could not restrict lower federal court jurisdiction on the basis of race. Such a statute would blatantly violate the equal protection clause. It is also plausible to argue that in other specific areas where there is a recognized constitutional right, removal of lower federal court jurisdiction over that subject would violate the corresponding constitutional provision. This analysis is strongest where it can be demonstrated that Congress has removed the jurisdiction for the very purpose of weakening the ability of citizens to vindicate a particular right.

In the final analysis, however, the fascinating constitutional dialogue is simply that—a fascinating dialogue. Even if we could resolve the question of whether Congress has the power, the more critical question is whether Congress ought to exercise it. Rather than constitutionality or emotion, what we need to do is pay far more attention to the public policy considerations of the various proposals.

The public policy debate

The argument in favor of the proposals to remove court jurisdiction goes something like this: The Supreme Court has acted unconstitutionally in reaching decisions—it has usurped the legislative function by expanding its own power under the Fourteenth Amendment. The school prayer cases are just one example of such court conduct.[9] When the court so acts, it is not only permissible, but appropriate, for the Congress to take the court out of the business of acting unconstitutionally.

The argument is based on the everyday analogy that if a child has used his BB gun to put a hole through a window at the Jones' house, then the parents should take the gun away. If he doesn't have a gun, he can't do any more damage.

The analogy breaks down immediately because the Congress and the courts are involved in something more akin to a marriage than a parental relationship. But even if one stays with the analogy, pending proposals amount to much more than the parents simply taking the gun away. The proposals amount to telling the child that he can never go over to the Jones' house again, even for some positive purpose like helping them mow their lawn. And it's important to note that keeping the child from ever going to the Jones' again does not replace the broken window.

Removal of court jurisdiction over specific subject matter does not repair any damage. The simple fact is that withdrawing the Supreme Court's jurisdiction over school prayer does not return prayer to the schools. Withdrawing court jurisdiction over abortion does not outlaw abortion. While this may seem obvious, it is a point that has escaped many who have engaged in the dialogue over this issue.

In fact, one can plausibly argue that not only do these jurisdictional bills not alter the substantive state of the law, but that they actually elevate Supreme Court decisions to the status of the "permanent" law of the land. The Court's school prayer decisions would not only be the law of the land today, but would be locked in stone as the last word from the Supreme Court.

Also possible is the situation where state courts might further restrict the scope of current Supreme Court rulings. For example, it is generally agreed that current Supreme Court rulings do not preclude school periods of silent meditation. If Supreme Court jurisdiction over school prayer were removed, individual state supreme courts would be free to declare periods of silent meditation in schools unconstitutional. In those states, citizens who support school prayer would have to live with an even more unacceptable state of the law than that which the Supreme Court has already declared.

Similarly, the opponents of abortion would have substantially damaged their own cause if they had attempted and succeeded in removing Supreme Court jurisdiction over abortion in the wake of *Roe v. Wade*.[10] The Court would have been unable to render its decision in the *McRae* case in which it held that Congress and state legislatures can constitutionally prohibit federal and state funding of abortions.[11] State supreme courts would have been free to declare that a state's funding of abortions was constitutionally required in that state.

Finally, consider the confusion created by a scheme where federal funding of abortions is constitutionally required in some states, not constitutionally required in others, and not reviewable by the Supreme Court. In such a situation, the removal of Supreme Court jurisdiction over abortion would have have aided those who opposed the Court's ruling in *Roe v. Wade*.

Impact on the judicial system

Not only do these proposals do so little to promote the cause of their proponents, they do much to upset many basic principles upon which our judicial system currently operates. Two of the primary principles at stake are those of judicial independence and the separation of powers. These proposals undermine the essential function of the courts to serve as the final protector and arbiter of the terms of the U.S. Constitution. As Alexander Hamilton stated in Federalist 78, it is the duty of the courts "to declare all acts contrary to the manifest tenor of the Constitution void. Without this, all reservations of particular rights or privileges would amount to nothing."[12] The court jurisdiction proposals envision a system of government in which the judicial branch's ability to protect constitutional rights and privileges can be removed by a simple majority of Congress.

The proponents argue that judicial usurpation of the legislative function is ample justification for their proposals. But they have clearly prescribed the legislative usurpation of the judicial function as the antidote. The end result of their proposals is that constitutional protections become illusory.

If Congress can determine which rights and privileges are to be reviewed, Congress has, in effect, decided which rights and privileges exist. The protections of the Constitution will only be what 51 percent of the House and 51 percent of the Senate say they are. This is not what was intended by the framers of our Constitution.

President Andrew Johnson made this exact point in his message of veto of the legislation that became the subject of the *McCardle* decision.

The legislation proposed (to foreclose constitutional review in the Supreme Court) is not in harmony with the spirit and intention of the Constitution . . . it establishes a precedent which, if followed, may eventually sweep away every check on arbitrary and unconstitutional legislation.

Thus far, during the existence of the government, the Supreme Court of the United States has been viewed by the people as the true expounder of their Constitution, and in the most violent party conflicts, its judgments and decrees have always been sought and deferred to with confidence and respect . . . any act which may be construed into or mistaken for an attempt to prevent or evade its decisions on a question which affects the liberty of the citizens and agitates the country cannot fail to be attended with unpropitious consequences.[13]

A third principle profoundly affected by such legislation is that of *stare decisis*. One of the most unfortunate aspects of these jurisdictional bills is that at their heart they depend on an erosion of the principle. The congressional sponsors of the legislation realize that they cannot directly reverse the Supreme Court school prayer decision, so instead they want to withdraw the Supreme Court's jurisdiction and give the state courts a knowing wink and say, "go ahead—they can't touch you now." This congressional wink is, in my view, not responsible legislation. It is an open invitation to the states to overrule decisions of the Supreme Court. Likewise it is an open invitation for the general disrespect of the rule of law.

A fourth principle that would be affected is that of uniformity of constitutional interpretation. Regardless of the intentions of the framers of the Constitution, Congress can, and should, make the judgment that today, in 1981, the First Amendment in Montana will offer the same protections as the First Amendment in North Carolina. The definition of the term "person" under the Fourteenth Amendment should be the same in Louisiana as it is in Illinois. Permitting 50 state courts to engage in setting 50 different definitions of constitutional terms destroys the ability of the Constitution to serve as a meaningful national document.

Impact on Congress

Many members of Congress have not only under-estimated the impact of these bills on the basic principles of our judicial system, but have also underestimated the impact on the Congress itself. If Congress decides to enter this arena, the pressure to respond to a wider range of constitutional issues will grow. Every constituency that feels victimized by an adverse constitutional ruling will come running to Congress for a jurisdiction withdrawal bill.

Anyone who argues that this jurisdiction removal approach would only be used in the most flagrant cases of "excessive" judicial decision making ought to examine the record created thus far in the 97th Congress. One bill was introduced to remove Supreme Court jurisdiction over sex bias in the Selective Service system.[14] This legislation was introduced prior to the Court's recent decision on the subject.[15] Now that the Court has ruled that a male-only military registration is not a denial of the equal protection clause, the need for removing the subject from the Court's jurisdiction no longer exists. Another court jurisdiction bill would go so far as to remove jurisdiction over "any order of a court of a state if such order is, will be, or was, subject to review by the highest court of the state."[16]

After reviewing all the bills introduced in this Congress, it is not wholly implausible to predict that jurisdiction withdrawal language will become a boiler-plate provision of much legislation. Any time a member of Congress was unsure whether the Supreme Court would uphold legislation, he or she could tack on a section denying the Court jurisdiction over that issue. This could apply to taxation and personal property as well as to social issues.

If the Supreme Court ever upheld legislation to withdraw jurisdiction over the issue of school prayer or abortion, there is no area of constitutional law which would be immune from congressional action. If one accepts the desirability of even a partial removal of substantive constitutional jurisdiction, then one is condoning the possibility of the removal of the entire Supreme Court appellate jurisdiction.

The proponents of these measures ought to contemplate future Congresses, who may have significantly different views on substantive issues, playing the jurisdictional withdrawal game as well. They should consider carefully whether we would like a pro-gun-control Congress to preclude the Supreme Court from interpreting the meaning of the right to bear arms.

Current restraints on the judiciary

Many in Congress are not concerned about these effects. They believe that without the enactment of these proposals, the Congress and the nation are defenseless against an "imperial" judiciary. I would suggest that our system of government does permit us to respond to fundamentally wrong or "unconstitutional" decisions of the Supreme Court. The framers of our Constitution wisely provided within Article 5 a mechanism for Congress and our citizenry to respond to such decisions. The Eleventh, Fourteenth, Sixteenth, and Twenty-Sixth Amendments were all responses to Supreme Court decisions. This country has had a long and consistent history of actively responding to constitutional decisions of the Supreme Court.

Furthermore, the president of the United States and 100 members of the U.S. Senate have been able to change the philosophical composition of the federal judiciary to respond to changes in public positions on major constitutional issues. Additionally, partial remedies are often available to those in Congress who want to respond to constitutional decisions of the Supreme Court. For example, many of those in Congress who opposed the court's ruling in *Roe v. Wade* exercised their constitutional power to eliminate federal funding over most abortions.

The Congress also has the power to fashion judicial remedies as long as it does not preclude the courts from vindicating constitutional rights. Finally, the court itself has the ability to review its own decisions, which has often served as a significant self-correcting mechanism.

It is my view that our constitutional amendment process, congressional control over the federal pocketbook, and congressional power to fashion judicial remedies gives Congress and our citizenry adequate tools with which to deal with controversial decisions of the Supreme Court. It would be unfortunate if in an effort to promote a specific social agenda, basic principles of governance that have served this country well for 200 years would be undermined.

The issue of federal court jurisdiction may be the single most important item on our nation's non-economic agenda in the 1980s. The outcome of this debate will determine the status of individual rights and liberties in this country for decades to come. It is my hope that future dialogue will help the Congress and the nation to re-examine what is really at stake in the court jurisdiction proposals.

NOTES

This article originally appeared in Volume 65, Number 4, October 1981, pages 185-189. It was adapted from an address delivered at the annual meeting of the American Judicature Society Board of Directors in New Orleans on August 8, 1981.

1. In 1957, Senator William E. Jenner introduced S. 2646, a bill designed to forbid the Supreme Court from reviewing cases that questioned any action of a congressional committee or any action of Congress against a witness charged with contempt of Congress or any state laws or regulations that combated subversive activities. A similar effort to remove the Court's jurisdiction occurred in 1968 when an amendment to the Omnibus Crime Control and Safe Streets Act proposed that the Supreme Court be restricted from reviewing state criminal proceedings involving *Miranda* issues. None of these efforts were successful. *See* S. 2646, 85th Cong., 1st Sess. (1957) and Title II of S. 917, 90th Cong., 2nd Sess. (1968), as amended in S. REP. No. 1097, 90th Cong., 2nd Sess. (1968).

2. *See* 125 CONG. REC. S. 4128-S. 4132 (April 5, 1979) and S. 4138-S. 4165 (April 9, 1979). S. 450 as amended passed the Senate but was never formally considered in the House.

3. *See* S. 158, 97th Cong.

4. *See* Johnston Amendment to S. 951, 97th Cong.

5. *See* S. 528, S. 1147, S. 1005, 97th Cong.

6. *See also* S. 481, H.R. 72, 73, 114, 326, 408, 761, 865, 867, 869, 989, 1079, 1180, 1335, 2347, 2365, 2791, 97th Cong.

7. 74 U.S., 7 Wall. 506 (1868).

8. United States v. Klein, 80 U.S., 13 Wall. 128 (1872).

9. *See* Engle v. Vitale, 370 U.S. 421 (1962) and Abbington School Dist. v. Schempp, 374 U.S. 203 (1963).

10. 410 U.S. 113 (1973).

11. Harris v. McRae, 448 U.S. 297 (1980).

12. *See* Hamilton, THE FEDERALIST, No. 78.

13. *See* Message of Veto, President Andrew Johnson, CONG.

Perspectives on court-Congress relations: the view from the Hill and the federal bench

An edited transcript of a panel presentation at the American Judicature Society's 1996 midyear meeting.

Robert A. Katzmann: Congressional scrutiny of the federal judiciary appears to be more intense than ever. The issues are far ranging: how judges should spend their time, how judges should spend their budget, how courthouses should be built, how circuit judicial conferences should be run, whether inspectors general should be lodged in the administrative office of the courts, the organization and size of the federal courts, federalism, sentencing policy, judicial discretion and independence, judicial discipline, and the confirmation process.

For the second year in a row Chief Justice William Rehnquist focused on the relationship between Congress and the courts in his year-end report, noting that the "past year's events make this an easy choice for a leitmotif again." While noting many positive aspects of the relationship, the chief justice cautioned against what he called a potentially "unwarranted and ill-considered effort to micro-manage the work of the federal judiciary."

The issues before us are not simply ones of dollars and cents, or of how the judiciary might better spend its budget. The issues are fundamentally about judicial independence and about the proper relationships between the judiciary and the other branches. And at the core of any such discussion must be some shared understanding of the unique roles of judges and legislators.

The Constitution clearly provides important roles for Congress. The Senate is charged, through the advice and consent provisions, with scrutinizing judicial nominees. The legislative branch determines the number of judgeships, the structure and function and procedures of the judiciary, and the jurisdiction of the courts, and it appropriates

funds for the Third Branch. Clearly, Congress's role is important and legitimate.

The founders also sought to create a system in which the independence of judges would be ensured. By providing for life tenure they substantially isolated federal jurists from public pressures, giving them freedom to make unpopular decisions. They recognized the peril of putting judges in positions that could compromise their impartiality. The very process of judging, as Frank Coffin has reminded us in his book, *On Appeal*, is grounded in the premise that decisions require, among other things, careful consideration of all views, appreciation of the particular facts in the law guiding a case, attention to detail and nuance, and painstaking, often painful reflection.

Independence, the founders appreciated, also requires requisite resources that enable justice to be dispensed effectively and fairly. Indeed, Congress recognized this, at least implicitly, when it enacted legislation in January 1996 [in the midst of a budget impasse] funding the courts through September 30.

What this all means is that the relationships between the judiciary and Congress must be finely tuned to take into account a variety of concerns and interests. On the one hand, the process must be structured so that Congress has enough information to make intelligent decisions, not just simply in confirming judges but also in ensuring that its work with regard to the administration of justice makes sense. On the other hand, the process must preserve the integrity of the judicial function.

With that in mind, we have assembled a distinguished panel of judges and legislators to examine the current state of relations between the

Moderator

Robert A. Katzmann, president of the Governance Institute; Walsh Professor of Government and Professor of Law and Public Policy, Georgetown University; visiting fellow, Brookings Institution.

Panelists

Richard S. Arnold, chief judge, U.S. Court of Appeals for the Eighth Circuit; chair, Committee on the Budget of the Judicial Conference of the United States; member, executive committee of the Judicial Conference.

Robert W. Kastenmeier, Distinguished Fellow of the Governance Institute; former chair, House Judiciary Subcommittee on Courts, Intellectual Property and the Administration of Justice; former chair, National Commission on Judicial Discipline and Removal.

Michael M. Mihm, chief judge, Central District of Illinois; member, executive committee of the Judicial Conference; former chair, Subcommittee on Long Range Planning of the Judicial Conference Committee on the Judicial Branch.

Carlos Moorhead, U.S. House of Representatives (R-California); chair, House Judiciary Subcommittee on Courts and Intellectual Property.

Paul Simon, U.S. Senate (D-Illinois); member, Committee on the Judiciary; author of *Advice and Consent*, a study of the judicial confirmation process.

Deanell R. Tacha, judge, U.S. Court of Appeals for the Tenth Circuit; former chair, Judicial Conference Committee on the Judicial Branch; judicial representative, U.S. Sentencing Commission.

branches and the prospects for those relationships.

Judge Arnold, if I might begin with you, how would you characterize the current status of judicial-legislative relations? Are things more intense than ever, or is it simply a case of a short view of history?

Richard S. Arnold: My main job is to chair the budget committee of the Judicial Conference, so I'm obsessed with money—getting it, and then spending it properly. I'm going to say something

you're not going to hear much—Congress is doing a good job. They have not given us everything we asked for, but that is not to be expected in the real world. They did give us a 5 percent increase for fiscal 1996 over 1995, and most importantly they separated us from the train wreck, the government shut-down, in early January and gave us our full appropriation for the entire fiscal year, even though the departments of Justice, State, and Commerce (which are in the same appropriations bill) have not yet been fully funded.

We have seen in the last few years a great increase in the interest level of Congress in the details of our operations, and that poses an opportunity and a problem. The opportunity is for us judges to realize that we work for the people, just as the members of Congress do, and if somebody, some taxpayer, even the taxpayer who's a member of Congress, wants to know what we are doing, they have a right to know. By the same token, there can be instances in which congressional interest becomes excessive. We hope that does not occur, and I have to say that in the time I've been budget chair I have never had an experience where some member of Congress has said to me, "We're not going to give you your money this year because we don't like your decisions."

Katzmann: Congressman Moorhead, as you look at the state of court-Congress relations, what's your assessment?

Carlos Moorhead: I think we have a very good relationship for the most part with the courts. This year there has been some controversy over the general effort to cut down on spending and balance the budget. And that brought about a so-called logjam. But the members of the Judiciary Committee realized the disaster that would occur if the courts couldn't operate in their normal way and were soon able to get the leadership to change their mind and support the judiciary with the adequate increase they needed to carry on their normal program.

A major issue that was somewhat controversial was the desire of some senators to split the Ninth Circuit. As I see it, the goal of the judiciary is to avoid conflict of decisions. I can't see how dividing the Ninth into two diverse circuits is going to help in achieving any kind of uniformity. If you're going to split up the circuits, it would be wise to consider all of them and to try to come closer to equalizing their populations and not do it according to the ideology of a particular area, which brings about conflict rather than uniformity in the long run.

Any congressman with judgment is not going to go to the courts and interfere with any case that's being heard, although we're urged to all the time by our constituents. More often the courts tell us what to do, but I think we also know what we need to do in those instances. We try to do the best we can to help the courts provide the best kind of justice.

Katzmann: Senator Simon, on the Senate side there appears to be an intense interest in the way the judiciary works. There is Senator Grassley's questionnaire to all federal judges and Senator Cohen's call for what appears to be a moratorium on construction of federal courthouses.* Does this reflect, in any way, a mood within the Senate as to the way the judiciary does its job?

Paul Simon: Let me be slightly less sanguine than Judge Arnold and my friend Carlos about the legislative-judicial relationship. There is micro-managing in areas where I think we should not be, and we're micro-managing, frankly, for political purposes. The issue of mandatory minimums is a great example. We can go back home and tell that Democratic or Republican rally we're for greater mandatory minimums and putting more people in prison to solve our crime problems, but it doesn't stand up under the right kind of scrutiny.

Plato, in his *Republic*, said, "Choose the right judges and then give them flexibility." I think that's the way we ought to be going. I think that frankly my colleague Chuck Grassley's questionnaire is related to an excessive amount of partisanship that has grown up over the years. I'm not suggesting that either Democrats or Republicans are responsible for this—both are. It has gradually grown, and it is not a good thing for the courts, it's not a good thing for the country, and ironically it's not a good thing for the two political parties. One of the reasons that people are cynical towards government and the two political parties is they see us playing political games too often.

Katzmann: Judge Mihm, as someone who's just chaired a committee trying to help developing countries with their judicial systems, do you think that if they looked at the state of judicial-legislative relations in our country they'd say, "What a great system?"

Michael M. Mihm: Indeed they do. In fact, my experience in dealing with judges from other countries is that they find our interaction truly remarkable. They're not convinced that in any one of their own countries they could succeed, to the extent we have. With that positive statement as a precursor, let me characterize the status of judicial-legislative relations somewhat melodramatically as the best of times and the worst of times, the summer of hope and the winter of discontent.

It's the best of times because there are a large number of people in the judiciary and in the legislative branch who treat each other with respect, work from a position of mutual concern about the public good, and really make an effort to build bridges between the branches. As an example of that, last month there was a meeting of representatives from all three branches of government. Several judges met with some of the leaders of Congress and the attorney general and her staff to discuss the role of the federal judiciary. The judges involved see that as a very positive step and an example of the type of bridge building that can occur.

It's the worst of times because not unlike society generally, there certainly are instances where it would be fair to characterize events as involving a high level of mutual distrust. The word micromanagement has been uttered here already today, and I'm sure it will be again. There are many judges, myself included, who feel that although Congress absolutely, unequivocally, categorically has the power to do many things regarding the judiciary, some things they should not do.

We've never experienced the degree of scrutiny that I think is going on right now. Some of it, of course, is the result of legitimate budget concerns. The concern of quite a few judges around the country is that the methods by which certain inquiries have been made to the judiciary could have been done differently. We see some things like the Grassley questionnaire as an unwarranted intrusion. Not that Senator Grassley does not have the power to do this, and certainly the type of information's that's sought, as Judge Arnold has rightly pointed out, is the kind of information that Congress is entitled to. Our disagreement is about how to go about gathering that information.

Katzmann: Judge Tacha, as a judge, scholar, and active member of the judicial hierarchy, how would you characterize the relationship?

Deanell R. Tacha: I like to call it a healthy tension. And it takes only a little bit of looking back at the history of Articles I, II, and III to understand that a healthy tension was a part of the original plan. The whole concept of micro-management and judicial independence and all of the discussions that seem to be at the root of the congressional-judicial relationship requires us to look at the two faces of judicial independence. On the one hand, we are a branch of government and therefore interdependent. In that respect, all of the budgetary issues that have already been referred to, all of the constraints that are on the entire government affect us. On the other hand we are an independent branch of government.

The other aspect of judicial independence is each face of the judiciary. The art of judging is very much an individual, analytical, independent endeavor. So I hope that as we talk about these relationships, the healthy respect that Mike talks about could be addressed in two ways. One is, what is our responsibility as a branch of government to participate in the travails, the economies, the joys, the legacies of a branch of government that enjoys a long history of flourishing vitality and must be responsive to the taxpayer? The other is the individual faces of each of the judges.

One only has to look at emerging republics around the world to understand that we must protect the ability of that judge to act independently and do his or her work in the way that works best. It's that that's made us such a flourishing branch of government and a beacon to the rest of the world. So, when we talk about micro-management, I like to think about the questions in those two ways. Is this a question about the whole branch and how we're economizing, or is this something that somehow erodes my ability to be the best judge I can be?

I live at the confluence of all three branches of government right now as a member of the Sentencing Commission. And I have had to learn things from a very different perspective. That which I would prefer as a judge may not be appropriate, given the political imperatives or the political mandates of the other two branches of government. But on all issues, particularly those related to crime, it seems to me that we all three have some very important interests that need to be shared.

The Executive Branch has some very important interests in the Sentencing Commission. We have

set up, much as the judiciary has set up, some mechanisms to try to talk about some of these issues, not the least of which of course are the concerns that we share with the Judicial Conference on mandatory minimums and the interplay between the sentencing guidelines and mandatory minimums.

Katzmann: As we conclude this round of opening views, I turn to Congressman Kastenmeier, who has a longer perspective on these issues than almost anybody. Congressman, what has changed since 1958 when you entered Congress?

Robert W. Kastenmeier: I see about three periods. The '60s were not a period in which Congress and the federal judiciary had a great deal of interaction, at least as far as administration was concerned. It really wasn't until the 1970s that we got into a very activist period. The '70s were a time in which we had a great deal of Great Society legislation, all of which necessitated an increase in numbers of judges. And we found that the federal judiciary was no longer a small group of 300 or so. Now, including senior judges in the system, it could be well over 1,000. It became a bureaucracy and necessitated a series of bills dealing in part with discipline, judicial behavior, and other aspects of the judiciary.

We also had a great deal of communication in those years—I'm talking about the 1970s and early 1980s. There were many organizations and commissions—the chief justice, Warren Burger, created the Williamsburg Conference that included key judges, members of the House and the Senate judiciary committees, and the executive branch as represented by the attorney general and other key officers. Many of us appeared twice a year at the Judicial Conference of the United States to report on what Congress was doing.

But ever since the late '70s congressional attention has moved away from the judiciary. We used to be able to get members to provide oversight of the federal judiciary. As Carlos well knows, it is very difficult to get members to do so any more. The number of subjects facing the average House member or senator has just increased enormously in 15 or 20 years. The amount of time he or she can spend in a given subcommittee looking at the judiciary is minimal. And so communication is a problem. Sometimes the results of lack of communication are adverse for the federal judiciary. Communication to get Congress re-interested in the judiciary as an institution, as a coordinate part of government, is needed.

Katzmann: I'd like to move on to a series of specific issues. The first is this question of communications, and the first dimension is communications in the confirmation process. What is the extent to which we can ever expect to have a consensus as to the kinds of questions that are appropriate to ask of judicial nominees? Senator Simon, there are those who say senators are now asking judicial nominees for specific answers as to how they're going to rule on issues, that they don't have a good sense of what the role of the judge is and the need to preserve impartiality. Is there any substance to that?

Simon: There are occasionally questions asked that should not be asked, that skirt very close to asking, "How would you rule on such and such?" The nominee has to use good sense and simply diplomatically evade answering those kind of questions. I think it is proper to ask someone his or her views on basic questions, particularly Supreme Court nominees where basic philosophy becomes very important. I also think it is appropriate to decline to answer.

It's interesting that in 1787 they were first going to have the House and the Senate elect federal judges, including Supreme Court members. Then it got down to the Senate only. Finally, on one of the last days of the Constitutional Convention, it shifted from the Senate electing judges to the president nominating them, with advice and consent of the Senate. When the first nominees came up, the Senate invited George Washington to meet with the Senate, but he said, "No, I don't want to. You ought to feel free, for whatever reason you want, to reject a nominee." As on a great many other things, George Washington, I think, exercised proper judgment and set a good precedent.

Katzmann: I've attended a number of confirmation hearings for lower court judges and the Judiciary Committee attendance is generally not very large. You may not have more than three or four senators attending the hearings.

Simon: In fact, there's usually only two. When I was a freshman member of the Judiciary Committee I had the job—at that point they assigned it all to one person—of being there for all the nominations except when I had a conflict. It is unusual when you have more than two people there.

Katzmann: Is that a good use of the hearing system?

Simon: Well, what's really important is the staff work. I've had discussions today with two senators about a judicial nominee from Illinois where staff work is taking place, where questions have arisen. This kind of informal discussion is taking place on something that, frankly, should not be public at this point. But when the staff work is done we get reports on all the nominees. So it is not quite as loose as it might appear when only two members are there.

Arnold: I just want to say that if you're a nominee for one of the lower courts and a lot of senators show up at your hearing, you're in trouble [laughter].

Tacha: I think that one thing AJS should be concerned about and one thing I'm concerned about is less what happens between the judicial nominee and the legislator, because I think there is a lot of understanding that much of what happens does not happen publicly. But what I think we all must be concerned about is an ever-decreasing level of understanding among the general populace about the role of each branch of government. One of the concerns is the extent to which questions somehow go to the impartiality of the judge, or the ability of the judge to make an independent decision out of the political process. The public then gets slightly misinformed about what it is a judge does, and what the role of Congress is.

I couldn't agree more with Senator Simon that the Senate has every right to ask a whole host of questions of nominees. But I'd like to see both judicial nominees and questioners give a little bit of thought to how much we educate the public when we ask a particular question about the role of the judge and the role of Congress. I think there's some real basic civics education that needs to go on about our constitutional scheme.

Katzmann: Moving on to another issue, the budget, my question for Judge Arnold is this: The judiciary, the Third Branch, is an independent branch. Couldn't a good case be made, just in terms of our understanding of constitutional theory, that the judiciary's budget should be treated separately?

Arnold: I take it by separately you mean that we should have an appropriations bill of our own, and perhaps an appropriations subcommittee of our own. In theory it sounds good. The year-end report by the chief justice this year suggested that, although I think the language in the chief justice's address was perhaps purposefully ambiguous, in the sense that it can be read as being a special plea for separation at that particular time when the other departments were involved in the government shutdown. In fact, the budget committee and the executive committee of the Judicial Conference have considered this in some detail, and we have concluded that it would not be practical for us to ask Congress to put us in a separate appropriations bill. My sense is the process works pretty well now.

Katzmann: Congressman Moorhead, any reaction to that? Do you think it would ever be practical for the judiciary to have its own appropriations bill and its own appropriations subcommittee?

Moorhead: I don't think in the long run it would make any difference. The judiciary has done very well in getting the amounts of money they have said were necessary to do their job. If you did create another subcommittee to handle that, or you tried to do it independently, the end result would be just about the same as it is now. We've got so many appropriation bills now it's hard to get them out on the floor in an adequate time, and I just think we'd have more problems than we do now.

Katzmann: Moving on to the issue of budget tightening, Judge Mihm, are there areas where you think the judiciary simply cannot absorb budget cuts?

Mihm: I think Congress has every right to very carefully scrutinize everything that we do, from our purchasing processes, to personnel, to the question of what work we're performing. For example, there's a move within the judiciary right now to get space utilization under control. The amount of space that the courts are renting has increased tremendously over the past few years. That is being very carefully looked at. How we use personnel, how we use magistrate judges, for example, has been very carefully looked at. I think there have been significant changes in the utilization of magistrates in recent years.

Some things, of course, are hard to reduce in the courts. It's hard to say, "Well, we're not going to have any more trials this year because we can't pay the jurors," or, "We're not going to have any more criminal trials because we've run out of money for the Criminal Justice Act attorneys who are appointed in indigent cases." But I think most people in the judiciary would accept, without question, that almost everything we do can be done more efficiently, and at a lower cost. So Congress is completely within its rights to take a careful look at us.

Katzmann: What about courthouse construction? There are a lot of newspaper accounts, television programs about beautiful courthouses being constructed—luxurious courthouses was a depiction in the media. How would the judiciary react to that charge in this era of budget tightening?

Mihm: There's been a lot of courthouse construction going on. I don't know the numbers, but it may well be one of the most active periods in our history. Just within the last few months, Congress asked the judiciary to prioritize its list of needed new courthouses. That was done. We had a committee of the Judicial Conference that was actively involved in that. There have been reports of courthouses that were extravagant, and I'm not here to defend those necessarily. There may be examples where what was done cannot be justified.

I would also take the position, however, that I don't think we want our federal courthouses to look like local traffic courts. For the work that we do in federal court I believe that the surroundings are very important. For example, my courthouse in Peoria was built in 1937. It's a beautiful courtroom, and everyone acts accordingly, including me because I'm in a very important place. The lawyers know that, the witnesses, the parties. I would say that there's almost a church-like feeling when you're in there. And that's a good thing. I would not want us to get too far from that idea, recognizing the realities of the budget. I would hope that we would continue to build courthouses like they should be built. I don't think anything that Congress has done has seriously detracted from the legitimate concerns that we have about what courthouses should look like.

Katzmann: Congressman Kastenmeier, the Judicial Conference has stated that it is strongly opposed to unlimited expansion of the federal judiciary, because a system that is too large often becomes unwieldy, and has difficulty maintaining consistency. What is your response?

Kastenmeier: I think the Judicial Conference is well advised to be concerned about the size of the federal judiciary. We were as early as the '70s looking at the size of the judiciary—realizing that it can't just be expanded without limit. You do pay in some untoward ways for creating that much of a bureaucracy. We probably have to expand the judiciary, but we need to look at other alternatives, such as whether all of the cases currently being reviewed need to be. There are alternatives to just expanding mathematically the number of judges.

Katzmann: Let's open it up to audience questions.

Audience member: I'd be very interested in the views of the panelists about responsibility for civil justice reform—procedural reform. There seems to have been a good deal of interest on the part of Congress—a good deal more interest in recent years than in the past—in civil justice reform. Cynics say it's because procedures became a political issue. Others less cynical say because people have stopped pretending that procedure doesn't have any substantive dimensions, Congress now recognizes that the way you do things may in fact determine the results. But in any event there's a good deal of consternation, certainly among the federal bench, and in academic circles, about who has responsibility, who should have responsibility for civil justice reform. Is this a topic that would benefit from the sort of interbranch discussions that have been mentioned? Is there any possibility that we could have more agreement about who does what and how in the future than we have in the recent past?

Moorhead: There's been a great deal of effort this year in the area of tort reform and product liability, but as far as telling the courts how to conduct the proceedings, there's been very little. You could argue about the number of jurors that have to be on one side or the other and things like that, but that hasn't been a matter of discussion. It's very difficult to get changes through the Congress however, and through the president.

One of the issues this past year was the loser-pays provision, which passed the House of Representatives but is sleeping very gently over in the Senate. I think the bill that passed is a rather modest one that would require more payment by those who refuse to negotiate, rather than those who really just lost the case. We've been working on legislation that would encourage other resolution methods, such as arbitration, rather than letting all these cases wait interminable months. I think we need to do everything we can to get people to negotiate, to get these issues settled without a long-delayed trial. A good judge can usually see that that

happens, but not all judges are good in that particular area. I think when you're taking up so much of the court's time with criminal justice problems, it's to everybody's interest that we find ways to speed up civil cases.

Tacha: This is one of the places where that healthy tension that I talked about really comes into play, and where, when we attempt to speak as a whole, in the judiciary and as individuals, the constraints of the ethical bounds of what is appropriate for a judge to speak out upon as a policy matter can come head on into the interests of the whole system. I think the Judicial Conference has done a very good job of trying to balance the appearance of impartiality for each judge and for the judiciary as a whole on issues that are real policy issues with recommendations for clear procedural rules. Some very important policy and political issues have confronted the conference and individual judges, and the conference has made some very thoughtful calls about drawing the lines.

Audience member: Congressman Kastenmeier, in the years you were in Congress, as I recall, the Judicial Conference always had to come to you to put out the fires, and you were very helpful. How often did they have to push you to do something, and how often did you really have to pull them to get them to do something?

Kastenmeier: I think it probably was a fairly even split on that score. I did work a great deal with the chief justice as well as the Judicial Conference and felt that we had sort of a common understanding, we probably didn't differ on very many things. Our committee decided these things, but often they were after consultation or even hearings in which we had members of the Judicial Conference and others, and we used judges as witnesses a great deal. I don't think the communication with senators and representatives exists as it did in years past. There is a tremendous turnover in members. New people coming in are not exposed to judges and the judiciary. That concerns me because I think Congress is more distant, not necessarily more hostile, but certainly not attuned to the problems of the judiciary.

Katzmann: The problem of communications that we've talked about seems like an uphill fight. With the increasing turnover among legislators could come a decrease in institutional memory and expertise needed to understand the problems of the judiciary.

I'd like to conclude by asking each of our panelists for a suggestion about how best to improve judicial-legislative relations.

Mimh: As I mentioned earlier, I think there are some initiatives underway that hold great promise—this three-branch structure that's been developed for us to come together and discuss the mission of the federal courts, I think, is excellent. At the meeting of that group last month, Chief Judge Gilbert Meritt of the Sixth Circuit, who is also chairman of the executive committee of the Judicial Conference, suggested to the members of Congress who were present that they consider the possibility of a small group of judges meeting with the bipartisan leadership in Congress to discuss the mission of the courts on a semi-regular basis. That suggestion was favorably received. That's the kind of institutional contact that I think would be very helpful.

Tacha: One more point is that a part of this tension is also built into the first three articles of the Constitution. By definition we judges work on a case or controversy basis, so we see a very small slice of what are much larger policy issues for Congress and indeed the Executive Branch. It seems to me that efforts to make us see where our interests converge, and how we might articulate better those convergences, will serve us all very well.

Arnold: I would like to see more contact between judges and members of Congress—personal contact, conversations, meetings like this. There is a misperception in each branch of the other. There are a lot of judges who think that members of Congress—all of them—are solely motivated by partisanship. That is not true. And there are a lot of members of Congress who think that judges are imperial monarchs who work half a day, and that is not true. I try to tell judges that some of their impressions of Congress are incorrect—for example, Congress is not treating itself better budget-wise than it treats us. A lot of judges think that, but that is not true. I think we should work to correct those misunderstandings.

Kastenmeier: I endorse what the three judges have said and what I indicated earlier. We need more communication, and some of the suggestions they made I surely endorse. In addition, we have to find a way to have members of Congress find time for these discussions, and that's difficult, that's a challenge.

Moorhead: More communication with all members of Congress would help. There's seldom a day I don't see a judge or two who comes by the office and has a suggestion of one kind or another. But the average member of Congress who isn't assigned to the court subcommittee probably doesn't see judges that often. And I would like to have them hear some of the problems that judges are having in the court system. Especially, the long trials and delays that could be avoided if they didn't have, for instance, minimum sentencing standards.

Katzmann: Thank you one and all for coming—judges, legislators, and citizens.

NOTES

This article originally appeared in Volume 79, Number 6, May-June 1996, pages 303-309.

*Editor's note: In January, Senator Charles Grassley (R-Iowa) sent a survey to all active and senior court of appeals and district court judges asking a series of questions dealing with judicial administration and workload, circuit conferences, and outside work activities. In his memo that transmitted the survey, Grassley said, "My intention is to begin a dialogue that will have positive results."

In November, Senator William S. Cohen (R-Maine) held a hearing to examine federal courthouse construction programs. He called for a moratorium on construction of new courthouses until tougher controls on costs were put in place.

The Courts and Their Publics
States and State Courts

INTRODUCTION

The United States is a federal system in which national supremacy was established over the state governments by the U.S. Constitution and its interpretation by John Marshall for the Supreme Court in the classic case of *McCulloch v. Maryland* in 1819. The American judiciary, too, is organized on a federal model with federal courts coexisting with their state court counterparts. The development of constitutional law has also established federal judicial supremacy as the rule for the relationships among American courts. Consequently, when examining the relationships between the Supreme Court and its "public," much attention must be paid to the interface of the Supreme Court, the states, and state courts.

In the wake of the dominance of conservatism on the Burger and Rehnquist courts in the rights and liberties domain in the past three decades, many voices have called for the active pursuit of "new judicial federalism," a phenomenon in which state courts rely increasingly on their own laws and constitutions to decide cases wherever possible. It was hoped by many that such an approach to adjudication could protect and, perhaps, expand upon the rights and liberties legacy of the Warren Court. Shirley Abrahamson and Diane Gutman offer us our first view of this topic in "The new federalism: state constitutions and state courts." The article develops the historical foundation of the relationship between federal and state courts while emphasizing the greater role that the state courts could play in the wake of the Supreme Court's 1983 decision in *Michigan v. Long*. In that case Justice Sandra Day O'Connor stated for the Court's majority that, "State courts will be presumed to be acting as 'federal forums,' unless they plainly state that they are not so acting…. If a state court plainly says that it is relying on state law, the Supreme Court will not review its decision."

Abrahamson and Gutman's analysis of *Michigan v. Long* emphasizes the case's potential for giving state courts "substantial freedom in determining the extent of their autonomy as long as their decisions do not violate federal law." If this suggests, however, that such "freedom" and the "new judicial federalism" have led to the widespread expansion in the scope of citizens' rights, Michael Esler's study

of "State supreme court commitment to state law," offers a cautionary note. Esler demonstrates that despite the rhetoric of the new
judicial federalism, "State supreme courts rely on federal law in the
vast majority of their decisions." Esler explains this finding by noting
that, "The conservatism of most state political systems and entrenched
legal and institutional barriers work against widespread development
of state constitutional law." In essence, predictions of an increasing
liberalism emerging from state court systems as they interpret their
own state constitutions generally fall before the realities of the political climate in which most state court systems operate.

Both Abrahamson and Gutman and Esler underline that federalism is a dynamic process in the American political system that is always in a state of "becoming." This has been made amply clear in
Supreme Court decisions in recent years. It is equally clear that federalism issues and the relationship between the Supreme Court, the
states, and state courts will remain high on the list of the American
judiciary's concerns for years to come

The new federalism: state constitutions and state courts

The "perplexing" idea of federalism has a long and complex history in the United States; jurists and commentators have grappled with its application to the state and federal court systems. The U.S. Supreme Court's Michigan v. Long *decision has opened up a new chapter in this struggle.*

by Shirley S. Abrahamson and Diane S. Gutmann

In 1984, Judge John Minor Wisdom, senior judge, U.S. Court of Appeals for the Fifth Circuit, commented, "It is striking indeed that so many . . . [who] write on the subject of 'Civil Rights and Federalism' have focused on the growing role of the *states* in protecting civil rights, in some cases going beyond Supreme Court guidelines."[1]

For a long time, few people seemed aware that protection of individual liberties could lie in the state constitution—and not solely in the U.S. Constitution. In the 1970s, state courts gradually reawakened to their legitimate authority to construe the rights that their state constitutions provide independently of the U.S. Supreme Court's construction of analogous rights in the federal Constitution. When a state court construes the state constitution in the same way that the U.S. Supreme Court construes the federal Constitution, or when a state court goes beyond the Supreme Court in the protection of human rights, there is no inherent conflict between nation and state. Conflict does arise when state standards fall short of federal standards.

Federal court of appeals Senior Judge J. Skelly Wright recently declared himself an "enthusiastic new convert to 'federalism' " and applauded "state judges who have resumed their historic role as the primary defenders of civil liberties and equal rights."[2]

Federalism has been a perplexing idea from its very inception. At the Constitutional Convention one of the framers expressed his confusion with the as yet not fully developed idea of federalism when he said, "I cannot conceive of a government in which there exist two supremes."[3] Although the Constitution explicitly makes the federal government supreme, the idea that the states remain in some sense sovereign or autonomous has retained vitality throughout our history.

As James Madison recognized in *Federalist 37*, no mathematical formula can tell us how to allocate power between the national government and the state governments. History shows that the allocation of authority between the states and the national government shifts over time. The tension between pressures for state autonomy and pressures for national supremacy is fundamental to federalism. This tension has led at times to conflict and at other times to dialogue and accommodation.

Some commentators use the term *new federalism* to refer to a new relationship between federal and state courts and between the federal and state constitutions. New federalism refers to the renewed willingness of state courts to rely on their own law, especially state constitutional law, in order to decide questions involving individual rights. In new federalism, the federal Constitution establishes minimum rather than maximum guarantees of individual rights, and the state courts determine, according to their own law (generally their own state constitutions), the nature of the protection against state government. New federalism also includes the potential for greater deference by federal courts to state court proceedings and decisions.

Federal and state courts work out their relationship with each other as they work out the relationship between the federal and state constitutions. The balance between state autonomy and national supremacy is vividly illustrated in the context of the protection of civil liberties.

In this article we examine, first, the historical background of the relationship between federal and state courts. Then, we turn to the experience of both court systems in the protection of civil liberties. Finally, we attempt to assess the impact on both court systems of incorporation, that is, applying many portions of the federal Bill of Rights to the states through the Fourteenth Amendment. We look at the U.S. Supreme Court reaction in *Michigan v. Long* (1983)[4] to the increased role of the state courts in the interpretation and application of the state and federal bills of rights.

Dual governments

The states predate the Constitution and its predecessor, the Articles of Confederation. Before the Declaration of Independence, members of the Continental Congress suggested that each colony form an independent state government. During the months preceding independence, colonists debated the uniformity of state constitutions but rejected such uniformity in favor of each state's calling a convention to draw up a constitution of its own. This individuality reflected a political reality that manifested itself in such incidents as the response of New Jersey soldiers to George Washington's attempt to get them to swear allegiance to the United States: "New Jersey is our country."[5]

At the time of the Constitutional Convention of 1787 in Philadelphia, the states were an independent and somewhat fractious lot loosely bound together by a central "government" backed only by the force of persuasion. Protective of state autonomy, the people waited nervously for the results of the convention, unaware that the delegates were laboring over an entirely new Constitution in apparent disregard of the mandate to meet "for the sole and express purpose of revising the Articles of Confederation."

The idea of unqualified state "sovereignty" lost some of its luster under the Articles of Confedera-

tion, but state sovereignty was to survive—albeit somewhat redefined—the framing and ratification of the Constitution.

A proposal at the convention that the existing governmental foundations be swept away in favor of a purely national government was not well received. The framers built the Constitution on the foundation of the states, rather than attempting to lay an entirely new foundation. The Constitution assumes the existence of states (mentioning them at least 50 times), state judiciaries (at least three times), and state constitutions (at least once). In structure and conception, the Constitution drew heavily on the constitutions of the states. As John Adams declared, "What is the Constitution of the United States, but that of Massachusetts, New York, and Maryland! There is not a feature in it which cannot be found in one or the other."[6]

Thus the document that emerged at Philadelphia presupposed two levels of government, each with its own constitution and governmental structure, each existing simultaneously in the same geographic territory, and each deriving its powers from and governing the same people. The states remained autonomous entities under the Constitution, instead of being reduced to mere administrative subdivisions of the central government. Like the people, the states retained whatever powers were not delegated to the central government. James Madison wrote in *Federalist 45*:

The powers delegated by the proposed Constitution to the federal government are few and defined. Those which are to remain in the State governments are numerous and indefinite . . . . The powers reserved to the several States will extend to all the objects which, in the ordinary course of affairs, concern the lives, liberties, and properties of the people, and the internal order, improvement, and prosperity of the State.

Although the states retained autonomous status, the United States was constituted as more than a federation, more than a league or an alliance between nations. The government established by the new Constitution acted on the people directly as well as on the states, in contrast to the Articles of Confederation, which were concerned only with relations between the states.

As Madison described it, the Constitution "is, in strictness, neither a national nor a federal Constitution, but a composition of both."[7] Alexis de Tocqueville put it aptly many years later: "Evidently this is no longer a federal government, but an incomplete national government, which is neither exactly national nor exactly federal; but the new word which ought to express this novel thing does not yet exist."[8] The Constitution established a hybrid national-federal government in which the national government was not to swallow up the states and the states were not to undermine the national government. The Constitution encased two political communities within one system, creating the potential for conflict as well as the potential for fruitful collaboration and dialogue.

A classic description of our federalism in this century comes from Justice Hugo Black. He described it as "a proper respect for state functions, a recognition of the fact that the entire country is made up of a Union of separate state governments, and a continuance of the belief that the National Government will fare best if the States and their institutions are left free to perform their separate functions in their separate ways."[9] The concept of federalism, observed Justice Black, requires neither "blind deference to States' Rights" nor the centralization of control over every important issue. Rather, each government must be sensitive to the legitimate interests of the other. Anxious though the national government may be to vindicate and protect national rights and national interests, it must do so in ways that will not impede legitimate state activities.

Federalism and individual rights have been intertwined in American constitutional history from the very beginning. The framers strove to bestow upon the national government authority to deal with national problems, while safeguarding state autonomy and individual liberty. As Madison wrote in *Federalist 51*, "In the compound republic of America, the power surrendered by the people is first divided between two distinct governments, and then the portion allotted to each subdivided among distinct and separate departments. Hence, a double security arises to the rights of the people. The different governments will control each other, at the same time that each will be controlled by itself."

With the division of powers between the national and state governments and the separation of powers, the framers of the Constitution, according to John Quincy Adams, gave us "the most complicated government on the face of the globe."[10]

Dual courts

In attempting to tell the story of the dual court system in condensed form, we begin with the ending. This country has two independent but interrelated judicial schemes: state and federal. The framers and Congress provided for a complex and intricate system of two sets of courts with overlapping jurisdiction. They did not attempt to simplify the dual judicial scheme by apportioning federal adjudicative powers solely to the federal courts and state adjudicative powers solely to the state courts. Rather, both the federal and state courts apply federal and state law.

Before exploring the interaction between state and federal courts as an aspect of our federalism, we will trace the origins of the dual system of courts. The dual judicial system grows out of the tension between two contending principles: national supremacy and state autonomy.

The federal judiciary seems so natural and inevitable now that it may be difficult to imagine a time when its establishment and existence were controversial. We have been schooled to think of constitutional governments as necessarily composed of three branches: the legislative, the executive, and the judicial. Our government would seem unbalanced without a judiciary.

Yet in order to comprehend the original understanding of the role of the federal judiciary, we must realize that a federal judiciary was not at all inevitable. There was no national judiciary under the Articles of Confederation. While not very controversial during the drafting process, the establishment of a federal judiciary became intensely controversial during the ratification process. The establishment of the federal judiciary was perceived as a threat to state autonomy. The resistance to this perceived threat did not succeed in blocking the establishment of a federal judiciary, but it did succeed in influencing its structure and jurisdiction.

The cornerstones of the present-day federal judicial system are Article III of the Constitution and the Judiciary Act of 1789.

The Convention: Article III. If we were to look to the records of the Constitutional Convention for information on the original understanding of the role of the federal judiciary and its relationship to the states, we would find surprisingly little on the subject. What controversy there was concerning the federal judiciary centered on the form it would take, not on whether it should exist at all.

The Convention quickly decided to establish a

federal judiciary separate from the existing state judicial systems, adopting Edmund Randolph's resolution "that a National Judiciary be established." The reason for this quick assent, Alexander Hamilton later explained, was that the framers were convinced that a national judiciary was an essential part of a government. This conviction must have rested in part on the belief that all properly formed governments have three branches. The national government would rely on the national judicial system to uphold federal laws (especially when the national and local policy were at variance) and to provide a more uniform system of justice than the state courts could. As Tocqueville later put it, "The object of creating a Federal tribunal was to prevent the state courts from deciding, each after its own fashion, questions affecting the national interests, and so to form a uniform body of jurisprudence for the interpretation of the laws of the Union."[11]

Although the framers were willing to limit state autonomy in order to ensure that the laws and the Constitution of the national government would be fairly and uniformly applied, they balked at setting up any federal courts other than the Supreme Court. Many feared that lower federal tribunals would unacceptably infringe on state autonomy and the integrity of the state judicial system. John Rutledge urged that "the State tribunals might and ought to be left in all cases to decide in the first instance, the right of appeal to the supreme national tribunal being sufficient to secure national rights & uniformity of Judgments: that it was making an unnecessary encroachment on the jurisdiction of the States and creating unnecessary obstacles to their adoption of the new system."[12] Some delegates viewed creating a national system of courts as expensive and as a possible impediment to the states' ratification of the Constitution if the states feared that lower federal courts would encroach on the jurisdiction of the state courts. Madison and other delegates, however, favored a provision in the Constitution creating lower federal courts with final jurisdiction.

After Rutledge's motion against lower federal courts carried, James Wilson and Madison urged that "there is a distinction between establishing such tribunals absolutely and giving a discretion to the Legislature to establish or not establish them."[13] They proposed the compromise that the convention adopted: The national legislature would be empowered to institute lower federal courts. Thus, because the framers were unable to reach a conclusion on the issue of lower federal courts, they decided to leave the matter to Congress.

To summarize what emerged from the convention concerning the judiciary, Article III of the Constitution expressly provides that the federal judicial power encompasses both the states and individuals as litigants. Furthermore, the federal judicial power, like the legislative and executive powers, is an enumerated power. The listed categories of cases that federal courts could hear may be viewed as restrictions on federal invasion of state judicial power. The federal judicial power of the United States extends to "all cases in law and equity arising under the Constitution," a broadly worded grant of jurisdiction, and to laws of the United States and to diversity jurisdiction, that is, to suits between citizens of different states.[14] Diversity jurisdiction was accepted without debate at the convention and without explanation of its purpose, although debate on this provision was extensive during ratification and has been intermittent ever since. Hamilton explained in *The Federalist* that because state courts could not be supposed to be impartial in cases pitting a citizen of their state against a citizen of another state, diversity jurisdiction was properly in the federal courts.[15]

The text of the Constitution clearly evinces concern for the independence of the federal judiciary, perhaps because the framers were aware that many state judges depended on state legislatures. This concern is evident in the method of judicial appointment (the president with the advice and consent of the Senate), the protection of judicial tenure (during good behavior), and the prohibition on diminishing judicial salary during continuance in office.

One issue the Constitution did not address directly, however, is the relation of the federal courts to the state courts.

The supremacy clause. A mechanism was needed to settle disputes over the respective spheres of state and federal judicial power, i.e., to ensure that the states did not undermine the national government and that the national government did not usurp state powers. To address that need, the framers adopted Article VI of the Constitution, the supremacy clause. The supremacy clause provides that the Constitution, laws, and treaties of the United States are the supreme law of the land, superior to state constitutions and state laws. State judges are bound by oath to support the Constitution and are "bound [by the Constitution], any thing in the Constitution or Laws of any State to the Contrary notwithstanding." The supremacy clause makes the Constitution enforceable in all the courts in the land.

Madison, in *Federalist 44*, vividly portrayed the need for the supremacy clause, stating that without it, "the world would have seen, for the first time, a system of government founded on an inversion of the fundamental principles of all government; it would have seen the authority of the whole society everywhere subordinate to the authority of the parts; it would have seen a monster, in which the head was under the direction of the members." In contrast to the constitutional mechanism to prevent the states from undermining the national government, the Constitution did not expressly provide a mechanism to thwart a central government's "natural tendency" to destroy state governments. Although scholars still debate the original understanding of the framers, the federal judiciary has had this power since *Marbury v. Madison* (1803).[16]

The framers did not try to resolve with finality the tension they had set up between national supremacy and state autonomy in the judicial sphere. Future generations would have to work that out by adjusting and readjusting the relationship between state and federal courts. As Hamilton said in *Federalist 82*, "Time only can mature and perfect so compound a system, liquidate the meaning of all the parts, and adjust them to each other in a harmonious and consistent WHOLE."

Ratification. The need for a federal judiciary, which had seemed so self-evident to the framers at the convention, became the center of controversy during the ratification debates. Some antifederalists feared the breadth of federal judicial power and argued that state courts were adequate. In fact, the antifederalists prophesied the demise of the state tribunals should the Constitution be ratified. According to George Mason, "the Judiciary of the United States is so constructed and extended, as to absorb and destroy the Judiciaries of the several States."[17]

In contrast to the gloomy picture painted by the antifederalists, some passages of *The Federalist Papers* paint a rosy picture in which the state and federal courts function as kindred systems and parts of a whole. Hamilton interpreted the Constitution as permitting state and federal courts concurrent jurisdiction, with both state courts and federal courts deciding questions of state and federal law arising in cases within their respective judicial powers.

According to Hamilton, the state courts would retain the jurisdiction they had, except where state jurisdiction was expressly prohibited. The state courts were not, according to Hamilton, divested of their "primitive jurisdiction" except for appeals.[18] Furthermore, except where expressly prohibited, the state courts would have concurrent jurisdiction in all cases arising under the laws of the union. Hamilton reasoned that the supremacy clause demonstrates the framers' assumption that state courts could adjudicate issues of federal law.

Hamilton concluded, however, that in instances of concurrent jurisdiction, the Supreme Court's appellate jurisdiction would extend to decisions of the state courts as well as the federal courts. Indeed, Hamilton saw a need for federal appellate jurisdiction over state courts. He claimed in *Federalist 81* that state judges could not be "relied upon for an inflexible execution of national laws" because, in all states, judges were to some degree dependent on the state legislatures through selection, salary, or term, and might not stand up to them. Hamilton found no impediment to permitting appeals from state courts to inferior federal courts. "The evident aim of the plan of the convention is," wrote Hamilton, "that all the causes of the specific classes shall, for weighty public reasons, receive their original *or* final determination in the courts of the union."

The prospect of a national court with ultimate authority to determine the final meaning of the supremacy clause was a frightening one for the antifederalists. Not only was the federal government deemed supreme, it was also empowered to decide what this supremacy meant. Federal courts were charged with the important responsibility of limiting the supremacy of the federal government and protecting state autonomy.

The Judiciary Act of 1789. Article III was not self-executing, and on September 24, 1789, the first Congress adopted "An Act to establish the Judicial Courts of the United States." The Judiciary Act of 1789 is weighty evidence of the true meaning of the Constitution, according to the U.S. Supreme Court, because it was passed by the first Congress assembled under the Constitution, many of whose members had taken part in the convention. Furthermore, the act set forth, to a large extent, the basic structure of the federal courts as we know it.

The Judiciary Act of 1789 established the Supreme Court, which has existed continuously ever since, although the number of associate justices has changed. More significantly, the act resolved the controversy over lower courts: Congress approved them. After a vigorous debate reminiscent of ratification, Congress decided that federal trial courts were necessary. The act set up two tiers of trial courts: district courts (at least one per state) and three circuit courts. The circuit courts, composed of two Supreme Court justices and one district court judge, were the weak spots in the system and were later abolished; separately constituted circuit courts of appeals were ultimately established.

Congress did not confer on the federal courts the full judicial power granted by the Constitution. Surprisingly, the act did not grant the federal trial courts jurisdiction over "federal question cases," that is, cases arising under the Constitution or laws of the United States in private civil litigation. The prevailing view was that state courts were the appropriate forum for the enforcement of federal law and that federal courts should be available to citizens who might be victims of bias in sister state courts. Accordingly, Congress granted diversity jurisdiction to the lower courts, concurrent with state courts, and authorized the removal of diversity actions from state court to federal court.

Federal district courts did not obtain "federal question" jurisdiction until 1875. Until that time, federal question cases, in the absence of diversity jurisdiction, could only be brought in state courts.

To ensure state court autonomy and a final determination by a federal court for all cases raising federal issues, the 1789 act provided for Supreme Court review of state courts' final judgments or decrees in matters of federal concern in three categories of cases in which the state court held *against* a federal claim:

• where the validity of a treaty, statute, or authority of the United States is drawn into question, and the state court decides against its validity;

• where the validity of a state statute or authority is challenged on the basis of federal law, and

the state court decides in favor of the validity of the state statutory authority;

• where a state court construes the U.S. Constitution, a U.S. treaty, statute, or commission and decides against a title, right, privilege, or exemption under any of them.[19]

The Supreme Court could not review state court decisions favorable to a claim of federal right until 1914, when Congress granted this review power to the Supreme Court. This amendment was prompted largely by a New York Court of Appeals decision holding a state workers' compensation law in conflict with the due process guarantees of both the federal and state constitutions.

During Reconstruction and thereafter, Congress broadened federal jurisdiction largely at the expense of state courts. Federal removal jurisdiction was expanded. The writ of *habeas corpus* empowered lower federal courts to test the legality of confinements by reviewing the judgments of state courts, even after they had been affirmed by the state's highest court. Thus, state criminal defendants could challenge their convictions in lower federal court and ultimately in the U.S. Supreme Court. Within this scheme, federal courts have a significant impact on state courts and cases.

The United States still has the dual system of courts it had initially. State courts retain the authority they possessed before the Constitution, plus the power to hear questions of federal law. In the Constitution and the Judiciary Act, the state courts appeared to be the primary guarantors of federal constitutional rights and in many instances actually have been the ultimate ones. Congress gave federal courts, existing side by side with their state counterparts, limited jurisdiction. The ability of federal courts to decide matters of state law was restricted to state law issues arising in cases in which federal jurisdiction was independently established. Thus, only the basic outline of the relationship between federal and state courts was set by the Constitution and the Judiciary Act. Much was left to be worked out in practice.

Protection of liberties

Although it initially lacked a bill of rights, the Constitution did not ignore the subject of individual liberties altogether. It guaranteed jury trial in criminal cases, freedom from both federal and state *ex post facto* laws and bills of attainder, and freedom from state laws impairing the obligation of contract. Missing, however, were the traditional clauses of a bill of rights, found in many state constitutions, protecting such individual liberties as freedom of religion, freedom of speech and press, and freedom from unreasonable searches and seizures or compulsory self-incrimination. Thomas Jefferson viewed the absence of a bill of rights securing the people's liberties against governmental power as a major obstacle to the acceptance of the Constitution. The champions of ratification, recognizing their political error, promised to amend the Constitution. The first session of the first Congress drafted a bill of rights in the form of a series of amendments, 10 of which were approved by the required number of states by December 15, 1791.

The federal Bill of Rights now protects individual liberties against the federal and state governments, while the state constitutions protect against the state government and sometimes against action by private persons. It has not always been so.

The federal Bill of Rights. Despite the presence of bills of rights in so many state constitutions, the delegates, with the notable exception of George Mason, seemed uninterested in appending a bill of rights to the Constitution. Mason objected: "There is no Declaration of Rights, and the laws of the general government being paramount to the laws and constitution[s] of the several states, the Declaration of Rights in the separate states are no security."[20] Until Mason raised it, James Wilson said, the issue of a bill of rights had never "struck the minds" of the delegates.[21]

To many of the delegates, the guarantees of individual liberty in the state constitutions appeared to be enough, in part because the Constitution, unlike the state constitutions, was a government of limited, enumerated powers. Roger Sherman apparently expressed the consensus of the convention when, in response to a question about the need to preserve the right to trial by jury, he said, "The State Declarations of Rights are not repealed by the Constitution; and being in force are sufficient."[22] Sherman's argument was that the Constitution could not be interpreted to authorize the federal government to violate rights that the states could not violate.

During the ratification process, the people were unpersuaded by federalist arguments against inclusion of a federal bill of rights in the Constitu-

tion: the state declarations of rights would adequately protect individual liberty; the state declarations of rights would wither away if a federal bill of rights were established; and the enumeration of rights in a federal declaration of rights might prejudice those rights not enumerated. The popular clamor for a bill of rights was so great that several states agreed to ratify the Constitution only on the understanding that a bill of rights would be added. The Constitution was ratified without a bill of rights, but Congress immediately took up the issue.

Abiding by promises made during ratification, James Madison, initially a staunch opponent of a federal bill of rights, supported the Bill of Rights in Congress. Arguing before Congress that fundamental rights should not depend on the "too uncertain" hope that the limited powers of the national government enumerated in the Constitution would be interpreted to protect individual liberties, Madison claimed that state declarations of rights would not be sufficient. Echoing Mason's argument at the convention, Madison noted that while a state bill of rights might protect an individual's rights from state interference, it might not prevent the national government from interfering with those same rights. Besides, some states had no bill of rights and bills of other states were defective.[23]

Although Madison's arguments in favor of a bill of rights restraining the national government prevailed, his proposal to have the federal bill of rights impose specific restraints on the state governments failed. Madison's proposed amendment no. XIV provided: "No State shall infringe the right of trial by Jury in criminal cases, nor the right of conscience, nor the freedom of speech or of the press." Although some states had no bill of rights, and although Madison reasonably argued that "if there were any reason to restrain the Government of the United States from infringing upon these essential rights, it was equally necessary that they should be secured against the State Governments,"[24] amendment no. XIV did not pass. A federal constitutional protection against state infringement of individual rights would have to wait until well after the adoption of the Fourteenth Amendment after the Civil War.

Separate and distinct spheres. The challenge after the ratification of the Bill of Rights was to reconcile its existence with the existence of state bills of rights. The Supreme Court responded to this challenge by confining the Bill of Rights to national governmental action. In *Barron v. Baltimore* (1833),[25] an owner of a wharf sought compensation from the City of Baltimore under the Fifth Amendment to the Constitution for destroying the commercial use of his property in making street improvements. The Supreme Court concluded that the owner had no Fifth Amendment protection, calling the issue a matter "of great importance, but not of much difficulty."

Overlapping spheres of the two constitutions. Reconstruction dramatically changed the scope of the Bill of Rights and changed the relations between the court systems. Adopted in 1868, the Fourteenth Amendment expressly limits states' interference with civil liberties. It is reminiscent of Madison's proposed amendment no. XIV, but Madison's proposal was restricted to certain specific rights; the language of the Fourteenth Amendment is more open-textured.

Section 1 of the Fourteenth Amendment prohibits the state from making or enforcing any law that abridges the privileges or immunities of citizens of the United States; deprives any person of life, liberty, or property without due process of law; or denies any person within its jurisdiction the equal protection of law. The last section of the amendment empowers Congress to enforce the amendment by appropriate legislation.

Between 1866 and 1877 Congress took steps to enforce the Fourteenth Amendment by adopting several major civil rights statutes that created new federal rights and remedies modifying existing state law. Congress also increased federal judicial jurisdiction. It opened the lower federal courts to civil rights claims, and, in 1875, to all cases founded on federal law. Thus, litigants could bypass state courts in federal question cases. Finally, Congress authorized the lower federal courts—as opposed only to the Supreme Court—to supervise or supersede the state courts in their implementation of federal law by *habeas corpus*, removal, and injunction.

The first test of the limits of the postwar restructuring of federal-state relationships came in the *Slaughterhouse Cases* (1873).[26] The Fourteenth Amendment provides that no state shall abridge "the privileges and immunities" of citizens of the United States. In the *Slaughterhouse Cases* a group of butchers challenged as a denial of one of the

protected privileges and immunities a Louisiana statute granting a monopoly of the slaughtering trade to a private corporation. The Court declared that the claim was not a federal right or privilege but rather a state right or privilege not within the ambit of the Fourteenth Amendment.

The Supreme Court construed the Fourteenth Amendment as extending against the states only those rights that were national in character: the right to travel, the right to petition for redress of grievances, the right to use the navigable waters of the United States, and other similar rights. This list of national rights remained short, because the Supreme Court refused to hold that the other guarantees enumerated in the Bill of Rights were among the privileges and immunities of citizens of the United States.

Although the Supreme Court read the privileges and immunities clause of the Fourteenth Amendment narrowly in the *Slaughterhouse Cases*, the Court later applied many of the first eight amendments to the states through the Fourteenth Amendment's due process clause, rather than the privileges or immunities clause. This application of the first eight amendments to the states through the Fourteenth Amendment is known as incorporation.

In 1897, the Court held that the Fourteenth Amendment proscribed the taking of private property for public use without payment of just compensation.[27] It was not until 1925, in *Gitlow v. New York*,[28] that the Court suggested in *dictum* that the rights guaranteed by the First Amendment are among the fundamental personal rights and liberties protected by the due process clause of the Fourteenth Amendment against the state government.

Thus, from 1787 to 1925, the Bill of Rights offered individuals little or no protection in their relations with state and local governments. The state constitutions provided those protection. During that period, however, the states' records in preserving individual rights were uneven within a state and among the states. For example, the states' records were good in appointing counsel for indigent criminal defendants at public expense. In 1859, the Wisconsin Supreme Court, as a matter of its own state constitutional law, required counties to appoint counsel for indigent felony defendants at county expense. It was not until 1963, 104 years after the Wisconsin Supreme Court had acted, that the U.S. Supreme Court required states, as a matter of Fourteenth Amendment due process, to provide counsel in state felony trials. By the time the U.S. Supreme Court imposed this requirement, most states appointed counsel at public expense, as called for by state constitutions, state laws, or state practice. In *Gideon v. Wainwright* (1963)[29] the U.S. Supreme Court brought only a few laggard states into line.

In other areas of individual rights, the states' records were poor. Many have argued that the failure of the states to provide better protection for individual rights created a void—one that the Supreme Court felt compelled to fill.

Incorporation after 1925. After 1925, the incorporation of the enumerated guarantees of the first eight amendments into the Fourteenth gained momentum, and the pace accelerated during the 1960s. The incorporation doctrine partly nationalized individual liberties and the doctrine coincided with technological, economic, and social changes that tended also toward nationalization.

Because many of the first eight amendments deal with the criminal process, the incorporation doctrine involves, to a large extent but not exclusively, a defendant's criminal procedural rights. The Fourteenth Amendment, for instance, now applies to the states the guarantees of the Sixth Amendment, including the rights to obtain a speedy trial, to have a public trial, to have an impartial jury, to confront one's accusers, to have compulsory process for obtaining witnesses in one's behalf, and to have the assistance of counsel. The Fourth Amendment right of freedom from unreasonable searches and seizures, including the federal exclusionary rule, which since 1914 has required federal judges to exclude illegally seized evidence from the trial, has been fully binding on the states since 1961. The Court made the Fifth Amendment prohibition of double jeopardy and the rule against compulsory self-incrimination fully binding upon the states as well. This privilege against self-incrimination became the basis of *Miranda v. Arizona* (1966),[30] requiring police to give warnings before custodial interrogation. Those rights in the federal Bill of Rights that are not incorporated in the Fourteenth Amendment remain dependent on state law.

The Supreme Court also expanded certain rights afforded by the Constitution as it was extending them against the states through the Fourteenth Amendment. The Court expanded not only the procedural rights of the criminal defendants

but also other civil liberties. For example, several decisions of the 1960s expanded First Amendment protections, thereby barring state-required prayers in public schools and limiting the extent to which public officials and public figures could avail themselves of state libel laws.

The incorporation doctrine gave prominence to the Constitution as a protection against invasions of individual liberties by either the state or national government. The combination of incorporation and expansion of rights increased state judges' obligations to apply federal law in state cases.

State courts, of course, were not total strangers to federal law. The two systems have always influenced each other, both directly and indirectly. Federal courts had always applied and developed state law, and state courts had always applied and developed federal law. As Justice John Harlan wrote in the 1884 *Robb v. Connolly* decision, "Upon the State courts, equally with the courts of the Union, rests the obligation to guard, enforce, and protect every right granted by the Constitution of the United States . . ."[31]

Nevertheless, the incorporation of much of the Bill of Rights through the Fourteenth Amendment, as well as the extension of the reach of federal law in general, made the state courts partners with the federal courts in the enforcement of federal law to an unprecedented extent. Working out the terms of this new partnership is one of the main challenges in adjusting federal-state court relations in the post-incorporation period.

Independent state grounds

The U.S. Supreme Court does not have a responsibility to review a state court interpretation of state law and will not do so unless an interpretation somehow implicates issues of federal law. In other words, if a state judgment rests on adequate and independent state grounds, the Supreme Court will not reach either the state or the federal issues in the case. While some commentators assert that neither the Constitution nor federal statutes requires this position, the adequate and independent state grounds doctrine is the generally accepted and traditional test for reconciling the respective claims of the state for independence of state law and of the national government for review of interpretations of federal law.

The genesis of the adequate and independent

state grounds test as a way of determining which state court decisions are subject to Supreme Court review lies in *Murdock v. City of Memphis* (1875).[32] Seventy years later, the Supreme Court more clearly explained its position in *Herb v. Pitcairn* (1945).[33] The doctrine is premised on the Court's respect for the independence of state courts and the Court's desire to avoid issuing advisory opinions, that is, opinions that discuss and answer legal questions unnecessary to the resolution of the case. The Court explained:

This Court from the time of its foundation has adhered to the principle that it will not review judgments of state courts that rest on adequate and independent state grounds. The reason is so obvious that it has rarely been thought to warrant statement. It is found in the partitioning of power between the state and federal judicial systems and in the limitations of our own jurisdiction. Our only power over state judgments is to correct them to the extent that they incorrectly adjudge federal rights. And our power is to correct wrong judgments, not to revise opinions. We are not permitted to render an advisory opinion, and if the same judgment would be rendered by the state court after we corrected its views of federal laws, our review could amount to nothing more than an advisory opinion.[34]

Complications arise when the state court opinion is ambiguous about whether the court relied on federal or state law. Determining whether an independent and adequate state ground exists is no easy task. Until 1983, when presented with an ambiguous state court decision, the Supreme Court could exercise one of several options. It could dismiss the case. It could vacate the decision and send the case back to the state court to clarify the grounds. It could order a continuance and direct the petitioner to obtain clarification from the state court. Finally, the Court itself could determine which constitution the state court relied upon.

In 1983, in *Michigan v. Long*, the Court admitted that it "had not developed a satisfying and consistent approach for resolving this vexing issue" and adopted a new approach to the independent and adequate state grounds test, concluding that its prior "ad hoc method of dealing with cases that involve possible adequate and independent state grounds is antithetical to the doctrinal consistency that is required when sensitive issues of federal-state relations are involved."

Michigan v. Long

Michigan v. Long involved the constitutionality of a protective police search of an automobile for weapons. During the search of the trunk, the police found 75 pounds of marijuana; the defendant moved to suppress the evidence. Citing the Michigan Constitution twice, but otherwise relying exclusively on federal law, the Michigan Supreme Court held "that the deputies' search of the vehicle was proscribed by the Fourth Amendment to the United States Constitution and art. I, sec. 11 of the Michigan Constitution."[35]

Writing for the five-member majority, Justice Sandra Day O'Connor stated that the Court was unconvinced that the Michigan decision rested upon independent state grounds. More important, the Court announced a new approach to its use of the adequate and independent state grounds doctrine in state cases in which the grounds for the decision are ambiguous. The Court would "accept as the most reasonable explanation that the state court decided the case the way it did because it believed that federal law required it to do so."

In other words, the Court set forth a presumption that the state decision rested on federal grounds. If the state court wanted to avoid this presumption, it

need only make clear by a plain statement in its judgment or opinion that the federal cases are being used only for the purpose of guidance, and do not themselves compel the result that the court has reached .... If the state court decision indicates clearly and expressly that it is alternatively based on bona fide separate, adequate, and independent grounds, we, of course, will not undertake to review the decision.[36]

The Court's justification for imposing the plain statement requirement was to protect the integrity of both federal and state law making. To the extent that a state court decision is based on federal law, federal review is required for doctrinal coherence, and for uniformity of federal constitutional law. State court systems and the federal courts develop and interpret federal constitutional law. Indeed, state courts turn out a larger body of criminal law cases than the federal courts. Justice O'Connor viewed the mixed federal-state opinions as threatening the federal system with a deluge of unauthoritative elaboration on federal law. The *Michigan v. Long* rule promotes uniformity by enabling the Court to review more state court decisions, because the Court now reviews decisions that are or *may* be based on federal law. The Supreme Court thus fulfills its role as the final arbiter of federal constitutional law.

Commentators assert that the *Michigan v. Long* presumption apparently rests on the Court's belief that the Constitution is the primary law in the state courts for protecting civil liberties. They say that the presumption relegates state constitutional law to a marginal role such that state judges may ignore it altogether and render judgment exclusively under federal law. The effect of the presumption is that the U.S. Supreme Court treats state courts as functional equivalents of federal courts unless the state courts expressly deny equivalency in a particular case.

In this sense, *Michigan v. Long* nationalizes state courts when their decisions are based on federal and state grounds. The Court will presume that state court decisions resolving federal and state issues rest on the resolution of the federal issues in the case. State courts will be presumed to be acting as "federal forums," unless they plainly state that they are not so acting.

In summary, in the interests of "efficiency," "uniformity," and "justice," and out of "respect for independence of state courts," the Court requires that state court opinions contain a "plain statement" that their judgments rest on adequate and independent state grounds if they do not wish to invite Supreme Court review. The judicial presumption, therefore, is that a state court's decision does *not* rest on adequate and independent state grounds, and a state court must clearly rebut that presumption if it wishes to insulate its decision from federal review.

Michigan v. Long also seeks to protect the integrity of the state. If a state court plainly says that it is relying on state law, the Supreme Court will not review its decision. The Court reaffirms the state court's opportunity to be the final arbiter of its own law and to divest the U.S. Supreme Court of jurisdiction to review. As Justice O'Connor explained in a speech, a state determines whether to "grant or withhold jurisdiction to the Supreme Court by the choice and articulation of the grounds for the state court decisions."[37] Furthermore, *Michigan v. Long* appears to encourage state courts to function more effectively by considering separately their functions as "federal courts" and as state courts. As author of the majority opinion, Justice O'Connor stated the goal as facilitating justice and judicial administration, not thwarting state constitutional development.

One effect of *Michigan v. Long*, therefore, is to shift the burden to the state courts to decide just how far they are going to be nationalized. If a state court feels it important to assert the state's autonomy by interpreting its constitution independently—not necessarily differently, just independently—then the court itself must ensure that its decisions are based on adequate and independent state grounds. Essentially, state courts must begin to develop their own philosophy of federalism from the state perspective.

Nonreviewability is the U.S. Supreme Court's acknowledgment of state autonomy. Reviewability is the affirmation of national supremacy.

The dissent

Justice John Paul Stevens viewed the case as raising "profoundly significant questions concerning the relationship between two sovereigns—the State of Michigan and the United States of America." He argued that historically the presumption was that adequate state grounds are independent unless it clearly appears otherwise. He favored retaining this policy of federal judicial restraint, thereby husbanding the limited resources of the Supreme Court. Justice Stevens expressed the belief that "a policy of judicial restraint—one that allows other decisional bodies to have the last word in legal interpretation until it is truly necessary for this Court to intervene—enables this Court to make its most effective contribution to our federal system of government."

Moreover, Justice Stevens reasoned, the Court has an interest in a case only when state standards fall short of federal standards and an individual has been deprived of a federal right. He believed the Court should not be concerned when the state court interprets federal rights too broadly and overprotects the individual. Justice Stevens complained of a "docket swollen with requests by States to reverse judgments that their courts have rendered in favor of their citizens."

Some commentators take issue with Stevens' contention that the majority's presumption of reviewability is not supported by any significant federal interest. They point out that cases that grant rights to the citizen against the state government affect important government functions that protect all of us and that Supreme Court review ensures that state courts will not hamper state officials by imposing erroneous federal constitutional requirements on them. Other commentators assert that the majority's presumption serves the federal interest in having effectively functioning states, because it eliminates a "dysfunction" caused by incorporation.[38] According to this dysfunction viewpoint, where a state court decision that erroneously relies on federal law to restrain state action goes unreviewed, because a state ground was also cited for the decision, there would be an error in the system that everyone would seem powerless to correct. The Supreme Court could not correct it because it could not review it. It would be beyond the reach of the state legislature as well.

The majority and dissent in *Michigan v. Long* agree that state courts may constitutionally develop an independent body of civil liberties law and that if no federally guaranteed rights are abridged in the process, state courts may apply state law to the exclusion of federal law. *Michigan v. Long* does not signal a change in the rule that state constitutions may provide more protections for the individual than those provided in the federal Constitution. It does remind the states that when they act like federal courts and interpret federal rights, they are potentially subject to review as a federal court.

The disagreement between Justice Stevens and Justice O'Connor is thus not whether to adopt a clear rule for determining whether a state decision is independent, but what that rule should be.

The aftermath

Michigan v. Long has engendered a large body of literature that ranges from praise for the decision to condemnation of the "plain statement" rule to questioning the constitutional, theoretical, and functional bases of the adequate and independent state grounds doctrine. The proponents of the decision support it as a workable, practical way for handling state decisions that fail to state clearly whether they rest on federal grounds or independent and adequate state grounds. They conclude that the U.S. Supreme Court ought to promote its federal lawmaking role and ought not to renounce its power to interpret federal law in favor of the nonauthoritative state court readings of federal law. They view *Michigan v. Long* as promoting the U.S. Supreme Court's maintaining uniformity and supremacy of federal law.

To its admirers, *Michigan v. Long* furthers federalism because it delineates clearly the respective spheres of state and federal law and possibly enhances the ability of state courts to experiment in developing principles of constitutional law suitable for that state's constitution and that state's people. They see the case as attempting to encourage states to construct their own inviolable sphere of state law. Some commentators conclude that the plain statement will be a burden only to those state courts that were purposely ambiguous in grounding their decision in federal and state law to evade Supreme Court review and to insulate the decision from the state political process.

Other commentators are more skeptical. They question whether *Michigan v. Long*, which was decided in the name of federalism, really encourages federal judicial interference with state courts' constitutional discretion. The detractors of *Michigan v. Long* view it as an artificial attempt to impose federal law on state courts. They suspect the case is not based on a natural principle of federalism but rather is a means of constraining civil liberties protection. They view *Michigan v. Long* as masking the Court's substantive goal of keeping state courts from interpreting their constitutions generously.

These commentators conclude that although, in theory, *Michigan v. Long* preserves the state court's ability to interpret its own constitution, in the real world the decision hinders state courts from developing state law. These writers argue that the state political climate might prevent state judges from interpreting state law more broadly than federal law. They say that a state court opinion that benefits a minority or runs against majoritarian preferences places a state judge, who is often an elected official, at risk. The detractors reason that a state judge who holds that state and federal law together compel an unpopular result is taking a safer political course than a judge who holds that state law gives greater rights than federal law. Moreover, these commentators point out that the people of the state can respond to an unpopular state court interpretation by amending the state constitution. Indeed, some states have amended their constitutions to require state courts to harmonize their interpretation of the state constitution with federal precedents. Putting a new twist on the old fear that state judges are "dependent" rather than independent and are not on a par with federal judges, some argue that state courts whose interpretations of the state constitutions will be subject to review by state legislators and the electorate will not be as receptive to claims that a constitutional right has been denied as would be a federal court that is independent from other branches of government and from the electorate at large. Thus, the argument goes, state courts will either interpret their constitutions restrictively or risk Supreme Court review so that the Court will take the blame for the increased protection of civil liberties.

Regardless of which view one takes of *Michigan v. Long*, the U.S. Supreme Court has itself made a plain statement. If a state court wishes to insulate its decision from Supreme Court review, it must express clearly the state law grounds for its decision and must, of course, not deny any federal right.

The advent of incorporation has required a readjustment of the relations between federal and state courts. Incorporation affects each system. It threatens the federal system with a loss of control over federal law, and it threatens the state system with nationalization. In *Michigan v. Long*, the Supreme Court apparently tried to stave off both these threats. The measure of its success will be seen in future state and federal court decisions involving civil liberties.

The impact

Michigan v. Long will be felt in federal district courts and circuit courts of appeals as well as in state courts. As we said earlier, federal courts may apply state law and thus function as state courts. In *City of Mesquite v. Aladdin's Castle, Inc.* (1982),[39] for example, the U.S. Supreme Court remanded a case to the Fifth Circuit to decide whether its opinion declaring a city ordinance violative of the constitutional guarantees of due process and equal protection rested on Texas law or federal law. The Supreme Court held that it would not decide this novel federal constitutional question if Texas law provided independent support for the courts of appeals judgment.

Similarly, in 1985 the Ninth Circuit set aside a city ordinance prohibiting the solicitation of donations in public areas used by a municipal stadium. The court began its analysis by stating that the challenge was based on both the federal and California constitutions and that if the California Constitution provides independent support for the claim, there is no need for a decision of the federal issue. There is no certification procedure in California for the federal court to ask the state supreme court to declare the state law issue. The Ninth Circuit decided the state law question, holding the ordinance violative of the California Constitution, and did not reach the federal question.

It is too early to judge the long-term impact of *Michigan v. Long* on state and federal courts. We can say, however, that many state courts remain unaffected by *Michigan v. Long*, and their decisions are like their pre-1983 decisions. Many still do not refer to state constitutions. Those that do often make no effort to separate the state and federal grounds upon which the decision is based. At the same time, a growing number of state high courts have been relying on their own constitutions. If a state court adopts federal interpretations as the interpretation of the state constitution, however, the state ground may not be sufficiently independent of federal law to insulate the decision from review.

If federal and state courts respond to *Michigan v. Long* in the future by increased reliance on state law, the number of cases in which the Court can articulate its views of federal constitutional law may be decreased. In this eventuality, *Michigan v. Long* may achieve disparity between federal and state interpretations of similar constitutional provisions.

Michigan v. Long does not mandate any particular approach to federal and state constitutional claims, although scholars are divided on whether Justice O'Connor's and Justice Stevens's opinions represent a debate over the interstitial and primacy approaches, which in turn represent different views toward federalism. For the present, however, hopes and fears will abound with regard to *Michigan v. Long*. Some will continue to fear that federal review of state court decisions that do not make clear whether they rest on federal or state grounds will become "advisory" in a new sense—that the U.S. Supreme Court will be advising the states how to construe their state constitutions. Such advice is not unprecedented. In a case predating *Michigan v. Long*, Chief Justice Burger criticized the Florida Supreme Court's construction of the Florida Constitution, saying that it was not rational law enforcement and suggesting that the people amend the state's laws or constitution to override state court opinions that extend individual rights.

Others will continue to hope that the presumption of reviewability will force state courts to make clear the grounds of their decisions and interpret their state constitutions. In that case, the Supreme

Court may also receive some unsolicited commentary, favorable or unfavorable, on its own opinions, such as that found in some recent state court opinions.

Perhaps such spirited mutual advice is not totally unwelcome in a federal system of which one of the chief virtues is the dialogue between the national and the state governments.

Conclusion

Federalism will continue to mean different things to different people. From the time the framers adopted the term *federalism*, there was confusion and disagreement about what the term meant. Deriving from *foedus*, meaning treaty or alliance, the term *federal* was, some assert, coopted by the proponents of the Constitution to refer to their quasi-national form of government. As Garry Wills puts it, "By a kind of pre-emptive verbal strike, the centralizers seized the word and cast the original federalists in the role of antifederalists."[40]

The term was born through a process of redefinition, and it has been continually redefined since that time. The genus federalism already includes a wide variety of species: dual federalism, cooperative federalism, interactive federalism, classical federalism, and dialectical federalism, to name just a few. We will not attempt to classify "new federalism" within any of these categories.

New federalism represents an attempt to reinvigorate the idea of federalism by reviewing the idea of state autonomy, an idea that some had declared dead during the incorporation period. The meaning of state autonomy and the proper role for states remain unsettled: state courts, among other institutions, will play a role in resolving these unsettled issues as they decide whether and how to apply the protections of civil liberties in their state constitutions. In this respect, new federalism is a return to the preference of the framers for a monolithic system tempered by pluralism.

New federalism is not an attempt to return to the nullificationist vision of the role of states. The proponents of new federalism do not suggest that state courts be the sole guardians of individual liberty or that the U.S. Supreme Court retreat from applying the Bill of Rights to state action. As Justice Brennan said, "One of the strengths of our federal system is that it provides a double source of protection for the rights of our citizens. Federalism is not served when the federal half of that protection is crippled."[41] The difficulty is to work out a system in which federal and state protections can coexist. The fundamental puzzle, as Professor Paul Bator notes, is to determine what the appropriate criteria are for deciding which questions the federal Constitution should be deemed to have made a matter of uniform national policy.[42]

State court approaches to the questions of when and how to interpret their state bills of rights will also tend to define their relationship with the federal courts. As *Michigan v. Long* seems to indicate, state courts will have substantial freedom in determining the extent of their autonomy as long as their decisions do not violate federal law. Thus, the great challenge for state courts in the post-incorporation era is to ground their decisions both in the protection of individual liberties and in the principles of federalism.

NOTES

This article originally appeared in Volume 71, Number 2, August-September 1987, pages 88-99. It is adapted from a paper presented at the 73rd American Assembly, Arden House, Harriman, New York, April 23-26, 1987, and which appears in its entirety in A WORKABLE GOVERNMENT?: THE CONSTITUTION AFTER 200 YEARS (New York: W.W. Norton, 1987).

The authors wish to thank Diana Balio, Sharon Ruhly, and Joel R. Wells for their assistance in the preparation of the manuscript.

1. Wisdom, *Foreword: The Ever-Whirling Wheels of American Federalism*, 59 NOTRE DAME L. REV. 1063, 1076 (1984).

2. Wright, *In Praise of State Courts: Confessions of a Federal Judge*, 11 HASTINGS CONST. L.Q. 165, 188 (1984).

3. Gouverneur Morris, quoted in Bowen, MIRACLE AT PHILADELPHIA 40 (1966).

4. 463 U.S. 1032 (1983).

5. Bowen, *supra* n. 3, at 7.

6. *Id.* at 199.

7. THE FEDERALIST PAPERS, No. 39.

8. De Tocqueville, DEMOCRACY IN AMERICA 164 (Henry Reeve Text as Revised by Francis Bowen, 1945).

9. Younger v. Harris, 401 U.S. 37, 44 (1971).

10. John Quincy Adams, "Jubilee of the Constitution: A Discourse Delivered at the Request of the New York Historical Society in the City of New York on Tuesday, the 30th of April, 1839, Being the Fiftieth Anniversary of the Inauguration of George Washington as President of the United States on Thursday, the 30th of April, 1789," p. 115 (1839).

11. De Tocqueville, *supra* n. 8, at 148.

12. 1 Farrand, THE RECORDS OF THE FEDERAL CONVENTION OF 1787, 124 (1966).

13. *Id.* at 125.

14. Art. III, Sec. 2, U.S. Const.

15. THE FEDERALIST PAPERS No. 80.

16. 1 Cranch 137, 2 L.Ed. 60 (1803).

17. 2 Farrand, THE RECORDS OF THE FEDERAL CONVNENTION OF 1787, 638 (1966).

18. FEDERALIST PAPERS No. 82.

19. Act of Sept. 24, 1789, 1 Stat. 73.

20. 2 Farrand, *supra* n. 17, at 637.

21. Wood, THE CREATION OF THE AMERICAN REPUBLIC 536

(1969).

22. 2 Farrand, *supra* n. 17, at 588.

23. 1 Kurland & Lerner, THE FOUNDERS' CONSTITUTION 479-484 (1987).

24. *Id.* at 492.

25. 32 U.S. (7 Pet.) 243 (1833).

26. 83 U.S. (16 Wall.) 36 (1873).

27. Chicago B. & Q.R.R. v. Chicago, 166 U.S. 226, 241 (1897).

28. 268 U.S. 652 (1928).

29. 372 U.S. 335 (1963).

30. 384 U.S. 436 (1966).

31. 111 U.S. 624 (1884).

32. 87 U.S. (20 Wall.) 590 (1875).

33. 324 U.S. 117 (1945).

34. *Id.* at 125-126 [citations omitted].

35. People v. Long, 413 Mich. 461, 320 N.W.2d 866, 870 (1982).

36. 463 U.S. 1032, at 1041 (1983).

37. O'Connor, *Our Judicial Federalism*, 35 CASE WEST RES. L. REV. 1, 5 (1984-85).

38. Althouse, *How to Build a Separate Sphere: Federal Courts and State Power*, 100 HARV. L. REV. 1485 (1987).

39. 455 U.S. 283 (1982).

40. Wills, EXPLAINING AMERICA: THE FEDERALIST 169 (1981).

41. Brennan, *State Constitutions and the Protection of Individual Liberties*, 90 HARV. L. REV. 489, 503 (1977).

42. Bator, *Some Thoughts on Applied Federalism*, 6 HARV. J. L. & PUB. POL'Y 51, 58 (1982).

State supreme court commitment to state law

Despite promotion of the New Judicial Federalism, state high courts continue to rely on federal law for most of their decisions.

by Michael Esler

For the last two decades, much interest has been paid to the development and use of state constitutions for protecting civil liberties and rights. While there are good reasons to believe that reliance on state law has grown in recent years, empirical evidence shows that the extent to which state courts rely on their own constitutions has been greatly overstated. One reason is that the predominant focus has been on case outcomes rather than on the decision-making process, often leaving questions about the actual level of reliance on state law unexamined.

Moreover, research that has examined the "use" question specifically is often misleading. Typically, this approach primarily examines decisions and courts that exemplify use of state law. The problem with this leading cases approach is that it ignores the much greater number of decisions based on federal law.

This article reports findings indicating that, at least through the first decade and a half of what has come to be called the New Judicial Federalism, state supreme courts rely on federal law in the vast majority of their decisions. Further, even state courts that base their decisions on state law usually do not do so in ways that will lead to the state law's development as a viable alternative to federal law. The results are best explained by the political, legal, and institutional barriers that limit the willingness of state courts to develop their own constitutions for issues that already have been decided by federal law.

The New Judicial Federalism

The essence of the New Judicial Federalism is the development of state constitutional law for deciding issues with parallel provisions in state and federal law. Most attention, however, has been directed toward the outcomes of decisions that rely on state law. This emphasis on outcomes corresponds to the perception that federal courts are no longer as committed to protecting individual rights as they were during the Warren Court era.[1] Many advocates of the New Judicial Federalism thus urge greater reliance on state law as a way to expand rights protections beyond the level required by federal law.[2] The legal means are provided by the independent and adequate state grounds doctrine, which obligates state courts to recognize rights established under federal law, but frees them to establish greater levels of protection as a matter of their own state law.[3]

Not surprisingly, most empirical research about the New Judicial Federalism has analyzed whether state courts have followed the advice of the advocates, and why some courts have been more willing than others to use state law for expanding liberties and rights. Generally, this research has not systematically compared significant numbers of decisions based on state law that both expand and decline to expand rights beyond the level required by federal law.

Many of these problems were avoided in a recent study by Latzer,[4] which is an improvement precisely because it accounts for decisions by all 50 state supreme courts and, more importantly, a full range of decisional outcomes based on state law. Latzer analyzed virtually every state high court criminal procedure decision based on state law from the late 1960s through 1989. He found that only about a third of the decisions based on state law expanded rights beyond the level required by federal law.[5]

This overall pattern of results corresponded to a state-by-state analysis. Here, Latzer found that only four state high courts (Alaska, California, Florida, and Massachusetts) consistently rejected U.S. Supreme Court doctrines in favor of more expansive rights protections on the basis of state law. Of the four, two (California and Florida) did so only until state constitutional amendments compelled conformity with federal law.[6] Thus, all but a small number of state high courts consistently adopted Supreme Court doctrines even when basing decisions on their own constitutions. Latzer presents compelling evidence that, in most cases, state high court decisions do not use state law to further criminal defendant rights beyond the level required by the U.S. Supreme Court. Moreover, very few state high courts consistently interpret their state law in such an expansive manner.

While considerable attention has been directed toward the outcomes of court decisions based on state grounds, relatively little scholarship has focused on what is arguably a more fundamental question: the frequency with which state courts base their decisions on state law. Most research on state court use of state law has involved studies of leading cases,[7] courts,[8] or a simple counting of the number of decisions based on state law for a selected area of law.[9] These approaches are useful for identifying exemplars among state courts, the justifications they provide for relying on state law, and a sense of the changes in absolute numbers of decisions based on state law for a given set of issues. Yet they do not account for the extent to which state courts rely on state law relative to the total number of decisions they make.[10]

Latzer's study is typical of most research. His data consisted solely of decisions based on state law. While this might be appropriate for his main interest—investigating the frequency with which state supreme courts use state law to expand criminal defendant rights beyond federal requirements—it says nothing about the extensiveness of state court reliance on state law. As a result, Latzer could only assume that reliance on state law is generally extensive.[11]

Turning his attention to individual states, Latzer ranked each state supreme court on the basis of its commitment to developing its own law. He did so, however, by simply counting the decisions each court grounded in state law.[12] This method of rank-

ing the "activism" of individual state supreme courts could not account for the number of decisions each court grounded in federal law. Consequently, it is impossible to tell if the most active courts are truly more committed to developing their own constitutions, or whether their ranking is just a function of the number of cases they hear.

The main objective of Latzer's study was to assess the extent to which state high courts use their constitutions to extend rights protections beyond the level required by federal law. His research is important for pointing out the limitations of much of the result-oriented literature as well as for providing a valid assessment of the results of state supreme court decisions.[13] Latzer's criticisms of the result-oriented research can be extended to much of the research that has examined the extent to which state courts rely on their own constitutions.

Measuring reliance on state law

The extent to which state courts rely on their own law can be measured by analyzing judicial decisions based on both state and federal law. The study reported here examined a set of issues related to the right against self-incrimination that were decided by all 50 state supreme courts.[14] Limiting the study to a common set of issues provided some assurance that the courts reacted to similar kinds of legal stimuli. This helped control for the influence of varying legal factors that combine to shape decisions in other cases.

Issues involving questions of self-incrimination were selected for a number of reasons. First, they were frequently litigated before the state high courts. On average, about 27 courts decided each issue. In all, 249 cases were analyzed. These issues also were selected because analogues exist to the Fifth Amendment's protection against self-incrimination in all but two state constitutions.[15] Consequently, state courts for these issues are free to base their decisions on either state or federal law.

Moreover, decisions by the post-Warren Supreme Court arguably have encouraged state high courts to rely on their own constitutions when deciding cases raising these issues. For each of these issues, the post-Warren Court has been less sympathetic to criminal defendant claims than its predecessor. This provides an incentive for state courts that favor more expansive protections for criminal defendants to ground their decisions in state law. State courts also are more inclined to turn to their own law when federal doctrines are undergoing transformation, regardless of the outcomes these courts might favor. Finally, previous research suggests that claims based on state law are more likely to occur in the area of criminal procedure.[16] Focusing on these issues, then, maximized the possibility of finding decisions based on state law.

The time frame of the study, 1981 to 1986, covers the early years of the New Judicial Federalism. This is a likely time for state courts to have turned to their own law when deciding self-incrimination issues. The U.S. Supreme Court decisions that signaled the post-Warren Court's retreat from more protective self-incrimination standards for each of the issues in this study were handed down between 1971 and 1982. The majority of these doctrinal shifts occurred in the years just prior to the period examined. As a consequence of these changes, large numbers of cases raising these issues were brought before the state high courts between 1981 and 1986. Given the unsettled legal status of these issues during this time, state courts had both the incentive and opportunity to base significant numbers of decisions on state law.

Further, this period generally has been identified as a time when state supreme courts began turning to their own constitutions for deciding a range of issues. For instance, research by Collins, Galie, and Kincaid indicates that between 1950 and 1986, the period of greatest reliance on state law by state supreme courts occurred from 1980 to 1986.[17] Much of the literature on the New Judicial Federalism similarly identifies this period as the time when state high courts first began to rely on their own law in significant numbers.[18] The nature of these issues and the time frame involved provide a generous test of the extent to which state courts rely on state law.

Methods

Each majority opinion was coded to measure two aspects of state court commitment to state law. The first was the extent to which state courts rely on state law in their opinions. The second, which focused specifically on the decisions based on state law, measured the strength of state court commitment to developing state law as a viable alternative to federal law.

Coding the reliance of state courts on state law was potentially problematic in that, in the majority of cases (64 percent), both state and federal

law were considered in the opinions. Ambiguously worded opinions by state courts is not a problem faced only by scholars. It also creates problems for the U.S. Supreme Court when it grapples with jurisdictional questions. The Court's decision in *Michigan v. Long*[19] was prompted partly by the failure of state courts to explicitly provide the legal bases of their decisions. In *Long*, the Court ruled that it would assume that ambiguously worded decisions were based on federal law unless state courts explicitly declared that their decisions rested on independent and adequate state grounds.

Scholars have used similar criteria when their research has required them to draw the same types of distinctions. For instance, Latzer defined a decision as grounded in state law, and thus selected it for his analysis, only if the majority opinion included a "plain statement" that it was based on state law, or an "exclusive citation to a state constitutional provision, or a citation to a state case which itself clearly rested upon a state provision . . . ."[20] Similarly, Fino coded a decision as based on state law only if it referred exclusively to state law, unless the reference to federal law was for purely rhetorical purposes or when the federal approach was discussed only to reject it.[21]

This study used similar, if less demanding, criteria for determining whether a decision rested on state law. Even if a decision discussed both state and federal law, it was coded as based on state law if a clear majority of the relevant part of the opinion was devoted to analysis of state law and the opinion otherwise indicated that federal law was not controlling. If it was unclear whether the decision rested on state or federal grounds, it was eliminated from further analysis. This approach was designed to maximize the possibility of finding decisions based on state law.

When a decision met the criteria for being defined as grounded in state law, it was further analyzed before it was finally coded as based on state law. If the opinion cited a state court precedent as the authority for the decision, the precedent, and any other state cases the precedent cited, were analyzed to determine their legal foundation. If any of the state court precedents ultimately were rooted in federal law, the decision was coded as based on federal law. This strategy revealed the ultimate basis of state court decisions, including those that preceded the starting point of this study.

Each majority opinion also was coded for the

strength of state court commitment to developing state law as an alternative to federal law. State courts may base their decisions on state law, but nevertheless lack the commitment to developing it in ways that would enable other courts in the state to use and build upon it as a viable alternative to federal law.

A useful measure for distinguishing different levels of state court commitment to developing state law involves the types of law state courts cite as the authority for their opinions. Decisions that rely on state court precedents typically cite the relevant cases without elaboration. Moreover, they rarely express any intent to develop state law as an alternative to federal law.

On the other hand, decisions based on provisions of state constitutions, statutes, or common law doctrines usually involve carefully developed analyses of the requirements of state law and how they are similar to or different from the requirements of federal law. As a result, they establish a foundation and provide a record for other courts in the state to build upon. In this sense, state court decisions based on provisions of state constitutions, statutes, or common law doctrines reflect a commitment to establishing state law as an alternative to federal law that is deeper than decisions authorized by state court precedents.

Three limitations of this study should be noted. First, since this study analyzed the commitment of state supreme courts to developing state law, the primary focus was on the type of law (state or federal) on which these courts base their decisions. The study, however, did not reach the important questions concerning the various state and federal legal influences that may have shaped these laws. Ultimately, both state and federal doctrines are the product of a complex set of relationships between state and federal law.

Second, the data include only decisions by high courts. Since 37 states have intermediate appeals courts, the study does not provide a complete picture of current constitutional law in the states. Still, these courts play a decidedly secondary role to high courts in creating legal doctrine. Therefore, focusing on state high courts provides a reasonably accurate account of legal policy in the states.

A final limitation is the study's focus on one relatively narrow set of legal issues dealing with self-incrimination. It could be that the results drawn from these data are not applicable to other areas

Table 1 Legal bases for decisions

	N	Percent of state law	Percent of total
State law	54		22%
State precedent	38	70%	15
State constitution	10	19	4
State statute	5	9	2
Common law doctrines	1	2	1

	N	Percent of federal law	Percent of total
Federal law	195		78%
Federal precedent	192*	98%	77
Federal constitution	3	2	1

*Includes 26 cases that originally cited state law but whose decisions ultimately were traced to U.S. Supreme Court precedent.

of state constitutional law. However, these issues probably are representative of criminal justice cases in general, which constitute the "overwhelming, everyday mass of all constitutional claims."[22] Moreover, the results of this study generally are consistent with the results of several other studies that analyzed different issues. Taken together, these studies cast serious doubt on the commitment of state supreme courts to the development of their own constitutions, at least through the early years of the New Judicial Federalism.

Results

Table 1 shows that state supreme courts based relatively few of the examined decisions on their own state law. Only slightly more than one in five decisions (22 percent) ultimately rely on state law, leaving the vast majority grounded in federal law. Of these decisions, virtually all (98 percent) defer to precedents established by the U.S. Supreme Court.

Table 1 also indicates that, even when they based their decisions on state law, state high courts seldom developed their states' law in ways that would establish it as a viable alternative to federal law. Of the decisions that rest on state law, 70 percent rely only on state court precedents. That is, fewer than a third of these decisions (or about 7 percent of all decisions) are based on state constitutions, statutes, or common law doctrines. Thus, focusing solely on the extensiveness of state supreme court reliance on state law actually overstates the commitment of high courts to developing their states' law, even though the data hardly indicate a strong commitment according to that measure. In short, both measures indicate that state supreme courts are not committed to developing state law, at least through the early years of the New Judicial Federalism.

These findings are consistent with the results of the three other studies, encompassing other issues, that have investigated the extent to which state supreme courts rely on state law. Fino analyzed all the decisions of six state high courts for the year 1975.[23] She found that 17 percent of all cases that raised constitutional issues were decided on the basis of state law.[24] The percentage dropped to 8 percent for constitutional issues that involved questions of criminal procedure.[25] In a separate study of cases involving constitutional issues that raised equal protection claims before the 50 state supreme courts between 1975 and 1984, Fino found that fewer than 7 percent of all cases were decided on the basis of state law (fewer than 5 percent for criminal cases that raised equal protection claims).[26] Finally, Emmert and Traut found that, between 1981 and 1985, about 16 percent of all state supreme court cases that involved challenges to state statutes were decided on the basis of state law (about 18 percent for criminal cases).[27] Although the actual figures vary, the studies that have analyzed the extent to which state courts rely on state law are consistent in showing that, across a range of issues, a relatively low percentage of all decisions are based on state law.[28]

A state-by-state analysis yielded results that support these general findings. Table 2 groups the 50 state supreme courts into four categories according to the percentage of their decisions grounded in federal law. "High support" courts are those that based at least half their decisions on state law. Only eight state supreme courts (or 16 percent of the total) are in this category. "Moderate support" courts based more than one-fourth, but fewer than half, of their decisions on state law. Eleven courts (22 percent of the total) may be described as providing moderate support for reliance on state law. "Low support" courts based at least one decision, but no more than one-fourth of their decisions, on state law. Seventeen courts (34 percent of the total) are in this category. Finally, the 14 courts (28 percent of the total) that did not base any of their decisions on state law are described as "zero support" courts. Clearly, most state supreme courts based a low percentage, if any, of their decisions on state law. On the other hand, only a small number of state high courts based as many as half their decisions on state law.

The state supreme courts that were most con-

Table 2 State supreme court commitment to use of state law

Level of commitment	Court		Percent of all states
High (At least half of decisions based on state law)	Alaska Arkansas Florida New Jersey	New York South Dakota Tennessee Texas	16%
Moderate (At least one-fourth of decisions based on state law)	California Georgia Illinois Michigan Montana Nebraska	New Hampshire New Mexico Oregon Utah Wyoming	22
Low (At least one decision based on state law)	Alabama Colorado Connecticut Idaho Indiana Iowa Louisiana Maine Massachusetts	Minnesota Mississippi Missouri North Carolina Pennsylvania Vermont Virginia West Virginia	34
Zero	Arizona Delaware Hawaii Kansas Kentucky Maryland Nevada	North Dakota Ohio Oklahoma Rhode Island South Carolina Washington Wisconsin	28

sistent in their use of state law included several courts, such as those of Alaska, New Jersey, and New York, that are often mentioned as leaders of the New Judicial Federalism. However, courts that usually are not considered leaders in the use of state law, such as those of Texas, South Dakota, Tennessee, Florida, and Arkansas, also based at least half the examined decisions on state law. The courts of California, Oregon, and Washington, usually recognized as leaders, fell short of basing a majority of the examined decisions on state law.

It is noteworthy that the few studies that took account of the relative mix of decisions grounded in state and federal law present an image of the New Judicial Federalism quite different from studies that did not consider a full range of decisions. Even the decisions based on state law reflect a general indifference toward establishing state law as a viable alternative to federal law. The data in this study not only raise questions about the overall commitment of state courts to the development of state law, but about the number of state supreme courts that are actively committed to developing their own constitutions, at least during the first decade and a half of the New Judicial Federalism.

Reliance on federal law

For more than a decade, legal scholars, attorneys,

and judges have championed the New Judicial Federalism. Advocates have called for increased reliance on state law both for result-oriented purposes and for ends that are unrelated to political outcomes. Despite the advocacy and a number of notable examples from some state courts, commitment to developing state law is still exceptional. While there is no single explanation for this state of affairs, a number of political, legal, and institutional theories of judicial decision making explain why state courts continue to look to federal law for guidance for the vast majority of their decisions.

As Latzer and others have shown, state supreme courts generally do not support the expansion of constitutional rights in their decisions.[29] Leaving aside the justices' own usually conservative attitudes,[30] groups such as prosecutors, police, corrections administrators, law-and-order legislators, and executives represent strong, organized voices for tougher standards for dealing with the accused.[31] The interests of criminal defendants rarely enjoy the same level of organized support. Electoral pressures and the proximity of state court judges to their constituents also sensitize them to prevailing opinion, which is generally conservative[32] and almost uniformly unsympathetic when it comes to the rights of the accused.[33] Not coincidentally, law enforcement has been the main theme of judicial campaigns for the last 20 years.[34]

Given the reality of state politics, it is hardly surprising that state courts have not been more active in expanding criminal defendant rights. It is one thing for state supreme courts to acknowledge criminal defendant rights when mandated by federal law. It is quite another for them to initiate the expansion of liberties and rights under state law. Judges who forget this fact of political life need only consider several highly publicized cases where the public has rebuked state courts that have used state law to promote the rights of the accused. The defeat of Chief Justice Rose Bird and Associate Justices Cruz Reynoso and Joseph Grodin in California sent a message to all state judges about the consequences of straying too far from prevailing opinion.[35]

Voters in California, Massachusetts, Pennsylvania, and Florida have used alternative, but no less clear, means to express displeasure with their high courts' liberal use of state law. In these states, voters used the power of the initiative to amend their constitutions to overturn defendants' rights decisions. Chief Justice Warren Burger even applauded the action of Florida voters in a 1983 opinion and encouraged voters in other states to overturn state court decisions with which they disagreed.[36] State legislatures also have proposed constitutional amendments, as well as exercised other powers they hold over the courts, when they have been displeased with liberal judicial decisions.[37] To the extent that political forces shape judicial decisions, conservative influences are usually decisive.[38] Since conservative results can be reached on the basis of federal law, state courts that are motivated by political goals have little incentive to base their decisions on state law.

Even courts that are not pursuing a particular political agenda or, for that matter, courts favoring a liberal agenda might also be dissuaded from basing decisions on state law. This follows from the perception that the primary reason for state courts to base their decisions on state law is to achieve liberal outcomes. Governor George Deukmejian promoted this idea when he was California's attorney general. In a widely circulated article, he criticized use of state constitutional law without sufficient theoretical justification. The message for many judges was to question the legitimacy of ever relying on state grounds.[39]

The perception that courts usually base decisions on state law to effect liberal results is shared by many scholars, even those who favor the development of state law for reasons that are not result-oriented.[40] Ironically, overemphasis by advocates of the New Judicial Federalism on the result-oriented uses of state law has contributed to the reluctance of even conservative state courts to develop and use their own law.

The U.S. Supreme Court also has played a role in discouraging development of state law. In several decisions, it has narrowed the definition of what constitutes an "adequate" and "independent" basis for state courts to claim their decisions are grounded in state law.[41] For instance, there has been speculation that the effect of the Court's decision in *Michigan v. Long* has been to make it more difficult for state courts to claim their decisions rest on independent state grounds.[42] By requiring them to issue a "plain statement" that their decisions are grounded in state law, the Court forced state courts to face potential criticism from conservative forces that see reliance on state law as a pretext for liberal activism.[43] In this sense, U.S.

Supreme Court decisions play a role in the reluctance of state courts to base decisions on state law.

Few political incentives exist for state courts to develop and use their own constitutions. State court judges who are driven by political considerations are likely to be conservative as a result of their own attitudes and in response to the dominance of conservative pressures that characterize most states. For these courts there is nothing to gain politically from relying on state law when federal law will do. The politics of using state law also are shaped by the mere perception that the purpose of using state law is to effect liberal results. Thus, even courts that might otherwise have an interest in developing their own state law might be reluctant to risk the potential political consequences that go with it.

Dominance of federal law

Politics are not all that work against reliance on state law. Legal and institutional factors also provide important reasons for why state courts continue to rely on federal law for the majority of their decisions. The development and expansion of the incorporation doctrine throughout this century has transformed federal judicial relations in a fundamental way. As the number of incorporated provisions in the U.S. Bill of Rights reached its peak during the Warren years, the dominance of federal law became practically complete.[44]

After decades of looking no further than federal requirements, state court reliance on federal law remains deeply entrenched. State courts continue to view federal law as the primary source for settling individual rights cases.[45] Deference to the rule of precedent is decisive for many state courts. The sheer weight of years of U.S. Supreme Court decisions is reason enough to look no further than federal law. To depart from federal precedent could create uncertainty about legal issues that had been thought to be settled.[46]

Moreover, many state court judges are unwilling to expend the resources, time, and effort to develop state law when an established body of federal law already exists. And, after so many years of neglect, some state courts lack the self-confidence to embark on an independent interpretation of their own law.[47] As a result, most state court judges view the appropriate role of state law as "reactive" or "supplemental."[48] Federal law is construed first, and state law is consulted only if federal law is found to be inadequate or when there are other reasons to justify turning to state law.[49]

Textual similarities between the federal and state bills of rights also work against independent and innovative interpretations of state law. State court judges often feel they must justify interpreting identically worded provisions in state constitutions differently from their federal analogues.[50] To do so could seem to undermine the idea that written law matters.

Some scholars have expressed concern that excessive concentration on state law could even retard development of federal law. It might "dampen the lively interaction between state and federal interpretations of the federal Bill of Rights . . . and thereby decrease the ability of the United States Supreme Court to select from a wide variety of innovative and well-considered interpretations of the federal charter."[51] Along these lines, a state-centered approach might call into question the meaning and importance of federal law.

State courts especially are unlikely to turn to state law in the area of criminal procedure. Given the relative complexity of criminal law, state courts often find it difficult enough to apply standards mandated by federal law. If state courts were to turn to standards based on state law, their problems could multiply. Prosecutors and police especially might find it difficult to operate under an array of state and federal rules. At least one prosecutor called it "an open invitation to confusion-and-error on the enforcement front."[52]

Federal and state law enforcement officers often work together on the same cases. When this occurs, state officials usually prefer to prosecute under federal laws because they are generally tougher on criminal defendants. Sometimes state prosecutors are even deputized by federal officials so that they can more effectively pursue their cases.[53] State courts may be reluctant to threaten these relationships by basing decisions on state law.

The powerful effect of decades of federal dominance retards development of state law in still another way. Even when state supreme courts are otherwise receptive to basing decisions on state grounds, institutional factors largely beyond their control often present significant obstacles to the development of state law. The general lack of historical records on the events and forces that shaped state constitutions creates problems for judges who wish to develop state law.[54] Moreover, the paucity of precedents grounded in state law and the federal bias that characterizes the legal training of their clerks often means that judges will be presented only with federal cases when writing opinions.[55]

Another factor is that attorneys often do not argue state grounds before state courts. When state grounds are not presented in legal arguments, it is difficult for judges to base their decisions on state law, since to do so they must develop their reasoning without benefit of counsels' briefs. However, there is an even more fundamental reason why the failure to raise state grounds often results in the underdevelopment of state law. Most state supreme courts refuse to base their decisions on legal grounds *sua sponte*, as a matter of principle.[56] Thus, the type of arguments that attorneys present to state courts plays a central role in the relatively low level of development of state law. Indeed, the failure of attorneys to raise state legal grounds is arguably as great a factor in the failure to develop state constitutional law as any lack of will on the part of judges.

Some judges have criticized the failure of attorneys to raise state grounds. Oregon Supreme Court Justice Robert E. Jones has gone as far as stating that any defense lawyer who relies solely on federal grounds when arguing constitutional issues before state courts should be found guilty of legal malpractice.[57] Placing the entire blame on attorneys, however, ignores the role of legal education in this process. Law schools focus scant attention on state law, much less offer courses in state constitutional law.[58] Without training in the substance and procedures of state constitutional law, newly minted lawyers hardly can be expected to present adequate state legal arguments.

For their part, law schools may be forgiven for not including courses in state constitutional law in light of its lack of development by state courts in recent decades. State courts must share some of the blame for generally failing to demand that attorneys raise state claims. Thus, the failure of state courts to develop state constitutional law is part of a self-perpetuating cycle. The typical law school curriculum produces lawyers who are not versed in raising claims under state constitutional law, which means that state grounds often are not presented in court. The result is that judges usually refuse to base their decisions on state law, which in turn discourages law schools from taking state

law seriously. This cycle is the basis for what Gardner recently described as the "poverty of state constitutional discourse."[59] This is the idea that state constitutional law lacks the basic language, conventions, and meanings that are required for participants to make intelligible claims to one another and thus build the foundation for its development.

In the final analysis, the powerful pull of precedent, the history of federal judicial dominance, and the interrelationship of many state and federal practices in the area of criminal law make it likely that state courts will look to federal law first. Given that many issues facing state courts already are settled as a matter of federal law; that constraints of time, resources, and energy confront all courts; and that institutional impediments stand as a barrier to its development, there is little wonder that state constitutional law remains relatively undeveloped. In combination with the potentially high political costs of invoking state law, legal and institutional factors work against the development of state constitutional law for issues that have been decided as a matter of federal law.

Conclusion

The literature on the New Judicial Federalism posits two types of motivations for state court judges to develop state law. One is to avoid conservative federal judicial rulings in pursuit of liberal outcomes. The other is to promote a more balanced system of judicial federalism without regard to substantive results. However, the conservatism of most state political systems and entrenched legal and institutional barriers work against widespread development of state constitutional law. The finding that state supreme courts rely on federal law for almost four of every five decisions is testimony to the importance of these three factors in shaping their behavior, at least through the first decade and a half of the New Judicial Federalism.

The movement toward increased development and reliance on state constitutions is still young, and advocates of the New Judicial Federalism have reason to be optimistic for the future. Although established legal and institutional barriers do not fall easily, they are not immutable. As law journals and other scholarly publications promote the idea of the New Judicial Federalism, law schools could begin to produce attorneys who are well versed in the principles of state constitutional law. As leading courts continue to render path-breaking decisions while insisting that attorneys argue state grounds in the cases they present, other state courts could follow the lead. As courts within particular states base greater numbers of decisions on state law, they could invite more claims to be brought on the basis of state law. In short, institutional pressures could play the decisive role in establishing doctrines that are rooted in carefully developed principles of state constitutional law.

It is unlikely, however, that any movement toward greater reliance on state law will be associated with liberal outcomes any time soon. Unless the level of federal protection falls below a threshold that state courts are not willing to go, they are unlikely to rush toward advancing new rights under the auspices of state law. Given the current political conditions of state politics, attempts to expand protections for criminal defendants represents too great a risk for most courts.

NOTES

This article originally appeared in Volume 78, Number 1, July-August 1994, pages 25-32.

1. Latzer, *The hidden conservatism of the state court "revolution,"* 74 JUDICATURE 195 (1991).

2. *See, e.g.,* Brennan, *State Constitutions and the Protection of Individual Rights,* 90 HARV. L. REV. 489 (1977). *See, also,* his dissent, joined by Marshall, in Michigan v. Mosely, 423 U.S. 96 (1975) and their concurring opinion in Oregon v. Kennedy, 456 U.S. 667, 680-681 (1982).

3. *See, e.g.,* Latzer, STATE CONSTITUTIONS AND CRIMINAL JUSTICE ch. 1 (1991); STATE CONSTITUTIONAL LAW: CASES AND MATERIALS 93-103 (1990); Greenhalgh, *Independent and Adequate State Grounds: The Long and Short of It,* in McGraw, ed., DEVELOPMENTS IN STATE CONSTITUTIONAL LAW 219 (1985); and Friedelbaum, *Independent State Grounds: Contemporary Invitations to Judicial Activism,* in Porter and Tarr, eds., STATE SUPREME COURTS: POLICYMAKERS IN THE FEDERAL SYSTEM (1982).

4. *Supra* n. 1. *See, also,* Latzer, *supra* n. 3.

5. *Id.* at 190, 192.

6. *Id.* at 193-194.

7. *See, e.g.,* Tarr, *State Constitutionalism and First Amendment Rights* in Friedelbaum ed., HUMAN RIGHTS IN THE STATES 21-48 (1988); Levinson, *Freedom of Speech and Right of Access to Private Property Under State Constitutional Law* in DEVELOPMENTS IN STATE CONSTITUTIONAL LAW, *supra* n. 3, at 51-70; Neuborne, *State Constitutional Protection of Free Speech and Establishment Clause Values* in Bamberger ed., RECENT DEVELOPMENTS IN STATE CONSTITUTIONAL LAW 205-230 (1985); Crosby, *Rights of Privacy* in RECENT DEVELOPMENTS IN STATE CONSTITUTIONAL LAW, *id.* at 231-236; Porter with O'Neill, *Personal Autonomy and the Limits of State Authority* in Friedelbaum ed., HUMAN RIGHTS IN THE STATES, *id.* at 73-96; Davis, *Gender Issues in the States: The Private Sphere and the Search for Equality* in HUMAN RIGHTS IN THE STATES, *id.* at 49-72; Williams, *Equality and State Constitutional Law* in DEVELOPMENTS IN STATE CONSTITUTIONAL LAW, *supra* n. 3, at 71-93; Galie, *Social Services and Egalitarian Activism* in HUMAN RIGHTS IN THE STATES, *id.* at 97-120; Fino, *Remnants of the Past: Economic Due Process in the States* in HUMAN RIGHTS IN THE STATES, *id.* at 145-162; Wilkes,

The New Federalism in Criminal Procedure in 1984: Death of the Phoenix? in DEVELOPMENTS IN STATE CONSTITUTIONAL LAW, *supra* n. 3, at 166-200; Kramer, *Reactions of State Courts to Pro-Prosecution Burger Court Decisions* in HUMAN RIGHTS IN THE STATES, *id.* at 121-144. Friedelbaum, *supra* n. 3, at 25-31.

8. Galie, *State Constitutional Guarantees and Protection of Defendants' Rights: The Case of New York, 1960-1978,* 28 BUFFALO L. REV. 157-194 (1978). Kramer and Riga, *The New York Court of Appeals and the U.S. Supreme Court, 1960-1978* in Porter and Tarr, *supra* n. 3, at 175-200. Porter, *State Supreme Courts and the Legacy of the Warren Court: Some Old Inquiries for a New Situation* in Porter and Tarr, *id.* at 3-22. Tarr and Porter, STATE SUPREME COURTS IN STATE AND NATION (1988).

9. See, e.g., Collins and Galie, *State Constitutional Rights Decisions,* National Law Journal, Sept. 29, 1986, at S-8-S-19. Actually, their count includes only decisions that are based on state law that expand rights. Yet it is often cited as evidence of increased reliance on state law, more generally.

10. Only a few studies account for a range of decisions that are based on both state and federal law. *See* Fino, THE ROLE OF STATE SUPREME COURTS IN THE NEW JUDICIAL FEDERALISM 70 (1987); Fino, *Judicial Federalism and Equality Guarantees in State Supreme Courts,* 17 PUBLIUS 53 (1987); and Emmert and Traut, *State Supreme Courts, State Constitutions, and Judicial Policymaking,* 16 JUST. SYS. J. 44, Table 2 (1982). However, even these studies do not focus specifically on the "use" question. Rather, as is typical of the literature on the New Judicial Federalism, the main focus is on analyzing the results of court decisions. Consequently, discussion about the extent to which state court decisions rely on state law is minimal. The possible exception here is Fino, in PUBLIUS at 66. These studies are valuable, however, for providing data on the extent to which state courts rely on state law for a range of legal issues.

11. For instance, Latzer refers to a "major upsurge in state court decisions predicated upon state . . . constitutional law," a "sizable and growing body of case law interpreting state constitutional provisions, especially the state bills of rights . . ." and an "extraordinary output" of state constitutional rulings over the last two decades. *Supra n.* 1, at 190, 197.

12. *Supra* n. 1, at 193, Tables 2 and 3.

13. *Id.* at 190.

14. The issues are: (1) using silence to impeach credibility when Miranda warnings have not been read; (2) using silence to impeach when Miranda warnings have been read; (3) refusal to stop interrogation; (4) denying counsel access to client; (5) errors in Miranda warnings; (6) when rights must be read; (7) using coercion to compel confessions; (8) using inadmissible statements to impeach credibility; (9) informing suspect about nature of the crime.

15. The two states are Iowa and New Jersey. Both states, however, have statutes that provide similar protections.

16. Collins, Galie, and Kincaid, *State High Courts, State Constitutions, and Individual Rights,* 16 PUBLIUS 153 (1986). *But see* State v. Earl, 716 P.2d 803 (1986).

17. *Supra* n. 16, at 142.

18. *Supra* n. 7 and 8.

19. 463 U.S. 1032 (1983).

20. *Supra* n. 1, at 192, n. 8.

21. Fino, THE ROLE OF STATE SUPREME COURTS, and PUBLIUS at 53, *supra* n. 10.

22. Linde, *Does the 'New Federalism' Have a Future?,* 4 EMERGING ISSUES IN STATE CONSTITUTIONAL LAW 251 (1991).

23. Included were the supreme courts of Arizona, Kentucky, California, Michigan, Nebraska, and New Jersey.

24. Fino, THE ROLE OF STATE SUPREME COURTS, *supra* n. 10, at 142.

25. *Id.* at 141.

26. Fino, PUBLIUS, *supra* n. 10, at 6.

27. Emmert and Traut, *supra* n. 10, at 44, Table 2.

28. Analysis of a sample of state supreme court opinions for issues involving self-incrimination claims that were decided between 1987 and 1992 indicates results consistent with these findings. Moreover, recent comments by two state supreme court judges who have been actively involved in promoting the New Judicial Federalism support the claim that state high court reliance on federal law in recent years is not significantly greater than during the earlier years of the movement. *See* Linde, *supra* n. 22; Utter, *The Practice of Principled Decision-Making in State Constitutionalism: Washington's Experience*, 65 TEMPLE L. REV. 1153 (1992).

29. *Supra* n. 1, at 190, 192.

30. Baum, *State Supreme Couts: Activism and Accountability*, in Van Horn, ed., THE STATE OF THE STATES 110 (1989).

31. *Supra* n. 1, at 197. Generally on the concept of intrastate pressures, see Tarr and Porter, *supra* n. 8, at 41-63.

32. A majority of citizens in all but one of the 48 contiguous states consider themselves to be more conservative than liberal. Wright, Erikson, and McIver, *Measuring State Partisanship and Ideology with Survey Data*, 47 J. POL. 469-489 (1985).

33. Baum, *supra* n. 30, at 120; Fino, PUBLIUS, *supra* n. 10, at 67.

34. Linde, *supra* n. 22, at 257.

35. Stumpf and Culver, THE POLITICS OF STATE COURTS 150 (1992).

36. Florida v. Casal, 462 U.S. 637 (1983). *See also*, Kincaid, *State Constitutions in the Federal System*, 496 ANNALS 18-20 (1988).

37. Baum, *supra* n. 30, at 115, 120-121.

38. Not all judicial decisions are shaped by political forces. However, it is well established that at least some judges hold "broad role conceptions." That is, they allow their decisions to be influenced by extra-legal factors such as their attitudes and the political forces in their environments. *See, e.g.*, Gibson, *Judges' Role Orientations, Attitudes, and Decisions*, 72 AM. POL. SCI. REV. 911-924 (1978).

39. Deukmejian and Thompson, *All Sail and No Anchor—Judicial Review under the California Constitution*, 6 HASTINGS CONST. L. Q. 975-1010 (1979). *See also* Utter, *Don't make a constitutional case out of it, unless you must*, 73 JUDICATURE 147 (1989).

40. *See, e.g.*, Collins and Galie, *Models of Post-Incorporation Judicial Review: 1985 Survey of State Constitutional Individual Rights Decisions*, 16 PUBLIUS 117-118 (1986).

41. Henry v. Mississippi, 379 U.S. 443 (1965), Delaware v. Prouse, 440 U.S. 648 (1979), Michigan v. Long, 463 U.S. 1032 (1983). *See also*, Latzer, *supra* n. 3, at 20-26.

42. *Supra* n. 3. *But see*, Abrahamson and Gutmann, *The new federalism: state constitutions and state courts*, 71 JUDICATURE 88, 97 (1987).

43. *Id.* at 98.

44. Utter, *supra* n. 28, at 1155. *See also*, Abraham, FREEDOM AND THE COURT 107 (1988).

45. Linde, *E Pluribus—Constitutional Theory and State Courts*, 18 GA. L. REV. 173-174 (1984); *Developments in the Law—The Interpretation of State Constitutional Rights*, 95 HARV. L. REV. 1356-1357 (1982).

46. Frohnmayer, *AGs' Mixed Emotions*, National Law Journal, Sept. 29, 1986 at S-4.

47. Tarr, *State Constitutionalism and 'First Amendment' Rights*, in Friedelbaum, ed., *supra* n. 7, at 39.

48. *Supra* n. 40, at 117.

49. *See, e.g.* Williams, *In the Supreme Court's Shadow: Legitimacy of State Rejection of Supreme Court Reasoning and Result*, 35 S.C. L. REV. 385-388 (1984).

50. *Supra* n. 22, at 258.

51. Although it is not his own, this viewpoint is discussed in Utter, *Freedom and Diversity in a Federal System: Perspectives on State Constitutions and the Washington Declaration of Rights*, in McGraw, ed., *supra* n. 3, at 248.

52. *Supra* n. 46.

53. Comments of Kaufman in *Judicial federalism: don't make a federal case out of it . . . or should you?*, 73 JUDICATURE 153 (1989).

54. Utter, *supra* n. 28, at 1156.

55. Linde, *supra* n. 22, at 259.

56. Collins, Galie, and Kincaid, *supra* n. 16, at 144-145, 154-156. *See also* Emmert and Traut, *supra* n. 10, at 42.

57. State v. Lowry, 295 Or. 337, 365 (1983) (Jones concurring).

58. Linde, *supra* n. 22, at 261. A search of The AALS Directory of Law Teachers reveals that only 22 of approximately 177 law schools in the United States offer courses in state constitutional law.

59. Gardner, *The Failed Discourse of State Constitutionalism*, 90 MICH. L. REV. 766 (1992).

Alternatives to Traditional Litigation

INTRODUCTION

It was not too many years ago when the topic of alternatives to traditional litigation would have been considered a frontier concern not worthy of inclusion in a course examining the workings of the American legal system. While such alternatives (including alternative dispute resolution or ADR) have not, in any sense, displaced courts as mechanisms for resolving civil disputes between citizens, multifaceted ADR processes and other "nontraditional" modes of processing legal claims are clearly here to stay and constitute an important component of the American system of justice. Indeed, situations now exist in which ADR mechanisms are not just vehicles for voluntary settlement but are, at times, ordered by courts to seek, in the words of John Cooley, "swift, inexpensive, simple justice." ADR has clearly become, over time, a more accepted means of dealing with court delay and case management problems in a highly litigious society.

In the first article in this section, John Cooley examines two ADR approaches in "Arbitration vs. mediation–explaining the differences." Cooley demonstrates that the techniques are utilized in different types of disputes and settings. Arbitration involves employment of a third-party decision maker, whereas mediation utilizes a facilitator to foster agreement and/or reconciliation among disputants. Thus, arbitration proceedings are pictured as analogous to a trial, whereas mediation more closely resembles a settlement conference.

In "ADR problems and prospects: looking to the future," Stephen Goldberg, Eric Green, and Frank Sander offer a critical assessment of alternative dispute resolution and ask why ADR has not spread more rapidly given its apparent success when utilized. Among the impediments to ADR that the authors examine are the lack of public knowledge about and acceptance of alternatives to litigation and the role of lawyers for whom litigation is often the path of least resistance. Critiques of ADR, particularly the "second-class justice" argument often attached to it, are explored, as is the emerging concern about the professionalization and institutionalization of ADR mechanisms. The authors are wary of some facets of professional institutionalization, supporting certification and training that serves ADR consumers, while opposing licensure, which they claim only serves professional self-interest. Much of the article is speculative in tone and clearly underlines the need for additional research in the ADR domain. Indeed, as Goldberg, Green, and Sander conclude:

What we need now is a multi-pronged effort to expand our limited present understanding of the field. This will require continued experimentation and research.... It will necessitate enhanced public education about the benefits to be derived from alternative modes of dispute settlement.... Above all, if the movement is to hold any significant promise of gaining a permanent foothold on the American scene, it will require the broadened involvement and support not only of the legal and legal education establishment but also the society at large.

Goldberg, Green and Sander highlight the seemingly vested interest that the legal profession has in constraining the range and scope of alternatives to utilizing traditional formal judicial processes and professional representation to pursue settlement of legal problems. Based on a study conducted in four locales where legal advocacy is performed by both attorneys and non-lawyers, Herbert Kritzer concludes in "Rethinking barriers to legal practice," that, "This systematic research makes it clear that non-lawyers can be effective advocates and, in some situations, better advocates than licensed attorneys." By no means is Kritzer calling for open season for providing legal advocacy, and caveat emptor for the consumer of legal services. Rather, he opines, "It is time instead to consider the nature of legal services in an age of specialized tasks and specialized training. All providers of legal services should be subject to appropriate regulation and discipline. Within the proper framework, the public can be well served by non-lawyer providers."

Much non-lawyer advocacy in our judicial system is practiced by individuals who represent themselves, a phenomenon examined by Jona Goldschmidt in "How are courts handling pro se litigants?" Goldschmidt documents the growth in pro se litigation while also underscoring how little we know about the consequences of the utilization of pro se processes. Goldschmidt's study relies, in part, on the responses of judges themselves to questions about the handling of pro se litigants and graphically highlights the judicial dilemma. As one judge put it, "Pro se litigants feel they are not being treated fairly if they are required to comply with rules of procedure with which they are not familiar. On the other hand, they are perceived as having an advantage if the procedural rules are not strictly enforced as they are against counseled parties." Interview responses underscore the widely divergent treatment and assistance that pro se litigants receive in our courts, and Goldschmidt finds "current judicial attitudes toward pro se litigants ranging from an acknowledgment of the courts' obligation to provide access to justice to firm opposition to any form of pro se litigation itself." He concludes that the difficulty of reaching an appropriate balance in handling pro se litigation, "will be lessened to the extent that out-of-court programs are established that educate pro se litigants to negotiate the labyrinths of litigation, thus reducing the necessity for the proactive judicial assistance that many pro se litigants expect from the court."

Arbitration vs. mediation—explaining the differences

by John W. Cooley

An amazing number of lawyers and business professionals are unaware of the difference between arbitration and mediation. Their confusion is excusable.

In the early development of the English language, the two words were used interchangeably. The *Oxford English Dictionary* provides as one historical definition of arbitration: "to act as formal arbitrator or umpire, to mediate (in a dispute between contending parties)." The Statutes of Edward III (1606) referring to what today obviously would be called a commercial *arbitration* panel, provided: "And two Englishmen, two of Lombardie and two of Almaigne shall (be) chosen to be mediators of questions between sellers and buyers."[1]

Modern labor relations statutes tend to perpetuate this confusion. As one commentator has observed:

Some statutes, referring to a process as "mediation" describe formal hearings, with witnesses testifying under oath and transcripts made, require reports and recommendations for settlement to be made by the neutral within fixed periods, and either state or imply the finality of the "mediator's recommendations." In one statute the neutral third parties are called, interchangeably, mediators, arbitrators and impasse panels.[2]

The Federal Mediation and Conciliation Service (note the absence of "arbitration" in its title) performs a basic arbitration function by maintaining a roster from which the service can nominate arbitrators to the parties and suggest "certain procedures and guides that [the service believes] will enhance the acceptability of arbitration."[3]

The National *Mediation* Board (emphasis added) performs important functions in the promotion of arbitration and the selection of arbitrators for the railroad and airline industries.[4]

Libraries also assist in perpetuating the arbitration/mediation definitional charade. Search under "mediation" and you will invariably be referred to "arbitration." In the midst of this confusion—even among congressional draftsmen—it is time to explain the differences between the processes.

The most basic difference between the two is that arbitration involves a *decision* by an intervening third party or "neutral"; mediation does not.

Another way to distinguish the two is by describing the processes in terms of the neutral's mental functions. In arbitration, the neutral employs mostly "left brain" or "rational" mental processes—analytical, mathematical, logical, technical, administrative; in mediation, the neutral employs mostly "right brain" or "creative" mental processes—conceptual, intuitive, artistic, holistic, symbolic, emotional.

The arbitrator deals largely with the objective; the mediator, the subjective. The arbitrator is generally a passive functionary who determines right or wrong; the mediator is generally an active functionary who attempts to move the parties to reconciliation and agreement, regardless of who or what is right or wrong.

Because the role of the mediator involves instinctive reactions, intuition, keen interpersonal skills, the ability to perceive subtle psychological and behavioral indicators, in addition to logic and rational thinking, it is much more difficult than the arbitrator's role to perform effectively.[5] It is fair to say that while most mediators can effectively perform the arbitrator's function, the converse is not necessarily true.

Besides these differences the two processes are generally employed to resolve two different types of disputes. Mediation is used where there is a reasonable likelihood that the parties will be able to reach an agreement with the assistance of a neutral. Usually, mediation is used when parties will have an ongoing relationship after resolution of the conflict. Arbitration, on the other hand, is generally appropriate for use when two conditions exist: there is no reasonable likelihood of a negotiated settlement, and there will not be a continuing relationship after resolution.[6]

If the two processes are to be used in sequence, mediation occurs first, and if unsuccessful, resort is made to arbitration.[7] Viewed in terms of the judicial process, arbitration is comparable to a trial and mediation is akin to a judicial settlement conference. They are as different as night and day.[8] The differences can best be understood by discussing them in terms of the processes of arbitration and mediation.

The arbitration process

Arbitration has had a long history in this country, going back to procedures carried over into the colonies from mercantile England. George Washington put an arbitration clause in his last will and testament to resolve disputes among his heirs. Abraham Lincoln urged lawyers to keep their clients out of court and himself arbitrated a boundary dispute between two farmers. Today, arbitration is being used more broadly for dispute settlement both in labor-management relations and in commercial transactions.

Aside from its well-known use in resolving labor disputes, arbitration is now becoming widely used to settle intercompany disputes in various industries, including textile, construction, life and casualty insurance, canning, livestock, air transport, grain and feed, and securities.[9]

Simply defined, arbitration is a process in which a dispute is submitted to a third party or neutral (or sometimes a panel of three arbitrators) to hear arguments, review evidence, and render a decision.[10] Court-annexed arbitration, a relatively new development, is a process in which judges refer civil suits to arbitrators to render prompt, nonbinding decisions. If a particular decision is not accepted by a losing party, a trial *de novo* may be held in the court system. However, adverse decisions sometimes lead to further negotiation and pretrial settlement.[11]

The arbitration process, court-annexed or otherwise, normally consists of six stages: initiation, preparation, prehearing conferences, hearing, decision making, and award.

Initiation. The initiation stage of arbitration consists of two substages: initiating the proceeding, and selecting the arbitrator. An arbitration proceeding may be initiated either by: submission; "demand" or "notice;" or, in the case of a court-annexed proceeding, court rule or court order.

A submission must be signed by both parties and is used where there is no previous agreement to arbitrate. It often names the arbitrator (or method of appointment), contains considerable detail regarding the arbitrator's authority, the procedure to be used at the hearing, statement of the matter in dispute, the amount of money in controversy, the remedy sought, and other matters.

On the other hand, where the description of a dispute is contained in an agreement and the parties have agreed in advance to arbitrate it, arbitration may be initiated unilaterally by one party serving upon the other a written "demand" or "notice" to arbitrate.

However, even where an agreement contains a "demand" or "notice" arbitration clause, parties sometimes choose also to execute a submission after the dispute has materialized. In the court-annexed situation, a lawsuit is mandatorily referred to an arbitration track and the parties must select an arbitrator from a court-maintained roster or otherwise by mutual agreement.[12]

Several types of tribunals and methods of selecting their membership are available to parties who wish to arbitrate. Parties may choose between the use of a "temporary" or "permanent" arbitrator. They can also choose to have single or multiple arbitrators. Since success of the arbitration process often hinges on the expertise of the tribunal, parties generally select a tribunal whose members possess impartiality, integrity, ability and experience in the field in which the dispute arises. Legal training is often helpful but not indispensable.

Information concerning the qualifications of some of the more active arbitrators is contained in the *Directory of Arbitrators*, prepared by the Bureau of National Affairs, Inc., and in *Who's Who* (of arbitrators) published by Prentice-Hall, Inc. Also, the Federal Mediation and Conciliation Service (FMCS), the National Mediation Board (NMB), and the American Arbitration Association (AAA) provide biographical data on arbitrators.[13]

Preparation. The parties must thoroughly prepare cases for arbitration. Obviously, a party must fully understand its own case to communicate effectively to the arbitrator. Depending on the nature of the case, prehearing discovery may be necessary, and its permissible extent is usually determined by the arbitrator. The advantages of simplicity and utility of the arbitration mode normally weigh against extensive discovery. During this stage, the parties also enter into fact stipulations where possible.[14]

Ordinarily, most or all of the arbitrator's knowledge and understanding of a case is based upon evidence and arguments presented at the arbitration hearing. However, the arbitrator does have some "preparation" functions. Generally, where no tribunal administrator (such as AAA) is involved, the arbitrator, after accepting the office, designates the time and place of the hearing, by mutual agreement of the parties if possible. The arbitrator also signs an oath, if required in the particular jurisdiction, and determines whether the parties will have representation, legal or otherwise, at the hearing.[15]

Prehearing conferences. Depending on the complexity of the matter involved, the arbitrator may wish to schedule a prehearing conference, which is normally administrative in nature.[16] Briefing schedules, if necessary, are set on motions attacking the validity of claims or of the proceeding. But generally, briefing is minimized to preserve the efficiency of the process. Discussion of the underlying merits of claims or defenses of the parties are avoided during a prehearing conference. *Ex parte* conferences between the arbitrator and a party are not permitted.[17]

The hearing. Parties may waive oral hearing and have the controversy determined on the basis of documents only. However, an evidentiary-type hearing in the presence of the arbitrator is deemed imperative in virtually all cases. Since arbitration is a private proceeding, the hearing is not open to the public as a rule but all persons having a direct interest in the case are ordinarily entitled to attend.

A formal written record of the hearing is not always necessary; use of a reporter is the exception rather than the general practice. A party requiring an interpreter has the duty to arrange for one. Witnesses testifying at the hearing may also be required to take an oath if required by law, if ordered by the arbitrator, or on demand of any party.[18]

Opening statements are made orally by each party in a brief, generalized format. They are designed to acquaint the arbitrator with each party's view of what the dispute is about and what the party expects to prove by the evidence. Sometimes an arbitrator requests each party to provide a short written opening statement and issue statement prior to the hearing. Occasionally, a respondent opts for making an opening statement immediately prior to presenting initial evidence.[19]

There is no set order by which parties present their cases in arbitration, although in practice the complaining party normally presents evidence first. The parties may offer any evidence they choose, including personal testimony and affidavits of witnesses. They may be required to produce additional evidence the arbitrator deems necessary to determine the dispute. The arbitrator, when authorized by law, may subpoena witnesses or documents upon his or her own initiative or by request of a party. The arbitrator also decides the relevancy and materiality of all evidence offered. Conformity to legal rules of evidence is unnecessary. The arbitrator has a right to make a physical inspection of premises.[20]

The parties make closing arguments, usually limited in duration. Occasionally, the arbitrator requests post-hearing briefs. When this occurs, the parties usually waive oral closing arguments.[21]

Decision making. When the issues are not complex, an arbitrator may render an immediate decision. However, when the evidence presented is voluminous and/or time is needed for the members of an arbitration panel to confer, it might require several weeks to make a decision.

The award is the arbitrator's decision. It may be given orally but is normally written and signed by the arbitrator(s). Awards are normally short, definite, certain, and final as to all matters under submission. Occasionally, they are accompanied by a short, well-reasoned opinion. The award is usually issued no later than 30 days from the closing date of the hearing. When a party fails to appear, a default award may be entered.[22] Depending on the nature of the award (i.e., binding), it may be judicially enforceable and, to some extent, reviewable. The losing party in a court-annexed arbitration is entitled to trial *de novo* in court.

The mediation process

Mediation is a process in which an impartial intervenor assists the disputants to reach a voluntary settlement of their differences through an agreement that defines their future behavior.[23] The process generally consists of eight stages: initiation, preparation, introduction, problem statement, problem clarification, generation and evaluation of alternatives, selection of alternative(s), and agreement.[24]

Initiation. The mediation process may be initiated in two principal ways: parties submit the matter to a public or private dispute resolution organization or to a private neutral; or the dispute is referred to mediation by court order or rule in a court-annexed mediation program.

In the first instance, counsel for one of the parties or, if unrepresented, the party may contact the neutral organization or individual and the neutral will contact the opposing counsel or party (as the case may be) to see if there is interest in attempting to mediate the dispute.

Preparation. As in arbitration, it is of paramount importance that the parties to a dispute in mediation be as well informed as possible on the background of the dispute, the claims or defenses and the remedies they seek. The parties should seek legal advice if necessary, and although a party's lawyer might attend a typical nonjudicial mediation, he or she normally does not take an adversary role but is rather available to render legal advice as needed.

The mediator should also be well-informed about the parties and the features of their dispute and know something about:
- the balance of power;
- the primary sources of pressure exerted on the parties;
- the pressures motivating them toward agreement as well as pressures blocking agreement;
- the economics of the industry or particular company involved;
- political and personal conflicts within and between the parties;
- the extent of the settlement authority of each of the parties.

The mediator sets the date, time and place for the hearing at everyone's convenience.[25]

Introduction. In the mediation process, the introductory stage may be the most important.[26] It is in that phase, particularly the first joint session, that the mediator establishes his or her acceptability, integrity, credibility, and neutrality. The mediator usually has several objectives to achieve initially.

They are: establish control of the process; determine issues and positions of the parties; get the agreement-forging process started; and encourage continuation of direct negotiations.[27]

Unlike a judge in a settlement conference or an arbitrator who wields the clout of a decision, a mediator does not, by virtue of position, ordinarily command the parties' immediate trust and respect; the mediator earns them through a carefully orchestrated and delicately executed ritual of rapport-building. Every competent mediator has a personal style. The content of the mediator's opening remarks is generally crucial to establishing rapport with the parties and the respectability of the mediator and the process.

Opening remarks focus on: identifying the mediator and the parties; explaining the procedures to be followed (including caucusing),[28] describing the mediation function (if appropriate) and emphasizing the continued decision-making responsibility of the parties; and reinforcing the confidentiality and integrity of the process.[29] When appropriate, the mediator might invoke the community and public interest in having the dispute resolved quickly and emphasize the interests of the constituents in the successful conclusion of the negotiations.[30]

Finally, the mediator must assess the parties' competence to participate in the process. If either party has severe emotional, drinking, drug, or health problems, the mediator may postpone the proceeding. If the parties are extremely hostile and verbally abusive, the mediator must endeavor to calm them, by preliminary caucusing if necessary.[31]

Problem statement. There are essentially two ways to open a discussion of the dispute by the parties: Both parties give their positions and discuss each issue as it is raised; or all the issues are first briefly identified, with detailed exposition of positions reserved until all the issues have been identified. The second procedure is preferred; the first approach often leads to tedious time-consuming rambling about insignificant matters, sometimes causing the parties to become more entrenched in their positions.[32]

Generally, the complaining party tells his or her "story" first. It may be the first time that the adverse party has heard the full basis for the complaint. The mediator actively and empathically listens, taking notes if helpful, using listening techniques such as restatement, echo and nonverbal responses. Listening is the mediator's most important dispute-resolving tool.[33]

The mediator also:

• asks open-ended and closed-ended questions at the appropriate time and in a neutral fashion;

• obtains important "signals" from the behavior and body movements of the parties;

• calms a party, as necessary;

• clarifies the narration by focused questions;

• objectively summarizes the first party's story;

• defuses tensions by omitting disparaging comments from the summary;

• determines whether the second party understands the first party's story;

• thanks the first party for his or her contribution.

The process is repeated with the second party.[34]

Problem clarification. It is in this stage that the mediator culls out the true underlying issues in the dispute. Often the parties to a dispute intentionally obfuscate the core issues. The mediator pierces this cloud cover through separate caucuses in which he or she asks direct, probing questions to elicit information that one party would not disclose in the presence of the other party. In a subsequent joint session, the mediator summarizes areas of agreement or disagreement, being careful not to disclose matters that the parties shared with the mediator in confidence. They are assisted in grouping and prioritizing issues and demands.[35]

Generation and evaluation of alternatives. In this stage, the mediator employs two fundamental principles of effective mediation: creating doubt in the minds of the parties as to the validity of their positions on issues; and suggesting alternative approaches that may facilitate agreement.[36] These are two functions that parties to a dispute are very often unable to perform by themselves. To carry out these functions, the mediator has the parties separately brainstorm to produce alternatives or options; discusses the workability of each option; encourages the parties by noting the probability of success, where appropriate; suggests alternatives not raised by the parties, and then repeats the three previous steps.[37]

Selection of alternative(s). The mediator may compliment the parties on their progress and use humor, when appropriate, to relieve tensions; assist the parties in eliminating the unworkable options; and help the parties determine which of the remaining workable solutions will produce the optimum results with which each can live.[38]

Agreement. Before the mediation is terminated, the mediator summarizes and clarifies, as necessary, the terms of the agreement reached and secures the assent of each party to those terms; sets a follow-up date, if necessary; and congratulates the parties on their reasonableness.

The mediator does not usually become involved in drafting a settlement agreement. This task is left to the parties themselves or their counsel. The agreement is the parties', not the mediator's.[39]

A mediator's patience, flexibility, and creativity throughout this entire process are necessary keys to a successful resolution.

The "neutral's" functions

To fully appreciate the differences (or the similarities) between the two processs, and to evaluate the appropriate use of either process, it is instructive to focus on considerations that exist at their interface—the function and power of the "neutral." This is a particularly important exercise to acquire a realistic expectation of the result to be obtained from each process.

The arbitrator's function is quasi-judicial in nature and, because of this, an arbitrator is generally exempt from civil liability for failure to exercise care or skill in performing the arbitral function.[40] As a quasi-judicial officer, the arbitrator is guided by ethical norms in the performance of duties. For example, an arbitrator must refrain from having any private (*ex parte*) consultations with a party or with an attorney representing a party without the consent of the opposing party or counsel.[41]

Moreover, unless the parties agree otherwise, the arbitration proceedings are private and arbitrators must take appropriate measures to maintain the confidentiality of the proceedings.[42] It has generally been held that an arbitrator may not testify as to the meaning and construction of the written award.[43]

In contrast, a mediator is not normally considered to be quasi-judicial, unless he or she is appointed by the court as, for example, a special master. Some courts have extended the doctrine of immunity to persons termed "quasi-arbitrators"—persons empowered by agreement of the parties to resolve disputes arising between them.[44] Although the law is far from clear on this point, a very persuasive argument may be advanced that mediators are generally immune from lawsuits relating to the performance of their mediation duties where the agreement under which they perform contains a hold-harmless provision or its equivalent.

In absence of such contractual provision, it would appear that a functionary such as a mediator, selected by parties to perform skilled or professional services, would not ordinarily be immune from charges of negligence but rather is required to work with the same skill and care exercised by an average person engaged in the trade or profession involved.[45]

Of course, weighing heavily against a finding of negligence on the part of a mediator is the intrinsic nature, if not the essence, of the mediation process which invests the parties with the complete power over their destiny; it also guarantees any party the right to withdraw from the process and even to eject the mediator during any pre-agreement stage.[46]

Also, in contrast to arbitrators, certain ethical restrictions do not apply to mediators. Mediators are permitted to have *ex parte* conferences with the parties or counsel. Indeed, such caucuses, as they are called, are the mediator's stock-in-trade. Furthermore, while one of the principal advantages of a privately-conducted mediation is the nonpublic or confidential nature of the proceedings, and although Rule 408 of the Federal Rules of Evidence and public policy considerations argue in favor of confidentiality, the current state of the law does not provide a guarantee of such confidentiality.[47] However, in most cases a strong argument can be made that the injury from disclosure of a confidential settlement proceeding is greater than the benefit to be gained by the public from nondisclosure.[48]

Finally, unlike the arbitrator, the performance of whose function may be enhanced by knowledge, skill, or ability in a particular field or industry, the mediator need not be an expert in the field that encompasses the subject of the dispute. Expertise may, in fact, be a handicap, if the parties look wrongly to the mediator as an advice-giver or adjudicator.[49]

Comparative power

The arbitrator derives power from many sources. The person may be highly respected in a particular field of expertise or widely renowned for fairness. But aside from these attributes, which emanate from personal talents or characteristics, the arbitrator operates within a procedural and enforcement framework that affords considerable power, at least from the perspective of the disputants. Under certain circumstances, arbitrators may possess broad remedy powers, including the power, though rare, to grant injunctive relief.[50] They normally have subpoena power, and generally they have no obligation to anyone, not even "to the court to give reasons for an award."[51]

In general, a valid arbitration award constitutes a full and final adjustment of the controversy.[52] It has all the force and effect of an adjudication, and effectively precludes the parties from again litigating the same subject.[53] The award can be challenged in court only on very narrow grounds. In some states the grounds related to partiality of the arbitrator or to misconduct in the proceedings, such as refusal to allow the production of evidence or to grant postponements, as well as to other misbehavior in conducting the hearings so as to prejudice the interests of a party.[54]

A further ground for challenge in some states is the failure of the arbitrator to observe the limits of authority as fixed by the parties' agreement— such as determining unsubmitted matters or by not dealing definitely and finally with submitted issues.[55] In Illinois, as in most states, a judgment entered on an arbitration award is enforceable "as any other judgment."[56] Thus, from a systemic perspective, the arbitrator is invested with a substantial amount of power.

In striking contrast, with the exception of a special master appointed by the court or a neutral appointed by some governmental body, the mediator has little if any systemic-based power. Most if not all of a mediator's power is derived from experience, demonstrated skills and abilities, and a reputation for successful settlements.

Any particular mediator may wield power by adopting a particular role on what might be described as a continuum representing the range of strengths of intervention: from virtual passivity, to "chairman," to "enunciator," to "prompter," to "leader," to virtual arbitrator.[57] The mediator who can adopt different roles on this continuum, changing strategies to fit changing circumstances and requirements of both the disputants and himself, is inevitably more effective in accumulating and wielding power that is real, yet often not consciously perceptible by the disputants themselves.[58]

Table 1   A comparison of arbitration/mediation processes

Arbitration	Mediation
1. Initiation Submission Demand or notice Court rules or order Selection of arbitrator	**1. Initiation** Submission Court rule or order Assignment or selection of mediator
2. Preparation Discovery Prehearing conference Motions Stipulations Arbitrator's oath Arbitrator's administrative duties Arbitrator does not seek out information about parties or dispute	**2. Preparation** Usually, no discovery Parties obtain background information on claims, defenses, remedies Mediator obtains information on parties and history of dispute Usually, no mediator oath
3. Prehearing conference Administrative Scheduling No discussion of underlying merits of claims or defenses No *ex parte* conference	**3. Introduction** Mediator: Conduct *ex parte* conferences, if necessary, for calming Gives opening descriptive remarks Develops trust and respect Emphasizes importance of successful negotiations Helps parties separate the people from the problem

4. Hearing
Not generally open to public
Written record, optional
Witnesses and parties testify under oath
  Opening statement
  Made orally
  Sometimes also in writing
  Order of proceedings and evidence
  Complaining party usually presents evidence first
  Arbitrator may subpoena witnesses
  Evidence rules relaxed
  Arbitrator rules on objections to evidence; may reject evidence
  Closing arguments
  Oral arguments normally permitted for clarification and synthesis
  Post-hearing briefs sometimes permitted
	4. Problem statement
	Confidential proceeding, no written record
	Parties do not speak under oath
	Issues identified
	Issues discussed separately, stories told
	Mediator listens; takes notes
	Mediator asks questions; reads behavioral signals
	Mediator calms parties; summarizes stories; defuses tensions
	Mediator determines whether parties understand stories
	Mediator usually has no subpoena power
	
	5. Problem clarification
	Mediator:
	Culls out core issues in caucus
	Asks direct, probing questions
	Summarizes areas of agreement and disagreement
	Assists parties in grouping and prioritizing issues and demands
	Helps parties focus on interests, not positions

5. Decision making If issues non-complex, arbitrator can issue an immediate decision If issues complex, or panel has three members, extra time may be required	**6. Generation and evaluation of alternatives** Mediator: Creates doubts in parties' minds as to validity of their positions Invents options for facilitating agreement Leads "brainstorming;" discusses workability; notes probability of success of options **7. Selection of alternative(s)** Mediator: Compliments parties on progress Assists parties in eliminating unworkable options Helps parties to use objective criteria Helps parties determine which solution will produce optimum results
6. Award Normally in writing, signed by arbitrator(s) Short, definite, certain and final, as to all matters under submission Occasionally a short opinion accompanies award Award may be judicially enforceable or reviewable	**8. Agreement** Mediator: Summarizes and clarifies agreement terms Sets follow-up date, if appropriate Congratulates parties on their reasonableness Usually does not draft or assist in drafting agreement Agreement is enforceable as a contract and subject to later modification by agreement

Since, in the ordinary case, the result of the mediation process is an agreement or contract not reduced to a court judgment,[59] the result is binding on the parties only to the extent that the law of contracts in the particular jurisdiction requires. And to the same extent, the result is enforceable by one party against another. As a practical matter, where a party breaches an agreement or contract that is the product of mediation and the agreement is not salvageable, prudence would seem to dictate that in most cases the underlying dispute—and not the breach of agreement—should be litigated.

Summary

It is clear that both the functions and the levels of power of arbitrators and mediators are dramatically different. Counsel must assess the nature of the dispute and the personalities of the disputants prior to determining which process, arbitration or mediation, has the best chance to achieve a successful resolution of the particular conflict.

For example, arbitration would probably prove to be the better dispute resolution choice where the dispute involves highly technical matters; a long-standing feud between the disputants; irrational and high-strung personalities; and no necessity of a continued relationship after resolution of the conflict.

On the other hand, mediation may prove to be the most effective choice where disputants are stubborn but basically sensible; have much to gain from a continued relationship with one another; and conflict resolution is time-critical.

Arbitration and mediation are two separate and distinct processes having a similar overall goal (terminating a dispute), while using totally different methods to obtain dissimilar (decisional vs. contractual) results. These differences are best understood by viewing the processes side-by-side in Table 1.

The benefits of arbitration and mediation to litigants, in terms of cost and time savings, are just beginning to be recognized by lawyers and business professionals alike. It is hoped that this discussion of the arbitration and mediation processes and their differences will help lawyers feel more comfortable with these two methods of dispute resolution and to use them to their clients' advantage in their joint pursuit of swift, inexpensive, simple justice.

NOTES

This article originally appeared in Volume 69, Number 5, February-March 1986, pages 263-269. It is adapted from a version that appeared in the CHICAGO BAR RECORD (January-February, 1985).

1. Robins, A GUIDE FOR LABOR MEDIATORS 6 (Honolulu: University Press of Hawaii, 1976).

2. *Id.*

3. Elkouri and Elkouri, HOW ARBITRATION WORKS 24 (Wash-

ington, D.C.: BNA, 3rd ed. 1973).

4. *Id.* at 25.

5. As one American professional mediator put it, the mediator "has no science of navigation, no fund inherited from the experience of others. He is a solitary artist recognizing, at most, a few guiding stars and depending mainly on his personal power of divination." Meyer, *Function of the Mediator in Collective Bargaining,* 13 INDUS. & LAB. REL. REV. 159 (1960).

6. In labor relations arbitration, of course, condition (2) is normally not present. Labor disputes are generally divided into two categories: rights disputes and interest disputes. Disputes as to "rights" involve the interpretation or application of existing laws, agreements, or customary practices; disputes as to "interests" involve controversies over the formation of collective agreements or efforts to secure them where no such agreement is yet in existence. Elkouri and Elkouri, *supra* n. 3, at 47.

7. Because of ethical considerations, the arbitrator and mediator normally are different persons. It should also be noted that mediation is frequently effective when it is attempted, with the concurrence of the parties, during the course of an arbitration with a neutral other than the arbitrator serving as the mediator. Often the unfolding of the opponent's evidence during arbitration leads to a better appreciation of the merits of their respective positions and hence an atmosphere conducive to settlement discussions.

8. The stark distinction between mediation and arbitration was well made by a professional mediator who became chairman of the New York State Mediation Board: "Mediation and arbitration . . . have conceptually nothing in common. The one [mediation] involves helping people to decide for themselves, the other involves helping people by deciding for them." Meyer, *supra* n. 5, at 164, as quoted in Gulliver, DISPUTES AND NEGOTIATIONS, A CROSS-CULTURAL PERSPECTIVE 210 (New York: Academic Press, 1979).

9. Cooley, *Arbitration as an Alternative to Federal Litigation in the Seventh Circuit,* REPORT OF THE SUBCOMMITTEE ON ALTERNATIVES TO THE PRESENT FEDERAL COURT SYSTEM, SEVENTH CIRCUIT AD HOC COMMITTEE TO STUDY THE HIGH COST OF LITIGATION 2 (July 13, 1978).

10. *Paths to Justice: Major Public Policy Issues of Dispute Resolution,* REPORT OF THE AD HOC PANEL ON DISPUTE RESOLUTION AND PUBLIC POLICY, Appendix 2 (Washington, D.C.: National Institute for Dispute Resolution, October, 1983).

11. *Id. See also* EVALUATION OF COURT-ANNEXED ARBITRATION IN THREE FEDERAL DISTRICT COURTS (Washington, D.C.: Federal Judicial Center, 1981).

12. Cooley, *supra* n. 9, at 4, Elkouri and Elkouri, *supra* n. 3, at 183-186. Domke on Commercial Arbitration. §§14:00-14:05 (Rev. Ed. 1984). Arbitrators, if chosen from a list maintained by an arbitration organization or court-maintained roster, are normally compensated at the daily rate fixed by the organization or the court. Arbitrators selected independently by the parties are compensated at the daily or hourly rate at which they mutually agree. In such cases, the parties equally share the expense of the arbitrator's services.

13. Elkouri and Elkouri, *supra* n. 3, at 24-25.

14. Elkouri and Elkouri, *supra* n. 3, at 197; (for preparation checklist *see* pp. 198-199); Domke, *supra* n. 12, §§24:01 and 27:01.

15. *Id.*

16. Some of the matters that might be discussed at a prehearing conference are: whether discovery is needed and, if so, scheduling of same; motions that need to be filed and briefed or orally argued; and the setting of firm oral argument and hearing dates.

17. Cooley, *supra* n. 9, at 4-5; Elkouri and Elkouri, *supra* n. 3, at 186-190.

18. Cooley, *supra* n. 9, at 5.

19. Elkouri and Elkouri, *supra* n. 3, at 224-225.

20. Cooley, *supra* n. 9, at 5; Elkouri and Elkouri, *supra* n. 3, at 223-228.

21. Elkouri and Elkouri, *supra* n. 3, at 225.

22. Cooley, *supra* n. 9, at 6.

23. Salem, *Mediation—The Concept and the Process*, in INSTRUCTORS MANUAL FOR TEACHING CRITICAL ISSUES (1984, unpublished). *See generally* Simkin, MEDIATION AND THE DYNAMICS OF COLLECTIVE BARGAINING 25 (BNA, 1971). Court-annexed mediation is a process in which judges refer civil cases to a neutral (mediator or master) for settlement purposes. It also includes in-court programs in which judges perform the settlement function fulltime.

24. *See generally* Ray, *The Alternative Dispute Resolution Movement*, 8 PEACE AND CHANGE 117 (Summer 1982). The process of mediation and the roles and strategies of mediators have been generally neglected in studies of negotiation. As one author remarked, "Mediation still remains a poorly understood process." Gulliver, *supra* n. 8.

25. Meagher, "Mediation Procedures and Techniques," 18-19 (unpublished paper on file in the Office of the General Counsel, FMCS, Washington, D.C.). Mr. Meagher is a former commissioner of FMCS.

26. The success of the introductory stage is directly related to two critical factors: (1) the appropriate timing of the mediator's intervention, and (2) the opportunity for mediator preparation. A mediator's sense of timing is the ability to judge the psychological readiness of an individual or group to respond in the desired way to a particular idea, suggestion, or proposal. Meagher, *supra* n. 25, at 5, *see also* Maggiolo, TECHNIQUES OF MEDIATION IN LABOR DISPUTES 62 (Dobbs Ferry, NY: Oceana Publications, 1971). The kinds of preparatory information needed by the mediator are discussed in the text *supra*. In many instances, such information is not available prior to intervention and thus it must be delicately elicited by the mediator during the introductory stage.

27. Meagher, *supra* n. 25, at 26-27. Wall, *Mediation, An Analysis, Review and Proposed Research*, 25 J. CONFLICT RES. 157, 161 (1981).

28. Caucusing is an *ex parte* conference between a mediator and a party.

29. Meagher, *supra* n. 25, at 28; Maggiolo, *supra* n. 26, at 42-44.

30. *Id.*

31. Ray, *supra* n. 24, at 121; Maggiolo, *supra* n. 26, at 52-54.

32. Meagher, *supra* n. 25, at 30; Maggiolo, *supra* n. 26, at 47.

33. Ray, *supra* n. 24, at 121; Salem, *supra* n. 23, at 4-5; Robins, *supra* n. 1, at 27; Maggiolo, *supra* n. 26, at 48-49.

34. Ray, *supra* n. 24, at 121.

35. *Id.* at 121-122; Meagher, *supra* n. 25, at 57-58; Robins, *supra* n. 1, at 43-44; Maggiolo, *supra* n. 26, at 49-50.

36. Maggiolo, *supra* n. 26, at 12. Other basic negotiation principles that some meditors use to advantage throughout the mediation process are found in Fisher and Ury, GETTING TO YES (New York: Penguin Books, 1983). Those principles are: (1) separate the people from the problem; (2) focus on interests, not positions; (3) invent options of mutual gain; (4) insist on using objective criteria.

37. Ray, *supra* n. 24, at 122. Meagher, *supra* n. 25, at 48-49, describes additional techniques of "planting seeds," "conditioning," and "influencing expectations."

38. Ray, *supra* n. 24, at 122.

39. *Id.*

40. Domke, *supra* n. 12, §23:01, at 351-353.

41. *Id.* §24:05, at 380.

42. *Id.*

43. *Id.* §23:02, at 355.

44. See Craviolini v. Scholer & Fuller Associated Architects, 89 Ariz. 24, 357 P.2d 611 (1960), where an architect was deemed to be a "quasi-arbitrator" under an agreement with the parties and therefore entitled to immunity from civil liability in an action brought against him by either party in relation to the architect's dispute-resolving function. *Compare* Gammell v. Ernst & Ernst, 245 Minn. 249, 72 N.W.2d 364 (1955), where certified public accountants, selected for the specific purpose of making an examination and of auditing the books of a corporation to ascertain its earnings, were held not to have acquired the status of arbitrators so as to create immunity for their actions in the performance of such service, simply because the report was to be binding upon the parties.

45. Domke, *supra* n. 12, §23:01, at 352-353.

46. As two professional mediators have commented: "Unlike arbitration and other means of adjudication, the parties retain complete control . . . If they do not like the mediator, they get another one. If they fail to produce results, they may end the mediation at any time." Phillips and Piazza, *How to Use Mediation*, 10 A.B.A. J. OF SECT. OF LIT. 31 (Spring, 1984).

47. *See* Grumman Aerospace Corp. v. Titanium Metals Corp., 91 F.R.D. 84 (E.D. N.Y. 1981) (court granted a motion to enforce a subpoena *duces tecum* involving a report prepared by a neutral fact-finder on the effects of certain price-fixing activities). *See generally* Restivo and Mangus, *Alternative Dispute Resolution: Confidential Problem-Solving or Every Man's Evidence? Alternatives to the High Cost of Litigation*, 2 LAW & BUS. INC./CTR. FOR PUBLIC RESOURCES 5 (May, 1984). Parties can assist the preservation of confidentiality of their mediation proceedings by reducing to writing any expectations or understanding regarding the confidentiality of the proceedings and by being careful to protect against unnecessary disclosure both within their respective constituencies and the outside world, *id.* at 9.

48. *See, e.g.*, NLRB v. Joseph Macaluso, 618 F.2d 51 (9th Cir. 1980); Pipefitters Local 208 v. Mechanical Contractors Assn. of Colorado, 90 Lab. Cas. (CCH) ¶12,647 (D. Colo. 1980).

49. Phillips and Piazza, *supra* n. 46, at 33.

50. In re Ruppert, 29 LA 775, 777 (N.Y. Ct. App. 1958); In re Griffin, 42 LA 511 (N.Y. Sup. Ct. 1964). *See generally* Elkouri and Elkouri, *supra* n. 3, at 241-251.

51. Domke, *supra* n. 12, §29:06, at 436.

52. Donoghue v. Kohlmeyer & Co., 63 Ill. App. 3d 979, 380 N.E.2d 1003, 20 Ill. Dec. 794 (1978).

53. Borg, Inc. v. Morris Middle School Dist. No. 54, 3 Ill. App. 3d 913, 278 N.E.2d 818 (1972).

54. Domke, *supra* n. 12, §33:00, 463.

55. *Id.* In Illinois, the court's power to vacate or modify arbitration awards is narrowly circumscribed. *See* ILL. REV. STAT. ch. 10, ¶¶112, 113 (1981).

56. ILL. REV. STAT. ch. 10, ¶114 (1981).

57. Gulliver, *supra* n. 8, at 220.

58. *Id.* at 226.

59. Where a settlement agreement is reduced to a judgment, for example, through intervention and assistance of a special master, the "consent judgment" is generally enforceable, if necessary, before the court in which the consent judgment is entered.

ADR problems and prospects: looking to the future

The alternative dispute resolution movement is at a critical turn in the road. What is needed now is a multipronged effort to expand understanding and promote increased involvement and support among all members of society.

by Stephen B. Goldberg, Eric D. Green, and Frank E.A. Sander

If alternative dispute resolution is an idea whose time has come, why has it not spread more rapidly and widely? Why is it that, although the users of neighborhood justice centers appear satisfied with the process, many of these centers are starving for business? Why is there such an abundance of individuals who want to provide mediation services, yet so few customers? In this article we will explore some of these questions, as well as possible answers. It should be noted at the outset, however, that much of our discussion will be based on speculation, for there is a dearth of reliable data concerning alternative dispute resolution mechanisms. Indeed, the absence of such data is itself a deterrent to the use of alternative processes.

Impediments to ADR use

The reason most frequently given for the failure of disputants to make greater use of mediation and other alterntives to the courts is that they don't know about their existence. Despite increasing publicity given to alternatives, we suspect that if a Gallup poll were taken today asking what an individual should do if he had a dispute with his neighbor which they could not resolve, most citizens would say "go to court" or "see your lawyer," rather than "visit your local neighborhood justice center." The emphasis given to courts and lawyers as the paradigm dispute resolvers in American society is simply too pervasive to be easily disturbed. One need only consider, by way of example, the consistent message conveyed by television—

"People's Court," "Miller's Court," and "Perry Mason." We have no programs entitled Perry Mediator, Miller's Neighborhood Justice Center, or People's Ombudsman.

Even if potential disputants are aware of alternatives to the court and live in a community where such mechanisms are available, it is often difficult to locate them because they have not been publicly institutionalized. This segregation of alternatives from the judicial process also has other adverse consequences, such as the common absence of public funding, which sometimes requires disputants to pay for alternative dispute resolution services even as the judicial ones are provided free. More subtle discouragement derives from the distrust that often accompanies processes that are new and unfamiliar and that appear to be unaccompanied by the legal protections that disputants have been taught over the years to value so highly. A related deterrent may be the absence of mechanisms for ensuring high standards in the provision of alternatives.

Psychological factors may also play a part in the gravitational pull of disputants toward the courts. Over 100 years ago de Tocqueville commented on the tendency in the United States of most social problems to devolve eventually into legal problems. Many disputants go to court because they want to challenge their adversaries rather than come to terms with them. In 20th century United States, lawsuits are the socially acceptable form of fighting.

In addition to these general explanations, special considerations may come into play in particular sectors of the disputing universe. For example, large institutional litigants may want a binding precedent to guide future disputes, which they can only get from a court. In bureaucratic organizations, such as the government, there is also the tendency towards following the path of least resistance and minimal risk. This means taking the tried-and-true route of dumping the problem into the court's lap, rather than risking criticism that might come from what some superior views as an unwise settlement.

The role of lawyers

No discussion of the impediments to the use of alternative dispute resolution processes would be complete without considering the role played by lawyers. For all the reasons alluded to above, most disputes that cannot be resolved by the disputants themselves are today presented to lawyers. In most instances, the client will, we suspect, be unaware of the existence of alternative dispute resolution processes. Hence, if such processes are to be utilized, it will typically be as a result of the lawyer's suggestion and encouragement.[1] The fact that alternative dispute resolution processes have not been more widely used suggests that lawyers have not been actively encouraging their use. Why not?

Initially, some of the factors that deter disputants from using alternative processes also deter lawyers from recommending them. While lawyers are more likely than their clients to be aware of the existence of alternatives, a surprising number of lawyers know very little about them, frequently confusing mediation and arbitration.[2] Hence, they are reluctant to suggest their use. The lack of institutionalization also has a deterrent effect. If a lawyer takes a case to court, she knows what she will find—a procedure that is specified by rules and that is familiar in every respect. If she opts for an alternative process, she frequently must decide what rules she wishes to apply and then obtain opposing counsel's agreement to those rules. The path of least resistance is to litigate. Finally, the lawyer is apt to have in common with her client the view that adversary combat in a judicial arena is the normal, socially acceptable, and psychologically satisfying method of resolving disputes. Indeed, most legal education is premised on an adversarial approach to dispute resolution.[3]

There are also psychological factors that discourage an enthusiastic acceptance of alternative processes by lawyers. Like most other professionals, lawyers frequently exert considerable control over their clients, which derives from the lawyer's ability to utilize a complex set of technical rules. This dominance is jeopardized by the use of dispute resolution methods like negotiation and mediation that place greater emphasis on client control over the outcome. These methods contemplate at times a diminished role for lawyers (e.g., as non-participating advisers in a divorce mediation) and at other times a different conceptualization of their role (e.g., as process facilitators who enable the parties themselves to arrive at the best possible solution). While these new roles may represent an exciting challenge to younger lawyers seeking to integrate their personal values with their professional training, they are regarded as threatening by many older lawyers who have become accustomed to the dominance and control inherent in much traditional legal practice.

Economic considerations may also constitute a significant impediment to the greater use of alternatives. Over the past decade, law firms have built up immense litigation departments. Even though some of the leading litigation practitioners are prominent in the alternatives movement because they see the advantages of accommodative problem-solving in many situations, the very existence of these expanding litigation empires constitutes a self-reinforcing movement towards more and more litigation.

Aside from these institutional forces, there are elements of the typical attorney compensation structure that militate against greater use of alternatives. The lawyer who gets paid on an hourly basis has no short-run economic interest in faster methods of dispute resolution. The plaintiff's lawyer who is paid on a contingent fee basis might, unless he will receive a higher proportion of a jury verdict than of a settlement. Under these circumstances, processes that encourage settlement may not be welcome.

Alternatives may also have an impact on future fees. If mediation, as advertised, deters future disputes so that people do not have to go to a lawyer as often, then lawyers may see the alternatives movement as disadvantageous to their economic interest. On the other hand, lawyers must be concerned about their competitive position vis-a-vis other lawyers; once clients become aware of the benefits of alternatives, they may bring pressure on their attorneys to use these methods or threaten to take their business elsewhere. Inasmuch as attorneys can buttress the case against the use of alternatives by the uncertain results and the absence of legal protections inherent in those processes, it may be only the client with considerable sophistication who will be capable of withstanding the countervailing pressures and insist upon the use of alternatives.

Even those attorneys who support alternative processes in principle, and would encourage their use in specific cases, may encounter difficulties. For example, some lawyers believe that a suggestion to opposing counsel that alternatives to litigation be explored may be taken as a sign of weakness (fear of litigation), which will negatively affect the lawyer's negotiating position. It is also possible that the Code of Professional Responsibility's emphasis on "zealous representation" deters some lawyers from proposing what has been called "a warmer way of disputing."[4] Furthermore, the lawyer who would not only advocate, but engage in, the provision of dispute resolution services must be concerned with the vague prohibitions of the Code against dual representation, which, to some uncertain extent, preclude lawyers from acting in a mediatory role.

There are also barriers to the provision of alternative dispute resolution services by those who are not lawyers. They must first acquire the necessary skills—no easy task at a time when the state of the art is still fairly primitive. Then they must turn these skills into a marketable career, which brings them up against the impediments earlier alluded to—a minimal demand compounded by the absence of institutional structures and public funding. Finally, there is the risk that in providing dispute resolution services they will run afoul of the prohibitions on the unauthorized practice of law. Indeed, there have already been a number of instances in which such prohibitions have been invoked against divorce mediators. To be sure, the extent to which nonlawyers should be free to provide dispute resolution services presents difficult issues. For present purposes, however, the point is that the unauthorized practice rules deter the provision of dispute resolution services by nonlawyers, and thereby to some extent discourage their use.

Needless to say, these barriers to the use of al-

ternatives have crosscutting and interlocking effects. For example, one reason for the shortage of empirical data is the shortage of research funds, but the shortage of persuasive research data in turn makes more difficult the procurement of additional funds to facilitate the enhanced institutionalization of alternative mechanisms.

In subsequent sections of this article, we will explore further some of these barriers and ways of ameliorating them. As regards the overriding goal of the need for enhanced education with respect to alternatives, perhaps the most promising efforts along these lines are presently being made through inclusion of conflict resolution units in the public school curriculum.[5] Only if people learn at an early age about the varied ways of resolving conflict can the prevailing emphasis on adversary dispute settlement be significantly moderated.

Critiques of mediation

The principal thrust of recent criticism of ADR has been aimed primarily at mediation, perhaps because that process blends third-party facilitation with disputant control of outcome, and hence is inherently imprecise and manipulable. In theory, mediation is a voluntary process whereby two or more disputants arrive at a mutually acceptable solution with the help of a neutral third party. In fact, some of these features are often lacking. Because of the not uncommon reluctance of one party to participate in mediation, overt or covert pressure is brought against the reluctant party.

As regards the element of coercion, a distinction should be drawn between coercion "into" and coercion "in" mediation. Although ideally a disputant should be able to make a knowing choice between going to mediation and going to court, a bit of a push towards mediation does not seem too serious, given the general ignorance of that process, as long as the disputants are free to choose any outcome they wish *in* the mediation proceeding.

In a recent piece, Professor Owen Fiss of Yale Law School launched a ringing attack on one of the fundamental premises of the alternatives movement—that settlement as a general rule is a social good.[6] Fiss contends that settlement necessarily involves a compromise of legal entitlements, which is of particular concern when there is a sharp power disparity between the parties.

The case against mediating disputes of the disadvantaged has been articulated with particular fervor by radical critics of the legal system, for they see the alternatives movement as a calculated effort by the establishment to discourage the disadvantaged from asserting their legal rights[7] and hence as simply another form of social control. By way of factual support, these critics point out that the three Neighborhood Justice Centers that were set up by the United States Department of Justice in the late seventies were in fact used predominantly by lower income disputants.[8]

Another argument raised on behalf of the lower income users of alternatives is that they are relegated to "second class" justice while the rich preempt the courts. Like most slogans, the term "second class" justice requires closer analysis. It appears to consist of three distinct ideas.

The first is that the thrust of the mediation process is towards a surrender of legal rights; its goal is settlement, not assertion of principle. This is the thesis that is so forcefully asserted by Fiss, not only from the perspective of the individual disputant but also in terms of the potential harm to society where socially important issues are at stake. To take a common example, if a consumer who has been victimized by a merchant sues in small claims court and then is referred to mediation, the case may be settled by having the vendor make some modest payment, without the consumer ever being apprised of his right to get treble damages under the applicable consumer protection act.

The second concern is that mediation lacks the legal protections associated with the adjudicatory process. Lawyers rarely participate in mediation, there are no evidentiary rules to prevent the introduction of unreliable or even prejudicial evidence, and in criminal-type cases no provision is made for the assertion of constitutional rights, such as the privilege against self-incrimination. In short, there is no guarantee of due process in mediation.

The assumption that underlies both preceding arguments—that many persons "relegated" to alternative processes would prefer to go to court—is dubious at best. When the disputants have an ongoing relationship, or the dispute is polycentric,[9] mediation may be far more responsive to the needs of the disputants than adjudication. Consider, for example, sexual harassment in the work place. While adjudication, if successful, would provide vindication, it might also create such tension that a continuation of the employment relationship

might, as a practical matter, be extremely difficult. In such a situation, employees might well prefer mediation to adjudication.

Another assumption of the "second-class" justice argument is that if lower-income disputants were not relegated to alternative processes, they would receive the procedural protections and full-blown trial inherent in the phrase "first-class" justice. In actuality, however, most "minor" disputes are shunted aside or mass-processed by the judicial system in a way that provides very little of the deliberative flavor that is the advertised hallmark of adjudication. Hence, the real choice may often be between mediation and surrogates for true adjudication. In this connection it is crucial to draw a sharp distinction between complex and pathbreaking litigation (such as a desegregation case that receives a disproportionate amount of judicial attention) and run-of-the-mill civil or criminal cases that are far more likely to be thoughtfully considered in the alternative processes.

A third implication of the "second-class" justice argument is that mediation, by focusing on accommodative resolutions of individual disputes, prevents aggregate solutions. For example, using the previous consumer fraud example, if a manufacturer has committed flagrant violations of the consumer protection laws, these wrongs will not be effectively redressed if the perpetrator is allowed to "buy off" individual complainants through settlements that do not address directly the legality of the underlying practice.

Here again the assumption that the asserted deficiency is necessarily avoided in court is open to question. To be sure, a class action may be brought, or an individual case may create a binding precedent, but the vast preponderance of cases in court are settled without addressing any broader recurring issue that may be involved. This is particularly true of the high volume lower-level courts where most of these cases are brought. Hence what may be best is a mechanism (such as a consumer protection bureau in an attorney general's office) that effectively blends redress of individual grievances (perhaps through mediation) with aggregate relief through adjudication for "pattern and practice" violations.

In the final analysis, the question is how best to bring about change by individual or by institutional defendants. Sometimes lawsuits represent the most promising way; at other times, institutional change is brought about best from within, through accommodative processes such as mediation.[10]

A need for empirical research

Notable progress has been made in demonstrating empirically some of the claimed advantages of alternative methods of dispute resolution, such as the greater satisfaction of disputants with mediation.[11] Most of the mediation research, however, has been carried out with disputants who mediated voluntarily. The obvious risk is that those disputants who were willing to mediate were particularly susceptible to a mediatory approach, and that if mediation were compulsory, as may be necessary to bring about its widespread use, its apparent advantages would disappear. For example, settlement rates, compliance, and participant satisfaction might all diminish if mediation were compulsory.

Another risk of compulsory mediation is that disputants who would otherwise resolve their disputes through direct negotiation might take advantage of the easy accessibility of mediation, each hoping to do better in mediation than in negotiation. If that would occur in a substantial proportion of cases, mediation would, as a practical matter, be a substitute for negotiation, and should be compared to it, not adjudication. Hence, research on the effects of compulsory mediation on settlements by negotiation is called for, as is research comparing compulsory mediation with adjudication.

The data on compulsory mediation are slim. McEwen and Maiman found that in the mediation of small claims, neither settlement rates nor compliance varied according to whether mediation was voluntary or compulsory.[12] However, their findings are weakened by the fact that in the small claims courts they studied, the assignment of cases to mediation was not random. Judges in some courts ordered disputants to mediation, while others made mediation voluntary. It is not clear whether those judges who imposed mediation did so in all cases, or only in those cases in which they thought the parties were susceptible to a mediatory approach. If the latter procedure were followed, the data regarding the effectiveness of compulsory mediation would be weakened.[13] A subsequent study, however, in which a six-month period of voluntary mediation of grievances arising under a collective bargaining contract was followed by a six-month

period of compulsory mediation, found that settlement rates at mediation were not affected by whether mediation was voluntary or compulsory. The same study found compulsory mediation associated with a decrease in directly negotiated settlements, although the existence of a causal relationship could not be determined.[14]

Considerably more research on the effects of compulsory participation in alternatives to litigation is needed. One opportunity for such research in the mediation context is presented by California's recent change from voluntary to compulsory mediation of child custody disputes. Data comparing mandatory mediation to voluntary mediation or adjudication of child custody disputes on each of the criteria discussed by Pearson would be extremely useful.[15] Obviously, any such study would have to be replicated in other contexts before we could generalize from it.

The spread of compulsory court-annexed arbitration provides ample opportunity for testing the extent to which this process is capable of resolving disputes more satisfactorily than they would be resolved by the traditional route of settlement negotiations followed by trial for those cases that do not settle. It is, of course, important in collecting data on this question that courts which are experimenting with arbitration do so in a truly experimental mode, assigning cases randomly to the arbitration route and the traditional route. Only then will we have a clear comparison of the two approaches. One problem with such research, however, is that it is unclear whether random assignment would constitute constitutionally impermissible disparate treatment.[16]

If the alternatives to adjudication have all the advantages claimed for them, why are they not more widely used? The answers to this question remain a matter of controversy. It is, however, an exceedingly important question. For, until we know why voluntary alternatives are not more used, any response to their underutilization will necessarily be based on speculation, with all the false starts and inefficient expenditure of resources that entails.

Researches have already determined what proportion of disputes result in court filings by tracking disputes from their origin to their final disposition.[17] However, that research does not disclose why those disputants who went to court did not utilize one of the alternatives to litigation. To answer the latter question, one might offer disputants their choice of adjudication or mediation. Those who chose adjudication rather than mediation could be questioned concerning their reasons. Additionally, the characteristics of those who chose mediation could be compared with those who chose adjudication. In conducting research of this type with individuals who accepted and rejected mediation of child custody disputes, Pearson, Thoennes, and Vanderkooi found that the lawyers' attitude toward mediation was the key factor in the choice of processes.[18] Similar research could be conducted in conjunction with the multidoor courthouse experiments described by Finkelstein elsewhere in this issue.[19]

Lack of knowledge

It is frequently asserted that a major reason for the failure to use alternatives to adjudication is lack of knowledge. One recent study, however, casts doubt upon this assertion. According to Merry and Silbey, who studied attitudes and behaviors of disputing in three neighborhoods, disputants do not use alternatives to the extent hoped for by their proponents because by the time they are willing to turn to an outsider for help, they do not want what alternatives have to offer.[20] They no longer wish to settle the dispute by discussion and negotiation; rather each wants vindication, protection of his or her rights, an advocate to help in the battle, or a third party who will declare the other party wrong.

Another approach to testing the hypothesis that lack of knowledge is a major barrier to the use of alternatives would be to compare the number of cases submitted to the judicial system and to, for example, the neighborhood justice center, in two closely matched communities, preceding and following an extensive education program, using both the media and the schools in one of those communities. Any significant difference in the proportion of cases submitted to the neighborhood justice center in the "educated" community compared with the control community could (absent other intervening variables) be attributed to the educational campaign; any significant increase in the total volume of cases presented to the neighborhood justice center and the courts combined in the "educated" community compared with the control community might also indicate that an effect of the education campaign was to reduce the frequency of "lumping it" or avoidance as a means

of dispute resolution.[21]

Another means to determine the extent to which lack of knowledge regarding alternatives explains their limited use is to provide such knowledge, together with encouragement to try an alternative in appropriate cases, and facilitate access to the alternatives. That is the approach being taken by the multi-door courthouse experiments.

What can research accomplish?

Can we develop a satisfactory taxonomy of dispute resolution processes, matching disputes to appropriate dispute resolution processes? To some extent, the success of the multidoor courthouse will depend on the capacity of its staff to direct disputants to a process that is appropriate for their dispute. However, to the best of our knowledge, there are no empirical data on this question. To generate such data, a laboratory experiment might be conducted in which the same dispute was dealt with in a variety of dispute resolution processes. Measures could then be taken of settlement rate, cost, speed, participant satisfaction with process and outcome, and other relevant variables. If such an experiment were conducted with a number of different types of disputes, varying in such criteria as subject matter, amount at issue, presence or absence of a continuing relationship, presence or absence of a substantial power disparity, etc., one would begin to develop some empirical basis for suggesting that a particular type of dispute might be best handled in a particular process. Laboratory experiments of this nature, in which the same dispute has been subjected to a variety of dispute resolution processes, and participant satisfaction measured in each, have been conducted by Thibaut and Walker, LaTour, et al. and Brett.[22]

Can we develop a sophisticated cost-benefit analysis for the various dispute resolution processes? Doing so presents substantial questions of measurement. Some items can be measured in financial terms, some in psychological terms, some not at all. For example, many of the costs to both the public and the parties of resolving a dispute in one process or another—attorneys' fees, dispute resolvers' salaries—are easily measurable in financial terms. Similarly, some benefits, such as increased compliance and deterrence of future disputes, can be translated into financial terms.

There are, however, some items, such as participant satisfaction, that can be measured only in psychological terms, and others that cannot be measured at all. What, for example, is the cost to the justice system or the parties of a dispute being settled in mediation, but no precedent being set, as it would be in adjudication?[23] Another problem of cost-benefit analysis in this context is the difficulty in determining the appropriate unit of measurement. If mediation does, indeed, lead to greater compliance and deterrence of future disputes, its benefits extend beyond the individual case in which it is used, and treating the case as the appropriate unit of measurement would be misleading. In sum, the most that research may be able to accomplish in this context is to provide a variety of measures on which to compare some of the costs and benefits of the various dispute resolution processes. Still, even those data, limited as they are, are preferable to sheer impressionism as a means for allocating limited funds among these processes.

Is there a danger that in our preoccupation with finding the appropriate dispute resolution *process*, we will lose sight of the need for fair outcomes? While one cannot engage in empirical research bearing directly on this speculative question, it is possible to design research with the aim of minimizing the danger that the need for fair outcomes will be overlooked. For example, in doing the research necessary to develop a taxonomy of dispute resolution processes, one could include among the measures to be examined both objective criteria such as the efficiency of the outcome (the extent to which joint gains have been maximized) and subjective criteria such as the parties' satisfaction with outcome, as distinguished from process. Indeed, considerable research has already been done on participant satisfaction. That research suggests that satisfaction with process is related to satisfaction with outcome—disputants who believe that a dispute resolution process was fair tend also to believe that the outcome was fair.

Is there a danger that the availability of alternatives will shunt low- and middle-income disputants to a form of second-class justice, consisting primarily of semi-coerced compromise settlements, while the so-called first-class justice offered by the courts becomes available only to the rich and powerful? To some extent, this question presents an issue of definition. What is first-class justice? If it is defined as a method of resolving disputes that includes legal representation, formal rules of procedure, and

a resolution based upon law, then those alternatives that are mediatory in nature will inevitably be labeled second-class, and the central question essentially answers itself. If, however, first-class justice is defined as that dispute resolution process which most satisfies the participants, research can be conducted by surveying the users of the alternative processes concerning their satisfaction with them, and comparing their responses with those of the users of the courts. Much of that research has been done, and uniformly concludes that participants in the alternative processes are as satisfied or more satisfied with those processes than are participants in court adjudication.[24]

There are undoubtedly other questions not mentioned here that are important for the future of the dispute resolution movement as a whole or for particular processes. The crucial point is that as such questions are identified they should be scrutinized to determine the extent to which they are susceptible to empirical research. Such research may, to be sure, have a limited effect on the resolution of the underlying legal and policy questions, a phenomenon frequently noted (and bemoaned) by social science researchers.[25] Still, empirical data can be influential in changing policy, particularly to the extent that existing policy is based on factual misconceptions. In a field as comparatively new as dispute resolution, such misconceptions are certain to abound. Hence, the opportunity exists for empirical researchers to make a significant contribution to removing at least some of the impediments to the expanded use of alternative dispute resolution processes.[26]

Creating a coherent scheme

It is implicit in the preceding discussion that dispute resolution mechanisms are dispersed all through the social fabric. Sometimes they are private; sometimes they are public. Sometimes they are mandatory; at other times they are optional. Wherever disputes arise between individuals and organizations, a complex network of possible grievance mechanisms appears to be available for the venting of these grievances.[27]

The question naturally arises what, if any, relationship there should be between the different types of mechanisms. This question assumes importance not only for the disputant who might benefit from some guidance concerning where to take any particular dispute but also from the point of view of society seeking to provide a coherent response to these requests.

One can certainly envision a system in which there is some kind of hierarchy and structure within the formal public dispute resolution system, but where that system is complemented in some vague way by a vast and ill-understood network of indigenous dispute mechanisms. Indeed, that, in essence, is our present system. Disputants may first try to utilize the vast array of informal mechanisms that are provided in the particular universe where the dispute arises, and then, as a last resort, take the dispute to the public forum, the court.[28] At least that is the paradigm. In fact, of course, informal private mechanisms often are not available, or if they are, they are not resorted to, and the typically American habit of taking the case immediately to court often becomes the prevailing practice. The net effect is that many disputes presented to court are not appropriate for court adjudication and could be better handled by some other mechanism.[29]

This situation led to a suggestion by one of the authors in a paper delivered at the Pound Conference in 1976[30] that, in lieu of the courthouse as we now know it, we might envision in years ahead a more comprehensive and diverse mechanism known as a Dispute Resolution Center, which would seek to provide a variety of dispute resolution processes, according to the needs of the particular dispute. Someone subsequently dubbed this concept "the multidoor courthouse."

The multidoor courthouse

What would such an institution look like? A provisional first-step type of multidoor courthouse could consist essentially of a screening and referral clerk who would seek to diagnose incoming cases and refer them to the most suitable process. Depending on the available mechanisms in the particular community, referrals might be made to mediation, arbitration, court adjudication, fact finding, malpractice screening, a media action line, or an ombudsman.[31]

One of the fringe benefits of such an institution is that it would provide an opportunity to learn more about what process is most appropriate for what kinds of disputes; it would also give helpful feedback concerning what "doors" were missing or not working effectively. That information could then be utilized to refine the model.

The potential benefits of such an approach are enhanced responsiveness and effectiveness, possible time and cost savings, and the legitimization of various alternative dispute resolution processes. What should result is less frustration among the populace in dealing with the vagaries of the legal system. An additional benefit would come from a better understanding of the peculiar advantages and disadvantages of particular processes for specific types of disputes.

There are also potential pitfalls. Not only will the success of a multidoor courthouse largely depend on the skill of the intake official, there is also a real danger—as with all administrative innovations—that it will become the genesis of a new bureaucracy that will result in Kafkaesque shunting of individuals from one "door" to another without any genuine effort to address the problems presented. In addition, there are some difficult questions that must be addressed such as whether the multidoor courthouse should be a centralized institution under one roof, or more akin to a wheel, with a core operation at the center, supplemented by satellite intake and referral offices. Another critical question—whether the referral should be mandatory or voluntary—is discussed below.

Institutionalization

It should be recognized that the multidoor courthouse is but one form of publicly provided alternative dispute resolution. The issues surrounding the public institutionalization of alternatives, or their private provision through public funding, are vital issues that warrant further discussion.

The case for public institutionalization of alternatives rests on a number of propositions. Since courts are publicly provided, why should an alternative process that might be more effective in particular cases not be publicly provided? Unless it is, society creates a financial disincentive to the use of the more effective process. Moreover, for better or worse, the courthouse is where most American citizens ultimately go if they cannot otherwise resolve their disputes. Hence, from the point of view of public education and exposure, as well as enhanced credibility, governmental provision of alternatives in the courthouse itself may be essential.

The question of mandatory use of alternatives raises different issues depending in large part on the effect to be given to the mandated process. As indicated earlier, coercion *into* mediation does not seem objectionable, as long as there is no coercion *in* mediation to accept a particular outcome, and as long as unsuccessful mediation does not serve as a barrier to adjudication. Similarly, we perceive no persuasive objection to mandating nonbinding arbitration as a precondition to litigation for small or middle-size money claims. If, however, participation in mandatory mediation or arbitration were to bar access to the courts, serious constitutional questions would be presented. Inasmuch, however, as no program for the mandatory use of alternatives has this effect, the more realistic question concerns the extent to which the outcome of a mandatory alternative should be allowed to affect the adjudication process (e.g., by financial preconditions on resort to court or use in court of the noncourt result).

Public institutionalization of alternatives involves their public funding; that is a powerful additional argument put forward by the proponents of institutionalization, who are all too mindful of the fact that private foundations are constantly searching for novel experiments, and are usually not interested in facilitating the continuation of successful pilot programs.[32]

But public funding does not necessarily imply public provision of dispute resolution services. Governments might make grants to private organizations; this is the path taken by New York State, which supports more than 30 privately operated community dispute resolution programs in the state. Texas, meanwhile, has developed a novel path for raising public funds for alternative dispute resolution; it has authorized counties to add a surcharge to the civil filing fee, with the accumulated funds to be used to fund alternative programs. The possibility of federal funding for dispute resolution programs was at least temporarily aborted when the Dispute Resolution Act of 1980 was not funded.

Institutionalization, whether public or private, carries with it potent dangers. Any attempt to make an experiment permanent and larger in scale is likely to result in increasing bureaucratization.[33] As the proportion of volunteers declines, the exuberance and excitement that initially pervaded the project may give way to routinization and burnout. Particularly where public funds are involved, bureaucratic job requirements are likely to be imposed, and political influences may come into play.

Whether an innovative program can withstand "success" by effectively making the transition to institutionalization may well be the ultimate test of the program.

A final question concerns the competing claims of alternatives and the courts for limited public funds. Ideally, the funds should go to that system which is more cost effective or qualitatively superior. But, as was noted earlier, we are only beginning to accumulate adequate sophisticated data to help make that judgment. Pending obtaining that data, we need to hedge our bets by encouraging experimentation with alternatives, coupled with careful research to determine their effectiveness.

Professionalization

As the practice of dispute resolution outside the courts expands, the question arises how to ensure high standards of practice and ethical behavior. A related question is how prospective users can find high-quality dispute resolution services suited to their needs.

These questions urgently require answers. In recent years, the number of persons and organizations offering mediation and other dispute resolution services has increased significantly. In addition to a dozen or more national and regional organizations that offer a broad range of dispute resolution services,[34] there are over 180 local mediation programs.[35] Further, both lawyers and other professionals are more often offering mediation as one of their services.

Ensuring high standards is also important at this time because the alternatives movement is in the early stages of professional development. According to Wilensky's[36] typology of the steps through which "occupations" pass on the way to becoming "professions," the alternatives movement is in the stage of professionalization in which people work at the occupation full-time, practitioners press for the establishment of training schools, enthusiastic leaders emerge who are the protagonists of some new technique, and activists engage in much soul searching on "whether the occupation is a profession, what the professional tasks are, how to raise the quality of recruits, and so on." As this occurs, there is "a self-conscious effort to define and redefine the core tasks of the occupation,"[37] and a struggle often ensues over whether the occupation will become fully professionalized with specialized degree programs and exclusionary licensing.

There are vigorous advocates of professionalization of mediation. Robert Coulson, president of the American Arbitration Association, has recently issued a call for "a full-fledged profession of Certified Public Mediator."[38] He visualizes a system in which local courts would regulate mediators as they now regulate lawyers, and litigation could not be undertaken without the assurance by a CPM that mediation had been fully utilized in an effort to avoid litigation. Although most CPMs would be lawyers certified by the court, there would be a role for nonlawyers in specialized substantive areas.[39]

Others oppose efforts to professionalize the alternatives movement. They contend that professionalization is inconsistent with the goal of community building through lay dispute resolution. They are also concerned that replacing volunteer mediators with paid professionals will increase costs and restrict the availability of alternatives.[40]

While at present there is no legal regulation of the private practice of dispute resolution, there is an increasing tendency by public agencies to set minimum education and experience requirements for mediators. The California, Connecticut, Nevada, and Oregon courts, for example, require that family mediators employed by them have a master's degree in counseling, social work, or a related field, as well as substantial experience. Other courts require that mediators working in court-established mediation programs be members of the bar or establish their expertise in the subject of the dispute.[41]

The pros and cons of such standards and of greater regulation of private mediation are discussed by Folberg and Taylor.[42] As they point out, some commentators argue that minimum education and experience requirements and licensure of practitioners are necessary to protect an unknowing public from incompetents and charlatans. These commentators point out that the quality of services cannot easily be judged by the results obtained, and that most clients will have little or no experience against which to evaluate the performance of a mediator or other dispute resolution practitioner. Further, the generally private, informal, and interdisciplinary nature of dispute resolution practice increases the danger that "bad" or unfair practices will occur and go undetected.

Codes and standards

A logical conclusion of this reasoning is not only to set minimum educational and experience requirements, but also to establish standards of practice that will enable clients to judge the quality of the services they receive. Such standards can serve as a set of expectations and minimally acceptable common practices for the service offered, thereby protecting both the client and the provider by defining what is "reasonable care."[43] Others, however, argue that alternative dispute resolution is still such a new field that it is difficult if not impossible to set standards of practice with any degree of confidence. In lieu of standards of practice, they would do no more than articulate basic ethical precepts, derived from fundamental notions of fairness, decency, and morality.

We doubt whether this distinction between standards of practice and ethical limitations—between "do's" and "don'ts" in Folberg and Taylor's terminology[44]—is easy to apply in practice or serves much purpose. Codes of ethics for arbitrators have been promulgated by the American Arbitration Association and other arbitration associations.[45] Standards of practice and codes of ethics have also been promulgated by interested and responsible groups in the fields of family and labor mediation. Others will undoubtedly follow. The real question is what use is to be made of such standards and codes. If they are used to educate novice practitioners and inform the public of what is generally considered good practice, and to serve as guidelines for agencies and courts when judging whether a practitioner has used reasonable care, then careful and flexible use of such standards will be beneficial. If, however, they are applied rigidly or for the purpose of protecting the turf of a particular group, then such standards are likely to retard desirable experimentation and growth.

It is therefore important to consider how standards might be enforced. There are four traditional options:

- regulation and licensing by government;
- self-regulation and licensing by a trade or professional organization with expulsion the ultimate sanction;
- liability principles, i.e., suits for malpractice or negligence;
- public disclosure and the operation of the marketplace, coupled, perhaps, with certification of expertise or education.

These options are not mutually exclusive. In most professions (e.g., law, medicine) standards of practice and ethical behavior are enforced in all of these ways. But these professions tend to be well-established, cohesive, and highly developed, as opposed to the emerging dispute resolution profession.

Moreover, even in the older, established professions, critics contend that professionalization, when coupled with standards and licensure, serve more to protect the turf of the powerful than the interests of the public. The tendency of professionals to create a monopoly by employing licensing standards in an economically self-interested manner is well documented.[46] Indeed, the "higher" stages of professionalization are characterized by this development and by the conflicts within the developing profession and with outsiders that this inevitably generates. According to Wilensky[47] and Pipkin and Rifkin,[48] a pecking order emerges that stratifies practitioners and creates conflict and internecine struggles between new and old cohorts of practitioners, and between practitioners of the new occupation and other occupations who claim the same territory. These final stages of professional development typically involve the formation of associations which seek the support of law to impose licensure restrictions on practitioners and thus protect the territory from outsiders and exclude the unqualified and unscrupulous. At some point in this process, the profession codifies its rules of ethics as a basis for self-regulation.

If the alternatives movement develops in the direction of licensure, the impetus is likely to come from public agencies that employ mediators and which must decide, in making employment decisions, who is qualified to be a mediator. California and other states with publicly supported mediation programs chose to specify formal training and degrees. Rather than specify the kind of degree a person had to have to be a mediator—an approach that is bound to engage the agency in a highly charged and broad-based turf battle between lawyers and those in the healing professions—Michigan chose instead to specify the *skills* that a mediator had to possess.

This approach may only serve to camouflage the conflict by specifying skills that go with a certain kind of education. Moreover, the likely result of specifying skills is the establishment of an industry offering to provide eager practitioners with such skills. There is still the problem of ensuring that practitioners actually possess the skills that their degrees advertise for them. Thus, either the teachers that train practitioners in these skills (or their schools) may have to be licensed (the same old problem), or practitioners will have to be tested. This raises the difficult question of whether it is possible at this time to do skills testing of dispute resolution practitioners.

We believe that it is possible to devise and administer a skills test that could effectively screen for basic mediator competency and ethics. Any such test would have to be carefully pretested and administered with flexibility, however, so as not to exclude practitioners on the basis of legitimate differences of theory or style.

Certification and training

A compromise between full-scale professionalization with licensure and no professionalization at all would be the establishment of certification and training programs for dispute resolution practitioners. Certification would indicate that the certified individual met the criteria established by the certifying organization, and so provide potentially useful information to users, but would not bar practice by noncertified persons. Although the same problems of defining good practice and skills testing exist with certification as with licensure, the absence of any occupational exclusionary power minimizes the problem. Many flowers can bloom and the public may learn to identify the flowers and choose among them. This appears to be the approach favored by the Ethics Committee of the Society of Professionals in Dispute Resolution, although the committee took no formal position on licensure, certification, or training.[49]

A form of certification program for arbitrators, pursuant to which lists of arbitrators certified as meeting minimum criteria are made available on request, is currently administered by the American Arbitration Association and the Federal Mediation and Conciliation Service. Similarly, the Center for Public Resources and the American Arbitration Association provide lists of prominent mediators and private judges. But certification or listing by these organizations is based essentially on recommendations or number of cases handled. There is no attempt at testing, and no effort to train those certified or to monitor their performance. Only a serious violation of ethical rules will cause a listed arbitrator to be removed from the AAA or FMCS lists.

A different approach to certification is offered by educational programs that offer training in dispute resolution skills, and certification based on that training. Some of these programs are university-based, others are free-standing. Some last as long as a year, others no longer than a weekend. Many of these programs do not attempt to evaluate the competency of participants, and others certify everyone who completes the program. Hence, there is apt to be little correlation between possessing a certificate from some of these programs and possessing the certified skills.

Despite those shortcomings, certification, together with the operation of market forces and legal liability for malpractice, appears to be a better approach than licensure for the dispute resolution field at the present time. Notwithstanding problems at the edges in defining standards of good practice and ethical limitations, and in ensuring quality training and monitoring of certified practitioners, certification by responsible organizations and well-established and operated training programs may be of some help to the inexperienced consumer. Licensure, on the other hand, adds little to certification in the way of consumer protection, and creates the very real danger that in enforcing licensing rules, professional self-interest will predominate over consumer protection. Whichever approach is taken, given the conceptual ferment in this field, it is important that standards and norms not be viewed as immutable precepts, but as subject to experience, debate, and modification.

Conclusion

The alternative dispute resolution movement is at a critical turn in the road. After 10 years or so of scholarly inquiry and practical experimentation, our knowledge of the field has been substantially enhanced and there is a far greater awareness, both among the general public and in the legal community, of the promise of alternative dispute settlement.

What we need now is a multipronged effort to expand our limited present understanding of the field. This will require continued experimentation and research, as well as further attempts to conceptualize the field. It will necessitate enhanced public education about the benefits to be derived from alternative modes of dispute settlement. Ways must be found to develop career paths and employment opportunities for talented individuals who wish to devote their lives to providing alternative dispute resolution services. This will probably require, at least in the short run, some infusion of public financing. Above all, if the movement is to hold any significant promise of gaining a permanent foothold on the American scene, it will require the broadened involvement and support not only of the legal education establishments but also of the society at large.

NOTES

This article originally appeared in Volume 69, Number 5, February-March 1986, pages 291-299. An initial version was presented by Professor Sander as a paper at a conference at Harvard Law School in October 1982. Portions of the revised paper are adapted from Goldberg, Green and Sander, DISPUTE RESOLUTION (Little, Brown and Co., 1985).

1. Pearson, Thoennes and Vanderkooi, *The Decision to Mediate: Profiles of Individuals Who Accept and Reject the Opportunity to Mediate Contested Child Custody and Visitation Issues*, 6 J. DIVORCE 17 (1982).

2. *See* Cooley, *Arbitration vs. mediation: explaining the differences*, 69 JUDICATURE 263 (1986).

3. Riskin, *Mediation and Lawyers*, 43 OHIO ST. L.J. 29 (1982).

4. Smith, *A Warmer Way of Disputing: Mediation and Conciliation*, 26 AM. J. COMP. L. (Supp.) 205 (1978).

5. Davis, *Justice Without Judges*, UPDATE ON LAW-RELATED EDUCATION (Chicago: American Bar Association Special Committee on Youth Education For Citizenship, 1984).

6. Fiss, *Against Settlement*, 93 YALE L.J. 1987 (1984).

7. Abel, *The Contradictions of Informal Justice*, in Abel, ed., THE POLITICS OF INFORMAL JUSTICE: THE AMERICAN EXPERIENCE 1 (New York: Academic Press, 1982); Auerbach, JUSTICE WITHOUT LAW? (New York: Oxford, 1983).

8. Cook, Roehl and Shepard, NEIGHBORHOOD JUSTICE CENTER FIELD TEST: FINAL EVALUATION REPORT (Washington, DC: U.S. Government Printing Office, 1980).

9. Fuller, *The Forms and Limits of Adjudication*, 92 HARV. L. REV. 353 (1979).

10. Singer, *Nonjudicial Dispute Resolution Mechanisms: The Effects on Justice for the Poor*, 13 CLEARINGHOUSE REV. 569 (1979); Rowe, *Predicting the Effects of Attorney Fee Shifting*, 47 LAW AND CONTEMP. PROBS. 139 (1984).

11. Pearson, *An Evaluation of Alternatives to Court Adjudication*, 7 JUST. SYS. J. 420 (1982).

12. McEwen and Maiman, *Small Claims Mediation in Maine: An Empirical Assessment*, 33 ME. L. REV. 237 (1981).

13. But see McEwen and Maiman, *Mediation in Small Claims Court: Achieving Compliance Through Consent*, 18 LAW & SOC'Y REV. 11, 22-28 (1984).

14. Brett and Goldberg, *Grievance Mediation in the Coal Industry*, 37 INDUS. AND LAB. REL. REV. 49, 56, 59-60 (1983).

15. Pearson, *supra* n. 11.

16. Federal Judicial Center, EXPERIMENTATION IN THE LAW: REPORT OF THE FEDERAL JUDICIAL CENTER ADVISORY COMMITTEE ON EXPERIMENTATION IN THE LAW (Washington, DC: U.S. Government Printing Office, 1981).

17. Miller and Sarat, *Grievances, Claims and Disputes: Assessing the Adversary Culture*, 15 LAW AND SOC'Y REV. 525 (1981).

18. Pearson, Thoennes and Vanderkooi, *supra* n. 1.

19. Finkelstein, *The D.C. multi-door courthouse*, 69 JUDICATURE 305 (1986).

20. Merry and Silbey, *What Do Plaintiffs Want? Reexamining the Concept of Dispute*, 9 JUST. SYS. J. 151 (1984).

21. Felsteiner, Abel and Sarat, *The Emergence and Transformation of Disputes: Naming, Blaming, Claiming*, 15 LAW AND SOC'Y REV. 631 (1981).

22. Thibaut and Walker, PROCEDURAL JUSTICE: A PSYCHOLOGICAL ANALYSIS (Hillsdale, NJ: Lawrence Erlbaum, 1975); LaTour, Houlden, Walker, and Thibaut, *Procedure: Transnational Perspectives and Preferences*, 86 YALE L.J. 258 (1976); Brett, *Procedural Justice* in Symposium, JUSTICE: BEYOND EQUITY THEORY (Convention, Academy of Management, 1983).

23. Fiss, *supra* n. 6.

24. Pearson, *supra* n. 11.

25. Weiss, USING SOCIAL SCIENCE RESEARCH IN PUBLIC POLICY MAKING (Lexington, MA: Lexington Books, 1977); Lindblom and Cohen, USABLE KNOWLEDGE (New Haven, CT: Yale University Press, 1979).

26. The need for additional empirical data is equaled by the need for careful analysis of both existing and newly-collected data. Galanter, *Reading the Landscape of Disputes: What We Know and Don't Know (and Think We Know) About Our Allegedly Contentious and Litigious Society*, 31 U.C.L.A. L. REV. 4 (1983).

27. Galanter, *Justice in Many Rooms*, 19 J. OF LEG. PLURALISM 1 (1981).

28. "At present, it is almost accidental if community members find their way to an appropriate forum other than the regular courts. Several other modes of dispute resolution already are available in many communities. Still, since they are operated by a hodge-podge of local government agencies, neighborhood organizations, and trade associations, citizens must be very knowledgeable about community resources to locate the right forum for their particular dispute." Johnson, *Toward a Responsive Justice System* in STATE COURTS: A BLUEPRINT FOR THE FUTURE 122 (Williamsburg, VA: National Center for State Courts, 1978).

29. Sander, *Varieties of Dispute Resolution*, 70 F.R.D. 111 (1976).

30. *Id.*

31. For a description of the way cases are handled in a multidoor courthouse, see Finkelstein, *supra* n. 19.

32. The National Institute for Dispute Resolution appears to be well aware of the problems of institutionalizing successful programs. Lacking the funds to achieve that goal itself, it has attempted to use its limited resources to leverage public-sector and other private-sector funds.

33. Edelman, *Institutionalizing Dispute Resolution Alternatives*, 9 JUST SYS. J. 134 (1984).

34. Marks, Johnson and Szanton, DISPUTE RESOLUTION IN AMERICA: PROCESSES IN EVOLUTION 69-74 (Washington, DC: National Institute for Dispute Resolution, 1984).

35. American Bar Association, DISPUTE RESOLUTION PROGRAM DIRECTORY (Washington, DC: American Bar Association, 1983).

36. Wilensky, *The Professionalization of Everyone?*, 70 AM. J. SOC. 137 (1964).

37. Pipkin and Rifkin, *The Social Organization in Alternative Dispute Resolution: Implications for Professionalization of Mediation*, 9 JUST SYS. J. 204, 205-206 (1984).

38. Coulson, PROFESSIONAL MEDIATION OF CIVIL DISPUTES (New York: American Arbitration Association, 1984).

39. *Id.* at 24-25, 32-33.

40. Pipkin and Rifkin, *supra* n. 37, at 207.

41. The issue also arises in connection with confidentiality statutes that seek to limit the individuals who are entitled to the statutory protections. See e.g., Mass. Ann. Laws c. 233, §23c (1985).

42. Folberg and Taylor, MEDIATION: A COMPREHENSIVE GUIDE TO RESOLVING CONFLICTS WITHOUT LITIGATION 244 (San Francisco, Jossey-Bass, 1984).

43. *Id.* at 250.

44. *Id.*

45. Hay, Carnevale, and Sinicropi, *Professionalization: Selected Ethical Issues in Dispute Resolution*, 9 JUST SYS. J. 228, 236 (1984).

46. Gellhorn, *Abuse of Occupational Licensing*, 44 U. CHI. L. REV. 6, 39 (1976).

47. Wilensky, *supra* n. 36.

48. Pipkin and Rifkin, *supra* n. 37.

49. Hay, Carnevale, and Sinicropi, *supra* n. 45, at 230, 236-240.

Rethinking barriers to legal practice

Instead of being prohibited from providing legal services, nonlawyers should be regulated and controlled, just like lawyers.

by Herbert M. Kritzer

Throughout the 20th century, the legal profession has worked hard to create an expansive definition of what constitutes the practice of law and to exclude all nonlawyers from activities falling within that definition. Critics maintain that the only real reason for restrictions on who can provide legal services is the protection of lawyers from competition. One witness at a public hearing of the American Bar Association Commission on Nonlawyer Practice referred to the profession as a "greedy lawyer cartel" that sells justice to the highest bidder.[1] Others have made similar, though less strident, observations. For example, law professor Richard Abel develops a strong case that historically the profession sought to limit both the "production of producers" of legal services (i.e., limiting entry into the profession) and the "production [of legal services] by producers" (i.e., limiting who provides services and the nature of what is provided).[2]

While the profession has largely lost control of the production of producers, lawyers continue to try to limit the opportunities for nonlawyers to provide legal services. The profession continues to fall back on the standard rhetoric about "protecting the public" from incompetent providers, even in the absence of systematic evidence that the quality of routine services delivered by nonlawyers is substantially below that delivered by lawyers. While lawyers can provide anecdotal evidence of errors by nonlawyers, professional disciplinary bodies can provide similar evidence of errors by lawyers. There is no evidence that the presence of a disciplinary body actually reduces the number of errors of legal ser-vice providers.

A recent detailed study of legal advocacy in four

settings in which lawyers and nonlawyers regularly appear examined the likelihood of success of various types of advocates, observed advocates at work in a variety of types of hearings, and interviewed advocates, adjudicators, and clients.[3] This systematic research makes it clear that nonlawyers can be effective advocates and, in some situations, better advocates than licensed attorneys. The assertions by members of the legal profession that the public is protected when only licensed attorneys provide legal services is not supported by what happens when specialized nonlawyers are permitted to represent clients.

Toward nonlawyer practice

Does this mean that anyone should be permitted to offer legal services? Some countries allow anyone to do exactly this, subject to very specific exclusions. In England, for example, one of the biggest providers of legal advice is the Citizens' Advice Bureau. The CABs are locally funded dispensers of a wide range of advice, much of which would, at least in the United States, be labeled legal advice. In fact, while the managers of CABs are usually salaried employees, trained volunteers handle most of the actual client contacts, with professionals (including volunteer solicitors) often available for backup or more specialized advice. The issue of unauthorized practice of law is not relevant, because anyone in England may dispense legal advice or assist with a claim pursued outside the courts.

Research shows that formal legal training is only one path to the skills and knowledge necessary for competent legal assistance and representation. The image of legal services still revolves around the general practitioner who is there to help individuals with the full range of legal needs. If, however, one thinks of legal practice in terms of specialized areas rather than as general practice, it is clear that a person can acquire specialized representational competency, both in terms of the legal substance and the legal process/procedures, through a variety of avenues. Furthermore, traditional legal training in the United States equips a person with only some parts of this competency, and that training primarily serves to prepare the practitioner to acquire specialized competency.

Specialized experience and training other than law school can probably be as effective in preparing a person to provide representation in a narrow, specific area. For many contexts, such as unemployment compensation, social security disability, tax appeals, and labor grievance arbitration, the key to effective representation is the combination of three types of expertise: knowledge about the substance of the area, an understanding of the procedures used, and familiarity with the other regular players in the process. The latter can come only with experience, but the first two (substantive and procedural expertise) could be imparted through one-year, specialized training programs for paralegals, legal technicians, and licensed advocates. The expertise necessary to handle specialized proceedings or tasks can also be acquired experientially, either through an apprentice-like process or by parallel experience.

Error and redress

Defenders of restrictions raise two questions about the idea of opening up specialized legal services to nonlawyers: Would the nonlawyers be more prone to error than are lawyers? In what ways should the non-lawyers be regulated, particularly with regard to recourse for dissatisfied clients?

In discussing nonlawyer practice, lawyers tell of such experiences as a client who had first gone to a nonlawyer who made errors the lawyer now had to clean up. The assumption is that a lawyer would not have made such mistakes. Interestingly, we know almost nothing about the frequency of "legal error," a term that parallels the idea of "medical error."

How frequent is error in the provision of legal services? The answer is simply unknown. One might speculate that in comparing three groups— nonlawyer specialists, lawyer specialists, and law-

yer generalists—the latter would be the most likely to make an error. If this speculation is correct, then the logic of excluding nonlawyers (assuming their error rate is higher than that for lawyer specialists) would also dictate allowing only lawyer specialists to handle matters within their area of specialization.

How might nonlawyer practitioners be regulated to provide redress for dissatisfied consumers? Can the regulation of lawyers provide a model for regulating nonlawyers? There are three separate mechanisms currently used to regulate lawyers:[4]

• Institutional controls, in which institutional forums within which the lawyers work take some responsibility for uncovering and sanctioning lawyer misconduct (in the federal courts this is exemplified by Rule 11 sanctions for filing frivolous cases, unsupported claims, and motions);

• Liability controls, in which disgruntled clients can seek compensation by bringing a claim for professional malpractice; and

• Disciplinary controls, in which independent agencies (often a part of the state bar) investigate and prosecute violations of rules of professional conduct (with the final disciplinary authority typically resting with the state supreme court).

All three of these are currently or potentially applicable to nonlaw-yer advocates.

Institutional controls

Many agencies already have the power to regulate both lawyers and nonlawyers who appear before them. For example, many federal administrative agencies, including the Social Security Administration, have broad latitude to regulate advocates (both in permitting nonlawyers to appear and in disciplining advocates who appear before them). State agencies often have similar powers. At least one state agency in Wisconsin, which handles appeals concerning unemployment compensation, has disciplinary powers in this sense. Another example of a state agency with extensive licensing and disciplinary powers is the New York State Workers' Compensation Board, which has procedures for examining, licensing, and disciplining nonlawyers who appear in its proceedings.

The experience of agencies with disciplinary power is interesting. The Wisconsin Unemployment Compensation Bureau's administrative rules were put into place years ago because of problems with one nonlawyer advocate, but no one at the bureau could recall the rules actually being invoked to discipline an advocate. The Social Security Administration initiates "only a few dozen cases each year,"[5] and there is no indication that there are more problems with nonlawyers than with lawyers. As of the mid-1980s nonlawyers constituted 16.5 percent of those registered to practice before the Trademark and Patent Office, and about one-sixth of the disciplinary matters initiated during that period pertained to nonlawyer practitioners.[6]

The New York State Workers' Compensation Board, whose procedures require nonlawyers to pass an examination covering workers' compensation law and procedures before being allowed to appear as representatives, initiates disciplinary proceedings against few nonlawyers. One official noted that there are probably more complaints about nonspecialist lawyers than about nonlawyers who have passed the board's examination. Thus, where there is experience with institutional regulation, there is no evidence that it is used disproportionately to discipline nonlawyers.

Liability controls

In principle, liability controls ought to be available in any venue for any type of representative, on simple consumer-protection grounds. In the same way that one would have recourse against a plumber who made a faulty repair that led to substantial expense, one could seek damages against an advocate who failed to provide competent services. The dilemma is that of standards against which to measure performance, but this is also a problem in legal malpractice because of the difficulty in separating performance of the advocate from the outcome of the matter. Obvious things, such as missing filing deadlines and the like, can be applied just as easily to nonlawyer advocates as to lawyer advocates.

The major reason that liability controls are not frequently used with regard to nonlawyers (except, perhaps, for accountants) is the question of available sources of compensation for damages. Lawyers (and many other professionals) typically carry professional liability insurance. In fact, many states require at least some types of service providers to carry insurance or to be bonded, although only one state—Oregon—requires that lawyers carry liability insurance.

Licensing often provides a mechanism for enforcing an insurance requirement. (In fact, this may well be the most important aspect of some licensing systems.) Devising some type of licensing system for nonlawyer advocates who offer their services to the public could be justified on the grounds of providing an insurance mechanism (but this would probably also require imposing an insurance requirement on attorneys). With an insurance mechanism in place covering the work of nonlawyer advocates, there is no reason that the liability system would work any less well for nonlawyers than it currently does for lawyers.

Disciplinary controls

The last mechanism, disciplinary controls, goes hand-in-hand with licensing. Here, however, the licensing authority assumes responsibility for discipline, while the liability system relies entirely upon the dissatisfied client. The central component of this system is some mechanism for identifying possible problems, investigating and prosecuting problems, and imposing disciplinary sanctions upon proof that the problems are real. As with the liability mechanism, disciplinary controls rely on the existence of some type of standards. For most professions and occupations subject to licensing and regulation, executive agencies of the various states handle the licensing and disciplinary process. In most states, the state supreme court oversees the licensing of legal professionals because they are deemed to be "officers of the court."

There are a variety of ways to organize the licensing and disciplining of nonlawyer advocates, either through some central agency or through venue-specific offices. One might complain that such mechanisms would be costly for the public, but there is no reason that the license fees could not be set at a level that covers the cost of administration. Nonlawyer advocates might object to bearing this cost on the ground that it would make their costs of practice so high that they could not compete with lawyers. If this is true, it in effect means that their current costs fail to reflect the "real costs" of their practice, because it does not take into account the need to protect clients from unethical behavior or to compensate clients for practitioner errors.

The politics of change

The need to regulate and control nonlawyer advocates is real; it is also feasible. The same types of mechanisms and protections for clients available with regard to legal professionals would work (and in some settings already exist) for nonlawyer advocates. The failure of these mechanisms to be further developed reflects the relatively small stakes involved in large numbers of cases, the absence of apparent and recurring problems with nonlawyer advocates, and continuing unwillingness of the legal profession to accept and deal with the reality of nonlawyer practice. The latter of these may be the most important: the continued focus on the idea that the work of nonlawyer advocates represents the unauthorized practice of law results in the pursuit of traditional responses (i.e., seeking to suppress such work), rather than systematically investigating the nature of problems created by such activities and designing mechanisms to regulate the providers and protect their clients.

Beginning in the late 1980s, various groups within the legal profession have considered nonlawyer practice. In California, bar committees studied the problems and potential of nonlawyer provision of legal services. Those committees generally concluded it is time to recognize both that such practice exists and that it should, and probably will, expand.

The response to these reports from the bar associations that spawned them have generally been hostile. In California, when the Commission on Legal Technicians developed proposals that would permit limited practice by nonlawyers and provide for the regulation of those practitioners, segments of the bar succeeded in blocking the proposals both before the bar and in the legislature.

In 1994 the American Bar Association Commission on Nonlawyer Practice published a document summarizing its findings that nonlawyer practice was already widespread and that there was no support for the traditional contention that such practice resulted in widespread abuse.[7] In response, and in anticipation of a formal report and recommendation, ABA members hostile to the direction the commission was moving mobilized in opposition. The National Caucus of State Bar Associations adopted a resolution against any plan that would permit legal technicians to offer their services to the public.[8]

The commission's final recommendations recognize the current reality, but refrain from strongly advocating major extensions of that reality, with one exception. The commission apparently was impressed that nonlawyer practice permitted under the federal Administrative Procedures Act had shown that nonlawyers could effectively practice in administrative agencies. This seems to have led to their recommendation that state administrative agencies be similarly opened to nonlawyer practice. Beyond this, the commission stated that nonlawyers could be effective, but recommended no action other than that the states take an "analytical approach" in considering whether to extend rights of nonlawyer practice and how to regulate that practice. Despite calls that the ABA act upon and adopt the commission's recommendations,[9] no action has been taken, and none appears contemplated. The commission's recommendations are quickly being forgotten.

*****

The research on which this essay is based produced findings that are consistent with those reported by the commission. Both the research and the commission's findings make it clear that it is time to abandon the existing rules regarding "unauthorized practice of law." It is time instead to consider the nature of legal services in an age of specialized tasks and specialized training. All providers of legal services should be subject to appropriate regulation and discipline. Within the proper framework, the public can be well served by nonlawyer providers. Consumers of legal services, from whatever source, must have suitable recourse should the services fall below some established standard. In this regard, nonlawyer providers are no different from members of the legal profession.

NOTES

This article originally appeared in Volume 81, Number 3, November–December 1997, pages 100-103.

1. Quoted in Nonlawyer Practice in the United States: Summary of the Factual Record Before the American Bar Association Commission on Nonlawyer Practice, discussion draft for comment (Chicago: American Bar Association, April 1994), A.TX-2.

2. *See* Abel, American Lawyers (New York: Oxford University Press, 1989).

3. The details appear in Kritzer, Legal Advocacy: Lawyers and Nonlawyers at Work (forthcoming, 1998).

4. Wilkins, *Who Should Regulate Lawyers?*, 105 Harv. L. Rev. 801-887 (1992).

5. *See* Wolf, *Nonlawyer Practice Before the Social Security Administration*, 37 Admin. L. Rev. 415 (1985).

6. Quigg, *Nonlawyer Practice Before the Patent and Trademark Office*, 37 Admin. L. Rev. 410 (1985).

7. *See supra* n. 1, at A.CA-8f.

8. *See* France, *Bar Chiefs Protect the Guild*, National Law Journal, August 7, 1995, at 28.

9. *See* Rhode, *Meet Needs with Nonlawyers: It Is Time to Accept Lay Practitioners—and Regulate Them,* ABA Journal, January 1996, at 82.

Recommendations of the ABA Commission on Nonlawyer Practice

• The range of activities of traditional paralegals should be expanded, with lawyers remaining accountable for their activities.

• States should consider allowing nonlawyer representation of individuals in state administrative agency proceedings. Nonlawyers should be subject to the agencies' standards of practice and discipline.

• The activities of nonlawyers who provide assistance, advice, and representation authorized by statute, court rule, or agency regulation should be continued, subject to review by the entity under whose authority the services are performed.

• With regard to the activities of all other nonlawyers, states should adopt an analytical approach in assessing whether and how to regulate varied forms of nonlawyer activity that exist or are emerging in their respective jurisdictions. Criteria for this analysis should include the risk of harm these activities present, whether consumers can evaluate providers' qualifications, and whether the net effect of regulating the activities will be a benefit to the public. State supreme courts should take the lead in examining specific nonlawyer activities within their jurisdictions with the active support and participation of the bar and public.

• The American Bar Association, state, local, and specialty bar associations, the practicing bar, courts, law schools, and the federal and state governments should continue to develop and finance new and improved ways to provide access to justice to help the public meet its legal and law-related needs.

• The American Bar Association should examine its ethical rules, policies and standards to ensure that they promote the delivery of affordable competent services and access to justice.

How are courts handling pro se litigants?

Litigation by people who represent themselves is a growing phenomenon that presents a variety of challenges to court staff and judges.

by Jona Goldschmidt

Pro se litigation (litigation by self-represented persons) is a growing phenomenon in American courts about which we know very little. Judges and court staff in general jurisdiction courts, accustomed to an adversarial procedure in which every litigant is represented by counsel, must now cope with growing numbers of unrepresented individuals who have little or no knowledge of legal substance or procedural requirements. As their presence in court increases, self-represented litigants are making increased demands for services from court staff, and the types of legal cases in which they appear are expanding.

The extent of the phenomenon

To learn more about the phenomenon of pro se litigation, the American Judicature Society and the Justice Management Institute, with funding from the State Justice Institute, conducted a national survey of judges and court managers. The survey collected information regarding attitudes of judges about pro se litigants, existing pro se assistance programs, policies regarding court staff assistance, and strategies judges use to handle self-represented litigants.

Previous data on the extent of pro se litigation indicate it is prevalent in certain types of cases. For example, a 1990 study for the American Bar Association of the domestic relations court in Maricopa County (Phoenix), Arizona, found that in 88 percent of these cases one party appeared pro se, and in 52 percent both parties appeared pro se. A study conducted by the National Center for State Courts of case data from 16 large urban trial courts during 1991 to 1992 found that, for all domestic rela-

tions cases, one party appeared pro se in 53 percent of the cases, and both parties appeared pro se in 18 percent of the cases. In contested domestic relations cases, one party appeared pro se in 19 percent of the cases, and both parties appeared pro se in 7 percent of the cases. The courts reported ranges from between 0 to 15 percent in which one party appeared pro se in general civil litigation. In tort cases, an average of 3 percent of the cases involved at least one self-represented litigant.

A report from the State Bar of California based on 1991 and 1995 data indicates that in California one party appeared pro se in 67 percent of all domestic relations cases and in 40 percent of all child custody cases. Courts reported a range of 10 to 53 percent for the proportion of pro se litigants in divorce cases. A 1996 report from the Circuit Court of Cook County (Chicago), Illinois, states that 30 percent of all new civil actions for less than $10,000 damages in 1994 were filed pro se, and that 28 percent of litigants in forcible entry and detainer cases appeared pro se. A report by the Minnesota Conference of Chief Judges acknowledged "the increased number of pro se litigants" in that state.

The Federal Judicial Center, in a study of data from 10 U.S. district courts during 1991 to 1994, reports that 21 percent of all filings were by pro se litigants. Nonprisoner pro se cases constituted 37 percent of all cases filed. Data from the Administrative Office of the U.S. Courts show that, between 1991 and 1993, the number of pro se litigants in the federal courts of appeals increased by 49 percent. In 1993, pro se appeals constituted 37 percent of all open and closed cases.

Previous writings

The literature regarding pro se litigation consists primarily of commentaries in law reviews, judicial journals, and bar journals. The popular press is also increasingly aware of the new challenge of pro se litigation.

Early writings merely focused on the benefits of procedures such as small claims courts, "where the little man has his day" in court, as one 1977 *Judicature* article's subtitle notes. The late 1980s, however, spawned a series of law review commentaries touching upon legal issues affecting the processing of cases involving pro se litigants. One commentator argued that the right to be heard in federal and state courts has little value to those who lack the knowledge to exercise their right in a meaningful or skillful way: "Provision of counsel need not be the only solution to the pro se litigant's dilemma: Lawyers and paralegals can assist the pro se litigant by educating her about her legal situation."[1] She recommended classroom instruction to "help the pro se litigant understand and effectively present her legal position in court."

Arguments for a greater recognition of the constitutional dimensions of pro se litigation, insofar as a "meaningful hearing" is required by the due process clause, have also been made.[2] Some commentaries focus on specific litigation contexts in which unfairness to self-represented litigants has been found, such as the granting of a summary judgment motion against a pro se plaintiff who is unaware of the obligation to respond to such motions.[3]

More recently, the popular press's attention has been drawn to the subject. *The Wall Street Journal* noted that pro se litigant "numbers are exploding.... As these hordes of non-lawyers stumble along, they clog systems that aren't designed to accommodate amateurs, creating a host of new challenges for court administrators."[4]

Judges and attorneys have also begun to acknowledge the reality of the situation and are struggling to address it within the existing boundaries of the adversary process. Some courts and bar associations have begun to address pro se litigation by forming task forces or committees consisting of representatives from the bench and bar. They have issued reports reflecting a sense of urgency regarding the pro se phenomenon.

This review of the literature would be incomplete without references to materials contained on the Internet. A search using the term "pro se" reveals some interesting items. For example, it appears pro ses are establishing their own organizations. The "Utopia Foundation" publishes a "Texas Pro Se's Creed" (an oath describing the pro se's obligations to "our legal system," "to him/herself," "to opposing counsel," and the "judge"), a long diatribe against attorneys, and materials from Texas law governing domestic relations cases. This and other sites, such as the American Pro Se Association, appear to have been developed by disgruntled litigants. There are also commercial sites, such as the one advertising "The Video Library for Self Litigation" ("You Can Be A Pro Se Litigant" for only $79), and sites that sell legal forms. In addition, courts and law schools, such as the Superior Court of Arizona in Maricopa County and the University of Maryland School of Law, are using the Internet to assist pro se litigants with court forms and other information.

Treatment of pro se litigants

Until recently, the U.S. Supreme Court's 1972 decision in *Haines v. Kerner*[5] was the only case that addressed the question of the extent of leniency that should be granted to a civil pro se litigant. *Haines* held that, in the case of a pro se prisoner, a complaint must be held "to less stringent standards than formal pleadings drafted by lawyers." Subsequently, the issue arose whether nonprisoner pro se litigants who had erred procedurally could also benefit from some liberality to excuse their oversight or ignorance of procedural rules not involving pleadings. Some of these cases arose in the context of summary judgment motions, in which the pro se litigant had not submitted a timely response to such a motion. While some courts found such noncompliance should be excused and held the court is required to instruct the pro se regarding the duty to respond, others have held to the contrary, limiting such rules to prisoner pro ses.[6]

Some courts in civil cases quote the following passage from 1984's *McKaskle v. Wiggins*, in which the Supreme Court refused to relieve a criminal defendant of his obligation to follow all applicable procedural and evidentiary rules: "A defendant does not have a constitutional right to receive personal instruction from the trial judge on courtroom procedure. Nor does the Constitution require judges to take over chores for a pro se defendant that would normally be attended to by trained counsel as a matter of course."[7] Judges are naturally concerned that if they unduly aid a pro se litigant they may be perceived as being an advocate for that litigant.

Although there are some exceptions, the general rule in the state case law is that pro se litigants are bound by the same procedural and evidentiary rules as are those with representation. For example, one court held:

A pro se litigant must comply with the rules and orders of the court, enjoying no greater rights than those who employ counsel.... Although pro se pleadings are viewed with tolerance..., a pro se litigant, having chosen to represent himself, is held to the same standard of conduct and compliance with court rules, procedures, and orders as are members of the bar.... [a party's] pro se status does not require us or the trial court to assume he must be led by the hand through every step of the proceeding he initiated.[8]

If, however, procedural errors arise that "threaten to impinge upon the substantive legal rights of others, whether committed by seasoned counsel or pro se litigants, the court is compelled to act to prevent injustice."[9]

Some courts, however, extend the principle of leniency announced for review of pro se pleadings in *Haines v. Kerner* to compliance with procedural rules. For example, one court held, "Once a pro se litigant has done everything possible to bring his action, he should not be penalized by strict rules which might otherwise apply if he were represented by counsel."[10] Other courts have held that failure to adhere to technical rules of procedure should be ignored to ensure that claims made by pro se litigants are given "fair and meaningful consideration."[11] Judge Posner has written, "It is unfair to deny a litigant a lawyer and then trip him up on technicalities."[12] And, as one court stated, "Courts will go to particular pains to protect pro se litigants against the consequences of technical errors if injustice would otherwise result."[13] For example, the sanction of dismissal cannot be exercised lightly with pro ses.[14]

Only one state supreme court apparently commended a trial judge for his conduct in "relax[ing] the rules of evidence and mak[ing] a special effort to facilitate the [pro se] plaintiff's presentation of his case."[15] In that case, the court followed a recommendation of an American Bar Association committee in declining to set any firm parameters regarding how far a judge should go to assist a pro se litigant:

The court is confronted by an especially difficult task when one of the litigants chooses to represent himself. The court's essential function to serve as an impartial referee comes into direct conflict with the concomitant necessity that the pro se litigant's case be fully and completely presented.

The proper scope of the court's responsibility [to a pro se litigant] is necessarily an expression of careful exercise of judicial discretion and cannot be fully described by a specific formula.[16]

A recent judicial ethics opinion addresses the issue of whether a judge may assist a pro se litigant in the context of a nonadversarial case. The Indiana Commission on Judicial Qualifications noted that judges often preside over cases such as default divorces or name changes in which a pro se litigant has not complied with a technical requirement of pleading or proof (for example, failure to allege and prove the county of residence, or that the name change petition is not brought for a fraudulent purpose). Some judges, the commission found, take an "unnecessarily strict" approach to these deficiencies. The commission held that a judge in such cases "violates the Code [of Judicial Conduct] by refusing to make any effort to help that litigant along, instead choosing to deny the litigant's request for relief.... Neither the interests of the court nor of the litigant are served by rejecting the petition on the basis of this type of deficiency.... A judge should make inquiry of the parties to establish this element of their petition, and proceed appropriately, rather than deny the petition and excuse the parties from the courtroom on the basis of their omission."

The latter opinion, it is hoped, will be a harbinger of a new perspective on the need to balance the judicial duty to provide a meaningful opportunity to be heard for all litigants with the obligation to maintain impartiality. Judges would benefit from further guidance of this nature from other judicial conduct organizations.

The judiciary's challenge

The challenges for courts presented by pro se litigation are well known. As non-lawyers, pro se litigants obviously have no knowledge of relevant procedural and evidentiary rules, and they are unaware of the necessary substantive elements of legal causes of action (or criminal defenses). The American Judicature Society/Justice Management

Institute survey asked judges whether they handled pro se cases in which one party was represented differently from those in which both parties appeared pro se. Many of the judges cited the ethical duty of maintaining judicial impartiality as the primary problem in cases where one party appears pro se. According to one judge, "Pro se litigants feel they are not being treated fairly if they are required to comply with rules of procedure with which they are not familiar. On the other hand, they are perceived as having an advantage if the procedural rules are not strictly enforced as they are against counseled parties." Judges struggle with the question, "How much should I help the pro se litigant to completely present his case?" At the same time, some judges are concerned with the obvious power and knowledge imbalance between a self-represented litigant and his or her attorney adversary. As one judge put it, "The lack of ability of the pro se requires the judge to be certain that the lawyer does not take advantage of the pro se, and still remain neutral."

Many judges make an effort to deter litigants from proceeding pro se. They draw a variety of analogies from other occupations when making their plea: "I tell them they have the same right to represent themselves in court as I have to the handling of my personal plumbing problems, i.e., I don't, they shouldn't." Another cautions pro se litigants that "doing your own legal work is like doing your own mechanic work. Most of us could do it if we had the time and the patience. But, you need to recognize that if it still doesn't run, you have to look at who did the work." Another judge asks pro se litigants, "Would a person elect to perform major medical surgery on themselves? Likewise, most pro se litigants should not be representing themselves."

Some judges have experienced some agonizing moments during the course of trials where one party is represented and one is pro se. One judge cited as problematic, "My own discomfort when it appears a different legal result could (likely would) occur if the pro se party took appropriate action." Another stated, "The principal problem is the unfairness of a pro se party who is not familiar with the law facing an adversary situation against an attorney. Usually [I] offer a continuance to allow [the] pro se party to obtain counsel."

The judges also commented on the feelings they perceived on the part of the pro se litigants. One observed that the "pro se person has [a] feeling of isolation—require[s] time to dispel," while another noted a "sense of unfairness, helplessness and futility by the pro se." One judge said that "the pro se feels the system is fixed." Another explained, "The overwhelming greatest problem is the inability of most pro se litigants to comply with the rules of evidence, which leads to a failure of proof in most cases, and an embittered pro se litigant." The perception of "the unrepresented party [is that] the court will come to his/her aid in prosecuting the case. Of course, this is not really true. This causes difficulty."

Some judges expressed concern regarding the conduct of attorneys toward pro se litigants. One judge was concerned with "the attorney attempting to take control, and overkill by the attorney. This is usually with younger lawyers." Another remarked that "attorneys want to assert technical objections at bench trials. The pro se litigant doesn't understand the objection. I spend time trying to explain why I cannot admit pro se's evidence so as not to appear that the court is a railroad. Attorneys get impatient and act as if the court is trying to represent the pro se—which I am not trying to do—but I want the pro se to feel they got a fair trial and the attorney too."

Attorneys are not, however, always trying to take advantage of the pro se litigant. There are times when pressing one's advantage may be counterproductive. As one judge observed, "Counsel for the opposing party often feels reluctant to press his/her advantage, especially in front of a jury, because it looks bad."

Surprisingly, some judges feel the rules of evidence become more of a hindrance in certain cases, as do the attorneys themselves. Several judges suggested a "need to relax the rules so that justice can be done." Sometimes, "the lawyer whines and complains that the other side doesn't follow the rules. That is true to a point, but the rule often gets in the way of the truth." One judge explained, "It's amazing how much evidence can be presented without attorneys. Much more effective. Lawyers try to hide evidence much of the time."

Where both parties appear pro se, some judges said the problems "just doubled." Others, in contrast, believe that this situation is "actually easier." As one judge put it, "I can ask questions of each sides' witnesses and conduct proceedings less formally and still get at the evidence so as to be able to make a fair ruling." Another observed: "When all the parties are pro se, I find it easier to resolve. We can usually handle domestic relations issues informally. The parties are usually willing to work it out."

Some judges mentioned the problems of the court having to do all the research for the parties, the time that is necessary to teach the parties court procedures, and the difficulty of controlling litigants. The latter includes keeping parties in some cases from getting into arguments. ("Emotions sometimes get out of hand.") These proceedings, as one judge wrote, "are very difficult to control. Also, it is difficult to shape the issues without acting as an attorney for either side and risk losing impartiality. These hearings tend to take longer and be more emotional." Sometimes judges are faced with the problem of "keeping the parties from getting into arguments with the witness such as calling the witness a liar." In addition, some cases are more volitile than others: "The potential for violence rises when lawyers are not present in domestic cases and spousal abuse cases."

Judges occasionally must deal with what they characterize as a "pest," a "nut," or a "kook." Some of these might be "frequent filers," or the self-described "constitutionalists." The latter are litigants who often have a militia-oriented, right-wing political agenda that includes non-recognition of the court's jurisdiction. Some of these individuals have gone so far as to establish their own "common law courts." Others often delay court proceedings with non-meritorious claims and contentions, or "irrelevant and incomprehensible positions," and some have been known to file suits or liens against judges who ruled against them.

The judges' suggestions reflect the seriousness with which they are taking these litigants. Their suggestions include: (1) have the sheriff present, "who is ready to place the obstructionist in jail"; (2) clear explanations as to when the contempt power will be utilized; (3) use of "extreme patience"; (4) "give them enough time to 'vent' and then politely, but firmly, shut them off"; (5) "keep them focused on the issues in the case and away from political issues"; (6) rule on the "barrage of motions brought"; (7) provide extra time for their trials; (8) "address each issue raised, no matter how farfetched"; (9) "Get the guns before they get into the courtroom"; and (10) "always take the matters under advisement, and then promptly rule by written order."

Handling pro ses

Given these responses, it was not surprising to learn from 91 percent of the judges that their courts had no general policy addressing the manner in which pro se litigants should be handled in the courtroom or in the litigation process generally. When asked to describe their individual policies, their responses fell into the following categories reflecting traditional, liberal, and reform philosophies toward pro se litigants:

• I do not give them legal advice or act as their attorney; I enforce the rules of procedure and evidence and give them no preferences; I give them cautionary admonitions regarding the necessity of legal counsel.

• I generally follow the rules of procedure or evidence, but the "reality" of the situation is such that I relax some rules in certain cases in order to do justice.

• I treat all litigants fairly and impartially. In order to ensure a fair hearing for all parties, I assist pro se litigants with the presentation of their claim or defense, and "protect" the pro se litigant who is being taken advantage of by an attorney.

As to handling pro se litigants during trial, many judges said they briefly explain trial procedures to self-represented litigants before the hearing, including the manner of presentation of evidence, the hearsay rule, marking exhibits, and other procedural matters. Some provide this explanation a week or more before trial. Other judges' policy is to presumptively admit all evidence, subject to stated objections. Judges themselves sometimes raise objections.

To take testimony, some judges ask questions of the witnesses themselves. One judge swears in both pro se parties and asks questions of each, "sometimes at the same time." Another judicial strategy is "nudging them along by asking if they want 'x' to be admitted." One judge described his procedure as follows: "If the pro se litigant testifies, I have him/her make a statement and dispense with questions and answers." Still others take a firmer approach: "I expect the rules of evidence will be enforced. I point out to the litigant that the rules must be the same for each side. Retain counsel or suffer the consequences."

The responses discussed to this point are interesting in that they denote a clear lack of unifor-

Table 1   Types of questions pro se litigants pose to court staff

	%
Requests for appropriate court forms	39
Requests for information regarding legal remedies	28
Logistical questions (e.g., directions)	27
Requests for assistance in filling out forms	3
Other requests	3

Table 2   Areas of law inquired about by pro se litigants

	%
Domestic relations	59
Traffic	12
Prisoner/civil rights	9
Small claims	8
Criminal	7
Post-trial/appeal	3
Landlord-tenant	1
Probate	1

mity across courts and judges with respect to the handling of pro se litigants, raising questions about the consistency and quality of justice administered to them. Some judges are truly sensitive to the "pro se's dilemma" and acknowledge the need to provide access to the court for the self-represented: "Most people need the courts for the ordinary things of life (adoption, divorce, child custody, minor civil damages, minor disputes, etc.). The courts should be able to help them without the necessity of expending large sums of money on attorneys' fees and still not being satisfied with the process." According to one judge, "Most of the pro se litigants have been honest and well-intentioned people who cannot afford an attorney. We should simplify our procedures in virtually all cases." Another progressive view was expressed by the judge who wrote: "From the outset they must be accorded respect and a fair opportunity to be heard. Judges and court staff must not treat them as though they are a nuisance and a waste of time. Pro ses deserve the same courteous, prompt, and fair service as those represented by the finest counsel." Or, as one judge succinctly put it, pro se litigants are "the symptoms of a lack of access to justice, the seeds of future revolution."

In addition to these progressive views, the judges' survey revealed some contrary, negative attitudes toward self-represented litigants. For example, when asked for their view regarding the "ideal" pro se assistance program, several judges expressed the view of one who said such programs would "open the floodgates and attorneys would revolt." Another stated that "we have already ad-

dressed the pro se litigants as far as possible." Other judges also feared that "soon virtually every litigant would seek to be included in it." If "too much attention" is given to pro se litigation, wrote one judge, "there will be a tremendous increase in pro se litigation, much of which will be by non-indigent parties."

Some judges went beyond the "floodgates" argument, evidencing a genuine anti-pro se litigant sentiment. One judge flatly objects to "babysitting the pro ses." Another bluntly stated: "No one likes pro se litigants—the jury does not have much sympathy for them at all—they put a real burden on the court staff, especially the clerk post verdict. They tend to think they are 'unique' and frequently call and pester staff long after the case is concluded."

As to whether specific rules should be developed for pro se litigation, one judge cautioned: "I would not suggest any rule changes which would only encourage more pro se activity and the added burdens attached thereto." One judge must have interpreted the question asking for suggestions for rule changes "relating to pro se litigation" as including a rule restricting it somehow: "I could not establish rules to eliminate pro se [litigation] until the problem is eradicated—that is, until a program is instituted to provide competent, legal assistance for those who cannot pay for counsel. Then if the reason for pro se representation is simply refusal to hire a lawyer despite his/her ability to pay on a sliding scale—I would make a rule outlawing pro se representation." The attitude of some judges frustrated with pro se litigants may be reflected by the comment, "I would do away with pro se representation altogether." The attitude of one judge is so negative that he even finds disturbing what pro se litigants do after leaving the courthouse: "Pro se litigants are an increasing problem because they get the ear of the media who then report inaccurate information that makes the judiciary look bad."

Court managers' views

The court managers surveyed were from a wide range of courts and jurisdictions. For the five years prior to administration of the survey, they observed, the overall proportion of pro se litigants increased either greatly (45 percent) or moderately (39 percent). Only 13 percent believe pro se litigation stayed about the same during that time, and only 2 percent believe it has decreased. Despite the dramatic growth of such litigation, only 23 percent of the court managers surveyed currently collect data on it in their court.

The growth of pro se litigation directly affects court staff functions. Traditionally, court staff are reluctant to answer many questions about litigation posed by pro se litigants due to the specter of an unauthorized practice of law charge. Only about half of the court managers' courts have a policy to guide court staff in rendering assistance to the public. Of those, only 38 percent are in writing. It appears that courts have done little by way of policy and training of court staff in anticipation of the rising tide of pro se litigation.

When asked about the average daily proportion of their staff time that is devoted to providing pro se assistance, 66 percent of the responding court administrators said that this proportion was from 1 to 25 percent; 23 percent said that it was 26 to 50 percent; and 11 percent said it took up between 51 to 100 percent of their time. Table 1 presents the types of assistance most frequently sought from court staff.

Overwhelmingly, pro se litigants are requesting court forms for the matters they wish to bring to the court's attention. However, many of these litigants are seeking information about their legal rights and remedies, for which court clerks are undeniably not suited, and for which there may be no form. Additionally, it is interesting to note that (at least according to the court managers surveyed) few pro se litigants request assistance in filling out forms, and that these litigants are not asking for attorney referrals.

Table 2 lists the areas of law most commonly inquired about, according to the court administrators surveyed. It is not surprising that domestic relations is the area of law about which pro se litigants ask the most questions. Nor is it surprising that traffic, prisoner matters, and small claims follow. What is surprising is that, with the exception of some inquiries about landlord-tenant and probate, so few other civil law areas are represented in Table 2. We had anticipated that pro se litigants would be asking questions in many other civil law areas, including torts, contracts, and injunctions, given the anecdotal data regarding the growth of pro se litigation in general jurisdiction courts.

Services
Of the 98 responding court administrators, 44 (45 percent) have established some form of pro se assistance program or service. These programs take a variety of forms that go beyond the counter assistance described above. They can be broadly categorized as taking the following forms, all of which are—to varying degrees—designed to educate the pro se litigant, but which differ by the degree of comprehensiveness of the services provided:

Informational. This basic, low-cost form of assistance consists of instructional brochures, kits with instruction sheets and accompanying court forms, and videotape programs. Some courts, especially in the domestic relations area, provide such materials in "plain English," in a bilingual format, or both. The Denver District Court's Information and Referral Office is an example of this type of program. It provides packets of "user friendly" forms, paralegal assistance from court staff in filling out the forms, and a videotape program on "How to Handle a Divorce."

Technology. Some programs consist of the use of technological devices such as a computer kiosk or the Internet. Arizona was one of the first states to utilize a computer kiosk ("QuickCourt") that went beyond the early uses of such kiosks for paying traffic and parking tickets. QuickCourt consists of a touch-screen computer with accompanying (bilingual) audio instructions that walk a pro se litigant through the steps needed to produce pleadings in such case types as small claims, child support, and landlord-tenant. A user fee for some of the services supports the vendor's maintenance of the 25-kiosk system statewide.

Clinics. These programs instruct pro se litigants on court procedures and appropriate court forms through instructional sessions led by pro bono attorneys, law students, paralegals, or court staff. They generally focus on a specific case type, usually domestic relations. Some clinics, such as the Family Law Pro Per Clinic in Ventura, California, enhance their accessibility by conducting evening sessions. That program conducts weekly clinics for up to 75 litigants. The session includes an orientation regarding the operations of the family court, followed by instructions for filling out forms presented through the use of an overhead projector by an attorney hired by the court as a "family court facilitator." Those who need no individuaized assistance are directed to self-help binders that contain appropriate forms and further instructions, and are assisted by volunteer family law attorneys, law students, and paralegals. A court clerk is available to review and file completed pleadings, eliminating the need for another trip to the courthouse during the workday.

Self-service centers. The best example of this comprehenive approach to pro se assistance is the well-known Maricopa County (Phoenix) Self-Service Center. This program, initiated by a State Justice Institute grant, is a multilevel program that combines all of the features of the previously described programs. In addition, it includes a web site that contains court forms and instructions, an automated telephone information service, a data bank containing names of mediators as well as attorneys who have agreed to provide unbundled legal services (i.e., assistance in discrete tasks, such as petition drafting or consultation only, at a modest fee), and personalized assistance from pro bono attorneys on site at the courthouse. In addition to the grant startup funds, a partnership including the court and the state court administrator's office, the state and county bar associations, legal services, the county lawyer referral service, the business community, domestic violence advocacy groups, and others supports the program through additional funds and services

Most pro se assistance programs are targeted toward a particular population and case type. Fifty-five percent of the court managers reported that the predominant area of law for such programs was domestic relations, including divorce, child support, paternity, visitation, and domestic violence. Additional case types include small claims, probate (e.g., guardianship, conservatorship, etc.), landlord-tenant, traffic, criminal, and civil case appeals from limited jurisdiction court judgments.

The court administrators noted that they had considered other pro se assistance programs, but, due to various obstacles, these plans were abandoned. The following barriers to pro se assistance program development were reported: funding (25 percent); the bar (16 percent); lack of personnel, equipment, or space (13 percent); the bench (12 percent); the line between legal advice and procedural advice (11 percent); untrained staff or staff resistance (8 percent); internal problems or coordination (8 percent); the difficulty of satisfying the pro se litigant (4 percent); and language barriers (3 percent).

The court administrators reported that funding for pro se assistance programs came from the following sources: the court (35 percent), state government (20 percent), local government (16 percent), the bar (12 percent), and other sources (such as pro bono services, grants, federal funds, United Way) (17 percent). Management of the programs primarily rests with the court (68 percent), but includes the bar (12 percent), volunteers (5 percent), or some combination thereof (15 percent). Staffing for the programs is provided by the court (60 percent), the bar (15 percent), volunteers (10 percent), or a combination thereof (15 percent).

*****

Maintaining public confidence in the courts and the constitutional right to due process requires that all litigants, whether represented or appearing pro se, be afforded a meaningful opportunity to be heard. Courts must be accessible to those with the funds to hire counsel, those who have the means to do so but elect not to retain counsel, and those who cannot afford counsel. Just as correctional institutions are required to afford adequate legal assistance to prisoners seeking judicial remedies, so do courts have an obligation to provide adequate legal assistance—by way of information, at a minimum—to all litigants. This is not to argue for a guarantee of legal representation (a "civil *Gideon*"), as such, but rather for a multifaceted approach to the establishment of pro se assistance programs like those described for litigants with varying levels of literacy and skill.

The data gathered in this study evidence current judicial attitudes toward pro se litigants ranging from an acknowledgement of the courts' obligation to provide access to justice to firm opposition to any form of pro se litigation itself. The judges holding the latter view have forgotten Thomas Paine's observation that self-representation is a natural right. Nevertheless, judges, charged with providing pro se litigants meaningful hearings, need guidance to carry out the "meaningful hearing" obligation consistent with their ethical duty of impartiality. The difficulty of balancing these obligations will be lessened to the extent that out-of-court programs are established that educate pro se litigants to negotiate the labrynth of litigation, thus reducing the necessity for the proactive judicial assistance that many pro se litigants expect from the court.

NOTES

This article originally appeared in Volume 82, Number 1, July-August 1998, pages 13-22.

The complete report of the project on which this article is based is found in Goldschmidt, Mahoney, Solomon and Green, *Meeting the Challenge of Pro Se Litigation: A Report and Guidebook for Judges and Court Managers* (Chicago: American Judicature Society, 1998). It is available for $25 plus $5 postage and handling. To order, contact Rodney Wilson at 312-558-6900 x147.

1. Kim, *Legal Education for the Pro Se Litigant: A Step Towards a Meaningful Right To Be Heard*, 96 Yale L. J. 1641-1660 (1987).

2. Bradlow, *Procedural Due Process Rights of Pro Se Civil Litigants*, 55 U. Chi. L. Rev. 659-683 (1988).

3. McLaughlin, *An Extension of the Right of Access: The Pro Se Litigants' Right to Notification of the Requirements of the Summary Judgment Rule*, 55 Ford. L. Rev. 1109-1137 (1987).

4. Woo, *More People Represent Themselves in Court. But is Justice Served?*, Wall Street Journal 1, 7 (August 17, 1993).

5. 404 U.S. 519, 520, 92 S.Ct. 594, 595 (1972).

6. Courts must accord "special attention" to pro se litigants faced with summary judgment motions. Ham v. Smith, 653 F.2d 628 (D.C.Cir. 1981). At the very least, a litigant is entitled to be warned that when he is confronted by a summary judgment motion, he must obtain counter-affidavits or other evidentiary material to avoid the entry of judgment against him. Timms v. Frank, 953 F.2d 281 (7th Cir. 1992); Roseboro v. Garrison, 528 F.2d 309 (4th Cir. 1975); Hudson v. Hardy, 412 F.2d 1091 (D.C.Cir. 1968).

Some circuits have limited this rule to prisoners. Brock v. Hendershott, 840 F.2d 339 (6th Cir. 1988); Jacobsen v. Filler, 790 F.2d 1362 (9th Cir. 1986) ("[a] litigant who chooses himself as legal representative should be treated no differently" than one with counsel, and requiring notice to non-prisoners of Rule 56 requirements "implicates the court's impartiality and discriminates against opposing parties who do have counsel.") However, Timms, 953 F.2d at 285, held that "the attempted distinction between prisoners and other pro se litigants with regard to this issue is unconvincing.... [T]he idea that non-prisoners do not deserve notice because they have chosen to proceed pro se ignores the fact that most litigants who sue without a lawyer do so because they cannot afford one.... Indigent plaintiffs have no more 'freedom of choice' as to legal representation than do prisoners. Also, even though non-prisoner plaintiffs may often be more educated than prisoners, that is no guarantee that a layman will understand the effects of a failure to respond to a summary judgment motion."

7. 465 U.S. 168, 183-84 (1984). In another criminal case, a federal court held that "[t]he trial court is under no obligation to become an 'advocate' for or to assist and guide the pro se layman through the trial thicket." U.S. v. Pinkey, 548 F.2d 305, 311 (10th Cir. 1977). *See also*, Faretta v. California, 422 U.S. 806, 835, n. 46, 95 S.Ct. 2525, 2540, n. 46 (1975) ("the right of self-representation is not a license to abuse the dignity of the courtroom. Neither is it a license not to comply with relevant rules of procedural and substantive law").

8. Newsome v. Farer, 708 P.2d 327, 331 (NM. 1985).

9. Cassell v. Shellenberger, 514 A.2d 163 (PA 1986) (dismissal proper where complaint lacks factual basis).

10. Ortiz v. Cornetta, 867 F.2d 146, 147 (2d Cir. 1989).

11. Matzker v. Herr, 748 F.2d 1142, 1146 (7th Cir. 1984).

12. Merritt v. Faulkner, 697 F.2d 761 (7th Cir. 1983) (Posner, concurring and dissenting).

13. United States v. Sanchez, 88 F.3d 1243 (D.C. Cir 1996).

14. "There are of course a wide variety of other sanctions short of dismissal.... The [trial court], however, need not exhaust them all before finally dismissing a case. The exercise of his discretion to dismiss requires only that possible and meaningful alternatives be reasonably explored." Von Poppenheim v. Portland Boxing and Wrestling Comm., 442 F.2d 1047, 1053-54 (9th Cir. 1971), cert. denied, 92 S.Ct. 715 (1972), cited with approval in Newsome v. Farer, supra. Dismissal for noncompliance with rules permissible where parties have "neglected their cases" or for "refusal to obey court orders." Factors to be considered are: (1) degree of actual prejudice to adverse party; (2) degree of interference with judicial process by the noncompliance; and (3) the culpability of the pro se litigant. Green v. Dorrell, 969 F.2d 915 (9th Cir. 1992) (dismissal for noncompliance not appropriate where "the infringement of the local rule was a single, unintentional incident, making the sanction of dismissal inappropriately severe").

15. Austin v. Ellis, 119 N.H. 741, 743 (1979).

16. Citing ABA Standards, Comm. On Standards of Judicial Administration, Sec. 2.23, at 45-47 (1976).

The survey

The American Judicature Society and the Justice Management Institute conducted a national survey of judges and court administrators regarding pro se litigation. The judges' survey was sent by mail to 612 judges non-randomly chosen from among all state court judges at all levels of courts in urban, rural, and suburban jurisdictions. Of the surveys mailed, 133 (22 percent) were completed and returned. Another mailed survey was sent to a sample of 237 court administrators in all levels of state trial courts who are members of the National Association for Court Management. Of these, 98 (41 percent) were returned. Although the judges' survey was not randomly administered and therefore not generalizable to the population of all judges, it did provide compelling information about this new phenomenon, illuminating the issues facing judicial policy makers and court managers.

Policy recommendations

The following recommendations appear in further detail in *Meeting the Challenge of Pro Se Litigation: A Report and Guidebook for Judges and Court Managers.*

General recommendations

Courts should provide self-represented litigants with information and services to enable them to use the court.

Courts should study the composition and greatest needs of the self-represented litigants they serve, and design services to effectively meet those needs.

Development of programs to assist self-represented litigants should be a collaborative effort of the bench, court staff, the bar, and the public.

Courts, in conjunction with the bar, should establish policies to guide court staff in assisting self-represented litigants.

State court systems and local courts should train court staff on how to assist self-represented litigants.

Simplified court forms should be developed for cases involving self-represented litigants, and judges should have the authority to relax procedural and evidentiary rules when necessary to ensure fairness.

For judges

Judges should provide reasonable assistance to self-represented litigants in the courtroom.

Each state should establish judicial protocols to guide judges assisting self-represented litigants.

State court systems and national judicial education providers should develop educational programs for judges on methods of handling self-represented litigants.

For the bar

The legal profession should assist the court in developing pro se assistance programs.

Rules governing the unauthorized practice of law should take into consideration the necessary assistance provided by court staff to self-represented litigants.

The bar should enhance the delivery of pro bono and unbundled or limited legal services, especially in family law.

For legislatures and local governments

Court staff should be protected by qualified immunity for acts taken to assist self-represented litigants.

Court funding at the state and local levels should be provided to establish programs to assist self-represented litigants.

Judicial Policy Making and Judicial Independence in the United States

INTRODUCTION   Throughout this anthology we have presented selections that offer the reader a slice of the American judicial process through articles examining a single topic or facet of our legal system. In the first edition of *Judicial Politics*, the final section of readings consisted of the first two selections appearing here. They were intended to offer a broad perspective on judicial politics, and to consider the place of the judiciary in the context of the larger fabric of American democracy. While that emphasis remains a focal point in the concluding readings in the second edition, it is important to underscore that, in the context of the renewed controversies that have swirled around American judges in recent years, particularly the vocal condemnation from conservative quarters aimed at perceived judicial activism on the federal bench, we have expanded this section to include material on the issue of judicial independence.

We begin with "The federal courts since 1787: stability and change in 200 years," an edited transcript of a panel discussion among judges, academicians, and attorneys that examines the relationship of the federal courts, particularly the Supreme Court, with the other components of our governmental system in the light of two centuries of experience. Among the topics considered are judicial review, the appropriate scope of judicial authority, judicial activism, and judicial independence. The panel discussion is a lively and provocative one, bringing together many of the concerns addressed throughout this volume and setting the stage for the pieces to follow.

Following the panel discussion is Stephen Wasby's thoughtful exposition in "Arrogation of power or accountability: judicial imperialism revisited." At bottom, Wasby offers a response to the criticism that the judiciary has become an "imperial" branch of American government that too often intervenes in American life and policy formulation. In Wasby's view, judges exercise powers that have been granted to them legitimately, and they are publicly and governmentally accountable in many ways. Further, Wasby asserts, judges have the capacity to deal with policy matters and, indeed, perform comparatively well when held to the standard of other policy makers in our system.

The next three articles put a more contemporary face on many of the issues addressed in the panel discussion and Wasby's challenging essay. These include Jon Newman's documentation of "The Judge Baer controversy," Stephen Bright's condemnation of "Political attacks on the judiciary," and Edwin Meese III and Rhett DeHart's retort, "Reining in the federal judiciary."

Newman's contribution, written while he was serving as chief judge of the U.S. Court of Appeals for the Second Circuit, presents a dramatic chronology through primary source documents of the crisis for judicial independence created in 1996 when more than 200 members of Congress, unhappy with a decision by district court Judge Harold Baer, wrote to President Clinton urging him to call for the judge's resignation. The documents presented detail the "Baer controversy" from both sides and serve to demonstrate how the judiciary became embroiled in ongoing presidential electoral politics as an "issue" that needed to be dealt with by President Clinton and candidate Bob Dole. In addition, the Baer controversy was also a stage upon which Clinton's difficulties with a Congress controlled by his political adversaries could be played out. The unfolding of the Baer controversy, as told through Newman's commentary and the documents he presents, is both fascinating reading and a real-world reminder of the precarious balance that is so difficult to achieve between judicial independence and judicial accountability.

Bright's essay goes beyond the Baer case study offered by Newman to discuss multiple examples across time of how attacks on judicial independence occur as judges come under attack for making decisions that are politically unpopular. While criticism of judicial decisions may often be appropriate, political attacks posing under the banner of legitimate criticism can undermine judicial power. Bright demonstrates how the votes of judges and the statements made in their opinions can often be taken out of context and distorted by people whose interest and motivation lies not in developments in the law per se but, rather, in their own political agenda. As Bright notes, "[I]t is important to determine the difference between fair criticism of judges and intimidation.... It is irresponsible for critics of the courts to argue that only results matter without regard for the legal principles that govern judicial decision-making."

The counterpoint to Bright's advocacy of judicial independence is offered by Meese and DeHart who opine that the role of the courts is to interpret the law and not to make policy, a distinction that clearly would be lost on those who feel that in every interpretation of law policy is indeed being "made" with the real issue one of who benefits and who loses from the specific interpretation. The article sugests a number of concrete steps that a Congress and, indeed, a country bent on reining in judicial policy making, could take. These include explicit efforts to confirm only "nonactivist" judges, diminishing the power of the organized bar in the confirmation process, limiting federal court jurisdiction, and allowing states to act without Congress to amend the Constitution.

We close the anthology with Barry Friedman's analysis of why, in his view, attacks on the judiciary and judicial independence historically have been and ultimately are destined not to succeed. Friedman demonstrates that judges have been attacked for their decisions for more than 200 years and that such attacks are invariably politically driven and motivated and almost always lack popular support. Ultimately, for Friedman, a political attack can be defined as one where, "no matter what members of Congress or the executive branch have said about why they are threatening judicial independence, they are doing it because they do not like the way judges are deciding particular cases."

According to Friedman, the controls that are necessary to "rein in" the judiciary, to speak in the language of Meese and DeHart, are already part and parcel of the "ordinary" processes of American governance that are "working" as they are supposed to. Friedman points, for example, to the hierarchical structure of American courts and the normal consequences of appellate processes where aberrant decisions will be overturned as they work their way up through the judicial system. He also underscores the moderating tendencies of the appointment and confirmation processes that judges go through as well as the noted tendency for Supreme Court justices to not be out of step too far or in the long run from the American public.

Certainly the articles presented in this final section of readings are advocacy efforts in their tone and provocative in their content. While they cannot "solve" for the reader the critical dilemmas that they address, they do offer considerable food for thought and debate about the role of the courts in the American democracy, an appropriate place to both begin and end our consideration of judicial politics.

The federal courts since 1787: stability and change in 200 years

At the annual meeting of the American Judicature Society on August 8, 1987, in San Francisco, a panel examined the relationship of the federal courts, and especially the Supreme Court, to the other braZnches of government in light of 200 years of experience. Here is an edited transcript of their remarks. Although space did not permit publication of the full transcript, every effort has been made to avoid distorting the participants' views.

Justice Christine Durham: I'd like to share with you a little passage that I found recently in an old book that belonged to my father-in-law, who was a political scientist and a university president. In one of the old treatises I found this passage—it was written in 1912. "It is then the consciousness of the American people that law must rest upon justice and reason. But the Constitution is a more ultimate formulation of the fundamental principles of justice and reason . . . . And the judiciary is a better interpreter of those fundamental principles than the legislature. It is this consciousness which has given such authority to the interpretation of the Constitution by the Supreme Court. I would not hesitate to call the government system of the United States the aristocracy of the robe, and I do not hesitate to pronounce this the truest aristocracy for the purposes of government which the world has produced." I suspect that we're here today to discuss the aristocracy of the robe, and the truth thereof.

Professor A.E. Dick Howard: What I want to do this morning is to think about certain features of the American judicial landscape. I want to take the long view and speak primarily of those features of the landscape which appear as you stand back and look over 200 years of American judicial history, especially as fashioned through the eyes and by the hands of the U.S. Supreme Court.

One must begin where law professors always begin, with *Marbury v. Madison* and the principle of judicial review. Without the Supreme Court's power to strike down legislative acts they think unconstitutional, a great deal of the other landscape features would not really make much difference. The striking thing about judicial review is that the Constitution nowhere mentions that power of the courts. Nowhere, in my judgment, is it possible to read the debates in Philadelphia or any diaries, letters, or other documents that came out of that meeting, and make the persuasive case that the founders clearly intended for the Court to have that power. I suppose the best evidence of their intention is found in Article VI's language—the supremacy clause—which says that those laws passed in pursuance of the Constitution shall be the supreme law of the land.

I think it is fair to say that much of the argument in support of *Marbury v. Madison* flows form the long path of Anglo-American constitutional history reaching back certainly to the 17th century to Dr. Bonham's case (1606), back to colonial experiences. It's probably fair to say that the ultimate rationalization for *Marbury* flows from the experience of the founding period—it was really the enactment of the Judiciary Act of 1789, the addition

The participants on the panel

Moderator: Honorable Christine M. Durham, associate justice, Utah Supreme Court. *Presenters:* A.E. Dick Howard, professor of law, University of Virginia School of Law; Lawrence Baum, professor of political science, Ohio State University. *Responders:* Honorable Stephen Reinhardt, a judge of the U.S. Court of Appeals for the Ninth Circuit; James J. Brosnahan, Esq., Morrison & Foerster, San Francisco.

to the Constitution of the Bill of Rights, events of that kind, which began to make much plainer the need that the courts had for the power which John Marshall said they should have in *Marbury*.

In my foreign travels, I have found that separation of powers, federalism, and a lot of other things are interesting to foreign audiences. But one feature that I think strikes them as the most important single contribution to American constitutionalism is the power of judicial review.

The second landmark that I observed as I sauntered across this constitutional landscape is the expansive interpretation by the court of national power—it fulfills the expectation of some framers that a national court system would inevitably have a tendency to favor national power. It's a historical trend that begins very early, in cases such as *McCulloch v. Maryland* where John Marshall gives a very generous reading to the "necessary and proper" clause, in effect, reading "necessary" as saying something like "convenient or appropriate."

Soon thereafter, in *Cohens v. Virginia*, Marshall established the Supreme Court's constitutional authority to review state supreme court judgments. That opinion has been called Marshall's great nationalist address. One of his critics was the chief justice of Virginia's supreme court, Spencer Roane. Roane called *Cohens* "a most monstrous and unexampled decision, which may be accounted for only from that love of power which history informs us corrupts all who possess it and from which even the upright and ermined judges are not exempt."

Examples of this expansive interpretation of national power are many—I'll simply remind you of the commerce powers as one example. We, of course, think about the most contemporary commerce clause cases, but you could go back to *Gibbons v. Ogden* in 1824 and read Marshall's description of the commerce power and I don't find modern dictum which describes that power any more broadly than Marshall did in *Gibbons v. Ogden*. The Court, to be sure, later tried to limit the commerce power, for example, by drawing distinctions between "production of goods" and "interstate traffic in goods," but since 1937, the Court has basically gotten out of the business of putting any substantial limitation at all on the commerce power. Indeed, the Court's current posture is that even when the states as states complain of Article I power being used by Congress, that is in effect, though

perhaps not technically stipulated, a political question. A few years ago, in the *Garcia* case, Justice Blackmun, writing for the majority, basically said to the states, "If you have a complaint about Congress' commerce power usage, then go to Congress—that's the forum to address, not the courts."

There is also, finally, a thread that runs through some of the modern Supreme Court cases, and that is an insensitivity to, or more fundamentally, a mistrust of states and their institutions. This phenomenon, I think, is most obvious in the Warren Court era. A great many of the Court's decisions at that time showed an obvious distrust of state courts. It's hard otherwise to explain the imposition upon the states of rules such as *Miranda* and the exclusionary rule. This is still a battleground; we have Brennan on the one hand and Rehnquist on the other currently battling over certain unstated premises about the extent to which state courts can in fact be trusted to enforce federal rights.

The "living" Constitution

Sauntering a bit further, the third landmark is the one that has come to be called the "living" Constitution. Because it does seem to be that in the battle between those who adhere to a very strict construction of the Constitution and those who would show a willingness to adapt and reinterpret constitutional language, at least for the moment, the "living" Constitution theory is the one very much paralleled. Once again, Marshall sets the stage, in the famous line, "We must never forget it is a (here he italicizes the word) *constitution* we are expounding." Yes, it is indeed a constitution. But in Marshall's language, a constitution intended to endure for ages to come and consequently to be adapted to the various crises of human affairs. Marshall obviously has contrasted the Constitution with ordinary legal documents such as contracts and wills.

There are many examples of this phenomenon. I suppose one of the best would be the Court's uses of the Fourteenth Amendment equal protection laws. A good example would be *Brown v. Board of Education* (1954). As you may recall, the Court ordered that case to be reargued in the 1953 term, having first heard the case in the 1952 term. And in the reargument the counsel were asked to investigate, as they did exhaustively, circumstances surrounding the adoption of the Fourteenth

Amendment; for example, the fact that the same Congress that approved the Fourteenth Amendment also appropriated funds for segregated schools in the District of Columbia. But in *Brown*, in the opinion written by Earl Warren, the Court found all this history and investigation, as Warren put it, inconclusive. More to the point, Warren found that education in 1954 was simply not the same as it had been in 1868. In approaching this problem, we cannot turn the clock back to 1868, when the amendment was adopted, or even 1896, when *Plessy v. Ferguson* was decided. We must consider public education in the light of its full development and its present place in American life. This is what I call the adaptation of the Fourteenth Amendment to the circumstances.

A fourth landmark, and this is really a corollary of what I call the "living" Constitution, is the court's ability to discover substantive constitutional rights, even in cases where there is no direct textual support for those rights. The most conspicuous historical example is the use of substantive due process in *Lochner v. New York* (1905), a famous case where Justice Peckham used the due process clause to strike down a New York statute limiting the hours that bakers could work at their trade. Peckham said that statutes "limiting the hours in which grown intelligent men may labor to earn their living are a mere meddlesome interference with the rights of the individual." Substantive use of the due process clause had fallen into ill repute since 1937 since the so-called constitutional revolution. But just as soon as people thought it was dead, it reemerged in a somewhat different context, beginning this time in 1965 with *Griswold v. Connecticut.* This is not the right of contract, but the right of privacy explicitly mentioned in the Constitution.

I'm sure most of you remember reading *Griswold.* And you remember Justice Douglas' painful effort not to admit that he was using substantive due process. He was obviously embarrassed by it. Just eight years later, in *Roe v. Wade*, Justice Blackmun, in talking about the right to privacy, said it comes from the Fourteenth Amendment's due process clause. All of this is familiar debating territory and I'm sure we'll be hearing more about this debate over unenumerated rights when the Senate Judiciary Committee begins its work with Judge Bork.

This dispute over the so-called "living" Constitution reflects, I would think, a tension between two traditions, both of which are very much a part of the American constitutional fabric. It is, on the one hand, looking to the Constitution's text as the ultimate point of reference. On the other hand, there is the need to adapt the Constitution to changing circumstances. This inevitably creates tension.

The equity power

Another landmark. This would be one that the layman would probably not appreciate as much as the lawyer, and that is the continued expansive use of federal courts' equity powers. The corollary of increasing rights as we all know them is more equity powers as well. This has come into its own in a year in which the class action has become the paradigm lawsuit.

There are those on the court, and I think Rehnquist would be foremost among them, who are battling valiantly to limit what they see as excessive use by federal and district courts of their equity powers. It may not have been a losing battle, but I would say that, by and large, the Supreme Court has been very permissive toward lower courts in their use of their power.

I think one of the features of this increasing use of institutional litigation as an approach to the courts (and the court's response, by the way, is to use more equity powers), has been to a trend away from what might in the framers' eyes have been the negative use of rights—what Hugo Black used to call the "thou shalt nots," which the Bill of Rights says government can't do. But the U.S. Constitution, unlike most foreign constitutions, simply doesn't talk about affirmative rights. You read a Third World country's constitution and you're likely to find rights, including the negative rights such as speech and religion, but you'll also find affirmative rights such as the right to a job. We don't have that in our Constitution's text, but in the work of the courts in these equity cases, there seems to be a slide in that direction, especially in education cases.

Let me add another feature of the landscape, and this is one that probably is more of an outgrowth of the Fourteenth Amendment that it is of the original Constitution. I think there is a fundamental and special concern and preoccupation in the eyes of the Supreme Court with minorities, and in particular with those who are without clout in the political process. You may remember Justice

Stone's famous *Carolene Products* case in 1938. Footnote 4 in that case is probably the most famous footnote in the Supreme Court's history. In it, some raised the question of whether there might be more searching judicial inquiry when the Court had reviewed statutes aimed at limiting the rights of minorities.

Well, footnote 4 has proved to be the font of an enormous amount of Supreme Court jurisprudence, especially in the area of race. For example, the first right of association case came out of the State of Virginia's effort to put the NAACP out of business back in the 1950s. The first right to counsel case was *Powell v. Alabama* back in the '30s involving the so-called Scottsboro boys. Think about First Amendment speech in public places in the '60s—I could give you a long list—but I think it fair to say that the doctrine has emerged in areas that don't seem to affect race.

Judicial supremacy

My last feature on the landscape brings me full circle. Having started with judicial review, I think the last feature on the landscape is what some call judicial supremacy. One recalls *Marbury*, in which Marshall left open the question whether the Supreme Court not only has the power to interpret the Constitution, but whether it also is the ultimate arbiter, the ultimate interpreter. It was in *Cooper v. Aaron* in 1958, the Little Rock school case, where state officials claimed that they were not bound by the ground rules, because they weren't parties to it. Well, in *Cooper v. Aaron*, all nine justices signed off on the opinion. That's most unusual on the Supreme Court. In *Aaron*, the Court quoted from *Marbury* that language which is often quoted, "it is emphatically the province and duty of the judicial department to say what the law is." In *Cooper v. Aaron*, the Court reinterpreted that language almost casually to mean, "the Federal Judiciary is supreme in the exposition of the law of the Constitution," as if it were some self-defining proposition. I suppose the lay public would assume that was the way things are, so that you can ask the average nonlawyer who has the final word and he would say the Supreme Court. Our attorney general has reminded us that there may be questions about the reach of Supreme Court authority.

What conclusion does all this lead to? It is interesting in this bicentennial year to recall that at the Philadelphia convention in 1787 the judicial power was the least debated. Most of the time was given to arguing over how powerful the executive should be. What should the respective relationship between the federal and state government be? Though the judiciary was by no means an afterthought, it simply didn't require the same kind of focused attention. And yet today it is the work of that branch of government which year in and year out stokes the most extensive debate over constitutional questions.

Certianly at no time in the past 200 years have appointments to the Supreme Court occasioned more national attention than in the last year or two. These confirmation hearings, to which we all shall be glued come September, are likely to have all the trappings of some medieval morality play. The forces of good and evil will battle each other while senators mount their horses in Washington. Underlying all of the political issues and all the hype and all the commentary, we'll be reminded again of the very pervasive place in American life of the American judiciary.

The other side

Professor Lawrence Baum: I would like to talk about the other side of what Dick Howard was discussing. Professor Howard outlines a sequence of events in court actions that at the beginning and increasingly over time enhanced the role and power and policy-making significance of the federal courts. My concern is how the other branches of government reacted to that growing role of federal courts.

We know that a good deal of what the federal courts have done over time, beginning even earlier than *Marbury v. Madison*, has aroused a good deal of unhappiness in the other branches of government. We also know that the other branches of government have the power to do a great many bad things to the federal courts should they choose to do so. The question is, how much *have* they chosen to do so? I want to suggest that given this tremendous array of powers held by the other branches, they have been remarkably forebearing in making use of their powers. Whatever we may conclude about the restraint of the courts, the really remarkable restraint is by Congress and the president.

I find the task of trying to talk about a period of 200 years quite impossible. So I want to take a shortcut and focus on a period of approximately the last 35 years in which the federal courts have taken, in many cases, strongly activist positions, primarily as defenders of civil liberties, most dramatically and most visibly in the Supreme Court, but also increasingly in the lower federal courts. This period since the 1950s is certainly not perfectly representative of our history as a whole, but I think it is representative of the general rule—that although the federal courts have often aroused a good deal of unhappiness in the other branches, they have been, I think, given the political power of the other branches, remarkably free and safe to follow their own course as decision makers and as policymakers.

Let me begin by reminding you of something with which you are all familiar, the tremendous activism of the federal courts since the 1950s. There are a lot of different ways in which to measure activism. If we simply look at the number of laws that have been declared unconstitutional, you all know that the numbers since 1960 have been unprecedented, that more than one-third of all the federal and state and local laws that have been struck down by the Supreme Court have come in the last 25 years.

In an even more dramatic way, consider the intervention of the Court in the operation of public institutions, whether it's schools or prisons or mental institutions. None of these things is unprecedented, none of those kinds of activities are new in the last quarter century, but their extent is probably unprecedented. I think it's easy enough to argue that there has been unprecedented activism since the 1950s and particularly the 1960s.

Certainly, we're also familiar with the fact that a great deal of what federal courts have done in this period has been highly unpopular in the country as a whole, but more relevantly in the other branches. Some of the Supreme Court's major civil liberties decisions have been quite popular—the right to counsel in *Gideon*, for example. But others have aroused a good deal of congressional and presidential wrath. Consider the school busing decisions, which have had relatively little support in the other branches. Or the school prayer decisions. The restrictions on police searches and questioning. Protections of people on the political left, particularly in the 1950s. If any of those decisions had come to a vote in Congress, there would have been very few votes for them on the merits. And yet, the other branches have not done a great deal

to attack either the decisions or the courts that made them.

Keep in mind all the various things that Congress and the president can do: Structural things, such as restricting the jurisdiction of federal courts; verbal attacks of various sorts which are the one thing that's easiest to do; limiting court size and budgets. Congress and the president also have a good deal of power over the implementation of court decisions. There is a lot of ammunition that the other branches have. And yet it's striking how little of that has been used since the 1950s. A great deal of verbal attack, some in very strong language; a lot of bills introduced, a lot of proposals made to restrict court jurisdiction. And yet, very little of that has become law. It's probably true that some of the restrictions on budgets and salaries have resulted from unhappiness with court decisions.

There were also symbolic bills on busing; there was a symbolic bill passed in 1968 to restrict *Miranda*. But that's about all. None of the proposed constitutional amendments have been adopted; none of the proposed limits on court jurisdiction have been adopted. Basically, all the unpopular things that the Supreme Court and the lower federal courts have done since the 1960s have been allowed to stand. That to me is more remarkable than the things that the courts themselves have done. It seems to me the question then is "why?" Given all this power, and all the unhappiness they have with so many decisions, why have Congress and the president basically let those decisions stand and left the courts unscathed? I don't think there is any one particularly good answer. But it does seem to me there are several bits and pieces.

Why court decisions stand

First of all, there has been some self-restraint by the courts themselves. It is easy enough to assume that because there has been so much active policymaking by the courts since the 1950s they acted without any sense of restraint at all. Clearly that is not the case. We have some subtle evidence of this from the papers of Supreme Court justices—the judges have recognized that they can push only so far. So, in part, I think the courts protected themselves with some degree of restraint.

Second, let me suggest that as unpopular as some court decisions have been, all of them have enjoyed some support, not only from society at large, but within Congress as well. Even the most unpopular decisions—school busing, school prayer—have enjoyed some basis of support in Congress. And so when the Court has been on the run, when there are strong efforts to overturn its decisions or to limit its jurisdiction, there have always been some members of Congress willing to support the Court.

Third, and this is something that is primarily a modern development, there has been an increasing acceptance in the other branches of government of the desirability of maintaining the autonomy of the courts. I don't mean to imply there is some awe of the courts. Rather, I think there is general public support for the independence of the courts, that the system requires that the courts be given a degree of autonomy. And this creates some restraint on the part of the president and members of Congress when they are considering curbing the courts.

I think the best example to illustrate this is proposals to restrict the Court's jurisdiction. Although there is some controversy about the extent of Congress' constitutional power to restrict Court jurisdiction, it has a great deal of such power—that much is clear. And all it needs to do is pass bills with simple majorities to restrict the Court's jurisdiction. And yet Congress has not done so since 1868, and certainly has not done so in the modern period of civil liberties support by the Supreme Court. I think this is because there's a feeling that trying to manipulate the Court by restricting its jurisdiction is going to be viewed by people as unacceptable.

In the 19th century it was quite common to increase or decrease the number of Supreme Court justices. And sometimes that was done in order to manipulate the Court. Of course, the effort to do that during the New Deal was defeated. And it's not even considered anymore because, again, I think there is a tinge of illegitimacy to it. I think there is an element of self-restraint based on a feeling that federal courts must be left alone, not because of anything mystical about them, but because the people demand it, and because the system seems to require it.

Finally, and to me the most interesting thing, there is a good deal of evidence that presidents, but even more, members of Congress, are grateful to the Court for taking burdens off themselves. Every controversial issue that is decided by the Court takes a good deal of heat off the Congress to deal with that issue. School integration is a good example. The decisions of the Supreme Court have largely left Congress powerless to deal with the issue in more than a peripheral and symbolic way. I think that for many members of Congress that's a great thing. It keeps them from having to deal with something that's going to make people on one side or the other very unhappy.

The issue of abortion is similar. Certainly many members of Congress feel very strongly that the Supreme Court's decisions on abortion have been quite wrong in both the legal and moral senses. And yet I think members of Congress, and even more state legislators, are grateful that they don't have to deal with the issue. Had *Roe v. Wade* never been decided, in every legislative session at both the national and state levels there would be tremendous battles over abortion. Should the Supreme Court reverse *Roe v. Wade*, we can be guaranteed those battles will be quite bloody. And so however much they disagree with *Roe*, as many legislators strongly do, nonetheless the Court has done them a favor by taking the issue out of their hands. I think there is a certain reluctance to wrest that power away from the Court and take the burdens back onto themselves.

Having emphasized the fact that the other branches have left the courts alone, let me say a couple of things to water that down a bit. First, there is a great deal of power over the courts simply through the appointment power. It's delayed power; it doesn't work perfectly, but it does rein in the courts to some degree. It may be that the Reagan administration has not brought about an overturning of any of the decisions of the Warren Court or even the Burger Court, but it has staffed much of the lower courts, and increasingly the Supreme Court, with judges who are more sympathetic to its point of view. That is an important control and it is one that we shouldn't lose sight of.

Even so, it seems to me that the most striking thing is the relative autonomy of the courts in practice. Despite what would seem to be a tremendous weakness, a tremendous subservience to the other branches, even in a time of great controversy such as the last 30 years, the federal courts have been largely left alone to chart active policymaking paths, paths that were often quite unpopular. Autonomy of the courts, rather than control of the courts, has been the primary feature of the system.

And that, given the legal and political subservience of the courts, strikes me as remarkable.

In perspective

Judge Stephen Reinhardt: I think what Professor Howard described as the experience of the courts has been the experience of the nation. In fact, I think it has also been the experience of the executive and legislative branches. We've come from a sleepy, rural society with 13 small states to a national, world power in a very complex, fast-moving society. To the same extent that the courts have become more important, more powerful, so have the president and the Congress. So I think it's important to put this picture of the growing power of the federal judiciary in perspective.

It would be hard for this country to function effectively in modern society if the federal judiciary hadn't, thanks to John Marshall and others such as Earl Warren, understood that this nation and its court system were compelled to keep moving, keep advancing, keep up with contemporary life, deal with different and modern problems, find solutions by adjusting our thoughts, our attitudes, our understanding of all the things that we learned over 200 years. Had this country simply said we won't do anything, or had our federal courts said we won't do anything that we can't find in somebody's notes taken 200 years ago, it would be a sad state of affairs indeed.

Therefore, there is really nothing very surprising about the fact that the powers of the federal courts have expanded. Whether that trend will continue or not is a different question—whether the Constitution will continue to stand for what it has for so long depends on whether we are ready and willing now, after 200 years, to accept that evolutionary development. Some may not be. I think there is a serious view that the Constitution doesn't mean what John Marshall said it meant, what we all grew up understanding it meant. I think there are people in prominent positions these days who think that the Bill of Rights doesn't mean anything, that it was a mistake.

Once you accept the premise that the Constitution means what the Supreme Court says it means, then if you have a Supreme Court that doesn't believe in rights, we're not going to have much of a Constitution and we're not going to have many rights. But it's very hard to resist the idea of evolution; it's very hard to resist the idea of growth. It would be very hard to transform this nation into what it was at a different time and a different era. *Back to the Future* was a nice movie, but it's really hard to believe that this nation can go back to the confederation that some might like it to become.

Distrust of courts

The next general area that Professor Howard mentioned is distrust of state courts. That is a sensitive subject, particularly for a federal judge—why federal courts are better than state courts. To me it doesn't seem particularly peculiar that federal courts should decide federal rights. It should be the body to decide what the federal Constitution means.

I'm all in favor of state courts determining their state constitutions, and affording broader protection—I think that states should absolutely have the right to do whatever they wish to protect people's rights. On the other hand, they have no business limiting people's rights that are protected under federal law. And to say that states may not limit federal rights, but that state courts should decide whether states have limited federal rights, doesn't make a lot of sense.

It seems to me fairly elementary that federal courts are there to protect federal rights. Historically, there may be some conceptual difficulties with that argument. It may not always have been thus. But as we grow in understanding of what the functions of courts are and the purposes of federalism, I don't have much difficulty with thinking that when you have a question of whether state legislation and state action is in violation of federal law, persons who feel that there is a violation should have the right to go to federal court to protect their federal rights.

It sounds very simple when I say it, but there are many people with a different view. The tension that Professor Howard mentioned between the text of the Constitution and the need to grow is not a problem. One of the nice things about our Constitution is you don't find the answers in the text frequently because it was understood that you can't answer constitutional questions in the text. You can only give general principles in the text, and those principles mean different things at different times as we learn more about life. The conflict is between the need to grow and how judges interpret those principles. One of the problems with the debate over the Constitution is that it is not so clear what the intent was.

The role of judges

Essentially, the real debate over the role of judges and over federal judges is in a basic difference in view over what law is and what a judge is. The extremes are that one of you believes that judges should not have discretion; that judges must act like some form of human computer where a judge can look at a case, look at a statute, and there is a clear answer. Well, sometimes there is and I suppose if you look at the volume of our caseload, you would find there are pretty clear answers to most of the cases.

But they're not as easy to decide as some people think. There are problems with more cases than some of my colleagues seem to think. There are judges who will tell you that 80 percent of the cases are easy, but I find that very few cases are easy. The ultimate outcome in a majority of cases may be fairly clear. But the cases that come to public attention are usually cases that are not so clear. The reason you have divided votes is because, normally, reasonable people can differ. There isn't an automatic, clear scientific answer to the problem. Law is not a science. It requires judgment, and the most important thing to know about a judge is how he goes about the process of applying judgment and what his values are.

I think President Reagan is absolutely correct in looking for judges who reflect his basic philosophical values. It is impossible to decide the kinds of cases the Supreme Court decides without applying one's values. Of course, there are all kinds of limits, and what the limits are is a matter of great disagreement. And it also happens to depend where you are at any particular time. I participated in a panel discussion like this with a representative from the Justice Department and some of President Reagan's appointees who have a rather broad view of overriding or disregarding precedent. And, rather surprisingly, the concept of precedent means very little to a Supreme Court justice. If you don't like the previous decision, that's enough—you just change it.

Justice Rehnquist said pretty much the same thing in *Garcia*, which one of our speakers alluded to. He made it very clear that the next time there was an appointment, the vote would be 5 to 4 the other way, instead of 5 to 4 the way *Garcia* came out. That was probably the most blatant explana-

tion of how courts reach decisions—"we needed one more vote," is what he said, "and we'll get it."

In any event, I don't understand quite why there is this much debate over judges exercising discretion. Sometimes that is referred to as being activist. Other times, it seems to me at least, it's just simply doing the job you are required to do—you are required to apply judgment, to make decisions involving fundamental powers. It is really the only branch of government that is free to apply the principles that we heard about earlier of justice and reason, without concern over any other consideration.

At least in the federal judiciary, we have the benefit of lifetime appointment and do not have to be concerned about any other consideration. The Constitution is there in large part to protect minorities against the temporary sentiments of the majority. It's thus quite clear why lifetime appointments are desirable. When a majority doesn't like what officeholders do, the majority throws out officeholders, and that's quite appropriate. It's not quite appropriate to throw out judges who are enforcing people's constitutional rights because you don't happen to like those constitutional rights. And that is a great danger in an electoral system. There is a question about how safe the federal judiciary really is these days, and I certainly agree with Professor Baum that we have been very fortunate. A lot could have been done to the federal judiciary that has not been done.

Free from threats

I think probably Professor Baum's predictions, optimistic as they are, are justified. There was a lot of talk several years ago about limiting the powers of the federal judiciary. There was a lot of talk about constitutional changes. Some of the societies that were established in the recent eight to ten years have published serious treatises on modifying our Constitution to change the federal system. Usually, with a little bit of time, those ideas disappear. A senator from California, who happens to be still sitting in the Senate, proposed when he ran for office the first time that we have direct elections of federal judges. Now that he's a senator and has won the election, I don't think he's likely to repeat that proposal. But there were other proposals seriously made by people who have a great impact on the California Supreme Court and who were very involved, long before the recent bloodbath in California, in an effort to change the basic system of replacing California judges in an orderly manner, when they decided and announced they would like to see the same approach applied on a national scale. I think that one of the things that happens, though, is that people who believe in that kind of change in the court system come to power and stay in power long enough so they take over the courts, and then they don't want to change it. In fact, they become the activists themselves, only they are active for a different social policy—instead of protecting individual rights, they protect property rights.

Either way, the system generally continues to go on free from serious external threats, and I think it likely that it will.

Judicial independence

James J. Brosnahan: Professor Howard started by saying that judicial review, *Marbury v. Madison*, is most important—we all agree with that. Over the last five or six years particularly, I've had some clients who have come from other systems. In the last couple of years, I've been talking to people who have fled other systems, and in all of that it seems to me that there is a great new challenge for us to make known to the world, and some American lawyers are trying to do it, what it is about our system that is good—even if we got it accidentally—even if at the convention in Philadelphia they didn't quite focus on it—nonetheless, we've got it.

The starting point is not judicial review, although that is so terribly important as Professor Howard said. What I've come to believe is that judicial independence is everything. In Africa, when judges are consulted, whether they like it or not, by the chief executive officer, there is no judicial independence. You can't have judicial review unless you have judicial independence. There is much to be learned as to what happened in California last year, because conservative or liberal, left or right, center or whatever, I think we would agree that judicial independence is the starting point.

Federal judges, indeed, are independent and have been all the way through, and as a result we have the system that we have. Looking back over 200 years, Professor Howard mentioned the period of national power. My theory is simply that the federal courts are independent, but society moves through those courts, reflecting whatever is hap-

pening in our society. The irony of the debate as to whether judges should ever put a little bit of themselves into what they're doing is that we revere the judges over the last 300 or 400 years who have done exactly that. Consider Lord Mansfield, who invented equity while reading one night a book on Roman law. He found that the Romans had edicts by which they could ameliorate the harshness of the law. Thus was equity born. And we remember Mansfield for that and many other things.

Indeed, when you look back on the federal courts, you find rights, as Professor Howard says, that may not spring right out, but that does not automatically mean they're not appropriate. For who will now say that the right to privacy should be struck down? The federal courts have become in recent years a great megaphone out of which rights could be declared, but the country, starting by my notes about April 10, 1973, has become quieter. We have been busy with economic matters, to beat the Japanese productively. Rights are still important, but they are not at the center of our particular thinking, although the equity power in federal courts remains very, very vigorous.

It is interesting to see that a pup fish can be defended with tremendous vigor by the federal courts, even though the lawyers and judges, before the case was filed, did not know, as I did not know, what a pup fish is. But in the Ninth Circuit over the last approximately seven years, in 24 cases, 16 have resulted in an injunction. And some of these judges, I think, could fairly be said to be nonactivist judges. And yet, when dependent Native Americans in Alaska are denied by some government agency the subsistence which they need to live over the next month, the judges move to deal with that.

I must say that one of the things that I have been privileged to see in the federal courts is the advancement of other ideas that have come in, including the representation of the poor, and of course there are now federal public defenders. There are judges of all stripes who participate in making the system what it is.

The legislature, I think, will not come after the federal courts, any more than they seem particularly capable of going after the executive branch. Because somewhere deep down in their hearts, they really know they ought to be doing the job. For example, the most telling point I ever heard was with regard to *Miranda*. Between approximately 1930 and the time that the Warren Court started to decide procedures for arrest, no state legislature passed any statute—good, bad or otherwise—on the subject of how people were to be advised of their rights. The legislature is good, they are well meaning, I like them, but they get terribly confused. And this is the great protector, I think, of our federal courts.

The final point I would like to mention is access to the courts, because every legal system is known for something. The Greeks invented the idea of lawyers. When their society died and their legal system crumbled, nonetheless, they had invented the idea of lawyers and courts, something that could go on. The Romans brought uniformity to it—as they brought it to their roads, to their army—a systemized body of law. And the English began the concept of rights. But only in this country has it been the idea, which we have approached, but not totally achieved, that people of the smallest and weakest position will have access to the courts. We haven't made it, because in the civil field we have no doctrine that a person is entitled to a lawyer in civil cases. Very good lawyers have argued that, but we have never succeeded. Yet, overall, our best thing is that everybody will get a chance to go to court to articulate his or her position. So, when doctrines come down in the federal courts whacking away at access, they are whacking away at our best thing. Access to the courts is what our society will be remembered for.

NOTE

This transcript originally appeared in Volume 71, Number 2, August-September 1987, pages 116-122.

Arrogation of power or accountability: "judicial imperialism" revisited

The "imperial judiciary" is an illusion. Judges only exercise power given them by others and remain accountable both to professional interests and the public.

by Stephen L. Wasby

In the last half-dozen years it has become increasingly popular to argue that judges, particularly federal judges, have become an "imperial judiciary" improperly intervening in American life. Both an intellectual argument, made most notably by Nathan Glazer and Raoul Berger,[1] and political efforts have developed to restrict courts' power, with the former used to bolster the latter. Proposed constitutional amendments would limit federal judges to a single 10-year term[2] or would directly overturn Supreme Court abortion and school desegregation rulings thought to result from improper activism. Methods for reversing the courts' invalidation of federal or state laws have also been proposed.[3]

Complaints come from within as well as outside the judiciary. Justice Rehnquist has asserted that "It is basically unhealthy to have so much authority concentrated in a small group of lawyers who have been appointed to the Supreme Court and enjoy virtual life tenure." And Justice Powell has characterized the lower courts' orders in the 1979 school desegregation cases as "wholesale substitution of judicial legislation for the judgments of elected officials and professional educators" and "social engineering that hardly is appropriate for the federal judiciary."[4]

One can certainly make a strong, but hardly new, case that courts play a large role in American policy making. The question is whether a critic is engaging in dispassionate treatment of judicial policy making capacity or simply arguing against such policy making on the basis of disliked results. As noted by Cavanagh and Sarat, "However cast, arguments about failures of competence or capacity tend to be political statements about the desirability of particular court decisions or aspects of legal doctrine."[5] In short, dislike of substantive results fully pervades the discussion of "judicial imperialism" and lack of judicial capacity, both explicitly as in Glazer's work or somewhat more thinly veiled as in Horowitz's oft-cited study.[6]

Arguments supporting a limited role for the judiciary are part of a long, honorable tradition of *normative* argument. Among several legitimate normative positions on the place of judges in the system, however, critics of "judicial imperialism" seem to recognize only passivity—at least when convenient to applaud it. (At other times, they often wish judges to retain a strong hand, for example, so that regulators can be restrained or so that some of their own substantive goals can be attained.)

In the social climate of the last decade, with reduced support for civil rights and endemic disaffection with the social programs of the 1960s, crossing over into result-oriented advocacy is especially easy. Arguments like those by Glazer and Horowitz are certainly legitimate social *criticism*, but one should be cautious about accepting them as neutral or objective accounts. "Judicial imperialism" is a useful rhetorical device, but the assertions accompanying it are seldom supported by hard analysis. As Monti notes, "Critics of judicial activism have not posed their arguments in a way that anticipates, much less permits, the introduction of information that could qualify or contradict their positions."[7]

In this essay, I raise questions about the "judicial imperialism" argument as rhetoric and ideology, maintaining that the argument that judges have arrogated power to themselves is seriously defective. Critics of the "imperial judiciary" ignore the genesis of judicial rulings and blame the messenger—the courts—for others' acts or omissions. Instead, judges exercise power given them by others and are accountable in many ways both to professional interests and the larger political system. Furthermore, despite claims often made along with attacks on "judicial imperialism," judges are not incapable of dealing with policy issues presented to them and, when compared with other institutions, do so well.

Judicial imperialism and incapacity

The "imperial judiciary" argument gives disproportionate attention to certain types of cases, reinforced by result-oriented selection of examples; fails to examine closely the causes of litigation, leading to a strong tendency to blame the messenger rather than the source; lacks systematic *comparative* examination of the capacity of courts and other political institutions to resolve policy disputes; and fails to examine ways in which judges, instead of arrogating power, are both potentially and actually accountable.

Selectivity of cases

The general tone of the "judicial imperialism" argument is set by the critics' selectivity in choosing types of cases to support their argument. Horowitz even dismisses the question of whether the cases in his study are representative by asserting—not showing—that they are not "aberrational" and by arguing that "frequency is not an issue in this study."[8] Yet how is one to know whether cases are "aberrational" without some baseline or idea of the frequency with which they occur?

Repeated emphasis on Judge Garrity's Boston school desegregation rulings and Judge Frank Johnson's Alabama prison and mental hospital decisions, with the former often misrepresented, has led many to expect incorrectly that those decisions are the norm. However, most judges are not "activist" but instead are "narrow-minded lawyers with little stomach for being creative or for second-guessing other government officers."[9]

With respect to school desegregation cases, on which critics often focus, "it is not at all clear that the courts are prepared to assume the responsibility of directing a far-reaching program of institutional reform in the public schools."[10] Concerning prison cases, Justice Brennan has pointed out that "no one familiar with litigation in this area could suggest that the courts have been overeager to usurp the task of running prisons."[11] More generally, "Even in an era in which 'landmark' decisions with broad social implications dominate much of the debate over the role of courts, most court decisions present no arguable infringement on legislative, executive, or electoral prerogatives."[12]

The selectivity of those arguing against "judicial imperialism" extends even further. The pejorative "judicial activism" is applied only to Warren Court decisions and not those of the Burger Court. But certainly, promises to appoint "strict constructionist" judges has not meant that President Nixon's appointees have acted in a consistently "self-restrained" manner when faced with legislation running counter to deeply-held values.

Nor have critics of activism showed concern when judges have acted imperiously in the absence of some large social issue. The critics' concerns would have been more heartening if they had joined dissent from the Supreme Court's ruling in *Stump v. Sparkman* that judges were immune from suit if acting within what appears to be formal jurisdiction.[13] Justice Stewart, objecting to immunity for actions judges have no constitutional or statutory authority to take, certainly has the better of the argument: "A judge is not free, like a loose cannon, to inflict indiscriminate damage whenever he announces that he is acting in his judicial capacity."[14]

Clearly, critics are unable to penetrate the rhetoric of "strict construction," "judicial policy making," an "unaccountable" judiciary, or "judicial imperialism." Certainly political scientists have raised serious questions about accepting at face value a judge's rhetoric on self-restraint;[15] those writing more recently can legitimately be expected to exercise more care in their use of labels. But the critics' inability—or unwillingness—raises the question of how the events leading to 1937, which certainly should have taught us that the courts are policy makers, ever occurred. If "judicial policy making" may still be used pejoratively, chances for serious public discussion of courts' operation are slim. Such a difficulty clearly infects *The Brethren*,[16] where the authors' breathless discussion of bargaining within the Court suggests a failure to accept the Court's role as a policy maker. What else would we expect from a major policy making institution but bargaining and compromise?

An aspect of the critics' biased selectivity is their lack of historical perspective. "Social policy" issues have long been placed in the courts' hands. Contemporary commentators forget that "commercial interests in diversity jurisdiction dominated circuit dockets in the beginning [of the U.S. Courts of Appeals, while] the Great Depression and World War II brought into court continuing relations with powerful social aggregates concerned with labor relations, taxation, and public regulation of basic industries"[17]—all definitely "social policy" matters. Perhaps what discomforts the neoconservatives is that "the deprived have joined the advantaged as users of [the judicial] route of grievance redress."[18] Whatever the reason, the critics confuse differences in substantive content—the presence on the docket of, for example, environmental issues—with differences in procedure and remedy, thus exaggerating changes in the latter.

The "imperial judiciary" critics also demonstrate a lack of historical perspective by failing to remind us of earlier judicial "activism"—interference with governmental regulation of the economy in the 1930s and earlier. Those earlier decisions, in aid of a conservative ideology, are conveniently not seen as activist. Moreover, the critics fail to deal with Dahl's argument that the Supreme Court has seldom been out of line with the nation's dominant political interest.[19] The Court, Dahl argued, has been able to do little without support from Congress and the president, although it could maneuver when the other branches were in disagreement. Neither his posture that the Court conferred legitimacy on the policies developed by the other branches, nor his critics' view that elites legitimize the Court rather than the reverse, support a view of judicial overreaching.[20]

Causes of judicial actions

Although some judicial rulings said to indicate an "imperial judiciary" are based on broad constitutional provisions concerning "equal protection" and "cruel and unusual punishment," many challenged decisions stem from interpretation and enforcement of statutes. Vague and ambiguous constitutional clauses and statutory provisions may allow judges to project their values into decisions. However, the judges are not to blame for either the existence of the provisions or their lack of clarity.

Justice Powell has reminded us that "Congress' failure to make policy judgments can distort our system of separation of powers by encouraging other branches to make essentially legislative decisions."[21] Yet the critics find it easier to blame courts for decisions based on statutes than to question the legislative action itself. Similarly, it is not the plethora of administrative regulations based on those statutes that are attacked but the greater judicial action necessary to resolve disputes stemming from the regulations.[22]

Critics forget that if judges misread congressional intent, Congress has the power to right the situation, just as it can scrutinize the regulations designed to implement its own statutes. Yet critics seldom question Congress' failure to review such regulations and to strike down those that it disapproves. Failing to acknowledge that oversight has often meant *overlook*, critics continue to attack the courts, not the Congress, for not exercising its responsibilities and delegating substantial policy making authority to the executive.[23]

Decisions attracting critics' particular attention restrain officials or require them to improve substantially the conditions in the facilities they direct. It is, however, the judges' actions rather than events leading to their rulings that are criticized. Perhaps the best example is the attention given Judge Garrity's schools desegregation rulings in Boston rather than the Boston School Board's adamant refusal to obey clear state law. Similarly, rulings ordering improvement in prison conditions get attention, not state officials' unwillingness to correct long-standing, appalling and clearly unconstitutional conditions. Wishing to make judges accountable, critics of judicial imperialism ignore institutional officials' desire to remain unaccountable or to criticize legislators and senior political executives for not keeping the officials accountable.

Intent on ignoring the causes of allegedly unprecedented and improper judicial actions, the critics imply that judges are imposing particular views concerning the prisons or schools rather than responding to complaints brought by others, often as a last resort. It is, after all, the litigants, not the courts, who have the "power to initiate legal action," so that "litigants, not judges, set court agendas."[24] People need not turn to courts to satisfy their claims. Perhaps their doing so is in part a reflection of larger social or cultural trends or of "the oft-noted litigiousness of the American people."[25] Perhaps it is because plaintiffs find the legislature or executive unresponsive and are not content to be denied their due. Such use of the courts "belies the assessment of the courts as somehow being immune to the vagaries of the political process"[26] and indeed shows not their imperious isolation but their *connectedness* to the political process.

The critics also do not realize that most judges act only when conditions have become so atrocious that even the most conservative among them are horrified. Such judicial hesitation results from deference paid the expertise of those administering the institutions, part of the older "hands-off" policy now revived and thoroughly ensconced in the Supreme Court's prisoners' rights rulings.[27] Similarly ignored is the fact that more severe judicial orders are provoked by state resistance to initial judicial action; the critics instead make further complaints about later orders, forgetting that intransigent parties have always had to be forced to comply with decrees.[28]

In any event, when judges do act, dire predictions about the potential consequences of their rulings seldom are borne out.[29] Officials' authority is *not* invariably destroyed by judicially-established monitoring of their activities and judicial action does lead defendant officials to undertake seriously their responsibilities, with resulting improvements in institutional conditions.

Critics of the judiciary also conveniently ignore the fact that some decrees are not judicially-written or imposed but are consent decrees to which the executive branch agrees. If the state later does not fully assume responsibility for the decree,[30] who is to blame if plaintiffs return to court and the judge orders implementation? It is also important to note that administrators may find it politically useful to be hauled into court, so they have a reason for agreeing to carry out politically unpopular actions.[31] As professionals, they may share plaintiffs' standards about proper conditions. More generally, "the interests of officials with direct operating responsibility—for example, institutional superintendents and their deputies—often overlap substantially with those of the plaintiffs."[32]

Perhaps all this is but another piece of evidence for the proposition that litigation is not only an end in itself but is part of a continuing disputing process and a wedge to negotiation when nothing else will attract the other side's serious attention. Indeed, "extended impact litigation does not displace negotiation and compromise but is frequently an essential precondition to it."[33]

The foregoing reinforces the point that judges are embedded in the governmental system, not external to it. Nor is this unusual. Shapiro points out that judging is "an integral part of the mainstream of political authority rather than . . . a separate entity."[34]

What, then, of the norm of "judicial independence" so highly touted in the American political system and so strongly adhered to because of the belief that the costs of a judiciary directly subservient to the political powers-that-be are much too great? At one level it refers to judges not being dependent on one of the parties to a lawsuit; at another level, it entails an institutional separation so that judges are not attached to the same part of the government with whom an individual may be having a dispute.[35] Such a separation, with the judiciary expected to check and balance the other branches, may result in the judiciary acquiring "substantial lawmaking and administering capabilities."[36]

An "independent judiciary" does not, however, mean one completely separate from the political system, and may well indicate a system serving certain broad societal interests, historically the "upper class and nationalizing interests rather than dominant local interests."[37] Among the interests the American federal judiciary has at time served has been the cause of minority rights. The critics forget that the judiciary's very task is to protect civil liberties, a task that, despite public perceptions created by Warren Court decisions, the courts have not often fulfilled. Without such action or "activism," there would be even further erosion of our liberties, "because of the substantial political and bureaucratic obstacles that hinder the implementation of the Court's decisions and blunt their impact." Put differently, "because the statements in the Bill of Rights are only rights in theory, they need all the help they can get if they are to survive in fact" because "pressures in the real world" against them are "substantial"—a consideration favoring the view that courts "lean harder in the direction of emphasizing our nation's constitutional ideals."[38]

Beyond rulings on the merits, judges must also attend to implementation of decrees. Without such "intrusive" implementation, judicial orders are likely to be ineffective, remaining "merely a paper victory for the plaintiffs."[39] If neoconservatives showed greater concern for alternative modes of securing the rights sought and implemented through the courts in this way, their criticism of judicial "activism" would carry more weight. Yet one hears only the criticism, not suggestions of alternative methods of resolving societal disputes.

Judicial incapacity

A last important element of the attack on "judicial imperialism" is the argument that courts lack the capacity to resolve complex social policy issues. (This argument is separate from the position that, regardless of competence, courts in a democracy should not be making decisions about complex social issues.) In making their argument, critics often suffer from indecision about whether to focus only on courts or to compare courts with the other branches of government. They usually settle for the former, taking cheap pot-shots at the courts while ignoring the possibility that the other branches suffer from some of the same defects claimed to affect or infect the judiciary.

An example of the faulty analysis by those claiming judicial incapacity is Horowitz's argument that courts "carve up and . . . treat as separate" related transactions when those transactions "are intertwined in social life."[40] We are also told that judges are preoccupied with individual cases, and thus do not think about whether the cases before them represent a typical situation, from which precedent for later cases might be properly derived, or are extremes and thus to be confined to their facts. Furthermore, attention to individual cases is said to produce piecemeal policy making.

Incremental decision making does characterize the judiciary, but it also characterizes *all* governmental policy making,[41] despite occasional instances of "speculative augmentation."[42] Administrative agencies as well as courts have long been criticized for predominant reliance on a case-by-case approach instead of using rule making—although rule making is also criticized when it produces disliked results.

Nor does reliance on a case-by-case approach

always entail ad hoc decision making, as the critics appear to assume. Legislators, administrators, and judges generally begin policy making with a problem presented by particular instances or cases. However, all contemplate to some degree other situations to which their rulings would apply. In particular, courts have regularly grouped cases involving common issues so as not to base decisions too narrowly on the specifics of an individual case. If courts are not self-starters, having to wait for cases to be filed or appealed, we must also remember that most legislative action does not commence until after a series of constituent or interest group complaints.

We are also told that courts cannot effectively make advance estimates of the magnitude or direction of the effects of their decisions. We are not told, of course, that legislatures and executives similarly fail to predict effectively. Judicial correction of policy is said to be intermittent. Yet it is equally the case that agencies charged with enforcing legislation do not continuously monitor many matters under their jurisdiction. The critics also do not recognize that, whatever the courts' difficulties with new subject-matter, other governmental institutions also have trouble processing new material effectively; however, for all institutions, courts included, time and preparation can overcome the problem.

To argue that judges are not prepared by training and experience to supervise administrative agencies like mental health and corrections departments or even to select appropriate masters whose work the judges are to supervise ignores the fact that legislators are generalists sharing problems "of being adequately informed about disputes and in their relations with experts,"[43] as well as in selecting specialist staff. Judges' supervision of agencies can be facilitated by requiring periodic reports and by reliance on complainants' attorneys to return to court if something is amiss. Beyond that, judicial appointment of masters can "compensate for judges' lack of familiarity with organizational routines and procedures in defendant institutions," and their use may be essential in securing compliance with judicial decrees.[44]

To engage in serious analysis of courts' capacity to resolve matters requires a set of well-defined criteria; Carter provides us with one. An institution's policy, to be effective, must "accord with fundamental, widely shared beliefs about acceptable governmental action" and must "carry some plausible hope of alleviating the problem." Moreover, the promulgation and implementation of the policy must not "destroy the position and authority of the position's source."[45] The criteria Carter suggests include technical competence, effective information processing, and political accountability:

(1) *familiarity* with the language in which a policy problem is articulated and an *understanding* about "cause and effect beliefs that define the existence of a problem in the first place";[46]

(2) *reliable access to information* bearing on the problem's causes, on all solutions proposed and their direct and indirect consequences, on targets, and on implementation strategies;

(3) the *ability to reformulate policy* when new information is obtained; and

(4) once there is agreement that a problem exists and on perceptions of the problem, the *public's belief* that the institution's authority and competence match the problem.

Once an institution (legislative, executive, or judicial) is seen to satisfy any one of these criteria, the question arises whether,

regardless of the skill of members of a given policy making institution (PMI), any other PMI is equally or better prepared to proceed, and whether alternative policy sources, even if they may be better equipped technically to proceed, will in fact do so.[47]

Use of the criteria and of this comparative formulation will produce different answers at different times as to the appropriateness of judicial action. What is important is that, by insisting that the second question be asked, Carter has properly focused attention on *comparative* capacity as well as on the crucial *will to proceed*, neither of which is addressed seriously by the "imperial judiciary" critics.

Judicial accountability

Advocates of the "judicial imperialism" position ignore ways in which the judiciary *is* accountable. To remedy this omission, it helps to stress not arrogation of power but accountability, defined to mean "keeping an institution's decisions in line with community political and social values and otherwise imposing constraints on the courts' exercise of discretion."[48] Means of judicial accountability may appear to be few or at times less than fully

effective, but that does not mean there is no accountability.

For one thing, despite American emphasis on judicial independence, courts are not fully independent or autonomous institutions. Their structure, jurisdiction, and resources, including their budget and personnel, are determined by the other branches of government. Courts are initially established, and often reorganized, by the legislature. And, as indicated by current debate over limiting the Supreme Court's appellate jurisdiction—or the jurisdiction of all federal courts—the legislature can limit what the courts hear.

Ironically, discussion of judicial imperialism, both by those attacking the judiciary and defenders, has itself contributed to accountability by producing more intellectual soul-searching by judges. In general, accountability of judges is of two principal types—within the legal system and to the broader political system. The former includes judges' socialization; precedent and the public nature of judicial action; reversal of lower court judges' decisions; and constraints imposed by courts' organizational needs. Political accountability derives from selection and removal of judges (also part of accountability within the legal community); the role of public opinion; and resistance to judges' decisions.

The socialization of judges

Given the limited amount of *formal* training of judges as judges, judges' most extensive socialization has been to their earlier role as lawyers. This includes socialization to the norm of judicial independence, the idea that judges ought not be accountable to the other branches of government. Thus, we find judges, as lawyers, socialized to norms about accountability itself. The lack of formal training for judges means that the most important direct socialization of judges is through contact with other judges; reliance on each other is reinforced by norms against consultation with those who are not judges and especially with nonlawyers. All this reinforces accountability within the judicial profession rather than to others.

Part of lawyers' socialization is to precedent. Lawyers also learn that, even when precedent is lacking, they should look to "the law," not popular feelings, as the source of their decisions. Precedent affects the process by which judges arrive at reasoned decisions: "We contain our judges by method, and demand justification of their results by reason."[49] In particular, we wish judges' rulings to be characterized by *formality*. The requirement of written opinions is part of the process of producing accountability. Believers in role theory will agree that judges' beliefs that they *should* follow precedent and that their decisional process *ought* to be a reasoned one, even if the true bases of their decisions are not in fact presented, will affect judges' actions.

Socialization to precedent can lead judges away from legislative and executive branches and toward their own colleagues. That has helped produce a consensus on how to decide many cases. That such a consensus exists in the Supreme Court is evident from the high degree of unanimity on which cases are appropriate for review and on the disposition of many other cases.[50] Such consensus suggests that "judicial role," not personal values about preferred policy goals, drives much judicial activity, although variations exist in the degree to which values and judicial role reinforce or crosscut each other.

Other forms of accountability

Coupled with precedent is the openness of the judicial decision process, at least at the result stage. Although most trial court opinions are not written or published, and despite federal appellate courts' increased use of not-for-publication opinions, people expect that judges will justify their rulings in published (or at least public) documents. However, serving to reduce accountability is the fact that judges' deliberations are private. Moreover, some courts have been slow to explain even their operating procedures, and Freedom of Information Act (FOIA) provisions do not extend to internal court documents. A penchant for secrecy seems apparent in the Administrative Office of the U.S. Courts' practice of masking judges' identities so that they cannot be matched with particular decisions.

If precedent and openness help produce accountability, so does the sanction of reversal by higher courts for not following precedent or for not viewing the law as the higher court does. Higher courts thus limit lower courts' freedom of action. However, appellate court review of lower court decisions is limited in several ways. Not all trial court decisions are appealed, because the decision to appeal is in lawyers', not judges', hands.

Moreover, the absence of controlling precedent also reduces appellate courts' ability to control lower courts, particularly in novel or changing areas of law. Similarly, the Supreme Court and other courts with discretionary jurisdiction cannot take all cases. Because of the limited number of cases they decide, they cannot establish controlling doctrine for all issues faced by lower courts.[51] Even lower appellate courts hearing a higher volume of cases may be hard pressed to issue controlling precedents for the trial courts.

Certain judicially-established standards—the "abuse of discretion" doctrine, for example—also limit higher courts' propensity to overturn lower courts. Not only are those tests flexible and work to affirm the lower courts' rulings, but high courts also cannot afford to antagonize the lower courts, on which they must rely if their precedential rulings are to be implemented. Frequency of reversal is thus not high, so that the *fear* of reversal—its symbolic effect—must be more important than actual reversal in achieving accountability. And, indeed, most judges do follow law developed by higher courts; at least they "go along" because higher court rulings on most topics fall within their "zone of indifference."[52]

Attention to the criminal trial courts has recently revealed another aspect of judicial accountability—lateral or horizontal accountability to norms of the "courtroom workgroup."[53] Organizational dynamics control many dispositions reached or recorded in the trial courts. Values shared by trial judges, prosecutors, defense attorneys and other court personnel often limit the effect of higher court rulings, particularly in crisis situations, such as major civil disturbances when some judges seem to suspend independent judgment almost completely.

Selection and public opinion

Methods of judicial selection may also help achieve judicial accountability. Although judges, once chosen, might go their own ways, continuing accountability would be less necessary if accountability were "built in" through selection of judges with characteristics and values thought appropriate by those to whom the judges were to be accountable. Which groups play a dominant role in judicial selection is thus quite important, because it is to the values of those groups that accountability will run. Thus the "merit system," in which lawyers play an explicit role, would increase accountability of judges within the legal system, while partisan election systems would increase accountability to political parties and the values represented by party leaders, that is, "political accountability."

Elections, whether in the merit system, which has led to non-retention (removal) of very few judges,[54] or in nonpartisan or partisan elections, do not substantially increase judicial accountability. Use of nonpartisan ballots makes it difficult for voters to tell "good" candidates from "bad" ones, particularly if the candidates lack previous public identity. Moreover, the norm that one should not run against sitting judges often leaves candidates unopposed. Stiff competition occurs infrequently, and voting in judicial elections is generally reduced by comparison with turnout in elections for other positions.[55]

The difficulty of holding judges accountable through methods of selection, coupled with accounts of improper personal or judicial behavior, has led most states to implement methods for judicial discipline, including removal.[56] Serious discussion of means short of impeachment for handling such problems at the federal level has led to proposals for a separate discipline court and to legislation, enacted in 1980, strengthening the role of the circuit councils in the discipline process, but leaving impeachment as the only means of removing a federal judge from office.[57]

Political accountability may also be achieved through public opinion. Despite the high value placed on judicial independence, public opinion does appear to affect judges. Judges politically active before becoming judges had both become familiar with public opinion and accustomed to responding to it. Although judges do differ in how strongly they adhere to local values, the continuing pull of constituency can be seen in numerous cases, for example, in the race relations area.[58]

Public opinion may, however, be less effective in promoting judicial accountability than it is in the legislative arena because the public, accepting the norm of judicial independence, generally leaves judges alone. At least until recently, negative public opinion about judicial decisions has seldom shown up as more than negative responses in public opinion surveys. More recently, however, "single-issue" interest groups have been pressing effectively for legislation to overturn especially disliked decisions or to remove the courts' jurisdiction over controversial areas. However, even without such activity and even in the absence of a high degree of public knowledge about the decisions, public opinion can affect judicial action. The absence of specific mechanisms for transmitting public opinion to the courts indicates not the absence of an effect of public opinion but only the presence of a noncoercive linkage between public opinion and judicial decisions.

If quiescence most often characterizes even negative reaction to the courts' ruling, there *are* notable instances in which the public resists judicial action. Such resistance, while not making judges directly accountable, certainly lessens the claimed effects of "judicial imperialism." Not only are rulings appealed, with reversal or modification producing some accountability, but, more important, they are at times ignored, resisted, attacked, and overturned in other arenas. Such action, whatever it may say about the presence of a "government of laws," is certainly an effective means of holding courts accountable to views of important segments of the public. This is true even if noncompliance may have received attention disproportionate to its occurrence.[59]

In all of this, however, we should be careful not to overestimate the effect of public opinion on judicial accountability. For one thing, as noted above, public knowledge of judicial decisions is limited. For another, if public opinion can produce accountability when it is clear and unidirectional, at many times opinion is confused, fragmented, and weak, thus providing courts considerable room in which to maneuver. When the public's view differs from views held by the organized bar, judges have freedom to choose between competing audiences.

As the above suggests the two basic types of accountability must be seen together. Those mechanisms providing accountability within the legal system and those providing political accountability at times seem to diverge. Within the legal system, judicial accountability is primarily to lawyers or to other judges, while political accountability propels judges toward the broader public or at least the more attentive members of the public. Despite these potentially divergent strains, some overlap exists because lawyers simultaneously play a large role in judicial selection and are members of the political elite.

Perhaps particularly important is that the values and attitudes of the elite constitute a large part of the environment in which judges function. Appellate judges developing legal doctrine base decisions in part on the political environment or "democratic subculture."[60] Lower court judges expected to follow appellate rulings will have absorbed values from that same political and legal culture before taking the bench and will continue to draw from it because of their greater exposure to the local community. This would suggest that, over the long run, important conjoint legal and political system constraints can operate to limit judges' discretion and thus to hold them accountable.

The burden of this essay has been that the "judicial imperialism" and "judicial incapacity" arguments are defective in a number of important ways. One is a failure to use terminology carefully; another is a lack of historical perspective, coupled with a biased selectivity in examples critics choose to make their case. Perhaps most serious is the critics' sole focus on selected judicial acts rather than on the sources of judicial action—in statutes and administrative regulations. Examination of judicial capacity solely in terms of the judiciary rather than through a comparison of differential institutional capacity is another serious weakness in the critics' argument. So is their attention solely to what they see as lack of judicial accountability without attention to the numerous important ways in which judges are accountable.

More, of course, is necessary than a critique of the critics' arguments. These arguments have, however, been so readily accepted that their defects must be exposed. The possibility for evenhanded analysis of the problems of judicial action in a political system and for thorough comparative analysis of institutional capacity has also been pointed to here, but it remains for others to carry such work forward.

NOTES

This article originally appeared in Volume 65, Number 4, October 1981, pages 209-219.

An earlier version of this article was presented at the American Political Science Association meeting in New York on September 4, 1981.

1. Glazer, *Toward an Imperial Judiciary*, 40 PUB. INT. 104-123 (Fall, 1975), and *Should Judges Administer Social Services?*, 50 PUB INT. 64-80 (Winter, 1980); Berger, GOVERNMENT BY JUDICIARY: THE TRANSFORMATION OF THE FOURTEENTH AMENDMENT (Cambridge, MA: Harvard University Press, 1977).

For other, rather different positions on judicial review, *see* Choper, JUDICIAL REVIEW AND THE NATIONAL POLITICAL PROCESS: A FUNCTIONAL RECONSIDERATION OF THE ROLE OF THE SUPREME COURT (Chicago: University of Chicago Press, 1980); and Ely, DEMOCRACY AND DISTRUST: A THEORY OF JUDICIAL REVIEW (Cambridge, MA: Harvard University Press, 1980).

2. S.J. Res. 24, 97th Cong. 1st Sess., CONG. REC. (Jan. 29, 1981) S 787 (Rep. Dornan).

3. H.R. 4111, 96th Cong. 1st Sess., CONG. REC. (Oct. 10, 1979), E 4953 (Rep. Dornan).

4. Richmond Newspapers v. Virginia, 100 S.Ct. 2814, 2843 (1980); Columbus Bd. of Educ. v. Penick, 443 U.S. 229 (1979).

5. Cavanagh and Sarat, *Thinking About Courts: Toward and Beyond a Jurisprudence of Judicial Competence*, 14 LAW & SOC'Y REV. 371, 386 (Winter, 1980).

6. Glazer, *supra* n. 1, and, particularly, AFFIRMATIVE DISCRIMINATION: ETHNIC INEQUALITY AND PUBLIC POLICY (New York: Basic Books, 1975), Horowitz, THE COURTS AND SOCIAL POLICY (Washington, D.C.: The Brookings Institution, 1977).

7. Monti, *Administrative Foxes in Educational Chicken Coops: An Examination of the Critique of Judicial Activism in School Desegregation Cases*, 2 LAW & POL'Y Q. 233, 242 (April, 1980).

8. Horowitz, *supra* n. 6, at 63.

9. Miller, *For Judicial Activism*, N.Y. TIMES, Nov. 10, 1979.

10. Monti, *supra* n. 7, at 252-253.

11. Rhodes v. Chapman, 101 S.Ct. 2392, 2403 (1981).

12. Cavanagh and Sarat, *supra* n. 5, at 372.

13. 435 U.S. 439 (1978). *See* Way, *A call for limits to judicial immunity: must judges be kings in their courts?*, 64 JUDICATURE 390 (April 1981).

14. 435 U.S., at 367.

15. *See, e.g.*, Grossman, *Role-Playing and the Analysis of Judicial Behavior: The Case of Mr. Justice Frankfurter*, 11 J. PUB. L. 285 (1962).

16. Woodward and Armstrong, THE BRETHREN (New York: Simon and Schuster, 1979).

17. Howard, COURTS OF APPEALS IN THE FEDERAL JUDICIAL SYSTEM: A STUDY OF THE SECOND, FIFTH, AND DISTRICT OF COLUMBIA CIRCUITS 17 (Princeton, NJ: Princeton University Press, 1981).

18. Monti, *supra* n. 7, at 236.

19. Dahl, *Decision-Making in a Democracy: The Role of the Supreme Court as a National Policy-Maker*, 6 J. PUB. L. 279 (Fall, 1957).

20. Adamany, *Legitimacy, Realigning Elections, and the Supreme Court*, 1973 WISC L. REV. 790.

21. Schweiker v. Wilson, 101 S.Ct. 1074, 1088 (1981).

22. *See* Greanias and Windsor, *Is judicial restraint possible in an administrative society?*, 64 JUDICATURE 400, 401 (April, 1981).

23. *Id.* at 410-411.

24. Howard, *supra* n. 17, at 13.

25. *Id.* at 17.

26. Monti, *supra* n. 7, at 235-236.

27. Bell v. Wolfish, 99 S.Ct. 1861 (1979); Jones v. North Carolina Prisoners' Labor Union, 433 U.S. 119 (1977).

28. Eisenberg and Yeazell, *The Ordinary and the Extraordinary in Institutional Litigation*, 93 HARV L. REV. 465, 492, 476-481 (January, 1980).

29. Harris and Spiller, AFTER DECISION: IMPLEMENTATION OF JUDICIAL DECREES IN CORRECTIONAL SETTINGS 21 (Washington, D.C.: LEAA, 1977), quoted in Rhodes v. Chapman, *supra* n. 11, at 2405 (Justice Brennan).

30. Hansen, *Willowbrook: Try, Try Again*, 10 SOC. POL'Y 41 (November/December 1979).

31. "Even prison officials have acknowledged that judicial intervention has helped them to obtain support for needed reform." Rhodes v. Chapman, *supra* n. 11, at 2406 (Justice Brennan).

32. Diver, *The Judge as Political Power Broker: Superintending*

Change in Public Institutions, 65 VA. L. REV. 43, 71 (February 1979).

33. Cavanagh and Sarat, *supra* n. 5, at 405.

34. Shapiro, COURTS: A COMPARATIVE AND POLITICAL ANALYSIS 20 (Chicago: University of Chicago Press, 1981).

35. *Id.* at 19, 27.

36. *Id.* at 31-32.

37. *Id.* at 24.

38. Wasby, CONTINUITY AND CHANGE: FROM THE WARREN COURT TO THE BURGER COURT 210-211 (Pacific Palisades, CA: Goodyear, 1976).

39. Special Project, *The Remedial Process in Institutional Reform Litigation*, 78 COLUM. L. REV. 785, 815 (May, 1978). See also Monti, *supra* n. 7, at 238, 241; Cavanagh and Sarat, *supra* n. 5, at 408; Rhodes v. Chapman, *supra* n. 11, at 2402.

40. Horowitz, *supra* n. 6, at 260.

41. Shapiro, *Stability and Change in Judicial Decision-Making: Incrementalism and Stare Decisis*, 2 LAW IN TRANS. Q. 134-157 (1965); see Lindblom, *The Science of 'Muddling Through'*, 19 PUB AD. REV. 79 (1959).

42. *See* Jones, *Speculative Augmentation in Federal Air Pollution Policy-Making*, 36 J. POL. 438 (May, 1974); Schulman, *Nonincremental Policy Making: Notes Toward an Alternative Paradigm*, 69 AM. POL. SCI. REV. 1354 (December, 1975).

43. Howard, *Adjudication Considered as a Process of Conflict Resolution: A Variation on the Separation of Powers*, 18 J. PUB. L. 339, 350 (1969).

44. Cavanagh and Sarat, *supra* n. 5, at 406; see also Nathan, *The Use of Masters in Institutional Reform Litigation*, 10 TOLEDO L. REV. 419 (Winter, 1979), and Special Project, *supra* n. 39, at 805-809.

45. Carter, *When Courts Should Make Policy: An Institutional Approach*, in Gardiner (ed.), PUBLIC LAW AND PUBLIC POLICY 145 (New York: Praeger, 1977).

46. *Id.*

47. *Id.* at 146.

48. Wasby, *Accountability of the Courts* 145, in Greer et al. (eds.), ACCOUNTABILITY IN URBAN SOCIETY (Beverly Hills: Sage, 1978). The following material draws on that article.

49. Dixon, *The "New" Substantive Due Process and the Democratic Ethic*, 1977 B.Y.U..L. REV. 43, 73 n. 134.

50. Provine, CASE SELECTION IN THE UNITED STATES SUPREME COURT (Chicago: University of Chicago Press, 1980).

51. See Howard, *supra* n. 17, at 41, 56.

52. Baum, *Lower-Court Response to Supreme Court Decisions: Reconsidering a Negative Picture*, 3 JUST SYS. J. 208, 216 (Spring, 1978).

53. See Eisenstein and Jacob, FELONY JUSTICE: AN ORGANIZATIONAL ANALYSIS OF THE CRIMINAL COURTS (Boston: Little, Brown, 1977).

54. Carbon, *Judicial retention elections: are they serving their intended purpose?*, 64 JUDICATURE 210 (November 1980).

55. Dubois, FROM BALLOT TO BENCH—JUDICAL ELECTIONS AND THE QUEST FOR ACCOUNTABILITY (Austin: University of Texas Press, 1980); Dubois, *Public Participation in Trial Court Elections*, 2 L. & POL'Y. Q. 133 (April, 1980).

56. Hoelzel, *No easy answers: a report on the national conference for judicial conduct organizations*, 64 JUDICATURE 279 (December-January 1981).

57. For a discussion of the new law, *see* Neisser, *The new federal judicial discipline act: some questions Congress didn't answer*, 65 JUDICATURE 142 (September, 1981).

58. See Peltason, FIFTY-EIGHT LONELY MEN (New York: Harcourt, Brace and World, 1961); Vines, *Southern State Supreme Courts and Race Relations*, 13 WEST POL. Q. 5 (March, 1965); Hamilton, THE BENCH AND THE BALLOT: SOUTHERN FEDERAL JUDGES AND BLACK VOTERS (New York: Oxford University Press, 1973).

59. Baum, *supra* n. 52.

60. Richardson and Vines, THE POLITICS OF THE FEDERAL COURTS (Boston: Little, Brown, 1970).

The Judge Baer controversy

Correspondence from the White House, Senator Dole, congressmen, and judges

by Jon O. Newman

With the presidential election behind us, it is now appropriate to publish correspondence concerning the extraordinary statements made during the campaign about a ruling by U.S. District Judge Harold Baer Jr.

Judge Baer, as many will recall, had suppressed evidence seized by New York City police officers under circumstances that aroused their suspicions of narcotics activity. The government, having presented a somewhat minimal case to support the warrantless seizure, moved for reconsideration. While the motion was pending, more than 200 members of Congress, led by Representatives Bill McCollum, Fred Upton, and Michael Forbes, wrote President Clinton the following letter, dated **March 20, 1996:**

Dear Mr. President:

The recent ruling by Federal District Judge Harold Baer Jr. of the Southern District of New York in a significant drug prosecution is a shocking and egregious example of judicial activism. In siding with drug traffickers and against hard-working police officers and the frightened residents of violence-ridden communities, Judge Baer has demonstrated a level of ideological blindness that renders him unfit for the proper discharge of his judicial duties. We respectfully request that you join us in calling for his resignation from the federal bench.

No amount of legal reasoning can justify Judge Baer's decision; indeed, *The New York Times* described it as "malpractice." His ruling prevented about 80 pounds of cocaine and heroin, with a street value of $4 million dollars, and a confession by a habitual drug trafficker from being used as evidence in a major drug trafficking case. The drugs were found in the back of a car with out-of-state tags, at 5:00 a.m., in a neighborhood overrun by drug traffickers, after police officers observed four men loading duffel bags in the trunk of the car and after at least one of the men fled upon seeing the police. Judge Baer managed to overlook or dismiss all of these facts in concluding that the police lacked "reasonable suspicion" to stop the car, in part because the corruption of police justifies running from them. According to *The New York Times*, the effect of his decision "was to undermine respect for the legal system, encourage citizens to flee the police and deter honest cops in drug-infested neighborhoods from doing their jobs."

Mr. President, you appointed Judge Baer to the federal bench. In doing so, you undoubtedly assumed he would support law enforcement and maintain an unbiased commitment to the rule of law. Judge Baer's negative view of police officers reveals the inaccuracy of your assumption. He has turned his back on the millions of residents of communities like the one in this case who are prisoners in their own homes because of violent drug traffickers.

You more than anyone else, Mr. President, have the right to call for the Judge's resignation. We respectfully request that you do so, and you can count on our support if you take this important step.

Sincerely,
Rep. Fred Upton
Rep. Michael Forbes
Rep. Bill McCollum

The White House responds

In response to a press conference inquiry about the letter, White House spokesman Michael McCurry said on March 21 that President Clinton would defer deciding upon whether to call for Judge Baer's resignation until the then-pending motion for reconsideration was decided. According to a page-one story in the *New York Times* the next day, "The White House put a federal judge on public notice today that if he did not reverse a widely criticized decision throwing out drug evidence, the President might seek his resignation....

"Asked about the Republican request that the President seek the resignation of his appointee, Mr. McCurry said, 'We would evaluate Judge Baer's record, as anyone legitimately should, on the full breadth of his cases.' But he added pointedly that 'we are interested in seeing how he rules' in his reconsideration of his decision.

"Asked if future action against the judge were possible, he then said, 'I think I made that pretty clear by that answer.'

"Pressed again, he said, 'I gave a good, appropriately elliptical answer.' "

On March 23, the president's opponent, Senator Bob Dole, was quoted in the *New York Times* as saying that Judge Baer "ought to be impeached instead of reprimanded. If he doesn't resign, he ought to be impeached."

Concerned that statements by the White House and Senator Dole far exceeded tolerable criticism of a judicial ruling and posed a threat to judicial independence, three former chief judges of the Second Circuit and I, as the current chief judge, issued a statement on **March 28** that was prominently reported in the New York Times and elsewhere nationwide. It read:

The recent attacks on a trial judge of our Circuit have gone too far. They threaten to weaken the constitutional structure of this Nation, which has well served our citizens for more than 200 years.

Last Friday, the White House press secretary announced that the President would await the judge's decision on a pending motion to reconsider a prior ruling before deciding whether to call for the judge's resignation. The plain implication is that the judge should resign if his decision is contrary to the President's preference. That attack is an extraordinary intimidation.

Last Saturday, the Senate Majority leader escalated the attack by stating that if the judge does not resign, he should be impeached. The Constitution limits impeachment to those who have committed "high crimes and misdemeanors." A ruling in a contested case cannot remotely be considered a ground for impeachment.

These attacks do a grave disservice to the principle of an independent judiciary, and, more significantly, mislead the public as to the role of judges in a constitutional democracy.

The Framers of our Constitution gave federal judges life tenure, after nomination by the President and confirmation by the Senate. They did not provide for resignation or impeachment whenever a judge makes a decision with which elected officials disagree.

Judges are called upon to make hundreds of decisions each year. These decisions are made after consideration of opposing contentions, both of which are often based on reasonable interpretations of the laws of the United States and the Constitution. Most rulings are subject to appeal, as is the one that has occasioned these attacks.

When a judge is threatened with a call for resignation or impeachment because of disagreement with a ruling, the entire process of orderly resolution of legal disputes is undermined.

We have no quarrel with criticism of any decision rendered by any judge. Informed comment and disagreement from lawyers, academics, and public officials have been hallmarks of the American legal tradition.

But there is an important line between legitimate criticism of a decision and illegitimate attack upon a judge. Criticism of a decision can illuminate issues and sometimes point the way toward better decisions. Attacks on a judge risk inhibition of all judges as they conscientiously endeavor to discharge their constitutional responsibilities.

In most circumstances, we would be constrained from making this statement by the Code of Conduct for United States Judges, which precludes public comment about a pending case. However, the Code also places on judges an affirmative duty to uphold the integrity and independence of the judiciary. In this instance, we believe our duty under this latter provision overrides whatever indirect comment on a pending case might be inferred from this statement (and we intend none).

We urge reconsideration of this rhetoric. We do so not because we doubt the courage of the federal judges of this Circuit, or of this Nation. They have endured attacks, both verbal and physical, and they have established a tradition of judicial independence and faithful regard for the Constitution that is the envy of the world. We are confident they will remain steadfast to that tradition.

Rather, we urge that attacks on a judge of our Circuit cease because of the disservice they do to the Constitution and the danger they create of seriously misleading the American public as to the proper functioning of the federal judiciary.

Each of us has important responsibilities in a constitutional democracy. All of the judges of this Circuit will continue to discharge theirs. We implore the leaders of the Executive and Legislative Branches to abide by theirs.

The ensuing correspondence

On **March 29,** Peter Erichsen, associate counsel to the president, responded:

Dear Chief Judge Newman:

In connection with the joint statement issued by you and other chief judges of the Second Circuit yesterday, I enclose a copy of the letter dated March 22, 1996 from Jack Quinn, the Counsel to the President, to Congressman McCollum and the other principal signatories of a letter reportedly signed by over 150 members of the House of Representatives requesting the President to call on Judge Baer to resign. Mr. Quinn's letter states that the President believes Judge Baer to have been mistaken in his ruling, but it also makes clear that the President shares your view that an independent judiciary is vitally important to the nation. The letter states the President's view that "the proper way for the Executive Branch to contest judicial decisions with which it disagrees is to challenge them in the courts, exactly as the Clinton Administration

is doing in this case."

Please do not hesitate to contact me if you are in need of further information about this matter.

    Sincerely,
    Peter C. Erichsen
    Associate Counsel to the President

The enclosed letter of **March 22** from Jack Quinn, counsel to the president, to Congressman Bill McCollum read:

Dear Congressman McCollum:

The President has asked me to respond to your letter of March 20, 1996, expressing your disapproval of the recent decision of United States District Judge Harold Baer of the Southern District of New York to suppress evidence in a drug trafficking case.

The President has made clear that he believes Judge Baer's decision is grievously wrong, not only in its result but also on its totally unjustified criticism of the New York City Police and its suggestion that it is acceptable behavior for anyone to run from the police. The President's views on this matter are represented by the U.S. Attorney for the Southern District, his chief law enforcement officer in Manhattan, who brought the prosecution in the first place and against whom Judge Baer ruled. Immediately after the decision, the President instructed me to ascertain that the U.S. Attorney was prepared to challenge the judge's decision vigorously. The U.S. Attorney is in fact vigorously challenging the Judge's order. And, it is only because of the U.S. Attorney's pursuit of this case that Judge Baer eventually agreed to rehear the motion and consider additional police testimony. The President hopes that Judge Baer will reverse his earlier decision. If he does not, the President will direct the Justice Department to appeal the decision.

The proper way for the Executive Branch to contest judicial decisions with which it disagrees is to challenge them in the courts, exactly as the Clinton Administration is doing in this case. The President supports the independence of the federal judiciary, which is established by the Constitution. Although comments in recent press reports may have led some to conclude otherwise, the President believes strongly that the issues now before Judge Baer should be resolved in the courts.

> **Sincerely**
> **Jack Quinn**
> **Counsel to the President**

On **April 1,** I sent the following letter to President Clinton:

Dear Mr. President:

Enclosed is the full text of the joint statement issued this past Thursday by myself and three former Chief Judges of the Court of Appeals for the Second Circuit.

Speaking for myself, I was heartened to read Mr. McCurry's reaction, as quoted in *The New York Times* of March 29, emphasizing the White House view that "the proper way to contest rulings that the executive branch disputes is through the courts." The absence of any renewal of his prior statement that a call for resignation would depend on the judge's decision on rehearing was especially noteworthy.

It was also gratifying to receive this morning the thoughtful letter from your associate counsel, Peter Erichsen, enclosing Mr. Quinn's letter to Congressman McCollum.

> **Respectfully,**
> **Jon O. Newman**
> **Chief Judge**

The same day I also sent the following letter to Senator Dole:

Dear Senator Dole:

Enclosed is the full text of the joint statement that was released this past Thursday by myself and three former Chief Judges of the United States Court of Appeals for the Second Circuit.

Speaking for myself, I drew some encouragement from the report in *The New York Times* of March 29, in which your spokesman, Nelson Warfield, though renewing criticism of Judge Baer's decision, refrained from the prior call for the Judge's impeachment. It was that call, not criticism of the initial decision, that prompted the Chief Judges' statement.

> **Sincerely,**
> **Jon O. Newman**
> **Chief Judge**

On **April 9** Senator Dole sent the following letter to Judges Lumbard, Feinberg, Oakes, and myself:

Your Honors:

It has come to my attention that you have issued a joint statement criticizing me for expressing my belief that U.S. District Court Judge Harold Baer's decision in *United States v. Bayless*, 1996 WL 23150 (S.D.N.Y Jan. 23, 1996), has no basis in law. I must say I was surprised to learn that you had commented publicly on a case that may well appear before you on appeal. Judges, unlike elected officials such as Senators, perform what your statement calls their "important responsibilities in a constitutional democracy" in the courtroom, not in the court of public opinion.

Although I share your concerns about maintaining the independence of the federal judiciary, I believe you were wrong to suggest that I overstepped my bounds in criticizing Judge Baer's ruling in the *Bayless* case. Simply put, judges are not the only ones in our constitutional system who have "important responsibilities" relating to the proper administration of justice in the federal courts. The Legislative Branch, along with the President, has a significant role to play in ensuring that judges, no less than other officers of the United States, faithfully perform their duties under the Constitution. That is why our Constitution gives the President the power to appoint judges, subject to the power of the Senate to "Advice and Consent" on each appointment. U.S. Const. art. II, sec. 2. That is also why Congress is given the solemn power under the Constitution, where warranted, to remove from office judges and other officers of the United States.

To be clear, I believe it would be inappropriate for an elected official to coerce a judge to change his or her ruling in a particular case, and I have not done so here. It is, however, perfectly proper for me to point out when a judge makes ridiculous and prejudicial statements demonstrating a deeply held disdain for the police.

Your statement argues that "[t]he Constitution limits impeachment to those who have committed 'high crimes and misdemeanors,'" and implies that no conduct—no matter how outrageous or contrary to the public interest—can be grounds for impeachment unless it constitutes a criminal act. With all due respect, I find your conclusion surprising. From the earliest days of our Republic, it has been understood that judges were subject to impeachment for grounds other than the commission of crimes. As Justice Story explained in his *Commentaries on the Constitution*, the concept of "misdemeanor" extends well beyond criminal acts to encompass other forms of misbehavior in the conduct of one's public office.[1] (That likewise was the conclusion of the House Judiciary Committee when it considered the impeachment of President Nixon in 1974[2]). A ruling in a case that exhibits improper bias or an abuse of power can be one example of such misbehavior.

You offer your opinion that "[a] ruling in a contested case cannot remotely be considered a ground for impeachment." Again, I must take exception. Only a few years ago, the Supreme Court held that matters of impeachment are left by the Constitution to the political branches of the federal government and that the courts are powerless to review impeachment decisions. *See Nixon v. United States*, 113 S. Ct. 732 (1993). It is thus for the Congress to decide what constitutes a proper basis under the Constitution for impeaching federal judges.

In any event, I trust that issues relating to the standards for impeachment will not obscure our focus on the larger, more fundamental issue on which I commented in relation to the *Bayless* case. That issue is whether justice is being done in our federal courts. I believe that the quality of justice meted out in our courts depends on the judges who serve on it. Because who sits on the federal bench is so vitally important to how well the federal courts serve the American people, it is entirely proper for those who seek or hold public office to criticize poor judicial appointment and poor rulings. In no area of law is this more true than in the case of the criminal law, which exists to protect law-abiding citizens from the depredations of criminals. Indeed, to quote the Supreme Court, "[t]he operation of the courts and the judicial conduct of judges are matters of utmost public

concern." *Landmark Communications, Inc. v. Virginia*, 435 U.S. 829, 839 (1978).

It was in this spirit that I addressed Judge Baer's ruling in *Bayless*. You are correct that it would be improper for you to comment on the merits of that ruling, but I think even you would agree that I had the right, indeed, the duty, to do so as an elected official and candidate for the highest office in the land. In *Bayless*, Judge Baer suppressed from evidence massive quantities of illicit narcotics in a drug trafficking prosecution—and the defendant's confession—on the ground that the search that produced the narcotics evidence was unreasonable. He ruled that New York police lacked reasonable suspicion that a crime was occurring when they witnessed four men, at 5:00 a.m. in an area notorious for drug dealing, walk across the street to a double-parked car, load four duffel bags into its trunk, walk away without talking with the driver, and then flee in different directions upon seeing the police. To the Judge, it was perfectly normal and not at all suspicious for the men to run when the police approached because he wrote, "residents in this neighborhood tended to regard police officers as corrupt, abusive and violent" and it would have been remarkable "had the men *not* run."

I strongly believe that his ruling is contrary to well-established Fourth Amendment law and to common sense. On even the most narrow reading of Fourth Amendment law, the police had more than ample cause to believe that a crime was in progress—and, in fact, 80 pounds of drugs were found in the duffel bags, and the driver of the car confessed to a long-standing involvement in drug trafficking. Moreover, it is obvious that fleeing from the police can constitute suspicious conduct and create "probable cause."

What I find most disturbing about the ruling, however, is that it rests on an apparent hostility to police officers who are honestly doing their jobs by apprehending criminals who make our neighborhoods and schools [un]safe. On the legal question, Judge Baer himself now apparently agrees with me, given recent reports that he has confessed error and reversed his prior decision.

Still, the larger question remains: what kind of judges has President Clinton appointed to our courts, and what kind of appointments can we expect from him if he is reelected this Fall? The ruling in *Bayless* remains relevant to this fundamental question. In fact, President Clinton has stated that he does not regret appointing Judge Baer to the federal bench.

It is my intention, both as Majority Leader and as the nominee of my party for President of the United States, to continue to call attention to judicial decisions, such as *Bayless*, that disregard the law.

I recognize that judicial ethics may preclude you from responding in substance to this letter. I thought it was important, however, to respond to your statement and address where I stand on the *Bayless* case.

Sincerely,
Bob Dole

On **April 19,** I responded to Senator Dole:
Dear Senator Dole:
Thank you for your letter of April 9, 1996 (received yesterday), in response to the statement issued on March 28, 1996 by me and three of my predecessors as Chief Judge of the Second Circuit.

It appears that a fundamental misunderstanding exists as to the point of our statement. Your letter states that we issued a statement "criticizing me for expressing my belief that U.S. District Court Judge Harold Baer's decision in *United States v. Bayless*, 1996 WL 23150 (S.D.N.Y. Jan. 23, 1996), has no basis in law."

On the contrary, as the enclosed text of our statement makes clear, "We have no quarrel with criticism of any decision rendered by any judge. Informed comment and disagreement from lawyers, academics, and public officials have been hallmarks of the American legal tradition."

We expressed concern, not about criticism of the judge's decision, but about statements relating to the judge's resignation or impeachment, statements that we believed constituted the very sort of coercion to change a ruling in a particular case that your letter agrees is "inappropriate." I am gratified by

the expression of your view on this important point.

On the issue of grounds for impeachment, our statement did not say, as you apprehend, that we thought impeachment was limited to criminal acts. We quoted, as you do, the Constitution's phrase "high crimes and misdemeanors." We did offer the view that a judge's decision in a contested case ought not to be considered grounds for impeachment, a view recently expressed by Chief Justice Rehnquist in remarks at the Washington College of Law. He cited the Senate's 1805 decision not to impeach Justice Samuel Chase as "assurance to federal judges that their judicial acts—their rulings from the bench—would not be a basis for removal from office by impeachment and conviction. And that has been the guiding principle of the House of Representatives and the Senate from that day to this...."

I appreciate having the benefit of your thoughts on the important issue of judicial independence.

Sincerely,
Jon O. Newman
Chief Judge

The aftermath

As for the case that provoked the episode, Judge Baer granted the government's motion for reconsideration, heard additional evidence, and issued a new ruling that denied the defendant's motion to suppress. Though the judge was widely criticized for changing his original ruling in response to political pressure, I believe this criticism was unwarranted.

Judge Baer acted in the finest traditions of an independent judiciary. In both his initial and subsequent decisions he ruled on the basis of the evidence then available to him. A judge concerned about public criticism might well have maintained his original ruling just to avoid condemnation by those unaware of the additional evidence presented at the rehearing. Regrettably, the second ruling drew as much criticism as the first one, though from different quarters.

The controversy evoked widespread comment, and the topic of judicial independence became a matter for editorial discussion across the country.

The issue even attracted international attention. A statement by Mr. Param Cumaraswamy, Special Rapporteur on the Independence of Judges and Lawyers, to the 52nd session of the United Nations Commission on Human Rights at Geneva on April 3, 1996, included the following:

> Threat to judicial independence appears all pervasive. As seen judicial independence was recently threatened in a developed country like the United Kingdom.
>
> What is of greater concern is the latest outburst in the United States over a decision of a federal judge given some two months ago to exclude certain evidence in a drugs related trial. From information received just two days ago, the President of the United States was reported to have said through his spokesman that if the judge did not change his ruling the President would call for the judge's resignation. Though attempts were made subsequently to distance the President from the words of his spokesman, the damage appears to have been done.
>
> It was further reported that Senator Dole had called for the same judge's impeachment.
>
> These political attacks led four judges of the Federal Appeals Court to come in defense of the judge concerned with a public statement which read, inter alia, "These attacks do a grave disservice to the principle of an independent judiciary and most significantly, mislead the public as to the role of judges in a constitutional democracy."
>
> ...Obviously the President and the Senator, in the heat of their political campaigns, lost sight of constitutionalism.

For their part, neither President Clinton nor Senator Dole renewed any mention of resignation or impeachment of a federal judge because of their disapproval of a judicial ruling. The episode is closed, but the struggle to maintain judicial independence as a cornerstone of our constitutional democracy will continue.

NOTE

This article originally appeared in Volume 80, Number 4, January-February 1997, pages 156-164.

Political attacks on the judiciary

Although fair criticism of judicial decisions can be healthy for democracy, distorted attacks for political gain endanger judicial independence and public confidence in the courts.

by Stephen B. Bright

Political attacks on the judiciary by both major political parties and by candidates for judicial office affect the independence of the judiciary and the public's confidence in it. Thus, it is important to determine the difference between fair criticism of judges and intimidation.

There is no question that fair criticism plays an important role in improving the quality of the courts. Every appeal, every petition for rehearing, every dissent is a criticism of a judicial decision. Decisions like *Dred Scott v. Sandford*, *Plessy v. Ferguson*, and *McCleskey v. Kemp* should be criticized. Citizens should ask if the decision was correct. What does the Constitution require? Should it be amended? If the case involved a matter of statutory interpretation, should Congress respond with legislation?

It is equally clear that everyone in the United States has a First Amendment right to be a demagogue and to make irresponsible criticisms. Given this, what is the appropriate response of those who care deeply about the independence and integrity of the judiciary and who want judges to be free to enforce the Bill of Rights? What response should we expect from political leaders and the bar, and what, if any, response should we expect from judges themselves? What steps are needed to insulate the judiciary from irresponsible attacks and demagoguery and ensure that decisions are based on the law and not political pressures?

There is a particular need for responsible criticism of judges because courts have a duty to protect the rights of minorities—political, racial, ethnic—no matter how unpopular their rulings may be. Legislators or executives may base their deci-sions on focus groups or public opinion polls, but judges may not. Judges are expected to enforce the law, whether it be the First Amendment right of the radical right or the radical left to publish political views that are distasteful to some, the right of the *New York Times* to publish the Pentagon Papers, or the right of a suspected child molester to a fair and impartial trial. As Edmund Burke put it, the judiciary is to serve as "safe asylum" during times of crisis. In the United States, we expect the courts to uphold the Bill of Rights regardless of whether the decision is popular at the time. No one has said it better than Justice Robert Jackson, writing in *West Virginia State Board of Education v. Barnette* (1943):

The very purpose of a Bill of Rights was to withdraw certain subjects from the vicissitudes of political controversy, to place them beyond the reach of majorities and officials and to establish them as legal principles to be applied by the courts. One's right to life, liberty, and property, to free speech, a free press, freedom of worship and assembly, and other fundamental rights may not be submitted to vote; they depend on the outcome of no elections.

This important concept seems to have been forgotten. Indeed, former federal judge Robert Bork, a self-described strict constructionalist, proposed in his new book, *Slouching Toward Gomorrah*, that Congress should be given the power to override court decisions. Alabama Governor Fob James has also expressed the view that the state legislature and governor should be able to override decisions of his state's highest court and, on the federal level, that the president and Congress should simply ignore court decisions they believe to be wrong.[1]

James' views are in accordance with a long history of defiance of judicial orders by Alabama governors, but most of us expect courts to uphold the fundamental principles enshrined in the Bill of Rights against the passions and prejudices of the moment. Judges are not expected to gauge public opinion in making their decisions, but, as Judge William Cranch wrote, decide the legal issues before them "undisturbed by the clamor of the multitude."

Going too far

There has been at least a grudging acceptance of this principle in the past. Politicians have long blamed judges for forcing them to take unpopular actions—for example, desegregating the schools or bringing prisons or mental health facilities up to minimal standards—but many of those politicians had enough respect for the courts that they were careful not to take their criticism too far. Today, however, politicians criticize judges for the purpose of removing them from office, intimidation, and getting certain results.

Immediately after Justice Penny White was voted off the Tennessee Supreme Court last August in a retention election that became a referendum on the death penalty, Tennessee Governor Don Sundquist said, "Should a judge look over his shoulder [when making decisions] about whether they're going to be thrown out of office? I hope so."[2] This contrasts sharply with a statement made by Florida Supreme Court Justice Ben Overton, who was quoted by U.S. Supreme Court Justice John Paul Stevens at the 1996 American Bar Association annual meeting: "It was never contemplated that the individual who has to protect our individual rights would have to consider what decision would produce the most votes."

Judges are increasingly coming under fire in our political system. When U.S. District Judge Harold Baer last spring suppressed drug evidence seized by New York City police officers, Republican presidential candidate Robert Dole called for his impeachment, and the Clinton White House suggested it would ask for his resignation if Baer did not reverse his ruling. Judge Baer subsequently reconsidered his ruling and upheld the seizure of the drugs.

As Senator Dole floundered about, looking for a theme for his presidential campaign, one tack he tried was to attack judges appointed by President Clinton. Even though Dole voted to confirm 97 percent of Clinton's judicial nominees, and most observers found most of Clinton's nominees to be moderate to conservative, Dole claimed that those judges were dismantling "guard rails that protect society from the predatory, the violent, the anti-social elements in our midst."

In response to these attacks by Dole and others, Third Circuit Judge H. Lee Sarokin resigned from the bench, saying in his resignation letter to Clinton that the efforts to "Willie Hortonize" him and other members of the federal judiciary made it impossible for him to carry out his responsibilities as a federal judge: "So long as I was the focus of criticism for my own opinions, I was resigned to take the abuse no matter how unfair or untrue, but the first moment I considered whether or how an opinion I was preparing would be used [politically] was the moment I decided that I could no longer serve as a federal judge."

Courts are not independent when state judges are voted off the bench because of unpopular decisions by their courts, and when federal judges reverse decisions or resign from the bench after a barrage of criticism.

Distortion

The most obvious example of irresponsible criticism and demagoguery is distortion of a judge's record or decision in a case. The most common example is the suggestion that a judge's decision indicates approval of the criminal behavior alleged in the case or that the judge "coddles criminals" or is "soft" on crime. Similarly, critics often suggest that the failure to impose the most severe sentence possible means a judge is not sympathetic to victims of crime.

Often those who criticize irresponsibly focus only on the result of a single decision while ignoring the underlying facts and the legal principles that governed the judge's ruling in the case or the judge's overall performance while in office. However, attacks increasingly include outright misrepresentations of what a judge decided.

For example, in the campaign to remove Justice Penny White from the Tennessee Supreme Court, the Tennessee Conservative Union sent out a letter that opened with the following description of crimes committed by Richard Odom:

78-year-old Ethel Johnson lay dying in a pool of blood. Stabbed in the heart, lungs, and liver, she fought back as best she could. Her hands were sliced to ribbons as she tried to push the knife away. And then she was raped. Savagely.

...But her murderer won't be getting the punishment he deserves. Thanks to Penny White.

The Republican party also mailed a brochure to voters titled, "Just Say NO!" with the slogan, "Vote for Capital Punishment by Voting NO on August 1 for Supreme Court Justice Penny White." Inside, the brochure described three cases to demonstrate that Justice White "puts the rights of criminals before the rights of victims." It described Odom's case as follows:

Richard Odom was convicted of repeatedly raping and stabbing to death a 78 year old Memphis woman. However, Penny White felt the crime wasn't heinous enough for the death penalty—so she struck it down.

Neither mailing disclosed that Odom's case was reversed because all five members of the Tennessee Supreme Court agreed that there had been at least one legal error that required a new sentencing hearing. The court affirmed Odom's conviction and remanded his case for a new sentencing hearing. No member of the court expressed the view that the crime was not heinous enough to warrant the death penalty. Indeed, the remand for a new sentencing hearing at which a jury would decide between the death penalty and life imprisonment made it clear that the court did not find the death penalty inappropriate for Odom. White did not write the majority opinion, a concurring opinion, or a dissenting opinion. Yet Tennessee voters were led to believe that she had personally struck down Odom's death penalty because she did not think the crime was "heinous enough."

Although the Odom case dominated the attacks against White, her opponents misrepresented her opinions in other cases as well. The Republican brochure criticized White for two cases she participated in as a member of the Tennessee Court of Criminal Appeals. The brochure told voters that White voted to reverse the aggravated sexual battery conviction of Edward Jones "[d]espite the child's graphic heart-breaking testimony of what Jones did to her." In fact, a panel of the court unanimously reversed the conviction because the state's expert made an improper comment on the credibility of the complaining witness.

The brochure also told voters that White "voted that John Henry Wallen shouldn't be tried for first degree murder when he shot to death Tennessee Highway Patrolman Doug Tripp." The Court of Criminal Appeals reversed the conviction. All three members of the panel concluded that evidence of other crimes was improperly admitted at trial and that statements obtained from the accused should have been suppressed. White dissented in part, expressing the view that while there was sufficient evidence of premeditation, there was insufficient evidence of deliberation as defined in Tennessee law and thus the defendant could be retried for a lesser crime, but not first degree murder.

In his race for the U.S. Senate in California in 1994, Michael Huffington attacked the incumbent, Diane Feinstein, for voting to confirm Rosemary Barkett for a seat on the U.S. Court of Appeals for the Eleventh Circuit. Huffington ran full-page advertisements that said, "Here are the facts in a *real* murder case. See if you agree with the judge's decision." The advertisement then described the facts of three cases. The first one reads:

Jacob Dougan brutally killed a teenage boy named Steven Orlando. After the murder, Dougan sent a tape to the boy's mother describing her son's murder....

Jacob Dougan was convicted and sentenced to death. But on appeal in 1992, a judge named Rosemary Barkett voted to spare Dougan the death penalty. Judge Barkett believed that a lifetime of discrimination explained Dougan's actions—so she let him off the hook.

The ad described the facts of two other cases and then compared Barkett with former California Chief Justice Rose Bird, who was voted off the state's supreme court in 1986, before concluding that "Michael Huffington opposes soft-on-crime judges like Rosemary Barkett and Rose Bird." The Dougan case was later cited by presidential candidate Dole when he nominated Barkett for his "judicial hall of shame."

In truth, Barkett concurred in a dissent in the Dougan case written by Justice Parker Lee McDonald, one of the most conservative justices on the Florida Supreme Court. A majority of the court upheld the death sentence. No one let Dougan "off the hook," as alleged in the Huffington advertisement and later by Dole.

The Huffington ad misrepresented Barkett's position in two other cases as well. The ad told readers that Barkett voted in *Adams v. State* to "spare the life of the killer of an eight-year-old girl because he had 'learning problems.'" However,

Barkett dissented from the majority because of the trial judge's failure to instruct the jury that it could consider nonstatutory mitigating circumstances in deciding punishment. Huffington's ad also told voters that in *Hall v. State* Barkett voted against the death penalty for a man who had "raped, beaten and killed a woman" because the killer had experienced "emotional deprivation." In a dissent expressing the view that imposition of the death penalty on a mentally retarded person violated the Florida Constitution, Barkett pointed out that Freddie Lee Hall "has an IQ of 60; he suffers from organic brain damage, chronic psychosis, a speech impediment, and a learning disability; he is functionally illiterate; and he has a short-term memory equivalent to that of a first grader."

Justice James Robertson was voted off the Mississippi Supreme Court in 1992. His opponent in the Democratic primary ran as a "law and order candidate" with the support of the Mississippi Prosecutors Association.[3] Robertson was attacked for a concurring opinion he had written expressing the view that the Constitution did not permit the death penalty for rape where there was no loss of life. However, Robertson and his fellow justices who had taken an oath to uphold the Constitution of the United States had no choice. The U.S. Supreme Court had held 10 years earlier, in *Coker v. Georgia*, that the Eighth Amendment did not permit the death penalty in such cases.

Robertson's opponents also told Mississippi voters that Robertson believed "a defendant who 'shot an unarmed pizza delivery boy in cold-blood' had not committed a crime serious enough to warrant the death penalty."[4] In truth, Robertson filed a dissent in the case, maintaining that because the trial court had failed to define the "heinous, atrocious or cruel" aggravating factor for the jury, it should be remanded for a new sentencing hearing. He did not suggest that the crime was not serious enough to warrant a death sentence.

The eventual disposition of the case vindicated the position taken in dissent by Robertson. The U.S. Supreme Court granted certiorari and remanded the case to the Mississippi Supreme Court because it could not tell how the majority of the Mississippi court had resolved the issue. On remand, the Mississippi Supreme Court reversed the case and remanded it to the trial court for a new sentencing hearing. Thus, had Robertson's view prevailed on the initial appeal, it would have saved four years and considerable costs before the resentencing. If anything, Robertson's dissent would appear to be an indication of his abilities as a judge and not a basis for removing him from the court.

But a critic can take a single decision—even, as in Justice Penny White's case, a decision she did not write—and ignore everything else a judge has done during her tenure on the bench. Rosemary Barkett participated in more than 12,000 decisions during her eight-year tenure on the Florida Supreme Court and wrote more than 3,000 opinions. Yet Huffington's advertisements condemned her for a dissenting opinion that another member of the court wrote.

Decisions in criminal cases are most susceptible to such distortion. Much of what judges do in other types of cases is of little concern to anyone except the litigants. But one can portray a judge's decision with regard to bail, the suppression of evidence, or imposition of sentence—no matter how little discretion the judge had under the law—as putting the entire community at risk. A single decision in one of these cases can be used to distort a judge's entire career.

For example, throughout their careers, some judges are called upon to make thousands of bail decisions. Often those decisions are made in very little time and with less than full information. Many citizens do not understand that the purpose of bail is to ensure presence, not to incapacitate the defendant. Out of those thousands of decisions, it is inevitable that someone released on bail will commit another crime and, on occasion, even a serious one. Unfortunately, it is impossible to predict in making the bail decision who those people will be, but it is very easy with hindsight for a politician to criticize a judge for granting bail to someone who commits an offense while on bail.

Similarly, judges presiding over criminal dockets are required to hear many motions that seek the suppression of evidence. The Fourth Amendment—what little is left of it—is still the law of the land. It serves important purposes in protecting the privacy of all citizens. But on occasion it may require the suppression of illegally obtained evidence. A trial judge—who has no authority under the law to overrule Supreme Court precedents—is eventually going to run across a bad search and, if the judge follows his or her oath, be required to suppress some evidence.

New York judges are frequently criticized by the mayor and others for their decisions on bail and suppression of evidence. The recent enactment of a death penalty statute will politicize the judiciary in New York even more. Governor George Pataki, who was elected on a promise to bring back the death penalty, has already attacked a prosecutor and removed him from a case after the prosecutor expressed reservations about seeking the death penalty. Once judges begin ruling on issues in capital cases they, too, will be attacked. As in other states, New York judges will be savaged for any ruling adverse to the prosecution. Appellate judges will be attacked for any reversals of capital cases. Candidates for governor of New York, like their counterparts in California, Tennessee, and elsewhere, will run promising to appoint judges who will uphold the death penalty.

Results, not justice

It is irresponsible for critics of the courts to argue that only results matter without regard for the legal principles that govern judicial decision making. It is irresponsible to attack a judge for the purpose of removing the judge from office so that a different political party may appoint the replacement, as was the effort against Justice White in Tennessee. And it is equally irresponsible to attack a judge for the purpose of intimidating those who remain on the bench to go along with a particular course of action.

Since the Supreme Court's decision in *Roe v. Wade*, candidates from both political parties have promised to appoint judges who would reach a certain result on the issue of abortion. However, the way to change constitutional law is by constitutional amendment, not by appointing judges who will produce a desired result.

Politicians promise results with regard to the outcomes of criminal cases as well. In 1986, California Governor George Deukmejian publicly warned two justices of the state's supreme court that he would oppose them in their retention elections unless they voted to uphold more death sentences. Obviously, he did not know the legal issues presented by those cases; all he was interested in was results. He had already announced his opposition to Chief Justice Rose Bird because of her votes in capital cases. Apparently unsatisfied with the subsequent votes of the other two justices, the governor carried out his threat. He opposed the

retention of all three justices and all lost their seats after a campaign dominated by the death penalty. Deukmejian appointed their replacements in 1987.

After a decision by the Texas Court of Criminal Appeals, reversing the conviction in a particularly notorious capital case, a former chairman of the state Republican party called for Republicans to take over the court in the 1994 election. The voters responded to the call. Republicans won every position they sought on the court that year.

Candidates for judicial office are not beyond promising results if elected. Stephen Mansfield campaigned for the Texas Court of Criminal Appeals in 1994 on promises of greater use of the death penalty, greater use of the harmless-error doctrine, and sanctions for attorneys who file "frivolous appeals especially in death penalty cases." Before the election it came to light that Mansfield had misrepresented his prior background, experience, and record, that he had been fined for practicing law without a license in Florida, and that—contrary to his assertions that he had experience in criminal cases and had written extensively on criminal and civil justice issues—he had virtually no experience in criminal law. Nevertheless, Mansfield received 54 percent of the vote in the general election, defeating the incumbent judge, a conservative former prosecutor who had served 12 years on the court and had been supported by both sides of the criminal bar.[5]

Those who have a role in nominating or confirming judicial nominees have also promised results. Candidates for office have promised to support a certain kind of judge if elected and attacked their opponents for decisions made by judges they may have nominated or voted to confirm. For example, Bill Frist, in his successful campaign to unseat Tennessee Senator Jim Sasser, attacked Sasser for voting to confirm Rosemary Barkett for a seat on the U.S. Court of Appeals for the Eleventh Circuit and for having recommended the nomination of a federal district judge who, two months before the election, granted habeas corpus relief to a death-sentenced man. Frist appeared at a news conference with the sister of the victim in that case. After the victim's sister criticized Sasser for recommending U.S. District Judge John Nixon for the federal bench, Frist said that Sasser's vote to confirm Barkett showed that he "still hasn't learned his lesson." In order to avoid such criticism, President Clinton has mostly avoided nominating any judges who might be controversial and provide campaign fodder for his opponents.

Those who led some of the recent attacks on judges have not been hesitant to acknowledge that their efforts are aimed at producing results by removing those with whom they disagree and by intimidating those who remain on the bench. Tennessee Governor Sundquist, in opposing the retention of Justice Penny White, promised that he would appoint to judgeships only those who support the death penalty. After White was voted off the court, Sundquist reiterated his pledge. He and other opponents of White also made it clear that their successful campaign against her was expected to influence the remaining members of the court.

The costs

The bashing of judges, the removal of some from office, and the efforts to stack courts with judges who will produce certain results, undermines the independence, integrity, and impartiality of the judiciary. A grievance similar to the one made against King George III in the Declaration of Independence could be leveled against those politicians who attack judges for their rulings: "He has made judges dependent on his Will alone, for the tenure of their offices...."

In the current political climate, judges undoubtedly realize that by upholding the Bill of Rights in a controversial case they may be signing their own political death warrants. The costs extend far beyond those who are removed from office or denied promotion. The greatest threat to the rule of law comes from those judges who remain on courts and make compromises in order to stay in office or advance to a higher court. Once a judge has compromised his or her oath as a judge by refusing to enforce the law in order to stay in office, both the judge and the court have been irreparably diminished.

In addition, unfair criticisms and distortions discourage those who we would most want to be judges from seeking or taking the bench. After what happened to Justice White in Tennessee or Justice Robertson in Mississippi, why would any conscientious lawyer want to accept a seat on one of those courts, knowing that one opinion may be used to misrepresent everything he or she may do as a judge? Do we want as judges those who will violate the canons of judicial ethics before even taking office by promising certain results to the

voters or an executive?

The credibility of the courts suffers when judges are perceived as giving in to political pressures. Regardless of why Judge Baer eventually changed his ruling with regard to the suppression of drug evidence, there will always be the appearance that he backed down due to the barrage of criticism he received. The defense lawyer in the case, the *Washington Post* reported, expressed the belief that the outside pressure influenced the judge, and one scholar compared the reversal to "a baseball umpire who reverses his call when the crowd boos," adding, "You always fear it was the booing that influenced the umpire."

The overall quality of justice is diminished when courts are composed of judges who are there to produce certain results. The California Supreme Court, which had been one of the most distinguished state supreme courts in the country, is now an undistinguished death mill known mostly for its various refinements of the harmless error doctrine. One scholar has pointed out that the court's harmless error decisions reflect "jurisprudential theory" less than a "desire to carry out the death penalty."[6] The steady erosion of the Fourth Amendment's protection against unreasonable searches and seizures in the quest to prosecute drug offenders has diminished everyone's right to privacy and security in their homes.

Most fundamentally, however, when judges must depend upon majority approval, courts are simply unable to perform one of their most important constitutional roles, described by Justice Hugo Black in *Chambers v. Florida* (1940), as serving as "havens of refuge for those who might otherwise suffer because they are helpless, weak, outnumbered, or because they are...victims of prejudice and public excitement." Today as politicians in both major political parties compete to see who can be the toughest on those who are most defenseless—poor people accused of crimes, immigrants, and those on welfare—there is a particularly urgent need for independent courts that will rely on the Constitution alone to decide whether politically popular measures pass constitutional muster.

What can be done?

There is little that judges can do when attacked. When Judge Baer was attacked, Chief Judge Jon O. Newman and three senior judges of the U.S. Court of Appeals for the Second Circuit issued a statement warning that the attacks "threaten to weaken the constitutional structure of this nation." The statement continued: "These attacks do a grave disservice to the principle of an independent judiciary and, more significantly, mislead the public as to the role of judges in a constitutional democracy." Chief Justice William Rehnquist, without mentioning Judge Baer, Senator Dole, or President Clinton, defended judicial independence in a speech at American University and reminded his audience that judges were not to be removed from their jobs because of unpopular rulings. Justice John Paul Stevens addressed the pressures on judges briefly in his speech to the American Bar Association meeting last August.

But judges do not command the media attention of a presidential candidate, a sitting president, a mayor, or a senator. Moreover, judges are prohibited from discussing pending cases by the canons of judicial ethics. However, it is imperative that someone tell the rest of the story about the decision in a particular case, put a single ruling by a judge in the broader perspective of a career, and, most important, point out how the role of judges is different from that of legislators or executives. Responsible public officials and members of the bar must step forward and respond to irresponsible attacks on judges. But there has been an absence of leadership in this area.

Some Republican officeholders should have responded to Dole's call for the impeachment of Baer by pointing out that it was irresponsible. They should have reminded Dole that impeachment of a federal judge is authorized only for a most serious offense after a very careful procedure. Where was Senator Orrin Hatch, a lawyer and the chairman of the Senate Judiciary Committee? Unfortunately, he was not defending the independence of the judiciary. After Baer reversed his ruling, Hatch told reporters, "Unfortunately, this sort of attention cannot be brought to bear on all of the other soft-on-crime decisions issued by other activists that President Clinton has appointed." Similarly, those in the Democratic party should have taken President Clinton—a former constitutional law professor—to task for the suggestion that he might call for Baer's resignation because he disagreed with Baer's decision.

When Dole was nominating Rosemary Barkett for his "judicial hall of shame," where was Florida Senator Connie Mack, who supported Barkett's nomination to the U.S. court of appeals? Mack could have told his former colleague of her distinguished career as a jurist, including service as the chief justice of Florida. When Dole singled out a few decisions for criticism, Mack could have reminded him that Barkett voted to uphold the death penalty in 275 cases, even on occasions when the court reversed; that she was endorsed for retention on the Florida Supreme Court in 1992 by the Fraternal Order of Police, by the Police Officers Benevolent Association, and the Peace Officers Association. But, much more important, Mack could have taught Dole and everyone else in his party a lesson about the importance of judicial independence and the responsibility of all of us, including public officeholders, to help preserve it.

The Bill of Rights is regularly denigrated in political discourse today as nothing more than a collection of technicalities. Someone needs to step forward and remind everyone that the procedural guarantees of the Bill of Rights are fundamental principles that distinguish the rule of law from the rule of the lynch mob.

Several steps should be taken to insulate judges from political pressure. The first and most fundamental is to end direct elections and retention elections for judicial office. The elimination of judicial elections is needed not only to prevent the problems discussed throughout this article but also because of the increasing tendency of special interest groups to buy judges by spending huge sums on judicial campaigns.[7] The recent election in Tennessee demonstrates that retention elections are no better than direct elections. Indeed, retention elections are particularly susceptible to completely negative attacks against a judge with no consideration of an alternative.

Judges should be appointed on the basis of merit by executives from a list of nominees provided by a nominating committee. They should be appointed for long terms or life. At the end of the term, the judge should be evaluated by a judicial qualifications commission based on the entire tenure in office. This type of merit selection of judges will be true merit selection only if there is diffuse citizen input and involvement in the nominating process. The members of the nominating committee must be appointed by various officeholders so that neither the executive nor the bar dominates the process.

Such a system will provide some insulation, but it is of course not guaranteed to always produce good judges. Any system is only as good as the honor of the people in charge of it. Regardless of what system is employed, there will still be presidents, governors, and mayors promising to obtain certain results with their judicial appointees. Thus, whatever system is employed, it will be essential for politicians, bar leaders, and journalists to remind citizens of the value of independent courts.

There is much we all can do. Whenever a politician launches an irresponsible attack on a judge's decision or calls for impeachment or replacement, all of us have a duty to write that official a letter expressing our disapproval. Bar associations should create strike forces to tell citizens in various ways—through press conferences, reports, op-ed pieces, letters to the editor, and in public forums—about the role of the courts and the importance of the independence of the courts. Law schools must instill in their students respect for the Bill of Rights and the rule of law.

Within individual cases, judges must disqualify themselves in cases in which they cannot be fair and impartial due to political pressures. And litigants must move for the disqualification of judges who come under such pressures or have engaged in campaigns that raise questions about their impartiality. As Justice Stevens pointed out at the ABA meeting, "A campaign promise to 'be tough on crime,' or to 'enforce the death penalty,' is evidence of bias that should disqualify a candidate from sitting in criminal cases."

An example of such leadership was provided recently by President Nelson Mandela of South Africa. When the Constitutional Court of South Africa struck down a law delegating broad powers to his administration, Mandela immediately made a public announcement that the court had spoken and its decision must be implemented. Unless we heed this lesson, we may applaud the results reached by our courts in the short run, but we will not have courts of justice.

NOTES

This article originally appeared in Volume 80, Number 4, January-February 1997, pages 165-173. It is adapted from the author's speech before the Association of the Bar of the City of New York, October 7, 1996.

1. *A Governor with a Mission,* TIME, Sept. 4, 1995, at 32 (reporting that James had introduced a bill that would allow the legislature and the governor to overturn rulings of the Alabama Supreme Court from which three or more judges dis-

sent); *James pushes restructuring of state's judicial branch,* Columbus (Ga.) Ledger-Enquirer, May 5, 1995, at B2 (describing the proposal and reporting that Gov. James "sees Alabama judges acting like schoolyard bullies"); *James: President, Congress should ignore Supreme Court,* Columbus (Ga.) Ledger-Enquirer, June 17, 1996, at B-2; *James apologizes for kowtowing to judiciary,* Columbus (Ga.) Ledger-Enquirer, Aug. 8, 1995, at B-2.

2. Wade, *White's defeat poses a legal dilemma: How is a replacement justice picked?,* Memphis Commercial Appeal, Aug. 3, 1996, at A1.

3. Case, *In Search of an Independent Judiciary: Alternatives to Judicial Elections in Mississippi,* 13 MISS. C. L. REV. 1, 15-20, (1992). The resolution of the prosecutors association asserted that Robertson's opponent "best represents the views of the law abiding citizens" and "will give the crime victims and the good, honest and law abiding people of this state a hearing that is at least as fair as that of the criminal in child abuse, death penalty, and other serious criminal cases." *Id.,* at 16 n.108.

4. *Id.,* at 18.

5. *See* Elliott and Connelly, *Mansfield: The Stealth Candidate; His Past Isn't What It Seems,* Tex. Law., Oct. 3, 1994, at 1, 32; Elliott, *Unqualified Success: Mansfield's Mandate; Vote Makes a Case for Merit Selection,* Tex. Law., Nov. 14, 1994, at 1; *Do It Now,* Ft. Worth Star-Telegram, Nov. 12, 1994, at 32 (editorial calling for reform of the judicial selection system in Texas and for an immediate challenge to Mansfield's election because he had "shaded the truth of virtually every aspect of his career"); *Q & A with Stephen Mansfield; 'The Greatest Challenge of My Life,'* Tex. Law., Nov. 21, 1994, at 8 (printing a post-election interview with Mansfield in which he "retracts" a number of statements made before and during the interview).

6. Kessler, *Death and Harmlessness: Application of the Harmless Error Rule by the Bird and Lucas Courts in Death Penalty Cases—A Comparison & Critique,* 26 U.S.F. L. REV. 41, 85, 89 (1991).

7. *See e.g.,* McNeil, *State Judges, Merit Selection, Not Partisan Politics,* LITIGATION, Summer 1996, at 1 (describing costs of judicial campaigns and the efforts of various groups to elect the judge of their choice).

The price a justice paid to uphold the law

How judicial elections are swayed by public opinion on the death penalty was the topic of Cable News Network's "CNN Today," broadcast October 17, 1996. One of the guests joining host Lou Waters was former Tennessee Supreme Court Justice Penny White, who recently had been defeated for retention. Following is an excerpt from that interview:

Waters: Judge White, you were appointed to the Tennessee Supreme Court in '94. Your first death penalty case, you upheld the conviction but overturned the death penalty. Why was that?

White: The five-member court overturned the death penalty because the trial judge didn't allow the defendant to put on his mitigation evidence in the sentencing phase. So the court believed that the defendant had a right to put on evidence so that the jury could determine whether to give death or life.

Waters: Would a pro-death penalty person call this a technicality?

White: I don't think so. It's pretty basic evidence law that both sides get to put on their evidence before the jury decides whether to give life or death in the case.

Waters: All right. Now, because of this decision, a group campaigned against you very—very vigorously, as I understand it, and you were routed in the next election. Is that how that worked?

White: Yes, that's right.

Waters: How do you feel about that?

White: Well, I feel it's unfortunate that a single issue is ever used to judge a judge, particularly. The basis of our justice system is that judges must be independent. They shouldn't be pro-death penalty or anti-death penalty. In fact, if they are either, I don't think they can be judges.

So it's unfortunate, and I hope that the electorate in other states will be aware of the danger of single-issue politics in judicial races.

Waters: As you have gone back over this in your head, and I assume that you have, could you have kept your job by voting not to overturn this death penalty?

White: Absolutely, but I couldn't have slept at night. And I hope that that's the way most of the judges in this country feel. You know, a judge's obligation is to uphold the law despite sometimes very emotional and public issues and sometimes despite public outcry. And probably to vote to uphold the death penalty in this case, I'd still be on the Supreme Court. But I certainly wouldn't feel very good about my job as a judge.

Reining in the federal judiciary

Federal judges have strayed far beyond their proper functions of interpreting and clarifying the law by reading their personal views and prejudices into the Constitution.

by Edwin Meese III and Rhett DeHart

America's founders created a democratic republic in which elected representatives were to decide the important issues of the day. In the framers' view, the role of the judiciary, although crucial, was to interpret and clarify the law—not to make law. The framers recognized the necessity of judicial restraint and the dangers of judicial activism. James Madison wrote in *The Federalist Papers* that to combine judicial power with executive and legislative authority was "the very definition of tyranny." Thomas Jefferson believed that "[i]t is a very dangerous doctrine to consider the judges as the ultimate arbiters of all constitutional questions. It is one which would place us under the despotism of an oligarchy."

Unfortunately, the federal judiciary has strayed far beyond its proper functions, in many ways validating Jefferson's warnings about judicial power. In no other democracy in the world do unelected judges decide as many vital political issues as they do in America. Supreme Court decisions based on the Constitution cannot be reversed or altered, except by a constitutional amendment. Such decisions are virtually immune from presidential vetoes or congressional legislation. Abraham Lincoln warned of this in his first inaugural address when he wrote:

[T]he candid citizen must confess that if the policy of the government, upon vital questions, affecting the whole people, is to be irrevocably fixed by decisions of the Supreme Court...the people will have ceased to be their own rulers, having, to that extent, practically resigned their government into the hands of that eminent tribunal.

When the most important social and moral issues are removed from the democratic process, citizenship suffers because people lose the political experience and moral education that come from resolving difficult issues and reaching a social consensus. At the swearing-in ceremonies for Chief Justice William Rehnquist and Associate Justice Antonin Scalia, President Reagan explained how judicial activism is incompatible with popular government:

The founding fathers were clear on this issue. For them, the question involved in judicial restraint was not—as it is not—will we have liberal courts or conservative courts? They knew that the courts, like the Constitution itself, must not be liberal or conservative. The question was and is, will we have government by the people?

Judicial excesses

When federal judges exceed their proper interpretive role, the result is not only infidelity to the Constitution, but very often poor public policy. Numerous cases illustrate the consequences of judicial activism and the harm it has caused our society. Activist court decisions have undermined nearly every aspect of public policy. Among the most egregious examples:

Allowing racial preferences and quotas. In *United Steelworkers of America v. Weber* (1979), the Supreme Court held for the first time that the Civil Rights Act of 1964 permits private employers to establish racial preferences and quotas in employment, despite the clear language of the statute that states: "It shall be an unlawful employment practice for any employer...to discriminate against any individual because of his race, color, religion, sex, or national origin...." The *Weber* decision is a classic example of how unelected government regulators and federal judges have distorted our civil rights laws from a colorblind ideal to a complex and unfair system of racial and ethnic preferences and quotas that perpetuate bias and discrimination.

Creating a right to public welfare assistance. In *Goldberg v. Kelly* (1970), the Supreme Court sanctioned the idea that welfare entitlements are a form of property under the Fourteenth Amendment. The Court's conclusion: Before a government can terminate benefits on the grounds that the recipient is not eligible, the recipient is entitled to an extensive and costly appeals process akin to a trial. Thanks to the Court, welfare recipients now have a right to receive benefits fraudulently throughout lengthy legal proceedings, and they do not need to reimburse the government if their ineligibility is confirmed. The decision has tied up thousands of welfare workers in judicial hearings and deprived the truly needy of benefits. By 1974, for example, New York City alone needed a staff of 3,000 to conduct *Goldberg* hearings.

Hampering criminal prosecution. In *Mapp v. Ohio* (1961), the Supreme Court began a revolution in criminal procedure by requiring state courts to exclude from criminal cases any evidence found during an "unreasonable" search or seizure. In so holding, the Court overruled a previous case, *Wolf v. Colorado* (1949), which had allowed each state to devise its own methods for deterring unreasonable searches and seizures. The Supreme Court in effect acted like a legislature rather than a judicial body. As a dissenting justice noted, the *Mapp* decision unjustifiably infringed upon the states' sovereign judicial systems and forced them to adopt a uniform, federal procedural remedy ill-suited to serve states with "their own peculiar problems in criminal law enforcement."

In fact, nothing in the Fourth Amendment or any other provision of the Constitution mentions the exclusion of evidence, nor does the legislative history of the Constitution indicate that the framers intended to require such exclusion. We should explore remedies that will deter police misconduct without acquitting criminals, such as civil lawsuits against reckless government officials and internal police sanctions such as fines and demotions.

In *Miranda v. Arizona*, the Supreme Court determined the rules for the admissibility of police interrogations in all criminal trials and radically changed the criminal procedure of every state and the federal government. The Court held that the Fifth Amendment requires what have become known as Miranda warnings whenever a witness in custody is subject to police questioning. Failure to deliver the warnings and obtain the suspect's consent automatically bars the use at trial of the suspect's statements, regardless of whether the suspect confessed or otherwise provided reliable information to authorities. In effect, the Court invented an absolute right for criminal suspects not to be questioned.

Not surprisingly, the costs of *Miranda* have been staggering. In a comprehensive study of the impact of *Miranda* in a 1996 *Northwestern Law Review* article, Professor Paul Cassell estimates that each year *Miranda* results in approximately 28,000 cases of violent crime and 79,000 cases of serious property crime that cannot be prosecuted successfully because of this decision.

Lowering hiring standards. In *Griggs v. Duke Power Co.* (1971), a plaintiff challenged a company's requirement that job applicants possess a high-school diploma and pass a general aptitude test as a condition of employment. The lawsuit argued that because the diploma and test requirements disqualified a disproportionate number of minorities, those requirements were unlawful under the Civil Rights Act of 1964 unless shown to be related to the job in question.

The Court ruled that under the act, employment requirements that disproportionately exclude minorities must be shown to be related to job performance, and it rejected the employer's argument that the diploma and testing requirements were implemented to improve the overall quality of its work force. Moreover, the Court held that "Congress has placed on the employer the burden of showing that any given requirement must have a manifest relationship to the employment in question."

In fact, the act explicitly authorizes an employer to use aptitude tests like the one challenged in *Griggs*. This insidious Court decision has lowered the quality of the U.S. workforce by making it difficult for employers to require high-school diplomas and other neutral job requirements. It also forced employers to adopt racial quotas in order to avoid the expense of defending hiring practices that happen to produce disparate outcomes for different ethnic groups.

Discovering a right to abortion. In *Roe v. Wade* (1973), the Supreme Court considered the constitutionality of a Texas statute that prohibited abortion except to save the life of the mother. Although the Court acknowledged that the Constitution does not explicitly mention a right of privacy, it held that the Constitution protects rights "implicit in the concept of ordered liberty." The Court ruled that "the right of personal privacy includes the abortion decision," and it struck down the Texas statute under the due process clause of the Fourteenth Amendment. The Court then went on, in a blatantly legislative fashion, to proclaim a precise framework limiting the states' ability to regulate abortion.

The dissenting opinion in *Roe* pointed out that, in order to justify its ruling, the majority had to somehow find within the Fourteenth Amendment a right that was unknown to the drafters of the amendment. When the Fourteenth Amendment was adopted in 1868, there were at least 36 state or territorial laws limiting abortion, and the passage of the amendment raised no questions at the time about the validity of those laws. "The only conclusion possible from this history," wrote the dissenting justices, "is that the Drafters did not intend to have the Fourteenth Amendment withdraw from the States the power to legislate with respect to this matter."

One of the most pernicious aspects of the *Roe* decision is that it removed one of the most profound social and moral issues from the democratic process without any constitutional authority. For the first 197 years of America's existence, the abortion issue was decided by state legislatures, with substantially less violence and conflict than has attended the issue since the *Roe* decision. No matter what one's view may be about abortion, it is clear that the founders did not establish the United States as a democratic republic to have unelected judges decide the most important issues of the day.

Overturning state referenda. In *Romer v. Evans* (1996), the Supreme Court actually negated a direct vote of the people. This case concerned an amendment to the Colorado constitution enacted in 1992 by a statewide referendum. "Amendment 2" prohibited the state or any of its political subdivisions from adopting any policy that grants homosexuals "any minority status, quota preference, protected status, or claim of discrimination." The Court ruled that the amendment was unconstitutional, claiming that Amendment 2 did not bear a "rational relationship" to a legitimate government purpose and thus violated the Equal Protection Clause of the Fourteenth Amendment.

The state of Colorado contended that this amendment protected freedom of association, particularly for landlords and employers who have religious objections to homosexuality, and that it only prohibited preferential treatment for homosexuals. The Court, however, rejected these arguments and offered its own interpretation of what motivated the citizens of Colorado, claiming that "laws of the kind now before us raise the inevitable inference that the disadvantage imposed is born of animosity toward the class of persons affected."

The dissenting opinion argued that Amendment 2 denied equal treatment only in the sense that homosexuals may not obtain "preferential treatment without amending the state constitution." The Court's decision, the dissent charged, "is an act not of judicial judgment, but of political will."

Critics argue that the *Romer* decision is the pinnacle of judicial arrogance because six appointed justices struck down a law approved by 54 percent of a state's voters in a direct election, the most democratic of all procedures. In one of the most egregious usurpations of power in constitutional history, the Supreme Court not only desecrated the principle of self-government, but set itself up as the moral arbiter of the nation's values.

Although this representative sample of Supreme Court decisions demonstrates the widespread impact of judicial activism, other federal courts have usurped executive and legislative functions within their jurisdictions. In nearly every state, district and appellate courts are substituting their judgment for that of local officials and are trying to manage everything from prisons and mental hospitals to grammar schools and athletic leagues. Often they are aided and abetted by extremist lawyers, funded at taxpayers' expense, who bring the cases that serve as the vehicles for judicial activism.

Turning the tide

Fortunately, Congress has a number of strategies at its disposal to confine the judiciary to its proper constitutional role:

The Senate should use its confirmation authority to

block the appointment of activist federal judges.

When a president appoints judges who exceed their constitutional authority and usurp the other branches of government, the Senate can properly restrain the judiciary by carefully exercising its responsibilities under the "advise and consent" clause of Article II, Section 2 of the Constitution.

Unfortunately, the confirmation process in recent years has been relatively perfunctory. The Senate has been reluctant to closely question a nominee to ascertain the candidate's understanding of the proper role of the judiciary. The Senate Judiciary Committee hearing provides an excellent opportunity to discern a judicial candidate's understanding of a constitutionally limited judiciary.

Senators, in carrying out this important responsibility, should ascertain a prospective judge's commitment to a philosophy of judicial restraint and constitutional fidelity. In doing so, they should review carefully all the opinions, legal articles, and other materials authored by the candidate; the report of the background investigation conducted by the Federal Bureau of Investigation; and information obtained from judges and other attorneys who have had opportunities to view a candidate's work.

In the name of efficiency, the full Senate sometimes votes to confirm judicial nominees in bundles. This practice should cease. Senators should vote on each nominee individually, in order to remind the prospective judge and the public of the awesome responsibility of each new member of the judiciary and to hold themselves accountable for every judge they confirm to the federal bench.

Congress should strip the American Bar Association of its special role in the judicial selection process.

The American Bar Association has shown itself to be a special-interest group, every bit as politicized as the American Civil Liberties Union or the National Rifle Association. In recent years, for example, the ABA officially supported federal funding for abortion services for the poor, racial and ethnic preferences, and a ban on assault weapons. Moreover, it opposed a ban on flag-burning, reform of the exclusionary rule and of death-penalty appeals, and a proposal to restrict AFDC payments for welfare mothers who have additional children. Hence it should be removed from any official role in evaluating judicial nominees. The ABA should still be free to testify before the Senate Judiciary Committee concerning the potential judge, but it should not have any special status or authority.

The Senate will always need the impartial assessment of judges and lawyers who have a detailed knowledge of the work and background of a judicial candidate. In place of the ABA, the Senate should appoint a special fact-finding committee in each of the 94 federal judicial districts. Members would be selected for their objectivity, ideological neutrality, and understanding of the constitutional role of the judiciary. They would obtain the detailed information the Senate needs to evaluate a candidate and would give that information directly to the Judiciary Committee without subjective comments or evaluation.

Congress should exercise its power to limit the jurisdiction of the federal courts.

Congress has great control over the jurisdiction of the lower federal courts. Article III, Section 1, of the Constitution provides that "[t]he judicial power of the United States, shall be vested in one supreme Court, and in such inferior Courts as the Congress may from time to time ordain and establish." It is well-established that since Congress has total discretion over whether to create the lower federal courts, it also has great discretion over the jurisdiction of those courts it chooses to create. In fact, Congress has in the past withdrawn jurisdiction from the lower federal courts when it became dissatisfied with their performance or concluded that state courts were the better forum for certain types of cases. The Supreme Court has repeatedly upheld Congress's power to do so.

Congress also has some authority to limit the jurisdiction of the Supreme Court and to regulate its activities. Article III, Section 2, of the Constitution states that the Supreme Court "shall have appellate jurisdiction, both as to law and fact, with such Exceptions, and under such Regulations as the Congress shall make." Although we recognize that the scope of Congress's power to regulate and restrict the Supreme Court's jurisdiction over particular types of cases is under debate, there is a constitutional basis for this authority.

In the only case that directly addressed this issue, the Supreme Court upheld Congress's power to restrict the Court's appellate jurisdiction. In *Ex Parte McCardle* (1869), the Court unanimously upheld Congress's power to limits its jurisdiction, stating:

We are not at liberty to inquire into the motives of the legislature. We can only examine into its power under the Constitution; *and the power to make exceptions to the appellate jurisdiction of this court is given by express words.* What, then, is the effect of the repealing act upon the case before us? We cannot doubt as to this. Without jurisdiction, the court cannot proceed at all in any case. [Emphasis added.]

Although some respected constitutional scholars argue that Congress cannot restrict the Supreme Court's jurisdiction to the extent that it intrudes upon the Court's "core functions," there is no question that Congress has more authority under the Constitution to act than it has recently exercised.

The 104th Congress displayed an encouraging willingness to assert its authority over the jurisdiction of the lower federal courts. For example, the Prison Litigation Reform Act of 1995 reduced the discretion of the federal courts to micromanage state prisons and to force the early release of prisoners. The act also makes it more difficult for prisoners to file frivolous lawsuits. (An incredible 63,550 prisoner lawsuits were filed in federal court in 1995 alone.) Congress also passed the Effective Death Penalty Act of 1995. This act limited the power of the federal courts to entertain endless habeas corpus appeals filed by prisoners in death row, significantly expediting the death-penalty process.

Other issues are due for some congressional muscle-flexing to restrain an activist judiciary:

Private-school choice. Some radical groups like the American Civil Liberties Union argue that the government would violate the First Amendment's establishment clause if it gave a tuition voucher to a family that uses it at a religious school. Under current Supreme Court precedents, school vouchers are almost certainly constitutional. Nevertheless, some federal judges have indicated they would invalidate private-school choice plans under the establishment clause. Moreover, if more activist justices are named to the Supreme Court, a liberal majority could crush one of the most promising educational initiatives in recent years by judicial fiat. To ensure that the issue of private-school choice is decided through the democratic process, Congress should consider restricting the Court's jurisdiction over this issue.

Judicial taxation. "Judicial taxation" refers to federal court orders that require a state or local government to make significant expenditures to pay for court-ordered injunctions. For example, one federal judge ordered the state of Missouri to pay for approximately $2.6 billion in capital improvements and other costs to "desegregate" the school districts of St. Louis and Kansas City, which in recent years had lost many white students. To attract white students back into the system, a federal judge required Kansas City to maintain the most lavish schools in the nation, and actually ordered the city to raise property taxes to pay for his court-ordered remedies.

There is a name for tax increases imposed by appointed, life-tenured federal judges: taxation without representation. Under the Constitution, only Congress can lay and collect taxes; our founders would be appalled at the thought of federal judges doing so. Congress should consider restricting the federal courts' authority to order any government at any level to raise taxes under any circumstance.

Use of special masters. Federal judges sometimes appoint special masters to micromanage prisons, mental hospitals, and school districts. In the past, these special masters have been appointed to carry out the illegitimate excursions of judges into the province of the legislative and executive branches. Moreover, the use of special masters has been a form of taxation, in that state and local governments are required to pay their salaries and expenses—which have often been extravagant. In some cases, special masters have hired large staffs to help execute the court order. Congress should outlaw special masters; without them, federal judges would be constrained by the limits on their time and resources from managing prisons or other institutions.

Same-sex marriage. No area of the law has been more firmly reserved to the states than domestic relations. Nevertheless, the Court's absurd reasoning in *Romer v. Evans* suggests the possibility that some federal judges will discover a constitutional right to homosexual marriage, and thus remove the issue from the democratic process.

The Hawaii Supreme Court recently indicated that it would soon recognize homosexual marriages, which all other states would then have to recognize under the full faith and credit clause of the Constitution (Article IV). This possibility motivated Congress to pass the Defense of Marriage Act, which authorized any state to refuse to recognize a same-sex marriage performed in another state. The act does not, however, prevent the federal judiciary from usurping this issue. Congress should consider going one step further to remove the jurisdiction of the lower federal courts over same-sex marriages to ensure that this cultural issue is decided by the legislative process in each state.

The states should press Congress to amend the Constitution in a way that will allow the states to ratify constitutional amendments in the future without the approval of Congress.

One reason judicial activism is so dangerous and undemocratic is that reversing or amending federal court decisions is so difficult. When a decision by the Supreme Court or a lower federal court is based on the Constitution, the decision cannot be reversed or altered except by a constitutional amendment. Such constitutional decisions are immune from presidential vetoes or congressional legislation.

The existing means of amending the Constitution, however, are seldom effective in halting judicial activism. The amendment procedure set forth in Article V of the Constitution is difficult and lengthy for good reason: to avoid hasty changes spurred by the passions of the moment. But history has shown that even the most egregious court decisions—particularly those that affect the balance of power between the national government and the states—have been impervious to correction by constitutional amendment. One reason for this is that Congress, which must initiate such amendments, is loath to give up federal power.

The amendment procedure of the U.S. Constitution led Lord Bryce to conclude in his 1888 study, *The American Commonwealth*, that "[t]he Constitution which is the most difficult to change is that of the United States." This difficulty has encouraged judicial activism and allowed the unelected federal courts to "twist and shape" the Constitution, as Jefferson predicted, as an "artist shapes a ball of wax." The reason that the difficult amendment procedure encourages judicial activism is simple: Life-tenured judges are less likely to show restraint when the possibility that their rulings will be rejected is slight.

Consequently, one strategy to reign in the federal judiciary is to revise the amendment procedure in Article V of the Constitution to allow the states to amend the Constitution without Congress's approval and without a constitutional convention.

Here is how it would work: When two-thirds of state legislatures pass resolutions in support of a proposed amendment to the Constitution, Congress would have to submit it to all the states for ratification. The proposal would then become part of the Constitution once the legislatures of three-fourths of the states ratify it. Congress's role would be purely ministerial. This process would give the states equal power with Congress to initiate an amendment and would further check the power of the federal courts and of Congress.

Congress should stop the federalization of crime and the expansion of litigation in federal court.

Whenever Congress enacts a new federal criminal statute or a statute creating a cause of action in federal court, it enlarges the power and authority of the federal courts and provides more opportunities for judicial activism. At the same time, the federalization of crimes that have traditionally concerned state and local governments upsets the balance between the national government and the states. The following steps can help reduce the federalization of the law and once again restore balance to the federal-state relationship.

Recodify the U.S. Code. In the present federal criminal code, important offenses like treason are commingled with insignificant offenses like the unauthorized interstate transport of water hyacinths. The Federal Courts Study Committee found that the current federal code is "hard to find, hard to understand, redundant, and conflicting." Ideally, Congress would start with a blank slate, recodifying only those offenses that truly belong under federal jurisdiction. Due to the highly political nature of crime, such an undertaking might require the creation of an independent commission, modeled after the recent commission for closing unneeded military bases.

Require a "federalism assessment" for legislation. This idea would require that all federal legislation offer a justification for a national solution to the issue in question, acknowledge any efforts the states have taken to address the problem, explain the legislation's effect on state experimentation, and cite Congress's constitutional authority to enact the proposed legislation.

Create a federalism subcommittee within the judiciary committees of the House and Senate. First proposed by President Reagan's Working

Group on Federalism, federalism subcommittees would attempt to ensure compliance with federalism principles in all proposed legislation.

*****

The framers of the Constitution intended that the federal judiciary play a vital role in America's representative democracy. None of the above material should be interpreted as an assault on the very existence of the judiciary. It is important to remember, however, that in no other democracy in the world do unelected judges decide as many vital political issues as they do in the United States. When viewed objectively, this is actually a nonpartisan issue. The "conservative" activist Supreme Court of the 1920s and 1930s, which struck down as unconstitutional minimum wage and other mild labor reforms, was as repugnant to constitutional democracy as the "liberal" activist Warren Court.

In recent decades, the legislative and executive branches have been very meek in responding to activist federal judges. As a result, perhaps no issue is more in need of attention and effort than restoring the judiciary's non-ideological role as interpreter and clarifier of the law. The strategies listed above illustrate some ways in which the judiciary can be restrained in a proper and constitutional manner. These and other strategies must be used to rein in the activist federal judiciary and return it to its rightful place in our democracy.

NOTES

This article originally appeared in Volume 80, Number 4, January-February 1997, pages 178-183. It is adapted from MANDATE FOR LEADERSHIP IV, published by The Heritage Foundation in January 1997.

Attacks on judges: Why they fail

In testimony last summer before a U.S. Senate subcommittee, the author recounts that the American people consistently reject challenges to an independent federal judiciary.

by Barry Friedman

Why are judges attacked at some times, but not others, as interfering with the popular will? The answer is not as obvious as one might think. Judges have been attacked often throughout history, but the complaint has not always been (as it is now) that judges are interfering with the proper workings of democracy.

To answer this question, I have spent the last three years studying the history of popular attacks on the judiciary. Rather than confining myself to academic tomes, my research materials have been newspapers, magazines, books written for the general public, congressional speeches and debates, cartoons, correspondence and speeches of political figures, and letters to the editor by ordinary citizens—in short, anything that would tell me as best as I could discern the state of public opinion about judges.

Attacks on the courts have occurred for some 200 years. My subject matter has been the Jeffersonian attacks on the Federalist judiciary, many similar attacks during the period of Jacksonian democracy, the vilification of the *Dred Scott* decision, challenges to judicial authority during Reconstruction, the large public outcry surrounding the *Legal Tender* decisions, the long period of Populist-Progressive attacks on the courts reaching from the late 1800s to the 1920s, the New Deal and the Court-packing controversy, challenges to the decisions of the Warren Court (such as *Brown v. Board of Education*, decisions favoring communists, and the controversial reapportionment or school prayer decisions), and, finally, some more recent controversies such as that surrounding the Supreme Court's decision in *Roe v. Wade*.

From 200 years of challenges to judicial independence, some fairly clear lessons have emerged. First, attacks on the judiciary throughout history are inevitably political. By this I mean they are launched to express dissatisfaction with the content of particular judicial decisions. Second, those attacks have come from every point on the ideological spectrum. Third, virtually every technique one might think of to limit judicial decision making has already been suggested or tried. Finally, and most important, almost invariably challenges to judicial independence fail, because the public does not support them. Once the citizens of this country pay attention to the debate, they are approving of judicial independence and disapproving of attacks on it. Unquestionably this popular sentiment has grown over the course of the more than two centuries of attacks on the federal judiciary. In the rare instances in which Congress has taken steps to influence judicial decision making, the almost invariable public response has been regret.

Attacks are political

The first lesson is that attacks on the judiciary are invariably political. Note that I say political, and not partisan, though the attacks often (but not always) are partisan as well. By political I mean that no matter what members of Congress or the executive branch have said about why they are threatening judicial independence, they are doing it because they do not like the way judges are deciding particular cases.

Sometimes there is a great deal of candor on the subject, but sometimes political actors try to wrap their motives in something their constituents might find a bit more palatable. The need for sugar coating seems to have increased in this century, as the public increasingly has become uncomfortable with attacks on judges.

An example of candor occurred in the early 1800s, when President Thomas Jefferson's Democrat-Republicans tried to impeach Supreme Court Justice Samuel Chase. This was the first and last time—until recently—that we have seriously considered impeaching federal judges because of unhappiness with the decisions rendered.

Chase, by almost any standard, was fit material for impeachment. He regularly engaged in partisan harangues, he browbeat witnesses and counsel, and he even refused to hear the legal arguments of counsel in some cases. But Chase's impeachment failed, largely because of the Democrat-Republicans' admission that they sought impeachment on the basis of the justice's views on the merits. As John Quincy Adams reported in his memoirs concerning the views of Representative William Branch Giles, one of the prime movers in the impeachment effort, "removal by impeachment was nothing more than a declaration by Congress to this effect: You hold dangerous opinions, and if you are suffered to carry them into effect you will work the destruction of the nation. *We want your offices*, for the purpose of giving them to men who will fill them better."

In contrast, when Franklin Roosevelt launched his attack on the federal judiciary with his now-infamous Court-packing plan, he felt forced to provide a nonideological cover for what was nonetheless obvious to all. Incidentally, this was not the first, but was assuredly the last, high-profile attempt to "pack" the membership of a federal court to achieve a desired result. When Roosevelt announced the plan on February 5, 1937, he justified it in terms of workload and judicial efficiency. For this he was attacked from all quarters as being disingenuous, and for having dictatorial tendencies. Newspapers around the country questioned Roosevelt's motives. Finally, Roosevelt had no choice but to be candid about his motives, which he did in a March 9 "fireside chat":

Last Thursday I described the American form of government as a three-horse team provided by the Constitution to the American people so that their field might be plowed. The three horses are, of course, the three branches of government—the Congress, the executive, and the courts. Two of the horses are pulling in unison today; the third is not.

Conservatives and liberals

History teaches that challenges to judicial independence have come from liberals as well as conservatives. It is easy to forget this, because in recent years complaints about judges generally have come from conservatives, concerned about what they perceive as liberal decisions. In the first half of this century, however, it was exactly the opposite. Perhaps it is for this very reason that Americans have developed a deep-seated caution about those attacks, concerned about creating a precedent that might come back to haunt them. Today it might be a liberal judicial ox that is gored, but tomorrow it might be a conservative one.

The issues confronting the United States in its first century were very different from what they are today. In the early 1800s, and again in the 1820s, the Supreme Court was attacked for its nationalizing tendencies. The causes for concern were often Supreme Court decisions that required the states to adhere to the policies of a national Congress and national Constitution. *Dred Scott*, of course, was attacked by Republicans for its pro-slavery outcome, and the notable instance of jurisdiction-stripping during Reconstruction represented a Radical and Republican attack on the Court, which—it was feared—would invalidate Reconstruction.

In this century the ideology is much more familiar. For the first half of this century it was Progressives and liberals who were attacking an entrenched conservative Court. Between the late 1800s and 1937, the Supreme Court invalidated the income tax, upheld the use of injunctions against the labor movement, and struck down numerous laws to protect worker safety, prohibit child labor, and regulate the hours and minimum wages of all employees. Then, of course, there was invalidation of many New Deal measures such as the Agricultural Adjustment Act.

Indeed, it is fair to say that during this century until the late 1950s defenders of judicial independence almost always were conservatives. Generally speaking, we did not really have a Supreme Court of liberal bent in this country until the 1950s. For most of history, conservatives defended the judiciary on the ground that it was the judiciary's job to protect constitutional values against rampant majorities. From the perspective of a constitutional historian, it is more than a little odd to see conservatives attacking the Supreme Court in the name of the people. When the courts were attacked by progressives for interfering with popular will, conservative response was simply to point out that that was the Court's function—to trump popular will in the name of the Constitution. Perhaps it is well to remember the election of 1924, in which Progressive party candidate Robert LaFollette gave a speech to a packed Madison Square Garden, arguing:

Either the court must be the final arbiter of what the law is, or else some means must be found to correct its decisions. If the court is the final and conclusive authority to determine what laws Congress may pass, then, obviously, the court is the real ruler of the country, exactly the same as the most absolute king would be.

Who was the judiciary's chief defender at the time? The Republican who won the presidential election in which judicial independence was a chief issue: Calvin Coolidge.

A road often traveled

Almost any imaginable technique to control the federal judiciary has been proposed. At times there were very serious efforts to implement such proposals, the vast majority of which failed. As we have proceeded through our 200-plus years of history, the American people seem to have ruled out the candidates one by one.

During the Jeffersonian Era, Congress took two direct swipes at the federal judiciary, one of which was the attempted impeachment of federal judges. First, it repealed the Circuit Judges Act of 1801, which had created numerous judgeships the Federalists rapidly filled before the Democrat-Republicans took office. The legislation, incidentally, was challenged on constitutional grounds and upheld by the Supreme Court. Second, there was the failed campaign to impeach federal judges.

One popular technique for dealing with unpopular decisions has been defiance. During Andrew Jackson's presidency, the states sometimes defied Supreme Court decisions, such as when Georgia went through with the execution by hanging of a Cherokee named Corn Tassels in the face of a Supreme Court order not to do so. Jackson was thought to lack the will to enforce federal court mandates. In another Cherokee controversy with Georgia, Jackson reputedly said, "John Marshall has made his decree, now let him enforce it." As one newspaper aptly reported, "We are sick of such

talks [of defiance]. If there is not power in the Constitution to preserve itself—it is not worth keeping." It is notable, however, that when John Calhoun launched the nullification movement, Jackson made it clear he stood behind the Court. The last widespread attempt at defiance was in response to *Brown v. Board of Education*, not a chapter in our history of which anyone today is especially proud.

Attempting to strip the courts of jurisdiction also has been popular. During Reconstruction, Congress succeeded in the only successful attempt to strip the Supreme Court of jurisdiction, passing legislation over a veto by President Andrew Johnson that deprived the Court of jurisdiction to hear *Ex parte McCardle*, in which, it was feared, the Court would strike down Reconstruction. Another attempt shortly thereafter to limit the Court's jurisdiction for similar reason failed, and the only other close attempt was in 1957, in response to Supreme Court decisions that seemed to protect communists. The Jenner-Butler bill, which aimed to strip the Court's power in many cases involving communists, was watered down to almost nothing and still failed. Since then numerous proposals have been made to strip the courts of power over busing, abortion, or school prayer decisions, none of which have gone anywhere.

Court packing also had its day. I already have discussed FDR's failed attempt to pack the New Deal Court, the last serious attempt to do so in our history. The only arguably successful Court-packing occurred on the heels of Reconstruction, when President Ulysses Grant put two new justices on the Supreme Court, thereby rapidly changing the result in the *Legal Tender* cases. I say arguably, because history suggests the appointments may simply have been fortuitous.

Although these are the most frequently used techniques to control the federal courts, numerous others have been proposed. Many of these proposals were made during the Populist-Progressive era, and many have resurfaced recently. Examples include requiring a unanimous or a two-thirds vote for the Supreme Court to overturn laws, limiting the jurisdiction of the lower courts to overturn laws, recall of judges, limited terms of judges, and reversal of judicial decisions by the Senate. About the only thing not seriously proposed has been the rack, although vituperative popular sentiment has been expressed, including burning Supreme Court justices in effigy during the New Deal.

Support for existing system

As the history related thus far suggests, almost every attempt to interfere with judicial independence has failed. There is a reason for this—the public has chosen regularly to support the system we have, warts and all. Often it takes time for the public to focus its attention fully on what is happening in Washington, D.C., and attempts to limit judicial independence have gone quite far before being derailed. But for the most part derailed is what they have been. Interestingly, those politicians who suggested aggressive treatment of the courts sometimes watched their political futures fail along with their proposals.

The only successful attempts to interfere with judicial independence met with subsequent popular unhappiness. Those "successes" were the stripping of the Supreme Court's jurisdiction to hear the *McCardle* case, and the arguable packing of the Court that heard the second *Legal Tender* decision. As noted above, a subsequent attempt to strip jurisdiction failed; the legislation was a matter of tremendous controversy, with many Republicans splitting off and opposing the measure. Similarly, even though the first *Legal Tender* decision—partially invalidating the government's printing of money during the Civil War—was met with widespread unhappiness, when the Court changed its mind in response to new membership, the second *Legal Tender* decision was met with even more widespread derision. It was one of the Supreme Court's lowest moments.

From the early days of the Republic until after the Civil War, judicial supremacy was not established. Once it was established in the minds of the American people, politicians tried varying techniques to control that supremacy. Some of the early attempts succeeded, but gradually over time the citizenry has expressed its view that the ordinary processes of judicial decision making and judicial attrition should run their course.

Although there is loud public clamoring at times to do something about judges, when push comes to shove and calmer minds prevail, the public has always stepped away from the abyss. In the meantime, some politicians have fallen into it. FDR, elected in one of history's largest popular mandates, fell quickly to his lowest approval when he proposed the Court-packing plan. Matters were so

bad Republicans stepped aside and permitted Democrats to take the lead in challenging the president, who might not have recovered his popularity absent a world war. Other examples include Teddy Roosevelt, whose broad attacks on federal judges and his Progressive attempts to regain the presidency both failed, as did those of Robert LaFollette.

Ordinary processes work

What final lesson can be drawn from all this? Perhaps that when all is said and done, the American people have come to feel that the ordinary processes for controlling judges and the judiciary should prevail.

What are these ordinary processes? The first, and most relevant to today's debates, is the normal appellate process. Today's complaints seem for the most part to be about the decisions of individual judges, not about the judiciary as a whole. That is why the word impeachment has been uttered so regularly. But why is this necessary? No one judge decides any important case. In the federal system at least a three judge appellate panel, and perhaps an en banc court, reviews any case that is important. And truly significant cases are almost certainly going to be heard by the Supreme Court.

Indeed, it is because of the availability of Supreme Court review—a likelihood in landmark cases—that today's debate is so unfathomable to some of us that watch from the sidelines. Of the nine members of the Supreme Court, seven were appointed by Republican presidents. It is hardly a radical Court, and certainly not a radically liberal one. After all, for the first time since the New Deal we are seeing a resurgence in federalism. The right to abortion, while still existent, has been narrowed. The Court recently lowered the wall between church and state somewhat. Many death sentences are being enforced. It is difficult to see what the concern is for individual decisions, when the mechanism to overturn any aberrant ones appears to be in good health.

Second, there is the ordinary appointment and confirmation process of federal judges. If there was any lesson from the failed Court-packing plan, it was the general public's sense that natural attrition was the correct constitutional way to influence the federal judiciary. It has worked reasonably well—about as well as any system in our government—for almost 200 years. The truly conservative course would seem to be reluctance in tinkering with it.

Indeed, it does seem that much of what is currently occurring reflects anxiety about the number of appointments to the federal bench President Clinton may make. But this too is unseemly and a bit incomprehensible. Historically, it reeks of the same motives that caused the Federalists to pack the judiciary before Jefferson took office. In more recent history, 12 years of Republican presidential leadership placed a majority of Republican judges on the bench. Now, President Clinton's appointments must be approved by a Republican Senate, and given the case backlog and numerous vacancies, one can only hope that nominations will be forthcoming and confirmations will occur at a reasonable pace after that. But by any measure reported in the popular press or academic journals, President Clinton's appointments have been quite moderate in their decision making. It is hard to see, again, what the fuss is about.

The third process is one seldom discussed, but plainly evident. It is, in large part, a function of the appointment process, as well as the fact that federal judges are American citizens like the rest of us, having grown up in the same culture. The result of this process, if one may call it that, is that federal judicial decisions rarely fall out of line with popular sentiment for very long. Political scientist Robert Dahl observed this 40 years ago at the height of the Warren Court controversy, and numerous other academics have made similar observations. Surely that is the case today. The courts have "moderated" (if that is the right word) their views on abortion, the death penalty, the rights of criminal defendants, and the wall between church and state.

It is hard to see many issues on which today's federal judiciary is far outside the mainstream of public opinion. There may be a few, but then that is what living under a Constitution is all about. My sense is that they are undoubtedly very few, so few that those who are suggesting otherwise might check their premises. And yes, there are going to be decisions with which many of us disagree, even bitterly. Some decisions will seem very, very wrong. But we do have a way of correcting those problems, and that system has worked powerfully well for a long time. History suggests attempts to tamper with it are not, even in the short run, met with much success or public approval.

NOTES

This article originally appeared in Volume 81, Number 4, January-February 1998, pages 150-155. It was adapted from the author's testimony before the U.S. Senate Judiciary Committee's Subcommittee on the Constitution, Federalism, and Property Rights, July 14, 1997.

Delving deeper

Senator John Ashcroft (R-Missouri), chairman of the Judiciary Committee's Subcommittee on the Constitution, Federalism, and Property Rights, and Senator Strom Thurmond (R-South Carolina) followed up on Professor Friedman's testimony with a letter containing additional questions. The following is an edited version of the professor's written response:

Would you agree that, as a general matter, it is a proper function for Congress to examine the proper allocation of jurisdiction between state and federal courts?

In general, the answer is yes. You undoubtedly are familiar with the "Madisonian Compromise," in which the framers of the Constitution gave Congress the power to create lower federal courts, but left it to Congress to decide whether to do so. Generally speaking, that power has been interpreted to give Congress leeway in deciding which lower courts to create and what jurisdiction to bestow upon them. Thus, as a practical matter Congress regularly decides whether to have federal courts hear specific causes of action, or whether to leave them in the hands of the state courts.

The simplicity of this general answer, however, betrays another question of great complexity regarding the extent to which the Constitution imposes limitations on Congress's power to control the jurisdiction of the federal courts. This is one of the most mooted questions in the academic literature, with scholars of great ability coming to very different answers. Some would accord Congress great authority, perhaps even to remove jurisdiction from the federal courts over virtually any question. Others advance varying theories that would limit Congress's power.* My own position is that the Constitution is unclear on this question, for better or for worse, and that answers will be worked out as a matter of repeated interaction among the branches of the federal government.

Which brings me to history, once again. Although the question is much-mooted, it tends to be an academic debate simply because Congress rarely has sought to exercise the power. The only "successful" example of jurisdiction stripping occurred when the Republican Congress—in an effort to fend off a decision regarding the constitutionality of Reconstruction—stripped the Supreme Court of its statutory authority to hear certain habeas corpus cases. I put the word "successful" in quotation marks because although the Supreme Court acquiesced in this removal of its jurisdiction, it hinted that other means of review were available, a state of affairs that quickly proved itself to be correct. I also put "successful" in quotations because even the Republican Congress resisted subsequent efforts to strip jurisdiction, necessary though they appeared to be to avoid a decision on Reconstruction. Moderate Republicans (and much of the public) were so put off by the shenanigans that led to the original withdrawal of jurisdiction that they recoiled from further attempts.

The latest major attempt to strip the Supreme Court of jurisdiction was in response to several decisions in 1957 that seemed pro-communist. The bill that was the subject of attention was the Jenner-Butler bill, ironic because in an earlier era Senator Butler had sought to amend the Constitution to protect the Supreme Court from any such incursions on its constitutional role. This only serves to reinforce the point I made in my original testimony: attacks on the Court tend to come when people disagree with the substantive content of judicial decisions. The Jenner-Butler bill attracted wide national attention. In its original form the bill would have stripped jurisdiction over a number of areas, such as state bar admissions. In response to criticism, the original legislation was watered down thoroughly. Nonetheless, it still was defeated in a close and closely watched debate in the Senate. Supreme Court opponents could not even muster the votes to overturn a Supreme Court decision holding that the federal sedition law preempted similar state laws.

The point we can glean from history is that it is important to distinguish between Congress's general power to see that jurisdiction is allocated in sensible fashion between the state and federal courts, and jurisdiction-stripping legislation enacted by Congress simply to reverse the trend of decisions with which it disagrees. I believe no one disputes the necessity of Congress exercising the former function, although they may have strong opinions as to whether Congress is doing a good

job or not, as we have seen during recent debates over congressional legislation federalizing crime. On the other hand, historical precedent would discount Congress's power to strike out at the federal courts in response to the substance of decisions. And for good reason. In all these cases the concern was that the independence of federal judges would be threatened.

During my testimony, you questioned whether the removal of jurisdiction over specific sorts of cases necessarily would threaten judicial independence, suggesting that judges would remain free to decide cases in any fashion they wished in the areas left open to them. I understand the logic of your position, but would disagree with its application in practice. I think my central point finds support in the very distinction I draw above. If Congress merely is doing its housekeeping job of allocating jurisdiction, I do not believe independence would be, or would seem to be, threatened. But stripping jurisdiction out of unhappiness with substantive outcomes makes it patent to judges and to the general public that if judges do not toe the line Congress would like to see followed, the judges simply will be removed from the picture. History suggests the public has seen such attempts for precisely what they are, as attacks on judicial independence, and such attacks have been resisted.

One historical example of a successful legislative reaction to perceived judicial activism is the Norris-La Guardia Act, which limits the ability of federal courts to issue injunctions against labor organizations. Do you consider that act to be an illegitimate intrusion on judicial independence?

This question raises a narrower issue than the question above, namely whether Congress has the power to remove a particular remedial tool from the federal courts. My answer turns on the principle widely accepted in this country and made plain by Chief Justice John Marshall in *Marbury v. Madison* that "[t]he very essence of civil liberty certainly consists in the right of every individual to claim the protection of the laws, whenever he receives an injury."

Generally speaking, I do not believe the remedial power of the federal courts can be limited to such an extent that those courts cannot act effectively to remedy constitutional violations. There is good reason for this. If federal courts lack the power to provide an effective remedy for violations of the citizenry's constitutional rights by the other branches of government, then our entire system of constitutional government is threatened.

The seminal case on the labor injunction provisions of the Norris-La Guardia Act is the Supreme Court's 1938 decision in *Lauf v. E.G. Shinner & Co.* As Professor Gordon Young made clear in a law review article (*A Critical Reassessment of the Case Law Bearing on Congress's Power to Restrict the Jurisdiction of the Lower Federal Courts*, 54 Md. L.Rev. 132 (1995)), some read the *Lauf* decision as approving of Congress's broad power to limit the federal courts' jurisdiction.

I believe, in agreement with Professor Young, that *Lauf* stands for a narrower principle, one consistent with the general principle I advanced above. The injunction provision challenged in *Lauf* did not forbid labor injunctions entirely; it merely curtailed their use unless specific (albeit stringent) conditions were met. To the extent that those conditions themselves permitted federal courts to issue injunctions when the Constitution required them, the decision is unproblematic. Moreover, there is every reason to suspect that at the time *Lauf* was decided, this was the case. *Lauf* was decided right after the Supreme Court famously switched direction on the question of economic rights. The employers' constitutional "right" to a labor injunction depended on substantive due process protection of property rights that by 1938 there was every reason to doubt the courts would afford. If this were the case, no constitutional right was threatened by the provisions of the Norris-La Guardia Act at issue, and the limitation on the remedy was unproblematic as well.

You state in your prepared testimony that "no one judge decides any important case." How do you respond to the concern that, as a practical matter, litigants often may not appeal activist decisions?

In answering this question, I would like to distinguish between the decision of a particular dispute between parties, and the resolution of a broader legal issue by the courts. The distinction is an important one, because in our society any important and controversial legal question is likely to arise in more than one case. Generally speaking, important questions tend to filter their way through the state and federal courts to the Supreme Court, gleaning the wisdom of many judges, rendered in disputes presented in adversarial fashion by several sets of lawyers.

As for the impact of a decision in any single case, however, I adhere completely to my view, which is that such a decision can be appealed. Appeal is of right, of course, to at least a three-judge panel of the court of appeals. After that, en banc review and review by the Supreme Court are available on a discretionary basis.

As litigants, some governments choose not to appeal. This, of course, is their decision. A government might decide to forego an appeal because the district court decision is persuasive, because it appears the weight of the law is against it, or even because the government's position is politically unpopular. It is difficult to hold the federal courts accountable for these governmental decisions. Indeed, because these governments are accountable to their citizens, it is difficult to complain about a government's decision not to appeal on the ground that the unappealed decision interferes with popular will.

It is possible that governments decide not to appeal because of the expense of litigation, a point which deserves response. This economic decision is one that every litigant faces. It is resolved by considering the cost of litigation, available resources, the importance of the case, and the likelihood of prevailing. These are the difficult decisions governments face every day. My own suspicion is that in the vast majority of cases that truly are of importance to a government, in which there is any chance of ultimate success, an appeal is taken.

Moreover, it is inaccurate to portray governments as standing alone in facing the resource question of whether to take an appeal. There are many organizations that assist governments in this regard. For example, I serve on the advisory board to the State and Local Legal Center, an organization that files briefs before the Supreme Court in matters of interest to state and local government.

I hope these answers are helpful to the subcommittee's further deliberations.

NOTE

* My own views are set out in Friedman, *A Different Dialogue: The Supreme Court, Congress and Federal Jurisdiction*, 85 Nw. U.L. Rev. 1 (1990), which also contains a summary of the diversity of opinion on the subject.

The Contributors

Shirley S. Abrahamson is chief justice of the Supreme Court of Wisconsin.

Arlin N. Adams is a retired judge of the U.S. Court of Appeals for the Third Circuit and a lecturer at the University of Pennsylvania School of Law.

James Austin is a professor in the Department of Sociology at George Washington University.

Christopher P. Banks is an assistant of political science at the University of Akron.

Lawrence Baum is a professor of political science at the Ohio State University.

Susan M. Behuniak is a professor of political science at Le Moyne College, Syracuse, New York.

Larry C. Berkson served as director of educational programs for the American Judicature Society from 1976-1982. He is currently in private business in New Hampshire.

Terry Bowen is an associate professor of political science at the University of North Florida.

William J. Bowers is principle research scientist at the College of Criminal Justice at Northeastern University.

Christopher N. Bratcher is a graduate student in the Department of Government at the University of Texas at Austin and an instructor at the University of the South.

William J. Brennan Jr. was an associate justice of the Supreme Court of the United States from 1956-1990.

Susan W. Brenner is associate dean and a professor at the University of Dayton School of Law.

Stephan B. Bright is director of the Southern Center for Human Right, Atlanta, and teaches at Yale, Harvard, and Emory law schools.

David J. Brown is an attorney in Lawrence, Kansas. He served as a research attorney for Kansas Court of Appeals Judge Mary Beck Briscoe from 1991 to 1992.

J. Louis Campbell III is an assistant professor of speech, theater, and the humanities at Missouri Western College.

Bradley C. Canon is a professor of political science at the University of Kentucky.

Robert A. Carp is a professor of political science at the University of Houston.

John Clark is a senior associate at the Pretrial Services Resource Center in Washington D.C.

Beverly Blair Cook is an emeritus professor of political science at the University of Wisconsin-Milwaukee.

John W. Cooley is an adjunct professor of law at Northwestern University School of Law. He is a former United States magistrate who has served as a settlement master, mediator, and arbitrator.

David Crump is a professor of law at the University of Houston.

Sue Davis is a professor of political science at the University of Delaware.

Rhett DeHart is special counsel at the Heritage Foundation.

Shari S. Diamond is a professor of psychology at the University of Illinois, Chicago, and a senior research fellow at the American Bar Foundation.

Michael Esler is an associate professor of politics and government at Ohio Wesleyan University.

Kevin M. Esterling is a research associate with the American Judicature Society and a Ph.D. candidate in political science at the University of Chicago.

Steven Flanders, an international court consultant, served as executive of the Second Judicial Circuit of the United States from 1980-1997.

Jason S. Fleming is an attorney with Thomas, Ison & Fleming in Hopkinsville, Kentucky.

Barry Friedman is a professor at Vanderbilt University School of Law.

Stephen B. Goldberg is a professor of law at Northwestern University School of Law.

Sheldon Goldman is a professor of political science at the Univesity of Massachusetts, Amherst.

Jona Goldschmidt is an associate professor of criminal justice at Loyola University Chicago.

Leslie Friedman Goldstein is a professor of political science at the University of Delaware.

Eric D. Green is a professor of law at Boston University.

Kimberly Greenfield is a costume designer for ballet and opera productions in Lexington, Kentucky.

Diane S. Gutmann is an attorney in Madison, Wisconsin.

Susan Haire is an assistant professor of political science at the University of Georgia.

Arthur D. Hellman is a professor of law at the Univesity of Pittsburgh School of Law.

D. Alan Henry is executive director of the Pretrial Services Resource Center.

Thomas Hensley is a professor of political science at Kent State University.

Marie Hojnacki is an assistant professor of political science at Penn State.

Joseph Ignagni is an associate professor of political science at the University of Texas at Arlington.

Christopher G. Jordan is business manager for the city of Galveston, Texas.

Kenneth R. Kay is chairman of Infotech Strategies, Washington, D.C.

Herbert M. Kritzer is a professor of political science and law at the University of Wisconsin, Madison.

Gerald B. Lefcourt is immediate past president of the National Association of Criminal Defense Lawyers.

Robert C. Luskin is an associate professor in the Department of Government at the University of Texas at Austin.

William Lyons is a professor of political science at the University of Tennessee, Knoxville.

George Mace was an associate professor and vice president at Southern Illinois University, Carbondale. He is currently in private enterprise in Carterville, Illinois.

Thomas R. Marshall is a professor of political science at the University of Texas at Arlington.

Robert McDuff is an attorney in Jackson, Mississippi.

Edwin Meese III, who served as U.S. attorney general from 1985 to 1988, is the Ronald Reagan Fellow at the Heritage Foundation.

Albert P. Melone is a professor of political science at Southern Illinois University, Carbondale.

Roger J. Miner is a Senior Judge of the U.S. Court of Appeals for the Second Circuit and adjunct professor of law at Albany Law School.

Richter H. Moore was a professor of political science and criminal science at Appalachian State University.

Norval Morris is the Julius Kreeger Professor of Law and Criminology Emeritus at the University of Chicago.

Laura Natelson is a Ph.D. candidate in the School of Public Affairs at American University.

Jon O. Newman is a senior judge on the U.S. Court of Appeals for the Second Circuit. At the time of the events of this article, he was chief judge.

David M. O'Brien is the Leone Reaves and George W. Spicer Professor of Government at the University of Virginia.

Nathan L. Posner was a partner in the Philadelphia law firm of Fox, Rothschild, O'Brien & Frankel and served as chancellor of the Philadelphia Bar Association, 1975-76.

D. Marie Provine is a professor of political science at Syracuse University.

Tracy K. Renner is a graduate student in the Department of Government at the University of Texas at Austin.

Wm. Bradford Reynolds, an attorney in Washington D.C., was Assistant Attorney General, Civil Rights Division, U.S. Department of Justice from 1981 to 1988, and counselor to the Attorney General of the United States in 1987–1988.

Jack E. Rossotti is a professor in the School of Public Affairs at American University.

Frank E. A. Sander is Bussey Professor and associate dean at the Harvard Law School.

John M. Scheb II is a professor of political science at the University of Tennessee, Knoxville.

Kris S. Seago is a graduate student in the Department of Government at the University of Texas at Austin.

Jeffrey A. Segal is a professor of political science at State University of New York, Stony Brook.

Jennifer A. Segal is an assistant professor of political science at the University of Kentucky.

Jeffrey M. Shaman is a professor of law at DePaul University.

Elliot E. Slotnick, editor of *Judicial Politics: Readings from Judicature*, is a professor of political science at The Ohio State University and associate dean of the graduate school.

Christopher E. Smith is a professor of criminal justice at Michigan State University.

Donald R. Songer is a professor of political science at the University of South Carolina.

Harold J. Spaeth is a professor of political science at Michigan State University and a member of the Michigan bar.

Peter W. Sperlich is a professor of political science at the University of California, Berkeley.

Diana Stech is a graduate student in economics at the University of Maryland.

John Paul Stevens is an associate justice of the Supreme Court of the United States.

Ronald Stidham is a professor of political science and criminal justice at Appalachian State University.

John Stookey is a member of the law firm Osborn Maledon and a former professor of political science at Arizona State University.

Mary Lou Stow, now Mary Lou Peters, is an attorney at Weil, Gotshal & Manges in New York.

Ruth Ann Strickland is an associate professor of political science and criminal justice at Appalachian State University.

Raymond Tatalovich is a professor of political science at Loyola University Chicago.

Michael Tonry is Marvin J. Sonosky Professor of Law and Public Policy at the University of Minnesota.

J. Clifford Wallace is a judge of the United States Court of Appeals for the Ninth Circuit.

Stephen L. Wasby is a professor of political science at the State University of New York, Albany.

George Watson is a political science professor in the Walter Cronkite School of Journalism at Arizona State University.

Ronald E. Weber is the Wilder Crane Professor of Government at the University of Wisconsin, Milwaukee.

Alissa Worden is a professor in the School of Criminal Justice at the State University of New York at Albany.

The American Judicature Society

The American Judicature Society (AJS), founded in 1913, is an independent, nonpartisan organization of judges, lawyers, and other members of the public who seek to improve the justice system.

AJS, which brings a public perspective to justice system issues, has the following mission:

★ To minimize the role of politics in judicial selection.

★ To support an independent judiciary that operates with the highest standards of ethics.

★ To enhance the role of the jury and the importance of jury service.

★ To increase public understanding and appreciation of the justice system.

★ To promote operational improvements in the courts.

★ To build knowledge through research on judicial issues.

Judicature, the Society's refereed bimonthly journal, is a forum for fact and opinion relating to all aspects of the administration of justice and its improvement. The journal has been published continuously since 1917.